Modern American Remedies

Cases and Materials

Modern American Remedies

Cases and Materials

Douglas Laycock

Fulbright & Jaworski Professor of Law
The University of Texas at Austin

Little, Brown and Company

Boston   Toronto

Library of Congress Catalog Card No. 84-82267
ISBN 0-316-51749-6

First Edition

MV

Published simultaneously in Canada
by Little, Brown & Company (Canada) Limited

Printed in the United States of America

For Terry and Joe Pete

They were always more important than the book —
but sometimes the book was more urgent,
and it was always less forgiving.

Summary of Contents

Contents

Preface

Why Another Casebook?

This didn't start out to be a casebook. I put together some materials to supplement another casebook, and they just kept growing. It gradually became apparent to me that the things that I wanted to do with my course couldn't be done with any of the other books on remedies. This book is designed to let me and other teachers so inclined do those things. Some features of this book appear in some other books, but I think its combination of features is unique. That is the only reason I would bring a new book to market.

Most important, the book reflects my belief that a course in remedies should not be a series of appendixes to the substantive curriculum. It contains no chapters on remedies for particular wrongs or particular kinds of injury. Such chapters are important, but their place is in the substantive courses to which they pertain. This book attempts to explore general principles about the law of remedies that cut across substantive fields and that will be useful to a student or lawyer encountering a remedies problem in any substantive context.

Second, the book tries to integrate the study of public and private law remedies. Public law has spawned dramatic remedial innovations during the last generation, and no course should ignore them. But public law remedies are built on traditional private law remedies. If we study public law remedies alone, we tear them from their roots and from a set of principles that can help guide the vast discretion courts exercise in public law cases. And of course, ordinary torts and contracts remain the bread and butter for most litigators.

Third, as the title suggests, the book emphasizes problems of contemporary importance. I have tried to place contemporary issues in historical context, but I have not devoted much ink to issues that have been largely mooted by recent developments. The merger of law and equity, the ambitious reach of modern American equity, the generous contemporary attitude toward measuring damages, the progress toward a general theory of restitution not based on procedural fictions — these and other less sweeping developments have reduced the significance of some issues that were important a generation ago.

Fourth, the book explores and tests the claims of the Chicago school of law and economics. It tries to do so in a way that is accessible to students who lack backgrounds in economics, that is fair to both sides, and that doesn't dominate the book. I believe that doctrine, fairness, and corrective justice are as important as economics and have given all these values equal treatment. But I think that the course in remedies is an especially important place to test the economic theory. One of that theory's central claims is that the law should and does encourage an optimal level of violations. If the law is serious about doing that, remedies must be primarily designed to provide the optimal level of deterrence. If remedies law does other things, and especially if it tries to eliminate violations without regard to their economic efficiency, the Chicago school has a problem.

Finally, this book tries to teach students as much as possible before class, so that class discussion has a strong base. I have tried to supply memorable cases, lots of structure, lots of leading questions, and lots of information. Most of the rest of this preface explains that pedagogical choice.

Some Notes on Pedagogy

This book is designed to teach basic principles and to help students think about difficult problems; it is not designed as a research tool. When there are highly visible decisions of the United States Supreme Court, I have made some effort to summarize the whole line of cases and make clear what "the law" is at that level. But most remedies law is not made at that level, and even when there are important Supreme Court cases, the states can make their own rules about remedies on state law claims. I have made no pretense of exploring all the resulting variations, or of presenting enough cases to enable a reader to determine what "the law" is on a particular point. However, I have been careful to ensure that principal cases are representative of dominant approaches and that any exceptions are plainly labeled as such.

The book's pedagogical theory is pragmatic. Most often, the notes ask questions of students, but sometimes they provide explanation, sometimes they summarize related cases, and sometimes they offer my own speculations. The style of the notes depends on the nature of the material being presented; I do not believe that any one of these approaches is intrinsically superior to the others.

Students may find that the notes raise more questions than they answer. But the questions are always leading questions. I ask questions because it is important to encourage students to think for themselves, but the questions are leading because there is no reason to believe students can regularly produce answers out of thin air. They must be given some raw material to think about. And the questions are always directed at important issues; I have carefully tried to avoid "hiding the ball." I believe what I said in reviewing another casebook: "Casebooks and instructors should channel [student] effort toward developing the most important skills and teaching the most important subject matter. We should bring students to the edge of insight as quickly and painlessly as possible. Then they should be asked to learn by the 'socratic' method, but not before. The law has plenty of real difficulties for students to grapple with; it is never necessary to create artificial ones." Laycock, A Case Study in Pedagogical Neglect, 92 Yale L.J. 188, 202 (1982).

The selection and editing of the cases also reflect the decisions to direct students' attention to central issues and not to write a reference book. I have tried to select opinions that focus squarely on an important issue, are clearly written, and have memorable facts. I have deleted everything that is not germane to the issue, and everything that does not either advance the analysis or provide an interesting error that is useful for teaching purposes. The deletions are designed to focus students' attention on the central issue, without requiring them to wade through excess verbiage and wonder whether it matters. There will be plenty of opportunity to develop that skill after they have mastered basic principles.

I have applied the same principles to citations. I have collected illustrations, but not citations. That is, I have generally taken the view that if the facts are not worth developing, the case is not worth citing. I have included citations to cases that students might recognize. And I do try to provide one good citation — to a case or article that will lead to others — for each important point. Readers who want more citations for research purposes should follow up on those leads and check the principal cases in the original reporter. I have deleted citations and footnotes, and corrected obvious typographical errors, without notation; I have marked textual deletions with ellipses. Footnotes retain their original numbers.

A Note to Teachers

You may occasionally fear that a set of notes has left you nothing to talk about in class — that the notes have "given too much away." That is not the students' view, and that has not been my experience. I have taught some of the cases in this book as many as eight times. Often, I started with a bare case, continued to teach the case as the materials evolved through skeletal, incomplete notes, and finally, in the last year or two, taught the case with something like the complete set of notes finally included in the book. Almost without exception, the more the students knew at the beginning of class, the better the class discussion. I could not pull as many rabbits out of hats, but many students never learn where those rabbits come from anyway. If teaching students is a higher goal than showing off, then extensive notes are a great advantage. If we want students to be thoughtful in class, we have to give them some advance notice of what to think about.

One of my colleagues who read the manuscript is not a remedies teacher. As a gifted teacher of contracts, she was quite familiar with the basic issues in damages, but knew almost nothing of injunctions. Her reaction to parts of chapter 2 was that I had given too much away. Her reaction to chapter 3 was that she didn't quite understand how everything fit together. The notes are just as leading in chapter 3, but she came to chapter 3 with a student's perspective instead of a teacher's. A leading question leads a teacher who already knows the answer much further than it leads a student who is trying to learn. Because of her reaction, I tightened the organization of chapter 3. I didn't try to hide anything in chapter 2.

One other important piece of advice: *Look at the teacher's manual,* even if you have never used one. I have tried to make it possible for you to tailor your own course the first time through the book, in the way you would tailor it the second or third time through. There are several sets of day-by-day assignments to choose from, each emphasizing different aspects of the course, and information on variations from those basic choices. There is advice on which cases to teach and which to skip if you want to sample more chapters than you can cover thoroughly. My views on how to teach particular cases are probably no better than yours, but I do know more about what's in this book. The teacher's manual tries to make that knowledge available to you.

A Note to Students

Most of my students have been enthusiastic about the notes, and I hope that you will be too. The notes provide much information and raise many questions. They are designed to help you learn a lot before you come to class. This allows class to start from a higher base; unprepared students will be at a greater disadvantage. Your teacher will probably pick a few of the issues raised by the cases and notes for further exploration in class. There won't be time to talk about every question raised in the notes; you are expected to think about some things on your own. Some teachers may assign whole sections to be read on your own, without class discussion. Reading alone is not as good as reading plus discussion, but reading this book should be a lot more helpful than reading a casebook written with a different philosophy.

I encourage you to take the questions in the notes seriously. They are all questions that you can answer or begin to answer with the information in the book and the hints in the leading questions. I have not tried to make leading questions do more than they can do. Where you need facts, I have given them to you; where there is a settled rule, I have told you about it. If a series of leading questions seems to suggest inconsistent answers, all the suggested answers are fairly arguable and there is no consensus in the cases. Your thoughtful opinion on such questions is as valuable as the next person's. I would only mislead you if I presented my opinion as the "right" answer.

Finally, the headings in this book *are* part of the text. Chapters and sections and subsections all have headings; every set of notes has a heading. Those headings are intended to help organize the material for you and to signal the main focus of each set of notes and the accompanying cases. All the headings are listed in the table of contents, which is a detailed outline of the book. Read the headings and use them; don't ignore them.

Douglas Laycock

April 1985

Acknowledgments

I am grateful to many people who helped this project in many ways. Two law schools supported this book with research leave. I collected my first set of supplemental cases in the fall quarter of 1976, on a leave supported by The University of Chicago Law School and arranged by Dean Norval Morris. I wrote chapter 6 in the fall semester of 1983, on a half-time leave supported by the Lidell, Sapp, Zively, Brown & LaBoon Professorship in Banking, Financial, Commercial, and Corporate Law, arranged by Dean John Sutton and approved by the Trustees of The University of Texas Law School Foundation.

My introduction to the academic study of remedies came from Owen Fiss, in his course in equity, at The University of Chicago. Owen's influence is apparent at many places in this book, although he is obviously not responsible for its contents. Indeed, I suspect he finds some of my recent work too positivist for his taste. Owen is not to blame for the arguably excessive number of pages this book devotes to the *Younger* cases. I knew Justice Black had his history wrong the first time I read the *Younger* opinion. I knew, with more certainty than was justified, from my undergraduate constitutional law courses at Michigan State University. The faculty there thought it important to note the procedural history of every case, and I knew I had briefed a lot of Supreme Court opinions deciding whether to enjoin enforcement of state statutes.

My introduction to the practical implementation of remedies came from Robert Plotkin and Aram Hartunian of the Chicago bar and Glen Wilkerson of the Austin bar, three tenacious litigators with whom I worked in practice. Lessons I learned from them show up in this book as well.

This book also reflects the influence of the Chicago school of law and economics. Much of what they explain with economic theory I prefer to explain as corrective justice. But a scholar is as much the intellectual

xxxi

product of those he reacts against as he is the product of those he follows. And somewhat to my surprise, I finish this book convinced that either economics or corrective justice can explain a wide range of remedies law. Only a few cases force us to choose between the theories.

I have repeatedly turned to my colleagues, both at Chicago and Texas, for help with the background of substantive law or with remedial problems that arise more frequently in one substantive field than in others. I have queried nearly every member of both faculties at one time or another. But the people I troubled most often on substantive matters were Bill Powers and Guy Wellborn in torts, Bob Hamilton in corporate and securities law, and Elizabeth Warren in contracts. Jay Westbrook and Elizabeth Warren have been endlessly helpful with respect to creditor's rights and bankruptcy, which I consider an important subdivision of remedies. Liz also read substantial portions of the draft manuscript and made more useful comments than I had time or space to implement. Dale Oesterle at Cornell provided the same service for chapter 6.

I also had lots of bibliographic help. As always, the staff of the Tarleton Law Library was magnificent. But others helped as well. Jim Treece tracked down a student note on remedies in intellectual property cases that saved days of research. Lino Graglia supplied an unpublished busing opinion. Art Curtis of the Chicago bar tracked down obscure parts of the history of the *Meatpackers Antitrust Decree.* Professor Hamilton Bryson and the reference librarian at the University of Richmond Law School sent me the briefs in Thompson v. Commonwealth, together with an analysis of their contents. The briefs clarify an otherwise inexplicable part of the opinion; the explanation is in the teacher's manual.

A series of research assistants worked on this project over the years. Those who made the most sustained and memorable contributions were Paul Beach and Joe Markowitz at Chicago and Jack Hohengarten, Rob Pacholski, Mary Sahs, David Brown, Maralene Martin, Jeff Horowitz, and Judy Weaver at Texas. An equally long series of secretaries worked on the manuscript, but Dianne Grandstrom, Ruth Fischer, and Pam Grisham did most of the secretarial work in the final push to completion.

Those who made the greatest sacrifice for this book, aside from the trees, were the students at Chicago and Texas who took the course from fuzzy photocopies of early drafts. I am grateful for their patience, their suggestions and insights, and their sometimes puzzled questions. Our students know a remarkable variety of things. For example, Bill Emmons at Texas first told me about the curious language of barge leasing, introduced me to the wondrously mysterious phrase "net net per diem gross," and suggested that the "net profits" of the *Helen B. Moran* might not be what they appeared.

Finally, I am grateful to copyright holders for permission to reprint excerpts from the following items:

Atiyah, Patrick, The Rise and Fall of Freedom of Contract (1979). Copyright © 1979 by Clarendon Press.

Chayes, Abram, The Role of the Judge in Public Law Litigation, 89 Harvard Law Review 1281 (1976). Copyright © 1976 by Abram Chayes.

Diver, Colin, The Judge as Political Power Broker: Superintending Structural Change in Public Institutions, 65 Virginia Law Review 43 (1979). Copyright © 1979 by the Virginia Law Review Association.

Dobbs, Dan B., Handbook on the Law of Remedies (1973). Copyright © 1973 by the West Publishing Co.

Eisenberg, Theodore, and Yeazell, Stephen C., The Ordinary and the Extraordinary in Institutional Litigation, 93 Harvard Law Review 465 (1980). Copyright © 1980 by the Harvard Law Review Association.

Fiss, Owen M., The Civil Rights Injunction (1978). Copyright © 1978 by Owen M. Fiss.

Frug, Gerald E., The Judicial Power of the Purse, 126 University of Pennsylvania Law Review 715 (1978). Copyright © 1978 by the University of Pennsylvania.

Fuller, L. L., and Perdue, William R., Jr., The Reliance Interest in Contract Damages, 46 Yale Law Journal 52 (1936). Copyright © 1936, 1937 by the Yale Law Journal, Inc.

Johnson, Frank M., The Constitution and the Federal District Judge, 54 Texas Law Review 903 (1976). Copyright © 1976 by Texas Law Review Publications, Inc.

Laycock, Douglas, Federal Interference with State Prosecutions: The Need for Prospective Relief, 1977 Supreme Court Review 193. Copyright © 1978 by the University of Chicago.

———, Federal Interference with State Prosecutions: The Cases *Dombrowski* Forgot, 46 University of Chicago Law Review 636 (1979). Copyright © 1979 by the University of Chicago.

———, Injunctions and the Irreparable Injury Rule, 57 Texas Law Review 1065 (1979). Copyright © 1979 by Texas Law Review Publications, Inc.

Macneil, Ian R., Efficient Breach of Contract: Circles in the Sky, 68 Virginia Law Review 947 (1982). Copyright © 1982 by Ian R. Macneil.

Maitland, Frederic, Equity 449 (2d ed. 1936). Copyright © 1920, 1936 by Cambridge University Press.

Nagel, Robert F., Separation of Powers and the Scope of Federal Equitable Remedies, 30 Stanford Law Review 661 (1978). Copyright © 1978 by the Board of Trustees of the Leland Stanford Junior University.

Posner, Richard A., Economic Analysis of Law (2d ed. 1977). Copyright © 1972, 1973, 1977 by Little, Brown and Company.

Wixon, Rufus, ed., Accountants' Handbook (4th ed. 1960). Copyright © 1956 by the Ronald Press Company. Reprinted by permission of John Wiley & Sons, Inc.

Modern American Remedies

Cases and Materials

CHAPTER 1

Introduction

THE ROLE OF REMEDIES

A remedy is anything a court can do for a litigant who has been wronged or is about to be wronged. The two most common remedies are judgments that plaintiffs are entitled to collect sums of money from defendants and orders to defendants to refrain from their wrongful conduct or to undo its consequences. The court decides under the substantive law whether the litigant has been wronged; it conducts its inquiry in accordance with the procedural law. The law of remedies falls somewhere between substance and procedure, distinct from both but overlapping with both.

Remedies give meaning to obligations imposed by the substantive law. Suppose Brown discovers that Smith claims the timber in Brown's forest and plans to cut it. Remedies law does not determine who owns the land, nor create the law's prohibitions of theft and trespass. But remedies law does determine the consequences of violating those prohibitions. Remedies law determines whether Brown can enforce the substantive law in advance, through an order to Smith to stay off the land, or whether he must wait until after his timber has been cut. If the timber is cut, remedies law determines whether Brown gets money and how much he gets. Brown conceivably may get a sum based on the recreational value of the forest, the value of the uncut trees, or the value of the finished lumber, or a sum not based on value at all, such as nominal damages or punitive damages. If Smith disobeys the order, or fails to pay the judgment, remedies law determines what Brown can do about that.

1

Remedies law can thus determine whether Brown gets $1, or $100,000, or an order that saves him from being harmed at all. Such a body of law is not sensibly thought of as procedural. But remedies law does not change Smith's underlying obligation to leave Brown's trees alone, so it is not easily thought of as substantive either.

However categorized, remedies law is of immense practical importance. Clients are typically more interested in the bottom line than in the principle of the thing. This book is about the bottom line. In every case, we will assume that the defendant's conduct is unlawful and ask what the court can do about it: What does plaintiff get? How much does he get? Why does he get that instead of something more, or less, or entirely different?

CLASSIFYING REMEDIES

Anglo-American law has developed a rich inventory of remedies. Most remedies fit rather easily into a small number of categories, and it is helpful to label those categories as a way of organizing thought and providing a common vocabulary. But students should not allow the classification scheme to control reality. Some remedies do not fit squarely into any of the categories, and it is rarely worthwhile to worry about how to classify such a remedy. The important question is always which remedies are available and what they offer, not where they fit in somebody's classification scheme.

The most important categories of remedies are compensatory remedies, coercive remedies, declaratory remedies, restitutionary remedies, punitive remedies, and ancillary remedies. Compensatory remedies are designed to compensate plaintiffs for harm they have suffered. The most important compensatory remedy is compensatory damages, a sum of money designed to make the plaintiff as well off as he would have been if he never had been wronged. In the example above, payment of the value of Brown's trees would be compensatory damages. Compensation for plaintiff's court costs and attorneys' fees are also compensatory remedies; for historical and doctrinal reasons, they are not thought of as damages.

Coercive and declaratory remedies are closely related. Both are designed to prevent harm before it happens, so that the issue of compensation never arises. It is sometimes helpful to combine these two categories and call them preventive remedies. The most important preventive remedy is the injunction. An injunction is an order from a court to litigants ordering them to do or to refrain from doing some specific thing. An order directing Smith to stay off Brown's land is a typical example. A specific performance decree, ordering defendants to perform their contract, is a specialized form of injunction. Courts also issue a variety of specialized orders that for one reason or another are not traditionally thought of as injunctions, such as writs of mandamus, prohibition, and habeas corpus. These too are designed to prevent harm to the plaintiff.

Injunctions and similar orders from courts are coercive remedies. A defendant who violates a direct order from a court is guilty of contempt. The court may impose escalating punishments until defendant obeys, or a fixed punishment for past disobedience. It is the direct order and the potential for punishing disobedience that distinguish coercive remedies from declaratory remedies.

Declaratory remedies authoritatively resolve disputes about the parties' rights, but they do not end in a direct order to the defendant. For example, Brown might sue Smith, asking the court to decide who owns the forest. If the court formally declared that Brown owned the forest, that would decide the matter, and Smith would probably honor the decision. If so, the declaration would prevent harm to Brown as effectively as an injunction. In general, declaratory remedies prevent harm to the litigants by resolving uncertainty about their rights before either side has been harmed by erroneously relying on its own view of the matter. Smith might be as eager as Brown to get a declaration of ownership; without it, he can cut trees only at the risk of incurring liability to Brown. The most important declaratory remedy is the declaratory judgment, but there are also older, more specialized declaratory remedies, such as bills to quiet title and cancellation of instruments.

It is somewhat misleading to describe declaratory remedies as noncoercive. It is more accurate to say that the coercive threat is implicit rather than explicit. If the court declares that Brown owns the forest, and Smith ignores that declaration and continues to cut trees, the court will enforce its declaration with sterner measures. The court will certainly award compensation to Brown, and it is nearly as certain to issue an injunction ordering Smith off the land. The distinction between declaratory and coercive remedies is largely one of form; if coercion turns out to be necessary, it will be applied.

Restitutionary remedies are designed to restore to plaintiff all that defendant gained at plaintiff's expense. In some cases, restitution and compensation are identical. If the court holds Smith liable for the market value of Brown's timber, it compensates Brown and simultaneously deprives Smith of what he gained at Brown's expense. But depending on how the court measures gains and losses, it may appear that Smith gained more than Brown lost. The court would probably measure Brown's loss by the value of the standing timber. It might measure Smith's gain the same way, but it might also measure Smith's gain by the higher value of the finished lumber. It seems unfair that Smith should keep a profit that he was able to earn only because he stole Brown's timber. Restitutionary remedies measure Brown's recovery by Smith's gain; Brown could proba-

bly recover Smith's profit. I say probably, because there are difficult allocation problems here and the rules are not clear. Smith's profit is partly
the product of Brown's forest, and partly the product of Smith's own
labor and investment in logging equipment and a sawmill. But at least if
Smith were a conscious wrongdoer, it is likely that most courts would
allow Brown to recover Smith's profits.

Consider a better settled example of restitution. Suppose Smith steals
Brown's shares of common stock in Stodgy Nogrowth Industries, worth
$1,000, sells them, and reinvests in Superflyer Hi-Tech Co. Suppose
further that by the time Brown finds out what has happened and sues, the
Superflyer Hi-Tech stock is worth $5,000, and the Stodgy Nogrowth stock
is still worth only $1,000. Brown would be fully compensated by $1,000 in
damages, but it is troubling to let Smith keep his $4,000 profit. Brown
could recover the Superflyer stock or its value.

Restitution has traditionally been administered through a variety of
separate remedial devices, such as quasi-contract, constructive trust,
equitable lien, accounting for profits, rescission, and subrogation. Courts
increasingly recognize that these are different labels for the same thing,
and speak simply of granting restitution.

Punitive remedies are designed to punish wrongdoers. Criminal prosecution, not civil liability, is the usual route to punishment. But there are
punitive civil remedies: The best known is punitive damages. If Smith
deliberately stole Brown's timber, a jury could award punitive damages in
addition to compensatory damages. If Smith erroneously thought the
forest belonged to him, even if he were negligent in checking title to the
land, punitive damages would not be available. A variety of statutes authorize minimum recoveries in excess of actual damages, or recovery of
double or triple plaintiff's actual damages; these may also be thought of as
punitive remedies. One may question whether punitive remedies are
remedies at all; they often do not remedy anything in the usual sense of
correcting, repairing, or fixing. But punitive damages or statutory minimum recoveries are sometimes necessary to make it economically feasible for private plaintiffs to enforce important rights.

Ancillary remedies are designed in aid of other remedies. Most ancillary remedies are designed to enforce the primary remedies. Thus, punishment for contempt is ancillary to coercive remedies. Various means of
collecting money are ancillary to all remedies that end in money judgments, including compensatory remedies and some restitutionary and
punitive remedies. When defendant does not pay voluntarily, the primary
means of collecting money are execution and garnishment. Under a writ
of execution, a sheriff will seize defendant's property, sell it, and use the
proceeds to pay plaintiff's judgment. In garnishment, the court will order
people who owe money to defendant to pay plaintiff instead; these payments will be applied to the judgment. Plaintiff is entitled to postjudgment discovery to find out about defendant's property, and other more

extraordinary collection devices are available if defendant has concealed his assets or removed them from the jurisdiction. Despite these remedies, many money judgments go uncollected. One should not assume that plaintiff wins when he gets a money judgment.

A more unusual ancillary remedy is the receivership. Sometimes it is necessary for the court to manage assets pending litigation. For example, Brown and Smith may agree that the timber should be cut, but disagree on who should control the operation and who should get the proceeds. Each of them may claim that the other would dissipate the proceeds if allowed to hold them until the case can be tried. If the court could not trust either side to manage the forest pending litigation, it might appoint a receiver to manage the forest until the rights of Brown and Smith could be determined. Receivership is an unusual and expensive remedy, but it is available when needed. Receivership is also sometimes used as an extraordinary collection device after judgment. But a receivership is never an end in itself; it is always ancillary to some other remedy.

LEGAL AND EQUITABLE REMEDIES

Remedies may also be classified as legal or equitable. For half a millennium or so, England had two separate sets of courts functioning side by side: courts of law and courts of equity. Each set of courts devised its own body of substantive rules, its own procedures, and its own remedies; there was a separate set of rules for determining which cases went to which set of courts. This country inherited separate courts of law and equity and their separate bodies of law.

By now, the separate courts have been merged in nearly all the states, although there are some important exceptions. The merged courts have largely combined the two sets of substantive rules and adopted a single set of procedures, except that the right to jury trial is generally guaranteed only in cases that would have been legal before the merger.

The line between law and equity is largely the result of a bureaucratic fight for turf; each set of courts took as much jurisdiction as it could get. Consequently, the line is jagged and not especially functional; it can only be memorized. Damages are the most important legal remedy; in general, compensatory and punitive remedies are legal. Injunctions and specific performance decrees are the most important equitable remedies; some of the specialized coercive remedies, such as mandamus, prohibition, and habeas corpus, are legal. Declaratory judgments were created by statute after the merger, so they are not classified either way; the older, more specialized declaratory remedies are generally equitable. Restitution was developed independently in both sets of courts; some restitutionary remedies are legal, some equitable, and some both. Receiverships are equitable.

Where the law/equity distinction is especially murky, as in restitution, lawyers and judges tend to overlook it, and the distinction becomes less and less important. But the distinction between damages (legal) and injunctions (equitable) remains clear and important. If Brown lets Smith cut his trees and then sues for damages, either party may demand a jury trial. If Brown sues for an injunction to prevent Smith from cutting his trees, neither side is entitled to a jury in federal court nor in most states. In addition, Brown will encounter one of the rules originally used to allocate cases between the separate courts of law and equity: He cannot have an equitable remedy if the legal remedy would be adequate. This rule is still good law everywhere, but often it does not seem to have much bite.

ORGANIZATIONAL NOTE

Part I of this book surveys the principal remedies and is organized on the basis of the classification scheme just outlined. We examine compensatory remedies in chapter 2, coercive remedies in chapters 3 and 4, declaratory remedies in chapter 5, restitutionary remedies in chapter 6, punitive remedies in chapter 7, and ancillary remedies in chapter 8.

Part II of the book examines problems that are best studied after you know all the basic types of remedies. That pedagogical judgment explains the somewhat miscellaneous appearance of part II. Chapter 9 considers two problems of implementing remedies: the limits of practicality and the drafting of decrees. Chapter 10 considers two problems of measuring what plaintiff is entitled to: attorneys' fees, and private agreements specifying in advance what the remedy will be if something goes wrong. Chapter 11 considers the equitable defenses. Chapter 12 considers two kinds of timing problems: time limits on bringing suit and the need to modify old decrees in light of changing circumstances. Chapter 13 considers some remedies issues that affect the allocation of political power.

NOTE ON THE NATURE OF REMEDIES

The first section of this introduction suggests that remedies law is neither procedural nor substantive, but somewhere in between. That suggestion is not entirely uncontroversial. To the extent that the argument is purely definitional, it is not worth pursuing. But the argument that remedies are the essence of substance casts light on the nature of remedies and of substance and the relationship between them.

There is a sense in which the remedy ultimately defines the substantive obligation. This suggestion requires a choice between two ways of looking at the law. One might say that the substantive law forbids the cutting of other people's trees, and that the usual remedy for a violation is a money judgment for the value of the trees. Or one might say that the law forbids nothing; it merely specifies the consequences of various choices. Thus, the law says that if Smith cuts Brown's trees, he will suffer a money judgment for their value; Smith has a free choice. Justice Holmes sometimes talked in these terms, and so do some of the modern scholars who apply classical economics to legal problems.

This second view effectively highlights the importance of remedies. It is certainly true that some individuals will obey the law only if the consequences of violation are more painful than obedience. The potential victims of such individuals have substantive rights, but those rights are not worth much unless the rights are backed up by effective remedies.

Even so, I find the attempt to define substance in terms of remedies unpersuasive. To do so denies the normative function of the law. To say that the law forbids Smith to cut Brown's trees is a meaningful statement, a statement with moral force, whether the remedy is an injunction or damages or criminal punishment or a slap on the wrist. That some individuals are unmoved does not eliminate the statement's moral force for the rest of us.

In addition, the view that prohibitions are no more than a choice between alternatives cannot stop with the first such choice. What does it mean to say that Smith must leave Brown's trees alone or suffer a money judgment? Not that Smith must leave the trees alone or pay, but only that if he does not pay, Brown can ask the sheriff to come seize Smith's assets. Smith is forbidden to conceal his assets, but again, that means only that he can choose between revealing assets or going to jail if Brown and the authorities are sufficiently diligent in their efforts to enforce the judgment. But again, if nothing is forbidden, his choice is not between revealing assets or going to jail, but between going to jail or going into hiding. I find it implausible to say that all this is merely the process of defining Smith's substantive obligation: that if the government will not spend as much as it takes to track Smith down, the law is indifferent between his leaving Brown's trees alone or cutting them and going into hiding.

Similarly, Smith may be able to discharge Brown's judgment in bankruptcy. The enactment of generous bankruptcy laws says something about the comparative importance a society attaches to the rights of plaintiffs and the distress of insolvent defendants. But such laws do not mean that if Smith is insolvent, he doesn't violate the substantive law when he cuts Brown's trees.

I chose the example of Brown and Smith because it can be used to illustrate all sorts of remedies without too much straining. But the example stacks the deck in favor of the view that substantive law has moral force independent of the remedies provided. If we assume it is clear that Brown owns the forest, then Smith is a thief, and it is hard to sympathize with him. It is easy to agree that theft is wrong, and forbidden, even though most thefts go unremedied because thieves are too hard to catch.

The case of Brown and Smith may look different if we assume that ownership is genuinely disputed, and that the court is still in doubt even when it makes its decision on the preponderance of the evidence. And there may be other legal rules with less independent moral force than the rules against theft. Those who take an economic view of law believe that parties to contracts should have an option to perform or pay compensatory damages, and, more generally, that profitable violations of law ought to be encouraged so long as the violators compensate their victims.

A course in remedies is a good place to test these views, and we will explore them intermittently throughout the book. I do not mean to prejudge them here when I say that the underlying substantive rules are analytically distinct from the remedies available to enforce them. Whether we design remedies that encourage profitable violations, or remedies that minimize violations, or remedies that serve some other purpose altogether, we are making choices distinct from the choices we make when we design the substantive law.

PART I

The Measure of Relief: A Survey of the Principal Remedies

CHAPTER 2

Paying for Harm: Compensatory Damages

A. THE BASIC PRINCIPLE: RESTORING PLAINTIFFS TO THEIR RIGHTFUL POSITION

UNITED STATES v. HATAHLEY
257 F.2d 920 (10th Cir. 1958)

[Plaintiffs are eight families of Navajo Indians who have lived for generations on open range land owned by the United States. Plaintiffs' livestock grazed on the public lands along with livestock owned by whites who held grazing permits. The United States and these white stockmen considered the Indians to be trespassers, and in separate litigation sought to have them ordered off the public lands.

While those lawsuits were pending, government agents rounded up plaintiffs' horses and burros and sold them to a glue factory. Federal law required that alleged trespassers be given notice and an opportunity to remove their animals before such a roundup: no such notice was given. The Supreme Court held that the roundup was a trespass under Utah law, actionable against the United States under the Federal Tort Claims Act. Hatahley v. United States, 351 U.S. 173 (1956). The Court remanded to the district court for further findings on the amount of damages. This is an appeal from the district court's decision on remand.]

10

Before BRATTON, Chief Judge, and MURRAH, PICKETT, LEWIS and BREITENSTEIN, Circuit Judges.

PICKETT, Circuit Judge. . . .

Upon remand, the District Court took additional evidence on the issue of consequential damages, and without an amendment of the complaint, entered a judgment against the United States for the total sum of $186,017.50. The value of each horse or burro taken was fixed at $395; each plaintiff was awarded $3,500 for mental pain and suffering; and damages were given for one-half of the value of the diminution of the individual herds of sheep, goats and cattle between the date the horses and burros were taken in 1952, and the date of the last hearing in 1957. . . .

The fundamental principle of damages is to restore the injured party, as nearly as possible, to the position he would have been in had it not been for the wrong of the other party. Applying this rule, the plaintiffs were entitled to the market value, or replacement cost, of their horses and burros as of the time of taking, plus the use value of the animals during the interim between the taking and the time they, acting prudently, could have replaced the animals.

The plaintiffs did not prove the replacement cost of the animals, but relied upon a theory that the animals taken were unique because of their peculiar nature and training, and could not be replaced. The trial court accepted this theory, and relying upon some testimony that a horse or a burro could be traded among Indians for sheep, goats or cattle worth a stated price, together with the owner's testimony of the value, arrived at a market value of $395 per head. No consideration was given to replacement cost. The court rejected evidence of the availability of like animals in the immediate vicinity, and their value. This, we think, was error. It is true that animals of a particular strain and trained for a special purpose are different from animals of another strain and not so trained, but that does not mean that they cannot be replaced by animals similarly developed and trained, or which may be trained after acquisition. Ordinarily every domestic animal is developed and trained for the purpose to which the owner intends to use it. This development and training adds to its usefulness and generally increases the market value of the animal. In arriving at a fair market value of destroyed animals, the court should consider evidence of the availability of like animals, together with all other elements which go to make up market value. In proper instances, parties and witnesses may be cross-examined on the subject.

Likewise, we think the court applied an erroneous rule, wholly unsupported by the evidence, in arriving at the amount of loss of use damage. There was testimony by the plaintiffs that because of the loss of their horses and burros they were not able to maintain and look after as much livestock as they had been able to before the unlawful taking, consequently the size of their herds was reduced. If the unlawful taking of the animals was the proximate cause of the herd reductions, the measure of damages would be the loss of profits occasioned thereby.

Applying the same formula to all plaintiffs, the court, without giving consideration to the condition, age or sex of the animals, found the value of the sheep and goats in 1952 to be $15 per head, and cattle to be $150 per head. The number of sheep, goats and cattle which each plaintiff had in 1952, as well as the number which each had at the date of the last hearing was established. This difference was multiplied by $15, in the case of sheep and goats, and by $150, in the case of cattle, and judgment was entered for one-half of the amount of the result. No consideration was given to the disposition of the livestock by the plaintiffs in reducing the herds. For example, the plaintiff Sakezzie had 600 sheep and goats and 101 head of cattle when his horses and burros were taken in 1952. At the date of the last hearing in 1957, he had 160 head of sheep and goats and 39 head of cattle. The dollar value of the difference at $15 per head for the sheep and goats, and $150 per head for the cattle, amounted to $15,900. The court found "that approximately fifty percent of this amount represents damages to the plaintiff proximately caused by deprivation of the use of plaintiff's horses, and on this basis plaintiff is entitled to recover $7,950.00 as consequential damages resulting from such deprivation." The result, insofar as it related to use damage, was arbitrary, pure speculation, and clearly erroneous. In United States v. Huff, 5 Cir., 175 F.2d 678, a case where the method of computing damages for loss of sheep and goats was strikingly similar to that used here, the court said:

> Moreover, there has been no sufficient showing of how much of the damage from the loss of the sheep and goats was proximately caused by the Government's failure to maintain and repair the fences under the lease, and how much of the damage resulted from the various other causes. There is no testimony whatever as to the specific dates of loss of any of the sheep and goats, or as to their age, weight, condition and fair market value at the time of the alleged losses. It therefore becomes patent that the evidence as to the loss of these animals in each case fails to rise above mere speculation and guess.

175 F.2d 680.

Plaintiffs' evidence indicated that the loss of their animals made it difficult and burdensome for them to obtain and transport needed water, wood, food, and game, and curtailed their travel for medical care and to tribal council meetings and ceremonies. Plaintiffs also testified that because of the loss of their animals they were not able to grow crops and gardens as extensively as before. These were factors upon which damages for loss of use could have been based. This does not exclude the right to damages for loss of profits which may have resulted from reduction of the number of livestock, or actual loss of the animals, if the unlawful acts of the defendant agents were the proximate cause of the loss and were proved to a reasonable degree of certainty.

But the right to such damages does not extend forever, and it is limited to the time in which a prudent person would replace the destroyed horses and burros. The law requires only that the United States make full reparation for the pecuniary loss which their agents inflicted.

The District Court awarded each plaintiff the sum of $3,500 for mental pain and suffering. There is no evidence that any plaintiff was physically injured when his horses and burros were taken. There was evidence that because of the seizure of their animals and the continued activity of government agents and white ranchers to rid the public range of trespassers, the plaintiffs and their families were frightened, and after the animals were taken, they were "sick at heart, their dignity suffered, and some of them cried." There was considerable evidence that some of the plaintiffs mourned the loss of their animals for a long period of time. We think it quite clear that the sum given each plaintiff was wholly conjectural and picked out of thin air. The District Court seemed to think that because the horses and burros played such an important part in the Indians' lives, the grief and hardships were the same as to each. The equal award to each plaintiff was based upon the grounds that it was not possible to separately evaluate the mental pain and suffering as to each individual, and that it was a community loss and a community sorrow.[5]

Apparently the court found a total amount which should be awarded to all plaintiffs for pain and suffering, and divided it equally among them. There was no more justification for such division than there would have been in using the total value of the seized animals and dividing it equally among the plaintiffs. Pain and suffering is a personal and individual matter, not a common injury, and must be so treated. While damages for mental pain and suffering, where there has been no physical injury, are allowed only in extreme cases, they may be awarded in some circumstances.

Any award for mental pain and suffering in this case must result from the wrongful taking of plaintiffs' animals by agents of the United States, and nothing else.

As the case must be remanded for a new trial as to damages, we are confronted with the contention of the United States that it cannot obtain a fair and impartial trial before the same Judge because of his personal feelings in the matter. . . .

5. The court's finding on this subject is as follows:

28. It is not possible for the extent of the mental pain and suffering to be separately evaluated as to each individual plaintiff. It is evident that each and all of the plaintiffs sustained mental pain and suffering. Nor is it possible to say that the plaintiffs who lost one or two horses sustained less mental pain and suffering than plaintiffs who lost a dozen horses. The mental pain and suffering sustained was a thing common to all the plaintiffs. It was a community loss and a community sorrow shared by all. On this basis, the Court finds and awards the sum of $3,500.00 to each of the plaintiffs as a fair and reasonable approximation of the mental pain and suffering sustained by each, as a proximate result of the taking of the horses by the defendant.

A casual reading of the two records leaves no room for doubt that the District Judge was incensed and embittered, perhaps understandably so, by the general treatment over a period of years of the plaintiffs and other Indians in southeastern Utah by the government agents and white ranchers in their attempt to force the Indians onto established reservations. This was climaxed by the range clearance program, with instances of brutal handling and slaughter of their livestock, which the Court, during trial, referred to as "horrible," "monstrous," "atrocious," "cruel," "coldblooded depredation," and "without a sense of decency." The Court firmly believed that the Indians were being wrongfully driven from their ancestral homes, and suggested Presidential and Congressional investigations to determine their aboriginal rights. He threatened to conduct such an investigation himself. A public appeal on behalf of the plaintiffs was made for funds and supplies to be cleared through the Judge's chambers. From his obvious interest in the case, illustrated by conduct and statements made throughout the trial, which need not be detailed further, we are certain that the feeling of the presiding Judge is such that, upon retrial, he cannot give the calm, impartial consideration which is necessary for a fair disposition of this unfortunate matter, and he should step aside.

Plaintiffs' claims are asserted under the Federal Tort Claims Act. In applying this Act, everyone should be treated the same. Racial differences merit no concern. Feelings of charity or ideological sympathy for the Indians must be put to one side. The deep concern which the executive and legislative branches of the government should have for the plaintiffs does not justify the court in giving them any better or worse treatment than would be given to anyone else. As Justice Jackson said in his concurring opinion in Northwestern Bands of Shoshone Indians v. United States, 324 U.S. 335, 355: "The Indian problem is essentially a sociological problem, not a legal one. We can make only a pretense of adjudication of such claims, and that only by indulging the most unrealistic and fictional assumptions." . . .

[W]e suggest that when the case is remanded to the District Court, the Judge who entered the judgment take appropriate preliminary steps to the end that further proceedings in the case be had before another Judge.

Reversed and remanded for a new trial as to damages only.

NOTES ON THE BASIC PRINCIPLE

1. *Hatahley*'s rule — that the fundamental principle of damages is to restore the injured party as nearly as possible to the position he would have been in but for the wrong — is the essence of compensatory damages. This chapter is largely devoted to working out the application of that principle: not by exploring every compensatory damage rule, but rather

by illustrating the workings of the basic principle and the most important questions that emerge in its application.

2.   We need a shorter phrase than "the position plaintiff would have been in but for the wrong." One possible alternative is "plaintiff's original position." That phrase is in common use, and I may not have revised it in all the places I used it in earlier drafts of this book. But I have come to think it is misleading. It suggests a position that plaintiff has already occupied. But often, defendant interfered with some improvement in plaintiff's position. Lost earnings are an obvious case. Personal injury defendants are liable for earnings plaintiff would have earned, even though plaintiff never had that money before. A better shorthand is "plaintiff's rightful position" — the position he rightfully would have come to but for defendant's wrong. I will try to use that phrase consistently. I intend "rightful position" to mean exactly the same thing as the more cumbersome "position plaintiff would have been in but for the wrong."

3.   What does it mean to restore plaintiffs to their rightful position? The court cannot resurrect their dead horses, or undo their mental pain. The remedy is to be in dollars, and the court's disagreement with the district judge is over how many dollars and how the number is to be determined. Damage remedies are often described as "substitutionary," because they substitute dollars for what plaintiff lost. Sometimes dollars are exactly what plaintiff lost, as in a suit for lost income. Sometimes dollars can be used to replace what was lost; plaintiffs in *Hatahley* can use their damage award to buy new horses. For losses like these, the substitution is quite direct, and a mandate to restore plaintiffs to their rightful position gives real guidance. What does it mean to restore plaintiffs to their rightful position with respect to mental anguish?

4.   Assuming we know what it means to restore plaintiffs to their rightful position, is it self-evident that that should be the standard? Did the district court purport to apply a different standard? In part, the disagreement between the trial and appellate court is over how precisely damages must be proven and found; the district court would restore plaintiffs to their rightful position, but would use average losses and approximations of loss to determine that position. At times, the court of appeals implies that the district judge thought his task was simply to require the payment of a sum of money that would be fair. Indeed, in the first trial, the judge awarded a lump sum of $100,000, the amount requested in the complaint, without any explanation of how the sum was calculated or how it was allocated among the various elements of damage or among the individual plaintiffs. And at times, the court of appeals implies that the district judge took the complaint about the slaughter of the horses as an occasion to remedy as many as possible of the Navajo's grievances against the United States and the white population of Utah. Is there anything to be said for either of these approaches? Until fairly

modern times, the standard jury instruction on damages was to give a fair or appropriate sum.

5. The traditional argument for restoring plaintiff to his rightful position is based on corrective justice. Plaintiff should not be made to suffer because of wrongdoing, and if we restore plaintiff to his rightful position, he will not suffer. To do less would leave part of the harm unremedied; to do more would confer a windfall gain.

More recently, a quite different justification has been offered for the same rule. Proponents of the economic analysis of law argue that in most contexts, the purpose of law is to maximize the value of conflicting activities. Economists view individual profit as a good proxy for societal value, because a seller or investor can make a profit only by persuading someone else to pay him more for his product, service, or capital than he has spent to produce it. He may do this by taking advantage of his customers or suppliers, but he often does it by conferring on his customers a benefit more valuable than the resources he has used. Economists emphasize the latter source of profits, and conclude that the person who makes the most profit is the one who confers the most benefits on society.

Those who apply this view to law believe that the law should generally encourage profitable activity, even if it is harmful to others, so long as the actor takes account of the harm he inflicts. If the profit from his proposed activity exceeds the costs to be inflicted on others, he should go ahead. In order not to discourage him from doing so, the law should not impose liability in excess of the costs he imposes on his victims. Activity that is profitable even after payment of all the costs it imposes on others is said to be efficient or economical; other activity is inefficient or uneconomical. The law is said to be efficient to the extent it encourages efficient activity and discourages inefficient activity. The most prominent school of law and economics believes that the law should always be efficient, and that judge-made law nearly always is efficient. Other scholars who apply economics to law make less sweeping claims. Some of them are concerned about the distribution of wealth as well as the creation of wealth; still others view economics as simply one tool among many for analyzing legal problems.

The following excerpt summarizes the economic explanation of the compensation principle in the context of negligently caused accidents, but the point is much more general. With respect to accidents, the economic view is that the amount spent on safety precautions should not exceed the costs that would be suffered if the accidents were allowed to happen.

The limitation to compensatory damages in negligence cases is consistent with the economic criterion. . . . If the defendant's liability exceeded the expected accident cost, he might have an incentive to incur prevention costs in excess of the accident cost, and this would be uneconomical. . . .

The association of negligence with purely compensatory damages has prompted the erroneous impression that liability for negligence is intended solely as a device for compensation. Its economic function is different; it is to deter uneconomical accidents. As it happens, the right amount of deterrence is produced by compelling negligent injurers to make good the victim's losses. Were they forced to pay more (punitive damages), some economical accidents might also be deterred; were they permitted to pay less than compensation, some uneconomical accidents would not be deterred. It is thus essential that the defendant be made to pay damages and that they be equal to the plaintiff's loss. But that the damages are paid *to the plaintiff* is, from an economic standpoint, a detail.

R. Posner, Economic Analysis of Law 142-143 (2d ed. 1977).

In a footnote, Judge Posner says that payment to the plaintiff is an *important* detail, but not for the traditional reasons. He thinks victims should be compensated because this helps produce the right level of enforcement activity, and because if potential victims knew they would not be compensated, they would take excessive safety precautions of their own to avoid being injured.

6.   Is it a detail from a legal standpoint that the damages are paid to the victim? From the perspective of justice? In the minds of voters who elect legislators and judges to create and enforce rules of law?

B.   DEFINING THE RIGHTFUL POSITION: RELIANCE OR EXPECTANCY?

NERI v. RETAIL MARINE CORP.
30 N.Y.2d 393, 285 N.E.2d 311 (1972)

GIBSON, Judge.

The appeal concerns the right of a retail dealer to recover loss of profits and incidental damages upon the buyer's repudiation of a contract governed by the Uniform Commercial Code. This is, indeed, the correct measure of damage in an appropriate case and to this extent the code (§2-708, subsection [2]) effected a substantial change from prior law, whereby damages were ordinarily limited to "the difference between the contract price and the market or current price." . . .

The plaintiffs contracted to purchase from defendant a new boat of a specified model for the price of $12,587.40, against which they made a deposit of $40. They shortly increased the deposit to $4,250 in consideration of the defendant dealer's agreement to arrange with the manufacturer for immediate delivery on the basis of "a firm sale," instead of the delivery within approximately four to six weeks originally specified. Some six days after the date of the contract plaintiffs' lawyer sent to defendant a letter rescinding the sales contract for the reason that plaintiff Neri was about to undergo hospitalization and surgery, in consequence of which, according to the letter, it would be "impossible for Mr. Neri to make any payments." The boat had already been ordered from the manufacturer and was delivered to defendant at or before the time the attorney's letter was received. Defendant declined to refund plaintiffs' deposit and this action to recover it was commenced. Defendant counterclaimed, alleging plaintiffs' breach of the contract and defendant's resultant damage in the amount of $4,250, for which sum defendant demanded judgment. Upon motion, defendant had summary judgment on the issue of liability tendered by its counterclaim; and Special Term directed an assessment of damages, upon which it would be determined whether plaintiffs were entitled to the return of any portion of their down payment.

Upon the trial so directed, it was shown that the boat ordered and received by defendant in accordance with plaintiffs' contract of purchase was sold some four months later to another buyer for the same price as that negotiated with plaintiffs. From this proof the plaintiffs argue that defendant's loss on its contract was recouped, while defendant argues that but for plaintiffs' default, it would have sold two boats and have earned two profits instead of one. Defendant proved, without contradiction, that its profit on the sale under the contract in suit would have been $2,579 and that during the period the boat remained unsold incidental expenses aggregating $674 for storage, upkeep, finance charges and insurance were incurred. . . .

The issue is governed in the first instance by section 2-718 of the Uniform Commercial Code which provides, among other things, that the buyer, despite his breach, may have restitution of the amount by which his payment exceeds: (a) reasonable liquidated damages stipulated by the contract or (b) absent such stipulation, 20% of the value of the buyer's total performance or $500, whichever is smaller (§2-718, subsection [2], pars. [a], [b]). As above noted, the trial court awarded defendant an offset in the amount of $500 under paragraph (b) and directed restitution to plaintiffs of the balance. Section 2-718, however, establishes, in paragraph (a) of subsection (3), an alternative right of offset in favor of the seller, as follows:

> (3) The buyer's right to restitution under subsection (2) is subject to offset to the extent that the seller establishes (a) a right to recover damages under the provisions of this Article other than subsection (1).

Among "the provisions of this Article other than subsection (1)" are those to be found in section 2-708, which the courts below did not apply. Subsection (1) of that section provides that the measure of damages for non-acceptance or repudiation by the buyer is the difference between the market price at the time and place for tender and the unpaid contract price together with any incidental damages provided in this Article (Section 2-710), but less expenses saved in consequence of the buyer's breach.

However, this provision is made expressly subject to subsection (2), providing:

(2) If the measure of damages provided in subsection (1) is inadequate to put the seller in as good a position as performance would have done then the measure of damages is the profit (including reasonable overhead) which the seller would have made from full performance by the buyer, together with any incidental damages provided in this Article (Section 2-710), due allowance for costs reasonably incurred and due credit for payments or proceeds of resale. . . .

The conclusion is clear from the record — indeed with mathematical certainty — that "the measure of damages provided in subsection (1) is inadequate to put the seller in as good a position as performance would have done" (Uniform Commercial Code, §2-708, subsection [2]) and hence — again under subsection (2) — that the seller is entitled to its "profit (including reasonable overhead) . . . together with any incidental damages . . . , due allowance for costs reasonably incurred and due credit for payments or proceeds of resale."

It is evident, first, that this retail seller is entitled to its profit and, second, that the last sentence of subsection (2), as hereinbefore quoted, referring to "due credit for payments or proceeds of resale" is inapplicable to this retail sales contract.[2] Closely parallel to the factual situation now before us is that hypothesized by Dean Hawkland as illustrative of the operation of the rules:

Thus, if a private party agrees to sell his automobile to a buyer for $2,000, a breach by the buyer would cause the seller no loss (except incidental damages, i.e., expense of a new sale) if the seller was able to sell the automobile to

2. The concluding clause, "due credit for payments or proceeds of resale," is intended to refer to "the privilege of the seller to realize junk value when it is manifestly useless to complete the operation of manufacture" (Supp. No. 1 to the 1952 Official Draft of Text and Comments of the Uniform Commercial Code, as Amended by the Action of the American Law Institute of the National Conference of Commissioners on Uniform Laws [1954], p. 14). The commentators who have considered the language have uniformly concluded that "the reference is to a resale as scrap under . . . Section 2-704" (1956 Report of N.Y. Law Rev. Comm., p.397; 1 Willier and Hart, Bender's Uniform Commercial Code Service, §2-708, pp. 1-180–1-181). Another writer, reaching the same conclusion, after detailing the history of the clause, says that "'proceeds of resale' previously meant the resale value of the goods in finished form; now it means the resale value of the components on hand at the time plaintiff learns of breach" (Harris, Seller's Damages, 18 Stanf. L. Rev. 66, 104).

another buyer for $2000. But the situation is different with dealers having an unlimited supply of standard-priced goods. Thus, if an automobile dealer agrees to sell a car to a buyer at the standard price of $2000, a breach by the buyer injures the dealer, even though he is able to sell the automobile to another for $2000. If the dealer has an inexhaustible supply of cars, the resale to replace the breaching buyer costs the dealer a sale, because, had the breaching buyer performed, the dealer would have made two sales instead of one. The buyer's breach, in such a case, depletes the dealer's sales to the extent of one, and the measure of damages should be the dealer's profit on one sale. Section 2-708 recognizes this, and it rejects the rule developed under the Uniform Sales Act by many courts that the profit cannot be recovered in this case.

Can go the other way too, I think.

(Hawkland, Sales and Bulk Sales [1958 ed.], pp. 153-154.)

The record which in this case establishes defendant's entitlement to damages in the amount of its prospective profit, at the same time confirms defendant's cognate right to "any incidental damages provided in this Article (Section 2-710)"[3] (Uniform Commercial Code, §2-708, subsection [2]). From the language employed it is too clear to require discussion that the seller's right to recover loss of profits is not exclusive and that he may recoup his "incidental" expenses as well. Although the trial court's denial of incidental damages in the uncontroverted amount of $674 was made in the context of its erroneous conclusion that paragraph (b) of subsection (2) of section 2-718 was applicable and was "adequate . . . to place the sellers in as good a position as performance would have done," the denial seems not to have rested entirely on the court's mistaken application of the law, as there was an explicit finding "that defendant completely failed to show that it suffered any incidental damages." We find no basis for the court's conclusion with respect to a deficiency of proof inasmuch as the proper items of the $674 expenses (being for storage, upkeep, finance charges and insurance for the period between the date performance was due and the time of the resale) were proven without objection and were in no way controverted, impeached or otherwise challenged, at the trial or on appeal. . . .

It follows that plaintiffs are entitled to restitution of the sum of $4,250 paid by them on account of the contract price less an offset to defendant in the amount of $3,253 on account of its lost profit of $2,579 and its incidental damages of $674. . . .

---

3. "Incidental damages to an aggrieved seller include any commercially reasonable charges, expenses or commissions incurred in stopping delivery, in the transportation, care and custody of goods after the buyer's breach, in connection with return or resale of the goods or otherwise resulting from the breach." (Uniform Commercial Code, §2-710).

FULD, C.J., and BURKE, SCILEPPI, BERGAN, BREITEL and JASEN, JJ., concur.

Ordered accordingly.

NOTES ON §2-708(2) AND ATTEMPTS TO CODIFY REMEDIES

1.   It is plain that the court's award of lost profits plus incidental damage is necessary to put Retail Marine in the position it would have been in had the contract been performed. It is also relatively clear that the framers of the Uniform Commercial Code intended this remedy for the volume seller. But it is almost impossible to get that result from the statute, which is astonishingly badly drafted. Why so astonishing?

2.   Are you persuaded by the court's efforts to explain away the last clause of §2-708(2)? A credit for the proceeds of resale makes perfect sense when a seller undertakes to make or procure specially ordered goods and the buyer repudiates. The seller has goods he would never have had but for the special order, and any resale is a sale he would not have made but for the special order followed by the repudiation. But is §2-708(2) needed in that case? Isn't the seller fully compensated under §2-708(1) or §2-706?

In *Neri*, a credit for the proceeds of resale renders §2-708(2) absurd and futile. Subsection 2 does not come into effect at all unless subsection 1 is "inadequate to put the seller in as good a position as performance would have done." Subsection 1 does not put the seller in that position on these facts, because the market price is equal to the contract price and that measure of damages does not allow for the fact that seller could have made two sales instead of one. It is absurd for subsection 2 to come into effect because of that inadequate result and then yield the identical result. The resale price is also equal to the contract price, and crediting plaintiff for proceeds of resale leaves seller in exactly the same inadequate position. Does it help to note that plaintiff is entitled only to "due credit" for proceeds of resale? That leaves to the court the power to decide how much credit is due on any set of facts.

No such argument can avoid the central problem: In the cases where the "due credit for proceeds of resale" clause makes sense, it never comes into effect; in cases where it comes into effect, it makes no sense. Are courts free to never apply part of a statute that seems to be a mistake? Compare United States v. Finn, 502 F.2d 938 (7th Cir. 1974), where the court convincingly concluded that Congress had inserted an extra negative, so that the statute was intended to mean exactly the opposite of what it said.

3.   Would the UCC drafters have done better to enact a general damages principle instead of detailed damages rules? How about, "The

amount of damages shall be that sum necessary to put the plaintiff in as good a position as if the defendant had fully performed." Won't there always be unforeseen situations in which detailed rules designed to implement such a principle fail to do so?

NOTES ON PROTECTING EXPECTANCIES

1.   As you undoubtedly learned in first-year contracts, the victim of a breach of contract is entitled to recover the profits he would have earned if the contract had been performed. But it is not obvious that that should be the remedy. If the Neris paid Retail Marine its $674 in incidental expenses, it would be as well off as if the contract had never been made. Awarding expected profits involves a choice. In remedies terms, the question is what we mean by rightful position: the position plaintiff occupied before he made the contract, or the position he would have occupied if the contract had been performed? This section asks why contract damages try to put plaintiff in the position defendant would have put him in instead of the position he would have occupied on his own, whether that is true only in contract, and if so, what is so special about contract.

2.   There is a third option. We could try to restore *defendant* to the position *defendant* occupied before the contract. The general principle of *Hatahley* commits us to a focus on the plaintiff's position, at least if he seeks compensatory damages. But plaintiff has the option of focusing on defendant's position, and that option is sometimes quite attractive. All three measures of recovery are recognized in the Second Restatement of Contracts. These three recoveries are based on three distinct interests first clearly identified in an extraordinarily influential article. It is helpful to begin by reviewing those three interests.

FULLER AND PERDUE, THE RELIANCE INTEREST IN CONTRACT DAMAGES
46 Yale L.J. 52, 53-56, 73-75 (1936)

It is convenient to distinguish three principal purposes which may be pursued in awarding contract damages. These purposes, and the situations in which they become appropriate, may be stated briefly as follows:

First, the plaintiff has in reliance on the promise of the defendant conferred some value on the defendant. The defendant fails to perform his promise. The court may force the defendant to disgorge the value he received from the plaintiff. The object here may be termed the prevention of gain by the defaulting promisor at the expense of the promisee; more briefly, the prevention of unjust enrichment. The interest protected may be called the *restitution interest*. . . .

Secondly, the plaintiff has in reliance on the promise of the defendant changed his position. For example, the buyer under a contract for the sale of land has incurred expense in the investigation of the seller's title, or has neglected the opportunity to enter other contracts. We may award damages to the plaintiff for the purpose of undoing the harm which his reliance on the defendant's promise has caused him. Our object is to put him in as good a position as he was in before the promise was made. The interest protected in this case may be called the *reliance interest.*

Thirdly, without insisting on reliance by the promisee or enrichment of the promisor, we may seek to give the promisee the value of the expectancy which the promise created. We may in a suit for specific performance actually compel the defendant to render the promised performance to the plaintiff, or, in a suit for damages, we may make the defendant pay the money value of this performance. Here our object is to put the plaintiff in as good a position as he would have occupied had the defendant performed his promise. The interest protected in this case we may call the *expectation interest.* . . .

If . . . the gain involved in the restitution interest results from and is identical with the plaintiff's loss through reliance, then the restitution interest is merely a special case of the reliance interest; all of the cases coming under the restitution interest will be covered by the reliance interest, and the reliance interest will be broader than the restitution interest only to the extent that it includes cases where the plaintiff has relied on the defendant's promise without enriching the defendant.

It should not be supposed that the distinction here taken between the reliance and expectation interests coincides with that sometimes taken between "losses caused" . . . and "gains prevented." . . . In the first place, though reliance ordinarily results in "losses" of an affirmative nature (expenditures of labor and money) it is also true that opportunities for gain may be foregone in reliance on a promise. Hence the reliance interest must be interpreted as at least potentially covering "gains prevented" as well as "losses caused." . . . On the other hand, it is not possible to make the expectation interest entirely synonymous with "gains prevented." The disappointment of an expectancy often entails losses of a positive character. . . .

In distinguishing between the reliance and the expectation interests we encounter . . . a miscellaneous group of cases which seem equally happy in either category. These two interests will furnish identical, or nearly identical, measures of recovery in at least three kinds of cases.

First, where the plaintiff's reliance takes the form of acts essential to the enforcement of the contract by him (such as partial performance of the contract or necessary preparations to perform) and the defendant breaks or repudiates the contract before complete performance has taken place, it is possible to classify the plaintiff's suit as resting either on the expectation interest alone, or on a combination of the expectation and reliance interests. If a building contractor has finished half the structure when the property owner puts an end to the contract the contractor's declaration may list two items of damage: (1) expenditures actually made in performing or preparing to perform, and (2) the profit which he would have made on the whole contract. This looks like a combination of the reliance and the expectation interests, and it will necessarily be so analyzed if we restrict the scope of the expectation interest to what may be called the net expectancy, in other words, if we make "the expectation interest" and "the lost profit" synonymous. But in cases where the plaintiff has undertaken performance or preparations to perform a profitable contract before the defendant's breach it involves no distortion to say that the plaintiff's expectancy is really twofold and includes (1) reimbursement for what has been done, and (2) a profit in addition. This broader expectancy we may call the _gross expectation interest._ Using this broader concept the contractor's suit in the case supposed will appear to be founded entirely on the expectation interest. The possibility of subsuming a recovery for the value of part performance under the expectation interest is indicated by the fact that it is possible to state, entirely in terms of the expectancy, measures of recovery which would, if all the relevant data were available, yield the same sum as the formula measuring recovery by the reasonable value of what has been done plus the profit. Examples of such measures would be: (a) payment for work done at the contract rate, plus the profit lost on the unperformed portion of the contract, (b) the full contract price less the cost of completion.

Secondly, where the reliance interest is conceived to embrace the loss of the opportunity to enter similar contracts with other persons, the reliance and expectation interests will have a tendency to approach one another, the precise degree of their correspondence depending upon the extent to which other opportunities of a similar nature were open to the plaintiff when he entered the contract on which suit is brought. The physician who by making one appointment deprives himself of the opportunity of making a precisely similar appointment with another patient presents a case of a complete correspondence between the reliance and expectation interests. The tendency of the expectation and reliance interests to coalesce in cases of this sort has the consequence that the same item of damages may often be classified under either heading. Thus where the defendant's breach of contract results in the plaintiff's property remaining idle for a period, the courts in awarding the plaintiff the rental value of the premises have sometimes considered that they were granting reimbursement for the loss of the opportunity to employ the property for other purposes (the reliance interest), and sometimes that they were granting compensation for the loss of the profits which would have been made had the defendant performed his promise (expectation interest).

Thirdly, the reliance and the expectation interests will coincide in those cases where the breach of a contract results not simply in the loss of the promised value but in some direct harm. A farmer buys a cow warranted to be free from disease. The cow is in fact diseased and contaminates the purchaser's whole herd. So far as the item of direct loss is concerned (the contamination of the herd) it is not possible to draw a distinction between the reliance and the expectation interests. This loss would not have occurred either if the defendant had not broken his contract, or if the plaintiff had not entered and relied on the contract.

MORE NOTES ON PROTECTING EXPECTANCIES

1. Fuller and Perdue recognize that reliance losses may include gains forgone, and that reliance losses may often equal expectancy losses. But reliance of this sort is difficult to prove. There has been a tendency to think of the reliance interest as the interest in recovering out-of-pocket losses, and of the expectancy interest as the interest in receiving the benefit of the bargain. Thus, most lawyers would call Retail Marine's $674 in expenses its reliance loss, and the $2,579 in lost profits its expectancy loss. This usage has practical benefits, even though Fuller and Perdue used the terms in a more sophisticated way.

The tendency of the reliance and expectancy interests to converge when pushed to their limits means that the distinction is useful primarily for focusing attention on whether plaintiff should be allowed to recover profits that he expected only because of the defendant's promise or representation. Once that question has been answered in the affirmative, the distinction is not very useful in actually calculating damages. It is far more important, and generally easier, to be sure that each element of loss is counted once and only once than to characterize each element of loss as reliance or expectancy damages.

But sometimes the expectancy cannot be recovered. One example is promissory estoppel, where plaintiff recovers what he lost by relying on a promise that turns out not to be an enforceable contract. Recovery usually is limited to reliance losses. In that situation, it becomes critical to distinguish reliance from expectancy.

2. _Neri_ also illustrates the restitution interest. The Neris partly performed their side of the contract when they paid the $4,250 deposit. That deposit made Retail Marine $4,250 better off. Their subsequent breach inflicted $3,253 damage on Retail Marine, but the court says they are still entitled to restitution of the difference — $997. We will consider the restitution interest much more extensively in chapter 6.

3. We still haven't decided why Retail Marine's damages are $3,253 instead of $674. That is, why does the law protect expectancies? The rule is well settled, but it is not entirely uncontroversial, and its applications

around the edges are not perfectly clear. We will consider the rationale for the basic rule first, and then some of the marginal applications.

4. Professor Atiyah believes that the expectancy remedy is largely unjustified and in decline. Just before the excerpt that follows, Atiyah has discussed two kinds of contract liability. "Benefit-based" liabilities are based on payment to the defendant, or some other benefit conferred on the defendant, and correspond to the Restatement's "restitution interest." "Reliance-based" liabilities are based on plaintiff's reliance on defendant's promise and correspond to the Restatement's "reliance interest."

P. ATIYAH, THE RISE AND FALL OF FREEDOM OF CONTRACT
2-5, 756-757, 759-763 (1979)

The third situation concerns a promise or a contract which has not been paid for, and which has not yet been relied upon. In the law such a contract or promise would be called "wholly executory." If such a promise or contract generates any liability, the liability must be promise-based, since it cannot be benefit-based or reliance-based. In the first two cases, distinct grounds exist for imposing the liability, apart altogether from the promise. In this case, no such distinct grounds exist. If the promise is held to be 'binding' or to create some liability, it must be for some reason which is inherent in the promise itself. . . . First, it may be said that a promise, even while executory, creates expectations, and that these expectations will be disappointed if the promise is not performed. In this sense, there is a similarity between a promise-based and a reliance-based liability. The promisee whose expectations are disappointed may feel he is worse off than he would have been if no promise had been made at all. Psychologically this may be true; but in a pecuniary sense, it is not. . . .

Secondly, it may be said that contracts and promises are essentially risk-allocation devices, like simple bets. The nature of this device is such that the transaction must generally remain executory prior to the occurrence of the risk, and the whole point of the transaction would be lost if the arrangement could not be made binding for the future.

The third possible ground for the enforcement of executory promises or contracts is that it may be desirable to uphold the *principle* of promissory liability, even in cases where the non-performance of the promise has little practical effect. The argument here comes to this, that if executory promises are held binding (whether in law or in social custom and morality) then people are more likely to perform promises which have been paid for, or relied upon. . . .

The protection of mere expectations cannot . . . rank equally with the protection of restitution interests (arising from benefit-based liability) or reliance interests (arising from reliance-based liability). A person whose expectations are disappointed, but who suffers no pecuniary or other loss from the failure to perform a promise, has surely a relatively weak claim for complaint or redress. No doubt if there is *no* excuse or justification at all for the failure to perform the promise or contract, the promisee may be felt entitled to some redress, but even then it does not follow that he should be entitled to demand full performance of the promise, or redress based on such an entitlement. Frequently, a promise-based claim is based on relatively short-lived expectations; for it is where the promisor has (for instance) made some mistake, or overlooked some fact, that he is most likely to attempt to withdraw a promise. Where the promisor does not do this, the probability is that some action in reliance (or some payment) will soon be performed by the promisee, and he can then claim the much greater protection due to reliance interests or restitution interests. . . .

Pure risk-allocation contracts are relatively rare, and it may be that special considerations do apply to them. . . . [E]ven in contracts of this nature an element of reliance is still needed before it becomes essential to maintain the integrity of the transaction. Even an executory insurance arrangement, for instance, could be made cancellable so long as the insured still has time to find alternative cover. . . .

The third ground for the creation of promise-based liabilities is also . . . very weak. . . . There are . . . great difficulties in arguing that promise-based liabilities should be observed even though there is no independent justification for their observance, in order that reliance-based and benefit-based obligations should be better observed. . . .

[T]here has been . . . a decline in the power of the executory contract, a growing belief that there is an important difference between a present and a future consent, a growing recognition that the opportunity to change one's mind is itself a valuable right which often outweighs the desirability of holding parties bound to some future arrangement. In the case of consumer contracts, at least, the evidence of this shift of opinion is quite striking, and has actually led to amendments of the law. In the Hire Purchase Act of 1964 provision was first made for a "cooling-off" period in certain limited circumstances, that is, where orders are obtained by door-to-door salesmen, and these provisions have been much extended by the Consumer Credit Act. But in actual practice, as opposed to law, the true position today appears to be that wholly executory consumer contracts are not in fact held binding on the consumer unless there is some specific agreement to the contrary, as for example, where an agreement provides that it is "non-cancellable." Generally speaking consumers today expect to have the right to cancel agreements, and while they are still wholly executory, such cancellation rights are almost invariably conceded. In some cases, extra-legal arrangements have been made which formalize (and limit) the right of cancellation. For instance, members of the British Travel Agents Association permit cancellation of holiday bookings up to six weeks before departure on forfeiture of any deposit paid. Thereafter, an increasing proportion of the price is levied, as the time of cancellation approaches the departure date. . . .

Airlines . . . are very tolerant of last-minute cancellations, or even of a simple failure to appear. Hotels rarely expect to charge anything, except perhaps for last-minute cancellations where a room may be vacant as a result. Thus they expect to be protected against reliance losses (that is, the loss of the opportunity to let the room to some other person) but not against bare expectation losses (that is, the loss whether or not they could have let the room again). . . .

Even when we turn to examine commercial arrangements, as opposed to consumer transactions, there are signs of the waning force of the executory contract. Certainly, there is evidence that in practice, businessmen, almost as much as consumers, often expect to have some sort of right to cancel executory contracts. Empirical studies, both in the United States, and in England, suggest that businessmen usually expect, and are usually conceded, the right to cancel orders for goods prior to any expenditure by the seller; and even after such expenditure, cancellation is often permitted subject to payment of the costs incurred by the seller. In other words, reliance interests are protected but bare expectations are not. . . .

It may well be that decisions of this character often reflect the real understanding of contracting parties more accurately than the classical model of the executory contract. It is clear that in many situations contracting parties, particularly, but not exclusively, consumers, do not regard a contract as involving mutual promises. The legal analysis of an agreement as one in which the parties both *promise* to carry out their part is often the invention of the Courts rather than the inevitable meaning of the arrangement. Parties often "agree" on the terms of a transaction, meaning thereby that, if and in so far as the transaction is carried out, the terms governing the performance will be those which they have agreed; such an agreement does not necessarily imply that the parties mean to commit themselves not to change their minds. This is, perhaps, particularly obvious in cases of long-term or continuing relationships. . . . The terms of a continuing arrangement may well amount to an agreement that, so long as the relation subsists, it is to be on the terms agreed; but the agreement does not necessarily carry an implication that [it] is to be permanent. Generally speaking, it is now held that, in the absence of express provision to the contrary, such continuing contracts are terminable, either at will, or on reasonable notice. . . .

Before leaving this topic, something should be said about the relationship between executory contracts and the protection of expectations. I have been at pains to stress that where a wholly executory contract is enforced by the Courts — no performance, no benefit, and no reliance having taken place — the Court is protecting a bare expectation. It is commonly said that one of the primary differences between the law of damages in contract and in tort is that expectation damages are only awarded in contract. . . .

The truth is that expectations are becoming more and more divorced from promises. On the one hand, certain expectations are today accorded greater recognition, because they are more powerfully held. These expectations do not necessarily arise from promises, still less from contract. They arise from the modern way of life. For example, expectations with regard to future employment and earnings are amongst the best protected of all expectations in modern times. The nature of the society in which we live means that many people tend to have very powerful expectations about their future earnings, and anything which interrupts those earnings is likely to cause serious disappointment, and even dislocation. But these expectations are not protected merely as a matter of contract. Even in tort law, damages for future earnings are awarded as a matter of everyday practice in personal injury actions; and such damages do not merely take account of what the plaintiff was earning when injured, but also what he might reasonably have expected to earn in the future (inflation apart). It is difficult to understand how the common idea has grown up that expectation damages cannot be awarded in a tort action. . . .

What it comes to, then, is that it is no longer possible to tie the protection of expectations so closely to contractual rights. Bare expectations, arising under executory contracts, may be less well protected; other expectations, not based on contracts or promises at all, may be better protected. Nevertheless, it remains true in current law that, generally speaking, expectations are the basis of the damages which will be awarded for breach of contract where such liability does exist. Even where there has been some element of reliance, or some benefit rendered, and where it might have been thought that the damages would be confined to the element of reliance or the value of the benefit, this is not generally the case. Doubtless, there are arguments for maintaining the traditional principle here, though it might be better to recognize them frankly for what they are. Frequently, the best justification for awarding such expectation damages is not that the plaintiff's expectations in fact deserve such handsome protection, but that proof of the losses flowing from reliance would be too difficult or costly, and that if the damages are excessive by way of compensation, then this is a deserved penalty on the defendant anyhow. But in view of the declining belief in the idea that the law should actually deter parties from breaking their contracts, it would not be surprising if future developments tend to show a still further whittling down of expectation damages. Only in cases where expectations tend already to be so powerful that the demand for their protection is overwhelming, as in the case of employment expectations, is it likely that there will be any increase in the protection afforded by the law.

STILL MORE NOTES ON PROTECTING EXPECTANCIES

1.   Does Professor Atiyah document a declining belief in contractual expectancy, a declining belief in contract generally, or merely a widespread business practice of promoting goodwill by not insisting on performance by customers? The right to cancel is often not dependent on whether there has been reliance. Consumers are often permitted to cancel even after performance, by returning the goods for a refund, and sellers do not collect the cost of preparing or packaging the goods for resale. Airlines' tolerance for cancellations and no-shows does not depend on whether other passengers have been turned away; the airlines protect themselves by overbooking, with the result that they sometimes turn away passengers who relied on "confirmed" reservations. Those passengers are offered rough and ready compensation. If there is a general casualness toward contractual obligation, does that help us decide what the remedy should be when contracts are enforced?

2.   Consider Atiyah's puzzlement about the notion that expectancies could not be recovered in tort. As he notes, lost wages are regularly recovered in tort, and this is certainly recovery of an expectancy. Lost profits are another example. But there is an important difference between the tort cases and the contract cases. In the contract cases, plaintiff is seeking to recover an expectancy that is itself a product of defendant's promise — an expectancy that never would have existed but for the defendant. In the typical tort case, plaintiff's expectancy is not derived from defendant. Plaintiff expected profits or earnings from his own efforts, and defendant interfered to defeat that expectancy. In that context, there can be no doubt that full compensation requires defendant to restore plaintiff's expectancy. The argument about expectancy versus reliance arises only when plaintiff seeks to collect on an expectancy that would never have existed at all but for the defendant's promise. That argument typically arises in contract cases, but as we shall see, it can arise in torts such as fraud and misrepresentation, where the tort is in the nature of a promise.

3.   The best defense of giving plaintiff an expectancy created by defendant is still Fuller and Perdue's. They concede that plaintiff's claim to his expectancy is weaker than his claim to restitution or reliance damages, and they comment that giving plaintiff "something he never had . . . seems on the face of things a queer kind of 'compensation.'" 46 Yale

L.J. at 53. But they ultimately conclude that such compensation is justified.

FULLER AND PERDUE, THE RELIANCE INTEREST IN CONTRACT DAMAGES
46 Yale L.J. 52, 57-63 (1936)

Why Should the Law Ever Protect the Expectation Interest?

Perhaps the most obvious answer to this question is one which we may label "psychological." This answer would run something as follows: The breach of a promise arouses in the promisee a sense of injury. This feeling is not confined to cases where the promisee has relied on the promise. Whether or not he has actually changed his position because of the promise, the promisee has formed an attitude of expectancy such that a breach of the promise causes him to feel that he has been "deprived" of something which was "his." Since this sentiment is a relatively uniform one, the law has no occasion to go back of it. It accepts it as a datum and builds its rule about it.

The difficulty with this explanation is that the law does in fact go back of the sense of injury which the breach of a promise engenders. No legal system attempts to invest with juristic sanction all promises. Some rule or combination of rules effects a sifting out for enforcement of those promises deemed important enough to society to justify the law's concern with them. Whatever the principles which control this sifting out process may be, they are not convertible into terms of the degree of resentment which the breach of a particular kind of promise arouses. Therefore, though it may be assumed that the impulse to assuage disappointment is one shared by those who make and influence the law, this impulse can hardly be regarded as the key which solves the whole problem of the protection accorded by the law to the expectation interest. . . .

[Another] solution of our difficulty lies in an economic or institutional approach. The essence of a credit economy lies in the fact that it tends to eliminate the distinction between present and future (promised) goods. Expectations of future values become, for purposes of trade, present values. In a society in which credit has become a significant and pervasive institution, it is inevitable that the expectancy created by an enforceable promise should be regarded as a kind of property, and breach of the promise as an injury to that property. In such a society the breach of a promise works an "actual" diminution of the promisee's assets — "actual" in the sense that it would be so appraised according to modes of thought which enter into the very fibre of our economic system. That the promisee had not "used" the property which the promise represents (had not

relied on the promise) is as immaterial as the question whether the plaintiff in trespass . . . was using his property at the time it was encroached
upon. . . .

The most obvious objection which can be made to the economic or
institutional explanation is that is involves a *petitio principii* [that is, it
begs the question]. A promise has present value, why? Because the law
enforces it. "The expectancy," regarded as a present value, is not the
cause of legal intervention but the consequence of it. . . . Promises were
enforced long before there was anything corresponding to a general system of "credit," and recovery was from the beginning measured by the
value of the promised performance, the "agreed price." It may therefore
be argued that the "credit system" when it finally emerged was itself in
large part built on the foundations of a juristic development which preceded it.

The view just suggested asserts the primacy of law over economics; it
sees law not as the creature but as the creator of social institutions. The
shift of emphasis thus implied suggests the possibility of [another] explanation for the law's protection of the unrelied-on expectancy, which we
may call *juristic*. This explanation would seek a justification for the normal rule of recovery in some policy consciously pursued by courts and
other lawmakers. . . .

What reasons can be advanced? In the first place, even if our interest
were confined to protecting promisees against an out-of-pocket loss, it
would still be possible to justify the rule granting the value of the expectancy, both as a cure for, and as a prophylaxis against, losses of this sort.

It is a cure for these losses in the sense that it offers the measure of
recovery most likely to reimburse the plaintiff for the (often very numerous and very difficult to prove) individual acts and forbearances which
make up his total reliance on the contract. If we take into account "gains
prevented" by reliance, that is, losses involved in foregoing the opportunity to enter other contracts, the notion that the rule protecting the
expectancy is adopted as the most effective means of compensating for
detrimental reliance seems not at all far-fetched. Physicians with an extensive practice often charge their patients the full office call fee for
broken appointments. Such a charge looks on the face of things like a
claim to the promised fee; it seems to be based on the expectation interest. Yet the physician making the charge will quite justifiably regard it as
compensation for the loss of the opportunity to gain a similar fee from a
different patient. This foregoing of other opportunities is involved to
some extent in entering most contracts, and the impossibility of subjecting this type of reliance to any kind of measurement may justify a categorical rule granting the value of the expectancy as the most effective way of
compensating for such losses. . . .

The rule measuring damages by the expectancy may also be regarded
as a prophylaxis against the losses resulting from detrimental reliance.

Whatever tends to discourage breach of contract tends to prevent the losses occasioned through reliance. Since the expectation interest furnishes a more easily administered measure of recovery than the reliance interest, it will in practice offer a more effective sanction against contract breach. It is therefore possible to view the rule measuring damages by the expectancy in a quasi-criminal aspect, its purpose being not so much to compensate the promisee as to penalize breach of promise by the promisor. The rule enforcing the unrelied-on promise finds the same justification, on this theory, as an ordinance which fines a man for driving through a stop-light when no other vehicle is in sight. . . .

There is . . . also a policy in favor of promoting and facilitating reliance on business agreements. As in the case of the stop-light ordinance we are interested not only in preventing collisions but in speeding traffic. Agreements can accomplish little, either for their makers or for society, unless they are made the basis for action. When business agreements are not only made but are also acted on, the division of labor is facilitated, goods find their way to the places where they are most needed, and economic activity is generally stimulated. These advantages would be threatened by any rule which limited legal protection to the reliance interest. Such a rule would in practice tend to discourage reliance. The difficulties in proving reliance and subjecting it to pecuniary measurement are such that the business man knowing, or sensing, that these obstacles stood in the way of judicial relief would hesitate to rely on a promise in any case where the legal sanction was of significance to him. To encourage reliance we must therefore dispense with its proof. . . .

The juristic explanation in its final form is then twofold. It rests the protection accorded the expectancy on (1) the need for curing and preventing the harms occasioned by reliance, and (2) on the need for facilitating reliance on business agreements. From this spelling out of a possible juristic explanation, it is clear that there is no incompatibility between it and the economic or institutional explanation. They view the same phenomenon from two different aspects. The essence of both of them lies in the word "credit." The economic explanation views credit from its institutional side; the juristic explanation views it from its rational side. The economic view sees credit as an accepted way of living; the juristic view invites us to explore the considerations of utility which underlie this way of living, and the part which conscious human direction has played in bringing it into being.

The way in which these two points of view supplement one another becomes clearer when we examine separately the economic implications of the two aspects of the juristic explanation. If we rest the legal argument for measuring damages by the expectancy on the ground that this procedure offers the most satisfactory means of compensating the plaintiff for the loss of other opportunities to contract, it is clear that the force of the argument will depend entirely upon the existing economic environment.

It would be most forceful in a hypothetical society in which all values were available on the market and where all markets were "perfect" in the economic sense. In such a society there would be no difference between the reliance interest and the expectation interest. The plaintiff's loss in foregoing to enter another contract would be identical with the expectation value of the contract he did make. The argument that granting the value of the expectancy merely compensates for that loss, loses force to the extent that actual conditions depart from those of such a hypothetical. These observations make it clear why the development of open markets for goods tends to carry in its wake the view that a contract claim is a kind of property. . . . He who by entering the contract passes by the opportunity to accomplish the same end elsewhere will not be inclined to regard contract breach lightly or as a mere matter of private morality. The consciousness of what is foregone reinforces the notion that the contract creates a "right" and that the contract claim is itself a species of property.

If, on the other hand, we found the juristic explanation on the desire to promote reliance on contracts, it is not difficult again to trace a correspondence between the legal view and the actual conditions of economic life. In general our courts and our economic institutions attribute special significance to the same types of promises. . . .

The inference is therefore justified that the ends of the law of contracts and those of our economic system show an essential correspondence. One may explain this either on the ground that the law (mere superstructure and ideology) reflects inertly the conditions of economic life, or on the ground that economic activity has fitted itself into a rational framework of the law. Neither explanation would be true. . . . The law measures damages by the expectancy *in part* because society views the expectancy as a present value; society views the expectancy as a present value *in part* because the law . . . gives protection to the expectancy.

ONE MORE VIEW OF WHY WE PROTECT EXPECTANCIES: NOTE ON EFFICIENT BREACH

Judge Posner finds it obvious why the law enforces expectancies. Recall the economic view that profitable violations of law should be encouraged as long as violators compensate their victims. In contract, this view leads to the concept of "efficient breach." To an economist, the purpose of contract is to move resources to more valuable uses. A contract to sell a machine for $100,000 indicates that the buyer values the machine more than the money, and the seller values the money more than the machine. It follows that the machine is more valuable in the buyer's hands. But circumstances may change; the seller may find an even more valuable use for the machine, or for the resources he would use to build it. If he can breach and come out ahead even after paying the buyer's damages, the breach is said to be efficient. Judge Posner argues that the only way to encourage efficient breaches and discourage inefficient breaches is to base damages on plaintiff's lost expectancy:

> Suppose A contracts to sell B for $100,000 a machine that is worth $110,000 to B, i.e., that would yield him a profit of $10,000. Before delivery C comes to A and offers him $109,000 for the machine promised B. A would be tempted to breach were he not liable to B for B's loss of expected profit. Given that measure of damages, C will not be able to induce a breach of A's contract with B unless he offers B more than $110,000, thereby indicating that the machine really is worth more to him than to B. The expectation rule thus assures that the machine ends up where it is most valuable.

R. Posner, Economic Analysis of Law 90 (2d ed. 1977).

This is a powerful explanation in cases to which it applies. But how wide a range of cases is that? Does Posner's example help explain why Retail Marine recovers its expectancy? Why Chatlos recovers its expectancy in the next principal case?

CHATLOS SYSTEMS v. NATIONAL CASH REGISTER
670 F.2d 1304 (3d Cir. 1982)

Before ALDISERT, ROSENN and WEISS, Circuit Judges.

PER CURIAM. . . .

Chatlos Systems, Inc., initiated this action . . . alleging, inter alia, breach of warranty regarding an NCR 399/656 computer system it had acquired from defendant National Cash Register Corp. . . . Following a nonjury trial, the district court determined that defendant was liable for breach of warranty and awarded $57,152.76 damages for breach of warranty and consequential damages in the amount of $63,558.16. . . . Defendant appealed and this court affirmed the district court's findings of liability, set aside the award of consequential damages, and remanded for a recalculation of damages for breach of warranty. . . . On remand, applying the "benefit of the bargain" formula of N.J. Stat. Ann. §12A:2-714(2) (Uniform Commercial Code §2-714(2)),[1] the district court deter-

---

1. Section 12A:2-714(2) states:

   The measure of damages for breach of warranty is the difference at the time and place of acceptance between the value of the goods accepted and the value they would have had if they had been as warranted, unless special circumstances show proximate damages of a different amount.

mined the damages to be $201,826.50,[2] to which it added an award of prejudgment interest. Defendant now appeals from these damage determinations, contending that the district court erred in failing to recognize the $46,020 contract price of the delivered NCR computer system as the fair market value of the goods as warranted, and that the award of damages is without support in the evidence presented. . . .

Waiving the opportunity to submit additional evidence as to value on the remand which we directed, appellant chose to rely on the record of the original trial and submitted no expert testimony on the market value of a computer which would have performed the functions NCR had warranted. Notwithstanding our previous holding that contract price was not necessarily the same as market value, . . . appellant faults the district judge for rejecting its contention that the contract price for the NCR 399/656 was the only competent record evidence of the value of the system as warranted. The district court relied instead on the testimony of plaintiff-appellee's expert, Dick Brandon, who, without estimating the value of an NCR model 399/656, presented his estimate of the value of a computer system that would perform all of the functions that the NCR 399/656 had been warranted to perform. Brandon did not limit his estimate to equipment of any one manufacturer; he testified regarding manufacturers who could have made systems that would perform the functions that appellant had warranted the NCR 399/656 could perform. He acknowledged that the systems about which he testified were not in the same price range as the NCR 399/656. Appellant likens this testimony to substituting a Rolls Royce for a Ford, and concludes that the district court's recomputed damage award was therefore clearly contrary to the evidence of fair market value — which in NCR's view is the contract price itself.

Appellee did not order, nor was it promised, merely a specific NCR computer model, but an NCR computer system with specified capabilities. The correct measure of damages, under N.J. Stat. Ann. §12A:2-714(2), is the difference between the fair market value of the goods accepted and the value they would have had if they had been as warranted. Award of that sum is not confined to instances where there has been an increase in value between date of ordering and date of delivery. It may also include the benefit of a contract price which, for whatever reason quoted, was particularly favorable for the customer. Evidence of the contract price may be relevant to the issue of fair market value, but it is not controlling. Appellant limited its fair market value analysis to the contract price of the computer model it actually delivered. Appellee de-

---

2. The district court found the fair market value of the system as warranted to be $207,826.50; from this it subtracted its determination of the value of the goods delivered, $6,000.

veloped evidence of the worth of a computer with the capabilities promised by NCR, and the trial court properly credited the evidence.

Appellee was aided, moreover, by the testimony of Frank Hicks, NCR's programmer, who said that he told his company's officials that the "current software was not sufficient in order to deliver the program that the customer [Chatlos] required. They would have to be rewritten or a different system would have to be given to the customer." . . .

Hicks recommended that Chatlos be given an NCR 8200 but was told, "that will not be done." . . . Gerald Greenstein, another NCR witness, admitted that the 8200 series was two levels above the 399 in sophistication and price. . . . This testimony supported Brandon's statement that the price of the hardware needed to perform Chatlos' requirements would be in the $100,000 to $150,000 range.

Essentially, then, the trial judge was confronted with the conflicting value estimates submitted by the parties. Chatlos' expert's estimates were corroborated to some extent by NCR's supporters. NCR, on the other hand, chose to rely on contract price. Credibility determinations had to be made by the district judge. Although we might have come to a different conclusion on the value of the equipment as warranted had we been sitting as trial judges, we are not free to make our own credibility and factual findings. We may reverse the district court only if its factual determinations were clearly erroneous. . . .

The judgment of the district court will be affirmed.

Rosenn, Circuit Judge, dissenting. . . .

I respectfully dissent because I believe there is no probative evidence to support the district court's award of damages for the breach of warranty in a sum amounting to almost five times the purchase price of the goods. The measure of damages also has been misapplied and this could have a significant effect in the marketplace, especially for the unique and burgeoning computer industry. . . .

II

A . . .

Chatlos presented its case under a theory that although, as a sophisticated purchaser, it bargained for several months before arriving at a decision on the computer system it required and the price of $46,020, it is entitled, because of the breach of warranty, to damages predicated on a considerably more expensive system. Stated another way, even if it bargained for a cheap system, i.e., one whose low cost reflects its inferior quality, because that system did not perform as bargained for, it is now entitled to damages measured by the value of a system which, although

capable of performing the identical functions as the NCR 399, is of far
superior quality and accordingly more expensive.

The statutory measure of damages for breach of warranty specifically
provides that the measure is the difference at the time and place of
acceptance between the value "of the goods accepted" and the "value
they would have had if they had been as warranted." The focus of the
statute is upon "the goods accepted" — not other hypothetical goods which
may perform equivalent functions. "Moreover, the value to be considered is the reasonable market value of the *goods delivered*, not the value
of the goods to a particular purchaser or for a particular purpose." KLPR–
TV, Inc. v. Visual Electronics Corp., 465 F.2d 1382, 1387 (8th Cir. 1972)
(emphasis added). The court, however, arrived at value on the basis of a
hypothetical construction of a system as of December 1978 by the plaintiff's expert, Brandon. The court reached its value by working backward
from Brandon's figures, adjusting for inflation. . . .

Although NCR warranted performance, the failure of its equipment to
perform, absent any evidence of the value of any NCR 399 system on
which to base fair market value, does not permit a market value based on
systems wholly unrelated to the goods sold. . . . NCR rightly contends
that the "comparable" systems on which Brandon drew were substitute
goods of greater technological power and capability and not acceptable in
determining damages for breach of warranty under section 2-714. Furthermore, Brandon's hypothetical system did not exist and its valuation
was largely speculation.

B . . .

First, ordinarily, the best evidence of fair market value is what a willing
purchaser would pay in cash to a willing seller. . . . In the instant case
we have clearly "not . . . an unsophisticated consumer," Chatlos Systems v. National Cash Register Corp., 479 F. Supp. 738, 748 (D.N.J.
1979), . . . who for a considerable period of time negotiated and bargained with an experienced designer and vendor of computer systems.
The price they agreed upon for an operable system would ordinarily be
the best evidence of its value. The testimony does not present us with the
situation referred to in our previous decision, where "the value of the
goods rises between the time that the contract is executed and the time of
acceptance," in which event the buyer is entitled to the benefit of his
bargain. *Chatlos*, supra 635 F.2d at 1088. On the contrary, Chatlos here
relies on an expert who has indulged in the widest kind of speculation.
Based on this testimony, Chatlos asserts in effect that a multi-national
sophisticated vendor of computer equipment, despite months of negotiation, incredibly agreed to sell an operable computer system for $46,020
when, in fact, it had a fair market value of $207,000.

Second, expert opinion may, of course, be utilized to prove market value but it must be reasonably grounded. Brandon did not testify to the fair market value "of the *goods* accepted" had they met the warranty. Instead, he testified about a hypothetical system that he mentally fashioned. He ignored the realistic cost advantage in purchasing a unified system as contrasted with the "cost of acquiring seven separate application components" from various vendors. . . .

Fourth, the record contains testimony which appears undisputed that computer equipment falls into one of several tiers, depending upon the degree of sophistication. The more sophisticated equipment has the capability of performing the functions of the least sophisticated equipment, but the less sophisticated equipment cannot perform all of the functions of those in higher levels. The price of the more technologically advanced equipment is obviously greater.

It is undisputed that in September 1976 there were vendors of computer equipment of the same general size as the NCR 399/656 with disc in the price range of $35,000 to $40,000 capable of providing the same programs as those required by Chatlos, including IBM, Phillips, and Burroughs. They were the very companies who competed for the sale of the computer in 1974 in the same price range. On the other hand, Chatlos' requirements could also be satisfied by computers available at "three levels higher in price and sophistication than the 399 disc." Each level higher would mean more sophistication, greater capabilities, and more memory. Greenstein, NCR's expert, testified without contradiction that equipment of Burroughs, IBM, and other vendors in the price range of $100,000 to $150,000, capable of performing Chatlos' requirements, was not comparable to the 399 because it was three levels higher. Such equipment was more comparable to the NCR 8400 series.

Fifth, when it came to the valuation of the hardware, Brandon did not offer an opinion as to the market value of the hypothetical system he was proposing. Instead, he offered a wide ranging estimate of $100,000 to $150,000 for a hypothetical computer that would meet Chatlos' programming requirements. The range in itself suggests the speculation in which he indulged.

III

The purpose of the N.J.S.A. 12A:2-714 is to put the buyer in the same position he would have been in if there had been no breach. See Uniform Commercial Code 1-106(1). The remedies for a breach of warranty were intended to compensate the buyer for his loss; they were not intended to give the purchaser a windfall or treasure trove. The buyer may not receive more than it bargained for; it may not obtain the value of a superior computer system which it did not purchase even though such a system can perform all of the functions the inferior system was designed to serve. . . .

Although it may be that the "benefit of the bargain" concept is applicable to situations involving other than periodic fluctuations in market prices, the cases cited by Chatlos stand only for the premise that the proved market value of the goods in question must be accepted. Thus, in Melody Home Manufacturing Co. v. Morrison, 502 S.W.2d 196 (Tex. Civ. App. 1973), where $5,300 was the price of a mobile home, the measure of damages for breach of warranty under U.C.C. §2-714(2) was the difference between $2,000, the value of the delivered home, and $6,000, the proved market value of the particular home. In Miles v. Lyons, 42 Mass. App. Dec. 77, 6 U.C.C. Rep. 659 (Dist. Ct. 1969), the defendants (Lyons) sued for conversion of furniture, impleaded Anita Miles, former wife of the plaintiff, from whom they had purchased the furniture. Mrs. Miles had sold it to the Lyons for $100, falsely asserting it belonged to her. The justice found for the plaintiff in the amount of $275, the value of the furniture at the time of conversion, but he found for the Lyons as third-party plaintiffs for $100. On appeal, the finding of $100 was vacated and judgment entered for $275, the loss resulting from the seller's breach of warranty of title. The Lyons were entitled, the court held, to the benefit of their bargain and the measure of damages under section 2-714. The bargain consisted of the value of the specific furniture they purchased — not other hypothetical furniture constructed in superior fashion or of superior materials.

Even if we were to accept plaintiff's theory that the value of other systems may be used to establish the value of the specific computer system purchased, the cases cited by Chatlos to support its theory are distinguishable. In Giant Food v. Jack I. Bender & Sons, 399 A.2d 1293 (D.C. App. 1979), when a seller, after three years, replaced carpet under warranty with new carpet of higher price, the buyer refused to pay the excess cost. The court agreed that the value of the replacement carpet represented the buyer's damages. However, the appellate court expressly noted that "[t]he trial court implicitly found that the *replacement* was a reasonable one — i.e., it was of substantially the same style, goods and character as that for which [the buyer] had originally contracted." Id. at 1306 n.26 (emphasis added). In the instant case, there was no testimony that the hypothetical system — apart from its ability to perform identical functions — was otherwise the same. Furthermore, as distinguished from this case, the goods were *actually replaced* by the seller. In Huyett-Smith Manufacturing Co. v. Gray, 129 N.C. 438, 40 S.E. 178 (1901), a pre-Code case, the vendor of a kiln represented that it had a capacity in excess of any kiln on the market. In measuring the damages claimed by the purchaser the court would not fix damages in excess of the contract by looking to a non-existent kiln stating that the purchaser "is not entitled to speculative damages for an ideal machine which was not on the market." Id. at 179. . . .

SMITH v. BOLLES
132 U.S. 125 (1889)

The court in its opinion, stated the case as follows:

Richard J. Bolles filed his petition against Lewis W. Smith . . . to recover damages for alleged fraudulent representations in the sale of shares of mining stock. . . . The amended petition set up five causes of action: First. That in the fall of 1879 defendant and one Joseph W. Haskins entered into a fraudulent combination to form an incorporated mining company based upon alleged mining property in the Territory of Arizona, and for the alleged purpose of mining silver ore therefrom and milling the same for market; . . . that in the month of February, 1880, the defendant applied to him to buy and subscribe for some of the stock, stating that he was interested in it, and that before acquiring an interest he had learned from Haskins the enormous value of the property, and to satisfy himself had gone to Arizona and thoroughly examined it; that he then represented to plaintiff a variety of facts as existing in respect to the mine, making it of great value, which representations are set forth in detail; and that having known the defendant for several years, and believing him to be a truthful and honest man, and without knowledge or suspicion that said representations were untrue, but believing and relying on the same, the plaintiff had, at the request of the defendant, in the month of February, 1880, agreed to buy of the defendant four thousand shares of the stock, at $1.50 per share, which contract was completed in the month of March, 1880, by the payment in full of the purchase price, to wit, six thousand dollars, to one H. J. Davis, who claimed to act as treasurer of the company, and from whom plaintiff received certificates for the stock. Plaintiff then alleged that said representations were each and all false and fraudulent, specifically denying the truth of each of them, and averring that

> said stock and mining property was then, and still is, wholly worthless; and that had the same been as represented by defendant it would have been worth at least ten dollars per share, and so plaintiff says that by reason of the premises he has sustained damages to the amount of forty thousand dollars. . . .

Mr. Chief Justice Fuller delivered the opinion of the court.

The bill of exceptions states that the court charged the jury "as to the law by which the jury were to be governed in the assessment of damages under the issues made in the case," that

> the measure of recovery is generally the difference between the contract price and the reasonable market value, if the property had been as represented to be, or in case the property or stock is entirely worthless, then its value is what it

meas. of damages

would have been worth if it had been as represented by the defendant, and as may be shown in the evidence before you.

In this there was error. The measure of damages was not the difference between the contract price and the reasonable market value if the property had been as represented to be, even if the stock had been worth the price paid for it; nor if the stock were worthless, could the plaintiff have recovered the value it would have had if the property had been equal to the representations. What the plaintiff might have gained is not the question, but what he had lost by being deceived into the purchase. The suit was not brought for breach of contract. The gist of the action was that the plaintiff was fraudulently induced by the defendant to purchase stock upon the faith of certain false and fraudulent representations. . . . If the jury believed from the evidence that the defendant was guilty of the fraudulent and false representations alleged, and that the purchase of stock had been made in reliance thereon, then the defendant was liable to respond in such damages as naturally and proximately resulted from the fraud. He was bound to make good the loss sustained, such as the moneys the plaintiff had paid out and interest, and any other outlay legitimately attributable to defendant's fraudulent conduct; but this liability did not include the expected fruits of an unrealized speculation. The reasonable market value, if the property had been as represented, afforded, therefore, no proper element of recovery.

Nor had the contract price the bearing given to it by the court. What the plaintiff paid for the stock was properly put in evidence, not as the basis of the application of the rule in relation to the difference between the contract price and the market or actual value, but as establishing the loss he had sustained in that particular. If the stock had a value in fact, that would necessarily be applied in reduction of the damages. . . .

For the error indicated, the judgment is reversed and the cause remanded with a direction to grant a new trial.

NOTES ON THE DISTINCTION BETWEEN TORT AND CONTRACT

1.   The conventional wisdom is that expectancy damages are recoverable only in contract, not in tort. That is why Chatlos recovers its expectancy and Bolles does not. What sense does that make? Why should plaintiff's right to recover his expectancy depend on whether he frames his complaint in fraud or breach of warranty? The anomaly is heightened by the difference between the mental element of the two wrongs — fraud requires deliberate misrepresentation or reckless disregard of the truth, but one is liable for breach of warranty even if his mistake were innocent and non-negligent.

2. Many states have responded to the anomaly by allowing plaintiffs to recover the value of what was promised to them, regardless of whether they sue in fraud or warranty. Many of the cases are collected in Thompson, The Measure of Recovery under Rule 10b-5: A Restitution Alternative to Tort Damages, 37 Vand. L. Rev. 349, 358 n.26 (1984). With respect to the sale of goods, the Uniform Commercial Code provides that "Remedies for material misrepresentation or fraud include all remedies available under this Article for non-fraudulent breach." §2-721. The Second Restatement of Torts provides that the victim of fraud may always recover his reliance damages: the difference between what he paid and the value of what he recieved, plus any incidental reliance expenses. In addition, "The recipient of a fraudulent misrepresentation in a business transaction is also entitled to recover additional damages sufficient to give him the benefit of his contract with the maker, if these damages are proved with reasonable certainty." §549. As the conflicting opinions in *Chatlos* suggest, there is plenty of room for disagreement over the "reasonable certainty" requirement.

3. The federal courts generally adhere to the rule of Smith v. Bolles in fraud cases, including cases under the securities statutes. But they have distinguished *Smith* and awarded expectancy damages in a few cases. In Osofsky v. Zipf, 645 F.2d 107 (2d Cir. 1981), plaintiffs alleged that they had sold their shares to a tender offeror who promised securities worth $62.50, but delivered securities worth only $59.88. As is typical in tender offers, even $59.88 was far in excess of the previous market value of plaintiffs' shares. Defendant argued that damages were therefore zero: Plaintiffs received more than they gave and had no out-of-pocket loss. The court held that on these facts, plaintiffs could recover expectancy damages, the difference between $62.50 and $59.88. The court said:

Smith v. Bolles [and a similar case] involved situations in which the representations as to what the buyers were receiving was highly speculative. . . . But the case of a defrauded securities buyer, whose gain was speculative, is surely different from the case of a seller who does not receive the price for which he had bargained. The distinction lies in the ability to determine the amount of damages with certainty.

645 F.2d 112.

4. Can tort and contract be distinguished on the ground that the two theories identify different parts of the transaction as wrongful? There is nothing wrongful about making a contractual promise; contract law identifies the breach as the wrong. Tort law identifies the misrepresentation as the wrong; fraud may consist of making a promise you do not intend to keep, or falsely representing the value of a promise. If the wrong is in lying about the existence of a silver mine, where would plaintiff be but for the wrong? The promise would not have been made, plaintiff would not

have invested, and he would still have his original money. He would not have a $10 per share profit. But if the wrong is failing to perform a lawful promise, where would plaintiff be but for the wrong? The promise would have been performed; he would have received his expectancy. Those deductions are unobjectionable as a matter of formal logic. Do they make any sense as a matter of policy?

NOTES ON EXCESSIVE EXPECTANCIES

1.   One curiosity of the fraud and breach of warranty cases is that the plaintiff who claims expectancy damages in excess of the price he paid is claiming that he expected to get more than he was paying for. If he expected only a little more than he was paying for, he may have thought he had found a legitimate bargain. *Chatlos* appears to be a case of an overeager salesperson exaggerating the abilities of his product to a buyer who knew little about computers. But Judge Rosenn was not persuaded of that, and the trial court found no bad faith by NCR.

2.   Did Chatlos recover too much? Don't make the legal issue go away by rejecting the findings of fact. The legal issue could be presented quite unambiguously. Suppose NCR made specific written representations that the computer would do X, and no computer under $207,000 would do X. Chatlos's expectancy was that it would get a computer that would do X for $46,000. That's a great deal, but it's what Chatlos expected. Does NCR's foolish promise entitle Chatlos to something it never could have gotten otherwise?

3.   Most puzzling are cases where plaintiff consciously expected far more than he paid for. Was it reasonable for Bolles to expect to buy $10 stock for $1.50? Suppose a contract to sell a Stradivarius violin for $4,000. If it's a fake, and a real Stradivarius costs $100,000, can plaintiff recover $100,000? The question is posed but not answered in Smith v. Zimbalist, 2 Cal. App. 2d 324, 38 P.2d 170 (1934). If a patent medicine man sells a "cancer cure" for $2.00, does he become liable for whatever a jury decides a cancer cure is worth? Isn't that what UCC §2-714(2) says? Should plaintiffs be limited to reasonable expectancies? Or is reasonableness just evidentiary on the question whether plaintiff really expected what he now claims? Should frauds who breach unbelievable warranties have less liability than honest businessmen who commit minor breaches? Keep in mind that one way for a fraudulent seller to overcome a victim's resistance is to offer a bargain.

4.   It is easy to imagine expectancy losses greater than reliance losses. There are also cases of reliance losses greater than expectancy losses. The most common examples are cases where plaintiff was losing money on a contract when defendant breached. Plaintiff may have spent large sums in reliance on the contract, and conferred substantial benefits on defen-

dant, even though his expectancy was negative. An old Supreme Court case holds that government contractors can recover their reliance costs, and says in a clear dictum that prospective losses from full performance should not be subtracted. United States v. Behan, 110 U.S. 338, 344-346 (1884). Learned Hand rejected *Behan*'s dictum in L. Albert & Son v. Armstrong Rubber Co., 178 F.2d 182 (2d Cir. 1949). *Albert* was a diversity case that turned on Connecticut law, so *Behan* did not control. Hand doubted that the Supreme Court would adhere to it in any event.

The Restatement of Contracts has always taken Hand's view. Section 349 of the Restatement Second provides that plaintiff can recover his reliance costs "less any loss that the party in breach can prove with reasonable certainty the injured party would have suffered had the contract been performed." The effect of this provision is to convert reliance recoveries into net expectancy recoveries in the only situation in which plaintiff would prefer to recover reliance costs. In the Restatement's view, reliance costs are to be recovered only when neither side can prove the expectancy.

A plaintiff with a losing contract can also sue for restitution of the benefit he has conferred on defendant. The Restatement says he can recover the value of the benefit without regard to his negative expectancy. The cases are mixed, but in general courts have been quite generous to plaintiffs seeking restitution for breach of contract. Consequently, most losing contract cases are decided on restitution grounds, and there are few cases that test whether a negative expectancy limits reliance damages. We will take a more intensive look at losing contracts in chapter 6.

C. VALUE AS THE MEASURE OF THE RIGHTFUL POSITION

O'BRIEN BROTHERS v. *THE HELEN B. MORAN*
160 F.2d 502 (2d Cir. 1947)

[Plaintiff's barge, the *Dayton*, was sunk in a collision with a Navy vessel. The United States was held liable for 80 percent of the damage. Under admiralty procedure at the time, the plaintiff was referred to as the "libellant."]

Before L. HAND, Augustus N. HAND, and CHASE, Circuit Judges.

Augustus N. HAND, Circuit Judge. . . .

The United States introduced evidence to the effect that the value of the barge at the time of the collision was $15,000 to $16,000. The libellant showed what the repairs had cost and what hire it received for its barge.

While the net of $101.85 per day, and an apparent likelihood of prolonged use, were some evidence of a greater value than $16,000, the United States introduced evidence that a similar barge could have been built new for $33,000 and that upon such an assumed cost there should be allowed a depreciation of $17,800 in order to obtain a proper valuation of a barge that was twelve years old at the time of the collision, as was the *Dayton*. The actual cost of the *Dayton* according to books of the libellant was $44,653, and the depreciation taken on the books was $28,212, leaving a book value of $16,441. Yet the Commissioner and the District Judge allowed $7,732.21 for expenses of raising the wreck, $37,014.99 for repairs, $6,230.23 for repairs still to be made, $3,423.91 for miscellaneous items of damage, and $6,620.25 for demurrage, making a total of $61,021.59, upon which the 80% allowed under the provision of the interlocutory decree was based, or a net of $48,817.27.

In *The Reno*, 2 Cir., 134 F. 555, 556, the owner of a vessel sunk in a collision had her raised and repaired. In a suit to recover damages for the collision this court, in an opinion by Judge Wallace, set forth the rule to be applied in such cases as follows:

> The damages sustained by the owner of a vessel which is sunk in a collision, when the vessel is a total loss, is her value at the time of the loss, to which interest may be added to afford complete indemnity; and to this may also be added the necessary expenses of raising her, when that is necessary to determine whether she can be repaired advantageously; and when she is sunk in a place where she is liable to be an obstruction to navigation, the expenses of removing her may also be added. If she was not a total loss, then the measure of damages is the reasonable expense of raising and repairing her to an extent sufficient to put her in as good condition as she was before the collision. The burden is upon the owner to prove the amount of his loss, either by showing the vessel to have been a total loss, actually or constructively, or by showing the extent and cost of the necessary repairs and the incidental expenses. . . .

The Commissioner appointed under the interlocutory decree for the ascertainment of the damages suffered by the libellant reported that: (1) The *Dayton* was not a total loss because she was capable of being repaired and was repaired; (2) The doctrine that a vessel owner may not spend on the repair of his vessel more than the amount for which a comparable or similar vessel can be purchased in the open market is based on the obligation of the party who has been wronged to minimize damages and there was no evidence indicating that the libellant could buy in an open market another vessel comparable to the *Dayton* for less than the cost of the repairs; (3) Under conditions existing at the time of the collision, the value of the *Dayton* greatly exceeded the sum of $16,000, and it was doubtful whether a seller of a lighter comparable to the *Dayton*, and in reasonably good condition, could have been found; (4) The burden of proving that the value did not exceed $16,000 was on the United States. . . .

In our opinion the holding of the Commissioner that the respondent had the burden of proving that the value of the barge at the time of the collision did not exceed $16,000 was erroneous. The court adopted that view because it considered that the sole issue was one concerning the duty of an injured party to "minimize damages." But that duty only applies in dealing with expenditures that should be allowed if found to be reasonable under the circumstances. It does not affect the ordinary rule that an injured party has the burden of proving the damages he has actually suffered. Here the libellant has merely shown what he has paid out for repairs and attendant expenses, while the respondent has shown, without contradiction, that those sums were expended on a vessel that was worth much less than the expenditures. It seems quite evident that the real loss involved no such amount if in fact the value of the vessel at the time of the collision was less than the sums expended to restore her to service. . . .

The libellant did show the extent of necessary repairs and their cost. That may be regarded as prima facie proof of the extent of damage to the barge for the reason that, in the absence of other evidence, it is reasonable to infer that it would not have made such expenditures if it could have recouped its loss otherwise. But it is only prima facie proof and was met by respondent's testimony that the ship after deduction of proper depreciation was only worth about $16,000. The libellant should have met this evidence by showing not merely that the worth was greater but what it actually was. This might have been founded upon (a) a capitalization of earning capacity, (b) the cost of a barge of a similar type in the open market, (c) the cost of constructing a new barge if that was feasible. In each case — i.e., of (a), (b) and (c) — there should be a deduction of proper depreciation due to the age and deterioration of the vessel involved in the collision. The least of these alternatives would furnish the measure of recovery because of the duty of the injured party to minimize damages. . . .

It was agreed by both parties that there was no open market at the time of the collision, and thus standard (b) could not be applied. The Commissioner made no finding as to standard (a) except to the effect that the value of the lighter based on its earning power was greater than $16,000. The only evidence as to standard (c) was introduced by respondent, but was deemed irrelevant by the Commissioner because, as he said, there was not a total loss. However, to determine whether or not the vessel should reasonably have been treated as a total loss, it was necessary to compare the estimated cost of repairs with the lowest valuation set by standards (a), (b) and (c). If the lowest valuation was lower than the cost of necessary repairs, then the vessel should have been regarded as a total loss and the lowest valuation set by the standards (a), (b) and (c) would properly be deemed the measure of damages.

If the value of the damaged vessel should prove to be greater than the reasonable cost of the repairs, the cost should be allowed as well as any demurrage occasioned by the reasonable time consumed in making the repairs. Such is the rule in the case of what is termed a partial loss. If, on the contrary, the value of the damaged vessel should prove to be less than the reasonable cost of the repairs there would be a constructive total loss and the damages would be the value of the vessel at the time of the collision less any value of the wreck as salvage, without any allowance of demurrage, but only interest on the net amount from the date of the collision. In the case of a claim against the United States interest can only run from the date of judgment. 46 U.S.C.A. §782.

At most, in case of a constructive total loss, only the anticipated profits of the particular voyage upon which the *Dayton* was engaged at the time of the collision could have been recovered as demurrage. In such a case, the Supreme Court has limited the anticipated profits recoverable holding that "if the vessel were under a charter which had months or years to run, the allowance of the probable profits of such charter might work a great practical injustice to the owner of the vessel causing the injury." *The Umbria*, 166 U.S. 404, 422. In the case at bar, the charter of the *Dayton* apparently had an indefinite time to run, while the service in carrying any given cargo was a day to day affair and everything due for the day on which the accident occurred was paid. In such circumstances it seems clear that in case of a constructive total loss nothing in the way of demurrage should be granted to the libellant.

The expenses of raising the barge were properly allowed inasmuch as she had to be raised in order to ascertain the extent of the damage and to remove her as an obstacle to the use of the slip in which she was sunk as a result of the collision. We hold that all of the sums allowed, except the cost of repairs and demurrage, were proper items of damage. We hold the cost of repairs and demurrage can only be allowed if such cost of repairs did not exceed the value of the barge at the time of the collision. That value must be established upon a further hearing in the District Court. In the event that the reasonable cost of repairs did not exceed the value of the barge at the time of the collision such cost may be allowed and demurrage for such reasonable time as might be necessary to make proper restoration. It is to be borne in mind that the record indicates a close relation between the libellant and the repair company so that the cost of the repairs should be carefully scrutinized and only what would be a fair amount should be allowed. . . .

The decree is reversed and the cause remanded with directions to proceed to determine the amount of damages upon the present record and such further competent evidence as the parties may introduce and in accordance with the foregoing opinion. The final decree to be entered shall allow all items of damage heretofore allowed except those attributed to the loss of the barge itself and except demurrage during a reasonable time consumed in making repairs if the value of the barge prior to the collision shall be found to be less than the reasonable cost of repairs.

Whatever amount is finally allowed as the total damage is, of course, subject to reduction in the final decree to 80% under the provisions of the interlocutory consent decree.

Decree accordingly.

NOTES ON DAMAGE TO PROPERTY

1. Assuming the court can get the numbers straight on remand, is there anything wrong in principle with the government's theory? Is there any reason to make the government pay for $43,000 in repairs if plaintiff could have built a new barge for $33,000? The cases generally agree that plaintiff can recover the lesser of value or repair costs. But there is disagreement over *The Helen B. Moran*'s insistence that plaintiff must prove both numbers. Even *Moran* says it is enough for plaintiff to prove one number unless defendant comes forward with evidence that that number is too high. But *Moran* apparently leaves the ultimate burden of persuasion on plaintiff; it rejects the notion that abandonment instead of repair or replacement is merely a mitigation of damages issue.

Compare Jenkins v. Etlinger, 55 N.Y.2d 35, 432 N.E.2d 589 (1982), where runoff from defendant's landfill silted in plaintiff's pond, which was used for recreation. Plaintiff recovered $6950, the cost of removing the silt. There was no evidence of the value of the pond. Defendant appealed on the ground that plaintiff had not proved his damages unless he proved both numbers. The court agreed that the measure of recovery was the lesser of value or cost of repair. But it held that the possibility that plaintiff had spent too much on repairs was a mitigation of damages issue, so that defendant bore the burden of proof. "Simply stated, the plaintiff need only present evidence as to one measure of damages, and that measure will be used when neither party presents evidence going to the other measure." 55 N.Y.2d at 39-40, 432 N.E.2d at 590-591.

2. *Demurrage* is an admiralty term. In the context of *The Helen B. Moran*, it means damages for loss of use. The court says that demurrage is recoverable if the barge should have been repaired, but not if the barge were a total loss. That makes sense if the barge is not replaced and the plaintiff tries to claim the value of the barge plus demurrage for the rest of its expected life. That would obviously be a double recovery, because the prospect of future earnings is the main thing that gives the barge value. But if plaintiff replaces the barge, there may be a delay pending replacement, and there is no reason not to award demurrage for that time. This has gradually been recognized, and most courts now award damages for the time it takes to replace destroyed property. These damages may be measured by lost earnings, the cost of renting a replacement, or interest on the value of the property destroyed. Many of the cases are collected in D. Dobbs, Handbook on the Law of Remedies §5.11 (1973).

3. In *The Helen B. Moran,* isn't there something wrong with the government's numbers? If it were possible to build a barge for $33,000 that would earn $101 per day, more people would be building barges. Investors could recoup the entire cost of construction in less than one year, with many years of profitable use remaining.

Part of the problem may be a misleading use of the term "net earnings." When a vessel is leased net, the lessee gets the vessel without a crew. But the owner may still be responsible for maintenance or other expenses. Thus net earnings of $101.85 per day might be gross earnings in ordinary English: rental payments on a net lease, out of which the owner must pay for maintenance.

Even so, the barge is earning far too much to be worth only $16,000. Some market distortion is required to explain the gap between the cost of building a barge and the value of this barge's capitalized earnings. One possible explanation is that all the shipyards were committed to other uses. The parties stipulated that it was impossible to buy a barge during the war; perhaps it was impossible to build one as well.

4. The capitalized earnings method of calculating value is sufficiently important to justify elaboration. Many students are unnecessarily put off by the arithmetic, which is really quite simple. Suppose that 75 percent of the earnings went to expenses, so that the barge earned $25 a day, that it was leased 320 days per year, and that it had a remaining life expectancy of ten years. Under these assumptions, the barge would earn $80,000 in its remaining life. However, that does not mean that the barge is worth $80,000. The $8,000 earned this year can be reinvested immediately, earning interest or profits, so it is worth more than $8,000 ten years from now. How much more depends on the interest rate. Assume an interest rate of 5 percent, which might not have been thought unreasonable for this purpose in 1943. Then the present value of earnings to be received a year from now is 5 percent less than the face amount, to allow for one year of interest. The value of earnings to be received two years from now is 5 percent less than that, to allow for two years of interest. And so on. If we introduce the simplifying assumption that all earnings are received in a lump sum at the end of the year, the calculation looks like this:

Year	Earnings		Discount Rate		Present Value
1943	$8,000	÷	1.05	=	$7,619.05
1944	8,000	÷	1.05^2	=	7,256.24
1945	8,000	÷	1.05^3	=	6,910.70
1946	8,000	÷	1.05^4	=	6,581.62
1947	8,000	÷	1.05^5	=	6,268.21
1948	8,000	÷	1.05^6	=	5,969.72
1949	8,000	÷	1.05^7	=	5,685.45
1950	8,000	÷	1.05^8	=	5,414.71
1951	8,000	÷	1.05^9	=	5,156.87
1952	8,000	÷	1.05^{10}	=	4,911.31
				Total	$61,773.88

Any business computer or sophisticated calculator can do the calculations instantly, or the answer can be found in a table of present value such as the one in the appendix. What is difficult about such calculations is not the arithmetic, but deciding what numbers go into the calculations in the first place. This requires informed judgment and generally requires expert testimony. How long will this barge last? How long will it be able to earn at its present rate? Will prices, or the number of days of use each year, be sharply reduced when the war ends? Or will earnings go up when wartime price controls are ended? What discount rate should be used? Not the interest rate on government bonds or insured savings, because earnings from a barge are more risky and less reliable than interest on such supersafe investments. Consequently, a barge that will earn $8,000 per year is probably not as valuable as a government bond that will pay $8,000 per year in interest. But how much less valuable? What is a fair rate of return for a barge investor? And what about the offsetting possibility that income from the barge may go up? A lawyer who hopes to rely on capitalized earnings must find answers to questions such as these and find ways of proving the answers. We will consider the present value of a stream of earnings in much more detail in section G.

5.   What about depreciation? The government did not want to pay even $33,000; it wanted to pay $15,000, because the barge was twelve years old. The theory is plain enough. If a new barge costs $33,000 and has a life expectancy of twenty-two years, then the owners of a twelve-year-old barge have already used up 12/22 of the value.

But the court says that depreciation must be deducted however value is calculated. This is surely a slip of the pen. In the calculation based on capitalized earnings in note 4 above, depreciation has already been accounted for by estimating remaining useful life. And under the open market method, the best proof would be the cost of buying a used barge approximately twelve years old. If that evidence were available it would obviously be improper to subtract depreciation from that price. Depreciation adjustments would be proper if the court used the price of a new barge or the price of a used barge substantially more or less than twelve years old.

UNITED STATES v. EBINGER
386 F.2d 557 (2d Cir. 1967)

Before FRIENDLY, KAUFMAN and ANDERSON, Circuit Judges.
FRIENDLY, Circuit Judge.
Appellant, Tobias Ebinger, who undertook an $880 plumbing job on the water cooling tower of a government building in Brooklyn in February 1960, finds himself on the paying end of a judgment for damage he is claimed to have done, in the amount of $34,867.84, along with interest from July 30, 1963, when the action was brought, and costs. . . .

Although Ebinger does not question that it was cheaper to procure a new tower than to repair the old one, he claims that the value of the tower before the fire constituted the limit of the Government's recovery. The cases on which he relies are based on the rationale that the plaintiff could have held its loss to the value of the property before the damage by abandoning rather than repairing it. This reasoning has no application when the damaged unit is an essential part of a larger whole. Despite the fact that the water tower was located above the building rather than within its four walls, it was a necessary and integral part of the building's air conditioning system. Under such circumstances it has been generally held that the defendant is not entitled to a credit merely because the plaintiff has acquired a new unit, presumably with a longer life expectancy than the old, if that was the cheapest course available. This can be justified by the consideration that the plaintiff should not be required to finance in part the premature replacement of equipment when there is no assurance that this will add to the realizable value of the property to which it appertains. It is true that, as Judge Chase noted in Shepard S.S. Co. v. United States, 111 F.2d 110, 113 (2d Cir. 1940), "much might be said logically to the contrary," and we are not sure we would apply the established rule when this would be clearly inequitable, e.g., in a case where the damaged part was scheduled for early replacement, long before the expiration of the useful life of the whole. Here, however, the judge found that the old tower had "a useful life expectancy of 20-25 years or perhaps longer" and while he estimated a somewhat longer useful life for the building, any increment in value by avoiding the possible need to replace the water tower a quarter of a century hence would be small and speculative.

On the other hand, the trial court should have allowed credit for the maintenance expenses the new tower will save. There was evidence that the old tower had been cleaned and lined in 1959 at a cost of $12,000, and the record suggests that this process might have to be repeated as frequently as every five years. With the new tower, on the other hand, a government witness testified that "the corrugated cement asbestos boards as opposed to the steel doesn't require any maintenance" and that "the hot dipped galvanized frame with the proper water treatment does not require any periodic painting such as a steel frame requires." On the basis of this testimony, the judge found that the new tower "was to some extent more economical to maintain." The Government should not have the benefit of this at Ebinger's expense, particularly since a saving of this sort would be reflected in the sale price of the building unless, of course, it were to be scrapped. The judge should thus have proceeded to determine as nearly as possible the amount of this saving and to deduct an amount not exceeding its capitalized value. . . .

The judgment as to liability is affirmed; the judgment as to damages is reversed in part and the cause remanded for a redetermination of damages in accordance with this opinion. . . .

MORE NOTES ON DEPRECIATION

1.   *Ebinger* raises additional questions about the rationale for reducing damages by the amount of depreciation. Why does it matter that the cooling tower was an essential part of the building? How is a cooling tower different from a barge? Apparently, the court believes that the government is required to replace the cooling tower to preserve the value of the building, but that plaintiff in *The Helen B. Moran* could choose not to replace the barge. Is that view of *The Helen B. Moran* consistent with the general remedial principle of restoring plaintiff to the position he would have been in but for the wrong? Isn't plaintiff entitled to a remedy that will give him a barge? Or is $15,000 really the same as a barge if we have confidence in our assessment of value? Should the adequacy of the remedy be tested on the assumption that plaintiff will put the $15,000 damage award in the bank and abandon or reduce the size of its business? Or on the assumption that plaintiff will add $18,000 of its own money and replace the barge?

2.   Consider the $15,000 judgment on the latter assumption. The judgment might still be defended on the ground that plaintiff had already lost $18,000 worth of the barge's value to wear and tear and obsolescence, and would eventually have had to spend that money anyway, quite aside from the tort. But plaintiff will have to spend its $18,000 ten years earlier than if the barge had not been wrecked and had served out its expected life. Shouldn't plaintiff be able to recover ten years' interest on that money? Is it a sufficient answer that during the ten years he doesn't have the money, he has a newer barge? What good is that to him? Judge Friendly implies in *Ebinger* that he might sell it. Then he would have his $18,000 back and ten years' interest in addition.

3.   The only case I know of that explicitly considers interest for early replacement is Freeport Sulphur Co. v. S/S Hermosa, 526 F.2d 300 (5th Cir. 1976). *Freeport* also makes an important point about calculating depreciation. The defendant ship crashed into plaintiff's dock, inflicting damage that cost $84,000 to repair. The dock was sixteen years old with an expected remaining life of twenty-five years; after repair, its expected remaining life was thirty-five years. The court held defendant responsible for 25/35 of the repair cost, or $60,000; plaintiff had to pay for 10/35 of the repairs itself, or $24,000. This is equivalent to allowing ten years' depreciation instead of sixteen. What really matters is not how old the property was, but how much its life is extended by repair or replacement.

Judge Rubin in the district court reasoned that because plaintiff had to spend its $24,000 twenty-five years ahead of schedule, it was entitled to compensation for the loss of its capital for twenty-five years. He treated the $24,000 as damages, and treated the savings of $24,000 twenty-five years later as an offsetting benefit. Then he discounted that benefit to present value at the statutory interest rate of 7 percent. That made the offsetting benefit worth only $4,320. So, he awarded $79,680. (Actually, he awarded a slightly different number because of other complexities not relevant to this discussion.)

The court of appeals reversed. In the majority's view, compensation for loss of use of capital due to premature replacement was too speculative on this record:

> There is nothing in the record to show: whether the dock might be rebuilt long before it crumbles into the water at the end of its estimated useful life; the extent to which a reasonable return may be obtained on the cost of the enhanced value as on other capital expenditures; the possible savings in the cost of extended useful life construction now as opposed to the possible future cost; the extent to which sinking fund commitments may be reduced by the extended life of the dock and the possible reduction of maintenance costs on the new structure, both of which would tend to lessen the diversion of funds from the operation; the effect on possible loss to the dockowner of the many other considerations that might be relevant to whether the dockowner will suffer any real damage from the early expenditure of funds. It may well be that full evaluation of the damage question would demonstrate no actual damage or that some of the considerations would be so speculative as to be incapable of the reasonable ascertainment required to sustain a damage award. In any event, the dockowner offered no proof on this item of damage and there is no support in the record for the conclusion that loss occurred as a result of premature extension costs. In view of the absence of factual support, a court should apply the general rule that a plaintiff is denied consideration for expenditure of repair costs beyond that necessary to restore its property to the condition it was in before the accident.

Id. at 307.

Judge Wisdom concurred on different grounds. He thought that plaintiff had offered sufficient proof of the cost of early replacement, and that most of the offsetting factors hypothesized by the majority were implausible, and that the burden of proving them should be on defendant. But he thought 7 percent was far too high a discount rate, because interest rates include a prediction of future inflation. It would have cost far more dollars to replace the dock in twenty-five years. In the absence of evidence on the question, Wisdom assumed that interest on the $24,000 spent today would be totally offset by the lower prices resulting from replacing today. We will take up the effect of inflation on damage awards in connection with Jones & Laughlin v. Pfeiffer, infra at 198.

The court granted rehearing en banc in *Freeport*, but no further opinion is reported. Presumably the case settled pending the rehearing.

4. The market in used goods provides another argument against interest on the uncompensated cost of early replacement. If plaintiff in *The Helen B. Moran* could have bought a new barge for $33,000, it presumably could also have bought a used barge for $15,000 and not spent any of its own money. Does buying someone else's used barge put plaintiff in as

good a position as if it still owned the original barge? Plaintiff had twelve years' experience with its own barge, and knows whether it had any problems; plaintiff has much less information about any used barge it might buy. Does plaintiff's fear of used barge salesmen justify shifting to defendant the cost of buying a new barge ten years early? In theory, defendant could be required to warrant the replacement used barge, or pay a premium to insure its quality. But such an insurance scheme would be unworkable. Plaintiff is entitled to a barge as good as the one that was wrecked and no better, but only plaintiff knows how good that is, and there is no good way to verify plaintiff's claims. Should we ignore the risks of buying used goods or avoid those risks by imposing a remedy that defendants will consider unnecessarily expensive?

Courts need not worry about the adequacy of a used replacement if there is no market in used goods of the kind destroyed. The most obvious examples are things that must be built on site for each installation. It is impossible to put on a used roof, and it may have been impossible to buy a used cooling tower in *Ebinger*. It was impossible to build a used dock in *Freeport Sulphur*, and it was probably impossible to make adequate repairs that did not extend the dock's useful life. Specialized products not widely used may yield other examples. Even for goods with an established resale market, an exact replacement may be unavailable. Suppose plaintiff cannot find a twelve-year-old barge and buys a six-year-old barge instead. Just like a brand new barge, the six-year-old model will cost more and last longer, and plaintiff will have to spend its part of the purchase price ten years early.

5. *Ebinger* notes the cost of financing premature replacement, but does not explore the possibility of interest on the depreciated portion as part of the measure of damage. Rather, it ignores depreciation altogether. Is this overcompensation? Or is it fair on the theory that the building would not bring any higher price with the new cooling tower than with the old one, and that the cooling tower could not be sold separately?

6. It generally takes more time and effort to shop for used goods than for new goods. Selection is spottier, and there is no manufacturer's catalog. If the measure of compensation assumes that plaintiff replaces in the used market, shouldn't he be compensated for the extra transaction costs of using that market?

7. Depreciation is not the only source of discrepancy between market value and replacement cost. Consider United States v. 50 Acres of Land, 105 S. Ct. 451 (1984). The United States acquired a landfill by eminent domain. The city that had owned the landfill apparently could not find a comparable site: The jury found that the market value of the condemned landfill was $225,000 and that the reasonable replacement cost was $724,000. The Court held that the just compensation clause was satisfied by an award of $225,000, reasoning that the city now owned a more valuable landfill. The Court might have reached the same result in a

private case, but this case was plainly affected by the rule that victims of eminent domain are not entitled to consequential damages.

Personal - furn.
Prop. ct's approach is hot
street m.v

WALL v. PLATT
169 Mass. 398, 48 N.E. 270 (1897)

Morton, J.

This is an action against the defendants, as receivers of the New York & New England Railroad Company. . . .

The statute under which action is brought is as follows:

> Every railroad corporation and street railway company shall be responsible in damages to a person or corporation whose buildings or other property may be injured by fire communicated by its locomotive engines. . . .

The remaining questions relate to the measure of damages. The defendant contends that it is the market value. . . . The damages consist — First, of buildings destroyed, or substantially destroyed, by the fire; secondly, of household furniture, personal effects, and other personal property contained in the buildings, and burned up by the fire; and, thirdly, of the injury to and destruction of fences, fruit, and shade trees, and sprout and grass land. . . .

The supplemental report states the amount of damages if the rule of market value is to be applied, and how it was arrived at in the case of the buildings. In the report the auditor states that, in estimating the value of the buildings, he has

> taken into consideration the original cost, the depreciation consequent upon the use to which they had been put, the condition in which they were, and also the cost of replacing them by other buildings of the same character, with a proper allowance for the difference between new buildings and the condition of the buildings in question on the day of the fire;

and on that basis he finds the damages to be $5,250. Their fair market value in connection with the land he finds to be $3,250. In determining the amount of damages sustained by the loss of the furniture and other personal property included in the second item, the auditor states that he has "taken into consideration the cost of the articles when used, the length of time they have been used, and the condition they were in at the time of the fire"; and on this basis he estimates the damages at $3,187.69. Their market value he finds to be $2,337.31. The report states the facts on which these findings are made. In regard to the buildings, the report, after describing them generally, proceeds as follows:

I find that the buildings were more expensive in character than is customary in the neighborhood in which they were situated, and that at no time could they probably have been sold for a price approximating the original cost of constructing them, or the cost of replacing them. The buildings were in reasonably good repair at the time of the fire, and there was little depreciation, beyond what would inevitably result from the lapse of time.

In regard to the articles included in the second item, the auditor, after stating that the defendant introduced evidence — as bearing on the measure of damages — to show that second-hand household furniture, effects, and other personal property of the kind destroyed was at the time of the fire commonly used in Boston, but that he did not find that they were commonly used in the town of Norfolk, continues as follows:

I also find that the price paid for second-hand articles is very much less than the price paid for them when new, by reason of the fact that they are second-hand, and without reference to whether they have depreciated by use or not; and I find that the difference between the price of household furniture and other personal property destroyed, when new, and the price at which it would be sold as second-hand articles, is very much greater than any difference in value occasioned by the use to which the articles had been put, or the condition in which they were at the time of the fire.

And he adds that, "under the circumstances," he has "not deemed that the plaintiff is limited to . . . the market value of the household furniture and other personal property as second-hand articles." . . .

No general rule can be laid down by which the amount of indemnity can be arrived at infallibly in all cases. In cases [involving] commodities which are bought and sold in the market in the ordinary course of trade or dealing, the market value . . . would seem to furnish the best measure. . . . In such cases market value usually is equivalent to market price, and the sum received . . . would enable [plaintiff] to replace the goods which he had lost with others equal to them in every respect, and thus restore him to as good a position as he was in before the fire occurred. But market value does not in all cases affirm a correct measure of indemnity, and is not, therefore, a "universal test." In some cases there is no market value, properly speaking; and in others, if there is, it plainly would not of itself afford full indemnity. . . .

Ordinarily, in determining the market value of buildings, they are valued either for the purpose of removal, or, as was the case here, in connection with the land on which they stand. The first, manifestly, would not afford just compensation in the present instance. In the second case the value depends on the location, and other considerations entering into the value of the land, and therefore would not necessarily constitute a just criterion of the loss actually sustained by the destruction of the buildings. Buildings adapted to the land on which they stand are not bought and sold in the market separate from the land. We think that the manner in which the auditor arrived at the damages approaches more nearly the correct rule, in cases like the present. We understand him to have assessed them according to the real value of the buildings at the time of the fire, and to have ascertained that, by taking into account the original cost and the cost of replacing them, and making such allowance as depreciation from use, age, and other like causes, and the condition in which they were, required. We think that this was correct. We also think that as to the furniture, personal effects, and other personal property, the market value, if there was one, would fail to furnish a satisfactory test of the actual loss. We assume that by "other personal property" is meant property of the same general description as the furniture and personal effects. It is true that the defendant offered testimony tending "to show that second-hand furniture, effects, and other personal property of the kind destroyed, was at the time of the fire commonly sold in Boston." But if we assume that Boston was the nearest place where such articles were bought and sold, and that the market value there would be evidence of the market value at the place of loss, we nevertheless think that a sum equal to the market value would not indemnify the plaintiff for the loss which she has sustained. Such a value would depend largely on considerations which would have nothing to do with the intrinsic value of the articles, or with their actual worth to the owner. And we think that, being in the plaintiff's possession, and used and kept for use by her in her house and about her person, without any intention or expectation on her part of selling them or of offering them for sale, they should be regarded as belonging, in a sense, to the person of the owner, and that the damages should be assessed according to the actual worth of the articles to her for use in the condition in which they were at the time of the fire, excluding any fanciful or sentimental considerations. We know of no more satisfactory way of arriving at this than to do as the auditor has done, namely, take the cost of the articles when new, the length of time they have been used, the condition they were in at the time of the fire, and from these facts determine what they were then worth to the owner. We do not understand that there is any dispute respecting the damages to which the plaintiff is entitled for the injury to, and destruction of, the grass and sprout land, fruit and shade trees, and fences. The result is that we think that the plaintiff is entitled to recover, and that judgment should be entered for the sum found due by the auditor in his report, namely, $8,939.69, with interest. So ordered.

NOTES ON CONSUMPTION GOODS

1.   What can the court mean by phrases such as "real value," "intrinsic value," and "actual worth to the owner . . . excluding any fanciful or

sentimental considerations?" Consider another formulation of the same idea:

> Worn wearing apparel in use and . . . household goods and effects owned and kept for personal use . . . cannot in any real sense be said to have a fair market value, unless it be in the second hand market where such goods are sold. And in such a market it must, of course, be conceded that full and fair market value cannot generally be obtained and that sales are usually at a sacrifice.

DeSpirito v. Bristol County Water Co., 102 R.I. 50, 53, 227 A.2d 782, 784 (1967). How can the market value be different from the price that would be paid in the market? How can the "real value" be different from the market value? Are these opinions just economic nonsense? Or is the nonsense in the economic view that market price is the only measure of value?

2. Perhaps there is a way to reconcile economic and judicial wisdom. Market value is the price that a willing buyer would pay and a willing seller would accept. Plainly, Ms. Wall is not a willing seller. She is presumably not in the habit of taking all her belongings into Boston and selling them in secondhand stores. Does this prove that the value of her belongings to her is greater than the market price? But then the government was not looking to sell its cooling tower, and the O'Brien Brothers were not interested in selling their barge. Can't they argue on the same logic that their property was worth more to them than market value? Why are they limited to some approximation of market value when Ms. Wall can recover "real value?" Is it that the judges are focusing on replacement cost? Professor Dobbs suggests that "No judge buys his clothing second hand and none would expect any owner to replace his clothing in a second hand store." D. Dobbs, Handbook on the Law of Remedies §5.12 at 397 (1973). Or is the distinction between "instrumental goods" and "consumption goods" — that is, between goods held only for their commercial or economic value and goods held for personal consumption, with respect to which noneconomic values may predominate?

3. What about the house? There, the discrepancy between "real" and market value arises not from any weakness in the secondhand market, but from the fact that construction cost is much higher than market value. Why should anyone spend more than $5,000 to build a house that, because of its location, will be worth only $3,250? Yet someone has done that in this case; the original owner who built the house has proven quite emphatically that despite the market's contrary judgment, the house is worth more than $5,000 to him. Does it matter whether Ms. Wall or her family were the original builders, or whether she bought it at the lower market price? Regardless of how she got it, one way she can be restored to her rightful position is by rebuilding the same house on the same lot, and that will cost more than $5,000. But suppose she builds a $3,000 house on

the lot, which will be worth $3,000, and puts the remaining $2,000 in the bank? Or suppose she sells the lot, buys another lot in a better neighborhood, and builds a $5,000 house that will be worth $5,000? Under either of these scenarios, hasn't she been made more than whole? In chapter 4, we will encounter a rule that money is never an adequate substitute for real estate. Does that rule have any application here? Should damages be measured on the assumption that she can make herself whole by selling her land or building a smaller house?

4. Wall v. Platt is plainly good law with respect to the secondhand furniture and clothing. Whether it is good law with respect to the house is more doubtful; that is an issue that arises less frequently, and there are cases going both ways. In chapter 11, we will examine cases where the discrepancy between market value and cost of repair or replacement is much more substantial.

5. What does the court mean when it excludes "any fanciful or sentimental considerations?" Suppose the house has special personal value to plaintiff because her family has owned it for many generations, and some of its furnishings were handmade by her ancestors. Can she recover for that? If not, why is that special value any different from the special value reflected in her decision to build a $5,000 house on a lot where it will be worth only $3,250? If yes — if she can recover for history that is valuable only to her — what is the sentimental value she can't recover for?

Suppose the handmade ancestral furnishings had market value as antiques. Or suppose the Mona Lisa were hanging in her library. Not all aesthetic values are "fanciful or sentimental," are they?

6. Plainly values verifiable in the market are not excluded sentimental values. It is not clear that all nonmarket values are excluded either. What if the thing lost or damaged has no substantial value other than sentimental value? Courts disagree on the answer. There is authority that the rule against recovering sentimental value does not apply in such cases. Some of the cases are collected in Brown v. Frontier Treaties, Inc., 369 S.W.2d 299 (Tex. 1963).

Mieske v. Bartell Drug Co., 92 Wash. 2d 40, 593 P.2d 1308 (1979), reached a similar result by a different route. Plaintiffs had thirty-two fifty-foot reels of home movies, depicting their wedding and honeymoon, all their vacations, their children while they were growing up, and relatives since deceased. They took them to defendant to be spliced into four larger reels. Defendant lost them. A jury instructed not to compensate sentimental or fanciful values awarded $7500. The court affirmed:

> What is sentimental value? The broad dictionary definition is that sentimental refers to being "governed by feeling, sensibility or emotional idealism. . . ." Webster's Third New International Dictionary (1963). Obviously that is not the exclusion contemplated by the statement that sentimental value is not to be compensated. If it were, no one would recover for the wrongful death of a

spouse or a child. Rather, the type of sentiment which is not compensable is that which relates to "indulging in feeling to an unwarranted extent" or being "affectedly or mawkishly emotional. . . ." Webster's Third New International Dictionary (1963).

Other courts have denied recovery in such cases. A good example is Carpel v. Saget Studios, 326 F. Supp. 1331 (E.D. Pa. 1971), involving lost wedding pictures.

Doesn't the Washington court have the best solution? Sentimental values are real values aren't they?

DECATUR COUNTY AG-SERVICES v. YOUNG
426 N.E.2d 644 (Ind. 1981)

PRENTICE, Justice . . . .

We adopt the statement of facts and issues as written by the Court of Appeals, as follows:

> The facts favorable to the appellee disclose that Young contracted with Decatur in the summer of 1976 for Decatur to aerially apply an insecticide to his eighteen acre soy bean field which was being attacked by grasshoppers. After the spraying, Young detected damage to his crop. As a result of the negligent spraying, the crop's growth was retarded and the field yielded approximately thirty one bushels per acre. Prior to the damage, this particular soy bean field was of above average quality, in fact of exceptional quality, and located on good farmland. The average yield that year for soy bean fields of above average quality in this locality was forty to fifty bushels of beans per acre with many outstanding fields exceeding fifty bushels per acre.
>
> Young harvested his soy beans and stored them in his own storage bins, which had a capacity of eleven hundred bushels. He held the beans for sale until after the planting period the following year, at which time he sold the beans for amounts ranging from $8.86 per bushel to $10.38 per bushel. Young transported the beans from storage to market in his own truck. He explained that his usual procedure was to store his soy beans until after the next year's planting before selling them. The trial judge found that Young would have realized a yield of fifty bushels of soy beans per acre if his crop had not been damaged. Thus, the difference between the potential yield and the actual yield for the eighteen acres was three hundred and forty two bushels of beans. The court further found that Young was entitled to $3,420 in damages, which was equal to a price of ten dollars per bushel for the lost portion of the crop.
>
> The sole issue on appeal is the propriety of the damages awarded. Decatur asserts that the damages were speculative, excessive, and contrary to law. Decatur bases this claim on three points. First, Decatur challenges the sufficiency of the evidence to support the trial court's determination that Young's undamaged crop would have yielded fifty bushels per acre and therefore,

[handwritten marginal notes: "31/acre", "not", "40-50/acre", "I"]

Decatur argues for the application of an alternative measure of damages based upon the rental value of the property. Second, Decatur asserts the trial court erred in determining the value of the lost portion of the crop based upon market prices at the time Young sold his crop rather than the prevailing market price at the time of harvest. . . .

Finally, Decatur argues that the trial court erred by failing to consider Young's reduced expenses for cultivating, marketing, and storing his crop, due to the reduced yield, when computing the damage award. . . .

We find ample evidence to support the trial court's determination that, but for the damage to the crop, Young would have realized a yield of fifty bushels of soy beans per acre. There was evidence introduced indicating the quality of the crop prior to damage, the quality of Young's farmland, and the yields for comparable crops in the locality. We also note that Decatur's authority for an alternative measure of damages involved a factual situation different than the case at bar. Jay Clutter Custom Digging v. English, (1979) Ind. App., 393 N.E.2d 230. In that case, the crop was never planted and so no determination of the crop's quality was possible.

The trial court and the Court of Appeals erred in holding that the plaintiff's damages could be ascertained with reference to the price obtained by him when he sold his diminished crop the following year, as was Plaintiff's custom.

The rule was correctly expressed in Cutler Cranberry Co. v. Oakdale Electric Cooperative, (1977) 78 Wis. 2d 222, 229 as follows:

> The measure of damages for injury to or partial destruction of a growing crop is the difference between the crop's value immediately before and after the injury or partial destruction. Under this rule, the most generally accepted method for determining damages for such injury to a crop is to compute the difference between the value at maturity of the probable crop if there had been no injury and the value of the actual crop at maturity, less the expense of cultivation, harvesting and marketing that portion of the probable crop which was prevented from maturing.

The above stated rule does limit the time for computing damages to the time of the crop's maturity or harvest. The purpose of damages is to compensate the injured party for the loss suffered. From the record the trial court could have found and did find that Defendant's negligent spraying deprived Plaintiff of three hundred forty-two (342) bushels of mature beans. Because many crops, in their immature state, have no market value, damages are computed at the time of harvest, when a market value first exists. To the extent that Plaintiff elected not to sell his harvest at the time it was first marketable, he was speculating that its market value would be greater at some subsequent date. The risk inherent in such speculation is not chargeable to the defendant. The lost beans could have been replaced from the market place at the time of harvest.

Whatever this market value was at that time was the gross loss and, in this case, the extent of Plaintiff's damages. . . .

The cause must be remanded to the trial court for a redetermination of damages consistent with this opinion.[3]

Finally, Decatur argues that the trial court erred in failing to deduct any saving to Young for reduced costs. "Although the costs of producing and marketing a crop should be deducted where it appears that costs were reduced by the lower yield, the evidence here indicates that no substantial cost reduction occurred." Wm. G. Roe & Co. v. Armour & Co., (5th Cir. 1969) 414 F.2d 862, 872 (applying Florida law).

Plaintiff harvested the beans himself. He provided his own storage, transportation and care of the crop, and the record discloses that Plaintiff realized no consequential savings because of the reduced yield.

The judgment of the trial court as to the damages owing is reversed and the cause is remanded to the trial court to redetermine such damages in accordance with this opinion.

GIVAN, C.J., and DeBRULER, HUNTER and PIVARNIK, JJ., concur.

NOTES ON PROPERTY THAT FLUCTUATES IN VALUE

1.   The standard rule is to value property at the time of the loss. That usually produces sensible results, but not in the case of crops; there, the time of harvest has emerged as the standard rule.

2.   A standard time for valuation works fine when values are stable, but may produce arbitrary results when values are subject to rapid change. Was Farmer Young restored to the position he would have occupied but for the wrong? Would his claim have been less plausible if he had not regularly held his beans until spring in recent years? If he thought the price would go up after harvest, was he obligated to buy beans to minimize his damages? Is investing cash in speculative beans economically equivalent to holding his own beans? Is it psychologically equivalent? What if he had no spare cash?

3.   The problem of fluctuating values has been most frequently litigated in cases where defendants deprived plaintiff of investment securities. Courts have responded in many ways, but there are three main approaches. A few states value the loss at the time of the wrong even in this context, but the decisions are old and might not be followed today. A larger group of states resolves doubts against defendant by awarding the highest value between the time of the wrong and the time of trial, the

---

3.   On cross-examination Plaintiff testified that beans were around seven dollars ($7.00) at harvest time.

time of filing suit, or some similar date. Finally, some states give plaintiff the highest value between the time he learned of the loss and a reasonable time thereafter in which he could have replaced the securities. Is that the best of the three approaches? The approaches, and their variations, are reviewed in more detail in D. Dobbs, Handbook on the Law of Remedies §5.14 at 403-405 (1972).

NOTES ON CHOOSING BETWEEN COMPETING MEASURES OF DAMAGES

1. Are you satisfied with the court's reason for choosing the lost yield measure of damages over the rental value of the land measure of damages? The court says that in Jay Clutter Custom Digging v. English, it was impossible to determine the quality of the crop because the crop was never planted. But the expected yield could have been proven by evidence that showed the quality of the land and the yield that year on similar land, just as it was proven in *Decatur County*. Is there any other basis for choosing between the two measures of damages?

2. In thinking about that question, consider the following: Farmer Young had incurred the cost of buying or renting his land, buying seed, planting, cultivating, and harvesting. He expected to recoup these costs, plus a profit, from the value of the crops. The lost yield measure of damages automatically compensates for all of his costs plus his profit. Giving him the rental value of the land would compensate for only one of his costs, and therefore would not make him whole. In *Jay Clutter*, because the crop was never planted, plaintiff may have incurred only one of these costs: the rental value of the land. He is not entitled to a lost yield measure of damages, unless there is an offset for the costs he saved: the costs of seed, planting, cultivating, and harvesting. He should have been entitled to his profit, but he apparently did not prove what that would have been.

3. Whenever damages depend on the value of work in progress, damages based on costs already expended plus a profit should equal damages based on value less cost of completion. If they don't, one of two things has happened. Either the value of the thing to be produced is not equal to the cost of producing it, or you have made a mistake. More generally, there will often be more than one way to calculate damages. If they don't yield approximately the same result, make sure you know why. What is being compensated by one measure that is not being compensated by the other? Or is some part of the loss being double counted in one of the two measures?

4. *Decatur County* also illustrates the convergence of the value approach and the reliance/expectancy approach to damages. The value of the lost crops is plaintiff's expectancy; he expected to earn a profit based

on fifty bushels per acre. Assuming there were other crop sprayers who would have done a competent job, plaintiff's reliance loss may be equal to his expectancy loss: If he had not hired Decatur County Ag-Services, he could have hired someone else who would have done the job right. But if Decatur County were the only crop sprayer available, then plaintiff's loss is a pure expectancy loss. But for his contract with Decatur County, he would have had however many beans the grasshoppers left. Decatur County's promise to spray created an expectancy that he could get a normal yield of fifty bushels per acre; its negligent performance of its contract defeated that expectancy.

5.   Suppose the proof of lost yield really were too speculative. In that event, plaintiff should be entitled to the rental value of the land as a second best measure of damage. But how speculative is too speculative? We will consider that question in section F.

NOTES ON THE VALUE OF TIME

1.   Plainly, defendant is entitled to an offset for any expenses plaintiff saved as a result of the lower yield. The court finds that plaintiff saved nothing because he did all the work himself. Does this mean that plaintiff's time has no value? Suppose plaintiff had worked many extra hours to save the part of the crop he saved. Should he be allowed to recover for the value of his extra labor? If you say yes to that question, don't you also have to say that defendant was entitled to an offset for the labor plaintiff saved? Should it matter whether the time plaintiff saved was used to take a part-time job that brought in income, or used for leisure? Does it make sense to say that unless the amount of time saved or the amount of extra time spent is quite substantial, the difficulties of proof and the small sums at stake make it not worth litigating over? Or is that up to the parties?

2.   The main obstacle to recovering the value of lost time is the difficulty of keeping records that document how much time was spent. A court that insists on detailed proof can make recovery impossible for all but the most meticulous plaintiff. Less exacting proof is more realistic, but it creates a potential for excessive claims. Consider two recent cases:

In Bunn v. Central Realty, 592 F.2d 891 (5th Cir. 1979), a housing discrimination case, the court awarded $500 for the unproved but presumed inconvenience of finding another apartment.

In Convoy Co. v. Sperry Rand Corp., 672 F.2d 781 (9th Cir. 1982), ✳ plaintiff recovered $82,281.63 for the time its salaried employees lost due to a defective computer. The court rejected the argument that plaintiff would have paid these salaries anyway; if the computer had worked, plaintiff would have gotten something for its money. The real problem was that there were no time records, and the trial was ten years after the events. The supervisors were allowed to "estimate" how much time they had spent, and to confirm each other's estimates. Not surprisingly, defendant offered no contradictory evidence. Is there any middle ground between denying recovery and accepting such estimates without question? How could a judge, jury, or defense lawyer test the reasonableness of such estimates?

HARRIS v. AMERICAN INVESTMENT CO.
523 F.2d 220 (8th Cir. 1975),
cert. denied, 423 U.S. 1054 (1976)

Before MATTHES, Senior Circuit Judge, BRIGHT and STEPHENSON, Circuit Judges.

BRIGHT, Circuit Judge. . . .

AIC stock is publicly traded on the New York Stock Exchange. Harris purchased his shares on August 4, 1969, at a price of $18⅞. The market for this stock remained fairly constant for a time, but by June 30, 1970, the stock had plunged to $7½. It recovered somewhat thereafter, and by April 8, 1971, the day preceding the filing of the complaint, AIC shares were sold on the New York Stock Exchange at a high of $16⅝ and a low of $16⅛.

Harris contends that in the fall of 1970 he came to believe that he had been the victim of an on-going scheme of misrepresentation and fraudulent concealment of information. At that time the market price of AIC stock had fallen to approximately $9 per share. He contends that he approached his attorneys at that time to discuss possible federal securities law violations. The attorneys prepared a complaint in the winter of 1970 and, as we have noted, filed it in early April of 1971.

I. Damages

The dispute in this case focuses upon whether the appellant individually sustained any recoverable damages from the defendants' alleged violations of §§10(b) and 18(a) of the Securities Exchange Act. In granting summary judgment, the district court ruled that Harris had suffered no damages. . . .

The district court noted that following Harris' purchase of the stock its price exceeded $18⅞ — his purchase price — for 47 days through May 31, 1971. Included in this period were 18 days out of the 30 days immediately subsequent to the commencement of this action. However, the record shows that between the fall of 1970, when plaintiff asserts that he first suspected fraud, and the filing of the lawsuit, the stock at no time equaled or exceeded the purchase price.

The validity of the district court's holding rests upon its legal determination that the defendants may be absolved from liability by showing that the plaintiff could have recouped his loss by selling his stock subsequent to his discovery of their alleged fraud, including sale after the institution of the lawsuit. We disagree with this determination. We hold that on the record presented in this case it cannot be concluded, for purposes of summary judgment, that plaintiff has suffered no damages.

A. Possible Dates for Fixing Damages

Although the federal securities laws in several instances offer greater protection to buyers and sellers of securities than do common law fraud concepts, common law fraud concepts underlie the securities laws and provide guidance as to their reach and application, particularly where, as here, Congress has not specified the remedies available to a defrauded buyer.

In cases arising under §10(b) and Rule 10b-5 the federal courts employ an out-of-pocket rule of damages borrowed from the tort action of deceit.

The Restatement of Torts (1938), at §549, measures damages under this rule as

(a) the difference between the value of the thing bought, sold or exchanged and its purchase price or the value of the thing exchanged for it. . . .

Thus, actual pecuniary loss rather than loss of bargain is the measure of damages. . . .

The federal courts have identified two dates at which damages under the out-of-pocket rule may be ascertained. Quoting from Sigafus v. Porter, 179 U.S. 116, 125 (1900), Judge Aldrich of the First Circuit has suggested that damages for a defrauded purchaser of securities coming within the coverage of §10(b) and Rule 10b-5 should be fixed as of the date of purchase:

[T]he damages are to be reckoned solely by "the difference between the real value of the property at the date of its sale to the plaintiffs and the price paid for it, with interest from that date, and, in addition, such outlays as were legitimately attributable to the defendant's conduct, but not damages covering 'the expected fruits of an unrealized speculation' [Smith v. Bolles, 132 U.S. 125, 130 (1889)]." [Janigan v. Taylor, 344 F.2d 781, 786 (1st Cir.), *cert. denied*, 382 U.S. 879 (1965).] The typical fact situation in these cases discloses an alleged fraudulent concealment or misrepresentation by a seller directed at the buyer-plaintiff only and not the public at large. Hence, the actual worth of the securities at the time of purchase by the plaintiff is readily ascertainable.

The Restatement of Torts observes that there may be difficulty ascertaining the value of the article transferred in connection with a misrepresentation where the misrepresentation affects the market price of the article. This is particularly true with respect to publicly-traded securities:

The value of the article is normally determined by the price at which it could be resold in an open market or by private sale if its quality or other characteristics which affect its value were known. However, the price which determines

the value of the article is not necessarily the price which it would bring at the
time the sale is made. In many cases this price is due to the widespread belief
of other buyers in misrepresentations similar to that made to the person seeking recovery, as where the market price of securities, such as bonds or shares, is
the result of widely spread misrepresentations of those who issue or market
them. The fact that the market price is inflated or depressed by such misrepresentations is the important factor which makes the price fictitious. . . .

[Restatement of Torts §549, comment c at 111.]

Thus, where a defendant's fraudulent conduct is alleged, as it is in this
case, to have caused an artificial market of long duration, damages have
been fixed, consistently with the Restatement's position, not at the date of
purchase but rather at the date of discovery of the fraud.

Although the Tenth Circuit has fixed damages as of the date that the
buyer actually discovered, or should have discovered, the seller's fraud,
Richardson v. MacArthur, 451 F.2d 35, 43-44 (10th Cir. 1971), we believe
that under the allegations made in the instant case the public discovery of
the fraud may be the proper date at which to ascertain damages. The
circumstances may disclose that only then did the market reflect the true
value of the stock, unaffected by what is alleged to have been the defendants' continuing fraud:

> [V]alue is determined by their [i.e., the securities'] market price after the fraud
> is discovered when the price ceases to be fictitious and represents the consen-
> sus of buying and selling opinion of the value of the securities as they actually
> are. . . .
>   In the majority of stock transactions the person seeking recovery discovers
> the falsity of the misrepresentations at the same time that it becomes known to
> the investing public and, therefore, at a time when the price of the stock is no
> longer inflated or depressed by the same or similar misrepresentations. It may
> be, however, that he discovers the falsity of the representations either earlier
> or later than the general public. In the first situation, his loss is determined by
> the actual value of the securities in question shown by their market price after
> the public discovery of the fraud brings the price into accord with the actual
> value. In the second situation, where the person seeking recovery does not
> learn of the falsity of the facts represented until sometime after the general
> public has discovered it, the value of the securities is fixed by the price at
> which they are selling at the time of his and not of the public's discovery.

[Restatement of Torts §549, comment c at 111, 112-13.]

The American Law Institute's Federal Securities Code draft adopts in
principle this same reasoning:

The measure of damages . . . is

> (A), if the plaintiff is a buyer, the difference between the amount that he paid
> and the value of the security determined as of the time specified in section

1402(e)(1) [i.e., when, inter alia, all material facts became generally available to the investing public].

[ALI, Federal Securities Code §1402(f)(1)(A) (Tent. Draft No. 2, 1973).] This proposed codification incorporates the common law rule for the date of ascertaining damages.

Thus, assuming, arguendo, the truth of Harris' claims that the actual value of the securities cannot be established at or near the date of purchase due to an artificially inflated market price of long duration attributable to defendants' fraudulent misrepresentations, Harris may be able at the trial to establish an alternate basis for recovery by introducing evidence of his damages as of the date of public discovery of the fraud.

If Harris cannot make out a case justifying this rule of damages, he may nevertheless be able to prove at trial that the actual value of the securities at the time of purchase was less than the market price that he paid for them. . . .

B. Mitigation of Damages

A defrauded buyer of securities may maintain an action for damages under §10(b) and, presumably, §18(a), even though he continues to hold the securities. At common law, a defrauded purchaser of securities is under no duty to sell them prior to maintaining an action for deceit but may hold them for investment purposes if he chooses. Thus, Harris was under no duty to sell his AIC stock, for mitigation of damages or any other purpose, prior to commencing this action.

Where one has bought securities for long-term investment, it would be inappropriate to apply a rule requiring him to sell them prematurely for the benefit of the defrauding defendant. As we have noted, Harris' damages may be measured as of the date of public discovery of the fraud. Under those circumstances,

> [t]he plaintiff will not be able to avail himself of any further decrease in the value of the security after that date. So also the defendant should not be able to avail itself of any increase in the value of the stock after that date. This is the only method in which a consistent measure of damages can be obtained.

[Cant v. Becker & Co., 379 F. Supp. 972, 975 (N.D. Ill. 1974).]

Consequently, we reject the appellees' contention that Harris was under a duty, after discovery of the fraud, to sell his AIC stock for the benefit of the appellees. By continuing to hold the stock after that date Harris has, in effect, made a second investment decision unrelated to his initial decision to purchase the stock. As the court observed in Cant v. Becker & Co., supra, 379 F. Supp. at 975, what happens after this second decision has no bearing whatsoever on the measure of plaintiff's damages. . . .

NOTES ON DAMAGES FOR SECURITIES FRAUD

1. Both holdings in *Harris* are controversial. If no other events have intervened, the market price after full disclosure may be the best evidence of the true value of the stock at the time of plaintiff's purchase. But what if stock prices generally rose or fell 30 percent in the meantime? Or what if some boon or disaster unrelated to the fraud has struck the company? Concerns such as these underlie a conflicting line of cases that insists that damages must be measured by the difference between the price paid and the true value of the stock on the day of purchase. There is a good statement of this view in Green v. Occidental Petroleum Corp., 541 F.2d 1335, 1341-1346 (9th Cir. 1976) (Sneed, J., concurring).

2. The problem is further complicated by plaintiff's need to file the case as a class action on behalf of all who purchased the security during the time the price was affected by the fraud; such cases are generally too expensive to litigate as individual claims. Judge Sneed would have the jury find the actual value of the security on every day that the fraud is alleged to have continued, which may be a period of many months or even years. He assumed that these values could be determined and plotted on a chart with the price of the stock; each investor's damage would be the difference between price and value on the day he bought. For regularly traded stocks, daily prices are readily available. But actual value is much more difficult to determine.

3. In Bonime v. Doyle, 416 F. Supp. 1372 (S.D.N.Y. 1976), the court adopted Judge Sneed's measure of damage but found it impossible to determine the actual value of the shares at any time during the fraudulent scheme. The impossibility of proving damage was a substantial factor in its approval of a $1.35 million class settlement in a case where even defendants estimated damages under the *Harris* formula at $40 million.* The court thought the *Harris* formula irrelevant, because the price of the stock had been depressed by many factors besides disclosure of the fraud. Which is worse: the risk that defendant will be held liable for losses not caused by the fraud, or the risk that damage determination will be so difficult that plaintiffs get only token compensation?

4. *Bonime* illustrates another common pattern in the cases. Often the fraud consists of failing to disclose a risk that may or may not come to fruition. In *Bonime*, the company announced that it had acquired rights to what appeared to be the largest copper deposit in the world. It did not disclose that it owned only the right to explore and the first opportunity to negotiate for mining rights. That is not as good as owning mining rights, but it is worth a great deal. Had the company disclosed the truth, the

---

* The author was one of those representing class members who objected to the settlement.

stock might have traded at a level only slightly below the inflated price it actually achieved. As it happened, negotiations for mining rights broke down, and the company lost the deposit. At that point, the price of the shares crashed. Suppose the shares were worth $15 if the company owned mining rights, $12 if it owned the right to negotiate for mining rights, and $5 if the negotiations fell through. What are the damages of an investor who bought at $15? Is the breakdown of negotiations an extraneous factor for which the company is not responsible? Or should it have to protect investors from risks it failed to disclose?

5.   Neither measure of damage bears much relation to the defrauded investor's view of his loss, but that is especially true of Judge Sneed's measure. If plaintiff buys at $15 and sells at $10, or holds shares worth $10 at the time of trial, he will think of his loss as $5 per share. He will be surprised to learn that the $10 figure has nothing whatever to do with his damages. What if he would never have bought the shares at all had he known the truth? In that case, there is authority for awarding the difference between purchase price and sale price. Chasins v. Smith, Barney & Co., 438 F.2d 1167, 1173 (2d Cir. 1970).

There is a similar award on somewhat different reasoning in Hotaling v. A. B. Leach & Co., 247 N.Y. 84, 159 N.E. 870 (1928). Plaintiff paid $980 for a bond issued by National Oil Co. Changed conditions in the oil industry drove National into receivership, and the bond was paid off for $5.84. Despite the changed conditions, the court awarded the difference between purchase price and sales price as damages: $974.16. The court reasoned that plaintiff *might* not have bought the bond if the company's prospects had not been exaggerated. The court also relied on a form of the argument raised in note 4: If the company had been as strong as the seller of the bond had claimed, it would have survived the changed conditions in the industry. *Chasins* and *Hotaling* are exceptional; *Harris* and Judge Sneed's opinion reflect the dominant views.

6.   Section 11(e) of the Securities Act, 15 U.S.C. §77k (1976), specifies a measure of damage closer to the investor's intuitive sense of what he lost. Section 11 applies only when a material misstatement or omission appears in a formal registration statement under the Securities Act of 1933. Plaintiff can recover the difference between the price he paid or the initial offering price, whichever is lower, and:

1.   the price at which he sold, if he sold before filing suit,
2.   the value of the shares on the day he filed suit, or
3.   the price at which he sells after filing suit but before judgment, if that is more than the value on the day he filed suit.

Recovery is reduced to the extent defendant proves that the decline in value resulted from causes other than facts misrepresented or not disclosed in the registration statement. The American Law Institute's proposed Federal Securities Code provides a similar defense. Is this allocation of the burden of proof an effective compromise between the *Harris* measure and Judge Sneed's measure? Should courts adopt it under other sections of the securities laws in which Congress did not specify the measure of damages?

7.   *Harris* also holds it irrelevant that the price of the shares subsequently rose above the price at which plaintiff purchased. That is consistent with Judge Sneed's view that damages are fixed on the day of purchase. Is there any reason to treat subsequent positive developments differently from subsequent negative developments? Is there anything to the argument that Harris hasn't lost anything? To the argument that he would have made an even bigger profit if he hadn't bought at an inflated price? What if he wouldn't have bought at all but for the fraud?

8.   What if Harris had sold before disclosure, while the market price was still inflated by the fraud? Wouldn't that give him a benefit from the violation? Shouldn't that be offset against his original loss? Judge Sneed thinks so; that is the one exception to his rule that damages are fixed from the moment of purchase.

D.   DAMAGES WHERE VALUE CANNOT BE MEASURED IN DOLLARS

BOTTA v. BRUNNER
26 N.J. 82, 138 A.2d 713 (1958)

[This was a suit for personal injuries arising out of an auto accident. The jury awarded $5,500 and defendant appealed.]

FRANCIS, J. . . .

In his closing argument to the jury, after speaking of actual monetary losses, plaintiff's counsel said:

> You must add to that, next, the pain and suffering and the disability that she has undergone from August 2nd, 1953 to now. Take that first. That is 125 weeks of pain and suffering. Now, that is difficult to admeasure, I suppose. How much can you give for pain and suffering? As a guide, I try to think of myself. What would be a minimum that a person is entitled to? And you must place yourself in the position of this woman. If you add that disability which has been described to you, and you were wearing this 24 hours a day, how much do you think you should get for every day you had to go through that harrowing experience, or every hour?
>
> Well, I thought I would use this kind of suggestion. I don't know. It is for you to determine whether you think I am low or high. Would fifty cents an hour for that kind of suffering be too high?

On objection, the court declared the argument to be improper as to "the measure of damages for pain and suffering" and directed that it be discontinued. . . .

For hundreds of years, the measure of damages for pain and suffering following in the wake of a personal injury has been "fair and reasonable compensation." This general standard was adopted because of universal acknowledgment that a more specific or definitive one is impossible. There is and there can be no fixed basis, table, standard, or mathematical rule which will serve as an accurate index and guide to the establishment of damage awards for personal injuries. And it is equally plain that there is no measure by which the amount of pain and suffering endured by a particular human can be calculated. No market place exists at which such malaise is bought and sold. A person can sell quantities of his blood, but there is no mart where the price of a voluntary subjection of oneself to pain and suffering is or can be fixed. It has never been suggested that a standard of value can be found and applied. The varieties and degrees of pain are almost infinite. Individuals differ greatly in susceptibility to pain and in capacity to withstand it. And the impossibility of recognizing or of isolating fixed levels or plateaus of suffering must be conceded.

It is just as futile to undertake to attach a price tag to each level or plateau which could be said to have a reasonable basis in scientific or economic fact. Any effort to do so must become lost in emotion, fancy and speculation.

As a consequence, the law has declared the standard for measuring damages for personal injuries to be reasonable compensation and has entrusted the administration of this criterion to the impartial conscience and judgment of jurors who may be expected to act reasonably, intelligently and in harmony with the evidence. This does not mean that jurors are free to fix what they would want as compensation if they had sustained the injuries or what the pain and suffering would be worth to them. The so-called "golden rule" may not be applied to such damages. Obviously, the quoted portion of plaintiff's summation here runs counter to this principle. However, we prefer to base our disposition of the appeal on a more extensive treatment of the problem.

But since the nature of the subject matter admits only of the broad concept of reasonable compensation, may counsel for the plaintiff or the defendant state to the jury, in opening or closing, his belief as to the pecuniary value or price of pain and suffering per hour or day or week, and ask that such figure be used as part of a mathematical formula for calculating the damages to be awarded? Without expressing a personal opinion, may he suggest that the valuation be based on so much per hour or day or week, or ask the jurors if they do not think the pain and suffering are fairly worth so much per hour or day or week — and then demonstrate, by employing such rate as a factor in his computation, that a verdict of a fixed amount of money would be warranted or could be justified?

Some jurisdictions have sanctioned such practice. Others, which we shall advert to, have condemned it. The precise question has not been passed upon by this court until now. Accordingly, we are free to adopt the rule which in our judgment best serves the cause of justice and its fair and orderly administration.

As has been indicated, pain and suffering have no known dimensions, mathematical or financial. There is no exact correspondence between money and physical or mental injury or suffering, and the various factors involved are not capable of proof in dollars and cents. For this reason, the only standard for evaluation is such amount as reasonable persons estimate to be fair compensation. In discussing the matter of a proposed mathematical formula for determining the allowance for future pain and suffering and inconvenience, the Eighth Circuit Court of Appeals said in Chicago & N.W. Ry. Co. v. Candler, 283 F. 881, 884, (1922): . . .

> At the best the allowance is an estimated sum determined by the intelligence and conscience of the jury, and we are convinced that a jury would be much more likely to return a just verdict, considering the estimated life as one single period, than if it should attempt to reach a verdict by dividing the life into yearly periods, setting down yearly estimates, and then reducing the estimates to their present value. The arbitrariness and artificiality of such a method is so apparent that to require a jury to apply it would, we think, be an absurdity.

In our neighboring state of Pennsylvania the rule assigning the admeasurement of damages for injuries to the jury has been adhered to over the years with the utmost fidelity. No suggestion of the character made in the present case either by court or counsel is tolerated; nor is reference to the ad damnum clause of the complaint permitted. Speaking on the subject in a fairly early opinion, the Supreme Court said:

> Pain and suffering are not capable of being exactly measured by an equivalent in money, and we have repeatedly said that they have no market price. The question in any given case is not what it would cost to hire someone to undergo the measure of pain alleged to have been suffered by the plaintiff, but what, under all the circumstances, should be allowed the plaintiff in addition to the other items of damage to which he is entitled, in consideration of suffering necessarily endured. . . . This should not be estimated by a sentimental or fanciful standard. . . .
>
> The word "compensation," in the phrase "compensation for pain and suffering," is not to be understood as meaning price or value, but as describing an allowance looking towards recompense for or made because of the suffering consequent upon the injury.

Goodhart v. Pennsylvania R. Co., supra [177 Pa. 1, 35 A. 192].

And in a case where plaintiff's counsel, in cross examining the defendant, called express attention to the ad damnum clause, the Federal Court for the Third Circuit, which follows the Pennsylvania rule, declared: . . .

> The amount of damages a party recovers is ascertained by the jury from evidence regularly offered and admitted by the court of such pertinent facts as will enable the jury to itself fix the money value of the injury sustained. While among those facts may, at times, be certain definite amounts in the way of medical, surgical, and nursing expenses, and other items capable of exact fixation, yet, when it comes to determining the amount of the damages to be awarded, this is the province of the jury alone, and of a jury uninfluenced by the figures or estimates of any other person as to the amount thereof. The law, therefore, permits no estimate to be given by either party to the jury, even under oath, of the money amount of such damages, and to get the same character of estimates before a jury by indirect methods is a reprehensible practice.

Vaughan v. Magee, 218 F. 630, 631 (3 Cir., 1914). . . .

There can be no doubt that the prime purpose of suggestions, direct or indirect, in the opening or closing statements of counsel of per hour or per diem sums as the value of or as compensation for pain, suffering and kindred elements associated with injury and disability is to instill in the minds of the jurors impressions, figures and amounts not founded or appearing in the evidence. . . .

If plaintiff's counsel is permitted to make such valuation suggestions to the jury, justice cannot be administered fairly in the trial of this type of case. Can defense counsel argue that pain and suffering are worth only $2.50 per day or $1 or any lesser sum? If he attempts to do so, he must necessarily inject as further factual suggestions valuations which again are incapable of proof. By doing so, he fortifies his adversary's implication that the law recognizes pain and suffering as having been evaluated and as capable of being evaluated on such basis. . . .

In Ahlstrom v. Minneapolis, St. Paul & Sault Ste. M.R. Co., 244 Minn. 1, (1955), . . . [t]he court said: . . . "Certainly no amount of money per day could compensate a person reduced to plaintiff's position, and to attempt such evaluation, as in this case, leads only to monstrous verdicts." . . .

An excellent expression of the fundamental doctrine to which we adhere is found in Braddock v. Seaboard Air Line Railroad Company, 80 So. 2d 662 (Fla. Sup. Ct. 1955):

> Jurors know the nature of pain, embarrassment and inconvenience, and they also know the nature of money. Their problem of equating the two to afford reasonable and just compensation calls for a high order of human judgment, and the law has provided no better yardstick for their guidance than their enlightened conscience. Their problem is not one of mathematical cal-

culation but involves an exercise of their sound judgment of what is fair and right. . . .

It is declared to be improper to send the complaint to the jury as a matter of course, since it contains the damages demanded. But our holding is not intended to interfere with use of the pleadings for other proper trial or evidentiary purposes.

Informing the jury of the ad damnum clause serves no useful or sound function. . . . In the hands of the jury, untrained in the trial of cases, it may very well raise confusing and difficult complications. It is a matter of common knowledge that ordinarily the amount of damages laid in the complaint is much in excess of any sum which the plaintiff hopes to receive.

WACHENFELD, J. (dissenting in part).

I am generally in accord with the majority opinion but cannot subscribe to that portion which [forbids counsel to suggest a total sum to the jury or inform the jury of the amount demanded in the complaint].

The practices . . . have prevailed for years and have resulted in no inequities or difficulties warranting our interference with them.

NOTES ON PAIN AND SUFFERING

1. At least four distinct practices are condemned by the *Botta* opinion:

a. The Golden Rule argument, which asks jurors how much they would want if they had suffered plaintiff's injuries, has been condemned everywhere. The appeal to put themselves in plaintiff's shoes is an appeal to abandon neutrality; defendant might as plausibly urge jurors to imagine how much they would want to pay if they had inflicted these injuries.

b. The argument that jurors should give the market value of the injuries, or the amount it would cost to hire someone to suffer these injuries, has also been uniformly rejected. Why should that be? Isn't it the measure that best implements the principle of making plaintiff as well off as he would have been but for the wrong? Isn't it the measure most analogous to the measure in property damage cases and other cases we have read? Obviously, the analogy is not entirely apt. In the property damage cases, there is a real market for such property. Evidence of prices in that market can be presented. But as the court notes, there is no market in pain and suffering. One can imagine hiring persons to undergo modest pain and suffering, in medical experiments for example, but such experimental subjects are generally people with very few other options. It is hard to imagine hiring a person to suffer permanent paralysis, blindness, or brain damage, for any sum of money. Is the jury better off without any guidance at all, or with the guidance of being instructed to imagine an unimaginable transaction? Should the fear of "monstrous verdicts" play any role in assessing this issue? Or should we expect monstrous verdicts only in cases of monstrous injuries?

c. Judges and commentators are badly split on whether plaintiff's counsel should be allowed to urge the jury to assess pain and suffering on a per diem or unit-of-time basis. In upholding the unit-of-time argument, the Fifth Circuit reasoned:

> The idea or worth of one year of pain may not be as understandable, real or persuasive to a juror as its equivalent, 365 days of pain and suffering. Whether the unit be cast in years or months, or weeks or days, is a mere matter of degree, and there is little logic in prohibiting the discussion of large units of time in terms of their smaller mathematical equivalents. It is merely a different way of talking about precisely the same thing. . . .

Baron Tube Co. v. Transport Insurance Co., 365 F.2d 858, 865 (5th Cir. 1966).

d. _Botta_ also holds that counsel cannot express any opinion at all on the amount of damages for pain and suffering, or mention the amount pleaded in the complaint, even if he refrains from the more controversial arguments discussed above. A few other states also follow this rule; most do not. Does it make any sense to insist that the jury be left utterly without any guidance at all on this issue? On the other hand, how much guidance does the jury really get from the argument of counsel?

2. As might be expected, those who take an economic approach to law tend to equate compensation with the market value of pain and suffering. Judge Posner notes that market compensation would produce much larger recoveries:

> The tendency of tort damages, although so often criticized as excessive, is in fact to undercompensate the victims of serious accidents. If damages fully compensated the victim, he would be indifferent about being injured or not being injured. . . .

R. Posner, Economic Analysis of Law 155 (2d ed. 1977). But he also concludes that this is an area in which society cannot afford full compensation. He uses the example of wrongful death, but the point is equally applicable to very serious injuries:

> Most people would not exchange their lives for anything less than an infinite sum of money, if the exchange were to take place immediately. . . . Yet it cannot be correct that the proper award of damages in a death case is infinite. This would imply that the proper rate of fatal accidents was zero, . . . and it is plain that people are unwilling individually or collectively to incur the costs necessary to reduce the rate of fatal accidents so drastically.

Id. at 150. Could this be what the court was afraid of when it talked about "monstrous verdicts?" Would truly compensatory damages shut down all industry, all transportation, and all other risky but valuable activities?

3.   What if plaintiff's injuries render him incapable of feeling pain? Should the comatose victim's recovery be limited to lost earnings and medical expenses? Even if he feels no pain, what about his loss of all capacity to enjoy life? Does it matter that he cannot derive any compensating pleasure from the recovery, so that in practical effect only his heirs will benefit from the compensation for his loss of capacity to enjoy life? Most courts would award substantial damages in such cases: some under the "pain and suffering" label, and some under the "loss of capacity to enjoy life" label. But some courts disagree.

The case of Michael Flannery is a dramatic example of the disagreement. An automobile accident left Flannery permanently comatose. A federal employee driving on government business caused the accident, so Flannery's personal representative sued the United States under the Federal Tort Claims Act. The act provides that the United States shall be liable for negligence and certain other torts under "the law of the place where the act or omission occurred," 28 U.S.C. §1346(b) (1982), "but shall not be liable for interest prior to judgment or for punitive damages," 28 U.S.C. §2674 (1982).

The trial judge awarded $1.3 million for loss of capacity to enjoy life. The government argued on appeal that there could be no recovery for loss of capacity to enjoy life, and the Fourth Circuit certified that question to the Supreme Court of Appeals of West Virginia. The state court answered that loss of capacity to enjoy life was a proper element of recovery under West Virginia law. Flannery v. United States, 297 S.E.2d 433 (W. Va. 1982).

Under the certification procedure, the state court answers the certified question of law and the federal court uses the answer to decide the case. When the case came back to the Fourth Circuit, the majority decided it had misunderstood the case. It held that because Flannery could get no benefit from the award for loss of capacity to enjoy life, it was punitive and not recoverable under the Tort Claims Act. Flannery v. United States, 718 F.2d 108, 110-111 (4th Cir. 1983). It didn't matter that West Virginia considered the award compensatory. One judge dissented.

If the key to the case was that Flannery couldn't get any benefit from the award, why weren't lost wages also punitive? The only money that benefitted Flannery was the money that paid his medical expenses.

SANCHEZ v. SCHINDLER
651 S.W.2d 249 (Tex. 1983)

SPEARS, J. . . .

Johnny Sanchez, age fourteen, was severely injured in a motorcycle-pickup truck collision in Key Allegro, Texas in 1979. Paramedics treated him on the scene and transported him to Memorial Medical Center in Corpus Christi. His parents were at home at the time of the accident, and were told of the collision by a neighbor. At the hospital, they were prevented from seeing their son, but caught glimpses of his bloody legs through the doorway. He died several hours later.

Mr. and Mrs. Sanchez brought suit for the damages they sustained, individually and as heirs of Johnny Sanchez, against Charles J. Schindler, Jr., a minor, and Charles J. and Jean Schindler, his parents. The jury awarded $50,000 for the pain and suffering endured by Johnny Sanchez prior to his death, $7,187.41 for Johnny's medical treatment, $4,000 for funeral and burial expenses, and $450 for damages to his motorcycle. The jury found that Mr. and Mrs. Sanchez sustained no pecuniary loss resulting from their son's death; however, they awarded $102,500 damages for the mental anguish suffered by Mrs. Sanchez. Upon defendants' motion, the trial court disregarded the answers to the special issues on mental anguish. Angelica Sanchez has appealed, seeking the jury award of $102,500 for her injuries.

The seminal question presented is whether damages for mental anguish are recoverable under the Texas Wrongful Death Act for the death of a child. Tex. Rev. Civ. Stat. Ann. art. 4671. More specifically, we must determine whether Texas should continue to follow the pecuniary loss rule as the proper measure of damages for the death of a child.

In the past a surviving parent's damages in an action for the death of a child under the Texas Wrongful Death Act have been limited to the pecuniary value of the child's services and financial contributions, minus the cost of his care, support and education. The Texas statute does not expressly limit recovery to pecuniary loss. Tex. Rev. Civ. Stat. Ann. article 4671 creates a cause of action for "actual damages on account of the injuries causing the death. . . ." Article 4677 provides that "[t]he jury may give such damages as they may think proportionate to the injury resulting from such death." Like most states, Texas patterned its wrongful death statutes after Lord Campbell's Act. The Fatal Accident Act, 9 & 10 Vict., ch. 93 §1 (1846). The English court ruled that Lord Campbell's Act limited recovery to pecuniary loss. Blake v. Midway Railway Co., 118 Eng. Rep 35 (Q.B. 1852). In March v. Walker, 48 Tex. 372, 375 (1877), this court held that since the language of the Texas Wrongful Death Act was based on Lord Campbell's Act, the measure of damages under the Texas statute would also be restricted to pecuniary loss.

Sanchez argues the pecuniary loss rule is based on an antiquated concept of the child as an economic asset, and should be rejected. We agree. It is time for this court to revise its interpretation of the Texas Wrongful Death statutes in light of present social realities and expand recovery beyond the antiquated and inequitable pecuniary loss rule. If the rule is literally followed, the average child would have a negative worth. Strict adherence to the pecuniary loss rule could lead to the negligent tortfeasor being rewarded for having saved the parents the cost and expense of rearing a child. The real loss sustained by a parent is not the loss of any financial benefit to be gained from the child, but is the loss of love, advice, comfort, companionship and society.

We, therefore, reject the pecuniary loss limitation and allow a plaintiff to recover damages for loss of companionship and society and damages for mental anguish for the death of his or her child. In this case, Mrs. Sanchez pleaded for the recovery of damages for mental anguish, and the jury awarded her $102,500 pursuant to the special issues on mental anguish. She has preserved her argument on appeal to this court.

Schindler argues that the responsibility of changing the recovery under the Wrongful Death statute belongs to the Texas Legislature. This court originally imposed the pecuniary loss rule as a limitation of the damages recoverable under the Texas Wrongful Death Act. It is, therefore, logical for this court to now act in response to the needs of a modern society, and abolish the antiquated rule in favor of recovery of loss of society and mental anguish. . . .

The legislature has attempted to amend the Texas Wrongful Death Act to allow damages for loss of society and mental anguish; however, none of the bills have passed. This court should not be bound by the prior legislative inaction in an area like tort law which has traditionally been developed primarily through the judicial process. Green, Protection of the Family Under Tort Law, 10 Hastings L.J. 237, 245 (1959). In his article, Dean Green stated that because the difficulties in reducing the refinements of tort law doctrines into statutory form often result in legislation which is either underinclusive or overbroad and which is frequently couched in ambiguous terms which the court must interpret, judicial decision is the best way to develop tort law. Id. at 246. Inaction of the legislature cannot be interpreted as prohibiting judicial reappraisal of the judicially created pecuniary loss rule. "[A] legislature legislates by legislating, not by doing nothing, not by keeping silent." Wycko v. Gnodtke, 105 N.W.2d 118, 121-22 (Mich. 1960).

This court has recognized previously that injuries to the familial relationship are significant injuries and are worthy of compensation. In Whittlesey v. Miller, 572 S.W.2d 665, 668 (Tex. 1978), we held that either spouse has a cause of action for loss of consortium suffered as a result of an injury to the other spouse by a tortfeasor's negligence. We held that loss of affection, solace, comfort, companionship, society, assistance, and sexual relations were real, direct, and personal losses and said that these losses were not too intangible or conjectural to be measured in pecuniary terms. Id. at 667. A parent's claim for damages for the loss of companionship of a child is closely analogous to the loss of consortium cause of action created in *Whittlesey*. . . .

Either by statute or judicial decision, thirty-five states allow recovery for loss of companionship and society in a wrongful death action brought by the parents. Presently, fourteen jurisdictions allow recovery for damages for loss of companionship and society under statutes containing language which traditionally had been interpreted as limiting recovery to pecuniary loss. Twenty-one states recognize recovery for loss of society and companionship by statute. Nine of these statutes were amended to include these elements after their existing statutes were judicially interpreted to include society and companionship.

Commentators are virtually unanimous in their criticism of the pecuniary loss limitation and advocate recovery for nonpecuniary losses.

The jurisdictions that do not limit recovery to pecuniary loss realize that damages for loss of companionship and society of a child are not too uncertain to be measured in pecuniary terms in an attempt to redress the actual loss which a parent suffers. These elements of damage are not too speculative to be given a monetary value. Recovery is allowed in other tort areas for injuries which are equally intangible; e.g., pain and suffering. The fear of excessive verdicts is not a sufficient justification for denying recovery for loss of companionship. The judicial system has adequate safeguards to prevent recovery of damages based on sympathy or prejudice rather than fair and just compensation for the plaintiff's injuries.

A parent's recovery under the wrongful death statute includes the mental anguish suffered as a result of the child's wrongful death. The destruction of the parent-child relationship results in mental anguish, and it would be unrealistic to separate injury to the familial relationship from emotional injury. Injuries resulting from mental anguish may actually be less nebulous than pain and suffering, or injuries resulting from loss of companionship and consortium. A plaintiff should be permitted to prove the damages resulting from a tortfeasor's negligent infliction of emotional trauma. This includes recovery for mental anguish.

In this case Mrs. Sanchez proved she is suffering from traumatic depressive neurosis. She presented testimony that she is despondent and disoriented, has been forced to seek mental attention for her neurosis and has frequent neck and shoulder pains and headaches. Mrs. Sanchez has proved that she suffered mental anguish, and therefore, is entitled to recover the $102,500 awarded to her by the jury for her mental anguish.[6]

Presently, the courts of several states allow recovery for mental anguish under statutes similar to Texas' statute. . . .

We, therefore, reverse the judgment of the court of appeals, and render judgment that Mrs. Angelica Sanchez recover $102,500 for the mental anguish she suffered as a result of her son's death in addition to the other damages awarded by the jury which have not been appealed.

---

6. Under the Wrongful Death Act there is no requirement that the plaintiff be within the zone of danger or have witnessed the accident in order to recover for mental anguish.

POPE, Chief Justice, dissenting. . . .

If we were dealing with the common law rather than the statute, I might be persuaded by the majority's reasoning. There is strong evidence, however, that the Texas Legislature intended to limit recovery to pecuniary losses when it enacted the Texas Wrongful Death Statute. The Texas statute was patterned after the English statute. Both statutes provided that "the jury may give such damages as they may think proportioned to the injury resulting from such death. . . ." The Fatal Accident Act, 9 & 10 Vict., ch. 93, §2 (1846); 1860 Tex. Gen. Laws, ch. 35, at 32, 4 H. Gammel, Laws of Texas 1394 (1898). When the Texas Legislature adopted the statute in 1860, the English statute and every American statute patterned after it had already been interpreted to limit recovery to pecuniary losses. The majority does not dispute that the Texas Legislature at the inception of the statute intended to apply the pecuniary loss rule to the Texas statute. The continued use of the same language for more than a century while the courts have time and again consistently held that mental anguish may not be recovered shows that the courts' construction is in accord with the legislature's intent.

There are times when we have properly stuffed new meaning into old words of some statute. We should proceed modestly, however, when the Texas Legislature has addressed the provisions of this specific statute many times since we handed down March v. Walker, 48 Tex. 372 (1877). The Texas Legislature had addressed the provisions of this specific statute many occasions since our decision in *March*. Article 4671 of the act, which authorizes the cause of action, has been amended five times. The Sixty-Third Legislature addressed the specific matter of damages under the statute and enacted article 4675a to permit proof of remarriage of the surviving spouse as evidence of reduced damages. Four bills introduced in the Sixty-Sixth Legislature and three bills introduced in the Sixty-Seventh Legislature would have expanded recovery to include mental anguish. None of these bills passed. . . .

An effective way of defeating a weak or bad bill is to avoid voting on it. The legislature's refusal to vote on the many proposals to change the measure of damages is an opinion of that branch of government that there is no pressing need to change the present law. Legislatures act affirmatively and negatively; but in either instance, the legislative will is expressed. For us to ignore defeated legislation is as misleading as it would be for a court to reject from our common law decisions those cases which hold for the defendant. When we refuse the claims of plaintiffs and hold for defendants, we are still handing down legal opinions and guidelines, just as the legislature makes a statement of its intent by defeating legislation. . . .

A second reading of the majority opinion shows that the many cases cited in support of its proposed new rule relate to loss of society, which is not here involved. It is not until we reach the penultimate paragraph of the majority opinion that we are told that the majority's new rule is actually supported only by "several states." According to the majority, three states allow recovery for mental anguish under statutes similar to Texas' statute: Arizona, South Carolina, and Washington.

The Washington Supreme Court quite properly applied the Washington Legislature's 1967 amended statute that provided for a parent's recovery. We do not have a statute, as Washington does, that says:

> damages may be recovered for the loss of love or companionship of the child and for injury to or destruction of the parent-child relationship. . . .

Wash. Rev. Code §4.24.010. The Arizona Supreme Court abandoned the precuniary loss rule as a result of a 1956 amendment which authorized

> such damages as it [the jury] deems fair and just with reference to the injury resulting from the death to the surviving parties who may be entitled to recover. . . .

Ariz. Rev. Stat. Ann. §12-613.

The South Carolina Supreme Court has always construed its statute to permit mental anguish damages. The important distinction is that none of these courts had to overturn an established statutory construction. The majority does not cite a single case in which a court has authorized damages for mental anguish by overruling a long-standing statutory construction that has been ratified by legislative re-enactment of the existing statute and ratified by legislative rejection of amendments authorizing mental anguish damages. Yet that is what the majority does today.

Other states that have achieved the result sought by the majority have waited until the statutory policy was changed by the legislature's amendment of the statute. A minority of eleven jurisdictions permit recovery for mental anguish, and ten of those jurisdictions declared their policy by amending their statutes. The majority can muster no substantial precedent for its in-house change of legislative policy.

The majority opinion does not clearly delineate the proof required to recover its newly created damages for mental anguish. Some of the language in the opinion suggests that any mental anguish, however slight, is compensable. The established threshold for recovering mental anguish damages requires proof of willful tort, gross negligence, willful and wanton disregard, or physical injury resulting from the mental anguish. This threshold is universally applied in the common law and statutory law of this state. . . . In this case, Mrs. Sanchez has satisfied the threshold for recovering mental anguish damages by proving a resulting physical injury. In future cases, we should continue to adhere to the universally established standard for mental anguish damages. . . .

I would affirm the judgments of the courts below.

McGEE and BARROW, JJ., join in this dissenting opinion.

RAY, Justice, concurring.

On Motion for Rehearing

I concur with the majority in overruling the Schindlers' motion for rehearing. I further concur with the majority of the Court in rejecting the pecuniary loss limitation in actions for the wrongful death of a child. In doing so, we join the modern trend in allowing recovery for loss of companionship, society, emotional support, love and felicity.

The opinion speaks only to recovery by a parent for the death of a *minor* child. Legal symmetry mandates that the class of beneficiaries affected by this decision not be limited to parents of minor children. The majority has aptly noted that "injuries to the familial relationship are significant injuries and are worthy of compensation." In future cases brought under the Texas Wrongful Death Act, I would permit recovery for the social losses and emotional injuries inflicted upon any beneficiary designated by statute.

We have permitted Mrs. Sanchez to recover damages for mental anguish, recognizing that "[a] plaintiff should be permitted to prove the damage resulting from a tortfeasor's negligent infliction of emotional trauma." Mrs. Sanchez introduced evidence that she is suffering from traumatic depressive neurosis and as a result must seek medical care for physical pains associated with her neurosis. While the majority opinion does not address the issue, I do not believe that proof of such physical manifestations should be a necessary predicate for recovery for mental anguish.

Mr. Chief Justice Pope, in his dissent to the majority opinion, states that "[s]ome of that language in the opinion suggests that any mental anguish, however slight, is compensable." While I agree with his observation, I disagree with his objection. The focus should be on compensating the bereaved for their harrowing experience resulting from the untimely, preventable and otherwise unnecessary death of one with whom they have shared a special emotional relationship. To this extent, I would overrule such cases as Speier v. Webster College, 616 S.W.2d 617, 618 (Tex. 1981). . . .

KILGARLIN, J., joins in this concurring opinion.

NOTES ON WRONGFUL DEATH

1. Texas joins the majority of jurisdictions in authorizing damages for loss of society and companionship, but is in the minority with respect

to mental anguish. The Supreme Court of the United States has summarized the state of wrongful death damage law as follows:

> Recovery for loss of support has been universally recognized, and includes all the financial contributions that the decedent would have made to his dependents had he lived. Similarly, the overwhelming majority of state wrongful-death acts and courts interpreting the Death on the High Seas Act have permitted recovery for the monetary value of services the decedent provided and would have continued to provide but for his wrongful death. Such services include, for example, the nurture, training, education, and guidance that a child would have received had not the parent been wrongfully killed. Services the decedent performed at home or for his spouse are also compensable.
>
> Compensation for loss of society, however, presents a closer question. The term "society" embraces a broad range of mutual benefits each family member receives from the others' continued existence, including love, affection, care, attention, companionship, comfort, and protection.[17] Unquestionably, the deprivation of these benefits by wrongful death is a grave loss to the decedent's dependents. Despite this fact, a number of early wrongful-death statutes were interpreted by courts to preclude recovery for these losses on the ground that the statutes were intended to provide compensation only for "pecuniary loss," and that the loss of society is not such an economic loss. . . .
>
> A clear majority of States, on the other hand, have rejected such a narrow view of damages, and, either by express statutory provision or by judicial construction, permit recovery for loss of society. . . .
>
> Finally, in addition to recovery for loss of support, services, and society, damages for funeral expenses may be awarded under the maritime wrongful-death remedy in circumstances where the decedent's dependents have either paid for the funeral or are liable for its payment. A majority of States provided for such recovery under their wrongful-death statutes.

17. Loss of society must not be confused with mental anguish or grief, which are not compensable under the maritime wrongful-death remedy. The former entails the loss of positive benefits, while the latter represents an emotional response to the wrongful death. The difference between the two is well expressed as follows:

> When we speak of recovery for the beneficiaries' mental anguish, we are primarily concerned, not with the benefits they have lost, but with the issue of compensating them for their harrowing experience resulting from the death of a loved one. This requires a somewhat negative approach. The fundamental question in this area of damages is what deleterious effect has the death, as such, had upon the claimants? In other areas of damage, we focus on more positive aspects of the injury such as what would the decedent, had he lived, have *contributed* in terms of support, assistance, training, comfort, consortium, etc. . . .
>
> The great majority of jurisdictions, including several which do allow damages for other types of nonpecuniary loss, hold that the grief, bereavement, anxiety, distress, or mental pain and suffering of the beneficiaries may not be regarded as elements of damage in a wrongful death action."

S. Speiser, Recovery for Wrongful Death §3.45, p.223 (emphasis in original) (footnotes omitted).

Sea-Land Services v. Gaudet, 414 U.S. 573, 584-587, 591 (1974).

2.   What is the value of society, services, companionship and similar elements of damage? In Norfolk & Western Railway v. Liepelt, infra at 185, the decedent was a railroad fireman. He was survived by a wife, two young children, and two older children by an earlier marriage. Plaintiff's expert estimated the decedent's lost earnings, plus the value of the services he would have performed for his family, less the amounts he would have spent on himself, to be $302,000. Defendant's estimate was substantially less. The jury returned a verdict for $775,000. Plaintiff argued "that the excess is adequately explained by the jury's estimate of the pecuniary value of the guidance, instruction and training that the decedent would have provided to his children." What does it mean to say that "guidance, instruction and training" is worth $473,000? That the father's guidance and training would have enabled the children to earn that much more during their lifetime? That the children would spend that much to purchase substitute guidance and training? Or does this verdict simply illustrate that juries will find a way to compensate for grief and mental anguish even though told not to?

Some courts equate loss of society with loss of "love and affection." An example is Faust v. South Carolina, 527 F. Supp. 1021, 1035 (D.S.C. 1981). That formulation edges closer to compensation for grief and further from traditional pecuniary measures; some of the questions in this note would be irrelevant to an award for loss of love and affection.

3.   Is there any reason to pretend that we do not compensate for grief and mental anguish in wrongful death cases? In Carey v. Piphus, infra at 100, the Supreme Court says that plaintiff can recover for the mental distress caused by being denied a hearing before being suspended from high school. The court comments that "distress is a personal injury familiar to the law. . . ." Why do we allow recovery for mental anguish in the context of constitutional and dignitary torts, but not for the death of a loved one? Is it the fear of monstrous verdicts again? The mere accident that wrongful death law was codified in the nineteenth century, when notions of proper compensation were less generous?

4.   Large verdicts like the one in *Liepelt* suggest that jurors compensate for grief even when they are told not to. But there are also small verdicts; some juries do as they are told and not as they are expected. Surely $10,000 verdicts for deaths of children (described in Table 2-1) were not intended to compensate parents for grief and mental anguish. And consider Green v. Bittner, 85 N.J. 1, 424 A.2d 210 (1980), where, with liability established, a jury found no damages for the wrongful death of a high school senior. The trial court denied a motion for new trial, and the Appellate Division affirmed. The Supreme Court found the judgment correct under existing law and commented on the "conscientious" jury. But it ordered a new trial on damages, holding that the measure of damages should be expanded to include the value of companionship and

advice the child might provide in the parent's old age, emphasizing that "its value must be confined to what the marketplace would pay a stranger with similar qualifications for performing such services." These losses must be discounted to present value. The new trial gave a second jury a chance to do justice, but wouldn't a "conscientious" jury still bring in a nominal verdict? Juries as "conscientious" as the one in *Green* are probably rare, but verdicts in the low five digits are fairly common. The denial of recovery for grief must be defended on the ground that it is just, not on the ground that it is ineffective. But why is it just?

5.   Should grief be noncompensable on the ground that death is inevitable and the grief would eventually be experienced anyway? That reasoning has not been applied to funeral expenses, which are recoverable even though they would also be incurred eventually. But suppose the premise is accepted. What about a claim that grief is worse when a loved one dies wrongfully and prematurely than when he dies naturally after a full life? And where the victim is a child, can't the parents claim that defendant inflicted grief that *they* would not have suffered, because in ordinary course they would have died before the child?

6.   Some jurisdictions compensate for distress caused by receipt of a false notification of death, but not for the distress caused by an actual death. Johnson v. State, 37 N.Y.2d 378, 334 N.E.2d 590 (1975). What sense does that make?

7.   Compare the *Sanchez* verdict with the damage assessments in Tables 2-1 and 2-2, all of which were reported in a single monthly issue of Verdicts & Settlements. Variations in awards for adult decedents may be partly explained by differences in earning capacity and life expectancy, or differences in the beneficiaries, although such factors cannot explain why the jury in Pierce v. Fairchild (Table 2-2) gave only four years pay to the widow and orphan of a young truck driver. In the children's cases, earning capacity and life expectancy make little or no difference, and all the beneficiaries are parents. What explains the differences there? The law of the jurisdiction? Whether the death was especially painful or lingering? Whether the defendants are especially culpable? Or especially appealing? The credibility of the competing lawyers? Can any list of factors legitimate such extraordinary variations in the valuation of human lives? Variations in pain and suffering verdicts appear to be as great.

8.   One solution to such variations is legislation specifying a fixed recovery. It is hard to imagine a statutory schedule for pain and suffering, because pain and suffering is itself infinitely variable. But what about a statute limiting wrongful death recovery to pecuniary losses narrowly conceived — financial support from lost earnings, plus services in the home that can be replaced in the market — plus $500,000, indexed for inflation, for bereavement, grief, mental anguish, love, affection, society, companionship, guidance, training, advice, and all similar concepts? Is it a sufficient objection to such uniformity that families vary greatly in their

TABLE 2-1
Representative Assessments of Damage for Wrongful Death of Children

Case	Decedent	Damages	Special Facts	Elements of Damage[a]
Jones v. Carrell, 641 P.2d 105 (Utah 1982)	Boy, 5	$10,000	Liability stipulated; defendant was decedent's uncle.	"Such damages as may be just," including lost society but apparently not including grief.[b]
Agee v. Solberg, — Ohio App. 2d — (1981) No. 1193 (2d Dist., Greene Co., 3/25/81)	Boy, 17	$10,000		"Pecuniary injury," not including lost society or grief.[c]
Frutiger v. State Farm Ins., No. 160-479 (Dane Co. Cir. Court, Wis. 1981)	Girl, 16	$14,490	Decedent was conscious and trapped in burning vehicle for 20 minutes; jury also awarded $70,000 for her pain and suffering.	$10,000 for lost society; $2,200 for lost services; $2,690 for funeral expense.
Addair v. Bryant, 284 S.E.2d 374 (W. Va. 1981)	Boy, 15	$25,000		$10,000 for "solatium" (solace) (statutory limit); $1,700 for funeral expense; $13,300 for pecuniary loss. Appealed as excessive; affirmed on basis of evidence that decedent did household chores, ran errands, and earned money from odd jobs.

Case	Description	Award	Outcome	Comments
Cassa v. Nicola, mem. 86 App. Div. 2d 785 (1982), N.Y.L.J. (1/22/82) at 12, col. 5	College student, 18	$100,000	Reduced to $44,000 for comparative negligence.	"Pecuniary injury," not including lost society or grief but including lost services;[d] jury awarded $200,000; reduced as excessive because decedent did not contribute to expenses at home.
Caldarera v. Eastern Airlines, 529 F. Supp. 634 (W.D. La. 1982)	Boy, 8	$154,320	Bench trial; decedent's mother and grandmother killed in same accident (see Table 2-2).	$150,000 for physical and mental anguish, lost companionship, love, and affection; $4,320 prorated from cost of triple funeral.
Wims v. Barkus, No. 80-10183 (Dade Co. Cir. Court, Fla. 1981)	Infant, 8 months	$2,500,000	Decedent born prematurely and dropped on floor at moment of birth; defendants claimed premature birth was cause of death; plaintiffs' final settlement demand was $850,000.	$2,250,000 to mother; $250,000 to father. Statute authorizes recovery for lost support, lost services, "mental pain and suffering from the date of injury," and medical and funeral expenses but not lost society or pain and suffering of decedent.[e]

Source: 2(1) Verdicts and Settlements (June 1982).
a. Elements of damage taken from opinion or jury instructions in case described when that is possible. Other sources of relevant state law are separately footnoted.
b. Grief and mental anguish are not mentioned in *Jones*. They are disallowed in Corbett v. Oregon Short Line R.R., 25 Utah 449, 455 (1903), a case that is apparently still good law.
c. Keaton v. Ribbeck, 58 Ohio St. 2d 443, 444-445 (1979). The Ohio statute was subsequently amended to allow recovery for mental anguish and loss of society. Ohio Rev. Code Ann. §2125.02 (Page 1982 Supp.).
d. N.Y. Estates, Powers & Trusts Law §5-4.3 (McKinney 1982 Supp.); Liff v. Schildkrout, 49 N.Y. 2d 622, 404 N.E. 2d 1288 (1980); Franchell v. Sims, 73 App. Div. 2d 1, 5 (1980).
e. Fla. Stat. §768.21 (1982 Supp.); Florida Clarklift, Inc. v. Reutimann, 323 So. 2d 640 (Fla. App. 1975); Metropolitan Dade County v. Dillon, 305 So. 2d 36 (Fla. App. 1974).

TABLE 2-2

Representative Assessments of Damage for Wrongful Death of Adults

Case	Decedent	Beneficiaries	Damages	Special Facts	Elements of Damage[a]
Pierce v. Fairchild, 641 F.2d 729 (9th Cir. 1981) (opinion withdrawn from bound volume)	Truck driver, 36	Wife, child	$75,000	Verdict equaled 4 years' salary; vacated as inadequate.	"Such damages as may be just," including lost society, but not including grief.[b]
Berns v. Pan Am Airlines, 667 F.2d 826 (9th Cir. 1982)	1. Father	Children age 17, 18, and 20; decedent's mother	$225,000	Plane crash in Canary Islands.	"All benefits heirs could expect to receive," including loss of society, but not including grief or loss of inheritance.
	2. Mother	Children age 17, 18, and 20	$225,000	"	"
Faust v. South Carolina, 527 F. Supp. 1021 (D.S.C. 1981)	School teacher, 40	Wife and 3 children age 5, 8, and 11	$499,069	Bench trial.	$229,112 lost earnings net of decedent's personal consumption; $58,734 lost services (10 hrs/wk at minimum wage); $58,742 lost training (present value of $1,500/child/yr to age 25); $150,000 lost society ($60,000 for wife; $30,000/child); $2,481 funeral expense.
Felus v. H. B. Alexander & Sons	Apparently a construction worker	Unreported	$500,000	Reduced to $400,000 for comparative negligence.	Unreported; jurisdiction also unreported.

Case			Amount	Comments
Caldarera v. Eastern Airlines, 529 F. Supp. 634 (W.D. La. 1982)	1. Mother	Husband, child	$938,431	Bench trial; decedent 1's son killed in same crash (see Table 2-1). In simultaneous trial against another joint tortfeasor, jury awarded $937,500 to husband for all 3 deaths and same amount to surviving child for death of his mother. Court let husband's verdict stand; reduced son's verdict to $600,000.
	2. Grand-mother	Adult son	$104,320	$400,000 loss of society to husband; $400,000 loss of society to child; $134,021 lost services; $4,320 prorated from cost of triple funeral; $100,000 loss of society; $4,320 prorated from cost of triple funeral.
Barron v. Transport of New Jersey		Bus passenger	Unreported	$1,100,000	Unreported; assuming New Jersey law applied, such damages as jury deems "fair and just with reference to the pecuniary injuries" plus medical and funeral expense; damages include lost services and advice of the sort available in the market but not lost society or grief.[c]

91

TABLE 2-2 *Continued*

Case	Decedent	Beneficiaries	Damages	Special Facts	Elements of Damage[a]
Bond v. Turner-Newall Ltd (No. 78-1345C(B), E.D. Mo.)	Unreported	Unreported	$1,400,000	Settlement; death from asbestosis 17 years after exposure.	Unreported; assuming Missouri law applied, such damages as jury deems "fair and just," including lost society and decedent's pain and suffering, but not including grief or bereavement.

Source: 2(1) Verdicts and Settlements (June 1982).

a. Elements of damage taken from opinion or jury instructions in case described when that is possible. Other sources of relevant state law are separately footnoted.

b. Idaho Code §5-311 (1979); Gavica v. Hanson, 101 Idaho 58, 608 P.2d 861 (1980).

c. N.J. Rev. Stat. §2A: 31-5 (1982 Supp.); Green v. Bittner, 85 N.J. 1, 424 A.2d 210 (1980).

d. Mo. Rev. Stat. §537.090 (1982 Supp.). The statute was enacted in 1979 and is quite precise for a wrongful death act. As this is written, it has not been construed by the Missouri Supreme Court. The federal court in which Bond was filed has implausibly read the act to authorize recovery for "mental anguish," distinguishing that loss from "grief" and "bereavement." Bergmann v. United States, 526 F. Supp. 443, 451 (E.D. Mo. 1981). Bond was filed in 1978, and it is not clear whether the 1973 or 1979 act would have applied. The 1973 act authorized "such damages as will fairly and justly compensate for any damages." 1973 Mo. Laws 498. This was perceived as liberalizing earlier laws, which had been construed as limited to pecuniary damages, not including loss of society, except when a husband sued for the death of his wife. Mitchell v. Buchheit, 559 S.W.2d 528, 532-533 (Mo. 1977); Wyatt v. United States, 470 F. Supp. 116, 118-120 (W.D. Mo.), aff'd, 610 F.2d 545 (8th Cir. 1979). The 1973 act was never construed by the Missouri Supreme Court except on a collateral issue not relevant here.

closeness? That the amounts may be set at unreasonably low (or high) levels?

Historically, legislation fixing wrongful death recoveries have set limits, rather than specific amounts. The limits have been perceived as unreasonably low and have been abandoned after interim periods in which they were raised repeatedly. Some states have constitutional prohibitions on such limits. A more common example of legislative schedules for personal injury or death is worker's compensation statutes. The Texas act provides that a permanently and totally disabled worker, or the survivors of a worker killed on the job, get his medical expenses and two-thirds of his lost pay, up to a limit about equal to the minimum wage. Tex. Stat. Ann. art. 8306, §§8, 10, 29 (Vernon 1983 Supp.). Except for six injuries specified in the statute, payments end after 401 weeks even if the total disability is permanent. Id. at §§10, 11a (Vernon, 1967, 1983 Supp.). Is there any theory under which such awards are compensatory? Do they make you optimistic about a legislatively determined wrongful death award?

9.   Note the discrepancy between the awards for the mother and grandmother in Caldarera v. Eastern Airlines, Table 2-2. Wrongful deaths of retired people present many of the same problems as wrongful deaths of children: Damages measured by lost earnings or financial support will usually be small or negative. Should recoveries for grief or loss of society also be smaller, on the ground that decedent's companionship could only have been enjoyed a few more years?

10.   What about decedent's loss of capacity to enjoy life? If a comatose victim can recover for that, why not the estate of a dead victim? Aren't the losses the same? Why do we focus on the survivors' derivative losses and ignore the primary loss, which was suffered by decedent? Is it because decedent can't benefit from the recovery? Because compensating decedent's loss would force us to explicitly put a number on the value of human life? Because no one voluntarily insures the value of his own life to himself, and no one should be forced to do so indirectly through the cost of goods and services or liability insurance?

NOTES ON WRONGFUL BIRTH AND WRONGFUL LIFE

1.   Many parents have conceived and delivered healthy children after ineffective attempts at sterilization. What should the measure of damages be when they sue the doctor for negligence? State supreme courts have been struggling with that question. Plaintiffs seek the full cost of child rearing. Some courts allow the cost of child rearing with an offset for the intangible benefits of parenting. The majority of courts assume as a matter of law that the benefits outweigh the costs. But nearly all courts allow

recovery of the medical expenses, lost wages, and pain and suffering associated with pregnancy and delivery. A typical case, with a good opinion and a strong dissent, is Cockrum v. Baumgartner, 95 Ill. 2d 193, 447 N.E.2d 385 (1983).

2. The Sanchezes claim to have been damaged by the death of a healthy child. The Cockrums claim to have been damaged by the birth of a healthy child. Common experience suggests that both claims are truthful, but the conflicting nature of the claims highlights the difficulty of measuring damages. The law generally attempts to determine the objective value of things, and perhaps that is what the courts are doing when they say as a matter of law that the benefits of child rearing exceed the costs. Yet many courts deny recovery for those intangible benefits if the child is killed. Moreover, if the benefits of child rearing exceed the costs, why don't the benefits also exceed the damages associated with childbirth? When the court allows recovery of those costs, isn't it saying that a child has a positive value to the Sanchezes and a negative value to the Cockrums?

3. Estimates of the cost of raising and educating a middle-class child range upward from $200,000. (For low-income parents, the cost would be smaller but the financial burden would be greater.) That is $200,000, and thousands of hours, the parents would not have had to spend but for the doctors' negligence. Most commonly, these are precisely the costs the operation was intended to avoid. One court has argued that the millions of couples who regularly use contraceptives indicate community rejection of the view that a child is always a benefit. Troppi v. Scarf, 31 Mich. App. 240, 253, 187 N.W.2d 511, 517 (1971).

Is it conclusive that plaintiffs did not abort or give the child up for adoption? Can they argue that they were conscientiously opposed to abortion, and that by the time of the birth they were too emotionally involved to give the child up for adoption, despite their continued belief that the costs of parenthood far outweigh the benefits? If the child is subsequently killed, can they also recover for its wrongful death?

4. The problems of valuation are even more difficult when the child is born with a serious birth defect. These cases typically arise when an obstetrician fails to advise high-risk parents to seek genetic counseling, or when genetic tests on the parents or fetus are negligently performed. The child is then born with some serious defect, and the parents say that they would have used contraception or obtained an abortion if they had known. In the wrongful birth cases, the parents seek damages for the costs of raising the child, including the extraordinary medical expenses associated with the defect, for emotional distress, for the expenses and pain of labor and delivery, sometimes for embarrassment and humiliation, and for funeral expenses where the defect is fatal. Courts have generally allowed a cause of action, but have measured damages in many

different ways. New York allows parents to recover the expenses of care and treatment, but not the value of emotional distress. Becker v. Schwartz, 46 N.Y.2d 401, 386 N.E.2d 807 (1978). New Jersey allows parents to recover for emotional distress, but not the cost of care and treatment. Berman v. Allan, 80 N.J. 421, 404 A.2d 8 (1979). Virginia allows parents to recover both. Naccash v. Burger, 23 Va. 406, 290 S.E.2d 825 (1982). Both the New York and New Jersey courts believed that there were benefits to being the parents of even a defective child; one court treated these benefits as offsetting medical expenses, and the other as offsetting emotional suffering.

In the wrongful life cases, the child has sued for its own pain, suffering, and humiliation. The gist of these claims is that the child would be better off to have never been born, and the courts have generally rejected such claims on public policy grounds. An example is Berman v. Allan, supra. When the position plaintiff would have occupied but for the wrong is to never have been conceived, or to have been aborted, is it possible to speak intelligently about the value of restoring him to that position? Must plaintiff mitigate damages by committing suicide? That question does not arise directly, because plaintiff is represented by his next friend, who could mitigate only by committing murder.

See supplement
Levka

THOMAS v. E. J. KORVETTE, INC.
329 F. Supp. 1163 (E.D. Pa. 1971)

Fullam, District Judge.

The plaintiff was employed as security manager of the King of Prussia store of the defendant when, on November 12, 1965, the defendant caused him to be arrested and prosecuted on a charge of larceny by employee. This criminal charge was later dismissed at a Justice of the Peace hearing, and the present action for false arrest, malicious prosecution and defamation of character followed.

Liability issues were tried first. The jury expressly found that there was no probable cause for plaintiff's arrest and prosecution, that the defendant was motivated by malice, and that certain disputed defamatory statements were made. Additional evidence was then presented on the damage issues, and the jury awarded compensatory damages in the sum of $250,000, and punitive damages in the sum of $500,000, making a total award of $750,000. The defendant has moved for judgment n.o.v. and for a new trial. . . .

Plaintiff testified that, since his arrest, he has been utterly unable to obtain employment in the security field. He obtained employment as a salesman of cosmetics, but, while engaged in this occupation, was asked to leave one of the defendant's stores, on the ground that he was a "security risk." In February of 1969, a prospective employer, checking with the defendant for references, was told: "If you want a thief working for you, go ahead." . . .

As indicated in the discussion thus far, I have concluded that the defendant's motion for a judgment n.o.v. must be denied. And while there is a distinction between the quantum of proof required to escape a directed verdict and the quantum of proof which would justify the refusal to grant a new trial on the basis of the weight of the evidence (admittedly, however, a somewhat elusive distinction), I have concluded that, on the liability issues, the jury's verdict should be permitted to stand. To set aside the verdict and grant a new trial in this case would mean disregarding the jury's evaluations of credibility, and substituting contrary evaluations. Credibility of witnesses is peculiarly within the province of the jury. The motions for judgment n.o.v. and for a new trial, insofar as they relate to liability issues, will be denied.

However, the jury's appraisal of damages is patently excessive, and cannot be permitted to stand. The evidence established that, up to the date of trial, plaintiff had sustained the following pecuniary losses:

Bail bond	$ 65.00
Attorney fee	350.00
Employment agency fee	310.00
Wages lost between jobs	950.00
Total	$1,675.00

In addition, plaintiff claimed loss of future earning capacity by reason of his inability to obtain employment in the security field. The difficulty with this assertion is that he has been earning more as a salesman than he was earning at Korvette's. However, there was evidence that employment in the security field, other than at Korvette's, would pay approximately $600 per year more than plaintiff's present income.

Obviously, plaintiff did sustain substantial general damages for such intangibles as injury to feelings, humiliation, embarrassment, damage to reputation, etc. His life has been substantially changed as a result of the arrest. Exclusion from his chosen field of endeavor, which he very much enjoyed and in which he was quite successful, is an element of damage of considerable magnitude, even though incapable of precise measurement.

Giving all these factors their appropriate weight, however, I find it impossible to justify an award of $250,000 as representing actual damages sustained by the plaintiff. In my judgment, the most that a reasonable jury could have awarded under these circumstances is $100,000, and even that may be generous. . . . It is my view that a generous compensatory award should not be further exaggerated by multiplication in computing punitive damages. Taking into consideration all of the appropriate factors, I have concluded that punitive damages in the present case should not be permitted to exceed $50,000. . . .

NOTES ON DIGNITARY TORTS

1. Dignitary torts, including assault, false imprisonment, malicious prosecution, intentional infliction of emotional distress, libel, slander, invasion of privacy, and batteries that are offensive but do no physical harm, present valuation problems comparable to those of pain and suffering. Valuation problems in these cases are more tolerable only because the amounts involved are generally smaller, not because the valuation is any more reliable. As in the pain and suffering cases, juries are given no more precise instruction than to do what is reasonable. In *Korvette*, the trial judge found the jury's award unreasonable and substituted his own assessment of what was reasonable, but it is rather clear that he had no operative standard either. He cannot explain his judgment except to say that any larger sum seems unreasonable to him. Consider the valuation problems in the following cases:

remitted

a. Plaintiff was mistakenly identified as the man who had recently cashed worthless checks in defendant's store; this resulted in plaintiff's being arrested, "objectionably interrogated by the police, and . . . kept incommunicado overnight in a filthy, roach-infested jail." There was no evidence of permanent harm comparable to Thomas's difficulties in finding a job in his chosen field. The court held that $10,000 compensatory damages was not excessive. National Food Stores v. Utley, 303 F.2d 284 (8th Cir. 1962).

b. Plaintiff, a married woman, alleged that defendant indecently assaulted her while she was alone in her home. She said that he "came over and put his . . . right hand on my hip and his other arm around my waist and shoulder and pushed the lower part of his body against my body and held me there, and he said, 'I won't hurt you, girl.' I pushed away from him then . . . and he asked me if I would let him come to see me when I moved . . . I told him that I wished he would leave. I was in a hysterical condition, and he did leave then." Plaintiff and her husband testified that she lay in bed and shook like a leaf for twenty-four hours, that her preexisting nervous condition was aggravated, and that she subsequently developed ulcers. There was no medical evidence to connect the ulcers to the assault. The jury's verdict of $250 was upheld. Edmisten v. Dousette, 334 S.W.2d 746 (Mo. App. 1960).

c. Plaintiff sold food from a truck outside the courthouse. A judge sent a deputy sheriff to buy coffee. Both the judge and the deputy thought that the coffee tasted "putrid," and the judge told the deputy to get the plaintiff and bring him "in front of me in cuffs." Plaintiff was handcuffed and marched through the courthouse in full view of dozens of people. The judge interrogated, threatened, and screamed at plaintiff for twenty minutes. Plaintiff testified that he was very upset by the incident, that he could not sleep, that he started to stutter and get headaches, that he required treatment at a hospital, that he could not work, and that his wife asked him to move out of the house. Plaintiff sued the judge, and the jury awarded $80,000 compensatory damages and $60,000 punitive damages. The compensatory award was not challenged, and the punitive award was upheld. Zarcone v. Perry, 572 F.2d 52 (2d Cir. 1978).

d. A federal statute, 18 U.S.C. §2520 (1982), authorizes victims of unauthorized wiretapping to recover "actual damages," but not less than liquidated damages computed at the rate of $100 a day for each day of violation or $1,000, whichever is higher.

e. A high school teacher sued the school principal for authorizing prayers at student assemblies held at Christmas and Easter. Plaintiff testified that "he was shocked by the Easter prayer and that the prayers were upsetting, embarrassing, and humiliating." He did not see a doctor, and the court concluded that his mental distress was of short duration. The trial judge awarded $300. Abramson v. Anderson, 50 U.S.L.W. 2462 (S.D. Iowa 1982).

Abramson provides a note on the inadequacy of legal remedies to control human relationships: Abramson was fired at the end of the 1982-1983 school year. He alleged that his termination was in retaliation for his opposition to school prayer. He filed civil rights suits seeking reinstatement and damages; those cases were still pending at last report. Abramson v. Council Bluffs Community School District, 4 Religious Freedom Rptr. 42 (1984) (describing pending cases).

f. A Michigan jury awarded $60,000 to seventeen relatives of a seventy-nine-year-old man whose coffin fell apart as it was being carried to the grave. His widow fainted when his body dropped onto the ground, and she was briefly hospitalized. Associated Press Report (1983).

A Florida jury awarded $240,000 in a similar incident. That body fell onto pavement. In addition, an employee of the funeral home tried to sell a gravesite to a mourner during the visitation, and the funeral director wanted to use the widow's station wagon instead of a hearse. Briefs, 70 A.B.A.J. 42 (May 1984).

g. A magazine incorrectly identified a novelist as one of the nude women in photographs of an orgy. An all-woman jury in New York City awarded her $7 million compensatory damages and $33 million punitive damages. It would have been a lot cheaper to kill her, wouldn't it? The court of appeals found the damages "grossly excessive"; it noted that plaintiff had not sought counseling or suspended her writing and that other juries in similar cases had awarded $1,500 and $25,000. Lerman v. Flynt Distributing Co., 745 F.2d 123, 141 (2d Cir. 1984).

2.   Some authorities have questioned the compensatory nature of such awards. Professor Dobbs notes that the nature of the defendant's conduct and motive, usually relevant only to punitive damages, becomes relevant to compensatory damages in these cases because the more outrageous the defendant's behavior, the more outraged and distressed the victim will be. He also suggests that damage awards in these cases are more important for deterrent than compensatory purposes. "It may well be that substantial damages are permitted in these cases partly in recognition that such public purposes are being served rather than in any belief that a person falsely arrested has suffered humiliation worth $100,000." D. Dobbs, A Handbook of the Law of Remedies §7.3 at 530-531 (1973). Dean Yudof agrees. Yudof, Liability for Constitutional Torts and the Risk-Averse Public School Official, 49 S. Cal. L. Rev. 1322, 1371-1373 (1976). However, Yudof reports that most tort professors of his acquaintance disagreed with his article; they insisted that compensatory awards in dignitary tort cases represent the real value of the victim's distress.

The Second Restatement of Torts takes an intermediate position:

§903.   COMPENSATORY DAMAGES — DEFINITION

Comment:

a.   When there has been harm only to the pecuniary interests of a person, compensatory damages are designed to place him in a position substantially equivalent in a pecuniary way to that which he would have occupied had no tort been committed. When, however, the tort causes bodily harm or emotional distress, the law cannot restore the injured person to his previous position. The sensations caused by harm to the body or by pain or humiliation are not in any way analogous to a pecuniary loss, and a sum of money is not the equivalent of peace of mind. Nevertheless, damages given for pain and humiliation are called compensatory. They give to the injured person some pecuniary return for what he has suffered or is likely to suffer. There is no scale by which the detriment caused by suffering can be measured and hence there can be only a very rough correspondence between the amount awarded as damages and the extent of the suffering. However, these damages, although frequently not segregated in a verdict, differ from punitive damages, both in the reasons for their existence and in the method of their computation.

NOTE ON THE RIGHT TO RECOVER FOR EMOTIONAL DISTRESS

Courts have granted recovery for emotional distress for a long time, but only in certain contexts. There has been a widespread fear of fraudulent claims, and courts have sought to protect against such claims by establishing formal prerequisites to any recovery for emotional distress.

The details of these prerequisites have varied from state to state and have gradually been liberalized, but some such prerequisites remain universal. The Texas prerequisites mentioned in Sanchez v. Schindler — willful tort, gross negligence, willful and wanton disregard, or physical injury resulting from the mental anguish — are illustrative. Another common rule has been that a victim of physical injury could recover for associated emotional distress, even if defendant were guilty only of simple negligence. Some jurisdictions have allowed plaintiffs who were not physically injured to recover for the emotional distress of seeing a loved one killed or seriously injured; some of these jurisdictions added the requirement that the plaintiff must have been within the "zone of danger" created by defendant's negligence. Some courts have now gone further, abandoning any requirement of physical injury but insisting that the emotional distress be "serious," Schultz v. Barberton Glass Co., 4 Ohio St. 3d 131, 136, 447 N.E. 2d 109, 113 (1983), or "medically diagnosable" and "medically significant," Bass v. Nooney Co., 646 S.W.2d 765, 772-773 (Mo. 1983). In *Bass*, plaintiff suffered a "severe anxiety reaction" and was hospitalized for five days as a result of being trapped in an elevator for thirty minutes.

It is worth emphasizing that most of the debate has centered on emotional distress that is caused negligently, or caused intentionally but not caused by one of the traditional intentional torts. Plaintiffs who prove assault, battery, false imprisonment, defamation, or invasion of privacy have always recovered for emotional distress, including embarrassment and humiliation, whether or not the distress was serious or medically significant or resulted in bodily harm. Constitutional torts have been assimilated to this model.

CAREY v. PIPHUS
435 U.S. 247 (1978)

MR. JUSTICE POWELL delivered the opinion of the Court.

In this case, brought under 42 U.S.C. §1983, we consider the elements and prerequisites for recovery of damages by students who were suspended from public elementary and secondary schools without procedural due process. The Court of Appeals for the Seventh Circuit held that the students are entitled to recover substantial nonpunitive damages even if their suspensions were justified, and even if they do not prove that any other actual injury was caused by the denial of procedural due process. We disagree, and hold that in the absence of proof of actual injury, the students are entitled to recover only nominal damages.

I

Respondent Jarius Piphus was a freshman at Chicago Vocational High School during the 1973-1974 school year. On January 23, 1974, during

school hours, the school principal saw Piphus and another student standing outdoors on school property passing back and forth what the principal
described as an irregularly shaped cigarette. The principal approached
the students unnoticed and smelled what he believed was the strong odor
of burning marihuana. He also saw Piphus try to pass a packet of cigarette
papers to the other student. When the students became aware of the
principal's presence, they threw the cigarette into a nearby hedge.

The principal took the students to the school's disciplinary office and
directed the assistant principal to impose the "usual" 20-day suspension
for violation of the school rule against the use of drugs. . . .

Piphus and his mother, as guardian ad litem, filed suit against the
petitioners in Federal District Court under 42 U.S.C. §1983 and its jurisdictional counterpart, 28 U.S.C. §1343, charging that Piphus had been
suspended without due process of law in violation of the Fourteenth
Amendment. The complaint sought declaratory and injunctive relief,
together with actual and punitive damages in the amount of $3,000.
Piphus was readmitted to school under a temporary restraining order
after eight days of his suspension.

[The Court then described the facts of a companion case involving
Silas Brisco, who was also suspended from school without a hearing.
Piphus and Brisco are referred to as respondents; the school officials are
referred to as petitioners.]

The District Court held that both students had been suspended without procedural due process. . . .

Despite these holdings, the District Court declined to award damages
because:

> Plaintiffs put no evidence in the record to qualify their damages, and the
> record is completely devoid of any evidence which could even form the basis
> of a speculative inference measuring the extent of their injuries. Plaintiffs'
> claims for damages therefore fail for complete lack of proof.

The court also stated that the students were entitled to declaratory
relief and to deletion of the suspensions from their school records, but for
reasons that are not apparent the court failed to enter an order to that
effect. Instead, it simply dismissed the complaints. No finding was made
as to whether respondents would have been suspended if they had received procedural due process.

On respondents' appeal, the Court of Appeals reversed and remanded.
It first held that the District Court erred in not granting declaratory and
injunctive relief. It also held that the District Court should have considered evidence submitted by respondents after judgment that tended to
prove the pecuniary value of each day of school that they missed while
suspended. The court said, however, that respondents would not be entitled to recover damages representing the value of missed school time if
petitioners showed on remand "that there was just cause for the suspen-

sion[s] and that therefore [respondents] would have been suspended even
if a proper hearing had been held."

Finally, the Court of Appeals held that even if the District Court found
on remand that respondents' suspensions were justified, they would be
entitled to recover substantial "nonpunitive" damages simply because
they had been denied procedural due process. . . . [T]he court stated
that such damages should be awarded "even if, as in the case at bar, there
is no proof of individualized injury to the plaintiff, such as mental distress. . . ." . . .

II

Title 42 U.S.C. §1983 provides:

> Every person who, under color of any statute, ordinance, regulation, cus-
> tom, or usage, of any State or Territory, subjects, or causes to be subjected,
> any citizen of the United States or other person within the jurisdiction thereof
> to the deprivation of any rights, privileges, or immunities secured by the
> Constitution and laws, shall be liable to the party injured in an action at law,
> suit in equity, or other proper proceeding for redress."

The legislative history of §1983 demonstrates that it was intended to "[cre-
ate] a species of tort liability" in favor of persons who are deprived of
"rights, privileges, or immunities secured" to them by the Constitution.
Imbler v. Pachtman, 424 U.S. 409, 417 (1976).

Petitioners contend that the elements and prerequisites for recovery of
damages under this "species of tort liability" should parallel those for
recovery of damages under the common law of torts. In particular, they
urge that the purpose of an award of damages under §1983 should be to
compensate persons for injuries that are caused by the deprivation of
constitutional rights; and, further, that plaintiffs should be required to
prove not only that their rights were violated, but also that injury was
caused by the violation, in order to recover substantial damages. Unless
respondents prove that they actually were injured by the deprivation of
procedural due process, petitioners argue, they are entitled at most to
nominal damages.

Respondents seem to make two different arguments in support of the
holding below. First, they contend that substantial damages should be
awarded under §1983 for the deprivation of a constitutional right *whether
or not* any injury was caused by the deprivation. This, they say, is appropriate both because constitutional rights are valuable in and of themselves, and because of the need to deter violations of constitutional rights.
Respondents believe that this view reflects accurately that of the Congress that enacted §1983. Second, respondents argue that even if the
purpose of a §1983 damages award is, as petitioners contend, primarily to

compensate persons for injuries that are caused by the deprivation of constitutional rights, every deprivation of procedural due process may be *presumed* to cause some injury. This presumption, they say, should relieve them from the necessity of proving that injury actually was caused.

A

Insofar as petitioners contend that the basic purpose of a §1983 damages award should be to compensate persons for injuries caused by the deprivation of constitutional rights, they have the better of the argument. Rights, constitutional and otherwise, do not exist in a vacuum. Their purpose is to protect persons from injuries to particular interests, and their contours are shaped by the interests they protect.

Our legal system's concept of damages reflects this view of legal rights. "The cardinal principle of damages in Anglo-American law is that of *compensation* for the injury caused to plaintiff by defendant's breach of duty." 2 F. Harper & F. James, Law of Torts §25.1, p.1299 (1956) (emphasis in original). . . .

To the extent that Congress intended that awards under §1983 should deter the deprivation of constitutional rights, there is no evidence that it meant to establish a deterrent more formidable than that inherent in the award of compensatory damages.[11]

B

It is less difficult to conclude that damages awarded under §1983 should be governed by the principle of compensation than it is to apply this principle to concrete cases. But over the centuries the common law of torts has developed a set of rules to implement the principle that a person should be compensated fairly for injuries caused by the violation of his legal rights. These rules, defining the elements of damages and the prerequisites for their recovery, provide the appropriate starting point for the inquiry under §1983 as well. . . .

In order to further the purpose of §1983, the rules governing compensation for injuries caused by the deprivation of constitutional rights should be tailored to the interests protected by the particular right in

---

11. This is not to say that exemplary or punitive damages might not be awarded in a proper case under §1983 with the specific purpose of deterring or punishing violations of constitutional rights. . . . [T]here is no basis for such an award in this case. The District Court specifically found that petitioners did not act with malicious intention to deprive respondents of their rights or to do them other injury. . . .

We also note that the potential liability of §1983 defendants for attorney's fees, 42 U.S.C. §1988, provides additional — and by no means inconsequential — assurance that agents of the State will not deliberately ignore due process rights. See also 18 U.S.C. §242, the criminal counterpart of §1983.

question — just as the common-law rules of damages themselves were defined by the interests protected in the various branches of tort law. We agree with Mr. Justice Harlan that "the experience of judges in dealing with private [tort] claims supports the conclusion that courts of law are capable of making the types of judgment concerning causation and magnitude of injury necessary to accord meaningful compensation for invasion of [constitutional] rights." Bivens v. Six Unknown Fed. Narcotics Agents, 403 U.S. at 409 (Harlan, J., concurring in judgment). With these principles in mind, we now turn to the problem of compensation in the case at hand.

C

The Due Process Clause of the Fourteenth Amendment provides:

> [N]or shall any State deprive any person of life, liberty, or property, without due process of law. . . .

This Clause "raises no impenetrable barrier to the taking of a person's possessions," or liberty, or life. Fuentes v. Shevin, 407 U.S. 67, 81 (1972). Procedural due process rules are meant to protect persons not from the deprivation, but from the mistaken or unjustified deprivation of life, liberty, or property. . . .

In this case, the Court of Appeals held that if petitioners can prove on remand that "[respondents] would have been suspended even if a proper hearing had been held," then respondents will not be entitled to recover damages to compensate them for injuries caused by the suspensions. The court thought that in such a case, the failure to accord procedural due process could not properly be viewed as the cause of the suspensions. The court suggested that in such circumstances, an award of damages for injuries caused by the suspensions would constitute a windfall, rather than compensation, to respondents. We do not understand the parties to disagree with this conclusion. Nor do we.

The parties do disagree as to the further holding of the Court of Appeals that respondents are entitled to recover substantial — although unspecified — damages to compensate them for "the injury which is 'inherent in the nature of the wrong,'" even if their suspensions were justified and even if they fail to prove that the denial of procedural due process actually caused them some real, if intangible, injury. Respondents, elaborating on this theme, submit that the holding is correct because injury fairly may be "presumed" to flow from every denial of procedural due process. Their argument is that in addition to protecting against unjustified deprivations, the Due Process Clause also guarantees the "feeling of just treatment" by the government. Anti-Fascist Committee v. McGrath, 341 U.S. 123, 162 (1951) (Frankfurter, J., concurring). They contend that the deprivation of protected interests without procedural due process, even where the premise for the deprivation is not erroneous, inevitably arouses strong feelings of mental and emotional distress in the individual who is denied this "feeling of just treatment." They analogize their case to that of defamation per se, in which "the plaintiff is relieved from the necessity of producing any proof whatsoever that he has been injured" in order to recover substantial compensatory damages. C. McCormick, Law of Damages §116, p.423 (1935).

Petitioners do not deny that a purpose of procedural due process is to convey to the individual a feeling that the government has dealt with him fairly, as well as to minimize the risk of mistaken deprivations of protected interests. They go so far as to concede that, in a proper case, persons in respondents' position might well recover damages for mental and emotional distress caused by the denial of procedural due process. Petitioners' argument is the more limited one that such injury cannot be presumed to occur, and that plaintiffs at least should be put to their proof on the issue, as plaintiffs are in most tort actions.

P's argument

We agree with petitioners in this respect. As we have observed in another context, the doctrine of presumed damages in the common law of defamation per se "is an oddity of tort law, for it allows recovery of purportedly compensatory damages without evidence of actual loss." Gertz v. Robert Welch, Inc., 418 U.S. 323, 349 (1974). The doctrine has been defended on the grounds that those forms of defamation that are actionable per se are virtually certain to cause serious injury to reputation, and that this kind of injury is extremely difficult to prove. Moreover, statements that are defamatory per se by their very nature are likely to cause mental and emotional distress, as well as injury to reputation, so there arguably is little reason to require proof of this kind of injury either. But these considerations do not support respondents' contention that damages should be presumed to flow from every deprivation of procedural due process.

First, it is not reasonable to assume that every departure from procedural due process, no matter what the circumstances or how minor, inherently is as likely to cause distress as the publication of defamation per se is to cause injury to reputation and distress. Where the deprivation of a protected interest is substantively justified but procedures are deficient in some respect, there may well be those who suffer no distress over the procedural irregularities. Indeed, in contrast to the immediately distressing effect of defamation per se, a person may not even know that procedures *were* deficient until he enlists the aid of counsel to challenge a perceived substantive deprivation.

Moreover, where a deprivation is justified but procedures are deficient, whatever distress a person feels may be attributable to the justified deprivation rather than to deficiencies in procedure. But as the Court of Appeals held, the injury caused by a justified deprivation, including distress, is not properly compensable under §1983. This ambiguity in causation, which is absent in the case of defamation per se, provides additional need for requiring the plaintiff to convince the trier of fact that he actually suffered distress because of the denial of procedural due process itself.

Finally, we foresee no particular difficulty in producing evidence that mental and emotional distress actually was caused by the denial of procedural due process itself. Distress is a personal injury familiar to the law, customarily proved by showing the nature and circumstances of the wrong and its effect on the plaintiff.[20] In sum, then, although mental and emotional distress caused by the denial of procedural due process itself is compensable under §1983, we hold that neither the likelihood of such injury nor the difficulty of proving it is so great as to justify awarding compensatory damages without proof that such injury actually was caused. . . .

III

Even if respondents' suspensions were justified, and even if they did not suffer any other actual injury, the fact remains that they were deprived of their right to procedural due process. . . .

Common-law courts traditionally have vindicated deprivations of certain "absolute" rights that are not shown to have caused actual injury through the award of a nominal sum of money. By making the deprivation of such rights actionable for nominal damages without proof of actual injury, the law recognizes the importance to organized society that those rights be scrupulously observed; but at the same time, it remains true to the principle that substantial damages should be awarded only to compensate actual injury or, in the case of exemplary or punitive damages, to deter or punish malicious deprivations of rights.

Because the right to procedural due process is "absolute" in the sense that it does not depend upon the merits of a claimant's substantive assertions, and because of the importance to organized society that procedural due process be observed, we believe that the denial of procedural due process should be actionable for nominal damages without proof of actual injury. We therefore hold that if, upon remand, the District Court determines that respondents' suspensions were justified, respondents

---

20. We use the term "distress" to include mental suffering or emotional anguish. Although essentially subjective, genuine injury in this respect may be evidenced by one's conduct and observed by others. Juries must be guided by appropriate instructions, and an award of damages must be supported by competent evidence concerning the injury.

nevertheless will be entitled to recover nominal damages not to exceed one dollar from petitioners.[25]

The judgment of the Court of Appeals is reversed, and the case is remanded for further proceedings consistent with this opinion.

It is so ordered.

MR. JUSTICE MARSHALL concurs in the result.

MR. JUSTICE BLACKMUN took no part in the consideration or decision of this case.

NOTES ON VALUING CONSTITUTIONAL RIGHTS

1. Does the Court ever answer plaintiffs' argument that "constitutional rights are valuable in and of themselves?" Does a judgment for $1.00 really "vindicate" the importance of constitutional rights?

2. The circuits are split on the meaning of *Carey*. Consider Herrera v. Valentine, 653 F.2d 1220 (8th Cir. 1981). *Herrera* was a police brutality case in which the jury was instructed to compensate plaintiff for her physical harm, her mental and emotional harm, the extent and duration of her injuries, *and* the violation of her constitutional rights. Elaborating on this last element of recovery, the district court said:

> The precise value you place upon any constitutional right which you find was denied to plaintiff is within your discretion. You may wish to consider the importance of the right in our system of government, the role which this right has played in the history of the republic, the significance of the right in the context of the activities which the plaintiff was engaged in at the time of the violation of the right.

Is that instruction consistent with *Carey?* Weren't all elements of damage permissible under *Carey* included in the instructions on physical and mental harm? The Eighth Circuit thought not; it said *Carey* applies only to procedural violations. It noted that the Supreme Court had approved substantial damages for loss of the right to vote in Nixon v. Herndon, 273 U.S. 536 (1927). Actually, *Herrera* limited *Carey* more severely than the Eighth Circuit acknowledged, because some of the rights violated in

---

25. Respondents contend that the Court of Appeals' holding could be affirmed on the ground that the District Court held them to too high a standard of proof of the amount of damages appropriate to compensate intangible injuries that are proved to have been suffered. It is true that plaintiffs ordinarily are not required to prove with exactitude the amount of damages that should be awarded to compensate intangible injury. But, as the Court of Appeals said, "in the case at bar, there is no proof of individualized injury to [respondents], such as mental distress. . . ." With the case in this posture, there is no occasion to consider the quantum of proof required to support a particular damages award where actual injury is proved.

Herrera were also procedural — the right to counsel and the right not to be punished without trial. Indeed, the right not to be punished without trial was precisely the right asserted in *Carey*, although the violation in *Herrera* was much more egregious, and was inextricably linked with the unconstitutional nature of the punishment inflicted.

By contrast, the Fifth Circuit found it "abundantly clear" that *Carey* applies to all constitutional rights, and allowed only nominal damages for violation of first amendment rights of political association. Familias Unidas v. Briscoe, 619 F.2d 391, 402 (5th Cir. 1980). Which view is the better reading of *Carey*?

3.   Which approach do you prefer? Does *Herrera* allow sentiment to justify excessive compensation? Or does *Carey* err in denying that constitutional rights have intrinsic value?

Plaintiff in *Carey* argued that he was entitled to recover the value of his lost hearing just as he would be entitled to recover the value of a stolen bicycle. Why not ask the jury to determine the value of a hearing? Is it a persuasive answer here, as in the pain and suffering cases, that there is no market in hearings? Plaintiff could not sell his right to a hearing to another student. But plaintiff could conceivably sell his right to the school. The school might pay a small sum of money to save the expense of a hearing, and the plaintiff might be willing to forgo his hearing and accept the suspension in exchange for such a payment, especially if he expected to be suspended at the hearing anyway. Could the court ask the jury to imagine that transaction and determine the sale value of plaintiff's right to a hearing? Would such a verdict be too speculative? Or is the whole idea offensive, contrary to public policy and notions of "inalienable rights?"

In the plea bargaining process, criminal defendants regularly exchange their right to trial for reductions in charge or sentence. Citizens rarely sell constitutional rights to the government for money. But consider the case of Clifford Olson, as reported in the Wall Street Journal, Jan. 27, 1982, p.24, col. 4. Canadian police were convinced Olson was guilty of a series of rapes and murders of children, but they didn't have enough evidence to convict him. Surveillance officers saw him pick up two female hitchhikers. They arrested him to save the lives of the hitchhikers, but they still didn't have enough evidence. The police inspector thought that with luck he could convict Olson of one second degree murder. Olson eventually concluded an apparently unprecedented bargain. The government paid $90,000 to Olson's wife and infant son; in exchange, Olson provided the evidence needed to convict him of eleven rapes and murders.

The Attorney General of British Columbia authorized the payment. He and other officials connected with the deal offered several justifications: It ensured a life sentence for Olson, it assured the people of Vancouver that there was only one murdering child molester at work, it ended the uncertainty of the victims' parents and gave their children "a

Christian burial," it prevented Olson from selling his information to the press, and it saved hundreds of thousands of dollars in police work. Some members of the public supported the transaction; others characterized it as a "reward for murder" and demanded the discharge of the responsible officials. The police inspector called it "probably the most difficult decision I have ever made."

Does Olson's transaction prove that the privilege against self-incrimination is worth $90,000? Or does it prove only that imprisonment for life is worth $90,000? If life in prison is worth only $90,000 in an arm's-length transaction, how can one night in jail be worth $10,000, and twenty minutes in handcuffs worth $60,000? Of course, one imprisoned unjustly may suffer more outrage and anguish than one imprisoned justly, but does this element alone change the value of imprisonment from $90,000 per lifetime to $10,000 per night? Note too that the price Olson could charge was limited by the risk that the authorities might somehow gather enough evidence on their own to convict him of an offense carrying life imprisonment even if he did not cooperate.

4. Dean Yudof argues that constitutional torts are a special case of dignitary torts. In his view, damages for dignitary torts are more than compensatory: "Juries and judges are saying that society's interest in human dignity is so great that the recovery may exceed any plausible estimate of economic injury." Yudof, Liability for Constitutional Torts and the Risk-Averse Public School Official, 49 S. Cal. L. Rev. 1322, 1379-1380 (1976). He refers to such damage rules as "superliability rules." Id. at 1379. He believes that they are justified by deterrent considerations, and he would apply the same rules to constitutional violations:

> Normal liability rules would not yield a sufficient degree of deterrence. These superliability rules would essentially allow for the recovery of "punitive" damages, however they are officially labeled. They would encourage persons suffering dignitary injuries to bring suit, and they would defray the costs of litigation. In contrast to the normal fashion in which punitive damages are justified, the critical element justifying recovery under a superliability rule is the significance of the interest that has been compromised, human dignity, rather than simply the willfulness or wantonness of the asserted misconduct. This may explain, in part, the tradition of labeling excessive recoveries in dignitary tort cases as compensatory damages, thereby avoiding a confrontation with traditional notions of punitive damages. . . .

Id. Is this the analysis reflected in the jury instruction in *Herrera*?

5. Re-read *Carey*'s treatment of emotional distress at footnote 20 and accompanying text. Does this incorporate the common law background on which Dean Yudof relies? Plainly, the Supreme Court would not accept his characterization of damage measures in dignitary tort cases as "superliability rules," but will this difference in characterization have any effect on awards?

6. If you represented plaintiffs, how would you prove the value of plaintiffs' mental distress? Assuming you could prove that a fair hearing would not have resulted in a suspension, how would you prove the value of eight days in the Chicago public schools? How would you approach these issues if you represented defendants?

7. *Carey* may not preclude large verdicts even in cases in which it is applied. Consider Laje v. R. E. Thomason General Hospital, 665 F.2d 724 (5th Cir. 1982). Dr. Laje sued the hospital after being discharged without a hearing. At a subsequent court-ordered hearing, his discharge was found to be justified on grounds of insubordination. "Dr. Laje and his wife both testified specifically that the summary proceedings surrounding his dismissal caused severe anxiety and distress, and that these feelings were not relieved until after the full hearing on his discharge. . . ." Id. at 728. The jury, instructed to ignore any harm from the discharge itself and consider only harm from the procedural violation, awarded $20,000 for mental anguish and emotional distress. The court of appeals affirmed. What are the ethical obligations of an attorney questioning his client about the sources of his emotional distress?

8. In defamation cases the common law presumed substantial general damages without proof, but the Court refuses to extend that practice to constitutional cases. The Court had already held that many applications of presumed damages are unconstitutional. Gertz v. Welch, 418 U.S. 323 (1974). The Court held that the free speech and free press clauses of the first amendment limit the liability that can be imposed on negligent defamers to proven compensatory damages. It said that presumed damages and punitive damages are unconstitutional except with respect to defendants who publish defamatory material with knowledge of its falsity or reckless disregard for the truth. 418 U.S. at 338-350.

Professor Anderson believes that the Court's attempt to restrict presumed damages has failed for two reasons. First, juries are too quick to find recklessness. Second, mental anguish counts as actual damages, and juries are prone to presume mental anguish. He would require plantiffs to prove actual damage to reputation as a precondition to recovery. If they proved that, they could also recover for accompanying mental anguish. But under his proposal, plaintiffs could not recover for mental anguish alone. Anderson, Reputation, Compensation, and Proof, 25 Wm. & Mary L. Rev. 747 (1984).

9. Note that the district court in *Carey* inexplicably found that plaintiffs were entitled to declaratory and injunctive relief, but dismissed the complaints without entering an order to that effect. This highlights a simple but important point: Remedies are given in judgments, not in opinions. Whatever a judge says in his opinion, the prevailing party must make sure that appropriate relief appears in the judgment. Typically, both sides will be asked to submit proposed drafts of any important orders.

E. CONSEQUENTIAL DAMAGES

BUCK v. MORROW
2 Tex. Civ. App. 361, 21 S.W. 398 (1893)

STEPHENS, J.

On the 1st day of May, 1886, H. C. Morrow leased to A. C. Buck a certain pasture in Wise county, for a term of five years, commencing with that date, for the sum of $125 per year, with the provision that after the second year, should Morrow have occasion to sell the land, he should compensate Buck for any or all losses occasioned by the sale. It was understood between the parties at the time that the land was being leased by Buck to graze cattle thereon. At the expiration of two years the land was sold, and appellant, Buck, dispossessed. He offered to prove on the trial, by the witness J. L. Campbell, that, at the time he was dispossessed, he had 140 head of cattle in the pasture, under the charge and control of said Campbell, and that he and Campbell had made diligent inquiry and search for another pasture for the cattle, but failed to find one; that said cattle were turned out of the pasture on the commons, and ran at large on the range for a period of five months before another could be procured; that during the time the cattle were on the range it required an extra hand to look after and keep them rounded up, at a cost of $1.50 per day, which was a reasonable charge; that all reasonable diligence was used to prevent said cattle from straying off, but during said time 15 of them were lost, reasonably worth $15 per head, and, after diligent search, could not be found. Further evidence was offered as to the expense of pasturing the cattle in another pasture thereafter procured. This testimony was all excluded, on the ground that it was immaterial, the measure of damages being the difference, if any, between the contract price and the rental value of the pasture for the unexpired term. The rule followed by the trial court in excluding this evidence is undoubtedly the correct rule for measuring the general damages incident to the breach of a covenant for quiet enjoyment in a lease. In addition to the difference between the rent to be paid and the actual value of the unexpired term, the tenant may also recover as special damages such extra expense and damage, if any, as are the natural and proximate result of the breach. The rule which confines the general damage to the difference between the rental value and the stipulated rent seems to rest upon the assumption that the tenant can go at once into the market and obtain like property. Where the reason of the rule does not exist, it would seem that the rule itself should not apply to the exclusion of all other considerations in estimating the damages. Special damages, in addition, have been allowed in many instances. It was held in De la Zerda v. Korn, 25 Tex. Supp. 194, that injury to the tenant's goods or stock in trade, in addition to the value of the use and occupation of the premises, should be considered in estimating the damages. Whatever special damage naturally and proximately resulted to appellant from the sale of the land and termination of the lease — whatever may reasonably be supposed to have entered into the contemplation of the parties at the time of the contract — he should recover. The items of expense which he sought to prove for pasturage elsewhere, we think, should be included in the general damages, measured by the difference between the market value of the residue of the term and the contract price, and that part of the evidence was perhaps properly excluded.

As to the extra expense and loss incident to a temporary holding of his cattle on the commons pending a diligent effort to secure another pasture, if the proof should show that these items were the proximate result of the sale of the land and termination at that time of the lease, and that thereby a loss was sustained, which otherwise would not have occurred, and that it was not the result of the want of proper care and diligence on the part of appellant, we think he would be entitled to recover the amount of loss thus sustained, as special damages. . . .

HEAD, J., disqualified, and not sitting.

NOTES ON GENERAL AND SPECIAL DAMAGES

1.   Plaintiff has expended $1.50 per day for five months, or $225. He has also lost fifteen cattle worth $15 per head, for another $225. In addition, his rent will be higher for the two years and seven months between the time he was able to rent alternative pasture and the time his original lease would have expired. The opinion does not indicate what the higher rent was, but the original rent was only $125 per year. Even with fairly substantial inflation, plaintiff's losses from the difference in rent would have been a small fraction of the $450 in extra wages and lost cattle. Assuming plaintiff acted reasonably and could not have found alternative pasture any sooner than he did, is there any theory under which he is restored to his rightful position without being compensated for the extra wages and lost cattle? What purpose is served by distinguishing the increase in rent (general damages) from the extra wages and lost cattle (special damages)? And why would any court ever say the special damages cannot be recovered?

2.   We have already encountered a number of cases in which the court awarded special or consequential damages, without noting any particular difficulty. In United States v. Hatahley, supra at 10, the court authorized recovery for plaintiffs' loss of sheep, goats, and cattle that resulted from the loss of their horses and burros. In Neri v. Retail Marine Corp., supra at 17, the seller recovered $674 for incidental expenses of storage, insurance, and maintenance of the unsold boat, and most law-

yers would characterize the profits from the lost sale as consequential damages. In *The Helen B. Moran*, supra at 45, plaintiff was allowed to recover, in addition to the value of the barge, the cost of raising the barge to clear the obstacle to navigation and to determine if the barge should be repaired. It seems clear that such losses result from defendant's wrongdoing, and that plaintiff must recover them if he is to be restored to his rightful position. Yet there is a long-standing suspicion of such damages, reflected in the trial court's judgment in Buck v. Morrow. The suspicion lingers even today, although the trend is certainly to award consequential damages more freely.

3. Consider §1-106(1) of the Uniform Commercial Code:

> The remedies provided by this Act shall be liberally administered to the end that the agreed party will be put in as good a position as if the other party had fully performed but neither consequential or special nor penal damages may be had except as specifically provided in this Act or by other rule of law.

The contrast between the two halves of this provision is sharp, and is made even sharper in the Official Comment:

> Subsection (1) is intended to . . . make it clear that compensatory damages are limited to compensation. They do not include consequential or special damages. . . .

Could the drafters really have believed that compensation is complete even though plaintiff is not reimbursed for his consequential losses? Perhaps not; the UCC frequently provides for consequential damages. Examples are §2-715 (Buyer's Incidental and Consequential Damages) and §4-402 (Bank's Liability to Customer for Wrongful Dishonor).

4. One area in which consequential damages are never awarded is eminent domain. The Court reaffirmed the rule in United States v. 50 Acres of Land, 105 S. Ct. 451 (1984).

5. The traditional reasons for hostility to consequential damages are that such damages are more speculative, less certain, more remote, and more likely to have been avoidable if the plaintiff had been more diligent. There are doctrines for dealing with each of these concerns; we will take them up in the next section. But there is a sense in many of the cases, especially the older cases, that such doctrines are not enough and must be supplemented by a general hostility to consequential damages, even at the cost of failing to achieve the goal of compensation. Here is a statement of the traditional view:

> For a wrong, the law's ideal, not always realized, is compensation, neither more nor less. Theoretically the loss to an injured party because of a broken contract is its value to him. Yet this rule may not always be safely applied. He may have in mind or claim that he had in mind some special object which

would make the contract of extraordinary value. It is well to avoid temptation. It is well to have some theory applicable to the majority of cases. The rule is therefore limited. As such value, for such loss, he may recover as damages only those that would naturally arise from the breach itself, or those that might reasonably be supposed to have been contemplated by the parties when the contract was made. True this is an arbitrary rule. By it full justice is not always done. But it has seemed a politic one.

Further, the methods by which the result is reached are often standardized. In the case of sales, where the articles may be purchased in the market, the value of the contract to the purchaser is the difference between the price at which in like quantities they may be bought at the time and place of delivery and the price which he would have had to pay under the contract.

Orester v. Dayton Rubber Manufacturing Co., 228 N.Y. 134, 136, 126 N.E. 510, 511 (1920).

You are not yet in a position to assess the adequacy of the doctrines that deal directly with certainty, remoteness, and avoidable consequences. But you can begin to think about whether those problems are avoided by emphasizing general measures of damage. How would you prove "the market value of the residue of the term" of the lease in Buck v. Morrow? Outside the special context of organized exchanges, market value is an abstraction. And note that the court takes the position that the price plaintiff agreed to pay for alternate pasture elsewhere is not admissible on the question of market value. We will explore that startling proposition in the next principal case. But suppose plaintiff's rent elsewhere is let in as the primary evidence of market value, or even as the general measure of damage. Defendant could still argue that plaintiff paid too much, or that the alternate pasture was better and more expensive than the pasture covered by the broken lease. Are these issues different in kind from whether plaintiff's extra wages and lost cattle could not have been avoided through greater diligence?

NOTES ON THE MEANING OF CONSEQUENTIAL AND SPECIAL

1.   Lawyers frequently talk about *special* damages and *general* damages; contracts regularly disclaim liability for *consequential* damages or *special* damages. But it is rarely clear what these terms mean. To the extent it is possible to identify customary usage, that usage does not match the customary definitions.

2.   Some of the early cases defined general damages as those that necessarily result from the violation complained of, or as damages that "the law implies or presumes." Howard Supply Co. v. Wells, 176 F. 512, 515 (6th Cir. 1910). Special damages were those that "proximately resulted, but do not always immediately result" from the violation com-

plained of. Id. To say that some damage always or necessarily resulted seemed fictional, and these standards were soon reformulated in terms of foreseeability and natural consequences. Restatement of Contracts §330, comment e, Special Notes (1932); Restatement of Torts §904 (1939). But this was a special kind of foreseeability; in practice, it retained the overtones of inevitability and necessity of the earlier formulations. The comments to the Restatement of Torts indicate that pain and suffering is so universally foreseeable as to be general damage but that medical expenses are special damages. The Restatement Second, promulgated in 1977, adhered to this position. §904, comments a and b.

As noted in Orester v. Dayton Rubber Manufacturing Co., supra at 114, the bench and bar tended to develop standardized measures of general damage. The difference between contract and market prices, the difference between the value of the goods as delivered and as warranted, and interest on detained money were such measures. Many lawyers mean only such standardized measures when they refer to "general" damages; in that usage, all other damages are "consequential" or "special," with "consequential" and "special" being more or less synonymous. But these standard formulas have only the most attenuated relationship to definitions based on foreseeability; consequential damages are often foreseeable.

3. The conflict is illustrated in Applied Data Processing v. Burroughs Corp., 394 F. Supp. 504 (D. Conn. 1975). Burroughs sold a defective computer, and ADP suffered substantial damages: downtime, work that had to be done over, translating programs to the language used by Burroughs, and then translating them back to IBM when ADP eventually replaced the Burroughs computer. Burroughs's form contract excluded consequential damages but didn't define the term. In addition, ADP had demanded and received a written warranty that the Burroughs computer would meet the needs of ADP's operation. Burroughs argued that the only recoverable damage was the difference between the contract price and the value of the computer if it had been as warranted, and that everything else was consequential.

The court took a different view. It quoted the following definition from Ruggles v. Buffalo Foundry & Machine Co., 27 F.2d 234, 235 (8th Cir. 1938):

> The distinction between general and special damages is not that one is and the other is not the direct and proximate consequence of the breach complained of, but that general damages are such as naturally and ordinarily follow the breach, whereas special damages are those that ensue, not necessarily or ordinarily, but because of special circumstances.

This definition apparently uses *naturally, ordinarily*, and *necessarily* as equivalents, contrasting all three with damages that result from *special circumstances*. The court focused on *ordinarily* and ignored *necessarily*. In this way, general damages became those that were foreseeable without any special information. And the court used *foreseeable* in its ordinary sense, without the usual overtones of inevitability and standardization. The court concluded that damages Burroughs could foresee without any special information about ADP were general, and recoverable, even if they did not fit any standardized formula. It concluded that damages Burroughs could foresee only because it had been told about ADP's operation were consequential, and excluded by the disclaimer. Not surprisingly, that test did not produce clear results when applied to the facts. Whether the case is a sport or an important evolutionary development remains to be seen. The court might have done better to say that the bargained for warranty implicitly amended the boilerplate disclaimer of liability. The warranty was plainly directed to ADP's special needs and might have been useless if those needs were irrelevant to the measure of damages.

4. Part of the confusion about the meaning of *general* and *special* damages is that the words are used in several quite distinct senses, without widespread recognition that the usages are different. One set of definitions is illustrated by *Applied Data* and the Restatements; it emphasizes natural consequences. A different definition is that special damages are damages that are reduced to a sum certain before trial. Thus, in the customary usage of personal injury lawyers, pain and suffering are general damages, and medical expenses and lost earnings are special damages. Note how this usage flips the usual prejudices; special damages are real, provable, and reliably measurable; it is general damages that are speculative and suspect. The Restatement's insistence that medical expenses are not sufficiently foreseeable to be general damages in personal injury cases may be an attempt to squeeze the personal injury bar's usage into the Restatement definition, without recognizing that the two usages may be entirely unrelated.

Special damages are also sometimes defined as those that must be specially pleaded, or as those that defendant must have notice of when he makes the contract. These usages are at least related to the natural consequences definitions, but they do not necessarily lead to the same answers. Harry Street notes four meanings of *special* and two meanings of *general*. He thinks all will be clear if we just keep track of which sense we mean and don't mistakenly assume that "that which is not special damage in some particular one of the four senses must be general damages in one of its two meanings." Principles of the Law of Damages 18 (1962). The other possible inference from his review is that we can't possibly communicate without a new set of terms.

The UCC defines *consequential* and *incidental* damages from contracts for the sale of goods. We'll examine those definitions in the next set of notes.

5. Should any rule of law depend on whether damages are character-ized as general or special, direct or consequential? Contracting parties should be able to limit liability for certain kinds of damage, but shouldn't they have to describe the excluded items of damage in comprehensible terms? Or would that put too much burden on the bargaining process? One advantage of terms such as *consequential* or *special* is that they are easily included in boilerplate, they suggest to the court that at least some items of damage should be excluded because liability was intended to be limited, and they avoid any need to focus on the problem until after the deal goes bad. Once litigation is threatened, the imprecision of such terms becomes a serious disadvantage. But it is their very imprecision that makes it possible for parties to gloss over problems that will probably never arise, thus simplifying the vast majority of contracts: those that are performed without serious dispute. But if this is what is going on, shouldn't clauses limiting liability for consequentials be read as saying: "The court shall decide the extent of liability for damages and plaintiff should not be fully compensated." Does it make sense to search for the intended meaning of a word that was chosen largely because it doesn't have much meaning?

6. Outside the context of contract clauses limiting damages, the im-portance of the distinction between general and special or direct and consequential damages has declined greatly. In my view, little of the traditional hostility to special or consequential damages remains. This is especially true in tort, but consequential damages are now much more likely to be awarded in contract as well. But not everyone thinks the trend has gone as far as these comments suggest. Here is Professor Dobbs's summary of the matter as of 1973:

> Courts are quite willing to award general damages but quite reluctant to award special damages. . . .
>
> [C]ourts are moving toward . . . a greater willingness to award special damages. . . .
>
> It is too soon to say how far this trend will go or what determinants will guide it. The trend . . . may suggest that substantial departures from value measures and general damages measures lie in the foreseeable future. This may well be so, but it is still true that courts tend to first use general measures of damages, usually based upon "value" as their point of departure.

D. Dobbs, Handbook on the Law of Remedies 138, 148 (1973).

Part of the difference between his sense of the situation and mine is that the trend we both recognize has progressed further since 1973. But I do not believe that even in 1973 I would have said that "courts are . . . quite reluctant to award special damages." Of course, Dobbs may be right and I may be wrong, and in any event, there are still lawyers and judges of the old school, representing clients and deciding cases. I would be de-lighted to abandon the distinction between general and special damages, but students can still expect to encounter people who consider it critical. And there are still cases where courts refuse to compensate consequential damages.

NOTE ON *ACTUAL* DAMAGES

Another term that is occasionally used, especially in statutes, is *actual* damages. The term might be helpful if it were consistently used in its ordinary English sense to exclude punitive damages and presumed damages. Plaintiff could recover for any losses he suffered, but he would have to prove that they were actually suffered. However, the term has also been used or construed in a wide variety of other ways, including most of the meanings associated with *special* damages. The United States argues that *actual* damages as used in the Privacy Act, 5 U.S.C. §552a (1982), means "out-of-pocket losses" and excludes all liability for mental or physical suffering. Of course, mental distress is the primary damage caused by invasions of privacy. The government lost in Johnson v. Department of Treasury, 700 F.2d 971 (5th Cir. 1983), and won in Fitzpatrick v. Internal Revenue Service, 665 F.2d 327 (11th Cir. 1982). Both courts agreed that the term has no "consistent legal interpretation."

WOLF v. COHEN
379 F.2d 477 (D.C. Cir. 1967)

Before DANAHER, Circuit Judge, BASTIAN, Senior Circuit Judge, and ROBINSON, Circuit Judge.
    BASTIAN, Senior Circuit Judge. . . .
    On August 31, 1962, Parkwood, Inc., the owner of a parcel of land in the District of Columbia, entered into a contract to sell the property to one Butler for $1,000,000. Thereafter, Parkwood, Inc., conveyed the property to the Cohens, subject to Butler's rights under his contract of purchase. Butler, in turn, assigned his rights under the contract to one Lovitz. It is clear that Lovitz was the straw party for the real parties in interest, Messrs. Wolf, Wolf, and Dreyfuss.
    In the complaint originating this action, filed November 7, 1962, the Cohens (as plaintiffs) alleged that there had been an anticipatory breach of the contract on August 31, 1962, and asked the court to declare the contract cancelled and void. Messrs. Wolf, Wolf, and Dreyfuss, et al., filed a counterclaim for specific performance of the original contract and for damages.
    On December 4, 1962, the date for the settlement of the contract, the Cohens and Parkwood, Inc. defaulted. Cross motions were filed in the

District Court and, on December 13, 1963, judgment was entered holding that there had been no anticipatory breach of the contract of August 31, 1962, and decreeing specific performance against the Cohens and Parkwood, Inc.[1] Appeal was taken from this judgment and, on December 14, 1964, we affirmed the judgment of the District Court, with costs.

On January 25, 1965, an amendment of the original judgment of the District Court was entered by that court, directing the specific performance of the written agreement of purchase and providing that all rents, taxes, water rent, insurance, interest on existing encumbrances, operating charges and other apportionable items should be adjusted to the date of the actual transfer of the property. The case was set for trial for determination of the damages, if any, to which Messrs. Wolf, Wolf, and Dreyfuss, et al., were entitled under the counterclaim as a result of the breach of contract by the Cohens and Parkwood, Inc. On February 5, 1965, the property was, pursuant to the decree of the District Court, conveyed to Messrs. Wolf, Wolf, and Dreyfuss.

From now on herein Messrs. Wolf, Wolf, and Dreyfuss, et al., will be denominated plaintiffs or appellants, and the Cohens and Parkwood, Inc., defendants or appellees.

After the filing of affidavits the case came on for hearing on the issue of damages on cross motions for summary judgment. It was claimed by plaintiffs that they were entitled to damages in the amount of $355,000, based on the following:

Under the contract of sale, the purchase price of the property was $1,000,000. Plaintiffs claimed that, prior to the original settlement date, they contracted to resell the property for $1,800,000 but, because of delay of performance, the prospective purchaser had withdrawn, as he had a right to do under his contract. Thus, plaintiffs claimed, they were deprived of a profit of $800,000. It appears without contradiction that the market value of the property was $1,000,000 on the date the contract of August 31, 1962, should have been settled, and that the market value on February 5, 1965, when the sale was finally completed, was $1,445,000. Thus plaintiffs claimed that the difference between this latter amount and $1,800,000, the price at which they claimed they could have sold the property on the originally scheduled date of conveyance, left them damaged in the sum of $355,000. Interest thereon from December 4, 1962, was claimed and they also sought reimbursement for counsel fees.

The District Court, after argument on the cross motions for summary judgment, filed its opinion on June 9, 1966, holding that plaintiffs were not entitled to receive damages for the delay in settlement. . . .

When the contract was breached, the case went forward as to the vendees' right to performance, and the claim for damages was severed.

1. The judgment reserved for a later trial the issue of damages.

Thereafter the vendees filed their statement of undisputed material facts pursuant to the District Court's Rule 9(h). They specifically alleged: "The fair market value of the real estate on the actual date of settlement, February 5, 1965 was $1,445,000."

Despite the value as thus represented, in amount $445,000 greater than the original price, the vendees contend that the District Court erred in denying their additional claim for what they alleged they might have received had there been timely settlement in the first place.

We do not agree. No matter what the rule in other jurisdictions may be, it has long been settled in this jurisdiction that the measure of damages for breach of a contract of sale is the difference between the contract price and the fair market value of the property. Here, as appears above, the *undisputed* evidence is that the value of the property was $1,000,000 at the time of the original settlement date, and that the value of the property as of February 5, 1965, the date the property was actually conveyed to appellants, was $1,445,000. . . .

In Quick v. Pointer, 88 U.S. App. D.C. 47, 186 F.2d 355 (1950), we had before us an appeal from a judgment of the District Court for breach of a contract to sell real estate. The contract price was $16,000. Some ten days after the contract was made, and before the settlement date, the purchaser made a contract for resale at $19,500. Because the original vendor did not have proper title, he was unable to conclude the sale and the vendee filed suit for damages. The District Court gave judgment for $3,500, the difference between the prices in the two contracts. In reversing, we held that the measure of damages for such a breach is the difference between the contract price and the fair market value of the property and, as there was before the court no evidence of the fair market value of the property, we reversed the judgment of the District Court.

In connection with its consideration of *Quick*, the District Court, in the judgment appealed from and in its opinion, note 2 supra, 255 F. Supp. at 305, used this language:

> No reason appears discernible for applying a different principle where damages are sought in addition to specific performance than where action is brought solely to recover damages.

Nor do we see any such discernible reason. If appellants had sued for damages they would not, under *Quick*, have been entitled to damages as the evidence is that the sale price was exactly the same as the value put on the property by the expert who testified and whose testimony is accepted by both sides. *Quick* would have been on all fours with the present case. The fact that appellants elected to take the property is to our minds a fortiori.

Accordingly, we deny plaintiffs' claim for damages for the delay in settlement. . . .

NOTES ON LOST RESALES AND RELATED PROBLEMS

1. Have the buyers in Wolf v. Cohen been restored to the position they would have occupied but for the sellers' breach? Is there any reason why they should not be restored to that position?

2. Wolf v. Cohen reflects the traditional measure of general damages in sale contracts and is still the law in some jurisdictions. The law in most jurisdictions is more generous to plaintiffs, but the majority rule probably would not lead to a different result in *Wolf* itself. The rule in most jurisdictions is that the difference between the contract price and the market price is the measure of general damages, but that profits from a lost resale can be recovered as special damages if the seller had reason to know of the resale contract. If the resale contract would have yielded an unusually large profit to the buyer, the seller is liable only if he were informed of this prospect when he made the original contract.

What result under that standard in Wolf v. Cohen? Is there any chance the buyers told the sellers they had a contract to resell for $1.8 million? If they had been told that, is there any chance the sellers would have agreed to sell for $1 million? In the absence of a special relationship of trust and confidence, or a direct question by the seller, a buyer would have no duty under the law of fraud to disclose that he had a contract to resell at an 80 percent profit. But might the prevailing damage rule reflect an unstated view that it is not entirely cricket for buyers to withhold such information? That rationale would be more persuasive if we were dealing with a special rule about lost resales. But the rule that sellers must be told about unusually profitable resale contracts is derived from the general rule of Hadley v. Baxendale: Obligors must be told about any unusual consequence that will result from their breach. (Surely you remember *Hadley*: broken crankshaft, "the mill is stopped," delay in carriage, no recovery for lost production? 156 Eng. Rep. 145 (1854).)

3. The Uniform Commercial Code adopts the majority rule for contracts for the sale of goods. Section 2-712(2) provides that the buyer may recover "the difference between the cost of cover and the contract price together with any incidental or consequential damages." To "cover" is to buy replacement goods elsewhere. Section 2-713(1) provides in the alternative that the buyer may recover "the difference between the market price . . . and the contract price together with any incidental and consequential damages." Section 2-715 defines incidental and consequential damages as follows:

(1) Incidental damages resulting from the seller's breach include expenses reasonably incurred in inspection, receipt, transportation and care and custody of goods rightfully rejected, any commercially reasonable charges, expenses or commissions in connection with effecting cover and any other reasonable expense incident to the delay or other breach.

(2) Consequential damages resulting from the seller's breach include
  (a) any loss resulting from general or particular requirements and needs of which the seller at the time of contracting had reason to know and which could not reasonably be prevented by cover or otherwise; and
  (b) injury to person or property proximately resulting from any breach of warranty.

The only one of these provisions that could authorize recovery of the profits of a lost resale is §2-715(2)(a), and it is limited to "loss resulting from . . . needs of which the seller at the time of contracting had reason to know."

4. Note the distinction between "incidental" and "consequential" damages in §2-715. Aren't incidental damages just a subset of what most lawyers would call consequential damages — a subset of consequences so universally foreseeable that the drafters thought it unnecessary to require a showing that defendant had reason to anticipate them? When the buyer breaches, more may turn on the distinction. The sections on seller's damages, §§2-706 and 2-708, authorize recovery of incidental damages but make no mention of consequentials. The conventional wisdom is that sellers cannot recover consequentials. But seller's incidental damages are defined more broadly than buyer's incidental damages. Section 2-710 provides:

> Incidental damages to an aggrieved seller include any commercially reasonable charges, expenses or commissions incurred in stopping delivery, in the transportation, care and custody of goods after the buyer's breach, in connection with return or resale of the goods or otherwise resulting from the breach.

Suppose seller is a wholesaler whose orders are just large enough to entitle him to a quantity discount from the manufacturer. Suppose further that one of his customers cancels a large order, with the result that he loses his quantity discount and has to pay a higher price for the goods sold to his other customers. Why isn't the higher price recoverable as incidental damages? Isn't it a "commercially reasonable . . . expense . . . otherwise resulting from the breach?" Could there ever be consequential damages that are not also incidental damages within this definition?

The courts think so. The court denied recovery of a lost quantity discount in Nobs Chemical, U.S.A. v. Koppers Co., 616 F.2d 212 (5th Cir. 1980). The court thought that §2-710 applied only to expenses "contracted by the seller after the breach and occasioned by such things as the seller's need to care for, and if necessary, dispose of the goods in a reasonable manner." Id. at 215. Doesn't that read "otherwise resulting from the breach" right out of the statute?

5. Recall the economic notion of efficient breach. Judge Posner says that the efficiency of contract law depends on measuring damages by the

plaintiff's lost profits. He assumes that the lost expectancy is always equivalent to the lost profits. R. Posner, Economic Analysis of Law 89-91 (2d ed. 1977). Is that view consistent with the law's residual hostility to consequential damages? With the rule that sellers who were not notified of any unusually profitable use for their product will not be liable for unusual lost profits if they breach? Is it reasonable to expect buyers bargaining over price to tell sellers about the large profits they expect to make with sellers' product? If not, shouldn't we expect lost profits to often go uncompensated? Is that efficient? Is it fair?

6.   In Wolf v. Cohen, why is it so clear to the parties and to the court that the market value of the land at the original closing date was $1 million? On that day, two contracts for the sale of that land were in effect: one for $1 million and one for $1.8 million. The vast discrepancy illustrates the difficulties of identifying *the* market value. Was the market value $1 million because most buyers and sellers would have agreed on that price and the buyer who offered $1.8 million was out of line? Or was the market value $1.8 million until that buyer withdrew, whereupon market value collapsed back to $1 million? Does the usual definition of market value help? Market value is said to be the price a willing buyer would pay a willing seller if neither were under any compulsion to buy or sell.

Whatever you ultimately decide market value is, shouldn't both contract prices at least be admissible on the issue? But note the court's description of its earlier decision in Quick v. Pointer: Although the record in *Quick* showed a contract to sell the land for $16,000, and another contract to resell it at $19,500, *Wolf* says "there was before the court no evidence of the fair market value of the property." The traditional view was that market value could not be proved by showing actual sale prices, but only by the opinion evidence of "witnesses who were acquainted with its market value." Latimer v. Burrows, 163 N.Y. 7, 57 N.E. 95 (1900). There were exceptions to the rule even in 1900, and most jurisdictions would probably now admit both kinds of evidence, but Wolf v. Cohen indicates that the traditional view has not entirely died out. Is there anything at all to be said for excluding evidence of actual prices? In *Latimer,* the court feared that litigants might enter into collusive resale contracts to establish misleading evidence of market value, and that the other side would have no way of detecting the collusion.

7.   The UCC rejects these fears in contracts for the sale of goods. Both buyers (§2-713) and sellers (§2-708(1)) can recover damages based on the difference between the contract price and the market price. In addition, each has an alternative. Seller can recover the difference between the contract price and the price at which he resells (§2-706(1)), and the buyer can recover the difference between the contract price and the cover price — the price at which he buys replacement goods (§2-712(1)). Buyer's cover must be "in good faith," "reasonable," and "without unreasonable delay" (§2-712(1)); seller's resale must be "in good faith and in a

commercially reasonable manner" (§2-706(1)). Is there any reason for the difference between the requirements for cover and the requirements for resale?

8. It is not always clear when or whether buyer covered or seller resold. Just as Retail Marine argued that its sale of the Neri's boat was a sale it would have made anyway (supra at 17), buyers sometimes argue that a particular purchase of goods similar to those not delivered under the contract was not cover, but a purchase they would have made anyway. In *Chatlos* (supra at 35), plaintiff had bought an IBM computer to do many of the same things the NCR had been intended to do, but Chatlos insisted that the IBM was not a substitute for the NCR.

Consider also the case of the volume buyer. Suppose a retailer who sells thousands of widgets per year and places frequent orders with several suppliers. One supplier fails to deliver on a contract for 500 widgets at an unusually low price. In the month following breach, the retailer places five orders, totaling 4,000 widgets, with four different suppliers, at three different prices. Defendant will want to argue that the 500 cheapest widgets were the substitutes for the undelivered order. Plaintiff may want to argue that the 500 most expensive widgets were the substitutes, or that none of them were substitutes because all 4,000 would have been ordered anyway. Is there any way to resolve such issues? If you were one of the lawyers in this case, what information would you seek in discovery?

9. The contract-market measure of damage is familiar to every first year law student. Yet it has been argued that, at least for buyers, "this damages measure makes no sense whatever" in real life. Childres, Buyer's Remedies: The Danger of Section 2-713, 72 Nw. L. Rev. 837, 841-842 (1978). Professor Childres argues that if the buyer covers, he should get the difference between the contract price and the cover price. If he does not cover, "he has not suffered market price-contract price differential damages, not having used the market. The only damages he *could* have suffered are the consequentials — what he would have made had he received the goods." Id. at 843-844.

Isn't his point equally applicable to sellers who don't resell? And isn't he right? Or do the difficulties of identifying cover, or of proving consequential losses, justify retaining the contract-market alternative? If buyer could have covered but didn't, recovery of consequentials would be limited to the difference between the contract price and the price at which he should have covered. Isn't the market price likely to be the best approximation of the hypothetical cover price? That may justify contract-market recoveries when consequentials are large. But when the contract-market difference exceeds the consequentials, isn't it a windfall to let a noncovering buyer recover contract-market damages? Or is market value the best measure of what buyer lost, even if he now decides he would rather have the money than the goods? If I negligently damage your car, and you choose not to repair it, is it a windfall for you to collect the cost of repair or the loss in value?

One case refusing to award contract-market damages is Nobs Chemi--
cal, U.S.A. v. Koppers Co., 616 F.2d 212 (5th Cir. 1980). Buyer breached
a contract to buy 1,000 tons of cumene for $540 per ton. Seller had
arranged to buy the cumene in Brazil for $400 per ton, but seller was able
to cancel his purchase when buyer breached. When buyer breached, the
Brazilian price had dropped to $264 per ton. The court awarded seller's
lost profits under §2-708(2), $140 per ton. It refused to award the contract-
market difference of $276 per ton, because seller could not have made
that much if the deal had been completed. Is that the right result? Or
does §2-708(1) guarantee seller at least the contract-market difference?
(Section 2-708 is reprinted in Neri v. Retail Marine, supra at 19.) Doesn't
Nobs imply that damages based on market price are unavailable whenever
damages can be based on the price in a particular transaction?

Seller in Nobs had at least some power to cancel his purchase. Suppose he had been able to cancel, repurchase at the new market price, and
perform his contract with buyer? Then should he get the contract-market
difference?

MEINRATH v. SINGER CO.
87 F.R.D. 422 (S.D.N.Y. 1980)

WEINFELD, District Judge.

Plaintiff Leopold Meinrath is a Belgian entrepreneur engaged in the
marketing and distribution of computers and computer-related products
principally in the Benelux countries and France. He commenced this suit
to recover payments of "bonus compensation" allegedly due under an
Agreement of Purchase and Sale . . . entered into among him, the four
"Unicard companies" in which he had controlling interests, and the defendant, The Singer Company. . . . His first claim is for $300,000 — the
difference between the amount he received in bonus compensation and
the maximum allowable amount, to which he claims entitlement. . . .

Meinrath claims "consequential damages" in the amount of U.S.
$770,000. This claim is based upon allegations that Singer knew at the
time it entered into the contract that Meinrath had substantial subsisting
business ventures that would survive the Agreement; that Meinrath repeatedly apprised Singer and its representatives of the necessity for
prompt payment of the bonus compensation as it became due in order to
provide working capital for his Unicard ventures; and that as a direct,
foreseeable result of Singer's failure to make timely payments to which he
claims he was entitled but defendant denies, Meinrath's other businesses
suffered substantial losses, which in turn injured him. . . .

[Singer has moved for summary judgment on the claim for consequential damages.]

Meinrath's claim for consequential damages consists of (1) losses of
approximately $648,000 in invested capital suffered as a result of the

liquidation of Unicard France in 1975, and of the forced sale of all assets of Unicard Nederland in 1974 for the nominal sum of $2, and (2) a $122,000 decline in the net worth of Unicard Belgique which Meinrath continues to own and operate, due to operating and tax losses allegedly attributable to the losses suffered by the other two Unicard companies. . . .

The essence of each of these claims is that at the time of the signing of their Agreement and even prior thereto, Singer had a special awareness of the Unicard companies' financial plight and their dire need for funds with a consequent obligation upon Singer to make timely payments of bonus compensation. In essence, plaintiff seeks to parlay Singer's knowledge of his and his companies' financial predicament into a claim that Singer was required to provide them with necessary financial capital by making prompt payment of all amounts due under the Agreement. The Agreement contains no such explicit or implicit undertakings; plaintiff was to be paid commission on revenues collected from sales and leases of equipment by Singer affiliates during a period of two and one-half years after September 1, 1973. No liquidated damages are specified in the event of nonpayment or late payment of bonus compensation. . . .

Singer does not dispute that for purposes of this motion, both before and after September 7, 1973, it had actual knowledge of Meinrath's other business ventures, and of his and their need for funds to finance these other enterprises. Moreover, Singer acknowledges that Meinrath made several unsuccessful demands for payment of bonus compensation he alleged was due him. We assume for purposes of this motion that in fact the payments were wrongfully withheld when due. Nonetheless, under these facts Singer is not liable for consequential damages for the failure of Meinrath's other business ventures, unrelated to the contract. Meinrath's essential claim is one for payment withheld although due; the consequential damages stemming from such a claim are not compensable. Almost one hundred years ago the Supreme Court in Loudon v. Taxing District[6] resolved the precise issue now before the Court and in the process formulated a rule which survives today. The plaintiff in *Loudon* had contracted with the City of Memphis to repair certain streets and public places. When the City failed to make payments upon the notes it had tendered, plaintiff was required to borrow funds at "exorbitant" rates of interest and to sell its securities at a discounted rate in order to meet its obligations. Having won a judgment on the notes, plaintiff sued to recover the interest paid and its other related losses as consequential damages. The Court limited plaintiff's relief to recovery of interest at the prevailing legal rate:

> [A]ll damages for delay in the payment of money owing upon contract are provided for in the allowance of interest, which is in the nature of damages for

6.   104 U.S. 771 (1881).

withholding money that is due. The law assumes that interest is the measure of all such damages.[7]

The rule of *Loudon* has been adopted by the New York courts, and is thus applicable to this contract, which by its terms invokes New York law. Moreover, all of the commentators have held that where the alleged breach of contract consists only of a failure to pay money, remedy for the breach is limited to the principal owed plus damages in the form of interest at the prevailing legal rate. As Professor Williston has noted:

> In an action by a creditor against his debtor for the non-payment of the debt, no other damages [than the sum of money itself with interest at the legal rate from the time when it was due] are ever allowed.

When a large order of goods is bought on credit from a seller known to have but little capital, it may be plainly foreseeable by the buyer when he enters into the transaction that failure to pay the price when it is due may ruin the seller financially, and such a consequence is both proximate and natural. . . . The universality of the rule limiting damages to interest is, therefore, based on the policy of having a measure of damages of easy and certain application, even though occasionally leading to results at variance with the general principle of compensation.[9]

In opposing the motion, plaintiff has not cited a single authority that supports the award of damages other than interest where the claim is for payments withheld. Our own independent search reveals none either. Instead, plaintiff strains to analogize this case to Spang Industries v. Aetna Casualty, 512 F.2d 365 (2d Cir. 1965), in which our Court of Appeals upheld the award of consequential damages to a construction company which incurred emergency expenses in completing construction of a bridge after its subcontractor had breached its obligation timely to deliver steel girders before the onset of winter. That case is distinguishable from the instant case. In *Spang* the contract was for the provision of a specialty item not easily replaceable or found elsewhere. Moreover, the damages suffered, which flowed from plaintiff's crash program to complete the bridge, were a natural outgrowth of the breach. They related solely to plaintiff's efforts to complete the breached contract and thereby mitigate damages. Likewise, in For Children, Inc. v. Graphics Int'l Inc.,[10] a case also cited by Meinrath, plaintiff recovered lost profits when the defendant failed to provide a unique article (children's "pop-up pictures") unobtainable elsewhere: The damages were suffered by the same enterprise that was injured by the breach. Those cases cannot be analogized to the facts of the instant case. Here the plaintiff's claim is not for a unique

---

7. Id. at 774.
9. S. Williston, 11 Contracts §1410, at 605-06 (3d ed. 1968) (footnotes omitted).
10. 352 F. Supp. 1280 (S.D.N.Y. 1972).

article, but only for payments withheld although allegedly due. More-over, the claimed loss was not related to the completion of the contract; instead, it was incurred in other, wholly unrelated ventures. Plaintiff's argument that his injury was foreseeable to Singer at the time of the contract is unavailing; if he wanted to impose liability upon Singer for the failure of his business empire because of nonpayment of amounts alleg-edly due under their contract, he could have bargained for that result by fixing liquidated damages for a breach. Accordingly, we hold that as a matter of law plaintiff's consequential loss is too remote from the main injury to be compensable and too speculative to be ascertainable; plaintiff is barred from recovering such damages.

As Professor Williston has noted, there are sound policy reasons for limiting recovery in cases such as this to lost interest. If allowed to assert the consequential damages claim, plaintiff would infuse the trial of a simple contract dispute with a vast array of evidence concerning his far-flung business empire.[12] To permit him to do so upon a claim of payments withheld is only one step less extreme than permitting him to prove that, had he received timely payments, he would have invested his money wisely and profited thereby. If such were the case every contract dispute would be rendered complex, limited only by counsel's imagination and conceptual theories of unrealized profits and opportunities.

Singer's motion for summary judgment on the issue of consequential damages is granted. . . .

NOTES ON CONSEQUENTIAL DAMAGES FROM FAILURE TO PAY MONEY

1. *Meinrath* presents the pure case of a court refusing to award con-sequential damages. The court says that Meinrath's consequential losses were too "remote" and "speculative," but these are merely labels for the conclusion that such damages should not be awarded. Defendant's mo-tion for summary judgment was decided on the basis of the undisputed facts, plus plaintiff's version of all disputed facts. On that view of the facts, is there any ordinary sense in which plaintiff's losses were remote and speculative? Even if there were, what about the usual rule that de-fendant is liable for unusual consequences if he had actual notice that his breach would cause them?

12. The parties appear to agree that the consequential damages claim, if permitted, would swallow the main claim of an alleged unpaid $300,000 bonus compensation and would extend the trial a period of a full month. Although this consideration can play no part in the disposition of the motion, if plaintiff is without a right to assert the consequential damages claim, the defendant should not be subjected to the burden and expense entailed in a protracted and intricate trial.

2. Does the court's flat rule make sense on a cover theory — that plaintiff could have borrowed the $300,000 to keep his business going until defendant paid? That rationale might explain many of the cases, especially the ones in which plaintiff claims that if he had been paid promptly he would have invested the money shrewdly. But a plaintiff like Meinrath, who claims that defendant's failure to pay drove him over the brink of insolvency, might have had great difficulty finding someone to loan him $300,000. And if he found such a loan only at exorbitant rates, Loudon v. Taxing District (described in *Meinrath*) says he could not even recover the extra interest he paid. There surely wouldn't be anything remote or speculative about that, would there?

3. Are you persuaded by the court's fear that a trial on Meinrath's consequential damage claim would dwarf the trial on the merits? Does it matter that in cases where plaintiff could not borrow elsewhere, causation would always be murky because of the risk that plaintiff's business would have failed anyway? Even so, why an absolute rule? There will be cases in which causation is clear: Professor Williston's example of a solvent small seller who borrows heavily to fill a very large order. If the buyer fails to pay, the seller will be ruined; if the buyer pays, or if the buyer had never placed the order at all, the seller would have been financially comfortable.

4. Suppose you conclude that we need an absolute rule that interest is the only measure of damage for failure to pay money. Do the traditional distinctions between direct and consequential damages, or general and special damages, make it any easier to reach or explain that rule?

5. On its facts, *Meinrath* would probably be good law everywhere. But there is some erosion in the strict rule of Loudon v. Taxing District. Courts have awarded unpaid sellers the actual interest they paid, instead of the legal rate, as incidental damages under UCC §2-710. See, e.g., Intermeat v. American Poultry, 575 F.2d 1017 (2d Cir. 1978) (applying New York law). A common law example is Ma v. Community Bank, 686 F.2d 459 (7th Cir.), *cert. denied*, 459 U.S. 962 (1982), decided under Wisconsin law. The bank refused to pay $30,000 owed to a depositor. The court awarded the higher interest he would have earned by reinvesting in an otherwise identical saving certificate. The court held that "loss of living comfort and ease" and damage to career and reputation were too speculative, but did not invoke any absolute rule against consequential damages.

6. Some cases have also denied consequential damages for breach of a contract to loan money. But the majority rule allows such damages where they are sufficiently foreseeable. An example is St. Paul at Chase Corp. v. Manufacturer's Life Insurance Co., 262 Md. 192, 278 A.2d 12 (1971), in which defendant breached its commitment to refinance an apartment building. Plaintiff could not refinance elsewhere, the original

lender foreclosed, and plaintiff suffered a $1.3 million deficiency judgment. That judgment had accrued $250,000 in interest. Plaintiff had also lost the benefit of several hundred thousand dollars spent in reliance on the loan commitment. Plaintiff recovered all these items, totaling nearly $2 million.

Why is a promise to pay money on condition that it be repaid so different from a promise to pay money absolutely?

7.   Another exception flourishes in suits against insurers for bad faith refusal to settle. The insured has no claim merely for failure to pay or delay in payment. But if the insurer refuses or delays in bad faith, knowing that it is liable, plaintiff can sue not only for interest, but for consequential damages, emotional distress, and punitive damages. An example in which the consequential losses were small and easily foreseeable is First Security Bank v. Goddard, 181 Mont. 407, 593 P.2d 1040 (1979). Goddard bought credit disability insurance to cover the payments on his new car. When he was disabled and the insurer denied coverage, the car was repossessed and sold for less than the amount still owing. A jury awarded damages of $4,227.95, $1,300 less than the price of the car; it is not clear how these damages were computed. In Silberg v. California Life Insurance Co., 113 Cal. Rptr, 711, 521 P.2d 1103 (1974), the insurer failed to pay medical bills under a hospitalization policy. The jury awarded $75,000 for physical and mental distress. Both state supreme courts upheld the verdicts. The Montana court also upheld $5,000 in punitive damages; the California court threw out $500,000 in punitives. The Notes on Punitive Damages for Breach of Contract, infra at 619, have other examples of punitive damages for failure to pay insurance benefits.

These cases typically involve consumers or small businesses, in desperate straits from their original loss, seemingly at the mercy of huge insurance companies. It is easy to understand why courts think there must be some remedy beyond collecting the amount due with interest. But the usual arguments against consequential damages for failure to pay money apply; it is no easier to measure damage or trace causation in these cases. Many insureds will be in desperate straits after a loss, but some won't be, and in a society that lives on credit, most people will be in bad shape if expected money doesn't arrive, whether it's insurance money or some other kind of money.

There has been little attention to the tension between the insurance cases and the loan cases on the one hand, and the supposed general rule on the other. The Montana case does address the issue, and implies that the rule against consequential damages for failure to pay money applies only in contract. Like most states, Montana says that an insurer's bad faith failure to pay is a tort.

8.   From the seller's perspective, what is a sales contract but a promise to pay money? Uniform Commercial Code §2-710 authorizes sellers to

recover incidental damages, but the language speaks only of "charges, expenses, or commissions . . . resulting from the breach." Is Meinrath's loss an expense arising from the breach? What about interest paid if the seller has to borrow money while waiting for the price?

9.   One argument for the general rule does not appear in *Meinrath*. If any delay in paying money triggered liability for consequential damages, the risks of negotiating or litigating disputed claims would be increased. Everyone who lost a lawsuit would potentially be liable for additional consequential damages caused by his failure to pay as soon as the claim was made. This would give creditors another bargaining chip with debtors. Our law encourages litigation; courts have been reluctant to deter disputes by imposing liability for asserting one's assumed rights. That is why insurers are liable only for bad faith failure to pay. But the failure-to-loan cases generally do not include a bad faith requirement.

F. LIMITS ON THE BASIC PRINCIPLE

There are a number of limits on the basic principle of restoring plaintiff to his rightful position. These limits are closely related to distinctions between direct and consequential, and general and special, damages. Rules about avoidable consequences, proximate cause, and certainty of damage are the primary tools for restricting recovery of consequential damages.

1. Avoidable Consequences, Offsetting Benefits, and Collateral Sources

S. J. GROVES & SONS CO. v. WARNER CO.
576 F.2d 524 (3d Cir. 1978)

Before ALDISERT, VAN DUSEN and WEIS, Circuit Judges.
   WEIS, Circuit Judge. . . .
   As part of a highway improvement program, the Pennsylvania Department of Transportation undertook the erection of the Girard Point Bridge in Southwest Philadelphia and selected American Bridge Company as the prime contractor. Plaintiff-appellant Groves was awarded a subcontract for the placement of the bridge's concrete decks and parapets and contracted with the defendant Warner for the delivery of ready-mixed concrete for use at the Girard Point site. Groves filed this lawsuit claiming extensive losses because of Warner's failure to deliver adequate supplies at scheduled times. The case was tried to the court and after

preparing detailed findings of fact and conclusions of law, the trial judge entered judgment in favor of the plaintiff in the amount of $35,401.28. Dissatisfied with the denial of a large part of its claimed damages, Groves appealed.

The contract at issue provided that Warner would supply approximately 35,000 cubic yards of ready-mixed concrete at a rate of 40 cubic yards per hour and at times specified by Groves. . . .

Groves expected to pour concrete for the decks of the bridge in the mornings and then to use some of the crew to construct parapets in the afternoons. This general plan was frustrated by Warner's frequent failures to make deliveries in compliance with Groves' instructions. As a result, deck pours originally scheduled for the mornings often extended into the afternoons and evenings and created overtime labor expense.

Concerned with its lagging progress, Groves considered securing other sources of concrete as early as 1971 but found no real alternatives. It was too expensive to build its own batching plant at the site and the only other source of ready-mixed concrete in the area was the Trap Rock Company, located near the Warner plant. Trap Rock, however, was not certified to do state work in 1971 and its price was higher than Warner's. Moreover, the production facilities at Trap Rock were limited, as was the number of trucks it had available. Meanwhile, Warner continued to assure Groves that deliveries would improve.

Despite its promises, Warner's performance continued to be erratic and on June 21, 1972, the Pennsylvania Department of Transportation ordered all construction at Girard Point halted until the quality of Warner's service could be discussed at a conference. A meeting took place the next day with state officials and representatives from Warner, Groves, and other contractors in attendance. Based on Warner's renewed assurances of improved performance, state officials allowed work to resume on June 26, 1972. From that date until July 20, 1972, Warner's delivery service improved significantly, although it still did not consistently meet Groves' instructions. In the months following and until completion in October of 1972, Warner's performance continued to be uneven and unpredictable.

On June 14, 1972, when Groves again approached Trap Rock, that firm maintained that it could service the job at the desired delivery rate but did not reduce its price. On July 11, 1972, Trap Rock was certified by the state and the next day agreed to accept the same price as Warner. Groves, nevertheless, decided to continue with Warner as its sole supplier.

The district judge found that Warner had acted in bad faith by deliberately overcommitting its ability to manufacture and deliver enough concrete, providing an inadequate number of trucks to service Groves' project, and following a policy of providing delivery at only 75 percent of the ordered rate. On that basis, the court stripped Warner of the protection offered by the no-claim-for-delay clause in its contract and awarded damages. In the court's view, on June 15, 1972 Groves had no reasonable expectation that Warner's performance would improve to "totally satisfactory levels" and by July 11, 1972, "there were no practical impediments to employing Trap Rock as a supplemental supplier." The court therefore concluded that "as of July 12, 1972, Groves had an obligation to utilize Trap Rock as a supplemental supplier . . . in order to mitigate any possible 'delay damages' resulting from Warner's service." Accordingly, the court did not award Groves all the delay damages it sought, allowing only $12,534 for overtime which had been paid on days when Warner's deliveries were late before, but not after, July 12, 1972. . . .

The district court determined that since the contract was essentially one for the sale of a product with an additional requirement of proper and timely delivery, the Uniform Commercial Code should govern.

The court described the transaction between Groves and Warner as an installment contract as that term is defined in Pa. Stat. Ann. tit. 12A, §2-612(1) (Purdon 1970), that is, an agreement to deliver goods in "separate lots to be separately accepted." Where there is non-conformity with respect to one or more installments which substantially impairs the value of the whole contract, there is a breach of the whole. §2-612(3). In the district court's view, such a breach occurred as of July 12, 1972 and should have been apparent to Groves. At that time Warner had been recertified by the Pennsylvania Department of Transportation and Trap Rock had also received state approval. . . .

Section 2-715 provides that the consequential damages a buyer may recover are those which "could not reasonably be prevented by cover or otherwise." Thus, generally, when a seller refuses to deliver goods, the buyer must attempt to secure similar articles elsewhere as a prerequisite to receiving consequential damages. "Cover" is defined in §2-712(1):

> After a breach . . . the buyer may "cover" by making in good faith and without unreasonable delay any reasonable purchase of or contract to purchase goods in substitution for those due from the seller. . . .

The requirement of cover or mitigation of damages is not an absolute, unyielding one, but is subject to the circumstances. Comment 2 to §2-712 says:

> [t]he test of proper cover is whether at the time and place the buyer acted in good faith and in a reasonable manner, and it is immaterial that hindsight may later prove that the method of cover used was not the cheapest or most effective.

Essentially the cover rules are an expression of the general duty to mitigate damages and usually the same principles apply. The burden of proving that losses could have been avoided by reasonable effort and expense must be borne by the party who has broken the contract.

Here, the court found that as of July 12, 1972, Groves had no reasonable expectation that Warner's performance would improve to totally satisfactory levels, that there were no practical impediments to employing Trap Rock as a supplemental supplier, and therefore Groves had a duty to contract with Trap Rock to mitigate delay damages. We do not think that the premises justify the conclusion.

In July, 1972, Groves found itself confronted with a breach by Warner and the consequent necessity to choose among a number of alternative courses of action. In the circumstances, Groves could have:

1. Declared the contract breached, stopped work, and held Warner liable for all damages. This was not a realistic alternative.
2. Set up its own cement batching plant at the job site. Time and expense made this impractical.
3. Accepted Warner's assurances that it would perform satisfactorily in the future, see §2-609(1).[6] The court, however, found that it would have been unreasonable to have any faith in continued assurances from Warner.
4. Substituted Trap Rock for Warner for the remainder of the contract. The court made no finding on the reasonableness of this choice but it appears questionable whether Trap Rock had the resources to meet all of Groves' requirements.
5. Engaged Trap Rock as a supplemental supplier; or
6. Continued dealing with Warner in the belief that though its performance would not be satisfactory, consequential damages might be less than if the other alternatives were adopted.

Of the six alternatives, Groves was seemingly faced with three practical ones — all subject to drawbacks. Groves had to: allow Warner to continue in the hope of averting even greater losses; substitute Trap Rock for all of Warner's work — a choice made doubtful by Trap Rock's ability to handle the project; or, lastly, use Trap Rock as a supplemental supplier.

The last choice — the option chosen by the district court — was subject to several difficulties which the court did not discuss. Even if Trap Rock supplied part of the contract with perfect scheduling, there would

---

6.   Section 2-609(1) reads in part:

When reasonable grounds for insecurity arise with respect to the performance of either party the other may in writing demand adequate assurance of due performance and until he receives such assurance may if commercially reasonable suspend any performance for which he has not already received the agreed return.

be no guarantee that Warner would do so. The element of erratic deliveries by Warner would not necessarily be cured, nor would the problems with the quality of concrete it delivered to the site. The presence of two independent suppliers acting separately might indeed pose problems more severe than those which existed before. Moreover, the record reveals that Trap Rock received some of its raw material from Warner and Groves suspected that Warner might not have been too cooperative if part of the Girard Bridge contract were taken away by Trap Rock.

Confronted with these alternatives, Groves chose to stay with Warner, a decision with which the district court did not agree. The court's preference may very well have been the best; that, however, is not the test. As Judge Hastie wrote in In re Kellett Aircraft Corp., 186 F.2d 197, 198-99 (3d Cir. 1950):

> Where a choice has been required between two reasonable courses, the person whose wrong forced the choice can not complain that one rather than the other was chosen.
>
> The rule of mitigation of damages may not be invoked by a contract breaker as a basis for hypercritical examination of the conduct of the injured party, or merely for the purpose of showing that the injured person might have taken steps which seemed wiser or would have been more advantageous to the defaulter. . . . One is not obligated to exalt the interest of the defaulter to his own probable detriment.

There are situations in which continuing with the performance of an unsatisfactory contractor will avoid losses which might be experienced by engaging others to complete the project. In such a setting, mitigation is best served by continuing existing arrangements. As the troubled Prince of Denmark once observed we " . . . rather bear those ills we have, Than fly to others that we know not of. . . ."

There is another unusual feature in this case. Engaging Trap Rock as an additional source of supply was a course of action open to Warner as well as Groves. Indeed, on other commercial work Warner *had* used Trap Rock as a supplemental supplier. When the Pennsylvania Department of Transportation approved Trap Rock, Warner could have augmented its deliveries to Groves by securing extra trucks and concrete from Trap Rock as needed. Such an arrangement by Warner would have had the distinct advantage of having one subcontractor directly answerable to Groves for proper delivery, timing and quality.

Where both the plaintiff and the defendant have had equal opportunity to reduce the damages by the same act and it is equally reasonable to expect the defendant to minimize damages, the defendant is in no position to contend that the plaintiff failed to mitigate. Nor will the award be reduced on account of damages the defendant could have avoided as easily as the plaintiff. The duty to mitigate damages is not applicable where the party whose duty it is primarily to perform a contract has equal opportunity for performance and equal knowledge of the consequences of nonperformance.

Here, where the alternative the court imposed upon Groves was available to Warner as well, Warner may not assert Groves' lack of mitigation in failing to do precisely that which Warner chose not to do. Particularly is this so in light of the finding that Warner breached the contract in bad faith.

Thus, either upon the ground that Groves should not be faulted for choosing one of several reasonable alternatives or upon the basis that Warner was bound to procure an additional supplier, we hold that the district court erred in imposing on Groves as a matter of law a duty to engage Trap Rock. Accordingly, we vacate that portion of the court's judgment which allowed damages for delay only until July 12, 1972. We remand for assessment of damages from that point to completion of the contract on the same basis as that used for the pre-July 12 delay damages.

NOTES ON AVOIDABLE CONSEQUENCES

1. The rule that defendant is not liable for avoidable consequences of his wrongdoing is closely related to doctrines of contributory and comparative negligence. But the avoidable consequences doctrine applies in contract and to non-negligent torts as well. It is often discussed in terms of plaintiff's duty to mitigate damages. But it is not quite accurate to say that plaintiff has a "duty" to mitigate. He can mitigate or not, as he chooses, but he cannot recover for losses he could have avoided.

2. Avoidable consequences is generally treated as an affirmative defense. But avoidable consequences cases slip imperceptibly into cases on the basic measure of damage. Recall the disagreement between *The Helen B. Moran* and Jenkins v. Etlinger, supra at 45, 49. *Jacobs* required defendant to prove that plaintiff should have mitigated damages by abandoning his property instead of by repairing it. *The Helen B. Moran* held that that was not a mitigation issue and that plaintiff must prove that repair costs did not exceed the value of his property.

3. How vigorous must plaintiff be in avoiding the consequences of defendant's wrongdoing? It is generally said that he need not take steps that are unreasonable.

a. The question is most frequently litigated in employment discharge cases, where plaintiff must look for other employment. Some of the cases turn on the diligence of his search. These blend into cases about what kind of work he must search for and what offers he must accept. Must he leave the geographic area if there are better opportunities elsewhere? Must he accept work outside his field, or inferior to the job from which he was discharged? Most courts answer each of these questions in the negative. The Supreme Court recently summarized the law as follows:

> This duty, rooted in an ancient principle of law, requires the claimant to use reasonable diligence in finding other suitable employment. Although the un- or underemployed claimant need not go into another line of work, accept a demotion, or take a demeaning position,[16] he forfeits his right to backpay if he refuses a job substantially equivalent to the one he was denied. Consequently, an employer charged with unlawful discrimination often can toll the accrual of backpay liability by unconditionally offering the claimant the job he sought, and thereby providing him with an opportunity to minimize damages.[18]

Ford Motor Co. v. EEOC, 458 U.S. 219, 231-312 (1982).

In what may be an extreme case, the California court held that the lead in a western to be filmed in Australia was not equivalent to the lead in a musical to be filmed in Los Angeles, and affirmed a judgment for the full $750,000 fee promised actress Shirley MacLaine. The majority also relied on the fact that plaintiff would have less artistic control over the western. Parker v. Twentieth Century-Fox Film Corp., 3 Cal. 3d 176, 474 P.2d 689 (1970).

   b.   Another recurring fact pattern is personal injury litigation in which plaintiff refuses allegedly corrective surgery. The principle in *Groves* should enable you to decide these cases. Isn't it a matter of deciding if the operation's reasonably certain benefits outweigh its risks and discomforts? Although many standards have been announced, most are variations of this basic approach.

An example with a twist is Small v. Combustion Engineering, 681 P.2d 1081 (Mont. 1984). Plaintiff refused low-risk knee surgery that had a 92 percent chance of restoring his ability to walk. The court found that choice objectively unreasonable, but reasonable for plaintiff. Plaintiff was manic-depressive, and because of his mental disorder, he considered only the risks and ignored the benefits. The court felt obliged to take the plaintiff's view. Is that the right result?

   c.   Occasionally, obvious steps to avoid damages are impossible for a particular plaintiff. In Valencia v. Shell Oil Co., 23 Cal. 2d 840, 147 P.2d 558 (1944), defendant negligently did $222 damage to a truck used in

---

16.   Some lower courts have indicated, however, that after an extended period of time searching for work without success, a claimant must consider taking a lower-paying position. . . .

18.   The claimant's obligation to minimize damages in order to retain his right to compensation does not require him to settle his claim against the employer, in whole or in part. Thus, an applicant or discharged employee is not required to accept a job offered by the employer on the condition that his claims against the employer be compromised.

plaintiff's business. But plaintiff was too broke to pay the repair bill, and defendant refused to pay it, so the truck sat in the shop pursuant to a mechanic's lien for seventeen months. Can plaintiff recover $250 per month for loss of use of the truck? The court said yes, affirming a judgment for $4,416. And consider Close v. State, 90 A.D.2d 599, 456 N.Y.S.2d 437 (1982), a suit for personal injuries. Plaintiff's obesity aggravated her pain and disability, and the Court of Claims denied recovery for harm she could have avoided by losing weight. The Appellate Division reversed, finding that she tried in good faith but could not stay on a diet, and that her injuries precluded exercise. Are you convinced? What result if she didn't even try to lose weight?

d.   Plaintiff need not avoid loss by submitting to defendant's illegitimate demands. A dramatic example is O'Brien v. Isaacs, 17 Wis. 2d 261, 116 N.W.2d 246 (1962). Defendant's negligence forced plaintiff to leave his car overnight in defendant's parking lot. In the morning defendant demanded $1.00 for overnight parking. Plaintiff refused to pay, rented a car for three days while he recovered his own car by a suit in replevin, and then successfully sued for the $41 rental charge.

4.   What about *Groves*'s alternate holding — that the defendant could have avoided the damages as effectively as plaintiff. Why should that matter? Defendant could have avoided all damages by performing its contract. Doesn't the avoidable consequences doctrine assume that defendant is a wrongdoer and go from there? How serious do you think the court is about its alternative rule? Reconsider *Valencia*, note 3c supra. Suppose plaintiff had been wealthy but refused to pay for repairs because it was defendant's responsibility. Could plaintiff recover for loss of use on the ground that defendant could have avoided that damage as easily as plaintiff could?

Suppose defendant negligently started a fire in plaintiff's house. Suppose plaintiff and defendant both stood by, each urging the other to call the fire department. Could plaintiff recover for damages that would have been avoided if he had promptly reported the fire?

Despite the skeptical tone of these questions, the *Groves* rule is frequently stated. Perhaps the cases that make it look silly don't arise very often.

5.   In *Groves*, suppose plaintiff had tried using Trap Rock as a supplemental supplier and it had not worked out. Suppose damages had been increased by the confusion resulting from having two suppliers instead of one. Could plaintiff recover those extra damages? If you say no, aren't you penalizing plaintiff for a reasonable choice from among the unsatisfactory alternatives available after defendant's breach? Doesn't the avoidable consequences rule imply that plaintiff can recover all reasonable expenses incurred attempting to avoid damages?

6.   In Ford Motor Co. v. Equal Employment Opportunity Commission, 458 U.S. 219 (1982), Ford refused to hire the female plaintiffs for

traditionally male jobs in its assembly plant. They sued, alleging sex discrimination. After some time had elapsed, there was one opening in the job category, and Ford offered it first to one of the plaintiffs, then to another. Each declined, in part because they did not want to be the only woman in the department, and in part because Ford did not offer retroactive seniority to the day they would have been hired but for the original discrimination. They had already found comparable work with General Motors, and they would have had to forfeit accrued seniority there to start over at Ford. When the GM plant subsequently closed, it became important to decide whether they had had a sufficient reason to turn down Ford's offer.

The Court said plaintiffs should have accepted Ford's offer and continued to sue for retroactive seniority, and that Ford was not liable for any wages lost after the date of its offer. The Court treated the case as an application of the avoidable consequences rule, which is codified in the employment discrimination laws. But as an avoidable consequences case, it is surely wrongly decided. Weren't plaintiffs more likely to minimize damages by staying at GM with seniority than by returning to Ford without seniority? And even if that were unclear, perhaps because there were rumors about the possibility of closing the GM plant, shouldn't plaintiffs be protected by the rule in Groves v. Warner? Didn't they make a reasonable choice between two alternative strategies for minimizing damages? Still, isn't it troubling to hold Ford responsible for GM's plant closing? Does the case make sense on the theory that Ford's culpability ended when it offered plaintiffs the job for which they had applied? On the theory that Ford's discrimination was not the proximate cause of wages lost after GM's plant closing? Or is it just wrong? Proximate cause and related matters are taken up in the next subsection.

7.   Compare *Ford Motor* with United States National Bank v. Homeland, Inc., 291 Or. 374, 631 P.2d 761 (1981). Homeland defaulted on a lease of office space. The landlord relet to a new tenant, Sebastian's, at a higher rent for a longer term. Sebastian's also defaulted, before the expiration date of Homeland's lease. The court had no difficulty concluding that Homeland was still liable for unpaid rent. Does it matter that the employment contracts in *Ford Motor* had no expiration date short of plaintiffs' retirement?

8.   The issue in *Homeland* could arise because Oregon is one of the growing minority of states that apply the avoidable consequences rule to leases. The common law rule treated a lease as a sale for a term of years. It was no business of the seller (landlord) if the buyer (tenant) abandoned his property; the purchase price (rent) was still due and there was no duty to sell the same term of years to another buyer (relet). A recent survey concludes that twenty-five states still apply the common law rule to residential leases and thirty-two states apply it to commercial leases. Weissenberger, The Landlord's Duty to Mitigate Damages on the Tenant's

Abandonment: A Survey of Old Law and New Trends, 53 Temp. L.Q. 1, 7-10 (1980). Is there any conceivable justification for exempting leases from the general rule?

NOTES ON OFFSETTING BENEFITS

1. We have already encountered several cases in which plaintiff's damages were reduced by some offsetting benefit that resulted from the wrong. The argument about volume sellers in Neri v. Retail Marine Corp., supra at 17, presupposes that damages should be reduced if defendant's breach of contract created an opportunity to make an otherwise impossible sale to someone else. All the arguments about depreciation in *The Helen B. Moran,* supra at 45, and United States v. Ebinger, supra at 51, are about how to account for the benefit of having new property instead of old. The most obvious such benefit is a longer wait before the next replacement; in *Ebinger,* the new property also had lower maintenance costs. In the wrongful birth cases, the courts have noted the offsetting benefits of parenthood. In Thomas v. E. J. Korvette, supra at 95, plaintiff's claim to his wages as a security guard were offset by the wages he earned as a salesman, a job he could not have held if he had still been a security guard. The offsetting benefits rule is closely related to the avoidable consequences rule, because often the benefit conferred is an opportunity that plaintiff must take advantage of if he wishes to be fully compensated.

2. In all the foregoing cases, it seemed obvious that the principle of restoring plaintiff to his rightful position required that offsetting benefits be taken into account. The arguments tended to be about valuation of the benefit, and occasionally over whether it were really a benefit. But there are curious limitations in some formulations of the offsetting benefit rule; only some benefits are taken into account. Consider the Restatement of Torts Second:

§920. BENEFIT TO PLAINTIFF RESULTING FROM
DEFENDANT'S TORT

When the defendant's tortious conduct has caused harm to the plaintiff or to his property and in so doing has conferred a special benefit to the interest of the plaintiff that was harmed, the value of the benefit conferred is considered in mitigation of damages, to the extent that this is equitable.

Comment

a. The rule stated in this Section normally requires that the damages allowable for an interference with a particular interest be diminished by the amount to which the same interest has been benefited by the defendant's

tortious conduct. Thus if a surgeon performs an unprivileged operation resulting in pain and suffering, it may be shown that the operation averted future
suffering. . . .

  b. *Limitation to same interest.* Damages resulting from an invasion of
one interest are not diminished by showing that another interest has been
benefited. Thus one who has harmed another's reputation by defamatory
statements cannot show in mitigation of damages that the other has been
financially benefited from their publication (see Illustration 4), unless damages
are claimed for harm to pecuniary interests. (See Illustration 5). Damages for
pain and suffering are not diminished by showing that the earning capacity of
the plaintiff has been increased by the defendant's act. (See Illustration 6).
Damages to a husband for loss of consortium are not diminished by the fact
that the husband is no longer under the expense of supporting the wife.

  Illustrations . . .

  4. A charges B with murder. In an action for defamation in which B
claims no special damages, the defendant cannot show in mitigation that the
business of B, a seller of soft drinks, has been increased as the result of the
charge.
  5. A charges B with being a member of a secret order. B brings an action
for defamation alleging as special damage the loss of income by B as a surgeon.
A can show in mitigation of damages that because of the false charge, B has
been enabled to attract crowds to lectures given by him, to his great profit.
  6. A tortiously imprisons B for two weeks. In an action brought by B for
false imprisonment in which damages are claimed for pain, humiliation and
physical harm, A is not entitled to mitigate damages by showing that at the end
of the imprisonment B obtained large sums from newspapers for writing an
account of the imprisonment.

  What sense do these limitations make? Suppose that in illustration 6,
plaintiff also sued for the two weeks' wages he lost while falsely imprisoned. Would the addition of that claim of lost income enable defendant
to offset the newspaper profits? That is the plain implication of illustration
5. If the newspaper profits exceed the lost wages, can the excess be applied to the damages for pain, humiliation, and physical harm? Recall the
courts' reliance on the benefits of parenthood in the wrongful birth cases,
supra at 93. Don't the emotional benefits accrue to a different "interest"
than the financial harm?
  One might be reluctant to allow offsets in cases like illustrations five
and six on the ground that defendant's conduct is reprehensible and the
offsetting benefit is a windfall that should be awarded to the victim rather
than the wrongdoer. One can balance that argument against the general
principle of restoring plaintiff to his rightful position, and different persons might respectably reach different conclusions. But what possible
difference does it make whether the "interest" benefited is the same as
the "interest" harmed?

There is no comparable limitation in the statement of the offsetting benefit rule in the Second Restatement of Contracts. See §§347 and 349.

3.   One much argued benefit is the remarriage of a plaintiff spouse in a wrongful death case. Under the conventional measure of damages in wrongful death cases, remarriage may eliminate all subsequent damage. Remarriage provides a new source of financial support, companionship, society, services, etc. It does nothing for plaintiff's grief, but that is theoretically not compensable anyway. No state denies recovery to plaintiffs that do not remarry or make reasonable efforts to do so. Most conceal the fact of remarriage from the jury, or instruct the jury to ignore it. But England and a small minority of states instruct juries to consider any actual remarriage and also the possibility of remarriage in assessing damage. What is the possibility of remarriage worth? If juries took that instruction seriously, wouldn't it be nearly equivalent to instructing that prolonged widowhood is an avoidable consequence for plaintiffs who could attract another mate? Is remarriage within the reasonableness limit of the duty to mitigate damages?

Jurisdictions that consider remarriage do not necessarily assume that marriages are fungible. See, e.g., Jensen v. Heritage Mutual Insurance Co., 23 Wis. 2d 344, 127 N.W.2d 228 (1964), rejecting an argument that the damages awarded were excessive in light of plaintiff's remarriage: "It is pure speculation that the new husband will be able to provide plaintiff with the same amount of support that the deceased husband would be likely to have provided. . . . [L]ikewise there is no assurance that plaintiff will be as happy in her new marriage as allegedly in the prior one." Id. at 355, 127 N.W.2d at 234. The court did not seem interested in evidence on these questions. Do we really want plaintiff testifying about the ways in which her new husband is inferior to the old?

HELFEND v. SOUTHERN CALIFORNIA RAPID TRANSIT DISTRICT
2 Cal. 3d 1, 465 P.2d 61 (1970)

TOBRINER, Acting Chief Justice.

Defendants appeal from a judgment of the Los Angeles Superior Court entered on a verdict in favor of plaintiff, Julius J. Helfend, for $16,400 in general and special damages for injuries sustained in a bus-auto collision. . . .

We have concluded that the judgment for plaintiff in this tort action against the defendant governmental entity should be affirmed. The trial court properly followed the collateral source rule in excluding evidence that a portion of plaintiff's medical bills had been paid through a medical insurance plan that requires the refund of benefits from tort recoveries.

1. The Facts . . .

Defendant requested permission to show that about 80 percent of the plaintiff's hospital bill had been paid by plaintiff's Blue Cross insurance carrier and that some of his other medical expenses may have been paid by other insurance. The superior court thoroughly considered the then very recent case of City of Salinas v. Souza & McCue Construction Company (1967) 66 Cal. 2d 217, distinguished the *Souza* case on the ground that *Souza* involved a contract setting, and concluded that the judgment should not be reduced to the extent of the amount of insurance payments which plaintiff received. The court ruled that defendants should not be permitted to show that plaintiff had received medical coverage from any collateral source. . . .

We must decide whether the collateral source rule applies to tort actions involving public entities and public employees in which the plaintiff has received benefits from his medical insurance coverage.

2. The Collateral Source Rule

The Supreme Court of California has long adhered to the doctrine that if an injured party receives some compensation for his injuries from a source wholly independent of the tortfeasor, such payment should not be deducted from the damages which the plaintiff would otherwise collect from the tortfeasor. . . .

Although the collateral source rule remains generally accepted in the United States, nevertheless many other jurisdictions[4] have restricted[5] or repealed it. In this country most commentators have criticized the rule and called for its early demise. In *Souza* we took note of the academic criticism of the rule, characterized the rule as "punitive," and held it inapplicable to the governmental entity involved in that case.

We must, however, review the particular facts of *Souza* in order to determine whether it applies to the present case. The City of Salinas

---

4. [T]he House of Lords has recently reaffirmed the rule. Most other western European nations have repudiated the rule.

5. The New York Court of Appeals has, for example, quite reasonably held that an injured physician may not recover from a tortfeasor for the value of medical and nursing care rendered gratuitously as a matter of professional courtesy. The doctor owed at least a moral obligation to render gratuitous services in return, if ever required; but he had neither paid premiums for the services under some form of insurance coverage nor manifested any indication that he would endeavor to repay those who had given him assistance. Thus this situation differs from that in which friends and relatives render assistance to the injured plaintiff with the expectation of repayment out of any tort recovery; in that case, the rule has been applied. On the other hand, New York has joined most states in holding that a tortfeasor may not mitigate damages by showing that an injured plaintiff would receive a disability pension. In these cases the plaintiff had actually or constructively paid for the pension by having received lower wages or by having contributed directly to the pension plan.

brought suit against Souza & McCue Construction Company, a public works contractor, and its pipe supplier for breach of a contract to construct a sewer pipe line. Souza cross-complained against the city, alleging fraudulent misrepresentation and breach of implied warranty of site conditions; and against the pipe supplier, alleging a guarantee of performance of the piping and a promise to indemnify Souza for any losses. The trial court found that the city materially misrepresented soil conditions by failing to inform Souza of unstable conditions known to the city, that with the city's knowledge Souza relied upon the misrepresentations in bidding, and that Souza should recover damages proximately caused by the city's fraudulent breach.

We held that the trial court improperly determined damages against the city by refusing to allow the city to show that the supplier had recompensed Souza for some of the damages caused by the city's breach. In this contract setting in which the supplier did not constitute a wholly independent collateral source,[7] we held that the collateral source rule cannot be applied against public entities because the collateral source rule appears punitive in nature[8] and punitive damages cannot be imposed on public entities.

Although *Souza*'s reasoning as to punitive damages might appear to apply to private tortfeasors as well as public entities and to torts as well as contract actions, we did not there consider the collateral source rule in contexts different from the specific contractual setting and particular relationship of the parties involved. We distinguish the present case from *Souza* on the ground that in *Souza* the plaintiff received payments from his subcontractor which, in the contractual setting of that case, did not constitute a truly independent source. Obviously, such a "source" differs entirely from the instant one, which derives from plaintiff's payment of insurance premiums. Here plaintiff received benefits from his medical insurance coverage only because he had long paid premiums to obtain them. Such an origin does constitute a completely independent source. Hence, although we reaffirm the holding in *Souza*, we do not believe that its reasoning either compels the abolition of the collateral source rule in

7. . . . [T]he rule applies only to payments that come from a source entirely independent of the tortfeasor and does not apply to payments by joint tortfeasors or to benefits the plaintiff receives from a tortfeasor's insurance coverage.

8. . . . *Souza* . . . cited Harper & James, The Law of Torts (1956), section 25.22, pages 1343-1354, which concluded:

If therefore a feeling of revenge and resentment has any place in the law at all, it should certainly be banished as far as possible from the law of civil recovery, practically as well as theoretically. In spite of this, we suggest, it has played a large — though unrecognized — part in justifying plaintiff's double recovery.

Although we recognize that in the past a primitive moralism may have engendered the collateral source rule to serve punitive ends, we suggest below that the rule today still serves not mere punitive purposes, but legitimate objectives that may or may not survive the spread of a philosophy of social insurance. . . .

all cases or requires an unwarranted exemption from the rule of public entities and their employees involved in tort actions. . . .

The collateral source rule as applied here embodies the venerable concept that a person who has invested years of insurance premiums to assure his medical care should receive the benefits of his thrift.[14] The tortfeasor should not garner the benefits of his victim's providence.

The collateral source rule expresses a policy judgment in favor of encouraging citizens to purchase and maintain insurance for personal injuries and for other eventualities. Courts consider insurance a form of investment, the benefits of which become payable without respect to any other possible source of funds. If we were to permit a tortfeasor to miti-gate damages with payments from plaintiff's insurance, plaintiff would be in a position inferior to that of having bought no insurance, because his payment of premiums would have earned no benefit. Defendant should not be able to avoid payment of full compensation for the injury inflicted merely because the victim has had the foresight to provide himself with insurance.

Some commentators object that the above approach to the collateral source rule provides plaintiff with a "double recovery," rewards him for the injury, and defeats the principle that damages should compensate the victim but not punish the tortfeasor. We agree with Professor Fleming's observation, however, that "double recovery is justified only in the face of some exceptional, supervening reason, as in the case of accident or life insurance, where it is felt unjust that the tortfeasor should take advantage of the thrift and prescience of the victim in having paid the premiums." (Fleming, Introduction to the Law of Torts (1967) p.131.) As we point out infra, recovery in a wrongful death action is not defeated by the payment of the benefit on a life insurance policy.

Furthermore, insurance policies increasingly provide for either subro-gation or refund of benefits upon a tort recovery, and such refund is indeed called for in the present case. Hence, the plaintiff receives no double recovery;[15] the collateral source rule simply serves as a means of bypassing the antiquated doctrine of non-assignment of tortious actions and permits a proper transfer of risk from the plaintiff's insurer to the tortfeasor by way of the victim's tort recovery. The double shift from the

14.   In Lewis v. County of Contra Costa (1955) 130 Cal. App. 2d 176, 278 P.2d 756, the court held that the collateral source rule prohibited the trial court from admitting evidence that at the time of the accident plaintiff had accumulated sufficient sick leave to cover the period of his disablement. The court reasoned that "In a very real sense of the term it is as if he had drawn upon his savings account in an amount equal to his salary during the period of his disablement." (130 Cal. App. 2d at pp. 178-179, 278 P.2d at p.758.)

15.   In reaffirming our adherence to the collateral source rule in this tort case involving a plaintiff with collateral payments from his insurance coverage, we do not suggest that the tortfeasor be required to pay doubly for his wrong — once to the injured party and again to reimburse the plaintiff's collateral source — as Smith v. City of Los Angeles (1969) 81 Cal. Rptr. 120, appears to require.

tortfeasor to the victim and then from the victim to his insurance carrier can normally occur with little cost in that the insurance carrier is often intimately involved in the initial litigation and quite automatically receives its part of the tort settlement or verdict.

Even in cases in which the contract or the law precludes subrogation or refund of benefits,[17] or in situations in which the collateral source waives such subrogation or refund, the rule performs entirely necessary functions in the computation of damages. For example, the cost of medical care often provides both attorneys and juries in tort cases with an important measure for assessing the plaintiff's general damages. To permit the defendant to tell the jury that the plaintiff has been recompensed by a collateral source for his medical costs might irretrievably upset the complex, delicate, and somewhat indefinable calculations which result in the normal jury verdict.

We also note that generally the jury is not informed that plaintiff's attorney will receive a large portion of the plaintiff's recovery in contingent fees or that personal injury damages are not taxable to the plaintiff and are normally deductible by the defendant. Hence, the plaintiff rarely actually receives full compensation for his injuries as computed by the jury. The collateral source rule partially serves to compensate for the attorney's share and does not actually render "double recovery" for the plaintiff. Indeed, many jurisdictions that have abolished or limited the collateral source rule have also established a means for assessing the plaintiff's costs for counsel directly against the defendant rather than imposing the contingent fee system. In sum, the plaintiff's recovery for his medical expenses from both the tortfeasor and his medical insurance program will not usually give him "double recovery," but partially provides a somewhat closer approximation to full compensation for his injuries.[20]

If we consider the collateral source rule as applied here in the context of the entire American approach to the law of torts and damages, we find that the rule presently performs a number of legitimate and even indispensable functions. Without a thorough revolution in the American approach to torts and the consequent damages, the rule at least with respect

---

17.   [Anheuser-Busch v. Starley, 28 Cal. 2d 347, 355 (Traynor, J., dissenting):]

Certain insurance benefits are regarded as the proceeds of an investment rather than as an indemnity for damages. Thus it has been held that the proceeds of a life insurance contract made for a fixed sum rather than for the damages caused by the death of the insured are proceeds of an investment and can be received independently of the claim for damages against the person who caused the death of the insured. The same rule has been held applicable to accident insurance contracts. . . .

20.   Of course, only in cases in which the tort victim has received payments or services from a collateral source will he be able to mitigate attorney's fees by means of the collateral source rule. Thus the rule provides at best only an incomplete and haphazard solution to providing all tort victims with full compensation. Depriving some tort victims of the salutary protections of the collateral source rule will, short of a thorough reform of our tort system, only decrease the available compensation for injuries.

to medical insurance benefits has become so integrated within our present system that its precipitous judicial nullification would work hardship. In this case the collateral source rule lies between two systems for the compensation of accident victims: the traditional tort recovery based on fault and the increasingly prevalent coverage based on non-fault insurance. Neither system possesses such universality of coverage or completeness of compensation that we can easily dispense with the collateral source rule's approach to meshing the two systems. The reforms which many academicians propose cannot easily be achieved through piecemeal common law development; the proposed changes, if desirable, would be more effectively accomplished through legislative reform. In any case, we cannot believe that the judicial repeal of the collateral source rule, as applied in the present case, would be the place to begin the needed changes.

Although in the special circumstances of *Souza* we characterized the collateral source rule as "punitive" in nature, we have pointed out the several legitimate and fully justified compensatory functions of the rule. In fact, if the collateral source rule were actually punitive, it could apply only in cases of oppression, fraud, or malice and would be inapplicable to most tort, and almost all negligence, cases regardless of whether a governmental entity were involved. We therefore reaffirm our adherence to the collateral source rule in tort cases in which the plaintiff has been compensated by an independent collateral source — such as insurance, pension, continued wages, or disability payments — for which he had actually or constructively paid or in cases in which the collateral source would be recompensed from the tort recovery through subrogation, refund of benefits, or some other arrangement. Hence, we conclude that in a case in which a tort victim has received partial compensation from medical insurance coverage entirely independent of the tortfeasor the trial court properly followed the collateral source rule and foreclosed defendant from mitigating damages by means of the collateral payments.

3. The Collateral Source Rule, Public Entities, and Public Employees

Having concluded that the collateral source rule is not simply punitive in nature, we hold, for the reasons set out infra, that the rule as delineated here applies to governmental entities as well as to all other tortfeasors. We must therefore disapprove of any indications to the contrary in City of Salinas v. Souza & McCue Constr. Co., supra.

Defendants would have this court create a special form of sovereign immunity as a novel exception to the collateral source rule for tortfeasors who are public entities or public employees. We see no justification for such special treatment. In the present case the nullification of the collateral source rule would simply frustrate the transfer of the medical costs from the medical insurance carrier, Blue Cross, to the public entity. The public entity or its insurance carrier is in at least as advantageous a position to spread the risk of loss as is the plaintiff's medical insurance carrier. To deprive Blue Cross of repayment for its expenditures on plaintiff's behalf merely because he was injured by a public entity rather than a private individual would constitute an unwarranted and arbitrary discrimination.

Furthermore, if we were to follow without careful analysis the *Souza* characterization of the collateral source rule as punitive in nature, we would immediately face a dilemma as to the proper treatment of the public employee's liability. In order to encourage public employees to perform their duties without the threat of untoward personal liability, we held in Johnson v. State of California (1968) 69 Cal. 2d 782, 791-792, 73 Cal. Rptr. 240, 447 P.2d 352, that a public entity must indemnify and defend its employees against civil liability, except in cases of conduct outside the scope of employment or acts performed with actual fraud, corruption, or malice.

If we were to conclude that the collateral source rule cannot apply to public entities, we would be forced to reach one of three equally implausible results: (1) Since the public entity is immune from the rule and enjoys a deduction in damages, but the driver possesses no such immunity, the driver must bear the cost of the extra damages equivalent to the collateral source increment, despite our rule in *Johnson.* (2) Since the public entity is immune from the rule and enjoys a deduction in damages, the driver would initially bear the cost of the extra damages equivalent to the collateral source increment, but under *Johnson* he would be indemnified by the public entity for all the plaintiff's tort recovery. Hence, by suing both the public entity and the public employee the plaintiff can bypass the purported *Souza* rule through the *Johnson* decision. (3) Finally, since the public entity is immune from the rule and enjoys a deduction in damages, the only way to avoid untoward personal liability for the driver under *Johnson* would be for this court to extend the collateral source rule immunity from the public entity to the public employee.

The first alternative would patently conflict with this court's approach to the civil liability of public employees in *Johnson.* . . . The second alternative would . . . totally undermine the effect of *Souza* by indirectly imposing the rule upon the public entity by means of the indemnification process. . . . Rather than adopting this circumvention, we must confront the issues at stake in determining whether the collateral source rule should apply to public entities and their employees. As stated above, we conclude that the rule is not simply punitive in nature and applies to public entities to the same extent as to other tortfeasors.

The third approach would extend the collateral source rule immunity from the public entity to its employees and increase the unjustified discrimination against tort victims who happen to be injured by public entities rather than private individuals. . . .

In view of the several legitimate and important functions of the collateral source rule in our present approach to the law of torts and damages, we find no appropriate justification for labelling the rule "punitive" or for not applying it to public entities and public employees. . . .

The judgment is affirmed.

NOTES ON THE COLLATERAL SOURCE RULE

1. The collateral source rule may be thought of as an exception to the offsetting benefits rule. How are insurance benefits different from other benefits made possible by wrongdoers? Payments from an insurer are no more independent of the wrongdoer than payments from a new employer or a new buyer of land. In each case, plaintiff would not have been able to collect the insurance, work for the new employer, or sell the land to the new buyer, but for the injury inflicted on him. That is, in each case the payments come from sources independent of the wrongdoer, but the opportunity to receive those payments is created by the wrongdoer. Why do we offset wages and resales but not insurance benefits?

The distinction is not just between contract and tort. Consider Thomas v. E. J. Korvette, supra at 95. There, plaintiff lost his job because of false arrest, malicious prosecution, and defamation of character. But no one suggested that the wages from his new job should not be offset. Nor is it a sufficient distinction that plaintiff earned the insurance benefits by paying premiums. He even more clearly earned the wages from the second job.

2. Perhaps the difference is that benefits traditionally thought to fall within the collateral source rule are payments intended by the payors to be compensatory. The insurer, the employer with a sick pay plan, the family members who chip in to pay medical bills, the welfare official who pays emergency subsistence, disability, or Medicaid benefits, and the doctor or hospital who provides free care — all are acting to help the plaintiff and compensate or ameliorate his injuries. By contrast, the new employer or the new buyer of the land is acting at arm's length and in his own self-interest. Perhaps it would be more precise to say that in the collateral source cases, the payments are made gratuitously or in fulfillment of a promise made in exchange for consideration paid earlier; in the other cases, the payment is made for fresh consideration. Should that make any difference?

3. A third party who received fresh consideration suffered no loss and has no plausible claim of his own against the wrongdoer. Nor does he have any right to stand in the shoes of the original plaintiff and assert his claim: that is, to be subrogated to the plaintiff's claim. Conversely, all those who gratuitously helped the plaintiff, and all the insurers and

others who made a contingent promise to help him if necessary, hoping it would never be necessary, are out-of-pocket because of defendant's conduct and may plausibly claim reimbursement. *Helfend* is such a case. There, defendant will pay plaintiff's medical expenses, and plaintiff will use the money to reimburse his health insurer. This is fully consistent with the remedial goal of restoring victims of wrongdoing to their rightful position. Plaintiff is made whole; his insurer is made whole; and defendant only has to pay once. If all cases resulted in reimbursement to the collateral source, the collateral source rule would be much less controversial. Even then, it would not be completely uncontroversial. Some critics have suggested that it is wasteful to litigate whether the loss should fall on plaintiff's insurer or defendant's insurer, because either insurer can spread the loss, and often, either insurer will spread the loss to substantially the same population. That argument is part of the larger argument whether a fault-based tort system still makes sense.

4.   Surprisingly, there are many cases in which the collateral source does not seek reimbursement, or is not awarded reimbursement even though he seeks it. One reason, of declining significance, is archaic restrictions on subrogation derived from common law notions about the nonassignability of claims. Another reason is simply industry habit. Subrogation clauses are almost universal in property damage insurance policies, traditionally rare but now appearing with some frequency in medical insurance policies, and rare or nonexistent in accident and life policies. Government social insurance programs rarely seek reimbursement or subrogation. It is in these cases, where part of the loss has been shifted to a third party who is not reimbursed, that the collateral source rule has its real bite. Then plaintiff recovers twice, once from the defendant and once from the collateral source. The double recovery that would be unthinkable if plaintiff had given fresh consideration for the offsetting benefit becomes routine when he gave past consideration or no consideration at all.

5.   The strength of the double recovery argument varies with the nature of the insurance. Even critics of the collateral source rule have distinguished whole life insurance policies on the ground that they are investments as well as insurance. They have a cash value that is lost when one collects on the policy. But the cash value is often much less than the face amount of the policy, and term policies have no cash value at all. Preserving the investment feature of life insurance is not a rationale that justifies payment of the full policy amount over and above the wrongful death judgment. Perhaps a better argument is that life is so intrinsically difficult to value that it is meaningless to speak of double recoveries. Whole life is also special in that the risk insured against is inevitable; only the timing is uncertain. The insured will eventually collect, either by dying or by cashing in the policy, and the insurer will eventually pay.

What the insured has gained and the insurer has lost from the wrongful death is not the face amount of the policy, but the present value of the premiums over the years until the unknown time at which the insured would have died from other causes.

6. The core case for the collateral source rule is one in which plaintiff recovers his medical expenses or lost wages from a medical or disability insurance plan, collects them again from the defendant, and does not reimburse the insurer. Does *Helfend* persuade you that this is just and not overcompensatory? Lawyers and claims adjustors often value pain and suffering by multiplying the medical expense, or the out-of-pocket losses, by three. Does that make any sense? *Helfend* hints that it is so important that jurors have to be told about medical costs in order to value pain and suffering. Assuming that is right, why not just let plaintiff prove his medical expenses as evidence of pain and suffering? Do we really have to allow double recovery as a way of getting information to the jury?

What about the argument that double recovery for medical payments and lost wages makes up for inability to recover attorney's fees? Is this a new doctrine of offsetting errors? Wouldn't it make more sense to allow recovery of attorney's fees, if that is appropriate, and deny double recovery in collateral source rule cases if that is appropriate? Or is the whole system in such delicate and interrelated balance that it makes sense as a whole even though some of its individual parts make no sense at all?

2. Proximate Cause and Related Problems

PRUITT v. ALLIED CHEMICAL CORP.
523 F. Supp. 975 (E.D. Va. 1981)

MERHIGE, District Judge.

Plaintiffs bring the instant action against Allied Chemical Corporation . . . for Allied's alleged pollution of the James River and Chesapeake Bay with the chemical agent commonly known as Kepone. . . .

Plaintiffs allegedly engage in a variety of different businesses and professions related to the harvesting and sale of marine life from the Chesapeake Bay. . . .[1] All claim to have suffered economic harm from defendant's alleged discharges of Kepone into the James River and thence into the Bay. . . .

Defendant moves to dismiss counts I, II, III, V, VII, VIII, IX, X and XII of the complaint as they apply to all plaintiffs other than those di-

---

1. Plaintiffs include commercial fishermen; seafood wholesalers, retailers, distributors and processors; restauranteurs; marina, boat tackle and baitshop owners; and employees of all the above groups.

rectly engaged in the harvesting of the Bay's marine life.[2] That is, defendant would dismiss these nine counts as to all plaintiffs except those
classified in paragraph 6.A of the complaint (generally, fishermen,
shellfishermen, and lessors of oysterbeds.) All plaintiffs subject to defendant's motion claim . . . lost profits resulting from their inability to sell
seafood allegedly contaminated by defendant's discharges, and from a
drop in price resulting from a decline in demand for seafood coming from
areas affected by Kepone. These plaintiffs can generally be described as
parties suffering only indirect harm to their property or businesses as the
result of Kepone pollution.[3] They or their possessions have not been
caused direct, physical damage by defendant. Instead, plaintiffs allege
that the stream of profits they previously received from their businesses or
employment has been interrupted, and they seek compensation for the
loss of the prospective profits they have been denied. As plaintiffs' claims
rely on various, radically different theories of liability, the Court considers each count, or group of similar counts, separately.

Negligence and Products Liability

Counts I, II and V allege that negligence, of some degree, by defendant
entitles plaintiffs to recover. Count III alleges that the effluents released
by defendant were "defective and unreasonably dangerous," and that
defendant should be strictly liable for any harm caused by its discharges.
All of these counts arise from the Court's diversity jurisdiction and rely on
theories of state tort law.

The Virginia Supreme Court has, to the Court's knowledge, never
directly considered the question of recovery for loss of prospective economic benefits. It is commonly stated that the general rule both in admiralty and at common law has been that a plaintiff cannot recover for
indirect economic harm. The logical basis for this rule is obscure. Although Courts have frequently stated that economic losses are "not foreseeable" or "too remote," these explanations alone are rarely apposite.
As one well-respected commentator has noted, "the loss to plaintiff in
each case . . . would be readily recoverable if the test of duty — or
remoteness — usually associated with the law of negligence were applied."[6]

2. Defendants would leave for further proceedings Counts IV (as now construed by
plaintiffs), VI and XI. Those counts allege, generally, malicious and intentional injury by
defendants and violation of Va. Code Ann. §18.2-499, 500 (conspiracy willfully to injure
business).
3. In fact, none of the plaintiffs has suffered direct harm to his or its property. As
discussed below, the plaintiffs not subject to defendants' motion to dismiss obviously do not
own the marine life that they harvest or the water in which that life flourishes.
6. James, Limitations of Liability for Economic Loss Caused by Negligence: A Pragmatic Appraisal, 25 Vand. L. Rev. 43 (1972).

The Court frankly acknowledges the fact that there exist a substantial number of cases that may be construed to establish a general rule favorable to plaintiffs. . . .

As noted by the Ninth Circuit in Union Oil Co. v. Oppen, 501 F.2d 558 (9th Cir. 1974), the general rule has found application in a wide variety of contexts:

> [T]he negligent destruction of a bridge connecting the mainland with an island, which caused a loss of business to the plaintiff who was a merchant on the island, has been held not to be actionable. . . . A plaintiff engaged in commercial printing has been held unable to recover against a negligent contractor who, while engaged in excavation pursuant to a contract with a third party, cut the power line upon which the plaintiff's presses depended. . . . A defendant who negligently injures a third person entitled to life-care medical services by the plaintiff is liable to the third person but not to the plaintiff. . . . The operators of a dry dock are not liable in admiralty to charterers of a ship, placed by its owners in the dry dock, for negligent injury to the ship's propeller where the injury deprived the charterer of the use of the ship.

501 F.2d at 563-64 (citations omitted).

Nevertheless, there also exist cases that conflict with this broadly recognized general rule. At least two of the minority cases deal with precisely the case present here: the loss of business opportunities due to pollution of streams adjoining a plaintiff's property. Moreover, even defendant concedes that a third case, Union Oil, supra, that provided compensation for fishermen for losses caused by pollution from oil spills, is correctly decided. Although defendant would distinguish Union Oil as limited solely to those who labor on the water (but not at its edge) the rationale for creation of this particular distinction is unclear.

Given the conflicting case law from other jurisdictions, together with the fact that there exists no Virginia law on indirect, economic damages, the Court has considered more theoretical sources in order to find a principled basis for its decision. There now exists a considerable amount of literature on the economic rationale for tort law. In general, scholars in the field rely on Judge Learned Hand's classic statement of negligence[11] to argue that a principal purpose of tort law is to maximize social utility: where the costs of accidents exceeds the costs of preventing them, the law will impose liability.

The difficulty in the present case is how to measure the cost of Kepone pollution. In the instant action, those costs were borne most directly by the wildlife of the Chesapeake Bay. The fact that no one individual claims

11.   See United States v. Carroll Towing Co., 159 F.2d 169, 173 (2d Cir. 1947), in which Judge Hand stated that a person's duty to prevent injuries from an accident "is a function of three variables: (1) The probability that [the accident will occur]; (2) the gravity of the resulting injury, if [it] does; (3) the burden of adequate precautions."

property rights to the Bay's wildlife could arguably preclude liability. The Court doubts, however, whether such a result would be just. Nor would a denial of liability serve social utility: many citizens, both directly and indirectly, derive benefit from the Bay and its marine life. Destruction of the Bay's wildlife should not be a costless activity.

In fact, even defendant in the present action admits that commercial fishermen are entitled to compensation for any loss of profits they may prove to have been caused by defendant's negligence. The entitlement given these fishermen presumably arises from what might be called a constructive property interest in the Bay's harvestable species. These professional watermen are entitled to recover despite any direct physical damage to their own property. Presumably, sportfishermen share the same entitlement to legal redress for damage to the Bay's ecology. The Court perceives no valid distinction between recognition of commercial damages suffered by those who fish for profit and personal harm suffered by those who fish for sport.

The claims now considered by the Court, however, are not those of direct users of the Bay, commercial or personal. Instead, defendant has challenged the right of those who buy and sell to direct users of the Bay, to maintain a suit.

Defendant would have the Court draw a sharp and impregnable distinction between parties who exploited the Bay directly, and those who relied on it indirectly. In *Union Oil*, the Ninth Circuit suggested that it might make such a distinction if it were ever required to decide the issue. The panel in *Union Oil*, however, did not have to decide the question now facing this Court — and the Court does not perceive that there exists so simple a distinction as defendant would urge it to construct.

None of the plaintiffs here — including commercial fishermen — has suffered any direct damage to his private property. All have allegedly suffered economic loss as a result of harm to the Bay's ecology. Apart from these similarities, the different categories of plaintiffs depend on the Bay in varying degrees of immediacy. The commercial fishermen here fit within a category established in *Union Oil*: they "lawfully and directly make use of a resource of the sea."[16] The use that marina and charterboat owners make of the water, though hardly less legal, is slightly less direct. (And indeed, businesses in similar situations have been held entitled to recover in other courts.) Still less direct, but far from nonexistent, is the link between the Bay and the seafood dealers, restauranteurs, and tackle shops that seek relief (as do the employees of these establishments).

One meaningful distinction to be made among the various categories of plaintiffs here arises from a desire to avoid doublecounting in calculating damages. Any seafood harvested by the commercial fishermen here would have been bought and sold several times before finally being purchased for consumption. Considerations both of equity and social utility

16. 501 F.2d at 570.

suggest that just as defendant should not be able to escape liability for destruction of publicly owned marine life entirely, it should not be caused to pay repeatedly for the same damage.

The Court notes, however, that allowance for recovery of plaintiffs' lost profits here would not in all cases result in double-counting of damages. Plaintiffs in categories B, C, D, E, and F[20] allegedly lost profits when deprived of supplies of seafood. Those profits represented a return on the investment of *each* of the plaintiffs in material and labor in their businesses, and thus the independent loss to each would not amount to double-counting. Conversely, defendants could not be expected to pay, as a maximum, more than the replacement value of a plaintiff's actual investment, even if the stream of profits lost when extrapolated into the future, would yield greater damages.

Tracing the stream of profits flowing from the Bay's seafood, however, involves the Court in other complexities. The employees of the enterprises named in categories B through F, for example, had no physical investment in their employers' businesses. Yet if plaintiffs' allegations are proven, these employees undoubtedly lost wages and faced a less favorable job market than they would have, but for defendant's acts, and they have thus been harmed by defendant. What is more, the number of parties with a potential cause of action against defendant is hardly exhausted in plaintiffs' complaint. In theory, parties who bought and sold to and from the plaintiffs named here also suffered losses in business, as did their employees. In short, the set of potential plaintiffs seems almost infinite.

Perhaps because of the large set of potential plaintiffs, even the commentators most critical of the general rule on indirect damages have acknowledged that some limitation to liability, even when damages are foreseeable, is advisable. Rather than allowing plaintiffs to risk a failure of proof as damages become increasingly remote and diffuse, courts have, in many cases, raised an absolute bar to recovery.

The Court thus finds itself with a perceived need to limit liability, without any articulable reason for excluding any particular set of plaintiffs. Other courts have had to make similar decisions.[22] The Court con-

---

20.   Respectively, seafood wholesalers, retailers, processors, distributors and restauranteurs.

22.   See e.g., Judge Kaufmann's opinion in Petition of Kinsman Transit Co., 388 F.2d 821, 824-25 (2d Cir. 1968) (hereinafter cited as *Kinsman II*), where the court noted that

in the final analysis, the circumlocution whether posed in terms of "foreseeability," "duty," "proximiate [sic] cause," "remoteness," etc. seems unavoidable

and then turned to Judge Andrews well-known statement in Palsgraf v. Long I.R. Co., 248 N.Y. 339, 162 N.E. 99, 104 (N.Y. 1928):

It is all a question of expediency . . . of fair judgment, always keeping in mind the fact that we endeavor to make a rule in each case that will be practical and in keeping with the general understanding of mankind.

cludes that plaintiffs who purchased and marketed seafood from commercial fishermen suffered damages that are not legally cognizable, because insufficiently direct. This does not mean that the Court finds that defendant's alleged acts were not the cause of plaintiffs' losses, or that plaintiffs' losses were in any sense unforeseeable. In fact, in part because the damages alleged by plaintiffs here were so foreseeable, the Court holds that those plaintiffs in categories G, H and I[23] have suffered legally cognizable damages. The Court does so for several reasons. The United States Court of Appeals for the Fourth Circuit has held, in admiralty, that a defendant should "pay . . . once, but no more" for damages inflicted.[24] While commercial fishing interests are protected by allowing the fishermen themselves to recover, it is unlikely that sportsfishing interests would be equally protected. Because the damages each sportsman suffered are likely to be both small[25] and difficult to establish, it is unlikely that a significant proportion of such fishermen will seek legal redress. Only if some set of surrogate plaintiffs is entitled to press its own claims which flow from the damage to the Bay's sportfishing industry will the proper balance of social forces be preserved. Accordingly, the Court holds that to the extent plaintiffs in categories G, H and I suffered losses in sales of goods and services to sportsfishermen as a result of defendant's tortious behavior, they have stated a legally cognizable claim.

Defendant hardly has reason to complain of the equity of the Court's holding. First, it benefited above from the Court's exclusion of the claims of innocent businessmen in categories B through F who are probable victims of their alleged acts. Here, the Court applies different restrictions on liability for reasons of equity and efficiency previously addressed. Second, the "directness" of the harm, at least to plaintiffs in categories G and I,[27] is high here. Both operate on the water or at its edge. . . . The Court's conclusion results from consideration of all these factors, and an attempt to tailor justice to the facts of the instant case. . . .

NOTES ON PROXIMATE CAUSE

1. The court reached substantially similar conclusions with respect to the admiralty and nuisance counts.

2. What is the source of the "perceived need to limit liability"? Why shouldn't defendants pay for all the damage they inflict? The court found that these damages were foreseeable and not duplicative of the damages to fishermen, boat and marina owners, and bait and tackle shops. Yet it

23. Boat, tackle and bait shop, and marina owners respectively.
24. *Venore*, supra, 583 F.2d at 710.
25. The net loss to any sportsman would have to take into account any enjoyment received from natural areas visited as a substitute to the Chesapeake Bay.
27. Generally boat and marina owners.

cut off liability at the water's edge. Doesn't it follow that the court failed to achieve the goal of encouraging defendant to spend as much to avoid pollution as the pollution would cost?

3. Despite the inability to draw sensible lines or even to articulate a rationale, the feeling that liability must end somewhere has been widespread. Tests have been formulated in terms of foreseeable and unforeseeable, proximate and remote, and direct and indirect. As *Pruitt* illustrates, these labels are not interchangeable. Here, the damages are found to be foreseeable but indirect. Presumably they are also remote. But why does that matter? Are we back to the fear of monstrous verdicts again? Keep thinking about these questions in light of the next principal case.

EVRA CORP. v. SWISS BANK CORP.
673 F.2d 951 (7th Cir.), *cert. denied*, 459 U.S. 1017 (1982)

Before SWYGERT, Senior Circuit Judge, and WOOD and POSNER, Circuit Judges.

POSNER, Circuit Judge.

The question — one of first impression — in this diversity case is the extent of a bank's liability for failure to make a transfer of funds when requested by wire to do so. The essential facts are undisputed. In 1972 Hyman-Michaels Company, a large Chicago dealer in scrap metal, entered into a two-year contract to supply steel scrap to a Brazilian corporation. [Hyman-Michaels subsequently changed its name to Evra Corp.] Hyman-Michaels chartered a ship, the *Pandora*, to carry the scrap to Brazil. The charter was for one year, with an option to extend the charter for a second year; specified a fixed daily rate of pay for the hire of the ship during both the initial and the option period, payable semi-monthly "in advance"; and provided that if payment was not made on time the *Pandora*'s owner could cancel the charter. Payment was to be made by deposit to the owner's account in the Banque de Paris et des Pays-Bas (Suisse) in Geneva, Switzerland.

The usual method by which Hyman-Michaels, in Chicago, got the payments to the Banque de Paris in Geneva was to request the Continental Illinois National Bank and Trust Company of Chicago, where it had an account, to make a wire transfer of funds. Continental would debit Hyman-Michaels' account by the amount of the payment and then send a telex to its London office for retransmission to its correspondent bank in Geneva — Swiss Bank Corporation — asking Swiss Bank to deposit this amount in the Banque de Paris account of the *Pandora*'s owner. The transaction was completed by the crediting of Swiss Bank's account at Continental by the same amount.

When Hyman-Michaels chartered the *Pandora* in June 1972, market charter rates were very low, and it was these rates that were fixed in the charter for its entire term — two years if Hyman-Michaels exercised its option. Shortly after the agreement was signed, however, charter rates began to climb and by October 1972 they were much higher than they had been in June. The *Pandora*'s owners were eager to get out of the charter if they could. At the end of October they thought they had found a way, for the payment that was due in the Banque de Paris on October 26 had not arrived by October 30, and on that day the *Pandora*'s owner notified Hyman-Michaels that it was canceling the charter because of the breach of the payment term. Hyman-Michaels had mailed a check for the October 26 installment to the Banque de Paris rather than use the wire-transfer method of payment. It had done this in order to have the use of its money for the period that it would take the check to clear, about two weeks. But the check had not been mailed in Chicago until October 25 and of course did not reach Geneva on the twenty-sixth.

When Hyman-Michaels received notification that the charter was being canceled it immediately wired payment to the Banque de Paris, but the *Pandora*'s owner refused to accept it and insisted that the charter was indeed canceled. The matter was referred to arbitration in accordance with the charter. On December 5, 1972, the arbitration panel ruled in favor of Hyman-Michaels. The panel noted that previous arbitration panels had "shown varying degrees of latitude to Charterers";

> In all cases, a pattern of obligation on Owners' part to protest, complain, or warn of intended withdrawal was expressed as an essential prerequisite to withdrawal, in spite of the clear wording of the operative clause. No such advance notice was given by Owners of M/V *Pandora*. . . .

Hyman-Michaels went back to making the charter payments by wire transfer. On the morning of April 25, 1973, it telephoned Continental Bank and requested it to transfer $27,000 to the Banque de Paris account of the *Pandora*'s owner in payment for the charter hire period from April 27 to May 11, 1973. Since the charter provided for payment "in advance," this payment arguably was due by the close of business on April 26. The requested telex went out to Continental's London office on the afternoon of April 25, which was nighttime in England. Early the next morning a telex operator in Continental's London office dialed, as Continental's Chicago office had instructed him to do, Swiss Bank's general telex number, which rings in the bank's cable department. But that number was busy, and after trying unsuccessfully for an hour to engage it the Continental telex operator dialed another number, that of a machine in Swiss Bank's foreign exchange department which he had used in the past when the general number was engaged. We know this machine received the telexed message because it signaled the sending machine at both the beginning and end of the transmission that the telex was being received.

Yet Swiss Bank failed to comply with the payment order, and no transfer of funds was made to the account of the *Pandora*'s owner in the Banque de Paris.

No one knows exactly what went wrong. One possibility is that the receiving telex machine had simply run out of paper, in which event it would not print the message although it had received it. Another is that whoever took the message out of the machine after it was printed failed to deliver it to the banking department.

At 8:30 A.M. the next day, April 27, Hyman-Michaels in Chicago received a telex from the *Pandora*'s owner stating that the charter was canceled because payment for the April 27-May 11 charter period had not been made. Hyman-Michaels called over to Continental and told them to keep trying to effect payment through Swiss Bank even if the *Pandora*'s owner rejected it. . . .

Hyman-Michaels did not attempt to wire the money directly to the Banque de Paris as it had done on the occasion of its previous default. Days passed while the missing telex message was hunted unsuccessfully. Finally Swiss Bank suggested to Continental that it retransmit the telex message to the machine in the cable department and this was done on May 1. The next day Swiss Bank attempted to deposit the $27,000 in the account of the *Pandora*'s owner at the Banque de Paris but the payment was refused.

Again the arbitrators were convened and rendered a decision. In it they ruled that Hyman-Michaels had been "blameless" up until the morning of April 27, when it first learned that the Banque de Paris had not received payment on April 26, but that "being faced with this situation," Hyman-Michaels had

> failed to do everything in [its] power to remedy it. The action taken was immediate but did not prove to be adequate, in that [Continental] Bank and its correspondent required some 5/6 days to trace and effect the lost instruction to remit. [Hyman-Michaels] could have ordered an immediate duplicate payment — or even sent a Banker's check by hand or special messengers, so that the funds could have reached owner's Bank, not later than April 28th.

By failing to do any of these things Hyman-Michaels had "created the opening" that the *Pandora*'s owner was seeking in order to be able to cancel the charter. It had "acted imprudently." The arbitration panel concluded, reluctantly but unanimously, that this time the *Pandora*'s owner was entitled to cancel the agreement. The arbitration decision was confirmed by a federal district court in New York.

Hyman-Michaels then brought this diversity action against Swiss Bank, seeking to recover its expenses in the second arbitration proceeding plus the profits that it lost because of the cancellation of the charter. The contract by which Hyman-Michaels had agreed to ship scrap steel to

Brazil had been terminated by the buyer in March 1973 and Hyman-Michaels had promptly subchartered the *Pandora* at market rates, which by April 1973 were double the rates fixed in the charter. Its lost profits are based on the difference between the charter and subcharter rates. . . .

[The district judge held Swiss Bank liable in negligence for $2.1 million: $16,000 for arbitration expenses; the rest for lost profits on the subcharter. Under Swiss law, the bank had no liability except to its own customers. The court did not resolve the choice of law issue because it found no liability under Illinois law either.]

When a bank fails to make a requested transfer of funds, this can cause two kinds of loss. First, the funds themselves or interest on them may be lost, and of course the fee paid for the transfer, having bought nothing, becomes a loss item. These are "direct" (sometimes called "general") damages. Hyman-Michaels is not seeking any direct damages in this case and apparently sustained none. It did not lose any part of the $27,000; although its account with Continental Bank was debited by this amount prematurely, it was not an interest-bearing account so Hyman-Michaels lost no interest; and Hyman-Michaels paid no fee either to Continental or to Swiss Bank for the aborted transfer. A second type of loss, which either the payor or the payee may suffer, is a dislocation in one's business triggered by the failure to pay. Swiss Bank's failure to transfer funds to the Banque de Paris when requested to do so by Continental Bank set off a chain reaction which resulted in an arbitration proceeding that was costly to Hyman-Michaels and in the cancellation of a highly profitable contract. It is those costs and lost profits — "consequential" or, as they are sometimes called, "special" damages — that Hyman-Michaels seeks in this lawsuit, and recovered below. It is conceded that if Hyman-Michaels was entitled to consequential damages, the district court measured them correctly. The only issue is whether it was entitled to consequential damages. . . .

The rule of Hadley v. Baxendale — that consequential damages will not be awarded unless the defendant was put on notice of the special circumstances giving rise to them — has been applied in many Illinois cases, and *Hadley* cited approvingly. In Siegel v. Western Union, the plaintiff had delivered $200 to Western Union with instructions to transmit it to a friend of the plaintiff's. The money was to be bet (legally) on a horse, but this was not disclosed in the instructions. Western Union misdirected the money order and it did not reach the friend until several hours after the race had taken place. The horse that the plaintiff had intended to bet on won and would have paid $1650 on the plaintiff's $200 bet if the bet had been placed. He sued Western Union for his $1450 lost profit, but the court held that under the rule of Hadley v. Baxendale Western Union was not liable, because it "had no notice or knowledge of the purpose for which the money was being transmitted." 312 Ill. App. at 93, 37 N.E.2d at 871.

The present case is similar, though Swiss Bank knew more than Western Union knew in *Siegel*; it knew or should have known, from Continental Bank's previous telexes, that Hyman-Michaels was paying the Pandora Shipping Company for the hire of a motor vessel named *Pandora*. But it did not know when payment was due, what the terms of the charter were, or that they had turned out to be extremely favorable to Hyman-Michaels. And it did not know that Hyman-Michaels knew the *Pandora*'s owner would try to cancel the charter, and probably would succeed, if Hyman-Michaels was ever again late in making payment, or that despite this peril Hyman-Michaels would not try to pay until the last possible moment and in the event of a delay in transmission would not do everything in its power to minimize the consequences of the delay. Electronic funds transfers are not so unusual as to automatically place a bank on notice of extraordinary consequences if such a transfer goes awry. Swiss Bank did not have enough information to infer that if it lost a $27,000 payment order it would face a liability in excess of $2 million.

It is true that in both *Hadley* and *Siegel* there was a contract between the parties and here there was none. We cannot be certain that the Illinois courts would apply the principles of those cases outside of the contract area. . . . The best we can do is to assume that the Illinois courts would look to the policies underlying cases such as *Hadley* and *Siegel* and, to the extent they found them pertinent, would apply those cases here. We must therefore ask what difference it should make whether the parties are or are not bound to each other by a contract. On the one hand, it seems odd that the absence of a contract would enlarge rather than limit the extent of liability. After all, under Swiss law the absence of a contract would be devastating to Hyman-Michaels' claim. Privity is not a wholly artificial concept. It is one thing to imply a duty to one with whom one has a contract and another to imply it to the entire world.

On the other hand, contract liability is strict. A breach of contract does not connote wrongdoing; it may have been caused by circumstances beyond the promisor's control — a strike, a fire, the failure of a supplier to deliver an essential input.

And while such contract doctrines as impossibility, impracticability, and frustration relieve promisors from liability for some failures to perform that are beyond their control, many other such failures are actionable although they could not have been prevented by the exercise of due care. The district judge found that Swiss Bank had been negligent in losing Continental Bank's telex message and it can be argued that Swiss Bank should therefore be liable for a broader set of consequences than if it had only broken a contract. But *Siegel* implicitly rejects this distinction. Western Union had not merely broken its contract to deliver the plaintiff's money order; it had "negligently misdirected" the money order. . . . Yet it was not liable for the consequences.

Siegel, we conclude, is authority for holding that Swiss Bank is not liable for the consequences of negligently failing to transfer Hyman-Michaels' funds to Banque de Paris; reason for such a holding is found in the animating principle of Hadley v. Baxendale, which is that the costs of the untoward consequence of a course of dealings should be borne by that party who was able to avert the consequence at least cost and failed to do so. In *Hadley* the untoward consequence was the shutting down of the mill. The carrier could have avoided it by delivering the engine shaft on time. But the mill owners, as the court noted, could have avoided it simply by having a spare shaft.

Prudence required that they have a spare shaft anyway, since a replacement could not be obtained at once even if there was no undue delay in carting the broken shaft to and the replacement shaft from the manufacturer. The court refused to imply a duty on the part of the carrier to guarantee the mill owners against the consequences of their own lack of prudence, though of course if the parties had stipulated for such a guarantee the court would have enforced it. The notice requirement of Hadley v. Baxendale is designed to assure that such an improbable guarantee really is intended.

This case is much the same, though it arises in a tort rather than a contract setting. Hyman-Michaels showed a lack of prudence throughout. It was imprudent for it to mail in Chicago a letter that unless received the next day in Geneva would put Hyman-Michaels in breach of a contract that was very profitable to it and that the other party to the contract had every interest in canceling. It was imprudent thereafter for Hyman-Michaels, having narrowly avoided cancellation and having (in the words of its appeal brief in this court) been "put . . . on notice that the payment provision of the Charter would be strictly enforced thereafter," to wait till arguably the last day before payment was due to instruct its bank to transfer the necessary funds overseas. And it was imprudent in the last degree for Hyman-Michaels, when it received notice of cancellation on the last possible day payment was due, to fail to pull out all the stops to get payment to the Banque de Paris on that day, and instead to dither while Continental and Swiss Bank wasted five days looking for the lost telex message. Judging from the obvious reluctance with which the arbitration panel finally decided to allow the *Pandora*'s owner to cancel the charter, it might have made all the difference if Hyman-Michaels had gotten payment to the Banque de Paris by April 27 or even by Monday, April 30, rather than allowed things to slide until May 2.

This is not to condone the sloppy handling of incoming telex messages in Swiss Bank's foreign department. But Hyman-Michaels is a sophisticated business enterprise. It knew or should have known that even the Swiss are not infallible; that messages sometimes get lost or delayed in transit among three banks, two of them located 5000 miles apart, even when all the banks are using reasonable care; and that therefore it should take its own precautions against the consequences — best known to itself — of a mishap that might not be due to anyone's negligence.

We are not the first to remark the affinity between the rule of Hadley v. Baxendale and the doctrine, which is one of tort as well as contract law and is a settled part of the common law of Illinois, of avoidable consequences. If you are hurt in an automobile accident and unreasonably fail to seek medical treatment, the injurer, even if negligent, will not be held liable for the aggravation of the injury due to your own unreasonable behavior after the accident. If in addition you failed to fasten your seat belt, you may be barred from collecting the tort damages that would have been prevented if you had done so. Hyman-Michaels' behavior in steering close to the wind prior to April 27 was like not fastening one's seat belt; its failure on April 27 to wire a duplicate payment immediately after disaster struck was like refusing to seek medical attention after a serious accident. The seat-belt cases show that the doctrine of avoidable consequences applies whether the tort victim acts imprudently before or after the tort is committed. Hyman-Michaels did both.

The rule of Hadley v. Baxendale links up with tort concepts in another way. The rule is sometimes stated in the form that only foreseeable damages are recoverable in a breach of contract action. So expressed, it corresponds to the tort principle that limits liability to the foreseeable consequence of the defendant's carelessness. The amount of care that a person ought to take is a function of the probability and magnitude of the harm that may occur if he does not take care. If he does not know what that probability and magnitude are, he cannot determine how much care to take. That would be Swiss Bank's dilemma if it were liable for consequential damages from failing to carry out payment orders in timely fashion. To estimate the extent of its probable liability in order to know how many and how elaborate fail-safe features to install in its telex rooms or how much insurance to buy against the inevitable failures, Swiss Bank would have to collect reams of information about firms that are not even its regular customers. It had no banking relationship with Hyman-Michaels. It did not know or have reason to know how at once precious and fragile Hyman-Michaels' contract with the *Pandora*'s owner was. These were circumstances too remote from Swiss Bank's practical range of knowledge to have affected its decisions as to who should man the telex machines in the foreign department or whether it should have more intelligent machines or should install more machines in the cable department, any more than the falling of a platform scale because a conductor jostled a passenger who was carrying fireworks was a prospect that could have influenced the amount of care taken by the Long Island Railroad. See Palsgraf v. Long Island R.R., 248 N.Y. 339, 162 N.E. 99 (1928).

In short, Swiss Bank was not required in the absence of a contractual undertaking to take precautions or insure against a harm that it could not measure but that was known with precision to Hyman-Michaels, which could by the exercise of common prudence have averted it completely. As Chief Judge Cardozo (the author of *Palsgraf*) remarked in discussing the application of Hadley v. Baxendale to the liability of telegraph companies for errors in transmission, "The sender can protect himself by insurance in one form or another if the risk of nondelivery or error appears to be too great. . . . The company, if it takes out insurance for itself, can do no more than guess at the loss to be avoided." Kerr S.S. Co. v. Radio Corp. of America, 245 N.Y. 284, 291-92, 157 N.E. 140, 142 (1927).

But *Kerr* is a case from New York, not Illinois, and Hyman-Michaels argues that two early Illinois telegraph cases compel us to rule in its favor against Swiss Bank. Postal Tel. Cable Co. v. Lathrop, 131 Ill. 575, 23 N.E. 583 (1890), involved the garbled transmission of two telegrams from a coffee dealer — who as the telegraph company knew was engaged in buying and selling futures contracts — to his broker. The first telegram (there is no need to discuss the second) directed the broker to buy 1000 bags of August coffee for the dealer's account. This got changed in transmission to 2000 bags, and because the price fell the dealer sustained an extra loss for which he sued the telegraph company. The court held that the company had had notice enough to make it liable for consequential damages under the rule of Hadley v. Baxendale. It knew it was transmitting buy and sell orders in a fluctuating market and that a garbled transmission could result in large losses. There was no suggestion that the dealer should have taken his own precautions against such mistakes. In Providence-Washington Ins. Co. v. Western Union Tel. Co., 247 Ill. 84, 93 N.E. 134 (1910), a telegram from an insurance company canceling a policy was misdirected, and before it turned up there was a fire and the insurance company was liable on the policy. This was the precise risk created by delay, it was obvious on the face of the telegram, and the telegraph company was therefore liable for the insurance company's loss on the policy. Again there was no suggestion that the plaintiff had neglected any precaution. Both cases are distinguishable from the present case: the defendants had more information and the plaintiffs were not imprudent.

The legal principles that we have said are applicable to this case were not applied below. Although the district judge's opinion is not entirely clear, he apparently thought the rule of Hadley v. Baxendale inapplicable and the imprudence of Hyman-Michaels irrelevant.

He did state that the damages to Hyman-Michaels were foreseeable because "a major international bank" should know that a failure to act promptly on a telexed request to transfer funds could cause substantial damage; but *Siegel* — and for that matter *Lathrop* and *Providence-Washington* — make clear that that kind of general foreseeability, which is present in virtually every case, does not justify an award of consequential damages.

We could remand for new findings based on the proper legal standard, but it is unnecessary to do so. The undisputed facts, recited in this opinion, show as a matter of law that Hyman-Michaels is not entitled to recover consequential damages from Swiss Bank. . . .

MORE NOTES ON PROXIMATE CAUSE
AND AVOIDABLE CONSEQUENCES

1. Could *Swiss Bank* have been decided as an avoidable consequences case, without any talk about foreseeability, consequential damages, and Hadley v. Baxendale? Or is Hyman-Michaels protected by the rule in S. J. Groves & Sons Co. v. Warner Co., supra at 131? Isn't a strongly emphasized instruction to the bank to persist in efforts to make payment a reasonable alternative in the face of Swiss Bank's mistake? If the damages sought were not so unforeseeable and disproportionate to the size of Swiss Bank's transaction, would you hold Hyman-Michaels barred simply because of its own imprudence?

2. How does Hyman-Michaels' imprudence interact with the talk about foreseeability and Hadley v. Baxendale? It's not just that Hyman-Michaels could have avoided the harm, but that part of the reason it was best able to avoid the harm was that it was most able to foresee the risk. It knew that the banks might lose its cable, but the banks did not know that Hyman-Michaels might lose its charter. That rationale has some appeal on the facts, doesn't it? Is it a standard that can be generalized? What result if that standard is applied to Pruitt v. Allied Chemical Corp.? Who could best foresee and avoid the risk that kepone might destroy the Chesapeake Bay shellfish industry? Do you prefer that approach to the one Judge Mehrige actually used?

3. One formulation of the standard in *Swiss Bank* is slightly different. At one point, the court says that "the animating principle . . . is that the costs of the untoward consequence of a course of dealing should be borne by that party who was able to avoid the consequence at least cost and failed to do so." How would that formulation apply to *Pruitt*? Perhaps it does not apply at all, because there was no "course of dealing" between Allied and the shellfish industry. But it seems unlikely that Judge Posner intended that phrase to limit his standard. Might he say that except for the fishermen themselves, the shellfish industry could best avoid the harm by arranging for other sources of supply? Would you at least want evidence on what would happen to profits if more remote plaintiffs started importing all their shellfish from other states? Is the difficulty of litigating such questions itself a reason for some sort of proximate cause doctrine?

4. The court distinguishes between general and specific foreseeability. It was not enough that Swiss Bank is regularly involved in very large deals, that it knew that some percentage of all such deals are shaky and

can fall through because of small details, and that very substantial damages might result when that happens. Yet Hyman-Michaels was held responsible for knowing that messages sometimes get lost. Why is Hyman-Michaels held responsible for risks that are generally foreseeable, while Swiss Bank is responsible only for things that were specifically foreseeable?

5. It is easy to say that Hyman-Michaels should have been more careful. But are customers the cheapest loss avoiders in the general run of cases? Doesn't the court's reasoning imply that bank customers should not rely on bank transfers, because they are bound to know that banks will make mistakes and not be held responsible for the resulting damage? Does the court have any way of knowing whether it is cheaper overall for banks to install more safeguards or buy liability insurance than for customers to surround every important transaction with hedges against the bank's negligence?

6. The court says that plaintiffs who failed to use seat belts cannot collect for injuries seat belts would have prevented. That is the minority view. A survey found that only eight states had cases so holding, and in some of them the issue was considered unsettled. In twenty states, evidence of failure to use seat belts was not admissible to reduce damages, and eight others had held such evidence inadmissible on contributory negligence. Note, The Seat Belt Defense: A Comprehensive Guide for the Trial Lawyer and Suggested Approach for the Courts, 56 Notre Dame Law. 272, 274 n.10 (1980). Is there any plausible justification for the majority rule? That plaintiff was not required to anticipate defendant's negligence and the resulting crash? Compare the crashworthiness doctrine, under which auto manufacturers are liable if the design of their cars aggravates injuries in a crash. That it must be reasonable not to wear seat belts because so few people do? Compare the rule that custom is no defense if the whole industry is negligent. Is the exclusion of seat belt evidence explainable only as a reflection of pro-plaintiff bias in personal injury cases? As part of a gradual conversion from fault principles to social insurance principles?

7. Compare *Pruitt* and *Evra* with the cases arising from an electrical blackout in New York City. The New York Court of Appeals held that the electric utility was liable only for gross negligence. Food Pageant v. Consolidated Edison Co., 54 N.Y.2d 157, 429 N.E.2d 738 (1981). But once that standard was met, liability was extensive. Food Pageant was a grocery chain that recovered for the loss of its frozen inventory. In the next case, the court held that Con Ed was collaterally estopped on liability issues, and that plaintiffs could recover for all "physical injury to persons and property directly resulting from the service interruption," and for damages from looting and vandalism by rioters if a jury found that the rioting was foreseeable. Koch v. Consolidated Edison Co., 62 N.Y.2d 548, 560, 468 N.E.2d 1, 7 (1984).

Is that liability any less open ended than the liability rejected in *Pruitt* and *Evra*? Who could best avoid those losses? Who could best insure against them?

Koch also held that New York City could not recover for overtime paid to police, fire, and hospital personnel as a result of the blackout, or for lost tax revenues, or for wagers not placed with the city-owned Off-Track Betting Corporation. The court placed this result on grounds of public policy rather than proximate cause, citing a rule that public expenditures made in the performance of governmental functions are not recoverable.

SOUTHWESTERN BELL TELEPHONE CO. v. NORWOOD
212 Ark. 763, 207 S.W.2d 733 (1948)

McHANEY, Justice.

Appellee, a resident of Benton, Arkansas, sued appellant to recover damages caused by a fire originating in the bathroom of his home in said City which quickly spread to other rooms. It is not alleged that appellant caused the fire, but that the operator was negligent in not answering promptly a call to notify the Fire Department made first by his wife and then by himself, which caused a delay of four or five minutes in reaching the Fire Department. He also alleged negligence of appellant in permitting its telephone system to become so obsolete, crowded and inadequate that it did not render prompt and efficient service. . . .

Trial to a jury resulted in a verdict and judgment against appellant for $1,500. . . .

The proof shows that appellee had a contract with appellant for telephone service in his residence at the rate of $1.75 per month. The telephone system in Benton is known as the magneto type, one where the subscriber has to crank his phone in order to contact central, and the hook that holds the receiver must be held down when ringing central.

Assuming that the evidence sufficiently established the allegations of the complaint, still we are of the opinion that there can be no recovery in this case and that the court should have directed a verdict for appellant at its request.

We have held in two cases that: "A telephone company is not liable for special damages for failure to furnish connection to a patron if it had no notice of the circumstances out of which the damages might arise." Southern Telephone Co. v. King, 103 Ark. 160, 146 S.W. 489; Southwestern Bell Telephone Co. v. Carter, 181 Ark. 209, 25 S.W.2d 448. The reason for the rule, which was first announced in the old English case of Hadley v. Baxendale, 9 Exch. 341, was well stated by Judge Riddick in Hooks Smelting Co. v. Planters Compress Co., 72 Ark. 275, 79 S.W. 1052, quoted in the *Carter* case, supra, as follows:

"Now, where the damages arise from special circumstances, and are so large as to be out of proportion to the consideration agreed to be paid for the services to be rendered under the contract, it raises a doubt at once as to whether the party would have assented to such a liability, had it been called to his attention at the making of the contract, unless the consideration to be paid was also raised so as to correspond in some respect to the liability assumed. To make him liable for the special damages in such a case, there must not only be knowledge of the special circumstances, but such knowledge 'must be brought home to the party sought to be charged under such circumstances that he must know that the person he contracts with reasonably believes that he accepts the contract with the special condition attached to it.' In other words [where there is no express contract to pay such special damages], the facts and circumstances in proof must be such as to make it reasonable for the judge or jury trying the case to believe that the party at the time of contract tacitly consented to be bound to more than ordinary damages in case of default on his part."

It is not claimed by appellee that he ever notified appellant that if it did not answer his calls for the Fire Department promptly, he would hold it liable for the resultant loss, and it is not reasonable to presume that appellant would have contracted to furnish him service at the small rate charged, if it should assume liability for damages caused by a fire for which it was in no wise responsible in its inception. . . .

The judgment is reversed and the cause is dismissed.

ROBINS, J., dissenting. . . .

We do not have here a breach of an undertaking entered into between parties occupying equal contractual positions. Public authority has granted to this company what amounts to a monopoly in telephone service in the area wherein it operates. Anyone therein who desires telephone facilities must obtain same from this company on its terms or do without service. Implicit in the situation thus created is the duty of the company to exercise at least reasonable care and diligence in furnishing proper service and also an obligation on its part to answer in damages to one of its subscribers who suffers loss or injury flowing proximately from breach of the company's duty.

Nor can it be said that the telephone company has no notice of damages such as the jury below found appellee incurred. The availability of the telephone for use in summoning aid in any sudden emergency — to call a physician in case of dangerous illness or injury, to call peace officers for protection against felonious intruders, and, as in the case at bar, to summon the fire department to put out a fire — is one of the great inducements for subscribing for telephone service. The company well knows that its telephones are commonly used for such purposes, and the result of failure of the subscriber, on account of lack of proper telephone service, to obtain the necessary aid, is equally well known.

McFADDIN, Justice (concurring). . . .

The rule announced in Hadley v. Baxendale has no application to this present case, because — by all the pleadings and evidence — this is an action in tort for negligence. Hadley v. Baxendale enunciated a rule that governs in actions for breach of contract. . . .

In tort actions, the negligent person is liable for all damages that flow as the direct and proximate result of the negligence, but is not liable for remote or speculative damages. Tested by that rule, the plaintiff cannot recover in the case at bar. The negligence of the telephone company was the failure to answer the signal from the plaintiff's telephone; but it requires considerable speculation to say that the plaintiff's damages would have been lessened if the telephone signal had been answered promptly. The plaintiff's case is built on a series of conjectures, to wit:

(1) *If* the telephone company had answered the signal promptly; and
(2) *If* the fire department had answered its phone promptly; and
(3) *If* the fire truck had reached the fire promptly; and
(4) *If* the water power had been satisfactory; and
(5) *If* the firemen had functioned efficiently; then, on these five "ifs," the plaintiff's damages would have been lessened from a fire already in progress when the plaintiff first attempted to call the telephone office. These five "ifs" demonstrate that the plaintiff's damages were speculative and remote, rather than direct and proximate; and it is entirely for this reason that I concur with the result reached by the majority. . . .

STILL MORE NOTES ON PROXIMATE CAUSE

1. Should the solution to proximate cause problems depend at all on whether the suit is in contract or tort? As Judge Posner notes, there is strict liability for breach of contract. But some torts are also strict liability, and it is often possible to find negligence or misrepresentation in a breach of contract. Are more generous recoveries in tort a reward for clever pleading, or are there real differences between negligent and non-negligent breaches of contract?

One rationale for insisting on very specific foreseeability in contract is that contract liability is based on agreement, and defendants cannot be assumed to have accepted a liability they did not know about. In *Southwestern Bell*, the court points to a gross disproportion between the liability and the contract price as evidence that defendant must not have agreed to such liability. This tacit agreement standard is not accepted by all courts in all contexts. It is rejected by the Uniform Commercial Code; sellers of goods are liable for consequential damages they "had reason to know" of "at the time of contracting." UCC §2-715(2). Doesn't the choice between the two standards determine the result in *Southwestern Bell*?

In *Evra*, plaintiff paid nothing for the bank's services. Swiss Bank might have collected a few francs if the transfer had been completed, or it may have handled such transfers in exchange for Continental's agreement to complete transfers initiated by Swiss Bank, with each bank charging its own customers. Would Swiss Bank knowingly accept a $2 million liability for mishandling a ten franc transaction? Plainly it would, if the law said it had to. It would buy insurance, raise the charge to twelve francs, and commerce would go on largely unaffected. Equally plainly, it would not if given the choice. Adhesion contracts routinely disclaim any liability for consequential damages. Should the court look to that practice to decide how the parties to this transaction probably would have allocated the risk if they had bargained over it?

2. Does Justice McFadden's concurrence give real content to "remote"? Are damages remote because there are several links in the chain of causation? Or are they remote only when critical links in that chain are uncertain, and the uncertainties are cumulative, so that it is impossible to say by a preponderance of the evidence that the wrong caused the harm?

3. The Certainty Requirement

BIGELOW v. RKO RADIO PICTURES
327 U.S. 251 (1946)

Mr. Chief Justice Stone delivered the opinion of the Court.

Petitioners brought this suit in the District Court for Northern Illinois under §§1, 2 and 7 of the Sherman Act and §§4 and 16 of the Clayton Act, for an injunction and to recover treble damages. Petitioners are owners of the Jackson Park motion picture theatre in Chicago. . . .

The gist of the complaint is that, by reason of the conspiracy, petitioners were prevented from securing pictures for exhibition in their theatre until after the preferred exhibitors had been able to show them in the earlier and more desirable runs, and that petitioners have thus been discriminated against in the distribution of feature films in favor of competing theatres owned or controlled by some of the respondents. Petitioners charged that in consequence they had been subjected to loss of earnings in excess of $120,000 during the five year period from July 27, 1937 to July 27, 1942. The matter of the injunction was reserved and the case went to trial solely on the question of damages. The jury returned a verdict for $120,000 in petitioners' favor. The trial court gave judgment for treble that amount, as prescribed by §4 of the Clayton Act. The

Circuit Court of Appeals for the Seventh Circuit reversed on the sole ground that the evidence of damage was not sufficient for submission to the jury, and directed the entry of a judgment for respondents *non obstante veredicto*. We granted certiorari because of the importance of the problem presented.

Respondents do not now assail the jury's verdict, so far as it found an unlawful conspiracy to maintain a discriminatory system of distribution. The sole question for decision here is whether the evidence of damage is sufficient to support the verdict. . . .

Rental contracts between distributors and exhibitors undertake to furnish films to the exhibitors for stipulated rentals. . . . In Chicago, these contracts uniformly provide that the larger theatres in the Chicago Loop, all owned, leased, or operated by one or more of the respondents, shall have the right to the "first run" of the motion pictures distributed by the respondents, for one week or such longer period as they may desire to exhibit them. Following the "first run," the motion picture may not be shown in any Chicago theatre outside the Loop for three weeks, a period known as "clearance." In the fourth week following the end of the Loop run, the film is released for exhibition in theatres outside the Loop for successive runs in various theatres, for periods known as the "A," "B" and "C" "pre-release weeks," followed by weeks of "general release." . . .

[P]etitioners' theatre was unable to obtain feature films until the first week of "general release," or ten weeks after the end of the Loop run. By that time most of respondent exhibitors' theatres, with several of which petitioners' theatre competes, and which enjoyed the prior "A," "B" or "C" pre-release runs, had finished their showings. Regardless of the price offered for rental of film, the respondent exhibitors, in execution of the conspiracy, refused to release films to petitioners' theatre except for the first week of "general release." . . .

Two classes of evidence were introduced by petitioners to establish their damage. One was a comparison of earnings during the five year period of petitioners' Jackson Park Theatre with the earnings of its competitor, the Maryland Theatre, the two being comparable in size, the Jackson Park being superior in location, equipment, and attractiveness to patrons. Under the discriminatory release system, the Maryland had been allowed to exhibit pictures in the C pre-release run, one week ahead of petitioners' first week of general release. The evidence showed that during the five year period, the Maryland's net receipts after deducting film rentals paid to distributors exceeded petitioners' like receipts by $115,982.34.

The second was a comparison of petitioners' receipts from the operation of the Jackson Park Theatre less cost of film for the five year period following July 1937, with the corresponding receipts for the four years immediately preceding, after making an allowance for the elimination of "Bank Night" receipts. The comparison shows a falling off of petitioners' receipts during the five year period aggregating $125,659.00, which was more than $5,000 in excess of the $120,000 damage demanded by petitioners' complaint. The significance of the comparison lies in the fact that during most of the four year period, and despite the operation of the release system as described, petitioners' theatre had been able to procure some films which had not already been shown in respondents' theatres, whereas petitioners were not able to procure such films during the five year period which followed, although there is evidence that they made diligent efforts to do so. The change is attributable to the introduction of the practice of "double features" (the showing of two films at a single performance) in theatres in the Chicago district. The evidence tended to show that when single features were being shown, exhibitors who had playing positions ahead of petitioners' . . . did not exhibit all of the films distributed, so that, despite their inferior playing position, petitioners were able to exhibit pictures which had not been shown elsewhere. With the advent of double featuring, theatres with playing positions ahead of petitioners' used nearly all of the films distributed, and the pictures which petitioners were able to exhibit in the first week of general release, by reason of the distribution system, had had prior showing in nearly every case. . . .

The circuit court of appeals concluded that the jury accepted the comparison of plaintiffs' earnings before and after the adoption of double billing as establishing the measure of petitioners' damage. But it held that this proof did not furnish a proper measure of damage for the reason that, while petitioners' earnings were known and proved for both the four and five year periods in question, it could not be proved what their earnings would have been during the five year period in the absence of the illegal distribution of films. It thought that the mere fact that earnings of the Jackson Park Theatre were greater before the adoption of double billing did not serve to show what petitioners' earnings would have been afterwards, in the absence of the release system.

Similarly, the court of appeals rejected the comparison between petitioners' receipts and those of the Maryland Theatre during the five years in question, since, as it thought, the comparison would not tend to prove what the earnings of either theatre would have been during the critical period under any system other than that which was the product of the unlawful conspiracy.

Upon the record in this case it is indisputable that the jury could have found that during the period in question a first or prior run theatre possessed competitive advantages over later run theatres, because of its greater capacity to attract patronage to pictures which had not been shown elsewhere, and its ability to charge higher admission prices than subsequent run theatres, and that, other things being equal, the establishment of the discriminatory release system was damaging to the petitioners, who were relegated by it to a playing position inferior to that of their competitors.

Each of the two classes of evidence introduced by petitioners tended to show damage. They were not mutually exclusive, as the courts below seem to have thought, since each, independently of the other, tended to show that petitioners' inability to obtain films for exhibition before they had been shown elsewhere adversely affected their receipts, in the one case by showing that those receipts decreased when petitioners could no longer purchase such films following the introduction of double features, and in the other, that petitioners' receipts from its theatre were less by substantially the same amount than receipts of its competitor, the prior-run Maryland Theatre, operated under conditions in other respects less favorable than those affecting petitioners.

Respondents' argument is, that notwithstanding the force of this evidence, it is impossible to establish any measure of damage, because the unlawful system which respondents have created has precluded petitioners from showing that other conditions affecting profits would have continued without change unfavorable to them during the critical period if that system had not been established, and petitioners had conducted their business in a free competitive market. . . .

[W]hen petitioners acquired their theatre, it was possible for them . . . to secure films which had not had prior showing and to exhibit them in competition with theatres having preferred playing positions. Whatever restraints respondents' distribution system may then have imposed, and whether the later adopted practice of showing double features was or was not itself a product of an unlawful conspiracy, petitioners were entitled, as of right, to continue to purchase and show films which had not had prior showing free of the restraints of the unlawful distribution system. The fair value of petitioners' right thus to continue their business depended on its capacity to make profits. And a fair measure of the damage to that right by respondents' unlawful distributing system was the loss of petitioners' admission receipts resulting from the application of that system to petitioners.

Respondents only answer is that, without the conspiracy, the conditions of purchase of films might not have been the same after as they were before July, 1937; that in any case it is not possible to say what those conditions would have been if the restraints had not been imposed, and that those conditions cannot be ascertained, because respondents have not removed the restraint. Hence, it is said, petitioners' evidence does not establish the fact of damage, and that further, the standard of comparison which the evidence sets up is too speculative and uncertain to afford an accurate measure of the amount of the damage.

The case in these respects is comparable to Eastman Kodak Co. v. Southern Photo Co., 273 U.S. 359, and Story Parchment Co. v. Paterson Co., 282 U.S. 555, in which precisely the same arguments now addressed to us were rejected. . . .

In each case we held that the evidence sustained verdicts for the plaintiffs, and that in the absence of more precise proof, the jury could conclude as a matter of just and reasonable inference from the proof of defendants' wrongful acts and their tendency to injure plaintiffs' business, and from the evidence of the decline in prices, profits and values, not shown to be attributable to other causes, that defendants' wrongful acts had caused damage to the plaintiffs. In this we but followed a well-settled principle. The tortious acts had in each case precluded ascertainment of the amount of damages more precisely, by comparison of profits, prices and values as affected by the conspiracy, with what they would have been in its absence under freely competitive conditions. Nevertheless, we held that the jury could return a verdict for the plaintiffs, even though damages could not be measured with the exactness which would otherwise have been possible.

In such a case, even where the defendant by his own wrong has prevented a more precise computation, the jury may not render a verdict based on speculation or guesswork. But the jury may make a just and reasonable estimate of the damage based on relevant data, and render its verdict accordingly. In such circumstances "juries are allowed to act upon probable and inferential, as well as direct and positive proof." Story Parchment Co. v. Paterson Co., supra, 561-4. Any other rule would enable the wrongdoer to profit by his wrongdoing at the expense of his victim. It would be an inducement to make wrongdoing so effective and complete in every case as to preclude any recovery, by rendering the measure of damages uncertain. Failure to apply it would mean that the more grievous the wrong done, the less likelihood there would be of a recovery.

The most elementary conceptions of justice and public policy require that the wrongdoer shall bear the risk of the uncertainty which his own wrong has created.

That principle is an ancient one, and is not restricted to proof of damage in antitrust suits, although their character is such as frequently to call for its application. . . . [I]n cases where a wrongdoer has incorporated the subject of a plaintiff's patent or trade-mark in a single product to which the defendant has contributed other elements of value or utility, and has derived profits from the sale of the product, this Court has sustained recovery of the full amount of defendant's profits where his own wrongful action has made it impossible for the plaintiff to show in what proportions he and the defendant have contributed to the profits.

"The constant tendency of the courts is to find some way in which damages can be awarded where a wrong has been done. Difficulty of ascertainment is no longer confused with right of recovery" for a proven invasion of the plaintiff's rights. Story Parchment Co. v. Paterson Co., supra, 565.

The evidence here was ample to support a just and reasonable inference that petitioners were damaged by respondents' action, whose unlawfulness the jury has found, and respondents do not challenge. The comparison of petitioners' receipts before and after respondents' unlawful action impinged on petitioners' business afforded a sufficient basis for the jury's computation of the damage, where the respondents' wrongful action had prevented petitioners from making any more precise proof of the amount of the damage. . . .

The judgment of the district court below will be affirmed and the judgment of the court of appeals is reversed.

Mr. Justice Jackson took no part in the consideration or decision of this case.

Mr. Justice Frankfurter, dissenting. . . .

[O]ur real question is whether the respondents' violation of the Sherman Law illegally injured the petitioners. This necessarily involves substantial proof that the petitioners' business would have been more profitable if the distribution of movie films in Chicago had been a free-for-all and if no factor of the scheme that constituted an illegal conspiracy had been in operation, than it was under the conditions that actually prevailed. . . . The record appears devoid of proof that, if competitive conditions had prevailed, distributors would not have made rental contracts with their respective exhibiting affiliates to the serious disadvantage of independents like the petitioners. They might individually have done so and not have offended the Sherman Law.

I agree that Eastman Kodak Co. v. Southern Photo Co., and Story Parchment Co. v. Paterson Co., should guide the disposition of this case. But I do not find that the decisive distinction made in those cases has been observed in deciding this case. The distinction is between proving that some damages were "the certain result of the wrong" and uncertainty as to the dollars and cents value of such injuring wrong. Such difficulty in ascertaining the exact amount of damage is a risk properly cast upon the wrong-doing defendant. But proof of the legal injury, which is the basis of his suit, is plaintiff's burden. He does not establish it merely by proving that there was a wrong to the public nor by showing that if he had been injured ascertainment of the exact amount of damages would have had an inevitable speculative element to be left for a jury's conscientious guess. This basic distinction was thus formulated in Story Parchment Co. v. Paterson Co.:

> The rule which precludes the recovery of uncertain damages applies to such as are not the certain result of the wrong, not to those damages which are definitely attributable to the wrong and only uncertain in respect of their amount.

282 U.S. at 562. In the *Eastman* and *Story* cases the plaintiffs established what their profit was when competitive conditions prevailed and that the subsequent loss properly became exclusively attributable to restraint of

such conditions. Such a comparison is not revealed by this record. It was wholly speculative, as the Circuit Court of Appeals properly held in applying the rule in the *Story Parchment Co.* case, whether the intake of petitioners would have been more profitable if the distribution of films in Chicago had been left wholly to the haggling of a free market. . . .

NOTES ON THE CERTAINTY REQUIREMENT

1.   The defense in *Bigelow*, as articulated by Justice Frankfurter, is that defendants could have found a legal way to inflict the same harm on plaintiff. Is that defense repulsive to your sense of justice? Or does it indicate that defendants are being held liable on a technicality? How does it fit in with the basic principle of restoring plaintiff to the position he would have occupied but for the wrong? Isn't Frankfurter saying that but for the wrong, defendants would have had the ability and every incentive to put plaintiff in exactly the position in which it now finds itself? If that is to be a defense, shouldn't it at least be an affirmative defense, with the burden of persuasion on defendants? Why would Frankfurter put that burden on plaintiff?

The majority's holding made it unnecessary to explore the facts of the defense that persuaded Frankfurter. But there is good reason to believe that defendants could not have inflicted the same harm legally. Paramount Pictures owned the Maryland Theatre, and undoubtedly the Maryland would get all Paramount movies before plaintiff. But in the absence of a conspiracy, the plaintiff would have been able to compete with the Maryland for movies from all other distributors. Indeed, it may be that cases in which all the same harms could have been inflicted legally are quite rare.

2.   The majority treats Frankfurter's defense as going to the amount of damages rather than to whether there was any damage at all. That brings the case within the rule that wrongdoers must bear the risk of uncertainty in the amount of damages. There are still cases that say the amount of special damages must be proved with certainty, but most of these cases are old and the rule seems to be dying. Recall the ways in which damages are assessed for pain and suffering, wrongful death, and constitutional and dignitary torts. There has never been a certainty requirement in those cases. The traditional explanation is that those are general damages, and that only special damages have to be proved with certainty. Does that make any sense at all? Isn't it a better explanation, and a better rule, to say that plaintiff must prove his damages with as much certainty as is reasonably possible under the circumstances, and no more? Variations of that formulation appear in many of the modern cases, and some of the older ones.

3.   Might there still be cases in which a claimed pecuniary loss is so unmeasurable that no damages can be allowed under any standard? Consider Shannon v. Shaffer Oil and Refining Co., 51 F.2d 878 (10th Cir. 1931). Plaintiff owned a royalty interest in a gas well, and presented evidence that the producer had negligently allowed gas to escape into the air. He argued that the measure of what had been wasted was the pumping capacity of the wells less the amount actually produced. But there was also evidence that some of the waste was unavoidable, that some of the gas was used to run the pump, and that steps taken to reduce waste caused the pump to run at less than capacity. The court denied any recovery, saying that "When these factors are considered, there is no substantial basis left from which a jury could make a rational estimate of the amount of avoidable waste." Id. at 882. It seems likely that an expert could have provided a reasonable estimate. If so, plaintiff should have produced such an expert instead of asking the court to guess. But suppose the expert could do no more than establish a range, and the range was very wide. For example, suppose the testimony is that the avoidable portion of the waste did not exceed $5,000, may have been zero, and was probably somewhere in the middle of that range. Should plaintiff be denied recovery because he did not prove with certainty that there was at least some damage? Is that unfair? Or is failure to prove one's case on damages just like failure to prove one's case on liability?

Suppose the expert said the damages were somewhere between $20 and $5,000, but that there was no way to estimate probabilities within that range. What should plaintiff recover? Nothing, because there is no basis for a reasonable estimate of damages? Twenty dollars, because he lost at least that much? Twenty-five hundred dollars, because the midpoint of the range is the most reasonable estimate? Or $5,000, because the risk of uncertainty should fall on the wrongdoer? How big a difference should it make that the expert is able to say "at least $20" rather than "maybe nothing at all"?

4.   Compare Shannon with Brink's Inc. v. City of New York, 717 F.2d 700 (2d Cir. 1983). New York hired Brink's to pick up change from parking meters. Brink's employees were caught stealing coins. When the City replaced Brink's with another company, collections went up a million dollars in the first ten months. Brink's argued that the comparison was useless, because several other things had changed about the same time: gas rationing ended, a transit strike began, some meters were relocated, the number of snow emergency days varied, and there was evidence of an upward trend in collections anyway. Because all these other factors were unmeasurable, Brink's argued that the comparison was more prejudicial than probative: It conveyed a delusion of precision when in fact the compensatory damages were speculative and unknowable. New York's expert witness claimed to have controlled for all the other factors to within a standard error of 10 percent; he apparently used some sort of

sampling technique. The court upheld the evidence and the jury's million dollar verdict.

5. One special case of uncertain damages, for which special rules have developed, is the problem of conversion, destruction, or damage of assets of fluctuating value, discussed at 63-64 supra.

6. Perhaps the most common source of litigation over certainty is claims of lost profits. The most common types of evidence are those offered in *Bigelow*: comparisons of plaintiff's profits before and after the wrong, and comparison of plaintiff's profits to similar businesses unaffected by the wrong. With the development of econometrics and economic forecasting, projections by experts have also become more important. But most courts sensibly put more weight on comparisons of real experience than on expert projections.

Many courts have had an absolute rule that a new business cannot recover lost profits. The theory has been that such damages are inherently speculative and uncertain because most new businesses fail and there is no way to know that any particular new business would have made a profit but for the wrong done to it. Some courts still adhere to that rule, but the trend is to abandon any per se rule and treat the risks of a new business as simply one more element of proof. There is a good survey in Comment, Remedies — Lost Profits as Contract Damages for an Unestablished Business: The New Business Rule Becomes Outdated, 56 N.C.L. Rev. 693 (1978).

7. We will examine uncertainty problems from a different perspective in the section on practicality in chapter 9. In some of the cases in that section, the issue is whether harm is so hard to measure that a traditional remedy, or even any remedy at all, is impractical.

4. Substantive Policy Goals

BRUNSWICK CORP. v. PUEBLO BOWL-O-MAT
429 U.S. 577 (1977)

MR. JUSTICE MARSHALL delivered the opinion of the Court.

This case raises important questions concerning the interrelationship of the antimerger and private damages action provisions of the Clayton Antitrust Act.

I

Petitioner is one of the two largest manufacturers of bowling equipment in the United States. Respondents are three of the 10 bowling centers owned by Treadway Companies, Inc. Since 1965, petitioner has acquired and operated a large number of bowling centers, including six in the markets in which respondents operate. Respondents instituted this action contending that these acquisitions violated various provisions of the antitrust laws.

In the late 1950's, the bowling industry expanded rapidly, and petitioner's sales of lanes, automatic pinsetters, and ancillary equipment rose accordingly. Since this equipment requires a major capital expenditure — $12,600 for each lane and pinsetter — most of petitioner's sales were for secured credit.

In the early 1960's, the bowling industry went into a sharp decline. . . . [P]etitioner experienced great difficulty in collecting money owed it; by the end of 1964 over $100,000,000, or more than 25%, of petitioner's accounts were more than 90 days delinquent. Repossessions rose dramatically, but attempts to sell or lease the repossessed equipment met with only limited success.

To meet this difficulty, petitioner began acquiring and operating defaulting bowling centers when their equipment could not be resold and a positive cash flow could be expected from operating the centers. During the seven years preceding the trial in this case, petitioner acquired 222 centers, 54 of which it either disposed of or closed. These acquisitions made petitioner by far the largest operator of bowling centers, with over five times as many centers as its next largest competitor. Petitioner's net worth in 1965 was more than eight times greater, and its gross revenue more than seven times greater, than the total for the 11 next largest bowling chains. Nevertheless, petitioner controlled only 2% of the bowling centers in the United States.

At issue here are acquisitions by petitioner in the three markets in which respondents are located: Pueblo, Colo., Poughkeepsie, N.Y., and Paramus, N.J. . . .

Respondents initiated this action in June 1966, alleging, inter alia, that these acquisitions might substantially lessen competition or tend to create a monopoly in violation of §7 of the Clayton Act, 15 U.S.C. §18. Respondents sought damages, pursuant to §4 of the Act, 15 U.S.C. §15, for three times "the reasonably expectable profits to be made [by respondents] from the operation of their bowling centers." Respondents also sought a divestiture order, an injunction against future acquisitions, and such "other further and different relief" as might be appropriate under §16 of the Act, 15 U.S.C. §26. . . .

To establish a §7 violation, respondents sought to prove that because of its size, petitioner had the capacity to lessen competition in the markets it had entered by driving smaller competitors out of business. To establish damages, respondents attempted to show that had petitioner allowed the defaulting centers to close, respondents' profits would have increased. . . .

The jury returned a verdict in favor of respondents in the amount of $2,358,030, which represented the minimum estimate by respondents of the additional income they would have realized had the acquired centers been closed. As required by law, the District Court trebled the damages. It also awarded respondents costs and attorneys' fees totaling $446,977.32, and, sitting as a court of equity, it ordered petitioner to divest itself of the centers involved here. Petitioner appealed.

The Court of Appeals, while endorsing the legal theories upon which respondents' claim was based, reversed the judgment and remanded the case for further proceedings. . . . The court . . . decided that the jury had not been properly charged and that therefore a new trial was required. It also decided that since "an essential predicate" for the District Court's grant of equitable relief was the jury verdict on the §7 claim, the equitable decree should be vacated as well. And it concluded that in any event equitable relief "should be restricted to preventing those practices by which a deep pocket market entrant harms competition. . . . [D]ivestiture was simply inappropriate."

Both sides petitioned this Court for writs of certiorari. . . . We granted Brunswick's petition.

II

The issue for decision is a narrow one. Petitioner does not presently contest the Court of Appeals' conclusion that a properly instructed jury could have found the acquisitions unlawful. Nor does petitioner challenge the Court of Appeals' determination that the evidence would support a finding that had petitioner not acquired these centers, they would have gone out of business and respondents' income would have increased. Petitioner questions only whether antitrust damages are available where the sole injury alleged is that competitors were continued in business, thereby denying respondents an anticipated increase in market shares.

To answer that question it is necessary to examine the antimerger and treble-damages provisions of the Clayton Act. Section 7 of the Act proscribes mergers whose effect "*may be* substantially to lessen competition, or *to tend to* create a monopoly." (Emphasis added.) It is, as we have observed many times, a prophylactic measure, intended "primarily to arrest apprehended consequences of intercorporate relationships before those relationships could work their evil. . . ." United States v. E. I. du Pont de Nemours & Co., 353 U.S. 586, 597 (1957).

Section 4, in contrast, is in essence a remedial provision. It provides treble damages to "[a]ny person who shall be injured in his business or property by reason of anything forbidden in the antitrust laws. . . ." Of course, treble damages also play an important role in penalizing wrongdoers and deterring wrongdoing, as we also have frequently observed. It nevertheless is true that the treble-damages provision, which makes awards available only to injured parties, and measures the awards by a multiple of the injury actually proved, is designed primarily as a remedy.[10]

Intermeshing a statutory prohibition against acts that have a potential to cause certain harms with a damages action intended to remedy those harms is not without difficulty. Plainly, to recover damages respondents must prove more than that petitioner violated §7, since such proof establishes only that injury may result. Respondents contend that the only additional element they need demonstrate is that they are in a worse position than they would have been had petitioner not committed those acts. The Court of Appeals agreed, holding compensable any loss "causally linked" to "the mere presence of the violator in the market." Because this holding divorces antitrust recovery from the purposes of the antitrust laws without a clear statutory command to do so, we cannot agree with it.

Every merger of two existing entities into one, whether lawful or unlawful, has the potential for producing economic readjustments that adversely affect some persons. But Congress has not condemned mergers on that account; it has condemned them only when they may produce anticompetitive effects. Yet under the Court of Appeals' holding, once a merger is found to violate §7, all dislocations caused by the merger are actionable, regardless of whether those dislocations have anything to do with the reason the merger was condemned. This holding would make §4 recovery entirely fortuitous, and would authorize damages for losses which are of no concern to the antitrust laws.

Both of these consequences are well illustrated by the facts of this case. If the acquisitions here were unlawful, it is because they brought a "deep pocket" parent into a market of "pygmies." Yet respondents' injury — the loss of income that would have accrued had the acquired centers gone bankrupt — bears no relationship to the size of either the acquiring company or its competitors. Respondents would have suffered the identical "loss" — but no compensable injury — had the acquired centers instead obtained refinancing or been purchased by "shallow pocket" parents as the Court of Appeals itself acknowledged, 523 F.2d, at 279.[12] Thus, respondents' injury was not of "the type that the statute was intended to forestall," Wyandotte Co. v. United States, 389 U.S. 191, 202 (1967).

But the antitrust laws are not merely indifferent to the injury claimed here. At base, respondents complain that by acquiring the failing centers

10. The discussions of this section on the floor of the Senate indicate that it was conceived of primarily as a remedy for "[t]he people of the United States as individuals," especially consumers. 21 Cong. Rec. 1767-1768 (1890) (remarks of Sen. George). Treble damages were provided in part for punitive purposes, but also to make the remedy meaningful by counterbalancing "the difficulty of maintaining a private suit against a combination such as is described" in the Act. Id., at 2456 (Sen. Sherman).

12. Conversely, had petitioner acquired thriving centers — acquisitions at least as violative of §7 as the instant acquisitions — respondents would not have lost any income that they otherwise would have received.

petitioner preserved competition, thereby depriving respondents of the benefits of increased concentration. The damages respondents obtained are designed to provide them with the profits they would have realized had competition been reduced. The antitrust laws, however, were enacted for "the protection of *competition* not *competitors*," Brown Shoe Co. v. United States, 370 U.S., at 320. It is inimical to the purposes of these laws to award damages for the type of injury claimed here.

Of course, Congress is free, if it desires, to mandate damages awards for all dislocations caused by unlawful mergers despite the peculiar consequences of so doing. But because of these consequences, "we should insist upon a clear expression of a congressional purpose," Hawaii v. Standard Oil Co., 405 U.S., at 264, before attributing such an intent to Congress. We can find no such expression in either the language or the legislative history of §4. To the contrary, it is far from clear that the loss of windfall profits that would have accrued had the acquired centers failed even constitutes "injury" within the meaning of §4. And it is quite clear that if respondents were injured, it was not "by reason of anything forbidden in the antitrust laws": while respondents' loss occurred "by reason of" the unlawful acquisitions, it did not occur "by reason of" that which made the acquisitions unlawful.

We therefore hold that [for] the plaintiffs to recover treble damages on account of §7 violations, they must prove more than injury causally linked to an illegal presence in the market. Plaintiffs must prove *antitrust* injury, which is to say injury of the type the antitrust laws were intended to prevent and that flows from that which makes defendants' acts unlawful. The injury should reflect the anticompetitive effect either of the violation or of anticompetitive acts made possible by the violation. It should, in short, be "the type of loss that the claimed violations . . . would be likely to cause." Zenith Radio Corp. v. Hazeltine Research, 395 U.S., at 125.[14]

III

We come, then, to the question of appropriate disposition of this case. At the very least, petitioner is entitled to a new trial, not only because of the instructional errors noted by the Court of Appeals that are not at issue here, but also because the District Court's instruction as to the basis for damages was inconsistent with our holding as outlined above. Our review of the record, however, persuades us that a new trial on the damages

14. This does not necessarily mean, as the Court of Appeals feared, that §4 plaintiffs must prove an actual lessening of competition in order to recover. The short term effect of certain anticompetitive behavior — predatory below-cost pricing, for example — may be to stimulate price competition. But competitors may be able to prove antitrust injury before they actually are driven from the market and competition is thereby lessened. Of course, the case for relief will be strongest where competition has been diminished.

claim is unwarranted. Respondents based their case solely on their novel damages theory which we have rejected. While they produced some conclusory testimony suggesting that in operating the acquired centers petitioner had abused its deep pocket by engaging in anticompetitive conduct, they made no attempt to prove that they had lost any income as a result of such predation. Rather, their entire proof of damages was based on their claim to profits that would have been earned had the acquired centers closed. Since respondents did not prove any cognizable damages and have not offered any justification for allowing respondents, after two trials and over 10 years of litigation, yet a third opportunity to do so, it follows that, petitioner is entitled, in accord with its motion made pursuant to Rule 50(b), to judgment on the damages claim notwithstanding the verdict.

Respondents' complaint also prayed for equitable relief, and the Court of Appeals held that if respondents established a §7 violation, they might be entitled to an injunction against "those practices by which a deep pocket market entrant harms competition." Because petitioner has not contested this holding, respondents remain free, on remand, to seek such a decree.

The judgment of the Court of Appeals is vacated, and the case is remanded for further proceedings consistent with this opinion.

It is so ordered.

NOTES ON REMEDIAL IMPLICATIONS OF SUBSTANTIVE POLICY

1. *Brunswick* is a dramatic illustration of a pervasive point. Remedies implement substantive policies, and any remedial principle, no matter how well settled, may have to be adapted or limited when applied in the context of a particular substantive violation.

2. Consider Sure-Tan, Inc. v. National Labor Relations Board, 104 S. Ct. 2803 (1984). Sure-Tan employed illegal aliens. When some of them organized a union, Sure-Tan reported them to the Immigration and Naturalization Service, and they were promptly deported. The NLRB found an unfair labor practice, and the Supreme Court agreed. An employer can report violations of the law, but he must do so evenhandedly; he cannot do so in retaliation for union activity.

The usual remedy would be reinstatement with back pay. But for the wrong, the victims would still have their jobs, would not have been caught, and would not have been deported. Must they be readmitted to the country even though they are not entitled to admission under the immigration laws? The Board ordered the employer to offer reinstatement; it avoided the immigration question by finding no evidence that the victims had not already reentered the country. The Court of Appeals held that the offer of reinstatement had to be conditioned on legal admission to the country with permission to work. It then ordered the employer to pay six months' back pay, on the theory that six months was a reasonable estimate of how long the victims could have kept working without detection but for the unfair labor practice. The Supreme Court agreed that the offers of reinstatement had to be conditioned on compliance with the immigration laws. It reversed the award of six months' back pay, holding that the Court of Appeals had no authority to order that remedy if the Board had not ordered it. It declined to decide whether the Board could have ordered it. Four dissenters would have affirmed the award of six months' back pay. On remand, should the Board adopt the Court of Appeals' remedy?

3. *Sure-Tan* raises the problem of what to do when the victim is also a wrongdoer. The most important example of that recurring problem is illegal searches and seizures. Suppose the police conduct two flagrantly illegal searches. In the first, they find no evidence of crime. In the second, they find evidence of murder, and that evidence identifies a new suspect and ultimately leads to the victim of the search being sentenced to life in prison. Suppose both victims sue the police for violating their fourth amendment rights. Should the murderer recover much more than the innocent citizen? Both suffered the same damage at the time of the search. But in addition, the murderer suffered life in prison. But for the illegal search, he wouldn't be there. Should he get compensation for that? Or is the murder, rather than the search, the legal cause of his imprisonment? Is imprisonment not "fourth amendment damage," in the same sense that the lost profits in *Brunswick* were not "antitrust damage"?

If the murderer shouldn't recover compensation for imprisonment, why should he escape imprisonment altogether because of the exclusionary rule? Isn't excluding the evidence from his criminal trial the remedial equivalent of compensating him for imprisonment? The exclusionary rule prevents the harm of imprisonment from happening, so that compensation is unnecessary.

4. One more example: Several courts have limited the contract liability of clients who discharge attorneys without cause. They hold that the attorney can recover only the reasonable value of his services performed up to the time of breach, and not the expectancy he would have earned by completing the services. The Supreme Court of Florida recently explained that "there is an overriding need to allow clients freedom to substitute attorneys without economic penalty as a means of accomplishing the broad objective of fostering public confidence in the legal profession." Rosenberg v. Levin, 409 So. 2d 1016, 1021 (Fla. 1982).

5. Substantive policy considerations are sometimes invoked generically when the tribunal wants to withhold complete relief but can't explain why. Consider Shepard v. National Labor Relations Board, 459 U.S. 344 (1983). Shepard owned and drove a dump truck. The local

Teamsters Union used an illegal secondary boycott to coerce him into joining the union. The NLRB ordered an end to the boycott, but refused to order reimbursement of Shepard's union dues and initiation fee. The Board's reasoning was not clear; it offered three somewhat inconsistent reasons, each stated in conclusory fashion. One of the reasons implied that remedies against unions should not be as thorough as remedies against employers.

The courts enforced the Board's order. The Supreme Court opinion emphasized discretion and the difference between agencies and courts. It concluded that nothing in the act required "complete relief" for every unfair labor practice. 459 U.S. at 352.

Should complete relief be available as of right unless there is some "good" reason to deny it? This is a question that will arise more directly in chapter 13, when we consider implied remedies for violation of statutes that provide limited remedies or do not specify what the remedy shall be.

G.   COLLATERAL MATTERS: TAXES, INTEREST, AND INFLATION

NORFOLK & WESTERN RAILWAY v. LIEPELT
444 U.S. 490 (1980)

MR. JUSTICE STEVENS delivered the opinion of the Court.

In cases arising under the Federal Employers' Liability Act, most trial judges refuse to allow the jury to receive evidence or instruction concerning the impact of federal income taxes on the amount of damages to be awarded. Because the prevailing practice developed at a time when federal taxes were relatively insignificant, and because some courts are now following a different practice, we decided to answer the two questions presented by the certiorari petition in this wrongful death action: (1) whether it was error to exclude evidence of the income taxes payable on the decedent's past and estimated future earnings; and (2) whether it was error for the trial judge to refuse to instruct the jury that the award of damages would not be subject to income taxation.

In 1973 a fireman employed by petitioner suffered fatal injuries in a collision caused by petitioner's negligence. Respondent, as administratrix of the fireman's estate, brought suit under the FELA to recover the damages that his survivors suffered as a result of his death. In 1976, after a full trial in the Circuit Court of Cook County, the jury awarded respondent $775,000. On appeal, the Appellate Court of Illinois held that it was "not error to refuse to instruct a jury as to the nontaxability of an award" and also that it "[was] not error to exclude evidence of the effect of income taxes on future earnings of the decedent."

The evidence supporting the damage award included biographical data about the decedent and his family and the expert testimony of an economist. The decedent, a 37-year-old man, was living with his second wife and two young children and was contributing to the support of two older children by his first marriage. His gross earnings in the 11 months prior to his death on November 22, 1973 amounted to $11,988. Assuming continued employment, those earnings would have amounted to $16,828.26 in 1977.

The expert estimated that the decedent's earnings would have increased at a rate of approximately five percent per year, which would have amounted to $51,600 in the year 2000, the year of his expected retirement. The gross amount of those earnings, plus the value of the services he would have performed for his family, less the amounts the decedent would have spent upon himself, produced a total which, when discounted to present value at the time of trial, amounted to $302,000.

Petitioner objected to the use of gross earnings, without any deduction for income taxes, in respondent's expert's testimony and offered to prove through the testimony of its own expert, an actuary, that decedent's federal income taxes during the years 1973 through 2000 would have amounted to about $57,000. Taking that figure into account, and making different assumptions about the rate of future increases in salary and the calculation of the present value of future earnings, petitioner's expert computed the net pecuniary loss at $138,327. As already noted, the jury returned a verdict of $775,000.

Petitioner argues that the jury must have assumed that its award was subject to federal income taxation; otherwise, it is argued, the verdict would not have exceeded respondent's expert's opinion by such a large amount.[4] For that reason, petitioner contends that it was prejudiced by the trial judge's refusal to instruct the jury that "your award will not be subject to any income taxes, and you should not consider such taxes in fixing the amount of your award."

I

In a wrongful death action under the FELA, the measure of recovery is "the damages . . . [that] flow from the deprivation of the pecuniary benefits which the beneficiaries might have reasonably received. . . ." Michigan Cent. R. Co. v. Vreeland, supra, 227 U.S., at 70. The amount of money that a wage earner is able to contribute to the support of his

---

4. Respondent argues that the excess is adequately explained by the jury's estimate of the pecuniary value of the guidance, instruction and training that the decedent would have provided to his children.

family is unquestionably affected by the amount of the tax he must pay to the Federal Government. It is his after-tax income, rather than his gross income before taxes, that provides the only realistic measure of his ability to support his family. It follows inexorably that the wage earner's income tax is a relevant factor in calculating the monetary loss suffered by his dependents when he dies.

Although federal courts have consistently received evidence of the amount of the decedent's personal expenditures, and have required that the estimate of future earnings be reduced by "taking account of the earning power of the money that is presently to be awarded," they have generally not considered the payment of income taxes as tantamount to a personal expenditure and have regarded the future prediction of tax consequences as too speculative and complex for a jury's deliberations.

Admittedly there are many variables that may affect the amount of a wage earner's future income tax liability. The law may change, his family may increase or decrease in size, his spouse's earnings may affect his tax bracket, and extra income or unforeseen deductions may become available. But future employment itself, future health, future personal expenditures, future interest rates, and future inflation are also matters of estimate and prediction. Any one of these issues might provide the basis for protracted expert testimony and debate. But the practical wisdom of the trial bar and the trial bench has developed effective methods of presenting the essential elements of an expert calculation in a form that is understandable by juries that are increasingly familiar with the complexities of modern life. We therefore reject the notion that the introduction of evidence describing a decedent's estimated after-tax earnings is too speculative or complex for a jury.

Respondent argues that if this door is opened, other equally relevant evidence must also be received. For example, she points out that in discounting the estimate of future earnings to its present value, the tax on the income to be earned by the damage award is now omitted. Logically, it would certainly seem correct that this amount, like future wages, should be estimated on an after-tax basis. But the fact that such an after-tax estimate, if offered in proper form, would also be admissible does not persuade us that it is wrong to use after-tax figures instead of gross earnings in projecting what the decedent's financial contributions to his survivors would have been had this tragic accident not occurred.

Respondent also argues that evidence concerning costs of litigation, including her attorneys' fees, is equally pertinent to a determination of what amount will actually compensate the survivors for their monetary loss. In a sense this is, of course, true. But the argument that attorneys' fees must be added to a plaintiff's recovery if the award is truly to make him whole is contrary to the generally applicable "American Rule." The FELA, however, unlike a number of other federal statutes, does not authorize recovery of attorneys' fees by the successful litigant. Only if the

Congress were to provide for such a recovery would it be proper to consider them. In any event, it surely is not proper for the Judiciary to ignore the demonstrably relevant factor of income tax in measuring damages in order to offset what may be perceived as an undesirable or unfair rule regarding attorneys' fees.[10]

II

Section 104(a)(2) of the Internal Revenue Code provides that the amount of any damages received on account of personal injuries is not taxable income. The section is construed to apply to wrongful death awards; they are not taxable income to the recipient.

Although the law is perfectly clear, it is entirely possible that the members of the jury may assume that a plaintiff's recovery in a case of this kind will be subject to federal taxation, and that the award should be increased substantially in order to be sure that the injured party is fully compensated.

In this case the respondents' expert witness computed the amount of pecuniary loss at $302,000, plus the value of the care and training that decedent would have provided to his young children; the jury awarded damages of $775,000. It is surely not fanciful to suppose that the jury erroneously believed that a large portion of the award would be payable to the Federal Government in taxes and that therefore it improperly inflated the recovery. Whether or not this speculation is accurate, we agree with petitioner that, as Judge Ely wrote for the Ninth Circuit,

> To put the matter simply, giving the instruction can do no harm, and it can certainly help by preventing the jury from inflating the award and thus overcompensating the plaintiff on the basis of an erroneous assumption that the judgment will be taxable.

Burlington Northern, Inc. v. Boxberger, 529 F.2d 284, 297 (C.A.9 1975).

We hold that it was error to refuse the requested instruction in this case. That instruction was brief and could be easily understood. It would not complicate the trial by making additional qualifying or supplemental instructions necessary. It would not be prejudicial to either party, but

---

10. The dissent takes the position that §104(a)(2) of the Internal Revenue Code, which makes personal injury awards nontaxable, "appropriates for the tortfeasor a benefit intended to be conferred on the victim or his survivors." But we see nothing in the language and are aware of nothing in the legislative history of §104(a)(2) to suggest that it has any impact whatsoever on the proper measure of damages in a wrongful death action. Moreover, netting out the taxes that the decedent would have paid does not confer a benefit on the tortfeasor any more than netting out the decedent's personal expenditures. Both subtractions are required in order to determine "the pecuniary benefits which the beneficiaries might have reasonably received. . . ." Michigan Cent. R. Co. v. Vreeland, supra, 227 U.S., at 70.

would merely eliminate an area of doubt or speculation that might have an improper impact on the computation of the amount of damages.

The judgment is reversed and the case is remanded to the Appellate Court of Illinois for further proceedings consistent with this opinion.

MR. JUSTICE BLACKMUN, with whom MR. JUSTICE MARSHALL joins, dissenting. . . .

In my view, by mandating adjustment of the award by way of reduction for federal income taxes that would have been paid by the decedent on his earnings, the Court appropriates for the tortfeasor a benefit intended to be conferred on the victim or his survivors. And in requiring that the jury be instructed that a wrongful death award is not subject to federal income tax, the Court opens the door for a variety of admonitions to the jury not to "misbehave," and unnecessarily interjects what is now to be federal law into the administration of a trial in a state court.

In this day of substantial income taxes, one is sorely tempted, in jury litigation, to accept the propriety of admitting evidence as to a tort victim's earnings *net* after estimated income taxes, and of instructing the jury that an award will be tax-free. This, it could be urged, is only common sense and a recognition of financial realities.

Ordinarily, however, the effect of an income tax upon the recipient of a payment is of no real or ultimate concern to the payer. Apart from required withholding, it just is not the payer's responsibility or, indeed, "any of his business."

I

The employer-petitioner argues, and the Court holds, that federal income taxes that would have been paid by the deceased victim must be subtracted in computing the amount of the wrongful death award. Were one able to ignore and set aside the uncertainties, estimates, assumptions and complexities involved in computing and effectuating that subtraction, this might not be an unreasonable legislative proposition in a compensatory tort system. Neither petitioner nor the Court, however, recognizes that the premise of such an argument is the nontaxability, under the Internal Revenue Code, of the wrongful death award itself.

By not taxing the award, Congress has bestowed a benefit. Although the parties disagree over the origin of the tax-free status of the wrongful death award, it is surely clear that the lost earnings could be taxed as income. In my view, why Congress created this benefit under one statute is relevant in deciding where the benefit should be allocated under another statute enacted by Congress.

While Congress has not articulated its reasons for not taxing a wrongful death award, it is highly unlikely that it intended to confer this benefit on the tortfeasor. Two more probable purposes for the exclusion are apparent. First, taxing the award could involve the same uncertainties and complexities noted by respondent and the majority of the courts of this country as a reason for not taking income taxes into account in computing the award. Congress may have decided that it is simply not worthwhile to enact a complex and administratively burdensome system in order to approximate the tax treatment of the income if, in fact, it had been earned over a period of time by the decedent. Second, Congress may have intended to confer a humanitarian benefit on the victim or victims of the tort. One District Court has reasoned:

> The court can divine no societal purpose that would be furthered by awarding wrongdoing defendants with the benefit of this Congressional largesse. A societal purpose would be served by benefiting innocent victims of tortious conduct.

Huddell v. Levin, 395 F. Supp. 64, 87 (N.J. 1975).

Whichever of these concerns it was that motivated Congress, transfer of the tax benefit to the FELA tortfeasor-defendant is inconsistent with that purpose. If Congress felt that it was not worth the effort to estimate the decedent's prospective tax liability on behalf of the public fisc, it is unlikely that it would want to require this effort on behalf of the tortfeasor. And Congress would not confer a humanitarian benefit on tort victims or their survivors in the Internal Revenue Code, only to take it away from victims or their survivors covered by the FELA. I conclude, therefore, that any income tax effect on lost earnings should not be considered in the computation of a damages award under the FELA.

II

The Court concludes that, as a matter of federal law, the jury in a FELA case must be instructed, on request, that the damages award is not taxable. This instruction is mandated, it is said, because "it is entirely possible that the members of the jury may assume that a plaintiff's recovery . . . will be subject to federal taxation, and that the award should be increased substantially in order to be sure that the injured party is fully compensated." The Court finds it "surely not fanciful to suppose" that the jury acted on that assumption in this case.

The required instruction is purely cautionary in nature. It does not affect the determination of liability or the measure of damages. It does nothing more than call a basically irrelevant factor to the jury's attention, and then directs the jury to forget that matter. Even if federal law governed such an admonition to the jury not to misbehave, the instruction required by the Court seems to me to be both unwise and unjustified, and almost an affront to the practical wisdom of the jury.

It also is "entirely possible" that the jury "may" increase its damages award in the belief that the defendant is insured, or that the plaintiff will be obligated for substantial attorney's fees, or that the award is subject to state (as well as federal) income tax, or on the basis of any number of other extraneous factors. Charging the jury about every conceivable matter as to which it should not misbehave or miscalculate would be burdensome and could be confusing. Yet the Court's decision today opens the door to that possibility. There certainly is no evidence in this record to indicate that the jury is any more likely to act upon an erroneous assumption about an award's being subject to federal income tax than about any other collateral matter. Although the Court suggests that the difference in the expert's estimation of the pecuniary loss and the total amount of the award represents inflation of the award for federal income taxes, this is pure surmise. The jury was instructed that it could compensate for factors on which experts could not place a precise dollar value, and it is "entirely possible" that these, instead, were the basis of the award.

NOTES ON TAXES

1.   Would the effect of taxes matter if personal injury awards were not tax exempt? Suppose plaintiff recovered five years' salary in a suit for wrongful discharge, or five years' lost profits in an antitrust suit. If you told the jury to figure losses on the basis of after tax income, you would plainly have to tell it that its award would be taxable. Wouldn't it be easier to figure damages on the basis of gross income and assume that the taxes on the judgment would balance out the taxes on the lost income? That was the Court's solution in an antitrust case, even though tax rates had been cut sharply in the interim. Hanover Shoe v. United Shoe Machinery Corp., 392 U.S. 481 (1968). Could plaintiff complain that he would be pushed into a higher tax bracket in the year of the judgment? At least one court has said no. McLaughlin v. Union-Leader Corp., 100 N.H. 367, 371-372, 127 A.2d 269, 273 (1956). Could defendant complain that an uninstructed jury would likely inflate the verdict to cover taxes, even though it had been given gross income data for computing the verdict?

2.   What about Justice Blackmun's argument that courts should not try to outwit congressional allocation of tax burdens? At one level, that is an argument that Congress should take judgments into consideration in writing tax laws, rather than have courts take tax laws into consideration in making judgments. That doesn't seem very realistic as a general matter, does it? Is he on stronger ground when he says that in the specific case of personal injury judgments, Congress has considered the problem and deliberately conferred a tax subsidy on plaintiffs? Is he treating the tax exempt status of personal injury judgments as a collateral source of compensation for tort victims?

3.   "[T]he *Norfolk & Western* case stands against a mountain of contrary state authority (circa 28 states do not consider tax impact; 6 do)."

Estate of Spinosa, 621 F.2d 1154, 1158-1159 (1st Cir. 1980). *Norfolk & Western* settles the law only for the Federal Employers Liability Act, a statute about injuries to railroad workers. Presumably it will control all other personal injury litigation in which federal substantive law controls; it may also establish a general principle of considering significant tax consequences in federal damage awards. But it does not change state law, and state court reaction to its persuasive power has been mixed. Alaska and West Virginia have adhered to the majority rule. Yukon Equipment v. Gordon, 660 P.2d 428 (Alaska 1983); Flannery v. United States, 297 S.E.2d 433 (W. Va. 1982). Maryland has adopted *Norfolk & Western's* cautionary jury instruction; whether to calculate gross or net earnings was not at issue. Blanchfield v. Dennis, 292 Md. 319, 438 A.2d 1330 (1982). The Seventh Circuit predicted that Illinois would follow *Norfolk & Western*; the First Circuit predicted that New Hampshire would not. In re Air Crash Disaster Near Chicago, Illinois on May 25, 1979, 701 F.2d 1189 (7th Cir. 1983); Estate of Spinosa, 621 F.2d 1154 (1st Cir. 1980).

4. You may recall that Flannery v. United States was a suit under the Federal Tort Claims Act, described in the Notes on Pain and Suffering, supra at 78. The FTCA incorporates state law but excludes punitive damages. The Fourth Circuit said that West Virginia's damages for a comatose patient's loss of capacity to enjoy life were punitive. In the same case, the West Virginia court adhered to the traditional rule ignoring tax consequences. The Fourth Circuit also held that damages for lost earnings were punitive unless taxes were subtracted out. There was a dissent.

Is the state measure of compensation punitive if it exceeds the federal measure in any detail? "To the extent that an award gives more than the actual loss suffered . . . , it is 'punitive' whether or not it carries with it the deterrent and punishing attributes typically associated with the word . . ." Flannery v. United States, 718 F.2d 108, 111 (4th Cir. 1983). Isn't that equivalent to saying that FTCA plaintiffs get state damages or federal damages, whichever is less? The Sixth Circuit disagrees: "Congress simply prohibited use of a retributive theory of punishment against the government, not a theory of damages which would exclude all customary damages awarded under traditional tort law principles which mix theories of compensation and deterrence together." Kalavity v. United States, 584 F.2d 809, 811 (6th Cir. 1978). In *Kalavity*, the government argued that it was punitive to disregard a widow's remarriage, because the support and companionship of the new husband completely replaced the lost support and companionship of the dead husband.

5. If the court adjusts for taxes on future wages, doesn't it also have to adjust for taxes on the projected income from investing the judgment? Some courts say yes. Shaw v. United States, 741 F.2d 1202, 1206 (9th Cir. 1984). *Flannery* said no, because the judgment might be invested in tax exempt securities. Is that a sufficient answer? Doesn't it matter that tax exempt bonds pay less interest than taxable bonds?

UNION BANK v. FIRST NATIONAL BANK
677 F.2d 1074 (5th Cir. 1982)

Before WISDOM, SAM D. JOHNSON and WILLIAMS, Circuit Judges.

SAM D. JOHNSON, Circuit Judge.

This Court is again asked to allocate losses sustained by banks victimized in a check-kiting scheme. On the first appeal, this Court reversed the district court and held the First National Bank in Mount Pleasant, Texas (Mount Pleasant), liable for failure to timely return twenty-four checks received from the Union Bank of Benton, Arkansas, . . . (Benton). . . .

It was on July 18, 1980, that the Fifth Circuit reversed the district court and remanded the case to the district court for entry of judgment against Mount Pleasant. On January 16, 1981, some five years after Mount Pleasant's wrongful return of the checks, the district court entered judgment for Benton in the sum of $58,077, plus postjudgment interest from July 18, 1980. The district court, however, declined to award prejudgment interest — thus this appeal.

I.   Award of Pre-Judgment Interest

Benton asserts that, under Texas law, it has a right to prejudgment interest on the payments wrongfully withheld.[3] Benton cites the well-settled rule in Texas that interest is recoverable as a matter of right from the date of the injury or loss, where damages are established as of a definite time and the amount thereof is definitely ascertainable.

Failure to pay an amount due at a specified time is clearly a definitely ascertainable loss.

In the instant case, Benton sent Mount Pleasant twenty-four checks between December 15, 1975 and January 5, 1976, with the explicit directive "Pay or return within twenty-four hours." This Court, in an earlier decision, determined that Mount Pleasant's failure to comply with these instructions was a violation of Tex. Bus. & Com. Code §4.302. The loss had become definitely ascertainable before Mount Pleasant returned the twenty-four checks to Benton on January 7, 1976; the loss was definitely ascertainable on January 6, 1976, when Mount Pleasant exceeded the twenty-four hour maximum time allowed for payment or return. Accordingly, Benton has a right to prejudgment interest as a matter of law.

The district court misreads the controlling law in its denial of prejudgment interest. According to the district court, Benton's claim is governed by Black Lake Pipe Line Co. v. Union Construction Co., Inc., 538 S.W. 2d 80 (Tex. 1976).

Black Lake involved a pipeline company which refused to pay a subcontractor for performing extra work not specifically covered by the con-

---

3.   In a diversity case such as this one, state law controls whether the recovery of interest prior to the date of judgment is a mandatory element of damages. . . .

tract. The Texas Supreme Court not only authorized recovery in *quantum meruit* for this extra work, but also allowed prejudgment interest on the amount recovered. In so doing, that court extended to *quantum meruit* recoveries the general rule that prejudgment interest is recoverable as a matter of right when the time and amount of damages are definitely ascertainable. In the case *sub judice*, the district court apparently misconstrued the holding in *Black Lake* to *limit* prejudgment interest to situations where the defendant is unjustly enriched. The district court, therefore, determined that Benton did not qualify for recovery, based on its finding that Mount Pleasant never benefitted unjustly from money or services provided by Benton.

The district court failed to recognize that Texas law allows an award of prejudgment interest not only as restitution for unjust enrichment, but also as compensation for damages sustained. Recovery on equitable grounds is not an exclusive remedy; it is concurrent with the common-law right to prejudgment interest for ascertainable damages. The equitable grounds for restitution actually broadens, rather than limits, the scope of recovery for prejudgment interest. . . .

II. Determination of Amount to Be Awarded

On remand, the district court must determine the rate of interest and the date of loss from which prejudgment interest is to be computed. Although Benton's pleadings failed to specify a prejudgment interest rate, it requested six percent prejudgment interest in its brief on appeal. During oral argument Benton suggested that the rate be left to the discretion of the district court. Benton did plead, however, that interest be computed from January 6, 1976.

During the time frame between December 15, 1975 and January 5, 1976 — when Mount Pleasant failed to timely return the twenty-four checks — a prejudgment interest rate of six percent per annum was specified by statute on all written contracts and open accounts. Tex. Rev. Civ. Stat. Ann. art. 5069-1.03 (Vernon 1971). Many Texas courts have found this statutory rate applicable by analogy to awards of interest as damages.

Several Texas appellate courts have explicitly stated that an award of prejudgment interest above the statutory rate is within the court's equitable discretion, even where the cause of action is based on a contract. At least two appellate courts have allowed nine percent prejudgment interest on breach of contract awards, even though the statutory rate in effect was only six percent.[11] . . .

_____

11. One reason why these courts have awarded prejudgment interest at higher than the statutory rate is that the Texas legislature changed the statutory rate for postjudgment interest to 9% per annum effective September 1, 1975, while failing to raise the prejudgment interest rate to 9%. Because this discrepancy had no apparent justification, the courts raised the prejudgment interest rate to 9% to be consistent with the postjudgment rate.

Recently, one appellate court allowed a ten percent prejudgment interest rate on a damages award for negligent mismanagement of properties held in trust. . . . As a result, the Fifth Circuit has determined that any interest rate, in excess of that statutorily applicable, is within the trial court's discretion. It is therefore necessary to remand the issue to the district court for its determination of what rate of interest, if any, is applicable above the statutory rate of six percent.

In awarding prejudgment interest, the district court must also establish the time when the interest should begin to accrue. Benton notes that technically, interest should accrue from the date each check was withheld. It is noted, however, that for simplicity of calculation Benton asks that January 6, 1976, be set as the date at which interest should be calculated. It was on this date that the twenty-four hour deadline passed for paying or returning the last of the twenty-four checks submitted to Mount Pleasant and the total loss became ascertainable. Prejudgment interest may be awarded from the time at which the "measure of recovery of [the] claim, and not necessarily the amount of damages, is fixed by conditions existing at the time the injury arose or was inflicted." Dallas-Fort Worth Regional Airport, 623 F.2d at 1040. Whether the actual amount of damages is disputed until trial is immaterial. Tex. Bus. & Com. Code §4.302 establishes the measure of recovery for checks wrongfully withheld as the value of the checks, and this Court has established the time of the wrongful withholding under section 4.302 as twenty-four hours after the receipt of each check. The district court may therefore allow interest to accrue either from January 6, 1976 when the total loss became ascertainable or for each separate check calculated from the time when each became due. . . .

Reversed and remanded.

NOTES ON INTEREST

1. The rule that prejudgment interest will be awarded only when damages are "ascertainable" is generally followed, except where modified by statute. But the meaning of *ascertainable* varies widely among the jurisdictions. The term *ascertainable* is unfortunate; by the time a judge or jury takes up the question of interest, it has already ascertained the amount of damages. *Ascertainable* in this context refers to the ease and certainty with which damages may be ascertained. All jurisdictions agree that personal injury and wrongful death damages are not ascertainable. Most hold that damages for breach of contract are nearly always ascertainable. A majority now hold that damages for injured or destroyed property are ascertainable. The *Black Lake Pipe* case, discussed in *Union Bank*, held that the reasonable value of extra work done on a pipeline construction project was ascertainable. General Facilities v. National Marine Service, 664 F.2d 672 (8th Cir. 1981), affirmed an award of pre-

judgment interest on the expenses of repairing a damaged dock and the extra expenses of fulfilling contractual commitments by using other docks; the court also affirmed the denial of interest on a recovery for profits lost while the dock was shut down.

The Indiana cases illustrate a much more restrictive view of ascertainability. There, the rule is said to be that "pre-judgment interest is proper where the trier of fact need not exercise its judgment to assess the amount of damages." Indiana Industries v. Wedge Products, 430 N.E.2d 419, 427 (Ind. App. 1982). Interest was denied in one Indiana case because the appraisers disagreed over the value of land and in another because the judgment differed substantially from the amount demanded in the complaint. City of Anderson v. Salling Concrete Corp., 411 N.E.2d 728, 735 (Ind. App. 1981).

2. Why should ascertainability matter? One answer given by the cases is that defendant should not be penalized by the assessment of interest unless he could have paid and failed to do so, and that he could not have paid unless the amount he owed was ascertainable. This rationale suggests that the test should be whether defendant could ascertain the damages. Another rationale, offered in a case involving mental and emotional injury, is that "interest on such damages adds uncertain conjecture to speculation." Greater West Chester Home Association v. City of Los Angeles, 26 Cal. 3d 86, 103, 603 P.2d 1329, 1338 (1979). Is either of these rationales persuasive? Does an assessment of interest really penalize the defendant? Or does it merely adjust for what he gained and plaintiff lost during the delays of litigation?

3. Awards of interest tend to be based on the "legal rate" specified in statutes providing for postjudgment interest or, as in the case of the Texas statute cited in *Union Bank*, providing for interest on contracts and open accounts where the parties do not themselves specify the rate. The rates provided by these statutes were far below market rates throughout the late 1970s and early 1980s. *General Facilities*, cited in note 1, is unusual in awarding prejudgment interest based on the prime rate during the period of delay — in that case, 15.75 percent.

4. The courts almost universally deny compound interest, usually without stating a reason. Cases defending the practice argue that interest on damages is not due and payable before judgment, so no interest can accrue on the interest before then. An example is City of Austin v. Foster, 623 S.W.2d 672 (Tex. Civ. App. 1981). Isn't that just a restatement of the conclusion? Why do any damages accrue interest before judgment? It is also said that in the absence of agreement by the parties, there is no way to decide how often to compound. A dissenter in *City of Austin* would have allowed compounding, but only when the statutory rate was far below the market rate. Most cases simply cite the well-settled rule. On tracing that rule back to its origins, one usually finds some statement such as the following from Chancellor Kent:

Interest upon interest, promptly and incessantly accruing, would, as a general rule, become harsh and oppressive. Debt would accumulate with a rapidity beyond all ordinary calculation and endurance. Common business cannot sustain such overwhelming accumulation. It would tend also to inflame the avarice and harden the heart of the creditor. Some allowance must be made for the indolence of mankind, and the casualties and delays incident to the best-regulated industry.

Connecticut v. Jackson, 1 Johns. Ch. 13, 17 (1814).

Compounding is occasionally allowed where an established course of dealing has included compound interest, e.g., Ma v. Community Bank, 686 F.2d 459, 466 (7th Cir. 1982); Young v. Hill, 67 N.Y. 162, 168 (1876), and in certain cases involving fiduciaries, Restatement (Second) of Trusts §207 and comment d (1959).

5.   Consider the combined effect of the rules pertaining to interest. No prejudgment interest in many cases, interest well below the market rate in most cases, and compounding in hardly any cases, add up to a substantial deviation from the general rule that plaintiff is to be restored to the position he would have occupied but for the wrong.

The rules also give defendants substantial incentive to delay in cases where the damages are large. That incentive is dramatically illustrated by the advent of retroactive insurance, and especially by the insurance dispute arising out of the 1980 MGM Grand Hotel fire in Las Vegas. After the fire, the hotel bought $170 million in liability insurance for claims arising from the fire. The policies cost only $37.5 million. When the hotel began settling claims in only two or three years, the insurers refused to pay. The policies made sense only on the assumption that they could invest the premiums for many years before paying claims. They claim that the hotel betrayed them and settled claims in a way that was not "businesslike." The dispute is described in Hertzberg, Hotel Insurers Are Disputing Novel Policy, Wall St. J., July 25, 1983, at 13, col. 2.

6.   The rules on interest date from a time when wealth was held in land and tangible property, when income could not always be immediately reinvested, and when medieval religious prohibitions on interest were a recent memory. Are they obsolete in an era of money market funds, interest bearing checking accounts, and continuous compounding? Certainly the trend is toward increasingly generous interpretation of the existing rules.

7.   There is also a trend to statutory liberalization. Debate on these statutes generally focuses on personal injury litigation, but there is little pattern to the statutes themselves. For example, Alaska allows interest from the day of harm in all cases in which interest does not duplicate the measure of damage (e.g., compensation for temporary loss of use of property). State v. Phillips, 470 P.2d 266, 272-274 (Alaska 1970), construing Alaska Stat. §§45.45.010 and 09.50.280. California allows interest if

plaintiff obtains a judgment more favorable than a settlement offer rejected by defendant; interest accrues from the day of the first such offer. Cal. Civ. Code §3291 (West Supp. 1985). The Colorado statute applies only to personal injuries; *compound* interest accrues from the day suit was filed. If an unsuccessful appeal is taken, interest accrues from the day of the injury. Col. Rev. Stat. §13-21-101 (1984 Supp.). North Carolina allows interest on any compensatory damages covered by liability insurance. N.C. Gen. Stat. §24-5 (1983 Supp.). Many states have raised the legal interest rate, but few have tied it to some measure of market rates.

The Court Improvements Act of 1982 provides for market interest on federal judgments, compounded annually. 28 U.S.C. §1961 (Supp. I 1983). The market rate selected is based on the most recent auction of fifty-two-week Treasury bills. But the statute applies only to postjudgment interest.

JONES & LAUGHLIN STEEL CORP. v. PFEIFER
462 U.S. 523 (1983)

JUSTICE STEVENS delivered the opinion of the Court.

Respondent was injured in the course of his employment as a loading helper on a coal barge. As his employer, petitioner was required to compensate him for his injury under §4 of the Longshoremen's and Harbor Workers' Compensation Act. As the owner *pro hac vice* of the barge, petitioner may also be liable for negligence under §5 of the Act. . . .

In November 1979, respondent brought this action against petitioner, alleging that his injury had been "caused by the negligence of the vessel" within the meaning of §5(b) of the Act. The District Court found in favor of respondent and awarded damages of $275,881.31. The court held that receipt of compensation payments from petitioner under §4 of the Act did not bar a separate recovery of damages for negligence.

The District Court's calculation of damages was predicated on a few undisputed facts. At the time of his injury respondent was earning an annual wage of $26,065. He had a remaining work expectancy of $12\frac{1}{2}$ years. On the date of trial (October 1, 1980), respondent had received compensation payments of $33,079.14. If he had obtained light work and earned the legal minimum hourly wage from July 1, 1979 until his 65th birthday, he would have earned $66,350.

The District Court arrived at its final award by taking $12\frac{1}{2}$ years of earnings at respondent's wage at the time of injury ($325,312.50), subtracting his projected hypothetical earnings at the minimum wage ($66,352) and the compensation payments he had received under §4 ($33,079.14), and adding $50,000 for pain and suffering. The court did not increase the award to take inflation into account, and it did not discount

the award to reflect the present value of the future stream of income. The *PA*
Court instead decided to follow a decision of the Supreme Court of
Pennsylvania, which had held "as a matter of law that future inflation
shall be presumed equal to future interest rates with these factors offsetting." Kaczkowski v. Bolubasz, 491 Pa. 561, 583, 421 A.2d 1027, 1038-1039
(1980). Thus, although the District Court did not dispute that respondent
could be expected to receive regular cost-of-living wage increases from
the date of his injury until his presumed date of retirement, the Court
refused to include such increases in its calculation, explaining that they
would provide respondent "a double consideration for inflation." For
comparable reasons, the Court disregarded changes in the legal minimum wage in computing the amount of mitigation attributable to respondent's ability to perform light work.

It does not appear that either party offered any expert testimony concerning predicted future rates of inflation, the interest rate that could be
appropriately used to discount future earnings to present value, or the
possible connection between inflation rates and interest rates. Respondent did, however, offer an estimate of how his own wages would have
increased over time, based upon recent increases in the company's
hourly wage scale.

The Court of Appeals affirmed. . . . It is useful at the outset to review
the way in which damages should be measured in a hypothetical inflation-free economy. We shall then consider how price inflation alters the
analysis. Finally, we shall decide whether the District Court committed
reversible error in this case.

I

In calculating damages, it is assumed that if the injured party had not
been disabled, he would have continued to work, and to receive wages at
periodic intervals until retirement, disability, or death. An award for impaired earning capacity is intended to compensate the worker for the
diminution in that stream of income. The award could in theory take the
form of periodic payments, but in this country it has traditionally taken
the form of a lump sum, paid at the conclusion of the litigation. The
appropriate lump sum cannot be computed without first examining the
stream of income it purports to replace.

The lost stream's length cannot be known with certainty; the worker
could have been disabled or even killed in a different, non-work-related
accident at any time. The probability that he would still be working at a
given date is constantly diminishing. Given the complexity of trying to
make an exact calculation, litigants frequently follow the relatively simple
course of assuming that the worker would have continued to work up
until a specific date certain. In this case, for example, both parties agreed
that the petitioner would have continued to work until age 65 (12½ more
years) if he had not been injured.

Each annual installment[11] in the lost stream comprises several elements. The most significant is, of course, the actual wage. In addition, the worker may have enjoyed certain fringe benefits, which should be included in an ideal evaluation of the worker's loss but are frequently excluded for simplicity's sake. On the other hand, the injured worker's lost wages would have been diminished by state and federal income taxes. Since the damages award is tax-free, the relevant stream is ideally of *after-tax* wages and benefits. See Norfolk & Western R. Co. v. Liepelt, 444 U.S. 490 (1980). Moreover, workers often incur unreimbursed costs, such as transportation to work and uniforms, that the injured worker will not incur. These costs should also be deducted in estimating the lost stream.

In this case the parties appear to have agreed to simplify the litigation, and to presume that in each installment all the elements in the stream would offset each other, except for gross wages. However, in attempting to estimate even such a stylized stream of annual installments of gross wages, a trier of fact faces a complex task. The most obvious and most appropriate place to begin is with the worker's annual wage at the time of injury. Yet the "estimate of loss from lessened earnings capacity in the future need not be based solely upon the wages which the plaintiff was earning at the time of his injury." C. McCormick, Damages §86 (1935). Even in an inflation-free economy — that is to say one in which the prices of consumer goods remain stable — a worker's wages tend to "inflate." This "real" wage inflation reflects a number of factors, some linked to the specific individual and some linked to broader societal forces.

With the passage of time, an individual worker often becomes more valuable to his employer. His personal work experiences increase his hourly contributions to firm profits. To reflect that heightened value, he will often receive "seniority" or "experience" raises, "merit" raises, or even promotions.[14] Although it may be difficult to prove when, and whether, a particular injured worker might have received such wage increases, they may be reliably demonstrated for some workers.

Furthermore, the wages of workers as a class may increase over time. Through more efficient interaction among labor, capital, and technology, industrial productivity may increase, and workers' wages may enjoy a share of that growth. Such productivity increases — reflected in real increases in the gross national product per worker-hour — have been a permanent feature of the national economy since the conclusion of World War II. Moreover, through collective bargaining, workers may be

11.   Obviously, another distorting simplification is being made here. Although workers generally receive their wages in weekly or biweekly installments, virtually all calculations of lost earnings, including the one made in this case, pretend that the stream would have flowed in large spurts, taking the form of annual installments.

14.   It is also possible that a worker could be expected to change occupations completely.

able to negotiate increases in their "share" of revenues, at the cost of reducing shareholders' rate of return on their investments. . . .

Of course, even in an inflation-free economy the award of damages to replace the lost stream of income cannot be computed simply by totaling up the sum of the periodic payments. For the damages award is paid in a lump sum at the conclusion of the litigation, and when it — or even a part of it — is invested, it will earn additional money. It has been settled since our decision in Chesapeake & Ohio R. Co. v. Kelly, 241 U.S. 485 (1916) that "in all cases where it is reasonable to suppose that interest may safely be earned upon the amount that is awarded, the ascertained future benefits ought to be discounted in the making up of the award." Id. at 490.

The discount rate should be based on the rate of interest that would be earned on "the best and safest investments." Id., at 491. Once it is assumed that the injured worker would definitely have worked for a specific term of years, he is entitled to a risk-free stream of future income to replace his lost wages; therefore, the discount rate should not reflect the market's premium for investors who are willing to accept some risk of default. Moreover, since under *Liepelt*, supra, the lost stream of income should be estimated in after-tax terms, the discount rate should also represent the after-tax rate of return to the injured worker.[21]

Thus, although the notion of a damage award representing the present value of a lost stream of earnings in an inflation-free economy rests on some fairly sophisticated economic concepts, the two elements that determine its calculation can be stated fairly easily. They are: (1) the amount that the employee would have earned during each year that he could have been expected to work after the injury; and (2) the appropriate discount rate, reflecting the safest available investment. The trier of fact should apply the discount rate to each of the estimated installments in the lost stream of income, and then add up the discounted installments to determine the total award.[22]

---

21. The arithmetic necessary for discounting can be simplified through the use of a so-called "present value table," such as those found in R. Wixon, Accountants' Handbook, at 29.58-29.59 (1956 ed.), or S. Speiser, Recovery for Wrongful Death 2d §8:4, at 713-718 (1975). These tables are based on the proposition that if i is the discount rate, then "the present value of \$1 due in n periods must be $1 / (1 + i)^n$." Wixon, supra, at 29.57. In this context, the relevant "periods" are years; accordingly, if "i" is a market interest rate, it should be the effective *annual* yield.

22. At one time it was thought appropriate to distinguish between compensating a plaintiff "for the loss of time from his work which has actually occurred up to the time of trial" and compensating him "for the time which he will lose in the future." C. McCormick, Damages §86 (1935). This suggested that estimated future earning capacity should be discounted to the date of trial, and a separate calculation would be performed for the estimated loss of earnings between injury and trial. Id., at §§86-87. It is both easier and more precise to discount the entire lost stream of earnings back to the date of injury — the moment from which earning capacity was impaired. The plaintiff may then be awarded interest on that discounted sum for the period between injury and judgment, in order to ensure that the award when invested will still be able to replicate the lost stream.

II

Unfortunately for triers of fact, ours is not an inflation-free economy. Inflation has been a permanent fixture in our economy for many decades, and there can be no doubt that it ideally should affect both stages of the calculation described in the previous section. The difficult problem is how it can do so in the practical context of civil litigation under §5(b) of the Act.

The first stage of the calculation required an estimate of the shape of the lost stream of future income. For many workers, including respondent, a contractual "cost-of-living adjustment" automatically increases wages each year by the percentage change during the previous year in the consumer price index calculated by the Bureau of Labor Statistics. Such a contract provides a basis for taking into account an additional societal factor — price inflation — in estimating the worker's lost future earnings.

The second stage of the calculation requires the selection of an appropriate discount rate. Price inflation — or more precisely, anticipated price inflation — certainly affects market rates of return. If a lender knows that his loan is to be repaid a year later with dollars that are less valuable than those he has advanced, he will charge an interest rate that is high enough both to compensate him for the temporary use of the loan proceeds and also to make up for their shrinkage in value.[23]

At one time many courts incorporated inflation into only one stage of the calculation of the award for lost earnings. In estimating the lost stream of future earnings, they accepted evidence of both individual and societal factors that would tend to lead to wage increases even in an inflation-free economy, but required the plaintiff to prove that those factors were not influenced by predictions of future price inflation. No increase was allowed for price inflation, on the theory that such predic-

---

23. The effect of price inflation on the discount rate may be less speculative than its effect on the lost stream of future income. The latter effect always requires a prediction of the future, for the existence of a contractual cost-of-living adjustment gives no guidance about how big that adjustment will be in some future year. However, whether the discount rate also turns on predictions of the future depends on how it is assumed that the worker will invest his award.

On the one hand, it might be assumed that at the time of the award the worker will invest in a mixture of safe short-term, medium-term, and long-term bonds, with one scheduled to mature each year of his expected work-life. In that event, by purchasing bonds immediately after judgment, the worker can be ensured whatever future stream of nominal income is predicted. Since all relevant effects of inflation on the market interest rate will have occurred at that time, future changes in the rate of price inflation will have no effect on the stream of income he receives. On the other hand, it might be assumed that the worker will invest exclusively in safe short-term notes, reinvesting them at the new market rate whenever they mature. Future market rates would be quite important to such a worker. Predictions of what they will be would therefore also be relevant to the choice of an appropriate discount rate, in much the same way that they are always relevant to the first stage of the calculation. We perceive no intrinsic reason to prefer one assumption over the other. . . .

tions were unreliably speculative. In discounting the estimated lost stream of future income to present value, however, they applied the market interest rate.

The effect of these holdings was to deny the plaintiff the benefit of the impact of inflation on his future earnings, while giving the defendant the benefit of inflation's impact on the interest rate that is used to discount those earnings to present value. Although the plaintiff in such a situation could invest the proceeds of the litigation at an "inflated" rate of interest, the stream of income that he received provided him with only enough dollars to maintain his existing *nominal* income; it did not provide him with a stream comparable to what his lost wages would have been in an inflationary economy. This inequity was assumed to have been minimal because of the relatively low rates of inflation.

In recent years, of course, inflation rates have not remained low. There is now a consensus among courts that the prior inequity can no longer be tolerated. There is no consensus at all, however, regarding what form an appropriate response should take.

Our sister common law nations generally continue to adhere to the position that inflation is too speculative to be considered in estimating the lost stream of future earnings; they have sought to counteract the danger of systematically undercompensating plaintiffs by applying a discount rate that is below the current market rate. . . . [I]n Australia, the High Court has adopted a 2% rate, on the theory that it represents a good approximation of the long-term "real interest rate."

In this country, some courts have taken the same "real interest rate" approach as Australia. They have endorsed the economic theory suggesting that market interest rates include two components — an estimate of anticipated inflation, and a desired "real" rate of return on investment — and that the latter component is essentially constant over time. They have concluded that the inflationary increase in the estimated lost stream of future earnings will therefore be perfectly "offset" by all but the "real" component of the market interest rate.[26]

26. What is meant by the "real interest rate" depends on how one expects the plaintiff to invest the award, see n.23, supra. If one assumes that the injured worker will immediately invest in bonds having a variety of maturity dates, in order to ensure a particular stream of future payments, then the relevant "real interest rate" must be the difference between (1) an average of short-term, medium-term, and long-term market interest rates in a given year and (2) the average rate of price inflation in *subsequent* years (i.e., during the terms of the investments).

It appears more common for "real interest rate" approaches to rest on the assumption that the worker will invest in low-risk short-term securities and will reinvest frequently. Under that assumption, the relevant real interest rate is the difference between the short-term market interest rate in a given year and the average rate of price inflation during that same year.

However one interprets the "real interest rate," there is a slight distortion introduced by netting out the two effects and discounting by the difference.

Still other courts have preferred to continue relying on market interest rates. To avoid undercompensation, they have shown at least tentative willingness to permit evidence of what future price inflation will be in estimating the lost stream of future income. . . .

Finally, some courts have applied a number of techniques that have loosely been termed "total offset" methods. What these methods have in common is that they presume that the ideal discount rate — the after-tax market interest rate on a safe investment — is (to a legally tolerable degree of precision) completely offset by certain elements in the ideal computation of the estimated lost stream of future income. They all assume that the effects of future price inflation on wages are part of what offsets the market interest rate. The methods differ, however, in their assumptions regarding which if any other elements in the first stage of the damages calculation contribute to the offset.

Beaulieu v. Elliott, 434 P.2d 665 (Alaska 1967), is regarded as the seminal "total offset" case. The Supreme Court of Alaska ruled that in calculating an appropriate award for an injured worker's lost wages, no discount was to be applied. It held that the market interest rate was fully offset by two factors: price inflation and real wage inflation.

[The Court then described a minor variation on the Alaska rule.]

Kaczkowski v. Bolubasz, 491 Pa. 561 (1980), took still a third approach, . . . concluding that the plaintiff could introduce all manner of evidence bearing on likely sources — both individual and societal — of future wage growth, except for predictions of price inflation. However, . . . it deemed the market interest rate to be offset by future price inflation.

The litigants and the amici in this case urge us to select one of the many rules that have been proposed and establish it for all time as the exclusive method in all federal trials for calculating an award for lost earnings in an inflationary economy. We are not persuaded, however, that such an approach is warranted. For our review of the foregoing cases leads us to draw three conclusions. First, by its very nature the calculation of an award for lost earnings must be a rough approximation. Because the lost stream can never be predicted with complete confidence, any lump sum represents only a "rough and ready" effort to put the plaintiff in the position he would have been in had he not been injured. Second, sustained price inflation can make the award substantially less precise. Inflation's current magnitude and unpredictability create a substantial risk that the damage award will prove to have little relation to the lost wages it purports to replace. Third, the question of lost earnings can arise in many different contexts. In some sectors of the economy, it is far easier to assemble evidence of an individual's most likely career path than in others.

These conclusions all counsel hesitation. Having surveyed the multitude of options available, we will do no more than is necessary to resolve the case before us. . . .

III . . .

In calculating an award for a longshoreman's lost earnings caused by the negligence of a vessel, the discount rate should be chosen on the basis of the factors that are used to estimate the lost stream of future earnings. If the trier of fact relies on a specific forecast of the future rate of price inflation, and if the estimated lost stream of future earnings is calculated to include price inflation along with individual factors and other societal factors, then the proper discount rate would be the after-tax market interest rate. But since specific forecasts of future price inflation remain too unreliable to be useful in many cases, it will normally be a costly and ultimately unproductive waste of longshoremen's resources to make such forecasts the centerpiece of litigation under §5(b). As Judge Newman has warned, "The average accident trial should not be converted into a graduate seminar on economic forecasting." Doca v. Marina Mercante Nicaraguense, S.A., 634 F.2d 30, 39 (C.A.2 1980). For that reason, both plaintiffs and trial courts should be discouraged from pursuing that approach.

On the other hand, if forecasts of future price inflation are not used, it is necessary to choose an appropriate below-market discount rate. As long as inflation continues, one must ask how much should be "offset" against the market rate. Once again, that amount should be chosen on the basis of the same factors that are used to estimate the lost stream of future earnings. If full account is taken of the individual and societal factors (excepting price inflation) that can be expected to have resulted in wage increases, then all that should be set off against the market interest rate is an estimate of future price inflation. This would result in one of the "real interest rate" approaches described above. Although we find the economic evidence distinctly inconclusive regarding an essential premise of those approaches,[30] we do not believe a trial court adopting such an

---

30.   The key premise is that the real interest rate is stable over time. It is obviously not perfectly stable, but whether it is even relatively stable is hotly disputed among economists. In his classic work, Irving Fisher argued that the rate is not stable because changes in expectations of inflation (the factor that influences market interest rates) lag behind changes in inflation itself. I. Fisher, The Theory of Interest 43 (1930). He noted that the "real rate of interest in the United States from March to April, 1917, fell below minus 70 percent!" Id., at 44. Consider also the more recent observations of Justice Stephen of the High Court of Australia:

Past Australian economic experience appears to provide little support for the concept of a relatively constant rate of "real interest." Year by year a figure for "real interest" can of course be calculated, simply by subtracting from nominal interest rates the rate of inflation. But these figures are no more than a series of numbers bearing no resemblance to any relatively constant rate of interest which lenders are supposed to demand and borrowers to pay after allowing for estimated inflation. If official statistics for the past twelve calendar years are consulted, the Reserve Bank of Australia's Statistical Bulletins supply interest rates on two-year Australian government bonds (non-rebatable) and the O.E.C.D. Economic Outlook — July 1980, p.105 and p.143, supplies annual percentage changes in consumer prices, which gives a measure of inflation. The difference figure

approach in a suit under §5(b) should be reversed if it adopts a rate between one and three percent and explains its choice.

There may be a sound economic argument for even further set-offs. In 1976, Professor Carlson of the Purdue University economics department wrote an article in the American Bar Association Journal contending that in the long run the societal factors excepting price inflation — largely productivity gains — match (or even slightly exceed) the "real interest rate." Carlson, Economic Analysis v. Courtroom Controversy, 62 A.B.A.J. 628 (1976). He thus recommended that the estimated lost stream of future wages be calculated without considering either price inflation or societal productivity gains. All that would be considered would be individual seniority and promotion gains. If this were done, he concluded that the entire market interest rate, including both inflation and the real interest rate, would be more than adequately offset.

Although such an approach has the virtue of simplicity and may even be economically precise,[31] we cannot at this time agree with the Court of Appeals for the Third Circuit that its use is mandatory in the federal courts. Naturally, Congress could require it if it chose to do so. And nothing prevents parties interested in keeping litigation costs under control from stipulating to its use before trial. But we are not prepared to impose it on unwilling litigants, for we have not been given sufficient data to judge how closely the national patterns of wage growth are likely to reflect the patterns within any given industry. The legislative branch of the federal government is far better equipped than we are to perform a comprehensive economic analysis and to fashion the proper general rule.

As a result, the judgment below must be set aside. In performing its damages calculation, the trial court applied the theory of *Kaczkowski*, supra, as a mandatory federal rule of decision, even though the petitioner

---

year by year, which should represent the "real interest" rate, averages out at a negative average rate of interest of −1.46, the widest fluctuations found in particular years being a positive rate of 2.58 percent and a negative rate of −6.61 percent. Nothing resembling a relatively constant positive rate of 2 percent–3 percent emerges. An equally random series of numbers, showing no steady rate of "real interest," appears as Table 9.1 in the recent Interim Report of the Campbell Committee of Inquiry (Australian Government Publication Service — 1980). For the period of thirty years which that Table covers, from 1950 to 1979, the average "implicit real interest rate" is a negative rate of −.7 percent with 4 percent as the greatest positive rate in any year and −20.2 percent as the greatest negative annual rate.

Pennant Hills Restaurants Pty. Ltd. v. Barrell Insurances Pty. Ltd., 55 A.L.J.R. 258, 267 (1981).

31. We note that a substantial body of literature suggests that the Carlson rule might even *under*compensate some plaintiffs. See S. Speiser, Recovery for Wrongful Death, Economic Handbook, 36-37 (1970) (average interest rate 1% below average rate of wage growth). But see Comment, 49 U. Chi. L. Rev. 1003, 1023, and n.87 (1982) (noting "apparent congruence" between government projections of 2% average annual productivity growth and real interest rate, and concluding that total offset is accurate). . . .

had insisted that if compensation was to be awarded, it "must be reduced to its present worth."

IV

We do not suggest that the trial judge should embark on a search for "delusive exactness."[33] It is perfectly obvious that the most detailed inquiry can at best produce an approximate result. And one cannot ignore the fact that in many instances the award for impaired earning capacity may be overshadowed by a highly impressionistic award for pain and suffering.[35] But we are satisfied that whatever rate the District Court may choose to discount the estimated stream of future earnings, it must make a deliberate choice, rather than assuming that it is bound by a rule of state law.

The judgment of the Court of Appeals is vacated and the case is remanded for further proceedings consistent with this opinion.

It is so ordered.

NOTES ON INFLATION AND DISCOUNTING TO PRESENT VALUE

1.   The common law practice has been to include all damages in a single judgment, even though some of them will not be suffered until far into the future. As the opinion indicates, all courts have responded by discounting future damages to present value. Determining the present value of a stream of future wages is mathematically identical to determining the value of an income-producing property by the capitalized earnings method. The discount — $1/(1 + i)^n$ — prescribed in footnote 21 of *Jones & Laughlin* is simply a formal statement of the calculation illustrated at page 50, supra, and in the appendix. Both the "capitalized value" and the "present value" refer to the amount of money that would produce the future stream of earnings if invested today. In either context, it is erroneous to ignore the effect of inflation on interest rates.

2.   The formula in *Jones & Laughlin* — $1/(1 + i)^n$ is the discount formula for compound interest. Is there any reason why plaintiff's future losses should be discounted to present value at compound interest rates, while plaintiff is compensated for his past losses with simple interest?

3.   In addition to the "real" interest rate and the expected inflation rate, nominal interest rates are traditionally thought to include a pre-

33.   Judge Friendly perceived the relevance of Justice Holmes' phrase in this context. See Feldman v. Allegheny Airlines, Inc., 524 F.2d, at 392 (Friendly, J., concurring dubitante), quoting Truax v. Corrigan, 257 U.S. 312, 342 (1921) (Holmes, J., dissenting).

35.   It has been estimated that awards for pain and suffering account for 72 percent of damages in personal injury litigation. 6 Am. Jur. Trials §24 (1967).

mium for the risk of default. The Court can ignore that component because disabled plaintiffs are entitled to avoid that risk by investing in government bonds or government insured certificates of deposit. Netting out the inflation component of the interest rate and the inflation component of future wage increases avoids the need to predict the inflation rate. It also reduces a potential credibility problem for the plaintiff. Consider the case of a semiskilled worker, age 29, earning $15,000 per year. If inflation persists at 6 percent, he would make $120,000 at age 65, before any allowance for productivity gains or any other source of wage increase. Some juries may find such claims hard to believe.

4.   Even if inflation is netted out, difficult predictions remain. Economists dispute the stability of the real interest rate, and those who consider it stable argue about its level. The real interest rate fluctuates notoriously in the short term; most claims of stability relate only to the long-term real interest rate. Yet most courts that have discussed the issue have assumed plaintiff will make short-term investments. Minor differences in the estimate of the real interest rate can make enormous differences in judgments. The Court sanctions any estimate between 1 and 3 percent. For our twenty-nine-year-old worker earning $15,000 per year, a 1 percent discount yields an estimate of $451,614 for the present value of lost wages. A 2 percent discount yields an estimate of $382,331; a 3 percent discount yields $327,479.

5.   Litigants and juries who net out inflation must also predict what plaintiff's real wages would have been — his wage at the time of injury plus all increases from sources other than inflation. Some wage increases result from productivity gains, and some are rewards for long service. The expected earnings of a second-year law student far exceed his summer clerk's salary. His productivity will increase vastly with education and experience, and his firm's compensation structure will be designed to reward those productivity increases as well as to reward partners with a share of the income produced by associates and staff. A middle-age loading helper such as Pfeifer will have less spectacular gains, but he will have some. He should at least share in overall productivity gains that arise from improved technology and similar factors. The best argument for the total offset rule is that overall productivity gains, which vary from year to year, have usually been within the range of estimates for the real interest rate. It is not unreasonable to expect this coincidence to continue, although there is no reason in theory that it should. Any sort of offset formula can deal only with such overall or average gains; it will always be necessary to take evidence on individual variations. And even the overall gains can be misleading; productivity gains are distributed unevenly across industries.

6.   Should Pfeifer's award for pain and suffering be discounted to present value? The Court seems to assume not, and this is typical. Some

courts ignore the issue; some instruct juries not to discount pain and suffering. But these losses will also continue far into the future; Pfeifer will receive money today for pain he will suffer in twenty years. Would failure to discount these losses be a fair trade-off for the refusal to award prejudgment interest on past pain and suffering? Such a trade-off would work to plaintiff's advantage in cases of long-term injuries, and to defendant's advantage in cases where most of the suffering is over before trial. In both groups of cases there would be a deviation from the compensatory ideal. Are these deviations defensible on the ground that adjustments for inflation and interest make little sense when the original number is picked as haphazardly as the compensation for pain and suffering? Or are they just wrong?

One case that assumes pain and suffering should be discounted is Abernathy v. Superior Hardwoods, 704 F.2d 963, 973-974 (7th Cir. 1983). Plaintiff's lawyer had suggested $10 per day for pain and suffering. The court assumed the jury could not have picked a higher figure, discounted that figure to present value at a real interest rate of 2 percent, and on the basis of this calculation found the jury's verdict excessive. It ordered a new trial unless plaintiff accepted a remittitur of $138,204.39. Should the plaintiff take the new trial and change his final argument?

7.   One wonders about the capacity of jurors to handle discount calculations with or without allowances for inflation and productivity. Witnesses can illustrate the calculations, but that may be little help if the jury does not accept all of the witness's assumptions. Astonishingly, some judges simply instruct jurors to discount to present value, without explaining what that means or how to do it. One argument in favor of the total offset rule is that it eliminates all but the simplest calculations; it is enough to multiply the current wage by the remaining work expectancy. Indeed, the Pennsylvania court claims, "We are able to reflect the impact of inflation in these cases without specifically submitting this question to the jury." Kaczkowski v. Bolubasz, 491 Pa. 561, 583, 421 A.2d 1027, 1039 (1980). How likely do you think it is that an uninstructed jury will ignore inflation?

8.   Do not forget that the predictions discussed in *Jones & Laughlin* and these notes presuppose another one: the prediction of how long plaintiff will be disabled. His recovery may be quicker or slower or more or less complete than any doctor or jury can predict.

9.   One way to substantially reduce the difficulties of predicting future losses and economic events is to determine and pay damages periodically. That is the practice in some foreign countries, and it is authorized in this country in administrative schemes such as worker's compensation laws. Why don't we do that in personal injury litigation? Is it just habit and tradition? Avoiding an administrative burden on the courts? Protecting the right to jury trial? Fear of creating incentives to malinger? Or

assuring the lawyer quick payment of his contingent fee? Does it matter that administrative schemes for periodic payment make much less individualized determinations of damage?

The increasing frequency of very large judgments has triggered experimentation with periodic *payment* of judgments. Some of these experiments have provided for periodic *determination* of the rate of inflation and of whether plaintiff is still alive. Some settlements have been funded with annuities that pay a guaranteed and inflatable sum for as long as the victim lives. But no one has undertaken any periodic determinations that would require periodic hearings.

NOTES ON DAMAGES IN FOREIGN CURRENCY

1.   Changes in the value of money are even more problematic in international litigation. Consider a U.S. suit by a Swiss seller against a U.S. buyer for a purchase price stated in francs. Courts have traditionally rendered judgment in their own currency, converting foreign currency obligations as of the day of breach or the day of judgment. Conversion as of the day of breach more nearly places him in the position he would have occupied had he been paid on time. Conversion as of the day of judgment more nearly places him in the position he would have occupied had he sued and collected in Switzerland. Which is preferable? Does it matter whether the franc is appreciating or depreciating against the dollar? Would it matter if the buyer were deliberately speculating on a decline in the value of francs? Should the seller have to know about that?

2.   The Treaty of Rome requires members of the European Common Market to render judgment for creditors of member countries in the creditor's home currency. The House of Lords has adopted that rule more generally, and has provided that if such a judgment is collected in the United Kingdom, currency will be converted as near as possible to the day of payment. Miliangos v. George Frank (Textiles), Ltd., [1976] A.C. 443. Does that restore the plaintiff to his rightful position even more effectively than conversion as of the day of breach? Or does that depend on whether plaintiff would have already spent the money?

3.   The foreign currency debt is the simplest possible foreign currency case. For a taste of the possible complexities, suppose a German manufacturer defaults on a contract to deliver machinery to a U.S.-owned factory in Milan. The buyer may have made partial payments in marks and suffered consequential damages in lira; both losses will show up on the bottom line in dollars, and the litigation may be before an arbitrator in London. There is no contract stating an obligation in a specific currency; seller's obligation was to deliver machinery. What currency

should buyer's losses be valued in? If that is not the currency of judgment or collection, as of what date should currency be converted?

4.   One of the few things that should be clear in this area is that the choice of currency should control the choice of interest rate. If Swiss interest rates are low because Swiss inflation is low, and British interest rates are high because British inflation is high, plaintiff should not be able to collect British interest rates on a loss measured in the more stable Swiss currency.

CHAPTER 3

Preventing Harm: The Measure of Injunctive Relief

Introductory Note

This chapter has two organizational schemes operating simultaneously. They are substantially parallel, so most things are in the right order for either organization. But the section headings can reflect only one of the two organizations.

The sections are entitled Preventive Injunctions, Reparative Injunctions, and Structural Injunctions. The three uses of injunctions are worth distinguishing, even though many of the same problems arise in all three contexts.

But the three section headings suggest a sharper distinction between the sections than really exists. The main point of the chapter appears in the chapter title: The Measure of Injunctive Relief. Just as chapter 2 asked how much money plaintiff gets in a damage case, this chapter asks how much injunction plaintiff gets in an injunction case.

A. PREVENTIVE INJUNCTIONS

HUMBLE OIL & REFINING CO. v. HARANG
262 F. Supp. 39 (E.D. La. 1966)

RUBIN, District Judge.

At the start of this litigation, the plaintiff seeks a preliminary injunction to prevent one of the defendants, Jack F. Harang, from destroying "any document, record, check, map or writing relating to" certain transactions entered into by Harang or by a corporation which he is alleged to control.

The complaint alleges that Harang or other persons acting at his command or urging will conceal, destroy, or otherwise place these documents beyond the reach of the court unless enjoined from doing so. It supports this allegation by an affidavit of one of the lawyers for the plaintiff which states:

> Affiant is informed and believes and hence states that Harang has already attempted to secure the destruction of certain records reflecting his connection with said ex-employee. Because of the nature of the frauds practiced upon plaintiff, the concealment already accomplished, and the destruction of records already sought, affiant verily believes and, therefore, states that Harang will attempt to conceal further written evidence against him. . . .

The charges made in the complaint are briefly as follows: Harang entered into a conspiracy with a geologist who was then an employee of the plaintiff and who had access to confidential geophysical and geological information belonging to the plaintiff. The geologist-employee (now of course no longer an employee) would advise Harang of the plaintiff's proposed operations or acquisitions in a given area so as to permit Harang individually or through an intermediary to take leases or farmouts before the plaintiff could do so. Harang would then cause his agent or lease broker to offer to sell the leases or farmouts to the plaintiff or to other operators. As a result, Harang and the ex-employee made large profits in a number of transactions and have also gained secret overriding royalty interests for which neither has accounted to anyone. To conceal his part in these transactions, the geologist-employee set up a controlled corporation, Tammany Enterprises, Inc., and Harang used a wholly owned corporation, Geological, Geophysical Associates, Inc. . . .

An injunction should be issued only to prevent irreparable injury, but the rush of a litigant to the courthouse to seek the court's aid in restraint of an adverse party is not justified merely because it is alleged that, in the absence of judicial prohibition, an event may occur, the consequences of which cannot be reversed. The necessity for the injunction must be demonstrated clearly. Injunctions will not be issued merely to allay the fears and apprehensions or to soothe the anxieties of the parties.

It is apparent that the plaintiff may be irreparably injured if the evidentiary documents necessary to prove its claim are destroyed or otherwise put beyond the reach of the court. But this is true in every situation in which proof of a claim rests on documentary evidence; the parties may be irreparably injured if the documents are destroyed. Were the fact that a party to a lawsuit would suffer irreparable injury if a document were destroyed the sole test for the issuance of an injunction to prevent its destruction, injunctions should issue in every case in which important documents are within the control of either party. Obviously, this is not done and it cannot and should not be done. When the party who seeks an injunction shows potential irreparable injury, he has established merely one essential condition for relief. He must demonstrate in addition that there is real danger that the acts to be enjoined will occur, that there is no other remedy available, and that, under these circumstances, the court should exercise its discretion to afford the unusual relief provided by its injunction.

It goes without saying that Rule 34 of the Federal Rules of Civil Procedure embodies the normal procedure for the discovery of documents. . . . Counsel for the plaintiff correctly points out that . . . Rule 37 provides no penalty if the defendant should destroy the records sought in this case before an order for their production can be obtained. The defendant, however, testified that he had all of the original records in his possession, and had no intention of destroying them. His counsel made an offer at the trial of the rule to exchange documents in an orderly discovery procedure. The plaintiff offered no proof that there was an imminent threat of destruction or concealment of the evidentiary documents before a satisfactory order could be obtained under Rule 34, except the otherwise unsupported affidavit already quoted. This proof was not adequate to meet the burden that rests upon the plaintiff to demonstrate that the extraordinary remedy sought by it should be granted in the face of the defendant's testimony and the offer of defendant's counsel. . . .

It is true that the injunction sought would cause no hardship to the defendant since it would command him merely to do what he testified in open court that he had every intention of doing. Nonetheless, the lack of hardship on the defendant is not of itself sufficient reason for granting an injunction. The proper case for an injunction must be made out by the plaintiff, and it does not suffice to say, "Issue it because it won't hurt the other party." . . .

NOTES ON RIPENESS AND PREVENTIVE INJUNCTIONS

1. The injunction against future violations of law seeks to maintain plaintiff in his rightful position — to ensure that he is not illegally made worse off. It seeks to prevent harm rather than compensate for harm already suffered. This is the hallmark of coercive relief, of which injunctions are by far the most important example.

An injunction is simply a court order to do or refrain from doing some particular thing. The injunction against future violations of law is the simplest use of the injunction. Defendants may be ordered not to discriminate in employment, not to fix prices, not to pollute a stream, not to build a dam, not to trespass on plaintiff's property, etc.

2. This chapter examines the scope of the injunction. With respect to both compensatory and coercive remedies, the goal is to restore or main-

tain plaintiff's rightful position. This leads to a presumption, subject to certain exceptions, that wrongdoers should compensate for all the harm they cause. But courts have never believed, even as an initial presumption, that they should prevent all the harm wrongdoers might cause. Plaintiff must first make a threshold showing that a preventive order is necessary.

3. One can imagine courts enjoining every resident of the United States from violating any rule of statutory or common law. Such an injunction would make any violation of law contempt of court. But would it have any real meaning? Would people inclined to violate the laws be any more likely to obey an injunction repeating them? One function of injunctions is to individuate the law's command, specifying its application to a particular defendant in a particular situation. A realistic threat of violation is generally held prerequisite to such individuation. But why should that be the rule? Why isn't it enough that someone make an individuated request?

4. In *Humble,* we have a real plaintiff who genuinely fears that unlawful activity is about to occur to his serious injury. Why does the court deny an injunction in that case? Why do we require plaintiff to prove a real danger? What harm is there in ordering a defendant not to destroy documents that he cannot lawfully destroy and does not intend to destroy anyway? Why would defendant resist the injunction if he does not intend to destroy the documents?

5. One reason may be that both sides are seeking tactical advantage in subsequent discovery disputes. Such disputes may arise in many ways. Defendant may be lying. That is, he may presently intend to destroy documents. He may not intend to now, but he may change his mind later. Someone may inadvertently destroy documents. If any documents turn up missing, plaintiff will suspect destruction. Defendant may claim the documents never existed, or that he never had them, or that they were innocently destroyed without any thought of litigation. Plaintiff may make unfounded charges, or even knowingly false charges, that defendant destroyed documents. The court must pass on such charges, and an injunction affects the relevant procedure. Chapter 8 will consider in detail the means of enforcing injunctions. But you have to know something about those means now, in order to understand what is at stake if an injunction is issued and if it is not.

6. *The contempt power.* Violating an injunction is contempt of court. Contempt is a criminal offense if done wilfully. Plaintiff may bring the offense to the attention of the court, and the court decides whether to ask the prosecutor to prosecute the contempt. Defendant is entitled to most of the protections of criminal procedure.

Plaintiff may also cite defendant for civil contempt. Civil contempt is a remedial proceeding, and plaintiff prosecutes it himself. In compensatory civil contempt, the court grants compensation for any harm plaintiff suffered as a result of defendant's violation of the injunction. Compensation in contempt generally includes attorneys' fees and generally is awarded without jury trial.

Most important is coercive civil contempt, in which the court imposes conditional penalties to coerce defendant into obedience. These penalties are civil, but they may include fines or imprisonment or both. There is no limit to the penalties that can be imposed in coercive civil contempt, but the penalties must be conditional: Defendant must be able to avoid them. The court often specifies what steps defendant must take to "purge himself of contempt" and thereby avoid coercive penalties. The effect is to make the original injunction more specific, and sometimes more demanding.

Thus, if the court found that defendant had destroyed some documents in violation of the injunction but that many documents remained, it might specify that the penalty for any further destruction would be a fine of $100 per page destroyed. Or it might order defendant to deliver the documents to the court for safekeeping, and impose a fine of $1,000 per day until the documents were delivered. Or it might imprison defendant until he revealed the location of the remaining documents and agreed to turn them over to the court. If defendant had already destroyed all or most of the documents, the court might conclude that there was little to be gained by further coercion and impose criminal punishment for the past offense instead. Or it could order compensation if it could find a way to measure plaintiff's losses. Or it could do all three: criminal punishment for past violations, civil coercion to achieve future compliance, and compensation for past harm.

This array of enforcement devices makes contempt a potentially powerful remedy. In addition, contempt citations often go to the head of docket. They can be adjudicated promptly and as summarily as the facts permit. This further increases the attractiveness of contempt as an enforcement device. But all of this is in the discretion of the court. The contempt power may be ruthless or toothless, depending on the individual judge and his reaction to the individual case.

7. Contempt remedies must be compared to the remedies that are available if no injunction issued. In the ordinary case of common law tort or statutory violation, plaintiff's remedy in the absence of an injunction would be an ordinary action for damages. In addition, once he has proven one violation, it will be much easier to get an injunction against any future violations.

In *Humble Oil*, the remedies are less clear. Destroying documents is apparently not a tort. Professor Oesterle surveyed remedies for document destruction and found all options inadequate. Oesterle, A Private Litigant's Remedies for an Opponent's Inappropriate Destruction of Relevant Documents, 61 Tex. L. Rev. 1185 (1983). Under most modern discovery rules, a litigant seeking documents simply sends a written request to the other side. The court becomes involved only if the other litigant refuses to honor the request. Then the requesting party can file a motion to compel production of the documents. Federal Civil Rule 37 authorizes sanctions, including contempt and barring of claims or defenses to which the documents were relevant, if a litigant violates an order to produce. But there is no explicit authorization for a remedy if a litigant shreds requested documents before the court issues an order to produce. Many state rules are identical. Some courts have stretched the rule or asserted inherent power to penalize litigants for destroying documents before an order to produce, but their authority to do so is sketchy. The court in *Humble Oil* assumes that no such power exists.

Destroying documents with intent to prevent a litigant from seeing them is a criminal offense — obstruction of justice. But Oesterle could find no prosecutions arising out of private litigation. There is also an evidentiary inference that documents would have revealed information adverse to the position of the party that destroyed them. But there are many restrictions on use of the inference. Since Oesterle wrote, one court has recognized a tort claim against defendants who intentionally destroy evidence after promising to preserve it. Smith v. Superior Court, 151 Cal. App. 3d 451, 198 Cal. Rptr. 829 (1984).

8.   Do tactical considerations justify the ripeness rule? Would plaintiff have too great a tactical advantage if he could get an injunction for the asking and file a contempt citation at the first violation? Or does the rule give defendant a free violation? It takes one violation or a serious threat to get an injunction, and a second to get any serious efforts at enforcement. Of course, if that first violation does any harm, plaintiff will usually have an ordinary action for damages. Destruction of documents is an atypical context; human defendants do not generally get the one free bite accorded the common law dog. Even in the discovery context, Oesterle found that some courts have ordered all parties not to destroy documents. These orders were generally entries in a larger order resulting from a discovery conference. Probably these orders were issued by consent. Or perhaps calling them discovery orders instead of injunctions seemed to shift the doctrinal context and defuse the ripeness issue.

9.   Tactical advantage may not be the only interest at stake in ripeness arguments. Might defendant fear that an injunction would injure his reputation by implicitly finding that he is the sort of person who would destroy evidence? Or is that circular? If the court enjoined violations routinely on plaintiff's mere request, an injunction would not indicate anything about the character of the defendant. But might people assume that where there's smoke there's fire, and that injunctions don't issue unnecessarily no matter what the rules are? Assuming that these are legitimate fears, how do they stack up against plaintiff's fears?

10.   The court in *Humble* does not rely on potential harm to defendant, and says the absence of such harm is irrelevant. Does that mean

there is no reason at all for the rule? Or only that the rule presumes harm to defendant? In Marshall v. Lane Processing, 606 F.2d 518 (8th Cir. 1979), another court held that harm to defendant is irrelevant. In that case, the government had shown some risk of future violations of the child labor laws. The court reversed the trial judge for balancing that risk against damage to defendant's reputation and credit worthiness and resulting financial hardship. On the other hand, in Securities & Exchange Commission v. Warren, 583 F.2d 115 (3d Cir. 1978), the court did consider harm to defendant's reputation and financial opportunities in vacating an old injunction based on a single incident ten years before. The court found the continuing risk of future violations quite small. One of the grounds for vacating a final judgment of injunction is that the injunction is causing undue hardship to defendant; that provided the occasion to talk explicitly about the concerns that apparently underlie the rule in *Humble*. The consequences of being enjoined are particularly serious in the securities business, because the injunction must be disclosed in any transaction defendant is associated with. Many issuers, tender offerors, and proxy contestants would understandably prefer to dissociate him.

11. The rule does not require that defendant already have committed one violation before he can be enjoined from committing another. Nor does it require that defendant explicitly threaten a violation or admit his intention to violate. It is enough that there be a substantial or realistic threat of violation. An interesting example is FMC Corp. v. Varco International, 677 F.2d 500 (5th Cir. 1982). Robert L. Witt resigned his position with plaintiff and went to work for Best Industries, a subsidiary of Varco and a competitor of plaintiff. Plaintiff sued Witt and Varco to prevent disclosure of its trade secrets. Best's president and Witt both testified that they planned to use none of plaintiff's trade secrets. Best's president testified that he would not restrict Witt's work, but would rely on Witt to preserve the trade secrets. The district court denied a preliminary injunction pending trial, but the court of appeals reversed. It said:

> Since Best does not intend to limit Witt and since Witt himself indicated that he does not know exactly what constitutes a trade secret, it appears very possible that a trade secret will be revealed in violation of Witt's agreement with FMC. Witt is employed by Best in a position where he will be constantly called upon to decide what he believes he can and cannot properly disclose to Best. Best will expect Witt to contribute new ideas to improve the efficiency of any manufacturing process that ultimately is developed for the swivel joints, and Best's president testified that Witt's compensation and future with Best are directly dependent upon how well he performs his assigned duties. . . .
>
> Even assuming the best of good faith, Witt will have difficulty preventing his knowledge of FMC's . . . techniques from infiltrating his work.
>
> We therefore REVERSE the order of the district court and GRANT the injunction. Pending a trial on the merits in this case, Robert L. Witt is enjoined from divulging any information constituting a trade secret that he acquired during

his work as an employee of the FMC Corporation, and Best Industries is enjoined from placing or maintaining Witt in a position that poses an inherent threat of disclosure or use of FMC's trade secrets.

Id. at 504-505.

12. The requirement that there be a substantial threat of unlawful conduct before an injunction will issue to prevent it is one aspect of the ripeness doctrine. In addition to a real threat of unlawful conduct, plaintiff must show a real threat that he personally will be harmed by it. A dramatic example is City of Los Angeles v. Lyons, 461 U.S. 95 (1983), in which plaintiff challenged a police practice of choking arrestees until they were unconscious. The police had already choked Lyons once. His damage suit for that incident was obviously ripe; damage claims hardly ever raise ripeness issues. (One exception is anticipatory repudiation of contracts.) But the Court held his suit to enjoin future chokings unripe, in part because he could not show any likelihood that he personally would be choked again. Id. at 111. There were four dissenters.

13. Ripeness is partly a matter of timing; unripe cases may ripen. It is sometimes said that the threatened harm must be imminent, or even immediate. That is true only in the sense that ripe threats are usually imminent threats; a threat of long-delayed harm is likely to be contingent and speculative. But where it is possible to say with substantial certainty that a harm will occur eventually, and the facts are sufficiently developed for reliable decision, a suit to enjoin that harm is ripe even if the harm is not imminent. An example is the Regional Rail Reorganization Act Cases, 419 U.S. 102 (1974). Special legislation and court decisions pursuant to it had set in motion a chain of events that would "inexorably" lead to conveyance of all the assets of the bankrupt Penn Central Railroad. Although the conveyance was still a long time off, the Court found it inevitable and decided three constitutional challenges to it.

14. The ripeness doctrine is essential to understanding the scope of preventive injunctions. It is also closely related to another important restriction on injunctions, the requirement that plaintiff be threatened with injury that is irreparable. We will consider the scope of injunctive relief in this chapter and the irreparable injury rule in chapter 4.

NICHOLSON v. CONNECTICUT HALF-WAY HOUSE
153 Conn. 507, 218 A.2d 383 (1966)

[Plaintiffs were property owners and residents of a middle-class residential block in Hartford. Defendant purchased one of the homes in the block for use as a halfway house for parolees from the Connecticut state prison.

Before the halfway house could begin operation, the trial court enjoined it as a nuisance. Defendant appealed.]

THIM, J., delivered the opinion of the court. . . .

A fair test of whether a proposed use constitutes a nuisance is "the reasonableness of the use of the property in the particular locality under the circumstances of the case." Wetstone v. Cantor, 144 Conn. 77, 80, 127 A.2d 70. To meet this test in the instant case, the evidence must show that the defendant's proposed use of the property under the circumstances is unreasonable.

Here the proposed use of the defendant's property, in and of itself, is lawful. The only factual grounds offered to support the relief granted are the fears of the plaintiffs that the residents of the defendant's halfway house will commit criminal acts in the neighborhood and the finding that the proposed use has had a depreciative effect on land values in this area. The first of these grounds goes to the core of the plaintiffs' complaint. The real objection of the plaintiffs is to the presence in the neighborhood of persons with a demonstrated capacity for criminal activity. They fear future manifestations of such activity in their neighborhood. This present fear of what may happen in the future, although genuinely felt, rests completely on supposition. The anticipation by the plaintiffs of the possible consequences of the defendant's proposed use of the property can be characterized as a speculative and intangible fear. They have neither alleged nor offered evidence to prove any specific acts or pattern of behavior which would cause them harm so as to warrant the drastic injunctive relief granted by the court.

It is clear that the power of equity to grant injunctive relief may be exercised only under demanding circumstances.

> No court of equity should ever grant an injunction merely because of the fears or apprehensions of the party applying for it. Those fears or apprehensions may exist without any substantial reason. Indeed they may be absolutely groundless. Restraining the action of an individual or a corporation by injunction is an extraordinary power, always to be exercised with caution, never without the most satisfactory reasons.

Goodwin v. New York, N.H. & H.R. Co., 43 Conn. 494, 500. The fears and apprehensions of the plaintiffs in the present case, based as they are on speculation, cannot justify the granting of injunctive relief.

The plaintiffs' claim of depreciated property values is likewise ineffective as a basis for supporting the issuance of an injunction. The mere depreciation of land values, caused in this case by the subjective apprehensions of neighboring property owners and their potential buyers, cannot sustain an injunction sought on the ground of nuisance.

The plaintiffs have cited Brainard v. West Hartford, 140 Conn. 631, 103 A.2d 135, for the proposition that an unreasonable use of property which is merely anticipatory may be enjoined. In that case, however, the proposed use, a town dump in a residential area, was a known quantity whose attributes as a nuisance could be readily adjudged prior to the undertaking.[1] A similar factual showing has not been produced in the present case. The plaintiffs have also cited Jack v. Torrant, 136 Conn. 414, 71 A.2d 705, in support of their overall position. That case involved the operation of an embalming and undertaking establishment in a residential district and is clearly distinguishable on its facts from the present situation.

Our conclusion is not intended to serve as a comment on the future operations of the defendant. We only hold that, under the present circumstances, there has been an insufficient factual showing that the defendant will make any unreasonable use of its property or that the prospective residents of its halfway house will engage in unlawful activities in the surrounding neighborhood. For the reasons already discussed, the granting of the injunction by the trial court was not justified at this time. . . .

MORE NOTES ON RIPENESS

1. The finding in Brainard v. Town of West Hartford, set out in footnote 1 of *Nicholson*, was based on experience at a similar dump operated by defendant. In Jack v. Torrant, also discussed in *Nicholson*, the court held that any funeral home in a residential area would be a nuisance, no matter how it was run, because it would depress the neighborhood residents by constantly reminding them of death. Does the explanation of these three cases turn on how certain the court is that the proposed use will actually be a nuisance? Would *Nicholson* have come out differently if plaintiffs had argued the halfway house would depress them by constantly reminding them of crime?

2. Different courts have formulated the required degree of certainty in different ways. See Davis v. Miller, 212 Ga. 836, 839, 96 S.E.2d 498, 502 (1957) (injunction against construction of service station denied; nuisance and harm must be "not merely possible, but to a reasonable degree certain"); Fink v. Board of Trustees of Southern Illinois University, 71 Ill. App. 2d 276, 281, 218 N.E.2d 240, 244 (1966) (injunction against discharge of sewage granted; test is whether "it clearly appears that a nuisance will necessarily result"); Brent v. City of Detroit, 27 Mich. App. 628, 631, 183 N.W.2d 908, 909 (1970) (injunction against construction of

---

1. The trial court in *Brainard* found that "[t]he establishment of a dump on the land purchased by the defendant would greatly depreciate the value of the plaintiffs' land, creating a noxious smoke, litter, offensive and unhealthy odors, rats, vermin, insects and fire danger."

swimming pool denied; "courts are reluctant to enjoin anticipatory nuisances absent a showing of actual nuisance or the strong probability of such result").

3. What purpose does the ripeness doctrine serve in *Nicholson* and similar cases? Isn't the key idea simply that socially useful enterprises that might be run lawfully and harmlessly should not be enjoined because of the possibility that they might be run unlawfully and harmfully? Does this suggest that the likelihood of harmful consequences should be balanced against the benefits to be created by the enterprise?

4. The ripeness doctrine cannot fully solve the problem of uncertainty about the future. Development of the halfway house in *Nicholson* must proceed subject to the risk of damage liability and the risk that operation will be enjoined if the court later concludes that a nuisance has been created. This is an incentive to careful operation, but even skillful and well-intentioned defendants may not be able to prevent a nuisance. What result on a second application for injunction if an inmate of the halfway house commits a serious crime against a neighborhood child in the first few months of operation? Suppose defendant alleged that it was unable to secure financing with the threat of a second lawsuit hanging over it, and sought a declaratory judgment that operation of the halfway house would be lawful. Would that case be ripe?

5. Suppose that instead of seeking to enjoin operation of the halfway house altogether, plaintiffs had sought an injunction conditioning its operation on certain safeguards, such as exclusion of sex offenders, drug addicts, alcoholics, and parolees without jobs. Would that case be ripe? Would ripeness depend on the evidence presented concerning the groups mentioned? Suppose plaintiffs simply sought an injunction ordering defendants to prevent the inmates from harming anyone? Would that case be ripe? Would the injunction do any good?

6. The court also held that depreciated property values, when caused by subjective apprehensions, are not grounds for an injunction. Is that a ripeness holding, or a holding on the merits? Will the complaint about depreciated property values ever be any riper?

NOTE ON CONSTITUTIONAL AND REMEDIAL RIPENESS

Ripeness is a constitutional and jurisdictional doctrine as well as an equitable and remedial one. Federal courts, and most state courts, have jurisdiction only over "cases and controversies"; an unripe dispute is held not to be a case or controversy.

Obviously the two ripeness doctrines are closely related, and a case that is not ripe under one is unlikely to be ripe under the other. But the doctrines serve different primary purposes and thus might occasionally have different content. The constitutional and jurisdictional ripeness doctrine primarily serves political values. The traditional explanation emphasizes allocation of power between courts and the other branches of government, and avoidance of premature decision of constitutional questions. See, e.g., A. Bickel, The Least Dangerous Branch (1962). Ripeness and related jurisdictional doctrines also help allocate power between today's courts and future courts, by postponing resolution of some legal issues. Brilmayer, The Jurisprudence of Article III: Perspectives on the "Case or Controversy" Requirement, 93 Harv. L. Rev. 297, 302-306 (1979). And such doctrines serve values of self-determination and adequate representation, by ensuring that a litigant with a present personal stake will be heard before he and others like him are bound by a new rule of law. Id. at 306-315. That is, it protects nonparties who could be affected by litigation that is motivated by ideology or paternalism rather than immediate self-interest.

How relevant are these concerns in cases like *Humble* and *Nicholson*? Is there any other potential plaintiff more directly affected than the actual plaintiffs? Is there any other branch of government with a better claim to power over the issue? There might be in *Nicholson*, if a zoning commission or the like has approved the project. Modern environmental and land use regulation does much of the work traditionally done by the common law of nuisance. But this development cannot explain the ripeness doctrine, which dates from a time when nuisance litigation was the only or at least primary source of regulation. Courts have accommodated nuisance law to modern regulation by adjusting its substantive content, not by inventing ripeness rules.

The concern for defendants and their legitimate activities in *Humble* and *Nicholson* is attenuated or irrelevant in some cases better explained by constitutional ripeness. For example, courts enjoin enforcement of unconstitutional statutes, but only if there is a threat of prosecution. If plaintiff fears prosecution but cannot prove the basis of his fears, the injunctive remedy is unavailable, and he must risk imprisonment to get a ruling on his constitutional rights. What explains the ripeness rule in that context? There's no social utility in enforcing unconstitutional statutes, is there? Is it likely that the injunction would hurt the prosecutor's reputation? Could there ever be a serious dispute about whether the prosecutor had violated such an injunction? Does that depend on whether the court enjoins all applications of the statute or only some?

The political explanations fit better: An injunction against enforcement of an unconstitutional statute seems to resolve a constitutional question, set aside a decision of the legislature, and restrict the operation of the executive. This is held to be unjustified in the absence of a ripe dispute — a plaintiff who can show himself to be directly affected. But how strong are those concerns when the prosecutor denies any intention to enforce the statute anyway? If the plaintiff is genuinely afraid to exercise his asserted constitutional rights, he is personally affected. Why not enjoin enforcement as to him, without deciding the constitutional issue, until and unless the prosecutor states a desire to enforce?

This note has emphasized the differences between the two ripeness doctrines because they are less apparent than the similarities. There is one argument for a ripeness rule that applies equally well to both constitutional and remedial ripeness. That is the argument that courts will make better decisions if the facts are fully developed. Could that argument have been used in either *Humble* or *Nicholson?*

Sec'y of Labor

MARSHALL v. GOODYEAR TIRE & RUBBER CO.
554 F.2d 730 (5th Cir. 1977)

Before GEWIN, RONEY and HILL, Circuit Judges.

GEWIN, Circuit Judge.

After unsuccessful informal attempts to resolve the dispute, the Secretary of Labor sued appellant Goodyear Tire & Rubber Company . . . alleging a violation of the Age Discrimination in Employment Act of 1967. . . . The allegation concerned the discharge of William G. Reed, Jr., and appellee sought to enjoin further violations and to recover Reed's lost wages. The district court found the violation alleged and granted the requested relief, including a nationwide injunction against further violations. . . .   * DC: granted injunctions

[margin note: Enjoin further viols. + recover lost wages.]

Appellant primarily complains of the scope of the injunction. The court found a single violation — Reed's discharge — involving only the actions of the Auburndale store manager. This limited finding does not warrant such broad injunctive relief. Issuance of an injunction rests primarily in the informed discretion of the district court. Yet injunctive relief is a drastic remedy, not to be applied as a matter of course.

In determining the limitations on a district court's discretion to issue an injunction, it is appropriate to look to the ADEA, to Fair Labor Standards Act cases, since the ADEA can be enforced through FLSA provisions, and to cases involving other federal statutes regulating employment discrimination. ADEA §7(b), 29 U.S.C. §626(b), states that "[i]n any action brought to enforce this chapter the court shall have jurisdiction to grant such legal or equitable relief *as may be appropriate* to effectuate the purposes of this chapter. . . ." (emphasis added). . . .

Equal Pay Act, FLSA, and ADEA cases all establish that a nationwide or companywide injunction is appropriate only when the facts indicate a company policy or practice in violation of the statute. For example, in the leading ADEA case of Hodgson v. First Federal, 455 F.2d 818 (5th Cir.

1972), we held that the evidence entitled the Secretary to a broader injunction than that issued by the district court. The employer had a main office and five branches, all in one county. Evidence indicated that the hiring was done centrally by one personnel officer and that he had rejected several applicants for tellers' positions because of their age. The district court enjoined future violations of the ADEA "with regard to the hiring of tellers." On appeal this court concluded that the Secretary's evidence indicated the existence of a *discriminatory hiring policy* by the employer. One of the applicants, for example, was rejected for any job, not just for a teller's position. Moreover, the employer had also placed a newspaper advertisement seeking a "young man" for the position of financial advertising assistant. Inasmuch as the proof showed a *company policy* of hiring discrimination *extending beyond* the category of tellers' positions, a broad injunction against the employer's future discriminatory hiring based on age was appropriate.

This approach is also seen in Brennan v. J. M. Fields, Inc., 488 F.2d 443, 449-50 (5th Cir.), *cert. denied*, 419 U.S. 881 (1974). There this court affirmed the district court's issuance of an injunction against the employer's entire operations, which included more than sixty retail outlets, on the basis of violations of the Equal Pay Act at three of them. The Secretary defended the injunction on the ground that the New York office's close centralized supervision of wage scales and pay policies indicated a company policy with regard to the pay differential. This court agreed with that contention. Conversely, the Second Circuit has held that "absent a showing of a policy of discrimination which extends beyond the plants at issue . . . , there is no basis for a nationwide injunction." Hodgson v. Corning Glass Works, 474 F.2d 226, 236 (2d Cir. 1973) (Friendly, C.J.), *aff'd on other grounds*, 417 U.S. 188 (1974). Accordingly, the court limited the injunction's effect to the three plants in Corning, New York, where violations were shown, lifting its effect from the 26 other branch plants.[6]

The Secretary contends that in the instant case there is sufficient proof of multiple violations to warrant a nationwide injunction, relying on the proof of a discriminatory job order placed by the Lakeland store. There are several difficulties in accepting this position. The principal difficulty is that the evidence as to the Lakeland incident is slight, the district court made no findings with respect to it, and the court did not rely on it in determining the scope of the injunction. The court relied solely on Reed's discharge for its order and judgment. It made no finding of discriminatory company policy or practice. Indeed, the district judge ex-

---

6. The case of Wirtz v. Ocala Gas Company, 336 F.2d 236 (5th Cir. 1964), noted the general rule that an injunction is warranted where there is a likelihood of further violations. The complementary rule is obviously that an injunction's scope should not exceed the likely scope of future violations.

pressed the view that "Goodyear itself is committed to the principles of the Age Discrimination Act" and that Reed's discharge was the isolated action of Auburndale manager Coleman, who "believes that he can best run an organization if he has just got young people around."[7] . . .

In sum, the district judge relied only on the isolated fact of Reed's discriminatory discharge in enjoining appellant nationwide. He not only did not find a discriminatory company policy, he apparently found that the discharge resulted from store manager Coleman's individual prejudices. The latter may suggest the need for some form of injunctive relief. In light of the authorities discussed above, such relief should be limited to the Auburndale store. Consequently, we remand the case for the district court's further consideration of the scope of injunctive relief. . . .

J/ remand.
to reconsider
scope

NOTES ON THE SCOPE OF PREVENTIVE INJUNCTIONS

1. There are two remedies in *Marshall*. One remedy is $3,000 in back pay to Reed. This is basically a damage remedy, but because the plaintiff is the Secretary of Labor rather than Reed himself, the court talks in terms of an injunction to pay money. The Secretary might also have sought reinstatement for Reed, but apparently did not. Presumably, Reed did not wish to be reinstated. The measure of relief for Reed is the familiar one of restoring him to the position he would have occupied but for the wrongful discharge.

2. The rest of the remedy in *Marshall* is like the injunction sought in *Humble*. The court holds that the scope of the past violation determines the scope of the remedy against future violations. Is that a straightforward application of the rule in *Humble*? Has the Secretary established a propensity to age discrimination in the Auburndale store that creates an actual threat of future violations there but not elsewhere?

3. Suppose the court found that Reed was discharged because of a new company policy that assistant managers be under thirty. Should it enjoin that policy? All age discrimination in hiring and firing? All violations of the Age Discrimination in Employment Act? All employment discrimination? What propensity does the assistant manager policy show? Should the courts be as afraid of unnecessarily enjoining an adjudicated wrongdoer as a defendant against whom nothing has been proved?

---

7. The district judge, in his remarks at the end of trial, faulted Goodyear for not better policing the hiring decisions of local store managers, and he apparently thought a broad injunction would encourage greater oversight. The ADEA, however, does not require centralized supervision of employment decisions. Under the Act and the authorities cited above, therefore, imposition of that burden on the Company is unwarranted absent proof, at least, of a company policy or numerous violations.

Here is the standard doctrinal answer:

> A federal court has broad power to restrain acts which are of the same type or class as unlawful acts which the court has found to have been committed or whose commission in the future, unless enjoined, may fairly be anticipated from the defendant's conduct in the past. But the mere fact that a court has found that a defendant has committed an act in violation of a statute does not justify an injunction broadly to obey the statute and thus subject the defendant to contempt proceedings if he shall at any time in the future commit some new violation unlike and unrelated to that with which he was originally charged. . . . The breadth of [a National Labor Relations Board] order, like the injunction of a court, must depend upon the circumstances of each case, the purpose being to prevent violations, the threat of which in the future is indicated because of their similarity or relation to those unlawful acts which the Board has found to have been committed by the employer in the past.

NLRB v. Express Publishing Co., 312 U.S. 426, 435-437 (1941). How much help is that? How great a propensity must there be? Isn't the practical content of such a rule largely in the discretion of trial courts?

4. Federal Civil Rule 65(d) provides an independent ground for objecting to injunctions that simply copy out the statute and forbid all violations. It provides:

> Every order granting an injunction and every restraining order shall set forth the reasons for its issuance; shall be specific in terms; shall describe in reasonable detail, and not by reference to the complaint or other document, the act or acts sought to be restrained. . . .

In Payne v. Travenol Laboratories, 565 F.2d 895 (5th Cir. 1978), the court vacated an injunction against "discriminating on the basis of color, race, or sex in employment practices or conditions of employment in defendant's Cleveland, Mississippi facility." The court said the injunction "clearly fails to satisfy" Rule 65(d). "The word 'discriminating,' like the word 'monopolizing' is too general. . . . Such 'obey the law' injunctions cannot be sustained." Id. at 897-898.

Yet "obey-the-law" clauses are nearly standard practice in civil rights injunctions and in many other substantive fields as well. It is in the plaintiff's interest to have some clauses of the injunction drafted as specifically as possible, to avoid arguments about coverage and fair notice, and to also have catchall clauses worded as broadly as possible to cover any new developments and anything inadvertently omitted from the specific clauses. That preference tends to be reflected in injunctions, both because the parties submit draft injunctions to the judge for approval, and because by the time he has decided to issue an injunction, the judge shares the plaintiff's interest in discouraging disobedience or evasion by the defendant. Defendants do not object to catchall clauses nearly as often as one would expect in light of cases like *Payne* and *Express Publishing*.

Drafting specific decrees is often a difficult task. We will examine some of the problems in chapter 9, section B.

NOTE ON INDIVIDUAL AND CLASS INJUNCTIONS

Suppose Reed sued on his own behalf, and did not file as a class representative, or that class certification was denied because there were so few employees at the Auburndale store. Then what injunction should issue? An order not to discriminate against Reed? Or an order not to discriminate against anyone at the Auburndale store? Does Reed have standing to seek an injunction protecting anyone else? Should the scope of the injunction depend on whether there was a class certification? The issue can arise any time a court enjoins continuation of a policy that could be applied to others in the same way it was applied to plaintiff.

Many courts would order defendant not to apply the policy to anyone; that is especially true in the discrimination cases. The leading case is Galvan v. Levine, 490 F.2d 1255 (2d Cir. 1973), a suit to enjoin New York from denying unemployment compensation to persons who returned to Puerto Rico after losing their New York jobs. Judge Friendly reasoned that it would be a waste of time to argue and decide a motion for class certification, because the injunction in the individual case could protect the entire putative class. Subsequent cases have held that a class protected by the injunction must be indistinguishable from the individual plaintiffs in all respects. For example, in Hurley v. Ward, 584 F.2d 609 (2d Cir. 1978), the court affirmed an injunction restricting strip searches of the plaintiff, but vacated a clause extending the same relief to all inmates of the New York prison system, because there was no showing that the issues with respect to other prisoners were "identical to those raised by the searches of Hurley." Id. at 612.

Other cases hold that unless there is a class certification, an injunction can protect only the individual plaintiffs. In Zepeda v. United States Immigration & Naturalization Service, 753 F.2d 719 (9th Cir. 1985), the district court had enjoined the INS from searching any home without "reasonable suspicion, based on articulable facts," that aliens illegally in the country would be found there. Because he had not certified a class, the court of appeals restricted the injunction to the homes of the ten plaintiffs. Judge Timbers wrote a similar opinion in a prison discipline case. McKinnon v. Patterson, 568 F.2d 930 (2d Cir. 1977). But Timbers also joined the majority in Galvan v. Levine. The cases are collected in the majority and dissenting opinions in *Zepeda*.

The restrictive view draws substantial support from a series of Supreme Court cases. Each case in the series arose when the parties or the trial court assumed that class certification was a meaningless formality and didn't bother with it. In each case something subsequently went wrong with the named plaintiffs' claim: They were students and they graduated; they were job applicants and they were proven unqualified. In each case plaintiffs' lawyers tried to keep litigating on behalf of the putative class. And in each case the Supreme Court said the lack of a class certification was fatal. East Texas Motor Freight System v. Rodriguez, 431 U.S. 395 (1977); Pasadena City Board of Education v. Spangler, 427 U.S. 424, 429-430 (1976); Board of School Commissioners v. Jacobs, 420 U.S. 128 (1975). Two of these cases were discrimination cases, which have often been treated as inherently class actions. In two other cases where the named plaintiff's claim was mooted *after* a class certification, the Court allowed litigation to proceed on behalf of the class. Franks v. Bowman Transportation Co., 424 U.S. 747, 752-757 (1976); Sosna v. Iowa, 419 U.S. 393, 397-403 (1975).

These cases at least mean that the court could not enjoin Goodyear's policy of discrimination if anything happened to moot Reed's individual claim. Do they also mean that even if Reed is successful on the merits, the court could not enjoin discrimination against anyone but Reed? Is a class certification as magic when plaintiff wins as when he loses? The Supreme Court seems to think so, although it has not squarely addressed the question. It has said in a related context that the class action is "an exception to the usual rule that litigation is conducted by and on behalf of the individual named parties only," and that class certification is "peculiarly appropriate" in a case challenging a uniform government policy, because it saves resources "by permitting an issue potentially affecting every social security beneficiary to be litigated in an economical fashion under Rule 23." Califano v. Yamasaki, 442 U.S. 682, 700-701 (1979).

Should the class certification be magic? Insisting on careful attention to class certification requirements may protect absent class members if the named plaintiff loses on the merits. But if he wins, is there any reason to issue an injunction that protects only him? One possible reason is suggested by East Texas Motor Freight System v. Rodriguez, 431 U.S. 395 (1977). There, the putative class voted to reject the very remedy the named plaintiffs were seeking.

UNITED STATES v. W. T. GRANT CO.
345 U.S. 629 (1953)

Mr. Justice Clark delivered the opinion of the Court.

For the first time since the enactment of the Clayton Act in 1914 the Court is called upon to consider §8's prohibitions against interlocking corporate directorates. The Government appeals from judgments dis-

missing civil actions brought against Hancock and three pairs of corporations which he served as a director, W. T. Grant Co. and S. H. Kress &
Co., Sears Roebuck & Co. and Bond Stores, Inc., and Kroger Co. and
Jewel Tea Co., Inc. Alleging that the size and competitive relationship of
each set of companies brought the interlocks within the reach of §8, the
complaints asked the court to order the particular interlocks terminated
and to enjoin future violations of §8 by the individual and corporate
defendants. Soon after the complaints were filed, Hancock resigned from
the boards of Kress, Kroger and Bond. Disclosing the resignations by
affidavit, all of the defendants then moved to dismiss the actions as moot.
Treated as motions for summary judgment, they were granted by the
District Judge. He concluded that there is not "the slightest threat that
the defendants will attempt any future activity in violation of Section 8 [if
they have violated it already]. . . ." . . .

Both sides agree to the abstract proposition that voluntary cessation of
allegedly illegal conduct does not deprive the tribunal of power to hear
and determine the case, i.e., does not make the case moot. A controversy
may remain to be settled in such circumstances, e.g., a dispute over the
legality of the challenged practices. The defendant is free to return to his
old ways. This, together with a public interest in having the legality of the
practices settled, militates against a mootness conclusion. For to say that
the case has become moot means that the defendant is entitled to a
dismissal as a matter of right. The courts have rightly refused to grant
defendants such a powerful weapon against public law enforcement.[5]

The case may nevertheless be moot if the defendant can demonstrate
that "there is no reasonable expectation that the wrong will be repeated."[6] The burden is a heavy one. Here the defendants told the court
that the interlocks no longer existed and disclaimed any intention to
revive them. Such a profession does not suffice to make a case moot
although it is one of the factors to be considered in determining the
appropriateness of granting an injunction against the now-discontinued
acts.

Along with its power to hear the case, the court's power to grant
injunctive relief survives discontinuance of the illegal conduct. The purpose of an injunction is to prevent future violations, and, of course, it can
be utilized even without a showing of past wrongs. But the moving party
must satisfy the court that relief is needed. The necessary determination
is that there exists some cognizable danger of recurrent violation, some-

---

5. "When defendants are shown to have settled into a continuing practice or entered
into a conspiracy violative of antitrust laws, courts will not assume that it has been abandoned without clear proof. . . . It is the duty of the courts to beware of efforts to defeat
injunctive relief by protestations of repentance and reform, especially when abandonment
seems timed to anticipate suit, and there is probability of resumption." United States v.
Oregon State Medical Society, 343 U.S. 326, 333 (1952).
6. United States v. Aluminum Co. of America, 148 F.2d 416, 448.

thing more than the mere possibility which serves to keep the case alive. The chancellor's decision is based on all the circumstances; his discretion is necessarily broad and a strong showing of abuse must be made to reverse it. To be considered are the bona fides of the expressed intent to comply, the effectiveness of the discontinuance and, in some cases, the character of the past violations.

The facts relied on by the Government to show an abuse of discretion in this case are these: Hancock's three interlocking directorates viewed as three distinct violations, his failure to terminate them until after suit was filed despite five years of administrative attempts to persuade him of their illegality, his express refusal to concede that the interlocks in question were illegal under the statute and his failure to promise not to commit similar violations in the future.

Were we sitting as a trial court, this showing might be persuasive. But the Government must demonstrate that there was no reasonable basis for the District Judge's decision. In this we think it fails. An individual proclivity to violate the statute need not be inferred from the fact that three violations were charged, particularly since it is only recently that the Government has attempted systematic enforcement of §8. The District Court was not dealing with a defendant who follows one adjudicated violation with others. The only material before the District Judge on the supposed five years of administrative persuasion could easily support an inference that during that time the defendant and the Department of Justice were each trying to determine the legality of his directorships. The Government's remedy under the statute was plain. Postponement of suit indicates doubt on the prosecutor's part as much as intransigence on the defendant's. How much contrition should be expected of a defendant is hard for us to say. This surely is a question better addressed to the discretion of the trial court. The same can be said of the limited disclaimer of future intent. . . .

We conclude that, although the actions were not moot, no abuse of discretion has been demonstrated in the trial court's refusal to award injunctive relief. Moreover, the court stated its dismissals "would not be a bar to a new suit in case possible violations arise in the future." The judgments are affirmed.

MR. JUSTICE DOUGLAS, with whom MR. JUSTICE BLACK concurs, dissenting. . . .

Mr. Hancock served as a director for each of three sets of companies which, on the state of the pleadings before us, we must assume to have been competitive. The fact that he resigned under the pressure of these proceedings should not dispose of the case. We are dealing here with professionals whose technique for controlling enterprises and building empires was fully developed and well known long before Mr. Justice Brandeis was crying out against the evils of "the money trust." Mr. Hancock is and has been for some years a partner in the investment banking firm of Lehman Bros. In 1940 he testified that when Lehman Bros. did financing for a company it was their "traditional practice" to ask for representation on the board of directors.

It therefore seems to me that a District Judge, faced with violations such as were involved here, would want to know *first*, how investment bankers built their empires; *second*, how this particular firm built its own empire; *third*, the effect of these banker empires on competition between the companies which are tied to them.

The fact that the Lehman partner resigned to avoid a decision on the merits has little, if any, relevancy to the issue in the case, for we are here concerned with the *proclivity* of the house to indulge in the practice.

The relevant issues have never been weighed in this case. The District Court's ruling would be entitled to a presumption of validity if those various factors had been considered. But the District Court made no such considered judgment. It disposed of the case on the basis of mootness, a ruling now conceded to be erroneous. The case should go back for a consideration of the nature and extent of the web which this investment banking house has woven over industry and its effect on the "elimination of competition" within the meaning of §8 of the Clayton Act. Unless we know that much, we are in no position to judge the service an injunction against future violations may do. . . . .

NOTES ON MOOTNESS

1. Note the distinction in *Grant* between mootness sufficient to end the case or controversy and deprive the court of jurisdiction, and likelihood of repetition so low that relief should be withheld as a matter of discretion. Although one doctrine is labeled "constitutional," and the other "equitable," both arise only with respect to preventive relief. A claim for damages is never moot; it is never impossible to compensate for past harm. See, e.g., Powell v. McCormack, 395 U.S. 486, 495-500 (1969).

2. Defendant's voluntary cessation of allegedly wrongful conduct is one common source of mootness. Voluntary cessation cases are really a variation on one kind of ripeness case — cases where the defendant says he doesn't intend to do the harmful act. Normally, the fact that he has already done it once is sufficient to cause the court to take seriously plaintiff's fear that he will do it again. But sometimes the defendant says he's quit and won't do it again. That is, he says the normal inference from past conduct is not true in his case, and anticipatory relief aimed at preventing future repetitions is premature. Plaintiffs win more voluntary cessation cases than they do ripeness cases, because the past conduct hurts defendant's credibility, and because it arguably justifies inconveniencing defendant to make sure plaintiff is protected.

3. Do you think you can tell the difference between the "no reasonable expectation" standard and the "some cognizable danger" standard? Is the "mere possibility" standard more workable if the Court is serious about distinguishing moot cases from cases where no remedy is necessary?

4. Justice Douglas is interested in the proclivities of Lehman Brothers; the Court seems interested only in the proclivities of Hancock. Which is the better approach? Does that depend on substantive antitrust law and the theory of the government's case?

5. In Marshall v. Goodyear, what if Goodyear fired Coleman? Would that so remove the threat of future discrimination that no preventive injunction should issue? Compare Spomer v. Littleton, 414 U.S. 514 (1974), in which plaintiffs sought to enjoin racial discrimination by a county prosecutor, Berbling. Berbling was succeeded by Spomer, and Spomer was substituted as a defendant under Supreme Court Rule 48(3). This rule is modeled on Fed. R. Civ. Proc. 25(d) and provides for automatic substitution of successors in suits against public officers in their official capacity. The Court did not question Spomer's substitution, but it doubted whether plaintiffs had any controversy with him:

> The injunctive relief requested against former State's Attorney Berbling . . . is based upon an alleged practice of willful and malicious racial discrimination evidenced by enumerated instances in which Berbling favored white persons and disfavored Negroes. The wrongful conduct charged in the complaint is personal to Berbling, despite the fact that he was also sued in his then capacity as State's Attorney. No charge is made in the complaint that the policy of the office of State's Attorney is to follow the intentional practices alleged, apart from the allegation that Berbling, as the incumbent at the time, was then continuing the practices he had previously followed. Nor have respondents . . . made any record allegations that Spomer intends to continue the asserted practices of Berbling of which they complain.

414 U.S. 521. The Court ordered the complaint dismissed unless on remand plaintiffs could show a threat of continuing discrimination.

B. REPARATIVE INJUNCTIONS

BELL v. SOUTHWELL
376 F.2d 659 (5th Cir. 1967)

Before BROWN, GOLDBERG and AINSWORTH, Circuit Judges.
JOHN R. BROWN, Circuit Judge.
  A Georgia election was conducted under procedures involving racial discrimination which was gross, state-imposed, and forcibly state-compelled. Nevertheless the District Court by summary judgment held it

could not set aside such election or order a new one even though in parallel cases the unconstitutional discriminatory practices were enjoined and all persons arrested were ordered discharged immediately. We reverse.

The underlying facts out of which the controversy grew may be quickly stated. The Justice of the Peace for the 789th Militia District in Americus, Sumter County, Georgia, died on June 23, 1965. The Ordinary on June 26, 1965, called a special election to fill the vacancy, which was held on July 20, 1965. Mrs. Mary F. Bell, one of the plaintiffs, a Negro, was a candidate as was the winner, J. W. Southwell, a defendant, and four other white men. Following Georgia procedure, the results of the election were canvassed and the defendant J. W. Southwell declared the winner. Of the 2,781 votes cast, Negroes actually voting numbered 403 out of a total of 1,223 registered and qualified Negro voters in the District. . . . [I]f all of the qualified Negroes not voting were added to the combined vote of Southwell's opponents, the result could not have been changed. . . .

The specific allegations fell in two categories, one relating to the election system and the second to specific acts of intimidation. In the first it was alleged that voting lists for the election were segregated on the basis of race. Likewise, voting booths were segregated according to race, with one booth for "white males," another for "white women," and a third for Negroes. During the course of the election, a number of qualified Negro women voters were denied the right to cast their ballots in the "white women's" booth. In the second group were charges that the officials barred representatives of candidate Bell from viewing the voting, another was physically struck by an election official and police allowed a large crowd of white males to gather near the polls thus intimidating Negroes from voting. In addition, the plaintiffs were commanded by a deputy sheriff, acting under directions of the Ordinary, to leave the white women's polling booth and after their respectful refusal to do so on the ground that they had the constitutional right to vote without being subjected to racial discrimination, they were arrested. With precision, through simultaneous motions for temporary restraining order, preliminary injunction, show cause orders, and the immediate release from arrest, the plaintiffs requested that the Court declare the defendant Southwell was not the legally elected Justice of the Peace, that he be enjoined from taking office, and that the Ordinary be ordered to call a new election. . . .

By the decrees in the companion cases which all properly consider to be a part of the matter presented additionally by this case, the trial Court in unmistakable terms and action characterized the practices as flagrant violations of the Constitution. These steps were taken, so the Judge said, "to insure that in the future, elections in Sumter County will be free from discrimination." Despite his determination that for the future these glaring racial discriminations could not go on, the trial Judge concluded that a Federal Court was either powerless — or at least ought not to exercise power — to set aside a State election. The Judge was apparently influenced by two factors. The first is one going to the existence of power or the propriety of its exercise. On the basis of Reynolds v. Sims, 1964, 377 U.S. 533, and other reapportionment cases, the trial Court recognizing that a prohibitory decree could look to the future, nevertheless held that it could not rectify the past since, as the Judge put it, "only a few minutes' reflection is needed to realize that the implications of such a decision would be staggering." The second slipped over into a Georgia reason that, granting the existence of this crude discrimination, there is no way to tell whether the result would have been different in its absence. Hence, no harm or injury is shown by these complainants. Neither of these factors warrant, in our view, the complete denial of relief.

Drastic, if not staggering, as is the Federal voiding of a State election, and therefore a form of relief to be guardedly exercised, this Court in Hamer v. Campbell, 5 Cir., 1966, 358 F.2d 215, cert. denied, 1966, 385 U.S. 851, expressly recognized the existence of this power. Of course as that opinion emphasizes, not every unconstitutional racial discrimination necessarily permits or requires a retrospective voiding of the election. But the power is present and Hamer, announced subsequent to the action of the District Court below, would require reversal without more for re-examination by the District Court of the appropriateness of injunctive relief.

As to the second we do not think the Court could justify denial of effective, present relief because of any assumed inability to demonstrate that the outcome would have been different. The appellants seem to suggest that the existence of such flagrant racial discrimination would raise a presumption that the vote of every actual and potential voter was affected. On that approach, it is not Negroes alone who suffer, it is the body politic as a whole, both Negro and white. And this is certainly true at least to the extent that the trial Court legally could not assume — as it evidently did — that all white voters would vote for white candidates, all Negroes for Negroes, or that no whites would vote for Negroes in a free, untainted election. . . .

[T]he Supreme Court gave full play to this approach in striking down the Louisiana law requiring the designation of the race of each candidate on the ballot. Anderson v. Martin, 1964, 375 U.S. 399. It takes little transposition to substitute for the ballot's written racial candidate label the state-supplied racial marker for places and manner of voting. In each situation it is ". . . placing a racial label . . . at the most crucial stage in the electoral process — the instant before the vote is cast. . . ." By each mechanism "the State furnishes a vehicle by which racial prejudice may be so aroused as to operate against one group because of race and for another." And in both situations this "is true because by directing the citizen's attention to the single consideration of race or color, the State indicates that . . . race or color is an important — perhaps paramount

— consideration in the citizen's choice, which may decisively influence the citizen to cast his ballot along racial lines." And as much for one as for the other, the ". . . vice lies not in the resulting injury but in the placing of the power of the State behind a racial classification that induces racial prejudice at the polls." 375 U.S. 399, 402. . . .

Although as earlier pointed out, injunctive relief setting aside the election was granted, we emphasized in *Hamer* that this "action does not mean that we necessarily would set aside every election in which a substantial number of citizens have been denied the right to vote." Going further, we remarked, "This is not a case where an election is challenged for the first time after it is held." 358 F.2d 215, 222. This leads the Georgia authorities to insist here that the relief sought was properly denied since the injunction was requested after the election was over.

But we certainly intended no such mechanical rule. In *Hamer* the vice sought to be corrected was the denial of the right to vote to Negroes through operation of the registration procedure. That was known to exist before the election was held. It was also known that the effects could not be eradicated except through equitable court relief. Here, of course, the vice occurred on election day upon the opening of the polls. It might be suggested that the Negro voters should have anticipated that the traditional practice of racially segregated lists and polling places would be maintained. But it was equally permissible for them to think that at this late date and in the atmosphere of that moment and the passage of successive Civil Rights statutes increasing protection against racial discrimination, that these Georgia authorities would measure up to the demands of the Constitution.

There was really no effective relief available before the election. The moment the election process began, there was a protest by these Negro voters and others seeking an eradication of the discrimination and an opportunity for all members of that race, indeed for all voters, to vote without regard to race or color. That this self-help was not successful, indeed resulted in the unwarranted arrest and detention of those who protested, does not fault them for want of diligence. And within but a few days after the result of the election was published, this suit was filed as a part of an attack on many fronts.

Considering the gross, spectacular, completely indefensible nature of this state-imposed, state-enforced racial discrimination and the absence of an effective judicial remedy prior to the holding of the election, this is far removed from a belated effort to set aside retrospectively an election held long before on the ground that re-examination of the circumstances indicates a denial of constitutional rights on the part of candidates or voters, or both. The parties here moved with unusual diligence and as was true in *Hamer,* relief ". . . if it is to be had, must perforce come from the Court or the voters must simply be told to wait four more years." Hamer v. Campbell, supra, 358 F.2d 215, 222. . . .

Equally lacking in merit is the Court's conclusion that setting aside the election would be ineffectual since, on his interpretation of the Georgia statute, §24-408, prescribes that when an election is held and is determined not to have been valid, no re-election is held, but rather the Ordinary appoints a Justice of the Peace for the required term. The Court assumed, with unquestioned basis probably, that the Ordinary would have appointed Southwell. Clearly, the Federal Constitution and the Federal Courts are not so helpless or unresourceful as to condemn in words only to let go by default in fact such an open breach of constitutional demands.

This leaves only a tag end. There is a suggestion that the District Court enjoining Southwell from taking office pursuant to the election would be powerless to grant affirmative relief requiring that the Ordinary call a special election. In this vital area of vindication of precious constitutional rights, we are unfettered by the negative or affirmative character of the words used or the negative or affirmative form in which the coercive order is cast. If affirmative relief is essential, the Court has the power and should employ it.

The cause must therefore be reversed and remanded for the entry of an appropriate order setting aside the election and requiring the calling of a special election.

Reversed with directions.

NOTES ON REPARATIVE INJUNCTIONS

1. The district judge apparently thought that he could enjoin future violations but could not undo the effects of past violations. It is not clear whether he adhered to this distinction as a general matter, or thought that elections were a special case. Whatever the merits of a special rule about elections, there is no rule precluding the use of injunctions to ameliorate the harm of past violations. Indeed, such injunctions are quite common.

2. It has also occasionally been thought that injunctions can only forbid conduct and cannot order defendant to do something. There is no basis for this notion; one of the earliest forms of injunction was the specific performance decree — an order to perform a contract. The notion was more commonly reflected in absurd verbal formula ("defendant is ordered to stop failing to build and repair the dam") than in actual denial of relief. The last paragraph of Bell v. Southwell disposes of an echo of that notion that apparently appeared in defendant's argument.

3. Professor Fiss coined the label "reparative" for injunctions like the one in Bell v. Southwell. He distinguishes such injunctions from preventive injunctions, like the ones examined in the last section. This distinction is useful, but it can be overstated, and the label *preventive* is slightly misleading. The distinction is between preventing the wrongful act (racial

intimidation on election day), and preventing some or all of the harmful consequences of that act (four years under an illegally elected justice of the peace). Both forms of injunction often appear in the same case, because a past violation is the best proof that the threat of future violations is ripe. Fiss distinguishes both preventive and reparative injunctions from structural injunctions. Structural injunctions attempt to restructure institutions that are systematically violating the law or whose very structure is unlawful. School desegregation cases and antitrust divestiture cases are typical examples. These distinctions are developed in O. Fiss, The Civil Rights Injunction 8–12 (1978).

LAYCOCK, INJUNCTIONS AND THE IRREPARABLE INJURY RULE
57 Tex. L. Rev. 1065, 1073-1075 (1979)

One strength of Fiss' analysis [O. Fiss, The Civil Rights Injunction (1978)] is its account of the practical differences between the various uses of injunctions. An order to quit stealing plaintiff's rocks differs in important ways from an order to rerun a tainted election, and both differ from a complex series of orders designed to fully integrate a public school system. Fiss would label these three examples preventive, reparative, and structural injunctions, respectively. The distinctions are a helpful and original contribution and a significant improvement over earlier attempts at such categorization.

Nevertheless, Fiss makes too much of his categories; they describe differences in degree, not in kind. The preventive injunction prevents a future harmful act. The reparative injunction prevents the future harmful effects of a past act. The structural injunction is simply a long series of preventive and reparative injunctions in a single case presenting a complex fact situation; each individual order is part of a continuing attack on a larger problem. Thus, all three categories serve the classic role of the injunction: all prevent future harm.

While he does not "wholly deny" this analysis, Fiss insists that it "is false" in an "important sense" and that it "strain[s] and obscure[s] the underlying social realities." He correctly insists that the future harm avoided by reparative and structural injunctions is derivative from some past wrongful act or from an institutional structure that is itself wrongful. Fiss and I do not disagree over that description, but over its significance. For him, what is important is that the harm is derivative from a wrong done or created in the past; for me, what is important is that the harm will accrue in the future.

Our disagreement is thus over a nuance, but it is not without potential consequences. Those consequences are suggested by the following sentence: "The reconceptualization of the reparative injunction [as preventing future harm] is no more persuasive than would be the claim that the damage award is preventive because it prevents the future wrong of leaving the victim uncompensated for his injuries." This equating of damages and injunctive relief ignores the difference between avoiding harm altogether and compensating for harm actually suffered. It carries potential for confusion in litigation about the scope of relief and about mootness, especially when damages and an injunction are sought in the same case.

A reparative injunction is appropriate only when plaintiff will suffer additional harm in the future — when the total accrued loss as of Tuesday will be greater than it is on Monday — and when it is possible to prevent that additional harm from happening. Damages may be substituted for a reparative injunction; the court may let the harm happen and order compensation. But the converse is not true: reparative injunctions cannot always substitute for damages. Damages alone can compensate for harm suffered prior to the court's order and for future harm that cannot be prevented, such as pain and suffering from a lingering injury.

This formulation makes clear, as Fiss' does not, that the overlapping purposes served by reparative injunctions and damages remain quite distinct. Plaintiff may obtain both in the same case, without necessarily, or even probably, receiving a double recovery. Were the injunctive claim rendered moot, the suit would survive, for damage claims can never be moot.

The election case will serve as an illustration. In Bell v. Southwell, the court ordered an election for justice of the peace rerun because of racial intimidation at the polling place. The injunction was reparative because it did not prevent the wrongful conduct. But neither did it compensate for the harm already done — the humiliation suffered by black voters on election day and their subjection to the authority of an illegally elected justice of the peace for the two years between his installation and the court's decision, and for the additional time between the injunction and the installation of his successor. Some of those harms might have been compensated, although inadequately, by damages; they appear, however, to have gone unremedied. In the absence of a damage award, the injunction did nothing about the "harm of remaining uncompensated" for those injuries. Rather, it prevented the harm of subjecting plaintiffs to the illegally elected justice of the peace for the rest of his term. It probably altered beneficially the balance of racial power in the community. But it could not undo the past; it could only prevent or ameliorate future effects. Like all injunctions, it was a future-oriented remedy.

A complete remedy would have required a second election plus damages. Had the case dragged on until the end of the official's term, the claim for a second election arguably would have been moot.[63] But if

63. But see Wirtz v. Local 153, Glass Bottle Blowers Ass'n, 389 U.S. 463 (1968) (suit by Secretary of Labor under Landrum-Griffin Act, challenging union election, not mooted by expiration of winner's term).

damage were measured by the length of time the illegally elected official served, and not by the number of elections in which the right to vote was denied, the delay would have maximized the damage recovery. A double remedy problem would have arisen only if plaintiffs had sought compensation for some item of damage that would be avoided by the injunction, such as damages for a full term of office despite an early second election.

A more familiar example of simultaneous compensatory and preventive relief is the combined claim for specific performance of the executory portion of a breached contract, and damages for the harm already suffered.

NOTE ON ORGANIZATION

The measure of preventive injunctions most often turns on ripeness issues. Ripeness is less of an issue in preventive and structural injunction cases. As in Bell v. Southwell, defendant has already violated the law and plaintiff has already been hurt. The primary issue is how much defendant should be ordered to do to avoid further harm to plaintiff. These issues often turn on how much of plaintiff's harm results from defendant's wrongdoing, an issue we saw repeatedly in damage cases. Fiss's analogy between reparative injunctions and damages thus helps in understanding these cases, even though I find that analogy incomplete.

The rest of this chapter focuses on the question, How much harm should the injunction prevent? Or if you prefer, How much harm should the injunction undo? We will consider that question first with respect to reparative injunctions, and then with respect to structural injunctions. But it is really the same question in both contexts.

WINSTON RESEARCH CORP. v. MINNESOTA MINING & MANUFACTURING CO.
350 F.2d 134 (9th Cir. 1965)

Before JERTBERG and BROWNING, Circuit Judges, and FOLEY, District Judge.

BROWNING, Circuit Judge.

The Mincom Division of the Minnesota Mining and Manufacturing Company developed an improved precision tape recorder and reproducer. Somewhat later, Winston Research Corporation developed a similar machine. Mincom alleged that the Winston machine was developed by former employees of Mincom, including Johnson and Tobias, by using confidential information which they had acquired while working on the Mincom machine, and sued for damages and an injunction. The district court granted Mincom an injunction, but denied damages. Both sides appealed.

I

Some background is required for an understanding of the issues.

For some uses of precision tape recorder/reproducers, the time interval between coded signals must be recorded and reproduced with great accuracy.

[Mincom developed a substantially improved solution to this problem.]

In May 1962, when Mincom had substantially completed the research phase of its program and was beginning the development of a production prototype, Johnson, who was in charge of Mincom's program, left Mincom's employment. He joined Tobias, who had previously been discharged as Mincom's sales manager, in forming Winston Research Corporation. In late 1962, Winston contracted with the government to develop a precision tape reproducer. Winston hired many of the technicians who had participated in the development of the Mincom machine to work on the design and development of the Winston machine.

In approximately fourteen months, Winston completed a machine having the same low time-displacement error as the Mincom machine. . . .

III . . .

The district court found, and Winston concedes, that Johnson and the other former Mincom employees based Winston's development program upon the same approach to the problem of achieving a low time-displacement error as they had pursued in developing the Mincom machine. The district court further found that this general approach was not a trade secret of Mincom's. Finally, the district court found that the particular embodiment of these general concepts in the Mincom machine was Mincom's trade secret, and had been improperly utilized by the former Mincom employees in developing the Winston machine. . . .

IV

The district court enjoined Winston Research Corporation, Johnson, and Tobias from disclosing or using Mincom's trade secrets in any manner for a period of two years from the date of judgment — March 1, 1964. The court also required the assignment of certain patent applications to Mincom. No damages were awarded. . . . Mincom argues that the injunction should have been permanent, or at least for a substantially longer period. Winston contends that no injunctive relief was appropriate.

Mincom was, of course, entitled to protection of its trade secrets for as long as they remained secret. The district court's decision to limit the duration of injunctive relief was necessarily premised upon a determination that Mincom's trade secrets would shortly be fully disclosed, through no fault of Winston, as a result of public announcements, demonstrations, and sales and deliveries of Mincom machines. Mincom has not seriously challenged this implicit finding, and we think the record fully supports it.

Mincom argues that notwithstanding public disclosure subsequent to its former employees' breach of faith, Mincom was entitled to a permanent injunction under the Shellmar rule. Winston responds that under the competing Conmar rule public disclosure of Mincom's trade secrets would end the obligation of Mincom's former employees to maintain the information in confidence, and that neither the employees nor their privies may be enjoined beyond the date of disclosure.[6]

Thus, Winston's argument would bar any injunction at all once there was public disclosure, and Mincom's argument would require an injunction in perpetuity without regard to public disclosure. The district court rejected both extremes and granted an injunction for the period which it concluded would be sufficient both to deny Winston unjust enrichment and to protect Mincom from injury from the wrongful disclosure and use of Mincom's trade secrets by its former employees prior to public disclosure.

We think the district court's approach was sound. A permanent injunction would subvert the public's interest in allowing technical employees to make full use of their knowledge and skill and in fostering research and development. On the other hand, denial of any injunction at all would leave the faithless employee unpunished where, as here, no damages were awarded; and he and his new employer would retain the benefit of a head start over legitimate competitors who did not have access to the trade secrets until they were publicly disclosed. By enjoining use of the trade secrets for the approximate period it would require a legitimate Mincom competitor to develop a successful machine after public disclosure of the secret information, the district court denied the employees any advantage from their faithlessness, placed Mincom in the position it would have occupied if the breach of confidence had not occurred prior to the public disclosure, and imposed the minimum restraint consistent with the realization of these objectives upon the utilization of the employees' skills. . . .

Mincom argues that in any event a two-year injunction from March 1, 1964, was not sufficient to overcome the wrongful advantage obtained by

----

6. The two rules take their names from Shellmar Prods. Co. v. Allen-Qualley Co., 87 F.2d 104 (7th Cir. 1936), and Conmar Prods. Corp. v. Universal Slide Fastener Co., 172 F.2d 150 (2d Cir. 1949).

Winston. Mincom points out that four years were required to develop its machine, whereas Winston developed its machine in fourteen months. For this reason, and because the injunction was stayed for some time, Mincom argues that injunctive relief should be granted for at least three years from the completion of appellate review.

As we have noted, the appropriate injunctive period is that which competitors would require after public disclosure to develop a competitive machine. The time (fourteen months) which Winston in fact took with the aid of the very disclosure and use complained of by Mincom would seem to be a fair measure of the proper period. The district court granted an injunction for a somewhat longer period, presumably because the Mincom machine was built in such a way as to require some time for persons unfamiliar with it to determine the details of its construction, and to compensate for delay which Mincom encountered in the final stages of its development program because Winston had hired away Mincom's key personnel. Whether extension of the injunctive period for the latter reason was proper we need not decide, for Winston has not raised that question. . . .

Mincom argues that the district court should have awarded money damages as well as injunctive relief. We think the district court acted well within its discretion in declining to do so. Since Winston sold none of its machines, it had no past profits to disgorge. The evidence as to possible future profits was at best highly speculative. To enjoin future sales and at the same time make an award based on future profits from the prohibited sales would result in duplicating and inconsistent relief, and the choice which the district court made between these mutually exclusive alternatives was not an unreasonable one. There was evidence that Winston would probably sell its machine and realize profits after the injunction expired, but these sales and profits, as we have seen, would not be tainted by breach of confidence, since Winston could by that time have developed its machine from publicly disclosed information.

We have examined the other bases upon which Mincom sought damages and are satisfied that they were either too remote and speculative, or that the injunction made Mincom as nearly whole as possible. Mincom argues that Winston gained a wide variety of advantages from the improper use of Mincom's trade secrets — such as obtaining financing for its development program, securing a government contract, shortening its development program, and reducing its development costs. There is an obvious difficulty in assigning a dollar value to such matters. The two-year injunction deprived Winston of any benefit it might have gained from these advantages and shielded Mincom from any potential harm from Winston's competition which these advantages may have rendered unfair. Mincom suggests that by hiring away Mincom's skilled employees Winston hindered Mincom's development program and increased its cost, but, as we have noted, the district court expressly considered this delay and extended the period of the injunction for an equivalent period. . . .

NOTES ON THE SCOPE OF REPARATIVE INJUNCTIONS

1.   *Winston* illustrates the slipperiness of the distinction between preventive and reparative injunctions. If the wrong is conceived of as stealing Mincom's trade secrets, then the injunction is reparative, because it is designed to prevent the consequences of that wrong. If the wrong is conceived of as selling products manufactured through the use of the trade secrets, then the injunction is preventive. No wrong has yet occurred, and the injunction will prevent the threatened sales. Fortunately, no one's rights turn on the distinction. Once courts decided that reparative injunctions could be issued, the distinction became practical and descriptive; it was no longer doctrinal or determinative of anything.

2.   In *Winston*, the trial judge could have denied the injunction and awarded damages for the sales Mincom lost to Winston as a result of Winston's theft. If the court had chosen that remedy, what would the measure of damages have been? Would Mincom have had any claim at all for damages based on sales Winston would make five or ten years after the trade secrets were publicly disclosed? If not, is there any basis for a perpetual injunction against Winston? Is there any reason for the injunctive remedy to be more draconian or lucrative than the damages remedy? Shouldn't both remedies be designed to put plaintiff in the position it would have occupied but for the wrong?

3.   The parties in *Winston* argued for competing rules based on the *Shellmar* and *Conmar* cases. In *Conmar*, Learned Hand described the perpetual injunction issued in *Shellmar* as a "penalty" for which there was no basis in principle. Whether or not there is a basis for it, it is a penalty, isn't it? Some courts are still attracted to such penalties. An example is Merrill Lynch, Pierce, Fenner & Smith, Inc. v. Stidham, 658 F.2d 1098 (5th Cir. 1981), in which the court perpetually enjoined defendants from using on behalf of their new employer information acquired while they worked for Merrill Lynch. Their contract with Merrill Lynch provided only that they would not disclose such information while they were employed there. The court held that the blatant breach of the temporary nondisclosure agreement justified the perpetual injunction against using the wrongfully disclosed information. The court probably would not have awarded punitive damages for breach of contract. Is that relevant to deciding whether a penalty should be built into an injunction?

4.   Hand gave no remedy at all in *Conmar*, perhaps because plaintiff

didn't argue that there would be a lag between lawful disclosure and defendant's exploitation of the disclosure; the opinion does not discuss the lag time issue.

5.   What about Bell v. Southwell? Is that consistent with the rightful position standard? There is no way to know whether Mary Bell would have been elected but for the wrong, although the odds were surely against it. But plaintiffs would have had an election free of racial intimidation. Does the appropriate remedy depend on whether you emphasize the result or the process?

BAILEY v. PROCTOR
160 F.2d 78 (1st Cir.), *cert. denied*, 331 U.S. 834 (1947)

[Aldred Investment Trust was a mutual fund organized before the Investment Company Act of 1940 and typical of the abuses that led to the act. Voting control of the trust was held by the owners of $150,000 in stock; the holders of $6 million in debentures provided most of the capital. A debenture is like a bond or promissory note: It is a promise to pay a fixed sum of money, usually on a date far in the future, and to pay periodic interest until the principal is paid. Debenture holders are fixed income investors, interested in a safe steady return.

The abuse in this capital structure is in its uneven and misleading distribution of risk and reward. If the trust performs badly, the stock holders can lose no more than $150,000; the debenture holders can lose $6 million. But if the trust does well, the debenture holders get only their interest; all the speculative profit goes to the stock holders. Their profits can be enormous as a percentage of their investment, because the $6,000,000 invested by the debenture holders is working for them. For example, if the debenture holders are promised 6 percent interest, and the trust actually earns 8 percent, that extra 2 percent of $6 million is $120,000. For the stock holders, that's an annual return of 80 percent. If the trust invests in speculative stocks and doubles its value, the debenture holders still get only 6 percent. But that $6 million profit is a 4,000 percent return to the stock holders. Consequently, the controlling stock holders have a great incentive to take risks with the debenture holders' money. The debenture holders are limited to their 6 percent return, but they don't get the safety they were seeking. On the other hand, 6 percent was considerably above market interest rates all through the 1930s and 1940s.

The Aldred trust became insolvent, and the control group was caught in fraud and self-dealing. For these reasons, a receiver was appointed at the request of the Securities and Exchange Commission. The court of appeals approved the appointment of the receiver in Aldred Investment Trust v. SEC, 151 F.2d 254 (1st Cir. 1945), *cert. denied*, 326 U.S. 795 (1946).

The original control group was led by a man named Hanlon. Bailey's group bought out Hanlon's group, and an enormous increase in the value of a racetrack investment made the trust solvent again. But the district court ordered the receiver to liquidate the trust. Bailey appealed, arguing that both reasons for the receivership had been eliminated, and that the court had no power to order liquidation in any event.]

Before MAGRUDER, MAHONEY, and WOODBURY, Circuit Judges.

MAHONEY, Circuit Judge.

Appellants' first argument is that the district court lacked jurisdiction to liquidate the Trust. In our view the jurisdiction of the district court to act in terminating the receivership by ordering liquidation is dependent upon the jurisdiction existing at the time the receivership was commenced. At that time the Trust was insolvent and the officers-trustees were guilty of "gross abuse of trust." We then upheld the district court's decree appointing receivers, as being within the court's general equity powers. Admittedly, however, at the time of that appeal the emphasis was on the power to appoint a receiver rather than the power to order liquidation as the end of the receivership. Therefore, rather than resting our present decision on the narrower ground of the "law of the case," we now hold that a court of equity has inherent power to appoint a receiver to liquidate a corporation or investment trust where fraud, mismanagement or abuse of trust is present whether or not insolvency is likewise present. . . .

The question now presented to us is whether or not the district court has lost that power by reason of intervening solvency and the removal of the officers-trustees guilty of abuse of trust and the impossibility of their now resuming such control of the Trust due to the transfer of the controlling shares to the present appellants. In the first place we do not believe that the perhaps temporary solvency of the Trust would necessarily affect the power of the court supervising the receivership. Other grounds for the appointment of a receiver having been present, the court's jurisdiction is not defeated by the supervening solvency. Since a receivership may be inaugurated for a solvent corporation, solvency, especially where it may be of a transient nature, does not terminate jurisdiction to continue a receivership created on grounds other than insolvency. Moreover, we believe that the jurisdiction existing at the time of creation of the receivership is a continuing jurisdiction and the questions of present solvency and removal from control of the offending officers and trustees pertain not to jurisdiction but to the propriety of the exercise of such jurisdiction. Once having properly assumed jurisdiction of a corporation or trust by appointing receivers under its general equity power, a court should not terminate its supervision until or unless it becomes satisfied that equity has been done to those whose interests the court had originally been asked to protect. The court upon examination of the plans for reorganization found that none was fair and feasible, and consequently, accepted liquidation as the only other alternative. The question before us is whether we can say that the court below abused its discretion in failing to order termination of the receivership by vesting control in the present common shareholders with the terms of the trust and the capital structure unchanged.

In considering the propriety of the order decreeing liquidation it must be remembered that reorganization of this Trust was considered, at least by the Securities and Exchange Commission, and undoubtedly by the court, a necessary prelude to any termination of the receivership other than by liquidation. Appellants at least recognized the advisability of a reorganization in their final petition before the district court.

Ordinarily, it is said that liquidation being a drastic remedy will only be decreed in an extraordinary case or where special and peculiar circumstances exist. Unfortunately the district court did not furnish us with an opinion in which it indicated the grounds for the exercise of its discretion. However, from the record we are able to garner facts which seem to us to support the manner in which such discretion was exercised.

Since 1937 the Aldred Trust assets have had a value substantially less than the principal amount of outstanding debentures. During the years 1940 to 1943 the earnings of the Trust were substantially insufficient to meet the interest charges on these debentures. Only as the result of the successful outcome of a highly speculative venture undertaken by Hanlon has the Trust been able to get its head out of water during the receivership. Temporary solvency was brought about by the sale of the Eastern Racing Association stock at a tremendous profit. Due to a postwar stock market inflation the other portfolio assets nearly doubled in value but were still less than the face amount of the outstanding debentures. The vagaries of the stock market are familiar to all of us. There seems to be doubt also as to the ability in the future of any portfolio to earn these interest requirements except by resort to speculative securities with the hope of capital appreciation.

The Securities and Exchange Commission indicated that the Aldred Trust security structure embodied the evils which led to the enactment of the Investment Company Act of 1940. The "free stock," representing only a small investment and often no equity, controlled the operations, policies and management of the almost $6,000,000 investment of the debenture holders. The inability to earn interest requirements induces the controlling shareholders to engage in capital appreciation investments or in speculative ventures to insure them a profit in one way or another, e.g., Hanlon's activities in the Eastern Racing Association stock. The present holders of the free stock, the appellants here, purchased control of Aldred, which has $5,900,000 principal amount of debentures, for $150,000. Their equity at present shows an appreciation of some $2,500,000 as a result of general market increases and the favorable sale of Eastern Racing Association stock.

The important question is not the personal honesty, integrity or ability of appellants or their proposed management, but rather the lack of balance and equality of control in the capital structure of the Trust. Specifically, the court could not feel assured that a recurrence of the events leading up to the present receivership was impossible. Insolvency was likely; lack of sufficient earnings to cover interest requirements was possible. In such event, nothing would prevent the controlling shareholders, either appellants or their successors, from embarking on new speculation to the detriment of the debenture holders. The court properly felt that the debenture holders were entitled now to the cash salvaged from what had appeared to be a doomed enterprise.

Finally, it was indicated at the argument before us that one of appellants' primary motives for the continuation of Aldred was to preserve its security structure, inasmuch as a similar trust could not now be created under the Investment Company Act. The Act itself does not require the liquidation or reorganization of existing investment companies which do not conform to the new statutory standards. But when a court of equity has exercised its jurisdiction to appoint receivers of an investment company pursuant to a complaint charging gross abuse of trust on the part of the trustees or officers, we deem it proper for the court, in determining what would be the appropriate remedy in order to afford complete relief, to take account of the fact that the capital structure is not in conformity with the standards and safeguards which Congress has now written into law. That fact, in conjunction with the other facts in the case, may well render it fair and equitable to require the liquidation of the company in the absence of an acceptable plan of reorganization.

No dissenting voice to the order of liquidation has arisen from the debenture holders who have the greater equity and whose interests the court was originally called upon to protect. It would seem that, if appellants are intent upon investing in an investment corporation or trust, they could form a new one and even solicit the present debenture holders for subscriptions. But it would be inequitable to allow them to force those with burnt fingers to remain investors in an enterprise of proven questionable value.

In view of the above considerations, we find it impossible to say that the order of liquidation was an improper exercise of equitable discretion but rather indicated a court of equity doing equity. . . .

The decision of the District Court is affirmed and the case is remanded to that court for further proceedings in accord with this opinion.

MORE NOTES ON THE MEASURE OF INJUNCTIVE RELIEF

1. What is the measure of relief in *Bailey*? That equity should be done? What position would the debenture holders have been in if the trust had never been insolvent and Hanlon had never engaged in self-

dealing? Wouldn't they have been debenture holders in a solvent trust with honest management and a risky over-leveraged financial structure that was protected by the grandfather clause in the Investment Company Act? What is the court remedying when it orders the trust liquidated?

2. The difference between *Bailey* on the one hand and *Bell* and *Winston* on the other is not that *Bailey* involves a receivership. We will take up receiverships in more detail in chapter 8; for present purposes, just treat the order to liquidate the trust as though it were an injunction. The talk about "an equity court doing equity" is equally common in injunction and receivership cases; both are equitable remedies, developed by the English chancellors in their equity court and not in the common law courts. There is long tradition that a suit in equity is an appeal to the chancellor's conscience. The modern successor to the chancellor is the trial judge, and there is still much talk about the flexibility of equity and the discretion of trial judges in equity cases.

Such talk led to the famous complaint that relying on the chancellor's conscience as a measure of justice is like relying on the chancellor's foot as the measure of length. But this reflects a common misunderstanding of the nature of equitable discretion. Courts of last resort have frequently reiterated that equitable discretion is discretion to consider all the relevant facts, not discretion for the trial judge to do whatever he wants. The U.S. Supreme Court made the point in connection with discretionary awards of back pay to victims of employment discrimination:

> However, such discretionary choices are not left to a court's "inclination, but to its judgment; and its judgment is to be guided by sound legal principles." United States v. Burr, 25 F. Cas. No. 14,692d, pp. 30, 35 (CC Va. 1807) (Marshall, C.J.). The power to award backpay was bestowed by Congress, as part of a complex legislative design directed at a historic evil of national proportions. A court must exercise this power "in light of the large objectives of the Act," Hecht Co. v. Bowles, 321 U.S. 321, 331 (1944). That the court's discretion is equitable in nature hardly means that it is unfettered by meaningful standards or shielded from thorough appellate review. In Mitchell v. Robert DeMario Jewelry, 361 U.S. 288, 292 (1960), this Court held, in the face of a silent statute, that district courts enjoyed the "historic power of equity" to award lost wages to workmen unlawfully discriminated against under §17 of the Fair Labor Standards Act. The Court simultaneously noted that "the statutory purposes [leave] little room for the exercise of discretion not to order reimbursement." 361 U.S., at 296.
>
> It is true that "[e]quity eschews mechanical rules . . . [and] depends on flexibility." Holmberg v. Armbrecht, 327 U.S. 392, 396 (1946). But when Congress invokes the Chancellor's conscience to further transcendant legislative purposes, what is required is the principled application of standards consistent with those purposes and not "equity [which] varies like the Chancellor's foot."[10] Important national goals would be frustrated by a regime of discretion

---

10. Eldon, L. C., in Gee v. Pritchard, 2 Swans. *403, *414, 36 Eng. Rep. 670, 674 (1818).

that "produce[d] different results for breaches of duty in situations that cannot be differentiated in policy." Moragne v. States Marine Lines, 398 U.S. 375, 405 (1970).

Albemarle Paper Co. v. Moody, 422 U.S. 405, 416-417 (1975).
3. The question remains what general principles are to guide the trial court's discretion in formulating injunctions or other equitable remedies. *Winston* represents one tradition, which is to restore the plaintiff as near as may be to the position it would have occupied but for the violation. That still leaves some room for discretion: for example, whether two years or eighteen months is the appropriate lead time to offset the effects of the violation is left to the discretion of the trial judge. Deference to the trial judge on that issue may not be much different from deference to the trial judge's application of the measure of damages.

Bailey represents a different tradition. At its extremes, that tradition says that once there is a violation that brings a case into the equity court, the chancellor has a roving commission to do good. He should see that equity is done to all within his jurisdiction; he should liquidate the trust because that is fair, even though it is not legally required and is not necessary to restore the plaintiffs to their original position. An academic formulation of this tradition "rejects the position that any simple, logical relationship between right and remedy can exist in most legal matters." Goldstein, A *Swann* Song for Remedies: Equitable Relief in the Burger Court, 13 Harv. C.R.-C.L.L. Rev. 1, 5, 23 (1978).

These two traditions can fairly be thought of as poles on a single continuum describing the extent of the trial judge's discretion. Bell v. Southwell may fall in between. Another case somewhere in the middle is Community Renewal Foundation v. Chicago Title & Trust Co., 44 Ill. 2d 284, 255 N.E.2d 908 (1970). That case presented a constitutional challenge to a statute and court decree authorizing repair of buildings found to be in violation of the building or housing codes. The repairs were to be financed by borrowing money and giving a mortgage that would have priority over earlier mortgages. One of the challenges to the decree was that the repairs authorized were more than necessary to correct the violations. The court rejected the argument:

> The appellant says . . . that the court's authority was limited to the ordering of only those repairs which would cause the building concerned to satisfy minimal requirements under the ordinance or plan. He argues that no improvement beyond this could be authorized, and that the order of the court should have specifically limited the rehabilitation. However, we do not believe that this narrow and restrictive interpretation is required, when one considers, as we do, the intendment of the legislature to be that deteriorated buildings be returned to economic life and acceptable usefulness. Even granting that in all cases the limits of minimal repairs could be nicely measured, as the appellant's argument supposes, we judge that the court should be given reasonable discretion to determine the repairs necessary to restore the buildings for acceptable

use within the legislative design. There is no evidence that the rehabilitation here proposed exceeds that necessary to return the building to economic life and acceptable usefulness.

Id. at 296, 255 N.E.2d at 915.

What was the court remedying under this rationale? Would it have had any power to restore a building to economic usefulness if there had not been a code violation? Is the code violation a trigger for generally doing good? Or is merely repairing the code violations futile, wasteful, and no remedy at all unless at least enough is done to make the building useful again?

C. STRUCTURAL INJUNCTIONS

A series of cases in the U.S. Supreme Court has highlighted the tension between these two approaches to the scope of injunctive relief. As it happens, the cases all involve structural injunctions. But the debate over the scope of injunctive relief is substantially applicable to preventive and reparative injunctions as well.

SWANN v. CHARLOTTE-MECKLENBURG BOARD OF EDUCATION
402 U.S. 1 (1971)

[This case involved desegregation of the Mecklenburg County, North Carolina, schools. The district was thirty-six miles long and twenty-two miles wide; it served 84,000 students in 1969. Twenty-four thousand students were black, 21,000 of whom attended schools in the city of Charlotte. The findings of illegal segregation were not challenged in the Supreme Court.

The school board proposed to desegregate by drawing wedge-shaped attendance zones pointed toward the central city. This would have placed most of the high school and junior high school students, but fewer than half the elementary school students, in integrated schools.

The court-appointed expert proposed a plan that adopted much of the board's proposal but also paired black and white schools not reached by the gerrymander, bused students between these schools, and made certain other additions. The district court adopted this plan, along with a guideline that, so far as practical, the racial makeup of each school should reflect the racial composition of the district as a whole. Defendants appealed, and the Supreme Court reviewed the details of an urban desegregation plan for the first time.

The opinion refers repeatedly to *Brown I, Brown II,* and *Green. Brown I* held that deliberately segregated schools were unconstitutional even if the black schools were equal to the white schools. 347 U.S. 483 (1954). *Brown II* held that district courts should work out school desegregation remedies "with all deliberate speed." 349 U.S. 294, 301 (1955). *Green* reviewed a desegregation plan from a rural county with one black school, one white school, and no housing segregation. 391 U.S. 430 (1968). Drawing two geographic attendance zones would have produced instant integration. Instead, the plan allowed each child to choose a school. All whites chose the white school, and most blacks chose the black school. In that fairly simple situation, the Court laid down the standards that it tries to apply in *Swann.*]

CHIEF JUSTICE BURGER delivered the opinion of the Court. . . .

None of the parties before us questions the Court's 1955 holding in *Brown II,* that . . .

> In fashioning and effectuating the decrees, the courts will be guided by equitable principles. Traditionally, equity has been characterized by a practical flexibility in shaping its remedies and by a facility for adjusting and reconciling public and private needs. These cases call for the exercise of these traditional attributes of equity power. At stake is the personal interest of the plaintiffs in admission to public schools as soon as practicable on a nondiscriminatory basis. To effectuate this interest may call for elimination of a variety of obstacles in making the transition to school systems operated in accordance with the constitutional principles set forth in our May 17, 1954, decision. Courts of equity may properly take into account the public interest in the elimination of such obstacles in a systematic and effective manner. But it should go without saying that the vitality of these constitutional principles cannot be allowed to yield simply because of disagreement with them.

Brown v. Board of Education, 349 U.S. 294, 299-300 (1955). . . .

III

The objective today remains to eliminate from the public schools all vestiges of state-imposed segregation. Segregation was the evil struck down by *Brown I* as contrary to the equal protection guarantees of the Constitution. That was the violation sought to be corrected by the remedial measures of *Brown II.* That was the basis for the holding in *Green* that school authorities are "clearly charged with the affirmative duty to take whatever steps might be necessary to convert to a unitary system in which racial discrimination would be eliminated root and branch." 391 U.S. at 437-438.

If school authorities fail in their affirmative obligations under these holdings, judicial authority may be invoked. Once a right and a violation have been shown, the scope of a district court's equitable powers to remedy past wrongs is broad, for breadth and flexibility are inherent in equitable remedies.

> The essence of equity jurisdiction has been the power of the Chancellor to do equity and to mould each decree to the necessities of the particular case. Flexibility rather than rigidity has distinguished it. The qualities of mercy and practicality have made equity the instrument for nice adjustment and reconciliation between the public interest and private needs as well as between competing private claims.

Hecht Co. v. Bowles, 321 U.S. 321, 329-330 (1944).

This allocation of responsibility once made, the Court attempted from time to time to provide some guidelines for the exercise of the district judge's discretion and for the reviewing function of the court of appeals. However, a school desegregation case does not differ fundamentally from other cases involving the framing of equitable remedies to repair the denial of a constitutional right. The task is to correct, by a balancing of the individual and collective interests, the condition that offends the Constitution.

In seeking to define even in broad and general terms how far this remedial power extends it is important to remember that judicial powers may be exercised only on the basis of a constitutional violation. Remedial judicial authority does not put judges automatically in the shoes of school authorities whose powers are plenary. Judicial authority enters only when local authority defaults.

School authorities are traditionally charged with broad power to formulate and implement educational policy and might well conclude, for example, that in order to prepare students to live in a pluralistic society each school should have a prescribed ratio of Negro to white students reflecting the proportion for the district as a whole. To do this as an educational policy is within the broad discretionary powers of school authorities; absent a finding of a constitutional violation, however, that would not be within the authority of a federal court. As with any equity case, the nature of the violation determines the scope of the remedy. In default by the school authorities of their obligation to proffer acceptable remedies, a district court has broad power to fashion a remedy that will assure a unitary school system. . . .

IV . . .

The construction of new schools and the closing of old ones are two of the most important functions of local school authorities and also two of the most complex. They must decide questions of location and capacity in light of population growth, finances, land values, site availability, through an almost endless list of factors to be considered. The result of this will be a decision which, when combined with one technique or another of student assignment, will determine the racial composition of the student body in each school in the system. Over the long run, the consequences of the choices will be far reaching. People gravitate toward school facilities, just as schools are located in response to the needs of people. The location of schools may thus influence the patterns of residential development of a metropolitan area and have important impact on composition of inner-city neighborhoods.

In the past, choices in this respect have been used as a potent weapon for creating or maintaining a state-segregated school system. In addition to the classic pattern of building schools specifically intended for Negro or white students, school authorities have sometimes, since *Brown*, closed schools which appeared likely to become racially mixed through changes in neighborhood residential patterns. This was sometimes accompanied by building new schools in the areas of white suburban expansion farthest from Negro population centers in order to maintain the separation of the races with a minimum departure from the formal principles of "neighborhood zoning." Such a policy does more than simply influence the short-run composition of the student body of a new school. It may well promote segregated residential patterns which, when combined with "neighborhood zoning," further lock the school system into the mold of separation of the races. Upon a proper showing a district court may consider this in fashioning a remedy. . . .

V

The central issue in this case is that of student assignment, and there are essentially four problem areas. . . .

(1)   Racial Balances or Racial Quotas . . .

If we were to read the holding of the District Court to require, as a matter of substantive constitutional right, any particular degree of racial balance or mixing, that approach would be disapproved and we would be obliged to reverse. The constitutional command to desegregate schools does not mean that every school in every community must always reflect the racial composition of the school system as a whole. . . .

[But here] the use made of mathematical ratios was no more than a starting point in the process of shaping a remedy, rather than an inflexible requirement. From that starting point the District Court proceeded to frame a decree that was within its discretionary powers, as an equitable remedy for the particular circumstances. As we said in *Green*, a school authority's remedial plan or a district court's remedial decree is to be judged by its effectiveness. Awareness of the racial composition of the whole school system is likely to be a useful starting point in shaping a remedy to correct past constitutional violations. In sum, the very limited use made of mathematical ratios was within the equitable remedial discretion of the District Court.

(2) One-Race Schools

The record in this case reveals the familiar phenomenon that in metropolitan areas minority groups are often found concentrated in one part of the city. In some circumstances certain schools may remain all or largely of one race until new schools can be provided or neighborhood patterns change. Schools all or predominantly of one race in a district of mixed population will require close scrutiny to determine that school assignments are not part of state-enforced segregation.

In light of the above, it should be clear that the existence of some small number of one-race, or virtually one-race, schools within a district is not in and of itself the mark of a system that still practices segregation by law. The district judge or school authorities should make every effort to achieve the greatest possible degree of actual desegregation and will thus necessarily be concerned with the elimination of one-race schools. No per se rule can adequately embrace all the difficulties of reconciling the competing interests involved; but in a system with a history of segregation the need for remedial criteria of sufficient specificity to assure a school authority's compliance with its constitutional duty warrants a presumption against schools that are substantially disproportionate in their racial composition. . . .

(3) Remedial Altering of Attendance Zones

The maps submitted in these cases graphically demonstrate that one of the principal tools employed by school planners and by courts to break up the dual school system has been a frank — and sometimes drastic — gerrymandering of school districts and attendance zones. An additional step was pairing, "clustering," or "grouping" of schools with attendance assignments made deliberately to accomplish the transfer of Negro students out of formerly segregated Negro schools and transfer of white students to formerly all-Negro schools. More often than not, these zones are neither compact nor contiguous; indeed they may be on opposite ends of the city. As an interim corrective measure, this cannot be said to be beyond the broad remedial powers of a court.

Absent a constitutional violation there would be no basis for judicially ordering assignment of students on a racial basis. All things being equal, with no history of discrimination, it might well be desirable to assign pupils to schools nearest their homes. But all things are not equal in a system that has been deliberately constructed and maintained to enforce racial segregation. The remedy for such segregation may be administratively awkward, inconvenient, and even bizarre in some situations and may impose burdens on some; but all awkwardness and inconvenience cannot be avoided in the interim period when remedial adjustments are being made to eliminate the dual school systems.

No fixed or even substantially fixed guidelines can be established as to how far a court can go, but it must be recognized that there are limits. The objective is to dismantle the dual school system. "Racially neutral" assignment plans proposed by school authorities to a district court may be inadequate; such plans may fail to counteract the continuing effects of past school segregation resulting from discriminatory location of school sites or distortion of school size in order to achieve or maintain an artificial racial separation. When school authorities present a district court with a "loaded game board," affirmative action in the form of remedial altering of attendance zones is proper to achieve truly nondiscriminatory assignments. In short, an assignment plan is not acceptable simply because it appears to be neutral. . . .

(4) Transportation of Students

The scope of permissible transportation of students as an implement of a remedial decree has never been defined by this Court and by the very nature of the problem it cannot be defined with precision. No rigid guidelines as to student transportation can be given for application to the infinite variety of problems presented in thousands of situations. Bus transportation has been an integral part of the public education system for years, and was perhaps the single most important factor in the transition from the one-room schoolhouse to the consolidated school. Eighteen million of the Nation's public school children, approximately 39%, were transported to their schools by bus in 1969-1970 in all parts of the country.

The importance of bus transportation as a normal and accepted tool of educational policy is readily discernible in this and the companion case. The Charlotte school authorities did not purport to assign students on the basis of geographically drawn zones until 1965 and then they allowed almost unlimited transfer privileges. The District Court's conclusion that assignment of children to the school nearest their home serving their grade would not produce an effective dismantling of the dual system is supported by the record.

Thus the remedial techniques used in the District Court's order were within that court's power to provide equitable relief; implementation of the decree is well within the capacity of the school authority.

The decree provided that the buses used to implement the plan would operate on direct routes. Students would be picked up at schools near

their homes and transported to the schools they were to attend. The trips
for elementary school pupils average about seven miles and the District
Court found that they would take "not over 35 minutes at the most." This
system compares favorably with the transportation plan previously operated in Charlotte under which each day 23,600 students on all grade
levels were transported an average of 15 miles one way for an average trip
requiring over an hour. In these circumstances, we find no basis for
holding that the local school authorities may not be required to employ
bus transportation as one tool of school desegregation. Desegregation
plans cannot be limited to the walk-in school.

An objection to transportation of students may have validity when the
time or distance of travel is so great as to either risk the health of the
children or significantly impinge on the educational process. District
courts must weigh the soundness of any transportation plan in light of
what is said in subdivisions (1), (2), and (3) above. It hardly needs stating
that the limits on time of travel will vary with many factors, but probably
with none more than the age of the students. The reconciliation of competing values in a desegregation case is, of course, a difficult task with
many sensitive facets but fundamentally no more so than remedial measures courts of equity have traditionally employed.

VI

The Court of Appeals, searching for a term to define the equitable remedial power of the district courts, used the term "reasonableness." In
Green, this Court used the term "feasible" and by implication, "workable," "effective," and "realistic" in the mandate to develop "a plan that
promises realistically to work, and . . . to work *now*." On the facts of this
case, we are unable to conclude that the order of the District Court is not
reasonable, feasible and workable. However, in seeking to define the
scope of remedial power or the limits on remedial power of courts in an
area as sensitive as we deal with here, words are poor instruments to
convey the sense of basic fairness inherent in equity. Substance, not
semantics, must govern, and we have sought to suggest the nature of
limitations without frustrating the appropriate scope of equity.

At some point, these school authorities and others like them should
have achieved full compliance with this Court's decision in *Brown I*. The
systems would then be "unitary" in the sense required by our decisions in
Green and *Alexander*.

It does not follow that the communities served by such systems will
remain demographically stable, for in a growing, mobile society, few will
do so. Neither school authorities nor district courts are constitutionally
required to make year-by-year adjustments of the racial composition of
student bodies once the affirmative duty to desegregate has been accomplished and racial discrimination through official action is eliminated

from the system. This does not mean that federal courts are without power to deal with future problems; but in the absence of a showing that either the school authorities or some other agency of the State has deliberately attempted to fix or alter demographic patterns to affect the racial composition of the schools, further intervention by a district court should not be necessary. . . .

The order of the District Court . . . is . . . affirmed. . . .

NOTES ON REMEDIES IN SCHOOL DESEGREGATION CASES

1.   In considering remedies for school desegregation, it is important to recall the Court's distinction between de facto and de jure segregation. De jure segregation is segregation deliberately caused by state authorities; de jure segregation violates the constitution and must be remedied. De facto segregation is segregation from all other causes except the deliberate conduct of state authorities. The Court has always held that de facto segregation does not violate the Constitution. Thus, for example, if the preferences of home buyers and renters, and discrimination by real estate brokers, landlords, and sellers create housing segregation, and that housing segregation creates school segregation, the resulting school segregation does not violate the constitution and need not be remedied. That at least is the theory, and the Court has never repudiated it. However, the theory is subjected to great stress in the remedies cases. All the opinions are written in terms of how to remedy de jure segregation, and the notes to the cases will examine them largely on their own terms. But you may well conclude that at least some of the judges are trying to remedy de facto segregation as well, and that that thinly disguised goal is the best explanation for some of the opinions.

2.   What is the Court remedying with its gerrymander of attendance zones? Why isn't it enough to draw racially neutral attendance zones? Is it because the school locations are themselves gerrymandered? Because segregated school assignments have contributed to segregated housing, by inducing people to live near their own schools? Are these things presumed, or must plaintiffs prove them in every case?

3.   How plausible is the assumption that housing would be much more integrated if the schools had not been segregated? A large body of social science evidence points the other way. Most dramatically, when southern schools were integrated, residential segregation increased. Residential segregation is reinforced by discrimination by public and private actors, including school boards, but "It occurs regardless of the character of local laws and policies, and regardless of the extent of other forms of segregation or discrimination. . . ." Taueber and Taueber, Negroes in Cities 35-36 (1965). Much of the social science evidence is summarized in

Wolf, Northern School Desegregation and Residential Choice, 1977 Sup. Ct. Rev. 63, 63-70.

4.   Might the Court be trying to produce visible desegregation in order to show the community that de jure segregation is really over? Might that need for a visible remedy justify eliminating de facto segregation as a remedy for de jure segregation?

5.   How long should the desegregation plan last? The order not to deliberately segregate lasts forever. But what about busing and gerrymandered attendance zones? The Court keeps talking about interim measures, and it says that year-by-year adjustments are not necessary "once the affirmative duty to desegregate has been accomplished and racial discrimination through official action is eliminated from the system." Can defendants bus for five years and then revert to a neutral assignment plan? Or must they keep busing until population shifts have changed the composition of the neighborhoods surrounding paired schools so that the current plan no longer has an integrative effect? Or must they keep it up until prolonged busing has integrated housing? That isn't likely to happen, is it?

6.   In a companion case, the Court said: "Having once found a violation, the district judge or school authorities should make every effort to achieve the greatest possible degree of actual desegregation, taking into account the practicalities of the situation." Davis v. Board of School Commissioners, 402 U.S. 33, 37 (1971). If "desegregation" means the elimination of de jure segregation, as the context would seem to require, the sentence states an obvious directive to give as complete a remedy as possible. But if "actual desegregation" means the elimination of segregation from all causes, the resulting remedy might make plaintiffs far better off than if there had never been a violation.

The courts of appeals enthusiastically adopted the second reading. As one frustrated trial court said on its third attempt to draft a satisfactory desegregation plan for a school district in Beaumont, Texas: "Regardless of the rhetoric employed, . . . plans that fail to produce a sufficient degree of integration are rejected, and plans that do produce a sufficient degree of integration are approved." United States v. Texas Education Agency, Civ. Action B-6819-CA (E.D. Tex. 1981). He construed the Fifth Circuit's most recent remand as based "exclusively on statistics" and as requiring "a satisfactory system-wide racial mix — nothing less." He responded by assigning children to schools randomly after the third grade, and this time he was affirmed. 699 F.2d 1291 (5th Cir. 1983).

The Sixth Circuit read Swann as requiring trial courts to do everything it said they might do in their discretion. For example, a district judge in Nashville adopted as a guideline that every school should have at least 15 percent whites and at least 15 percent blacks, and ordered that in kindergarten through fourth grade there should be neighborhood schools with attendance zones gerrymandered to maximize integration without busing. He was reversed for ignoring *Swann*, ordered to use the population ratio of 68:32 as his guideline, and to bus in all grades. Kelley v. Metropolitan Board of Education, 687 F.2d 814 (6th Cir. 1982). That's not what *Swann* said, is it? On the other hand, is it a·plausible extension in light of the explanation of equitable discretion in *Albermarle Paper*, supra at 250? It doesn't make any sense to have the scope of busing depend on the personal preferences of each local judge, does it?

7.   The two cases described in note 6 also illustrate the potential life span of these cases. The Beaumont case was filed in 1970, the Nashville case in 1955. Consider this comment on "the nature of modern suits in equity."

> [T]he finding of a constitutional violation is in a practical sense only the preliminary hurdle. The heart of the lawsuit is the remedial stage, where the parties struggle, often for years, over the scope and details of injunctive relief. Under such circumstances it is not uncommon for the parties to take no appeal from the initial liability determination . . . because they recognize the wisdom of husbanding their energy and resources for the true battleground.

Gautreaux v. Chicago Housing Authority, 690 F.2d 601, 609-610 (7th Cir. 1982).

Is it sound strategy not to appeal the liability determination? If remedies are supposed to restore plaintiffs to the position they would have occupied but for the wrong, isn't it important to define the wrong with care? Some liability determinations go unappealed, but it is not as common as the court implies. Even so, the quotation usefully highlights the fallacy of assuming that all the important things happen at the liability stage.

MILLIKEN v. BRADLEY
418 U.S. 717 (1974)

[Plaintiffs sought desegregation of the Detroit public schools. The lower courts found that state and local officials had deliberately maximized school segregation by gerrymandering attendance zones and redrawing them in response to racial change, creating optional attendance zones in residentially changing neighborhoods, segregating feeder-school patterns, constructing new schools in locations and sizes that assured segregated student bodies, and busing black students from overcrowded schools past white schools with available space to more distant black schools. The state legislature had intervened to prevent voluntary desegregation as proposed by the local school board. These findings were not at issue in the Supreme Court.

The lower courts also found that desegregation within Detroit was impossible. This finding was based on the high percentage of black students in Detroit as a whole, the likelihood of white flight to the suburbs, and the distance between black and white neighborhoods in Detroit: Many of the black neighborhoods were closer to the white suburbs. The lower courts ordered fifty-three suburban school districts to be made parties and ordered the parties to submit proposals for a metropolitan desegregation plan and their objections to such plans. Certiorari was granted at this point, before any decision concerning particular metropolitan plans.]

CHIEF JUSTICE BURGER delivered the opinion of the Court. . . .

Here the District Court's approach to what constituted "actual desegregation" raises the fundamental question, not presented in *Swann*, as to the circumstances in which a federal court may order desegregation relief that embraces more than a single school district. The court's analytical starting point was its conclusion that school district lines are no more than arbitrary lines on a map drawn "for political convenience." Boundary lines may be bridged where there has been a constitutional violation calling for interdistrict relief, but the notion that school district lines may be casually ignored or treated as a mere administrative convenience is contrary to the history of public education in our country. No single tradition in public education is more deeply rooted than local control over the operation of schools; local autonomy has long been thought essential both to the maintenance of community concern and support for public schools and to quality of the educational process. Thus, in San Antonio School District v. Rodriguez, 411 U.S. 1, 50 (1973), we observed that local control over the educational process affords citizens an opportunity to participate in decision-making, permits the structuring of school programs to fit local needs, and encourages "experimentation, innovation, and a healthy competition for educational excellence."

The Michigan educational structure involved in this case, in common with most States, provides for a large measure of local control and a review of the scope and character of these local powers indicates the extent to which the interdistrict remedy approved by the two courts could disrupt and alter the structure of public education in Michigan. The metropolitan remedy would require, in effect, consolidation of 54 independent school districts historically administered as separate units into a vast new super school district. Entirely apart from the logistical and other serious problems attending large-scale transportation of students, the consolidation would give rise to an array of other problems in financing and operating this new school system. . . .

It may be suggested that all of these vital operational problems are yet to be resolved by the District Court, and that this is the purpose of the Court of Appeals' proposed remand. But it is obvious from the scope of the interdistrict remedy itself that absent a complete restructuring of the laws of Michigan relating to school districts the District Court will become first, a de facto "legislative authority" to resolve these complex questions, and then the "school superintendent" for the entire area. This is a task which few, if any, judges are qualified to perform and one which would deprive the people of control of schools through their elected representatives.

Of course, no state law is above the Constitution. School district lines and the present laws with respect to local control, are not sacrosanct and if they conflict with the Fourteenth Amendment federal courts have a duty to prescribe appropriate remedies. But our prior holdings have been confined to violations and remedies within a single school district. We therefore turn to address, for the first time, the validity of a remedy mandating cross-district or interdistrict consolidation to remedy a condition of segregation found to exist in only one district.

The controlling principle consistently expounded in our holdings is that the scope of the remedy is determined by the nature and extent of the constitutional violation. Before the boundaries of separate and autonomous school districts may be set aside by consolidating the separate units for remedial purposes or by imposing a cross-district remedy, it must first be shown that there has been a constitutional violation within one district that produces a significant segregative effect in another district. Specifically, it must be shown that racially discriminatory acts of the state or local school districts, or of a single school district have been a substantial cause of interdistrict segregation. Thus an interdistrict remedy might be in order where the racially discriminatory acts of one or more school districts caused racial segregation in an adjacent district, or where district lines have been deliberately drawn on the basis of race. In such circumstances an interdistrict remedy would be appropriate to eliminate the interdistrict segregation directly caused by the constitutional violation. Conversely, without an interdistrict violation and interdistrict effect, there is no constitutional wrong calling for an interdistrict remedy.

The record before us, voluminous as it is, contains evidence of de jure segregated conditions only in the Detroit schools; indeed, that was the theory on which the litigation was initially based and on which the District Court took evidence. With no showing of significant violation by the 53 outlying school districts and no evidence of any interdistrict violation or effect, the court went beyond the original theory of the case as framed by the pleadings and mandated a metropolitan area remedy. To approve the remedy ordered by the court would impose on the outlying districts, not shown to have committed any constitutional violation, a wholly impermissible remedy based on a standard not hinted at in *Brown I* and *II* or any holding of this Court.

In dissent, Mr. Justice White and Mr. Justice Marshall undertake to demonstrate that agencies having statewide authority participated in maintaining the dual school system found to exist in Detroit. They are apparently of the view that once such participation is shown, the District Court should have a relatively free hand to reconstruct school districts outside of Detroit in fashioning relief. Our assumption, arguendo, that state agencies did participate in the maintenance of the Detroit system, should make it clear that it is not on this point that we part company.[21] The difference between us arises instead from established doctrine laid down by our cases. *Brown, Green, Swann, Scotland Neck,* and *Emporia* each addressed the issue of constitutional wrong in terms of an established geographic and administrative school system populated by both Negro and white children. In such a context, terms such as "unitary" and "dual" systems, and "racially identifiable schools," have meaning, and the necessary federal authority to remedy the constitutional wrong is firmly established. But the remedy is necessarily designed, as all remedies are, to restore the victims of discriminatory conduct to the position they would have occupied in the absence of such conduct. Disparate treatment of white and Negro students occurred within the Detroit school system, and not elsewhere, and on this record the remedy must be limited to that system.

The constitutional right of the Negro respondents residing in Detroit is to attend a unitary school system in that district. Unless petitioners drew the district lines in a discriminatory fashion, or arranged for white students residing in the Detroit district to attend schools in Oakland and Macomb Counties, they were under no constitutional duty to make provisions for Negro students to do so. The view of the dissenters, that the existence of a dual system in *Detroit* can be made the basis for a decree requiring cross-district transportation of pupils cannot be supported on the grounds that it represents merely the devising of a suitably flexible remedy for the violation of rights already established by our prior decisions. It can be supported only by drastic expansion of the constitutional right itself, an expansion without any support in either constitutional principle or precedent. . . .

Accordingly, the judgment of the Court of Appeals is reversed and the case is remanded for further proceedings consistent with this opinion leading to prompt formulation of a decree directed to eliminating the segregation found to exist in Detroit city schools, a remedy which has been delayed since 1970.

Reversed and remanded.

MR. JUSTICE WHITE, with whom MR. JUSTICE DOUGLAS, MR. JUSTICE BRENNAN, and MR. JUSTICE MARSHALL join, dissenting. . . .

I am even more mystified as to how the Court can ignore the legal reality that the constitutional violations, even if occurring locally, were committed by governmental entities for which the State is responsible

---

21. Since the Court has held that a resident of a school district has a fundamental right protected by the Federal Constitution to vote in a district election, it would seem incongruous to disparage the importance of the school district in a different context. Kramer v. Union Free School District No. 15, 395 U.S. 621, 626 (1969). . . .

and that it is the State that must respond to the command of the Four-teenth Amendment. An inter-district remedy for the infringements that occurred in this case is well within the confines and powers of the State, which is the governmental entity ultimately responsible for desegregating its schools. The Michigan Supreme Court has observed that "[t]he school district is a State agency," Attorney General ex rel. Kies v. Lowrey, 131 Mich. 639, 644, 92 N.W. 289, 290 (1902), and that " '[e]ducation in Michi-gan belongs to the State. It is no part of the local self-government inher-ent in the township or municipality, except so far as the legislature may choose to make it such. The Constitution has turned the whole subject over to the legislature. . . .' " Attorney General ex rel. Zacharias v. De-troit Board of Education, 154 Mich. 584, 590, 118 N.W. 606, 609 (1908). . . .

No "State" may deny any individual the equal protection of the laws; and if the Constitution and the Supremacy Clause are to have any sub-stance at all, the courts must be free to devise workable remedies against the political entity with the effective power to determine local choice. . . .

The Court draws the remedial line at the Detroit School District boundary, even though the Fourteenth Amendment is addressed to the State and even though the *State* denies equal protection of the laws when its public agencies, acting in its behalf, invidiously discriminate. The State's default is "the condition that offends the Constitution," Swann v. Charlotte-Mecklenburg Board of Education, at 16, and state officials may therefore be ordered to take the necessary measures to completely elimi-nate from the Detroit public schools "all vestiges of state-imposed segre-gation." Id., at 15. I cannot understand, nor does the majority satisfactorily explain, why a federal court may not order an appropriate inter-district remedy, if this is necessary or more effective to accomplish this constitutionally mandated task. . . . [T]here is no acceptable reason for permitting the party responsible for the constitutional violation to contain the remedial powers of the federal court within administrative boundaries over which the transgressor itself has plenary power. . . .

Finally, I remain wholly unpersuaded by the Court's assertion that "the remedy is necessarily designed, as all remedies are, to restore the victims of discriminatory conduct to the position they would have occu-pied in the absence of such conduct." In the first place, under this prem-ise the Court's judgment is itself infirm; for had the Detroit school system not followed an official policy of segregation throughout the 1950's and 1960's, Negroes and whites would have been going to school together. There would have been no, or at least not as many, recognizable Negro schools and no, or at least not as many, white schools, but "just schools," and neither Negroes nor whites would have suffered from the effects of segregated education, with all its shortcomings. Surely the Court's rem-edy will not restore to the Negro community, stigmatized as it was by the dual school system, what it would have enjoyed over all or most of this period if the remedy is confined to present-day Detroit; for the maximum remedy available within that area will leave many of the schools almost totally black, and the system itself will be predominantly black and will become increasingly so. Moreover, when a State has engaged in acts of official segregation over a lengthy period of time, as in the case before us, it is unrealistic to suppose that the children who were victims of the State's unconstitutional conduct could now be provided the benefits of which they were wrongfully deprived. Nor can the benefits which accrue to school systems in which schoolchildren have not been officially segregated, and to the communities supporting such school systems, be fully and immediately restored after a substantial period of unlawful segregation. The education of children of different races in a desegregated environment has unhappily been lost, along with the social, economic, and political advantages which accompany a desegregated school system as compared with an unconstitutionally segregated system. It is for these reasons that the Court has consistently followed the course of requiring the effects of past official segregation to be eliminated "root and branch" by imposing, in the present, the duty to provide a remedy which will achieve "the greatest possible degree of actual desegregation, taking into account the practicalities of the situation." It is also for these reasons that once a constitutional violation has been found, the district judge obligated to provide such a remedy "will thus necessarily be concerned with the elimination of one-race schools." These concerns were properly taken into account by the District Judge in this case. Confining the remedy to the boundaries of the Detroit district is quite unrelated either to the goal of achieving maximum desegregation or to those intensely practical considerations, such as the extent and expense of transportation, that have imposed limits on remedies in cases such as this. The Court's remedy, in the end, is essentially arbitrary and will leave serious violations of the Constitution substantially unremedied. . . .

MR. JUSTICE MARSHALL, with whom MR. JUSTICE DOUGLAS, MR. JUSTICE BRENNAN, and MR. JUSTICE MARSHALL join, dissenting. . . .

The State must also bear part of the blame for the white flight to the suburbs which would be forthcoming from a Detroit-only decree and would render such a remedy ineffective. Having created a system where whites and Negroes were intentionally kept apart so that they could not become accustomed to learning together, the State is responsible for the fact that many whites will react to the dismantling of that segregated system by attempting to flee to the suburbs. Indeed, by limiting the District Court to a Detroit-only remedy and allowing that flight to the suburbs to succeed, the Court today allows the State to profit from its own wrong and to perpetuate for years to come the separation of the races it achieved in the past by purposeful state action.

The majority asserts, however, that involvement of outlying districts would do violence to the accepted principle that "the nature of the violation determines the scope of the remedy." *Swann*, 402 U.S., at 16. Not only is the majority's attempt to find in this single phrase the answer to the complex and difficult questions presented in this case hopelessly simplistic but more important, the Court reads these words in a manner which perverts their obvious meaning. The nature of a violation determines the scope of the remedy simply because the function of any remedy is to cure the violation to which it is addressed. In school segregation cases, as in other equitable causes, a remedy which effectively cures the violation is what is required. No more is necessary, but we can tolerate no less. To read this principle as barring a district court from imposing the only effective remedy for past segregation and remitting the court to a patently ineffective alternative is, in my view, to turn a simple common-sense rule into a cruel and meaningless paradox. Ironically, by ruling out an interdistrict remedy, the only relief which promises to cure segregation in the Detroit public schools, the majority flouts the very principle on which it purports to rely. . . .

Though not resting its holding on this point, the majority suggests that various equitable considerations militate against interdistrict relief. The Court, for example, refers to financing and administrative problems, the logistical problems attending large-scale transportation of students, and the prospect of the District Court's becoming a "de facto 'legislative authority'" and "'school superintendent' for the entire area." The entangling web of problems woven by the Court, however, appears on further consideration to be constructed of the flimsiest of threads. . . .

The State clearly has the power, under existing law, to effect a consolidation if it is ultimately determined that this offers the best prospect for a workable and stable desegregation plan. And given the 1,000 or so consolidations of school districts which have taken place in the past, it is hard to believe that the State has not already devised means of solving most, if not all, of the practical problems which the Court suggests consolidation would entail.

Furthermore, the majority ignores long-established Michigan procedures under which school districts may enter into contractual agreements to educate their pupils in other districts using state or local funds to finance nonresident education. . . . The metropolitan plan would not involve the busing of substantially more students than already ride buses. . . .

With respect to distance and amount of time travelled, 17 of the outlying school districts involved in the plan are contiguous to the Detroit district. The rest are all within 8 miles of the Detroit city limits. The trial court, in defining the desegregation area, placed a ceiling of 40 minutes one way on the amount of travel time, and many students will obviously travel for far shorter periods. As to distance, the average statewide bus trip is 8½ miles one way, and in some parts of the tri-county area, students already travel for one and a quarter hours or more each way. In sum, with regard to both the number of students transported and the time and distances involved, the outlined desegregation plan "compares favorably with the transportation plan previously operated. . . ." *Swann*, at 30. . . .

Since no inventory of school buses existed, a Detroit-only plan was estimated to require the purchase of 900 buses to effectuate the necessary transportation. The tri-county area, in contrast, already has an inventory of 1,800 buses, may of which are now under-utilized. Since increased utilization of the existing inventory can take up much of the increase in transportation involved in the interdistrict remedy, the District Court found that only 350 additional buses would probably be needed. . . .

[JUSTICE DOUGLAS also filed a separate dissent; JUSTICE STEWART filed a separate concurrence.]

MORE NOTES ON THE MEASURE OF INJUNCTIVE RELIEF

1. Plaintiffs in *Milliken* were black schoolchildren in the city of Detroit. The majority and dissenters disagree in part over what position they would have occupied but for the wrong. Justice White says that but for the wrong, black and white children would have gone to school together. Would the *plaintiffs* have gone to school with white children but for the wrong? Or would it have been some other black children, ten or twenty years before, when there were still enough whites in Detroit for a Detroit-only plan to have worked? Is Justice White ignoring the plaintiffs in search of a remedy for "the black community"? Or is he assuming that school segregation in Detroit is responsible for the movement of whites to the suburbs and the concentration of blacks in the city? That assumption isn't very plausible, is it? If plaintiffs could prove that assumption, would that be an interdistrict violation requiring interdistrict relief under the majority's test?

2. The majority's view is that but for the wrong, plaintiffs would have been going to school in Detroit, in a largely black system, but without any artificial separation of the whites and blacks who remained. That would seem to dispose of the case. Why does the opinion talk at such length about the political and administrative difficulties of a metropolitan remedy and the traditions of local control? Is that all an irrelevant rhetorical flourish? An alternate ground for decision? Or an essential part of a decision announcing a balancing test rather than an absolute rule?

3. If desegregation within the neutrally drawn boundary of the Detroit district is satisfactory, why wouldn't desegregation within neutrally drawn attendance zones have been satisfactory in *Swann?* To put it the

other way, if the remedy in *Swann* had to take account of the effects of school segregation on housing patterns, is there any reason to assume that those effects end at the school district line? Might the problem simply be that plaintiffs didn't provide those effects in *Milliken?* Of course, they didn't prove those effects in *Swann* either.

4.   Chief Justice Burger wrote both *Swann* and *Milliken.* Is his emphasis on restoring plaintiffs to the positions they would have occupied but for the wrong and his insistence that "the scope of the violation determines the scope of the remedy" consistent with all the rhetoric about the breadth, flexibility, and practicality of equity?

5.   Recall the statute in Bell v. Southwell providing for appointment of a justice of the peace in the event an election were declared invalid. The court overrode that statute and ordered a new election. Is that order suspect under *Milliken*'s emphasis on the scope of the violation? The appointment statute was not unconstitutional, was it? How is the appointment statute different from the statute creating the boundaries of the Detroit school district? Both were enacted long before the present controversies arose and without any illegal intent. Is the difference simply that but for the violation, the appointments statute in *Bell* would never have come into play?

MILLIKEN v. BRADLEY
433 U.S. 267 (1977)

[After *Milliken I,* the district court ordered a Detroit-only busing plan. That part of the order was not reviewed by the Supreme Court. The district court also ordered the local school board to provide a broad range of new or modified educational programs as part of the desegregation plan, and ordered the state to pay half the cost. Only the state defendants objected. A settlement was worked out concerning several of the educational programs, but the state defendants sought review of orders to help finance remedial reading and communication skills training for victims of segregated schools, in-service training for teachers and administrators on how to perform in an integrated system, design of testing programs free from racial, ethnic, and cultural bias, counseling for students adjusting to integration, and career guidance for students considering new vocational programs provided for in the settlement.]

CHIEF JUSTICE BURGER delivered the opinion of the Court. . . .

II

This Court has not previously addressed directly the question whether federal courts can order remedial education programs as part of a school desegregation decree. However, the general principles governing our resolution of this issue are well settled by the prior decisions of this Court. In the first case concerning federal courts' remedial powers in eliminating de jure school segregation, the Court laid down the basic rule which governs to this day: "In fashioning and effectuating the [desegregation] decrees, the courts will be guided by equitable principles." Brown v. Board of Education, 349 U.S. 294, 300 (1955).

A

Application of those "equitable principles," we have held, requires federal courts to focus upon three factors. In the first place, like other equitable remedies, the nature of the desegregation remedy is to be determined by the nature and scope of the constitutional violation. The remedy must therefore be related to "the *condition* alleged to offend the Constitution. . . ." *Milliken I,* 418 U.S., at 738. Second, the decree must indeed be *remedial* in nature, that is, it must be designed as nearly as possible "to restore the victims of discriminatory conduct to the position they would have occupied in the absence of such conduct." Third, the federal courts in devising a remedy must take into account the interests of state and local authorities in managing their own affairs, consistent with the Constitution. In *Brown II* the Court squarely held that "[s]chool authorities have the *primary* responsibility for elucidating, assessing, and solving these problems. . . ." 349 U.S. at 299. (Emphasis supplied.) If, however, "school authorities fail in their affirmative obligations . . . judicial authority may be invoked." *Swann,* at 15. Once invoked, "the scope of a district court's equitable powers to remedy past wrongs is broad, for breadth and flexibility are inherent in equitable remedies." Ibid.

B

In challenging the order before us, petitioners do not specifically question that the District Court's mandated programs are designed, as nearly as practicable, to restore the schoolchildren of Detroit to the position they would have enjoyed absent constitutional violations by state and local officials. And, petitioners do not contend, nor could they, that the prerogatives of the Detroit School Board have been abrogated by the decree, since of course the Detroit School Board itself proposed incorporation of these programs in the first place. Petitioners' sole contention is that, under *Swann,* the District Court's order exceeds the scope of the constitutional violation. Invoking our holding in *Milliken I,* petitioners claim that, since the constitutional violation found by the District Court was the unlawful segregation of students on the basis of race, the court's decree must be limited to remedying unlawful pupil assignments. This contention misconceives the principle petitioners seek to invoke, and we reject their argument.

The well-settled principle that the nature and scope of the remedy are to be determined by the violation means simply that federal-court decrees must directly address and relate to the constitutional violation itself. Because of this inherent limitation upon federal judicial authority, federal-court decrees exceed appropriate limits if they are aimed at eliminating a condition that does not violate the Constitution or does not flow from such a violation, or if they are imposed upon governmental units that were neither involved in nor affected by the constitutional violation. But where, as here, a constitutional violation has been found, the remedy does not "exceed" the violation if the remedy is tailored to cure the "'condition that offends the Constitution.'" *Milliken I*, supra, at 738. (Emphasis supplied.)

The "condition" offending the Constitution is Detroit's de jure segregated school system, which was so pervasively and persistently segregated that the District Court found that the need for the educational components flowed directly from constitutional violations by both state and local officials. These specific educational remedies, although normally left to the discretion of the elected school board and professional educators, were deemed necessary to restore the victims of discriminatory conduct to the position they would have enjoyed in terms of education had these four components been provided in a nondiscriminatory manner in a school system free from pervasive de jure racial segregation. . . .

C

In light of the mandate of *Brown I* and *Brown II*, federal courts have, over the years, often required the inclusion of remedial programs in desegregation plans to overcome the inequalities inherent in dual school systems. . . .

[T]he decree before us was aptly tailored to remedy the consequences of the constitutional violation. Children who have been thus educationally and culturally set apart from the larger community will inevitably acquire habits of speech, conduct, and attitudes reflecting their cultural isolation. They are likely to acquire speech habits, for example, which vary from the environment in which they must ultimately function and compete, if they are to enter and be a part of that community. This is not peculiar to race; in this setting, it can affect any children who, as a group, are isolated by force of law from the mainstream.

Pupil assignment alone does not automatically remedy the impact of previous, unlawful educational isolation; the consequences linger and can be dealt with only by independent measures. In short, speech habits acquired in a segregated system do not vanish simply by moving the child to a desegregated school. The root condition shown by this record must be treated directly by special training at the hands of teachers prepared for that task. This is what the District Judge in the case drew from the record before him as to the consequences of Detroit's de jure system, and we cannot conclude that the remedies decreed exceeded the scope of the violations found.

Nor do we find any other reason to believe that the broad and flexible equity powers of the court were abused in this case. The established role of local school authorities was maintained inviolate, and the remedy is indeed remedial. The order does not punish anyone, not does it impair or jeopardize the educational system in Detroit. . . .

The judgment of the Court of Appeals is therefore affirmed.

[JUSTICE POWELL concurred separately.]

STILL MORE NOTES ON THE MEASURE OF INJUNCTIVE RELIEF

1. What about past graduates of segregated schools? If they asked for remedial adult education, wouldn't their claim be even stronger than that of the current students, because they suffered through more years of segregated education?

2. Are the Court's three factors a good distillation of its cases? What does it mean to require that "the remedy . . . be related to 'the *condition* alleged to offend the Constitution'"? What does that add to the requirement that the remedy be "designed as nearly as possible 'to restore the victims of discriminatory conduct to the position they would have occupied in the absence of such conduct'"? The third factor, taking "into account the interests of state and local authorities in managing their own affairs," explicitly separates the federalism concerns that have run through these cases. General Building Contractors Association v. Pennsylvania, infra at 287, implies that the other two factors are applicable to private defendants. So does the statement in *Milliken I*: "the remedy is necessarily designed, as all remedies are, to restore the victims . . . to the position they would have occupied. . . ." There's no reason to distinguish public and private defendants with respect to that standard is there?

3. *Milliken II* was decided the same day as Dayton Board of Education v. Brinkman, 433 U.S. 406 (1977). The court of appeals had mandated citywide busing without modifying the district court's findings of rather limited violations. The Supreme Court vacated and remanded, holding that the remedy exceeded the scope of the violation, and giving the following instructions:

> The duty of both the District Court and the Court of Appeals in a case such as this, where mandatory segregation by law of the races in the schools has long since ceased, is to first determine whether there was any action in the conduct of the business of the school board which was intended to, and did in

fact, discriminate against minority pupils, teachers, or staff. All parties should be free to introduce such additional testimony and other evidence as the District Court may deem appropriate. If such violations are found, the District Court in the first instance, subject to review by the Court of Appeals, must determine how much incremental segregative effect these violations had on the racial distribution of the Dayton school population as presently constituted, when that distribution is compared to what it would have been in the absence of such constitutional violations. The remedy must be designed to redress that difference, and only if there has been a systemwide impact may there be a systemwide remedy.

433 U.S. at 420. "Incremental segregative effect" sure has a different ring than "greatest possible degree of actual desegregation." But if the Court is committed to restoring victims to the position they would have occupied but for the wrong, doesn't "incremental segregative effect" have to be the standard?

4.   Does *Dayton* mean that existing housing segregation should be taken as a given in school cases, and relief limited to drawing neutral attendance zone lines? That would overrule most of *Swann* sub silentio, wouldn't it? *Swann* noted that school segregation affects housing choices; does *Dayton* require the lower courts to determine what housing patterns would have looked like if there had never been deliberate school segregation, and then order busing to achieve the school attendance patterns that would have resulted from drawing neutral attendance zones on that housing pattern? Must the court allow for the effect on housing patterns of the higher socioeconomic status blacks would now enjoy if there had never been discrimination in education? How would you litigate such an issue? Or should courts ignore that effect because it is too uncertain, or too remote? Should there be a proximate cause limit on the harm that will be repaired by injunction, analogous to the proximate cause limit on compensation?

5.   In cases like *Milliken II*, does *Dayton* require the lower courts to distinguish educational deficiencies caused by racial discrimination from deficiencies caused by incompetent educators, inadequate funding, economic deprivation, and all other causes, and remedy only those caused by racial discrimination?

6.   On remand in *Dayton*, the district court dismissed the complaint. Brinkman v. Gilligan, 446 F. Supp. 1232 (S.D. Ohio 1977). It held that plaintiffs had failed to prove any current incremental segregative effect from the intentionally segregative acts committed in a few neighborhoods many years before.

The court of appeals reversed and reinstated the original citywide busing plan. Brinkman v. Gilligan, 583 F.2d 243 (6th Cir. 1978). The court used a chain of presumptions to avoid detailed analysis of the sort apparently contemplated by *Dayton I*. In combination, the presumptions effectively attributed all segregation anywhere in the city to the proven acts of deliberate segregation. These presumptions were rebuttable in theory. But the obvious line of rebuttal — that much school segregation was caused by residential segregation — was apparently inadequate.

The Supreme Court affirmed, specifically endorsing the chain of presumptions. Dayton Board of Education v. Brinkman, 433 U.S. 526 (1979). Dayton II's holdings about the proof of violations and causal relationships leave Dayton I's holding about remedy intact but largely irrelevant. There were four dissents.

HUTTO v. FINNEY
437 U.S. 678 (1978)

MR. JUSTICE STEVENS delivered the opinion of the Court.

After finding that conditions in the Arkansas penal system constituted cruel and unusual punishment, the District Court entered a series of detailed remedial orders. On appeal to the United States Court of Appeals for the Eighth Circuit, petitioners challenged two aspects of that relief: (1) an order placing a maximum limit of 30 days on confinement in punitive isolation; and (2) an award of attorney's fees to be paid out of Department of Correction funds. The Court of Appeals affirmed and assessed an additional attorney's fee to cover services on appeal. 548 F.2d 740 (1977). We . . . affirm.

This litigation began in 1969; it is a sequel to two earlier cases holding that conditions in the Arkansas prison system violated the Eighth and Fourteenth Amendments.[2] Only a brief summary of the facts is necessary to explain the basis for the remedial orders.

The routine conditions that the ordinary Arkansas convict had to endure were characterized by the District Court as "a dark and evil world completely alien to the free world." Holt v. Sarver, 309 F. Supp. 362, 381 (E.D. Ark. 1970) (Holt II). That characterization was amply supported by the evidence.[3] The punishments for misconduct not serious enough to

2. This case began as Holt v. Sarver, 300 F. Supp. 825 (E.D. Ark. 1969) (Holt I). The two earlier cases were Talley v. Stephens, 247 F. Supp. 683 (E.D. Ark. 1965), and Jackson v. Bishop, 268 F. Supp. 804 (E.D. Ark. 1967), vacated, 404 F.2d 571 (C.A.8 1968).

3. The administrators of Arkansas' prison system evidently tried to operate their prisons at a profit. Cummins Farm, the institution at the center of this litigation, required its 1,000 inmates to work in the fields 10 hours a day, six days a week, using mule-drawn tools and tending crops by hand. The inmates were sometimes required to run to and from the fields, with a guard in an automobile or on horseback driving them on. They worked in all sorts of weather, so long as the temperature was above freezing, sometimes in unsuitably light clothing or without shoes.

The inmates slept together in large, 100-man barracks, and some convicts, known as "creepers," would slip from their beds to crawl along the floor, stalking their sleeping enemies. In one 18-month period, there were 17 stabbings, all but 1 occurring in the barracks. Homosexual rape was so common and uncontrolled that some potential victims dared not sleep; instead they would leave their beds and spend the night clinging to the bars nearest the guards' station.

result in punitive isolation were cruel,[4] unusual,[5] and unpredictable.[6] It is the discipline known as "punitive isolation" that is most relevant for present purposes.

Confinement in punitive isolation was for an indeterminate period of time. An average of 4, and sometimes as many as 10 or 11, prisoners were crowded into windowless 8′ × 10′ cells containing no furniture other than a source of water and a toilet that could only be flushed from outside the cell. At night the prisoners were given mattresses to spread on the floor. Although some prisoners suffered from infectious diseases such as hepatitis and venereal disease, mattresses were removed and jumbled together each morning, then returned to the cells at random in the evening. Prisoners in isolation received fewer than 1,000 calories a day;[7] their meals consisted primarily of 4-inch squares of "grue," a substance created by mashing meat, potatoes, oleo, syrup, vegetables, eggs, and seasoning into a paste and baking the mixture in a pan.

After finding the conditions of confinement unconstitutional, the District Court did not immediately impose a detailed remedy of its own. Instead, it directed the Department of Correction to "make a substantial start" on improving conditions and to file reports on its progress. When the Department's progress proved unsatisfactory, a second hearing was held. The District Court found some improvements, but concluded that prison conditions remained unconstitutional. Again the court offered prison administrators an opportunity to devise a plan of their own for remedying the constitutional violations, but this time the court issued guidelines, identifying four areas of change that would cure the worst evils: improving conditions in the isolation cells, increasing inmate safety, eliminating the barracks sleeping arrangements, and putting an end to the trusty system. The Department was ordered to move as rapidly as funds became available.

---

4. Inmates were lashed with a wooden-handled leather strap five feet long and four inches wide. Although it was not official policy to do so, some inmates were apparently whipped for minor offenses until their skin was bloody and bruised.

5. The "Tucker telephone," a hand-cranked device, was used to administer electrical shocks to various sensitive parts of an inmate's body.

6. Most of the guards were simply inmates who had been issued guns. Although it had 1,000 prisoners, Cummins employed only eight guards who were not themselves convicts. Only two nonconvict guards kept watch over the 1,000 men at night. While the "trusties" maintained an appearance of order, they took a high toll from the other prisoners. Inmates could obtain access to medical treatment only if they bribed the trusty in charge of sick call. As the District Court found, it was "within the power of a trusty guard to murder another inmate with practical impunity," because trusties with weapons were authorized to use deadly force against escapees. "Accidental shootings" also occurred; and one trusty fired his shotgun into a crowded barracks because the inmates would not turn off their TV. Another trusty beat an inmate so badly the victim required partial dentures.

7. A daily allowance of 2,700 calories is recommended for the average male between 23 and 50. National Academy of Sciences, Recommended Dietary Allowances, Appendix (8th rev. ed. 1974). Prisoners in punitive isolation are less active than the average person; but a mature man who spends 12 hours a day lying down and 12 hours a day simply sitting or standing consumes approximately 2,000 calories a day. Id. at 27.

After this order was affirmed on appeal, Holt v. Sarver, 442 F.2d 304 (C.A.8 1971), more hearings were held in 1972 and 1973 to review the Department's progress. Finding substantial improvements, the District Court concluded that continuing supervision was no longer necessary. The court held, however, that its prior decrees would remain in effect and noted that sanctions, as well as an award of costs and attorney's fees, would be imposed if violations occurred. Holt v. Hutto, 363 F. Supp. 194, 217 (E.D. Ark. 1973) (*Holt III*).

The Court of Appeals reversed the District Court's decision to withdraw its supervisory jurisdiction, Finney v. Arkansas Board of Correction, 505 F.2d 194 (C.A.8 1974), and the District Court held a fourth set of hearings. 410 F. Supp. 251 (E.D. Ark. 1976). It found that, in some respects, conditions had seriously deteriorated since 1973, when the court had withdrawn its supervisory jurisdiction. Cummins Farm, which the court had condemned as overcrowded in 1970 because it housed 1,000 inmates, now had a population of about 1,500. The situation in the punitive isolation cells was particularly disturbing. The court concluded that either it had misjudged conditions in these cells in 1973 or conditions had become much worse since then. There were twice as many prisoners as beds in some cells. And because inmates in punitive isolation are often violently antisocial, overcrowding led to persecution of the weaker prisoners. The "grue" diet was still in use, and practically all inmates were losing weight on it. The cells had been vandalized to a "very substantial" extent. Because of their inadequate numbers, guards assigned to the punitive isolation cells frequently resorted to physical violence, using nightsticks and Mace in their efforts to maintain order. Prisoners were sometimes left in isolation for months, their release depending on "their attitudes as appraised by prison personnel."

The court concluded that the constitutional violations identified earlier had not been cured. It entered an order that placed limits on the number of men that could be confined in one cell, required that each have a bunk, discontinued the "grue" diet, and set 30 days as the maximum isolation sentence. The District Court gave detailed consideration to the matter of fees and expenses, made an express finding that petitioners had acted in bad faith, and awarded counsel "a fee of $20,000.00 to be paid out of Department of Correction funds." The Court of Appeals affirmed and assessed an additional $2,500 to cover fees and expenses on appeal. 548 F.2d, at 743.

I . . .

Petitioners do not . . . disagree with the District Court's original conclusion that conditions in Arkansas' prisons, including its punitive isolation cells, constituted cruel and unusual punishment. Rather, petitioners single out that portion of the District Court's most recent order that forbids the Department to sentence inmates to more than 30 days in punitive isolation. Petitioners assume that the District Court held that indeterminate sentences to punitive isolation always constitute cruel and unusual punishment. This assumption misreads the District Court's holding.

Read in its entirety, the District Court's opinion makes it abundantly clear that the length of isolation sentences was not considered in a vacuum. In the court's words, punitive isolation "is not necessarily unconstitutional, but it may be, depending on the duration of the confinement and the conditions thereof." It is perfectly obvious that every decision to remove a particular inmate from the general prison population for an indeterminate period could not be characterized as cruel and unusual. If new conditions of confinement are not materially different from those affecting other prisoners, a transfer for the duration of a prisoner's sentence might be completely unobjectionable and well within the authority of the prison administrator. It is equally plain, however, that the length of confinement cannot be ignored in deciding whether the confinement meets constitutional standards. A filthy, overcrowded cell and a diet of "grue" might be tolerable for a few days and intolerably cruel for weeks or months.

The question before the trial court was whether past constitutional violations had been remedied. The court was entitled to consider the severity of those violations in assessing the constitutionality of conditions in the isolation cells. The court took note of the inmates' diet, the continued overcrowding, the rampant violence, the vandalized cells, and the "lack of professionalism and good judgment on the part of maximum security personnel." The length of time each inmate spent in isolation was simply one consideration among many. We find no error in the court's conclusion that, taken as a whole, conditions in the isolation cells continued to violate the prohibition against cruel and unusual punishment.

In fashioning a remedy, the District Court had ample authority to go beyond earlier orders and to address each element contributing to the violation. The District Court had given the Department repeated opportunities to remedy the cruel and unusual conditions in the isolation cells. If petitioners had fully complied with the court's earlier orders, the present time limit might well have been unnecessary. But taking the long and unhappy history of the litigation into account, the court was justified in entering a comprehensive order to insure against the risk of inadequate compliance.[9]

---

9. . . . In this case, the District Court was not remedying the present effects of a violation in the past. It was seeking to bring an ongoing violation to an immediate halt. Cooperation on the part of Department officials and compliance with other aspects of the decree may justify elimination of this added safeguard in the future, but it is entirely appropriate for the District Court to postpone any such determination until the Department's progress can be evaluated.

The order is supported by the interdependence of the conditions producing the violation. The vandalized cells and the atmosphere of violence were attributable, in part, to overcrowding and to deep-seated enmities growing out of months of constant daily friction. The 30-day limit will help to correct these conditions.[11] Moreover, the limit presents little danger of interference with prison administration, for the Commissioner of Correction himself stated that prisoners should not ordinarily be held in punitive isolation for more than 14 days. Finally, the exercise of discretion in this case is entitled to special deference because of the trial judge's years of experience with the problem at hand and his recognition of the limits on a federal court's authority in a case of this kind. Like the Court of Appeals, we find no error in the inclusion of a 30-day limitation on sentences to punitive isolation as a part of the District Court's comprehensive remedy. . . .

The judgment of the Court of Appeals is accordingly affirmed.

MR. JUSTICE REHNQUIST, dissenting.

The Court's affirmance of a District Court's injunction against a prison practice which has not been shown to violate the Constitution can only be considered an aberration in light of decisions as recently as last Term carefully defining the remedial discretion of the federal courts. Dayton Board of Education v. Brinkman, 433 U.S. 406 (1977); Milliken v. Bradley, 433 U.S. 267 (1977). . . .

I

No person of ordinary feeling could fail to be moved by the Court's recitation of the conditions formerly prevailing in the Arkansas prison system. Yet I fear that the Court has allowed itself to be moved beyond the well-established bounds limiting the exercise of remedial authority by the federal district courts. . . .[1]

---

11. As early as 1969, the District Court had identified shorter sentences as a possible remedy for overcrowding in the isolation cells. The limit imposed in 1976 was a mechanical — and therefore an easily enforced — method of minimizing overcrowding, with its attendant vandalism and unsanitary conditions.

1. The Court suggests, ante, at n.9, that its holding is consistent with Milliken II, because it "was not remedying the present effects of a violation in the past. It was seeking to bring an ongoing violation to an immediate halt." This suggestion is wide of the mark. Whether exercising its authority to "remed[y] the present effects of a violation in the past," or "seeking to bring an ongoing violation to an immediate halt," the court's remedial authority remains circumscribed by . . . Milliken II. If anything, less ingenuity and discretion would appear to be required to "bring an ongoing violation to an immediate halt" than in "remedying the present effects of a violation in the past." The difficulty with the Court's position is that it quite properly refrains from characterizing solitary confinement for a period in excess of 30 days as a cruel and unusual punishment; but given this position, a "remedial" order that no such solitary confinement may take place is necessarily of a prophylactic nature, and not essential to "bring an ongoing violation to an immediate halt."

The District Court's order limiting the maximum period of punitive isolation to 30 days in no way relates to any condition found offensive to the Constitution. It is, when stripped of descriptive verbiage, a prophylactic rule, doubtless well designed to assure a more humane prison system in Arkansas, but not complying with the limitations set forth in *Milliken II*. Petitioners do not dispute the District Court's conclusion that the overcrowded conditions and the inadequate diet provided for those prisoners in punitive isolation offended the Constitution, but the District Court has ordered a cessation of those practices. The District Court found that the confinement of two prisoners in a single cell on a restricted diet for 30 days did not violate the Eighth Amendment. While the Court today remarks that "the length of confinement cannot be ignored," it does not find that confinement under the conditions described by the District Court becomes unconstitutional on the 31st day. It must seek other justifications for its affirmance of that portion of the District Court's order.

Certainly the provision is not remedial in the sense that it "restore[s] the victims of discriminatory conduct to the position they would have occupied in the absence of such conduct." Milliken v. Bradley, 418 U.S. 717, 746 (1974). The sole effect of the provision is to grant future offenders against prison discipline greater benefits than the Constitution requires; it does nothing to remedy the plight of past victims of conditions which may well have been unconstitutional. A prison is unlike a school system, in which students in the later grades may receive special instruction to compensate for discrimination to which they were subjected in the earlier grades. Nor has it been shown that petitioners' conduct had any collateral effect upon private actions for which the District Court may seek to compensate so as to eliminate the continuing effect of past unconstitutional conduct. See Swann v. Charlotte-Mecklenburg Board of Education, 402 U.S. 1, 28 (1971). Even where such remedial relief is justified, a district court may go no further than is necessary to eliminate the consequences of official unconstitutional conduct.

The Court's only asserted justification for its affirmance of the decree, despite its dissimilarity to remedial decrees in other contexts, is that it is "a mechanical — and therefore an easily enforced — method of minimizing overcrowding." Ante, at n.11. This conclusion fails adequately to take into account the third consideration cited in *Milliken II*: "the interests of state and local authorities in managing their own affairs, consistent with the Constitution." 433 U.S., at 281. The prohibition against extended punitive isolation, a practice which has not been shown to be inconsistent with the Constitution, can only be defended because of the difficulty of policing the District Court's explicit injunction against the overcrowding and inadequate diet which have been found to be violative of the Constitution. But even if such an expansion of remedial authority could be justified in a case where the defendants had been repeatedly contumacious, this is not such a case. The District Court's dissatisfaction with petitioners' performance under its earlier direction to "make a substantial start" on alleviating unconstitutional conditions cannot support an inference that petitioners are prepared to defy the specific orders now laid down by the District Court and not challenged by the petitioners. A proper respect for "the interests of state and local authorities in managing their own affairs," *Milliken II*, 433 U.S., at 281, requires the opposite conclusion.

The District Court's order enjoins a practice which has not been found inconsistent with the Constitution. The only ground for the injunction, therefore, is the prophylactic one of assuring that no unconstitutional conduct will occur in the future. In a unitary system of prison management there would be much to be said for such a rule, but neither this Court nor any other federal court is entrusted with such a management role under the Constitution. . . .

ONE LAST TIME: MORE NOTES ON THE MEASURE OF INJUNCTIVE RELIEF

1. Is *Hutto* an aberration? Or is it the busing cases that are aberrational? Or is the whole line of cases from *Swann* to *Hutto* consistent?

2. Recall the two traditions reflected in the section on reparative injunctions: the tradition of restoring plaintiff to his rightful position as precisely as possible and the tradition of equitable discretion. The *Milliken* line of cases lends force to the argument that only the first tradition is legitimate; *Hutto* may suggest that the Court did not mean to completely kill off the second tradition. But how much of it is left? Is Bailey v. Proctor, supra at 246, still good law? Or had "each element of the violation" already been remedied there, and if so, does that matter? Does *Hutto* suggest limits that leave courts some discretion but constrain that discretion far more than "power to do complete equity in the case"? Albermarle Paper Co. v. Moody, supra at 250, suggests that the guide to discretion is "the large objectives" of the substantive law being enforced. Do *Hutto* and the *Milliken* line of cases constrain discretion more than that?

3. Does the majority concede that punitive isolation for indefinite terms would be constitutional if defendants complied with all of the injunction except the thirty-day clause? Is *Hutto* limited to situations like Community Renewal Foundation v. Chicago Title & Trust, supra at 251, in which the line between legality and illegality is hard to find and hard to monitor? Even if it is, doesn't that category include nearly all the constitutional law cases?

4. Does Justice Rehnquist mean to abolish the discretionary element in equitable remedies by insisting that courts determine exactly what the Constitution requires and order exactly that, neither more nor less? Or

does he think that there will often be more than one way to achieve compliance with the Constitution without exceeding its minimum requirements? Or does he see discretion as a one-way street, allowing discretion to deny a complete remedy but not to safeguard a remedy with prophylactic rules? In his concurring opinion in Albermarle Paper Co. v. Moody, he emphasized the importance of retaining equitable discretion to refuse back pay in employment discrimination cases. Does his view of federalism require that discretion be transferred from the court to the wrongdoer when the wrongdoer is a state or local government?

5. The *Hutto* argument over prophylactic orders can arise even with respect to fairly simple preventive injunctions. A typical example is Bundy v. Jackson, 641 F.2d 934 (D.C. Cir. 1981). There, plaintiff proved that supervisors were sexually harassing female employees in violation of the employment discrimination laws. The court enjoined further sexual harassment. It also ordered defendant to explain the policy against sexual harassment in posted notices and individual letters to all employees, to develop disciplinary measures for harassers, and "to develop other appropriate means of instructing employees . . . of the harmful nature of sexual harassment." Id. at 947 n.15. These provisions are reasonably designed to protect plaintiff from further illegal harassment. But they also order more than the statute requires of its own force. Should Justice Rehnquist vote to vacate them for exceeding the scope of the violations? Would that make any sense? Should it matter whether defendant were a private corporation or the head of a government department?

HILLS v. GAUTREAUX
425 U.S. 284 (1976)

[This case involved racial segregation in public housing operated by the Chicago Housing Authority. After prolonged efforts to implement a remedy within Chicago, the Court of Appeals ordered consideration of a metropolitan plan. 503 F.2d 930 (7th Cir. 1974). The opinion distinguished Milliken v. Bradley as based on a balancing of all relevant factors, including difficulties of administration and traditions of local control which were less pronounced in a public housing case.]

JUSTICE STEWART delivered the opinion of the Court. . . .

II . . .

Although the *Milliken* opinion discussed the many practical problems that would be encountered in the consolidation of numerous school districts by judicial decree, the Court's decision rejecting the metropolitan area desegregation order was actually based on fundamental limitations on the remedial powers of the federal courts to restructure the operation of local and state governmental entities. That power is not plenary. It "may be exercised 'only on the basis of a constitutional violation.'" 418 U.S., at 738. Once a constitutional violation is found, a federal court is required to tailor "the scope of the remedy" to fit "the nature and extent of the constitutional violation." 418 U.S., at 744. In *Milliken*, there was no finding of unconstitutional action on the part of the suburban school officials and no demonstration that the violations committed in the operation of the Detroit school system had had any significant segregative effects in the suburbs. The desegregation order in *Milliken* requiring the consolidation of local school districts in the Detroit metropolitan area thus constituted direct federal judicial interference with local governmental entities without the necessary predicate of a constitutional violation by those entities or of the identification within them of any significant segregative effects resulting from the Detroit school officials' unconstitutional conduct. Under these circumstances, the Court held that the interdistrict decree was impermissible because it was not commensurate with the constitutional violation to be repaired.

Since the *Milliken* decision was based on basic limitations on the exercise of the equity power of the federal courts and not on a balancing of particular considerations presented by school desegregation cases, it is apparent that the Court of Appeals erred in finding *Milliken* inapplicable on that ground to this public housing case. The school desegregation context of the *Milliken* case is nonetheless important to an understanding of its discussion of the limitations on the exercise of federal judicial power. As the Court noted, school district lines cannot be "casually ignored or treated as a mere administrative convenience" because they separate independent governmental entities responsible for the operation of autonomous public school systems. 418 U.S., at 741-743. The Court's holding that there had to be an interdistrict violation or effect before a federal court could order the crossing of district boundary lines reflected the substantive impact of a consolidation remedy on separate and independent school districts. The District Court's desegregation order in *Milliken* was held to be an impermissible remedy not because it envisioned relief against a wrongdoer extending beyond the city in which the violation occurred but because it contemplated a judicial decree restructuring the operation of local governmental entities that were not implicated in any constitutional violation.

III

The question presented in this case concerns only the authority of the District Court to order HUD to take remedial action outside the city limits of Chicago. HUD does not dispute the Court of Appeals' determination that it violated the Fifth Amendment and §601 of the Civil Rights Act of 1964 by knowingly funding CHA's racially discriminatory family public housing program, nor does it question the appropriateness of a remedial order designed to alleviate the effects of past segregative practices by requiring that public housing be developed in areas that will afford respondents an opportunity to reside in desegregated neighborhoods. But HUD contends that the *Milliken* decision bars a remedy affecting its conduct beyond the boundaries of Chicago for two reasons. First, it asserts that such a remedial order would constitute the grant of relief incommensurate with the constitutional violation to be repaired. And, second, it claims that a decree regulating HUD's conduct beyond Chicago's boundaries would inevitably have the effect of "consolidat[ing] for remedial purposes" governmental units not implicated in HUD's and CHA's violations. We address each of these arguments in turn.

A

We reject the contention that, since HUD's constitutional and statutory violations were committed in Chicago, *Milliken* precludes an order against HUD that will affect its conduct in the greater metropolitan area. The critical distinction between HUD and the suburban school districts in *Milliken* is that HUD has been found to have violated the Constitution. That violation provided the necessary predicate for the entry of a remedial order against HUD and, indeed, imposed a duty on the District Court to grant appropriate relief. Our prior decisions counsel that in the event of a constitutional violation "all reasonable methods be available to formulate an effective remedy," North Carolina State Board of Education v. Swann, 402 U.S. 43, 46, and that every effort should be made by a federal court to employ those methods "to achieve the greatest possible degree of [relief], taking into account the practicalities of the situation." Davis v. School Comm'rs of Mobile County, 402 U.S. 33, 37. As the Court observed in Swann v. Charlotte-Mecklenburg Board of Education: "Once a right and a violation have been shown, the scope of a district court's equitable powers to remedy past wrongs is broad, for breadth and flexibility are inherent in equitable remedies." 402 U.S. at 15.

Nothing in the *Milliken* decision suggests a per se rule that federal courts lack authority to order parties found to have violated the Constitution to undertake remedial efforts beyond the municipal boundaries of the city where the violation occurred. As we noted in Part II, supra, the District Court's proposed remedy in *Milliken* was impermissible because of the limits on the federal judicial power to interfere with the operation of state political entities that were not implicated in unconstitutional conduct. Here, unlike the desegregation remedy found erroneous in *Milliken*, a judicial order directing relief beyond the boundary lines of Chicago will not necessarily entail coercion of uninvolved governmental units, because both CHA and HUD have the authority to operate outside the Chicago city limits.

In this case, it is entirely appropriate and consistent with *Milliken* to order CHA and HUD to attempt to create housing alternatives for the respondents in the Chicago suburbs. Here the wrong committed by HUD confined the respondents to segregated public housing. The relevant geographic area for purposes of the respondents' housing options is the Chicago housing market, not the Chicago city limits. To foreclose such relief solely because HUD's constitutional violation took place within the city limits of Chicago would transform *Milliken*'s principled limitation on the exercise of federal judicial authority into an arbitrary and mechanical shield for those found to have engaged in unconstitutional conduct.

B

The more substantial question under *Milliken* is whether an order against HUD affecting its conduct beyond Chicago's boundaries would impermissibly interfere with local governments and suburban housing authorities that have not been implicated in HUD's unconstitutional conduct. In examining this issue, it is important to note that the Court of Appeals' decision did not endorse or even discuss "any specific metropolitan plan" but instead left the formulation of the remedial plan to the District Court on remand. . . . HUD's contention that any remand for consideration of a metropolitan area order would be impermissible as a matter of law must necessarily be based on its claim at oral argument "that court-ordered metropolitan relief in this case, no matter how gently it's gone about, no matter how it's framed, is bound to require HUD to ignore the safeguards of local autonomy and local political processes" and therefore to violate the limitations on federal judicial power established in *Milliken*.

A remedial plan designed to insure that HUD will utilize its funding and administrative powers in a manner consistent with affording relief to the respondents need not abrogate the role of local governmental units in the federal housing-assistance programs. Under the major housing programs in existence at the time the District Court entered its remedial order pertaining to HUD, local housing authorities and municipal governments had to make application for funds or approve the use of funds in the locality before HUD could make housing-assistance money available. An order directed solely to HUD would not force unwilling localities to apply for assistance under these programs but would merely reinforce the regulations guiding HUD's determination of which of the locally authorized projects to assist with federal funds.

The Housing and Community Development Act of 1974 . . . significantly enlarged HUD's role in the creation of housing opportunities. Under the §8 Lower-Income Housing Assistance program, which has largely replaced the older federal low-income housing programs, HUD may contract directly with private owners to make leased housing units available to eligible lower income persons. As HUD has acknowledged in this case, "local governmental approval is no longer explicitly required as a condition of the program's applicability to a locality.". . . In most cases the Act grants the unit of local government in which the assistance is to be provided the right to comment on the application and, in certain specified circumstances, to preclude the Secretary of HUD from approving the application. Use of the §8 program to expand low-income housing opportunities outside areas of minority concentration would not have a coercive effect on suburban municipalities. For under the program, the local governmental units retain the right to comment on specific assistance proposals, to reject certain proposals that are inconsistent with their approved housing-assistance plans, and to require that zoning and other land-use restrictions be adhered to by builders.

In sum, . . . [the] order would have the same effect on the suburban governments as a discretionary decision by HUD to use its statutory powers to provide the respondents with alternatives to the racially segregated Chicago public housing system created by CHA and HUD.

Since we conclude that a metropolitan area remedy in this case is not impermissible as a matter of law, we affirm the judgment of the Court of Appeals remanding the case to the District Court "for additional evidence and for further consideration of the issue of metropolitan area relief." Our determination that the District Court has the authority to direct HUD to engage in remedial efforts in the metropolitan area outside the city limits of Chicago should not be interpreted as requiring a metropolitan area order. The nature and scope of the remedial decree to be entered on remand is a matter for the District Court in the exercise of its equitable discretion, after affording the parties an opportunity to present their views.

The judgment of the Court of Appeals remanding this case to the District Court is affirmed, but further proceedings in the District Court are to be consistent with this opinion.

NOTES ON RELIEF AGAINST THIRD PARTIES

1. The court of appeals in *Hills* rather clearly contemplated that the suburbs would be coerced into accepting housing if that were necessary. The Supreme Court disagreed, but was able to affirm because a new federal program abandoned the local consent requirement.

2. *Hills* says a wrongdoer can be ordered to take action that will affect innocent third parties. Does that mean the *Milliken* plaintiffs are entitled to an order directing the state of Michigan, an adjudicated wrongdoer, to provide metropolitan relief by using its powers to restructure and consolidate local school districts? Why not? Is the real difference

a discretionary judgment about the *extent* to which third parties will be affected? Does it matter that the Court goes out of its way to insist that *Milliken* was not based on a balancing test?

3. Does *Hills* mean that innocent third parties cannot be ordered to help remedy the defendant's violation? Some commentators so read it, going so far as to suggest that police could not be ordered to protect students and school officials from opponents of desegregation orders, especially where the school district is a separate political entity from the municipality. See Comment, Community Resistance to School Desegregation: Enjoining the Undefinable Class, 44 U. Chi. L. Rev. 111, 154-161 (1976). Wouldn't a strict prohibition of any relief against innocent third parties be inconsistent with the presuppositions of Federal Civil Rule 19(a), providing for the joinder of parties in whose absence "complete relief cannot be accorded among those already parties"?

4. In United States v. Board of School Commissioners, 637 F.2d 1101 (7th Cir.), *cert. denied sub nom.* Owen v. Buckley, 449 U.S. 838 (1980), the court approved a metropolitan school desegregation plan for Indianapolis. The interdistrict violation was consolidating the city and its suburbs for all purposes except schools; suburban school districts were kept separate. The state legislature enacted the consolidation legislation, and only the state was found guilty. The court did not order the school districts consolidated; instead, it ordered that some children be transferred to districts other than the one they lived in. Is that consistent with *Milliken I* and *Hills*? Would a consolidation order also have been permissible? Or would that be an impermissible restructuring of "innocent" third parties?

By statute, the state volunteered to pay half the cost of any court-ordered metropolitan plan, and allocated half the cost to the affected school districts. The suburban school districts asked the court to order the state to pay the entire cost, because it was the only adjudicated wrongdoer. The court granted the motion, ordering payment in addition to all other aid to the affected school districts, and ordering that aid to those districts not be discriminatorily reduced as compared to aid to other districts. United States v. Board of School Commissioners, 677 F.2d 1185 (7th Cir.), *cert. denied sub nom.* Orr v. Board of School Commissioners, 459 U.S. 1086 (1982). Judge Posner dissented. He thought Indiana's financing scheme was none of the federal court's business as long as the financial burden were not placed on the black children of Indianapolis, and he argued forcefully that the suburban school districts, who had lobbied hard to be excluded from metropolitan government, were not entitled to equitable relief even if they had not been found guilty of the resulting violation. Who has the better of that argument? There wasn't anything unconstitutional about making the suburban school districts pay, was there?

GENERAL BUILDING CONTRACTORS ASSOCIATION v. PENNSYLVANIA
458 U.S. 375 (1982)

JUSTICE REHNQUIST delivered the opinion of the Court.

Respondents, the Commonwealth of Pennsylvania and a class of racial minorities who are skilled or seek work as operating engineers in the construction industry in Eastern Pennsylvania and Delaware, commenced this action under a variety of federal statutes protecting civil rights, including 42 U.S.C. §1981. The complaint sought to redress racial discrimination in the operation of an exclusive hiring hall established in contracts between Local 542 of the International Union of Operating Engineers and construction industry employers doing business within the Union's jurisdiction. Respondents also alleged discrimination in the operation of an apprenticeship program established by Local 542 and several construction trade associations. Named as defendants were Local 542, the trade associations, the organization charged with administering the trade's apprenticeship program, and a class of approximately 1,400 construction industry employers. Petitioners, the defendant contractors and trade associations, seek review of a judgment granting an injunction against them. . . .

I . . .

Under the terms of the agreement, the Union was to maintain lists of operating engineers, or would-be engineers, classified according to the extent of their recent construction experience. Signatory employers were contractually obligated to hire operating engineers only from among those referred by the Union from its current lists. Workers affiliated with the Union were barred from seeking work with those employers except through Union referrals. Thus, the collective bargaining agreement effectively channeled all employment opportunities through the hiring hall.

Among the means of gaining access to the Union's referral lists is an apprenticeship program established in 1965 by Local 542 and the trade associations. The program, which involves classroom and field training, is administered by the Joint Apprenticeship and Training Committee (JATC), a body of trustees half of whom are appointed by the Union and half by the trade associations.

The District Court . . . found that the hiring hall system established by collective bargaining was neutral on its face. But the court found that Local 542, in administering the system, "practiced a pattern of intentional discrimination and that union practices in the overall operation of a hiring hall for operating engineers created substantial racial disparities."

The court made similar findings regarding the JATC's administration of the job training program. . . . [T]he court found that the plaintiffs had failed to prove "that the associations or contractors viewed simply as a class were actually aware of the union discrimination," and had failed to show "intent to discriminate by the employers as a class." [The Supreme Court held that the employers and trade associations had not violated the statutes.]

IV

In a separate portion of their brief, respondents urge several independent bases for the issuance of an injunction against the petitioners and the allocation to them of a portion of the costs of the remedial decree. . . . The issue before us, therefore, is whether a party not subject to liability for violating the law may nonetheless be assessed a proportionate share of the costs of implementing a decree to assure nondiscriminatory practices on the part of another party which *was* properly enjoined.

We find respondent's arguments based on the traditional equitable authority of courts to be unpersuasive. In Milliken v. Bradley, 433 U.S. 267 (1977), upon which respondents rely, and which we believe to be the case most closely in point, we expressly noted that the state petitioners had been found guilty of creating at least a portion of the constitutional violation which the order challenged in that case was designed to remedy. [The state of Michigan had been ordered to pay half the cost of the remedy in *Milliken II*.] Thus our holding there was consistent with our opinion in Hills v. Gautreaux, 425 U.S. 284 (1976), where we explained the relationship between our holding in the first *Milliken* case, Milliken v. Bradley, 418 U.S. 717 (1974), and our opinion in Swann v. Charlotte-Mecklenburg Board of Education, 402 U.S. 1 (1971). We read these earlier decisions as recognizing "fundamental limitations on the remedial powers of the federal courts." 425 U.S., at 293. Those powers could be exercised only on the basis of a violation of the law and could extend no farther than required by the nature and the extent of that violation. This principle, we held, was not one limited to school desegregation cases, but was instead "premised on a controlling principle governing the permissible scope of federal judicial power, a principle not limited to a school desegregation context." Id., at 294, n.11.

We think that the principle enunciated in these cases, transposed to the instant factual situation, offers no support for the imposition of injunctive relief against a party found not to have violated any substantive right of respondents. This is not to say that defendants in the position of petitioners might not, upon an appropriate evidentiary showing, be retained in the lawsuit and even subjected to such minor and ancillary provisions of an injunctive order as the District Court might find necessary to grant complete relief to respondents from the discrimination they suffered at the hands of the Union. But that sort of minor and ancillary relief is not the same, and cannot be the same, as that awarded against a party found to have infringed the statutory rights of persons in the position of respondents.

The order of the District Court, insofar as it runs against petitioners, cannot be regarded as "minor" or "ancillary" in any proper sense of those terms. First, it imposes considerable burdens on the employers and associations. It directs the employers to meet detailed "minority utilization goals" in their hiring, keyed to the number of hours worked. If they are unable to do so through referrals from Local 542, they are required to hire minority operating engineers who are not affiliated with the Union. If the goals are still not satisfied, the employers must recruit and hire unskilled minority workers from the community and provide on-the-job training. The employers are also obligated to make quarterly reports detailing the extent of their compliance with these directives. Finally, the District Court imposed on the employers and the associations a share of the financial cost incidental to enforcement of the remedial decree as a whole. According to petitioners, the expense of the decree in the first year of its five-year life exceeded $200,000.

Absent a supportable finding of liability, we see no basis for requiring the employers or the associations to aid either in paying for the cost of the remedial program as a whole or in establishing and administering the training program. Nor is the imposition of minority hiring quotas directly upon petitioners the sort of remedy that may be imposed without regard to a finding of liability. If the Union and the JATC comply with the decree by training and referring minority workers, we see no reason to assume, absent supporting evidence, that the employers will not hire the minority workers referred pursuant to the collective bargaining agreement, and employ them at wages and hours commensurate with those of non-minority workers. If experience proves otherwise, the District Court will then have more than sufficient grounds for including the employers within the scope of the remedial decree.

To the extent that the remedy properly imposed upon the Union and the JATC requires any adjustment in the collective bargaining contract between petitioners and the Union, it is entirely appropriate for the District Court to fashion its injunctive remedy to so provide, and to have that remedy run against petitioners as well as the Union and the JATC. But the injunctive decree entered by the District Court as presently drawn treats petitioners as if they had been properly found liable for the Union's discrimination. A decree containing such provisions, we hold, is beyond the traditional equitable limitations upon the authority of a federal court to formulate such decrees.

Nor does the All Writs Act, 28 U.S.C. §1651(a), support the extensive liability imposed upon petitioners by the District Court. The District Court did not rely upon this Act, and we think it completely wide of the mark in justifying the relief granted by the District Court. That Act was most recently considered by this Court in United States v. New York Telephone Co., 434 U.S. 159 (1977), where we said: "This Court has repeatedly recognized the power of a federal court to issue such commands under the All Writs Act as may be necessary or appropriate to effectuate and prevent the frustration of orders it has previously issued in its exercise of jurisdiction otherwise obtained. . . ." In *New York Telephone*, we held that the All Writs Act was available to require a third party to assist in the carrying out of a district court order pertaining to the installation of pen registers, and in doing so we noted that "[t]he order provided that the Company be fully reimbursed at prevailing rates, and compliance with it required minimal effort on the part of the Company and no disruption to its operations." Id., at 175.

An examination of our cases which have relied on the All Writs Act convinces us that respondents are simply barking up the wrong tree when they seek to support the injunctive order of the District Court against petitioners on the basis of the provisions of that Act. There was no need for the District Court to treat petitioners as strangers to this lawsuit, and therefore to rely upon some extraordinary form of process or writ to bring them before the court. Petitioners had been named as defendants by respondents in their complaint, and they litigated the injunctive liability phase of the action before the District Court. Petitioners were parties to the action in every sense of the word, and subject to the jurisdiction of the District Court both as to the imposition of liability and as to the framing of a remedial decree. The difficulty faced by respondents in supporting the decree of the District Court insofar as it grants affirmative relief and requires payment toward the cost of implementing the decree is not that petitioners would otherwise be strangers to the action. The difficulty lies instead with the fact that on the record before the District Court the petitioners could not properly be held liable to any sort of injunctive relief based on their own conduct.

JUSTICE O'CONNOR, with whom JUSTICE BLACKMUN joins, concurring. . . .

II

Regarding the scope of a federal court's equitable powers to afford full relief, I agree with the Court's holding that "a party not subject to liability for violating the law [may not] be assessed a proportionate share of the costs of implementing a decree to assure nondiscriminatory practices on the part of another party which *was* properly enjoined." I also agree with the Court's ancillary holding that the District Court may not require quarterly reports from the employers detailing their compliance with the court's ill-founded injunction. Of course, since the employers are not liable for general injunctive relief, such reports are unnecessary.

Under the appropriate circumstances, however, I believe other reports properly could be required of the employers, for example, to aid the court by charting the changes resulting from the injunction imposed on the Union and the JATC. Quite recently, in Zipes v. Trans World Airlines, Inc., 455 U.S. 385 (1982), this Court held that §706(g) of Title VII authorizes a federal court to order retroactive seniority relief over the objections of a union that was not guilty of discrimination. The Court stated that:

> Teamsters v. United States, 431 U.S. 324 (1977), . . . makes it clear that once there has been a finding of discrimination by the employer, an award of retroactive seniority is appropriate even if there is no finding that the union has also illegally discriminated. In *Teamsters*, the parties agreed to a decree which provided that the District Court would decide "whether any discriminatees should be awarded additional equitable relief such as retroactive seniority." 431 U.S., at 331, n.4. Although we held that the union had not violated Title VII by agreeing to and maintaining the seniority system, we nonetheless directed the union to remain in the litigation as a defendant so that full relief could be awarded to the victims of the employer's post-act discrimination.

455 U.S. at 400. As the Court acknowledges today, it is entirely possible that full relief cannot be granted without subjecting the petitioners to some incidental or ancillary provisions of the court's injunctive order. It is thus conceivable, for example, that quarterly reports providing employment statistics necessary for the court to ascertain whether its injunctive decree is being properly implemented could be ordered under the court's equitable powers to effectuate its decree.

[JUSTICES MARSHALL and BRENNAN dissented on the ground that the employers and trade associations had violated the statute. They agreed with Justice O'Connor "that the Court's opinion does not prevent the District Court from requiring petitioners to comply with incidental or ancillary provisions contained in its injunctive order."]

MORE NOTES ON RELIEF AGAINST THIRD PARTIES

1. A pen register is a wiretapping device that records the numbers called but does not record the conversations. In United States v. New York Telephone, discussed in *General Building Contractors*, the United States sought an injunction ordering the telephone company to place the pen register for it. The Court found power to issue the injunction in the All Writs Act, which authorizes federal courts to "issue all writs necessary or appropriate in aid of their respective jurisdictions and agreeable to the usages and principles of law." 28 U.S.C. §1651(a) (1982).

2. *General Building Contractors* also relies on Zipes v. Trans World Airlines and Teamsters v. United States. In those cases, the Court held

that plaintiffs were entitled to be employed with seniority retroactive to the day on which they would have been hired but for the employer's discrimination. Plaintiffs would then get whatever rights the existing seniority rules provided to an employee with that much seniority. The Court held that plaintiffs were not entitled to the broader relief they sought in *Teamsters*, which would have modified the seniority rules themselves. Even within the framework of the existing seniority rules, plaintiffs could not use retroactive seniority to displace incumbent workers. But as vacancies arose, plaintiffs could use their retroactive seniority to compete for those vacancies, jumping ahead of incumbents who had longer actual service. The effect was to freeze incumbents in the position they held at the time of the decree until plaintiffs reached their "rightful place": the position they would have occupied but for the discrimination. Perhaps the implementing orders directed to the union were "minor and ancillary," but the effect on incumbent workers was substantial.

3.   Combining the Court's stated rules with the factual results of its cases, the law seems to be that innocent third parties can be affected (*Hills*) substantially (*Zipes, Teamsters*), but not to the point of being restructured (*Milliken I*), by orders to defendants who violated the law. Innocent third parties may also be subjected to "minor and ancillary" orders themselves (*New York Telephone, General Building Contractors*). Is that a workable set of rules? Can you apply it to the following third parties?

a.   Schoolchildren who are involuntarily reassigned under the remedy approved in *Milliken*.

b.   Police who are needed to protect students and staff from opponents of desegregation. See note 3 following Hills v. Gautreaux.

c.   Statewide education officials who did not participate in local segregation but can be helpful in devising remedies. See Morgan v. Kerrigan, 509 F.2d 580, 582-583 n.4 (1st Cir. 1974) (refusing to dismiss as to such defendants) (pre-*Milliken*).

d.   Sellers in corporate acquisitions resulting in antitrust violations by the buyer. Section 7 of the Clayton Act forbids only the purchase and not the sale; sellers have objected to rescission orders on the ground that no relief can be ordered against them. See United States v. Coca-Cola Bottling Co., 575 F.2d 222 (9th Cir. 1978) (upholding power to order rescission) (not citing *Milliken* or *Hills*); United States v. E. I. du Pont de Nemours & Co., 366 U.S. 316, 334-335 (1961), and 353 U.S. 586, 608 (1957) (holding issue open).

e.   In a suit alleging sale of corporate control at an improper premium, a title company serving as cotrustee of a trust of assets beneficially owned by one of the defendants, including stock in an affiliated company. See Beverly Hills Federal Savings & Loan Association v. Webb, 406 F.2d 1275, 1279-1280 (9th Cir. 1969) (reversing dismissal as to title company).

f.   Developers engaged in construction pursuant to an allegedly illegal permit, where wrongdoing is charged only against the officials who issued the permit. See League to Save Lake Tahoe v. Tahoe Regional Planning Agency, 558 F.2d 914 (9th Cir. 1977) (reversing dismissal as to developers) (*Milliken* and *Hills* not cited).

g.   The sheriff in a suit to enjoin an eviction, where the real parties in interest are the landlord and tenant, and the sheriff is routinely executing a writ.

4.   In Bradley v. Detroit Board of Education, 577 F.2d 1032 (6th Cir. 1978), the court vacated an injunction against locating a halfway house for state prisoners next to a magnet school designed to attract students from all over the city as part of the desegregation program. The court of appeals found the threat to integration speculative. The building was owned by the Salvation Army, which had agreed to sell it to the Michigan Department of Corrections; the Salvation Army was joined as an additional defendant. Assuming that plaintiffs could show a real threat to integration, must they also show that the Salvation Army and Department of Corrections were each independently violating the Constitution? This isn't a "minor or ancillary" order, is it? Would the court have to order the school board to buy the land? Or at least compensate the Salvation Army for the lost sale?

5.   What if the litigants attempt to settle the case in a way that affects the rights of nonconsenting third parties? This issue has received its most extensive development in employment discrimination law. There, employers and minority employees frequently agree to consent decrees setting quotas for future hiring and promotion. There is rarely anyone to speak for future white applicants affected by hiring quotas, but unions and white incumbents often object to promotion quotas. These quotas often override rights under collective bargaining agreements and civil service laws.

Until 1984, most courts gave objectors very limited rights, approving "reasonable" settlements without proof of a violation or the relationship between the violation and the remedy. A typical case was Stotts v. Memphis Fire Department, 679 F.2d 541 (6th Cir. 1982), *rev'd in part, on other grounds, sub nom.* Firefighters Local Union No. 1784 v. Stotts, 104 S. Ct. 2576 (1984). The court of appeals held that a consent decree providing for quotas could be approved over the objections of affected nonminorities. Id. at 552. It said that requiring the union to consent to a decree overriding a collective bargaining agreement would undermine the policy in favor of settlements. Id. at 564-567.

Is it still a consent decree if everyone doesn't consent? Aren't nonconsenting third parties entitled to full litigation of every element of the claim that their rights can be overridden? The Fifth Circuit apparently so held. *United States v. City of Miami*, 664 F.2d 435 (5th Cir. 1981).

6. The Supreme Court's partial reversal casts substantial doubt on the doctrines reflected in the court of appeals opinion in *Stotts*. The Supreme Court considered only one small part of the decree. The trial court had modified the consent decree to require quota layoffs, reasoning that this was necessary to protect the consent decree from the effects of a crisis in the city's finances. The court of appeals had affirmed. However, not even the city had consented to the modification. The Supreme Court held that the modification could not be justified as a settlement because the city had not consented, and that it could not be justified as a litigated injunction because no one had proven a violation that would justify a layoff quota. The opinion does not directly say anything about the need to obtain the consent of affected third parties, but the opinion is plainly hostile to quota remedies in general. We will examine that part of the opinion in the Notes on Fluid Class Recoveries and Affirmative Action, infra at 798.

See also W. R. Grace & Co. v. Local 759, United Rubber Workers, 461 U.S. 757 (1983). *Grace* enforced an arbitrator's award of back pay to male employees who were laid off pursuant to a settlement agreement and in violation of their collective bargaining agreement. *Grace* says nothing about the validity of the settlement. But it holds that the employer's settlement agreement does not release its obligations under the collective bargaining agreement. An employer may make inconsistent contracts, but when he inevitably breaches one of the two contracts, the employer must pay compensation. Justice O'Connor, concurring in *Stotts*, infers from *W. R. Grace* that "if innocent employees are to be required to make any sacrifices" in a consent decree, they must have "full participation rights in the negotiation process." 104 S. Ct. at 2593 n.3.

D. THE DEBATE OVER STRUCTURAL INJUNCTIONS

CHAYES, THE ROLE OF THE JUDGE IN PUBLIC LAW LITIGATION
89 Harv. L. Rev. 1281, 1282-1284, 1293-1294, 1298-1303 (1976)

We are witnessing the emergence of a new model of civil litigation and, I believe, our traditional conception of adjudication and the assumptions upon which it is based provide an increasingly unhelpful, indeed misleading framework for assessing either the workability or the legitimacy of the roles of judge and court within this model.

In our received tradition, the lawsuit is a vehicle for settling disputes between private parties about private rights. The defining features of this conception of civil adjudication are:

(1)   The lawsuit is *bipolar*. Litigation is organized as a contest between two individuals or at least two unitary interests, diametrically opposed, to be decided on a winner-takes-all basis.

(2)   Litigation is *retrospective*. The controversy is about an identified set of completed events: whether they occurred, and if so, with what consequences for the legal relations of the parties.

(3)   *Right and remedy are interdependent*. The scope of the relief is derived more or less logically from the substantive violation under the general theory that the plaintiff will get compensation measured by the harm caused by the defendant's breach of duty — in contract by giving plaintiff the money he would have had absent the breach; in tort by paying the value of the damage caused.

(4)   The lawsuit is a *self-contained* episode. The impact of the judgment is confined to the parties. If plaintiff prevails there is a simple compensatory transfer, usually of money; but occasionally the return of a thing or the performance of a definite act. If defendant prevails, a loss lies where it has fallen. In either case, entry of judgment ends the court's involvement.

(5)   The process is *party-initiated* and *party-controlled*. The case is organized and the issues defined by exchanges between the parties. Responsibility for fact development is theirs. The trial judge is a neutral arbiter of their interactions who decides questions of law only if they are put in issue by an appropriate move of a party.

This capsule description of what I have called the traditional conception of adjudication is no doubt overdrawn. It was not often, if ever, expressed so severely; indeed, because it was so thoroughly taken for granted, there was little occasion to do so. Although I do not contend that the traditional conception ever conformed fully to what judges were doing in fact, I believe it has been central to our understanding and our analysis of the legal system.

Whatever its historical validity, the traditional model is clearly invalid as a description of much current civil litigation in the federal district courts. Perhaps the dominating characteristic of modern federal litigation is that lawsuits do not arise out of disputes between private parties about private rights. Instead, the object of litigation is the vindication of constitutional or statutory policies. The shift in the legal basis of the lawsuit explains many, but not all, facets of what is going on "in fact" in federal trial courts. For this reason, although the label is not wholly satisfactory, I shall call the emerging model "public law litigation."

The characteristic features of the public law model are very different from those of the traditional model. The party structure is sprawling and amorphous, subject to change over the course of the litigation. The traditional adversary relationship is suffused and intermixed with negotiating and mediating processes at every point. The judge is the dominant figure in organizing and guiding the case, and he draws for support not only on the parties and their counsel, but on a wide range of outsiders — masters, experts, and oversight personnel. Most important, the trial judge has increasingly become the creator and manager of complex forms of ongoing relief, which have widespread effects on persons not before the court and require the judge's continuing involvement in administration and implementation. School desegregation, employment discrimination, and prisoners' or inmates' rights cases come readily to mind as avatars of this new form of litigation. But it would be mistaken to suppose that it is confined to these areas. Antitrust, securities fraud and other aspects of the conduct of corporate business, bankruptcy and reorganizations, union governance, consumer fraud, housing discrimination, electoral reapportionment, environmental management — cases in all these fields display in varying degrees the features of public law litigation. . . .

The comparative evaluation of the competing interests of plaintiff and defendant required by the remedial approach of equity often discloses alternatives to a winner-takes-all decision. An arrangement might be fashioned that could safeguard at least partially the interests of both parties, and perhaps even of others as well. And to the extent such an arrangement is possible, equity seems to require it. . . . The result has often been a decree embodying an affirmative regime to govern the range of activities in litigation and having the force of law for those represented before the court.

At this point, right and remedy are pretty thoroughly disconnected. The form of relief does not flow ineluctably from the liability determination, but is fashioned ad hoc. In the process, moreover, right and remedy have been to some extent transmuted. The liability determination is not simply a pronouncement of the legal consequences of past events, but to some extent a prediction of what is likely to be in the future. And relief is not a terminal, compensatory transfer, but an effort to devise a program to contain future consequences in a way that accommodates the range of interests involved. . . .

The centerpiece of the emerging public law model is the decree. It differs in almost every relevant characteristic from relief in the traditional model of adjudication, not the least in that it *is* the centerpiece. The decree seeks to adjust future behavior, not to compensate for past wrong. It is deliberately fashioned rather than logically deduced from the nature of the legal harm suffered. It provides for a complex, on-going regime of performance rather than a simple, one-shot, one-way transfer. Finally, it prolongs and deepens, rather than terminates, the court's involvement with the dispute.

The decree is also an order of the court, signed by the judge and issued under his responsibility (itself a shift from the classical money judgment). But it cannot be supposed that the judge, at least in a case of any complexity, composes it out of his own head. How then is the relief formulated?

The reports provide little guidance on this question. Let me nonetheless suggest a prototype that I think finds some support in the available materials. The court will ask the parties to agree on an order or it will ask one party to prepare a draft. In the first case, a negotiation is stipulated. In the second, the dynamic leads almost inevitably in that direction. The draftsman understands that his proposed decree will be subject to comment and objection by the other side and that it must be approved by the court. He is therefore likely to submit it to his opponents in advance to see whether differences cannot be resolved. Even if the court itself should prepare the initial draft of the order, some form of negotiation will almost inevitably ensue upon submission of the draft to the parties for comment.

The negotiating process ought to minimize the need for judicial resolution of remedial issues. Each party recognizes that it must make some response to the demands of the other party, for issues left unresolved will be submitted to the court, a recourse that is always chancy and may result in a solution less acceptable than might be reached by horse-trading. Moreover, it will generally be advantageous to the demanding party to reach a solution through accommodation rather than through a judicial fiat that may be performed "in a literally compliant but substantively grudging and unsatisfactory way."[81] Thus, the formulation of the decree in public law litigation introduces a good deal of party control over the practical outcome. Indeed, relief by way of order after a determination on the merits tends to converge with relief through a consent decree or voluntary settlement. And this in turn mitigates a major theoretical objection to affirmative relief — the danger of intruding on an elaborate and organic network of interparty relationships.

Nevertheless it cannot be supposed that this process will relieve the court entirely of responsibility for fashioning the remedy. The parties may fail to agree. Or the agreement reached may fail to comport with the requirements of substantive law as the judge sees them. Or the interests of absentees may be inadequately accommodated. In these situations, the judge will not, as in the traditional model, be able to derive his responses directly from the liability determination, since, as we have seen, the substantive law will point out only the general direction to be pursued and a few salient landmarks to be sought out or avoided. How then is the judge to prescribe an appropriate remedy?

81. Eisenberg, Private Ordering through Negotiation: Dispute-Settlement and Rulemaking, 89 Harv. L. Rev. 637, 676 (1976).

If the parties are simply in disagreement, it seems plausible to suppose that the judge's choice among proposals advanced by the *quondam* negotiators will be governed by his appraisal of their good faith in seeking a way to implement the constitutional or statutory command as he has construed it. The interest in a decree that will be voluntarily obeyed can be promoted by enforcing a regime of good faith bargaining among the parties. Without detailed knowledge of the negotiations, however, any attempt to enforce such a regime can rest on little more than an uneasy base of intuition and impression. Where a proposed decree is agreed among the parties, but is inadequate because the interests shared by the litigants do not span the range that the court thinks must be taken into account, resubmission for further negotiation may not cure this fundamental defect. Here too, the judge will be unable to fill the gap without a detailed understanding of the issues at stake in the bargaining among the parties.

For these reasons, the judge will often find himself a personal participant in the negotiations on relief. But this course has obvious disadvantages, not least in its inroads on the judge's time and his pretentions to disinterestedness. To avoid these problems, judges have increasingly resorted to outside help — masters, amici, experts, panels, advisory committees — for information and evaluation of proposals for relief. These outside sources commonly find themselves exercising mediating and even adjudicatory functions among the parties. They may put forward their own remedial suggestions, whether at the request of the judge or otherwise.

Once an ongoing remedial regime is established, the same procedure may be repeated in connection with the implementation and enforcement of the decree. Compliance problems may be brought to the court for resolution and, if necessary, further remediation. Again, the court will often have no alternative but to resort to its own sources of information and evaluation.

I suggested above that a judicial decree establishing an ongoing affirmative regime of conduct is pro tanto a legislative act. But in actively shaping and monitoring the decree, mediating between the parties, developing his own sources of expertise and information, the trial judge has passed beyond even the role of legislator and has become a policy planner and manager. . . .

The public law litigation model portrayed in this paper reverses many of the crucial characteristics and assumptions of the traditional concept of adjudication:

(1) The scope of the lawsuit is not exogenously given but is shaped primarily by the court and parties.

(2) The party structure is not rigidly bilateral but sprawling and amorphous.

(3) The fact inquiry is not historical and adjudicative but predictive and legislative.

(4) Relief is not conceived as compensation for past wrong in a form logically derived from the substantive liability and confined in its impact to the immediate parties; instead, it is forward looking, fashioned ad hoc on flexible and broadly remedial lines, often having important consequences for many persons including absentees.

(5) The remedy is not imposed but negotiated.

(6) The decree does not terminate judicial involvement in the affair: its administration requires the continuing participation of the court.

(7) The judge is not passive, his function limited to analysis and statement of governing legal rules; he is active, with responsibility not only for credible fact evaluation but for organizing and shaping the litigation to ensure a just and viable outcome.

(8) The subject matter of the lawsuit is not a dispute between private individuals about private rights, but a grievance about the operation of public policy.

In fact, one might say that, from the perspective of the traditional model, the proceeding is recognizable as a lawsuit only because it takes place in a courtroom before an official called a judge. But that is surely too sensational in tone. All of the procedural mechanisms outlined above were historically familiar in equity practice. It is not surprising that they should be adopted and strengthened as the importance of equity has grown in modern times.

EISENBERG AND YEAZELL, THE ORDINARY AND THE EXTRAORDINARY IN INSTITUTIONAL LITIGATION
93 Harv. L. Rev. 465, 481-491 (1980)

For a number of centuries the courts have engaged in the sort of long-term supervision of affairs that has occasioned comment in analyses of recent institutional cases. Moreover, in some instances they have created specialized tribunals, or specialized branches of general tribunals, to conduct such supervision. Because of this specialization, those of us who do not deal frequently with particular substantive areas tend to forget that they too are parts of the law and that their courts are parts of the judicial universe. A survey of some of the activities in these areas may help to dispel the impression that supervisory burdens assumed in institutional cases present a dramatically new phenomenon. . . .

Probate . . . frequently requires that the court supervise the conduct of some continuing enterprise to preserve certain assets pending their final disposition. Thus, while the personal representative of the decedent may operate the decedent's business, incur debts, invest estate funds, enter into leases, and buy and sell property, in appropriate circumstances he may need a court's approval to do so. Judges supervise businesses — not as an extraordinary event, but as an incident of the entirely routine probate of an estate. . . .

The law of trusts has long recognized that the wealthy find it useful to divest themselves — at least partially — of control of their assets even before death forces them to do so. The courts have played a significant role in supervising the management of these trust assets. Trusts rest on the assurance that courts will be willing to step in to supervise the disposition and management of property by trustees who may be tempted to divert resources to themselves. To prevent trustee improprieties, courts have developed a body of substantive law designed to force the trustee to manage the assets at least as carefully as if they were his own. Courts enforce this fiduciary duty rule by insisting that the trustee render periodic accountings, and by requiring judicial approval of certain unusual or inherently suspicious transactions. These procedures involve the courts in the administration of complex and large bodies of assets on a continuing basis, and require judicial evaluation of the loyalty of the trustee, the prudence of an investment, and the propriety of self-dealing that the trustee claims will benefit the beneficiary.

A few examples reveal the complexity and length of some trust and probate matters. The disposition of one $17,000,000 estate took twenty-three years, required consideration of 26,000 claims, and led to 390 volumes of testimony. Another will contest involved 2,303 fortune hunters. . . .

Modern bankruptcy procedures spring both from the demise of the view that insolvency is the result of a moral failure and from the desire to reduce the nasty squabbling of too many creditors for too few assets. Bankruptcy law tries to ensure that at least some portion of each creditor's demands are satisfied, and helps restore hopeless insolvents to the ranks of the economically viable. In the process of applying this law, courts have become involved in operating the Penn Central Railroad as well as many other considerably more modest enterprises.

Bankruptcy administration requires the courts to play two roles. First, courts assist in the operation of an enterprise prior to liquidation and distribution of assets to the creditors; the court aids a trustee or receiver whose role is similar to that of the personal representative of a decedent who operates a business until the court can approve a plan of sale. Second, in more complex cases, the courts attempt to reestablish the business on a different financial footing, to reorganize it in a manner both fair to its creditors and financially sound. It is worth stressing that courts routinely handle such difficult reorganization cases, passing on aspects of financial structure that are unlikely to be second nature to most judges.

They struggle through with a little help from the briefs, but at least since the 1930s there have not been many suggestions that judicial supervision of these complex financial transactions is illegitimate. . . .

Critics recognizing the similarities set out above between the old and the new litigation might nevertheless contend that the judicial action taken in many institutional cases cannot be justified absent legislative authorization. . . .

Though often unarticulated, this statutory-nonstatutory distinction lies at the heart of much of the commentary on the new litigation. The argument from statutory authorization, however, is not compelling. . . . Institutional litigation is frequently brought under a civil rights statute, section 1983, which instructs the nation's courts to grant legal and equitable relief for violations of federal constitutional and statutory law. . . . [T]he underlying rights and the open-ended text of section 1983 suggest that many institutional cases should be viewed as judicial efforts to enforce a congressional mandate rather than as attempts to wrest power from the legislature. . . .

But even if it is conceded that there is no statutory authorization for much of the new litigation, there is a nagging inconsistency in the criticism of such cases. To the extent that institutional litigation is viewed as questionable because judges lack the capacity and resources to make policy for large institutions and to supervise their administration, it is difficult to understand why the existence of a relevant statute would make a difference. A legislative enactment does not magically enhance judges' administrative and policymaking abilities. The judges of the Railroad Reorganization Court do not suddenly become vested with detailed knowledge about locomotives and debt-equity ratios merely because they proceed under a statutory scheme. Yet, for the most part, critics of prison and mental hospital cases are strangely silent about judicial capacity to run large businesses, estates, or trusts. Arguments about statutory authorization obscure the more fundamental issue of whether judges actually have the capacity intelligently to authorize broad remedial measures. . . .

Statements about the novelty of courts assuming complex administrative tasks without statutory authority also encounter a formidable obstacle of historical fact. . . .

Courts have developed and administered, almost entirely on their own, significant bodies of remedial law requiring them to engage in continuing supervision of enterprises. Perhaps the best example of this judicially developed supervisory remedy is the law of trusts. . . . The Chancellor stood ready to enforce the duties created by a trust, including the quite common duty of establishing and faithfully running religious institutions. It can scarcely be said that a modern exercise of equitable power to correct conditions in a prison, hospital, or school is a newfangled addition to the judicial arsenal. . . .

Similarly, in probate cases, the ecclesiastical courts, whose powers were enforced and later assumed by Chancery, exercised "a strict supervision over executors, calling for accounts, examining them, and directing the work of administration generally."[125] Moreover, the church courts did so without the benefit of any particularized legislation, implying the powers required for elaborate supervision from their jurisdiction over wills in general. . . . The American colonies and their successor states embraced much of the British law of trusts, estates, and writs in their common law systems. And in the relatively recent American past, courts, without direct statutory authority, have become deeply involved in the affairs of that most complex institution — the modern business corporation. Both the newly enacted and the recently superseded bankruptcy acts contain detailed instructions for assisting financially troubled businesses. It is easy to forget, however, that these provisions, unlike much of the rest of bankruptcy law, derive from court-made bankruptcy law predating the country's first business reorganization legislation. Those first statutes built upon reorganization practices developed by federal courts without statutory guidance during late nineteenth- and early twentieth-century equitable receiverships. In the course of such receiverships courts involved themselves in the minute details of running large complicated businesses. . . .

NAGEL, SEPARATION OF POWERS AND THE SCOPE OF FEDERAL EQUITABLE REMEDIES
30 Stan. L. Rev. 661, 661-666, 680-681, 708-709 (1978)

In recent years, both popular and academic attention has begun to focus on the innovative and expansive remedies that federal courts have utilized with increasing frequency, especially against state governments. These forms of relief raise the question whether the judiciary has begun to tolerate in itself a blending of functions that would never be tolerated in another branch of government. Federal district courts largely have assumed the duties of administering a state mental health system and a state prison. Many federal courts are intimately involved with operating public school systems, and one court has placed a public high school directly under judicial control. For some years, of course, courts have mandated state apportionment schemes. One court has ordered the reorganization of an entire city government. In short, courts have exercised traditionally executive functions by appointing executive and quasi-executive officers responsible to the judiciary and by determining administrative processes in elaborately detailed decrees; they have exercised legislative functions by setting policy standards for the operation of state and federal programs, including the setting of budgetary requirements. . . .

---

125. T. Plucknett, A Concise History of the Common Law 742 (5th ed. 1956).

Not surprisingly, perhaps, in light of the judiciary's institutional needs and biases, the Supreme Court has held that the constitutional doctrine of separation of powers has no bearing on the problem of defining the limits of federal courts' equitable powers against state governments. The more extreme implications of this position are unacceptable by nearly any standard. As applied at the federal level, the fundamental assumption behind separation of powers is that because no branch of government can be trusted in its use of power, the power of each branch must be limited by some degree of functional specialization.

The federal judiciary is not immune from the need for limitations based on functional differentiation. James Madison observed that if the judicial power were joined with the legislative and executive powers, the judge "might behave with all the violence of *an oppressor*."[15] Subsequent history provides sobering examples of inadequate self-discipline by the judiciary in defining the limits of its own authority. . . .

The need for discipline in defining the authority of each branch does not evaporate when the federal government exercises power against state governments. It is not merely recent experience with malapportionment, segregation and inhuman prison conditions that demonstrates the extreme pressures that can exist for using the federal courts as substitutes for the other institutions of government. In the last century it became fairly obvious that under certain circumstances of fiscal mismanagement the constitutional protection against the impairment of contracts could be vindicated only by placing substantially all of the governmental functions of a bankrupt city into judicial receivership. The Supreme Court rejected the conclusion that the Constitution permits, much less requires, the right of self-government to be suspended in order to effect a particular constitutional guarantee,[21] and the conclusion should be equally rejected today. The substitution of government by the federal judiciary for local self-government involves dangerous disproportionality; it sacrifices fundamental democratic values in order to vindicate particular constitutional rights. Specific rights of specific plaintiffs are secured by autocratic mechanisms of broad impact. . . .

Professor Gunther has described the principle of separation of powers as a "horizontal" division of power among the three branches of the *national* government.[24] The "vertical" distribution of power between the national government and the states is thought to be encompassed sufficiently by the concept of "federalism."[25] The current position of the Supreme Court appears to be that this dichotomy is so neat as to liberate

---

15. The Federalist No. 47, at 326 (J. Madison) (J. Cooke ed. 1961) (quoting Montesquieu).

21. Meriwether v. Garrett, 102 U.S. 472, 520-521 (Field, Miller, and Bradley, JJ., concurring in the judgment).

24. G. Gunther, Cases and Materials on Constitutional Law 400 (9th ed. 1975) (emphasis added).

25. Id.

federal courts entirely from any formal constitutional constraints against assuming the functions of state executive or legislative departments. . . .

The distinction between vertical and horizontal separation of powers assumes that the power of judicial review inherently authorizes federal courts to do whatever is necessary to protect constitutional rights from infringement by less-than-coordinate branches of government. The assumption has been that if a state legislature or executive does not cooperate to achieve the objectives of a federal judicial decree, the need to enforce the constitutional mandate must take precedence over concern for maintaining the separate definition of their functions. . . .

Fully redressing violations of constitutional rights may often require the efforts of more than one branch of government, particularly if "redress" is defined broadly enough. If detailed standards need to be adopted and executive officers need to be employed to protect the people's rights, the Constitution provides the appropriate mechanisms, and it is not unimaginable that some of those mechanisms do not lie within the "judicial Power." The federal legislature and executive can and have supplemented the powers of the judiciary in order more fully to protect constitutional rights. If neither Congress nor the executive has the *legal authority* in a particular instance to supplement the judicial remedy, then the desired remedy simply constitutes a form or degree of redress that the Constitution does not authorize. If neither Congress nor the executive nor the state institutions have the *will* to cooperate with the judiciary to achieve the degree or form of redress desired by the court, then it is entirely possible that the court's objective is unwise. The great structural divisions of power in the Constitution were, after all, designed on the assumption that no single decisionmaker should be trusted.

The dimensions of what is being suggested must be understood. The issue is not whether federal courts can authoritatively declare federal law nor whether they can take action to redress violations of that law. The issue is whether the principle of separation of powers defines relevant, and perhaps even flexible, limits to the judiciary's unilateral power to seek complete correction of the consequences of a constitutional violation. Although "the moralist will find it difficult to sacrifice his aims in favor of structure and process," structure and process are "the essence of the theory and practice of constitutionalism."[111] . . .

The tendency to find very specific requirements in the Constitution's general language has increased greatly since 1960, especially among the lower courts. The Supreme Court has defined the precise warning that must be given criminal defendants to assure the voluntariness of confessions and has determined the nature of the states' interests in unborn life at each stage of pregnancy, but the lower courts have gone much further. They have relied on the due process clause to impose a precise staff-

___

111. A. Bickel, The Morality of Consent 30 (1975).

patient ratio in a mental health facility and to set the specific content necessary for an adequate individualized medical treatment plan. In prohibiting cruel and unusual punishment, a lower court has established standards for the minimum number of square feet in a prisoner's cell (60), the number of minutes of daily outdoor exercise for prisoners in isolation (30), the number of urinals to be provided (one urinal or foot of urinal trough per every 15 inmates), and such miscellany as a requirement that each dietary supervisor have at least a bachelor's degree in dietetics. . . .

When the constitutional language is broad, the judicial function is to articulate the broad policies contained in the Constitution, and to determine whether existing conditions are in compliance. The classical function of the executive is to decide detailed questions about how to implement constitutional policies. Therefore, a judicial decree specifying in detail how policy should be implemented intrudes deeply into the executive function. Alternatively, although detail is not necessarily unrelated to the purposes of constitutional adjudication, the plausibility that the injunctive language is necessary to fulfill the courts' constitutional function decreases as the gap between the generality of the constitutional language and the specificity of the injunctive language increases.

CHAYES, THE ROLE OF THE JUDGE IN PUBLIC LAW LITIGATION
89 Harv. L. Rev. 1281, 1307-1309 (1976)

[W]e have invested excessive time and energy in the effort to define — on the basis of the inherent nature of adjudication, the implications of a constitutional text, or the functional characteristics of courts — what the precise scope of judicial activity ought to be. Separation of powers comes in for a good deal of veneration in our political and judicial rhetoric, but it has always been hard to classify all government activity into three, and only three, neat and mutually exclusive categories. In practice, all governmental officials, including judges, have exercised a large and messy admixture of powers, and that is as it must be. That is not to say that institutional characteristics are irrelevant in assigning governmental tasks or that judges should unreservedly be thrust directly into political battles. But such considerations should be taken as cautionary, not decisive; for despite its well rehearsed inadequacies, the judiciary may have some important institutional advantages for the tasks it is assuming:

First, and perhaps most important, is that the process is presided over by a judge. His professional tradition insulates him from narrow political pressures, but, given the operation of the federal appointive power and the demands of contemporary law practice, he is likely to have some experience of the political process and acquaintance with a fairly broad range of public policy problems. Moreover, he is governed by a professional ideal of reflective and dispassionate analysis of the problem before him and is likely to have had some experience in putting this ideal into practice.

Second, the public law model permits ad hoc applications of broad national policy in situations of limited scope. The solutions can be tailored to the needs of the particular situation and flexibly administered or modified as experience develops with the regime established in the particular case.

Third, the procedure permits a relatively high degree of participation by representatives of those who will be directly affected by the decision, without establishing a *liberum veto.*

Fourth, the court, although traditionally thought less competent than legislatures or administrative agencies in gathering and assessing information, may have unsuspected advantages in this regard. Even the diffused adversarial structure of public law litigation furnishes strong incentives for the parties to produce information. If the party structure is sufficiently representative of the interest at stake, a considerable range of relevant information will be forthcoming. And, because of the limited scope of the proceeding, the information required can be effectively focused and specified. Information produced will not only be subject to adversary review, but as we have seen, the judge can engage his own experts to assist in evaluating the evidence. Moreover, the information that is produced will not be filtered through the rigid structures and preconceptions of bureaucracies.

Fifth, the judicial process is an effective mechanism for registering and responding to grievances generated by the operation of public programs in a regulatory state. Unlike an administrative bureaucracy or a legislature, the judiciary *must* respond to the complaints of the aggrieved. It is also rather well situated to perform the task of balancing the importance of competing policy interests in a specific situation. The legislature, perhaps, could balance, but it cannot address specific situations. The bureaucracy deals with specific situations, but only from a position of commitment to particular policy interests.

Sixth, the judiciary has the advantage of being non-bureaucratic. It is effective in tapping energies and resources outside itself and outside the government in the exploration of the situation and the assessment of remedies. It does not work through a rigid, multilayered hierarchy of numerous officials, but through a smallish, representative task force, assembled ad hoc, and easily dismantled when the problem is finally resolved.

The foregoing enumeration is admittedly one-sided. It surely does not warrant unqualified endorsement of the public law litigation model in its present form. For one thing, the returns are not all in, and those we have show varying degrees of success. Legislative apportionment, although bitterly opposed as an arena of judicial intervention, seems to have worked out reasonably well. School segregation, on the other hand, seemed obviously appropriate for judicial reform under the Constitution, but the results are at best mixed. And some heralded efforts at management of state institutions may turn out to be pretty thoroughgoing failures. What experience we have with administrative resistance to intrusive court decrees is not particularly encouraging.

There are also counter-instances and counter-arguments for each of the advantages of the public law model suggested above. Can the disinterestedness of the judge be sustained, for example, when he is more visibly a part of the political process? Will the consciously negotiated character of the relief ultimately erode the sense that what is being applied is law? Can the relatively unspecialized trial judge, even with the aid of the new authority and techniques being developed in public law litigation, respond adequately to the demands for legislative and predictive fact-finding in the new model? Against the asserted "responsiveness" of the courts, it may be argued that the insensitivity of other agencies represents a political judgment that should be left undisturbed. And although the courts may be well situated to balance competing policy interests in the particular case, if as is often true the decree calls for a substantial commitment of resources, the court has little basis for evaluating competing claims on the public purse.

FRUG, THE JUDICIAL POWER
OF THE PURSE
126 U. Pa. L. Rev. 715, 715-717, 788-792 (1978)

The most dramatic examples of this exercise of judicial power have occurred in the fields of corrections and care of the mentally ill and mentally retarded, fields in which a substantial portion of current budgets are now mandated not by legislative choice but by orders of lower federal courts. Finding that existing conditions violate constitutional standards, federal courts have ordered prisons throughout the nation to improve markedly their physical facilities and their level of services. They have ordered such extensive improvements in the level of care provided the mentally ill and mentally retarded that, in one case, the amount allegedly necessary to comply with the court's decree equalled sixty percent of the state budget, excluding school financing. . . .

The existence of lower federal court orders seeking to remedy constitutional violations by controlling, in part, the power of the purse does not, of course, mean that this exercise of power is legitimate. The Supreme Court has not yet reviewed any of the orders that significantly increase government expenditures for prisons or mental institutions. . . .

This is not to say that the Supreme Court itself has never affirmed a lower court order mandating increased government expenditures. It has done so in cases concerning school desegregation and access to the courts. But the orders that the Supreme Court has affirmed have been much more limited than those orders, as yet unreviewed, affecting prisons and mental institutions. Thus the reason that the Supreme Court has never set limits on federal equitable power to command the purse may be that no case yet decided required it to do so. The Court so far has been able to rely simply on such delphic propositions as "the nature of the violation determines the scope of the remedy" and "breadth and flexibility are inherent in equitable remedies." But when the Court reviews the increasing efforts of lower federal courts to remedy constitutional violations by requiring significant additional government expenditures, it will have to decide what limits there are, if any, to the judicial power of the purse. . . .

The principal practical reality that the courts must accept in shaping their remedies in the institution cases is that money is a constraint. They cannot continue their insistence on strict compliance regardless of the amount of money available, because the limits on government resources are no less applicable in the courtroom than outside of it. The Supreme Court recognizes this reality, as its procedural due process and equal protection cases demonstrate. A recognition that government resources are finite does not allow the government to refuse to enforce constitutional rights because it is too expensive to do so. The issue in the institution cases is not whether there will be compliance with the Constitution — of that there should be no doubt — but rather the timing of achieving that compliance. Because of myriad demands for limited government resources, only a certain amount of money can be allocated in any particular year for a new expenditure, no matter how intense the need for it. A judicial decision that institutional conditions are unconstitutional requires that money be found to correct them, but the amount of money to be applied each year is a legislative decision; this decision must be accepted by the courts if, in the words of the desegregation cases, it is made "in good faith." A court cannot weigh the competing demands for government resources to determine how much can be raised for the institutions, nor should it try to force the legislature to raise the necessary money regardless of competing considerations. The judicial impact on the purse is acceptable only if the legislature retains its discretion to raise and allocate money, a discretion limited by the need to meet the judicial order but not eliminated by it. Judicial requirements of expenditures must, in short, meet the test of feasibility, and feasibility is in the first instance a legislative judgment, subject to the requirement that the legislature's attempt to meet the constitutional standard is in good faith. If the courts allow the legislature this time to comply, interference with democratic decisionmaking will be minimized to the point that judicial confrontations with legislative power will become unlikely.

Courts must also recognize that detailed orders containing hundreds of specifications that the executive must implement are unworkable. The courts cannot effectively decide how many registered nurses or square feet per patient are constitutionally required. Moreover, this level of detail necessitates continual federal judicial supervision of the state's day-to-day management of its institutions; the court must intervene to ensure that its plan is being carried out. But state institutions are too complex to be administered under court order; there are too many variables for a court to consider and comprehend. It is no answer for the court to appoint a master to make these decisions. Basic administration must be left in the hands of executive officials, mandated to comply with the Constitution, but allowed the flexibility to do so as long as they proceed in good faith. A federal court's insistence on literal compliance with its own scheme ought to be recognized as having the potential to undermine, as well as to enhance, the executive's ability to improve conditions for institutionalized patients. Decisions mandating improved mental hospital facilities can divert money needed to deinstitutionalize patients and provide them with outpatient care. A new prison mandated by court order might be an undesirable substitute for small, community-based facilities. . . .

It might be argued that such a "good faith" standard would be meaningless and ineffectual and that only a detailed order and timetable, implemented under judicial supervision and requiring strict compliance regardless of the financial impact, would achieve the desired results. This need not be so, however. If, for example, a court were to decide that the Constitution requires "provision of basic medical care to all patients in the institution," it could then require the state to draft a plan indicating (1) what the state will do, in the setting of the institution in question, to meet such a standard and (2) how, and over what period of time, the state will implement its plan. The court would retain the power to review and criticize the state's particularization of the constitutional standard, but agreement is likely due to widespread acceptance of what constitutes minimally adequate care. In fact, the court can avoid deciding whether the precise ingredients of the plan amount to constitutionally adequate care by treating the state's plan as provisional only. If the plan makes major improvements in presently indefensible conditions, the court need not bless that plan as constitutional. The major issue is not what has to be done to complete the job — that is a long way off — but how the job can be begun. After the first steps are taken, the plan can, and no doubt will, be altered as problems arise in its implementation and as changes of judgment occur as to the type of care needed. It is the direction and rate of change that is important, not the details of timing, staffing, and planning for capital construction. These details should not become the business of the courts.

It is a mistake to assume that judicial power to ensure that the states are implementing necessary changes as fast as they can derives from the details of court orders or the extent of intervention in the local democratic process. The fact that general cooperation with the thrust of the court orders in the institution cases has occurred to date stems instead from the use of the courts' principal enforcement tool: their power publicly to make illegitimate the maintenance of intolerable conditions in the institutions. The power to declare conditions unconstitutional is a potent weapon, as demonstrated not only by the institution cases but also by those involving Presidents and Congress as well. Indifference to the institutional conditions is made impossible by the judicial order, publicly stated, that the outrageous conditions must be ended; its order that action be taken arms the reform movement to achieve the desired political result. Indeed, it is this kind of voluntary compliance that the court seeks, not a confrontation with legislative or executive power. But if the power of the courts rests principally on their declaration that current conditions are illegitimate, they must take care not to issue orders that make noncompliance excusable, and thus legitimate. The likelihood of compliance is undermined, not enhanced, by the detailed orders that fail to recognize the constraints on the political process. If the courts order the legislators and executives to do more than is possible, they invite understandable resistance rather than compliance; that resistance invites further orders, and the ensuing confrontation will lead not to better institutions but to political crisis.

If the courts invite confrontation, they will face a practical impediment to effectuating their orders more important than any yet mentioned. These judicial orders are unenforceable. Only the legislature can provide the necessary money, and only the executive can administer the spending of that money. The courts cannot imprison the legislature for contempt unless it raises or reallocates the necessary money, nor jail an executive official to ensure implementation of a government program. Courts ultimately lack the power to force state governments to act. Unless the courts are willing to do what no responsible government official would do — close the institutions, and let the prisoners and the mentally ill, dangerous or otherwise, go free — if the courts are unwilling to play a game of "chicken" with state officials, as they should be, they should face the fact that these orders will be complied with, if at all, voluntarily, absent federal executive action to enforce them. Recognition of this practical limit on judicial power does not render the courts powerless to enforce the Constitution. It merely restricts them to their real, and not their imagined, power. "The Court's authority — possessed of neither the purse nor the sword — ultimately rests on sustained public confidence in its moral sanction."[413]

413. Baker v. Carr, 369 U.S. 186, 267 (1962) (Frankfurter, J., dissenting).

JOHNSON, THE CONSTITUTION AND THE FEDERAL DISTRICT JUDGE
54 Tex. L. Rev. 903, 903-915 (1976)

[Judge Frank Johnson was United States District Judge for the Middle District of Alabama from 1956 to 1979. He issued and supervised many structural injunctions against Alabama officials. In 1979 he was elevated to the Court of Appeals.]

As governmental institutions at all levels have assumed a greater role in providing public services, courts increasingly have been confronted with the unavoidable duty of determining whether those services meet basic constitutional requirements. . . .

The reluctance with which courts and judges have undertaken the complex task of deciding such questions has at least three important sources. First, one of the founding principles of our Government . . . is that the powers of government should be separate and distinct, lest all the awesome power of government unite as one force unchecked in its exercise. . . .

Second, our Constitution and laws have strictly limited the power of the federal judiciary to participate in what are essentially political affairs. . . .

Last, federal judges properly hesitate to make decisions either that require the exercise of political judgment or that necessitate expertise they lack. . . . In an ideal society, elected officials would make all decisions relating to the allocation of resources; experts trained in corrections would make all penological decisions; physicians would make all medical decisions; scientists would make all technological decisions; and educators would make all educational decisions. Too often, however, we have failed to achieve this ideal system. Many times, those persons to whom we have entrusted these responsibilities have acted or failed to act in ways that do not fall within the bounds of discretion permitted by the Constitution and the laws. When such transgressions are properly and formally brought before a court — and increasingly before federal courts — it becomes the responsibility of the judiciary to ensure that the Constitution and laws of the United States remain, in fact as well as in theory, the supreme law of the land.

On far too many occasions the intransigent and unremitting opposition of state officials who have neglected or refused to correct unconstitutional or unlawful state policies and practices has necessitated federal intervention to enforce the law. Courts in all sections of the Nation have expended and continue to expend untold resources in repeated litigation brought to compel local school officials to follow a rule of law first announced by the Supreme Court almost twenty-two years ago. In addition to deciding scores of school cases, federal courts in Alabama alone have ordered the desegregation of mental institutions, penal facilities, public parks, city buses, interstate and intrastate buses and bus terminals, airport terminals, and public libraries and museums. Although I refer to Alabama and specific cases litigated in the federal courts of Alabama, I do not intend to suggest that similar problems do not exist in many of our other states. . . .

Desegregation is not the only area of state responsibility in which Alabama officials have forfeited their decisionmaking powers by such a dereliction of duty as to require judicial intervention. Having found Alabama's legislative apportionment plan unconstitutional, the District Court for the Middle District of Alabama waited ten years for State officials to carry out the duty properly imposed upon them by the Constitution and expressly set out in the court's order. The continued refusal of those officials to comply left the court no choice but to assume that duty itself and to impose its own reapportionment plan. State officers by their inaction have also handed over to the courts property tax assessment plans; standards for the care and treatment of mentally ill and mentally retarded persons committed to the State's custody; and the procedures by which such persons are committed.

Some of these cases are extremely troublesome and time consuming for all concerned. I speak in particular of those lawsuits challenging the operation of state institutions for the custody and control of citizens who cannot or will not function at a safe and self-sustaining capacity in a free society. Ordinarily these cases proceed as class actions seeking to determine the rights of large numbers of people. As a result, the courts' decisions necessarily have wide-ranging effect and momentous importance, whether they grant or deny the relief sought.

A shocking example of a failure of state officials to discharge their duty was forcefully presented in a lawsuit tried before me in 1972, Newman v. Alabama, which challenged the constitutional sufficiency of medical care available to prisoners in the Alabama penal system. The evidence in that case convincingly demonstrated that correctional officers on occasion intentionally denied inmates the right to examination by a physician or to treatment by trained medical personnel, and that they routinely withheld medicine and other treatments prescribed by physicians. Further evidence showed that untrained inmates served as ward attendants and X-ray, laboratory, and dental technicians; rags were used as bandages; ambulance oxygen tanks remained empty for long periods of time; and unsupervised inmates without formal training pulled teeth, gave injections, sutured, and performed minor surgery. In fact, death resulting from gross neglect and totally inadequate treatment was not unusual.

A nineteen-year-old with an extremely high fever who was diagnosed as having acute pneumonia was left unsupervised and allowed to take cold showers at will for two days before his death. A quadriplegic with bedsores infested with maggots was bathed and had his bandages changed only once in the month before his death. An inmate who could not eat received no nourishment for the three days prior to his death even though intravenous feeding had been ordered by a doctor. A geriatric inmate who had suffered a stroke was made to sit each day on a wooden bench so that he would not soil his bed; he frequently fell onto the floor; his legs became swollen from a lack of circulation, necessitating the amputation of a leg the day before his death.

Based on the virtually uncontradicted evidence presented at trial, the district court entered a comprehensive order designed to remedy each specific abuse proved at trial and to establish additional safeguards so that the medical program in Alabama prisons would never again regress to its past level of inadequacy. The State was ordered to bring the general hospital at the Medical and Diagnostic Center (now Kilby Corrections Facility) up to the minimum standards required of hospitals by the United States Department of Health, Education, and Welfare for participation in the medicare program. The court also directed the Alabama State Board of Health to inspect regularly for general sanitation all the medical and food processing facilities in the prison system. Finally, the court decreed that all inmates receive physical examinations by physicians at regular intervals of not more than two years.

One of the most comprehensive orders that I have entered concerning the operation and management of state institutions relates to the facilities maintained by the Alabama Department of Mental Health for the mentally ill and mentally retarded. Plaintiffs in Wyatt v. Stickney . . . produced evidence showing that Bryce Hospital, built in the 1850s, was grossly overcrowded, housing more than 5000 patients. Of these 5000 people ostensibly committed to Bryce for treatment of mental illness, about 1600 — almost one-third — were geriatrics neither needing nor receiving any treatment for mental illness. Another 1000 or more of the patients at Bryce were mentally retarded rather than mentally ill. A totally inadequate staff, only a small percentage professionally trained, served these 5000 patients. The hospital employed only six staff members qualified to deal with mental patients — three medical doctors with psychiatric training, one Ph.D psychologist, and two social workers with master's degrees in social work. The evidence indicated that the general living conditions and lack of individualized treatment programs were as intolerable and deplorable as Alabama's rank of fiftieth among the states in per patient expenditures would suggest. For example, the hospital spent less than fifty cents per patient each day for food.

The evidence concerning Partlow State School and Hospital for the retarded proved even more shocking than the evidence relating to the mental hospitals. The extremely dangerous conditions compelled the court to issue an interim emergency order requiring Partlow officials to take immediate steps to protect the lives and safety of the residents. The Associate Commissioner for Mental Retardation for the Alabama Department of Mental Health testified that Partlow was sixty percent over-crowded; that the school, although it had not, could immediately discharge at least 300 residents; *and that seventy percent of the residents should never have been committed at all.* The conclusion that there was no opportunity for habilitation for its residents was inescapable. Indeed, the evidence reflected that one resident was scalded to death when a fellow resident hosed water from one of the bath facilities on him; another died as a result of the insertion of a running water hose into his rectum by a working resident who was cleaning him; one died when soapy water was forced into his mouth; another died of a self-administered over-dose of inadequately stored drugs; and authorities restrained another resident in a straitjacket for *nine years* to prevent him from sucking his hands and fingers. Witnesses described the Partlow facilities as barbaric and primitive; some residents had no place to sit to eat meals, and coffee cans served as toilets in some areas of the institution.

With the exception of the interim emergency order designed to elimi-nate hazardous conditions at Partlow, the court at first declined to devise specific steps to improve existing conditions in Alabama's mental health and retardation facilities. Instead, it directed the Department of Mental Health to design its own plan for upgrading the system to meet constitu-tional standards. Only after two deadlines had passed without any signs of acceptable progress did the court itself, relying upon the proposals of counsel for all parties and amici curiae, define the minimal constitutional standards of care, treatment, and habilitation for which the case of Wyatt v. Stickney has become generally known.

During the past several years conditions at the Partlow State School for the retarded have improved markedly. It was pleasing to read in a Montgomery newspaper that members of the State Mental Health Board (the *Wyatt* defendants) recently met at Partlow and agreed that "what they saw was a different world" compared to four years ago; that "things are now unbelievably better," with most students "out in the sunshine on playground swings or tossing softballs[,] . . . responding to a kind word or touch with smiles and squeals of delight"; and that "enrollment has been nearly cut in half, down from 2,300 to just under 1,300 while the staff has tripled from 600 to 1,800."

Persons incarcerated in state and local prison and jail facilities around the Nation increasingly have attacked the conditions of their confine-ment as unconstitutional. In recent years, federal courts in Alabama, Arkansas, Florida, Maryland, Massachusetts, and Mississippi, among others, have been forced to declare that the constitutional rights of in-mates are denied by the mere fact of their confinement in institutions that inflict intolerable and inhuman living conditions. In Texas a federal judge has held unconstitutional the detention of juveniles in certain facil-ities maintained by the Texas Youth Council because of the extreme brutality and indifference experienced in these institutions. In fashioning appropriate remedies in these cases, the courts have exhibited sensitivity to the real but not the imagined limitations imposed on correctional officials forced to operate penal facilities with the meager sums appropriated by legislators who see few or no political rewards in supporting constitutional treatment of prisoners. Some courts have ordered that entire institutions be closed and abandoned; others have required substantial improvements in facilities and services as a precondition to their continued operation.

Knowing firsthand the considerable time, energy, and thought that must precede any decision affecting mental hospital or prison conditions, I seriously doubt that any judge relishes his involvement in such a controversy or enters a decree unless the law clearly makes it his duty to do so. The Fifth Circuit adheres to the well-settled rule that federal courts do not sit to supervise state prisons or to interfere with their internal operation and administration. The American system of justice, however, equally acknowledges that inmates do not lose all constitutional rights and privileges when they are confined following conviction of criminal offenses.

James v. Wallace, a recent class action tried before me objecting to conditions in Alabama's state penal facilities, presents another graphic example. . . . The *James* trial began last August following extensive pretrial discovery, which included more than 1000 facts stipulated to by all parties and filed with the court. At the close of the defendants' case, the lead counsel for the Governor and the State Board of Corrections acknowledged in open court that "the overwhelming majority of the evidence . . . shows that an Eighth Amendment violation has and is now occurring to inmates in the Alabama prison system."

Plaintiffs in *James* demonstrated the intolerability of life in Alabama's prisons by proof of both general living conditions and commonplace incidents. Fighting, assault, extortion, theft, and homosexual rape are everyday occurrences in all four main institutions. A mentally retarded twenty-year-old inmate, after testifying that doctors had told him he had the mind of a five-year-old, told in open court how four inmates raped him on his first night in an Alabama prison.

The evidence showed that most prisoners found it necessary to carry some form of homemade or contraband weapon merely for self-protection. One prisoner testified that he would rather be caught with a weapon by a prison guard than be caught without one by another prisoner. Seriously dilapidated physical facilities have created generally unsanitary and hazardous living conditions in Alabama's prisons. Roaches, flies, mosquitoes, and other vermin overrun the institutions. One living area in Draper prison housing over 200 men contained one functioning toilet.

A United States public health officer, testifying as an expert witness after having inspected the four major prisons, pronounced the facilities wholly unfit for human habitation according to virtually every criterion used for evaluation by public health inspectors. He testified that as a public health officer, he would recommend the closing of any similar facilities under his jurisdiction because they presented an imminent danger to the health of the exposed individuals. Moreover, all the parties to the lawsuit agreed that severe overcrowding and understaffing aggravated all these other difficulties. At the time of trial over 3500 prisoners resided in facilities designed for no more than 2300. The Commissioner of the Alabama Board of Corrections testified that although the prison system required a minimum staff of 692 correctional officers, it then employed 383. Correctional experts testified that such an overflow of prisoners, coupled with the shortage of supervisory personnel, precludes any meaningful control over the institutions by the responsible officials. The facts bore out that conclusion. Prison guards simply refused to enter some dormitories at night, and one warden testified that he would not enter a certain dormitory at his institution without at least four guards by his side. . . .

Alabama prisons do not have a working classification system, an essential ingredient of any properly operated penal system. A functioning classification system enables officials to segregate for treatment and for the protection of other[s] prisoners not able or willing to function in any social setting. Currently, mentally disturbed inmates receive no special care or therapy, and are housed and treated like the general prison population. Consequently, violent and aggressive prisoners live together with those who are weak, passive, or otherwise easily victimized. For example, when the twenty-year-old inmate I spoke of earlier reported the rape to prison officials, the warden of the institution told him that he, the warden, could do nothing about it. . . .

Based on the overwhelming and generally undisputed evidence presented at trial, the court granted immediate partial relief to plaintiffs in the form of two interim orders, which remain in effect. One order enjoined the State from accepting additional prisoners, except escapees and parole violators, until each State prison facility decreases its population to its design capacity. The second ruling banned the use of isolation and segregation cells that fail to meet minimum standards. Before this order, as many as six inmates were confined in four-by-eight foot cells with no beds, no lighting, no running water, and a hole in the floor for a toilet that only a guard outside could flush.

The final opinion and order entered in *James* in January 1976 established a broad range of minimum standards designed to remedy the broad range of constitutional deprivations proven at trial and conceded to exist by the State's lawyers. The standards govern staffing; classification of prisoners; mental and physical health care; physical facilities; protection of inmates; and educational, vocational, recreational, and work programs. . . .

[S]tate officials have frequently raised the tenth amendment's reservation of powers to the states as a defense to the exercise of federal jurisdiction over actions alleging state violations of constitutional rights. While the tenth amendment clearly preserves for the states a wide and important sphere of power, it does not permit any state to frustrate or to ignore the mandates of the Constitution. *The tenth amendment does not relieve the states of a single obligation imposed upon them by the Constitution of the United States.* Surely the concept of states' rights has never purported to allow states to abdicate their responsibility to protect their citizens from criminal acts and inhumane conditions. . . .

The cornerstone of our American legal system rests on recognition of the Constitution as the supreme law of the land, and the paramount duty of the federal judiciary is to uphold that law. Thus, when a state fails to meet constitutionally mandated requirements, it is the solemn duty of the courts to assure compliance with the Constitution. One writer has termed the habit adopted by some states of neglecting their responsibilities until faced with a federal court order "the Alabama Federal Intervention Syndrome," characterizing it as

> the tendency of many state officials to punt their problems with constituencies to the federal courts. Many federal judges have grown accustomed to allowing state officials to make political speeches as a prelude to receiving the order of the district court. This role requires the federal courts to serve as a buffer between the state officials and their constituencies, raising the familiar criticism that state officials rely upon the federal courts to impose needed reforms rather than accomplishing them themselves.[71]

As long as those state officials entrusted with the responsibility for fair and equitable governance completely disregard that responsibility, the judiciary must and will stand ready to intervene on behalf of the deprived. . . . We in the judiciary await the day when the Alabama Federal Intervention Syndrome, in that State and elsewhere, will become a relic of the past. To reclaim responsibilities passed by default to the judiciary — most often the federal judiciary — and to find solutions for ever-changing challenges, the states must preserve their ability to respond flexibly, creatively, and with due regard for the rights of all.

EISENBERG AND YEAZELL, THE ORDINARY AND THE EXTRAORDINARY IN INSTITUTIONAL LITIGATION
93 Harv. L. Rev. 465, 493-494 (1980)

In many cases characterized as institutional, the judicial role was far less intrusive. Some cases considered to be part of the new litigation are little

---

71. McCormack, The Expansion of Federal Question Jurisdiction and the Prisoner Complaint Caseload, 1975 Wis. L. Rev. 523, 536 (footnotes omitted).

more than judicial opinions blessing settlements negotiated by the parties. At least one decision adopted the remedial scheme proposed by the defendant health authorities instead of that proposed by plaintiff patients. In such cases it can scarcely be said that courts are seizing power from reluctant officials. In another case, the only issue decided was drastic overcrowding in a state prison system. The district court allowed two years of study before ordering measures calculated to reduce the inmate population to acceptable levels; it then gave the state another two years to achieve the required population levels. In many cases in which judicial intervention occurs, the intervention is at least initially mild, allowing the defendants to devise programs that will square institutional conditions with constitutional requirements. These are not courts hell-bent on remaking society.

Admittedly, courts should pause before ordering relief that will involve judges in continuous supervision of unfamiliar institutions. . . . [C]ourts do pause. But once intransigence and the complex nature of the institutions involved make detailed decrees and some level of supervision inevitable, courts are not on nearly such new ground as the commentary suggests. Courts often have had to monitor executors and various kinds of trustees, including some operating large, complex businesses. Moreover, courts have shown willingness to participate in the continuous supervision of large enterprises for reasons no more compelling than that such arrangements are useful to those who have more property than they can conveniently manage or dispose of themselves. By comparison, it does not seem to be an outrageous abuse of judicial authority for courts to supervise state and local authorities in order to ensure that these officials protect the constitutional rights of prisoners, patients, and school children. Courts should be able to demand sufficient alteration in the supervision of mental patients to keep them from drowning in their own vomit.

NOTES ON THE DEBATE OVER STRUCTURAL INJUNCTIONS

1. Professors Nagel and Frug are on their strongest ground when the courts order freewheeling discretionary remedies in the tradition of Bailey v. Proctor. Aren't their objections considerably weaker when the courts try in good faith to restore plaintiffs to the position they would have occupied but for the wrong? Despite its indeterminacy in constitutional cases, doesn't that standard constrain discretion far more than a principle that equity courts should do equity? Isn't judicial power to order compliance with minimum constitutional standards a necessary corollary of Marbury v. Madison? And isn't any injunction necessary to that limited goal within the judicial power, even if it directs the expenditure of

money or the administration of details? Isn't the history of judicial supervision of institutions sketched by Professors Eisenberg and Yeazell relevant to the meaning of "judicial power"?

2. Despite their disclaimers, aren't Frug and Nagel proposing that
states be allowed to violate the constitution? Their separation of powers
limits on constitutional remedies have no necessary correlation with the
substantive scope of constitutional rights. If the proposed limits have any
independent content, don't they mean that violations will go unremedied
when a remedy requires too much judicial supervision of legislative or
executive decisions?

3. Defendants always have the option to close the institution if they
are unable or unwilling to run it constitutionally. See Palmer v. Thompson, 403 U.S. 217 (1971), upholding the decision of Jackson, Mississippi,
to close its swimming pools rather than integrate them. How much does
that option reduce separation of powers problems? Is it completely irrelevant, because shutting down is not a realistic choice for anything more
important than a swimming pool? Does an order to "run it my way or shut
it down" interfere with the very same choices as an order to "run it my
way," even if shutting down *is* a realistic choice? Or is it important that
the choice to spend more money or none at all remains with the legislature, even if legislators don't find those choices very attractive? What
about partial shutdowns? Might there be a realistic choice between
spending the same money incarcerating fewer people or more money
incarcerating as many people as before?

4. Frug fears that the essence of democratic government is sacrificed
when judges control too much of the budget. Surely he is right that
legislatures should generally set priorities and spending patterns. They
can choose to support schools more than prisons, or even mortgage subsi-
dies for the middle class more than aid for impoverished children. But
isn't the point of the underlying constitutional rights in these cases that
there are some limits on that discretion? Doesn't the cruel and unusual
punishment clause mean, for example, that states can't decide to incar-
cerate people under the conditions Judge Johnson describes — that the
democratic process denied itself that option when the state legislatures
ratified the eighth and fourteenth amendments? Still, if the legislature
suddenly has to come up with a lot of money for some constituency that
has been unconstitutionally neglected, who is likely to bear the burden of
budget balancing? Other relatively neglected groups, or the majority that
has been doing the neglecting while voting benefits for itself?

5. Professor Chayes predicted that remedies in structural cases would
often be negotiated. An empirical study of selected cases tends to confirm
that prediction, and even finds that key legislative committees are occasionally involved in the negotiations. M. Rebell and A. Block, Educational Policy-Making and the Courts: An Empirical Study of Judicial
Activism (1982). How much should this pattern alleviate Frug and Nagel's

concerns? Doesn't it conform pretty well to Nagel's proposal that judges announce constitutional requirements in broad terms and leave the details of implementation to the executive? Does it violate separation of powers for the judge to mediate the negotiations or indicate whether he considers a proposed remedy adequate? What of the case where remedy can't be negotiated because defendants refuse to cooperate? Is the court required to give up at that point? If detailed supervision is the only effective way to deal with uncooperative defendants, and if detailed supervision were forbidden, wouldn't defendants have every incentive to be uncooperative?

6.   Whatever the doctrinal answers to Frug and Nagel, and however great the need for judicial intervention, aren't they right about the risk that power will be abused? Separation of powers was designed to restrain bad men and excessively zealous good men; the bench surely has some of each. There is a potential for abuse when one life-tenured judge tries to run an entire prison system, housing authority, or school district. Are appellate review, the pressure of public opinion, and the theoretical threat of impeachment sufficient safeguards?

7.   The Supreme Court obliquely addressed some of Frug's concerns in Hutto v. Finney. That opinion also affirmed an award of attorney's fees against the state. The Court rejected the state's claim that a fee award was barred by the eleventh amendment, which has been construed to make states immune from damage judgments in federal court. The opinion also included the following footnote:

> The Attorney General has not argued that this award was so large or so unexpected that it interfered with the State's budgeting process. Although the Eleventh Amendment does not prohibit attorney's fees awards for bad faith, it may counsel moderation in determining the size of the award or in giving the State time to adjust its budget before paying the full amount of the fee. In this case, however, the timing of the award has not been put in issue, nor has the State claimed that the award was larger than necessary to enforce the court's prior orders.

437 U.S. 678, 692 n.18 (1978).

8.   The order in *Milliken II* cost Michigan $6 million. The Detroit school board was delighted to get an extra $6 million in state aid; it sided with the plaintiffs on that issue and led Justice Powell to describe the case as largely a friendly suit. Similarly, conscientious officials of prisons, mental hospitals, and other institutions may view an injunction against themselves as a means of getting more money from the legislature. How much should we worry that these conflicting incentives on the defense side erode the adversary process? Recall the concession of unconstitutionality in the Alabama prison case. If the state's executives occasionally concede unnecessarily, should we care? Isn't the vigor with which elected

officials represent the majority a matter that really is for the political process?

HISTORICAL NOTES: THE MUNICIPAL BOND CASES

1. Professor Nagel notes that in Meriwether v. Garrett, 102 U.S. (12 Otto) 472 (1880), the Supreme Court refused to let a receiver take possession of the property of the city of Memphis on behalf of unpaid bondholders. That is an accurate statement of the case, but you should not infer that *Meriwether* typifies a lost sense of restraint in which judges readily acknowledged their inability to remedy violations of the constitution.

2. The municipal bond cases make an extraordinary story; they take up two chapters in the Holmes Devise History of the Supreme Court. C. Fairman, Reconstruction and Reunion 1864-88, Part One 918-1116 (1971). The Supreme Court decided more than two hundred cases of defaulted municipal bonds, beginning in the late 1850s and continuing to the end of the century. The great bulk of these cases involved bonds issued to subsidize the construction of railroads. Municipalities issued bonds in exchange for stock in railroad companies whose promoters promised to build lines serving the area; some municipalities gave bonds to promoters outright. The promoters raised money by selling the bonds in the financial markets.

Many municipalities issued bonds far in excess of their ability to pay, hoping to grow dramatically with the coming of the railroad. Public officials issued bonds without regard to formalities affecting their authority and without reasonable protections against default by the promoters. In many cases the promoters bribed local officials. Many of the railroads were never built, and those that were rarely produced sudden wealth for the towns and counties along the line. In some cases, the promoters changed the route and bypassed towns that had subsidized construction. Many municipalities repudiated railroad bonds and bitterly resisted efforts at collection.

The bondholders sued in federal court. They were generally East Coast and European financiers, claiming to be holders in due course without notice of any defenses. The defendants were generally small towns and counties, mainly in the South and Midwest. Memphis was a minor metropolis at 35,000; other defaulting litigants included Watertown, Wisconsin, and Coloma, Illinois.

With few exceptions, the Supreme Court enforced the bonds. Sometimes it held that repudiation violated the contract clause. But often, the defense was that the municipality lacked authority to issue the bonds, and that the state supreme court had held the obligations void under the state constitution. A court decision that the bonds were void from their inception did not violate the contract clause. Railroad Co. v. Rock, 71 U.S. (4 Wall.) 177 (1866). In those cases, the Court invoked its asserted power to declare the general law in diversity cases. Swift v. Tyson, 41 U.S. (16 Pet.) 1 (1842). Incredibly, it refused to be bound by state supreme court interpretations of state constitutions; it held that municipalities had power to issue railroad bonds even when the relevant state court said they didn't. Township at Pine Grove v. Talcott, 86 U.S. (19 Wall.) 666 (1874). Most of the criticism of these cases has focused on the substantive issues and on the abuse of the diversity jurisdiction. See Powe, Rehearsal for Substantive Due Process: The Municipal Bond Cases, 53 Tex. L. Rev. 738 (1975).

3. There has been less attention to the remedies used to enforce these decisions. Defendants did not pay just because they had lost their case in the Supreme Court. There were mass meetings and threats of violence against tax collectors and federal marshalls. In Iowa, stout unionist Republicans freshly home from the Civil War made speeches urging state nullification. Some Missouri counties quit using dollars: They paid their bills in scrip, let the merchants sell the scrip, and accepted the scrip in payment of taxes. The result was that the county never had any money to pay judgments with. In some small towns in Wisconsin, local officials resigned from office every time a marshall came to serve a writ. Watertown apparently did without public officials until the statute of limitations ran out.

How did the Court respond to this resistance? It was not absolutist, but neither was it so restrained as Nagel's simple statement of the Memphis example might suggest. The Court did reverse a decree putting Memphis into federal receivership, but the trial judge had plausibly thought he had power to issue such a decree, three justices would have affirmed, and the majority could agree only on a terse statement of conclusions. In other cases, the Court affirmed remedies that Nagel would likely find too intrusive.

The Court ordered local officials to issue warrants on municipal treasuries. The warrants would entitle the judgment creditor to all the money in the treasury ahead of any expenses subsequently incurred. United States v. County of Clark, 96 U.S. (6 Otto) 211 (1877). (The United States was not a party to any of these cases, but actions for mandamus were often brought in the name of the United States.)

The Court ordered local officials to raise taxes to the maximum rate permitted by state law. Macon County v. Huidekoper, 134 U.S. 332 (1890). The Court implied power to levy special taxes to pay bonds from the legislation authorizing issuance of the bonds. Then it ordered local officials to levy this implicitly authorized tax. And it held that statutes "purporting to take away . . . the power to levy taxes to meet the payments" were unconstitutional as applied to bonds issued earlier. Ralls County Court v. United States, 105 U.S. (15 Otto) 733 (1881). The Court ordered local officials to levy such taxes even though a state court had ordered them not to. It promised to release the officials on writs of habeas corpus if they were imprisoned for violating the state court injunction. Riggs v. Johnson County, 73 U.S. (6 Wall.) 166 (1867).

Perhaps most extraordinary, the Court appointed the federal marshall for the District of Iowa to levy and collect local taxes. Supervisors v. Rogers, 74 U.S. (7 Wall.) 175 (1868). The Court relied on a section of the Iowa mandamus statute, which said that if a defendant refused to do the act ordered by mandamus, the court could appoint someone to do it. A federal statute said that federal courts should use state procedures to enforce judgments. Neither statute mentioned levying taxes, but the Court did not appear to doubt that general language was sufficient.

4.   *Rogers* was as far as the Court went. It refused to order the federal marshall to levy and collect taxes in Wisconsin, because Wisconsin had no statute like the one in Iowa. Rees v. City of Watertown, 86 U.S. (19 Wall.) 107 (1873). It thought that courts had no inherent power to levy taxes, even in Watertown, where officials who did have that power resigned from office to avoid the court's orders. The Court also refused to levy on the property of individual citizens of Watertown.

5.   *Watertown* goes far toward explaining the Memphis case. First, the lower court purported to turn all the property of the city over to the receiver, except for property essential to the public such as streets, wharves, and fire wagons. Thus, this receivership went further even than the order allowing the federal marshall to levy taxes in Iowa. And the Court found no statutory authorization.

The case also involved a repeal of taxing authority in Memphis. The Court was considerably more deferential to that repeal than it had been in other cases where taxing authority was repealed, and the distinctions offered do not appear to reconcile the cases. But another distinction leaps off the page to a modern reader, even though the Court did not explicitly rely on it.

The repeal of taxing authority was part of a broader state plan to clean up the fiscal mess in Memphis. The Tennessee legislature had revoked the city's charter and replaced the city with a special taxing district tightly under state control. Another statute had created a state receiver to collect back taxes and earmarked those taxes for payment of the bonds. Memphis had collected only 60 percent of its taxes for several years. These back taxes were the primary target of the federal receivership. To uphold the federal court order would eviscerate the state repayment plan. The bondholders plausibly believed that the federal court would collect more than the state plan; the legislation made the new taxing district immune from old claims against the city. But compared to massive defiance in many other states, Tennessee may have looked like a paragon of fiscal responsibility.

The Court reaffirmed the availability of mandamus to order levy and collection of taxes in appropriate cases. It noted that federal mandamus could run against the state receiver if he failed to do his duty, but it held that such a claim would require a separate lawsuit. And it reserved the question whether a federal receiver could collect taxes levied pursuant to contract or judicial decree "if there be no public officer charged with authority from the legislature to perform that duty." 102 U.S. (12 Otto) at 501.

6.   There are many lessons to be learned from the municipal bond cases. The most salient for our purposes is that intrusive remedies against defiant local governments are not new, and that deference to good faith efforts by state and local government is not new either.

7.   Another result of this episode was the formalization of the municipal bond business. Independent counsel now write opinions confirming the municipality's authority with respect to each new bond issue. Bonds to subsidize private ventures are typically payable only out of the revenue produced by the venture.

But the lure of new technology can still lead to disaster. In 1974, municipally owned utilities in Washington guaranteed bonds to pay for two nuclear power plants to be built by the Washington Public Power Supply System. They promised to pay whether the plants were built or not. Both plants suffered huge cost overruns and were cancelled long before completion. Once again, bonds were in default and there was widespread public resistance to payment. Despite the opinions of bond counsel at issuance, many of the municipalities repudiated the bonds on the ground that they had no authority to promise to pay for unbuilt power plants. The Supreme Court of Washington agreed and held the bonds void. Chemical Bank v. Washington Public Power Supply System, 99 Wash. 2d 772, 666 P.2d 329 (1983). This time the Supreme Court did not get involved. The Court no longer makes general commercial law in diversity cases. Erie Railroad v. Tompkins, 304 U.S. 64 (1938). And there was no viable constitutional claim. It is still the rule that a judicial decision invalidating a contract does not violate the contracts clause. Railroad Co. v. Rock, 71 U.S. (4 Wall.) 177 (1866), has never been questioned.

CHAPTER 4

The Relationship between Legal and Equitable Remedies: The Irreparable Injury Rule and Related Matters

A. PERMANENT INJUNCTIONS

PARDEE v. CAMDEN LUMBER CO.
70 W. Va. 68, 73 S.E. 82 (1911)

[Plaintiff sued to enjoin defendant from cutting timber on plaintiff's land.]

POFFENBARGER, J. . . .

In 1874, in the case of McMillan v. Ferrell, 7 W. Va. 223, this court prescribed, as being essential and indispensable to a bill to prevent the cutting of timber, averments of good title in the plaintiff, trespass by the defendant, and the insolvency of the latter or some other circumstance, rendering an action for damages futile or unavailing, and that doctrine has been uniformly maintained ever since. However, this rule seems not to have commanded uniform approval by the public, nor by the members of the legal profession, and in later years, under conditions greatly enhancing the value of timber and altering, to a considerable extent, the method of handling it, the dissatisfaction has grown in extent and intensified in degree. Out of the great disfavor into which the rule has thus fallen, an insistent demand for its abolition has brought forth earnest, able, and laborious inquiry as to the soundness of the reasoning upon which it was established, resulting in increased dissatisfaction, which has extended even to members of this court, as will appear from official expressions of personal disapproval of the doctrine or principle of the line of decisions just mentioned.

Under these circumstances, we feel it our duty to re-examine the proposition and thoroughly test its soundness by the application of legal and equitable principles. . . .

Supposed adequacy of the legal remedy for the cutting of timber, regarded as a mere trespass upon land, constitutes the basis of the rule. If the legal remedy is not adequate, the whole doctrine necessarily fails. Whether it is must be determined by reference to the general policy of the law as disclosed by its application in analogous and related cases. In other words, we must see to what extent the remedies afforded by courts of law and equity protect and vindicate the right of an owner of property to keep it in such condition as he desires. If we find the general object to be the maintenance of this right, respecting all other kinds of property, we must necessarily say it ought to extend to the right of an owner of timber to allow it to stand upon his land in its natural state as long as he desires it to do so. Timber cut down and converted into mere logs and lumber is plainly not the same thing as standing timber. It is equally manifest that the legal remedies are wholly inadequate to reconvert logs and lumber into live, standing, growing trees. Our rule permits a mere trespasser to utterly destroy the forest of his neighbor, provided he is solvent and able to respond in damages to the extent of the value thereof. It can neither restore the forest, nor prevent its destruction. It allows the property to be wholly altered in nature and character, or converts it into a mere claim for damages. After the timber has been cut, the owner may recover possession thereof by an action of detinue, or, waiving that, may recover its value, but this does not in either case restore the property to its former state, nor replace it by the return of an equivalent. The general principles of English and American jurisprudence forbid such a result. They guarantee to the owner of property the right, not only to possession thereof and dominion over it, but also its immunity from injury, unless it be of such character that it may be substantially replaced. On the theory of adequacy of the legal remedy an injunction to prevent the sale or destruction of certain kinds of personal property will be refused, but the principles upon which this conclusion stand cannot be extended to all forms of property either real or personal, and the courts do not attempt so to extend it. Compensation in damages is adequate in all those instances in which the property injured or destroyed may be substantially replaced with the money recovered as its value. For instance, the world is full of horses, cattle, sheep, hogs, lumber, and many other articles. Ordinarily, one of these may be replaced by another just as good. This principle is applied in a proceeding for specific performance of contracts for the sale of corporate stocks. If the stock belongs to a class found generally in the market for sale, equity refuses specific performance of the contract, because other stock of the same kind can be purchased with the money recovered as damages. If, on the other hand, the stock is limited and unobtainable in the market, specific performance will be enforced. Similarly, as no two pieces of land can be regarded as equivalent in value and character in all respects, equity will always enforce specific performance of a valid contract for the sale thereof. If personal property possesses a value peculiar to its owner, . . . equity will vindicate and uphold the right to the possession thereof and immunity from injury by the exercise of its extraordinary powers. We observe, also, that the law gives a remedy for the possession of personal property, however trivial its value or character may be. It does not limit the owner to a claim for damages, unless the property has gone beyond the reach of its process. As equity follows the law, and, as far as possible, supplies omissions therein, so far as may be necessary to the effectuation of substantial justice, it vindicates the right of an owner to enjoy his property without injury or molestation by the exercise of its preventive powers; but, harmonizing with the great divine rule of help to those who help themselves, equity goes no further than is necessary. Therefore, if a man threatens to take away or kill his neighbor's horse, a court of equity will not interfere by injunction, because the owner may recover the value of that horse and buy another in the general market of substantially the same kind or value. For the same reason, it refuses to enforce specific performance of a contract of sale of a horse. But, if a man is about to destroy his neighbor's heirlooms, things having a peculiar value and insusceptible of replacement by purchase in the market, the legal remedy is not adequate, and a court of equity will, therefore, protect the possession and title of the owner by the exercise of its extraordinary powers. . . .

Such being the general policy of the law, do we not violate it by denying to the owner of standing timber his clear and indisputable legal right to have it remain upon his land until such time as he shall see fit to convert it into a different kind of property? Moreover, standing timber is everywhere regarded as part of the real estate upon which it grows. The cutting thereof converts it into personal property, and wholly changes its legal nature and incidents. Being a part of the land itself, it has no legal equivalent in nature or value, for no two pieces of land are alike in all respects, nor is a piece of land, stripped of its timber, with a right of action for the felled timber or for damages, the equivalent of the same land with the timber on it. Courts universally hold that all contracts relating to real estate are subjects of equitable cognizance, because they relate to real estate. A distinction is made between contractual rights respecting real estate and liability growing out of trespasses thereon. . . . Of course, the legal remedy is adequate, if the trespass amounts to nothing more than the trampling of the grass or throwing down of the fences, acts in no way affecting the substance of the estate, but the adequacy of the remedy in such cases does not argue efficacy in those cases in which part of the real estate is actually severed and carried away, to the injury and detriment of the inheritance. In Whitehouse v. Jones, 60 W. Va. 680, 690, 55 S.E. 730, 734, Judge Brannon condemned the rule now under consideration in the following terms: "It seems to me that this doctrine is now, always has been, unsound. Timber is of such inestimable value for building and repairing houses and fences, for fuel, and other purposes. It takes half a century or more to regrow it when once removed. A trespasser, without title, cuts it to-day, to-morrow, and on. Must you sue him in suit after suit for each day's or week's depredation? Or will you wait until he gets through, then have a long lawsuit? The timber is gone forever. The party has become insolvent. The remedy is not full and adequate."

Upon the principles and considerations here stated, we are of the opinion that the adoption of this rule was a deviation from fundamental principles of our jurisprudence. It is no doubt attributable to a lack of appreciation of the true character of timber, due to its former abundance and comparative worthlessness. In early days it was regarded as an incumbrance and burden upon lands. Having nothing but forests, the chief object or purpose of landowners everywhere was to get rid of the forests, and prepare their lands for agriculture. There was an abundance of timber, and no market for it. The soil was untillable because of the timber. Hence it was a common practice for owners to cut down the finest of timber, faultless oak, poplar, pine, walnut, and hickory, and burn it upon the premises in log heaps, upon the theory of a disposition of an incumbrance and obstacle to the growth and development of agriculture as a pursuit. Anybody who desired to cut a tree on his neighbor's land in the pursuit of wild animals or the search for deposits of honey had a tacit permission to do so. Forest fires were not regarded as evils, unless they happened to destroy fences, buildings, or other improvements or agricultural implements or products. Timber was not regarded as anything more than an ordinary commercial article, and almost worthless because of its abundance. . . . The error, thus born, has been revealed by the great change of conditions. Timber having become scarce and of great value, the layman, lawyer, and judge has in recent years given the subject more careful, critical, and profound consideration, with the result that the error is practically admitted everywhere.

Violative of principle, as we think, the rule is also contrary to the great weight of authority. In the general struggle for relief from it, courts have in some instances based distinctions upon the relative values of the timber and the land, saying the cutting of timber, constituting the chief value of the land, will be enjoined, but we think a clear case of trespass by the cutting of timber should always be enjoined. In one sense a small quantity of timber on land is more indispensable to its enjoyment than a large quantity. . . .

For the reasons here stated, the decree complained of will be reversed, the injunction reinstated, and the cause remanded.

BRANNON, J., filed a separate concurrence.

O. FISS, THE CIVIL RIGHTS INJUNCTION
1, 38-43 (1978)

Traditionally the relationship among remedies has been hierarchical. Remedies are ranked. Those near the top are the ones preferred. Those near the bottom may be utilized, but only if certain special conditions are met — conditions that are not placed on the other remedies.

This notion of a hierarchy of remedies has been one of the hallmarks of our legal system. Even more striking is the fact that in this hierarchy the injunction has classically been assigned a subordinate position. The injunction has been deemed an "extraordinary" remedy, to be used only if all else fails. . . . This hierarchical relationship and the subordination of the injunction is . . . primarily the handiwork of the irreparable injury requirement. That requirement makes the issuance of an injunction conditional upon a showing that the plaintiff has no alternative remedy that will adequately repair his injury. . . .

This hierarchical relationship among remedies . . . derives from several other doctrines as well, although they are of less general scope. One is the prior restraint doctrine, applicable to injunctions against speech. . . . For the injunction to issue, the speech not only must be unprotected but also must be so in some dramatic, clear, and special way, as exemplified in the troop movement paradigm: . . . an injunction against speech might be allowed if and only if the speech sought to be prevented was as *clearly* unprotected as that disclosing the movements of troops at time of war.[2] Speech falling short of that standard but nonetheless constitutionally unprotected might be the subject of other legal instruments, such as a criminal prohibition or prosecution, but not the injunction. In our culture the prior restraint doctrine is tied to the constitutional guarantee of freedom of speech, but the same sentiment is expressed in the traditional equitable maxim that equity will not enjoin a libel.

Another traditional maxim, to the effect that equity will not enjoin a crime, also might be viewed as a subordinating doctrine. When the conduct sought to be restrained is also proscribed by a criminal prohibition, the court will not issue an injunction even if there be a coordinate source of illegality (e.g., a civil nuisance law), unless the plaintiff demonstrates

2. Near v. Minnesota, 283 U.S. 697, 716 (1931).

the inadequacy of the criminal remedy. A preference is thereby expressed for the criminal remedy. . . .

The last of the subordinating doctrines — the one that confines injunctions to the protection of property interests — need not detain us. It is so devoid of justification — indeed I cannot think of a single argument in support of it — that we may treat it as having already been repudiated. No one takes it seriously. . . . The classic citation for repudiation, Kenyon v. City of Chicopee,[5] is a 1946 case, one in which Jehovah's Witnesses sought an injunction against authorities interfering with the distribution of handbills. The Massachusetts court put the doctrine to rest by capitalizing on the emerging consensus on the importance of constitutionally based human rights. . . . The court reasoned: "If equity would safeguard their right to sell bananas it ought to be at least equally solicitous of their personal liberties guaranteed by the Constitution."[6]

The other subordinating doctrines are of continuing vitality. This is obviously true of the prior restraint doctrine, which seems to be invoked with increasing frequency. I also think the equity-does-not-enjoin-a-crime doctrine and the more generalized irreparable injury requirement are alive and well. They continue to be invoked and affirmed. Indeed, the irreparable injury requirement — the principal object of my attack — seems to have received a new lease on life in Douglas v. City of Jeannette,[7] another 1940s case involving the Jehovah's Witnesses, and it was reinvigorated with a vengeance by a line of cases that begins in 1971 with Younger v. Harris.[8] . . .

I recognize the usual problem of the "gap": the subordinating doctrines express formal rules, and there may be a gap between actual judicial practice and formal rules. Indeed, it was the discordance between doctrine and practice that fueled this intellectual enterprise: doctrines required subordination, and yet the injunction was the primary remedy. In truth the civil rights plaintiff was not put to the task of establishing the inadequacy of alternative remedies, and that led me to inquire into the justification of the doctrine.

NOTES ON THE RULES THAT SUBORDINATE EQUITABLE REMEDIES

1. There is disagreement over the continuing importance of the subordinating doctrines. Professor Fiss recognizes the gap between theory and practice, but he thinks there are recent cases reinvigorating the tradi-

5.   320 Mass. 528, 70 N.E.2d 241 (1946).
6.   Id. at 533-34, 70 N.E.2d at 244.
7.   319 U.S. 157 (1943).
8.   401 U.S. 37 (1971).

tional rules. Other commentators tend to view those cases as isolated and explained by special considerations that only sometimes have anything to do with the choice of remedy. Professor Dobbs suggests that the irreparable injury rule is invoked only sporadically and not taken very seriously. D. Dobbs, A Handbook on the Law of Remedies, §2.5 at 61 (1973). And in a section subtitled "The Triumph of Equity," Professor Chayes says

> One of the most striking procedural developments of this century is the increasing importance of equitable relief. It is perhaps too soon to reverse the traditional maxim to read that money damages will be awarded only when no suitable form of specific relief can be devised. But surely, the old sense of equitable remedies as "extraordinary" has faded.

Chayes, The Role of the Judge in Public Law Litigation, 89 Harv. L. Rev. 1281, 1292 (1976).

2. To evaluate these arguments, students must decide what purposes subordinating doctrines serve. To do that, it is necessary to know a little of the history of equity.

F. MAITLAND, EQUITY
1-7 (2d ed. 1936)

[The chapters of this book were originally delivered as lectures at Cambridge in 1906.]

What is Equity? We can only answer . . . by giving some short account of certain courts of justice which were abolished over thirty years ago. In the year 1875 we might have said "Equity is that body of rules which is administered only by those Courts which are known as Courts of Equity." The definition of course would not have been very satisfactory, but now-a-days we are cut off even from this unsatisfactory definition. We have no longer any courts which are merely courts of equity. Thus we are driven to say that Equity now is that body of rules administered by our English courts of justice which, were it not for the operation of the Judicature Acts, would be administered only by those courts which would be known as Courts of Equity.

This, you may well say, is but a poor thing to call a definition. Equity is a certain portion of our existing substantive law, and yet in order that we may describe this portion and mark it off from other portions we have to make reference to courts that are no longer in existence. Still I fear that nothing better than this is possible. The only alternative would be to make a list of the equitable rules and say that Equity consists of those rules. This, I say, would be the only alternative, for if we were to inquire what it is that all these rules have in common and what it is that marks them off from all other rules administered by our courts, we should by way of answer find nothing but this, that these rules were until lately administered, and administered only, by our courts of equity.

Therefore for the mere purpose of understanding the present state of our law, some history becomes necessary.

In Edward I's day, at the end of the thirteenth century, three great courts have come into existence, the King's Bench, the Common Bench or Court of Common Pleas and the Exchequer. Each of these has its own proper sphere, but as time goes on each of them attempts to extend its sphere and before the middle ages are over a plaintiff has often a choice between these three courts and each of them will deal with his case in the same way and by the same rules. The law which these courts administer is in part traditional law, in part statute law. Already in Edward I's day the phrase "common law" is current. It is a phrase that has been borrowed from the canonists — who used "*jus commune*" to denote the general law of the Catholic Church; it describes that part of the law that is unenacted, non-statutory, that is common to the whole land and to all Englishmen. It is contrasted with statute, with local custom, with royal prerogative. It is not as yet contrasted with equity, for as yet there is no body of rules which bears this name.

One of the three courts, namely, the Exchequer, is more than a court of law. From our modern point of view it is not only a court of law but a "government office," an administrative or executive bureau; our modern Treasury is an offshoot from the old Exchequer. What we should call the "civil service" of the country is transacted by two great offices or "departments"; there is the Exchequer which is the fiscal department, there is the Chancery which is the secretarial department, while above these there rises the king's permanent Council. At the head of the chancery stands the Chancellor, usually a bishop; he is we may say the king's secretary of state for all departments, he keeps the king's great seal and all the already great mass of writing that has to be done in the king's name has to be done under his supervision.

He is not as yet a judge, but already he by himself or his subordinates has a great deal of work to do which brings him into a close connexion with the administration of justice. One of the duties of that great staff of clerks over which he presides is to draw up and issue those writs whereby actions are begun in the courts of law — such writs are sealed with the king's seal. A man who wishes to begin an action must go to the Chancery and obtain a writ. Many writs there are which have been formulated long ago; such writs are writs of course (*brevia de cursu*), one obtains them by asking for them of the clerks — called Cursitors — and paying the proper fees. But the Chancery has a certain limited power of inventing new writs to meet new cases as they arise. That power is consecrated by a famous clause of the Second Statute of Westminster authorizing writs *in consimili casu*. Thus the Chancellor may often have to consider whether the case is one in which some new and some specially worded writ should be framed. This however is not judicial business. The Chancellor does not hear both sides of the story, he only hears the plaintiff's application, and if he grants a writ the courts of law may afterwards quash that writ as being contrary to the law of the land.

But by another route the Chancellor is brought into still closer contact with the administration of justice. Though these great courts of law have been established there is still a reserve of justice in the king. Those who can not get relief elsewhere present their petitions to the king and his council praying for some remedy. Already by the end of the thirteenth century the number of such petitions presented in every year is very large, and the work of reading them and considering them is very laborious. In practice a great share of this labour falls on the Chancellor. He is the king's prime minister, he is a member of the council, and the specially learned member of the council. It is in dealing with these petitions that the Chancellor begins to develop his judicial powers. . . .

Very often the petitioner . . . complains that for some reason or another he can not get a remedy in the ordinary course of justice and yet he is entitled to a remedy. He is poor, he is old, he is sick, his adversary is rich and powerful, will bribe or will intimidate jurors, or has by some trick or some accident acquired an advantage of which the ordinary courts with their formal procedure will not deprive him. The petition is often couched in piteous terms, the king is asked to find a remedy for the love of God and in the way of charity. Such petitions are referred by the king to the Chancellor. Gradually in the course of the fourteenth century petitioners, instead of going to the king, will go straight to the Chancellor, will address their complaints to him and adjure him to do what is right for the love of God and in the way of charity. Now one thing that the Chancellor may do in such a case is to invent a new writ and so provide the complainant with a means of bringing an action in a court of law. But in the fourteenth century the courts of law have become very conservative and are given to quashing writs which differ in material points from those already in use. But another thing that the Chancellor can do is to send for the complainant's adversary and examine him concerning the charge that has been made against him. Gradually a procedure is established. The Chancellor having considered the petition, or "bill" as it is called, orders the adversary to come before him and answer the complaint. The writ whereby he does this is called a subpoena — because it orders the man to appear upon pain of forfeiting a sum of money, e.g., *subpoena centum librarum.* . . . The defendant will be examined upon oath and the Chancellor will decide questions of fact as well as questions of law.

I do not think that in the fourteenth century the Chancellors considered that they had to administer any body of substantive rules that differed from the ordinary law of the land. They were administering the law but they were administering it in cases which escaped the meshes of the ordinary courts. The complaints that come before them are in general complaints of indubitable legal wrongs, assaults, batteries, imprisonments, disseisins and so forth — wrongs of which the ordinary courts take cognizance, wrongs which they ought to redress. But then owing to one thing and another such wrongs are not always redressed by courts of law. In this period one of the commonest of all the reasons that complainants will give for coming to the Chancery is that they are poor while their adversaries are rich and influential — too rich, too influential to be left to the clumsy processes of the old courts and the verdicts of juries. However this sort of thing can not well be permitted. The law courts will not have it and parliament will not have it. Complaints against this extraordinary justice grow loud in the fourteenth century. In history and in principle it is closely connected with another kind of extraordinary justice which is yet more objectionable, the extraordinary justice that is done in criminal cases by the king's council. Parliament at one time would gladly be rid of both — of both the Council's interference in criminal matters, and the Chancellor's interference with civil matters. And so the Chancellor is warned off the field of common law — he is not to hear cases which might go to the ordinary courts, he is not to make himself a judge of torts and contracts, of property in lands and goods.

But then just at this time it is becoming plain that the Chancellor is doing some convenient and useful works that could not be done, or could not easily be done, by the courts of common law. He has taken to enforcing uses or trusts. . . . I must ask you not to believe that either the mass of the nation or the common lawyers of the fourteenth and fifteenth centuries looked with disfavour upon uses. No doubt they were troublesome things, things that might be used for fraudulent purposes, and statutes were passed against those who employed them for the purpose of cheating their creditors or evading the law of mortmain. But I have not a doubt that they were very popular, and I think we may say that had there been no Chancery, the old courts would have discovered some method of enforcing these fiduciary obligations. That method however must have been a clumsy one. A system of law which will never compel, which will never even allow, the defendant to give evidence, a system which sends every question of fact to a jury, is not competent to deal adequately with fiduciary relationships. On the other hand the Chancellor had a procedure which was very well adapted to this end. To this we may add that very possibly the ecclesiastical courts (and the Chancellor you will remember was almost always an ecclesiastic) had for a long time past been punishing breaches of trust by spiritual censures, by penance and excommunication. And so by general consent, we may say, the Chancellor was allowed to enforce uses, trusts or confidences.

Thus one great field of substantive law fell into his hand — a fruitful field, for in the course of the fifteenth century uses became extremely popular. . . . And then there were some other matters that were considered to be fairly within his jurisdiction. An old rhyme allows him "fraud, accident, and breach of confidence" — there were many frauds which the stiff old procedure of the courts of law could not adequately meet, and "accident," in particular the accidental loss of a document, was a proper occasion for the Chancellor's interference. No one could set any very strict limits to his power, but the best hint as to its extent that could be given in the sixteenth century was given by the words "fraud, accident and breach of confidence." On the other hand he was not to interfere where a court of common law offered an adequate remedy. A bill was "demurrable for want of equity" on that ground.

NOTE ON THE HISTORY OF EQUITY IN THE UNITED STATES

Article III of the Constitution authorizes equity jurisdiction for the federal courts, and Congress conferred it in 1789. Although the same federal judges exercised both law and equity powers, these powers were still conceived of as rigidly separate. Federal district courts had a law side and an equity side, and a case had to be on one side or the other; it could not be on both.

A serious movement for merger of law and equity began in the states in the mid-nineteenth century, beginning with the Field Code of 1848. Only four states still have separate courts of equity, although the merger in some other states is less than complete. The Federal Rules of Civil Procedure, adopted in 1938, accomplish complete merger in federal courts. But equitable doctrines and remedies are still identifiable in the merged practice, and they have become increasingly important in complex modern litigation.

NOTES ON THE REASONS FOR THE IRREPARABLE INJURY RULE

1. The irreparable injury rule is rooted in the beginnings of equity as a royal dispensation from the failings of the common law. Irreparable injury began as a rationale for the equity court's separate existence and consequently became the rationale for defining and limiting the court's jurisdiction. For if the equity court sat to correct the common law's inadequacies, it followed that there was no need for equity in cases in which the common law was satisfactory.

This history shows the equivalence of the inadequate remedy and irreparable injury formulations. It is sometimes said that equity will not act if there is an adequate legal remedy; and alternatively, that equity will act only to prevent injury that is irreparable, i.e., irreparable at law.

Despite occasional attempts to distinguish these statements, they are simply two formulations of the same rule. "The very thing which makes an injury 'irreparable' is the fact that no remedy exists to repair it." Bannercraft Clothing Co. v. Renegotiation Board, 466 F.2d 345, 356 n.9 (1972), *rev'd on other grounds*, 415 U.S. 1 (1974).

The defects in the common law to which equity responded were many and varied. Sometimes the problem was procedural clumsiness, sometimes harsh, antiquated, or inflexible substantive rules, sometimes the law's narrow range of remedies with its emphasis on money damages. Today, the typical application of the irreparable injury rule is to a comparison between some equitable remedy that will prevent a threatened injury, and money damages that will compensate for the injury after it has occurred. If money damages will be "adequate," then the injury is not irreparable and will not be prevented.

Modern irreparable injury decisions rarely turn on procedural clumsiness or inadequate substantive rules. This is partly due to the merger; equitable doctrines and procedural devices can now be used at law. But it is also due to the way the equity judges construed limits on their power. The limiting aspect of the irreparable injury rule was never applied to substantive equity. Equity will hear any trust case, any mortgage case. For example, a creditor foreclosing on a mortgage may have a perfectly adequate remedy by suing at law on the debt and levying on the debtor's assets. That has never been considered relevant; foreclosing mortgagees are not required to show that the mortgagor is insolvent. Substantive equitable rights could always be enforced in equity because they could not be enforced at law; it made no difference that some legal right was just as good. 1 J. Pomeroy, Equity Jurisprudence §219 (1st ed. 1881). Similarly, once the chancellors began to grant a particular remedy, they continued to grant it even if it later became available at law. Thus, a plaintiff seeking restitution can often find substantially equivalent remedies in both law and equity. The adequacy question now focuses on remedies such as damages, which were always the province of the law and never of equity.

2. A rule designed to preserve the jurisdictional boundaries between two courts that have long been merged should die unless it serves some modern purpose. Would any purpose be served in Pardee v. Camden Lumber by denying the injunction and making plaintiff sue for the value of the lost timber?

a. It is sometimes said that injunctions impose a greater burden on the court, because they have to be enforced over time. A damage judgment results in a one-time transfer of money, after which the court's involvement is over. Certainly there is something to that in the case of structural injunctions, and some reparative injunctions as well. But is there anything to it in *Pardee*? Is there any reason to believe it will always, or even usually, be harder to enforce an injunction than to collect a damage judgment? We will examine the means of enforcing injunctions and collecting judgments in chapter 8, and you should reconsider the irreparable injury rule then. But as a starting point, note that the damage judgment requires an affirmative act: Money or property must be transferred from defendant to plaintiff. The injunction in *Pardee* requires only that defendant refrain from certain conduct; no one is required to do anything. Which judgment is likely to be harder to enforce?

And what about the original litigation? The injunction eliminates the need to measure damages in money; a whole issue is removed from the trial. Measuring damages isn't always easy. If defendant hauled the timber to its sawmill and cut it up, how would you prove the value of the original standing timber?

b.   It is sometimes said that the injunction is a greater intrusion on defendant's liberty. This is partly because the injunction orders him to do or refrain from specified conduct; the damage remedy leaves him free to proceed if he is willing to pay the cost. And it is partly because the injunction can be enforced by coercive or punitive measures, including imprisonment. The damage remedy is enforced only by seizing defendant's property; the court will not try to make him write a check.

How persuasive is that? Do we want to preserve liberty to cut down other people's trees? To the extent the damage remedy preserves that liberty for defendant, doesn't it equally reduce plaintiff's liberty to grow trees? Should we preserve liberty by minimizing substantive restrictions on conduct, or by facilitating violations of the rules we find necessary? Would the liberty argument have more punch if the government were seeking the injunction?

c.   Is the rule justified by the different timing of preventive and compensatory litigation? To prevent the harm, the court must resolve the liability issue before the harm has happened. As we shall see, there are procedures for granting interim relief, pending a full trial on the merits, but these procedures cannot fully avoid the problems of hasty decision. Compensation can be litigated at leisure, after the harm is done. Timing might not matter much in cases like *Pardee* if defendant were clearly a thief. But true thieves tend not to act publicly or notify their victims in advance. In most cases where plaintiff is able to seek an injunction, defendant has some colorable claim of right to do what he is doing, or a colorable claim that he is not doing what plaintiff accuses him of. The court needs to control its calendar; it needs time to reflect and decide; and defendant needs time to prepare a defense. Do these needs justify making plaintiff accept damages if damages appear to be "good enough"? Do they carry much weight with respect to reparative and structural injunctions? What about preventive injunctions where defendant is not in a hurry? Even when the burden on the court's calendar is real, how much should that matter if the injunction is a better remedy otherwise? Does the court sit for its own convenience or to dispense justice? The timing argument has not been much relied on by proponents of the irreparable injury rule.

d.   In most jurisdictions, there is a right to jury trial in at law but not in equity. Thus, it is often said that the irreparable injury rule protects the right to jury trial. We will explore that proposition in connection with Willing v. Mazzocone, infra at 347, and again in chapter 13.

e.   Recall the economic view that profitable violations of law should be encouraged if the violator compensates his victims. Is that a reason for the irreparable injury rule? If the timber is more valuable to the lumber company than to the landowner, why shouldn't the lumber company be encouraged to take it now and worry about paying for it when the land-owner complains? Not even the most hard-line proponents of law and economics go that far. The following explanation of the economic view is based on a famous article, Calabresi and Melamed, Property Rules, Liability Rules, and Inalienability: One View of the Cathedral, 85 Harv. L. Rev. 1089, 1124-1127 (1972), and on R. Posner, Economic Analysis of Law 27-52 (2d ed. 1977).

The lumber company has no reason to cut the timber without asking; it can arrange to buy it from the landowner. If the landowner agrees to sell at a price the lumber company agrees to pay, we can be sure the timber has been transferred to a more valuable use. But if we ask a jury to decide the value of the timber, we introduce a risk of error. The jury will be told to award the market value of the timber; the possibility that the landowner personally values the timber at more than its market value is considered too speculative for the jury to consider, even if he previously refused to sell at the market price. If the timber is more valuable to the plaintiff than to the market, or if the jury underestimates the market value, the landowner will be undercompensated. If the timber is less valuable to plaintiff than to the market, or if the jury overestimates value, the lumber company will have to pay too much.

Economic purists do not care about the unfairness of these results. Their concern is that if lumber companies expect juries to undercompensate landowners, they will take timber even when their own use for it is not the most valuable, and if they expect juries to overcompensate, they will not take timber when they ought to. Litigation is not as reliable as market transactions for directing resources to their highest and best use. And litigation, threats of litigation, and settlement negotiations are expensive. So even if it is profitable for the lumber company to steal the timber, it should be discouraged from doing so if it could negotiate directly with the landowner. An injunction against cutting forces the lumber company to buy the timber at a price acceptable to the landowner. If the landowner refuses to sell, that means he values the timber more than the lumber company does.

Where the cost of negotiating a voluntary transaction would be high, proponents of the economic view of law would deny the injunction and leave victims to their damage remedy. There are many sources of high transaction costs, but two are the most common. One is transactions with so many parties that it is difficult or impossible to reach agreement among them all. This includes situations where an actor's conduct puts many people at risk and there is no way to know who the victims will be.

The other common source of high transaction costs is bilateral monopoly. Bilateral monopoly exists in situations where the parties have no alternative but to deal with each other. If Pardee wanted to sell, there would be no bilateral monopoly in Pardee v. Camden Lumber Co. Camden Lumber could buy timber from someone else if Pardee demanded too high a price, and Pardee could sell to someone else if Camden Lumber offered too low a price. If both sides wanted to complete the transaction, the existence of market alternatives makes it likely that they would quickly agree on something close to the market price. But if the dispute were that pollution from the lumber mill was harming Pardee's trees, their negotiations would be a bilateral monopoly. Pardee could not buy a promise that Camden Lumber would quit polluting from anyone but Camden Lumber. And Camden Lumber could not buy the right to poison Pardee's trees from anyone but Pardee. There would be no market alternative to guide their bargaining behavior, and they might have great difficulty reaching agreement. Litigation always involves bilateral monopoly; the parties cannot settle with anyone but each other. Settlement negotiations are guided by predictions about what the court will do if the case is tried; if the two parties make different predictions, settlement will be difficult or impossible.

To summarize the economic view: Where transaction costs are high, the usual remedy should be damages; where transaction costs are low, the usual remedy should be injunction. Does that justify the irreparable injury rule? As we examine the defects that make legal remedies inadequate, think about whether there is any correspondence between the adequacy of plaintiff's legal remedies and the level of transaction costs in the underlying situation.

NOTES ON THE CONTENT OF THE IRREPARABLE INJURY RULE

1. What makes a legal remedy inadequate? *Pardee* says damages are inadequate because plaintiff can't use the money to replace the trees. How sweeping is that principle? Doesn't it mean that money is never adequate in itself — that it is adequate only when it can be used to replace the very thing that plaintiff lost?

2. How identical must the replacement be? Surely there were other timberlands in West Virginia that plaintiff could have bought. Why aren't they adequate? Is it because no other land will have exactly the same number, size, and species of trees? Because no other land could be brought to the same place? Does it matter how plaintiff owned and used

the land? If the land were his ancestral home, or he used it only for hunting, fishing, and camping, his claim to that very land and no other looks pretty strong, doesn't it?

What if he is a commercial timber grower? If he owns the land only to earn dollars, why aren't dollars adequate compensation? Or at least, why isn't any timberland of equal value an adequate replacement? Is it because defendant interfered with his business judgment about when to harvest? Is it merely because the rule says all real estate is unique and the court won't look behind the rule? Or is it because, despite the contrary implications of the irreparable injury rule, it doesn't make much sense to let wrongdoers inflict harm first and pay for it later?

3. Why is the rule different for personal property? Isn't it as plausible to say every horse is unique as to say every piece of land is unique? There may not be much difference between two healthy plow horses, but there isn't much difference between two tract houses either. If the Indians in United States v. Hatahly, supra at 10, had found out in advance about the government's plan to round up their horses, should the court have denied an injunction because "the world is full of horses"? Because there would be high transaction costs if the government tried to negotiate removal of the horses? There were many separate owners, and it seems likely that each was in a situation of bilateral monopoly with the government. No one else could authorize the government to remove their horses, and the government appears to have owned all or nearly all the accessible open range land.

4. What about property that is truly fungible, such as mass-produced manufactured goods, or grain commingled in an elevator? The rule that damages are adequate makes the most sense there, doesn't it? But even there, why should plaintiff have to go to the trouble of collecting damages and buying a replacement?

5. Recall Professor Fiss's observation that injunctions are the standard remedy in civil rights cases, despite the irreparable injury rule. Doesn't the rationale of *Pardee* explain that? Victims can't replace civil rights in the market, can they? And wouldn't the sense that plaintiffs should not have to sell irreplaceable rights for cash be strongest in civil rights litigation, with our traditional sense of "inalienable" rights? *Pardee* also explains why injunctions are the standard remedy in environmental cases, doesn't it?

6. The courts have not accepted the economic view that injunctions should be withheld when transaction costs are high. Class action injunctions are common, especially in civil rights, environmental, and consumer cases, although the costs of buying a release from the injunction from every class member are plainly prohibitive.

The rule that damages are inadequate unless plaintiff can go to the market and replace the very thing he has lost turns the economic advice nearly upside down. If he cannot replace the thing he has lost, either he has the only one and it is about to be destroyed, or defendant will be the only source of supply. Either way, one of the parties is a monopolist, at least temporarily. Thus, monopoly is the law's most common reason for granting injunctions. But in the economic view, monopoly should be a warning flag against injunctions. If one party is a monopolist, we are halfway to bilateral monopoly. And bilateral monopoly is a source of high transaction costs. Thus, some of the cases in which plaintiff cannot replace the thing he lost are cases in which the economic wisdom is to deny injunctions. One scholar sympathetic to the economic view has suggested an explanation in a related context: When the plaintiff can easily replace what he has lost at the market price, it is easy to value his losses and the usual litigation risks of over or undercompensation are minimized. Kronman, Specific Performance, 45 U. Chi. L. Rev. 351, 355-365 (1978). Is that a sufficient explanation?

7. How inadequate must the legal remedy be? The standard answer is discussed in the following excerpt.

LAYCOCK, INJUNCTIONS AND THE IRREPARABLE INJURY RULE
57 Tex. L. Rev. 1065, 1071-1072 (1979)

The verbal formulation of the irreparable injury rule has tended to exaggerate the true extent of the preference for legal remedies. . . .

Adequacy is a matter of degree, and the normal statement of the general rule does not specify how inadequate the legal remedy must be. That question is left to a related rule — well-settled but less well-known . . . : no legal remedy is adequate unless it is "as complete, practical and efficient as that which equity could afford."[45] Although this rule is sometimes overlooked and sometimes willfully ignored, it is the overwhelmingly dominant statement of the law in opinions that raise the question.

Thus, the full statement of the traditional rule is as follows:

1. Equity will not act if there is an adequate remedy at law.
2. "Adequate remedy" means a remedy as complete, practical, and efficient as the equitable remedy.

This rule could be reformulated as follows:

1. Plaintiff is entitled in all cases to the most complete, practical, and efficient remedy.
2. If a legal and an equitable remedy are equally complete, practical, and efficient, the legal remedy shall be used.

45. Terrace v. Thompson, 263 U.S. 197, 214 (1923).

Although the two formulations are logically equivalent, they are not rhetorically equivalent, especially if one assumes that under either formulation the broader first rule of the pair will be more widely known than the narrower second rule. The second formulation would make clear that the irreparable injury rule is simply a tie-breaker, and that the plaintiff is not to be disadvantaged because of it. The first formulation suggests a stronger prejudice against equity; it is responsible for judicial statements that injunctions are an extraordinary remedy.

The rule that legal remedies are inadequate unless they are as complete, practical, and efficient as equitable remedies is easily explained historically. It was the chancellors who passed on the adequacy of legal remedies, in the course of deciding motions to dismiss suits in equity. Not surprisingly, they defined adequacy in a way that maximized their jurisdiction. Is it the right definition today? Doesn't that depend on the strength of the arguments for preserving the irreparable injury rule at all?

HART v. WAGNER
184 Md. 40, 40 A.2d 47 (1944)

Before MARBURY, C.J., and DELAPLAINE, COLLINS, GRASON, MELVIN, BAILEY, CAPPER, and HENDERSON, JJ.

MELVIN, Judge.

The bill of complaint in this case was filed by the appellant in Circuit Court No. 2 of Baltimore City, seeking an injunction to restrain the appellees from maintaining an alleged nuisance affecting the use and enjoyment of appellant's residence property in Baltimore City. The appellees' demurrer to this bill was sustained by the Chancellor, without leave to amend, and the bill dismissed. The present appeal is from that decree.

The sole question here is, therefore, whether or not the allegations of the bill of complaint are sufficient to entitle the appellant to relief in equity by way of injunction.

These allegations are, in substance, that the appellant is the owner and occupant of property, No. 4302 Roland Avenue, Baltimore City, which he acquired by inheritance from his mother on October 13, 1938; that the respondents (appellees) are the owners and occupants of the property designated as No. 4306 Roland Avenue, which they acquired in 1921; that immediately in the rear of the said properties there is situated an alley, twelve feet in width, and laid out for the use in common with other property owners abutting thereon; that the respondents (appellees)

> habitually burn trash, leaves and other inflammable matter in the aforesaid alley in a careless manner and in violation of law, and leave the dust and ashes

caused by the aforesaid fires in the said alley to be blown later by the wind into and upon the property owned and occupied by your orator, and constitute a nuisance;

that the aforesaid burning endangers Your Orator's property and depreciates the value thereof by damaging the paint on both the inside and outside of his property by the smoke and the dust and ashes which permeate the air while the burning is in progress, and for days after each unlawful burning, and also furniture and wallpaper and other personal property in the home owned and occupied by Your Orator, as aforesaid. . . .

The bill of complaint attempts to set up a case for injunction on the basis of a private nuisance by charging, in effect, that the respondents are habitually committing acts which deprive the complainant of the reasonable enjoyment of his own property and cause injury to it. . . . A conspicuous omission from the bill is any allegation as to personal discomfort or injury to health, although it is stated by appellant, both in his brief and in his oral argument on appeal, that the nuisance complained of made living in his home "almost intolerable because their (appellees') acts deprived them of the comfortable enjoyment thereof." Whether or not the present averments of the bill and their reasonable implications, if duly proven, are sufficient to invoke the restraining power of a court of equity is the question now before us. . . .

The appellees here contend, however, that the appellant has a full, complete and adequate remedy at law and that if he has any complaint at all he should have "turned for relief to the enforcement of the provisions of the city ordinances prohibiting the committing of nuisances in the alleys of the city." If, under the allegations of the bill, this were a public nuisance, the complainant's remedy would necessarily be by indictment, but such is not the case here. The principles applicable to private nuisances are the ones that apply, and these are clearly set forth in the case of Block v. Baltimore, 149 Md. 39, 59, 129 A. 887, 894.

The nuisance there was of an aggravated nature incident to the transfer of Baltimore city's garbage to a reduction company's plant on a creek in Anne Arundel County. One of the results of this operation was the giving off of offensive and noxious fumes, vapors, smoke and dust, which prevented the comfortable enjoyment by the complainants of their residence properties. It was contended there, as it is here, on a demurrer to the bill that the complainants had an adequate and complete remedy at law. In disposing of this contention this Court, through Judge Offutt, said:

. . . It is true that they could bring an action at law for such damages, if any, as they may have suffered as a result of the alleged nuisance, and that they could have perhaps applied to the state board of health for its abatement. But those remedies are obviously insufficient to meet such a case as this. The appellants might, in an action at law, be sufficiently compensated for any depreciation in the value of their property, but it would be difficult, if not impracticable, for them to recover definite and adequate compensation for such intangible injuries as loss of sleep, nausea, or even for the impairment of their health. Such damages would be hard to prove and harder to measure.

See, also, Townsend Grace & Co. v. Epstein, 93 Md. 537, 557, 49 A. 629, 633, wherein a suit for injunction was filed alleging irreparable injury to plaintiff's lot by the obstruction of the light and air caused by the defendant's building. There it was contended that the complainant's only redress was by way of a suit or suits at law for consequential damages. In rejecting this contention, the court pointed out that the obstruction was a continuing one and that, although the plaintiffs were entitled to recover damages at law for the injury and loss to which they were subjected, they could not recover for the whole damage, past and prospective, in one suit, but only for damages to the time of suit brought. "These damages," the court said, "would be difficult to estimate, and in any one case would be comparatively trivial. In seeking redress at law, therefore, they would be driven to a multiplicity of vexatious and unprofitable suits and continuous litigation. To tell them that this is the only redress they can have, would be to say that all the law can do for them is to aggravate the nuisance from which they are already suffering."

The court also quotes in this connection from Elliott on Roads and Streets at page 497, where, speaking of the phrase, "irreparable injury," it said:

> It does not necessarily mean, as used in the law of injunction, that the injury is beyond the possibility of compensation in damages nor that it must be very great. And the fact that no actual damages can be proved so that in an action at law the jury could award nominal damages only, often furnishes the very best reason why a court of equity should interfere in cases where the nuisance is a continuous one.

While the injuries complained of in the case at bar and the indicated consequential damages are undoubtedly very much less than those in the cases cited, the difference is one of degree and not of kind, and the same general principles of equity apply to all cases coming within this classification of nuisance.

The appellees rely strongly on their contention that certain city ordinances would afford relief to the complaint from the alleged nuisance. The one ordinance to which appellees refer is codified under the title "Nuisances and the Prevention of Diseases." In the instant case the bill does not allege, or even suggest, that the nuisance complained of has any relation to the subject of "disease," so that the ordinance referred to is irrelevant.

The only other ordinances that could have any possible application to the case at bar are the two which are mentioned by the appellant himself in his brief. The first of these two has reference solely to the emission or discharge of black or dark smoke from smokestacks or chimneys within the city limits, and the other, under the title "Pavements — Protection," makes it unlawful for any person to make, or cause to be made, any fire on any sheet asphalt, block or any improved cobblestone pavement on any street, lane or alley in the City. It is not clear from the bill that either of these ordinances could be invoked to abate the particular nuisance alleged here. . . .

[The court vacated and remanded for further proceedings, ordering that plaintiff be allowed to amend the complaint to provide more details and to "verify" the allegations. A "verified" complaint is a complaint that has been sworn to; Maryland and some other states require verified complaints in suits for injunctions.]

MORE NOTES ON THE IRREPARABLE INJURY RULE

1. The difficulty of measuring damages is a common ground for holding the legal remedy inadequate. Isn't that also sufficient to explain why injunctions are the standard remedy in civil rights and environmental cases? Do *Hart* and *Pardee* really recognize two aspects of the same source of inadequacy? Aren't damages always hard to measure when there is no market for the thing that was lost?

2. Should it matter that the injury in *Hart* was small? The court says no, and that is the dominant view. But judges occasionally suggest that *irreparable* means especially severe or serious, so that little injuries are not worth preventing by injunction. See, e.g., Myers v. Caple, 258 N.W.2d 301, 305 (Iowa 1977), described infra at 920. That's not the historical meaning; is there anything to it as a matter of policy? The extent of harm is relevant to whether the fires are a nuisance at all. And there may be something to the old maxim that the law does not take notice of trifles. But if we once decide that these fires justify gearing up the judicial machinery, is there any reason to say the harm is great enough for damages but not for an injunction? Isn't the damage remedy inadequate if the damages are too small to deter repetition? The answer might be different if the injunction harms defendant more than it helps plaintiff; we will consider that possibility in chapter 11.

3. Another standard ground for holding the legal remedy inadequate is that it would require multiple suits. But that ground does not arise as often as *Hart* implies. The dictum on damages in Townsend Grace & Co. v. Epstein, summarized in *Hart*, is an aberration. Because there is little prospect that a building cutting off light and air will be torn down volun-

tarily, most jurisdictions would hold it a permanent nuisance if a nuisance at all. (The building in *Townsend Grace* was held a nuisance because it bridged the public right-of-way.) The usual rule is that a plaintiff who seeks damages for a permanent nuisance can and must claim in a single action all the damages that will ever accrue. The usual measure is the difference in the value of plaintiffs' property before and after the creation of the nuisance.

By contrast, most states would say the nuisance in *Hart* is a temporary nuisance. Defendant might stop building the fires at any time. Similarly, the trespass in *Pardee* could stop at any time. Plaintiff can collect only for damage done up to the time of his suit; he cannot collect now for future fires that might never be built or trees that might never be cut. It is in these situations that the damage remedy is inadequate because plaintiff must sue repeatedly. And the rule has the most bite when the damages are too small to deter repeated violations.

4. Defendants argue that plaintiff has an adequate remedy because the city might abate the nuisance under local ordinances. The court rejects that argument because it is not clear that any of the ordinances apply. But suppose they did? Would they offer an adequate remedy *for plaintiff?* Surely the city officials have discretion to enforce or not to enforce. What if they refuse to act? Is there anything to be said for a rule that plaintiff can go to court himself only if he has tried and failed with complaints to the city? That remedy isn't as practical and efficient as going directly to court, is it?

5. How would the city abate the nuisance? If it sought a court order prohibiting the fires, how would that order be any different from the injunction plaintiff sought? If it tried to deter the fires with criminal prosecutions, isn't that a pretty indirect way of helping plaintiff? Should he have to criminally prosecute his neighbor to settle a civil dispute? Compare the Supreme Court's view that a crime victim has no "judicially cognizable interest in the prosecution" of the criminal. Linda R. S. v. Richard D., 410 U.S. 614, 619 (1973), infra at 1084.

NOTES ON BILLS OF PEACE AND OTHER EQUITABLE DEVICES FOR AVOIDING MULTIPLE LITIGATION

1. One reason for holding the legal remedy inadequate in Hart v. Wagner is that plaintiff would have to sue repeatedly. This is a classic source of irreparable injury; the phrase was that equity courts would take jurisdiction to avoid a "multiplicity of suits."

2. Another remedy for multiple litigation is a specialized injunction traditionally known as the bill of peace. Bills of peace are of two types. One responds to the same situation as the typical plaintiff's class action,

but it gives the initiative to the litigant who would normally be the defendant. He can sue all the claimants, alleging that he is threatened with multiple litigation on claims that share common issues and that the claims are without merit. The court can enjoin the claimants from filing claims anywhere but in response to the bill of peace, and it can adjudicate all the claims. An example is Yuba Consolidated Gold Fields v. Kilkeary, 206 F.2d 884 (9th Cir. 1953), in which a mining company accused of causing a flood brought a bill of peace against some two thousand flood victims.

This form of bill of peace has become less important under modern merged procedure; defendants can often accomplish the same purpose by motions to consolidate or, in the federal courts, by recourse to the Judicial Panel on Multi-District Litigation. See 28 U.S.C. §1407 (1982). In *Yuba*, consolidation was impossible, because plaintiffs were filing in state court in separate counties, and California had no procedure for intercounty transfer of cases.

The other kind of bill of peace is used to enjoin a chronic litigant who has filed repeated frivolous suits against the bill of peace plaintiff. Such a litigant can be ordered to file no more motions in the same proceeding, no more suits on the same subject matter, or no suits at all without permission of the court. A good example is In re Hartford Textile Corp., 681 F.2d 895 (2d Cir. 1982). This kind of bill of peace has become more common with the increase in pro se litigation. But the phrase "bill of peace" is dying out. The order in a bill of peace proceeding is simply an injunction against frivolous or scattered litigation, and courts are abandoning the more specialized label.

3.   Other equitable innovations for avoiding multiple litigation have been absorbed into merged procedure. Modern joinder rules, consolidation of related lawsuits, class actions, and interpleader all originated in equity. In all these cases, inability to join all the same parties at law rendered the legal remedy inadequate. The maxim was that "Equity delights in doing justice and not by halves." Today, in most jurisdictions, all these devices are available for both legal and equitable claims.

WILLING v. MAZZOCONE
482 Pa. 377, 393 A.2d 1155 (1978)

MANDERINO, Justice.

On Monday, September 29, and Wednesday, October 1, 1975, appellant, Helen Willing, demonstrated in the . . . well traveled pedestrian pathway between the two court buildings located at City Hall and at Five Penn Center Plaza. While engaged in this activity, which lasted for several hours each day, appellant wore a "sandwich-board" sign around her neck. On the sign she had hand lettered the following:

LAW-FIRM
of
QUINN-MAZZOCONE

Stole money from me — and

Sold-me-out-to-the
INSURANCE COMPANY

As she marched back and forth, appellant also pushed a shopping cart on which she had placed an American flag. She continuously rang a cow bell and blew on a whistle to further attract attention.

Appellees in this case are two members of the legal profession, Carl M. Mazzocone and Charles F. Quinn, who are associated in the two member law firm of Mazzocone and Quinn, p.c. When appellant refused appellees' efforts to amicably dissuade her from further activity such as that described above, appellees filed a suit in equity in the Court of Common Pleas of Philadelphia County seeking to enjoin her from further demonstration. Three hearings were held, at which the following factual history emerged.

In 1968, appellees, who have specialized in the trial of workmen's compensation matters for several years, represented appellant in such a case. Pursuant to appellees' representation, appellant was awarded permanent/partial disability benefits which she collected for a number of years. At the time of the initial settlement distribution with appellant, appellees deducted the sum of $150.00 as costs of the case. This sum, according to appellees' evidence, was paid in full to Robert DeSilverio, M.D., a treating psychiatrist who testified on appellant's behalf in the Workmen's Compensation matter. Appellees presented copies of their records covering the transaction with Dr. DeSilverio. A cancelled check for the amount of the payment, and the testimony of Dr. DeSilverio himself, confirmed appellees' account of the transaction. Appellant offered no evidence other than her testimony that the cause of her antagonism towards appellees was not any dissatisfaction with the settlement, but rather, her belief that appellees had wrongfully diverted to themselves $25.00 of the $150.00 that was supposed to have been paid to Dr. DeSilverio.

Based on this evidence, the equity court concluded that appellant was ". . . a woman firmly on the thrall of the belief that [appellees] defrauded her, an *idee fixe* which, either by reason of eccentricity or an even more serious mental instability, refuses to be dislodged by the most convincing proof to the contrary." The Court then enjoined appellant from

> . . . further unlawful demonstration, picketing, carrying placards which contain defamatory and libelous statements and or uttering, publishing and declaring defamatory statements against the [appellees] herein.

On appeal, the Superior Court modified the trial court's order to read,

> Helen R. Willing, be and is permanently enjoined from further demonstrating against and/or picketing Mazzocone and Quinn, Attorneys-at-Law, by uttering or publishing statements to the effect that Mazzocone and Quinn, Attorneys-at-Law stole money from her and sold her out to the insurance company. . . .

This case raises serious and far reaching questions regarding the exercise of the constitutional right to freely express oneself. We believe the orders issued by the Superior Court and by the trial court in the instant case are clearly prohibited by Article I, Section 7 of the Pennsylvania Constitution and by Goldman Theatres v. Dana, 405 Pa. 83, 173 A.2d 59, *cert. denied*, 368 U.S. 897 (1961).

Article I, Section 7, . . . reads in relevant part:

> The free communication of thoughts and opinions is one of the invaluable rights of man, and every citizen may freely speak, write and print on any subject, being responsible for the abuse of that liberty.

As we emphasized in *Goldman Theatres*, Article I, Section 7, of the Pennsylvania Constitution is designed

> . . . *to prohibit the imposition of prior restraints upon the communication of thoughts and opinions*, leaving the utterer liable only for an abuse of the privilege. (Emphasis added.)

405 Pa. at 88, 173 A.2d at 62.

History supports the view that the framers of our state constitution intended to prohibit prior restraint on Pennsylvanians' right to speak.

> After the demise in 1694 of the last of the infamous English Licensing Acts, freedom of the press, at least freedom from administrative censorship, began in England, and later in the Colonies, to assume the status of a "common law or natural right." See State v. Jackson, Or. 1960 [224 Or. 337], 356 P.2d 495, 499. Blackstone so recognized (circa 1767) when he wrote,

>> The liberty of the press is indeed essential to the nature of a free state; but this consists in laying no previous restraints upon publications, and not in freedom from censure for criminal matter when published. Every freeman had an undoubted right to lay what sentiments he pleases before the public; to forbid this is to destroy the freedom of the press; but if he publishes what is improper, mischievous, or illegal, he must take the consequence of his own temerity. To subject the press to the restrictive power of a licenser, as was formerly done, both before and since the revolution, is to subject all freedom of sentiment to the prejudices of one man, and make him the arbitrary and infallible judge of all controverted points in learning, religion, and government. . . .

405 Pa. at 88, 173 A.2d at 62.

A majority of the Superior Court concluded that appellant's conduct could be restrained without violating any federal constitutional prohibition. Our conclusion that the equity court violated appellant's state constitutional right to freely speak her opinion — regardless of whether that opinion is based on fact or fantasy — regarding appellees' professional integrity obviates the need for any discussion here of federal law.

Our resolution should also render unnecessary any discussion of the Superior Court's proposed exception to the so-called traditional view that equity lacks the power to enjoin the publication of defamatory matter. We do believe, however, that the Superior Court's observation that "in the present case an action for damages would be a pointless gesture since [appellant] is indigent," 246 Pa. Super. at 104, 369 A.2d at 832, requires specific comment. We cannot accept the Superior Court's conclusion that the exercise of the constitutional right to freely express one's opinion should be conditioned upon the economic status of the individual asserting that right. Conditioning the right of free speech upon the monetary worth of an individual is inconsistent not only with fundamental principles of justice developed by the Supreme Court of the United States and guaranteed by the Federal Constitution, but also violates our own Constitution's express admonitions that "[a]ll men are born equally free and independent, and have certain inherent and indefeasible rights . . ." (Art. I, Section 1), and that "[n]either the Commonwealth nor any political subdivision thereof shall deny to any person the enjoyment of any civil right, nor discriminate against any person in the exercise of any civil right." (Art. I, Section 26.)

In Pennsylvania the insolvency of a defendant does not create a situation where there is no adequate remedy at law. In deciding whether a remedy is adequate, it is the remedy itself, and not its possible lack of success that is the determining factor. "The fact, if it be so, that this remedy may not be successful in realizing the fruits of a recovery at law, on account of the insolvency of the defendants, is not of itself a ground of equitable inference." Heilman v. Union Canal Co., 37 Pa. 100, 104 (1860).

The order of the Superior Court, modifying and affirming the decree of the trial court, and the decree of the trial court are reversed.

POMEROY, J., filed a concurring opinion.
EAGEN, C.J., filed a dissenting opinion.
NIX and LARSEN, JJ., dissent.

ROBERTS, Justice, concurring.

I agree with the opinion of Mr. Justice Manderino that appellant's indigency does not justify the Superior Court's radical departure from the long-standing general rule that equity will not enjoin a defamation. In Heilman v. Union Canal Company, 37 Pa. 100, 104 (1860), this Court said:

The fact, if it be so, that this remedy may not be successful in realizing the fruits of a recovery at law, on account of the insolvency of the defendants, is not of itself a ground of equitable interference. The remedy is what is to be looked at. If it exist [sic], and is ordinarily adequate, its possible want of success is not a consideration.

Money damages are adequate to recompense the plaintiffs for any losses they have suffered as a consequence of the defendant's defamatory publication. Thus, it was improper to grant equitable relief based on appellant's presumed inability to pay a money judgment.

As a consequence of holding that the defendant's indigency creates equitable jurisdiction, the Superior Court conditions appellant's right to trial by jury on her economic status. One of the underlying justifications for equity's traditional refusal to enjoin defamatory speech is that in equity all questions of fact are resolved by the trial court, rather than the jury. Thus, it deprives appellant of her right to a jury trial on the issue of the truth or falsity of her speech. The right to trial by jury is more than mere form. Indeed the right to a jury trial is guaranteed by this Commonwealth's Constitution. . . .

O'Brien, J., joins in this concurring opinion.

NOTES ON PRIOR RESTRAINTS

1. As the court's quotation from Blackstone indicates, the prior restraint rule is derived from the days when freedom of speech consisted only of freedom from prior restraints. We have long since abandoned the notion that imprisoning a speaker for what he said does not violate freedom of speech, although prosecution is still permitted for "unprotected" speech, including libel if the speaker knowingly lied or spoke with reckless disregard for the truth. Garrison v. Louisiana, 379 U.S. 64 (1964). Pennsylvania had a criminal libel statute until 1972, and prosecutions under it coexisted with the ban on prior restraints. In New York Times v. Sullivan, 376 U.S. 254 (1964), the Court recognized that some damage judgments for defamation violate freedom of speech. But we are left with the notion that prior restraints are somehow special and require more justification than punishment for speech or damage judgments for speech. The special hostility to prior restraints is read into state and federal constitutions; the same policy is reflected in the nonconstitutional rule that equity will not enjoin a libel. What is the basis for this policy? Is the injunction really a greater threat to free speech?

2. In *Willing*, because defendants' statements were made in reckless disregard of the truth, the Supreme Court would permit a judgment against her for "compensatory" damages, which could be presumed in the absence of proof, plus punitive damages. See Gertz v. Welch, 418

U.S. 323, 348-350 (1974). If her statements are unprotected to that extent, why can't the court order her not to repeat them? Conversely, if the Constitution protects her statements, why can a jury punish her for making them? Would the rules make a little more sense if defamation judgments were limited to compensation for damages actually suffered and proved?

3. Isn't a damage judgment an inadequate remedy for defamation under the rules illustrated in *Pardee* and *Hart?* Plaintiff can't use the money to restore his reputation, can he? And damages are certainly hard to measure. But this may work out to plaintiff's advantage: Jury verdicts in defamation cases are often vastly greater than any plausible estimate of actual damage.

4. There is some appeal to the court's notion that rich and poor should have the same rights of free speech. But enjoining the rich speaker would go as far toward that goal as not enjoining the poor speaker. Does the court really think damage judgments have the same effect on all social classes? Those who are completely judgment proof may be undeterred, if they are sophisticated enough to understand their dubious advantage. But for those who are a little better off — who are not rich but have some nonexempt assets — a damage judgment can be a catastrophe. Doesn't the reliance on defamation judgments deter their speech far more than it deters the speech of a large corporation or a truly wealthy individual? Recall the general argument that injunctions restrict liberty more than damage judgments. Doesn't that have the most bite for the very rich and the judgment-proof?

NOTE ON THE RIGHT TO JURY TRIAL

The court says the damage remedy preserves Willing's right to jury trial. The point is not limited to prior restraint cases; it is often offered in defense of the irreparable injury rule generally. Equity courts traditionally sat without juries, and this tradition is reflected in most guarantees of jury trial. There are some important exceptions, but injunctions are generally issued and enforced without the aid of juries. How important is that? Is a jury more likely to decide for defendant than a judge? Is it enough that Willing would be more suspicious of a judge than a jury? Would she even get to the jury, or would she lose on a motion for summary judgment?

Undoubtedly there are cases where defendant may expect more sympathy from a jury than a judge. But how general a problem is that? Is there any reason to predict that juries would favor defendants in Hart v. Wagner? In Pardee v. Camden Lumber? What if plaintiffs' claim to the land were based on a "technicality"? What if plaintiff were a large corporate absentee landowner, and defendant were a local individual? Do such predictions matter if jury trial is a constitutional right? Or does that beg the question? If the case is properly in equity, there is no right to jury trial. Isn't the question whether the case is properly in equity? Anyway, if we are really concerned about civil jury trial, why not try the injunction suit to a jury, submitting special issues if necessary? Why must we deprive plaintiff of his preferred remedy to preserve defendant's right to jury trial?

Does it matter that jury trial is generally thought to be a bigger advantage to plaintiffs than to defendants? Most plaintiffs' lawyers prefer juries because they believe juries are more likely to act out of sympathy if liability is unclear, and because they believe that a jury's assessment of damages is likely to be bigger than a judge's. This view is especially strong in defamation cases, where judges regularly set aside or reduce jury verdicts. Do you suppose Willing really wanted a jury trial or wanted to deprive plaintiff of his only effective remedy?

There is a large body of law on the right to jury trial in cases where plaintiff seeks some combination of legal and equitable relief, or seeks equitable relief in the absence of irreparable injury. Those cases will be easier to understand if we complete some other material first, so we will take them up in chapter 13.

NOTES ON UNCOLLECTIBLE DAMAGES

1.   Quite apart from the speech issues, the court says that defendant's insolvency does not make plaintiffs' damage remedy inadequate. Does that make any sense at all? The Pennsylvania rule is very much in the minority; recall that *Pardee* treated defendant's insolvency as an uncontroversial ground for holding the damage remedy inadequate. Is there any reason to let defendant cut down plaintiff's trees if we know defendant won't be able to pay for the damage?

2.   But what if the trees have already been cut, and plaintiff seeks an injunction ordering defendant to turn over his few remaining assets to plaintiff in compensation? Might defendant's other creditors object to that? If defendant doesn't have enough assets to go around, the legal remedy is still inadequate, but there are other reasons not to prefer one creditor over all the others. Suppose plaintiff seeks a reparative injunction, e.g., one that orders defendant to plant a new generation of trees. Doesn't that harm other creditors just as much as an order to pay plaintiff first?

3.   There is an equitable remedy for the case of too many creditors fighting over too few assets. That remedy is bankruptcy. In bankruptcy, the debtor's assets are distributed among his creditors. The distribution to similarly situated creditors is equal. But the Bankruptcy Code creates many separate classes of creditors, so the distribution is often quite unequal in practice.

4. Most of the Pennsylvania cases are the kind described in note 2, in which one creditor seeks compensation ahead of all the others. But *Willing* is really a case where they let plaintiff do harm she can't pay for. So is the *Heilman* case, cited in *Willing*. There, the court refused to enjoin diversion of water from plaintiff's stream. Defendant had been paying for the water for many years, and he had built a mill in reliance on the diversion, which may have influenced the court. But the holding was that defendant could divert water without any prospect of paying for it, and that the damage remedy was adequate even if useless. Whatever the reasons for the decision, wasn't it just wrong to say the damage remedy was adequate? If special considerations cause the court to withhold the injunction despite the inadequacy of the legal remedy, shouldn't the court say so?

5. Damages may also be unavailable because defendant is immune from damage actions. But many immune defendants are not immune from injunctions. Not surprisingly, the nonexistent damage remedy has been held inadequate. An example is Toomer v. Witsell, 334 U.S. 385 (1948), in which the trial court enjoined South Carolina officials from discriminating against out-of-state shrimp fishermen. The Supreme Court affirmed. It said that compliance with the discriminatory statutes

> required payment of large sums of money for which South Carolina provides no means of recovery, that defiance would have carried with it the risk of heavy fines and long imprisonment, and that withdrawal from further fishing until a test case had been taken through the South Carolina courts and perhaps to this Court would have resulted in a substantial loss of business for which no compensation could be obtained.

Id. at 392. By contrast, plaintiffs' challenge to the South Carolina income tax was dismissed, because the state had waived its immunity to tax refund suits.

6. *Toomer* also alludes to the risk of imprisonment if one defies legislation he believes to be unconstitutional. This is another common source of irreparable injury. Because it has become enmeshed in controversy about the proper role of the federal courts, we will consider it in chapter 13. That chapter will also take up the source and scope of immunities from suit.

CITY OF CHICAGO v. FESTIVAL THEATRE CORP.
91 Ill. 2d 295, 438 N.E.2d 159 (1982)

WARD, Justice. . . .

The plaintiff, the city of Chicago, filed a complaint for injunctive relief on August 29, 1978. The complaint alleged that the defendants, Festival

Theatre Corporation and Liang, on three occasions presented exhibitions that consisted of live sex acts in violation of the criminal obscenity statute (Ill. Rev. Stat. 1977, ch. 38, par. 11-20). The city alleged that the performances were harmful to its citizens, and that it had no adequate remedy at law. . . . The complaint petitioned for the issuance of an injunction against such performances at the theater.

Testimony)

The court conducted a hearing on September 25, 1978, at which several Chicago police officers testified to the following. On July 26, 1978, and August 14, 1978, plainclothes police officers paid fees of five dollars to enter the theater. On both occasions, there was a live stage show involving two women. In the July 26 show, the women danced and completely disrobed to music. On both occasions, though the shows differed in some respects, the women kissed and fondled each other, and engaged in deviate sexual acts during the performances. After the performances, the women were arrested for obscenity and public indecency. The manager, Liang, was arrested for obscenity and for city ordinance violations.

On August 23, 1978, the stage show, which was witnessed by police officers, involved only one of the women and a man. The woman told the audience that she had to change her "act" because of previous arrests. Again she danced and removed her clothes. She was soon joined on stage by the man, who removed his clothes, and they engaged in actual or simulated intercourse and deviate acts. Both were arrested for obscenity and public indecency.

Criminal proceedings were begun after the arrests, but at the time of the hearing no dispositions had been made of them. The record does not indicate the eventual dispositions. . . .

[The trial court held that the performances were a common law nuisance. It issued an injunction forbidding certain kinds of live performances at the theater. The conduct was described in detail, and was limited to conduct that was obscene within the meaning of the criminal statutes on the subject. The appellate court vacated the injunction on first amendment grounds. It held that the concept of common law nuisance was too vague to support restraints on expression. The city appealed.]

The Public Nuisance Act does not displace common law actions to abate public nuisances. Rather, equitable jurisdiction to abate public nuisances is said to be of "ancient origin," and it exists even where not conferred by statute, where the offender is amenable to the criminal law, and where no property rights are involved. (Stead v. Fortner (1912), 255 Ill. 468, 475-79, 99 N.E. 680.) Too, in a common law action, the extent of the concept of public nuisance is not limited to those activities the legislature has declared public nuisances. . . .

A theater presenting obscene performances fits within the common law concept of public nuisance. . . .

That conduct may be subject to the sanctions of the criminal law does not, of course, foreclose a common law nuisance abatement action against the conduct. The General Assembly has also provided in section 1-4 of the Criminal Code of 1961:

> This Code does not bar, suspend, or otherwise affect any right or liability to damages, penalty, forfeiture, or other remedy authorized by law to be recovered or enforced in a civil action, for any conduct which this Code makes punishable; and the civil injury is not merged in the offense. . . .

We cannot accept the appellate court's observation that the procedures of a civil nuisance action make it unsuitable in obscenity cases. Specifically, the court noted the absence of a right to a jury trial and suggested that the civil standard of proof might not be appropriate. The Supreme Court has approved the use of adversary civil injunctive proceedings against obscenity. It has not held that jury trials are necessary in civil obscenity proceedings. We recognize that a jury may be useful in determining whether a performance in a given case is obscene according to contemporary community standards. But we recognize too that in not every case could reasonable minds differ as to whether a performance was obscene. Too, under our civil procedure the court is authorized to call an advisory jury to assist it where the court deems it necessary. . . .

The appellate court held also that the injunction is a prohibited prior restraint on expression. The court said that the circuit court's order listed prohibited activities, such as simulated intercourse. Therefore, the defendant is enjoined from presenting performances that involve the proscribed acts in any form or context. Because arguably one or more of the proscribed acts could be performed in a show that is not obscene, the appellate court concluded that this injunction covers even protected expression. . . .

[T]he court cited Vance v. Universal Amusement Co. (1980), 445 U.S. 308. There, the Supreme Court held that an injunction under a Texas public nuisance abatement statute would operate as an improper prior restraint. Under the statute a court could enjoin the exhibition of films at theaters that habitually had been used for the showing of obscene movies. The court said:

> As the District Court and the Court of Appeals construed Art. 4667(a), when coupled with the Texas Rules of Civil Procedure, it authorizes prior restraints of indefinite duration on the exhibition of motion pictures that have not been finally adjudicated to be obscene. Presumably, an exhibitor would be required to obey such an order pending review of its merits and would be subject to contempt proceedings even if the film is ultimately found to be nonobscene. Such prior restraints would be more onerous and more objectionable than the threat of criminal sanctions after a film has been exhibited, since nonobscenity would be a defense to any criminal prosecution.

445 U.S. 308, 316.

[handwritten margin notes: "no prob - prior rest."; "order"]

We judge that the injunction here did not present a problem of prior restraint. While the injunction does list a variety of sexual acts, it does not proscribe the performance of those acts in all contexts and unconditionally. The order says that the defendants are "permanently enjoined and restrained . . . from performing or permitting the performance of lewd acts of live persons, *in violation of applicable City Ordinances and State Statutes* . . . for the entertainment, sexual arousal, or viewing by and of members of the public; including, but not limited to, the following of such acts. . . ." (Emphasis added.) . . . The injunction does no more than order the defendants not to violate the criminal laws against obscenity at the theater. Unlike the order in *Vance*, the defendants here could not be held in contempt unless it were shown that they staged a performance that was obscene. In short, the order did not touch protected expression. Any effect it could have produced relating to the first amendment was no greater than that produced by the obscenity provisions of the Criminal Code. . . .

Although we have found no constitutional defect in the injunction, we do consider that it was improvidently granted. . . .

It is a principle of equity that an injunction will not issue except where there is no adequate remedy at law. Here, the activity complained of was the presenting of live obscene exhibitions, and those conducting such exhibitions are amenable to prosecution under the criminal obscenity laws. We deem that issuance of the injunction was error because it was not shown that criminal prosecution fails to afford an adequate remedy for the harm caused.

As we have previously noted, the fact that the activity complained of in a public nuisance action may give rise to a criminal prosecution does not foreclose the bringing of the action for equitable relief. The criminality of the conduct is a relevant factor, however, in determining whether an injunction should issue. The purpose of giving equity jurisdiction in public nuisance actions is to offer remedies more complete than those available at law. To permit a public body to obtain an injunction in a public nuisance action where there is an equally effective criminal law against the conduct would give rise to strong policy objections, such as were advanced in Commonwealth v. Stratton Finance Co. (1941), 310 Mass. 469, 38 N.E.2d 640. There, the court, in decrying any general use of equity in aid of criminal statutes, stated:

> The objections to "criminal equity" are that it deprives the defendant of his jury trial; that it substitutes for the definite penalties fixed by the Legislature whatever punishment for contempt a particular judge may see fit to exact; that it is often no more than an attempt to overcome by circumvention the supposed shortcomings of jurors; and that it may result, or induce the public to believe that it results, in the arbitrary exercise of power and in "government by injunction." These objections are substantial. They should cause a court to

hesitate to extend the use of the injunction into the criminal field without express legislative sanction.

310 Mass. 469, 474, 38 N.E.2d 640, 643.

For a legal remedy to be deemed adequate, "the remedy 'must be clear, complete, and as practical and efficient to the ends of justice and its prompt administration as the equitable remedy.'" Bio-Medical Laboratories, Inc. v. Trainor (1977), 68 Ill. 2d 540, 549, quoting K.F.K. Corp. v. American Continental Homes, Inc. (1975), 31 Ill. App. 3d 1017, 1021. This court has consistently recognized that the criminal law is not such a remedy where it is shown ineffective to prevent the continuance of the nuisance. City of Chicago v. Cecola (1979), 75 Ill. 2d 423, 27 Ill. Dec. 462, 389 N.E.2d 526 (maximum fine of $200 insufficient to dissuade defendants from maintaining establishment offering sexual massages); Village of Spillertown v. Prewitt (1961), 21 Ill. 2d 228, 171 N.E.2d 582 (defendant, having been arrested twice, claimed before village board he would continue stripmining despite imposition of fines under ordinance); People ex rel. Kerner v. Huls (1934), 355 Ill. 412, 189 N.E. 346 (criminal prosecution inadequate remedy where defendant's statements showed that he would pay statutory penalties but still not submit his cattle for tuberculin test); People ex rel. Dyer v. Clark (1915), 268 Ill. 156, 108 N.E. 994 (numerous criminal convictions of keeper of brothel did not deter her from continuing the activity).

It was not shown here that criminal prosecution would not lend a remedy as clear, complete, practical, and effective as the equitable remedy. The city argues and the appellate court held that there was no adequate legal remedy because the defendants presented an allegedly obscene performance on August 23, 1978, despite the two previous arrests. The appellate court found it of significance that the record does not show any dispositions of the criminal actions begun following the arrests. These factors, though, do not persuade us that a conclusion that there was no adequate legal remedy available may be drawn.

The injunction issued was coextensive with the criminal statute, so it did not seek to affect conduct beyond the reach of the statute. There is no contention by the city of Chicago that conviction and imposition of penalties available under the criminal obscenity law, which makes the first offense a misdemeanor and a second offense a felony, would be ineffective to deter the defendants' activities. The injunction was issued within a few months of even the first arrest at the theater and before the criminal proceedings were completed. It is not claimed that this is a case where a risk to public health would require expedited action by a court acting through its equity powers. We do not hold that an injunction action may not be hereafter brought against the defendants. We judge only that in this action it was not shown that criminal prosecution would be an inadequate remedy. . . .

NOTES ON INJUNCTIONS AGAINST CRIMES

1. In Chicago v. Festival Theatre, the irreparable injury rule protects the right to a jury trial in criminal cases. Is the criminal jury generally more important than the civil jury? The Supreme Court has held that the due process clause requires criminal juries but not civil juries in state courts. Compare Duncan v. Louisiana, 391 U.S. 145 (1968), with Walker v. Sauvinet, 92 U.S. 90 (1876).

2. General preferences aside, might jury trial really matter in *Festival Theatre*? To convict for obscenity, the jury must find that the show is patently offensive, and it is instructed to consider community standards. Many jurors would be deeply offended by the sexual entertainment described in *Festival Theatre*. But many other jurors would enjoy such entertainment, and others might be inclined to tolerate it. Given the deep divisions of opinion, and the vague definition of obscenity, isn't there a substantial chance of a hung jury? Might that be why the city is seeking an injunction instead of pursuing the criminal prosecutions? If a series of hung juries nullified the obscenity laws, would that make the criminal remedy inadequate? Or is the potential for jury nullification of unpopular criminal laws an important civil liberty?

Would you give the same answer if the example were jury nullification of civil rights laws? There is a clear tension between protection of minorities and deference to the jury as a popular but majoritarian institution. Consider Bose Corp. v. Consumers Union, 104 S. Ct. 1949 (1984). That opinion reviews cases in which, to protect one litigant's constitutional rights, the Supreme Court has independently re-examined the facts found by a jury or trial judge.

3. The civil injunction proceeding has other advantages for the city. It will almost certainly be quicker and cheaper than a criminal jury trial. Coercive contempt sanctions can be imposed by the judge alone in a summary procedure. Requests for preliminary injunctions and citations for contempt generally go to the top of the civil docket; a criminal prosecution would wait its turn with thousands of other cases. Are these reasons to find the criminal remedy inadequate? Or are they reasons to prefer the criminal remedy if it works at all?

4. Another suggestion in *Festival Theatre* is that proceeding by injunction and the contempt power allows a judge to change the penalties fixed by the legislature. If the court is serious, why does it also say that the injunction is available whenever the legislative penalty is insufficient to deter? Does the legislative penalty control except when it really matters? Or does the court mean that effective deterrence of repeated violations is essential, even though legislative judgment is conclusive on the question of appropriate retribution?

5. Recall the economic notion that the goal of law is not to deter all violations, but to deter only those violations that are unprofitable after

considering the costs to victims. Some proponents of that view apply it to criminal law as well, suggesting that "optimal" punishments for violating regulatory statutes would inflict costs on the criminal just equal to the costs he imposed on society. See R. Posner, Economic Analysis of Law 164-167 (2d ed. 1977). For crimes with identifiable victims, where the criminal could have bought what he wanted if he valued it more than the victim, Judge Posner would add to the fine the cost of adjudicating the criminal's case: "the cost of using the legal system as a surrogate for the market." Id. at 166. Do the cases enjoining crimes where the legislated penalty is inadequate to deter reject that view? Don't they assume that no violator should ever decide his crime is still profitable after he pays the fine? Who's right? The economists or the courts? Are legislators likely to approve profitable violations?

6. Compare United States v. Zenon, 711 F.2d 476 (1st Cir. 1983), affirming an injunction against trespass on a naval base used for weapons testing. The court rejected the argument that criminal prosecution would be an adequate remedy, apparently on the ground that immediate compliance was necessary.

7. Why isn't immediate compliance always necessary? How can a remedy be adequate if it requires the government to stand by and let a crime happen? Does punishing the criminal undo the crime in the way that buying a new widget undoes the loss of the old widget? Is criminal prosecution ever as complete, practical, and efficient as the injunction? Isn't defendant's whole point that criminal procedure is not as efficient for the government, and that those inefficiencies are an important protection for defendants? Does irreparable injury mean the same thing in *Festival Theatre* that it meant in *Pardee*?

8. The reluctance to enjoin crimes has little effect in litigation to order compliance with statutes perceived as regulatory, even if the statutes also carry criminal penalties. Many cases say that if the statute authorizes an injunction, plaintiff need not show irreparable injury or other equitable prerequisites. An example is South Central Bell Telephone Co. v. Louisiana Public Service Commission, 744 F.2d 1107, 1120 (5th Cir. 1984). Even if the statute does not explicitly authorize an injunction, there is a strong tendency to enjoin violations, especially when the government is the plaintiff. But there are also occasional decisions refusing to enjoin statutory violations.

The leading case is Hecht Co. v. Bowles, 321 U.S. 321 (1944). The government showed many violations of price controls in Hecht's department stores, and the statute provided that an injunction or other order "shall be granted" for a violation. But the Court refused to read the statute as eliminating equitable discretion. It denied the injunction, not on grounds of irreparable injury, but on grounds of futility. Hecht showed vigorous efforts to comply, and the district court found that an injunction would have no effect. The problem was that Hecht sold so many items that violations were inevitable. The Supreme Court adopted the findings and denied the injunction. More recent cases go both ways, but the Court has narrowly confined discretion to not enjoin statutory violations. The cases are analyzed in Farber, Equitable Discretion, Legal Duties, and Environmental Injunctions, 45 U. Pitt. L. Rev. 513 (1984).

Many of these regulatory statutes include criminal penalties. How are they different from the statute in *Festival Theatre*? Is it that criminal prosecution is the extraordinary remedy in the regulatory context? Criminal prosecution is generally reserved for a few of the most egregious regulatory violations. If the realistic alternative to an injunction is some other means of civil enforcement, or perhaps nonenforcement, how relevant are *Festival Theatre*'s concerns about the right to criminal procedure and a legislatively determined sentence?

MORE NOTES ON PRIOR RESTRAINTS

1. Obscenity, like malicious libel, is unprotected speech. *Festival Theatre* holds that it is unprotected even from prior restraints. The United States Supreme Court has also upheld injunctions against obscene expression, provided that there is an adjudication of obscenity prior to the injunction or, if later, after the "shortest fixed period compatible with sound judicial resolution." Freedman v. Maryland, 380 U.S. 51, 59 (1965).

2. The Court has also upheld other injunctions against unprotected speech.

a. Pittsburgh Press Co. v. Pittsburgh Commission on Human Relations, 413 U.S. 376 (1973): The Court upheld an order to stop printing help-wanted ads that segregated "male" and "female" jobs. It said: "The special vice of a prior restraint is that communication will be suppressed, either directly or by inducing excessive caution in the speaker, before an adequate determination that it is unprotected by the First Amendment." Id. at 390. Here, it was clear that the speech would be unprotected, so it could be forbidden. There were four dissents, all relying on the rule against prior restraints; two of the dissenters apparently thought the speech was protected against subsequent punishment as well.

b. Snepp v. United States, 444 U.S. 507 (1980) (reprinted infra at 479): Snepp published a book based on his work in Vietnam for the CIA. He had not submitted the manuscript to the CIA for prepublication approval as his employment contract required. The government stipulated that the book contained no classified information and that Snepp was free to publish unclassified information. But it got an injunction against further violations of the preclearance rule. The Supreme Court summarily affirmed.

The restraint in *Snepp* is not just an injunction against unprotected speech. All publications that relate to the CIA in any way must be submitted to an administrative censorship process, even though the relevant category of forbidden speech is much narrower. There are no provisions clearly requiring the censors to act promptly, and it is quite unrealistic to expect them to act within the few days apparently contemplated by the obscenity cases. This is the classic prior restraint as it existed in Stuart England: Nothing can be published until the censors approve. Whatever one's view of the merits, it is hard to believe that the difference between prior restraint and subsequent punishment made the slightest difference.

c.   Seattle Times Co. v. Rinehart, 104 S. Ct. 2199 (1984): In this suit against the Seattle Times for defamation and invasion of privacy, the trial court ordered the Times not to publish private information obtained through discovery from the plaintiffs. The Supreme Court upheld the injunction, not because publication would have been unprotected, but because the Times could never have gotten the information at all but for discovery. The court that granted access to the information could limit its use to the purposes for which discovery was granted.

3.   These cases suggest that the traditional rule against prior restraints is of declining significance. But other Supreme Court cases from the same period relied on the rule strongly.

a.   Vance v. Universal Amusement Co., 445 U.S. 308 (1980), and Southeastern Promotions, Ltd. v. Conrad, 420 U.S. 546 (1975): *Vance* invalidated a nuisance statute authorizing injunctions ordering theaters to close for a year if they had regularly shown obscene films in the past. *Southeastern* held that a municipal auditorium could not refuse to allow a touring company to present the musical "Hair," which included nudity, profanity, and sexual gestures. Both cases argued that prior restraints inevitably preclude speech that would have been protected, because it is impossible to know in advance what the speaker would have said. That argument was plausible in *Vance*, where the films were changed regularly, but not in *Southeastern*, where the company did the same show at every stop.

b.   Nebraska Press Association v. Stuart, 427 U.S. 539 (1976): *Nebraska Press Association* invalidated an injunction ordering the press not to report confessions or other facts "strongly implicative" of the accused in a widely reported trial for multiple murder. The Court thought other remedies were adequate; its examples were remedies that do not restrain speech at all, such as changing venue or sequestering jurors. It seems unlikely that the Court would permit the press to be punished or held liable in damages for publishing truthful reports that prejudiced a defendant's right to a fair trial.

c.   New York Times v. United States, 403 U.S. 713 (1971): *New York Times* invalidated an injunction against publishing The Pentagon Papers, a secret study of the war in Vietnam. The government claimed that publication would endanger national security. A majority of the

Court apparently contemplated that the Times could be criminally prosecuted; no such prosecution was ever filed.

d. Organization for a Better Austin v. Keefe, 402 U.S. 415 (1971): *Organization for a Better Austin* invalidated an injunction forbidding defendants to distribute leaflets in Westchester, Illinois, a suburb of Chicago. The leaflets charged a Westchester real estate broker with racial blockbusting in Chicago; the state court held that distributing them near his home and church invaded his privacy.

The Supreme Court reversed. The opinion emphasizes the traditional hostility to prior restraints, but that was probably unnecessary to the decision. The record also seems inadequate to support a damage judgment. And the injunction was plainly overbroad. It forbad all leaflets on any subject, not just the leaflets that had been found to invade the broker's privacy.

4. We are left with at least two lines of cases. In one line the Court affirms injunctions against unprotected speech. In the other, the Court says injunctions against speech are especially suspect even if the speech is otherwise unprotected. Is there any distinction between the two lines of cases? One answer is that in the second group, the speech was really protected against subsequent restraints as well, so that reliance on the rule against prior restraints was merely dictum. In this view, the Court may be expected to waive the rule against prior restraints whenever it encounters a carefully drafted injunction against speech that has properly been found unprotected. That may be a good prediction, and *Pittsburgh Press* actually says that, but that is not how the Court wrote the opinions. If the prediction is accurate, the rule is radically different from the traditional understanding invoked in *Willing*. It is no longer a rule against restraints prior to publication; it is a rule against restraints prior to adjudication.

Snepp goes even further. It upheld a restraint prior to adjudication, and implies that such restraints are permissible whenever the government's need is great enough. It was important to the Court that Snepp would not have gotten his information if he had not promised to submit to censorship; perhaps the government cannot show sufficient need for a censorship system any other way.

5. The most common justification for the rule against prior restraints is mentioned in *Festival Theatre*. An injunction that forbids protected speech must be obeyed; the unconstitutionality of the injunction is not a defense to a prosecution for contempt. This rule — called the collateral bar rule because it bars collateral attacks on injunctions — is not unique to speech cases. We will consider it more generally when we examine the contempt power in chapter 8.

If we take the collateral bar rule as a given, does it justify the rule against prior restraints? Doesn't *Festival Theatre* solve the problem by incorporating the constitutional defense into the injunction? If the speech is protected, it doesn't violate the injunction, and that is obviously a defense to a contempt prosecution. Can't the court issuing the injunction always write it in a way that waives the collateral bar rule? If the injunction is written that way, does it add anything to the underlying substantive law? Didn't the theater already know it wasn't supposed to put on obscene shows?

6. The strongest defense of the rule against prior restraints is Blasi, Toward a Theory of Prior Restraint: The Central Linkage, 66 Minn. L. Rev. 11 (1981). Professor Blasi rejects the traditional argument that injunctions deter more speech than liability rules and criminal statutes. But he finds other justifications for the traditional rule. He believes that the government is more likely to sue for an injunction than to prosecute criminally, because the injunction litigation is likely to be quicker, cheaper, and easier. And he believes that prosecutors and courts are more likely to find speech unprotected in an injunction suit. If asked to predict whether speech is likely to be so harmful that it loses its first amendment protection, Blasi believes that prosecutors and courts are prone to imagine possible consequences too horrible to risk, and err on the side of caution by issuing the injunction. But if there is a rule against injunctions, the speech will occur and often do little or no harm. Then courts are more likely to hold it protected. Does this seem plausible enough to justify the rule, at least in national security cases and incitement to violence cases? Is it consistent with experience in defamation cases, where plaintiffs sue and juries return large verdicts?

7. For a strong statement of the arguments against prior restraint doctrine, see Jeffries, Rethinking Prior Restraint, 92 Yale L.J. 409 (1983). Jeffries would abandon the doctrine as an obstacle to clear thinking. He thinks that such a wide variety of techniques for censorship have been labeled prior restraints that the concept no longer has any meaning, and that even in the fairly clear case of the injunction against speech, it is impossible to generalize: Sometimes injunctions are a greater threat to free speech, but more often they are not.

B. SPECIFIC PERFORMANCE OF CONTRACTS

CAMPBELL SOUP CO. v. WENTZ
172 F.2d 80 (3d Cir. 1948)

Before BIGGS, Chief Judge, and GOODRICH and O'CONNELL, Circuit Judges.

GOODRICH, Circuit Judge. . . .

On June 21, 1947, Campbell Soup Company, . . . a New Jersey corporation, entered into a written contract with George B. Wentz and Harry

T. Wentz, who are Pennsylvania farmers, for delivery by the Wentzes to Campbell of all the Chantenay red cored carrots to be grown on fifteen acres of the Wentz farm during the 1947 season. . . . The prices specified in the contract ranged from $23 to $30 per ton according to the time of delivery. The contract price for January, 1948 was $30 a ton.

The Wentzes harvested approximately 100 tons of carrots from the fifteen acres covered by the contract. Early in January, 1948, they told a Campbell representative that they would not deliver their carrots at the contract price. The market price at that time was at least $90 per ton, and Chantenay red cored carrots were virtually unobtainable. The Wentzes then sold approximately 62 tons of their carrots to the defendant Lojeski, a neighboring farmer. Lojeski resold about 58 tons on the open market, approximately half to Campbell and the balance to other purchasers.

On January 9, 1948, Campbell, suspecting that Lojeski was selling it "contract carrots," refused to purchase any more, and instituted these suits against the Wentz brothers and Lojeski to enjoin further sale of the contract carrots to others, and to compel specific performance of the contract. The trial court denied equitable relief.[1] . . .

A party may have specific performance of a contract for the sale of chattels if the legal remedy is inadequate. Inadequacy of the legal remedy is necessarily a matter to be determined by an examination of the facts in each particular instance.

We think that on the question of adequacy of the legal remedy the case is one appropriate for specific performance. It was expressly found that at the time of the trial it was "virtually impossible to obtain Chantenay carrots in the open market." This Chantenay carrot is one which the plaintiff uses in large quantities, furnishing the seed to the growers with whom it makes contracts. It was not claimed that in nutritive value it is any better than other types of carrots. Its blunt shape makes it easier to handle in processing. And its color and texture differ from other varieties. The color is brighter than other carrots. The trial court found that the plaintiff failed to establish what proportion of its carrots is used for the production of soup stock and what proportion is used as identifiable physical ingredients in its soups. We do not think lack of proof on that point is material. It did appear that the plaintiff uses carrots in fifteen of its twenty-one soups. It also appeared that it uses these Chantenay carrots diced in some of them and that the appearance is uniform. The preservation of uniformity in appearance in a food article marketed throughout the country and sold under the manufacturer's name is a matter of considerable commercial significance and one which is properly considered

---

1.   The issue is preserved on appeal by an arrangement under which Campbell received all the carrots held by the Wentzes and Lojeski, paying a stipulated market price of $90 per ton, $30 to the defendants, and the balance into the registry of the District Court pending the outcome of these appeals.

in determining whether a substitute ingredient is just as good as the original.

TC:
Not unique

The trial court concluded that the plaintiff had failed to establish that the carrots, "judged by objective standards," are unique goods. This we think is not a pure fact conclusion like a finding that Chantenay carrots are of uniform color. It is either a conclusion of law or of mixed fact and law and we are bound to exercise our independent judgment upon it. That the test for specific performance is not necessarily "objective" is shown by the many cases in which equity has given it to enforce contracts for articles — family heirlooms and the like — the value of which was personal to the plaintiff.

App ct:

J/aff'd

Judged by the general standards applicable to determining the adequacy of the legal remedy we think that on this point the case is a proper one for equitable relief. There is considerable authority, old and new, showing liberality in the granting of an equitable remedy. We see no reason why a court should be reluctant to grant specific relief when it can be given without supervision of the court or other time-consuming processes against one who has deliberately broken his agreement. Here the goods of the special type contracted for were unavailable on the open market, the plaintiff had contracted for them long ahead in anticipation of its needs, and had built up a general reputation for its products as part of which reputation uniform appearance was important. We think if this were all that was involved in the case specific performance should have been granted.

K too
one sided

The reason that we shall affirm instead of reversing with an order for specific performance is found in the contract itself. We think it is too hard a bargain and too one-sided an agreement to entitle the plaintiff to relief in a court of conscience. For each individual grower the agreement is made by filling in names and quantity and price on a printed form furnished by the buyer. This form has quite obviously been drawn by skilful draftsmen with the buyer's interests in mind.

Paragraph 2 provides for the manner of delivery. Carrots are to have their stalks cut off and be in clean sanitary bags or other containers approved by Campbell. This paragraph concludes with a statement that Campbell's determination of conformance with specifications shall be conclusive.

The defendants attack this provision as unconscionable. We do not think that it is, standing by itself. We think that the provision is comparable to the promise to perform to the satisfaction of another and that Campbell would be held liable if it refused carrots which did in fact conform to the specifications.

The next paragraph allows Campbell to refuse carrots in excess of twelve tons to the acre. The next contains a covenant by the grower that he will not sell carrots to anyone else except the carrots rejected by Campbell nor will he permit anyone else to grow carrots on his land.

Paragraph 10 provides liquidated damages to the extent of $50 per acre for any breach by the grower. There is no provision for liquidated or any other damages for breach of contract by Campbell.

The provision of the contract which we think is the hardest is paragraph 9. . . . Campbell is excused from accepting carrots under certain circumstances. But even under such circumstances the grower, while he cannot say Campbell is liable for failure to take the carrots, is not permitted to sell them elsewhere unless Campbell agrees. . . . What the grower may do with his product under the circumstances set out is not clear. He has covenanted not to store it anywhere except on his own farm and also not to sell to anybody else.

We are not suggesting that the contract is illegal. Nor are we suggesting any excuse for the grower in this case who has deliberately broken an agreement entered into with Campbell. We do think, however, that a party who has offered and succeeded in getting an agreement as tough as this one is, should not come to a chancellor and ask court help in the enforcement of its terms. That equity does not enforce unconscionable bargains is too well established to require elaborate citation.

The plaintiff argues that the provisions of the contract are separable. We agree that they are, but do not think that decisions separating out certain provisions from illegal contracts are in point here. As already said, we do not suggest that this contract is illegal. All we say is that the sum total of its provisions drives too hard a bargain for a court of conscience to assist.

This disposition of the problem makes unnecessary further discussion of the separate liability of Lojeski, who was not a party to the contract, but who purchased some of the carrots from the Wentzes.

The judgments will be affirmed.

NOTES ON SPECIFIC PERFORMANCE

1.   A specific performance decree is simply a specialized form of injunction, an order to defendant to actually perform his contract. It typically requires affirmative conduct, but as we have seen, that does not make it unusual. Its availability is conditioned on a showing of irreparable injury, and the sources of irreparability examined in the previous section are important in specific performance cases as well. In addition, other specialized conditions and defenses have been attached to requests for specific performance. This section will examine those rules and continue to explore the irreparable injury rule.

2.   Why does it matter whether Chantenay red cored carrots are unique? Isn't it the principle of Pardee v. Camden Lumber again — that money is an adequate remedy only if it can be used to replace the very thing that plaintiff lost? If some other kind of carrot is just as good, then

damages will suffice, because Campbell can use the money to buy carrots. But if no other carrots are like these carrots, money cannot replace what Campbell has lost.

3.   *Campbell* is not a fluke. Courts frequently grant specific performance of contracts for the sale of ordinary goods if scarcity, time constraints, or the sheer size of the contract make it difficult or impossible to cover. Some examples, old and new:

a.   Kaiser Trading Co. v. Associated Metals & Minerals Corp., 321 F. Supp. 923 (N.D. Cal. 1970): The court specifically enforced a long-term contract for the sale of four thousand tons of cryolite, a chemical essential to aluminum production. The world supply was limited, and much of it was committed to other long-term contracts. Defendant showed only that a few hundred tons were available on the open market.

b.   Eastern Airlines v. Gulf Oil Corp., 415 F. Supp. 429 (S.D. Fla. 1975): The court specifically enforced a contract to supply Eastern's jet fuel requirements at specified airports. Eastern procured 10 percent of its total fuel needs, or about one hundred million gallons per year, through the contract. Fuel was in short supply because of the 1973 Arab-Israeli war and the resulting Arab embargo of oil sales to nations that supported Israel. The court did not specifically find that cover was impossible. It did say that breach would cause "chaos and irreparable damage" and that "in the circumstances, a decree of specific performance becomes the ordinary and natural relief rather than the extraordinary one." Id. at 443.

c.   Curtis Brothers Co. v. Catts, 72 N.J. Eq. 831, 66 A. 935 (1907): The court specifically enforced a contract for the sale of a tomato crop. Plaintiff had a factory and all supplies for canning one million cans of tomatoes in the six-week packing season. The court doubted that a reliable supply was available on the open market; it reasoned that "the very existence" of preharvest contracts for the sale of whole crops "proclaims their necessity to the economic management of the factory." Id. at 833-834, 66 A. at 936.

4.   Compare Duval & Co. v. Malcom, 233 Ga. 784, 214 S.E.2d 356 (1975), a suit to specifically enforce a contract for the sale of a cotton crop. Drought had caused a shortage of cotton. Affirming a denial of cross-motions for summary judgment, the court said:

> Buyer has alleged that it "cannot go into the market and replace said cotton due to the uniqueness which now exists in the market." We note here that the mere fact that cotton prices soared after this alleged contract is not in itself adequate to show buyer entitled to specific performance.

Id. at 359. Is there a difference between the buyer's statement that cover is impossible and the court's statement that the price has soared? In economic theory, cover is never absolutely impossible; the price should rise until supply and demand are restored to balance. In practice, the market cannot reach equilibrium so quickly, especially if much of the supply is committed to long-term contracts. The market will always be in turmoil in the shortage cases; how clear will it be whether cover was truly impossible? If plaintiff decides to cover at any cost, won't defendant resist the damage claim on the ground that the cover price was unreasonable? How important is it that plaintiff wanted a long-term contract so he wouldn't have to scramble in the spot market? The incidental damages — the time and other resources spent arranging for cover — are hard to measure, aren't they?

In a case decided six weeks later, arising out of the same drought, the parties had stipulated that the cotton was unique. The court specifically enforced the contracts with a cf. citation to *Duval*. R. L. Kimsey Cotton Co. v. Ferguson, 233 Ga. 962, 214 S.E.2d 360 (1975). Do you suppose the shortage was any more severe in one case than in the other? *Duval* appears to be the deviant case; federal district courts in South Carolina, Georgia, Alabama, and Louisiana and the supreme court of Mississippi, all specifically enforced contracts for the sale of 1973 cotton crops.

5.   Recall Justice Holmes's famous description of contract:

> The duty to keep a contract at common law means a prediction that you must pay damages if you do not keep it, — and nothing else. If you commit a tort, you are liable to pay a compensatory sum. If you commit a contract, you are liable to pay a compensatory sum unless the promised event comes to pass, and that is all the difference.

Holmes, The Path of the Law, 10 Harv. L. Rev. 456, 462 (1897). He dismissed specific performance as so exceptional that it did not affect the general theory. Is that view consistent with *Campbell* and similar cases? Isn't it more accurate to say that a contract entitles a promisee to the thing he was promised, and that he has to accept damages only when he can use the money to replace the thing? Was Campbell entitled to money or carrots?

6.   One argument against specific performance is that the spot buyers offering $90 for carrots may have a more valuable use for them, and forcing a sale to Campbell for $30 may cause the carrots to be wasted in a less valuable use. This is based on the economic view that individual willingness to pay is a good proxy for societal value. The buyer who will pay the most for carrots expects to recover his investment plus a profit, and he can do that by conferring a benefit on his customers that exceeds the price he paid for the carrots. But the spot buyer's higher bid proves only that the price has gone up since Campbell's contract. Campbell was also paying $90 for spot carrots. No matter how much they value carrots, all buyers will pay about the market price. The only way to find out who values carrots more is to sell at auction in time of shortage. The damage remedy leaves sellers free to do that, although there is no indication Lojeski and the Wentzes did so.

Specific performance makes Campbell the potential auction seller. If other buyers value carrots more than Campbell, they can offer to buy them from Campbell. But Campbell may pursue its long-term interest in the soup business instead of taking a one-time profit in carrot speculation. It may refuse to sell carrots at any price a buyer is likely to offer, even though it might have dropped out at a lower price if forced to bid against that buyer in an auction. Would that mean specific performance has put the carrots to a less valuable use? Or does it just uncover an ambiguity in the economists' assumption that price is the measure of value? If Campbell will pay any price up to $120 but won't sell for less than $200, what is the value of carrots to Campbell? Does a buyer who would pay up to $150 have a more or less valuable use of the carrots than Campbell? What if that buyer wouldn't sell for less than $225 if he owned the carrots? What if that buyer also wants the carrots for soup, but is willing to pay more because he is richer than Campbell, or because he is trying to reduce Campbell's market share? Individual price is a quite imperfect proxy for societal value isn't it?

Even if we assume that allowing the Wentzes to sell the carrots to the highest bidder produces some economic gains, is there any reason to believe those gains exceed the economic losses from making long-term contracts less reliable? Wasn't the risk of shortage the most important reason Campbell wanted a long-term contract? If Campbell failed to cover because it was outbid at an auction, how would it prove the damages it suffered from using nonuniform carrots? Is this a good case for arguing that the UCC was right to preserve contract-market damages?

7.   Would specific performance be any more expensive or burdensome to the Wentzes than damages, if it were not for the liquidated damage clause? Won't contract-market damages, or contract-cover damages, equal the Wentzes' extra profits from selling at the new market price? What if the Wentzes manage to sell for $92 and Campbell manages to cover for $88? Should we deny specific performance to protect the Wentzes' opportunity for such profits? Does the $92 price prove that the Wentzes' new buyer had a more valuable use for the carrots than Campbell? Or just that there are minor variations around the new price because few markets are ever in perfect equilibrium?

8.   Suppose the Wentzes' new buyer really does have a more valuable use for the carrots. Does it follow even then that specific performance should be denied? Proponents of the economic view of law often speak of the need to encourage efficient breach, and this suggests a hostility to specific performance. Is that hostility consistent with the economists' preference for voluntary transactions? Why shouldn't the Wentzes or their new buyer have to buy Campbell's rights to the carrots at a price agreeable to Campbell, instead of breaching and forcing Campbell to accept a jury's estimate of its loss? Judge Posner suggests that buying Campbell's rights to the carrots imposes additional transaction costs. R. Posner, Economic Analysis of Law 96 (2d ed. 1977). Are those costs likely

to exceed the costs of settling Campbell's damage claim against the Wentzes?

Transaction costs are likely to be high either way. If carrots are in sufficiently short supply, the Wentzes have the power of a monopolist. Only Campbell has the right to buy those carrots for $30 per ton. Thus, there is a bilateral monopoly. Indeed, if there is only one other buyer willing to pay more than Campbell, there may be a trilateral monopoly. Suppose the carrots are worth $90 to Campbell and $110 to the new buyer, and that all three parties know these values. The market provides no basis for allocating the $20 difference. The new buyer would like to buy for $91 and make a $19 profit. The Wentzes would like to buy Campbell's rights for $61, forfeit the $30 due under the contract, and sell to the new buyer for $110, increasing their profit by $19. Campbell would like to buy the carrots for $30 and sell to the new buyer for $110, making a $20 profit after absorbing its $60 damages. (It could accomplish the same thing more simply by selling its contract rights to the new buyer for $80.) The parties may haggle indefinitely over the $20 surplus value created by the appearance of the new buyer.

A specific performance decree cuts out the Wentzes and leaves Campbell to haggle with the new buyer. A damage remedy cuts out Campbell and leaves the Wentzes to haggle with the new buyer. Either solution involves litigation between two of the parties and a voluntary transaction between two of the parties. Is there any basis for a general prediction about which will involve higher transaction costs?

9.   None of these problems arise in the absence of shortage. If there is no shortage, the new buyer with a more valuable use will buy at the market price. He will not need to outbid Campbell, and efficient breach analysis is irrelevant. Similarly, if there is no shortage, Campbell will have other sources of supply, so the price of cover will inform any negotiations for cancellation of Campbell's contract; those negotiations will not involve bilateral monopoly.

10.   Recall the general economic preference for injunctive remedies where transaction costs are low and damage remedies where transaction costs are high. Doesn't that suggest a rule exactly opposite to the courts' rule — that buyers ought to get specific performance when supplies are adequate, and be limited to damages when supplies are short? None of the proponents of law and economics have suggested that implication of their premises. Might that be because the courts have the more attractive solution?

11.   In *Campbell*, the carrots have long since been sold and the parties are fighting over money. Why does Campbell get more money if it is entitled to specific performance than if it is limited to damages? Did you figure the contract-market damages? Did you figure the damages under the liquidated damage clause? Did Campbell outsmart itself?

12.   There are many cases in which specific performance is burden-

some to defendant. The most obvious example is where defendant is unable to perform, but the contract is not excused for impossibility or frustration of purpose. But the irreparable injury rule does not solve these cases; whether plaintiff's legal remedy is adequate has little to do with whether specific performance would be a hardship on defendant. In chapter 11 we will consider a rule that speaks directly to defendants' hardship.

13. The UCC codified specific performance of sales contracts "where the goods are unique or in other proper circumstances." §2-716(1). The Official Comment says that the section "seeks to further a more liberal attitude" and that "inability to cover is strong evidence of 'other proper circumstances.'"

Why is inability to cover only "strong evidence"? Did the drafters mean to imply that sometimes damages are adequate despite inability to cover? Or only that sometimes hardship to defendant or some other competing consideration might lead a court to deny specific performance despite plaintiff's inability to cover?

Once goods are identified to the contract, §2-716(3) allows the buyer to replevy the goods if he can't cover. Replevin is a legal remedy, not subject to the irreparable injury rule or general notions of equitable discretion. Its traditional use is to recover plaintiff's property when possession is wrongfully withheld. Its use in §2-716(3) is an extension; the obvious intent is to create a nondiscretionary right to specific performance when the subsection's requirements are met. Most commonly, goods are identified to the contract when the seller ships them or marks specific items for delivery to the buyer. §2-501.

14. What if plaintiff is financially unable to cover? Consider Stephan's Machine & Tool v. D & H Machinery Consultants, 65 Ohio App. 2d 197, 417 N.E.2d 579 (1979). Plaintiff borrowed $96,000 to pay for a machine that didn't work. Defendant agreed to replace the machine and then failed to do so. Meanwhile, plaintiff was unable to conduct its business and defaulted on its loan. The court specifically enforced the replacement agreement, finding that plaintiff's financial straits made it impossible to buy a second machine elsewhere. The court awarded consequential damages for the same reason: Plaintiff could not have avoided those losses by cover because cover was impossible. Those are the right results, aren't they?

MACNEIL, EFFICIENT BREACH OF CONTRACT: CIRCLES IN THE SKY
68 Va. L. Rev. 947 (1982)

[This excerpt takes a second look at the debate over efficient breach and its relevance to the choice between damages and specific performance.

The article refers repeatedly to Peter Linzer's hypothetical with characters from The Three Musketeers. As the case is modified in the course of Macneil's article, Athos has a contract to make 100,000 chairs for Porthos at $10 per chair. Aramis asks Athos to make 50,000 tables for $40 per table. Athos cannot handle both jobs at once. If he makes the chairs, he will make a $250,000 profit. If he breaches, Porthos will suffer $250,000 in damages, in part because he will have to pay extra to get chairs on short notice from D'Artagnan (the fourth Musketeer). But Athos will make a $750,000 profit on the table contract. Efficiency theorists believe Athos should breach, pay Porthos's damages, and be left with $500,000 instead of $250,000. Both Linzer and Macneil quote Judge Posner's famous formulation: "if damages are limited to loss of expected profit, there will be an incentive to commit a breach. There should be." R. Posner, Economic Analysis of Law 89-90 (2d ed. 1977).]

I. Fallacy of Simple-Efficient-Breach Analysis

The simple-efficient-breach analysis is fallacious. The assumption that it is economically efficient for Athos to build tables rather than chairs by no means leads to the conclusion that breach is the economically efficient result. Rather, that result is obtained through the *nonperformance* of the contract to build chairs, and the substitution of the contract to build tables.[14] Since breach is far from the only way to avoid performance of the chair contract, no conclusion can be deduced that breach is any more (or less) efficient than other ways of securing the efficient result of nonperformance.

[Macneil shows that if there were no transaction costs, the parties would always reach the efficient result. Under a damage rule, Athos would breach and pay Porthos's damages. Under a specific performance rule, Athos or Aramis would pay Porthos to surrender his rights.]

II. Effect of Transaction Costs

[Macneil then considers three examples to test the effects of transaction costs: the costs of terminating the chair contract, compensating Porthos, and entering into the table contract with Aramis. Those costs may depend in part on the legal rule; the costs of breaching and paying Porthos's damages may not be the same as the costs of paying Porthos to surrender his right to specific performance.

---

14. . . . Even the conclusion that nonperformance is the efficient result is highly suspect although accepted arguendo in this article. If Porthos has a right of specific performance and actually enforces the chair contract, the neoclassical microeconomic model provides no basis for stating that this is an inefficient result. The very act of securing enforcement shows that Porthos puts a higher utility on the chairs than on all other opportunities available to him, assuming that transaction costs are not distorting the picture. . . .

In Macneil's first example, the transaction costs exceed $250,000 under either rule. Recall that $250,000 is the extra profit from making tables instead of chairs. On that assumption, Athos will make chairs no matter what the legal rule is.

In Macneil's second example, transaction costs are less than $250,000 under either rule. On that assumption, Athos will make tables no matter what the legal rule is. The more efficient rule is the one with the lowest transaction costs.

In Macneil's third example, transaction costs exceed $250,000 under a specific performance rule but not under a damage rule. On that assumption, Athos will make tables under a damage rule; he will make the less profitable chairs under a specific performance rule. So on this assumption, the damage rule is more efficient, but only because of its associated transaction costs, not because of its substance. If we assume that transaction costs exceed $250,000 under a damage rule but not under a specific performance rule, then the specific performance rule is more efficient.]

In sum, the correct statement of efficient breach in circumstances where a contractor has better opportunities is as follows:

> Whether an expectation damages rule or a specific performance rule is more efficient depends entirely upon the relative transaction costs of operating under the rules. Where, as will most generally be the case, transaction costs under either rule will exceed gross efficiency gains made possible by scrapping one contract in favor of another, each rule is equally (in)efficient. Where both rules will permit substituting a more productive contract for a less productive contract, the difference in efficiency of the rules will be measured exactly by the difference in their respective transaction costs. Where one rule will permit substitution and the other will not, the difference in efficiency will be measured by the difference in respective transaction costs, but subject to an upper limit consisting of the hypothetical net efficiency gain under the rule with the lower transaction costs. None of the transaction costs can be deduced by use of the microeconomic model, but can only be determined inductively from empirical evidence.

The principle of efficient breach also needs to be renamed if analytical error such as that of the simple-efficient-breach theorists is to be avoided; it should be called the principle of *efficient termination-and-remedy*.

I do not intend to make the investigations necessary to reach even slightly definitive conclusions about the transaction costs of the two rules. But the broad scope of the inquiry required before even slightly definitive conclusions could be suggested should be stressed. The pertinent transaction costs cannot be limited to one or two supplemental matters. Rather the inquiry must be addressed to *all* transaction costs respecting each rule. This includes some costs of initial planning in the *first* contract (including negotiations essential to the mutual planning required in contracting), costs of planning (again including negotiations) after the new opportunity comes along, costs of potential or actual litigation (including costs of delay), information costs, costs of inertia, costs of uncertainty, relational costs, such as damage to reputation and loss of future opportunities to deal, and undoubtedly others. All of these may vary depending upon which rule governs.

In addition, two other factors must be taken into account: negative transaction costs and externalities. Negative transaction costs are consequences of a rule which may lessen losses. For example, in the Four Musketeers, Porthos has to pay an added $200,000 to D'Artagnan "because of his distress situation" to enable him to buy substitute chairs. If one of the rules encourages early communication from Athos more than does the other, such distress losses may be reduced by that rule, thereby increasing its efficiency. Relational costs are another type of costs likely to vary a great deal depending upon the rule. If the damages rule encourages breaches without consultation, whereas the specific performance rule encourages consultation and mutually beneficial agreement, relational costs will be lower under the specific performance rule. In the real world it makes a great deal of difference whether a breach occurs, or is even threatened, or whether negotiations are viewed as leading towards mutually beneficial allocations of the increased productivity offered by the new opportunity. Unless the economic modeler explicitly treats this factor, the microeconomic model fails to take into account the difference between negotiating over what is viewed as an allocation of losses, and what is viewed as the allocation of potential gains. . . .

The other essential factor to consider is externalities. To the extent that whoever decides not to perform the first contract can avoid paying all the costs of that decision, the likelihood of his making inefficient decisions is increased. It is therefore necessary to weigh the two rules (in the wide range of circumstances to which they apply) in these terms. The consequences of uncertainty in measuring damages, of the American rule leaving most costs of litigation on the party initially incurring them, of costs of litigation generally, and of the costs of inertia, may enable the Athoses of the world to shift losses of termination of the first contract to the Porthoses in such a way that significant external costs escape their decision making. One way to limit the effect of this is to require joint decision making concerning termination of the first contract. The bargaining fostered by the specific performance rule in these circumstances seems ideally designed to prevent omission from the decisional calculus of the costs of either party.

III.   Origin and Bias of the Fallacy . . .

Suppose Athos has completed the chair contract by delivering the chairs to a public warehouse (as agreed in the contract) and has been paid. The chairs now belong to Porthos. Shortly afterwards Richelieu offers Athos

$2,000,000 for immediate delivery of 100,000 chairs. Athos, not having any chairs, forges a warehouse receipt, goes to the warehouse, takes Porthos's chairs, and sends Porthos a certified check for $1,250,000. Athos delivers the chairs to Richelieu and is paid, for a net efficiency gain of $750,000. If Porthos's liability for damages is limited to the amount of the check, there will be an incentive for Athos to commit the theft. There should be. To be sure, Athos could have gone to Porthos and negotiated a deal, but that would have involved added transaction costs.

The simple-efficiency theorists would probably consider the foregoing simple-efficient-theft argument a parody. But why? The answer lies in their assumption of efficiency-neutral ironbound property rights at the beginning and end of the changes being studied in the model. Once the magic words "my property" are spoken over the chairs on behalf of Porthos, he is entitled to them, or if they are gone, to their value, which in this case has been demonstrated by the Richelieu deal to be $2,000,000. But that answer leaves the simple-efficient-breach theory in considerable trouble. The magic "his property" can just as well be attributed to the holder of an effective right of specific performance or its true equivalent in damages as to the holder of possession, title, or both.

The very question in issue in the simple-efficient-breach theory is at what time do property rights in the chairs (or in the productive facilities to make them) become ironbound in Porthos? . . . [T]here is no a priori basis for selecting any particular time or event for determining that the transaction is closed, that new property rights are now established, and that with them a new, efficiency-neutral status quo has been achieved. . . .

[T]ransactions of this kind neither open nor shut precisely. After all, they open with negotiations (if not earlier in prior relations), often involve some performance (e.g., supplying samples) before a deal is clearly established, often drift through stages when it is difficult to ascertain if neither, one, or both parties are bound in legal or other ways (and if so, how much), commonly involve installment deliveries and various credit arrangements, and go through the noninstantaneous process of acceptance of the goods. Moreover, even after the chairs are delivered and accepted, and the price is paid in full, the transactions are subject to important "tagends" involving returns, claims for defective items, and potential warranty claims that may go on for years. . . . [J]ust as such contracts themselves "grow," so too the law governing grows with them. And in doing so this law reflects increasing buyer ownership and decreasing seller ownership as the contract follows common courses of development. For example, identification of goods confers on the buyer both a special property and an insurable interest in goods. In a case like the Four Musketeers, identification typically occurs when the chairs are "shipped, marked or otherwise designated by the seller as goods to which the

[Athos-Porthos] contract refers."[58] Had this happened, Porthos would have acquired a right to replevy the chairs — a recognition of his legal ownership — but, under the UCC, only if he were unable to effect cover or could show that an effort to do so would be unavailing. This particular effect of identification might be seen as simply a quirk of Anglo-American legal history, but insurable interest is hardly so easily dismissed, nor is the following buyer's right under UCC §2-503. Where the buyer has "paid a part or all of the price of goods in which he has a special property" under §2-502, he may, on making and keeping good a tender of any unpaid portion of the price, recover the goods from the seller if the seller becomes insolvent within ten days after receipt of the first installment on the price.

Identification and its effects are but one example of how the law reflects the fact that even a simple contract for the sale of goods grows between offer and acceptance and its final complete performance. Others include acceptance of goods, passage of title, risks of loss, rejection, cure, and tender. . . .

We thus find ourselves in the in-between mode of complex legal remedies throughout every transaction. In this in-between mode, the issue is not (apart from transaction costs) a matter of expectation damages vs. specific performance, as the simple-efficient-breach theory suggests. It is, rather, a question of rights of ownership, which the model (again apart from transaction costs in the creation of those rights) is powerless to describe as either efficient or inefficient, except in terms of transaction costs. Thus, under the expectation damages rule, Porthos has already acquired many of the rights of ownership of the chairs (and prior to their existence, of Athos's facilities for building them), namely the speculative market risks of such ownership. But the question is, how much ownership? It is perfectly conceivable that a rule of law could give Porthos legal rights in Athos's productive facilities from the time of the contract, but enforceable only by damages, not by specific performance.[69] Porthos would then be entitled to damages equal to the market value of those facilities during the time he is "owner" of them. In the Four Musketeers, that would give him the added $250,000 net efficiency gain from the Aramis table contract. A simple-efficient-breach analyst would, presumably, consider such a result just as inefficient as specific performance. . . .

There is a fundamental problem for the economic model here. No way exists to keep the exchanging processes themselves free of the idea of

----

58. UCC §2-501(1)(b).

69. If Porthos had leased Athos's facilities, expertise, and labor force, rather than ordered chairs, and then found himself shut out while Athos made tables for Aramis, this is just what would likely happen in many American jurisdictions, since American courts might be loath to enforce such a contract specifically due to alleged difficulties of supervision. This reluctance would not, however, affect Porthos's right to full expectation damages.

entitlements. Each change in legal rights occurring as the exchanging process goes on is a new set of legal entitlements, with just as much right as the preceding or succeeding one to be considered a new, efficiency-neutral status quo. Nor are the "normal" beginning or ending states of legal entitlements so ironbound and unfuzzy that the in-between stages can readily be distinguished as somehow fundamentally different. The existence of specific performance as a remedy illustrates this, since it can as readily be viewed as establishing a new, ironbound property right as it can be viewed as a remedy in the middle of the exchanging process.[70]

In sum, the economic model provides no basis for an a priori conclusion about the efficiency of passage of ownership at any given stage of a transaction. Moreover, the passage of ownership, a legal entitlement, cannot be separated analytically (except for analyzing transaction costs and the kinds of issues raised by Calabresi and Melamed [supra at 338–339]) from remedies for breach of contract. Thus, in the complex move from one property right status quo to another that occurs in an exchange, efficiency of particular rules can, once again, be ascertained not by their substantive content affecting ownership, but only by examining their pertinent transaction costs and externalities.

The final question is the nature of the bias of the simple-efficient-breach theory. That bias is in favor of individual, uncooperative behavior as opposed to behavior requiring the cooperation of the parties. The whole thrust of the Posner analysis is breach first, talk afterwards. Indeed, this may be an overstatement of the level of cooperation, since Posner pays singularly little attention to talking afterwards. Although he stresses the transaction costs of negotiations needed to reach efficient results under the specific performance rule, he pays no attention to the transaction costs of talking after a breach. And this is so despite the fact that "talking after a breach" may be one of the more expensive forms of conversation to be found, involving, as it so often does, engaging highpriced lawyers, and gambits like starting litigation, engaging in discovery, and even trying and appealing cases.

The bias against cooperation demonstrated by the simple-efficient-breach theory should surprise no one familiar with the neoclassical model. Such a bias is not limited to this particular fallacy, but is one towards which the neoclassical model inevitably and always tends. That model postulates individuals acting as if the relations in which those individuals exist have no effect on their behavior. Cooperative behavior postulates relations. A model assuming away relations slips with the great-

70.   Indeed, that is exactly how it was (and often still is) viewed in traditional equity; the existence of a right to specific performance was viewed as transferring equitable title to land, for example. *See* Stone, Equitable Conversion by Contract, 13 Colum. L. Rev. 369 (1913).

est of ease at any stage into favoring uncooperative and — ironically enough — highly inefficient human behavior.

NOTES ON MACNEIL'S VIEW OF EFFICIENT BREACH

1. Professor Macneil distinguishes "simple efficient breach theory" from economic analyses of breach that focus on transaction costs. There have been many such analyses, and they have come to conflicting conclusions. We will encounter some of them in the notes to the next principal case, arguing whether specific performance should be available when cover is possible. Macneil believes that it is almost impossible to consider all transaction costs, and that it is easy to consider mainly those transaction costs that support the result the analyst wants to reach. He also questions the value of the whole enterprise:

> The unrealistic figures given in the Athos illustration tend to obscure the fact that in real life a vast number of otherwise "more efficient" possibilities will be precluded, because they are not sufficiently more efficient to overcome the transaction costs to Athos of non-performance of the first contract. This will be true no matter what legal rule is in effect. It thus seems likely that the intellectual outpouring on this subject applies to only a relative handful of actual situations. If so, should the legal system burden itself with the kinds of high-cost analysis, producing very high transaction costs, both to parties and society generally, required by microeconomic analysis of this kind? Or would it not be far better to ignore all the sophistication in favor of historical or more intuitive solutions?

The answer to Macneil's rhetorical questions depends in part on how often you believe opportunities for efficient breach are still profitable after paying plaintiff's losses *and* all the transaction costs. That is an empirical question, but a very difficult one to answer. Ironically, both sides of the debate face a theoretical dilemma. Economists believe that in reasonably efficient markets, most contracts will produce about the same profit, and that the margin of profit will be small. That suggests very few opportunities for unusually profitable breach. Proponents of the economic approach to law generally think that most markets function efficiently; their critics generally disagree. Thus, Macneil's argument that the debate over efficient breach affects too few cases to bother with should have more appeal to proponents of the economic view than to its critics. But the critics can escape the dilemma more easily: They can argue that there is no reason not to pursue corrective justice if efficiency effects are uncertain.

2.   Macneil accuses the proponents of the economic view of law of using magic words — *property* and *contract* — to explain when profitable violations should be encouraged and when potential violators should be encouraged to buy what they want instead. He argues that there is no distinction between the two except in terms of transaction costs. Most proponents of the economic view of law recognize that, although Macneil wishes they would be more explicit about it. So Macneil's criticism of the economic distinction between property and contract turns on the same point as his criticism of the simple-efficient-breach theory: Everything depends on transaction costs, and there are too many of them to ever take them into account. Are you persuaded?

3.   What do you think of Macneil's suggestion that the transaction costs of negotiating after breach are always greater than the transaction costs of negotiating before breach? Are "efficient" violations of law inherently inefficient?

NOTES ON UNCONSCIONABILITY AND RELATED DEFENSES

1.   Unconscionability was an equitable defense, a defense developed by the chancellors before the merger. It is rooted in the notion that a suit in equity was an appeal to the king's conscience; recall too, that the early chancellors were usually bishops.

The chancellors enforced some equitable defenses at law as well as in equity. For example, fraud was an equitable defense not recognized at law in suits on bonds or other promises under seal. But the debtor could file his own suit in equity and prove the fraud there, and the equity court would enjoin the creditor from suing on the instrument at law, or from enforcing his judgment if he already had one. Just such a case led to a historic clash between law and equity in 1615. Lord Coke, Chief Justice of the King's Bench, attempted to have the debtor's lawyers and the officials of the equity court indicted under a statute originally intended to prevent Roman Catholic ecclesiastical courts from reviewing common law judgments. King James I decided the case himself, relying on a lengthy opinion from his attorney general, Sir Francis Bacon, and permanently established the power of equity to enjoin proceedings at law.

But the chancellors did not take all equitable defenses as seriously as they took fraud. Unconscionability was a defense in equity, a ground for denying specific performance, but it was not a ground for enjoining a suit at law. That tradition is reflected in *Campbell*'s distinction between unconscionable and illegal contracts: The contract is too one-sided to be specifically enforced, but Campbell might be entitled to damages. That rule might have been a reasonable accommodation when law and equity were separate courts fighting for turf. It might even have made sense in

Campbell as a compromise, relegating Campbell to the undercompensatory liquidated damage clause without denying it relief altogether. But does it make any sense in the run of cases? Consider *Campbell* without the liquidated damage clause. Does it make any sense to say the court won't order the Wentzes to sell $90 carrots for $30, but it will levy a $60 damage judgment against them if they refuse? Is one order any harsher than the other? How often do you suppose a court that considered a contract too unconscionable to specifically enforce actually entered a damage judgment?

The UCC codified unconscionability and made it a defense at law as well as in equity in contracts for the sale of goods. §2-302.

2. It is often said that there are other defenses to specific performance that are not defenses to damage actions. Common examples are inadequate consideration, unilateral mistake, and ambiguous terms. Some cases go beyond creating defenses. They put the burden of proof on plaintiff, and emphasize that specific performance is a discretionary remedy. One finds statements such as the following:

> Specific performance will be decreed only if it is clearly established that the contract is just, reasonable, and free from misapprehension or misrepresentation.

Lannon v. Lamps, 80 Ill. App. 3d 318, 324, 399 N.E.2d 712, 716 (1980).

There are plenty of cases on both sides of these propositions. In *Lannon*, the court refused to specifically enforce an option to lease land at an interstate highway interchange for ninety-nine years. The rent was fixed at $200 per acre per year; plaintiffs testified that that was a reasonable rent at the beginning of the five-year option period. Plaintiffs had purchased the option for $10 from two feeble octogenarians. Contrast *Lannon* with Bliss v. Rhodes, 66 Ill. App. 3d 895, 384 N.E.2d 512 (1978), specifically enforcing a contract to sell a farm for less than half its fair market value. The seller was severely depressed and alcoholic when he agreed to the sale. The legal description was inadequate and, to the extent it described anything, erroneous. Both *Lannon* and *Bliss* cited Illinois Supreme Court cases in support of their holdings.

3. Don't all these defenses go to the substance of the contract and not the remedy? Shouldn't they either be defenses or not? Does it make any sense at all to say they preclude specific performance but not damages? What would the damages be in *Lannon*? Might the court be counting on juries not to award those damages?

4. These defenses should be contrasted with defenses that focus on the remedy. For example, it is said that some contracts are too complicated for the court to supervise performance. We will consider that possibility in chapter 9, with other examples of remedies alleged to be impractical.

THOMPSON v. COMMONWEALTH
197 Va. 208, 89 S.E.2d 64 (1955)

SMITH, J., delivered the opinion of the court.

On May 16, 1950 the Commonwealth of Virginia filed this suit against Charles F. Thompson, Marshall F. Thompson and International Roll-Call Corporation, . . . for the purpose of obtaining a decree of specific performance of a contract between the parties dated May 23, 1945, wherein the defendants agreed to "prepare, build, construct, and deliver" certain electrical units for the Commonwealth. This contract was made for the purpose of settling a dispute between the parties arising out of earlier dealings with respect to electrical voting systems installed by Charles F. Thompson for the House of Delegates and the Senate of Virginia in their respective chambers. . . .

The remaining question is whether a court of equity may properly decree specific performance of this contract. In general, equity will grant specific performance of a contract when the remedy at law is inadequate and the nature of the contract is such that specific enforcement of it will not involve too great practical difficulties. Accordingly, contracts for the sale of personal property are not normally enforced specifically because the remedy at law is generally adequate. "While the doctrine is well established that a court of equity will not, in general, decree the specific performance of contracts relating to chattels, yet it will do so where the remedy at law is inadequate to meet all the requirements of a given case, and to do complete justice between the parties." Stuart v. Pennis, 91 Va. 688, 692, 22 S.E. 509, 510. Thus where the chattel which is the subject of the contract is unique or not purchasable in the market, equity will decree specific performance. Indeed, "The modern disposition is to be less technical in the application of this principle, and where a special need on the part of the plaintiff, and at least a temporary monopoly on the part of the defendant, justify its application, the remedy is allowed for breach of contracts for the sale of personal property for which damages might otherwise be adequate." 5 Williston, Contracts, rev. ed., §1419, pp. 3954, 3955. . . .

While the defendants allege in their answer that the Commonwealth "cannot go into the market and purchase" the equipment sued for, in their brief they admit that "any first class machine shop, of which there are several around Richmond, can build the counters and recorders, as well as the defendants can." . . .

Thus the question presented is whether the remedy at law is adequate where the Commonwealth, after receiving a money judgment, must take the responsibility of finding a first class machine shop which could, without original plans and specifications, manufacture the required equipment from an examination of similar equipment items with which it has had no prior experience.

If there were several machine shops experienced in manufacturing electrical voting equipment from which the Commonwealth could in the ordinary course of business order the equipment, then the remedy at law would be adequate and specific performance would not be granted. However, there are no other experienced manufacturers of such equipment as testified to by Marshall F. Thompson as follows: "I do not think there is any other corporation today that builds spare counters and spare recorders for roll call systems except International Roll Call Corporation. . . ." Thus if specific performance were denied, the Commonwealth would have to assume the responsibility and risk which properly belong to defendants. If anyone is to search for a manufacturer it should be defendants and not the Commonwealth.

The defendants contend, however, that "the uncontradicted evidence shows that the chattels which it is sought to force these defendants to build, construct and deliver under a decree of specific enforcement would require the personal attention and labor of two of your defendants for many months and therefore would place them in a position tantamount to involuntary servitude." It is generally true that "courts of equity will not entertain suits to enforce specifically contracts for personal services, or acts involving skill, labor and judgment." 17 Michie's Jur., Specific Performance, §66, p.101. But there is no need to apply that principle here or to determine whether the facts of this case fall under any exceptions to the general rule. Defendants have said that "any first class machine shop . . . can build the counters and recorders." It is unnecessary therefore to compel defendants to render any "personal services or acts involving skill, labor and judgment." If they be so advised, they may avoid personal services by contracting with one of the "first class machine shops" around Richmond or elsewhere to build the counters and recorders which defendants have contracted to deliver to the Commonwealth.

Accordingly, the trial court is directed to modify its decree of Sept. 15, 1954 so as to require the defendants to prepare, build, construct and deliver or cause to be prepared, built, constructed and delivered to the Clerks of the Senate and House of Delegates, the property specified in that decree. As thus modified, the decree is affirmed and the case remanded for such proceedings as may be necessary to carry out the views herein expressed.

Modified and affirmed.

NOTES ON SPECIFIC PERFORMANCE WHERE COVER IS POSSIBLE

1. Could the court have said it is impossible for plaintiff to buy elsewhere because defendant is the only supplier? Would that make the case

just like *Campbell?* Is it a significant extension to say that plaintiff could buy elsewhere but the burden and risk of selecting an alternate supplier justify specific performance? How great must the burden be? Isn't it always a chore to select a seller on a major purchase?

(2)   There has been a spirited academic debate over making specific performance available even when damages could be used to cover. Professor Schwartz argues that damages are generally undercompensatory:

> Although promisees are entitled to incidental damages, such damages are difficult to monetize. They consist primarily of the costs of finding and making a second deal, which generally involve the expenditure of time rather than cash; attaching a dollar value to such opportunity costs is quite difficult. Breach can also cause frustration and anger, especially in a consumer context, but these costs also are not recoverable.

Schwartz, The Case for Specific Performance, 89 Yale L.J. 271, 276 (1979). He thinks it wastes resources to litigate damage issues that specific performance would avoid. Of course, plaintiff could still claim damages resulting from the delay. Are those damage issues any easier to litigate than the damage issues Schwartz would avoid? Perhaps more telling, Schwartz thinks that a request for specific performance proves the inadequacy of damages. If buyer prefers coerced performance, available only after a lawsuit, from a disgruntled promisor who has already breached at least once, to immediate cover and subsequent reimbursement, his need for specific performance must outweigh the cost of delay and the risks of further unsatisfactory performance.

Professor Yorio responds that damages could be made more compensatory, and that compensation isn't the only goal of remedies law anyway; the competing interests of defendants and courts must be considered. Yorio, In Defense of Money Damages for Breach of Contract, 82 Colum. L. Rev. 1365 (1982). He argues that it is generally cheaper for disappointed buyers to cover than for breaching sellers to cover for them, so that damages will generally be a cheaper remedy to administer. Schwartz sees no reason that should be true. If replacement carrots existed in *Campbell,* who was better able to find and buy them? Who was better able to pick a machine shop capable of building roll call voting machines? Isn't any general assumption about comparative cover costs likely to be inaccurate in particular cases? Does the cost of case-by-case litigation justify a general rule, even if the general rule is often mistaken?

3.   Wheelock v. Noonan, 108 N.Y. 179, 15 N.E. 67 (1888), is a famous injunction case with reasoning similar to that in *Thompson.* Plaintiff gave defendant permission to store "a few stones" on plaintiff's land until spring. Id. at 184, 15 N.E. at 68. Defendant covered the land eighteen feet deep with huge boulders and refused to remove them. The court ordered him to do so. It indignantly rejected the argument that plaintiff should remove them himself and sue for the expense; that would "burden" the

owner, "compelling him to do in advance for the trespasser what the latter is bound to do." Id. at 185, 15 N.E. at 68.

FIRST NATIONAL STATE BANK v. COMMONWEALTH FEDERAL SAVINGS & LOAN ASSOCIATION
610 F.2d 164 (3d Cir. 1979)

[Mathema Developers built the Glen Oaks Shopping Mall in Camden County, New Jersey.]

Before ADAMS, ROSSENN and WEIS, Circuit Judges.

ADAMS, Circuit Judge. . . .

I . . .

As with most real estate developments, the financing here was to take place in two stages: a short-term construction loan and a long-term permanent loan. The construction loan was to finance the actual construction of the project and the permanent loan, or mortgage loan, was designed to replace or "take out" any short-term borrowings. A permanent loan is generally obtained from a savings institution or insurance company, while a construction lender usually is a commercial bank. A standby commitment obligates the permanent lender to refinance the construction loan if called upon to do so by the developer, but in addition generally provides the borrower with the option to search for an alternative lender with more advantageous terms. The premium paid for this option is a nonrefundable fee, and the commitment enables a developer to seek short term construction financing. . . .

[Commonwealth Savings made a standby commitment for a $3.5 million permanent loan. First National Bank made a $3.6 million construction loan in reliance on Commonwealth's standby commitment. Mathema assigned the commitment to First National.

The mall was an economic disaster from the beginning. When construction was completed, it was only 25 percent rented; by the time of trial, it was 50 percent rented. Commonwealth refused to make a permanent loan, claiming that its commitment had expired before construction was completed. The court ultimately rejected that defense on the merits.]

When the builder was unable to keep up its loan payments, First National proceeded with foreclosure, and it has operated the shopping mall ever since at a substantial loss. Both Mathema and First National brought suit in the New Jersey state court for specific performance of the loan. Both actions were removed to federal district court and consolidated for trial, but Mathema's claim was dismissed at trial for failure to prosecute.

Following trial, . . . Commonwealth was ordered to perform its obligation under the commitment, to pay interest at eight percent on the amount of the loan from the time the loan should have been made until such the time as the money is turned over to First National, and to reimburse with interest the amount First National has lost in operating the mall. . . .

IV

We come now to what appears to be the most provocative issue on this appeal, namely whether the decree of specific performance was proper. . . .

Traditionally, courts have been reluctant to grant specific performance of agreements to lend or borrow money, inasmuch as money is intrinsically fungible. The more recent cases, however, and especially those involving construction loans, have shown a greater recognition that specific performance may be justified in exceptional circumstances. Scholarly commentary is in general agreement with this trend, at least insofar as the borrower's remedy is concerned.

The district judge . . . found that New Jersey law supported the principle that a contract for the financing of a shopping center is unique, in the sense that the term has been used in cases granting specific performance, because the subject matter itself is "unavailable in similar form." Further, he ascertained that the damages suffered by First National were not susceptible to accurate calculation and that "an award of damages would fail to make plaintiff whole."

In so holding, the trial judge placed principal reliance on Selective Builders, Inc. v. Hudson City Savings Bank, 137 N.J. Super. 500, 349 A.2d 564 (Ch. Div. 1975), a case from a New Jersey trial court with facts strikingly similar to those sub judice. . . . Selective Builders is said to be distinguishable because the developer there had tried without success to secure other mortgage financing, while there is no evidence here that First National made any such effort. But the court in Selective Builders quoted approvingly from a decision of Maryland's highest court that emphasized the futility of seeking alternative mortgage financing for an obviously failed project:

[T]he would be permanent mortgage lender must contemplate that if, at the last minute, it cancels its commitment such action would be disastrous to the borrower; that in such event obtaining a new permanent mortgage loan would be well-nigh impossible, for the reason that whatever brought about the cancellation would in all likelihood prevent another lender from entering the fray. . . .

137 N.J. Super. at 507-08, 349 A.2d at 509 (ellipsis in original) (quoting St.

Paul at Chase Corp. v. Manufacturers Life Ins. Co., 262 Md. 192, 278 A.2d 12, 36 (1971)).

After noting that neither Mathema nor First National had sought to find another lender to fund the project in this case, the trial judge stated that "it is reasonable to infer from the nature of the agreement, and the notable lack of success of this shopping mall, that there is no hope of obtaining similar financing." Since both parties agree that the shopping mall is a financial failure, it would appear paradoxical for Commonwealth to insist that First National should have attempted to persuade some other mortgage lender to take over a bad investment. We therefore reject Commonwealth's assertion that specific performance was improper because First National should have attempted to mitigate its damages by obtaining substitute performance at a higher interest rate.[20]

There is ample evidence in the record to support the district court's conclusion that accurate calculation of damages was impracticable in this case. The basic measure of such damages would be to subtract from the amount of the permanent loan the estimated value of the shopping mall. However, the distinct qualities of such a property preclude a definitive estimate. The trial judge would have been forced to choose among widely disparate appraisals of the value of the mall. For tax purposes the property was appraised at $1,070,000. First National's expert witness testified that at the time of trial the fair market value of the mall was $1,500,000, while Commonwealth's expert gave three valuations, all based on at least a ninety percent occupancy rate. They ranged from $2,500,000 ("pessimistic") through $2,800,000 ("most probable") to $3,500,000 ("optimistic").

If it were necessary, of course, the trial judge could choose a figure among these estimates predicated on his assessment of the witnesses' relative credibility. It is apparent from the difficulty of choosing among the estimates, though, that a decree of specific performance was appropriate because it would "'do more perfect and complete justice.'"[21] Commonwealth, the party breaching the agreement, would then have the burden of owning the shopping mall and would realize the true market value either by operating the mall or selling it.[22] . . .

We recognize that the result in this case will work substantial hardship

---

20. We attach little credibility to the concern that failure to require the borrower to seek substitute performance in this type of case will significantly relax the requirements for specific performance. It will still be in the borrower's self-interest to refinance through alternative lenders if such are available and if alternative financing plus legal damages are truly sufficient compensation.

21. Fleischer v. James Drug Stores, 1 N.J. 138, 146, 62 A.2d 383, 387 (1948) (quoting Wilson v. Northampton & Banbury Junction Ry. Co., L.R. 9 Ch. App. 279, 284 (1874)).

22. That First National would be inclined to default on the loan was recognized in the district court's final judgment, ordering First National to turn over title to the property to Commonwealth Federal.

on Commonwealth, but any alternative would work an equal hardship on
First National inasmuch as neither wants to be in the business of operating a shopping center. Because Commonwealth agreed to be the permanent lender, and because it is the party that breached the commitment,
we cannot say that the trial judge abused his discretion in requiring
Commonwealth to shoulder the burden.

V

Commonwealth's final point on appeal is that the district court erred in
granting incidental damages in addition to specific performance. The
object of a remedy for breach of contract is to make the aggrieved party
whole. When a court decrees specific performance, it should also adjust
the equities to place the parties as far as possible in the same position that
they would have occupied had the agreement been completed on the
prescribed day. If Commonwealth had "taken out" the construction loan
on the prescribed date, First National would have had the benefit of
interest derived from the money paid to it by Commonwealth at that
time. It is equally clear that had the loan come through on time, Commonwealth, rather than First National, would have had to foreclose on
Mathema's debt and would have become the owner of the shopping mall.
Consequently, we cannot say that it was improper for the trial court to
award damages incidental to the breach covering reimbursement for interest and for losses sustained in operating the mall.

The judgment of the district court will be affirmed.

MORE NOTES ON SPECIFIC
PERFORMANCE

1. We have seen before that damages are inadequate if they are too
difficult to measure. *First National* applies that rule in a commercial
context. Are you persuaded? First National's losses aren't like smoke in
the house, or pain and suffering; these losses are suffered directly in
dollars. First National has lost $3.6 million plus interest and gained a
shopping mall. The shopping mall is an offsetting benefit, but how much?
Doesn't the value of the mall depend on predictions about future rental
income? Aren't those predictions especially uncertain in this case, where
the mall is struggling to survive?

On the other hand, why can't First National liquidate its loss by selling
the mall? Wouldn't a good faith sale after diligent search for the highest
bidder settle the question of market value? Even if the only bid were $10?
Might First National have thought it imprudent to sell under the distressed conditions existing before trial? Would an imprudent sale settle

the question of market value? Is the burden of selling a half-empty shopping mall one that defendant should not be able to shift to plaintiff?

Compare Johnson v. Swank, 128 Wis. 68, 107 N.W. 481 (1906), described in more detail infra at 450. Plaintiff was fraudulently induced to give a promissory note for a worthless horse. The issue was whether he could get a decree cancelling the note or could raise fraud only as a defense to a suit on the note. Plaintiff argued that the defensive remedy was inadequate because defendant might not sue on the note for a long time. Plaintiff feared a long period of uncertainty; he also complained that, meanwhile, he had to feed the horse. With respect to the second argument, the court held that he could resell the horse for defendant's account, with notice to defendant. *Johnson* reflects a solicitude for defendant's right to jury trial that is rare in more modern cases.

2.   Won't damages be difficult to measure any time plaintiff expects to lose profits? That argument is strongest when the contract is for a long term. The leading nineteenth century treatise said courts would specifically enforce contracts to sell goods to be delivered and paid for over a period of years. To deny specific performance would compel plaintiff "to sell his profits at a price depending upon a mere guess." J. Pomeroy, A Treatise on the Specific Performance of Contracts §15 at 20 (1879). An expert witness can often do better than guessing, but not always; expert projections based on assumptions are just a fancy way of guessing unless the assumptions are justified. The ultimate question in these cases is how much uncertainty about damages we are willing to tolerate to avoid granting specific performance.

3.   Unfortunately, the long-term contracts in which damages are most uncertain also present the greatest potential burden of supervision if the court orders specific performance. Courts have gradually become more ambitious about what they will supervise. They were enforcing long-term sales contracts in Pomeroy's day. For a time they thought cooperative marketing contracts were too difficult, but then, with some statutory encouragement, courts began to enforce such contracts. Poultry Producers v. Barlow, 189 Cal. 278, 208 P. 93 (1922), illustrates the older view; Fleischer v. James Drug Stores, 1 N.J. 138, 62 A.2d 383 (1948), illustrates the more modern view.

Fleischer had been expelled from an association of independent drug stores that provided cooperative purchasing, advertising, and other services. The court found the damages too hard to measure and the contract easy to supervise. It did not undertake to resolve disputes about how the cooperative should be run; it simply ordered that Fleischer be treated the same as other members. But what if it just happens that Fleischer's orders get delayed, and occasionally lost altogether or filled incorrectly? Does the difficulty of supervision depend on how obstinate and clever defendant is? Should the court balance these risks against the degree of uncertainty in the measure of damage?

Courts are still reluctant to specifically enforce construction contracts, although some courts have done so. The *Fleischer* solution is unavailable; there's no way to reduce a construction contract to an equal protection clause. Still, how does a construction contract compare to the typical structural injunction? We will take a second look at the construction contract problem in chapter 9, when we focus on practicality problems.

4.   *Fleischer* also said that even accurately calculated damages would be inadequate because the "subject matter of the contract . . . has a peculiar and special value to the party demanding performance. . . . Complainant has a right to his business." Id. at 148, 62 A.2d at 388. What does that mean? Is a small business like the right to vote: something no one should be compelled to sell? Is the court assuming plaintiff gets more than profit from his business? What if the court gave him enough in damages to buy a new business? Is every small business unique?

NOTE ON MUTUALITY OF REMEDIES

The mutuality rule flourished briefly in the late nineteenth and early twentieth centuries. Properly called the negative mutuality rule, the rule held that plaintiff could not get specific performance if defendant could not have gotten specific performance had plaintiff been the one to breach the contract. That is, if damages would have been adequate for defendant, plaintiff should be denied specific performance; if plaintiff's performance would have been too difficult to supervise, he must be denied specific performance against defendant. The rule produced absurd opinions with lengthy discussions of hypothetical lawsuits that had not been filed.

The doctrine co-existed with an older doctrine of affirmative mutuality. It held that if defendant could have gotten specific performance had plaintiff been the one to breach, plaintiff could get specific performance even if he did not otherwise qualify for it. The purpose of this rule seems to have been to give the equity court jurisdiction over all real estate contracts.

The existence of two mutuality rules only highlighted the absurdity of the mutuality notion. Both mutuality rules dealt with cases where one party would be entitled to specific performance and one would not. One rule said neither could get specific performance; the other said both could get it. In combination, they made plaintiff's remedy completely dependent on defendant's hypothetical remedy in a hypothetical lawsuit. Understandably, few judges ever referred to both doctrines in the same opinion.

Today, both doctrines are substantially dead. What remains is the notion that a court should not order defendant to perform if it will not be able to assure that plaintiff will perform in return. In Judge Cardozo's famous formulation:

> What equity exacts today as a condition of relief is the assurance that the decree, if rendered, will operate without injustice or oppression either to plaintiff or to defendant. Mutuality of remedy is important in so far only as its presence is essential to the attainment of that end.

Epstein v. Gluckin, 233 N.Y. 490, 494, 135 N.E. 861, 862 (1922).

Where plaintiff's performance is prior to or simultaneous with defendant's, there is almost never a mutuality problem. The issue arises when plaintiff is to perform long after defendant. Consider Thompson v. Commonwealth, where defendant said it would take two years to build the roll call voting machines. Suppose the price were $500,000, payable on delivery. If plaintiff were a private citizen, and not the Commonwealth of Virginia, defendants might spend $450,000 building the machines and then discover that plaintiff had become insolvent. It probably would have been much cheaper to pay damages and not spend any money building machines. The court can avoid this risk by denying specific performance, or by granting specific performance on condition that plaintiff post bond or pay in installments as the work progresses. Such a condition would be appropriate in *Thompson* itself if Virginia would be free to renege and claim immunity from Thompson's claim to reimbursement.

Even when defendant cannot get performance in return, he may be ordered to perform where the rights of third parties are affected. In *First National*, it is clear that no one is ever going to repay the loan that Commonwealth is forced to make. But it is equally clear that the contract allocated to Commonwealth the risk that the developer would complete construction and then be unable to repay the permanent loan. A damage remedy would impose that loss on Commonwealth, and except for the possibility that damages will be erroneously assessed, specific performance leaves it in the same position.

AMERICAN BROADCASTING COMPANIES
v. WOLF
52 N.Y.2d 394, 420 N.E.2d 363 (1981)

[Warner Wolf was a colorful and well-known sportscaster for ABC. His contract ran until March 4, 1980. He agreed to negotiate in good faith for an extension. He also agreed not to accept a competing offer in the first ninety days after March 4 without first giving ABC a chance to match it. He agreed to stay at ABC if it matched the competing offer. This clause is called a right-of-first-refusal clause.

On February 4 Wolf signed a contract with CBS. ABC sued, seeking specific performance of the right-of-first-refusal clause and an injunction against Wolf broadcasting for CBS. The court held that Wolf violated the good faith negotiation clause. It held that he did not violate the right-of-first-refusal clause, because he signed with CBS before the beginning of the ninety-day period.]

COOKE, Chief Judge. . . .

III

A

Courts of equity historically have refused to order an individual to perform a contract. Originally this rule evolved because of the inherent difficulties courts would encounter in supervising the performance of uniquely personal efforts. For practical, policy and constitutional reasons, therefore, courts continue to decline to affirmatively enforce employment contracts. During the Civil War era, there emerged a more compelling reason for not directing the performance of personal services: the Thirteenth Amendment's prohibition of involuntary servitude. It has been strongly suggested that judicial compulsion of services would violate the express command of that amendment.

Over the years, however, in certain narrowly tailored situations, the law fashioned other remedies for failure to perform an employment agreement. Thus, where an employee refuses to render services to an employer in violation of an existing contract, and the services are unique or extraordinary, an injunction may issue to prevent the employee from furnishing those services to another person for the duration of the contract. Such "negative enforcement" was initially available only when the employee had expressly stipulated not to compete with the employer for the term of the engagement. Later cases permitted injunctive relief where the circumstances justified implication of a negative covenant. In these situations, an injunction is warranted because the employee either expressly or by clear implication agreed not to work elsewhere for the period of his contract. And, since the services must be unique before negative enforcement will be granted, irreparable harm will befall the employer should the employee be permitted to labor for a competitor.

B

After a personal service contract terminates, the availability of equitable relief against the former employee diminishes appreciably. Since the period of service has expired, it is impossible to decree affirmative or negative specific performance. Only if the employee has expressly agreed not to compete with the employer following the term of the contract, or is threatening to disclose trade secrets or commit another tortious act, is injunctive relief generally available at the behest of the employer. Even where there is an express anticompetitive covenant, however, it will be rigorously examined and specifically enforced only if it satisfies certain established requirements. Indeed, a court normally will not decree specific enforcement of an employee's anticompetitive covenant unless necessary to protect the trade secrets, customer lists or good will of the employer's business, or perhaps when the employer is exposed to special harm because of the unique nature of the employee's services. And, an otherwise valid covenant will not be enforced if it is unreasonable in time, space or scope or would operate in a harsh or oppressive manner. There is, in short, general judicial disfavor of anticompetitive covenants contained in employment contracts.

Underlying the strict approach to enforcement of these covenants is the notion that, once the term of an employment agreement has expired, the general public policy favoring robust and uninhibited competition should not give way merely because a particular employer wishes to insulate himself from competition. Important, too, are the "powerful considerations of public policy which militate against sanctioning the loss of a man's livelihood." At the same time, the employer is entitled to protection from unfair or illegal conduct that causes economic injury. The rules governing enforcement of anticompetitive covenants and the availability of equitable relief after termination of employment are designed to foster these interests of the employer without impairing the employee's ability to earn a living or the general competitive mold of society.

C

Specific enforcement of personal service contracts thus turns initially upon whether the term of employment has expired. If the employee refuses to perform during the period of employment, was furnishing unique services, has expressly or by clear implication agreed not to compete for the duration of the contract and the employer is exposed to irreparable injury, it may be appropriate to restrain the employee from competing until the agreement expires. Once the employment contract has terminated, by contrast, equitable relief is potentially available only to prevent injury from unfair competition or similar tortious behavior or to enforce an express and valid anticompetitive covenant. In the absence of such circumstances, the general policy of unfettered competition should prevail.

IV

Applying these principles, it is apparent that ABC's request for injunctive relief must fail. There is no existing employment agreement between the parties; the original contract terminated in March, 1980. Thus, the negative enforcement that might be appropriate during the term of employment is unwarranted here. Nor is there an express anticompetitive covenant that defendant Wolf is violating, or any claim of special injury from tortious conduct such as exploitation of trade secrets. In short, ABC seeks to premise equitable relief after termination of the employment upon a simple, albeit serious, breach of a general contract negotiation clause. To grant an injunction in that situation would be to unduly interfere with an individual's livelihood and to inhibit free competition where there is no corresponding injury to the employer other than the loss of a competitive edge. Indeed, if relief were granted here, any breach of an employment contract provision relating to renewal negotiations logically would serve as the basis for an open-ended restraint upon the employee's ability to earn a living should he ultimately choose not to extend his employment. Our public policy, which favors the free exchange of goods and services through established market mechanisms, dictates otherwise.

Equally unavailing is ABC's request that the court create a noncompetitive covenant by implication. Although in a proper case an implied-in-fact covenant not to compete for the term of employment may be found to exist, anticompetitive covenants covering the postemployment period will not be implied. Indeed, even an express covenant will be scrutinized and enforced only in accordance with established principles.

This is not to say that ABC has not been damaged in some fashion or that Wolf should escape responsibility for the breach of his good-faith negotiation obligation. Rather, we merely conclude that ABC is not entitled to equitable relief. Because of the unique circumstances presented, however, this decision is without prejudice to ABC's right to pursue relief in the form of monetary damages, if it be so advised. . . .

[Judge FUCHSBERG dissented on the ground that the contract clearly contemplated that Wolf would not sign with a competitor before his contract with ABC had expired; allowing him to do so made the ninety day right-of-first-refusal useless. He agreed that the remedy ABC sought was too harsh. He would have enjoined Wolf from broadcasting for ninety days. He reasoned that the ninety day right-of-first-refusal was intended to keep Wolf off the air for ninety days if he changed networks, so that ABC could accustom viewers to his replacement.]

NOTES ON PERSONAL SERVICE CONTRACTS

1. What would the measure of damages be in ABC v. Wolf? Could ABC show that its ratings dropped six points after Wolf left, and recover

the resulting loss in advertising revenues? Isn't that likely to be a huge sum? In Lemat Corp. v. Barry, 80 Cal. Rptr. 240 (Cal. App. 1969), the trial court found that the loss of basketball star Rick Barry cost the San Francisco Warriors $365,000 the first year. The court compared that year's average increase in attendance at National Basketball Association games with the substantial decline in attendance suffered by the Warriors.

2.   Which remedy is a greater intrusion on the employee's liberty? Would Wolf rather work for ABC and keep his paycheck? Or work for CBS and turn most of his money over to ABC? Are you convinced that specific performance of personal service contracts holds employees in involuntary servitude but threatening them with huge damage judgments does not? And even if we prefer not to make people work against their will, do these cases really have anything to do with the thirteenth amendment? Warner Wolf voluntarily signed a contract; slaves never had that choice.

3.   The history of debt peonage casts light on these issues. Employers have found ways to hold workers to permanent labor by contract almost as effectively as slave owners held them by status. The employer loaned money or sold goods on credit in exchange for a promise to repay the loan with labor or through wage withholding. If wages were low relative to prices, the employee could never get out of debt and never end his obligation to work for the employer. States enforced such contracts with criminal penalties. The system flourished among the Spanish population in the southwest, and it flourished in the southeast after the Civil War. Congress was also aware that long-term apprenticeships had replaced slavery in the West Indies, with little benefit to the former slaves. The phrase "involuntary servitude" was intended to make clear that all these arrangements were banned along with formal slavery. Pursuant to its power to enforce the thirteenth amendment by appropriate legislation, Congress enacted criminal statutes prohibiting peonage. The surviving statute is now codified at 18 U.S.C. §1581 (1982).

The Supreme Court invalidated criminal punishment for workers who quit their jobs without paying debts to their employers. Bailey v. Alabama, 219 U.S. 219 (1911). The majority had no doubt that labor coerced by threat of criminal punishment was involuntary, even though the employee had voluntarily promised to perform that very labor. The majority also had no doubt that the employee could be held liable for contract damages without violating either the constitution or the peonage laws. Justice Holmes dissented. He rejected the distinction between damages and criminal punishment; both tended to coerce performance.

> I do not blink the fact that the liability to imprisonment may work as a motive when a fine without it would not, and that it may induce the laborer to keep on when he would like to leave. But it does not strike me as an objection to a law that it is effective. If the contract is one that ought not to be made, prohibit it.

> But if it is a perfectly fair and proper contract, I can see no reason why the
> state should not throw its weight on the side of performance.

Id. at 247. He defined peonage as forcing employees to work by "bodily
compulsion" inflicted by a "private master." Id. at 246, 247. The majority
considered the criminal law a more powerful compulsion than any private guard.

The congressional intent to ban debt peonage surely justifies the majority's conclusion that labor coerced by criminal punishment is involuntary. But what about its approval of damage liability? Is Holmes right
when he says the two sanctions are indistinguishable? Or is it dispositive
that criminal punishment had been widely used to create a system that
was like slavery in practice, and that damage judgments had not been so
used? That a debtor with no assets and no prospect of acquiring any is
largely unaffected by a damage judgment? That the damage judgment
could be discharged in bankruptcy? Does it matter that discharge in bankruptcy had not existed for much of the nineteenth century and that its
permanence was not yet established in 1910? That there are recurring
proposals in Congress to repeal the discharge for debtors who could make
partial payments out of future income?

4.   Specific performance has always been put on the criminal punishment side of the line drawn in *Bailey*, because the specific performance
decree can be enforced by punishment for criminal contempt. But does
Warner Wolf have anything else in common with Alonzo Bailey? ABC
wanted to make Wolf work for $450,000 per year. Is Wolf's plight enough
like slavery to involve the language or policies of the thirteenth amendment?

5.   The coercive effect of damage judgments for breach of employment contracts may be more theoretical than real. It is very difficult to
find cases granting or denying such damages. In Lemat Corp. v. Barry the
damages calculated were not actually awarded. The court had enjoined
Barry from playing for the rival Oakland Oaks, and he had sat out the
season. The court said that was a complete remedy and damages would
be double relief. That reasoning is surely wrong. The injunction did not
make Barry perform his obligation to play for the Warriors, and the trial
court found that if he had played for the Oaks, the Warrior's losses would
have been even greater. The court also said that the damages might be
too uncertain and speculative. Would they be too uncertain if the court
weren't so reluctant to enforce personal service contracts against employees? For whatever reason, employers do not file many damage actions
against breaching employees.

6.   Thompson v. Commonwealth rejected the involuntary servitude
argument on the ground that defendants could delegate the work to
someone else. But the court had already said that finding someone else
would be difficult; searching for someone else was a form of personal

service. With the possible exception of a contract to sell finished goods that the buyer will pick up, any contract requires some personal service. Should all specific performance decrees and all affirmative injunctions be forbidden, at least against individuals? Or does the involuntary servitude problem arise only when the contract is "primarily" for personal service? Or when defendant is an employee and not an independent contractor?

7. *Wolf* also notes the difficulty of supervising personal service contracts. Difficulty of supervision was once thought to be a reason not to specifically enforce personal service contracts against employers or employees. But the equivalent of specific performance against employers is now routine; reinstatement is the standard remedy for employees discharged in violation of the labor laws and employment discrimination laws. Supervision problems have been negligible. But most of the cases involve typical employees doing routine jobs. Might supervision be more difficult if the employee is sufficiently unique that the employer can plausibly claim he is irreplaceable? The courts have worried that they can't tell if performers are giving their best effort. Is it enough to rely on the employee's incentive to do his best if he performs at all? Would a Warner Wolf or a Rick Barry jeopardize his future income by deliberately having a mediocre season?

C. PRELIMINARY RELIEF

LOS ANGELES MEMORIAL COLISEUM COMMISSION v. NATIONAL FOOTBALL LEAGUE
634 F.2d 1197 (9th Cir. 1980)

Before WALLACE and POOLE, Circuit Judges, and MACBRIDE, Senior District Judge.

POOLE, Circuit Judge.

The National Football League (NFL) and certain of its members appeal from a preliminary injunction which restrained them from applying section 4.3 of the League's Constitution and Bylaws to a proposed transfer by the Oakland Raiders Ltd., football team (Raiders) of their home game playing site from Oakland to the Los Angeles Memorial Coliseum (the Coliseum). Suit was filed by the appellee, the Los Angeles Memorial Coliseum Commission (Commission), seeking an adjudication that by adopting and enforcing section 4.3 the League and its members had violated the antitrust laws of the United States and asking that the defendants be enjoined from applying that rule. The district court granted a preliminary injunction prohibiting the League from invoking section 4.3 to prevent transfer of an NFL franchise to Los Angeles. . . .

Legal Standards for Granting and Reviewing the Preliminary Injunction

We deem it important to emphasize at the outset in this highly publicized dispute that we are reviewing the grant of a *preliminary injunction*, not a final decision on the merits. We start with the general principle that an order issuing or denying a preliminary injunction will normally be reversed only if the lower court abused its discretion or based its decision upon erroneous legal premises. William Inglis & Sons Baking Co. v. ITT Continental Baking Co., 526 F.2d 86 (9th Cir. 1975).

Under the Clayton Act which is involved here injunctive relief is provided under the same conditions and principles as such relief is granted generally by courts of equity. A fundamental principle applied in such courts is that the basic function of a preliminary injunction is to preserve the *status quo ante litem* pending a determination of the action on the merits. The traditional equitable criteria for granting preliminary injunctive relief are (1) a strong likelihood of success on the merits, (2) the possibility of irreparable injury to plaintiff if the preliminary relief is not granted, (3) a balance of hardships favoring the plaintiff, and (4) advancement of the public interest (in certain cases). In this circuit, the moving party may meet its burden by demonstrating either (1) a combination of probable success on the merits and the possibility of irreparable injury or (2) that serious questions are raised and the balance of hardships tips sharply in its favor. These are not separate tests, but the outer reaches "of a single continuum." Benda v. Grand Lodge of Machinists, 584 F.2d 308, 315 (9th Cir. 1978), *cert. dismissed*, 441 U.S. 937 (1979).

The district court concluded that the plaintiff was unlikely to show that the balance of hardships tipped sharply in its favor, and it therefore rested its grant of preliminary injunction on a finding that plaintiff qualified for relief under the first half of this alternate formulation. We conclude that the court erred in issuing a preliminary injunction because there was no showing of irreparable injury. . . .

Irreparable Injury

[The court first held that the Coliseum had shown no threat of injury because it had not shown that the NFL owners would in fact deny permission to move the Raiders to Los Angeles.]

Even if some significant threat of injury be hypothesized, it was neither found nor shown to be *irreparable*. The basis of injunctive relief in the federal courts is irreparable harm and inadequacy of legal remedies. The district court specifically stated that the reason plaintiff had demonstrated the requisite possibility of irreparable injury was:

> because the managing partner of the Raiders has indicated both that his club desires to play its home games in Los Angeles, and that the only significant

obstacle to reaching an agreement with the Coliseum is the possible invocation of section 4.3.

The court identified "the alleged injury to the Coliseum in the absence of
an injunction" as "lost revenues due to its failure to acquire an NFL
team." It is well established, however, that such monetary injury is not
normally considered irreparable. . . . The Coliseum's lost revenues
would be compensable by a damage award should the Commission ultimately prevail on the merits. The district court, therefore, proceeded
upon the further erroneous legal premise that the type of injury it identified was irreparable and abused its discretion in improperly granting a
preliminary injunction on the basis of such threatened injury.
   Other than the threat of lost revenues, the plaintiff did not demonstrate any threat of harm that would have supported a finding of irreparable injury. The amended complaint alleged that without injunctive relief,
the Commission would suffer "a diminution of revenues, a diminution of
the market value of plaintiff's property and the loss of substantial goodwill
normally attached to a profitable enterprise." In support of its motion the
Commission argued that without a preliminary injunction it would be
unable to enter into a lease agreement, begin stadium renovations, obtain
financing for the renovations, or respond to the Raiders' alleged demand
for a nonrefundable advance payment to cover transfer expenses. All of
these are but monetary injuries which could be remedied by a damage
award. The Commission also claimed that it would lose its only opportunity to obtain a professional football tenant, since the Raiders were the
only team not already committed by long-term leases and would have to
enter into another long-term lease in Oakland if not allowed to move to
Los Angeles. There was, however, no factual showing that the Raiders
would indeed be forced into a long-term commitment in Oakland or that
the Coliseum would be unable in the near future to obtain another transfer team or new franchise as a tenant. Nor did the Commission contend
or show that loss of the Raiders as a tenant threatened to put it or the
Coliseum out of business. It was undisputed that the Coliseum continues
to have strong football attractions including the teams of the University
of Southern California and the University of California, Los Angeles.
The plaintiff simply did not make the requisite showing of irreparable
harm.

Balancing Hardships

The district court not only failed to identify the essential of irreparable
injury to plaintiff, but also failed to identify the harms which a preliminary injunction might cause to defendants and to weigh these against
plaintiff's threatened injury. In its only finding on the balance of hardships, the court stated:

plaintiff is required to show that the balance of hardships tips sharply in its favor. Such a showing seems unlikely in this case since the alleged injury to the Coliseum in the absence of an injunction, i.e., lost revenues due to its failure to acquire an NFL team, is nearly evenly balanced by the financial injury that granting the injunction could cause to a *third* party, the Oakland Coliseum, due to its possible loss of the Raiders. (Emphasis added.)

Whatever may be the rationale of balancing the injury of a third party against plaintiff's, the court could have reached no balance of harms favoring the Commission without considering the potential injury to the NFL and its members. This it did not do.

Traditional standards for granting a preliminary injunction impose a duty on the court to balance the interests of all parties and weigh the damage to each, mindful of the moving party's burden to show the possibility of irreparable injury to itself and the probability of success on the merits. *Inglis* clarified and added flexibility to understanding the burden carried by the moving party; it did not eliminate the requirement that some balance of hardships favoring that party be established by the record.

Under the continuum or sliding scale articulated in *Benda* a minimal showing on the merits is required even when the balance of harms tips decidedly toward the moving party. Conversely, at least a minimal tip in the balance of hardships must be found even when the strongest showing on the merits is made. Here a preliminary injunction was granted "[a]lthough the court consider[ed] the question [on the merits] to be close," and without finding a balance of harms favoring plaintiff. Such a combination is clearly insufficient under *Benda.* . . .

Reversed.

WALLACE, Circuit Judge, concurring in result. . . .

Because failure to show irreparable injury is a clear and sufficient ground for reversal, I would not reach the other issues addressed by the majority.

NOTES ON PRELIMINARY INJUNCTIONS

1. Suppose that after trial the court decides that the NFL violates the antitrust laws when it prevents the Raiders from moving to Los Angeles. Would it deny a permanent injunction, leave the Raiders in Oakland, and compensate the Coliseum's losses in money? Or would it say that the injury is irreparable because money can't buy another football team? Or that the revenue losses are too difficult to predict?

2. If loss of the Raiders would be irreparable after trial, why isn't it irreparable before trial? No amount of damages will buy a football team

for the season or more between the preliminary injunction hearing and the trial. Is it just that consequential damages for one season are easier to measure than consequential damages for the indefinite future? Or is the court applying a higher standard of irreparability because it doesn't yet know whether the NFL has done anything unlawful? Is there any basis for deciding whether Oakland or Los Angeles should go without pro football for a year, short of at least tentatively deciding the underlying dispute?

3.   *Coliseum* lists four "traditional equitable criteria" for granting preliminary relief. Some opinions tend to treat these criteria as four separate requirements. But the balancing test set out in *Coliseum* has very early roots, and the recent cases overwhelmingly apply some variation of it.

The Supreme Court applied a balancing test in Ohio Oil Co. v. Conway, 279 U.S. 813, 815 (1929). The trial court had refused a preliminary injunction against collection of a new oil severance tax. The Supreme Court reversed without predicting success on the merits. It found that a "real dispute" existed over the constitutionality of the tax that could not be resolved without trial, that any taxes paid pending trial could never be recovered because of the state's sovereign immunity, and that the state's interest in eventually collecting the tax if it were upheld could be protected by requiring plaintiff to post bond sufficient to cover all taxes likely to accrue before trial.

But dicta in more recent cases are ambivalent. A plurality appears to have endorsed a balancing test in Atchison, Topeka, & Santa Fe Railway v. Wichita Board of Trade, 412 U.S. 800, 822 n.15 (1973). But two more recent cases seem to say that plaintiff must separately prove likelihood of success and irreparable injury. Doran v. Salem Inn, 422 U.S. 922, 931 (1975); Sampson v. Murray, 415 U.S. 61, 90 n.63 (1974) (reprinted infra at 410). The choice between separate requirements and considerations to be balanced did not affect the result in any of the three cases from the seventies, and none of the three opinions focused on this issue.

4.   Won't the Court ultimately have to approve some version of the balancing approach now prevalent in the courts of appeals? Suppose the Camden Lumber Co. threatens to cut down all the trees around Pardee's personally designed custom-built vacation home. Shouldn't the court issue a preliminary injunction if Pardee has any chance of success at all? Doesn't Pardee have some chance of success until the court has reached final judgment? Wasn't Ohio Oil Co. v. Conway an equally clear case?

5.   Professor Leubsdorf has offered the most precise formulation of the balancing standard.

the preliminary injunction standard should aim to minimize the probable irreparable loss of rights caused by errors incident to hasty decision. . . . The court, in theory, should assess the probable irreparable loss of rights an injunction would cause by multiplying the probability that the defendant will prevail by the amount of the irreparable loss that the defendant would suffer if enjoined from exercising what turns out to be his legal right. It should then make a similar calculation of the probable irreparable loss of rights to the plaintiff from denying the injunction [multiplying plaintiff's probability of success by the irreparable loss plaintiff would suffer without the injunction].

Leubsdorf, The Standard for Preliminary Injunctions, 91 Harv. L. Rev. 525, 540-542 (1978). Why is this only right "in theory"? Is it because irreparable loss is inherently difficult to measure in dollars? And how do you quantify the probability of success? Leubsdorf claims only to offer an analytic framework; he does not envision much actual multiplication.

LAKESHORE HILLS v. ADCOX
90 Ill. App. 3d 609, 413 N.E.2d 548 (1980)

CRAVEN, Justice.

The defendant brings this interlocutory appeal from the trial court's grant of a preliminary injunction compelling him to remove a pet, a 12-year-old, 575-pound Canadian black bear, from his property — a lot in the subdivision. The plaintiff, a corporation, sold the subdivision lot to the defendant; persons who buy lots become shareholders in the corporation and are obligated to follow recorded restrictive covenants.

When the defendant bought his lot during the summer of 1979, convenant 12(a) permitted residents to keep on their property only household pets not raised for commercial purposes; the covenant did not define "household pets." At a shareholders' meeting held in February 1980, this covenant was amended to specifically exclude from the category of "household pets" bears, as well as certain other animals, such as lions and pythons, "usually found caged in a professional zoo." In April 1980, the plaintiff sued to enjoin the bear's continued presence in the subdivision. . . .

[T]he other residents are sharply divided in their feelings toward the bear; the defendant's immediate neighbors have no fear of the animal, but others are afraid of him. The bear is kept in a cage within a cage. The defendant, an experienced animal-keeper, testified that his pet is quite gentle — he is a fifth-generation captive — and bears no animosity toward humans, including young children. . . .

McCormick v. Empire Accounts Service, Inc. (1977), sets forth the conditions for granting a preliminary injunction; the party seeking the injunction must prove by a preponderance of the evidence four points:

(i) that he has no adequate remedy at law and will be irreparably injured if the injunction is not granted; (ii) that the threatened injury to him will be immediate, certain and great if the injunction is denied while the loss or inconvenience to the opposing party will be comparatively small and insignificant if it is granted; (iii) that he has a reasonable likelihood of prevailing on the merits of the case; and (iv) that granting the preliminary injunction will not have an injurious effect upon the general public.

49 Ill. App. 3d 415, 417.

(1)   The plaintiff here has no adequate legal remedy; monetary damages will not prevent the harm that the plaintiff fears. Although denial of the injunction would not necessarily have led to irreparable injury, the trial court correctly concluded that the better course was to enjoin the keeping of the bear and not risk the harm.

(2)   The threat of harm outweighs the inconvenience to the defendant. . . .

(3)   . . . Although only the amended version of covenant 12(a) expressly excludes bears, the limitation in the original version to "household pets" is also narrow enough to exclude them. The plaintiff is reasonably likely to prevail in seeking a permanent injunction.

(4)   Granting the preliminary injunction did not harm the general public but rather was designed to protect the public.

The injunction here altered rather than preserved the status quo. However, this does not require reversal. The trial court simply acknowledged that it is contrary to the nature of people to live with or in the immediate vicinity of bears. It is likewise contrary to the nature of bears to live in a cage in a yard busy with the incidents of suburban life. The injunction seeks to recognize the normal propensities of each. The bear, named Yogi, lacks claws, fangs, and is a fifth-generation captive. Yet Yogi is a bear and not a domestic household animal. The injunction is affirmed. . . .

TRAPP, P.J., and WEBBER, J., concur.

NOTES ON PRESERVING THE STATUS QUO

1.   Recall the statement in Coliseum Commission v. NFL that "the basic function of a preliminary injunction is to preserve the status quo." Indeed, it is often said that a preliminary injunction cannot change the status quo. The "rule" has shown remarkable hardiness despite repeated criticism. But *Lakeshore Hills* is not the only case to squarely reject it.

2.   What is the status quo when the parties are engaged in continuous activity? Consider Rees v. Panhandle Eastern Pipe Line Co., 176 Ind. App. 597, 377 N.E.2d 640 (1978), in which the pipeline company was

clearing trees and brush to widen its right-of-way on Rees's land, and Rees was threatening violence if the company continued. The trial court preliminarily enjoined Rees from interfering; it thought the status quo was that the company was at work. The appellate court disagreed; it thought the status quo was that some of the trees were still standing. The appellate court affirmed the preliminary injunction in *Rees* despite its definition of the status quo. It found an imminent risk of irreparable harm from gas leaks if the right of way could not be cleared to permit aerial inspection. It held that this risk justified a preliminary injunction that changed the status quo.

3. Can there ever be a status quo of activity? What about City of Chicago v. Festival Theatre, supra at 354? Would a preliminary injunction prohibiting real or simulated sex acts on stage preserve the status quo by preventing the further infliction of nuisance? Or is the status quo one of daily shows?

4. In *Festival Theatre*, does it matter how long the shows had been going on before the city complained? Assuming we know what the status quo is, shouldn't courts be less inclined to disturb a long-established status quo than a recently created one? Can potential defendants make themselves immune to preliminary injunctions by wrongfully changing the status quo before plaintiff can sue? Courts have responded to that risk by redefining the status quo to be preserved: It is the last peaceable uncontested status quo that counts. Otherwise, the court said in Rees v. Panhandle Pipe Line, the right to a preliminary injunction would depend on whether "the disputed or wrongful conduct is discovered in the contemplative or preparatory stage." 176 Ind. App. at 605, 377 N.E.2d at 646.

5. The last peaceable uncontested status quo is a concept subject to manipulation. In DeNoie v. Board of Regents, 609 S.W.2d 601 (Tex. Civ. App. 1980), the court used that concept to affirm a preliminary injunction against selling sandwiches on a street corner in the middle of a university campus. Defendants had sold sandwiches there for four years before the university complained and for nine years before it filed suit. But the court said the last uncontested status quo was defendants not selling sandwiches. Defendants were trespassers, and "status quo can never be a course of conduct which is a prima facie violation of law." Id. at 603. Was the court defining the status quo or deciding that plaintiff had a strong probability of success on the merits? How could it know defendants were trespassers without deciding the merits?

6. Isn't the question what condition the court should maintain pending final judgment? Shouldn't that depend on the probability of success, balance of irreparable injury, and public interest? Can any variation of the status quo test add anything useful? If not, why does the test persist? As a practical matter, isn't it unlikely that a peaceable uncontested status quo will inflict much irreparable injury? Does that make the status quo a

good guide to the irreparable injury issue? Or does it just prove that talk about the status quo will be harmless error except in unusual cases?

7.   A variation of the status quo rule is that a preliminary injunction should not give plaintiff all the relief he would receive after a full trial. This rule seems to be no more observed than the status quo rule. As Professor Leubsdorf asks, "Why is it worse to enjoin tomorrow's parade when that is the only relief plaintiff seeks than it is to enjoin tomorrow's parade when the plaintiff wants to enjoin next month's parade as well?" Leubsdorf, The Standard for Preliminary Injunctions, 91 Harv. L. Rev. 525, 545-546 (1978). Is it a sufficient answer that tomorrow's parade is less important if it is one of a series of similar parades? That there can be a fuller hearing before next month's parade but that hearing will never be held if the dispute relates only to tomorrow's parade? Is the lack of opportunity for further hearing relevant to the scope of the hearing that should be held today? Shouldn't the court explicitly recognize that it is deciding the merits, and not merely the plaintiff's probability of ultimate success? Wouldn't it be more accurate to call the hearing an emergency or accelerated trial, and not a preliminary injunction hearing? Whatever you call it, isn't it clear that injunctions disposing of the entire case sometimes have to be issued after very limited hearings?

8.   Recall the argument in *Coliseum* that the Raiders were about to be forced into another long-term lease at Oakland. Suppose they were. Would they have to move to Los Angeles to avoid that? Why not enjoin the city and the team from signing any lease longer than a year? Wouldn't that preserve the status quo and avoid granting the full relief sought in a preliminary injunction? Do we need those rules to reach that result? Should the real principle be not to do more than necessary to minimize the risk of irreparable harm pending trial?

CARROLL v. PRESIDENT OF PRINCESS ANNE
393 U.S. 175 (1968)

MR. JUSTICE FORTAS delivered the opinion of the Court.

Petitioners are identified with a "white supremacist" organization called the National States Rights Party. They held a public assembly or rally near the courthouse steps in the town of Princess Anne, the county seat of Somerset County, Maryland, in the evening of August 6, 1966. The authorities did not attempt to interfere with the rally. Because of the tense atmosphere which developed as the meeting progressed, about 60 state policemen were brought in, including some from a nearby county. They were held in readiness, but for tactical reasons only a few were in evidence at the scene of the rally.

Petitioners' speeches, amplified by a public address system so that they could be heard for several blocks, were aggressively and militantly racist. Their target was primarily Negroes and, secondarily, Jews. It is sufficient to observe with the court below, that the speakers engaged in deliberately derogatory, insulting, and threatening language, scarcely disguised by protestations of peaceful purposes; and that listeners might well have construed their words as both a provocation to the Negroes in the crowd and an incitement to the whites. The rally continued for something more than an hour, concluding at about 8:25 P.M. The crowd listening to the speeches increased from about 50 at the beginning to about 150, of whom 25% were Negroes.

In the course of the proceedings it was announced that the rally would be resumed the following night, August 7.

On that day, the respondents, officials of Princess Anne and of Somerset County, applied for and obtained a restraining order from the Circuit Court for Somerset County. The proceedings were ex parte, no notice being given to petitioners and, so far as appears, no effort being made informally to communicate with them, although this is expressly contemplated under Maryland procedure. The order restrained petitioners for 10 days from holding rallies or meetings in the county "which will tend to disturb and endanger the citizens of the County." As a result, the rally scheduled for August 7 was not held. After the trial which took place 10 days later, an injunction was issued by the Circuit Court on August 30, in effect extending the restraint for 10 additional months. The court had before it, in addition to the testimony of witnesses, tape recordings made by the police of the August 6 rally.

On appeal, the Maryland Court of Appeals affirmed the 10-day order, but reversed the 10-month order on the ground that "the period of time was unreasonable and that it was arbitrary to assume that a clear and present danger of civil disturbance and riot would persist for ten months.". . .

We agree with petitioners that the case is not moot. . . .

In Southern Pacific Terminal Co. v. ICC, 219 U.S. 498 (1911), this Court declined to hold that the case was moot although the two-year cease-and-desist order at issue had expired. It said: "The questions involved in the orders of the Interstate Commerce Commission are usually continuing . . . and their consideration ought not to be, as they might be, defeated, by short term orders, capable of repetition, yet evading review. . . ." Id., at 515.

These principles are applicable to the present case. The underlying question persists and is agitated by the continuing activities and program of petitioners: whether, by what processes, and to what extent the authorities of the local governments may restrict petitioners in their rallies and public meetings.

This conclusion — that the question is not moot and ought to be adjudicated by this Court — is particularly appropriate in view of this Court's decision in Walker v. Birmingham, 388 U.S. 307 (1967). In that case, the Court held that demonstrators who had proceeded with their protest march in face of the prohibition of an injunctive order against such a march, could not defend contempt charges by asserting the unconstitutionality of the injunction. The proper procedure, it was held, was to seek judicial review of the injunction and not to disobey it, no matter how well-founded their doubts might be as to its validity. Petitioners have here pursued the course indicated by Walker; and in view of the continuing vitality of petitioners' grievance, we cannot say that their case is moot. . . .

We need not decide the thorny problem of whether, on the facts of this case, an injunction against the announced rally could be justified. The 10-day order here must be set aside because of a basic infirmity in the procedure by which it was obtained. It was issued ex parte, without notice to petitioners and without any effort, however informal, to invite or permit their participation in the proceedings. There is a place in our jurisprudence for ex parte issuance, without notice, of temporary restraining orders of short duration; but there is no place within the area of basic freedoms guaranteed by the First Amendment for such orders where no showing is made that it is impossible to serve or to notify the opposing parties and to give them an opportunity to participate. . . .

The Court has emphasized that "[a] system of prior restraints of expression comes to this Court bearing a heavy presumption against its constitutional validity." Bantam Books v. Sullivan, 372 U.S. 58, 70 (1963); Freedman v. Maryland, 380 U.S. 51, 57 (1965). And even where this presumption might otherwise be overcome, the Court has insisted upon careful procedural provisions, designed to assure the fullest presentation and consideration of the matter which the circumstances permit. . . .

Measured against these standards, it is clear that the 10-day restraining order in the present case, issued ex parte, without formal or informal notice to the petitioners or any effort to advise them of the proceeding, cannot be sustained. . . .

In the present case, the record discloses no reason why petitioners were not notified of the application for injunction. They were apparently present in Princess Anne. They had held a rally there on the night preceding the application for and issuance of the injunction. They were scheduled to have another rally on the very evening of the day when the injunction was issued. And some of them were actually served with the writ of injunction at 6:10 that evening. In these circumstances, there is no justification for the ex parte character of the proceedings in the sensitive area of First Amendment rights.

The value of a judicial proceeding, as against self-help by the police, is substantially diluted where the process is ex parte, because the Court does not have available the fundamental instrument for judicial judgment: an adversary proceeding in which both parties may participate. The facts in any case involving a public demonstration are difficult to ascertain and even more difficult to evaluate. Judgment as to whether the facts justify the use of the drastic power of injunction necessarily turns on subtle and controversial considerations and upon a delicate assessment of the particular situation in light of legal standards which are inescapably imprecise. In the absence of evidence and argument offered by both sides and of their participation in the formulation of value judgments, there is insufficient assurance of the balanced analysis and careful conclusions which are essential in the area of First Amendment adjudication.

The same is true of the fashioning of the order. An order issued in the area of First Amendment rights must be couched in the narrowest terms that will accomplish the pin-pointed objective permitted by constitutional mandate and the essential needs of the public order. In this sensitive field, the . . . order must be tailored as precisely as possible to the exact needs of the case. The participation of both sides is necessary for this purpose. Certainly, the failure to invite participation of the party seeking to exercise First Amendment rights reduces the possibility of a narrowly drawn order, and substantially imperils the protection which the Amendment seeks to assure.

Finally, respondents urge that the failure to give notice and an opportunity for hearing should not be considered to invalidate the order because, under Maryland procedure, petitioners might have obtained a hearing on not more than two days' notice. But this procedural right does not overcome the infirmity in the absence of a showing of justification for the ex parte nature of the proceedings. The issuance of an injunction which aborts a scheduled rally or public meeting, even if the restraint is of short duration, is a matter of importance and consequence in view of the First Amendment's imperative. The denial of a basic procedural right in these circumstances is not excused by the availability of post-issuance procedure which could not possibly serve to rescue the August 7 meeting, but, at best, could have shortened the period in which petitioners were prevented from holding a rally.

We need not here decide that it is impossible for circumstances to arise in which the issuance of an ex parte restraining order for a minimum period could be justified because of the unavailability of the adverse parties or their counsel, or perhaps for other reasons. In the present case, it is clear that the failure to give notice, formal or informal, and to provide an opportunity for an adversary proceeding before the holding of the rally was restrained, is incompatible with the First Amendment. . . . Because we reverse the judgment below on this basis, we need not and do not decide whether the facts in this case provided a constitutionally permissible basis for temporarily enjoining the holding of the August 7 rally.

Reversed.

MR. JUSTICE BLACK concurs in the result.

MR. JUSTICE DOUGLAS, while joining the opinion of the Court, adheres to his dissent in Kingsley Books, Inc. v. Brown, 354 U.S. 436, 446-447, and to his concurring opinion in Freedman v. Maryland, 380 U.S. 51, 61-62.

[In those opinions, Justice Douglas argued that no temporary restraining order could constitutionally restrain speech, no matter how great the procedural safeguards.]

NOTES ON TEMPORARY RESTRAINING ORDERS

1. Temporary restraining orders (TROs) are designed to prevent irreparable harm that will occur even before a preliminary injunction hearing can be held. In a sufficiently urgent case, a judge will issue a TRO from home, in the middle of the night. Federal Civil Rule 65 puts tight restrictions on preliminary orders without notice:

(a) *Preliminary injunction*

(1) *Notice.* No preliminary injunction shall be issued without notice to the adverse party. . . .

(b) *Temporary restraining order; notice; hearing; duration*

A temporary restraining order may be granted without written or oral notice to the adverse party or his attorney only if (1) it clearly appears from specific facts shown by affidavit or by the verified complaint that immediate and irreparable injury, loss, or damage will result to the applicant before the adverse party or his attorney can be heard in opposition, and (2) the applicant's attorney certifies to the court in writing the efforts, if any, which have been made to give the notice and the reasons supporting his claim that notice should not be required. Every temporary restraining order granted without notice shall be indorsed with the date and hour of issuance; shall be filed forthwith in the clerk's office and entered of record; shall define the injury and state why it is irreparable and why the order was granted without notice; and shall expire by its terms within such time after entry, not to exceed 10 days, as the court fixes, unless within the time so fixed the order, for good cause shown, is extended for a like period or unless the party against whom the order is directed consents that it may be extended for a longer period. The reasons for the extension shall be entered of record. In case a temporary restraining order is granted without notice, the motion for a preliminary injunction shall be set down for hearing at the earliest possible time and takes precedence of all matters except older matters of the same character; and when the motion comes on for hearing the party who obtained the temporary restraining order shall proceed with the application for a preliminary injunction and, if he does not do so, the court shall dissolve the temporary restraining order. On 2 days' notice to the party who obtained the temporary restraining order without notice or on such shorter notice to that party as the court may prescribe, the adverse party may appear and move its dissolution or modification and in that event the court shall proceed to hear and determine such motion as expeditiously as the ends of justice require.

2. What is now Rule 65(b) originated in the Clayton Antitrust Act in 1914. Its appearance there was a response to injunctions against labor strikes. TROs without notice and of indefinite duration had effectively broken strikes without a hearing on their legality. Such injunctions had often been based on the antitrust laws. Congress responded by exempting labor unions from the antitrust laws and by restricting all TROs without notice. Most states have similar statutes or procedural rules.

3. Does *Carroll* constitutionalize the substance of Rule 65(b)? Is there any reason to believe *Carroll* is limited to free speech cases? The essence of due process is notice and opportunity to be heard. Can those rights be denied without a showing of necessity?

4. How often will notice of a TRO hearing be impossible? Even a TRO cannot be obtained instantly; plaintiff's lawyer must prepare a complaint, a motion for TRO, one or more affidavits setting out the facts, an injunction bond, and a proposed order. And he must find defendant after the TRO is issued to tell him it exists; defendant is not bound by an order he doesn't know about. If plaintiff can find the defendant then, isn't it likely he could have found him while the papers were being prepared?

5. Suppose plaintiff's lawyer knows where defendant or his lawyer is. Is it ethical to delay giving notice until after preparing all the papers and just before leaving for the courthouse? Is it sound tactics? If it becomes apparent that notice was delayed, will the court think plaintiff had reason to fear a defense? What if plaintiff fears that if he gave prompt notice, the threatened act could be completed more quickly than the papers?

SAMPSON v. MURRAY
415 U.S. 61 (1974)

Mr. Justice Rehnquist delivered the opinion of the Court.

Respondent is a probationary employee in the Public Buildings Service of the General Services Administration (GSA). In May 1971, approximately four months after her employment with GSA began, she was advised in writing by the Acting Commissioner of the Public Buildings Service, W. H. Sanders, that she would be discharged from her position on May 29, 1971. She then filed this action in the United States District

Court for the District of Columbia, seeking to temporarily enjoin her
dismissal pending her pursuit of an administrative appeal to the Civil
Service Commission. The District Court granted a temporary restraining
order, and after an adversary hearing extended the interim injunctive relief in favor of respondent until the Acting Commissioner of the
Public Buildings Service testified about the reasons for respondent's dismissal. . . .

I . . .

The underlying dispute between the parties arises over whether the more
limited procedural requirements applicable to probationary employees
were satisfied by petitioners in this case. . . . Commonly a Government
agency may dismiss a probationary employee found unqualified for continued employment simply "by notifying him in writing as to why he is
being separated and the effective date of the action." More elaborate
procedures are specified when the ground for terminating a probationary
employee is "for conditions arising before appointment." In such cases
the regulations require that the employee receive "an advance written
notice stating the reasons, specifically and in detail, for the proposed
action"; that the employee be given an opportunity to respond in writing
and to furnish affidavits in support of his response; that the agency "consider" any answer filed by the employee in reaching its decision; and that
the employee be notified of the agency's decision at the earliest practicable date. . . .

   The letter which respondent received from the Acting Commissioner,
notifying her of the date of her discharge, stated that the reason for her
discharge was her "complete unwillingness to follow office procedure and
to accept direction from [her] supervisors." After receipt of the letter,
respondent's counsel met with a GSA personnel officer to discuss her
situation and, in the course of the meeting, was shown a memorandum
prepared by an officer of the Public Buildings Service upon which
Sanders apparently based his decision to terminate respondent's employment. The memorandum contained both a discussion of respondent's
conduct in her job with the Public Buildings Service and a discussion of
her conduct during her previous employment at the Defense Intelligence
Agency. Relying upon the inclusion of the information concerning her
previous employment, respondent's counsel requested . . . the procedures to which she would be entitled under the regulations if in fact the
basis of her discharge had been conduct during her previous employment. This request was denied. . . .

   At the hearing on the temporary injunction, the District Court expressed its desire to hear the testimony of Sanders in person, and refused
to resolve the controversy on the basis of his affidavit which the Government offered to furnish. When the Government declined to produce

Sanders, the court ordered the temporary injunctive relief continued, stating that "Plaintiff may suffer immediate and irreparable injury, loss and damage before the Civil Service Commission can consider Plaintiff's claim." The Government, desiring to test the authority of the District Court to enter such an order, has not produced Sanders, and the interim relief awarded respondent continues in effect at this time.

II

While it would doubtless be intellectually neater to completely separate the question whether a District Court has authority to issue any temporary injunctive relief at the behest of a discharged Government employee from the question whether the relief granted in this case was proper, we do not believe the questions may be thus bifurcated into two watertight compartments. . . .

III . . .

The District Court, exercising its equitable powers, is bound to give serious weight to the obviously disruptive effect which the grant of the temporary relief awarded here was likely to have on the administrative process. When we couple with this consideration the historical denial of all equitable relief by the federal courts in cases such as White v. Berry, 171 U.S. 366 (1898), the well-established rule that the Government has traditionally been granted the widest latitude in the "dispatch of its own internal affairs," Cafeteria Workers v. McElroy, 367 U.S. 886, 896 (1961), and the traditional unwillingness of courts of equity to enforce contracts for personal service either at the behest of the employer or of the employee, we think that the Court of Appeals was quite wrong in routinely applying to this case the traditional standards governing more orthodox "stays." Although we do not hold that Congress has wholly foreclosed the granting of preliminary injunctive relief in such cases, we do believe that respondent at the very least must make a showing of irreparable injury sufficient in kind and degree to override these factors cutting against the general availability of preliminary injunctions in Government personnel cases. . . .

IV . . .

In form the order entered by the District Court now before us is a continuation of the temporary restraining order originally issued by that court. It is clear from the Court of Appeals' opinion that that court so construed it. But since the order finally settled upon by the District Court was in no way limited in time, the provisions of Fed. Rule Civ. Proc. 65 come into play. . . .

The Court of Appeals whose judgment we are reviewing has held that

a temporary restraining order continued beyond the time permissible *O.K.*
under Rule 65 must be treated as a preliminary injunction, and must
conform to the standards applicable to preliminary injunctions. We believe that this analysis is correct, at least in the type of situation presented
here, and comports with general principles imposing strict limitations on
the scope of temporary restraining orders. A district court, if it were able
to shield its orders from appellate review merely by designating them as
temporary restraining orders rather than as preliminary injunctions,
would have virtually unlimited authority over the parties in an injunctive
proceeding. In this case, where an adversary hearing has been held, and
the court's basis for issuing the order strongly challenged, classification of
the potentially unlimited order as a temporary restraining order seems
particularly unjustified. Therefore we view the order at issue here as a
preliminary injunction. . . .

Respondent's unverified complaint alleged that she might be deprived
of her income for an indefinite period of time, that spurious and unrebut-
ted charges against her might remain on the record, and that she would
suffer the embarrassment of being wrongfully discharged in the presence
of her coworkers. The Court of Appeals intimated that either loss of
earnings or damage to reputation might afford a basis for a finding of
irreparable injury and provide a basis for temporary injunctive relief. We
disagree.[63]

Even under the traditional standards of Virginia Petroleum Jobbers   *Temp. loss of*
Ass'n v. FPC, 259 F.2d 921 (D.C. Cir. 1958), it seems clear that the   *$ not*
temporary loss of income, ultimately to be recovered, does not usually   *irrep.*
constitute irreparable injury. In that case the court stated: *injury —*

> The key word in this consideration is *irreparable*. Mere injuries, however
> substantial, in terms of money, time and energy necessarily expended in the
> absence of a stay, are not enough. The possibility that adequate compensatory
> or other corrective relief will be available at a later date, in the ordinary course
> of litigation, weighs heavily against a claim of irreparable harm.

This premise is fortified by the Back Pay Act. . . . This Act not only
affords monetary relief which will prevent the loss of earnings on a periodic basis from being "irreparable injury" in this type of case, but its
legislative history suggests that Congress contemplated that it would be
the usual, if not the exclusive, remedy for wrongful discharge.

---

63. We have no doubt that a district court in appropriate circumstances may be justified in resolving against a party refusing to produce a witness under his control the relevant
issues upon which that witness' testimony might have touched. But it is clear from the
record that the testimony of the witness Sanders was desired to test the basis upon which
respondent was discharged, testimony which, of course, would go to the issue of respondent's ultimate chances for success on the merits. While the District Court may well have
been entitled to resolve *that* issue against the Government at that stage of the proceeding,
this conclusion in no way dispenses with the necessity for a conclusion that irreparable
injury will occur, since that is a separate issue that must be proved to the satisfaction of the
Court by the person seeking equitable relief.

Respondent's complaint also alleges, as a basis for relief, the humiliation and damage to her reputation which may ensue. As a matter of first impression it would seem that no significant loss of reputation would be inflicted by procedural irregularities in effectuating respondent's discharge, and that whatever damage might occur would be fully corrected by an administrative determination requiring the agency to conform to the applicable regulations. . . .

Assuming for the purpose of discussion that respondent had made a satisfactory showing of loss of income and had supported the claim that her reputation would be damaged as a result of the challenged agency action, we think the showing falls far short of the type of irreparable injury which is a necessary predicate to the issuance of a temporary injunction in this type of case.[68] We therefore reverse the decision of the Court of Appeals which approved the action of the District Court.

MR. JUSTICE DOUGLAS, dissenting. . . .

Both the District Court and the Court of Appeals were alert to the necessity to show irreparable injury before an injunction issues.

On that issue there is more than meets the eye.

Employability is the greatest asset most people have. Once there is a discharge from a prestigious federal agency, dismissal may be a badge that bars the employee from other federal employment. The shadow of that discharge is cast over the area where private employment may be available. And the harm is not eliminated by the possibility of reinstatement, for in many cases the ultimate absolution never catches up with the stigma of the accusation. And we cannot denigrate the importance of one's social standing or the status of social stigma as legally recognized harm.

There is no frontier where the employee may go to get a new start. We live today in a society that is closely monitored. All of our important acts, our setbacks, the accusations made against us go into data banks, instantly retrieved by the computer. Moreover, this generation grew up in the age where millions of people were screened for "loyalty" and "security"; and many were discharged from the federal service; many resigned rather than face the ordeal of the "witch hunt" that was laid upon us. Discharge from the federal service or resignation under fire became telltale signs of undesirability. Therefore, the case of irreparable injury for

---

68. We recognize that cases may arise in which the circumstances surrounding an employee's discharge, together with the resultant effect on the employee, may so far depart from the normal situation that irreparable injury might be found. Such extraordinary cases are hard to define in advance of their occurrence. We have held that an insufficiency of savings or difficulties in immediately obtaining other employment — external factors common to most discharged employees and not attributable to any unusual actions relating to the discharge itself — will not support a finding of irreparable injury, however severely they may affect a particular individual. But we do not wish to be understood as foreclosing relief in the genuinely extraordinary situation.

an unexplained discharge from federal employment may be plain enough on a hearing.

MR. JUSTICE MARSHALL, with whom MR. JUSTICE BRENNAN concurs, dissenting.

In my view no appealable order has been entered in this case, and both the Court of Appeals and this Court accordingly lack jurisdiction.

The orders issued by the District Court are both temporary restraining orders. The first, issued on May 28 and captioned "Temporary Restraining Order," enjoined Mrs. Murray's dismissal until the determination of her application for an injunction. The second, issued on June 4 and also captioned "Temporary Restraining Order," provides "that the Temporary Restraining Order issued by this Court at twelve o'clock P.M., May 28, 1971, is continued until the appearance of the aforesaid W. H. Sanders."

It is well settled that the grant or denial of a temporary restraining order is not appealable, except in extraordinary circumstances, not present here, where the denial of the temporary restraining order actually decides the merits of the case or is equivalent to a dismissal of the suit.

The Court holds, however, that since the temporary restraining order was extended by the District Court beyond the time limitation imposed by Fed. Rule Civ. Proc. 65(b), it became an appealable preliminary injunction. I cannot agree. Fed. Rule Civ. Proc. 52(a) expressly provides that "in granting or refusing interlocutory injunctions the court shall . . . set forth the findings of fact and conclusions of law which constitute the grounds of its action." This Rule applies to preliminary injunctions, and as no findings of fact and conclusions of law have yet been filed in this case, no valid preliminary injunction was ever issued.

Nor would it make sense for this Court to review the District Court's order in this case as the grant of a preliminary injunction. Where the District Court has not entered findings of fact and conclusions of law under Rule 52(a), meaningful review is well-nigh impossible. . . .

It is suggested that if an indefinitely extended temporary restraining order remained unappealable, the District Court would have virtually unlimited authority over the parties in an injunctive action. At the outset, this cannot justify this Court's reaching the merits of Mrs. Murray's claim for a preliminary injunction. Even if the order entered by the District Court is appealable, it should be appealable only for the purposes of holding it invalid for failure to comply with Rule 52(a).

In addition, the Government had other courses it could have taken in this case. In view of the District Court's error in granting a restraining order of unlimited duration without complying with the requirements for a preliminary injunction, the Government could have moved the District Court to dissolve its order indefinitely continuing the temporary restraining order. . . . Had the Government followed this course, the District Court could have corrected its error and gone on to resolve the issues presented by the application for a preliminary injunction. The end result would have been the grant or denial of a preliminary injunction, with findings of fact and conclusions of law, which we could meaningfully review.

Here, instead, we find the Supreme Court determining that although the District Court had jurisdiction to grant injunctive relief, the equities of Mrs. Murray's case did not support a preliminary injunction, when neither the District Court nor the Court of Appeals has yet confronted the latter issue. . . .

Since the majority persists in considering the merits of Mrs. Murray's claim for injunctive relief, some additional comment is in order. I agree with the majority's conclusion that Congress did not divest federal courts of their long-exercised authority to issue temporary injunctive relief pending the exhaustion of both administrative and judicial review of an employee's claim of wrongful dismissal. I cannot accept, however, the way in which the majority opinion then proceeds to take away with the left hand what it has just given with the right, by precluding injunctive relief in all but so-called "extraordinary cases," whatever they may be.

At the outset, I see no basis for applying any different standards for granting equitable relief in the context of a discharged probationary employee than the long-recognized principles of equity applied in all other situations. See Virginia Petroleum Jobbers Ass'n v. FPC, 259 F.2d 921 (D.C. Cir. 1958). Indeed, it appears that the factors which the majority would have courts weigh before granting injunctive relief are all encompassed within the traditional formulations. The adequacy of backpay as a remedy, for example, is relevant in determining whether the party seeking relief has shown that "without such relief, it will be irreparably injured." 259 F.2d, at 925. Likewise, the possible disruptive effect which temporary injunctive relief might have on the office where respondent was employed or on the administrative review process itself relates to whether "the issuance of a stay [will] substantially harm other parties interested in the proceedings." Ibid.

However one articulates the standards for granting temporary injunctive relief, I take it to be well settled that a prerequisite for such relief is a demonstrated likelihood of irreparable injury for which there is no adequate legal remedy. But I cannot accept the majority's apparent holding, buried deep in a footnote, that because of the Back Pay Act, a temporary loss in income can never support a finding of irreparable injury, no matter how severely it may affect a particular individual. Many employees may lack substantial savings, and a loss of income for more than a few weeks' time might seriously impair their ability to provide themselves with the essentials of life — e.g., to buy food, meet mortgage or rent payments, or procure medical services. Government employees might have skills not readily marketable outside the Government, making it difficult for them to find temporary employment elsewhere to tide themselves over until the lawfulness of their dismissal is finally determined. In some instances, the likelihood of finding alternative employment may be further reduced by the presence on the employee's records of the very dismissal at issue. Moreover, few employers will be willing to hire and train a new employee knowing he will return to his former Government position if his appeal is successful. Finally, the loss of income may be "temporary" in only the broadest sense of that word. Not infrequently, dismissed federal employees must wait several years before the wrongful nature of their dismissal is finally settled and their right to backpay established.

The availability of a backpay award several years after a dismissal is scant justice for a Government employee who may have long since been evicted from his home and found himself forced to resort to public assistance in order to support his family. And it is little solace to those who are so injured to be told that their plight is "normal" and "routine." Whether common or not, such consequences amount to irreparable injury which a court of equity has power to prevent.

Nor can I agree with the majority's analysis of Mrs. Murray's claim of damaged reputation. It is argued that Mrs. Murray can suffer no significant loss of reputation by procedural irregularities in effectuating her discharge because her claim is not that she could not as a matter of statutory or administrative right be discharged, but only that she was entitled to additional procedural safeguards in effectuating the discharge.

Mrs. Murray does not seek a hearing as an end in itself, but rather to correct what she believes is a mistaken impression the agency had about her conduct in her prior job, in the hope that with the record straight, the agency would not discharge her. She seeks to save her job and to avoid the blot on her employment record that a dismissal entails, and it is in this sense that she claims her dismissal would injure her reputation.

Whether the likelihood of irreparable injury to Mrs. Murray if she is not allowed to retain her job pending her administrative appeal, when balanced against the Government's interests in having her out of the office during this period, supports equitable relief in the present case is a question I would leave for the District Court. Because of Mr. Sanders' absence, the District Court cut short its hearing on the application for a preliminary injunction before either the Government or Mrs. Murray had an opportunity to present witnesses or other evidence. Mrs. Murray still has not had her day in court to present evidence supporting her allegation of irreparable injury, and what that evidence would be were she given that opportunity we can only speculate.

NOTES ON THE PROCEDURE FOR
GRANTING PRELIMINARY RELIEF

1. Was the order in *Sampson* a temporary restraining order or a preliminary injunction? The Court relies on the ten-day limit in Rule 65(b), but that limit applies only to TROs without notice. Here, the district

court purports to have issued a TRO with notice. How does such an order fit into the scheme of Rule 65? It can't be unappealable *and* of unlimited duration, can it? Does Rule 65 ever define the difference between TROs and preliminary injunctions?

2. Two weeks after *Sampson*, the Court took another look at the problem. This time Justice Marshall wrote the opinion:

> Although by its terms Rule 65(b) . . . only limits the duration of restraining orders issued without notice, we think it applicable to the order in this case even though informal notice was given. The 1966 Amendment to Rule 65(b), requiring the party seeking a temporary restraining order to certify to the court in writing the efforts, if any, which have been made to give either written or oral notice to the adverse party or his attorney, were adopted in recognition of the fact that informal notice and a hastily arranged hearing are to be preferred to no notice or hearing at all. But this informal, same-day notice, desirable though it may be before a restraining order is issued, is no substitute for the more thorough notice requirements which must be satisfied to obtain a preliminary injunction of potentially unlimited duration. The notice required by Rule 65(a) before a preliminary injunction can issue implies a hearing in which the defendant is given a fair opportunity to oppose the application and to prepare for such opposition. The same-day notice provided in this case before the temporary restraining order was issued does not suffice.

Granny Goose Foods v. Brotherhood of Teamsters, 415 U.S. 423, 433-434 n.7. In *Granny Foods*, the Court held that defendants were not in contempt of the TRO with notice, because it had expired ten days after its issuance and before they allegedly violated it.

The Supreme Court of Illinois reached the opposite result under a state statute identical to Rule 65(b). Kable Printing Co. v. Mount Morris Bookbinders Union Local 65-B, 63 Ill. 2d 514, 349 N.E.2d 36 (1976). The Illinois court thought it quite clear that the ten-day limit applies only to ex parte orders; it held a TRO with notice equivalent to a preliminary injunction and unlimited in duration. Might it matter that TROs are appealable in Illinois?

3. Are *Sampson* and *Granny Goose Foods* consistent? *Granny Goose Foods* says a TRO with notice, not limited by its terms to ten-days' duration, is still a TRO and expires in ten days. Doesn't *Sampson* say that such an order is really a preliminary injunction, appealable because of its indefinite duration? Did the government have the option to ignore the TRO in *Sampson* after ten days? Or is the *Sampson* order a preliminary injunction because defendant had longer notice and a fuller hearing? Should the choice between appeal and defiance after ten days turn on the adequacy of the hearing?

There are risks to defying a TRO that lasts more than ten days. A defiant defendant is in contempt of court, even if the order is erroneous, unless the order is void for lack of jurisdiction. Walker v. City of Birmingham, 388 U.S. 307 (1967), reprinted infra at 656. Should defiance ever be authorized? Why not require defendants to move to vacate the TRO on the ground it had lasted too long and make denial of that motion an appealable order? Doesn't there have to be some provision for TROs with notice to last more than twenty days? What should the court do in a case like Jurco v. Stuart, 110 Ill. App. 3d 405, 407, 442 N.E.2d 633, 635 (1982), where there was "a six-month backlog to hear preliminary injunctions"? Is the answer that such a backlog cannot be tolerated?

4. The usual federal rule is that no order is appealable before final judgment. But 28 U.S.C. §1292(a)(1) (1982) authorizes appeals from "interlocutory orders . . . granting, continuing, modifying, refusing or dissolving injunctions, or refusing to dissolve or modify injunctions." Most states have similar provisions. An interlocutory order is an order before final judgment. The rationale of these statutes is that interlocutory orders granting or denying injunctions may do irreparable harm before any appeal from a final judgment can be heard.

5. The broad statement that TROs are unappealable is misleading. The statute authorizing appeal from interlocutory orders granting or denying injunctions would seem to include TROs. But the courts have held orders granting or denying TROs unappealable because they last such a short time and because the trial judge has heard so little of the merits. See, e.g., Connell v. Dulien Steel Products, 240 F.2d 414, 418 (5th Cir. 1957), cert. denied, 356 U.S. 968 (1958). The trial judge can give relief from an erroneous order on a TRO application much more quickly than an appellate court. If that is true, why do litigants appeal orders granting and denying TROs? Might appellants plausibly interpret some dispositions as reflecting hostility to their position, so that giving the trial judge more information will not change the result?

Whatever the merits of the rule against appeals from orders granting or denying TROs, its rationales do not apply when the TRO lasts longer and the trial judge refuses to dissolve it or hold the preliminary injunction hearing. In that event, shouldn't the TRO be appealable? Isn't that what Sampson holds? Is there any need to call it a preliminary injunction in order to make it appealable?

6. There are also a few cases holding that orders granting or denying TROs are appealable as final judgments when they effectively dispose of the entire case. The most widely cited example is United States v. Wood, 295 F.2d 772 (5th Cir. 1961), cert. denied, 369 U.S. 850 (1962). There, the United States unsuccessfully sought a TRO against Mississippi's prosecution of a civil rights worker. The United States argued that the prosecution would discourage blacks from registering to vote, and that the prosecution would be complete before a motion for preliminary injunction could be heard.

Should that be enough to make the order appealable? Consider Judge Feinberg's argument that such an exception will "swallow up the

rule. . . . Erroneous denial of a temporary restraining order, by hypothe-
sis, leaves a plaintiff unprotected from immediate and irreparable injury."
Wirtz v. Powell Knitting Mills Co., 360 F.2d 730, 733-734 (2d Cir. 1966)
(Feinberg, J., concurring). Is he right? Is his argument as applicable to
TROs as to orders denying them? Should plaintiffs be more able to appeal
than defendants?

7.   Even with interlocutory appeals, an erroneous injunction order
may do irreparable harm before the appeal can be heard. The procedural
response to that problem is that judges at all levels of the judiciary can
stay an injunction until it can be reviewed, or can issue an injunction
until an order denying it can be reviewed.

A litigant seeking a stay or injunction pending appeal must generally
request it first from the district court. Only if that is denied can he seek it
from the court of appeals, and only if that is denied can he ask the
Supreme Court. In an emergency, a single judge may act for the court of
appeals. Under Supreme Court Rule 51, application to a single justice is
the usual practice, but the justices informally consult the rest of the
Court before ruling on such applications.

The standards for stays and injunctions pending appeal are the same as
for preliminary injunctions, modified to include appropriate deference to
the decision below. In the Supreme Court, probability of success depends
not only on the merits, but on the probability that four justices will
consider the case important enough to review.

8.   One cost of interlocutory appeals is that litigants are tempted to
devote their energy to the appeal of the preliminary order rather than the
trial of the case. Both can proceed simultaneously, but lawyers often
think there is no point proceeding in the trial court until they hear from
the appellate court. This can delay the case indefinitely, and the appellate
opinion may not be worth much. It is likely to say only that the trial court
did or did not abuse its discretion in assessing probabilities on a preliminary record. Unless they can get an injunction pending appeal, plaintiffs
will often do better to push the case to trial than to appeal denial of a
preliminary injunction.

9.   The scope of the hearing on a motion for TRO or preliminary
injunction depends on the complexity and urgency of the case. In Lektro-
Vend Corp. v. Vendo Co., 660 F.2d 255 (7th Cir. 1981), *cert. denied*, 455
U.S. 921 (1982), the preliminary injunction hearing lasted five days; the
judge heard four witnesses and admitted eighty-nine exhibits. The trial
on the merits lasted twenty-three days; the judge heard eleven witnesses
and admitted 2,762 exhibits. That proportion between the two hearings is
not unusual, but if there is sufficient urgency, even complex cases can be
compressed much more. The trial judge has great discretion here, but
must be evenhanded about it. Judges occasionally get impatient after the
plaintiff's case and cut the defendant off without an equal chance to be
heard; that is nearly always reversible. An example is Visual Sciences v.

Integrated Communications, 660 F.2d 56 (2d Cir. 1981). Affidavits are commonly admitted to establish undisputed facts, but witnesses must be called on any genuine factual dispute material to a preliminary injunction. See, e.g., Syntex Ophthalmics v. Tsuetaki, 701 F.2d 677, 682 (7th Cir. 1983). Evidence admitted at a preliminary injunction hearing may be considered at the trial of the case and need not be repeated. Fed. R. Civ. Proc. 65(a)(2). The judge may consolidate the trial with the preliminary injunction hearing, id., but only if both parties clearly understand that he has done so. University of Texas v. Camenisch, 451 U.S. 390, 395 (1981).

Hearings on motions for TROs tend to be much shorter. Sometimes there is a real hearing, with key witnesses explaining the key facts; sometimes there is only an informal conference with the judge. But the facts must be sufficiently developed to permit an intelligent decision. Justice Marshall's dissent in *Sampson* implies that findings of fact and conclusions of law are not required for TROs, and undoubtedly many TROs are issued without them. Rule 52(a) applies to all orders "granting or refusing interlocutory injunctions"; perhaps he assumes that a TRO is not an injunction. But at least one court has vacated a TRO issued without findings and conclusions. Newark Stereotypers' Union No. 18 v. Newark Morning Ledger Co., 353 F.2d 510 (3d Cir. 1965). At the very least, a TRO must comply with Rule 65(d), which provides that "Every order granting an injunction and every restraining order shall set forth the reasons for its issuance."

MORE NOTES ON IRREPARABLE INJURY

1. Would the majority in *Sampson* ever issue a preliminary injunction reinstating a government employee? What kind of "genuinely extraordinary situation" could there be that did not derive from "an insufficiency of savings or difficulties in obtaining other employment"? What if the mortgage company were about to foreclose on plaintiff's house? Recall the rule disallowing consequential damages for failure to pay money. Doesn't that make the loss of plaintiff's house, or any other consequence you can imagine, as irreparable as injury can be? Does Justice Rehnquist really mean that the government's interest in the efficiency of the service outweighs plaintiff's injury however severe?

2. Compare Rehnquist's opinion for the Court in Doran v. Salem Inn, 422 U.S. 922 (1975). A district court preliminarily enjoined criminal prosecutions of topless dancers and the corporate owner of the bar where they danced. The owner alleged a risk of bankruptcy if the local ordinance were enforced pending trial. The Supreme Court affirmed. "Certainly [bankruptcy] meets the standards for granting interim relief, for otherwise a favorable final judgment might well be useless." Id. at 932. Is bankruptcy more irreparable for a business than an employee?

COYNE-DELANY CO. v. CAPITAL
DEVELOPMENT BOARD
717 F.2d 385 (7th Cir. 1983)

Before ESCHBACH and POSNER, Circuit Judges, and DUMBAULD, Senior District Judge.

POSNER, Circuit Judge.

The principal questions for decision are the extent of the district court's power to deny damages to a defendant injured by the issuance of a preliminary injunction that is later reversed on appeal, and the proper standard for exercising that power.

The genesis of this case is an otherwise unrelated civil rights suit brought by inmates of the Illinois state prison at Stateville complaining about living conditions. A decree was entered requiring the prison to replace all of the plumbing fixtures in one of the prison's cellhouses. The state's Capital Development Board let a contract for the first of two projected phases of the work to Naal Plumbing & Heating Co., which subcontracted with Coyne-Delany Company for the flush valves required in the project. (Coyne-Delany is one of the nation's two principal manufacturers of flush valves for toilets, the other being the Sloan Company.) The valves were installed, and malfunctioned. After Coyne-Delany shipped redesigned valves which also malfunctioned, the prison authorities asked the Capital Development Board to designate another valve subcontractor in the bidding specifications for the second phase of the contract. The Board complied, designating Sloan.

Bids were received, but on May 7, 1979, two days before they were to be opened, Coyne-Delany sued the Board under section 1 of the Civil Rights Act of 1871, 42 U.S.C. §1983, and on May 8 it obtained a temporary restraining order against the Board's opening the bids. The state asked that Coyne-Delany be ordered to post a $50,000 bond, pointing out that the temporary restraining order was preventing it from proceeding with the entire project and that indefinite delay could be extremely costly. But Judge Perry, the emergency motions judge, required a bond of only $5,000, in the belief that the temporary restraining order would be in effect for only a week until Judge Bua could hear the motion for a preliminary injunction. However, at the preliminary-injunction hearing Judge Bua issued the injunction but refused to increase the bond.

Although the terms of the bond are limited to the damages caused by the temporary restraining order, which presumably were trivial, and a TRO bond does not automatically apply to a subsequently issued preliminary injunction, the parties stipulated that the "bond was continued for the preliminary injunction." We shall therefore assume that the bond secures the Board against its damages from the preliminary injunction as well as from the temporary restraining order.

The premise of Coyne-Delany's civil rights suit against the Capital

Development Board was that under Illinois law as expounded by the Illinois Appellate Court in Polyvend, Inc. v. Puckorius, 61 Ill. App. 3d 163, 377 N.E.2d 1160 (1978), Coyne-Delany, as an indirect bidder on the plumbing contract for the Stateville cellhouse, had a property right of which it was deprived without due process of law by the Board's requiring Naal to use Sloan valves merely because the prison authorities had determined — unreasonably in Coyne-Delany's opinion — that Coyne-Delany's valves were defective. When he issued the preliminary injunction Judge Bua said that Coyne-Delany was likely to prevail on the merits, especially given the Board's refusal to submit the dispute over the quality of Coyne-Delany's valves to an impartial expert for binding determination, as Coyne-Delany had proposed. This court reversed the grant of the preliminary injunction, however. Noting that Polyvend had been reversed by the Illinois Supreme Court, 77 Ill. 2d 287, 395 N.E.2d 1376 (1979), after Judge Bua had granted the preliminary injunction to Coyne-Delany, we held that under Illinois law a bidder, and a fortiori an indirect bidder, has no property right in being allowed to bid on a public contract and that Coyne-Delany therefore had no claim against the Board under the Fourteenth Amendment.

Our decision came down on February 22, 1980, and a few days later the Board at last opened the bids that had been submitted back in May 1979. Naal was the low bidder, with a bid of $214,000, but its bid had lapsed because of the passage of time, and the Board had to solicit new bids. The new bids were opened on May 9, 1980. Although Naal's new bid, $270,000, was higher than its old bid had been, Naal was again the low bidder and was awarded the contract.

The Board then joined Hanover Insurance Company, the surety on the injunction bond, as an additional defendant in Coyne-Delany's civil rights suit, pursuant to Rule 65.1 of the Federal Rules of Civil Procedure, and moved the district court to award the Board damages of $56,000 for the wrongfully issued preliminary injunction and statutory costs (filing fees and the like, see 28 U.S.C. §1920) of $523 which the Board had incurred in the district court. Judge Bua refused to award either costs or damages. His opinion states, "the Court must weigh the equitable factors of the case, including whether the case was filed in good faith or is frivolous. . . . [T]he parties have stipulated that the case was filed in good faith and without malice. Further, it is apparent that the case was not frivolous. The law as it existed at the time the case was filed clearly favored the plaintiffs. It would be unreasonable to require a party to anticipate a change in the law and would be unconscionable to label a suit filed in good faith as frivolous where there is such a subsequent change."

There is no dispute over the amount of costs claimed by the Board; and while Coyne-Delany has not conceded that the Board incurred damages of $56,000 as a result of the delay of the project and the district court made no finding with respect to those damages, they undoubtedly exceeded $5,000, the amount of the injunction bond. . . .

Although the district court has unquestioned power in an appropriate case not to award costs to the prevailing party and not to award damages on an injunction bond even though the grant of the injunction was reversed, the district court's opinion suggests that the court may have believed it had to deny both costs and damages because the lawsuit had not been brought in bad faith and was not frivolous. This would be the proper standard if the question were whether to award a prevailing defendant his attorney's fees (we disregard, since the Board has not requested an award of attorney's fees, the provision in 42 U.S.C. §1988 for awarding fees to prevailing parties in civil rights cases). In the absence of statute, an award of attorney's fees is proper only where the losing party has been guilty of bad faith, as by bringing a frivolous suit — frivolousness connoting not just a lack of merit but so great a lack as to suggest that the suit must have been brought to harass rather than to win.

The rule is different for costs. Rule 54(d) of the Federal Rules of Civil Procedure provides that "costs shall be allowed as of course to the prevailing party unless the court otherwise directs. . . ." This language creates a presumption in favor of awarding costs. The district judge can decline to award them but not just because an award of attorney's fees would not have been warranted — that is, not just because the losing party was acting in good faith. . . .

The language of Rule 65(c), governing damages on an injunction bond, is only a little less clear than that of Rule 54(d): "No restraining order or preliminary injunction shall issue except upon the giving of security by the applicant, in such sum as the court deems proper, for the payment of such costs and damages as may be incurred or suffered by any party who is found to have been wrongfully enjoined or restrained." The court is not told in so many words to order the applicant to pay the wrongfully enjoined party's damages. But it is told to require a bond or equivalent security in order to ensure that the plaintiff will be able to pay all or at least some of the damages that the defendant incurs from the preliminary injunction if it turns out to have been wrongfully issued. The draftsmen must have intended that when such damages were incurred the plaintiff or his surety, pursuant to Rule 65.1's summary procedure, which despite its wording is applicable to the principal as well as the surety on the bond, would normally be required to pay the damages, at least up to the limit of the bond.

Yet some courts treat the district court's discretion to award or deny damages under an injunction bond as completely open-ended unless the plaintiff acted in bad faith in seeking the preliminary injunction. The principal cases, Page Communications Engineers, Inc. v. Froehlke, 475 F.2d 994 (D.C. Cir. 1973) (per curiam), and H & R Block, Inc. v. McCaslin, 541 F.2d 1098 (5th Cir. 1976) (per curiam), rely on Russell v.

Farley, 105 U.S. 433 (1882), where the Supreme Court stated that "in the absence of an imperative statute to the contrary, the court should have the power to mitigate the terms imposed [in granting the injunction], or to relieve from them altogether, whenever in the course of the proceedings it appears that it would be inequitable or oppressive to continue them." Id. at 441-42. Although the statement partakes of dictum because the injunction had not been dissolved completely, see id. at 446-47, a more important point is the absence, at the time the case was decided, of any statute or rule of court dealing with security for federal court injunctions. The Court discussed state statutes and rules, precursors of Rule 65(c), requiring injunction bonds, and only then stated that because of the absence of a federal statute or rule the federal courts "must *still* be governed in the matter by the general principles and usages of equity." Id. at 441 (emphasis added). The implication is that a rule requiring an injunction bond would have changed the Court's result — would have been the "imperative statute" to which it referred.

Page and *H & R Block* do not consider this reading of *Russell* or cite Houghton v. Cortelyou, 208 U.S. 149, 160 (1908), where the Court narrowed the discretion that *Russell* had given district courts to relieve from liability under an injunction bond. And they dismiss Rule 65(c)'s requirement of a bond or other security by pointing out that the district court can require a bond of nominal amount in appropriate cases, for example if the plaintiff is indigent. But it is one thing to say that the requirement of a bond can in effect be waived when there is a good reason for doing so — a dispensation narrowly construed in this circuit — and another to say that where a substantial bond is clearly required by the equities of the case the district court nevertheless has carte blanche to excuse the plaintiff from paying any damages on the bond.

Most cases hold, contrary to *Page* and *H & R Block*, that a prevailing defendant is entitled to damages on the injunction bond unless there is a good reason for not requiring the plaintiff to pay in the particular case. We agree with the majority approach. Not only is it implied by the text of Rule 65(c) but it makes the law more predictable and discourages the seeking of preliminary injunctions on flimsy (though not necessarily frivolous) grounds.

When rules prescribe a course of action as the norm but allow the district court to deviate from it, the court's discretion is more limited than it would be if the rules were nondirective. Rules 54(d) and 65(c) establish what Judge Friendly recently called "a principle of preference" guiding the exercise of the district judge's discretion. Friendly, *Indiscretion About Discretion*, 31 Emory L.J. 747, 768 (1982). The judge must have a good reason for departing from such a principle in a particular case. It is not a sufficient reason for denying costs or damages on an injunction bond that the suit had as in this case been brought in good faith. That would be sufficient only if the presumption were against rather than in favor of awarding costs and damages on the bond to the prevailing party, as it would be if the issue were attorney's fees under the American rule, which in the absence of bad faith leaves each party to bear his own attorney's fees. The award of damages on the bond is not punitive but compensatory.

A good reason for not awarding such damages would be that the defendant had failed to mitigate damages. The district court made no reference to any such failure in this case and we can find no evidence that there was any; the Board's requesting and obtaining a 30-day extension of time for filing its appeal brief, the factor stressed by Coyne-Delany, did not create material or unreasonable delay. A good reason not for denying but for awarding damages in this case, unmentioned by the district court, was that the bond covered only a small fraction of the defendant's damages. The Board asked for and should have been granted a much larger bond; and when the heavy damages that the Board had predicted in asking for the larger bond materialized, it had a strong equitable claim to recover its damages up to the limit of the bond. Nor could $5,000 be regarded as excessive because the plaintiff was a poor person. The plaintiff is not a poor person but a substantial corporation that will not be crushed by having to pay $5,523 in damages and costs. It is particularly difficult in the circumstances of this case to understand the judge's refusal to award *any* damages, or the trivial amount of costs, conceded to be reasonable in amount, asked by the defendant.

In deciding whether to withhold costs or injunction damages, not only is the district court to be guided by the implicit presumption in Rules 54(d) and 65(c) in favor of awarding them, but the ingredients of a proper decision are objective factors — such as the resources of the parties, the defendant's efforts or lack thereof to mitigate his damages, and the outcome of the underlying suit — accessible to the judgment of a reviewing court. In the spectrum of decisions embraced by the overly broad and unfortunately named "abuse of discretion" standard (on which see Judge Friendly's recent article, supra), the decision to deny costs and injunction damages is near the end that merges into the standard of simple error used in reviewing decisions of questions of law.

Although the district court's decision cannot stand, both because it applies an incorrect standard and because it fails to consider and evaluate the full range of factors (which might in an appropriate case include, but is not exhausted by, the plaintiff's good faith) that would be relevant under the proper standard, we are not prepared to hold that the Board is entitled as a matter of law to its costs and to its injunction damages up to the limit of the bond. The district court did allude to one factor, besides mere absence of bad faith, that supported its ruling — the change in the applicable law after the preliminary injunction was issued. The law on which the court had relied in issuing the injunction was contained in an intermediate state appellate court decision and of course such decisions are reversed with some frequency. We do not believe that a change in the law is always a good ground for denying costs and injunction damages to a prevailing party, but it is a legitimate consideration, perhaps especially where the prevailing party is a state agency that benefited from a change in the law of its state. In a sense, this is a case where one state agency (the Board) is seeking to benefit from the confusing signals sent out by another state agency (the court system) — though we do not mean to suggest that the Illinois Supreme Court was rushing fraternally to the aid of another state agency when it reversed *Polyvend*. In any event, a remand is necessary to allow Judge Bua to consider and weigh all the relevant factors identified in this opinion — bearing in mind the principle of preference that we have indicated should guide his equitable determination.

It remains to consider whether on remand the Board should be allowed to seek injunction damages above the limit of the bond. The surety cannot be required to pay more than the face amount of the bond, but it is a separate question whether the plaintiff can be. However, the Ninth Circuit has held in a scholarly opinion that the bond is the limit of the damages the defendant can obtain for a wrongful injunction, even from the plaintiff, provided the plaintiff was acting in good faith, which is not questioned here. Buddy Systems, Inc. v. Exer-Genie, Inc., 545 F.2d 1164, 1167-68 (9th Cir. 1976). (Another exception might be where the plaintiff was seeking restitution rather than damages.) The Supreme Court has cited *Buddy Systems* in dictum for the proposition that "a party injured by the issuance of an injunction later determined to be erroneous has no action for damages in the absence of a bond." W.R. Grace & Co. v. Local Union 759, United Rubber Workers, 461 U.S. 757, 770 n.14 (1983).

Rightly or wrongly, American common law, state and federal, does not attempt to make the winner of a lawsuit whole by making the loser reimburse the winner's full legal expenses, even when the winner is the defendant, who unlike a prevailing plaintiff does not have the consolation of a damage recovery. In noninjunctive suits, except those brought (or defended) in bad faith, the winner can recover only his statutory costs, invariably but a small fraction of his expenses of suit. It would be incongruous if a prevailing defendant could obtain the full, and potentially the staggering, consequential damages caused by a preliminary injunction. The preliminary injunction in this case halted work on a major construction project for a year; it could easily have been two or three years, and the expenses imposed on the defendant not $56,000 but $560,000. It might be a very great boon to the legal system of this country to discourage injunction suits by putting plaintiffs at such risk, but we do not see how such an approach can be squared with the general attitude toward litigation implied by the American rule on attorney's fees. Although that rule may soon have to be curtailed to cope with the flood of litigation in the state and federal courts today, we are not authorized to curtail it, in the face of the Supreme Court's position in *Grace* and especially in Alyeska Pipeline Service Co. v. Wilderness Society, 421 U.S. 240 (1975). . . .

A right to injunction damages potentially unlimited in amount would be in one sense a more extreme remedy against a losing litigant than allowing the winner to have his attorney's fees reimbursed. Not only would the amounts involved be much greater in some cases (though appropriately greater: the costs of the litigation would be greater to the defendant than if no injunction had been issued) but the burden of the rule would fall entirely on plaintiffs; the English and Continental rule, which requires the loser to reimburse the winner's attorney's fees, benefits prevailing plaintiffs as well as prevailing defendants. Of course, having to post a bond is also a deterrent just to plaintiffs. But if the plaintiff's damages are limited to the amount of the bond, at least he knows just what his exposure is when the bond is set by the district court. It is not unlimited. If the bond is too high he can drop the suit.

A defendant's inability to obtain damages in excess of the bond unless the plaintiff was acting in bad faith can have unfortunate results, which are well illustrated by this case where the district court required too small a bond. But a defendant dissatisfied with the amount of bond set by the district court can, on appeal from the preliminary injunction, ask the court of appeals to increase the bond, which the defendant here did not do. We may suggest without having to decide that a defendant who wanted the court of appeals to increase the bond would have to ask for accelerated consideration of his request in order to mitigate his damages and thus reduce the plaintiff's exposure. But these observations are immaterial to the question of the defendant's right to obtain damages up to the limit of the bond set by the district court. . . .

Reversed and remanded.

NOTES ON INJUNCTION BONDS

1. Who should bear the risk of error in an interlocutory order? Is it plaintiff's fault that the trial court erred? Is it plaintiff's responsibility because plaintiff asked the court to issue an order without a full trial? In considering that question, do not think only of the intervening change in law in *Coyne-Delany*. In the most common fact pattern, the judge decides at trial that he got the facts wrong at the preliminary injunction hearing. An example is Atomic Oil Co. v. Bardahl Oil Co., 419 F.2d 1097 (10th Cir. 1969). There, Atomic charged Bardahl with infringing its "Savmotor" trademark. The court issued a preliminary injunction forbidding Bardahl to sell its "Savoil" product in any of the thirty states where Atomic did business. At full trial, the court decided that consumers recognized Atomic's trademark in only three states, and denied an injunction as to the other twenty-seven. The court of appeals enforced the

$50,000 preliminary injunction bond. Should we hold plaintiff responsible for that sort of error more readily than for an intervening change of law? Or should defendant have to bear his own losses, just as he bears his own litigation expenses, as the cost of preserving plaintiff's access to justice?

The conventional wisdom in the federal courts, and in nearly all the states, is that plaintiff is liable, but only up to the amount of the bond. As *Coyne-Delany* suggests, there are many variations on that basic rule. There are at least three distinct issues. First, is there liability anytime the permanent injunction is not as broad as the preliminary injunction, or must the preliminary injunction have been erroneous on the record as it then stood? Second, is the liability mandatory or discretionary? Third, is the decision to require bond in the first place mandatory or discretionary?

2. Federal Civil Rule 65(c) requires a bond to pay the damages of any party "wrongfully enjoined or restrained." Was the Capital Development Board "wrongfully enjoined"? Was Bardahl? Is a preliminary injunction "wrongful" if it is proper on the record compiled at the time of its issuance? If the purpose of the rule is to protect defendants from the risk of error in preliminary decisions on incomplete hearings, aren't the cases right to focus on the ultimate disposition?

University of Texas v. Camenisch, 451 U.S. 390 (1981), casts light on this question. Plaintiff was a deaf student. A preliminary injunction ordered the university to provide a sign-language interpreter for him. The university appealed the preliminary injunction, but plaintiff had graduated by the time the case reached the Supreme Court. Plaintiff said the case was moot, but the university sought to recover on the bond for the cost of the interpreter. The Court held that the preliminary injunction appeal was moot, because liability on the bond could only be determined after a trial on the merits. The Court remanded the case for trial. Does *Camenisch* implicitly resolve the "wrongfully enjoined" issue? Would you need a full trial if liability depended on identifying some error at the preliminary injunction hearing?

3. Another approach is to impose liability only if a preliminary injunction is vacated before decision on the permanent injunction, or if a TRO is vacated before decision on the preliminary injunction. Stocker Hinge Manufacturing Co. v. Darnel Industries, 94 Ill. 2d 535, 447 N.E.2d 288 (1983). Under that standard, there would have been liability in *Atomic Oil*, but not in *Coyne-Delany*. Illinois is one of the few states where liability is not limited to the amount of the bond; its stricter standard for imposing liability tempers that rule. But a strong dissent in *Stocker* argues that the Illinois rule encourages wasteful appeals from preliminary orders and leaves defendants inadequately protected.

4. Some courts claim broad discretion not to enforce the bond. *Coyne-Delany* acknowledges very narrow discretion; *Atomic Oil* appears

to say that once the preliminary injunction is narrowed or vacated, enforcement of the bond is mandatory. The leading case for broad discretion is Page Communications Engineers v. Froehlke, discussed in *Coyne-Delany*. There, the court preliminarily enjoined the U.S. Army from awarding a defense contract to plaintiff's competitor. The court ultimately ruled for the army, but it declined to enforce plaintiff's $100,000 bond. The court said plaintiff proceeded in good faith and raised "some solid questions," that "this was not a frivolous lawsuit," that the army's ambiguous procedure raised "doubts as to the fairness of the procurement," and that the army had not mentioned its comparative cost study at the preliminary injunction hearing, although the study had been completed at the time and was "significant" to the ultimate decision on the merits. Id. at 996-997. What does this leave of the bond? If the lawsuit were frivolous and not in good faith, plaintiff would be liable for malicious prosecution quite apart from the bond. How often will plaintiff get a preliminary injunction without raising "some solid questions"? Does the case turn on the army's failure to produce its strongest evidence? Was that the army's "fault" or the natural consequence of holding the hearing on short notice?

What if a TRO is proper on the merits but vacated because of a subsequently enacted statute? Kansas ex rel. Stephan v. Adams, 705 F.2d 1267 (10th Cir. 1983), refuses to impose liability in that situation. The opinion cites the Page v. Froehlke line of cases; it does not cite Atomic Oil v. Bardahl, the earlier Tenth Circuit case.

5.   The Supreme Court has not said anything definitive since Russell v. Farley, discussed in *Coyne-Delany*. The Court distinguished *Russell* on the facts (fairly so) in Houghton v. Meyer, 208 U.S. 149 (1908). It cited *Russell* and restated *Russell*'s rule in a casual dictum in Lawrence v. St. Louis-San Francisco Railway, 278 U.S. 228, 233 (1929). But a dictum in Public Service Commission v. Brashear Freight Lines, 312 U.S. 621 (1941), implies that liability on the bond is not discretionary — that discretion extends only to the choice between enforcing the bond on motion in the original action (as authorized by Federal Civil Rule 65.1), or in a separate action (as authorized by 28 U.S.C. §1352 (1976)). University of Texas v. Camenisch does not appear to imply anything about whether liability on the bond is mandatory or discretionary.

6.   More courts claim discretion not to require a bond in the first place. Federal Civil Rule 65(c), quoted in *Coyne-Delany*, says that no preliminary injunction can issue without a bond "in such sum as the court deems proper." *Atomic Oil* says the bond is mandatory. Is it? Should it be? How many plaintiffs can post a $50,000 bond? For many plaintiffs, injunction bonds are unavailable at any price. The bond is a surety agreement, not a liability policy; plaintiff remains primarily liable for any damages imposed. Thus, insurers who write injunction bonds do not care about the risks of litigation, but about the risk that plaintiff will

not be able to pay. They will write bonds only for plaintiffs with healthy financial statements. Among plaintiffs who can post a bond, how many can afford the risk of liability if some court later decides the preliminary injunction was wrongfully issued? A truly mandatory bonding rule would make preliminary relief generally unavailable in civil rights, environmental, and consumer litigation, to workers in labor litigation, and, in general, to nonwealthy plaintiffs.

The federal courts have responded by making the bond requirement discretionary. The most common explanation is that the amount of the bond is discretionary, and so a nominal bond could be required; if that is so, waiving bond altogether is no different. City of Atlanta v. Metropolitan Atlanta Rapid Transit Authority, 636 F.2d 1084, 1094 (5th Cir. 1981).

Are you convinced? Rule 65(c) is copied almost verbatim from the Clayton Antitrust Act; it was another part of Congress's attack on antilabor injunctions. Do you suppose Congress meant to leave the bond to the discretion of the judges it was trying to control? Doesn't the rule mean that the court has discretion only to estimate defendant's likely costs and damages, and must require bond in that sum? Would Congress want that rule applied to all litigants today? Have the courts made a better rule than the rulemakers? In some of the states, the rule or statute explicitly makes the bond discretionary.

7. Assuming bond is discretionary, what factors should guide the court's discretion? Potential loss to defendant, financial hardship to plaintiff, and the public importance of the right being enforced are the most commonly cited. Crowley v. Local 82, Furniture & Piano Moving, 679 F.2d 978, 1000 (1st Cir. 1982), rev'd on other grounds, 104 S. Ct. 2557 (1984). In City of Atlanta, the court temporarily restrained a fare increase expected to raise $43,000 per day. The court waived bond, in part because the case was "public-interest litigation." Should that matter if plaintiff cannot show financial hardship? Is there any reason to believe the transit authority was in better financial shape than the city? Other plaintiffs were a union of domestic workers and a class of "paupers." Should we have a rule that encourages the city to withdraw and leave the case to plaintiffs who plainly cannot post bond?

8. Should preliminary relief be easier to get for plaintiffs who can post bond? Doesn't harm to defendant that can be compensated by a bond drop out of the balancing test? Is that enough to encourage financially responsible plaintiffs to stay in a case like City of Atlanta?

9. Assuming liability, defendant still must show damages. The main issue here is whether defendant can recover attorneys' fees. Some jurisdictions disallow all fees; some allow fees for seeking dissolution of the preliminary order. Some of the latter also allow fees for contesting the preliminary order before it was issued, and some allow fees for defending the case on the merits. The federal courts disallow fees, citing Oelrichs v. Spain, 82 U.S. (15 Wall.) 211 (1872). Like Russell v. Farley, that case has

been questioned on the ground that it pre-dates the antecedents of Rule 65(c). Dobbs, Should Security Be Required as a Pre-Condition to Provisional Injunctive Relief?, 52 N.C.L. Rev. 1091, 1133-1136 (1974).

10.   There are three exceptions to the rule that plaintiff has no liability apart from the bond. First, a few states impose such liability by statute. See, e.g., the Illinois Injunction Act, Ill. Rev. Stat. ch. 69, par. 12. Second, courts occasionally waive bond for plaintiffs who are plainly able to pay damages. These plaintiffs are held liable as though they had filed bond in an unlimited amount. Monroe Division, Litton Business Systems v. DeBari, 562 F.2d 30 (10th Cir. 1977). (If you were representing a plaintiff, would you ever seek a waiver on this ground?)

Finally, plaintiff is liable if there is some independent ground of liability, such as malicious prosecution or abuse of process. Plaintiff may be liable in restitution for benefits conferred by the preliminary order. For example, when a preliminary injunction allows a regulated carrier to collect higher rates than those ultimately approved, the carrier must make restitution of the surcharge. Middlewest Motor Freight Bureau v. United States, 433 F.2d 212 (8th Cir. 1969). Commerce Tankers Corp. v. National Maritime Union, 553 F.2d 793 (2d Cir. 1977), illustrates a more unusual independent liability. There, the union got a preliminary injunction enforcing a contract; the contract itself violated the antitrust laws. The court held that the damage done by the preliminary injunction could be recovered in the employers' antitrust suit, without regard to the bond.

11.   As Judge Posner notes, whether plaintiff should be liable for the damages inflicted by a preliminary injunction is related to whether he should be liable for defendant's attorneys' fees. Because the attorneys' fee issue can arise with respect to any remedy, we will take it up again in chapter 10.

D. COERCIVE RELIEF AT LAW

The most common legal remedy is damages. But in certain circumstances the law courts gave coercive relief through specialized writs, and some of those remedies are still available.

1. Mandamus

Mandamus is an order to a public or corporate official, directing him to perform a ministerial duty. For example, mandamus can be used to force corporate officers to call a special meeting requested by the requisite number of shareholders, Auer v. Dressel, 306 N.Y. 427, 118 N.E.2d 590 (1954), to force prison officials to hold hearings before putting prisoners in isolation cells, Workman v. Mitchell, 502 F.2d 1201 (9th Cir. 1974), to require government contractors to pay the prevailing wage, Carpet, Linoleum & Resilient Tile Layers, Local Union No. 419 v. Brown, 656 F.2d 564 (10th Cir. 1981), or to compel the Secretary of State to issue a commission to a newly appointed judge, Marbury v. Madison, 5 U.S. (1 Cranch) 137, 168-173 (1803). These orders are indistinguishable from mandatory injunctions in practical effect. Often either remedy is available; sometimes, for reasons of history, local practice, or quirks in the jurisdiction and venue statutes, one is available and one is not. The federal statute grants federal jurisdiction over "any action in the nature of mandamus to compel an officer or employee of the United States or any agency thereof to perform a duty owed to the plaintiff." 28 U.S.C. §1361 (1982).

There are two principal limits on mandamus. First, it is not available against a private individual; it lies only to compel performance of official duty. Second, the duty must be clear and nondiscretionary; the court cannot substitute its policy judgment for the official's. But difficult legal questions do not preclude mandamus if the official's duty is clear once the legal questions have been answered. 13th Regional Corp. v. United States Department of Interior, 654 F.2d 758 (D.C. Cir. 1980).

In addition, mandamus is generally said to be discretionary and governed by equitable considerations. Id. Thus, mandamus is not available if plaintiff has some other adequate remedy. It makes no sense to deny mandamus because an injunction would be adequate or vice versa. But courts deny mandamus where there is some more specific provision for judicial review of the officer's decision, Cartier v. Secretary of State, 506 F.2d 191, 199-200 (D.C. Cir. 1974), or where damages would be adequate and the government has waived its immunity from suit, American Science & Engineering v. Califano, 571 F.2d 58, 64 (1st Cir. 1978).

2. Prohibition

Prohibition is an order to an inferior court or quasi-judicial agency to prevent it from exceeding its jurisdiction or abusing its authority. It is much like an injunction against filing or prosecuting a lawsuit, but with two essential differences. First, a court with equity powers can enjoin suits in courts that are in no sense inferior to it, including courts of other jurisdictions, and courts of law before the merger. Second, the equity court will never enjoin the other court or its judge; the injunction is addressed only to the plaintiff. The writ of prohibition is addressed to the inferior tribunal as well as the parties.

In modern legal systems, prohibition is a substitute for interlocutory appeal, and its availability depends on the strength of the jurisdiction's commitment to the final judgment rule. In some jurisdictions, such as California, prohibition is rather freely available to review all sorts of interlocutory orders. In the federal courts, the writ is usually called mandamus instead of prohibition. Mandamus to federal district judges is supposed to be available only in extraordinary circumstances, where the judge has usurped authority or clearly abused his discretion, and where no other remedy is available. Kerr v. United States, 426 U.S. 394 (1976). But the appellate court often discusses the merits in deciding whether there has been a clear abuse of discretion. Thus, even when mandamus is denied, the parties often get an effective advisory opinion from the court of appeals. The practice is carefully reviewed in Berger, The Mandamus Power of the United States Courts of Appeals: A Complex and Confused Means of Appellate Control, 31 Buffalo L. Rev. 37 (1982).

3. Habeas Corpus

Habeas corpus is an order to a person holding another in custody, directing him to bring the prisoner to court and justify his further detention. If the detention is not justified, the court will order the prisoner's release. Like injunction, mandamus, and prohibition, habeas corpus is in the form of a personal command to the defendant.

Both state and federal constitutions guarantee the right to habeas corpus. Whenever governments try to imprison people without charges or trial, the writ is a critical safeguard against tyranny; as long as it is obeyed, no one can be imprisoned without judicial review.

The most common use of the writ today is to permit further judicial review of criminal convictions. After a criminal defendant has exhausted his appeals, he can renew constitutional and jurisdictional attacks on his conviction in a petition for habeas corpus. This use of the writ is more controversial. A person unjustly imprisoned should be released no matter when the error is discovered, but multiple rounds of judicial review are expensive, and only a tiny portion of habeas petitioners are actually released. Further judicial review of a criminal conviction already reviewed may be a good thing, but it is not as essential to our liberties as judicial review of imprisonments imposed solely by the executive branch.

Habeas corpus is also used in child custody cases when a person having physical control of a child refuses to release the child.

E.   REPRISE ON IRREPARABLE INJURY

Professor Fiss has suggested that the irreparable injury rule be abolished. O. Fiss, The Civil Rights Injunction 90-91 (1978). He would have the court choose the best remedy in each case, without a presumption for or against any remedy. I endorsed that proposal in my review of his book. Laycock, Injunctions and the Irreparable Injury Rule, 57 Tex. L. Rev. 1065, 1084 (1979).

Many civil law jurisdictions go even further. They give plaintiff a free choice between damages or preventive relief, except where there is some strong reason to restrict that choice. Thus, in Louisiana, specific performance is the remedy for breach of contract, "except when it is impossible, greatly disproportionate in cost to the actual damage caused, no longer in the creditor's interest, or of substantial negative effect upon the interests of third parties." J. Weingarten, Inc. v. Northgate Mall, 404 So. 2d 896, 901 (La. 1981). The law is similar in "the overwhelming majority of civil-law systems." R. Schlesinger, Comparative Law 615 (4th ed. 1980). Orders to prevent threatened torts are generally available as well, although there are more exceptions. Preventive relief is most fully developed in systems influenced by German law. French courts will issue preventive orders, but only after the harm has already begun. Italian courts will issue preventive orders but will not coerce obedience; defendants can violate such orders and pay compensatory damages. Preventive relief is largely unknown in Japan, Norway, Sweden, and the Soviet Union. But no system uninfluenced by Anglo-American law appears to have anything like the irreparable injury rule. H. Stoll, Consequences of Liability: Remedies, in 11 International Encyclopedia of Comparative Law, ch. 8 at 150-154 (1973). Curiously, Louisiana has adopted the irreparable injury rule for injunctions against tort. La. Code Civ. Proc. Ann. art. 3601 (West 1961).

Which is preferable: the irreparable injury rule, the Fiss proposal, or the civil law practice? How often do these three approaches produce different results? Can't you find something inadequate about the legal remedy anytime your client has a reasonable ground for preferring the equitable remedy? Aren't courts much more inclined to find the legal remedy adequate when there is good reason to avoid the equitable remedy? Aren't they making the comparison Fiss suggests, at least de facto? Don't the civil law rules also lead to the court granting the best remedy, with plaintiff's choice as the tie breaker?

My personal view is that no version of the irreparable injury rule describes what the courts do or what they should do. The statement that equitable remedies are extraordinary and unavailable if legal remedies are inadequate suggests a general presumption against equity that does not exist in fact and should not exist. The clarification that the legal remedy is not adequate unless it is a complete, practical, and efficient as the equitable remedy suggests the opposite bias. This rule focuses attention only on the defects of the legal remedy. If there is anything wrong with it, plaintiff is entitled to the equitable remedy, even if that remedy has some other defect. That is not what courts do either, and it should not be.

There are countervailing rules that take account of some of the defects in equitable remedies. Equitable relief will be denied if it is impractical, imposes undue hardship on defendant, or requires personal services. Under the usual formulation of these rules, equitable relief is supposed to be denied no matter how inadequate plaintiff's legal remedy is. That is not what courts do either, and it should not be.

No rule explicitly authorizes courts to compare the legal remedy's problems with the equitable remedy's problems, unless it is implied by the slogan that all equitable remedies are discretionary. And no rule explicitly takes account of variations in the strength of our preference for jury trial, or says that courts should apply a stricter standard of irreparability at a preliminary hearing than at a trial, although these considerations can arguably be derived from explicit rules.

Regardless of what the opinions say, the courts in fact are doing what they always do, balancing competing interests and picking the solution they think is best. The cases in this chapter are not deviant or unusual, and they cannot be explained in any other way. The City of Chicago is remitted to a less complete, less practical, and less efficient remedy, although the court denies it, because the court cares about defendants' right to criminal procedure. A much less serious defect makes the legal remedy inadequate in Thompson v. Commonwealth, because the court does not take defendants' involuntary servitude claim seriously and nothing else is at stake. ABC is left with hardly any remedy at all, because the court takes Warner Wolf's involuntary servitude claim very seriously. Wolf would have to perform himself; Thompson can delegate the task. You should be able to identify other examples.

Aren't the courts doing what Fiss wants them to do? Is there any reason for the courts not to acknowledge what they're doing?

CHAPTER 5

Preventing Harm without Coercion: Declaratory Remedies

A. DECLARATORY JUDGMENTS

NASHVILLE, CHATTANOOGA & ST. LOUIS RAILWAY v. WALLACE
288 U.S. 249 (1933)

MR. JUSTICE STONE delivered the opinion of the Court.

Appellant brought suit in the Chancery Court of Davidson County, Tennessee, under the Uniform Declaratory Judgments Act of that state, to secure a judicial declaration that a state excise tax levied on the storage of gasoline is, as applied to appellant, invalid under the commerce clause and the Fourteenth Amendment of the Federal Constitution. A decree for appellees was affirmed by the Supreme Court of the State, and the case comes here on appeal.

After the jurisdictional statement required by Rule 12 was submitted, this Court, in ordering the cause set down for argument, invited the attention of counsel to the question "whether a case or controversy is presented in view of the nature of the proceedings in the state court." This preliminary question, which has been elaborately briefed and argued, must first be considered, for the judicial power with which this Court is invested by Art. 3, §1 of the Constitution, extends by Art. 3, §2, only to "cases" and "controversies"; if no "case" or "controversy" is presented for decision, we are without power to review the decree of the court below.

In determining whether this litigation presents a case within the appellate jurisdiction of this Court, we are concerned, not with form, but with substance. Hence, we look not to the label which the legislature has attached to the procedure followed in the state courts, or to the description of the judgment which is brought here for review, in popular parlance, as "declaratory," but to the nature of the proceeding which the statute authorizes, and the effect of the judgment rendered upon the rights which the appellant asserts.

Section 1 of the Tennessee Declaratory Judgments Act confers jurisdiction on courts of record "to declare rights . . . whether or not further relief is or could be claimed" and provides that "no action or proceeding shall be open to objection on the ground that a declaratory judgment or decree is prayed for. The declaration may be either affirmative or negative in form and effect and such declaration shall have the force and effect of a final judgment or decree." By §2 it is provided that "any person . . . whose rights, status or other legal relations are affected by a statute . . . may have determined any question of construction or validity arising under the . . . statute . . . and obtain a declaration of rights . . . thereunder."

Under §6, the Court may refuse to render a declaratory judgment where, if rendered, it "would not terminate the uncertainty or controversy giving rise to the proceeding." Declaratory judgments may, in accordance with §7, be reviewed as are other orders, judgments or decrees, and under §8 "further relief based on a declaratory judgment or decree may be granted whenever necessary or proper." Section 11 requires that "when declaratory relief is sought all persons shall be made parties who have or claim any interest which would be affected by the declaration, and no declaration shall prejudice the rights of persons not parties to the proceeding."

This statute has often been considered by the highest court of Tennessee, which has consistently held that its provisions may only be invoked when the complainant asserts rights which are challenged by the defendant, and presents for decision an actual controversy to which he is a party, capable of final adjudication by the judgment or decree to be rendered. . . .

Proceeding in accordance with this statute, appellant filed its bill of complaint in the state Chancery Court, joining as defendants the appellees, the Attorney General and the state officials charged with the duty of collecting the gasoline privilege tax imposed by the Tennessee statute. The complaint alleged that appellant is engaged in purchasing gasoline outside the state, which it stores within the state pending its use within and without the state in the conduct of appellant's business as an interstate rail carrier; that appellees assert that the statute taxes the privilege of storing gasoline within the state and is applicable to appellant; that they have demanded payment of the tax in a specified amount and have determined to enforce their demand and that, under the circumstances alleged, the statute as applied to appellant is invalid under the commerce clause and the Fourteenth Amendment. The relief prayed was that the taxing act be declared unconstitutional as applied to appellant. The Chancery Court sustained the appellees' demurrer to the sufficiency in law of the allegations relied on to establish the unconstitutionality of the tax. Its final decree dismissing the bill on the merits has been affirmed by the highest court of the state.

That the issues thus raised and judicially determined would constitute a case or controversy if raised and decided in a suit brought by the taxpayer to enjoin collection of the tax cannot be questioned. The proceeding terminating in the decree below was between adverse parties, seeking a determination of their legal rights upon the facts alleged in the bill and admitted by the demurrer. . . .

[V]aluable legal rights asserted by the complainant and threatened with imminent invasion by appellees, will be directly affected to a specific and substantial degree by the decision of the question of law; the question lends itself to judicial determination and is of the kind which this Court traditionally decides. The relief sought is a definitive adjudication of the disputed constitutional right of the appellant, in the circumstances alleged, to be free from the tax, and that adjudication is not subject to revision by some other and more authoritative agency. Obviously the appellant, whose duty to pay the tax will be determined by the decision of this case, is not attempting to secure an abstract determination by the Court of the validity of a statute or a decision advising what the law would be on an uncertain or hypothetical state of facts. Thus the narrow question presented for determination is whether the controversy before us, which would be justiciable in this Court if presented in a suit for injunction, is any the less so because through a modified procedure appellant has been permitted to present it in the state courts, without praying for an injunction or alleging that irreparable injury will result from the collection of the tax.

While the ordinary course of judicial procedure results in a judgment requiring an award of process or execution to carry it into effect, such relief is not an indispensable adjunct to the exercise of the judicial function. This Court has often exerted its judicial power to adjudicate boundaries between states, although it gave no injunction or other relief beyond the determination of the legal rights which were the subject of controversy between the parties, and to review judgments of the Court of Claims, although no process issues against the Government. As we said in Fidelity Nat. Bank v. Swope, 274 U.S. 132,

Naturalization proceedings, suits to determine a matrimonial or other status; suits for instruction to a trustee or for the construction of a will, bills of interpleader so far as the stakeholder is concerned, bills to quiet title where the plaintiff rests his claim on adverse possession, are familiar examples of judicial proceedings which result in an adjudication of the rights of litigants, although execution is not necessary to carry the judgment into effect, in the sense that no damages are required to be paid or acts to be performed by the parties.

The issues raised here are the same as those which under old forms of procedure could be raised only in a suit for an injunction or one to recover the tax after its payment. But the Constitution does not require that the case or controversy should be presented by traditional forms of procedure, invoking only traditional remedies. The judiciary clause of the Constitution defined and limited judicial power, not the particular method by which that power might be invoked. It did not crystalize into changeless form the procedure of 1789 as the only possible means for presenting a case or controversy otherwise cognizable by the federal courts. Whenever the judicial power is invoked to review a judgment of a state court, the ultimate constitutional purpose is the protection, by the exercise of the judicial function, of rights arising under the Constitution and laws of the United States. The states are left free to regulate their own judicial procedure. Hence, changes merely in the form or method of procedure by which federal rights are brought to final adjudication in the state courts are not enough to preclude review of the adjudication by this Court, so long as the case retains the essentials of an adversary proceeding, involving a real, not a hypothetical controversy, which is finally determined by the judgment below. . . .

As the prayer for relief by injunction is not a necessary prerequisite to the exercise of judicial power, allegations of threatened irreparable injury which are material only if an injunction is asked, may likewise be dispensed with if, in other respects, the controversy presented is, as in this case real and substantial. . . . Accordingly, we must consider the constitutional questions raised by the appeal. . . .

We cannot say that the tax is a forbidden burden on interstate commerce because appellant uses the gasoline, subsequent to the incidence of the tax, as an instrument of interstate commerce. . . .

Affirmed.

NOTES ON DECLARATORY JUDGMENTS AND RIPENESS

1. The Uniform Act has been very widely adopted in the states. Congress responded to *Wallace* by enacting a two-section federal declaratory judgment act in 1934, loosely based on §§1 and 8 of the Uniform Act (both quoted in *Wallace*). 28 U.S.C. §§2201-2202. The federal act explicitly requires an "actual controversy" and does not authorize declarations of status. It was upheld against constitutional attack in Aetna Life Insur-

ance Co. v. Haworth, 300 U.S. 227 (1937), in which the insurer sought a declaration that four policies had lapsed for nonpayment. The Court said that the statute and the Constitution used "controversy" in the same sense, and that "actual" was in the statute for emphasis only, so that the statute enacted the constitutional ripeness requirement.

2. Public Service Commission v. Wycoff, Co., 344 U.S. 237 (1952), contains the classic description of an unripe declaratory judgment action. Wycoff sought a declaration that its hauling business was interstate commerce. The Court said:

> The complainant in this case does not request an adjudication that it has a right to do, or to have, anything in particular. It does not ask a judgment that the Commission is without power to enter any specific order or take any concrete regulatory step. It seeks simply to establish that, as presently conducted, respondent's carriage of goods between points within as well as without Utah is all interstate commerce. One naturally asks, "So what?"

Id. at 244. Unfortunately, this appears to be a more accurate description of the plaintiff's inept pleadings and argument than of the underlying dispute. Justice Douglas, dissenting, and Justice Reed, concurring on other grounds, both found a clear controversy. The Commission threatened to shut Wycoff down for lack of an intrastate hauling license, which it had refused to grant. But the majority found no evidence the Commission was moving to carry out its threat. And it thought that if the Commission ever did take action, the facts might have changed in the meantime so that any declaration it issued would have become absolute without resolving the dispute.

3. Are you convinced that there is a difference of constitutional significance between *Wycoff* and *Wallace*? Isn't the declaratory judgment plaintiff most in need of relief when the party who would normally initiate the litigation delays doing so? Isn't elimination of prolonged uncertainty the main good of declaratory judgment acts? Even so, courts shouldn't grant declaratory judgments to resolve law professors' hypotheticals should they? Probably a line must be drawn, but it should not surprise you to learn that the line has never been consistent. Especially where ripeness turns on the likelihood that defendant will assert the rights plaintiff is challenging, or on the political considerations that underlie the case or controversy requirement, the ripeness doctrine is as amorphous and unpredictable in declaratory cases as in any other context. For further analysis and examples, see the note on constitutional and remedial ripeness, supra at 223, and Younger v. Harris and the notes following it, infra at 1182, 1211.

4. Reconsider the ripeness cases in chapter 3. Would it have mattered to those cases if plaintiffs had sought declaratory judgments instead of injunctions? Could Humble have gotten a declaratory judgment that Harang was not entitled to destroy the documents? Harang didn't dispute

that, did he? Wasn't Humble looking for coercion instead of clarification? What about Nicholson v. Connecticut Halfway House? Could the court have declared anything useful?

5.　Section 6 of the Uniform Act says the declaratory judgment may be denied if it "would not terminate the uncertainty or controversy giving rise to the proceeding." Is that a functional test that gives some content to the ripeness requirement?

A good example of a §6 case is Dodson v. Maroney, 15 Mass. App. 982, 447 N.E.2d 1256 (1983). Plaintiff sought a declaratory judgment that Mae Askling's will was invalid for undue influence and lack of testamentary capacity. Mae Askling was still alive. The court said the controversy could not be resolved, because she could revoke the will and write another at any time. It also said that no "exceptional circumstance" justified litigation before the usual opportunity for a will contest following Askling's death. Id. at 1257. What if Askling sued for a declaratory judgment that her will was valid? What if she alleged that she would not be around to testify and let the judge observe her sound mind when the time for a will contest arrived?

NOTES ON DECLARATORY JUDGMENTS AND IRREPARABLE INJURY

1.　Is there any practical difference between a declaratory judgment that the tax is unconstitutional and an injunction ordering the state authorities not to collect the tax? Both remedies are designed to protect plaintiff from having to pay the tax. The injunction would include a personal command; the declaratory judgment would not. How significant is that? Don't forget §8's provision that "further relief based on a declaratory judgment or decree may be granted whenever necessary or proper."

2.　As *Wallace* notes, plaintiff need not show irreparable injury to get a declaratory judgment. The only reference to other remedies in the Uniform Act is §1, which says courts can declare rights "whether or not further relief is or could be claimed." The Federal Rules are more explicit: "The existence of another adequate remedy does not preclude a judgment for a declaratory relief in cases where it is appropriate." Fed. R. Civ. Proc. 57. There are occasional decisions applying an irreparable injury rule anyway, but *Wallace* states the dominant view.

If declaratory relief serves the same preventive functions as coercive relief, should the same irreparable injury rule apply to both kinds of remedy? Do the surviving reasons for the irreparable injury rule not apply to declaratory judgments? Or do the declaratory judgment acts indirectly repeal the irreparable injury rule? If defendants ignored the declaratory judgment and plaintiff sought an injunction under §8, should he have to show irreparable injury then?

3. Even without an irreparable injury rule, the existence of other remedies is not wholly irrelevant. When is a declaratory judgment "appropriate"? Section 12 of the Uniform Act says that the act's purpose is "to settle and to afford relief from uncertainty and insecurity with respect to rights, status and other legal relations," that the act is remedial, and that it is to be liberally construed. Doesn't plaintiff have to show some need to have his uncertainty relieved? How different is that from irreparable injury properly understood? Whatever the answer to that question, there is a psychological difference that affects both judges and litigants. *Irreparable injury* has a more formidable ring than *uncertainty*. The proponents of declaratory judgment acts argued that declaratory judgments would be available where injunctions were not.

4. Consider two insurance coverage disputes that cast some light on when a declaratory judgment is appropriate. In the first case, Travelers issued a liability insurance policy to Superior Heating Co. A customer bought a furnace from Sears Roebuck, and Superior installed it. When the customer's house burned down, Sears payed the damages and sued Superior. Travelers denied coverage and refused to defend the lawsuit.

Superior sued for a judgment declaring the scope of the policy. This is a routine use of declaratory judgments. But the trial court denied relief on the ground that another remedy was available. Superior could pay a lawyer, pay Sears if it lost, and then sue for reimbursement. Is that an adequate remedy? What if Superior couldn't afford a lawyer? What if it could afford a lawyer, but settled with Sears because it couldn't afford the risk of a judgment for the full amount claimed? Even if Superior could afford the trial court's remedy, is it as practical and efficient as having Travelers defend? The Supreme Court reversed, holding that Superior need not show the inadequacy of other remedies. Friestad v. Travelers Indemnity Co., 452 Pa. 417, 306 A.2d 295 (1973).

5. Compare *Friestad* with Liberty Mutual Insurance Co. v. Bishop, 211 Va. 414, 177 S.E.2d 519 (1970). Liberty was one of three insurers arguably responsible for Bishop's liability in a wrongful death case. Liberty denied coverage; Bishop and the other two insurers settled the claim and paid decedent's estate. Then they sought a declaratory judgment that Liberty's policy was the primary coverage. The trial court so declared; the Supreme Court of Appeals reversed on the ground that declaratory judgment was an inappropriate remedy. But it said the insurers could have gotten a declaratory judgment before they settled. Before they settled, a declaratory judgment might have resolved uncertainty. But once plaintiffs had paid the claim, they were in effect seeking a money judgment for reimbursement. The claim for reimbursement was ripe, and there was no reason to merely declare that the money was owed. Is that the right result under §12 of the Uniform Act? Would a declaratory judgment serve any purpose in *Bishop*? Once it had been granted, did a reversal serve any purpose? Is there any reason to doubt that the trial court reached the

same result in a damage suit on remand? If not, why did the parties litigate this procedural issue to the Supreme Court of Appeals?

The answer may lie in procedural intricacies of Virginia insurance law that were in flux when *Bishop* was decided. The court had recently decided that an insurer who paid a claim could not sue another insurer for reimbursement. General Accident Fire & Life Assurance Corp. v. Aetna Casualty & Surety Co., 208 Va. 467, 158 S.E.2d 750 (1968). The legislature promptly enacted corrective legislation, but the new statute was arguably inapplicable to *Bishop*. The plaintiff insurers might have thought a declaratory judgment was the only way to get around *General*; defendant might have thought it could escape liability altogether if it could defeat the declaratory judgment action procedurally.

6. How should the court respond when plaintiff files a declaratory judgment action to avoid obstacles to relief in more traditional remedies? If the rule in *General* served a purpose, should plaintiffs have been allowed to avoid it by a declaratory judgment action? If it did not serve a purpose, shouldn't it be abolished?

Compare Lister v. Board of Regents, 72 Wis. 2d 282, 240 N.W.2d 610 (1976), in which four recent law graduates sued for a declaratory judgment that the Regents had erroneously charged them out-of-state tuition. A direct suit for a refund would have been barred by sovereign immunity; the court held that the state's immunity could not be evaded by a declaratory suit against university officials. Isn't that the right result if the state is serious about sovereign immunity?

7. Defendant has little reason to contest plaintiff's right to a declaratory judgment unless doing so will give him some advantage. Shouldn't the availability of declaratory relief turn on whether defendant is fairly entitled to the benefit of that advantage? Forum selection is one of the most common reasons for filing a declaratory judgment action. For example, in Wirkman v. Wirkman, 392 Pa. 63, 139 A.2d 658 (1958), the court refused to declare the meaning of a contract because the parties had agreed to submit all disputes to arbitration. Isn't the right to arbitration different from the hope that suffering damage and suing for reimbursement will be a remedy too expensive to pursue?

B. BILLS TO QUIET TITLE AND RELATED ACTIONS

NEWMAN MACHINE CO. v. NEWMAN
275 N.C. 189, 166 S.E.2d 63 (1969)

The hearing below was on demurrer. The . . . allegations may be summarized as follows: . . .

3.   George F. Newman, Jr., owned 64.77% of all the issued and outstanding shares of capital stock of plaintiff corporation. In March 1950 he
made a gift of certain of his shares to himself as trustee for his children.
Thereafter and until February 6, 1959, he owned individually 53.299% of
the capital stock and owned *as trustee for his children* 11.477% of said
shares. In addition, he also owned individually 65% of the outstanding
shares of capital stock of three affiliated corporations. . . .

5.   On February 6, 1959, George F. Newman, Jr., sold to the plaintiff
corporation at $135.25 per share all of its shares of stock which he owned.
This included both the 53.299% he owned individually and the 11.477%
he owned as trustee. The total purchase price was $785,802.50. . . .

8.   On February 5, 1965, defendant [George F. Newman, Jr.] notified
plaintiff by letter that defendant's attorneys were investigating the transaction involving the sale of the stock. On August 27, 1965, defendant
requested copies of plaintiff's audit report for the years 1957, 1958, 1959
and 1960; and on November 17, 1965, defendant's attorneys examined
copies of said audit reports at plaintiff's offices. Thereafter, on March 24,
1966, defendant's attorneys wrote plaintiff the following letter. . . .

[The letter said that the audit reports showed that Newman had been
defrauded and that the price paid for his shares had been "grossly inadequate." The attorneys said that they had advised Newman that he was
entitled to rescind the transaction or sue for damages, and that he was
legally obligated to sue with respect to the shares he owned as trustee.
They said that Newman had requested them to file suit, but that they
would be willing to discuss settlement first.]

9.   Defendant, through his attorneys, continued to make demands on
plaintiff and to threaten legal action against plaintiff, including threat of
receivership. These threats have seriously jeopardized plaintiff's corporate existence, hampered long-range planning, and seriously affected
plaintiff in the conduct of its business affairs.

10.   William M. York, Sr., President of plaintiff corporation, is 70
years of age and will be a material witness in any litigation. His evidence
should be preserved.

11.   A real controversy exists between plaintiff and defendant. The
threats constitute a cloud on the title to the shares of stock purchased by
plaintiff from George F. Newman, Jr., Trustee, and this action is brought
for the purpose of settling the controversy and removing the cloud on
plaintiff's title to the stock in question. . . .

12.   Plaintiff prays the court for judgment declaring that it has good
title to the 11.477% of its shares of stock purchased from defendant
trustee and for costs of the action. . . .

Huskins, Justice.

A demurrer tests the sufficiency of a pleading, admitting, for that
purpose, the truth of factual averments well stated and such relevant
inferences of fact as may be deduced therefrom. . . . Demurrers in de-

claratory judgment actions are controlled by the same principles applicable in other cases. Even so, it is rarely an appropriate pleading to a petition for declaratory judgment. If the complaint sets forth a genuine controversy justiciable under the Declaratory Judgment Act, it is not demurrable even though plaintiff may not be entitled to prevail on the facts alleged in the complaint. This is so because the Court is not concerned with whether plaintiff's position is right or wrong but with whether he is entitled to a declaration of rights with respect to the matters alleged.

The complaint and demurrer present these questions:

(1)   Does the complaint state a cause of action justiciable under the Declaratory Judgment Act?
(2)   Does the complaint state a cause of action in equity to quiet title to personal property?

Plaintiff contends for an affirmative answer to both questions, while defendant argues that an action to quiet title to personalty cannot be maintained in this jurisdiction because there is statutory provision for such suits only with respect to real property. G.S. §41-10. Defendant further contends that the type of dispute pictured by the complaint does not qualify for consideration under the Declaratory Judgment Act because (a) a genuine controversy does not exist, (b) the action does not include all necessary parties, (c) the action involves primarily issues of fact rather than questions of law, and (d) the object of the action is "to bag" in advance an impending lawsuit by becoming plaintiff now so as to avoid becoming defendant later.

The excellent briefs of the parties are largely devoted to discussions of whether the complaint states a cause of action justiciable under the Declaratory Judgment Act. We find it unnecessary to decide the first question, however, in view of the conclusion we have reached on the second.

We hold that the complaint states a cause of action to remove cloud and quiet title to personalty and that such action may be maintained in this State. Since the courts generally apply the same principles when title to personalty is involved as they do when title to land is clouded, brief reference to some of the requirements in equity suits to remove cloud and quiet title to realty prior to enactment of G.S. §41-10 is helpful to an understanding of the question before us.

Under the old equity practice,

> [a] bill *quia timet* was intended to prevent future litigation, by removing existing causes which might affect the plaintiff's title. If one in possession of land under a legal title knew that another was claiming an interest in the land under a title adverse to him, there was no adequate remedy at law for such occupant to test the validity of such claim. Being in possession, he could not

sue at law, and the adverse claimant would not sue, so that the adverse claim might be asserted at some future time when the evidence to rebut it might be lost, or at any rate the existence of such claim cast a cloud upon his title which would affect its value. His remedy was a bill in equity against the adverse claimant to have the cloud removed by a decree of the court and thereby quiet his title.

McIntosh, N.C. Practice and Procedure in Civil Cases §986 (1929); Holland v. Challen, 110 U.S. 15 (1883). . . .

Prior to 1893, in equity suits to remove cloud or quiet title to realty plaintiff was required to allege and show: (1) that he had no adequate remedy at law; (2) that he was in rightful possession of the land in question; and (3) that the defendant's adverse claim was such as to affect plaintiff's title injuriously. In Busbee v. Macy, 85 N.C. 329 (1881), plaintiff sought to remove a cloud upon the title to land alleging that a deed under which defendant claimed was void on its face by reason of the uncertain description of the land therein contained. The court held that since the illegality of defendant's deed appeared upon its face, a court of equity should dismiss the action and decline to declare an instrument to be a void deed which upon its face is no deed at all. . . .

Because the General Assembly considered *Busbee* an inconvenient or unjust application of the equitable doctrines involved, it enacted G.S. §41-10, providing, inter alia, that "[a]n action may be brought by any person against another who claims an estate or interest in real property adverse to him for the purpose of determining such adverse claims. . . ." That enactment was designed to avoid some of the limitations imposed upon the remedies formerly embraced by a bill of peace or a bill *quia timet*, and to establish an easy method of quieting titles of land against adverse claims.

Since we have no statute regarding suits in equity to remove cloud or quiet title to personalty, we apply to such suits the same principles which obtained prior to enactment of G.S. §41-10 when title to land was involved.

Although such suits were usually brought only in cases involving real property, "the generally accepted view is that a bill to quiet the title or to remove a cloud on the title to personal property may be maintained in equity, in the absence of statutory authorization, where, by reason of exceptional circumstances, there is no adequate remedy at law." Annot., 105 A.L.R. 291 (1936). In Loggie v. Chandler, 95 Me. 220, 49 A. 1059, it was held that a cloud upon the title to personal property in the form of a recorded chattel mortgage could not be removed; but Pomeroy says ". . . there seems no good reason for thus restricting the jurisdiction, and the instances are not infrequent where it has been exercised, in cases of void recorded chattel mortgages, spurious issues of shares of stock, etc." 5 Pomeroy, Equity Jurisprudence §2151 (4th ed. 1919). To like effect is

Thompson v. Emmett Irr. Dist., 227 F. 560 (9th Cir. 1915), where plaintiff, a purchaser of bonds issued by an irrigation district, alleged that defendant had defaulted in the payment of interest on all of the bonds on the ground that some of the bonds, without designating such bonds by number or otherwise, had been sold without consideration. Defendant demurred and moved to dismiss. Held: The allegations of the bill state a case for the removal of a cloud upon the title to personal property and such a case is within the jurisdiction of a court of equity. . . .

Even though there is no statute in North Carolina authorizing suits to quiet title to personalty, we adhere to the general rule that such suits may be maintained in equity where, due to exceptional circumstances, there is no adequate remedy at law. Here, plaintiff is in possession of the stock it purchased from defendant trustee, and defendant is claiming an interest in it adverse to plaintiff. Being in possession plaintiff cannot sue at law, and defendant will not sue — at least he has not done so during almost two years of threats and demands. His adverse claim may be asserted in court at some future time when plaintiff's evidence to rebut it may be lost. The existence of such a claim casts a cloud upon plaintiff's title to the stock and may adversely affect its value. Under these circumstances plaintiff is entitled to invoke the equitable assistance of the court to remove this cloud and quiet the title to ownership of said stock when defendant, for whatever reasons of his own, continues to threaten but refuses to act. With the ever increasing importance of personal property in the business world of today, especially stocks, bonds, and other intangibles, there is no sound reason why this equitable remedy should not be available to quiet title to personalty as well as realty. . . .

NOTES ON BILLS TO QUIET TITLE AND RELATED ACTIONS

1. Wouldn't a declaratory judgment have worked just as well in *Newman*? Is there any difference at all between a judgment quieting title in plaintiff and a judgment declaring plaintiff to be the owner? Why is the court still bogged down discussing the defects of the common law actions to try title?

2. The most important common law actions in disputes over real property were ejectment and trespass. Neither was available unless defendant had interfered with plaintiff's possession. Ejectment was essentially a restitutionary action; its aim was to restore plaintiff to possession. Its availability was expanded by elaborate fictional pleadings, but the plea that defendant was in possession could not be fictional. An owner who lost a chance to sell his property because a third party falsely cast doubt on his title could sue for slander of title and recover damages. But that action would not lie against a defendant who claimed title in himself.

There were no reasons for these restrictions that would be persuasive to modern lawyers; all these actions were artificially encumbered for reasons having much more to do with history than with logic, and it rarely occurred to the common law to question such limitations.

A claimant in disputed possession of personal property faced similar obstacles. If he were out of possession, he could sue in replevin, detinue, trover, or conversion, and recover damages, possession, or both. But as long as he remained in possession, the common law provided no remedy. Ejectment, replevin, and similar actions to recover possession are taken up infra at 578.

3. The equity court responded to the defects in the legal remedies with the bill to remove cloud on title. A cloud on title is any document tending to prove title, or a lien, in someone other than the plaintiff. The bill to remove cloud traditionally raised only the validity of the document, not the general question of who owned the property. If plaintiff prevailed, the court would order the document rescinded, cancelled, or reformed. In *Newman*, the bill is used to determine adverse claims not supported by any document.

The bill to quiet title is generally a statutory action that improves on the bill to remove cloud on title. The judgment usually determines ownership, not merely the validity of a single claim. The statutory actions can usually be brought by a plaintiff in or out of possession. But in some states, whether the plaintiff is in possession determines the right to jury trial. If defendant is in possession, the action is analogized to ejectment, and either party can demand a jury; if not, the action is analogized to removing a cloud on title and said to be equitable. Thompson v. Thompson, 7 Cal. 2d 671, 62 P.2d 358 (1936).

What some states call a bill to remove cloud may be called a bill to quiet title in other states. Sometimes the phrase bill to determine adverse claims is used.

4. All these nonpossessory actions represent early efforts to provide declaratory relief in situations where such relief is especially needed. Sometimes these actions were coercive in form; for example, defendant would be ordered to physically cancel his deed and, if necessary, imprisoned until he did so. But they were always declaratory in purpose and effect. They resolved questions of ownership before there was a trespass or ouster or even a threat of either, before a suit for damages or a conventional injunction or an order at law for possession would lie. In short, they removed uncertainty by declaring rights. Increasingly, these actions are declaratory in form. In most jurisdictions, it is no longer necessary to coerce the losing litigant into physically giving effect to the court's determination; the decree is self-executing.

5. Cancellation is an equitable remedy closely related to the bill to remove a cloud on title, and sometimes indistinguishable from it. Some modern examples: Miller v. San Sebastian Gold Mines, 540 F.2d 807, 809

(5th Cir. 1976), cancelling common stock issued without consideration; Citizens National Bank v. Pearson, 67 Ill. App. 3d 457, 384 N.E.2d 548 (1978), cancelling deed from mentally incompetent grantor; Blaising v. Mills, 176 Ind. App. 141, 374 N.E.2d 1166 (1978), cancelling deed from ex-husband, procured by false promise of reconciliation.

Some jurisdictions took the view that cancellation was not available if it would be an adequate remedy to wait to be sued on the instrument and then defend that lawsuit. A leading example is Johnson v. Swanke, 128 Wis. 68, 107 N.W. 481 (1906). Johnson paid for a horse with a non-negotiable promissory note for $3,000. The horse was worthless, and the sellers had fraudulently misrepresented its value. The court denied cancellation, finding no reason plaintiff could not wait to be sued on the note. The court noted the defect in the legal remedy:

> he would necessarily suffer embarrassment and anxiety by having [the note] outstanding against him, till the holder might see fit to enable him to show its true character and obtain a judicial decree in respect thereto by way of defense. Most men would so tire of such a situation as to be constrained to buy their peace, rather than to have it postponed till such time as their adversary might see fit to attack.

Id. at 482. But the Wisconsin precedents held that this defect was outweighed by the note holder's right to jury trial.

The English cases had made cancellation routinely available in fraud cases; the American cases were divided. Probably very few courts would follow Johnson v. Swanke today. Even the *Johnson* court implied that it would cancel a *negotiable* note in otherwise identical circumstances. A negotiable note could have been sold to a holder in due course, who would take the note free of Johnson's fraud defense unless he had notice of it. That would eliminate Johnson's defensive legal remedy, although he could sue the sellers for reimbursement if he were required to pay the note. But they were alleged to be insolvent.

6.   Rescission is often indistinguishable from cancellation. There is no practical difference between rescinding and cancelling a wholly executory contract. If the contract is wholly executory, a party can simply announce that he is rescinding, and wait to see if the other side does anything. If he sues for rescission, he is in effect seeking a declaratory judgment that he is entitled to rescind. Rescission is also available when the contract has been wholly or partly performed, but only if each party returns to the other all that he has received under the contract. In these circumstances, rescission is a restitutionary remedy; we will consider it in chapter 6.

7.   The opposite of cancellation is also available. Equity will order re-execution of a lost instrument if there is clear proof of its original execution and terms. An example is Smith v. Lujan, 588 F.2d 1304 (9th

Cir. 1979). This remedy is also essentially declaratory; it anticipates the dispute that would inevitably arise when something came to turn on whether the instrument had ever existed.

8.   The general declaratory judgment statute is a twentieth-century invention. It is not limited to specific subjects or contexts, and it seems capable of replacing all the more specialized declaratory remedies discussed in this section. But there does not seem to be much prospect of its actually doing so anytime soon. This is largely because lawyers and judges are familiar with the earlier forms and the body of authority concerning them. It is partly because the earlier forms seem to grant more relief, although it is hard to think of any practical difference between, for example, an order to surrender an instrument for cancellation and a declaratory judgment that the instrument is without effect and creates neither rights nor duties.

But even if the older forms of action persist, it seems likely that the availability of the declaratory judgment action to fill any gaps will lead to less and less litigation of the *Newman* sort, in which the parties argue over the precise scope of the older remedies.

9.   Consider defendant's four objections to maintenance of a declaratory judgment action in *Newman*. We are not told who the allegedly necessary party is, so we can't evaluate that. Is there anything to the other three? Do you have any doubt about the existence of an actual controversy? Don't most declaratory judgment actions involve potential defendants as plaintiffs? Is there anything wrong with that? Finally, why should issues of fact be a barrier to declaratory relief? If plaintiff is uncertain about his rights, should it matter whether the uncertainty derives from factual questions or legal questions? The objection that factual issues must be decided is often made, and occasionally made successfully, in declaratory litigation. The argument was summarily rejected in the very first case under the federal act. Aetna Life Insurance Co. v. Haworth, 300 U.S. 227, 242 (1937).

C.   REFORMATION

PARRISH v. CITY OF CARBONDALE
61 Ill. App. 3d 500, 378 N.E.2d 243 (1978)

JONES, Justice.

This is an appeal by the city of Carbondale . . . from a judgment of the circuit court of Jackson County, allowing the reformation of an agreement for an easement and denying the relief sought by the city in its countercomplaint.

The easement agreement involved was entered into between appellees, Gordon A. and Violet Parrish, and the city on November 1, 1965. By its terms the above mentioned appellees granted the city a perpetual easement across their land, which was located north of and outside the corporate limits of the city and used as a mobile home park, for the purpose of the construction of a water main and for its permanent maintenance and repair. A similar easement was executed in 1964 with respect to sanitary sewers. Both easements traversing the property of the Parrishes were obtained so that the city could supply utility services to an industrial park area being developed to the north of the Parrishes' mobile home park.

The 1965 water easement expressly reserved to the Parrishes the right to tap on to the line as necessary to develop their land, provided they pay the usual and customary charges for such taps. As a result of a preexisting city rule requiring any person whose property was not located within the corporate limits of the city but supplied with utility services to execute an annexation agreement, an annexation agreement was also entered into between these parties contemporaneously with the water easement.

The annexation agreement was limited to a five year period as presumably required by statute, and basically provided that the Parrishes (or their heirs, successors or assigns) would annex their land to the city upon its becoming contiguous thereto and that, in the meantime, the landowners could attach to and use the water and sanitary sewer facilities as required "and at the water and sewer rates as are established from time to time for all users thereof." Apparently, the property never became contiguous during the agreement's life. No complaint was made with respect to a party's meeting any obligations imposed under the annexation agreement.

Count I of the Parrishes' complaint, granted by the instant judgment, sought reformation of the easement on the basis of mutual mistake, alleging that the agreement as executed did not reflect the parties' agreement as to service charges and that such failure was the result of a scrivener's error. It further alleged that the true agreement was that in consideration of the Parrishes' execution of the easement, the city would furnish water and sewer service to the property of the Parrishes at the same water and sewer rates being charged, from time to time, to users located within the corporate limits of the city. The court agreed and ordered such a reformation.

The city's countercomplaint (and third party complaint) sought recovery of the difference between the water and sewer charges assessed "outside" users pursuant to a 1971 city ordinance ($1\frac{1}{2}$ times the rate of city users), which rate the city alleged was applicable to the Parrishes, and the city or "inside rates" which appellees had persisted in paying since June 30, 1972. This countercomplaint was grounded on the assertion that the agreement to charge city rates expired with the annexation agreement. The court found against the city as to the countercomplaint.

The main contention of the city on appeal is that the appellees did not meet their burden of proof in establishing that a mutual mistake of fact did occur and what the original agreement of the parties was. In other words, they contend that the trial court's factual determinations were erroneous. After consideration, we find that the trial court did not err in this respect. . . .

Reformation of a written instrument should be allowed only when clear and convincing evidence compels the conclusions that the instrument as it stands does not properly reflect the true intention of the parties, and that there has been either a mutual mistake or mistake by one party and fraud by the other. Both elements must be present: The mistake must be mutual and an agreement other than that expressed in the writing must have been reached. A reformation action rests upon the theory that the parties came to an understanding but in reducing it to writing, through mutual mistake or by mistake on one side and fraud on the other, some provision agreed upon was omitted, and the action is brought to so change the instrument as written so as to conform to a contract agreed upon by inserting the omitted provisions or striking out the one inserted by mutual mistake. In a reformation suit, the plaintiff has a higher burden of proof than in an ordinary civil lawsuit, and must prove a case by very strong, clear and convincing evidence.

Whether the evidence offered to support plaintiffs' claim of mutual mistake is sufficient to overcome the presumption that the written instrument expressed the true intent of the parties is primarily a question that the trier of fact must determine. A reviewing court will not disturb the decision of the trial court unless it is manifestly against the weight of the evidence. In the present case, the court found, after hearing the witnesses and viewing the exhibits, that the proof was clear and convincing that a mutual mistake was made by omission in that the parties agreed that in consideration of the plaintiffs granting a perpetual water easement to the city, the city would reciprocate by granting the plaintiffs a perpetual right to attach to and use its water and sanitary facilities at the same rates as established from time to time for all users in the city limits of Carbondale. We cannot say that the court was incorrect in so holding.

Gordon Parrish testified at the trial and the plaintiffs also produced the testimony of five others, including the former city attorney who negotiated the agreement, the former mayor and two former city councilmen. All of these witnesses stated that the easement did not contain the whole agreement in that it failed to mention the agreement that the plaintiffs be charged the same rates for water and sewer service as in-city users.

The former city attorney, J. Edward Helton, testified that in 1965 all users of these utilities paid the same rates but there had been discussion about charging higher rates to those outside the city limits and that Mr. Parrish wanted to be sure that paying the city rates was part of the consideration for the easement. In fact, the rates were discussed because

Parrish decried, "I won't grant it [the easement] unless you agree that you won't charge me any more for the rates than they do the people inside the city." Although Mr. Helton could not remember specifically telling Mr. Parrish that the right to such rates was to be perpetual, it was clearly understood that the benefit was to be for the period during which the land was outside the corporate limits.

In addition, Gordon Parrish testified that after discussing the duration of the right to city rates with Helton it was his understanding that the benefit was forever. Former mayor Miller testified that the easement agreement was not limited as to time and that it was his understanding that the agreement as to rates was to last as long as the easement existed.

With respect to how this provision of the agreement came to be left out of the written easement, the testimony reveals that the city attorney Helton's preparation of the easement was interrupted by someone who took the agreement to the Parrishes' attorney, W. Troy Barrett, for inspection. Mr. Helton did not see the easement again until after its passage, at which time he noticed that it did not contain the total agreement. The easement was not reformed at that time presumably because of the general belief that the land would be annexed shortly, mooting the efficacy of the provision omitted. Attorney Barrett, who was not privy to the negotiations or the specifics of the agreement between the parties, merely added some provisions not relevant to this appeal.

In view of this evidence, the findings of the court were correct, and the reformation was properly granted by addition of the instant terms. . . .

Affirmed.

EBERSPACHER, P.J., and GEORGE J. MORAN, J., concur.

NOTES ON REFORMATION

1. Suppose you were representing the Parrishes. How would you prove their case if there had not been a change of administration? If the parties agree that the written contract does not reflect their actual agreement, they can reform it themselves. If litigation is required, plaintiff must prove by clear and convincing evidence that both sides originally intended something that defendant denies ever having intended and that is inconsistent with what they wrote down. Testimony of third parties, such as lawyers and brokers, is often crucial. Defendant's employees may be willing to testify that the original understanding was different from what their employer now claims, but that cannot always be expected. The problem is not so much deliberate perjury, although there is some of that. Perhaps more important, it is easy for a witness to convince himself that he has always believed what it is now in his interest to believe. And of course, plaintiffs often think defense witnesses must be lying when the problem is that the parties failed to agree in the first place: Plaintiff

thought one thing and defendant another, and there was no agreement inconsistent with the writing. It is not enough for plaintiff to prove that there was a mistake or that the writing is inaccurate; plaintiff must prove what the actual agreement was. Neither the statute of frauds nor the parol evidence rule prohibits testimony on these issues.

2. Could plaintiff ever prove a case by clear and convincing evidence if the only evidence were his own and the defendant's inconsistent testimony? What if the judge simply doesn't believe defendant? What if defendant's story were shifting and contradictory? What if defendant's story were objectively implausible? Suppose the purchase price were half a million dollars. And suppose plaintiff testified that he agreed to buy a 640 acre farm, but that the contract and deed described a nearby section of swamp worth only $10,000. Is that clear and convincing, if defendant owns both sections? What if the case were in Mississippi, where plaintiff has to prove his case beyond a reasonable doubt? Sprow v. Hartford Insurance Co., 594 F.2d 418 (5th Cir. 1979). Don't juries disbelieve criminal defendants beyond a reasonable doubt every day?

3. What if the writing accurately states the parties' agreement but their agreement is itself based on a mutual mistake? Suppose that both buyer and seller thought the land they were trading was fertile farmland, that the contract and deed accurately described the land they meant, but that it turned out to be swamp of little value? Is that any different from the misdescription case in note 2? Can either side reform the contract to reflect the price they would have agreed on had they known they were dealing with swamp? Isn't deciding what they would have agreed on but for the mistake a lot chancier than deciding what they actually agreed on but failed to write down? The buyer may be able to rescind this contract for mutual mistake, but neither side will be able to reform the contract and enforce it as reformed. Rescission would leave the parties with no contract, their money refunded, and no obligations to each other. Reformation leaves them both obligated on a contract. Reformation is available for only one kind of mistake: where the writing misstates the parties' actual agreement. The theory is that the court is determining the parties' real agreement, not making an agreement for them.

4. What if both parties intended the same thing, but they never expressed that intent to each other and it is not reflected in the writing? American Employers Insurance Co. v. St. Paul Fire & Marine Insurance Co., 594 F.2d 973 (4th Cir. 1979), involved a marine liability policy. The question was whether St. Paul was liable for $500,000 per occurrence or $500,000 per vessel; three of the insured's vessels were involved in the accident. The policy, which was written by a trainee at St. Paul, provided per vessel coverage. But St. Paul's regional manager, and the insured's insurance agent, both testified that they meant to write per occurrence coverage. Neither had mentioned that to the other, and there was no settled usage in the industry. But St. Paul never wrote per vessel coverage

unless explicitly asked to. And the insured did not need per vessel coverage; it had another policy, from American, which would cover any excess liability. The trial court denied reformation for lack of an agreement inconsistent with the writing; the court of appeals reversed. That was the right decision, wasn't it?

5. *American* also raises the question of third party rights. The court reformed a contract between St. Paul and the vessel owner, because of their mutual mistake. That decision cost American a million dollars, but American was not party to the mistake and didn't know about it. Should that be enough to prevent reformation? What if American didn't know about the contract either, or didn't rely on it? In that case, isn't American seeking a million dollar windfall from the mistake? The standard for protecting third parties is formulated in varying ways, but reliance is usually the essential element.

6. Reformation is also available if the writing is inaccurate because of unilateral mistake plus fraud or inequitable conduct by the other party. The easy cases are where one party is blind or illiterate, or at least infirm, and the other party misrepresents the tenor of the instrument. But what about Anderson, Clayton & Co. v. Farmers National Bank, 624 F.2d 105 (10th Cir. 1980)? The bank held a security interest in all of a farmer's hogs. A company called Acco was selling hog feed on credit and held a security interest in the same hogs. The bank agreed to subordinate its interest to Acco's with respect to some of the hogs; the written subordination agreement applied to all the hogs. Acco drafted it, and the bank president signed it without reading it. He testified that he trusted Acco and had no reason to suspect that the writing didn't conform to the oral agreement. Is the bank entitled to reformation? The court said yes. It said that bankers ought to read before signing, but that this banker had sufficient reason for not doing so.

Should the case come out the other way if the bank president had thought Acco was sleazy from the beginning? The court quoted the Restatement standard: If Acco knew what the bank intended, and knew that the contract did not correctly state that intention, the bank is entitled to reformation. Why isn't that enough? Why did the court go on to say that reformation would be barred if the bank's negligence were sufficiently culpable or inexcusable? Whether or not you think plaintiff's negligence should bar reformation when the facts are clear, might plaintiff's negligence affect the clarity of the facts? If plaintiff claims to have made an unusually stupid mistake, isn't the judge less likely to believe he really made it, or less likely to believe defendant knew about it?

7. Most of these notes have discussed substantive law: When has plaintiff made out a sufficient case for reformation? When plaintiff is entitled to reformation on the merits, the remedy itself is so simple there is not much to say about it. The court's judgment states the terms of the

reformed contract. The writing may be physically modified, but that is not necessary. Either side may then enforce the contract as reformed.

Reformation looks most like a declaratory judgment when one party discovers the mistake and sues for reformation before any other dispute on the contract has arisen. Then the contract can be reformed in an action solely for that purpose; the parties can go on to perform or breach under the reformed contract, and there may or may not ever be further litigation. There does not seem to be any ripeness or irreparable injury requirement for reformation, although there are not many cases filed in which these issues could plausibly be raised. Usually, the mistake is not discovered, or no one is motivated to do anything about it, until some other dispute has arisen. Thus, it is quite common to see suits for reformation and breach of the contract as reformed, suits for breach of the contract as written and counterclaims for reformation, or, as in *Parrish*, suits for reformation and counterclaims for breach of the contract as written.

D. DECLARATORY RELIEF AT LAW

1. Nominal Damages

Recall part 3 of Carey v. Piphus, supra at 100. The Court said that violations of the due process clause were so important that plaintiff could recover $1.00 even if he had not been injured. Why would anyone sue for nominal damages? And why would the courts allow such suits? The most obvious purpose was to obtain a form of declaratory relief in a legal system with no general declaratory judgment act. When a landowner sued his neighbor for nominal damages in trespass, he presumably was not interested in the dollar, but in the court's determination that the neighbor was trespassing. The suit for nominal damages might resolve an underlying dispute about the location of a boundary, or an easement entitling the neighbor to cross the land. The common law courts would not declare such matters directly, but the suit for nominal damages allowed them to do so indirectly. Suits for nominal damages can still be used in this way today, although it is rarely necessary to do so.

In Carey v. Piphus, nominal damages were the consolation prize in an action for actual damages that plaintiff failed to prove. Here too they can be said to serve a declaratory function. The court might have been reluctant to issue a declaratory judgment that the school board had once violated plaintiff's right to due process; if no other charges were pending against plaintiff, the question could easily be considered moot. Awarding $1.00 allows the court to decide that the school board violated the due process clause and embody that decision in a judgment. But it is easy to overstate the importance of this. An opinion saying that the school board violated the due process clause but plaintiff proved no actual damages would guide the school board's future behavior as effectively as a judgment for nominal damages. And the unavailability of formal declaratory relief is least troubling where there is formally no continuing controversy; if either side could show a need for a declaratory judgment to eliminate uncertainty, the court would probably issue it.

The other function of nominal damages in a case like Carey v. Piphus is to make plaintiff the prevailing party. Liability for costs and attorneys' fees often depends on who is the prevailing party. Thus, although the court has considerable discretion in the matter, the $1.00 in nominal damages can be the key to many thousands of dollars in fees. We will examine whether that makes sense in chapter 10, when we take up attorneys' fees more generally.

2. Quo Warranto

Quo warranto is a specialized writ for determining the right to hold a public office or corporate franchise. In practical effect, it leads to a declaratory judgment that defendant is or is not entitled to the position he claims. Like mandamus, prohibition, and habeas corpus, quo warranto is a relic of the writ system that has survived to the present. The action is typically brought in the name of the state, or the attorney general, but in most states there are procedural devices that allow a competing claimant to the office to initiate and control the action.

The most obvious use of quo warranto is to contest the results of an election. It is still available for that purpose in some states; in others, it has been replaced or supplemented by statutory procedures for election contests. But a disputed election is only one of the many reasons why an incumbent may not be entitled to office. Here are some other examples:

Town of Cheshire v. McKenney, 182 Conn. 253, 438 A.2d 88 (1980): McKenney was a member of the town council and a public school teacher in the town. The town charter precluded any person who held a "position of profit" with the town from serving on the council. The town sued in quo warranto, and the court declared that his teaching job was a "position of profit."

Rogers v. Medical Association, 244 Ga. 151, 259 S.E.2d 85 (1979): A Georgia statute directed the governor to appoint members of the State Board of Medical Examiners from lists of nominees submitted by the Medical Association. Rogers sued on behalf of all doctors who were not members of the association, alleging that they were excluded from consideration and that it was unconstitutional to vest the exclusive nominating power in a private body. The court characterized his claim as a quo warranto suit, because it alleged that the incumbent examiners had been illegally appointed. In a judgment that highlights the declaratory nature of the remedy, the court held the nomination procedure unconstitutional but limited its holding to future appointments; it did not displace the incumbent examiners.

Gwinn v. Kane, 19 Pa. Commw. 243, 339 A.2d 838, *aff'd*, 465 Pa. 269, 348 A.2d 900 (1975): Pennsylvania appointed a special prosecutor to investigate political corruption in Philadelphia. The investigation resulted in Gwinn's indictment for perjury. Gwinn sued in quo warranto, alleging that the statute authorizing special prosecutors was unconstitutional, so that the office could have no legal existence and no one could occupy it. The Commonwealth Court agreed that quo warranto was the proper remedy, but it rejected plaintiff's claims on the merits. The Supreme Court affirmed on the merits without deciding whether quo warranto was the proper remedy. Quo warranto is generally said to be subject to the requirement that there be no other adequate remedy; it is not clear why a motion to dismiss the indictment would not have worked here.

Burns v. Kurtenbach, 327 N.W.2d 636 (S.D. 1982): Kurtenbach beat Burns in an election for school board. But Burns sued in quo warranto, alleging that Kurtenbach's nominating petitions had been defective. The court agreed and held Burns elected because he was the only legal candidate. Query whether democracy was served on the merits, but the use of the remedy was clearly appropriate.

State by Lockert v. Knott, 631 S.W.2d 124 (Tenn. 1982): Knott was elected county road engineer with 70 percent of the vote. But state law required county road engineers to have a high school diploma or equivalent; Knott had only an eighth-grade education. The court held him ineligible for office in a quo warranto action. You may feel better about this result if you know that Knott apparently filed a forged general equivalency diploma just before the election.

In the corporate area, quo warranto is sometimes used to forfeit corporate charters as a penalty for illegal conduct. In this application, the writ is punitive rather than declaratory. An example is Attorney General v. Diamond Mortgage Co., 414 Mich. 603, 327 N.W.2d 805 (1982), in which the attorney general sought to revoke Diamond's corporate charter for repeated violations of the usury and consumer protection laws. The court held that quo warranto was the proper remedy and remanded for further proceedings.

CHAPTER 6

Benefit to Defendant as the Measure of Relief: Restitution

A. THE BASIC PRINCIPLE: PREVENTING UNJUST ENRICHMENT

INTRODUCTORY NOTES

1. The law of restitution is both substantive and remedial. It creates causes of action and it provides a different measure of recovery. A restitutionary cause of action is often available in cases of ordinary tort and breach of contract, and electing the restitutionary claim leads to the restitutionary measure of recovery. But a plaintiff may have a cause of action in restitution even when no more traditional cause of action is available.

Recall the facts of Neri v. Retail Marine, supra at 17. The Neris put down a $4,250 deposit on a contract to buy a boat. Then they breached the contract and sued to recover the deposit. The first time we encountered the case, we focused on the seller's counterclaim for lost profits. This time, focus on the Neris' claim. What is the basis of their suit? They breached the contract; Retail Marine did not. Retail Marine certainly didn't commit a tort. It has done nothing wrong. But if it has been unjustly enriched, the Neris may recover the amount of the enrichment. Put the other way around, Retail Marine must restore to the Neris the benefit it received from them. Retail Marine is entitled to full compensation, but if the deposit exceeds its damages, it must refund the excess.

Under the Uniform Commercial Code, a defaulting buyer is entitled to restitution of his deposit to the extent it exceeds reasonable liquidated damages or actual damages. §2-718. For contracts without a liquidated damage clause, the UCC provides a statutory sum: 20 percent of the price or $500, whichever is less. Vines v. Orchard Hills, Inc., 181 Conn. 501, 435 A.2d 1022 (1980), is a common law case applying substantially similar rules to a contract for the sale of real estate.

2. The most distinctive feature of restitution is that liability is based on, and recovery is usually measured by, benefit to defendant rather than harm to plaintiff. Sometimes this is done by restoring to plaintiff the very thing that defendant unlawfully acquired from him, or some other thing that defendant acquired with plaintiff's thing, together with any profits defendant earned with plaintiff's thing. Sometimes it is done by requiring defendant to pay for benefits he received from plaintiff.

3. Substance and remedy are so thoroughly integrated in restitution that it is difficult to study one without studying the other. Unfortunately, it is no more feasible to seriously study the substantive law of restitution in a survey of remedies than it would be to seriously study the substantive law of contract or tort. Whole courses are taught on restitution, and there are multivolume treatises on the subject.

This chapter must necessarily focus on the ways in which restitutionary remedies differ from other remedies, and especially on how restitution differs from damages. The key question is, What can plaintiffs get from restitution that they could not get otherwise? But that question naturally leads back to the substantive question, When can the plaintiff elect restitution? These notes offer a superficial introduction to substantive restitution.

4. Retail Marine's damages were $3,253; the Neris' deposit was $4,250. So the final judgment was that the Neris recover $997 from Retail Marine. If Retail Marine didn't do anything wrong, what does it mean to say it was unjustly enriched? That it has plaintiffs' money without any justification and ought to give it back? Is there anything more to it than that?

Does the reason for plaintiffs' breach matter? What if Mr. Neri had not been hospitalized, but he simply found another boat he and his wife liked better? What if he breached because he took an irrational dislike to a Retail Marine salesperson? Would that make Retail Marine's enrichment more just? Does the justice of the breach affect the justice of the enrichment? Some courts have been reluctant to award restitution to plaintiffs who breached "willfully."

5. The substantive law of restitution is largely devoted to distinguishing between just and unjust enrichments, or more precisely, unjust and not unjust enrichments. General formulations are not too helpful, even in the hands of great judges. Justice Cardozo said the test is whether a benefit "was received in such circumstances that the possessor will give

offense to equity and good conscience if permitted to retain it." Atlantic
Coast Line Railroad v. Florida, 295 U.S. 301, 309 (1935). The concept
is in fact undefinable, but a few categories account for most of the
cases:

a. Cases where defendant acquired a benefit from plaintiff
through an unlawful act, such as theft, conversion, fraud, extortion, or
breach of fiduciary duty. Where the unlawful act is a tort, plaintiff can
generally elect either the damage remedy or the restitution remedy. But
many cases of duress and breach of fiduciary duty were not recognized as
torts; for them, the only remedy was in equity, and it was generally some
form of restitution. And acts not sufficiently culpable to support a damage action may be a ground for restitution. The unlawful act may be no
more than collecting charges under an administrative rate order later
held to be excessive. Democratic Central Committee v. Washington Metropolitan Area Transit Commission, 485 F.2d 786, 824-826 (D.C. Cir.
1973), cert. denied, 415 U.S. 935 (1974). Similarly, as noted in chapter 4,
plaintiff can get restitution of benefits conferred by an erroneous preliminary injunction.

b. Cases where plaintiff conferred a benefit on defendant pursuant to an actual or supposed contract. *Neri* is an example. Cases where
defendant breached after part performance by plaintiff are more obvious
examples. Perhaps most important substantively are cases where the contract is not binding but this is not discovered until after part or full
performance by plaintiff. Thus, if a contract is void under the statute of
frauds, or is discharged for impossibility or frustration, a party who partly
performed can get restitution of the benefits he conferred.

c. Cases where a benefit is conferred by mistake. Examples are
where plaintiff mistakenly pays money he doesn't owe, or a third party
who owes money to plaintiff mistakenly pays it to defendant, or plaintiff
mistakenly improves property belonging to defendant. Bryan v. Citizens
National Bank, 628 S.W.2d 761 (Tex. 1982), illustrates a common pattern. The bank mistakenly paid a $10,000 check despite a stop payment
order from its customer. The bank is entitled to restitution if the payee is
not entitled to the money, that is, if the bank's customer had a legally
sufficient reason for stopping payment.

6. Restitution is administered through a number of more specific
remedies. Each has a separate origin and its own set of historical limitations. It is only in this century and in the United States that lawyers have
begun to think of restitution as a general principle uniting these separate
remedies. But unification is not yet complete, and it is still necessary to
know something of quasi-contract, constructive trust, accounting for
profits, rescission, equitable lien, subrogation, indemnity, contribution,
replevin, and ejectment. Replevin and ejectment are not generally
thought of as based on unjust enrichment, but I include them here
because they provide a form of specific restitution.

This chapter will introduce these strange terms one by one, with a case and a set of explanatory notes for each. At this point, I want to explain only the relationship between this set of terms and the term *restitution*. Some of these terms are surviving relics of the writ system and the forms of action. Some are labels for fictional explanations that enabled courts to reach just results without fully confronting some doctrine that stood in the way. Each of them is a device for accomplishing restitution — for restoring unjust gain to its rightful owner. It may help to think of them as procedural devices instead of separate remedies.

Some of these procedural devices remain quite specialized. Others, especially quasi-contract and constructive trust, have been generalized and become available in all sorts of factual situations. The best cases, and the best statutes, simply talk in terms of restitution and unjust enrichment, without explaining the result in terms of one of the procedural devices.

7. A final word on organization. Unavoidably, this chapter asks you to do three things at once. The primary organizational scheme is based on the restitutionary measure of recovery and the reasons plaintiffs sometimes find restitution more lucrative than damages. But each case will also cast a little more light on the substantive grounds of restitution. And each case will illustrate one of the specific restitutionary remedies or procedural devices. The notes should help you keep all three balls in the air.

OLWELL v. NYE & NISSEN CO.
26 Wash. 2d 282, 173 P.2d 652 (1946)

MALLERY, Justice.

On May 6, 1940, plaintiff, E. L. Olwell, sold and transferred to the defendant corporation his one-half interest in Puget Sound Egg Packers, a Washington corporation having its principal place of business in Tacoma. By the terms of the agreement, the plaintiff was to retain full ownership in an "Eggsact" egg-washing machine, formerly used by Puget Sound Egg Packers. The defendant promised to make it available for delivery to the plaintiff on or before June 15, 1940. It appears that the plaintiff arranged for and had the machine stored in a space adjacent to the premises occupied by the defendant but not covered by its lease. Due to the scarcity of labor immediately after the outbreak of the war, defendant's treasurer, without the knowledge or consent of the plaintiff, ordered the egg washer taken out of storage. The machine was put into operation by defendant on May 31, 1941, and thereafter for a period of three years was used approximately one day a week in the regular course of the defendant's business. Plaintiff first discovered this use in January or February of 1945 when he happened to be at the plant on business and heard the machine operating. Thereupon plaintiff offered to sell the machine to defendant for $600 or half of its original cost in 1929. A counter offer of $50 was refused and approximately one month later this action was commenced to recover the reasonable value of defendant's use of the machine. . . .

The theory of the respondent was that the tort of conversion could be "waived" and suit brought in quasi-contract, upon a contract implied in law, to recover, as restitution, the profits which inured to appellant as a result of its wrongful use of the machine. With this the trial court agreed and in its findings of facts found that the use of the machine

> resulted in a benefit to the users, in that said use saves the users approximately $1.43 per hour of use as against the expense which would be incurred were eggs to be washed by hand; that said machine was used by Puget Sound Egg Packers and defendant, on an average of one day per week from May of 1941, until February of 1945 at an average saving of $10.00 per each day of use.

[Judgment was entered for $1,560, covering use of the machine within the three-year statute of limitations.]

In substance, the argument presented by the assignments of error is that the principle of unjust enrichment, or quasi-contract, is not of universal application, but is imposed only in exceptional cases because of special facts and circumstances and in favor of particular persons; that respondent had an adequate remedy in an action at law for replevin or claim and delivery; that any damages awarded to the plaintiff should be based upon the use or rental value of the machine and should bear some reasonable relation to its market value. Appellant therefore contends that the amount of the judgment is excessive.

It is uniformly held that in cases where the defendant *tort feasor* has benefited by his wrong, the plaintiff may elect to "waive the tort" and bring an action in assumpsit for restitution. Such an action arises out of a duty imposed by law devolving upon the defendant to repay an unjust and unmerited enrichment.

It is clear that the saving in labor cost which appellant derived from its use of respondent's machine constituted a benefit. . . .

It is also necessary to show that while appellant benefited from its use of the egg-washing machine, respondent thereby incurred a loss. It is argued by appellant that since the machine was put into storage by respondent, who had no present use for it, and for a period of almost three years did not know that appellant was operating it and since it was not injured by its operation and the appellant never adversely claimed any title to it, nor contested respondent's right of repossession upon the latter's discovery of the wrongful operation, that the respondent was not damaged because he is as well off as if the machine had not been used by appellant.

The very essence of the nature of property is the right to its exclusive use. Without it, no beneficial right remains. However plausible, the appellant cannot be heard to say that his wrongful invasion of the respondent's property right to exclusive use is not a loss compensable in law. To hold otherwise would be subversive of all property rights since his use was admittedly wrongful and without claim of right. The theory of unjust enrichment is applicable in such a case. . . .

Respondent may recover the profit derived by the appellant from the use of the machine. . . .

NOTES ON QUASI-CONTRACT

1.   Many wrongful acts do not benefit the wrongdoer. The negligent driver may inflict great damage, but he does not profit by his wrong, and his victim can sue only for damages. In another large group of cases, plaintiff's loss is exactly equal to defendant's gain. For example, in the typical conversion case, the converted property is no more valuable in defendant's hands than it was in plaintiff's. In these cases, the choice between compensatory damages and restitution of unjust enrichment does not affect the amount of the judgment. But sometimes defendant's gain exceeds plaintiff's loss, or at least exceeds plaintiff's loss as the law would measure it. It is in this third class of cases that restitution is most attractive to plaintiffs. *Olwell* is a dramatic example.

2.   Both law and equity developed remedies for granting restitution in such cases. The law implied a fictional promise to pay for the benefit. Under the writ system, the damage action was under some tort writ, such as case or trespass; the restitution action was in general assumpsit. (A suit on an actual contract was in special assumpsit.) The courts said plaintiff could waive the tort and sue in assumpsit. Today, it is more common to speak of quasi-contract than assumpsit, but talk of waiving the tort is still with us.

3.   It is essential to understand two things. First, a quasi-contract is not a contract and has nothing to do with enforcing agreements. Defendant rarely intended to pay, and it does not matter if he explicitly intended not to. In cases like *Olwell*, quasi-contract is simply a remedy for tort. Instead of suing for his own losses from the conversion, plaintiff sues for defendant's gains. Quasi-contracts are sometimes called contracts implied in law, to distinguish them from cases where the parties' words and actions reveal a real but tacit agreement — a contract implied in fact. Second, talk of waiving the tort is quite misleading. If plaintiff really waived the tort, he would have nothing left to sue for; it is the tort that makes defendant's enrichment unjust.

4.   Sometimes quasi-contract is a source of liability as well as a remedy, but there is still no real contract, or if there is, it does not support liability. Quasi-contract includes a group of actions historically called the

common counts, of which the most important for our purposes were money had and received, quantum meruit, and quantum valebant. These were for the recovery of money paid, the value of services performed, and the value of goods delivered, respectively, when there was no contract to pay but it was unjust for defendant not to pay. Some of the cases involve situations where defendant would have agreed to pay had he been able to agree; the doctor who treats an unconscious patient is the classic example. In re Crisan's Estate, 362 Mich. 569, 107 N.W.2d 907 (1961). But the law also implies the promise to pay in cases like *Neri*, cases where the benefit is conferred by mistake, and cases where the benefit is conferred pursuant to a contract that is not legally binding.

NOTES ON RECOVERING MORE THAN PLAINTIFF LOST

1.   Consider *Olwell* as the court apparently considered it: Assume that but for the wrong, the egg washer would have gathered dust in the back room. Is the remedy consistent with the goal of restoring plaintiff to his rightful position? It's a $1,500 windfall for him, isn't it? Does the remedy restore *defendant* to the position *it* would have occupied but for the wrong?

2.   Is *Olwell* consistent with the economic explanation of law? Isn't it more productive to use the egg washer every day than to let it sit idle? Why shouldn't Nye & Nissen be encouraged to use the egg washer? Even if Olwell were harmed, wouldn't the economic theory limit him to compensatory damages? If the law followed the economic theory, why would it ever allow recovery based on a defendant's profits?

3.   A similar case is Edwards v. Lee's Administrator, 265 Ky. 418, 96 S.W.2d 1028 (1936). Edwards discovered the entrance to a cave on his land and developed it as a tourist attraction. One third of the cave was under Lee's land. Lee's part of the cave was inaccessible to him, but it belonged to him under Kentucky law. Lee sued for restitution of the profits Edwards earned from showing Lee's part of the cave. The court granted restitution. It noted other kinds of cases in which plaintiff suffered no losses, nominal losses, unprovable losses, or losses less than defendant's profits, including the commercially important unfair competition cases.

> The law, in seeking an adequate remedy for the wrong, has been forced to adopt profits received, rather than damages sustained, as a basis of recovery. . . . The philosophy of all these decisions is that a wrongdoer shall not be permitted to make a profit from his own wrong.

Id. at 427, 96 S.W.2d at 1032. That is the traditional rationale for making defendant repay a benefit in excess of plaintiff's loss. Isn't that a moral judgment? Indeed, doesn't it reject the essence of the economic explanation of law — that profitable violations should be encouraged? At the very least, doesn't it choose morality over economics in a case where the two conflict? Is the law soft-headed and wrong here? Or is the economic explanation too singlemindedly focused on one important consideration to the exclusion of all others?

4.   Judge Posner's basic textbook on law and economics has very little to say about restitution, and nothing to say about cases where plaintiff recovers more than he lost. Other proponents of the economic explanation of law are similarly silent. But might the economic preference for voluntary transactions help explain restitution on their terms? Judge Posner certainly thinks so. He encountered restitution of profits in a copyright case, Taylor v. Meirick, 712 F.2d 1112 (7th Cir. 1983). Here was his response:

> It is true that if the infringer makes greater profits than the copyright owner lost, because the infringer is a more efficient producer than the owner or sells in a different market, the owner is allowed to capture the additional profit even though it does not represent a loss to him. It may seem wrong to penalize the infringer for his superior efficiency and give the owner a windfall. But it discourages infringement. By preventing infringers from obtaining any net profit it makes any would-be infringer negotiate directly with the owner of a copyright that he wants to use, rather than bypass the market by stealing the copyright and forcing the owner to seek compensation from the courts for his loss. Since the infringer's gain might exceed the owner's loss, especially as loss is measured by a court, limiting damages to that loss would not effectively deter this kind of forced exchange. This analysis also implies that some of the "windfall" may actually be profit that the owner would have obtained from licensing his copyright to the infringer had the infringer sought a license.

Id. at 1120.

5.   Recall that with respect to injunctions and criminal punishment, the economic explanation and the actual legal rules took different approaches to cases with high transaction costs. One source of high transaction costs is bilateral monopoly: the situation where plaintiff and defendant have no one to deal with but each other. Plainly there was a bilateral monopoly in Edwards v. Lee's Administrator; Lee had the cave, and Edwards had the entrance. There may have been bilateral monopoly in Olwell. We do not know whether anyone else would have wanted plaintiff's egg washer, or what they would have paid for it; plaintiff does not appear to have been looking for buyers. Nor do we know whether defendant had other sources of supply; egg washer factories might have been converted to war production. If the parties were effectively in a bilateral monopoly, they might have had great difficulty agreeing on a

price for sale or lease of the egg washer. Their inability to agree on a price after Olwell discovered the conversion is some evidence that bilateral monopoly actually existed, but it is not conclusive. Olwell's anger at being wronged, and Nye & Nissen's anger at being accused, might have caused those negotiations to break down so quickly. Recall Professor Macneil's suggestion that committing profitable violations of law is itself a source of high transaction costs.

It seems likely that a sale of the egg washer from Olwell to Nye & Nissen would have been profitable for both sides. Yet the parties could not complete the sale. That is the greatest risk in situations with high transaction costs. If the law were really committed to making sure resources are moved to their most valuable use, wouldn't it deny restitution in cases like *Olwell* and *Edwards*? Don't these cases treat the prevention of wrongful profits as a more important goal?

Where transaction costs are low, theories of corrective justice and theories of economic efficiency may both be able to explain a wide range of restitution cases.

6. Compare *Olwell* and *Edwards* with Vincent v. Lake Erie Transportation Co., 109 Minn. 456, 124 N.W. 221 (1910). Defendant's ship had just finished unloading at plaintiff's dock when an unusually severe storm arose. The captain kept the ship tied up and did $500 damage to the dock. The court found no negligence, but it held that having used plaintiff's property to save its own, the shipowner should be liable for the damage.

Is *Vincent* consistent with *Olwell*? Isn't defendant's profit the value of the ship, if it would have been lost, or the cost of repairing the harm that would have been done to it, if it could have been refloated and repaired? Didn't the court allow defendant to profit from its violation of plaintiff's right to exclusive use of the dock? Is that any different from Nye & Nissen's violation of Olwell's right to exclusive use of his egg washer? Is it sufficient to say that the shipowner in *Vincent* was not a wrongdoer, or that its enrichment was not unjust? That seemed to be the court's attitude, but how did the court know that? An economist would say that the dock's most valuable use that day was to save the ship. Is that why the shipowner was not a wrongdoer? On that theory Nye & Nissen was not a wrongdoer either. Many people find the cases distinguishable, but what exactly is the distinction? Is it the amount of the difference in value? That human life might have been at risk? That saving property from destruction is a better justification than making new profits, even if the profits and the property are of equal value? Avoiding greater harm is a common ground for creating privileges to do otherwise unlawful things. If the distinction is between avoiding harm and making profits, does it matter that the "profits" in *Olwell* were a savings of wasted labor?

Might it matter that in *Vincent* there was less time for a voluntary transaction? What if there had been time to negotiate, and plaintiff had explicitly denied permission to remain at his dock? The court implied that

that would not have affected its reasoning, citing a similar case where the dock owner was held liable for untying the ship, Ploof v. Putnam, 81 Vt. 471, 71 A. 188 (1908).

The court did not have to explain why plaintiff recovered only $500, because that was all plaintiff sought; he did not ask for the value of defendant's benefits. And the court did not specify whether it was granting damages or restitution. The American Law Institute read the case as based on unjust enrichment; Professor Palmer thinks it is better explained as awarding damages for strict liability in tort. 1 G. Palmer, Law of Restitution §2.10 at 139-140 (1978).

7.   So far we have considered *Olwell* on the assumption that but for the wrong, the egg washer would have sat idle. Why isn't it equally plausible to assume that if defendant had not converted it, defendant would have bought it or rented it from plaintiff, or bought or rented a similar machine from someone else? Suppose the fair market rental were $10 per month. Of course, if there were a bilateral monopoly, the rent would be indeterminate. In theory, defendant might have paid any rent up to $1,559 to save $1,560 in labor costs. But if there were a market, or price controls, $10 per month is a reasonable rent to assume. On that assumption, defendant has saved $1,560 in labor costs by converting plaintiff's egg washer, but it could have made the same savings honestly by paying $360 in rent. How much has it been enriched? How much of the enrichment is unjust? Why does the court so casually reject rental value as the measure of recovery?

8.   On the assumption in note 7, $360 is the value of the egg washer as such for three years; $1,200 is the surplus value created by putting it to use in defendant's business. Restitution of $360 might be thought of as equivalent to $360 damages for lost rents. Sometimes the law treats the problem in this way; for example, the patent statute provides that victims of infringement shall recover damages, "in no event less than a reasonable royalty." 35 U.S.C. §284 (1976). But courts are often reluctant to treat hypothetically lost payments as damages when there was no chance for a real transaction in which the payments would have been made. Thus, in University Computing Co. v. Lykes-Youngstown Corp., 504 F.2d 518 (5th Cir. 1974), the court found that plaintiff suffered no damages from the theft of its secret computer program, id. at 536, even though it measured restitution by the amount of royalty that a willing buyer would have paid a willing seller, id. at 540.

However one considers the $360, the bigger argument is over what to do with the $1,200 created by putting the egg washer to a new use. Is this value created by defendant's wrongful conversion or by his industry? Isn't it created by both? Does the propriety of awarding the whole $1,560 depend on causation, or on how strongly we disapprove of the conversion? Is the argument that defendant could have achieved the same savings honestly like Justice Frankfurter's argument that antitrust conspirators could have inflicted the same losses legally? See Bigelow v. RKO Radio Pictures, supra at 175.

9. One theme in the cases is that the measure of restitution depends on the defendant's culpability. A conscious wrongdoer is likely to be liable for all his profits, including those that result from putting plaintiff's property to defendant's more profitable use. A defendant who acted negligently, or illegally but in good faith, or with some justification not quite sufficient to exonerate him completely, is likely to be liable only for plaintiff's losses. If the recovery is in restitution, the measure of benefit is likely to be the amount saved by not paying plaintiff for the property used — the fair market value of the use.

The law of restitution is too unformed to have many clear rules, and you would misunderstand the previous paragraph if you took it as formulating rules. But it states a tendency for which there is much support. It is reflected in Vincent v. Lake Erie Transportation, supra note 6. It is reflected in the Restatement of Restitution, which distinguishes "conscious wrongdoer[s]" and defendants guilty of "consciously tortious conduct" from "innocent converter[s]," "gratuitous transferee[s]," and "non-tortious recipient[s] not more at fault than claimant[s]." §§150-155, 202-204 (1937). A clear example appears in Roberts v. Sears, Roebuck & Co., 573 F.2d 976 (7th Cir.), cert. denied, 439 U.S. 860 (1978). Roberts was a Sears employee who invented a wrench. Sears told him his invention wasn't worth much, bought all his rights for $10,000, and sold millions of the wrenches at a substantial profit. Roberts sued for restitution of Sears's profits in three counts, alleging breach of a confidential relationship, fraudulent misrepresentation, and negligent misrepresentation, respectively. All three counts were submitted to a jury. The judge told the jury that if it found for Roberts under either of the first two counts, it should award all the profits Sears had made from the invention, but if it found for Roberts only under the third count, it should award the value of a reasonable royalty on each wrench Sears sold. The distinction was lost on the jury; it brought in identical million dollar verdicts on all three counts.

10. The distinction between profits and a reasonable royalty in Sears corresponds to the distinction between profits and fair rental value in Olwell. Similarly, the court in Edwards v. Lee could have awarded the fair rental value of Lee's part of the cave, instead of defendant's full profits. The choice inheres in any case in which defendant's profits exceed the fair market value of the thing taken. Neither courts nor legislatures have made the same choice consistently.

In note 9, I suggested that defendant's culpability often explains the choice between restitution of profits and restitution of fair market value. Professor Palmer agrees. 1 G. Palmer, Law of Restitution §2.12 at 157, 164-166 (1978). Professor Dawson disagrees. He thinks that defendant's culpability is and should be largely irrelevant, that the Restatement provisions were "invented in the smoke-filled rooms of academia" and that they have been largely ignored by the courts. Dawson, Restitution without Enrichment, 61 B.U.L. Rev. 563, 614 (1981). For Dawson, restitution of full profits depends more on the importance of plaintiff's rights and on tracing the profit to a violation of those rights. He thinks that innocent wrongdoers are rare birds, that they appear most commonly in fiduciary duty cases, and that all fiduciaries are held to account for all their profits.

Dawson and Palmer are undoubtedly the two leading American restitution scholars; their disagreement on such a fundamental issue illustrates the unsettled nature of the field. But it is easy to exaggerate their disagreement. Palmer agrees that the importance of plaintiff's right matters; he claims only that defendant's culpability also matters.

11.   Palmer and Dawson both think *Olwell* is wrong. They both think that savings of expense is not a reliable measure of profits. Dawson at 611-612; Palmer §2.12 at 162. In addition, Palmer thinks the savings are more fairly attributable to defendant's business than to his conversion. Id. at 160-161. Each of them would award the fair rental value instead. So would the Restatement, which suggests that fair market value has "crystallized" as the measure of restitution for conversion of chattels. If defendant had resold the machine at a profit, the Restatement would determine value as of the time of resale, but it would never allow plaintiff to recover defendant's profits from the use of the machine. Restatement of Restitution §157, comment e (1937).

Professor Oesterle would generalize this provision of the Restatement, although he reports that it is not supported by the cases. He would always measure restitution by the market value of the thing taken. Oesterle, Restitution and Reform, 79 Mich. L. Rev. 336, 356-357 (1980). One can appreciate the reasons for that proposal, but why call it restitution? Wouldn't that make the restitutionary measure of recovery indistinguishable from the damage measure? He concedes that would be so except in "rare" cases.

MAIER BREWING CO. v. FLEISCHMANN DISTILLING CORP.
390 F.2d 117 (9th Cir. 1968)

[Plaintiffs Buchanan and Fleischmann distill and distribute Black and White scotch whisky. The Black and White trademark is registered and well established with consumers; the scotch is the one of the leaders in the market. Defendant Maier began brewing a cheap beer under the Black and White label. Maier distributed the beer exclusively through defendant Ralph's Grocery Co. The court found that plaintiffs' trademark was infringed, that there was no competition between the two products, but that consumers might be confused and that sales of Black and White beer might harm the reputation of Black and White scotch.]

Before BROWNING and DUNIWAY, Circuit Judges, and BYRNE, District Judge.

BYRNE, District Judge. . . .

The present appeal is from the awarding by the District Court of an accounting by the defendants of their profits ($34,912 from Maier Brewing and $29,849 from Ralph's Grocery Company) accrued from the sale of beer under the name Black & White, the trade name registered to the plaintiffs. . . .

The appellants next contend that even if the District Court had jurisdiction to enter an order for an accounting of profits, the making of such an order in this case was not merited by the facts. Appellants allege that the appellees have claimed, and that the District Court granted, an accounting of profits as a matter of right upon the finding of an infringement and the granting of an injunction. This must be so, they argue, since the appellees have shown no injury to themselves, no diversion of sales from them to the appellants, no direct competition from which injury may be inferable, and no palming off or fraudulent conduct. The equitable limitation upon the granting of monetary awards under the Lanham Act, 15 U.S.C. §1117, would seem to make it clear that such a remedy should not be granted as a matter of right. It therefore becomes appropriate for us to examine the remedy of an accounting of profits as provided by §35 of the Lanham Act, and to determine its applicability to the facts in this case.

Section 35 of the Lanham Act, 15 U.S.C. §1117, provides that a trademark registrant shall be entitled, upon the finding of an infringement and "subject to the principles of equity,"

> to recover (1) defendant's profits, (2) any damages sustained by the plaintiff, and (3) the costs of the action. The court shall assess such profits and damages or cause the same to be assessed under its direction. In assessing profits the plaintiff shall be required to prove defendant's sales only; defendant must prove all elements of cost or deduction claimed. In assessing damages the court may enter judgment, according to the circumstances of the case, for any sum above the amount found as actual damages, not exceeding three times such amount. If the court shall find that the amount of the recovery based on profits is either inadequate or excessive the court may in its discretion enter judgment for such sum as the court shall find to be just, according to the circumstances of the case. Such sum, in either of the above circumstances shall constitute compensation and not a penalty.

This language apparently confers a wide scope of discretion upon the district judge in the fashioning of a remedy for a violation of the Act. The exercise of this discretion is expressly made "subject to the principles of equity" and, although such a limitation would appear easy to implement, it is apparently the source of much of the confusion surrounding the application of section 35 of the Act.

Although the Lanham Act would appear to provide three distinct elements of compensation or recovery to the registrant of the infringed mark, i.e., the defendant's profits accrued from the use of the mark, plaintiff's damages, and the costs of the action, the case law which has developed under this section of the Act has been far from clear in defining the scope of the relief granted by the Act. This is particularly true as to the right of the plaintiff to an accounting of the defendant's profits.

There appear to be two distinct views as to the basis for awarding an accounting of profits. The majority of cases seem to view an accounting of profits by the defendant as a method of shifting the burden of proof as to damages for lost or potentially lost sales from the plaintiff to the defendant. The minority view, which is apparently the more recent trend, bases the accounting of profits on the equitable concepts of restitution and unjust enrichment. The rationale behind this view, as expressed in Monsanto Chemical Co. v. Perfect Fit Products Mfg. Co., 349 F.2d 389 (2d Cir. 1965), the leading case in this trend, is that the infringer has taken the plaintiff's property as represented by his trade-mark and has utilized this property in making a profit, and that if permitted to retain the profit, the infringer would be unjustly enriched.

Those courts which utilize an accounting of profits as a means of compensating the plaintiff for sales which he has lost as a result of his customers being diverted to the infringer, have, as a result of this premise, required that there be competition between the parties before this recovery can be granted. Clearly, if there is no competition, there can be no diversion of customers. It does not necessarily follow, however, that just because there is no direct competition an accounting of profits can serve no reasonable end.

The legislative history of the Lanham Act expressly states the purpose of the Act:

> This bill, as any other proper legislation on trade-marks, has as its object the protection of trade-marks, securing to the owner the good will of his business and protecting the public against spurious and falsely marked goods. The matter has been approached with the view of protecting trade-marks and making infringement and piracy unprofitable.

S. Rep. No. 1333, 79th Cong., 2d Sess. 1-2 (1946). (Emphasis added.)

It is unnecessary for this court to determine whether all of the decisions under the Lanham Act which have viewed an accounting of profits as merely a method of compensating the trade-mark registrant for his lost or diverted sales have fulfilled these goals. The question which we must answer is whether such a restrictive approach to an accounting of profits fulfills these goals today. We think it does not; and apparently the district court judge, in holding that the appellants would be unjustly enriched if an accounting were denied, thought it did not.

Earlier in our country's history it may have been necessary to copy both the trade-mark and the product of another in order to obtain a free ride on the good reputation of that product and its maker. In such an instance requiring direct competition between the parties as a prerequisite to the granting of an accounting of profits would have been both just and logical. This, however, is the age of television and mass communications. Fortunes are spent in publicizing a name, often with only slight reference to the real utility of the product. The theory behind this modern advertising is that once the name or trade-mark of a product is firmly associated in the mind of the buying public with some desired characteristic — quality, social status, etc. — the public will buy that product. . . .

need
not
compete

Although courts will protect this psychological value of the trade-mark by means of an injunction against infringement, even where the products are of different descriptive qualities and are, therefore, not in competition, those courts which treat an accounting solely as a method of compensating for the diversion of customers fail to fully effectuate the policies of the Act. Such courts are neither "securing to the owner the good will of his business [nor] protecting the public against spurious and falsely marked goods." See Monsanto Chemical Co. v. Perfect Fit Products Mfg. Co., supra, 349 F.2d at 395-396.

These courts are protecting the trade-mark owner from only the most obvious form of damages — the diversion of sales, and are not in fact providing protection to the value of the good will built up in the trademark itself. No recognition is given to the possibility that customers who believe that they are buying a product manufactured by the plaintiff — whether such product is competitive or non-competitive — may be so unhappy with that product that they will never again want to buy that product or any other product produced by the same manufacturer, who they believe to be the plaintiff. Nor do these opinions recognize that, even if the infringing product is of higher quality than that bearing the registered trade-mark, the trade-mark registrant has been deprived of his right to the exclusive use and control of the reputation of his product. . . .

[A]lthough the granting of an injunction, upon the finding that a confusion of source may exist between the trade-marked product and the infringing product, protects the public from buying this particular falsely marked product from this particular infringer in the future, it does not necessarily protect them from similar future acts of commercial piracy by the same party. To accomplish this, the courts must, as was recognized in the legislative history of the Act quoted above, make acts of trade-mark infringement, or at the very least acts of deliberate trade-mark piracy, unprofitable. As the court in *Monsanto* recognized, it is possible for a party to adopt a deliberate business pattern of trade piracy — selling his product under the trade-mark of one reputable company until enjoined and then merely adopting the trade-mark of another company and continuing his fraudulent activities.

Since it is fairly apparent that the use of an accounting of profits solely as a means of compensating the trade-mark registrant for sales which have been diverted to the infringer is somewhat less than wholly effective in fulfilling the goals of the Lanham Act, we must determine whether the utilization of the unjust enrichment rationale is in fact more effective, and if it is, whether such a utilization is permissible under the Act.

Initially it should be noted that there is nothing in the Lanham Act which would seem to preclude the use of the unjust enrichment rationale for an accounting of profits. Indeed the language of §1117 would seem to provide that "a plaintiff is specifically entitled 'to recover (1) defendant's profits' and . . . that he need 'prove defendant's sales only,' leaving to the defendant to 'prove all elements of cost or deduction claimed.' In addition, a plaintiff may recover '(2) any damages sustained by the plaintiff.'" *Monsanto*, supra at 397.

Thus, it must be determined if the concept of unjust enrichment, utilized "subject to the principles of equity," will properly serve to effectuate the policies of the Lanham Act. It would seem that it would. The utilization of this concept will not of course make an accounting of profits automatic. Situations will exist where it would be unduly harsh to grant such recovery. Cases exist where the infringement is entirely innocent; where rather than attempting to gain the value of an established name of another, the infringer has developed what he imagined to be a proper trade name only to find out later that his name caused confusion as to the source of, and therefore infringed, a product with a registered trade-mark. In such a case an injunction fully satisfies both the policy of the Act and the equities of the case.

Where, however, the infringement is deliberate and wilful, and the products are non-competitive, both the trade-mark owner and the buying public are slighted, if the court provides no greater remedy than an injunction. As the court said in Admiral Corp. v. Price Vacuum Stores, Inc., 141 F. Supp. 796, 801 (E.D. Pa. 1956):

> It seems scarcely equitable . . . for an infringer to reap the benefits of a trade-mark he has stolen, force the registrant to the expense and delay of litigation, and then escape payment of damages on the theory that the registrant suffered no loss. To impose on the infringer nothing more serious than an injunction when he is caught is a tacit invitation to other infringement.

It would seem fairly evident that the purposes of the Lanham Act can be accomplished by making acts of deliberate trade-mark infringement unprofitable. In the case where there is direct competition between the parties, this can be accomplished by an accounting of profits based on the rationale of a returning of diverted profits. In those cases where there is infringement, but no direct competition, this can be accomplished by the use of an accounting of profits based on unjust enrichment rationale. Such an approach to the granting of accountings of profits would, by removing the motive for infringements, have the effect of deterring future infringements. The courts would therefore be able to protect the intangible value associated with trade-marks and at the same time be protecting the buying public from some of the more unscrupulous members of our economic community.

All this, of course, would be carried out subject to the principles of equity. In certain cases an injunction will fully effectuate the policies of the Act; others will arise when there will be sufficient provable damages to effectuate the policies of the Act without the granting of an accounting for profits; and in still other cases only the granting of an accounting of profits will effectuate the policies of the Act. . . .

We conclude that the District Court reached the correct and proper conclusion when, upon finding that the appellants "knowingly, wilfully and deliberately infringed the said trade-mark 'Black & White,'" it granted the appellees an accounting of the appellants' profits.

The appellants make further arguments to the effect that . . . the award was of the profits of both Maier Brewing and Ralph's Grocery Company and hence constitutes more than a single full satisfaction of the appellees. . . . [T]his contention is based upon the assumption that the accounting of profits in this action was utilized as a method of compensating the appellees for diversion of sales. As our resolution of the question as to the appellees' right to an accounting indicates, this was not the basis for the accounting in this action. The dollar amount of the recovery in an accounting for profits under the unjust enrichment rationale has no relation to the damages, if any, sustained by the plaintiff in the action.

The decision of the District Court is affirmed.

MORE NOTES ON RECOVERING MORE THAN PLAINTIFF LOST

1. *Maier* is included for the benefit of those inclined to dismiss *Olwell* and Edwards v. Lee as insignificant cases on freakish facts. Trademark litigation is commercially significant, and there is nothing unusual about *Maier*'s facts. Indeed, it is rarely the case that defendant's profits closely match plaintiff's losses. Even in cases of direct competition, plaintiff would have made only some of defendant's sales. Sometimes plaintiff and defendant compete directly only in the overlap between two quite different distribution areas. The older cases that awarded defendant's profits only when they bore some relationship to plaintiff's losses did not worry too much about the closeness of the relationship. Any showing of compe-

tition was generally enough to trigger an accounting for all the profits. The only extension of liability in *Maier* and *Monsanto* (discussed in *Maier*) is to award profits where there is no competition at all between the two products. Is that a good rule? Is it required by the congressional intent to make trademark infringement "unprofitable"?

2.   In *Monsanto*, the court found that defendant Perfect Fit had carried out four separate promotions involving deliberate mislabeling with a popular brand name. "Perfect Fit has, it appears, taken up trademark infringement as its principal line of business. . . . It may be said to be a commercial racketeer." 349 F.2d at 396. The court thought an accounting for profits was essential because injunctions against each violation were insufficient to deter new violations. Does that make the award of profits look more attractive? In all cases, or only against repeat offenders? There can be no claim that Perfect Fit's profitable violations were efficient: Perfect Fit earned its profits by deceiving its customers, and there is no economic presumption that involuntary or misunderstood transactions are value maximizing. Deceiving a customer bypasses the market as much as stealing from him. Should accounting for profits be limited to such cases?

3.   Certainly no customers who bought the beer in *Maier* thought they were getting scotch. At worst, some consumers would think the distillers of Black and White scotch brewed Black and White beer. If they were disappointed with the beer, they might think less of the scotch. Whatever the value of that damage, defendants' profits don't measure it very well. Could a jury put a number on the harm to plaintiffs' reputation? Or is the damage too uncertain and speculative to be recoverable? Is no recoverable damage the same as no damage? Haven't we seen in the irreparable injury cases that the law will take account of damage it can't measure?

4.   One way to estimate plaintiffs' damage is to ask how much they would have charged for a license to use their mark. The answer probably is that the parties could not have agreed on a license fee. Plaintiffs would probably say that no amount of money would induce them to license their mark for a cheap beer. They would change their mind for a high enough price, but that price would probably far exceed defendants' profits, so the deal would never be struck. If that speculation is plausible, is restitution of profits undercompensatory? Should the court value damage to plaintiffs' reputation at the price it would have cost to inflict that damage in a voluntary transaction? Or is that figure so speculative, and so subject to plaintiffs' inflated estimates of the risk of harm to their product's reputation, that attempts to estimate it would be more misleading than helpful? Is the problem like estimating the cost of paying someone to endure pain and suffering?

5.   There is no violation of the trademark laws if there is no possibility of confusion. Thus, the court noted that a Black and White Dry Cleaners

would not have to account to Fleischmann for its profits. That substantive rule ensures at least the possibility that plaintiff will have been damaged. But it doesn't create any relationship between defendant's profits and plaintiff's loss.

6. How much of defendants' profit is derived from the trademark violation? One way to consider that is to ask what it would have cost them to buy a license to use the trademark. Other approaches suggest quite different results. How much did defendants' profits exceed what they would have been if they had sold the same beer under a different label? Did the Black and White label enable them to raise the price? Did it enable them to sell more six packs? Doesn't it seem likely that they would have earned most of the same profits anyway — that most of their profits came from the beer and not from the label? We will consider attempts to allocate profit between stolen and legitimate parts of the product in Sheldon v. Metro-Goldwyn Pictures Corp., infra at 497.

7. Statutory remedies for unfair competition and misuse of intellectual property are not entirely consistent. Patent infringers are liable only for damages, "in no event less than a reasonable royalty." 35 U.S.C. §284 (1976). Copyright infringers are liable for all their profits. 17 U.S.C. §504(b) (1977 Supp.). The trademark statute is quoted in *Maier*; infringers are liable for all their profits, but the court has express statutory discretion to award more or less than that. This discretion is entirely unguided by the statute.

As the dictum in *Maier* suggests, courts have used this discretion to distinguish degrees of culpability: Only willful or deliberate infringers must account for all their profits. The leading case denying an accounting for less culpable infringement is Champion Spark Plug Co. v. Sanders, 331 U.S. 125 (1947). Defendant sold reconditioned Champion Spark Plugs without authority from Champion. The Court held that to label such plugs as Champion was not an infringement, so long as the plugs were also clearly labelled *repaired* or *used*. Defendant had labelled its plugs *renewed*, and not as conspicuously as the Court thought necessary. The Court implied that defendant's efforts to comply were reasonable, and said that the likelihood of damage to Champion was slight, and that therefore an injunction would "satisfy the equities of the case." Id. at 132.

SNEPP v. UNITED STATES
444 U.S. 507 (1980)

PER CURIAM.   CIA

In No. 78-1871, Frank W. Snepp III seeks review of a judgment enforcing an agreement that he signed when he accepted employment with the Central Intelligence Agency. . . . In No. 79-265, the United States conditionally cross petitions from a judgment refusing to find that profits attributable to Snepp's breach are impressed with a constructive trust. We grant the petitions for certiorari in order to correct the judgment from which both parties seek relief.

I

Based on his experiences as a CIA agent, Snepp published a book about certain CIA activities in South Vietnam. Snepp published the account without submitting it to the Agency for prepublication review. As an express condition of his employment with the CIA in 1968, however, Snepp had . . . pledged not to divulge *classified* information and not to publish *any* information without prepublication clearance. The Government brought this suit to enforce Snepp's agreement. It sought a declaration that Snepp had breached the contract, an injunction requiring Snepp to submit future writings for prepublication review, and an order imposing a constructive trust for the Government's benefit on all profits that Snepp might earn from publishing the book in violation of his fiduciary obligations to the Agency.[2]

The District Court found that Snepp had "willfully, deliberately and surreptitiously breached his position of trust with the CIA and the [1968] secrecy agreement" by publishing his book without submitting it for prepublication review. The court also found that Snepp deliberately misled CIA officials into believing that he would submit the book for prepublication clearance. Finally, the court determined as a fact that publication of the book had "caused the United States irreparable harm and loss." The District Court therefore enjoined future breaches of Snepp's agreement and imposed a constructive trust on Snepp's profits.

The Court of Appeals accepted the findings of the District Court and agreed that Snepp had breached a valid contract.[3] . . . [T]he court upheld the injunction against future violations of Snepp's prepublication obligation. The court, however, concluded that the record did not sup-

2. At the time of suit, Snepp already had received about $60,000 in advance payments. His contract with his publisher provides for royalties and other potential profits.

3. The Court of Appeals and the District Court rejected each of Snepp's defenses to the enforcement of his contract. In his petition for certiorari, Snepp relies primarily on the claim that his agreement is unenforceable as a prior restraint on protected speech.

When Snepp accepted employment with the CIA, he voluntarily signed the agreement that expressly obligated him to submit any proposed publication for prior review. . . . Moreover, this Court's cases make clear that — even in the absence of an express agreement — the CIA could have acted to protect substantial government interests by imposing reasonable restrictions on employee activities that in other contexts might be protected by the First Amendment. The Government has a compelling interest in protecting both the secrecy of information important to our national security and the appearance of confidentiality so essential to the effective operation of our foreign intelligence service. The agreement that Snepp signed is a reasonable means for protecting this vital interest.

port imposition of a constructive trust. The conclusion rested on the court's perception that Snepp had a First Amendment right to publish unclassified information and the Government's concession — for the purposes of this litigation — that Snepp's book divulged no classified intelligence. In other words, the court thought that Snepp's fiduciary obligation extended only to preserving the confidentiality of classified material. It therefore limited recovery to nominal damages and to the possibility of punitive damages if the Government — in a jury trial — could prove tortious conduct.

Judge Hoffman dissented from the refusal to find a constructive trust. The 1968 agreement, he wrote, "was no ordinary contract; it gave life to a fiduciary relationship and invested in Snepp the trust of the CIA." Prepublication clearance was part of Snepp's undertaking to protect confidences associated with his trust. . . . We agree with Judge Hoffman that Snepp breached a fiduciary obligation and that the proceeds of his breach are impressed with a constructive trust.

II

Snepp's employment with the CIA involved an extremely high degree of trust. . . .

Whether Snepp violated his trust does not depend upon whether his book actually contained classified information. The Government does not deny — as a general principle — Snepp's right to publish unclassified information. Nor does it contend — at this stage of the litigation — that Snepp's book contains classified material. The Government simply claims that, in light of the special trust reposed in him and the agreement that he signed, Snepp should have given the CIA an opportunity to determine whether the material he proposed to publish would compromise classified information or sources. Neither of the Government's concessions undercuts its claim that Snepp's failure to submit to prepublication review was a breach of his trust. . . .

When a former agent relies on his own judgment about what information is detrimental, he may reveal information that the CIA — with its broader understanding of what may expose classified information and confidential sources — could have identified as harmful. In addition to receiving intelligence from domestically based or controlled sources, the CIA obtains information from the intelligence services of friendly nations and from agents operating in foreign countries. The continued availability of these foreign sources depends upon the CIA's ability to guarantee the security of information that might compromise them and even endanger the personal safety of foreign agents. . . . In view of this and other evidence in the record, both the District Court and the Court of Appeals recognized that Snepp's breach of his explicit obligation to submit his material — classified or not — for prepublication clearance has irreparably harmed the United States Government.[9]

III

The decision of the Court of Appeals denies the Government the most appropriate remedy for Snepp's acknowledged wrong. Indeed, as a practical matter, the decision may well leave the Government with no reliable deterrent against similar breaches of security. No one disputes that the actual damages attributable to a publication such as Snepp's generally are unquantifiable. Nominal damages are a hollow alternative, certain to deter no one. The punitive damages recoverable after a jury trial are speculative and unusual. Even if recovered, they may bear no relation to either the Government's irreparable loss or Snepp's unjust gain.

The Government could not pursue the only remedy that the Court of Appeals left it without losing the benefit of the bargain it seeks to enforce. Proof of the tortious conduct necessary to sustain an award of punitive damages might force the Government to disclose some of the very confidences that Snepp promised to protect. The trial of such a suit, before a jury if the defendant so elects, would subject the CIA and its officials to probing discovery into the Agency's highly confidential affairs. . . . When the Government cannot secure its remedy without unacceptable risks, it has no remedy at all.

A constructive trust, on the other hand, protects both the Government and the former agent from unwarranted risks. This remedy is the natural and customary consequence of a breach of trust. It deals fairly with both parties by conforming relief to the dimensions of the wrong. If the agent secures prepublication clearance, he can publish with no fear of liability. If the agent publishes unreviewed material in violation of his fiduciary and contractual obligation, the trust remedy simply requires him to disgorge the benefits of his faithlessness. Since the remedy is swift and sure, it is tailored to deter those who would place sensitive information at risk. And since the remedy reaches only funds attributable to the breach, it cannot saddle the former agent with exemplary damages out of all proportion to his gain. . . . We therefore reverse the judgment of the Court of Appeals insofar as it refused to impose a constructive trust

---

9. Although both the District Court and the Court of Appeals expressly found otherwise, Mr. Justice Stevens says that "the interest in confidentiality that Snepp's contract was designed to protect has not been compromised." Thus, on the basis of a premise wholly at odds with the record, the dissent bifurcates Snepp's 1968 agreement and treats its interdependent provisions as if they imposed unrelated obligations. Mr. Justice Stevens then analogizes Snepp's prepublication review agreement with the Government to a private employee's covenant not to compete with his employer. A body of private law intended to preserve competition, however, simply has no bearing on a contract made by the Director of the CIA in conformity with his statutory obligation to "protec[t] intelligence sources and methods from unauthorized disclosure." 50 U.S.C. §403(d)(3).

on Snepp's profits, and we remand the cases to the Court of Appeals for reinstatement of the full judgment of the District Court.

So ordered.

MR. JUSTICE STEVENS, with whom MR. JUSTICE BRENNAN and MR. JUS-TICE MARSHALL join, dissenting.

In 1968, Frank W. Snepp signed an employment agreement with the CIA in which he agreed to submit to the Agency any information he intended to publish about it for prepublication review. The purpose of such an agreement, as the Fourth Circuit held, is not to give the CIA the power to censor its employees' critical speech, but rather to ensure that classified, nonpublic information is not disclosed without the Agency's permission.

In this case Snepp admittedly breached his duty to submit the manuscript of his book, Decent Interval, to the CIA for prepublication review. However, the Government has conceded that the book contains no classified, nonpublic material. Thus, by definition, the interest in confidentiality that Snepp's contract was designed to protect has not been compromised. Nevertheless, the Court today grants the Government unprecedented and drastic relief in the form of a constructive trust over the profits derived by Snepp from the sale of the book. Because that remedy is not authorized by any applicable law and because it is most inappropriate for the Court to dispose of this novel issue summarily on the Government's conditional cross-petition for certiorari, I respectfully dissent.

I

The rule of law the Court announces today is not supported by statute, by the contract, or by the common law. Although Congress has enacted a number of criminal statutes punishing the unauthorized dissemination of certain types of classified information, it has not seen fit to authorize the constructive trust remedy the Court creates today. Nor does either of the contracts Snepp signed with the Agency provide for any such remedy in the event of a breach. The Court's per curiam opinion seems to suggest that its result is supported by a blend of the law of trusts and the law of contracts. But neither of these branches of the common law supports the imposition of a constructive trust under the circumstances of this case.

Plainly this is not a typical trust situation in which a settlor has conveyed legal title to certain assets to a trustee for the use and benefit of designated beneficiaries. Rather, it is an employment relationship in which the employee possesses fiduciary obligations arising out of his duty of loyalty to his employer. One of those obligations, long recognized by the common law even in the absence of a written employment agreement, is the duty to protect confidential or "classified" information. If Snepp had breached that obligation, the common law would support the implication of a constructive trust upon the benefits derived from his misuse of confidential information.

But Snepp did not breach his duty to protect confidential information. Rather, he breached a contractual duty, imposed in aid of the basic duty to maintain confidentiality, to obtain prepublication clearance. In order to justify the imposition of a constructive trust, the majority attempts to equate this contractual duty with Snepp's duty not to disclose, labeling them both as "fiduciary." I find nothing in the common law to support such an approach.

Employment agreements often contain covenants designed to ensure in various ways that an employee fully complies with his duty not to disclose or misuse confidential information. One of the most common is a covenant not to compete. Contrary to the majority's approach in this case, the courts have not construed such covenants broadly simply because they support a basic fiduciary duty; nor have they granted sweeping remedies to enforce them. On the contrary, because such covenants are agreements in restraint of an individual's freedom of trade, they are enforceable only if they can survive scrutiny under the "rule of reason." That rule requires that the covenant be reasonably necessary to protect a legitimate interest of the employer (such as an interest in confidentiality), that the employer's interest not be outweighed by the public interest, and that the covenant not be of any longer duration or wider geographical scope than necessary to protect the employer's interest.

The Court has not persuaded me that a rule of reason analysis should not be applied to Snepp's covenant to submit to prepublication review. Like an ordinary employer, the CIA has a vital interest in protecting certain types of information; at the same time, the CIA employee has a countervailing interest in preserving a wide range of work opportunities (including work as an author) and in protecting his First Amendment rights. The public interest lies in a proper accommodation that will preserve the intelligence mission of the Agency while not abridging the free flow of unclassified information. When the Government seeks to enforce a harsh restriction on the employee's freedom, despite its admission that the interest the agreement was designed to protect — the confidentiality of classified information — has not been compromised, an equity court might well be persuaded that the case is not one in which the covenant should be enforced.

But even assuming that Snepp's covenant to submit to prepublication review should be enforced, the constructive trust imposed by the Court is not an appropriate remedy. If an employee has used his employer's confidential information for his own personal profit, a constructive trust over those profits is obviously an appropriate remedy because the profits are the direct result of the breach. But Snepp admittedly did not use confidential information in his book; nor were the profits from his book in any sense a product of his failure to submit the book for prepublication review. For, even if Snepp had submitted the book to the Agency for prepublication review, the Government's censorship authority would surely have been limited to the excision of classified material. In this case, then, it would have been obliged to clear the book for publication in precisely the same form as it now stands. Thus, Snepp has not gained any profits as a result of his breach; the Government, rather than Snepp, will be unjustly enriched if he is required to disgorge profits attributable entirely to his own legitimate activity.

Despite the fact that Snepp has not caused the Government the type of harm that would ordinarily be remedied by the imposition of a constructive trust, the Court attempts to justify a constructive trust remedy on the ground that the Government has suffered *some* harm. The Court states that publication of "unreviewed material" by a former CIA agent "can be detrimental to vital national interests even if the published information is unclassified." . . .

The Court . . . relies . . . on the Government's theory at trial that Snepp caused it harm by flouting his prepublication review obligation and thus making it appear that the CIA was powerless to prevent its agents from publishing any information they chose to publish, whether classified or not.

[Justice Stevens thought that this danger had not been proved.]

In any event, to the extent that the Government seeks to punish Snepp for the generalized harm he has caused by failing to submit to prepublication review and to deter others from following in his footsteps, punitive damages is, as the Court of Appeals held, clearly the preferable remedy "since a constructive trust depends on the concept of unjust enrichment rather than deterrence and punishment."

II . . .

[T]he Government specifically stated . . . that it was cross petitioning only to bring the entire case before the Court in the event that the Court should decide to grant Snepp's petition. The Government explained that "[b]ecause the contract remedy provided by the court of appeals appears to be sufficient in this case to protect the Agency's interest, the government has not independently sought review in this Court." . . . Despite the fact that the Government has specifically stated that the punitive damages remedy is "sufficient" to protect its interests, the Court forges ahead and summarily rejects that remedy on the grounds that (a) it is too speculative and thus would not provide the Government with a "reliable deterrent against similar breaches of security," and (b) it might require the Government to reveal confidential information in court. . . . It seems to me that the Court is foreclosed from relying upon either ground by the Government's acquiescence in the punitive damages remedy. Moreover, the second rationale is entirely speculative and, in this case at least, almost certainly wrong. . . . [U]nder the Court of Appeals' opinion the Government would be entitled to punitive damages simply by proving that Snepp deceived it into believing that he was going to comply with his duty to submit the manuscript for prepublication review and that the Government relied on these misrepresentations to its detriment. I fail to see how such a showing would require the Government to reveal any confidential information or to expose itself to "probing discovery into the Agency's highly confidential affairs."

III

The uninhibited character of today's exercise in lawmaking is highlighted by the Court's disregard of two venerable principles that favor a more conservative approach to this case.

First, for centuries the English-speaking judiciary refused to grant equitable relief unless the plaintiff could show that his remedy at law was inadequate. Without waiting for an opportunity to appraise the adequacy of the punitive damages remedy in this case, the Court has jumped to the conclusion that equitable relief is necessary.

Second, and of greater importance, the Court seems unaware of the fact that its drastic new remedy has been fashioned to enforce a species of prior restraint on a citizen's right to criticize his government.[17] Inherent in this prior restraint is the risk that the reviewing agency will misuse its authority to delay the publication of a critical work or to persuade an author to modify the contents of his work beyond the demands of secrecy. The character of the covenant as a prior restraint on free speech surely imposes an especially heavy burden on the censor to justify the remedy it seeks. It would take more than the Court has written to persuade me that that burden has been met. . . .

NOTES ON CONSTRUCTIVE TRUSTS AND ACCOUNTING FOR PROFITS

1. A trust is a device for separating the legal ownership and control of property from its beneficial enjoyment. Property owners deliberately create express trusts for a wide variety of reasons. An owner conveys property to a trustee for the benefit of one or more named beneficiaries; the trustee agrees to hold subject to the trust. Before the merger of law and equity, law courts would not enforce the trust. The equity courts would acknowledge the trustee as the legal owner, but they would order him to

---

17. . . . In view of the national interest in maintaining an effective intelligence service, I am not prepared to say that the restraint is necessarily intolerable in this context. I am, however, prepared to say that, certiorari having been granted, the issue surely should not be resolved in the absence of full briefing and argument.

manage and distribute the property in accordance with the directions in the trust instrument. Lawyers still speak of the trustee as the legal owner and the beneficiary as the equitable owner, the beneficial owner, or the owner of the beneficial interest. Trusts can be used to avoid taxes, to avoid probate, to avoid creditors, to provide professional money management, to consolidate control, to divide the beneficial interest among multiple beneficiaries, and for many other purposes.

2.   A trustee is constantly subject to the temptation to use trust assets for his own purposes. The equity courts developed strict rules of fiduciary duty to combat that temptation. Trustees can collect fees for their services in amounts approved by the court, but they are not permitted to profit from the trust in any other way. They must account to the beneficiary for their management of the trust and for any profits earned with trust assets. Except in the case of charitable trusts, which are permitted to last forever, the trustee must eventually turn the assets over to the beneficiary entitled to become the legal owner at the termination of the trust.

3.   The trust provides an obvious analogy for courts faced with a defendant who has acquired the legal ownership of assets in a way that the court considers unjust. Declare him a trustee for the plaintiff, and the whole body of trust law becomes applicable, including the duty to account for profits and the duty to turn trust assets over to the beneficiary. This is the basic technique of the constructive trust. In the earliest cases, constructive trusts were used to plug loopholes in express trusts: If a trustee sold trust assets to a buyer who knew that the sale was a breach of trust, the courts would hold that the buyer took title as a constructive trustee. Then they imposed constructive trusts on other kinds of fiduciaries, such as agents and employees. In all these cases, there was a real fiduciary relationship, voluntarily assumed by the defendant. *Snepp* is such a case. But the constructive trust has also become a generalized remedy for wrongdoing.

4.   Perhaps the most prominent case in this transition was Newton v. Porter, 69 N.Y. 133 (1877). Thieves stole bearer bonds, sold them, invested the proceeds in new securities, and transferred the new securities to the attorneys who defended them in the criminal case. The attorneys knew that the securities were proceeds of the theft. By the time of trial, the attorneys had sold the new securities for cash. The victim of the theft sued the attorneys, arguing that the thieves had held the stolen bonds as constructive trustees, that the trust attached to the new securities as identifiable proceeds of the trust assets, that the attorneys took subject to the trust, and that they must account for their profits from sale of the trust property. The attorneys argued that the thieves could not possibly be trustees: They never had any intention to hold for the benefit of the plaintiff. The court thought it would be anomalous if victims of theft had fewer remedies than victims of dishonest fiduciaries; it ordered the attorneys to account as trustees.

Newton illustrates three important things about constructive trusts. First, a constructive trust is no more a trust than a quasi-contract is a contract. The trust is a fiction, created by the court, to move assets to the person who is fairly entitled to them. It is simply a remedy. Second, the constructive trust can be used to trace the proceeds of specific assets through a series of exchanges. Third, the constructive trust is very useful when some or all of the defendants are insolvent. A judgment against the thieves would have been uncollectible. But the constructive trust remedy let plaintiff reach assets in the hands of third parties. Moreover, the identifiable assets of the trust are thought of as equitably belonging to the beneficiary — the plaintiff. If the substitute securities had still been identifiable in the hands of the thieves or the attorneys, plaintiff could have recovered them even if the trustees — the defendants — were insolvent and their other creditors unpaid. These two characteristics of the constructive trust — tracing through exchanges and preferences in insolvency — are the main subject of section C.

5. Accounting for profits is closely related to the constructive trust. Beneficiaries of an express trust or other fiduciary relationship could sue in equity for an accounting of the trustee's profits. This became a natural part of the constructive trust remedy as it developed. But courts sometimes order an accounting for profits without first going through the fictional step of imposing a constructive trust. Maier Brewing v. Fleischmann Distilling is an example. There is one important practical difference between the two remedies. An accounting for profits ends in an ordinary money judgment; plaintiff gets no preference if defendant is insolvent. A constructive trust gives a preference in insolvency, but only to the extent that the very property taken or the identifiable proceeds of that property can still be found.

6. The choice between restitution of full profits and restitution of market value is sometimes expressed in terms of the choice between constructive trust or accounting for profits on the one hand, and quasi-contract on the other. Quasi-contract proceeds on the fiction of an implied promise to pay for the benefit. If there were a real promise, it would probably be to pay the market value, and the implied promise is analogized to that. There is nothing inherent about this; the promise is fictional and the court can imply whatever it thinks fair, as *Olwell* illustrates.

The fictions of constructive trust are filled in by analogy to the law of express trusts, and the express trustee is always liable for all his profits. Thus, a decision to impose a constructive trust is generally a decision to grant restitution of all the wrongdoer's profits. There is the same tendency in the accounting for profits cases. But it is only a tendency, and it gets weaker as accounting for profits is separated from constructive trust. Thus, as noted, in the patent, trademark, and copyright cases, accounting for profits sometimes means all profits, sometimes means a reasonable royalty, and sometimes means a substitute measure of plaintiff's damages.

7. All the fictional talk of quasi-contracts and constructive trusts seems unnecessary at best and sometimes gets in the way of sound analysis. Courts would surely do better to talk generically of restitution, and focus specifically on the question of when to award all profits and when to award the market value of what was taken. But it is hard to get away from the fictions, and as Professor Palmer says, the "constructive trust idea stirs the judicial imagination" and helps courts reach unjust enrichments that would otherwise go unremedied. 1 G. Palmer, Law of Restitution §1.3 at 16 (1978).

NOTES ON IRREPARABLE INJURY

1. Both constructive trust and accounting for profits are equitable remedies, so at least in theory they are subject to the irreparable injury rule. The dissenters invoke that rule in *Snepp*, and the majority ignores it. There is a certain irony in both positions. In chapter 13, we will read a series of cases in which speakers seek injunctions against criminal prosecutions for their speech. In those cases, the *Snepp* majority uses the irreparable injury rule to deny relief to speakers, and the *Snepp* dissenters would ignore or minimize the rule. Both sides invoke the irreparable injury rule for substantive purposes.

2. The dissenters relied on the possible adequacy of the government's punitive damages remedy. We will consider punitive damages in chapter 7; at this point, you need to know that punitive damages are in the discretion of the jury. A jury might award far more than Snepp's profits; it might award nothing.

Justice Stevens wanted to "wait[] for an opportunity to appraise the adequacy of the punitive damages in this case." What was he waiting for? Did he want to see how much a jury awarded and decide whether that was adequate? Did he want to see if the verdict deterred Snepp from future unreviewed publication? He seems to be analogizing to the cases on injunctions against crime, where criminal punishment is generally presumed adequate until experience shows it to be inadequate.

Isn't a remedy that might legitimately result in nothing inadequate when compared to a remedy that will produce $60,000 if properly applied? Can there be any doubt that an immediate constructive trust is more "complete, practical, and efficient" than Stevens' two-step remedy? Is Stevens asking whether punitive damages will be just as good as the constructive trust? Or is he trying to identify the weakest remedy that will protect the government's interests?

3. It is not unusual for the irreparable injury rule to be ignored in constructive trust cases. The damage remedy is often inadequate anyway, because the damages are unmeasurable or uncollectible. The tracing feature of constructive trusts is not available in any legal remedy. But where plaintiff seeks restitution from a solvent defendant, quasi-contract

will often yield the same recovery as constructive trust, and where there are no profits other than the value of the thing taken, damages will work as well. Occasionally courts say that plaintiff must use one of the legal remedies, thus protecting defendant's right to jury trial. Other courts disagree. Both views are illustrated by Fur & Wool Trading Co. v. George I. Fox, Inc., 219 A.D. 398, 219 N.Y.S. 625, rev'd, 245 N.Y. 215, 156 N.E. 670 (1927). A thief stole furs from plaintiff and sold them to defendant, who took with knowledge. Defendant resold them at a profit. Plaintiff wanted defendant to account for the proceeds as a constructive trustee. But the resale profits were recoverable in quasi-contract, and defendant was solvent, so the Appellate Division held the legal remedy adequate and dismissed the bill for an accounting. The Court of Appeals reversed. It held that equity would always order a trustee to account, and it made no difference whether the trust were actual or constructive. Professor Palmer finds the cases in disarray, but with the irreparable injury doctrine being invoked less and less over time. 1 G. Palmer, Law of Restitution §1.6 (1978).

NOTES ON RESTITUTION OF THE PROFITS FROM AN EFFICIENT BREACH OF CONTRACT

1. The government conceded that Snepp's book contained no classified information. It is not clear whether the government believed that, or whether the government feared it would have to reveal more secrets if it tried to show that Snepp had revealed secrets. Either way, didn't the government concede that it would have been obliged to approve the book if Snepp had submitted it? If so, wouldn't Snepp have published later and earned all the same profits? Should restitution be limited to interest for the time the review process would have taken? Is the Court assuming that, despite the government's concession, the CIA would have refused permission to publish?

2. In *Snepp* the Court awards restitution of substantial profits earned by breaching a contract, even though plaintiff proved no damages. If this were a fair description of the case, it would strike at the very heart of the efficient breach theory. But it is clear that the Court would have decided *Snepp* the same way without the contract, and that it believed the United States had suffered great damages even though it could not prove them. So a proponent of the economic view of law can probably live with *Snepp*. But *Snepp* is not the only case to impose a constructive trust on the profits from a breach of contract.

3. The largest group of cases involves land sale contracts. Suppose a contract to sell land for $10,000. Before the closing, seller sells to a third

party for $15,000. Many courts will impose a constructive trust on the $5,000 profit from the sale. Timko v. Useful Homes Corp., 114 N.J. Eq. 433, 168 A. 824 (1933). If courts would consistently say that market value cannot be lower than $15,000 on these facts, plaintiff's damages would be $5,000, and the constructive trust remedy would be no more lucrative. But as we saw in Wolf v. Cohen, supra at 118, courts may find that the market value is less than $15,000. One way to view the constructive trust in these cases is that it avoids litigation over market value. But if we take seriously the notion that market value might be only $12,000, so that plaintiff has suffered only $2,000 in damages, the constructive trust deters an efficient breach by taking all the profit out of it.

The most common explanation of these cases is that the right to a constructive trust is a corollary of the right to specific performance. If he had filed suit in time, the buyer could have compelled a conveyance despite seller's opportunity to commit an efficient breach. The right to specific performance of a land sale contract was so automatic for so long that it became natural to think of the land as already belonging to plaintiff and not just promised to him. Doctrinally, courts said the buyer was the equitable owner of the land from the moment the contract was signed. Once a court said that the seller held the land in trust for the buyer, it followed easily that the trust attached to the proceeds of the sale.

4. *Snepp* is an unusual example of another group of cases: those where a former employee violates a promise to protect trade secrets or other confidential information. Here there are multiple theories and multiple remedies. As in the other intellectual property cases, courts sometimes award defendant's full profits, sometimes a reasonable royalty for use of the secret, and sometimes plaintiff's losses. It is often unclear whether the courts are enforcing the employment contract or the fiduciary duty created by law. One case that is clear is Structural Dynamics Research Corp. v. Engineering Mechanics Research Corp., 401 F. Supp. 1102 (E.D. Mich. 1975). The court found that defendants had violated the contract but not the fiduciary duty. It decided that plaintiff should recover defendants' profits. But defendants didn't have any profits, so the court awarded a reasonable royalty on defendants' sales. Whether one thinks of this as restitution of the secret's value to defendants, or as an indirect way of measuring damages, economists can easily absorb the award of a reasonable royalty into the efficient breach theory.

5. Another group of cases involves various forms of covenants not to compete. Here courts sometimes order defendant to account for his profits from the breach, as in Automatic Laundry Service v. Demas, 216 Md. 544, 552, 141 A.2d 497, 501 (1958), and sometimes treat defendant's profits as evidence of the profits plaintiff lost, as in Cincinnati Siemens-Lungren Gas Illuminating Co. v. Western Siemens-Lungren Co., 152 U.S. 200 (1894). Other cases attempt to calculate the victim's actual damages more precisely, considering how many of the wrongdoer's sales

the victim could have made, and considering the victim's profit margin rather than the wrongdoer's. Uinta Oil Refining Co. v. Ledford, 125 Colo. 429, 435-437, 244 P.2d 881, 884-885 (1952). Not all the cases are clear on the measure or theory of recovery, but damages appear to be more common than restitution.

6. If constructive trust is a generalized remedy for wrongdoing, why isn't it generally available to recover the profits from breach of contract? The doctrinal answer is that many of the profits of breach of contract are not conferred by the plaintiff. The restitution interest is the interest in restoring benefit or enrichment unjustly transferred from plaintiff to defendant. If defendant breaches his contract with plaintiff and earns a large profit on a substitute contract with someone else, the traditional view is that the profit comes from the third party and cannot be restored to plaintiff. Restatement (Second) of Contracts §370, comment a (1981).

Doesn't the doctrinal answer beg the question? In the land sale contracts, courts say that buyer is entitled to the land, so that when seller sells the land to someone else, he is selling something that belongs to buyer, and a constructive trust attaches to the proceeds. Why can't courts just as easily say in any other contract that plaintiff is entitled to whatever of defendant's time and resources are needed to perform? It would follow that when defendant devotes the same time and resources to performing for someone else, he is selling something that belongs to plaintiff, and a constructive trust would attach to the proceeds. Recall Professor Macneil's suggestion that seller's factory might "belong to" buyer for however long it took to make buyer's chairs. Supra at 377. Why do we think of defendant's property as plaintiff's in the land cases and not in other cases? Is it just because of the right to specific performance? Macneil would probably say yes. He implies that the only analytic difference between the kinds of rights we call property and the kinds of rights we call contract is that property rights are more fully protected by remedies, with criminal penalties, specific performance, or constructive trusts in addition to damages. But why does the difference in remedies exist? Why is a defendant unjustly enriched when he profits from a tort or a breach of fiduciary duty, but not when he profits from a breach of contract?

7. Whether or not there is an analytic difference that can distinguish marginal cases, most people have an intuitive sense of difference between something they already own and something they have been promised. That difference is at the core of the debate over whether contract plaintiffs ought to recover their expectancies. We began our study of damages by asking whether the expectancy is too much — whether plaintiff has really lost anything when he loses only an expectancy. Now we are asking whether the expectancy is too little — whether the means of producing his expectancy is so much plaintiff's that he ought to get all the profits of diverting it. Courts seem to have an intuitive sense that the expectancy is

just right. Is there any analytic basis for that intuitive sense? Professor Dawson thinks not: "It may well be that the obstacle is nothing more than that well-known ailment of lawyers, a hardening of the categories. . . . Perhaps another way to express the idea is that the prevention of profit through mere breach of contract is not yet an approved aim of our legal order, as it is with breach of 'fiduciary' duties." Dawson, Restitution or Damages?, 20 Ohio St. L.J. 175, 187 (1959). He doubts that restitution of profits from breach of contract is likely to become customary any time soon, but he suspects that a desire to recapture most of the profits of breach has contributed to the unquestioned acceptance of the expectancy measure of damages. Professor Jones, the leading English authority on restitution, has collected a disparate set of cases in which the courts have stretched to measure contract damages in a way that captures defendant's profit from the breach. Jones, The Recovery of Benefits Gained from a Breach of Contract, 99 L.Q. Rev. 443 (1983). The cases come from both sides of the Atlantic, and from New Zealand as well. He suggests that plaintiffs be given an action for profits earned by breach, but that the courts retain discretion to deny restitution when it seems inappropriate.

8. Note 7 suggests that intuitive distinctions between promises and property may explain the courts' failure to grant restitution for breach of contract. These intuitions about ownership may have parallels in intuitions about morality. How many people consider breaking a promise to be as serious an offense as stealing? Our sense of morality may be partly derived from our sense of ownership; the thief (or converter) deprives his victim of a more strongly held entitlement. We may also be more forgiving of broken promises because of the likelihood that changed circumstances contributed to the breach.

9. The economic justification for restitution of profits is that it forces defendants to buy what they want in voluntary transactions. Why shouldn't they have to buy releases from contracts in voluntary transactions as well? The answer may be that economists have the same intuitions as judges in these matters. Or there may be a wholly economic answer, but it may emerge only tentatively, from an endless analysis of transaction costs. One response for the economists is that in the cases where a breach could be really profitable, negotiations for release from the contract are likely to involve bilateral monopoly. But as we have seen, negotiations to settle the ensuing lawsuit will also involve bilateral monopoly.

10. Consider one possible elaboration on the intuition that buyer does not own seller's productive resources. In Macneil's example, Porthos's claim on Athos's factory is only for a particular purpose. He is entitled to have the factory used to make chairs. But he is not entitled to change his mind and demand tables; that would change the contract and require seller's agreement. Does it follow that he does not own the fac-

tory, even temporarily, for the purpose of making tables or taking advantage of any other opportunities that come along? It is purely fortuitous that Athos's big chance to make a killing in tables came during the time of the Porthos's chair contract, but it is not fortuitous that a new customer wants Athos and his factory to make tables. And what if Athos can handle six contracts at a time, and he is committed to Porthos and five other customers when he gets the request for tables? Who owns the right to his capacity to make tables then?

11.   Professor Kronman has argued that the constructive trust should follow as a matter of course whenever specific performance is economically justified. Kronman, Specific Performance, 45 U. Chi. L. Rev. 351, 376-382 (1978). He equates irreparable injury with an undue risk of undercompensation, and suggests that specific performance guards against that risk by giving plaintiff a property right in the thing he was promised. The constructive trust gives him the nearest equivalent of this property right — the proceeds of his property. He also argues that the constructive trust is necessary to deter potential defendants from preempting specific performance decrees by making performance impossible. Otherwise, seller could unilaterally change buyer's right to specific performance to a right to possibly undercompensatory damages.

Kronman discusses only the land cases. But his analysis is more general. If a buyer of tomatoes is entitled to specific performance because he needs a reliable supply to keep his cannery running at full capacity, and the seller sells all his tomatoes to an innocent third party, should the contract buyer get the proceeds through a constructive trust? If only one of Athos's six customers is entitled to specific performance, perhaps because he has ordered unique patented chairs, should only that one be entitled to a constructive trust if Athos breaches his contract? Doesn't it make sense to deal more harshly with breaches that cause irreparable harm than with breaches that cause compensable harm? How far can you push that idea if "irreparable harm" means only that specific performance is at least a little better than damages?

NOTES ON RESTITUTION OF MONEY NOT SPENT ON SAFETY

1.   The other core case for the economic approach to law is negligence, and restitution has not been applied there either. Recall Judge Posner's view that accidents should be allowed to happen if that is cheaper than prevention. See Notes on the Basic Principle, supra at 16-17. Suppose a manufacturer could prevent ten serious injuries each year by adding a $20 safety device to its product. Suppose juries would value the injuries at $100,000 each and that the manufacturer produces 100,000

units per year. On those numbers, it would have to spend $2 million to prevent the injuries, but it can let them happen and pay only $1 million in damages.

Judge Posner would presumably say that no recovery should be allowed at all because the manufacturer was not negligent. But his views are not the law in this area; plaintiffs probably could recover their damages either in negligence or in strict liability for defective products. But why should plaintiffs be limited to damages? Why not award restitution of the $2 million the manufacturer saved by injuring them? If we say it was wrongful to distribute the product without the safety device, and if we only award $1 million in damages, aren't we allowing the manufacturer to profit from its wrong? Saved expense was the measure of profit in *Olwell*; why not here?

As in the cases on profit from breach of contract, there is the doctrinal obstacle that the manufacturer's profits do not seem to have been taken from the consumers. But again, that depends on how we conceptualize the problem. It is easy enough to say the consumers are entitled to a safe product and that the manufacturer deprived them of it.

2. I do not know of a single case that raises that possibility. Judge Keeton anticipated the question a quarter century ago, but he gave it only a single sentence, and no one has followed his lead. Keeton, Conditional Fault in the Law of Torts, 72 Harv. L. Rev. 401, 412 (1959). Professor Friedman, who supports restitution of profits from some breaches of contract, backs away at restitution of savings from cutting corners on safety. Friedman, Restitution of Benefits Obtained through the Appropriation of Property or the Commission of a Wrong, 80 Colum. L. Rev. 504, 531, 554-555 (1980).

3. Is there any reason for restitution to be unthinkable in this area? One problem is that consumers may have already received part of the $2 million in the form of lower prices. Had the manufacturer added the safety device, it probably would have increased the price. But under competitive or even partially competitive conditions, it could not have increased the price by $20, and even if it could, a higher price would mean fewer sales. And it is easy to imagine cases in which the price could not be increased at all. So manufacturers will generally be enriched by not adding safety devices, but the enrichment may be hard to measure. But as we shall see, measurement difficulties have not precluded restitution in cases where it is thought appropriate. And isn't there an argument for saying the manufacturer was enriched by the full $2 million in saved expense, whether or not some of it could be passed on in the form of higher prices?

4. Is restitution good policy in such cases? Do we want to go to that length to deter accidents, or are we content to let profitable accidents happen? To the Posnerians, it is clear we should let the accidents happen. Others probably find it equally clear that the accidents should be pre-

vented. For many, it may depend on the cost and value of the product. Adding a $20 safety device to a car looks reasonable; adding it to a $15 hand tool may look disproportionate; adding it to a 39-cent firecracker is prohibitive. If the cost of preventing the accidents is prohibitive, some of us will be willing to do without firecrackers; some won't. Hardly any of us would have the society do without automobiles or bridges. Some might find restitution more appealing when the manufacturer made a deliberate cost/benefit decision to let the accidents happen than when he failed to foresee the accidents. In short, this question leads directly to a consideration of substantive tort law, reminding us once again that remedies serve substantive policies.

5.　Restitution in this area would also pose problems of standing and of allocating the award: Who is entitled to the manufacturer's savings? Should the first plaintiff get the whole savings? Should every plaintiff get an amount equivalent to the whole savings? That's multiple liability, isn't it? Should the savings go into a fund, with each victim to recover a fraction of the fund based on some estimate of the total number of victims? Courts are grappling with these problems with respect to punitive damages in products liability; we will consider the judicial response in chapter 7.

6.　Juries sometimes consider defendant's savings when awarding punitive damages. In Sturm, Ruger & Co. v. Day, 594 P.2d 38 (Alas. 1979), a defective pistol had discharged and injured its owner while he was unloading it. There was evidence that if the pistol had been redesigned to eliminate the defect, the extra manufacturing cost would have been $1.93 per unit. Defendant had sold more than 1,501,000 pistols of the type that injured plaintiff. The jury awarded $2,895,000 in punitive damages, which is exactly $1.93 x 1.5 million. In Grimshaw v. Ford Motor Co., infra at 594, the jury apparently took the same approach to punitive damages, although the facts are less clear.

In both cases, judges found the award excessive and ordered most of it remitted. In the Ford case, the trial court reduced the jury's $125 million verdict to $3.5 million. In the gun case, the Supreme Court of Alaska reduced the award to $250,000; on rehearing, it allowed $500,000. 615 F.2d 621 (1980). None of the opinions evaluates the jury's procedure; the arithmetic that explains what the jury did in the gun case is found in a dissenting opinion. There is one allusion in the majority opinion:

> The jurors apparently responded to an invitation to punish Sturm, Ruger for all wrongs committed against all purchasers and users of its products, rather than for the wrong done to this particular plaintiff.

594 F.2d at 48.

Does that mean they should have given him $1.93? The court's $500,000 figure is obviously based on some intermediate approach.

B. MEASURING THE BENEFIT

SHELDON v. METRO-GOLDWYN PICTURES CORP.
309 U.S. 390 (1940)

MR. CHIEF JUSTICE HUGHES delivered the opinion of the Court. . . .

Petitioners' complaint charged infringement of their play "Dishonored Lady" by respondents' motion picture "Letty Lynton," and sought an injunction and an accounting of profits. The Circuit Court of Appeals, reversing the District Court, found and enjoined the infringement and directed an accounting. Thereupon the District Court confirmed with slight modifications the report of a special master which awarded to petitioners all the net profits made by respondents from their exhibitions of the motion picture, amounting to $587,604.37. The Circuit Court of Appeals reversed, holding that there should be an apportionment and fixing petitioners' share of the net profits at one-fifth. . . .

Petitioners' play "Dishonored Lady" was based upon the trial in Scotland, in 1857, of Madeleine Smith for the murder of her lover, — a *cause célèbre* included in the series of "Notable British Trials" which was published in 1927. The play was copyrighted as an unpublished work in 1930, and was produced here and abroad. . . . There had been negotiations for the motion picture rights in petitioners' play, and the price had been fixed at $30,000, but these negotiations fell through.

As the Court of Appeals found, respondents in producing the motion picture in question worked over old material; "the general skeleton was already in the public demense. A wanton girl kills her lover to free herself for a better match; she is brought to trial for the murder and escapes." But not content with the mere use of that basic plot, respondents resorted to petitioners' copyrighted play. They were not innocent offenders. From comparison and analysis, the Court of Appeals concluded that they had "deliberately lifted the play"; their "borrowing was a deliberate plagiarism." It is from that standpoint that we approach the questions now raised. . . .

The District Court thought it "punitive and unjust" to award all the net profits to petitioners. The court said that, if that were done, petitioners would receive the profits that the "motion picture stars" had made for the picture "by their dramatic talent and the drawing power of their reputations." "The directors who supervised the production of the picture and the experts who filmed it also contributed in piling up these tremendous net profits." The court thought an allowance to petitioners of 25 percent of these profits "could be justly fixed as a limit beyond which complainants would be receiving profits in no way attributable to the use of their play in the production of the picture." But, though holding these views, the District Court awarded all the net profits to petitioners, feeling bound by . . . Dam v. Kirk La Shelle Co., 175 F. 902, 903, a decision which the Court of Appeals has now overruled.

The Court of Appeals was satisfied that but a small part of the net profits was attributable to the infringement, and, fully recognizing the difficulty in finding a satisfactory standard, the court decided that there should be an apportionment and that it could fairly be made. The court was resolved "to avoid the one certainly unjust course of giving the plaintiffs everything, because the defendants cannot with certainty compute their own share." The court would not deny "the one fact that stands undoubted," and, making the best estimate it could, it fixed petitioners' share at one-fifth of the net profits, considering that to be a figure "which will favor the plaintiffs in every reasonable chance of error."

First. Petitioners insist fundamentally that there can be no apportionment of profits in a suit for a copyright infringement; that it is forbidden both by the statute and the decisions of this Court. We find this basic argument to be untenable.

The Copyright Act in §25(b) provides that an infringer shall be liable —

> (b) To pay to the copyright proprietor such damages as the copyright proprietor may have suffered due to the infringement, as well as all the profits which the infringer shall have made from such infringement, . . . or in lieu of actual damages and profits, such damages as to the court shall appear to be just. . . .

We agree with petitioners that the "in lieu" clause is not applicable here, as the profits have been proved and the only question is as to their apportionment.

Petitioners stress the provision for recovery of "all" the profits, but this is plainly qualified by the words "which the infringer shall have made from such infringement." This provision in purpose is cognate to that for the recovery of "such damages as the copyright proprietor may have suffered due to the infringement." The purpose is thus to provide just compensation for the wrong, not to impose a penalty by giving to the copyright proprietor profits which are not attributable to the infringement.

Prior to the Copyright Act of 1909, there had been no statutory provision for the recovery of profits, but that recovery had been allowed in equity both in copyright and patent cases as appropriate equitable relief incident to a decree for an injunction. That relief had been given in accordance with the principles governing equity jurisdiction, not to inflict punishment but to prevent an unjust enrichment by allowing injured complainants to claim "that which, *ex aequo et bono*, is theirs, and nothing beyond this." Livingston v. Woodworth, 15 How. 546, 560. Statutory provision for the recovery of profits in patent cases was enacted in 1870. . . .

In passing the Copyright Act, the apparent intention of Congress was to assimilate the remedy with respect to the recovery of profits to that already recognized in patent cases. Not only is there no suggestion that Congress intended that the award of profits should be governed by a different principle in copyright cases but the contrary is clearly indicated by the committee reports on the bill. As to §25(b) the House Committee said: . . .

> The provision that the copyright proprietor may have such damages as well as the profits which the infringer shall have made is substantially the same provision found in section 4921 of the Revised Statutes relating to remedies for the infringement of patents. The courts have usually construed that to mean that the owner of the patent might have one or the other, whichever was the greater. . . .

We shall presently consider the doctrine which has been established upon equitable principles with respect to the apportionment of profits in cases of patent infringement. We now observe that there is nothing in the Copyright Act which precludes the application of a similar doctrine based upon the same equitable principles in cases of copyright infringement.

Nor do the decisions of this Court preclude that course. Petitioners invoke the cases of Callaghan v. Myers, 128 U.S. 617, and Belford v. Scribner, 144 U.S. 488. In the _Callaghan_ case, the copyright of a reporter of judicial decisions was sustained with respect to the portions of the books of which he was the author, although he had no exclusive right in the judicial opinions. On an accounting for the profits made by an infringer, the Court allowed the deduction from the selling price of the actual and legitimate manufacturing cost. With reference to the published matter to which the copyright did not extend, the Court found it impossible to separate the profits on that from the profits on the other. And in view of that impossibility, the defendant, being responsible for the blending of the lawful with the unlawful, had to abide the consequences, as in the case of one who has wrongfully produced a confusion of goods. A similar impossibility was encountered in Belford v. Scribner, a case of a copyright of a book containing recipes for the household. The infringing books were largely compilations of these recipes, "the matter and language" being "the same as the complainant's in every substantial sense," but so distributed through the defendants' books that it was "almost impossible to separate the one from the other." The Court ruled that when the copyrighted portions are so intermingled with the rest of the piratical work "that they cannot well be distinguished from it," the entire profits realized by the defendants will be given to the plaintiff. . . .

[T]hese cases do not decide that no apportionment of profits can be had where it is clear that all the profits are not due to the use of the copyrighted material, and the evidence is sufficient to provide a fair basis of division so as to give to the copyright proprietor all the profits that can be deemed to have resulted from the use of what belonged to him. Both the Copyright Act and our decisions leave the matter to the appropriate exercise of the equity jurisdiction upon an accounting to determine the profits "which the infringer shall have made from such infringement."

Second. The analogy found in cases of patent infringement is persuasive. There are many cases in which the plaintiff's patent covers only a part of a machine and creates only a part of the profits. The patented invention may have been used in combination with additions or valuable improvements made by the infringer and each may have contributed to the profits. . . .

The principle as to apportionment of profits was clearly stated in the case of Dowagiac Co. v. Minnesota Co., 235 U.S. 641. . . .

In the Dowagiac case, we . . . referred to the difficulty of making an exact apportionment and . . . observed that mathematical exactness was not possible. What was required was only "reasonable approximation" which usually may be attained "through the testimony of experts and persons informed by observation and experience." Testimony of this character was said to be "generally helpful and at times indispensable in the solution of such problems." The result to be accomplished "is a rational separation of the net profits so that neither party may have what rightfully belongs to the other." Id., p.647.

We see no reason why these principles should not be applied in copyright cases. . . .

Petitioners stress the point that respondents have been found guilty of deliberate plagiarism, but we perceive no ground for saying that in awarding profits to the copyright proprietor as a means of compensation, the court may make an award of profits which have been shown not to be due to the infringement. That would be not to do equity but to inflict an unauthorized penalty. To call the infringer a trustee *ex maleficio* merely indicates "a mode of approach and an imperfect analogy by which the wrongdoer will be made to hand over the proceeds of his wrong." Larson Co. v. Wrigley Co., 277 U.S. 97, 99, 100. . . . Where there is a commingling of gains, he must abide the consequences, unless he can make a separation of the profits so as to assure to the injured party all that justly belongs to him. When such an apportionment has been fairly made, the copyright proprietor receives all the profits which have been gained through the use of the infringing material and that is all that the statute authorizes and equity sanctions. . . .

Third. The controlling fact in the determination of the apportionment was that the profits had been derived, not from the mere performance of a copyrighted play, but from the exhibition of a motion picture which had its distinctive profit-making features, apart from the use of any infringing material, by reason of the expert and creative operations involved in its production and direction. . . . And, in this instance, it plainly appeared that what respondents had contributed accounted for by far the larger part of their gains.

Respondents had stressed the fact that, although the negotiations had not ripened into a purchase, the price which had been set for the motion picture rights in "Dishonored Lady" had been but $30,000. And respondents' witnesses cited numerous instances where the value, according to sales, of motion picture rights had been put at relatively small sums. But the court below rejected as a criterion the price put upon the motion picture rights, as a bargain had not been concluded and the inferences were too doubtful. The court also ruled that respondents could not count the effect of "their standing and reputation in the industry." The court permitted respondents to be credited "only with such factors as they bought and paid for; the actors, the scenery, the producers, the directors and the general overhead."

The testimony showed quite clearly that in the creation of profits from the exhibition of a motion picture, the talent and popularity of the "motion picture stars" generally constitutes the main drawing power of the picture, and that this is especially true where the title of the picture is not identified with any well-known play or novel. Here, it appeared that the picture did not bear the title of the copyrighted play and that it was not presented or advertised as having any connection whatever with the play. It was also shown that the picture had been "sold," that is, licensed to almost all the exhibitors as identified simply with the name of a popular motion picture actress before even the title "Letty Lynton" was used. In addition to the drawing power of the "motion picture stars," other factors in creating the profits were found in the artistic conceptions and in the expert supervision and direction of the various processes which made possible the composite result with its attractiveness to the public.

Upon these various considerations, with elaboration of detail, respondents' expert witnesses gave their views as to the extent to which the use of the copyrighted material had contributed to the profits in question. The underlying facts as to the factors in successful production and exhibition of motion pictures were abundantly proved, but, as the court below recognized, the ultimate estimates of the expert witnesses were only the expression "of their very decided opinions." These witnesses were in complete agreement that the portion of the profits attributable to the use of the copyrighted play in the circumstances here disclosed was very small. Their estimates given in percentages of receipts ran from five to twelve percent; the estimate apparently most favored was ten percent as the limit. One finally expressed the view that the play contributed nothing. There was no rebuttal. But the court below was not willing to accept the experts' testimony "at its face value." The court felt that it must make an award "which by no possibility shall be too small." Desiring to give petitioners the benefit of every doubt, the court allowed for the contribution of the play twenty percent of the net profits.

Petitioners are not in a position to complain that the amount thus allowed by the court was greater than the expert evidence warranted. . . . Nor can we say that the testimony afforded no basis for a finding.

What we said in the *Dowagiac* case is equally true here, — that what is required is not mathematical exactness but only a reasonable approximation. That, after all, is a matter of judgment; and the testimony of those who are informed by observation and experience may be not only helpful but, as we have said, may be indispensable. Equity is concerned with making a fair apportionment so that neither party will have what justly belongs to the other. Confronted with the manifest injustice of giving to petitioners all the profits made by the motion picture, the court in making an apportionment was entitled to avail itself of the experience of those best qualified to form a judgment in the particular field of inquiry and come to its conclusion aided by their testimony. We see no greater difficulty in the admission and use of expert testimony in such a case than in the countless cases involving values of property rights in which such testimony often forms the sole basis for decision. . . .

The judgment of the Circuit Court of Appeals is affirmed.

MR. JUSTICE McREYNOLDS took no part in the decision of this case.

NOTES ON APPORTIONING PROFITS

1. The movie starred Joan Crawford and Robert Montgomery. MGM sold it to theaters as "Production No. 208, Joan Crawford No. 2." The trial court considered the sums paid other authors as evidence of the value of plaintiff's contribution. Novelist Margaret Mitchell got $50,000 for the movie rights to "Gone With the Wind." But the author of "Peter Pan" got 7 percent of the movie's gross receipts, which would be much more than 7 percent of the profits.

2. Is *Sheldon* consistent with the decisions it distinguishes? If a ballpark estimate is sufficient, why would it ever be impossible to apportion the profits between infringing and noninfringing components? Why not just count the proportion of stolen recipes in Belford v. Scribner and prorate the profits? That would be analogous to the solution in Edwards v. Lee, supra at 467, where the Kentucky court prorated profits on the basis of linear feet in the cave. And surely the uncopyrighted decisions were more important than the copyrighted headnotes to the court reporters in Callaghan v. Myers. Why not have an expert testify to that effect and give an opinion that the headnotes contributed 10 or 20 percent of the profits? Defendants did not offer such evidence in the earlier cases, and perhaps the Court was unwilling to make estimates without expert guidance. But it seems likely that the judges who decided *Callaghan* and *Belford* would have found apportionment impossible in *Sheldon* as well.

3. Two years after *Sheldon*, the Court took a quite different approach to apportionment in a trademark case. Mishawaka Rubber & Woolen Manufacturing Co. v. S. S. Kresge Co., 316 U.S. 203 (1942). *Sheldon* had

tried to allocate profits to factors of production. *Mishawaka* tried to apportion profits on the basis of sales. The Court held that defendant need not account for profits from sales to consumers who were not confused by the mislabeling. But defendant bore the burden of proving how many such consumers there were. The Court recognized that this burden is "as often as not impossible to sustain."

Could defendant meet its burden with a marketing survey showing how many of a random sample of customers were confused by the label? That was tried in Truck Equipment Service Co. v. Fruehauf Corp., 536 F.2d 1210 (8th Cir.), *cert. denied*, 429 U.S. 861 (1976). The survey showed that only 20 percent of defendant's customers purchased for reasons having anything to do with plaintiff's infringed product. The court rejected the survey's relevance without passing on its evidentiary sufficiency. Id. at 1222-1223. It thought that allowing an infringer to keep 80 percent of its profits from sales of infringing items was "clearly inadequate" to deter infringement. The decision appears to squarely conflict with *Mishawaka*. Is the case just wrong? Or does apportionment on the basis of sales look more attractive in theory when it is impossible in fact? The court said it was especially hesitant "to limit the award on the basis of the fine-tuned results of a post-infringement market survey" because defendant acted in bad faith and its conduct threatened to destroy plaintiff, which was a much smaller company. But its deterrence rationale did not appear to be limited to cases with these special factors.

4. Could the court apportion profits in Maier Brewing v. Fleischmann Distilling? Presumably, experts could testify about how much brewers or distributors would pay for a well-known label. Would that be enough under *Sheldon*?

5. The profit attributable to plagiarizing the play is not equivalent to the fair market value of rights in the play, although in theory, the difference should be small. Movie producers expect a reasonable return on each investment they make in a movie; when they pay for a plot or a script, this investment should pay for itself and generate a profit margin in addition. Competition among writers should make it unnecessary to pay more; competition among producers should make it impossible to pay less. The theory is problematic in practice. It is difficult to predict movie fans' reaction to a plot or script, and it is difficult to separate its contribution to the finished movie. Because market participants do not have good information at any point in the process, the market can be expected to work somewhat inefficiently. Producers will buy some plots cheap and make huge profits; they will pay too much for others and suffer losses. In a more efficient market, profits from a factor of production would equal cost plus the competitive margin of profit.

6. It is important to distinguish two closely related questions. In the notes to *Olwell*, we focused on the choice between restitution of profits and restitution of the market value of the thing taken. *Sheldon* chooses

between profits from the entire enterprise and profits from the thing taken. The two choices are not the same. *Olwell* dramatically illustrates the difference. The court awarded the profits from using the egg washer, which substantially exceeded its market value. But no one suggested that Olwell should recover the entire profits of the egg business for the three years Nye & Nissen used his egg washer. The court tried to award profits from the egg washer, not profits from the whole business.

But whenever one sees profits far in excess of the market value of the thing taken, it is prudent to ask whether profits from some other factor of production have been included. Professor Palmer thinks some of the profits in *Olwell* must have been fairly attributable to the rest of the business. 1 G. Palmer, Law of Restitution §2.12 at 160-161 (1978). Certainly the egg washer was much more valuable with the addition of an egg business, just as the play in *Sheldon* was much more valuable with the addition of Joan Crawford and MGM. Could the *Sheldon* approach be used to apportion profits between the egg washer and the other components of Nye & Nissen's business? Or did the court have a more direct measure in *Olwell*? The labor savings presumably went straight to the bottom line; the court could figure exactly what Nye & Nissen's profits would have been without the egg washer. When that is true, is any other basis for apportionment defensible?

7.   Courts generally do not determine profits by adding a profit margin to the value of the thing taken, although some evidence of that kind was considered in *Sheldon*, and there is no rule against it. But the other evidentiary approach in *Sheldon* has dominated. The court determines the gross receipts from infringing sales and subtracts the expenses of producing those sales. If necessary, this profit is then apportioned between infringing and noninfringing parts of the product. Apportionment questions also arise in measuring expenses; the same people and equipment often work on both infringing and noninfringing products. In the trademark and copyright cases, plaintiffs need prove only gross receipts; defendant has the burden of proving its expenses.

8.   Defendants in *Sheldon* were given expense credit only for things they "bought and paid for," with no allowance for the contribution of their "standing and reputation" in the industry. Perhaps more important, the "bought and paid for" standard excludes the value of defendants' labor. In *Callaghan*, discussed in *Sheldon*, the Court reasoned that plaintiff should not have to pay for the time defendants spent infringing his copyright.

Corporate infringers like MGM pay for labor and get to deduct salaries under the "bought and paid for" standard. Thus, that standard is in tension with the rationale that plaintiff should not have to pay for work done by infringers. *Callaghan* disallowed salaries paid to partners. But Rubber Co. v. Goodyear, 76 U.S. (9 Wall.) 788, 802-803 (1869), allowed salaries to corporate officers. Neither case explains the distinction. Perhaps the thought was that corporate salaries are really salaries but that partnership salaries are a form of profits; partnership law has traditionally not distinguished between profits and salaries. Whatever the rationale, the distinction is generally followed. *Rubber Co.* disallowed excessive salaries that looked like disguised profit distributions, and that practice has also been followed.

9. Suppose Leonardo da Vinci stole paints, canvas, and brushes from a hardware store and then painted the Mona Lisa. Could the store owner recover the painting or its value, with no allowance for the value of Leonardo's labor or reputation? Should the result be different if a patron of the arts stole the supplies and paid Leonardo a salary to paint the Mona Lisa? A similar but less flamboyant example appears in dictum in *Janigan v. Taylor*, 344 F.2d 781 (1st Cir. 1965). The court suggests that the result should differ in the two cases. In the second case, the court implies that the agreed salary would determine the value of Leonardo's contribution, and that neither he nor his patron could claim any more. But in the first case, the court would apparently value Leonardo's contribution independently, and, contrary to *Callaghan*, give him credit for it.

When the wrongdoer's labor contributes most of the profit, denying credit for the value of that labor begins to look like a penalty and not an effort to take away the profit of his wrongdoing. If that is so, isn't it equally a penalty to deny credit for labor that adds only marginally to the value of what was taken? But is it a penalty in either case? Or is the opportunity for employment one of the things the wrongdoer misappropriated?

What if Leonardo didn't intentionally steal the paint, but took it by mistake?

SECURITIES & EXCHANGE COMMISSION v. MACDONALD
699 F.2d 47 (1st Cir. 1983)

Before COFFIN, Chief Judge, ALDRICH, CAMPBELL, BOWNES and BREYER, Circuit Judges. . . .

ALDRICH, Senior Circuit Judge.

In this proceeding brought by the Securities and Exchange Commission . . . , defendant James E. MacDonald, Jr. was ordered by the district court to disgorge profits of $53,012 realized on the purchase and subsequent sale of 9,600 shares of Realty Income Trust (RIT) stock. The court, sitting without jury, found that defendant violated the antifraud provisions of the Securities Exchange Act of 1934, section 10(b), 15 U.S.C. §78j(b), and SEC Rule 10b-5 promulgated thereunder, 17 C.F.R. §240.10b-5, by making the purchases without disclosing certain material inside information learned in his capacity as chairman of RIT's board of trustees. . . . We affirm, except as to the amount.

RIT is a real estate investment trust whose stock is traded on the

American Stock Exchange. The present controversy revolves around defendant's knowledge of RIT's acquisition of the Kroger Building, a twenty-five story office building in Cincinnati, Ohio, and its likely negotiation of a profitable long-term lease of vacant space therein to Kenner Products. . . .

The land under the Kroger Building had been owned by RIT since 1962. Until December 1975, the building was owned and managed by City Center Development Company. Both the land and the building were subject to a first mortgage to Prudential Insurance Company. Under the terms of its ground lease, City Center was obligated to pay ground rent to RIT and mortgage payments to Prudential, but in 1975 it defaulted on both accounts. To protect its investment and avoid foreclosure, RIT advanced mortgage payments to Prudential, and then, on December 2, 1975, filed suit against City Center seeking reimbursement and the appointment of a receiver. The suit was publicly announced on December 4. On December 12, the case was settled by City Center's surrendering to RIT ownership of the Kroger Building. The news of the settlement was reported in a local Cincinnati paper but was not otherwise made available to the investing public. That day, however, RIT did release its quarterly financial report, which, basically, contained nothing but bad news.

Meanwhile, Kenner Products had been looking for a new home, its previous one having been acquired by the city. A tentative decision was made to move into the Kroger Building, and negotiations between City Center and Kenner ensued. After its acquisition of the building, RIT took over the negotiations. A report on the proposed terms of the lease was made to the trustees, including defendant, on December 15. The next day his wife, acting in his behalf, put in an order with her broker for the purchase of up to 20,000 shares of RIT stock at a price of $4\frac{1}{4}$. One hundred shares were purchased at that price. On December 23, defendant went personally to the broker's office and raised the purchase limit to $5 per share. This resulted in the purchase of 9,500 shares that day at $4\frac{5}{8}$.

The following day, December 24, RIT issued a press release, publicly announcing for the first time the acquisition of the Kroger Building, and referring to Kenner, that

> the Trust expects to sign a lease almost immediately for 105,000 square feet of space in the building with a major new tenant. The lease will bring occupancy in the building up to 95%, which would indicate a market value of the building of approximately $8,500,000 which is approximately $2,000,000 more than the existing first mortgage and RIT's investment in the property.

The price of RIT stock then jumped from $4\frac{5}{8}$ to $5\frac{1}{2}$ in two days of trading — a rise of 19% — and closed the year at $5\frac{3}{4}$. Defendant held on to the stock until 1977 when it was sold at an average price of over $10 per share. . . .

The district court ordered defendant to disgorge, for restitution to defrauded shareholders, the sum of $53,012 representing the profits he realized upon reselling the 9,600 shares of stock in early 1977 at roughly $10 per share. The court noted that since the essence of defendant's inside information was made public on December 24, 1975, "any changes in the market after a fairly reasonable period of time after the 24th of December were because of other developments." But it felt that it would be "inequitable to permit the defendant to retain the benefits of a bargain that was . . . clearly illegal, and that he should be required to disgorge the entire profits." . . . [T]here was no evidence that this subsequent increase in value was attributable to any action of the defendant, nor was there any evidence as to why defendant continued to hold the shares. In other words, there were no special circumstances affecting what should be the normal result in this situation. . . .

[W]e must consider the principles, and the entire picture to which any decision must interrelate. We accordingly put four hypotheticals, predicated on the assumption that an insider fraudulently bought shares at $4.00, and that, throughout the entire month after the undisclosed information became public, the stock sold at $5.00.

(1)　Insider sold forthwith for $5.00.
(2)　Stock declined thereafter and insider sold at $3.00.
(3)　Stock rose a year later to $10.00, but then declined, and insider ultimately sold at $3.00.
(4)　When the stock rose to $10.00, insider sold at $10.00.

The Commission would, properly, seek $1.00 in case (1). It would also seek $1.00 in case (2), its given reason being that the $1.00 profit "could have been realized." It adds, and we agree, that if the insider were to be permitted credit for the loss, he would have an investment "cushion," a "heads-I-win-tails-I-win" proposition. In case (3) the Commission concedes that it is entitled to only $1.00. In case (4) the present case, it claims the $6.00 as being "ill-gotten gains."

Before discussing the subject generally, we note two immediate seeming inconsistencies in the Commission's reasoning. If "could have been realized" is the test in case (2), equally a $6.00 profit "could have been realized" in case (3). Secondly, if the Commission does not claim the full realizable profit in case (3), as against case (4) is it not permitting the insider a "heads-I-win-tails-I-win cushion" which the Commission rejects in case (2)? We do not agree with the Commission's reasoning, or its conclusion in case (4). . . .

To start at the beginning, in our earlier case of Janigan v. Taylor, 1 Cir., 1965, 344 F.2d 781, *cert. denied*, 382 U.S. 879, approved by the Court in Affiliated Ute Citizens of Utah v. United States, 1972, 406 U.S. 128, 155, the president of a closely held corporation, by fraudulently misrepresenting the company's prospects, bought out "virtually all" its outstanding stock for approximately $40,000. Two years later he sold it for $700,000. The increase was well beyond what could have been foreseen, on the true facts, by the fraudulent buyer. Nevertheless, we held that in the case of property,

> not bought from, but sold to the fraudulent party, future accretions not foreseeable at the time of the transfer even on the true facts, and hence speculative, are subject to another factor, viz., that they accrued to the fraudulent party. It may, as in the case at bar, be entirely speculative whether, had plaintiffs not sold, the series of fortunate occurrences would have happened in the same way, and to their same profit. However, there can be no speculation but that the defendant actually made the profit and, once it is found that he acquired the property by fraud, that the profit was the proximate consequence of the fraud, whether foreseeable or not. It is more appropriate to give the defrauded party the benefit even of windfalls than to let the fraudulent party keep them.

344 F.2d at 786.

At the same time we recognized that "[t]here are, of course, limits to this principle." Id., at 787. While not discussed there, one of the limits that has emerged in cases following *Janigan* is that where the fraudulently obtained securities are publicly traded, and hence readily available, the defrauded sellers can recover only those accretions occurring up to a reasonable time after they discovered the truth. As Judge Friendly has pointed out,

> The reason for this, in the case of marketable securities, is obvious. Once the seller has discovered the fraud, he can protect against further damage by replacing the securities and should not be allowed to profit from a further appreciation, while being protected against depreciation by his right to recover at least the difference in value at the time of his sale.

Gerstle v. Gamble-Skogmo, Inc., 2 Cir., 1973, 478 F.2d 1281, 1306 n.27. Conscious hedging aside, when a seller of publicly traded securities has learned of previously undisclosed material facts, and decides nevertheless not to replace the sold securities, he cannot later claim that his failure to obtain subsequent stock appreciation was a proximate consequence of his prior ignorance. "If he has failed to reinvest, . . . he must suffer the consequences of his own judgment." Mitchell v. Texas Gulf Sulphur Co., 446 F.2d 90, 105 (10th Cir.), *cert. denied*, 404 U.S. 1004 (1971). Consistent with this position, the ALI proposed Federal Securities Code (1978 Official Draft and 1981 Supp.), which is said to codify *Janigan*, Comment (3) to section 1708(a), initially limits an insider's liability for profits in a case like the present one to "his ill-got gains," Comment 2 to section 1708(b)(4) (1981 Supp.), defined as the excess over the insider's purchase price of the "value of the security as of the end of the reasonable period after . . . the time when all material facts . . . became generally available." Sections 1708(a)(2) and 1703(h)(1)A; see sections 1703(b) and 1708(b).

When a fraudulent buyer has reached the point of his full gain from the fraud, viz., the market price a reasonable time after the undisclosed information has become public, any consequence of a subsequent decision, be it to sell or to retain the stock, is res inter alios, not causally related to the fraud. The dissent would acknowledge this reasoning as "unanswerable if we view the case as one between two private individuals, one defrauded and the other defrauding," but says the result should be different if the Commission is the plaintiff.

The Commission's rule would depart from the principle of "equal footing," SEC v. Shapiro, 494 F.2d 1301, 1309 (2d Cir. 1974), and measure assessments by purely fortuitous circumstances. If two fraudulent insiders bought at the same time and price, but, well after public disclosure, sold at different times and prices, their assessments would be measured by their selling dates, choices they made entirely independent of the fraud. To call the additional profits made by the insider who held until the price went higher "ill-gotten gains," or "unjust enrichment," is merely to give a dog a bad name and hang him. The dissent's measure, "damage done to investor confidence and the integrity of the nation's capital markets," if a measure at all, is the same for each of the fraudulent investors hypothesized in examples 1-4, ante. Granted that it may add to the deterrent effect of the Act every time the Commission conceives of a ground for assessing greater liability, to charge one class of insiders more than others who had committed precisely the same fraudulent act does not seem to us to meet any definition of "equitable." . . . We see no legal or equitable difference, absent some special circumstances, none of which was found here, between an insider's decision to retain his original investment with the hope of profit and a decision to sell it and invest in something else. In both cases the subsequent profits are purely new matter. There should be a cut-off date, both ways, in cases where, unlike *Janigan*, the sellers have an opportunity to take remedial action.

This is essentially the approach taken in SEC v. Shapiro, ante, where the court required defendant to disgorge profits accrued from the rise in price caused by the disclosure, despite a price drop some time later, since had the price risen after the cut-off date, "he could [have kept] subsequent profits." Id. at 1309. . . . Since, in the present case, there is no evidence of other material events during the period in question, the market itself may be the best indicator of how long it took for the investing public to learn of, and react to, the disclosed facts. The natural effect of public disclosure would be to increase the demand for, and correspondingly, the price of, RIT stock, and once investors stopped reacting to the good news, the price could be expected temporarily to level off.

Therefore, upon remand, in determining what was a reasonable time after the inside information had been generally disseminated, the court should consider the volume and price at which RIT shares were traded following disclosure, insofar as they suggested the date by which the news had been fully digested and acted upon by investors. And, although we have distinguished *Janigan* on the facts, we do not depart from the principle that doubts are to be resolved against the defrauding party.

The order requiring the disgorgement of $53,012 is reversed. On remand the district court should determine a figure based upon the price of RIT stock a reasonable time after public dissemination of the inside information. Under the circumstances, assessment of pre-judgment interest on the amount to be disgorged, commencing on the valuation date chosen by the court, would be appropriate. . . .

COFFIN, Chief Judge, with whom BOWNES, Circuit Judge, joins, dissenting in part. . . .

I disagree with the holding of the court en banc that a district court may not, absent special circumstances, require an insider who fraudulently trades on the basis of undisclosed material information to disgorge all of his ill-gotten gains in a suit by the SEC.

The court's opinion seems to me unanswerable if we view the case as one between two private individuals, one defrauded and the other defrauding. It does not, however, seem persuasive to me in this case in which the opposed interests are the investing community as a whole, represented by the SEC, and an individual who has seriously broken the rules of that community to his significant advantage. I concede that there is no case or other authority clearly sanctioning full disgorgement as "equitable." But to analyze this case in terms of a seller's ability to repurchase securities after the public disclosure of inside information seems to me to assume that the public instrumentality created to monitor the securities markets for the good of all stands in shoes no larger than those of a defrauded individual. Although what we might call *private* equity can give adequate protection to the individual, it seems to me that *public* equity in the contemporary world should permit a court, in the exercise of its discretion under 15 U.S.C. §78u(d), to safeguard the integrity of the securities markets as a whole by imposing, in a proper case, the civil sanction of full disgorgement of the actual profits of an illegal bargain. I see no authority barring this result and every reason of public policy justifying it.

Unlike a private plaintiff, the SEC does not sue for injury to itself; nor does it sue solely for the losses of sellers immediately injured by the defendant's fraud. Rather, it sues for the whole injury inflicted by the fraud. That injury includes the damage done to investor confidence and the integrity of the nation's capital markets, and is necessarily greater than the profits at issue in a private suit. I agree that the SEC in a civil enforcement action may seek only "remedial" and not punitive relief. But even if disgorgement must be strictly "compensatory" to be "remedial" (and I believe it need not be), society simply is not made whole by the court's measure of disgorgement. Although the broader social damage of an inside trade is diffuse, even diffuse damage may be large in the aggregate, and it is a settled principle of even private equity that where the nature of a wrong makes damage calculations difficult, as here, it is better to give the plaintiff a windfall than to permit the wrongdoer to profit from his wrong. See Janigan v. Taylor.[2] At the very least, the burden is on the wrongdoer to prove the appropriateness of a lower measure. These principles apply with added force here, for the plaintiff is not a private party pursuing a personal windfall, but a public agency enforcing broad public interests.

My disagreement with the court's measure of disgorgement is sharpened by my view of its inadequacy as a deterrent.[3] Since disgorgement only deprives the wrongdoer of his profit, even full disgorgement, without more, cannot deter all insider trading, for the risk of detection is less than 100 percent and the insider can never lose more than he stands to gain. Full disgorgement will, however, deter insiders like appellant where, as here, the additional profits subject to disgorgement under a full disgorgement rule are substantial. Under the court's approach, an insider like appellant who anticipates $1 per share in profit from inside information and $5 per share in later appreciation has nothing to lose from inside trading, because he keeps $5 in profit even if he is caught. A rational insider would not engage in inside trading, however, if he faced full disgorgement, for he would not rationally risk $5 in otherwise lawful profits for the sake of an extra $1 in ill-gotten gain.

I find the SEC enforcement cases cited by the court to be no barrier to the approach I urge. In *Texas Gulf*, disgorgement was not an issue; moreover, there is no negative pregnant to be derived from the sanction of partial disgorgement imposed there. As for *Shapiro*, ignoring losses after disclosure of the inside information does not require that gains after disclosure also be ignored. The purpose of the *Shapiro* rule is to avoid giving the wrongdoer an incentive to wrongdoing — to avoid giving him a "heads-I-win-tails-you-lose" opportunity by allowing him to "keep subsequent profits but not suffer subsequent losses." 494 F.2d at 1309. Given this purpose, I see no reason not to put the SEC in the position of winning whether the wrongdoing is followed by losses or profits. . . .

Nor does the court's reliance on the ALI's proposed Federal Securities Code persuade me. First, the provisions cited by the court deal with private damage actions, not suits in equity by the SEC. Second, although

---

2. Accord, Bigelow v. RKO Radio Pictures, Inc., 327 U.S. 251, 265-66 (1946).
3. Contrary to the court's assertion, deterrence is not penalty, but a legitimate and recognized end of equity in cases of conscious wrongdoing.

the Code states that a defrauded seller's damages should generally be determined by the value of the securities at the end of a reasonable period following full disclosure, the Code also authorizes a district court to award 150 percent of the ordinary figure to provide a deterrent against trading which fouls the public marketplace where, as here, an insider has fraudulently traded on the basis of inside information. ALI Federal Securities Code §1708(b)(4) (1981 Supp.) & comment 2. Moreover, under section 1702(e), a seller victimized by a "non-fraud-type" violation may recover as damages the value of the security *on the date of the judgment*, less the amount he received for the security. In effect, the innocent party has a right to rescind the transaction.[7] Like the 150 percent provision of section 1708, the aim of section 1702 is to deter violations. ALI Federal Securities Code §1708 introductory comment 5(d). From the SEC's perspective, a transaction is just as illegal whether it is a fraud-type violation or a non-fraud-type violation. In addition, once the principle of deterrence is recognized, section 1708's suggested limitation of 150 percent of profits to the time of disclosure is arbitrary: although such a cap may be appropriate in a private suit, where deterrence and enforcement incentives must be balanced against the inequity of giving a plaintiff an undue windfall, an artificial limit on disgorgement is wholly inappropriate in a public enforcement action by the SEC, where the policy against windfall awards is absent. Without attempting a formula for all cases, I would hold that on this record a district court should have power to order disgorgement of any amount up to the wrongdoer's full actual profits from the fraudulently acquired securities, its discretion in exercising that power to depend on the particular need for deterrence presented by the offender and the offense, and the equities of the case. Indeed, the Code explicitly recognizes a district court's power generally to adjust damages in this fashion. §1723(e). Finally, full disgorgement leaves the wrongdoer in exactly the same financial position as rescission; if rescission is equitable, so is full disgorgement.

In the present case, it is not unreasonable to view *all* of appellant's profits as "ill gotten." Absent an opportunity to trade on inside information, there is no evidence in the record that appellant would ever have purchased the stock. Having made the illegal purchase, appellant may have decided to hold the stock to take advantage of capital gains treatment under the tax laws, to avoid disgorgement of short-swing profits under 15 U.S.C. §78p(b), to diminish the risk of detection, or to avoid an appearance of disloyalty to his company — reasons unrelated to the sort of independent investment decision posited by the court. *Janigan* dictates that this uncertainty be resolved against the fraudulent party.

In short, I see more vitality than my brothers in *Janigan*, where the

---

7. Present law is equally if not more emphatic, declaring "void" all contracts "made in violation of any provision" of the Securities Exchange Act. 15 U.S.C. §78cc(b).

court held that once it is found that a defendant acquired property by fraud, "[i]t is more appropriate to give the defrauded party the benefit even of windfalls than to let the fraudulent party keep them." 344 F.2d at 786. Although, as the court notes, several courts have refused to apply *Janigan* in private damage actions where the fraudulently purchased securities are publicly traded, the SEC's remedial powers are not so restricted. The possibility that a defrauded *seller* could hedge his losses by reinvesting after full disclosure does not transform the profits subsequently made by the *buyer* as a result of the illegal trade into legitimate gains. In an SEC enforcement action, a court can legitimately seek to "disgorge ill-gotten gains or to restore the status quo, or to accomplish both objectives," SEC v. Commonwealth Chemical Securities, Inc., 574 F.2d 90, 95, 102 (2d Cir. 1978) (Friendly, J.), or to deter future violations of the securities laws.

Perhaps the real difference between my approach and the court's is merely a matter of burden of proof. Perhaps, in a given case, full disgorgement would be inappropriate, inequitable even in a public sense. But in such a case it seems only fair for the burden to be on the wrongdoer. Here, there is no question but that serious, willful wrong was done, with no mitigating circumstances. I see no reason why the SEC should, as the court evidently contemplates, have the burden of proving a negative (i.e., lack of independent investment motive) where it has already proven a serious infringement of public trust. I respectfully dissent.

NOTES ON PROFITS FROM INSIDER TRADING

1. This suit was filed by the Securities and Exchange Commission and not by MacDonald's victims. The Securities Exchange Act authorizes the SEC to sue for injunctions against violations of the act, and the courts have held that the Commission has power to seek additional relief as well. When the SEC recovers defendant's profits in an insider trading case, it holds them for five years to pay any claims filed by private plaintiffs. At the end of five years, any remaining funds are turned over to the insider's corporation. This procedure was devised as part of a settlement with one defendant in SEC v. Texas Gulf Sulphur Co., 446 F.2d 1301, 1307 (2d Cir. 1971), and has since been applied to contested litigation, including the suits against the nonsettling defendants in *Texas Gulf.*

A similar remedy is available in some jurisdictions through a shareholder's derivative suit. New York and Delaware, the two most important states in corporate and securities law, have held that a corporation is entitled to restitution of the profits of insider trading in its securities, and that a shareholder can assert this claim on the corporation's behalf. Diamond v. Oreamuno, 24 N.Y.2d 494, 248 N.E.2d 910 (1969); Brophy v.

Cities Service Co., 31 Del. Ch. 241, 70 A.2d 5 (1949). These cases both rely on the theory that inside information is a corporate asset and that the corporation is entitled to any profits derived from the information. But other jurisdictions have not agreed. The Seventh Circuit predicted that Indiana would not follow these cases, noting that it would also violate the securities laws for the corporation to trade on inside information. Freeman v. Decio, 584 F.2d 186 (7th Cir. 1978). The Florida Supreme Court took the much less defensible position that there could be no derivative suit without damage to the corporation. Schein v. Chasen, 313 So. 2d 739 (Fla. 1975).

The SEC does not need the corporate asset theory, and it has not emphasized it. The SEC demands defendant's profits pursuant to its statutory mandate to enforce the securities laws. The SEC's theory for giving the profits to the corporation appears to be that no more plausible recipient is available and that insider trading hurts the corporation's reputation. This unmeasurable harm to the corporation is mentioned in both *Diamond* and *Texas Gulf.*

Diamond argued that the derivative remedy is needed because the victims of insider trading are often unidentifiable and rarely sue. Presumably, this also explains why the SEC regularly sues for insider profits and rarely sues for damages to identifiable victims.

2. Many investors sold shares of RIT on the days MacDonald bought. None of them knew they were selling to MacDonald; none relied on a belief that he was not buying. It is entirely fortuitous whose sell orders were matched with MacDonald's buy orders, it would be difficult or impossible to find out, and the investors who sold to MacDonald got the same price as everyone else.

Whatever harm sellers suffered resulted from the lawful failure to disclose the Kenner deal, and not from MacDonald's unlawful predisclosure purchase. Everyone who sold that day would have sold anyway, and his purchases helped support the price at which they sold. Indeed, many proponents of the economic view of law believe that insider trading helps move stock prices toward the stocks' true values, and that it should be lawful. But the dominant view has been that insider trading is unfair to outsiders and erodes confidence in the integrity of markets; its illegality is well-established. That substantive debate is of only marginal concern to this course. As long as it is illegal, insider trading raises interesting remedies questions, because it creates large profits while doing no measurable damage to any identifiable victim.

In some of the cases, including *Texas Gulf*, the inside trades followed a misleading announcement from the company. The misleading announcement, and the failure to disclose all facts necessary to make the facts disclosed not misleading, are independent violations of the securities laws. In those cases, outside investors have damage claims based on the announcement; these claims are independent of any claim for profits from insider trading. *MacDonald* presents the profits claim without any damage claim, because RIT said nothing about the Kenner deal. Silence was lawful as long as no insiders traded in the shares and no one made misleading partial disclosures.

3. In Janigan v. Taylor, discussed in *MacDonald*, Janigan was the chief operating officer of a closely held corporation. He bought all the shares after falsely stating that there was no change in the business; in fact, there were signs of an upturn. Reasonable allowance for the effect of the misrepresentation suggests that the stock was worth only marginally more than the $40,000 he paid. But the upturn vastly exceeded all expectations; two years later, Janigan sold the stock for $700,000. The court awarded restitution of all his profits from the resale.

Judge Aldrich wrote both *MacDonald* and *Janigan*. In *MacDonald*, he distinguished *Janigan* by saying that MacDonald's unidentified victims could have repurchased in the open market after full disclosure; Janigan's victims could not, because he owned substantially all the shares. It is easy to see how that matters to a private plaintiff's damages. A plaintiff who sells on misleading news can avoid further losses by repurchasing after disclosure. This was the reasoning on the damage issues in Mitchell v. Texas Gulf Sulphur and Gerstle v. Gamble-Skogmo, the main precedents relied on in *MacDonald*. Both cases held on *other* grounds that there had been no unjust enrichment greater than plaintiffs' damages. *MacDonald* takes their analysis of plaintiff's damage and uses it to measure defendant's profits. But what does a victim's repurchase opportunity have to do with defendant's profits? MacDonald's victims can repurchase in the market, but they can't force him to resell; why should his profits be measured any differently from Janigan's?

4. There is no indication in *Janigan* that the truth about the company was disclosed before Janigan's $700,000 resale. Can the two cases be reconciled on the theory that they both awarded restitution based on the market value following disclosure? To test that theory, suppose plaintiffs in *Janigan* had learned the truth six months after they sold, when the stock was worth $100,000, and that during the subsequent litigation, Janigan resold for $700,000. Should he still have to disgorge the entire $660,000 profit? Or only $60,000, the amount of the profit earned before disclosure?

What is the significance of the $100,000 value on the day of disclosure? We know that MacDonald could have bought shares at 5½ after disclosure, because there was an active market. There was no active market in *Janigan*; instead, there were significant elements of bilateral monopoly. We don't know whether Janigan could have bought after disclosure, or at what price; that depends entirely on how the small group of investors would have reacted to full disclosure. The $100,000 figure, or any other valuation, would be based on the court's judgment and not on a market transaction. Did Judge Aldrich just have the wrong reason for emphasizing that the stock in *Janigan* was closely held? He thought it mattered that sellers couldn't repurchase after disclosure. Might the true significance be that defendant might not have been able to buy after disclosure? Should the court be reluctant to decide what deal the parties would have made if there had been full disclosure?

The court did just that in Gerstle v. Gamble-Skogmo, quoted in *Mac-Donald*. Plaintiffs alleged fraud in a proxy statement that induced shareholders to vote for a merger. Judge Friendly concluded that if the proxy statement had been truthful, the merger would have occurred anyway, perhaps on terms more favorable to the plaintiffs. Thus, he concluded, defendants would still have profited from the subsequent appreciation in the stock they acquired in the merger. Plaintiffs argued that the merger would not have been approved at all if there had been full disclosure, but the court disagreed. If the trier of fact finds that plaintiffs would not have sold at all if they had known the truth, should they get the benefit of subsequent appreciation?

5. The choice between recovery based on subsequent appreciation and recovery based on true value on the day of sale showed up in a different way in *Janigan*. The sellers there relied on a misrepresentation and could have sued for damages. It would not be implausible to say they lost $660,000, because all the gain would have accrued to them if they had not sold. But the court assumed that their damages were the small difference between the price and the actual value on the day of the sale. That is the dominant rule, although some courts use the market value following disclosure as the best evidence of actual value on the day of sale. See Harris v. American Investment Co., supra at 66. Measuring a defrauded seller's damage by the price he would have paid to repurchase as soon as the truth was disclosed is a slightly different rationale for the *Harris* measure.

Why should subsequent events be relevant to defendant's profits but not to plaintiff's losses? Should defendant's profits exceed plaintiff's losses if both are properly measured? Or is there a justification for different measures? Is it reasonable to measure losses more conservatively where defendant didn't gain from his wrong and has to dig into other assets to pay damages? At least for actively traded stocks, *MacDonald* appears to end the discrepancy; it applies the *Harris* standard to the measurement of profits. The SEC initially viewed the matter the same way. In *Texas Gulf*, all it asked for was the profits earned up to the time of disclosure.

6. The strongest argument for *MacDonald* is that only the profits up to the time of disclosure were derived from inside information; all the subsequent profits resulted from subsequent events. MacDonald could have earned the subsequent profits in an unquestionably legal way by buying at $5\frac{1}{2}$ after disclosure; deciding to keep shares after disclosure is no different from deciding to buy them after disclosure. How plausible is that? Is there any reason to believe MacDonald would have suddenly

bought 9,600 shares if he had not had inside information? Aren't the dissenters pretty persuasive that once he had bought the shares illegally, he was committed to keeping them for a while? Then why do the dissenters say the majority would be right if the plaintiff were MacDonald's seller instead of the SEC?

Does it make sense to say that only the predisclosure profits were a proximate consequence of insider trading? Does it make sense legally even if it is inaccurate factually? Is it better to have a bright-line causation rule than to speculate about what might have been? Sometimes, defendant really will make an independent decision to keep the shares after full disclosure. Of course, *Janigan* had a bright-line rule too — all the profits are unjust. Which bright line is better?

A similar causation problem lurks on the damage side. In the *Texas Gulf Sulphur* litigation, many plaintiffs sold after a misleadingly pessimistic announcement on April 12. The company disclosed the truth on April 16, and courts said that all plaintiffs should have repurchased within a reasonable time thereafter. The Tenth Circuit suggested May 1 as the cutoff. Mitchell v. Texas Gulf Sulphur Co., 446 F.2d 90, 105 (10th Cir. 1971). Is that as reasonable as the court assumes? How is an investor to know which announcement to believe? How can he know he has the whole truth, when the company lied to him four days earlier? Might a reasonable investor decide that the safest course is to avoid this company's shares because it can't be trusted? Wouldn't such a decision be a proximate consequence of the fraud? Enormous sums can turn on the answer. With a May 1 cutoff date, Texas Gulf's potential liability to investors who sold during the four days between announcements was over $16 million; without a cutoff date, the liability would have been $84 million. With an April 17 cutoff date, the liability would have been less than $5 million. The data for these calculations appear in Ruder, *Texas Gulf Sulphur* — The Second Round: Privity and State of Mind in Rule 10b-5 Purchase and Sale Cases, 63 Nw. U.L. Rev. 423, 428-429 (1968).

7. Judge Aldrich assumed that but for the wrong, MacDonald would have bought at 5½ after disclosure. Judge Friendly found that but for the wrong, Gamble-Skogmo would have completed its merger at a higher price. Is this like finding or assuming that Nye & Nissen would have rented the egg washer if it hadn't taken it without permission? Is it another way of saying defendants could have made the same profits legally?

8. Might differences in culpability help explain these cases? In *Janigan*, the representation was "consciously" false. 344 F.2d at 783. In *Gerstle*, it was not shown to be worse than negligent. 478 F.2d at 1298-1301. In *MacDonald*, there was no misrepresentation at all. But it would be a mistake to make too much of this pattern. Both the SEC and the courts used the *MacDonald* measure of profits in *Texas Gulf*, where there was a serious and conscious misrepresentation.

9. One analogy not mentioned in any of these cases is the liability of

a converter who resells at a profit. It is well settled that the victim can recover the proceeds of the resale in restitution. It doesn't matter that the resale was at a large profit. Fur & Wool Trading Co. v. George I. Fox, Inc., 245 N.Y. 215, 156 N.E.2d 670 (1927). Should that rule be applied in *MacDonald*? Or are the cases different because the converter's possession is always illegal, but MacDonald's ownership was no longer illegal after the Kenner deal had been disclosed?

10. Some of the puzzle of these cases results from the intrinsic difficulty of deciding how much profit resulted from the wrong. Some of the puzzle results from failure to adequately distinguish damages from restitution; many of the cases confuse the two. *MacDonald*'s definition of profit is now codified in the Insider Trading Sanctions Act of 1984, 15 U.S.C. §78u(d)(2)(C). That act authorizes the SEC to recover a civil penalty of up to three times defendant's profit.

CHERRY v. CRISPIN
346 Mass. 89, 190 N.E.2d 93 (1963)

Before WILKINS, C.J., and SPALDING, CUTTER, KIRK and SPIEGEL, JJ.
  SPIEGEL, Justice.
  This is a suit in equity in which the plaintiffs seek rescission of a conveyance of real estate alleging fraud and misrepresentation on the part of the defendants. The defendants have appealed from a final decree granting, in effect, rescission of the conveyance. . . .
  The defendants, husband and wife, were the owners of a parcel of land with a dwelling and garage thereon in the town of Cohasset. On December 11, 1959, they entered into a purchase and sale agreement with the plaintiffs, also husband and wife, whereby the property was to be sold to the plaintiffs for $21,000, and conveyance to be made on or before February 11, 1960. The agreement provided that the sale was contingent upon the plaintiffs acquiring a so called "G.I." mortgage. . . . An essential condition to such approval was satisfaction of the Veterans' Administration's (V.A.) requirement that "The Seller shall furnish Veteran Purchaser prior to settlement a written statement (or certification) from a recognized exterminator that there is no evidence of termites or other wood boring insects in the property." . . . William Matthews, an employee of the broker in the transaction, . . . communicated with an exterminator, whom he had engaged on prior occasions, and requested "the usual certificate" from him. The examination and inspection of the premises by this exterminator "was done, if at all, in a very careless manner." Although there was extensive and obvious evidence of "termite and wood borer activity in various parts of the house, inside and out," on February 4, 1960, the day he claims to have made the examination, he stated in a letter addressed to Crispin, but sent to Matthews: "There is no evidence

of termite or wood-borer activity in the structures." The exterminator knew or should have known that conditions on the premises would not have satisfied the V.A. requirement involved. . . .

On February 10, 1960, papers were "passed" in the office of the bank's lawyers. The exterminator's letter was referred to in the presence of the defendants during this closing, and read by Cherry who "relied upon its contents in going through with the sale." At the closing and at the time the purchase and sale agreement was executed, the defendants "had reason to believe that termites and wood-borer insects had infested parts of the house." They "knowingly permitted and acquiesced in the false representation made at the passing of papers to the effect that there was 'no evidence of termites or wood-borer insects.'" The Home Savings Bank was relying upon the V.A. approval in making the loan, and the V.A. would not have approved the mortgage without the certificate from the recognized exterminator.

The Cherrys moved into the house on March 11, 1960, and, within a few days, saw evidence of termites and "wood-borer insects." "The . . . work necessary to relieve the premises of termites and wood-borers and install termite control will cost $1,500." Since acquiring the property the plaintiffs have spent about $40 on the garage and painted the inside of the house.

One who has relied upon a misrepresentation as to a material fact, intentionally made and knowingly false, is entitled to rescission of the disputed transaction. "The test is the same as that applied in actions of tort for deceit." Yerid v. Mason, 341 Mass. 527, 529, 170 N.E.2d 718, 719. The defendants make no contention that the evidence fails to support the finding that they knowingly acquiesced in the false representation upon which the plaintiffs relied. They argue, rather, that the plaintiffs have suffered no "legal damage" because the misrepresentation merely "induced them to do what they were already legally bound to do," i.e., perform the purchase and sale agreement. They point out that the contingency of V.A. approval of the mortgage was satisfied, thus requiring the plaintiffs to accept conveyance of the deed. We are unable to agree with this line of reasoning. The contingency of V.A. approval of the mortgage was "a condition inserted in the contract for the benefit of the buyer." de Freitas v. Cote, 342 Mass. 474, 477, 174 N.E.2d 371, 373. The plaintiffs were bound to accept the deed only if the V.A. approved. They had the right to expect that this "approval" would be untainted by the fraudulent representation later found to have existed. . . . In completing the purchase the plaintiffs were damaged and they are entitled to relief by means of rescission of the conveyance.

Although rescission is an appropriate remedy on the facts found, the final decree entered must be modified. "Ordinarily one seeking rescission of a transaction must restore or offer to restore all that he received under it." Bellefeuille v. Medeiros, 335 Mass. 262, 266, 139 N.E.2d 413, 415.

The final decree before us orders, inter alia, a reconveyance from the plaintiffs to the defendants, payment of the full purchase price with interest to the plaintiffs by the defendants, and also reimbursement for the $40 expended by the plaintiffs on the garage. No mention is made, however, of payment to the defendants of the fair rental value of the premises during the plaintiffs' occupancy, a consideration necessary for full restoration of the status quo. See Restatement: Restitution, §§156-159. Such restoration also requires a determination of amounts to be credited to either of the parties by way of adjustments of taxes paid, improvements made, and so forth. The court has the power to impose such equitable conditions upon the relief granted the plaintiffs as will amply protect the rights of the defendants. . . .

The case is remanded to the Superior Court and the final decree is to be modified after further proceedings consistent with this opinion. . . .

NOTES ON RESCISSION

1.   Suppose plaintiffs had sued for damages instead of rescission. How much would they have recovered? Why wouldn't that be adequate? And why didn't the adequacy of the damage remedy matter? Courts almost never suggest that the irreparable injury rule applies to rescission; it is well settled that plaintiff has a free choice between the two remedies. Is that because it is reasonable for plaintiffs to decide they no longer want this house, even if it is repaired at defendants' expense? Is this the flip side of specific performance and injunctions? If injunction plaintiffs are entitled to the very thing they lost, should these plaintiffs be able to get rid of the very thing they don't want? Should they have to buy a house for a jury's estimate of value?

2.   The modern tendency is to treat rescission as equitable, but rescission was sometimes available at law. If plaintiff had paid money, or had delivered goods, he could rescind by tendering whatever he had received from defendant and suing at law to recover his money or replevy his goods. But if he had delivered a promissory note, or securities, or conveyed real estate, rescission required the court to cancel the instruments or compel defendant to reconvey. Such relief was available only in equity. Cherry v. Crispin is not unusual in ignoring the distinction; in Lipsky v. Commonwealth United Corp., 551 F.2d 887 (2d Cir. 1976), the court questioned whether the distinction survives. However silly the distinction, there is always the possibility of demanding jury trial on the ground that a particular case involves legal rather than equitable rescission.

3.   When a contract is wholly executory, a rescission decree amounts to a declaratory judgment that neither side is bound by the contract. When the contract has been wholly or partly performed, the decree or-

ders restitution as well: Each party must return to the other all that he received under the contract. If a benefit cannot be returned, such as the fresh paint in Cherry v. Crispin, the litigant who received the benefit must pay for it. What happens if he doesn't consider it a benefit? Can defendants say the old paint was fine, but the new colors are so ugly that *they* now have to repaint? What if plaintiffs had spent $10,000 building an addition before they discovered the termites. There does not appear to be any rule that disproportionate improvements bar rescission. In Nixon v. Franklin, 289 S.W.2d 82 (Mo. 1956), plaintiffs successfully rescinded after adding $6,000 to $8,000 in improvements to a farm they bought for $11,550.

4. One obstacle to rescission is that defendants may not be able to refund plaintiff's money. They may have spent it, or invested it in a new home that is exempt from execution. There is nothing unusual about an uncollectible judgment, but rescission often aggravates the problem. Plaintiff is more likely to collect a $1,500 damage judgment than the $21,000 purchase price for the whole house. The problem is further aggravated if plaintiff has made substantial improvements. Courts have responded to this risk by holding that when plaintiff reconveys the house to defendants, defendants take subject to an equitable lien to secure the refund of the purchase price. An equitable lien is like a constructive trust or a quasi-contract: It is a lien created by the court. If plaintiffs can't recover their money any other way, they can foreclose on the lien and wind up with the house after all.

5. If damages are measured by the difference between the contract price and the actual value of the property, and if the property to be restored does not change in value between the transaction and its rescission, then rescission is no more lucrative than damages. It is clear that plaintiffs' loss and defendants' gain are equal, even if we don't know exactly how much they are. But if the value of the property changes, then issues similar to those in SEC v. MacDonald arise.

Consider Seneca Wire & Manufacturing Co. v. A. B. Leach & Co., 247 N.Y. 1, 159 N.E. 700 (1928). Plaintiffs bought corporate notes from a securities dealer, relying on a representation that they would be listed on the New York Stock Exchange. In fact there was no intention to list them. Unlisted notes would generally be slightly less valuable, because they can be conveniently resold only to dealers who make their profit by buying at a discount and selling at a markup. Some investors would not want unlisted notes at all, for fear they would be unable to resell; other investors would not see this as a significant risk. The issuer of the notes subsequently went bankrupt, and plaintiffs successfully sued for rescission.

Suppose that at the time of purchase the notes were worth $10,000 listed and $9,800 unlisted, and that they were worthless after the bankruptcy. How much of plaintiffs' loss is because of the misrepresentation?

How much did defendant gain, and how much of that gain is because of the misrepresentation? But for the misrepresentation, would the dealer have held the notes until the bankruptcy, or sold them to someone else who didn't care whether they were listed? There's no way to know, is there? On these numbers, plaintiffs' damages were $200; rescission gave them a full refund. Is the damage measure wrong, or is rescission wrong? Note one more irony: Plaintiff and the court both assumed that the misrepresentation had been negligent at worst. Rescission is generally available for either fraudulent or innocent misrepresentations; damages are generally available only for fraud. Should plaintiffs be able to recover $10,000 on a lesser showing than it would take to recover $200?

6.   Suppose that in Janigan v. Taylor, plaintiffs had sued for rescission before Janigan sold his shares. Wouldn't plaintiffs get the shares, whatever they were worth? Wouldn't that be true even if other shares were outstanding and publicly traded? Or suppose MacDonald bought privately from an identifiable seller. If that seller sued for rescission, wouldn't he get the shares, even if they had continued to rise in value after full disclosure? The answer is, it depends. Plaintiffs who want rescission must demand it promptly after learning of the fraud, at least if the property is of a kind that fluctuates in value. A defrauded seller cannot wait until the statute of limitations is about to expire, and then sue for damages if the stock has gone down and rescission if it has gone up. That is a form of speculation in which defendant bears all the risk and plaintiff reaps all the gain. Baumel v. Rosen, 412 F.2d 571, 574-575 (4th Cir. 1969). But what if the defrauded seller had demanded rescission immediately on learning of the fraud, when the stock was worth $5.50 per share? When he finally got a rescission decree a year or more later, he would get the stock itself, even if it had doubled in the meantime. If that is true, why couldn't the SEC recover $10 per share if it promptly announced its intention to seek recovery based on rescission?

7.   In addition to fraud, rescission is available for innocent misrepresentation, Grimes v. Adelsperger, 67 Ill. App. 3d 582, 384 N.E.2d 537 (1978); material breach, Lipsky v. Commonwealth United Corp., 551 F.2d 887 (2d Cir. 1976); mutual mistake of fact, Sherwood v. Walker, 66 Mich. 568, 33 N.W. 919 (1887); and duress, Country Cupboard v. Texstar Corp., 570 S.W.2d 70 (Tex. Civ. App. 1978). The Uniform Commercial Code codifies rescission for buyers of goods in §2-711(1).

NOTES ON RESTITUTION FOR BREACH OF A LOSING CONTRACT

1.   Consider Boomer v. Muir, 24 P.2d 570 (Cal. App. 1933). Muir was the general contractor, and Boomer a subcontractor, on a contract to build a hydroelectric plant. Boomer was to build one dam for the project,

and Muir was to supply Boomer with materials and equipment. There were delays and cost overruns from the beginning, which each side blamed on the other. Finally, with Boomer's dam 95 percent complete, he abandoned the work. A jury found that Boomer's withdrawal was justified by Muir's material breach in failing to deliver materials.

The court doesn't give all the relevant numbers in *Boomer*; the numbers here include some reasonable assumptions. The contract price was $333,000. Boomer had received $313,000 in progress payments, and would have been entitled to another $20,000 if he finished the job. Boomer had spent $571,000 building as much as he did, not counting any waste that was his own fault. It would have cost another $29,000 to finish the job, making a total construction cost of $600,000.

How much should Boomer recover? His expectancy was negative; if the contract had been fully performed he would have lost $267,000. But the court said he could rescind the contract and sue for the value of the benefit he had conferred on Muir — the value of a nearly finished dam. He recovered $258,000, the difference between what he had been paid already and what he had spent.

2. Why should Muir have to pay $571,000 for a benefit he was promised for less than $333,000? Would he be unjustly enriched if he got such valuable work for such a bargain price? Is his enrichment unjust because the contract itself is unjust? Or is his enrichment unjust because he breached the contract? If the contract allocated to Boomer the risk that the work might cost more than expected, and if the court would not set aside the contract for unconscionability or mutual mistake, why does Storrie's breach justify reallocating the risk? Is restitution a penalty for breach?

3. *Boomer* raises two quite different questions. The one that has gotten the most attention is whether Boomer can sue for restitution instead of his expectancy. But if we say Boomer can sue for restitution, a harder question arises: What is the value of the benefit? How do we know the dam is worth $571,000 instead of 95 percent of $333,000? The court instructed the jury to award the "cost or expense of performing the work." Section 371 of the Restatement (Second) of Contracts would award (1) the amount "it would have cost" to obtain the work "from a person in the claimant's position," or (2) the amount by which defendant's property increased in value or "his other interests advanced." The court is to choose between these two measures "as justice requires." The first measure suggests the market price, but construction jobs tend to be unique, so the plaintiff's cost is important evidence of what it would have cost to obtain the benefit from another. What about the second measure? Does it make sense to ask what the benefit is worth to defendant? What if $600,000 for the dam makes the project economically unfeasible?

Most courts also hold that the contract price is admissible evidence on the value of the benefit. Why isn't it the best evidence? A court unhappy with the *Boomer* rule can avoid it without rejecting it by finding that the value of the benefit is equal to the contract price. An example is Constantino v. American S/T *Achilles*, 580 F.2d 121 (4th Cir. 1978). There was a strong dissent.

4. There are a few cases limiting plaintiff to the pro-rated contract price, but *Boomer* reflects the dominant view. The American Law Institute debated the issue hotly before adopting §371 of the Restatement. A compromise that is occasionally suggested is giving restitution up to the contract price as a limit. Suppose Boomer had spent $340,000 completing 60 percent of the work. Wouldn't a recovery of the full contract price raise the same problems as recovery of $571,000 for 95 percent of the work?

5. In *Boomer*, each side accused the other of breach. The jury authoritatively resolved the issue, but the jury may have been wrong. It commonly happens that both parties complain about the other's performance, exchanging escalating charges and countercharges until one side accuses the other of substantial breach and terminates the contract. Which side is in breach depends on a judgment call: on whether there was adequate cause for termination. And the party finally held in breach may be no more to blame than the other for the series of disputes that led up to the termination. Indeed, a party facing large losses may try to goad the other into a breach that will justify termination. But who owes whom how much can shift dramatically on the basis of the court's uncertain decision that there was or was not adequate cause to terminate the contract, especially where there is a large difference between the contract price and actual cost. The *Boomer* rule aggravates this problem. If Boomer can provoke a breach, he not only gets out of having to finish, he gets reimbursed for all his expenses.

6. Suppose Boomer had fully performed and Muir breached by refusing to pay. Should Boomer be able to recover the contract price, or the reasonable value of the work? The traditional answer has been that if plaintiff has fully performed and defendant owes only money, plaintiff is limited to the contract price and cannot recover restitution. Restatement (Second) of Contracts §373(2). Does the distinction between full and part performance make any sense? If defendant's breach justifies reallocating risks, why does the breach have to come before plaintiff has fully performed? The rule can force plaintiffs to denigrate their own performance to prove they never finished. An example is United States ex rel. Harkol, Inc. v. Americo Construction Co., 168 F. Supp. 760 (D. Mass. 1958); despite his own allegations of incomplete and faulty performance, plaintiff really had finished the work.

7. *Boomer* says that a plaintiff seeking restitution rescinds the contract and sues in quantum meruit, a form of quasi-contract. Muir can't rely on the contract price because the contract has been rescinded. How helpful is that? Is rescinding the contract here like waiving the tort in

Olwell? Suppose there really were no contract. Suppose Boomer just showed up one day and started building a dam on Muir's property. Should Muir have to pay for that? Obviously, one cannot go about conferring unwanted benefits on unwilling recipients and then demanding payment. The law recognizes this in the rule that "mere volunteers" or "officious intermeddlers" can't demand restitution. Doesn't Boomer have to rely on the contract to show that he is not an officious intermeddler? Doesn't he have to show that his work complies with the contract specifications to show that it is a benefit? As Professor Perillo notes in making a broader point about litigating quasi-contract liability in a transaction where the parties tried to make a real contract, "at every step and turn questions of fact and questions of law are definitively or partially resolved by reference to the contract." Perillo, Restitution in a Contractual Context, 73 Colum. L. Rev. 1208, 1216 (1973). The more modern cases and commentators have abandoned the fiction of rescission. The Restatement acknowledges restitution of the value of part performance as an alternate remedy on the contract. §§344, 345, 371, 373.

NOTES ON THE BENEFIT REQUIREMENT

1. In most of the cases we have read, there was clearly a benefit to defendant, whatever the difficulties of valuing it. But sometimes that is not clear at all. Suppose that an architect draws plans for a building, and that the architect's contract is terminated before the plans are used or even before they are delivered. Did the architect's customer benefit from the plans. Some courts and commentators would say yes. Consider three such cases collected in Dawson, Restitution or Damages?, 20 Ohio St. L.J. 175, 190-191 (1959). One of them explicitly finds a fictional benefit. Sterling v. Marshall, 54 A.2d 353 (D.C. Mun. Ct. 1947). One grants recovery for the "reasonable value" of the services without talking about benefits. Polak v. Kramer, 116 Conn. 688, 166 A. 396 (1933). The third also talks of reasonable value, but it explicitly links it to reliance; the architect is entitled to "restoration for that which is owing for [his] reliance on the contract," "regardless of the value received by the breaching party." Parrish v. Tahtaras, 7 Utah 2d 87, 91, 318 P.2d 642, 645 (1957). Professor Dawson cites all three as restitution cases, although *Parrish* is more easily read as a reliance case. *Polak*'s judgment for "reasonable value" seems to sound in restitution, but that too appears to be a reliance opinion in light of the Connecticut precedents, especially Kearns v. Andree, 107 Conn. 181, 139 A. 695 (1928).

2. Professor Dawson did not misunderstand the three cases in his footnote. Rather, his citation reflects a different conception of the law. He would eliminate the benefit requirement altogether in cases of restitution after part performance of a contract. He thinks the point of restitu-

tion in these cases is to reverse the transaction, not to avoid unjust enrichment, and that the language of "enrichment" and "benefit" has come to be misleading. Dawson, Restitution without Enrichment, 61 B.U.L. Rev. 563 (1981). In effect, he would equate restitution with reliance. Compare Professor Palmer's statement in another context: To measure restitution by the damage inflicted on plaintiff "almost wholly obliterates the distinction between gain to the defendant and loss to the plaintiff, a distinction which is fundamental in the law of restitution." 1 G. Palmer, Law of Restitution §2.10 at 140 (1978).

3.   The issue produced a furious debate in Farash v. Sykes Datatronics, 59 N.Y.2d 500, 452 N.E.2d 1245 (1983). Plaintiff had remodeled a building to defendant's specifications. But defendant reneged on an oral agreement to lease the building, and the contract was unenforceable under the statute of frauds. The majority held that plaintiff could recover his remodeling expenses in quasi-contract. After quoting some commentators who said this was a recovery of reliance damages, and others who said it was restitution of a benefit, the court held it didn't matter. The authorities disagreed on terminology but not on result. The dissenters insisted that there had been no benefit and that hence there could be no recovery in restitution. They thought the result could be explained as a recovery of reliance damages on a promissory estoppel theory, but they insisted that New York's version of promissory estoppel could not reach this case.

4.   In the losing contract cases, it may matter a great deal whether plaintiff seeks his own reliance damages or defendant's unjust enrichment. Recall the Restatement provision limiting reliance recoveries to plaintiff's expectancy. Re-read note 4 supra at 44-45. Under the Restatement rule, Boomer's reliance recovery would be his reliance expenses of $571,000, less his expected loss of $267,000, or a net of $304,000. Since he had already been paid $313,000 in progress payments, he would recover nothing; presumably, he would not have to give $9,000 back.

Does it make any sense to distinguish reliance from restitution so dramatically? Aristotle thought that the moral claim for a remedy is strongest when there is both a loss to plaintiff and a benefit to defendant. But doesn't the moral force of such distinctions depend on the benefit being real? Shouldn't courts either treat reliance and restitution identically, or insist on a real benefit if restitution recoveries are to be more generous or more freely available?

NOTES ON ELECTION OF REMEDIES

1.   One unfortunate consequence of holding that restitution is not a remedy on the contract was the election of remedies doctrine. The theory was that there is either a contract or there is not, and if there is, plaintiff

could either affirm it or rescind it. An affirmance was generally held to be irrevocable. Thus, if the plaintiff sued on the contract, orally affirmed its existence, or even delayed in claiming rescission, the restitution remedy became unavailable. Curiously, a decision to rescind did not necessarily preclude a subsequent suit on the contract. A decision to rescind could generally be revoked until defendant relied on it, until plaintiff recovered what he had given up under the contract, or until a judgment was entered. And most courts allowed plaintiff to plead in the alternative. Some jurisdictions required him to elect before trial, and some before submission to the jury. Some would submit the case to the jury in the alternative.

2. In some of the contract cases, there is a real inconsistency between the remedies, of a sort that requires plaintiff to choose. The parties either will or will not return the very things they received under the contract. For example, in Cherry v. Crispin, plaintiffs can either give back the house and recover all their money, or keep the house and recover only their damages. At some point they must choose, and the only argument is over how soon they must choose and whether their first choice is irrevocable.

But the election doctrine has also been applied to cases like *Olwell*, where plaintiff "waives" a tort and sues in quasi-contract. There are cases saying that once he waives the tort, plaintiff cannot change his mind and sue for tort damages. In these cases, plaintiff's choice is purely theoretical. Plaintiff has gotten nothing from defendant and will not have to return anything under either theory. The election rule has been criticized in this context as well, and the cases go both ways.

3. The doctrine often led to harsh results when the damage action turned out to be a loser, or when the damage recovery turned out to be much smaller than the restitutionary recovery. In a case in which the suit for contract damages was barred by limitations but the restitution remedy was not, Judge Cardozo showed the way out of the doctrine. He said that plaintiff's election was conditioned on actually collecting the contract damages, and that it was not binding if those damages were not paid. His language was much broader than the facts of the case; he implied that plaintiff could change his mind at any time before defendant paid. Schenck v. State Line Telephone Co., 238 N.Y. 308, 144 N.E. 592 (1924).

Cardozo's conditional election theory has not led to the doctrine's elimination. But increasingly, the cases hold plaintiff to an initial election only when defendant would be prejudiced by a change in theories. Some courts have adopted Professor Bogert's formulation, limiting election of remedies doctrine to three situations: "where (1) double compensation of the plaintiff is threatened or (2) the defendant has actually been misled by the plaintiff's conduct or (3) res adjudicata can be applied." Altom v. Hawes, 63 Ill. App. 3d 659, 380 N.E.2d 7 (1978), quoting 4 G. Bogert, Trusts and Trustees §946 (1935). The election doctrine is restated without qualification in the Restatement (Second) of Contracts §§380-382 (1981). But the black letter rule is misleading, because Judge Cardozo's rule-swallowing exception is tucked into an illustration, id. at §380, comment b, illus. 3. With respect to the sale of goods, §§2-720 and 2-721 of the UCC squarely reject the doctrine.

4. An example with interesting facts but a confused procedural history is Roberts v. Sears, Roebuck & Co., 573 F.2d 976 (7th Cir.), cert. denied, 439 U.S. 860 (1978), and Roberts v. Sears, Roebuck & Co., 617 F.2d 460 (7th Cir.), cert. denied, 449 U.S. 975 (1980). Roberts was a Sears employee who invented a wrench. Sears told him it wasn't worth much, bought the rights for $10,000, and made millions. The court instructed that Roberts was entitled to only a reasonable royalty if Sears negligently misrepresented the invention's value, but that it was entitled to all Sears's profits if Sears deliberately misrepresented its value. The case illustrates an argument for election in addition to Bogert's three concerns. If plaintiff is not required to elect before the case goes to the jury, there is a risk that the jury will be confused by alternative instructions. That apparently happened in *Sears*; the jury brought in identical verdicts on all counts. But if the facts are unclear and the jury's reaction unpredictable, requiring an election before verdict seriously prejudices plaintiff. He must either forfeit his right to a larger recovery if he proves more than negligence, or he must make an all or nothing gamble, forfeiting his right to a smaller recovery if negligence is all he proves.

In *Sears*, no one argued that the case should not have been submitted in the alternative. The Seventh Circuit had previously held that it is error to require an election before submission, and had suggested that if the trial judge had any difficulty submitting the case to the jury, he use special verdicts or interrogatories to simplify the jury's task. Berry Refining Co. v. Salemi, 353 F.2d 721, 722 (7th Cir. 1965).

The issues that were argued in *Sears* went to res judicata and double recovery concerns. After the jury verdict, plaintiff asked the court for rescission. It turned out that plaintiff sought two things by that motion. First, plaintiff wanted the judge to redetermine Sears's profits and award an amount much higher than the jury verdict. Not surprisingly, the Court of Appeals found that maneuver "completely unfair" to Sears. Second, plaintiff wanted his patent back, so that Sears would have to buy the right to use it in the future. The Court of Appeals allowed that. Rescission for the future involved neither double recovery nor second guessing the jury, because the jury had found Sears's profits only up to the day of trial.

5. A plaintiff claiming restitution may have incidental or consequential damages that are not compensated by recovery of what he gave to defendant. For example, a buyer may have paid shipping costs in addition to the price. When the sale is rescinded and the purchase price returned, he has still lost the shipping costs. Or he may have spent money trying to

repair the goods before rescinding, or the defective goods may have damaged his other property. Sellers and parties to other kinds of contracts may suffer similar losses. Finally, the party who rescinds loses his expected profit from the contract. Courts have held that plaintiff's election to rescind precludes recovery of his expected profits, but does not preclude recovery of any other nonduplicative damages. The explanation is formalistic: The right to expected profits is based on the contract, and the contract has been rescinded. The cases are reviewed in 1 G. Palmer, Law of Restitution §3.9 (1978). With respect to contracts for the sale of goods, §2-721 of the UCC provides that rescission does not bar recovery of damages; there is no exception for lost profits.

A nonfictional solution to this problem would ask whether plaintiff is getting a double recovery. But that question is not always easy to answer. When we ask whether two measures of damage include the same loss, we ask a question that is conceptually clear, even if the facts are ambiguous. But when we ask whether a restitutionary recovery duplicates a damage recovery, we are comparing apples and oranges. Is it a double recovery for plaintiff to get back his part performance and also get the profit he would have earned by performing? Is it a double recovery for a victim of copyright infringement to recover his own losses and also recover defendant's profits?

6. Consider the three situations covered by Professor Bogert's formulation in note 3. The general rule against double recoveries protects defendant from the grant of duplicative remedies. Equitable estoppel provides a ready model for a rule against changing theories if that would be prejudicial because of defendant's reliance or a material change of facts. (We will take up equitable estoppel in chapter 11.) And res judicata and collateral estoppel protect defendant from relitigation in pursuit of a different remedy. Does the election of remedies doctrine add anything useful?

C. TRACING DEFENDANT'S UNJUST ACQUISITIONS: RESTITUTION AND INSOLVENCY

HICKS v. CLAYTON
67 Cal. App. 3d 251, 136 Cal. Rptr. 512 (1977)

[Plaintiffs Richard and Mafalda Hicks sued defendants Howard and Virginia Clayton for rescission, restitution, and constructive trust with respect to real property known as Costebelle. Howard Clayton was the Hickses' lawyer. He swindled them out of Costebelle in exchange for worthless stock and his unsecured promissory note. The Hickses remained personally liable on three mortgage notes to their savings and loan. Clayton failed to make payments on his note, so the Hicks were unable to pay the savings and loan. At the time of trial, the savings and loan notes were thirteen months in arrears. In addition, the Internal Revenue Service filed a lien on Costebelle for the Claytons' unpaid taxes.

The trial court found Clayton guilty of fraud and gross abuse of fiduciary duty. But he denied rescission of the transaction, a constructive trust on Costebelle, or any other form of restitution. Instead, he awarded money damages. Plaintiffs appealed.]

STANIFORTH, J. . . .

Where a breach of fiduciary duty occurs, a variety of equitable remedies are available, including imposition of a constructive trust, rescission, and restitution, as well as incidental damages. . . .

The trial court considered use of the equitable remedies, but rejected them in favor of damages. Whether a trial court may deny equitable relief in a case authorizing the intervention of equity — as here, where a breach of fiduciary duty is shown — depends upon the adequacy, the completeness of the remedy at law. . . . The remedy of damages, in the context and circumstances of this case, is not an adequate and complete remedy. It does not reach the mischief done by Clayton to the Hicks, nor does it secure their whole right. A fair inference from the uncontested facts here is that the money judgment is uncollectable. . . .

The presence of the enormous tax lien dashes cold water on any hope of recovery by levy on Costebelle. To the Internal Revenue Service lien a homestead must be added, placed by the Claytons on Costebelle. The picture of nonpayment on the three trust deed notes in the foreclosure actions now pending raises no spectre, but a solid reality of personal liability of the Hicks on three deeds of trust and a deficiency judgment against them if, upon foreclosure, the property does not net enough to pay off these trust deeds. The Hicks are in no way protected from these very real harms by a damage judgment. The continuing obligations of the Claytons under the contract to Hicks is both unsecured and unlikely of payment if past performance is any gauge. Thus the money judgment granted does not resolve any of the just-recited problems. A money judgment leaves the problem unsolved and the mischief actually aggravated.

It is true that the propriety of granting equitable relief in a particular case by way of cancellation, rescission, restitution or impressment of a constructive trust, generally rests upon the sound discretion of the trial court exercised in accord with the facts and circumstances of the case. However, that discretion is not an arbitrary one, but should be exercised in accord with the principles and precedents of equity jurisprudence. Sound discretion is not based upon whimsy. Judicial discretion to grant relief becomes judicial duty to grant it under some circumstances, and the grace which equity should bestow then becomes a matter of right. Further, where, as here, remedies both legal and equitable are available, the Hicks have the right to elect the kind of relief they seek. The facts of this case require the intervention of equity, the highest skill and discretion of the chancellor, to the end that the Hicks be restored, to the extent equity can fashion a decree restoring them, to the position in which they stood before the execution of the April 30, 1971, agreement. This would necessarily involve, if equity is to be done by wholes and not by piecemeal, entering into the area of the values received by the Claytons in the use of the property . . . over the years, the value of the improvements made by the Claytons on the premises during their occupancy, and the expenses and the costs incurred by the Hicks to protect themselves from the various harms arising from this contract.

The judgment is reversed with directions to the trial court to hold *J/rev'd* further proceedings in the light of this opinion.

BROWN (Gerald), P.J., and COLOGNE, J., concurred.

NOTES ON RESTITUTION FROM AN INSOLVENT DEFENDANT

1. Why is rescission better than a money judgment? The court obviously assumes that if it orders defendants to give the house back, plaintiffs will really get the house, but if it awards a money judgment, plaintiffs will lose to other creditors and never collect anything. Why should that be true? Why should an award of rescission, or of constructive trust, have a higher priority against other creditors than an award of money damages?

The court doesn't say; to the court, the result seems too obvious to require explanation. The next two cases provide some explanation. But nearly all the cases in this area assume a basic premise without fully explaining it. In Hicks v. Clayton, that premise is that the Hickses are not merely creditors, but the true owners of Costebelle. An award of damages treats them as creditors, but an award of rescission or constructive trust recognizes their status as true owners. If they are the true owners, then Costebelle doesn't belong to the Claytons at all, and the Claytons' creditors have no claim to it.

This equitable ownership theory works against general creditors and against the Claytons' trustee in bankruptcy, as the next case illustrates. It generally would not work against bona fide purchasers for value who take from the Claytons without notice of the Hickses' claims. Whether it would work against the IRS tax lien is less settled. Federal law would control over state law. The federal Tax Lien Act (26 U.S.C. §6321 et seq. (1982)) generally recognizes state law claims, but it does not address restitutionary claims of equitable ownership. The state court's theory is that the Hickses are the true owners, so that the IRS lien for the Claytons' taxes never attached to the property. Plainly, the court assumes that theory will work, and it probably would, but the IRS might disagree.

2.   The *Hicks* opinion relies on the Claytons' insolvency to show the inadequacy of the legal remedy. At one point, the court says that the constructive trust could be denied if the legal remedy were adequate; at another, it says that plaintiff has a free choice of remedies. The point is not discussed much in the cases, but the practice is to give plaintiffs a free choice. Professor Palmer reports that he could not find a single case in which plaintiff's claim of equitable ownership of a specific asset had been denied solely because of the adequacy of the legal remedy. 1 G. Palmer, Law of Restitution §2.19 at 220 (1978).

IN RE TELTRONICS
649 F.2d 1236 (7th Cir. 1981)

Before SPRECHER and BAUER, Circuit Judges, and CAMPBELL, Senior District Judge.

BAUER, Circuit Judge.

Drawn for battle, a state court receiver and a bankruptcy trustee challenge each other's power over funds of the bankrupt, Teltronics, Ltd. The issue here is whether money held by a state court receiver under the Illinois Consumer Fraud and Deceptive Business Practices Act, Ill. Rev. Stat. ch. 121½, §261 et seq., is property of the bankrupt's estate and thus subject to surrender to the bankruptcy trustee. The district court held that the money was not the "property" of the bankrupt under the Bankruptcy Act, 11 U.S.C. §11(a)(21), because it was acquired by fraud. We affirm.

I

Dennis Roberts, doing business as Teltronics, Ltd., defrauded thousands of consumers when they responded to magazine advertisements offering digital watches. The watches were never delivered. Roberts collected about $1,700,000 in prepaid orders and absconded with $1,300,000, still not recovered. He was later found guilty of fifty counts of mail fraud.

On December 26, 1976, the Illinois Attorney General filed an action in the Circuit Court of Cook County under the Consumer Fraud Act against Dennis Roberts, Teltronics, and other defendants.

Section 267 of the Act authorized the Attorney General to seek an injunction in state court to restrain violations of the Act. Section 267 also permits the court to appoint a receiver. Circuit Court Judge O'Brien entered a preliminary injunction, freezing about $836,000 held in Teltronic's checking accounts. On January 13, 1977, he appointed defendant-appellee George Kemp as receiver and placed the funds in his possession.

On January 24, 1977, certain business creditors of Roberts d/b/a

Teltronics filed a petition for involuntary bankruptcy, asserting claims of approximately $15,000. Bankruptcy Judge James appointed plaintiff-appellant Glenn Heyman as receiver in bankruptcy on December 5, 1977. On December 20, 1977, Teltronics was adjudicated a bankrupt.

On January 20, 1978, the bankruptcy receiver filed a complaint against the state court receiver, seeking turnover of all assets, books, and records of the bankrupt. On June 26, 1979, Judge James entered a judgment in favor of the bankruptcy receiver and ordered the state court receiver to turn over the funds, books, and records. The district court reversed on review, and the bankruptcy trustee appeals.

II

A

The Bankruptcy Act authorizes the bankruptcy court to order a person in possession of property of the bankrupt to turn that property over to the trustee. In particular, section 2(a)(21) of the Act gives the bankruptcy court jurisdiction to:

> [r]equire receivers . . . appointed in proceedings not under this title . . . to deliver the property in their possession or under their control to the receiver or trustee appointed under this title. . . .

11 U.S.C. §11(a)(21) [now 11 U.S.C. §543 (1982)]. That power, however, is limited, by definition, to property that is part of the bankrupt's estate. As noted by the district court, it is settled that property obtained by fraud of the bankrupt is not part of the bankrupt's estate. Roberts' conviction of mail fraud collaterally estops Teltronics from contesting that fraud occurred here; in any event, appellant does not seriously question the finding of fraud. This appeal, then, appears quickly resolved: since the property is not part of the bankrupt's estate, the bankruptcy trustee has no power over it.

Appellant, however, launches several attacks on the state court receiver's powers. Appellant asserts that Roberts' fraud also vitiates the state receiver's right to the property, since he represents the bankrupt. . . .

The rule that property obtained by fraud is not part of the bankrupt's estate represents the policy that property should remain in the hands of its rightful owners, no matter how legitimate the claims of creditors. The Illinois Consumer Fraud Act furthers this end by establishing a receiver to manage the claims of the defrauded rightful owners. It can hardly be said that the receiver is powerless to give the consumers their money back because of the very fraud which took it from them. The bankruptcy rule simply does not apply to a receivership under the Consumer Fraud Act. . . .

B

Retreating from a frontal attack on the state court receiver's powers, appellant next attempts to ambush Nicklaus v. Bank of Russellville, 336 F.2d 144 (8th Cir. 1964), the leading case establishing that the bankrupt's estate does not include property obtained by fraud. The bankrupt in *Nicklaus* had swindled some bonds from the Bank of Russellville. By the time of bankruptcy, however, the bank had gotten the bonds back. The bank answered, in response to the bankruptcy trustee's turnover suit, that it possessed the very bonds the bankrupt had swindled. Here the property cannot be so easily identified. Since Roberts deposited the money in several bank accounts over a period of time, a customer can only roughly identify which money is his or hers. According to appellant, these circumstances violate the tracing rule of Cunningham v. Brown, 265 U.S. 1 (1924).

Cunningham held that a rescission for fraud creates a resulting trust in favor of the defrauded person. However, to recover the trust funds, the defrauded person must be able to trace his money to where the *cestui que trustent* applied it, the Court held.

The Court further held that tracing money to a fund "wholly made up of the fruits of the frauds perpetrated against a myriad of victims" was insufficient. According to the Court, a victim had to follow his actual deposits into and out of a bank account. If the victim was unable to so identify his funds, he had to participate as a general creditor in the bankrupt's estate. These stringent requirements have defeated the claims of consumers suing as a class to rescind contracts for fraud.

Even *Cunningham*, however, recognized that the tracing rule could be avoided *if* abandoning the rule resulted in equal treatment of the defrauded customers. *Cunningham* considered applying an exception that

> where a fund was composed partly of a defrauded claimant's money and partly of that of the wrongdoer, it would be presumed that in the fluctuations of the fund it was the wrongdoer's purpose to draw out the money he could legally and honestly use rather than that of the claimant, and that the claimant might identify what remained as his *res* and assert his right to it by way of an equitable lien on the whole fund, or a proper pro rata share of it.

The Court refused to apply the exception because, under the circumstances, it would violate the policy of equality. Some investors learned of the scheme prior to bankruptcy, rescinded their contracts, and received full refunds from Charles Ponzi, the bankrupt. The available funds were depleted before all the investors were satisfied. Since all the funds were obtained by fraud, to allow some investors to stand behind the fiction that Ponzi had legitimately withdrawn money to pay them "would be carrying the fiction to a fantastic conclusion." If the exception were applied, some investors would have kept full refunds of their money, while others got nothing. The Court refused to apply the exception because it would violate the fundamental policy that "equality is equity . . . [t]his is the spirit of the bankrupt[cy] law."

The present case also calls for an exception to the tracing requirement. The funds held by the state court receiver are those of the consumers. Fraud is established. Unlike the common law exception rejected in *Cunningham*, however, the Illinois Consumer Fraud Act provides a mechanism by which the consumers will share equally in the fund. The receivership is expressly designed to fairly distribute a fund among customers. Application of the Illinois Consumer Fraud Act thus realizes the equitable result sought by *Cunningham*. Where such a procedure is provided, an exception to the tracing requirement should be recognized. Otherwise, as noted in In re Paragon Securities Co., 589 F.2d 1240 (3d Cir. 1978), the creditors would obtain a windfall at the expense of the defrauded customers, who did not enter into their contracts with a creditor's acceptance of the risk of failure of the debtor.

Appellant rejoins that the Illinois statute creates an unlawful preference for one group of creditors. In practice, however, the statute does no such thing. Since the monies were obtained by fraud, the receiver administers monies that are not properly part of the bankrupt's estate. Cases to the contrary cited by the appellant involved no fraud or only alleged fraud. . . .

IN RE ERIE TRUST CO.
326 Pa. 198, 191 A. 613 (1937)

Argued before KEPHART, C.J., and SCHAFFER, MAXEY, DREW, LINN, STERN, and BARNES, JJ.

STERN, Justice.

In the estate of W. W. Gingrich, deceased, the orphans' court of Erie county filed an adjudication surcharging Erie Trust Company, the executor, in the sum . . . of $25,819.80, representing cash taken from the estate by the company as commissions, to which, as the court held, it was not entitled. Erie Trust Company having become insolvent, and the Secretary of Banking having taken possession as receiver, the beneficiaries of the Gingrich estate sought priority in distribution for the amount of this surcharge. The court of common pleas denied their right to a preference over general creditors. . . .

Where improperly converted assets of a trust estate are traced into the fund for distribution, a preference has always been allowed on the theory that such assets never have become a part of those of the trustee but at all times have remained, whether in their original or substituted form, the property of the cestui que trust, and therefore the trustee's general creditors are not entitled to any share in their distribution. The claim of the trust beneficiary in such a case is not really for a preference, or to establish an equitable lien, but rather for the reclamation of his own property. . . . An illustration of a claim on an *unpreferred* surcharge would be one based upon an act of negligence or mismanagement on the part of the trustee, as, for example, a failure to dispose of nonlegal securities in the trust, or allowing trust funds to remain uninvested for an undue period of time. But in the present case the claim of appellants is to recover, as their own property either in its original or changed form, cash actually taken from their estate by the trustee. . . .

We thus come to the principal question involved: Have appellants been able to trace the converted cash of the estate into the assets in the hands of the receiver for distribution? The court below held that this requirement had not been met. The $25,819.80 taken by Erie Trust Company from the Gingrich estate was placed in the general cash funds of the company. The lowest amount of actual cash in those funds from the time when the money was taken from the estate until the receiver was appointed was $3,865.40, together with "cash items" of $1,937.63. The lowest amount of the company's deposits in other banks was $6,373.23. During this period the company deposited a large amount of cash in another bank, and also invested some general cash funds in various securities (Church of the Covenant bonds and the "Leichner" mortgage). The bonds were in the possession of the company at the time the receiver took possession; the mortgage had been foreclosed and the mortgaged premises purchased by the company. . . . It is the contention of appellants that in tracing the cash taken from the Gingrich estate and mingled by Erie Trust Company with its own general cash funds, the commingled fund is to be considered as being coextensive with all of the cash on hand, cash items and cash on deposit with other banks, and therefore the balance on hand of all such items is impressed with the trust and subject to recapture as representing appellants' property; moreover, that the securities purchased from any such funds after the conversion of appellants' money, and now before the court for distribution, are likewise so subject as constituting a substituted form of the cash originally converted by the trustee.

The principles underlying the tracing of trust funds have been the subject of so much confusion in the law, and their formulation has had such a checkered history, that it is frequently impossible to reconcile decisions in the same jurisdiction, much less to harmonize those in the courts of different states. Although it may be said in general that the tendency has been toward a gradual liberalization of the requirements of identification of the trust res, the progress in that regard has been far from continuous. While from early times equity allowed a cestui que trust to follow the trust property through any change in form or species into which it may have been transmuted, this privilege originally was not extended to the case of money unless the beneficiary could identify the particular bills or coin which had constituted the trust res. But in the famous case of Knatchbull v. Hallett, L.R. 13 Ch. Div. 696, Sir George Jessel, M.R., . . . established the principle that not only could a cestui que trust trace a cash asset of the trust into a fund in which it had become commingled with moneys of the trustee, but that, where the latter made withdrawals from the mixed account, the presumption was that the money thus withdrawn was his own, and the cestui que trust could claim that the balance represented the trust property. There evolved the generally accepted doctrine that the beneficiary was entitled to the lowest balance to which the commingled fund at any time became depleted, such minimal residue being considered sufficiently identified as constituting the trust fund. The variance in later decisions arose from differences in viewpoint as to the boundaries properly to be ascribed to the "commingled fund." If a defaulting trustee mingled trust assets with his own, did the mixed fund embrace his general assets, or consist only of the specific assets with which the trust res had been mingled? More particularly, in the case of a bank which had improperly transferred to its own funds cash from an estate of which it was trustee, could the cestui que trust reclaim his property from the general assets of the bank, or only from its general cash funds, or, adopting a still more rigid requirement, only from the exact cash fund or particular bank deposit in which the cash of the estate was placed or deposited? There are some jurisdictions which hold that the trust property, even without any special identification, and even though the beneficiary cannot show that it came in some form or other into the hands of the receiver, can be reclaimed out of the general assets of the bank; the theory being that those assets were augmented and the bank unjustly enriched by its appropriation of the trust property, and its general creditors should have no right to profit thereby. This doctrine, however, has been discarded in several of the states which originally adopted it, and the view which presently prevails in most jurisdictions is that the cestui que trust must identify the trust res by tracing it into some *specific* funds or assets of the bank; the problem remaining to determine *how* specifically the commingled fund must be differentiated from the general assets. . . .

[I]n Pennsylvania, . . . it is not sufficient for a cestui que trust merely to show that the general assets of the trustee have been increased by an unauthorized appropriation of trust property, but he must also identify the trust res by tracing it into some specific property, funds, or assets. We have no hesitation in holding in the present case that the deposits of the trustee company in other banks are to be considered, together with the cash on hand and the cash items, as constituting a single fund, sufficiently differentiated from the company's general assets to meet the requirements of the law in regard to the tracing of trust property. We are led to this conclusion by the fact that banks and individuals alike generally regard cash on hand and deposits in banks as a unit of cash resources distinct from assets consisting of securities and other forms of personal property. To insist upon a separate tracing of cash funds and credit balances in banks would be to dissociate legal principles from practicalities. The intricacies of bookkeeping and accounting systems, the complexities of banking usage, the difficulty of identifying cash through a series of transactions, the frequency with which balances are shifted from one bank to another and indiscriminate withdrawals made therefrom, are such that ordinarily it would be virtually impossible to distinguish between cash, cash items, and deposits in other banks. Indeed, as a legal proposition, there is as little reason to attempt such a differentiation as there would be to establish one between moneys kept in different vaults of the same bank, compartments of a cash register, or pockets of a purse. Therefore, even though appellants have not in this case traced the money from their estate into any particular fund or bank deposit, they are, in our opinion, entitled to the lowest level of the cash and cash items, and funds of Erie Trust Company on deposit in other banks, reached between the time when the conversion occurred and when the secretary of banking took possession of the assets of the company.

It follows as a necessary corollary from this ruling that investments made by the trust company, after the time of the conversion, from funds on deposit in other banks, are also subject to the claim of appellants in this proceeding. If the deposits themselves are to be considered part of the fund into which the trust res has been sufficiently traced, any securities into which such deposits were transmuted must be regarded as merely substituted forms of the trust property. As early as In re Oatway, [1903] 2 Ch. 356, it was held that where a trustee commingled trust moneys with his own, from the mixed account purchased an investment in his own name, and subsequently dissipated the balance of the fund, the beneficiary could impress the trust upon such investment. The fictional presumption that the money withdrawn from a commingled fund is the trustee's own should not be applied to defeat the cestui que trust's rights where the balance left is insufficient to meet the trust obligation. The most satisfactory rule would seem to be that formulated in Restatement of Law of Trusts, §202(1)h, as follows:

> Where the trustee wrongfully mingles trust funds with his individual funds in one indistinguishable mass, and subsequently makes withdrawals from the mingled fund, the beneficiary is entitled to a proportionate share both in the part which remains and in the part which is withdrawn, or, at his option he is entitled to an equitable lien upon both parts to secure his claim for reimbursement.

The application of this rule to the present case entitles appellants, in addition to their rights in the general cash funds already stated, to pursue the balance of their claim of $25,819.80 into the Church of the Covenant bonds and the "Leichner" mortgage (subsequently foreclosed and now held in the form of real estate) purchased by Erie Trust Company out of its general cash funds after the conversion by it of the trust money. . . .

The decree of the court below is reversed, and the record remitted, with directions to enter a decree in accordance with this opinion; costs to be paid out of the general assets of Erie Trust Company in the hands of the receiver.

MORE NOTES ON RESTITUTION FROM INSOLVENT DEFENDANTS

1. A trustee in bankruptcy is appointed to represent the creditors of a bankrupt debtor. The trustee's job is to gather all the assets of the bankrupt, convert them to cash, and divide the proceeds among the creditors. Secured creditors generally get to keep their collateral. In addition, Congress has explicitly conferred special priority on some kinds of unsecured claims, such as unpaid taxes and wages. Each remaining creditor gets a pro rata share of all the assets that are left after secured creditors and priority creditors have been paid. The basic principle of bankruptcy is that all unsecured nonpriority creditors should share equally.

2. *Teltronics* and *Erie Trust* illustrate an uncodified exception to this principle of equality. Victims of fraud or misappropriation who can identify their property get preferred over all other creditors. The court says that their property never belonged to the bankrupt, so it does not belong to the trustee. In *Teltronics*, the result is that the fraud victim's money is not available for distribution to creditors through the bankruptcy court. In *Erie Trust*, the money is distributed through the receivership, a state law substitute for bankruptcy, but the victims of misappropriation get paid first and do not have to share with other creditors. The economic result is the same in each case. Moreover, the victims get the benefit of fictional tracing rules to help them identify their property. We will examine those rules in a separate set of notes. For now, focus on the holding that the victims of fraud or misappropriation have an exclusive right to their property, and that the wrongdoer's other creditors have no claim to it at all.

3. The rule is that a plaintiff with a right to constructive trust, who can identify the property that he lost, can recover that property and does not have to share with other creditors. Note that there are two requirements. A plaintiff with a right to constructive trust gets no preference if he cannot identify his property. And an ordinary creditor gets no preference even if he can identify his property. If the Hickses had not been defrauded — if they had had independent legal advice and had sold

Costebelle for an unsecured promissory note — they could not recover the property when the Claytons failed to pay.

4. What is the basis for this preference? The explanation is fictional — that a constructive trust is imposed and that of course the beneficiary of the trust is entitled to the trust property. But what fuels the fiction? Why do judges do this?

a. The requirement that the property be identifiable seems to rest on the notion that if a victim can find the very thing he lost, it's still his. Consider what might be considered the clearest case. A thief picks your pocket on the steps of the courthouse and walks through the door to the bankruptcy court. He has your wallet with your cash and ten pieces of identification bearing your name. You have missed your wallet and are in hot pursuit, but he files for bankruptcy just before you catch up to him. Should your wallet and its cash be part of the bankrupt estate, so that you share with all his other creditors? Or should the law honor your claim that "That is *my* wallet!"?

One of my colleagues who teaches bankruptcy says that you should share pro rata. "How are you any different from hundreds of other victims whose pockets he picked but who can't identify their cash. It is the merest fortuity that you can identify the property that you lost, and that fortuity should have no legal significance."

Is the law recognizing a fortuity, or is it recognizing widely shared intuitions about ownership? If the latter, can the law successfully ignore such intuitions in a democratic society? But even if those intuitions are dispositive in the case of the stolen wallet, how forceful are they when identification becomes more attenuated? What if identification depends on fictional assumptions about the wrongdoer's intent, as in *Erie Trust*?

b. The requirement that there be a cause of action for constructive trust serves to separate victims of fraud and misappropriation from other creditors. Why should they get special treatment? The court in *Teltronics* says that other creditors accepted the risk of insolvency when they extended credit, but that victims of fraud did not. How persuasive is that?

In the hypothetical about the pickpocket, the victim never agreed to transfer his wallet at all; he plainly did not assume the risk that the pickpocket would go broke and be unable to return it. Similarly, in a case like *Erie Trust*, where the bank was managing trust assets in a segregated account, it is plausible to say that the beneficiaries of the trust did not assume the risk of the bank's insolvency. The trust's assets and the bank's assets were supposed to be separate; if the bank went broke, the trust was supposed to still be there. That plan broke down when the bank improperly transferred money from the segregated trust account to its own account.

But what of the consumers in *Teltronics*? They paid cash in advance for watches to be delivered later. They may not have thought of themselves as lenders, but they were; they assumed the risk that Teltronics would go broke and not be able to deliver the watches. That could have happened without fraud. It happens whenever a merchant goes bankrupt. There are nearly always customers who have paid in advance for goods on order, or have put down deposits, or have made part payments on goods in layaway, or have paid in advance for service contracts. How are the victims in *Teltronics* different from these customer creditors? It is even clearer that the Hickses accepted the risk of the Claytons' insolvency; the Hickses took a promissory note from the Claytons.

Suppose the court said that the risk of fraud is qualitatively different from the risk of bankruptcy. The consumers in *Teltronics* cannot be protected from the risk of insolvency, but they can be protected from the risk that the man who controlled the company planned to spend their money on high living and never even try to deliver watches. Does it make sense to say that those who suffered fraud or misappropriation are not similarly situated with those who merely made bad loans? Then why the requirement that fraud victims identify their property? If they are simply more deserving, why not give them a priority claim to all the assets? And why distinguish between fraud victims who can identify what they lost and fraud victims who can't? The identification requirement seems to be a rough and ready compromise between the interests of fraud victims and the interest of other creditors, and one effect of that compromise is to create two classes of fraud victims.

c.   *Teltronics* also says that other creditors would get a windfall at the expense of fraud victims if the other creditors were allowed to share in the proceeds of the fraud. How persuasive is that? Should creditors have any right to expect that debtors will engage in crime or tort to get the funds to repay their loans? If not, should creditors get paid out of the proceeds of any crimes or torts the debtor does commit?

5.   So far we have accepted the courts' assumption that there is a clear distinction between the victim of fraud and the ordinary creditor. But how valid is that assumption? Would creditors have loaned to Teltronics if they had known that Teltronics was engaged in a massive fraud on its customers? The simpleminded fraud in *Teltronics* was certain to be disclosed, and the disclosure was certain to destroy the business. Realistically, aren't all the creditors victims of the fraud?

Erie Trust might be different. The misappropriation of fees was presumably a minor part of a substantial banking business. Had the bank not failed, the fee dispute would have probably been resolved in the Orphan's Court with no significant effects on the bank's depositors or other creditors. If these assumptions are realistic, then it is plausible to say that the other creditors were not victims of the misappropriation, and that they would benefit from it if the trust beneficiaries were not preferred. But what if the misappropriation had gone on for a long time, and other creditors had relied on financial statements showing the "fees" collected by the trust department?

NOTES ON TRACING

Neither the fraud victims in *Teltronics* nor the misappropriation victims in *Erie Trust* can identify their property in the way that the Hickses could identify Costebelle. Yet in each case the court invokes tracing rules that enable the victims to identify particular dollars or monetary obligations as the ones they lost. Some tracing rules are realistic; some are fictional.

1. *The tracing rules in* Teltronics. The *Teltronics* victims paid by cash or check or money order, and the money from thousands of victims was commingled in several bank accounts. It is common to think of money being "deposited" and thereafter resting "in" a bank account, but even this is a fiction. Legally, a bank account is a debt that the bank owes to the depositor, and practically, the bank uses the deposited money for its own purposes or lends it to other customers. All rules for tracing cash through bank accounts start with the fiction that the victims' dollars are "in" the account. Courts could reach the same results by noting that the victim's dollars were exchanged for the bank's obligation to repay, but the conventional fiction is less cumbersome.

In *Teltronics*, much of the money was spent, and there is no way to know which victims' money was spent and which victims' money was still in the accounts. The court considers it sufficient that all the money in the accounts came from victims, and that the state receivership proceeding will enable all the victims to share pro rata in the money that remains. But the court's conclusion that the "funds held by the state court receiver are those of the consumers" is inconsistent with its statement of the facts. The court says that Roberts collected $1.7 million from the fraud victims, and that $1.3 million of this is unrecovered. That would seem to leave $400,000 of identifiable proceeds of the fraud, but without explanation the court upholds the state receiver's claim to $836,000. As the court states the facts, it seems clear that $436,000 of this came from some source other than the fraud victims. Either the facts are not fully or correctly stated, or the case creates a preference that goes far beyond the usual tracing rules. Because the opinion does not focus on whether the funds in the accounts can be traced to the fraud victims, it would be a mistake to attach much significance to the apparent expansion of the preference.

2. *The tracing rules in* Cunningham. Cunningham v. Brown involved Charles Ponzi, who gave his name to a whole category of frauds known as Ponzi schemes. In December 1919, Ponzi advertised that he

would borrow money from anyone willing to lend. He promised that in ninety days he would repay $150 for every $100 lent. He claimed that he could pay such exorbitant rates by exploiting distortions in exchange rates resulting from World War I. To boost the confidence of potential victims, he also offered to refund money on demand before the ninety days were up. By July of 1920, Ponzi was taking in a million dollars per week from small investors.

He accumulated the money in checking accounts. He used the money received from later victims to pay the promised 50 percent return to earlier victims. This feature — using principal from new victims to pay the promised income to earlier victims — is the essence of Ponzi schemes. Such a scheme can work for as long as the pool of victims continues to expand; sooner or later it must collapse when there is not enough new money to pay off old obligations.

On August 2, a Boston newspaper disclosed the fraud and reported that Ponzi was hopelessly insolvent. Thousands of victims demanded their money back, and Ponzi honored their claims until his funds were exhausted on August 9. Thousands of others were left unpaid; they filed claims in Ponzi's bankruptcy.

One obvious way to evade the bankruptcy policy of equal shares to all unsecured nonpriority creditors is to obtain payment just before the bankruptcy is filed. The law of preferences is designed to close that escape route. A creditor who is paid in the last ninety days before the bankruptcy petition is said to have received a voidable preference; such a creditor can be required to return his payment to the trustee in bankruptcy and accept a pro rata share of the bankrupt's assets.

Cunningham v. Brown was an attempt by Ponzi's trustee in bankruptcy to recover as preferences the refunds Ponzi paid out in the first nine days of August. The victims who had received refunds defended on the theory illustrated in *Hicks* and *Teltronics*: that they had rescinded for fraud and that their money did not belong to Ponzi or his estate. The Supreme Court recognized the theory but held it inapplicable. The Court apparently would have preferred fraud victims over ordinary creditors, just as the court of appeals did in *Teltronics*. But in *Cunningham*, the contest was between two groups of fraud victims: those who had received refunds and those who had not. Both groups of victims had an equal claim to be true owners rather than mere creditors, and the Court refused to hold that a fraud victim staked his claim as a true owner by getting a preferential refund. The victims who had obtained refunds were required to return them to the trustee in bankruptcy and share pro rata with all the other victims.

3. *The tracing rules in* Erie Trust. *Teltronics* and *Cunningham* involved commingling the property of different victims. *Erie Trust* is more difficult. First, the victims' property was commingled with property that was lawfully acquired and plainly belongs to the bankrupt. Second,

money that the court held to be the victims' property was invested, and some of those investments were exchanged for other investments. The court allows the victims to trace their property through the commingled account and through the subsequent exchanges. The opinion illustrates all the important tracing fictions that are widely accepted.

a. *Tracing through commingled accounts: the presumption that the wrongdoer spends his own money first.* If the bank takes the victims' money and puts it in the bank's own account, along with other money lawfully belonging to the bank, and doesn't spend anything from the account, it is fairly easy to say that the victims' money is in the account. But what happens when the bank spends something from that account? Courts irrebuttably presume that the bank, being conscious of its fiduciary duties, intended to spend its own money first. Thus, as long as the amount in the account exceeds the amount of misappropriated funds that were deposited there, all the victims' money is still in the account. If the balance in the account falls below the amount of misappropriated funds that were deposited there, whatever is left in the account belongs to the victims. The presumption is obviously contrary to fact; the bank thought it had lawfully collected its fees and was not aware of any fiduciary duty whatever with respect to this account. The fictions have even been applied when the wrongdoer said explicitly that he was withdrawing the money to keep the victim from getting it. Universal C.I.T. Credit Corp. v. Farmers Bank, 358 F. Supp. 317 (E.D. Mo. 1973).

New money lawfully acquired by the bank and deposited in the account is not treated as replacing earlier withdrawals of the victims' money, unless the wrongdoer actually so intended. This is why the rule is often referred to as the lowest intermediate balance rule: If the balance in the account is less than the sum taken from the victims, the lowest balance between two deposits of money from the victims is the amount of money belonging to the victims just before the second deposit.

b. *Tracing through commingled accounts: the presumption that the wrongdoer invests the victims' money first.* The presumption in note 3a benefits victims where the money withdrawn from the account is dissipated. But it works against victims where the money withdrawn is invested in a valuable asset; often victims would rather claim the asset than the lowest intermediate balance left in the account. The tracing fictions let them do so. The bank bought Church of the Covenant bonds and the Leichner mortgage with money from the commingled accounts, so the victims get to claim the bonds and the mortgage as "their" property. The bank's other creditors cannot claim a share, because these investments "never belonged to the bank."

Again, the fictional presumption is allowed to defy the wrongdoer's probable intention, but it is not allowed to defy chronological possibilities. Thus, victims cannot claim investments that were purchased before their funds were deposited in the account. And if the balance in the account falls below the sum taken from the victims and is subsequently replenished with the wrongdoer's own funds, the lowest intermediate balance rule limits the victims' claim to any subsequent investments. The victims can claim a share of the investment equal to the fraction that could have been purchased with the lowest intermediate balance. For example, if $1,000 of the victims' money remained in the account under the lowest intermediate balance fiction, and the investment cost $3,000, the victims can claim to own one-third of the investment.

The combined effect of these two tracing fictions is that the wrongdoer is presumed to dissipate his own money and preserve the victims' money. Commingled assets that can still be found, in or out of the commingled account, belong to the victims; assets that have disappeared belonged to the wrongdoer. But for any property to belong to the victims, it must be possible for it to have been purchased with the victims' money. Once the victim traces his money into a commingled account, anything that was possible is presumed in his favor, however unlikely, but the impossible is not presumed.

c. *Tracing exchanges of identifiable property.* By using the fiction that the victims' money was withdrawn from the commingled account to make investments, the court identifies the Leichner mortgage as the victims' property. But the Leichner mortgage has been foreclosed; now the bank has the Leichner real estate instead. It is easy enough to say that the real estate belongs to the victims too, and the court so holds. Tracing through such a direct exchange does not even require an additional fiction. The victims can trace through as many such exchanges as have occurred, so long as they can identify the property at each step. Thus, if the real estate were sold and the money invested in General Motors stock, the victims could claim the stock. If the General Motors stock were sold and the money deposited in a commingled account, and then money from the account were used to buy IBM stock, the victims could use the tracing fictions for commingled accounts again to reach the IBM stock. In theory, there is no limit to the number of exchanges that can be traced. In practice, every additional step increases the difficulty of identifying the property and the court's skepticism at efforts to do so.

d. *Defining a commingled account.* In *Erie Trust*, the victims did not trace their money into any particular account. The most they can say is that the bank misappropriated cash, so the bank must have put their cash into one of the places where it kept cash. Unfortunately for the victims, the bank kept cash in several places, and the victims did not prove which account received their funds. Perhaps they couldn't find out, or perhaps they found out and didn't like the answer. If their cash went into an account that had been entirely dissipated, tracing through it would produce no recovery. For whatever reason, tracing seems to fail at the very first step in *Erie Trust*: If the cash is not traced into an account, there is no opportunity to apply the fictions about withdrawals from the account.

The court avoids all these problems by treating all the bank's cash accounts as one. The court suggests that it would be unrealistic to treat each cash account as separate. Undoubtedly that is true, but it is hard to see why that matters; if we were being realistic, we wouldn't have any of these tracing fictions in the first place.

Some courts went even further during the Great Depression, when there were many bank failures. Under the swelling of assets theory, all the wrongdoer's assets were treated as a single account. This nearly eliminated the tracing requirement altogether. The swelling of assets theory applied the lowest intermediate balance rule to the wrongdoer's gross assets. Unless gross assets were at some point less than the amount misappropriated, claims of fraud and misappropriation were paid before other claims. That straightforward preference has generally been repudiated; other creditors have successfully insisted on the tracing requirement as a limit on the special treatment of fraud and misappropriation victims.

4. Even without the swelling of assets theory, identification has come a long way from the victim in hot pursuit of the pickpocket. How sensible are the tracing rules as a means of balancing the interests of misappropriation victims against the interests of other creditors? It can be said in their favor that the tracing rules are fictions only with respect to withdrawals; for the most part, the victim must actually identify deposits in the ordinary English sense of "identify." But elasticity in the definition of account allows some slippage even from that requirement; the Gingrich heirs never did identify exactly what happened to their money in *Erie Trust*.

The strongest argument against the tracing fictions is that they tend to produce arbitrary results in all but the simplest cases. How much the victim recovers depends on the history of the account subsequent to the misappropriation — on deposits and withdrawals that have nothing to do with the wrong. If a large check clears just before a large deposit is made, the lowest intermediate balance may be close to zero; if the deposit comes in first, the lowest intermediate balance may exceed the full amount of the loss, so that the entire sum taken is still in the account. The result may depend on whether the court considers only the balance at the end of each day, or also considers fluctuations during a single day. Banks rarely have accurate records of the order in which items were paid or credited during a day, so the better reasoned cases rely at least initially on closing daily balances. But the cases hold out the possibility that a showing based on closing daily balances may be rebutted by a showing of the actual order in which items were handled, and testimony has been taken on that issue. The cases are collected in 1 G. Palmer, Law of Restitution §2.16(a) at 200-201 (1978).

This arbitrariness in complex cases is the direct consequence of rules that seem fairer in simple cases. If one hundred stolen dollars are added to fifty legitimately earned dollars, and then fifty dollars are spent, it is easy to say the remaining hundred dollars were stolen. Once you say that, it is easy to say that if ten more dollars are spent, the remaining ninety were stolen. This is the essential leap in the tracing fictions; if you don't like the fictions, you have to say that the ninety dollars is unidentifiable. If fifty more legitimately earned dollars are then deposited, it is easy — and not even fictional — to say they were earned and are not the money that was stolen. Once you say that, you have the whole lowest intermediate balance rule with all its sometime arbitrariness.

5. The strongest critic of tracing rules is Professor Oesterle. He thinks that the whole concept of tracing is fundamentally misguided in both its realistic and its fictional manifestations. Oesterle, Deficiencies of the Restitutionary Right to Trace Misappropriated Property in Equity and in UCC §9-306, 68 Corn. L. Rev. 172 (1983). He poses a series of cases such as the following: Wrongdoer steals a silver teapot from Victim 1 and a similar silver teapot from Victim 2. He trades Victim 1's teapot for a guitar; he trades Victim 2's teapot for wine, which he drinks. Under current rules, Victim 1 gets the guitar. Oesterle finds it arbitrary to prefer Victim 1 over Victim 2. Wrongdoer could just as easily have traded Victim 2's teapot for the guitar and Victim 1's teapot for the wine. There may be testimony that if Wrongdoer had stolen only one teapot, he would have traded it for wine. Thus, there would not have been any guitar, and Victim 1 could not have traced, unless Victim 2's teapot had also been stolen.

Oesterle suggests two possible solutions. It appears that his first choice is to abandon all tracing rules and decide which claimants to prefer solely on the basis of the nature of the claim. He suggests that we might prefer victims of misappropriation or we might not, but tracing should have nothing to do with it. Alternatively, if tracing is to be kept, he would trace on the basis of causation rather than physical transactions. Thus, he would not ask which teapot was traded for the guitar. Instead, he would ask whether each misappropriation contributed to the acquisition of the guitar. If the guitar would have been acquired anyway, neither victim could trace. If either could have been used to acquire the guitar, or if the guitar would not have been acquired at all if there had been only one misappropriation, both victims could trace and share the guitar pro rata. He suggests some presumptions to reduce the difficulties of litigating causation.

Even Oesterle is not wholly uninfluenced by a victim's ability to identify his property. He attacks only the tracing rules, and not the underlying notion of ownership. Thus, if Wrongdoer kept Victim 1's teapot, and traded Victim 2's teapot for wine and drank the wine, Oesterle would allow Victim 1 to recover his teapot. Oesterle, Restitution and Reform, 79 Mich. L. Rev. 336, 361 (1980). Is this any less arbitrary than letting Victim 1 recover the guitar in Oesterle's original hypothetical? What if there were testimony that if Wrongdoer had stolen only one teapot, he would have traded it for wine?

ADVANCED TRACING PROBLEMS: TRACING INTO ASSETS WORTH MORE THAN PLAINTIFF LOST, AND THE TRACING RULES OF THE RESTATEMENT

1.   We have seen that restitution awards wrongdoers' profits to their victims, even when those profits exceed the victims' losses. Tracing is one way to do this; defendant may use misappropriated property to acquire more valuable property. Suppose that in *Erie Trust* the Leichner property were suddenly worth $50,000 because of an oil strike on the adjacent land. If the Gingrich heirs are the true owners of the land, shouldn't the whole $50,000 belong to them? Even though they only lost $25,000? That is the logical conclusion of the constructive trust fiction, and most courts would probably reach that result if the wrongdoer is solvent. Otherwise defendant could profit from his own wrong. Such windfall gains are rare, and solvent defendants nearly as rare, so the issue has not been widely litigated.

2.   In *Erie Trust*, the wrongdoer was bankrupt. Should the heirs still recover $50,000 through a constructive trust? Professor Palmer reports that "although the issue is seldom noted in the cases, . . . almost as a matter of course" the courts award no more than the victim's actual losses when other creditors remain unpaid. 1 G. Palmer, Law of Restitution §2.14(c) at 183-184 (1978). This can be explained in fictional terms as an equitable lien rather than a constructive trust: Victims get a judgment for the amount of their loss and a lien on the traced asset to secure the judgment.

3.   The Restatement tracing rules differ in several ways from those applied by the courts. The differences are subtle and can only be understood through examples. Suppose Wrongdoer deposits $2,000 of Victim's money in an account with $1,000 of his own money. Then suppose he invests $1,500 of the commingled fund in IBM stock. Then suppose that he dissipates all but $10 of the money remaining in the account, and that the IBM stock increases in value to $2,500. Under the usual tracing rules, Victim can trace $1,500 of his money into the stock, saying that only $500 of his money was left in the account. Thus, Victim can claim a constructive trust in the stock, and also can claim the $10 remaining in the account, for a total of $2,510. If defendant were insolvent, the courts would limit him to an equitable lien in the amount of his original loss, $2,000.

The Restatement gives Victim a different choice. He can take an equitable lien on both the stock and the account, collecting $2,000 in total. Or he can elect a constructive trust on a pro rata portion of each. That is, he can claim $\frac{2}{3}$ of the stock and $\frac{2}{3}$ of the money in the account, so that he gets $1,333.33 from the stock and $6.67 from the account, for a total of $1,340. Obviously he would choose the equitable lien and $2,000. This choice is not affected by Wrongdoer's insolvency. Thus, if Wrongdoer were solvent, the customary tracing rules would give Victim a larger recovery. If Wrongdoer were insolvent, on these facts Victim would get $2,000 under either set of rules.

Now suppose the same facts, except that the IBM stock increased in value to $5,000. Under the customary rules, Victim would get a constructive trust in the stock if Wrongdoer were solvent, collecting $5,010, and an equitable lien if Wrongdoer were insolvent, collecting $2,000. Under the Restatement rules, Victim would claim a constructive trust in $\frac{2}{3}$ of the stock and $\frac{2}{3}$ of the account, collecting $3,340. He could make this choice even if Wrongdoer were insolvent. Restatement of Restitution §202, comments c and e (1937).

The Restatement's equitable lien provisions also appear to differ slightly from the customary formulations. Suppose again that Wrongdoer deposits $2,000 of Victim's money in an account with $1,000 of his own money. Then suppose he invests $1,500 of the commingled fund in IBM stock and $1,500 in General Motors stock. Now suppose that the IBM stock declines in value to $500 and the GM stock declines to $1,000. The customary formulation would let Victim trace $1,500 of his money into the GM stock, leaving $500 in the account. Thus, he can trace only $500 into the IBM stock. So he gets all the GM stock and $\frac{1}{3}$ of the IBM stock, collecting $1,166.67 in all. It would not matter which stock was bought first. The Restatement formulation appears to say that he gets an equitable lien on everything purchased from the commingled fund, so that he can claim all of both stocks, $1,500 in all. The apparent reason for this formulation is an aversion to the fiction that the commingled fund can be separated into Victim's money and Wrongdoer's money. The effect is to increase the preference to victims of fraud and misappropriation in cases where all investments decline in value.

The Restatement choice between an equitable lien on everything or a constructive trust in a pro rata share appears in Restatement of Trusts §202 (1935), Restatement of Restitution §211 (1937), and Restatement (Second) of Trusts §202 (1959). Professor Scott was the Reporter for all three of these Restatements, and he was the primary exponent of the Restatement formulation. In his treatise, he lamented the courts' refusal to adopt it. 5 A. Scott, Law of Trusts §§517-517.2 (3d ed. 1967). The opinion in *Erie Trust* quotes the rule from the Restatement of Trusts, not noticing that it differs from the rules in the rest of the opinion.

4. The apparent reason for the Restatement's insistence on pro rata constructive trusts is to limit windfalls. Allowing the victim to review all investments made from the fund and pick the one that turned out to be most lucrative may produce a windfall that is harsh even as against a conscious wrongdoer. What if $2 from the fund was used to buy a winning lottery ticket worth a million dollars? Forcing victims to take a pro rata share of all investments limits the windfall, although in an arbitrary manner.

Because the proportion of Victim's money and Wrongdoer's money changes with every transaction, the pro rata allocation rule greatly increases the random effects of the order of events. If Wrongdoer makes profitable investments early, Victim benefits; if he makes them late, Victim loses. When there are many deposits and withdrawals, the calculations get monstrously complex. Professor Palmer could not find a single case supporting the Restatement rule in a complicated case, and very few even in simple cases. 1 G. Palmer, Law of Restitution §2.17 (1978).

In fairness, there are not many cases that squarely force courts to choose between the Restatement formulation and their own. In the most common case there are mainly losses and no tracing rule produces more than Victim lost.

5. An early draft of the new Restatement attacks the problem of undue windfall directly, giving courts discretion to limit tracing when "the extent of the relief sought is grossly disproportionate to any loss on which the claimant's right to restitution is based." Restatement (Second) of Restitution §41(b) (Tentative Draft No. 2, 1984). Will that solve the problem of the lottery ticket?

6. The Restatement tracing rules limit windfalls but don't eliminate them. When they occur, Victim gets the windfall even if Wrongdoer is insolvent. Is there any reason to give the victim of fraud or misappropriation windfall profits while other creditors go unpaid? Professor Scott, the Reporter for the Restatement, answers that the creditors have no interest in the trust assets, and are not entitled to benefit from their debtor's wrong. A stronger argument for the Restatement position is that Wrongdoer is allowed to profit from his wrong if any of the proceeds are used to pay his debts. That is not very compelling if Wrongdoer is being liquidated, as in *Erie Trust*, or if the debts are being discharged in bankruptcy. Wrongdoer will be relieved of his debts in any event; he gets no further benefit if profits from his wrongdoing go to his creditors.

But some debts, such as unpaid taxes, are not dischargeable. And unlike corporations, live human debtors are never liquidated. An individual emerges from bankruptcy still owing his nondischargeable debts. If profits from his wrong are used to pay those debts, he plainly benefits. Should we worry about that? Or is our desire to prevent that benefit simply outweighed by the competing interests of the unpaid creditors? A tentative provision in the Second Restatement would generally limit tracing in insolvency to the amount of the victim's loss. Restatement (Second) of Restitution §43(2) (Tent. Draft No. 2, 1984).

7. The new Restatement's provisions on disproportionate recoveries and insolvent wrongdoers seem to make the pro rata constructive trust rule unnecessary; excessive windfalls and hardship to other creditors can be policed directly instead of by arbitrary arithmetic limitations. But §37(2) of the new draft retains the pro rata rule in limited form.

8. Professor Oesterle thinks that tracing systematically mismeasures the wrongdoer's profit in cases where he acquires a valuable asset. Once again, he thinks the source of the problem is a misguided focus on transactional rather than causal connections. Suppose Wrongdoer steals $10 from Victim and has $10 of his own. Suppose he deposits $10 in a bank and earns $1.00 in interest, and uses the other $10 to buy a silver teapot that turns out to be worth $100. If Victim's $10 went into the account, he can recover his $10 plus the $1.00 of interest. If Victim's $10 were used to buy the $100 teapot, he can recover that. If Victim can't tell which $10 were used for what, even with the help of tracing fictions, he cannot trace into anything; he must sue for damages instead.

Not surprisingly, Oesterle finds these results arbitrary. He would ask whether Wrongdoer would have bought the teapot if he had not stolen Victm's $10. If he would have bought the teapot anyway, then his profit from the wrongdoing is the stolen $10 plus the $1.00 of interest. If he would have borrowed to buy the teapot, his profit from the theft is the stolen $10 plus the interest he didn't have to pay on the borrowing. Whether he would have bought the teapot anyway is a difficult question to litigate; Oesterle would apparently presume that Wrongdoer would have bought the teapot anyway if he were wealthy enough to make that plausible.

This sounds a lot like the argument that defendant could have earned the same profit legally. But it is not like arguing that Nye & Nissen could have bought the egg washer from Olwell; Oesterle's argument presumes that the original misappropriation was wrongful. His point is simply that it makes no sense to ask which dollar bills were used to acquire the more valuable asset. In his view, Wrongdoer's profit should not be generally measured by his most attractive investment, or by the investment that can be physically traced to the misappropriation, but by his least attractive investment — the investment he would have given up if he had not had the misappropriated funds. Is that question reasonably answerable, at least with the help of presumptions? Is it a more accurate measure of Wrongdoer's real profit? Is the additional accuracy worth the additional litigation uncertainty?

Oesterle attacks only the customary formulation. He ignores the Restatement rules, but they are no better from his perspective. The Restatement produces the same results as the customary formulation if the stolen ten dollars and the original $10 are not commingled. But if they were commingled, the Restatement would give Victim his $10 back, *or* a half interest in the teapot, $5 from the account, and fifty cents of interest. Does that have anything to recommend it as a middle ground?

9.   Sometimes it is defendant's labor that makes the misappropriated asset more valuable. We encountered this problem in connection with Sheldon v. Metro-Goldwyn Pictures, supra at 497. There we asked whether all the profits from the movie were profits from the wrong of plagiarizing plaintiffs' script. Tracing poses this question slightly differently: If plaintiffs are the true owners of the script, are they also the true owners of the movie? An affirmative answer is not very intuitively plausible; defendants had plainly added things that did not belong to plaintiff. The notes to that case raised the hypothetical of Leonardo's stolen paints, brushes, and canvas. Given the traditional emphasis on tracing through physical exchanges, the victim could conceivably claim to be the true owner of those items even though they had been rearranged into the Mona Lisa. And if the stolen thing is changed less dramatically — if Wrongdoer merely cleans and repairs the stolen teapot — then Victim's claim to be the true owner looks quite plausible. Should Victim recover the teapot without having to pay for the improvements? After all, Wrongdoer knew he was spending his time or money on someone else's teapot.

If plaintiff can claim an identifiable asset, that tends to change the results in some ways and not in others. In Sheldon v. Metro-Goldwyn Pictures, defendants got to keep a share of the profits proportionate to their contribution. A wrongdoer who spends $50 repairing a teapot does not thereby become a co-owner; he is quite unlikely to get a proportionate share of future appreciation or of new property acquired with the teapot. He is likely to get credit for the $50 he spent, but if he did the work himself, he is not likely to get credit for his labor. The distinction between cash and labor is the same one we saw in *Sheldon*.

SIMONDS v. SIMONDS
45 N.Y.2d 233, 380 N.E.2d 189 (1978)

Chief Judge BREITEL.

Plaintiff Mary Simonds, decedent's first wife, seeks to impress a constructive trust on proceeds of insurance policies on decedent's life. The proceeds had been paid to the named beneficiaries, defendants Reva Simonds, decedent's second wife, and their daughter Gayle. Plaintiff, however, asserts as superior an equitable interest arising out of a provision in her separation agreement with decedent. Special Term granted partial summary judgment to plaintiff and impressed a constructive trust to the extent of $7,000 plus interest against proceeds of a policy naming the second wife as beneficiary, and the Appellate Division affirmed.[*] Defendant Reva Simonds, the second wife, appeals.

The separation agreement required the husband to maintain in effect, with the wife as beneficiary to the extent of $7,000, existing life insurance policies or, if the policies were to be canceled or to lapse, insurance policies of equal value. The issue is whether that provision entitles the first wife to impress a constructive trust on proceeds of insurance policies subsequently issued, despite the husband's failure to name her as the beneficiary on any substitute policies once the original life insurance policies had lapsed.

Prop. Rt.

There should be an affirmance. The separation agreement vested in the first wife an equitable right in the then existing policies. Decedent's substitution of policies could not deprive the first wife of her equitable interest, which was then transferred to the new policies. Since the proceeds of the substituted policies have been paid to decedent's second wife, whose interest in the policies is subordinate to plaintiff's, a constructive trust may be imposed.

On March 9, 1960, decedent Frederick Simonds and his wife of 14 years, plaintiff Mary Simonds, entered into a separation agreement which, on March 31, 1960, was incorporated into an Illinois divorce decree granted to plaintiff on grounds of desertion. . . .

On May 26, 1960, less than two months after the divorce, decedent husband married defendant Reva Simonds. Defendant Gayle Simonds was born to the couple shortly thereafter.

Sometime after the separation agreement was signed, the then existing insurance policies were apparently canceled or permitted to lapse. It does not appear from the record why, how, or when this happened, but the policies were not extant at the time of decedent husband's death on August 1, 1971. In the interim, however, decedent has acquired three other life insurance policies, totaling over $55,000, none of which named plaintiff as a beneficiary. . . . The first two policies named Reva Simonds, defendant's second wife, as beneficiary, and the third policy named their daughter. Hence, at the time of decedent's death he had continuously violated the separation agreement by maintaining no life insurance naming the first wife as a beneficiary.

The first wife, on March 11, 1972, brought an action against the second wife for conversion of $7,000 and to recover $13,600 in back alimony payments. This action was dismissed, essentially on the ground that the causes of action alleged could properly be brought only against decedent's estate, not against the second wife. The estate, however, is insolvent.

Subsequently, the first wife brought this action against both the sec-

---

[*] Special Term dismissed the cause of action against defendant Gayle Simonds. No appeal of that dismissal was taken to the Appellate Division.

ond wife and the daughter, seeking to impose a constructive trust on the insurance proceeds to the extent of $7,000. . . .

There is no question that decedent breached his obligation to maintain life insurance with his first wife as beneficiary. Consequently, the first wife would of course be entitled to maintain an action for breach against the estate. The estate's insolvency, however, would make such an action fruitless. Thus, the controversy revolves around plaintiff's right, in equity, to recover $7,000 of the insurance proceeds.

Law without principle is not law; law without justice is of limited value. Since adherence to principles of "law" does not invariably produce justice, equity is necessary (Aristotle, Nichomachean Ethics, Book V, ch. 9, pp. 1019-1020 [McKeon, ed. Oxford: Clarendon Press, 1941]). Equity arose to soften the impact of legal formalisms; to evolve formalisms narrowing the broad scope of equity is to defeat its essential purpose.

Whatever the legal rights between insurer and insured, the separation agreement vested in the first wife an equitable interest in the insurance policies then in force. An agreement for sufficient consideration, including a separation agreement, to maintain a claimant as a beneficiary of a life insurance policy vests in the claimant an equitable interest in the policies designated. This interest is superior to that of a named beneficiary who has given no consideration, notwithstanding policy provisions permitting the insured to change the designated beneficiary freely.

This is not to say that an insurance company may not rely on the insured's designation of a beneficiary. None of this opinion bears on the rights or responsibilities of the insurer in law or in equity.

Obviously, the policies now at issue are not the same policies in existence at the time of the separation agreement. But it has been held that mere substitution of policies, or even substitution of insurance companies, does not defeat the equitable interest of one who has given sufficient consideration for a promise to be maintained as beneficiary under an insurance policy. The persistence of the promisee's equitable interest is all the more evident where the agreement expressly provides for a change in policies, and in effect provides further that the promisee's right shall attach to the new policies.

For a certainty, the first wife's equitable interest would be easier to trace if the new policies were quid pro quo replacements for the original policies. The record does not reveal whether this was so. But inability to trace plaintiff's equitable rights precisely should not require that they not be recognized, much as in the instance of damages difficult to prove. The separation agreement provides nexus between plaintiff's rights and the later acquired policies. The later policies were expressly contemplated by the parties, and it was agreed that plaintiff would have an interest in them. No reason in equity appears for denying plaintiff that interest, so long as no one who has given value for the policies or otherwise suffered a detriment is involved. The second wife's innocence does not offset the wrong by the now deceased husband.

The conclusion is an application of the general rule that equity regards as done that which should have been done. Thus, if an insured, upon lapse or cancellation of insurance, followed by replacement with new insurance, has a contractual obligation to designate a particular person as beneficiary, equity will consider the obligee as a beneficiary.

In this case, then, the first wife's interest in the original policies extended as well to the later acquired policies. The husband, upon lapse or cancellation of the earlier policies, had by virtue of the separation agreement an obligation to name her as beneficiary on the later policies, an obligation enforceable in equity despite the husband's failure to comply with the terms of the separation agreement. Due to the husband's failure to do what he should have done, the first wife acquired not only a right at law to sue his estate for breach of contract, a right now worthless, but also an equitable right in the policies, a right which, upon the husband's death, attached to the proceeds.

And, since the first wife was entitled to $7,000 of the insurance proceeds at the time of the husband's death, she is no less entitled because the proceeds have already been converted by being paid, erroneously, to the named beneficiaries. Her remedy is imposition of a constructive trust.

In the words of Judge Cardozo, "[a] constructive trust is the formula through which the conscience of equity finds expression. When property has been acquired in such circumstances that the holder of the legal title may not in good conscience retain the beneficial interest, equity converts him into a trustee" (Beatty v. Guggenheim Exploration Co., 225 N.Y. 380, 386). Thus, a constructive trust is an equitable remedy. It is perhaps more different from an express trust than it is similar (5 Scott, Trusts [3d ed.], §461). As put so well by Scott and restated at the Appellate Division, "[the constructive trustee] is not compelled to convey the property because he is a constructive trustee; it is because he can be compelled to convey it that he is a constructive trustee" (id., §462, at p.3413).

More precise definitions of a constructive trust have been termed inadequate because of the failure to recognize the broad scope of constructive trust doctrine (id., at p.3412). As another leading scholar has said of constructive trusts, "[t]he Court does not restrict itself by describing all the specific forms of inequitable holding which will move it to grant relief, but rather reserves freedom to apply this remedy to whatever knavery human ingenuity can invent" (Bogert, Trusts and Trustees [2d ed. rev., 1978], §471, at p.29).

Four factors were posited in Sharp v. Kosmalski (40 N.Y.2d 119, 121). Although the factors are useful in many cases constructive trust doctrine is not rigidly limited. For a single example, one who wrongfully prevents a testator from executing a new will eliminating him as beneficiary will be held as a constructive trustee even in the absence of a confidential or fiduciary relation, a promise by the "trustee," and a transfer in reliance by the testator (see, e.g., Latham v. Father Divine, 299 N.Y. 22, 26-27). As then Judge Desmond said in response to the argument that a breach of a promise to the testator was necessary for imposition of a constructive trust (at p.27), "[a] constructive trust will be erected whenever necessary to satisfy the demands of justice . . . [I]ts applicability is limited only by the inventiveness of men who find new ways to enrich themselves unjustly by grasping what should not belong to them."

It so happens, as an added argument, if it were necessary, that the four factors enumerated in Sharp v. Kosmalski are perceptible in this case: a promise, a transfer in reliance on the promise, the fiduciary relation between decedent and his first wife, and the "unjust enrichment" of the second wife. Because decedent and plaintiff were husband and wife, there is a duty of fairness in financial matters extending even past the contemplated separation of the spouses. Hence, a separation agreement based on one party's misrepresentation of financial condition is voidable. A similar rule applies in Illinois, where the instant separation agreement was made. Thus, at the time of the separation agreement decedent and plaintiff remained in a confidential or fiduciary relationship.

It is agreed that the purpose of the constructive trust is prevention of unjust enrichment.

Unjust enrichment, however, does not require the performance of any wrongful act by the one enriched. Innocent parties may frequently be unjustly enriched. What is required, generally, is that a party hold property "under such circumstances that in equity and good conscience he ought not to retain it" (Miller v. Schloss, 218 N.Y. 400, 407). A bona fide purchaser of property upon which a constructive trust would otherwise be imposed takes free of the constructive trust, but a gratuitous donee, however innocent, does not.

The unjust enrichment in this case is manifest. At a time when decedent was, certainly, anxious to remarry, he entered into a separation agreement with his wife of 14 years. As part of the agreement, he promised to maintain $7,000 in life insurance with the first wife as beneficiary. Later he broke his promise, and died with insurance policies naming only the second wife and daughter as beneficiaries. They have collected the proceeds, amounting to more than $55,000, while the first wife has collected nothing. Had the husband kept his promise, the beneficiaries would have collected $7,000 less in proceeds. To that extent, the beneficiaries have been unjustly enriched, and the proceeds should be subjected to a constructive trust.

Moreover, the second wife's complaint, if that it be, over the distinction drawn below between her daughter and herself is to no avail. The first wife's equitable interest attached to all the substituted insurance policies, whether they named the second wife or the daughter as beneficiary. At the time each substituted policy was issued, decedent had an obligation to make the first wife a beneficiary. None of the named beneficiaries can escape the superior equitable interest of the first wife by pointing to other policies. True, plaintiff might also be entitled to impose a constructive trust on the policy naming the daughter as beneficiary. But that provides no cause for prorating the constructive trust. The beneficiaries are jointly and severally liable, if the analogy applicable to express trusts be applied. Plaintiff's choice not to appeal the dismissal against the daughter should not bar her from collecting in full against the second wife, who may have a right of contribution against the daughter, a question not before the court and not passed on.

The issues in this case should not generate significant controversy. The action is in equity, and the equities are clear. True, some courts have decided the issues differently (Rindels v. Prudential Life Ins. Co. of Amer., 83 N.M. 181; Lock v. Lock, 8 Ariz. App. 138, 143; see also, Larson v. Larson, 226 Ga. 209, 211). Those cases, however, rely heavily on formalisms and too little on basic equitable principles, long established in Anglo-American law and in this State and especially relevant when family transactions are involved. "A court of equity in decreeing a constructive trust is bound by no unyielding formula. The equity of the transaction must shape the measure of relief" (Beatty v. Guggenheim Exploration Co., 225 N.Y. 380, 389 [Cardozo, J.], supra).

Accordingly, the order of the Appellate Division should be affirmed, with costs.

JUDGES JASEN, GABRIELLI, JONES, WACHTLER, FUCHSBERG and COOKE concur.

NOTES ON RESTITUTION FROM THIRD PARTIES

1. Reva Simonds, the second wife, is not the wrongdoer. She might be thought guilty of inducing the divorce, but that is not the theory of the action. Gayle Simonds, the daughter, is not guilty of anything. They owe restitution because they were innocently but unjustly enriched by Frederick Simonds's breach of his obligations under the separation agreement.

2. Is Simonds a tracing case, or is it simply a case of unjust enrichment? Or is it something in between? Mary Simonds, the first wife, might plausibly claim to be the equitable owner of the original insurance policies, which named her as beneficiary. But there is no effort to trace the money from those policies into the later policies collected by Reva and Gayle. Suppose that Frederick had died uninsured, but that in his life had given $7,000 to Reva. (Assume that he was solvent when he made the gift, so that Mary could not recover the gift as a fraudulent conveyance. We'll

consider that possibility in the next set of notes.) Would the court impose
a constructive trust on the cash gift? Or is there something special about
insurance proceeds? What if the separation agreement had not explicitly
said anything about replacement policies? Would the obligation to name
Mary as beneficiary still attach to any insurance Frederick bought?

3.   As the court notes, a substantial number of cases refuse to impose
a constructive trust on similar facts. These cases tend to rely on plaintiff's
inability to identify any specific policy as the one that was intended to be
for her. In such cases, the first wife can sue the dead husband's estate for
breach of contract or conversion. But life insurance proceeds are generally exempt from the decedent's creditors, and there are often no other
assets to collect from.

4.   Another dispute over life insurance does turn on tracing. Suppose
Wrongdoer misappropriates $500 from Victim and uses the money to buy
a $100,000 life insurance policy on himself, naming Widow as beneficiary.
If he promptly dies, the investment is extraordinarily profitable. Invoking
standard tracing doctrine, Victim can argue that he is the true owner of
the policy, because it was bought with his money; therefore, he is entitled
to the whole $100,000. Widow cannot complain, because she is a mere
donee; she is not a good faith purchaser for value or even a creditor. She
is unjustly enriched because, but for the misappropriation, she would not
have gotten this $100,000.

Are you persuaded? Lots of cases touch on the issue, most suggesting
that Victim should get the whole $100,000. But Professor Palmer could
find only one case squarely raising the issue; in terms of the example used
here, it granted Victim the whole $100,000. Baxter House v. Rosen, 27
A.D.2d 258, 278 N.Y.S.2d 442 (1967). In most of the other cases, Wrongdoer had misappropriated other money from Victim that could not be
traced. Thus, Victim got the whole insurance proceeds, but that was less
than his total loss. The cases are collected in 1 G. Palmer, Law of Restitution §2.15(b) at 187-193 (1978). He finds *Baxter House* outrageous, but he
notes that Dean Ames and Professor Bogert both argued for that result.

5.   The life insurance cases are only one example of constructive
trusts imposed on property in the hands of third parties. The constructive
trust continues on the property so long as it is identifiable, in the hands of
whoever might come to own it, so long as it is not acquired by a good faith
purchaser, for value, without notice of plaintiff's claim. Thus, in Newton
v. Porter, summarized supra at 487-488, thieves used the identifiable
proceeds of stolen property to pay their attorneys. Because the attorneys
knew the source of the property, they were not good faith purchasers.
General creditors who do not take an interest in any specific asset are not
good faith purchasers, even if they rely on the misappropriated property
in assessing Wrongdoer's general credit worthiness. But a lender who
takes a mortgage on property subject to a constructive trust is a good faith
purchaser if he gives new value and has no reason to know of plaintiff's
claim.

6. *Simonds* cites Sharp v. Kosmalski for a four-part test for imposing a constructive trust. Drawing on earlier cases, *Sharp* said there must be a confidential relation, a promise, a transfer in reliance, and unjust enrichment. That formula seems inconsistent with the view of constructive trust as a generalized remedy. Do not be misled; the factors are at most fictional. In Newton v. Porter, the case of the stolen bonds, there was no confidential relation, no promise, and no reliance. There was simply a theft that caused unjust enrichment. In *Sharp* itself, it was clear that the promise was fictional. *Simonds* says the factors are useful but that constructive trust doctrine is not rigidly limited. Certainly the second half of that sentence is true. The four factors may be more misleading than useful.

NOTES ON CONSTRUCTIVE TRUSTS AND FRAUDULENT CONVEYANCES

1. The use of tracing to pursue property in the hands of third parties is closely related to fraudulent conveyance law. Indeed, I think it is fair to say that fraudulent conveyance law provides a form of restitution, although it is not usually thought of in those terms. It is a fraudulent conveyance for an insolvent debtor to give property away or sell property for less than reasonably equivalent value. It is also a fraudulent conveyance for anyone to transfer property on any terms with actual intent to hinder his creditors. Creditors who are prejudiced by a fraudulent conveyance can undo it, recovering the transferred property from the third party.

2. Thus, cases of insolvent wrongdoers giving away misappropriated property can be reached by either fraudulent conveyance or constructive trust law. And there is presumably some overlap between cases where a transferee takes misappropriated property with notice of the victim's claim and cases where the wrongdoer makes the transfer to hinder his creditors. But each theory reaches some cases not reached by the other.

   a. In Newton v. Porter, supra at 487-488 and 558, the attorneys who were paid with stolen property presumably performed legal services in return. Because they gave fair consideration, fraudulent conveyance law would not have reached the property in their hands. But constructive trust law did, because they took with notice of plaintiffs' claims.

   b. Fraudulent conveyance law does not reach gifts or sales for inadequate value unless at the time of the transfer it was at least foreseeable that the debtor would become insolvent. Only a constructive trust or equitable lien can trace misappropriated property through the hands of a solvent wrongdoer, even if he later becomes insolvent.

   c. Fraudulent conveyance law is available to ordinary creditors as well as victims of fraud and misappropriation.

d. Fraudulent conveyance law applies to all property of the debtor or wrongdoer; there is no need to trace the specific property plaintiff lost.

e. Under fraudulent conveyance law, creditors can recover only the amount of their loss; only a constructive trust enables them to claim more valuable assets acquired with their lost property. But the two theories can be combined. In Baxter House v. Rosen, supra at 558, plaintiffs were ordinary creditors who had no basis for restitution from their debtor. But the insolvent debtor spent substantial sums to buy $2 million of life insurance. Then he died and his adult daughters collected the $2 million. The creditors successfully argued that his purchase of the policies was a gift to the daughters at a time when he was insolvent — a fraudulent conveyance. This made the creditors victims of fraud, and they invoked constructive trust theory to claim a pro rata share of the insurance proceeds.

ROBINSON v. ROBINSON
100 Ill. App. 3d 437, 429 N.E.2d 183 (1981)

UNVERZAGT, J., delivered the opinion of the court.

This action was brought by the plaintiff, Ann M. Robinson, to obtain a dissolution of marriage from Wylie Robinson, and against his parents, Earl J. and Alice M. Robinson, to establish her rights in certain property owned by them, known as the Johnson Road property. . . .

The novel question presented by this appeal is whether one who improves real property which she knows to be owned by others, who neither request nor encourage the improvement but merely give their permission for the improvement, is entitled to restitution. . . .

The trial on the dissolution issues was on a bifurcated basis with the grounds being tried first. The court found Ann proved grounds for dissolution without contest by Wylie. Thereafter, the other dissolution issues were set for hearing along with five counts in which Ann alleged an interest in the real estate owned by Earl and Alice. . . .

After hearing all of the evidence, the able and experienced trial judge made a finding that all issues of credibility are found against Earl and Wylie, based upon the many inconsistencies in their testimony. The trial court entered judgment for dissolution of marriage finding that both husband and wife are self-supporting, in good health, and have sufficient income and assets that neither was entitled to maintenance. The trial court gave custody of the two minor children to Ann and required Wylie to pay child support, and found that he was then $980 in arrearage. The trial court determined that Wylie's Teacher's Retirement Pension Fund was a marital asset and awarded Ann one-half of its current value and also awarded Ann $3,000 in legal fees. The judgment also assigned to the parties various items of furniture, furnishings, other personal property, automobiles, bank accounts and insurance policies.

The judgment further determined that Ann and Wylie each had a one-half interest in the house constructed on the land owned by Earl and Alice and known as the Johnson Road property. The court valued the house and improvements at $71,000 and determined that there was a construction loan for the house amounting to $15,000 and that the value of the lot upon which the house was constructed was $12,000.

The judgment went on to provide for the disposition of the Johnson Road property by two alternate methods to be determined by the election of Earl and Alice. The first method was that the house and lot be sold, sale expenses be paid, the construction loan be paid, then Earl and Alice be paid the value of the land and the remaining sale proceeds be divided between Ann and Wylie. A lien was imposed on Wylie's one-half in favor of Ann in an amount equal to the court's determination of the amount owed for her child support arrearages, attorney's fees and her one-half interest in Wylie's Teacher's Retirement Pension Fund.

Alternatively, the judgment provided that if Earl and Alice do not elect to have the house and lot sold then they are to pay Ann $28,000 representing her one-half interest in the house, and pay the bank $7,500 representing one-half of the amount due on the construction loan and, further, Wylie was required to hold Ann harmless and indemnify her as to any liability on the other $7,500 due on that loan. This alternative also provided that Ann would have a lien on Wylie's one-half interest in the house in the amount he was required to pay her for child-support arrearages, attorney's fees and one-half of the teacher's retirement fund. Upon receipt of the above-described funds, Ann was to quitclaim her interest in the property to Earl and Alice. They, however, rejected both alternatives. The trial court appointed a receiver for the property, but the receiver declined appointment. . . .

Wylie grew up on a farm in Kendall County. He is the only child of Earl and Alice. They owned the farm upon which they lived and, in addition, owned another farm of 160 acres some five miles away known as the Johnson Road property, which is the focus of the controversy here.

Wylie and Ann were married in 1966. . . . They lived off of Wylie's salary and saved Ann's salary to build a home. . . .

Early in the spring of 1969, . . . Wylie asked his father if he and Ann could build their home on the Johnson Road property. Earl agreed. . . . Alice also consented. . . .

Wylie testified he selected the site for the house. . . . Wylie drew the plans for the house. He surveyed and staked out the site. . . .

Wylie and Ann had saved $4,000. They borrowed $18,000 from the local bank as a construction loan and told the president of the bank that when they completed the home that the land would be theirs and a regular mortgage would be placed on the property for purposes of security. The note was renewed on a yearly basis, and monthly payments reduced the debt to $15,000.

Wylie and Ann began construction of the house in the spring of 1969 and occupied it in 1970. The construction work was done mainly by Wylie with substantial help from friends and family including Earl, Alice and Ann's father. Ann sanded and finished woodwork and cabinets. After the home was occupied, additional improvements in the amount of $5,000 were made. These included carpeting, drapes, kitchen cabinets, linoleum and paint.

All of the parties knew that the house was Wylie's and Ann's home and treated it as such. They did all of the landscaping and planted shrubbery. They repaired it and maintained it. They made all of the loan payments and treated the interest thereon as a deduction on tax returns. They insured the house with a homeowner's policy. They had the only keys to the house and never paid or were asked for rent on it. The one connection Earl and Alice had with the house was that it was included on the farm tax bill since the lot was not subdivided. Earl and Alice paid the real estate tax bill. In exchange for that payment, Wylie worked additional time for his parents on their farm. . . .

There was no written agreement between the young and older Robinsons as to a transfer of title to the property. . . .

Marital discord arose in 1977 and Wylie moved to his parents' home where he resided at the time of the hearing. From the relationship of the parties it can thus be seen that the younger Robinsons would have every expectation of eventual ownership of the home they constructed. However, the testimony was in strong disagreement on this point. . . . According to Ann, it was made understood to Wylie and her that the house was sitting on property that would be theirs. She testified that Earl said they would sign it over to them.

Wylie testified that his father did not promise to transfer the house or sell it to him. His mother never promised anything, and neither parent ever said he would inherit all their property. Wylie acknowledged that the agreement was that he could live in the house.

Earl testified that he never had a conversation with Wylie and Ann about transferring the property to them. He never promised to transfer title or give Wylie the property, and he never told Wylie he was going to leave him the property by will or inheritance.

Alice testified that her husband gave Wylie and Ann permission to build a building, but that there were no representations that they were going to transfer an interest in the property to the younger Robinsons. . . .

The trial judge concluded that it would unjustly enrich Earl and Alice to gain the house without compensation to Ann.

A person who has been unjustly enriched at the expense of another is required to make restitution to the other. A person is enriched if he has received a benefit. A person is unjustly enriched if the retention of the benefit would be unjust. A person obtains restitution when he is restored to the position he formerly occupied either by the return of something he formerly had or by the receipt of its equivalent in money. . . .

Earl and Alice argue that the evidence at trial did not establish recovery under a theory of unjust enrichment. They argue that as a general rule, improvements of a permanent character, made upon real estate, and attached thereto, without consent of the owner of the fee, by one having no title or interest, become a part of the realty and vest in the owner of the fee. (Williams v. Vanderbilt (1893), 145 Ill. 238.) But, as the supreme court pointed out years ago:

> . . . [C]ourts of equity have not hesitated to soften the harshness and rigor of the rule of law, when the circumstances of the case and the relation of the parties required it to be done to meet the ends of justice.

Cable v. Ellis (1887), 120 Ill. 136, 152.

In Olin v. Reinecke (1929), 336 Ill. 530, 534, the court said:

> In equity, however, if the owner stands by and permits another to expend money in improving his land he may be compelled to surrender his rights to the land upon receiving compensation therefor, or he may be compelled to pay for the improvements. In such cases there is always some ingredient which would make it a fraud in the owner to insist upon his legal rights. Such an ingredient may consist in the owner encouraging the stranger to proceed with the improvement, or where one party acts ignorantly and without the means of better information and the other remains silent when it is in his power to prevent the expenditure of the money under a delusion. It has been held in such cases that to permit one to take advantage of the mistake of another would be revolting to every sentiment of justice. The exercise of such a judicial power, however, unless based upon some actual or implied culpability on the part of the party subjected to it, is a violation of constitutional rights.

In Pope v. Speiser (1955), 7 Ill. 2d 231, 240, where the plaintiff placed valuable improvements on the defendant's farm with the knowledge and consent of the defendant and after repeated statements by the defendant that the farm would belong to the plaintiff upon the defendant's death, the court granted plaintiff an equitable lien in the land, after the defendant attempted to sell the farm to a third person.

These cases support the trial court's ruling granting Ann an interest in the Johnson Road property. The improvements were made with the knowledge, co-operation and approval of Earl and Alice. . . .

We determine that while he did not denominate it as such, the interest awarded to Ann in the Johnson Road property by the trial judge was an equitable lien. As this court stated in Calacurcio v. Levson (1966), 68 Ill. App. 2d 260, 263:

The trend of modern decisions is to hold that in the absence of an express contract, a lien based upon the fundamental maxims of equity may be implied and declared by a court of equity out of general considerations of right and justice as applied to the relationship of the parties and the circumstances of their dealing. An equitable lien is the right to have property subjected in a court of equity to payment of a claim. It is neither a debt nor a right of property, but a remedy for a debt.

The next question posed by this case is the extent or amount of the equitable lien. The trial court ruled that Ann was entitled to one-half of the appraised value of the improvements less the value of the land after making provision for payment of the construction loan.

Earl and Alice argue that if Ann is entitled to restitution her recovery should be measured by the subjective value to them or the value of the labor and materials that went into the house, and not the increased value of the land resulting from the addition of the house.

One scholar has suggested that when one builds a house on another's land, there are at least two feasible objective measures of restitution and one subjective measure. They are (1) the objective value of the labor and materials which went into the house; (2) the increased value of the land resulting from the addition of the house to it; and (3) the personal value to the defendant landowner for his particular purposes. (See Dobbs, Remedies §4.5, at 261 (1973).) We have been supplied no case which has adopted the latter approach perhaps because of the almost impossibility of determining the subjective approach.

The Illinois cases have variously given an equitable lien for (1) the cost of the improvements, or (2) the enhanced value of the premises, or (3) a right to purchase the premises if the owner elects to sell. . . .

From the foregoing, we conclude there was an implied promise by Earl and Alice to deed the land in question to Wylie and Ann and that the trial court was correct in imposing an equitable lien on the premises amounting to the value of the improvements that Ann and Wylie constructed thereon, in order to prevent unjust enrichment to Earl and Alice. . . .

It is the opinion of this court that the trial court properly directed defendants Earl and Alice to perform their implied contract to pay the plaintiff one-half of the reasonable value of the permanent improvements placed on the premises by the plaintiff and her husband and on their failure or refusal so to do, the trial court correctly ordered the property sold to foreclose plaintiff's equitable lien.

Ann asserts that the trial court erred in not finding that Earl and Alice had either made an irrevocable gift of the Johnson Road lot to Wylie and Ann or had promised to make a gift of the lot and were estopped from refusing to complete the gift. In reviewing the evidence in this case, we find it insufficient to establish the existence of a gift of the lot. The trial court was correct in its rulings in this regard.

Earl and Alice next assert that the trial court erred in attaching a lien for Wylie's debts on the Johnson Road property. The trial court placed a lien on one-half of the property for Ann's attorney's fees, child-support arrearage and one-half interest in the teacher's retirement plan. We agree that this was erroneous because an equitable lien is a remedy and not a property right. As was said in Watson v. Hobson (1948), 401 Ill. 191, 201, in discussing the nature of an equitable lien:

> An equitable lien is the right to have property subjected, in a court of equity, to the payment of a claim. It is neither a debt nor a right of property but a remedy for a debt. It is simply a right of a special nature over the property which constitutes a charge or encumbrance thereon, so that the very property itself may be proceeded against in an equitable action and either sold or sequestered under a judicial decree, and its proceeds in one case, or its rents and profits in the other, applied upon the demand of the creditor in whose favor the lien exists.

We have found no case in which a lien was imposed on an equitable lien under such circumstances, as if the latter were a piece of property. Wylie has disclaimed any interest in the Johnson Road property. No matter how obstinate or intractable the trial court may have felt his action was in disclaiming the interest, the trial court cannot create a lien upon an equitable lien where none is sought. That portion of the judgment is reversed. . . .

Affirmed in part; reversed in part and remanded.

SEIDENFELD, P.J., and LINDBERG, J., concur.

NOTES ON EQUITABLE LIENS

1. It is important not to confuse Ann's claim for restitution with her suit for divorce. The claim against the older Robinsons is not part of the division of the younger Robinsons' marital property. The court must first decide on the basis of unjust enrichment that the younger Robinsons have a claim to the house or its value. Only then can it award 50 percent of that claim to Ann as part of the division of marital property.

The court says that Ann cannot collect other money Wylie owes her out of his share of the equitable lien on the house, because he waived his claim to the equitable lien. How much of an obstacle is that? If his other assets are insufficient to pay what he owes her, isn't it a fraudulent conveyance to waive his claim? Isn't it a gift to his parents, while insolvent, and probably with actual intent to hinder Ann, his primary creditor?

2. What is the basis for choosing equitable lien over constructive trust? It is not just that the house is built on land to which the younger Robinsons are not entitled. The court could have solved that problem with a prorated constructive trust, awarding Ann one-half of $\frac{56}{68}$ of the property. What is the difference between that and the equitable lien actually awarded? Under each remedy, what happens if the value of the

house and land increases to $102,000 after trial and before the house is sold? The answer, for those of you who don't like arithmetic, is that under the constructive trust, she would get $34,500; under the equitable lien she would still get $28,000.

3. As the example illustrates, equitable liens limit plaintiff's claim to the amount of her loss. An equitable lien does not give her anything in excess of that even if she can trace into something more valuable. This raises another variation on the basic question raised at the beginning of this chapter: When should plaintiff recover profits in excess of her loss?

Neither court focused on that question in *Robinson*. Perhaps the trial court contemplated a quick sale before much appreciation could occur. Perhaps the court of appeals considered that Ann's entitlement was fixed at the moment of divorce and could not expand thereafter. Perhaps it considered that the older Robinsons were not sufficiently culpable to justify imposing a constructive trust. Or perhaps it followed the specific rule of the Restatement, which limits the mistaken improver to an equitable lien. Restatement of Restitution §170 (1937).

Courts often fail to distinguish between constructive trusts and equitable liens, or simply award one or the other without considering the choice. When they do consider the choice, they sometimes focus on defendant's culpability. And sometimes they focus on the logic of the fictions. That argument would run this way: Ann cannot be a true owner, because none of her property was used to buy the land. At most she can have an equitable lien for what she subsequently added to property that is indisputably the older Robinsons'. How persuasive is that? Does that use of the fiction capture something important, or is it mindless formalism?

4. The strongest remedy courts can give plaintiff is a choice between constructive trust and equitable lien. If plaintiff can trace property worth more than she lost, she will elect the constructive trust. If the traceable property is worth less than she lost, she will seek a money judgment for the full amount of the loss and an equitable lien on the traceable property to secure the judgment. Then she can claim the property under the equitable lien, and still have a personal judgment for the rest of her loss. In effect, gains go to the victims, and losses fall on the wrongdoer. This choice is generally available to victims of a conscious wrongdoer or misappropriating fiduciary. There is an allusion to it in In re Erie Trust, supra at 538; some of the cases are collected in Provencher v. Berman, 699 F.2d 568, 570 (1st Cir. 1983).

5. In *Robinson*, the decree authorized Ann to foreclose her lien promptly if she were not paid. But courts sometimes create liens that cannot be foreclosed, typically when immediate foreclosure would cause hardship to a defendant who is not especially culpable. Such liens are usually collected only when the property is sold.

An example is Jones v. Sacramento Savings & Loan Association, 248 Cal. App. 2d 522, 528, 56 Cal. Rptr. 741, 747 (1967). An unidentified lender loaned a builder money to buy lots in a subdivision. The lender recorded a first mortgage, but that mortgage had a clause providing that it would be subordinated to a construction mortgage under certain conditions. Sacramento Savings loaned substantially more money to build houses on the lots. It filed its mortgage second, relying on the first mortgage's subordination clause. The builder completed the houses and then defaulted on both loans.

At this point, Jones bought the first mortgage from the first lender for a fraction of its face value. Both lenders foreclosed and bought the lots at their own foreclosure sale. The court held that Sacramento had failed to satisfy the conditions of the subordination clause, so that Jones had first priority and his foreclosure sale cut off Sacramento's junior interest. And it held that Jones had done nothing improper. Sacramento's failure to satisfy the conditions had left the first lender with substantially less protection than it had bargained for, and Sacramento could have protected itself by fully meeting the conditions, paying off the smaller first mortgage, or buying the houses at Jones's foreclosure sale.

The effect was that Jones had bought finished houses for a fraction of the cost of the undeveloped lots. The court held that this was unjust enrichment and awarded Sacramento an equitable lien. But it severely restricted Sacramento's right to enforce the lien:

> Equity imposes a lien here not to vindicate a wrong but to prevent unjust enrichment. The objective may be accomplished by a decree impressing the lien but without demanding an immediate sale. Equitable liens in favor of Sacramento Savings should be paid off at such times and under such circumstances as will avoid undue hardship on Jones. . . . Framing of an appropriate decree to protect the parties' respective interests should await further inquiry and consideration by the trial court.
>
> The circumstances do not call for an award of interest as part of the lien, either before or after judgment. . . . The judgment imposing the lien will not be a money judgment, will simply establish a charge on property and will not bear interest in favor of the equitable lienholder. We leave open the question whether interest would run in the event the landowner failed to pay off the equitable liens in compliance with such conditions as the trial court might embody in the judgment.

6. *Jones* also illustrates the use of equitable liens to save bungled transactions that were intended to create real liens. There are lots of simpler cases in which a borrower promises to give a mortgage but the parties forget to sign the mortgage documents, or the lender forgets to record the mortgage. As between the borrower and lender, it is easy to say the borrower is unjustly enriched. He has gotten the loan without giving the mortgage. The temptation to give the lender a mortgage anyway has been almost irresistible.

But the costs of creating an equitable lien typically fall on other creditors. A good example is In re Destro, 675 F.2d 1037 (9th Cir. 1982), decided under the Bankruptcy Act of 1898, enforcing an equitable lien in bankruptcy even though no mortgage had ever been signed. Other creditors could have been paid out of the property that Destro intended to mortgage but didn't. What is the basis for preferring the lender who wanted a mortgage but bungled the deal over other creditors who deliberately loaned unsecured? The lender seeking an equitable lien in these cases is not the victim of fraud or overreaching; he is the victim of his own incompetence. To recognize his claim undermines the recording statutes, which are designed to give other potential creditors notice of all outstanding liens. There have been repeated efforts to stamp out this use of equitable liens. With respect to security interests in personal property, the Official Comments to the Uniform Commercial Code say that unless the lender complies with the formalities of the Code, his security interest "is not enforceable even against the debtor, and cannot be made so on any theory of equitable mortgage or the like." UCC §9-203 Comment 5. Section 544(a) of the Bankruptcy Code of 1978, 11 U.S.C. §544(a) (1982), is cleverly designed to invalidate equitable liens that are substitutes for bungled security transactions, without invalidating equitable liens or constructive trusts in other contexts. These provisions should eliminate cases like In re Destro; whether they will succeed remains to be seen.

Jones is a somewhat less controversial example, because Jones had full notice of Sacramento's claim, no one else appears to have been affected, and there seems to be little doubt that Jones will get back all the money he loaned and more. But those who want to maximize the reliability of the rules relating to mortgages and security interests would object even to *Jones*.

An early draft of the Second Restatement takes the position that equitable liens to save bungled secured loans depend on intention rather than unjust enrichment, and hence they are wholly different from the restitutionary equitable liens described in the Restatement. Restatement (Second) of Restitution §30, comment j (Tent. Draft No. 2, 1984).

D. OTHER RESTITUTIONARY REMEDIES

1. Subrogation, Indemnity, and Contribution

AMERICAN NATIONAL BANK & TRUST CO.
v. WEYERHAEUSER CO.
692 F.2d 455 (7th Cir. 1982)

[American Bank held 40,000 shares of Weyerhaeuser common stock. American held the shares as agent or trustee for the Illinois State Board of Investment. The shares were actually registered in the name of Bivest, a nominee for American. There are references to Bivest in the opinion, but the court ultimately concludes that Bivest can be ignored.

Weyerhaeuser offered to purchase up to 3.5 million shares of its own stock. The offer provided that if more than 3.5 million shares were tendered, Weyerhaeuser would make pro rata purchases from each tendering shareholder.

The Investment Board told American to tender its shares, and American did so. Because the offer was oversubscribed, Weyerhaeuser bought 61 percent of the shares properly tendered. It rejected American's tender on behalf of the Board because someone had checked a box indicating that the Board did not want to sell any shares if it could not sell all 40,000. Had the box not been checked, Weyerhaeuser would have bought 24,400 of the Board's shares at $32.00 per share.

American claimed that it did not check the box and that the box must have been checked erroneously by First Jersey National Bank, which had handled the tender offer for Weyerhaeuser. Weyerhaeuser and First Jersey claimed that the form had arrived with the box already checked. That issue was unresolved at the time of this opinion. If First Jersey or Weyerhaeuser made the mistake, Weyerhaeuser would be liable to the Board for breach of contract. If American made the mistake, it would be liable to the Board.

American learned on September 6 that its tender had been rejected. On September 7, to make its customer whole, it bought 24,400 shares of Weyerhaeuser from the Board for $32.00. After confirming that Weyerhaeuser would not honor the tender, American resold the shares for about $29.12, suffering a loss of nearly $70,000.

American then filed this suit against Weyerhaeuser and First Jersey. The district court dismissed for lack of standing, holding that American was not the real party in interest.]

Before CUDAHY and ESCHBACH, Circuit Judges, and TEMPLAR, Senior District Judge.

CUDAHY, Circuit Judge. . . .

II

American seeks to assert the rights or claims of nonparties (i.e., the Board and Bivest) against Weyerhaeuser and First Jersey. But American lacks standing to assert such claims on its own behalf unless it is "the real party in interest." Fed. R. Civ. P. 17(a). To determine American's standing as the real party in interest, we must look to the applicable state substantive law. . . .

The district court here apparently applied Illinois law in concluding that American could not assert the rights of the Board and Bivest under principles of agency, assignment or subrogation. Construing as we must the record evidence most favorably to American in reviewing a grant of summary judgment, we believe that the district court erred by concluding that American was not, under Illinois law, subrogated to the claims of the Board against the appellees.

    "Legal" subrogation is an equitable right which arises by operation of law and not by contract. . . .[12] "Where property of one person is used in discharging an obligation owed by another . . . , under such circumstances that the other would be unjustly enriched by the retention of the benefit thus conferred, the former is entitled to be subrogated to the position of the obligee. . . ." Restatement of Restitution §162 (1937). Illinois courts have stated that "[t]he doctrine of subrogation is broad enough to include every instance in which one person, not a mere volunteer, pays a debt for which another is primarily liable and which in equity and good conscience should have been discharged by the latter." Bost v. Paulson's Enterprises, Inc., 36 Ill. App. 3d 135, 343 N.E.2d 168, 171-72 (2d Dist. 1976). Indeed, the Illinois Supreme Court has admonished us that "the policy of this court [is] to apply the expanding doctrine of subrogation, which originated in equity, and is now an integral part of the common law, in all cases where its essential elements are present, and where it effectuates a just resolution of the rights of the parties, irrespective of whether the doctrine has previously been invoked in the particular situation." Dworak v. Tempel, 17 Ill. 2d 181, 161 N.E.2d 258, 263 (1959).

    Notwithstanding the Illinois policy favoring a liberal application of subrogation principles, there are several requirements a potential subrogee (in this case, American) must satisfy before it may assert a right of subrogation. One such requirement (as to which there is no dispute here) is that the claim or debt under which the subrogee asserts his rights must have been paid in full. American purchased 24,400 of the shares tendered by the Board at the tender price, thereby paying in full whatever claim the Board or Bivest might assert.

    Another requirement of subrogation is that the subrogee must have paid a claim or debt for which a third party — not the subrogee — is primarily liable either in law or equity. This requirement is grounded in the principle that equity will permit only parties free from wrongdoing themselves to assert rights of subrogation against third parties. It is, of course, a matter of dispute whether the putative subrogee, American, or the third parties, Weyerhaeuser and First Jersey, are responsible for en-

---

12. Subrogation which is grounded in equity and applied as a matter of law is typically denominated "legal" subrogation. On the other hand, subrogation that is founded upon an express or implied agreement (e.g., on an insurance contract where the insurer is subrogated to any recovery for injuries received directly from a tortfeasor) is termed "conventional" subrogation. Various equitable principles, such as the denial of subrogation to a volunteer or to a subrogee who has not paid the claim in full, are not applicable to conventional subrogation. In this case, we are concerned only with legal subrogation as defined in equity and which arises by operation of law. There is no evidence of an express or implied agreement for subrogation among any of the parties whose claims are at issue here. . . .

tering the figure "40,000" in the "Conditional Tender" box. Since the parties have stipulated that this is a contested issue of fact, summary judgment based on a right of subrogation could not now be entered on the ultimate merits of American's claim. But if this factual question is resolved against the third parties, then the requirement that the claim paid was one for which a third party was primarily liable would be met.

A third requirement for proceeding by subrogation is that the subrogor must possess a right which he could enforce against a third party and that the subrogee seeks to enforce the subrogor's right. This requirement is based upon the principle that the subrogee's rights are derived from and dependent upon the rights of the subrogor. Illinois courts commonly express this needed element by saying that the subrogee must step into the shoes of, or be substituted for, the subrogor.

In the case before us there are two potential subrogors — Bivest and the Board — either of whom could have maintained an action against Weyerhaeuser and First Jersey. . . . [T]he Board could have maintained an action against First Jersey and Weyerhaeuser because its agent, American, purported to enter into a contract with these third parties on its behalf. "[W]hen a person puts his property in the hands of another to keep or manage, he creates, as between him and that other, the relation known as principal and agent." In re Mory's Estate, 17 Ill. App. 3d 6, 307 N.E.2d 669, 671 (1st Dist. 1973). In this case, the Board placed 40,000 shares of Weyerhaeuser stock in the hands of Bivest and American to tender pursuant to Weyerhaeuser's tender offer (which Bivest and American attempted to do). The parties here do not dispute that American and Bivest acted as the Board's agents when they tendered the stock. The Board, as the undisclosed principal of its agents, Bivest and American, could therefore have maintained an action on the contract with Weyerhaeuser.

Of course, the district court may ultimately determine that American (and not First Jersey or Weyerhaeuser) was in fact responsible for the rejection of the tendered shares, in which case Bivest and the Board, despite their right to sue, could not recover damages from the appellees. But, for the purpose of determining whether subrogation rights may be asserted by American, we need only conclude that either Bivest or the Board could have, in the absence of the satisfaction of their claim by American, stated a claim for relief against First Jersey or Weyerhaeuser. Under the equitable doctrine of subrogation, that claim is saved for the benefit of the party (in this case, American) that made the Board whole. We conclude that both Bivest and the Board, in the *absence* of satisfaction by American, could have stated claims for relief against Weyerhaeuser and First Jersey, and that, since instead there *has* been satisfaction by American, *American* can now state these claims for relief.

A final, and crucial, requirement for exercising the right of subrogation, which the district court found dispositive here, is that the potential subrogee must not have acted as a "volunteer" in paying a claim of the subrogor properly lying against a third party. Although Illinois courts have formulated this requirement in various ways, it may be succinctly stated as follows:

> It is well settled that a mere stranger or volunteer can not, by paying a debt for which another is bound, be subrogated to the creditor's rights in respect to the security given by the real debtor. But if the person who pays the debt is compelled to pay for the protection of his own interest and rights, then the substitution should be made. . . . In [Bennett v. Chandler, 199 Ill. 97, 64 N.E. 1052 (1902),] it was said that "a stranger within the meaning of this rule is not necessarily one who has had nothing to do with the transaction out of which the debt grew. Any one who is under no legal obligation or liability to pay the debt, is a stranger, and, if he pays the debt, a mere volunteer."

Ohio National Life Insurance Co. v. Board of Education, 387 Ill. 159, 55 N.E.2d 163, 171, *cert. denied*, 323 U.S. 796 (1944). The district court concluded that American "was under no legal obligation to either Bivest or to the Illinois Board to purchase the Weyerhaeuser shares, but did so without compulsion and as a mere volunteer."

But this is an overly narrow interpretation of the term "legal obligation" and ignores the agency relationship between American and the Board, under which American was legally obligated to the Board. One can be subrogated to the rights of another even if the debt in question is not paid pursuant to an unconditional or fully choate requirement of law, such as might be represented by a provision of a binding contract or by a final judgment. Both the Illinois courts and federal courts applying Illinois law have not required for subrogation compulsion similar to that of a final judgment or of an enforceable contract; rather, the *potential* for legal liability to the subrogor, as well as the disruption of normal relations and the frustration of reasonable expectations can, in many cases, supply sufficient compulsion to support subrogation. Indeed, to require an unconditional or fully choate legal liability is, to a degree, inconsistent with the nature of legal subrogation, which is *not* dependent upon a contract, statute or judgment but instead arises out of equitable principles as a matter of law. Rather than emphasizing the form of the legal compulsion, Illinois decisions involving rights of subrogation demand careful analysis of the nature of the relationship between the putative subrogee (American) and the subrogor (either Bivest or the Board) to determine whether the subrogee paid the debt "'pursuant to a legal liability.'" National Cash Register Co. v. UNARCO Industries, Inc., 490 F.2d 285, 286 (7th Cir. 1974) (quoting Geneva Construction Co. v. Martin Transfer & Storage Co., 4 Ill. 2d 273, 122 N.E.2d 540, 546 (1954)). . . .

We believe that the required legal obligation or compulsion must be based on American's status as an agent of its undisclosed principal, the Board, in the transfer of the stock certificates and the sending of the letter of transmittal to First Jersey. . . .

The existence of this agency relationship suggests that American acted under a "legal obligation" when it purchased the Board's Weyerhaeuser stock. For the Board, as principal, could presumably have sued its agent, American, for the loss sustained by the Board based on the colorable allegation that American negligently (or otherwise improperly) caused the loss by failing to tender unconditionally the 40,000 shares of Weyerhaeuser stock. When, as here, the agent reimburses his principal for a loss suffered by the principal for which the agent *may* be legally liable, the agent is entitled to be subrogated to the rights of the principal against third parties who *may also, or alternatively*, be legally liable for the loss. The agent, as subrogee, may sue the third parties to determine who must bear the ultimate burden of the loss. Ultimate liability is, in this instance, conditional upon a determination of whose improper conduct (including negligence, if any) caused the loss.

Moreover, American may also, under Illinois trust principles, be legally liable to the Board. . . . Because American as either an agent or a trustee could be reasonably charged with legal liability to the Board for the improper tender of the Board's Weyerhaeuser stock, we believe that American purchased the Board's stock under "compulsion" and under a "legal obligation," entitling American to exercise rights of subrogation.

It would serve no purpose to deny standing to American in this case. . . . Under the facts of this case, it makes sense that the innocent party be made whole now for its losses by the one of the potential wrongdoers who was its agent; subsequently this reimbursing party should be authorized to institute suit to determine who, among the three potential wrongdoers, should in equity be required ultimately to bear the loss. To frustrate this result by invocation of the "volunteer" doctrine may result in the one clearly innocent party (here the Board) needlessly bearing the heavy costs and enduring the uncertainties of litigation.

Second, the historical concerns which underlie the volunteer rule are not present in this case. These concerns were best summarized in Hult v. Ebinger, 222 Or. 169, 352 P.2d 583, 592 (1960), as follows:

> It has been suggested that the origins of the "volunteer" rule are in the individualistic bent of the English national character and in the common law regard for privity of contract. . . . The rule has been traced to the case of Grymes v. Blofield, Cro. Eliz. 541 (1598), which held that a debt could not be satisfied by a stranger, and more generally to the fear of champerty and maintenance which found expression in the early common law restricting the assignability of choses in action. . . . It is obvious that the modern practice which permits free alienability of choses has robbed the "volunteer" rule of much of its rational justification.

Privity of contract is a concern which we have already dealt with under the rubric of real party in interest. Concerns about champerty and maintenance are not relevant here.

Finally, to deny American standing in this case by some formalistic application of a volunteer rule would be inconsistent with the purpose of equity: to secure substantial justice. The Illinois courts, in recognition of this goal, have expressly broadened the area in which the remedy of subrogation is available. See Dworak v. Tempel, 17 Ill. 2d 181, 161 N.E.2d 258, 263 (1959). . . .

Reversed and remanded.

NOTES ON SUBROGATION

1.   We first encountered subrogation as an alternative to the collateral source rule. See note 3 in Notes on the Collateral Source Rule, supra at 149. The collateral source rule allows an injured plaintiff to recover from his insurer and also from the tortfeasor. One way to avoid that double recovery is to require plaintiff to reimburse his insurer. Subrogation attacks the problem directly, by giving plaintiff's cause of action to his insurer. Subrogation is common in some kinds of insurance, and rare in others.

2.   *American Bank* is also a case of reimbursement from a collateral source; once again, subrogation avoids the need to choose between double recovery and exoneration of the wrongdoer. Both exoneration and double recovery can be characterized as unjust enrichment. Weyerhaeuser would be unjustly enriched if American discharged its liability to the Board (assuming Weyerhaeuser is liable). And the Board would be unjustly enriched if it could sue and collect from Weyerhaeuser after being paid by American. The court avoids both of those results by giving the Board's rights to American.

3.   Subrogation may be thought of as a tracing remedy in which plaintiff traces through the rights of someone other than defendant. American gets exactly the rights the Board could have claimed, subject to all defenses Weyerhaeuser had against the Board. An identifiable asset — typically a claim or lien against an alleged wrongdoer or common debtor — is transferred to plaintiff. But subrogation differs from more conventional tracing claims in that the asset acquired by subrogation was not in any sense taken from the plaintiff. The Board's claim, and Weyerhaeuser's liability, are based on breach of contract. American did not create the claim; it existed before American paid the Board. The transfer of the claim is based on unjust enrichment, but the claim itself can be based on anything. Common cases are insurers who have paid their insureds and junior lienholders who pay off senior liens.

NOTES ON VOLUNTEERS

1.   Is there any reason to deny subrogation to "volunteers"? Does the volunteer sound less deserving if we call him an "officious intermeddler"?

We first encountered the volunteer concept in note 7 of Notes on Restitution for Breach of a Losing Contract, supra at 524. It is easy to understand why a volunteer cannot build an unwanted dam and then demand that the property owner pay for the "benefit." But how is Weyerhaeuser prejudiced if the Board's rights are asserted by American instead of the Board? As long as Weyerhaeuser's liability is not expanded, why should it care?

Should we be concerned that volunteers will pay dormant claims and file litigation that would otherwise go unfiled? They can do that anyway by taking an explicit assignment of the claim, and they might be able to buy the whole claim at a discount. A subrogation plaintiff recovers only what he paid. It is a rare case when a complete stranger officiously pays good money for a chance to file a lawsuit that at most will get the same money back. Instead, volunteer cases nearly always involve some sort of mistake or disputed liability.

2.) There is an astonishing amount of litigation over the volunteer requirement, and not all the cases have happy endings. Consider Armco v. Southern Rock, 696 F.2d 410 (5th Cir. 1983), decided under Mississippi law. Armco manufactured and delivered pipe for a new sewer system in Richland, Mississippi. When the sewers leaked, Armco promptly paid for repairs. Meanwhile, it investigated to determine whether the leaks were caused by faulty pipe or faulty installation. Concluding that the contractor who laid the sewers was at fault, Armco sued to recover the money it spent on repairs. The court denied recovery on the ground that Armco was a volunteer.

On the facts the case is indistinguishable from *American Bank*. Plaintiff's theory was different, but that should not matter. Armco did not sue as subrogee on the city's claim against the contractor. Instead, it sued in quasi-contract to recover money paid by mistake. In this context, subrogation and quasi-contract are simply different explanations for the very same thing. If Mississippi would deny relief in quasi-contract, it should also deny subrogation; the label should not control the availability of restitution.

The court noted that Mississippi defines a voluntary payment as one made "without compulsion, fraud or mistake of fact." Id. at 412. Conscious ignorance is not the same as mistake; for example, a party who enters a contract while consciously ignorant of a material fact cannot rescind for mistake when he learns the fact. Restatement (Second) of Contracts §154, Comment c (1979). Consequently, the court held that Armco had not paid by mistake, and that it thus was a volunteer. One can only speculate whether Armco led the court in this direction by framing its complaint in terms of money paid by mistake instead of subrogation.

In defense of its result, the court said:

A basic tenet of contract law is that courts should honor voluntary arrangements. This concern lies at the heart of the rule that voluntary payments cannot be recouped in the absence of fraud, compulsion, or mistake of fact. [Under Armco's proposed rule,] any voluntary settlement reached before culmination of a complete investigation could be judicially undone.

696 F.2d at 413.

Which policy analysis is more persuasive — *American Bank*'s or *Armco*'s? Was there a settlement in Armco, or simply a payment on account to avoid harm to the one clearly innocent victim?

3.   *American Bank* is more typical of the courts' attitudes toward mistaken or disputed payments. But the district court had rejected the subrogation claim, forcing a pretrial appeal. The volunteer argument still succeeds often enough to make it worth defendant's while. Isn't that all the more reason to get rid of it?

4.   The volunteer argument plays out differently when junior lienholders pay off senior liens. No one claims that junior lienholders are required to make such payments. Rather, the junior lienholder is protecting his own interest. Suppose real estate worth $90,000 is subject to a first mortgage of $40,000, a second mortgage of $30,000, and a third mortgage of $20,000. And suppose that the first mortgage is in default. Because foreclosure sales rarely bring full value, the third mortgagee is likely to receive little if the first mortgagee forecloses. The third mortgagee may want to pay the first mortgage himself to prevent foreclosure. To the extent that he does so, he is subrogated to the rights of the first mortgagee. The second mortgagee is not prejudiced; there was a $40,000 mortgage ahead of him, and there still is. Only the identity of the mortgagee has changed.

No court would hold the third mortgagee a volunteer. Even more interesting, the lender seeking subrogation need not have been a third mortgagee. He can be a new lender who voluntarily agrees to refinance the first mortgage. Even if he neglects to take an assignment of the first mortgagee's rights, he is still subrogated to the first mortgagee's priority, and even though his loan was voluntary, he is not a volunteer. French Lumber Co. v. Commercial Realty & Finance Co., 346 Mass. 716, 718-719, 195 N.E.2d 507, 509-510 (1964). Perhaps in this context *officious intermeddler* is a better phrase. The debtor presumably requested the refinancing; the new lender is not butting into someone else's business uninvited.

NOTES ON INDEMNITY AND CONTRIBUTION

1.   Indemnity and contribution are restitutionary remedies closely related to subrogation. In the Restatement's formulation, a person who discharges a duty that he owes, but "which as between himself and an-

other should have been discharged by the other," is entitled to indemnity, "unless the payor is barred by the wrongful nature of his conduct." Restatement of Restitution §76 (1937). A right to indemnity generally arises from some relationship between the indemnitor and indemnitee. Common cases are principal and agent, contractor and subcontractor, active and passive tortfeasors, and accommodation parties and makers on notes. In all these relationships, the wrongful act of one party may create vicarious or passive liability for the other, and the active wrongdoer would be unjustly enriched if the passive wrongdoer paid the liability. Sometimes the parties have a contractual agreement for indemnity, but that is not necessary. However, an indemnity contract will often be enforced where the facts are not clear enough to give rise to indemnity based on unjust enrichment.

2. Indemnity overlaps with subrogation. But there are some differences, and sometimes they are important. An indemnitor and indemnitee must both be liable to the same third party. But a subrogee may claim not to be liable at all, as in *American Bank*.

The most practical difference is illustrated by Great American Insurance Co. v. United States, 575 F.2d 1031 (2d Cir. 1978). Great American insured a house that was rented to federal witnesses under the protection and supervision of United States marshalls. When the witnesses moved out of the house, they allegedly took the fixtures with them, doing $19,000 worth of damage. The owner of the house filed a claim with Great American, and Great American denied coverage. The owner sued on the policy and recovered a judgment two years later. Great American then sued the United States for reimbursement.

Great American first claimed to be subrogated to the rights of the owner. But a subrogee gets exactly the rights of his subrogor and no more. The owner's claim was barred by a two-year statute of limitations that had run from the day of the damage. So Great American claimed a right of indemnity. In indemnity, the statute of limitations runs from the day of payment, or the day payment was due, whichever is later. But the court held indemnity unavailable. Great American was liable not because of its relationship to the United States, but because of its contract with the owner. Although the court did not put it in these terms, Great American and the owner had no power to make a contract that deprived the United States of the statute of limitations.

3. Contribution can be thought of as partial indemnification. If two or more parties are jointly liable for the same obligation, and one pays more than his share, he is entitled to contribution from the others, so that each pays his share. His "share" may be fixed by agreement in the original obligation, or by comparative fault, or by a presumption of equal responsibility. The remedy is universally available when two or more parties are liable on a contract. But the traditional rule was that there could be no contribution or indemnity between joint tortfeasors. That rule has been

in the process of repudiation for some time, in part because modern concepts of negligence and strict liability have made it possible to be a tortfeasor without being very blameworthy. Justice Stevens surveyed the field in 1981 and reported that thirty-nine states then permitted contribution between joint tortfeasors. Northwest Airlines v. Transport Workers Union, 451 U.S. 77, 88-89 n.17 (1981).

But the Supreme Court has been reluctant to allow contribution between parties who jointly violate statutes. In *Northwest Airlines*, the airline sought contribution from its unions for Equal Pay Act violations; contribution was denied. In Texas Industries v. Radcliff Materials, 451 U.S. 630 (1981), one party to a price-fixing conspiracy sought contribution from the others; contribution was denied. Both decisions were unanimous.

There has been a vigorous and inconclusive debate over the wisdom of contribution in antitrust cases, but the Court did not join in the debate. Indeed, neither decision suggests hostility to contribution as such. Rather, each appears to be a product of the Court's recent hostility to judge-made remedies for statutory violations. Apparently, if Congress wants contribution, it has to say so. In chapter 13, we will consider more generally whether courts or legislatures should bear primary responsibility for specifying remedies.

The Court has approved contribution between joint tortfeasors in admiralty. Cooper Stevedoring Co. v. Fritz Kopke, Inc., 417 U.S. 106 (1974). And it has approved apportionment of damages between an employer and a union when the employer discharges an employee and the union breaches its duty to fairly represent the employee. Bowen v. United States Postal Service, 459 U.S. 212 (1983).

2. Actions to Recover Specific Property: Replevin, Ejectment, and the Like

BROOK v. JAMES A. CULLIMORE & CO.
436 P.2d 32 (Okla. 1967)

[Brook gave Cullimore a security interest in personal property, securing a promissory note for some $8,000. Brook defaulted on the note. Cullimore brought this action in replevin to recover the collateral. Plaintiff alleged that the collateral was worth $2,500.

Brook paid $2,500 into court and asked the court to enter judgment for that amount. Cullimore demanded the property instead. The trial court entered judgment for possession of the property, and Brook appealed.]

McINERNEY, Justice.

The question dispositive of this appeal is whether in a replevin action the defeated litigant in possession of property whose recovery is sought may 1) elect to retain that property as his own, against the will of the successful party; 2) impose his election by requiring the trial court to render an alternative money judgment against him; and 3) avoid delivery of the property by tendering its value as set forth in the affidavit for replevin.

Cullimore sued Brook in replevin claiming a special interest in multiple items of personal property by virtue of a chattel mortgage securing a note in the sum of $8,147.26 and sought possession of the personalty. As disclosed by the petition and the affidavit for replevin, the aggregate value of this property was $2,500.00. Cullimore sought judgment

> for the immediate possession of said property, or in lieu thereof the value of the same in the sum of . . . $2,500.00 in the event delivery cannot be had in substantially the same condition as at the time of the filing of this action, and for the costs of this suit, including an attorney's fee of . . . $1,160.44. . . .

Brook gave a redelivery bond. He later offered to confess judgment for the alleged value of the property and a "reasonable" attorney's fee. Concurrently with this offer Brook attempted to satisfy the judgment he so sought to confess. He remitted all the accrued court costs and, by separate checks paid into the clerk's office, he deposited $2,500.00 — the alleged value of the property — as well as $1,160.44 — the amount of the attorney's fee Cullimore sought to recover. The latter sum was "tendered under protest" pending trial court's determination of a reasonable fee to be taxed as costs. Refusing to accept this offer of confession, Cullimore moved for a hearing "to determine whether said property is available" for delivery and "if found to be available that judgment be rendered . . . [for Cullimore] for immediate possession of said property" and that "the court determine a reasonable attorney fee."

At the hearing on Cullimore's motion Brook renewed his prior offer to confess a money judgment. He took the position the property whose possession was demanded could not be delivered "in substantially the same condition as at the time of filing of this action." Cullimore once again declined to assent to this confession. The issues to be tried were confined to determining whether the property can be delivered by Brook "in substantially the same condition" as at the time the action was commenced and to ascertaining the amount of counsel fee. The trial court adjudged, inter alia, that Brook deliver to Cullimore the property whose recovery was sought. Brook was authorized to withdraw the deposits made to the clerk's office. No alternative money judgment was rendered against Brook. He urges on appeal that the case should be remanded with directions "to take evidence of the value of the property sought by replevin, and [to] enter a money judgment" for its value.

At common law, the right to possession of the property at the time action was commenced formed the sole issue in replevin. If the property could not be returned, there was no method by which the prevailing party could recover a judgment for the value thereof. For procurement of a money judgment in lieu of possession the successful litigant was relegated to the remedy of trover. Our statute, 12 O.S. 1961 §1580, has provided a cumulative or supplemental remedy in favor of one who succeeds in a replevin action. By the terms of this enactment, if the losing party has retained possession of the property under a redelivery bond, the successful litigant is entitled to a judgment not only for his costs and for the recovery of possession, but also, if he so chooses, to an alternative money judgment for the value of the property. In the event possession cannot be given for any reason, the prevailing party may then proceed to enforce his money judgment. An alternative money judgment affords a new remedy given by the provisions of our Code of Civil Procedure. One on whom a new remedy is conferred may elect which course to pursue. He need not avail himself of the new remedy unless he so chooses, and if he does not, he is not barred from pursuing the old. The primary object of statutory replevin is the recovery of specific personal property and not of money. . . .

If a return of the property sought by replevin is possible, it *must* be returned. The defeated litigant is not granted an option to either relinquish possession or pay the value of the property. This rule applies with equal force when, as here, the successful plaintiff prays judgment for possession of the property or for its value as set forth in the affidavit. The alternative prayer is not to be treated as an election to accept money damages in lieu of the return of the property. The alternative remedy of a money judgment in replevin is extended solely for the benefit of the wronged party and affords a measure of relief only when the property cannot be returned. It may be waived by him either expressly or by failure to adduce proof tending to show the value of the property. An alternative money judgment is not deemed indispensable to the validity of an adjudication in replevin. In fact, it is error to render a money judgment where there is no evidence showing the value of the property. . . . Even if there had been evidence as to the value of the property, Brook could not complain of the trial court's failure to render an alternative money judgment. Such omission would have constituted error prejudicial to Cullimore and not to Brook. The unsuccessful litigant in replevin has no right to the cumulative remedy of an alternative money judgment since, we reiterate, that remedy avails to the wronged party only.

The defeated party in a replevin action, and his sureties on redelivery bond, are under an affirmative duty to take active measures to return all the property, whose recovery is adjudged, in as good condition as at the time action was commenced and free from material depreciation in its value. If the property has become deteriorated and worthless, the successful party is not required to accept it but may seek his remedy on the redelivery bond. But if property having a substantial value is available for delivery, the successful party should be required to accept it in partial satisfaction of his judgment. In such event the sureties are liable only for the difference in the value of the property when taken under the writ and the value at the time of its return.

Brook, against whom judgment for possession was rendered, did not have the power to retain the property and pay its value as stated in the affidavit for replevin. The property shown to be available for delivery was of substantial value. It was far from being worthless or materially deteriorated. Cullimore was willing to accept it. As prevailing party, he had a right to insist on its return. . . .

Affirmed. . . .

D. DOBBS, HANDBOOK ON THE LAW OF REMEDIES
399-402 (1972)

§5.13 Conversion and Detention of Chattels — Specific Relief

Replevin and Equitable and Statutory Substitutes

The owner of personal property wrongfully taken or detained may wish to recover damages; or he may prefer to recover the property in specie. Two common law actions, *Detinue* and *Replevin*, were designed to allow recovery of the property itself. The forms of action, of course, have long since been abolished, but a civil action for the recovery of personal property is recognized by statute in all states. Terminology about this civil action varies slightly; some states speak in terms of the old forms of action and call the suit one in "detinue" or "replevin"; others speak of a "claim and delivery," action. Georgia and Louisiana are each unique in referring to "bail" and "sequestration" respectively. "Replevin," not in the sense of the old forms of action, but in the sense of a generic label for actions to recover property, is probably the most commonly used term and is used here for convenience to include all such actions.

Replevin statutes adhere generally to the scheme provided in the old common law writ. The plaintiff files his action to recover personal property and claims the right to have it delivered to him immediately by posting a bond. The bond guarantees that the defendant will be reimbursed certain damages if, on final hearing on the merits, the court decides the property belongs to the defendant. The sheriff or other officer upon receiving the bond and any formal orders required by the statute, then seizes the property in the possession of the defendant and usually serves notice upon the defendant personally as well. The property so seized is then held for a stated period of time by the officer, during which period the defendant may attempt to require a bond in a higher amount or with better qualified sureties. Virtually all states are agreed in this much of the general scheme of replevin. All but a handful of states then go on to provide a second step. In this second step, the defendant may post a "counter bond" or "re-delivery bond," in which he and his sureties guarantee to pay certain damages to the plaintiff should it be finally adjudged that the plaintiff is the owner of the property. With this guarantee, the property is then re-delivered to the defendant, and a final determination as to title or possession is then made in the ordinary course of judicial events, which is to say, much later. When a final determination is made on the merits, appropriate orders are then made as to possession of the property and damages.

The whole process affords an analogy at law to the temporary restraining orders and interlocutory injunctions in equity; the cumbersome business of bonds and counterbonds in effect allows some preliminary adjustments before the merits can be reached on final hearing. Nevertheless, the statutory process of replevin is not particularly efficient for this purpose, and in some cases it fails utterly to meet the needs of the property owner. Of course, if the property is in no way unique or special, either objectively or in the eyes of the owner-plaintiff, the replevin statutes are adequate. Indeed, in that case, damages would be adequate. However, if the property is unique, or if it cannot be adequately compensated for in money, or if it has a "price of affection" on it, then the plaintiff wants the property and not a substitute for it. In addition, the plaintiff may have an urgent and not merely an eventual need for the property, for example, to use in his business. In these cases, the statutory replevin action may fall short of doing justice to the owner's needs. First, there is almost always a delay in getting the property, even if it is immediately found and seized by the sheriff, since it is held by the sheriff for several days to give the defendant an opportunity to object to the sureties on the plaintiff's bond or to post a bond himself. Second, the property may not be found immediately by the sheriff; indeed, it may never be found if the defendant secretes it, or carries it out of the jurisdiction, or commingles it with like property so that it cannot be identified, or, like the piqued husband from Texas, flushes it down the toilet where it can ride forever 'neath the streets of Houston. Third, in those states where a re-delivery bond is permitted, the defendant can defeat plaintiff's recovery of the property until final hearing, and of course he may destroy, damage or secrete the property during that period so as to defeat the plaintiff's recovery completely. In such a case, the plaintiff has a remedy on the bond posted by the defendant, but this will not give him his property.

These inadequacies in replevin statutes led the late Professor Van Hecke to support wide use of "equitable replevin."[12] This was simply a preliminary mandatory injunction issued by a court having equity powers and ordering delivery of the property to the plaintiff. It was issued where the replevin remedy was not adequate because of the danger that defendant might harm or hide the property or delay its recovery under the replevin statute. The advantage of the equitable replevin is twofold. First, there is an order requiring defendant to deliver the property, and it would be backed by equity's power to punish for contempt if it were disobeyed. Second, it would avoid the statutory delay and the statutory right of the defendant in most states to get re-delivery of the property until final judgment.

A number of cases support the use of equitable replevin. The primary issue in such cases is whether replevin is an adequate remedy, since if it is, equity will not intervene. . . . [T]he statutory remedy is inadequate when goods are either unique or irreplaceable and when there is a danger that the statutory remedy will fail to force a return of the goods in specie,[15] or where damages can not be measured or where the replevin remedy is inadequate because it will result in a multiplicity of suits.[16] On the other hand, the statutory replevin is usually quite adequate. Usually there is no suggestion that defendant might destroy or secrete the goods and they are often in no way especially unique. Since equity will not act when the remedy at law is adequate, the plaintiff in such cases is left to the statutory remedy in replevin.

NOTES ON REPLEVIN

1. In *Brook*, replevin is used to judicially repossess collateral under a security interest. That is probably the most common use of replevin. But the writ is also available for its original use in cases of theft, conversion, or other forms of outright dispossession. If Nye & Nissen had refused to return the egg washer, Olwell could have recovered it in replevin.

2. The owner also has the option to treat the taking as permanent and sue in conversion for damages, typically measured by the value of the thing taken. Or he can sue for the profits defendant earned from the

---

12. M. Van Hecke, Equitable Replevin, 33 N.C.L. Rev. 57 (1954).

15. E.g., Burton v. Rex Oil & Gas. Co., 324 Mich. 426, 36 N.W.2d 731 (1949) (goods not available in market, defendant refused to disclose whereabouts so that sheriff could not take them on replevin writ, equitable replevin allowed).

16. See Steggles v. National Discount Corp., 326 Mich. 44, 39 N.W.2d 237 (1949). The plaintiff sought return of a car from a finance company by way of mandatory injunction. This was granted. The court pointed out that if plaintiff were forced to sue in replevin, he might for some reason lose the case; if so, he would still have a damage action against the car dealer who allegedly got possession of the car for the finance company by fraud. This possibility was characterized by the court as a risk of "multiplicity of suits," and justified the injunction partly on that ground.

taking. If he gets the property back, either voluntarily or through re-plevin, he can sue for damages for the detention, measured by his actual consequential damages, or by the fair rental value of the property, or by both where that is not a double recovery.

3.   Replevin and similar remedies are not usually thought of as resti-tutionary. Replevin is an ancient common law writ; it has no historical link to quasi-contract, constructive trust, or the other fictional devices associated with restitution. And there is no special focus on defendant's unjust enrichment. Typically, defendant's gain and plaintiff's loss are identical.

But replevin is restitutionary in the literal sense that it restores the very thing that plaintiff lost. In *Brook* the property is apparently worth more than $2,500; both sides would rather have the property. Perhaps the prop-erty has increased in value during the trial. But more likely, the $2,500 figure in plaintiff's pleadings was artificially low to start with. The reason doesn't matter; plaintiff is entitled to get his property back. Replevin is a legal remedy; there is no need to show that the property is unique or that money would be inadequate for any other reason.

4.   Why would the complaint underestimate the value of the collat-eral? Underestimating value allows plaintiff to file a smaller bond. And the value stated in the complaint has no other significance to a secured creditor; even if the property disappears, Cullimore can still get an $8,000 judgment on the underlying debt.

Underestimating value would be riskier if plaintiff's only claim were that the property had been wrongfully taken. Then if the property disap-pears, plaintiff's damages will be the value of the property. He should not be bound by the amount stated in the complaint, but that amount would surely be admissible against him if he tried to prove a higher value at trial.

NOTES ON EJECTMENT AND FORCIBLE DETAINER

1.   Ejectment is the writ for recovery of land. Like replevin, it ends in a judgment for possession, and the sheriff will restore plaintiff to posses-sion if defendant does not leave voluntarily. Plaintiff can also recover either damages for the use of the land during the period of repossession, or restitution of the value of its use. Either damages or restitution for-merly required a separate action called mesne profits, but in modern procedure one action is sufficient. Similarly, the elaborate fictional plead-ings required at common law have been abolished by modern pleading rules. In Texas the writ itself has been abolished, and a statutory action called trespass to try title has been created instead. Tex. Prop. Code Ann. §22.01 (Vernon's 1983 Supp.).

2.   Ejectment does not have a preliminary remedy like the one in

replevin. Instead, there is a separate summary remedy for possession in simple cases, usually known as forcible detainer, or sometimes unlawful detainer. The remedy is statutory, and the statutes usually define two wrongs and two remedies. The statutes are generally known as forcible entry and detainer statutes, and that phrase is sometimes also used to describe one or both of the actions created.

Forcible entry is a damage action for forcibly entering land and dispossessing the occupant. Even the true owner can be liable for forcible entry, because the emphasis is on the use of private force and the associated risk of violence.

Forcible detainer is the summary action for possession. In most states, it can be used only against certain kinds of defendants, generally those who have no colorable claim of title. For example, under the 1983 recodification in Texas the remedy is available only against tenants at will, tenants whose leases have expired, and persons who have made forcible entries. Tex. Prop. Code Ann. §24.002 (Vernon's 1983 Supp.).

The action is typically heard in a court of very limited jurisdiction, such as a justice of the peace court. Courts generally say that title is not at issue. That is misleading; one obvious way to prove your right to possession is to prove title. What is true is that determinations of title in forcible detainer have no res judicata effect. If there is a serious title dispute, one must sue in ejectment or quiet title to get it resolved. Quiet title is a declaratory action to determine ownership; it is illustrated by Newman v. Newman Machine Co., supra at 444.

NOTES ON CONSTITUTIONAL RESTRICTIONS ON SUMMARY ACTIONS FOR POSSESSION OF PROPERTY

1. Professor Dobbs analogizes preliminary relief in replevin to temporary restraining orders and preliminary injunctions. The analogy is somewhat misleading, because writs of replevin issue without a preliminary hearing, without a showing that irreparable injury will occur before trial, without notice to defendants, and without any explanation why notice should not be given.

Over the years, replevin was streamlined for the benefit of creditors. In many states, plaintiff could get possession merely by filing a bond and filling out a form that alleged in conclusory fashion that he was entitled to the property. A clerk would issue the writ. In theory, this was merely a preliminary determination; defendant could file a redelivery bond and demand a hearing. But often the automatic issuance of the writ by a clerk ended the matter. Defendants did not respond, either because they had no defense, or did not know they could still assert a defense, or did not know how to assert a defense. Even if a defendant eventually recovered his property, he had been deprived of it in the meantime. And in many states, there was no guarantee that the hearing would be promptly scheduled.

In Fuentes v. Shevin, 407 U.S. 67 (1972), the Supreme Court invalidated the replevin statutes of Florida and Pennsylvania. The Court held that these statutes authorized the taking of property without due process of law, and said that the state could not take a defendant's property without a "fair prior hearing." Id. at 96. The Court did not specify the nature of the required hearing.

Two years later, the Court upheld the Louisiana sequestration law. Mitchell v. W.T. Grant Co., 416 U.S. 600 (1974). Louisiana required the plaintiff to state the details of his claim to the property in an affidavit or verified complaint. It required a judge to review the plaintiff's statement and sign the writ. And it provided that defendant could recover his property either by filing a bond, or by demanding a prompt hearing at which the burden of proof would be on the plaintiff.

Fuentes was decided 4 to 3. Mitchell was decided 5 to 4; the entire Fuentes majority dissented. Some thought that the distinctions between the two cases were too tiny to matter, and predicted that the new majority would soon overrule Fuentes. That has not happened, and most states have conformed their procedures to the minimum standard approved in Mitchell.

2.   Forcible detainer procedures came under constitutional attack in Lindsey v. Normet, 405 U.S. 56 (1972). All forcible detainer statutes guarantee the tenant some sort of hearing before eviction, but the hearing is often quite limited. Under the Oregon statute at issue in Lindsey, the hearing could be held on as little as two days' notice to the tenant. The tenant could get an additional two-day continuance, but he could not get a longer continuance unless he filed a bond to cover rent as it accrued. The issues were limited to whether the allegations of the complaint were true. The tenant could not raise any affirmative defenses, although he could sue for breach of the lease in a separate action. The Supreme Court upheld both of these provisions.

The Oregon statute also provided that the tenant could not appeal unless he filed a bond for double the amount of the rent that would accrue between commencement of the action and final judgment. If the tenant lost the appeal, he forfeited the entire bond whether or not the landlord had suffered any damage. The Court struck down this provision as a discriminatory burden on the right to appeal.

CHAPTER 7

Punitive Remedies

A. PUNITIVE DAMAGES

WALKER v. SHELDON
10 N.Y.2d 401, 179 N.E.2d 497 (1961)

FULD, Judge.

This appeal, here by permission of the Appellate Division on a certified question, calls upon us to decide whether punitive damages may be allowed in a fraud and deceit action.

The complaint alleges that the plaintiff was induced to enter into a contract with the defendant Comet Press and pay it $1,380 by means of a number of false and fraudulent representations made by the individual defendants who are officers of Comet. The representations, as well as the respects in which they are false, are set forth at some length. The complaint also alleges that the misrepresentations were made "in the regular course of [defendants'] business, and as the basis of their business knowing that plaintiff would, as other similarly situated had in the past, act upon said representations." Consequently, the plaintiff seeks, in addition to compensatory damages of $1,380, punitive damages in the amount of $75,000. . . .

It was the conclusion of the Appellate Division that, if the plaintiff is able to prove (what in effect she alleges) that the defendants were engaged in carrying on "a virtually larcenous scheme to trap generally the unwary," a jury would be justified in granting punitive damages. We agree with that view.

Punitive or exemplary damages have been allowed in cases where the wrong complained of is morally culpable, or is actuated by evil and reprehensible motives, not only to punish the defendant but to deter him, as well as others who might otherwise be so prompted, from indulging in similar conduct in the future. Moreover, the possibility of an award of such damages may not infrequently induce the victim, otherwise unwilling to proceed because of the attendant trouble and expense, to take action against the wrongdoer. Indeed, such self-interest of the plaintiff has been characterized as "Perhaps the principal advantage" of sanctioning punitive damages because it "leads to the actual prosecution of the claim for punitive damages, where the same motive would often lead him to refrain from the trouble incident to appearing against the wrongdoer in criminal proceedings." (McCormick, Damages [1935], pp. 276-277.) The list of actions in which punitive damages have been permitted in this State is long for, as this court observed in the Hamilton case (53 N.Y. 25, 30), "It is not the form of the action that gives the right to the jury to give punitory damages, but the moral culpability of the defendant."

Although they have been refused in the "ordinary" fraud and deceit case (Oehlhof v. Solomon, 73 App. Div. 329, 334, 76 N.Y.S. 716, 719), we are persuaded that, on the basis of analogy, reason and principle, there may be a recovery of exemplary damages in fraud and deceit actions where the fraud, aimed at the public generally, is gross and involves high moral culpability. And this court has — in line with what appears to be the weight of authority — sanctioned an award of such damages in a fraud and deceit case where the defendant's conduct evinced a high degree of moral turpitude and demonstrated such wanton dishonesty as to imply a criminal indifference to civil obligations. (See Kujek v. Goldman, 150 N.Y. 176, 44 N.E. 773.) . . .

Exemplary damages are more likely to serve their desired purpose of deterring similar conduct in a fraud case, such as that before us, than in any other area of tort. One who acts out of anger or hate, for instance, in committing assault or libel, is not likely to be deterred by the fear of punitive damages. On the other hand, those who deliberately and cooly engage in a far-flung fraudulent scheme, systematically conducted for profit, are very much more likely to pause and consider the consequences if they have to pay more than the actual loss suffered by an individual plaintiff. An occasional award of compensatory damages against such parties would have little deterrent effect. A judgment simply for compensatory damages would require the offender to do no more than return the money which he had taken from the plaintiff. In the calculation of his expected profits, the wrongdoer is likely to allow for a certain amount of money which will have to be returned to those victims who object too vigorously, and he will be perfectly content to bear the additional cost of litigation as the price for continuing his illicit business. It stands to reason that the chances of deterring him are materially increased by subjecting him to the payment of punitive damages.

It may be difficult to formulate an all-inclusive rule or principle as to what is an appropriate case for the recovery of punitive damages, but it is our conclusion that the allegations of the complaint before us, if proved, would justify such an award. The pleading charges that defrauding the general public into entering publishing contracts, such as the one involved in the present case, was the very basis of the defendants' business. What is asserted is not an isolated transaction incident to an otherwise legitimate business, but a gross and wanton fraud upon the public. It follows, therefore, that the courts below were thoroughly justified in refusing to strike the allegations which pertain to punitive damages. . . .

VAN VOORHIS, Judge (dissenting).

In our view the rules for the allowance of punitive or exemplary damages should not be extended to the facts of this case. The very circumstance that plaintiff asks for compensatory damages of $1,380 and punitive damages in the amount of $75,000 is an excellent illustration of the reasons on account of which the award of punitive damages should be restricted rather than extended to situations where they are not as yet traditionally allowed. In Dain v. Wycoff, 7 N.Y. 191, 193-194 the court used language which is applicable to the present situation:

> There can be no reason why twelve men wholly irresponsible should be allowed to go beyond the issue between the parties litigating, and after indemnifying the plaintiff for the injury sustained by him proceed as conservators of the public morals to punish the defendant in a private action for an offence against society. If the jury have the right to impose a fine by way of example, the plaintiff has no possible claim to it, nor ought the court to interfere and set it aside, however excessive it may be. In ordinary cases of misdemeanor, the legislature have restricted the power of the court in the imposition of penalties within certain definite limits. But a jury in civil actions have by this hypothesis an unlimited discretion to determine the crime and upon the measure of redress demanded by the public interest. The right stands upon no principle nor, in reference to actions of this character upon any authority.

The rule is firmly established in this State that punitive or exemplary damages are not allowed in fraud cases (Lane v. Wilcox, 55 Barb. 615; Oehlhof v. Solomon, 73 App. Div. 329, 76 N.Y.S. 716). Those cases consider the subject carefully and at length, stating the particular instances where punitive damages are granted and others in which they are denied.

The case of Kujek v. Goldman, 150 N.Y. 176, 44 N.E. 773, cited in the majority opinion, is not an exception to the denial of punitive damages in the ordinary fraud case. The best proof that they are not allowed is that damages of that nature are almost never demanded in instituting actions based on fraud. It is true that the majority opinion, following language adopted by the Appellate Division, aimed to distinguish the present appeal from the usual fraud case by purporting to limit punitive damages to what is alleged to have been "a virtually larcenous scheme to trap generally the unwary in which event punitive damages may be recoverable on the theory of wanton and malicious conduct." This language of the Appellate Division is based on the circumstance that the complaint alleges that the sum of $1,380 was obtained from plaintiff by misrepresentation for the purpose of a business which was illusory. It may well be that others than plaintiff were similarly mulcted and that this was merely what in popular terms is called a racket. If it was "larcenous," however, as the Appellate Division said, then it may be punishable under the criminal law, and to permit the award of punitive damages in a civil action may render the defendants liable to both civil and criminal punishment by way of admonishment and entirely without relation to whatever damages plaintiff has suffered. The time-honored rule of damages for fraud in business dealings is the actual pecuniary loss sustained.

The reasons against extending the coverage of punitive or exemplary damages are manifold, and many of them are patent under the facts of this case. McCormick on Damages (1935 ed., p.276) says that it is probable that, in the framing of a model code of damages today, for use in a country without previous legal tradition, "the doctrine of exemplary damages would find no place." His reasons are the double jeopardy involved in subjecting a defendant to both criminal prosecution and to punishment in the form of civil punitive damages for the same act, in violation of the spirit, if not the letter, of the constitutional prohibitions against punishing a man twice for the same offense, and the limitation of exemplary damages "only by the caprice of jurors, subject to a review by the judges only in a rare case where the judge can find impropriety of motive or gross disproportion, and that this want of a guiding measure leads to excess and injustice." Other reasons against extending the coverage of punitive damages in tort cases are stated in a learned article (44 Harv. L. Rev., pp. 1173-1209). Among these objections are the difficulty of apportioning punitive damages where, as in this case, there are several defendants possibly guilty of moral turpitude in varying degrees, and also that in the prosecution of such actions the proper admonition of a defendant need not involve the payment of money in as large an amount as can be obtained by a plaintiff by inflaming the passions of the jury. The motivation of plaintiffs in prosecuting such suits is likened to the situation which would exist if a District Attorney were paid according to the number of convictions that he was able to secure. The plaintiff profits more by heavy punishment than by light, even in instances where light punishment might have better admonitory value. The injustice is, of course, mentioned of lining the pocket of a plaintiff with money taken from a defendant in the interest of society, in addition to any loss which the plaintiff may have actually sustained. If it be thought that such a plaintiff should be recompensed not only for his damages but also for the expense of prosecuting a lawsuit for fraud, then the allowance of punitive damages is an inept manner of doing so. The jury are not instructed that the plaintiff's expenses of suit are a measure of the exemplary damage, but, rather, that whatever amount be awarded should be computed in such sum as would represent the payment of a defendant's debt to society. All of this is more properly the function of the criminal law.

For these reasons we consider that the law of punitive damage should be kept within its present boundaries, and not extended to cases to which it does not presently relate. The limitation on the extension of such coverage to fraud cases, suggested by the Appellate Division and adopted by the majority of this court, will, in practice, be difficult if not impossible to apply. In the ordinary case it is enough to try one lawsuit instead of a multiplicity of actions in order to determine to what extent a defendant is defrauding other members of the public besides the plaintiff. . . .

DESMOND, C.J., and DYE and BURKE, JJ., concur with FULD, J.

VAN VOORHIS, J., dissents in an opinion in which FROESSEL and FOSTER, JJ., concur.

NOTES ON PUNITIVE DAMAGES

1. Because fraud is an intentional tort, it is usually included in standard lists of wrongs for which punitive damages are available. Punitive damages are also generally available for torts committed recklessly. In addition, the modern reluctance of judges to control juries has led to recklessness being found in more and more contexts. A survey of civil judgments in Chicago and its near suburbs found punitive damages in "virtually all areas of civil liability," including breach of contract. Priest, Punitive Damages and Enterprise Liability, 56 So. Cal. L. Rev. 123, 123 (1982).

Punitive damages have even been awarded in a slip-and-fall case. Nolin v. National Convenience Stores, 95 Cal. App. 3d 279, 157 Cal. Rptr. 32 (1979). Defendant allowed gasoline and oil to accumulate around self-serve gasoline pumps. Defendant had not provided supplies or equipment for cleanup, despite requests from employees, and defendant's supervisor had ordered employees to take down warning signs and quit announcing warnings over a loudspeaker.

These developments largely moot the argument that fraud cases are generically inappropriate for punitive damages, although it is apparently still true that New York restricts punitive damages more than most jurisdictions. Outside New York, Walker v. Sheldon is interesting not for its holding, but for its general debate on punitive damages.

2.   In our study of restitution, we asked why it is ever necessary to make plaintiff more than whole. Punitive damages raise that question more starkly. Restitution sometimes exceeds plaintiff's loss; punitive damages always do. Moreover, punitive damages do not merely prevent defendant from profiting by his wrong. They usually exceed defendant's gain, and they are often awarded where defendant has no measurable gain at all; reckless driving is an obvious example. What is the rationale for such a remedy?

3.   The majority in *Walker* relies on the need for deterrence and punishment. Both rationales recur in the cases from early times to the present. Punitive damages first arose in cases of dignitary torts. Under early common law rules, mental suffering was not compensable, but juries awarded large sums and courts upheld the verdicts. Courts developed the theory of punitive damages to explain what they were doing; such damages were needed to deter and punish wrongdoing that might otherwise go unpunished and undeterred because it did not do compensable harm. Courts also feared that plaintiffs would take matters into their own hands if the law provided no effective remedy. That is still a real fear; it was a greater fear at a time when government was struggling to stamp out dueling. This history is reviewed in Ellis, Fairness and Efficiency in the Law of Punitive Damages, 56 So. Cal. L. Rev. 1, 12-20 (1982).

4.   If deterrence is the rationale, one must ask why compensatory damages do not provide sufficient deterrence. The dignitary tort cases provide one answer: Sometimes the law systematically underestimates damages. Should we solve those problems with punitive damages, or by fixing the compensatory damage rules? Mental distress is now generally compensable in intentional tort cases, but punitive damages are still available. Is it necessary to do both? Isn't it still true that outrageous conduct sometimes inflicts very little measurable harm? Punitive damages may be most appealing in that kind of case. More controversially, if there is a widespread sense that victims of serious personal injury are not really made whole by compensatory damages, then we may want punitives to get more deterrence.

Walker focuses on another risk of underdeterrence: Many claims for compensatory damages go unenforced. Some wrongs are hard to detect; fraud is the classic example. Some cases are too expensive to litigate; some plaintiffs choose not to sue for other reasons. Not all suits are successfully prosecuted. Even if one believes that profitable violations of law should be encouraged, paying compensatory damages only in cases successfully prosecuted does not provide enough deterrence.

Professor Ellis identifies one other source of underdeterrence. Some wrongdoers count profits from the violation that the law does not recognize. An angry assailant may take great pleasure from smashing his enemy in the face, great enough that he will do it even if he stops to think about the cost of compensatory damages. But the law does not recognize his pleasure as legitimate; we want to deter him no matter how much he enjoys it. Ellis, supra note 3, at 31-32. Most plausible examples of this source of underdeterrence are also appropriate for criminal prosecution. But the criminal justice system is already badly overloaded, and prosecutors may ignore minor crimes or plea bargain for probation. The risk of punitive damages may be a better deterrent. But all this assumes that people who need to be deterred know about the risk.

5. The dissent in *Walker* raises important procedural objections to punitive damages. These objections go to punitive damages in any form, but they are strongest if punishment is the primary rationale. Should punishment be inflicted without any standard and without the protections of criminal procedure? The argument about lack of standards may not get the dissenters very far; there's no standard for criminal sentencing either. But there are maximums, and parole boards can even out disparate sentences, so it's possible that punitive damages are even more standardless than criminal sentencing. The real problem seems to be that punishment is inherently standardless. We can measure losses caused, or gains accrued, but how do we measure blameworthiness in dollars?

6. The argument for procedural protections is harder to dismiss, although few modern judges have been troubled by it. The general rule is to treat punitive damage issues just like any other civil issue: Plaintiff can prove his case by a bare preponderance of the evidence, and judges will not interfere if there is some evidence to support the verdict. But there has been some recent trend toward a higher standard. Indiana and Wisconsin adopted a clear and convincing evidence standard in the early 1980s. Travelers Indemnity Co. v. Armstrong, 442 N.E.2d 349 (Ind. 1982); Wangen v. Ford Motor Co., 97 Wis. 2d 260, 300, 294 N.W.2d 437, 458 (1980). Both courts were responding to their own decisions making punitive damages more widely available — for breach of contract in Indiana, for products liability in Wisconsin — but neither court limited its new rule to those contexts. Here is what the Indiana court said:

> In determining whether or not we should stray from the traditional "preponderance of the evidence" standard, it should be particularly noted that there is no right to punitive damages. We have repeatedly said that such damages may be awarded in an appropriate case, as a punishment for the offense and to deter similar misconduct. It has never been implied that a plaintiff has any entitlement to such damages. Rather, he is merely the fortunate recipient of the "windfall." It cannot be said, therefore, that a plaintiff seeking such a bonus is denied any right, if he be held to a degree of proof higher than is required in other actions. In fact, it is incongruous to permit a recovery of that to which there is no entitlement upon evidence that barely warrants a recovery of that which is the plaintiff's absolute right. Yet, that is precisely what may occur when the inference of obduracy, from which punitive damages may flow, is permissible, but not compelled, from the same conduct from which compensatory damages flow, as a matter of right. To

avoid such occurrences, punitive damages should not be allowable upon evidence that is merely consistent with the hypothesis of malice, fraud, gross negligence or oppressiveness. Rather some evidence should be required that is inconsistent with the hypothesis that the tortious conduct was the result of a mistake of law or fact, honest error of judgment, over-zealousness, mere negligence or other such noniniquitous human failing. For, just as we agree that it is better to acquit a person guilty of crime than to convict an innocent one, we cannot deny that, given that the injured party has been fully compensated, it is better to exonerate a wrongdoer from punitive damages, even though his wrong be gross or wicked, than to award them at the expense of one whose error was one that society can tolerate and who has already compensated the victim of his error. The public interest cannot be served by a policy that favors the latter over the former. And, just as the requirement of proof beyond a reasonable doubt furthers the public interest with respect to criminal cases, a requirement of proof by clear and convincing evidence furthers the public interest when punitive damages are sought.

442 N.E.2d 349, 362-363.

GRIMSHAW v. FORD MOTOR CO.
119 Cal. App. 3d 757, 174 Cal. Rptr. 348 (1981)

TAMURA, Acting P.J.

A 1972 Ford Pinto hatchback automobile unexpectedly stalled on a freeway, erupting into flames when it was rear ended by a car proceeding in the same direction. Mrs. Lilly Gray, the driver of the Pinto, suffered fatal burns and 13-year-old Richard Grimshaw, a passenger in the Pinto, suffered severe and permanently disfiguring burns on his face and entire body. Grimshaw and the heirs of Mrs. Gray (Grays) sued Ford Motor Company and others. Following a six-month jury trial, verdicts were returned in favor of plaintiffs against Ford Motor Company. Grimshaw was awarded $2,516,000 compensatory damages and $125 million punitive damages; the Grays were awarded $559,680 in compensatory damages. On Ford's motion for a new trial, Grimshaw was required to remit all but $3½ million of the punitive award as a condition of denial of the motion. [Both sides appealed.] . . .

Facts . . .

Design of the Pinto Fuel System

In 1968, Ford began designing a new subcompact automobile which ultimately became the Pinto. Mr. Iacocca, then a Ford vice president, conceived the project and was its moving force. Ford's objective was to build a car at or below 2,000 pounds to sell for no more than $2,000.

Ordinarily marketing surveys and preliminary engineering studies precede the styling of a new automobile line. Pinto, however, was a rush project, so that styling preceded engineering and dictated engineering design to a greater degree than usual. Among the engineering decisions dictated by styling was the placement of the fuel tank. It was then the preferred practice in Europe and Japan to locate the gas tank over the rear axle in subcompacts because a small vehicle has less "crush space" between the rear axle and the bumper than larger cars. The Pinto's styling, however, required the tank to be placed behind the rear axle leaving only 9 or 10 inches of "crush space" — far less than in any other American automobile or Ford overseas subcompact. In addition, the Pinto was designed so that its bumper was little more than a chrome strip, less substantial than the bumper of any other American car produced then or later. The Pinto's rear structure also lacked reinforcing members known as "hat sections" (two longitudinal side members) and horizontal cross-members running between them such as were found in cars of larger unitized construction and in all automobiles produced by Ford's overseas operations. The absence of the reinforcing members rendered the Pinto less crush resistant than other vehicles. Finally, the differential housing selected for the Pinto had an exposed flange and a line of exposed bolt heads. These protrusions were sufficient to puncture a gas tank driven forward against the differential upon rear impact.

Crash Tests

During the development of the Pinto, prototypes were built and tested. . . . These prototypes as well as two production Pintos were crash tested by Ford to determine, among other things, the integrity of the fuel system in rear-end accidents. Ford also conducted the tests to see if the Pinto as designed would meet a proposed federal regulation requiring all automobiles manufactured in 1972 to be able to withstand a 20-mile-per-hour fixed barrier impact without significant fuel spillage and all automobiles manufactured after January 1, 1973, to withstand a 30-mile-per-hour fixed barrier impact without significant fuel spillage.

The crash tests revealed that the Pinto's fuel system as designed could not meet the 20-mile-per-hour proposed standard. . . .

The Cost to Remedy Design Deficiencies . . .

The vulnerability of the production Pinto's fuel tank at speeds of 20 and 30-miles-per-hour fixed barrier tests could have been remedied by inexpensive "fixes," but Ford produced and sold the Pinto to the public without doing anything to remedy the defects. Design changes that would have enhanced the integrity of the fuel tank system at relatively little cost per car included the following: Longitudinal side members and cross members at $2.40 and $1.80, respectively; a single shock absorbant "flak suit" to protect the tank at $4; a tank within a tank and placement of

the tank over the axle at $5.08 to $5.79; a nylon bladder within the tank at
$5.25 to $8; placement of the tank over the axle surrounded with a protective barrier at a cost of $9.95 per car; substitution of a rear axle with a
smooth differential housing at a cost of $2.10; imposition of a protective
shield between the differential housing and the tank at $2.35; improve-
ment and reenforcement of the bumper at $2.60; addition of eight inches
of crush space at a cost of $6.40. Equipping the car with a reinforced rear
structure, smooth axle, improved bumper and additional crush space at a
total cost of $15.30 would have made the fuel tank safe in a 34 to 38-mile-
per-hour rear-end collision by a vehicle the size of the Ford Galaxie. If, in
addition to the foregoing, a bladder or tank within a tank were used or if
the tank were protected with a shield, it would have been safe in a 40 to
45-mile-per-hour rear impact. If the tank had been located over the rear
axle, it would have been safe in a rear impact at 50 miles per hour or
more.

Management's Decision to Go Forward with Knowledge
of Defects

The idea for the Pinto, as has been noted, was conceived by Mr.
Iacocca, then executive vice president of Ford. The feasibility study was
conducted under the supervision of Mr. Robert Alexander, vice president
of car engineering. Ford's Product Planning Committee, whose members
included Mr. Iacocca, Mr. Robert Alexander, and Mr. Harold Mac-
Donald, Ford's group vice president of car engineering, approved the
Pinto's concept and made the decision to go forward with the project.
During the course of the project, regular product review meetings were
held which were chaired by Mr. MacDonald and attended by Mr. Alexander. As the project approached actual production, the engineers responsible for the components of the project "signed off" to their
immediate supervisors who in turn "signed off" to their superiors and so
on up the chain of command until the entire project was approved for
public release by Vice Presidents Alexander and MacDonald and ultimately by Mr. Iacocca. The Pinto crash tests results had been forwarded
up the chain of command to the ultimate decision-makers and were
known to the Ford officials who decided to go forward with production.

Harley Copp, a former Ford engineer and executive in charge of the
crash testing program, testified that the highest level of Ford's management made the decision to go forward with the production of the Pinto,
knowing that the gas tank was vulnerable to puncture and rupture at low
rear impact speeds creating a significant risk of death or injury from fire
and knowing that "fixes" were feasible at nominal cost. He testified that
management's decision was based on the cost savings which would inure
from omitting or delaying the "fixes."

Mr. Copp's testimony concerning management's awareness of the
crash tests results and the vulnerability of the Pinto fuel system was cor-

roborated by other evidence. . . . Mr. Kennedy, who succeeded Mr. Copp as the engineer in charge of Ford's crash testing program, admitted that the test results had been forwarded up the chain of command to his superiors.

Finally, Mr. Copp testified to conversations in late 1968 or early 1969 with the chief assistant research engineer in charge of cost-weight evaluation of the Pinto, and to a later conversation with the chief chassis engineer who was then in charge of crash testing the early prototype. In these conversations, both men expressed concern about the integrity of the Pinto's fuel system and complained about management's unwillingness to deviate from the design if the change would cost money. . . .

Punitive Damages . . .

(1)   "Malice" under Civil Code Section 3294

The concept of punitive damages is rooted in the English common law and is a settled principle of the common law of this country. . . . When our laws were codified in 1872, the doctrine was incorporated in Civil Code section 3294, which at the time of trial read: "In an action for the breach of an obligation not arising from contract, where the defendant has been guilty of oppression, fraud, or malice, express or implied, the plaintiff, in addition to the actual damages, may recover damages for the sake of example and by way of punishing the defendant."[11]

Ford argues that "malice" as used in section 3294 and as interpreted by our Supreme Court in Davis v. Hearst (1911) 160 Cal. 143 [116 P. 530],

---

11.   Section 3294 was amended in 1980 to read:

(a)   In an action for the breach of an obligation not arising from contract, where the defendant has been guilty of oppression, fraud, or malice, the plaintiff, in addition to the actual damages, may recover damages for the sake of example and by way of punishing the defendant.

(b)   An employer shall not be liable for damages pursuant to subdivision (a), based upon acts of an employee of the employer, unless the employer had advance knowledge of the unfitness of the employee and employed him or her with a conscious disregard of the rights or safety of others or authorized or ratified the wrongful conduct for which the damages are awarded or was personally guilty of oppression, fraud, or malice. With respect to a corporate employer, the advance knowledge, ratification, or act of oppression, fraud, or malice must be on the part of an officer, director, or managing agent of the corporation.

(c)   As used in this section, the following definitions shall apply:

(1)   "Malice" means conduct which is intended by the defendant to cause injury to the plaintiff or conduct which is carried on by the defendant with a conscious disregard of the rights or safety of others.

(2)   "Oppression" means subjecting a person to cruel and unjust hardship in conscious disregard of that person's rights.

(3)   "Fraud" means an intentional misrepresentation, deceit, or concealment of a material fact known to the defendant with the intention on the part of the defendant of thereby depriving a person of property or legal rights or otherwise causing injury.

requires animus malus or evil motive — an intention to injure the person
harmed — and that the term is therefore conceptually incompatible with
an unintentional tort such as the manufacture and marketing of a defectively designed product. This contention runs counter to our decisional
law. As this court recently noted, numerous California cases after Davis
v. Hearst have interpreted the term "malice" as used in section 3294
to include, not only a malicious intention to injure the specific person harmed, but conduct evincing "a conscious disregard of the probability that the actor's conduct will result in injury to others." Dawes v.
Superior Court (1980) 111 Cal. App. 3d 82, 88 [168 Cal. Rptr. 319], hg.
den. 12/17/80. . . .

In Taylor v. Superior Court, 24 Cal. 3d 890 (1979), our high court's
most recent pronouncement on the subject of punitive damages, the
court [said] . . . : "In order to justify an award of punitive damages on
this basis, the plaintiff must establish that the defendant was aware of
the probable dangerous consequences of his conduct, and that he wilfully and deliberately failed to avoid those consequences." (Id., at pp.
895-896.) . . .

The interpretation of the word "malice" as used in section 3294 to
encompass conduct evincing callous and conscious disregard of public
safety by those who manufacture and market mass produced articles is
consonant with and furthers the objectives of punitive damages. The
primary purposes of punitive damages are punishment and deterrence of
like conduct by the wrongdoer and others. In the traditional noncommercial intentional tort, compensatory damages alone may serve as an effective deterrent against future wrongful conduct but in commerce-related
torts, the manufacturer may find it more profitable to treat compensatory
damages as a part of the cost of doing business rather than to remedy the
defect. Deterrence of such "objectionable corporate policies" serves one
of the principal purposes of Civil Code section 3294. Governmental safety
standards and the criminal law have failed to provide adequate consumer
protection against the manufacture and distribution of defective products. Punitive damages thus remain as the most effective remedy for
consumer protection against defectively designed mass produced articles.
They provide a motive for private individuals to enforce rules of law and
enable them to recoup the expenses of doing so which can be considerable and not otherwise recoverable.

We find no statutory impediments to the application of Civil Code
section 3294 to a strict products liability case based on design defect.

(2) Constitutional Attacks on Civil Code
Section 3294 . . .

The argument that application of Civil Code section 3294 violates the
constitutional prohibition against double jeopardy is equally fallacious.

This prohibition like the ex post facto concept is applicable only to criminal proceedings.

The related contention that the potential liability for punitive damages in other cases for the same design defect renders the imposition of such damages violative of Ford's due process rights also lacks merit. Followed to its logical conclusion, it would mean that punitive damages could never be assessed against a manufacturer of a mass produced article. No authorities are cited for such a proposition; indeed, as we have seen, the cases are to the contrary. We recognize the fact that multiplicity of awards may present a problem, but the mere possibility of a future award in a different case is not a ground for setting aside the award in this case, particularly as reduced by the trial judge. If Ford should be confronted with the possibility of an award in another case for the same conduct, it may raise the issue in that case. We add, moreover, that there is no necessary unfairness should the plaintiff in this case be rewarded to a greater extent than later plaintiffs. As Professor Owen has said in response to such a charge of unfairness:

> This conception ignores the enormous diligence, imagination, and financial outlay required of initial plaintiffs to uncover and to prove the flagrant misconduct of a product manufacturer. In fact, subsequent plaintiffs will often ride to favorable verdicts and settlements on the coattails of the firstcomers.

(Owen, Punitive Damages in Products Liability Litigation, 74 Mich. L. Rev. 1258, 1325 (1976).) That observation fits the instant case.

(3) Sufficiency of the Evidence to Support the Finding of Malice and Corporate Responsibility

Ford contends that its motion for judgment notwithstanding the verdict should have been granted because the evidence was insufficient to support a finding of malice or corporate responsibility for such malice. The record fails to support the contention. . . .

Through the results of the crash tests Ford knew that the Pinto's fuel tank and rear structure would expose consumers to serious injury or death in a 20- to 30-mile-per-hour collision. There was evidence that Ford could have corrected the hazardous design defects at minimal cost but decided to defer correction of the shortcomings by engaging in a cost-benefit analysis balancing human lives and limbs against corporate profits. Ford's institutional mentality was shown to be one of callous indifference to public safety. There was substantial evidence that Ford's conduct constituted "conscious disregard" of the probability of injury to members of the consuming public.

Ford's argument that there can be no liability for punitive damages because there was no evidence of corporate ratification of malicious misconduct is equally without merit. California follows the Restatement rule that punitive damages can be awarded against a principal because of an action of an agent if, but only if,

> "(a) the principal authorized the doing and the manner of the act, or (b) the agent was unfit and the principal was reckless in employing him, or (c) the agent was employed in a managerial capacity and was acting in the scope of employment, or (d) the principal or a managerial agent of the principal ratified or approved the act." (Rest. 2d Torts (Tent. Draft No. 19, 1973) §909.)

The present case comes within one or both of the categories described in subdivisions (c) and (d).

There is substantial evidence that management was aware of the crash tests showing the vulnerability of the Pinto's fuel tank to rupture at low speed rear impacts with consequent significant risk of injury or death of the occupants by fire. There was testimony from several sources that the test results were forwarded up the chain of command; vice president Robert Alexander admitted to Mr. Copp that he was aware of the test results; vice president Harold MacDonald, who chaired the product review meetings, was present at one of those meetings at which a report on the crash tests was considered and a decision was made to defer corrective action; and it may be inferred that Mr. Alexander, a regular attender of the product review meetings, was also present at that meeting. Mac-Donald and Alexander were manifestly managerial employees possessing the discretion to make "decisions that will ultimately determine corporate policy." (Egan v. Mutual of Omaha Ins. Co., 24 Cal. 3d 809, 823.) There was also evidence that Harold Johnson, an assistant chief engineer of research, and Mr. Max Jurosek, chief chassis engineer, were aware of the results of the crash tests and the defects in the Pinto's fuel tank system. Ford contends those two individuals did not occupy managerial positions because Mr. Copp testified that they admitted awareness of the defects but told him they were powerless to change the rear-end design of the Pinto. It may be inferred from the testimony, however, that the two engineers had approached management about redesigning the Pinto or that, being aware of management's attitude, they decided to do nothing. In either case the decision not to take corrective action was made by persons exercising managerial authority. Whether an employee acts in a "managerial capacity" does not necessarily depend on his "level" in the corporate hierarchy. (Id., at p.822.) As the Egan court said: "'Defendant should not be allowed to insulate itself from liability by giving an employee a nonmanagerial title and relegating to him crucial policy decisions.'" (Id., at p.823, quoting conc. and dis. opn. in Merlo v. Standard Life & Acc. Ins. Co., 59 Cal. App. 3d 5, 25.) . . .

(4) Instructions on Malice

In its instructions to the jury, the trial court defined malice as follows: "'Malice' means a motive and willingness to vex, harass, annoy or injure another person. Malice may be inferred from acts and conduct, such as by showing that the defendant's conduct was wilful, intentional, and done in conscious disregard of its possible results." The court also instructed the jury that plaintiff Grimshaw had the burden of proving "[t]hat the defendant acted with malice which may be inferred from defendant's conduct if the conduct was wilful, intentional, and done in conscious disregard of its possible results."

On appeal, Ford contends that the phrase "conscious disregard of its possible results" used in the two instructions would permit a plaintiff to impugn almost every design decision as made in conscious disregard of some perceivable risk because safer alternative designs are almost always a possibility. Ford argues that to instruct the jury so that they might find "malice" if any such "possibility" existed was erroneous; it maintains that an instruction on "malice" in products liability must contain the phrase "conscious disregard of [the probability/a high probability] of injury to others," in order to preclude prejudicial error. . . .

The instruction on malice as given by the court was former BAJI No. 14.71 with a one-word modification. The instruction as given merely substituted the word "conscious" for the word "reckless."[13] The phrase "wilful, intentional and done in reckless disregard of its possible results" used in former BAJI No. 14.71 seems to have made its first appearance in Toole v. Richardson-Merrell Inc., 251 Cal. App. 2d 689, 713. . . .

In Dawes v. Superior Court, 111 Cal. App. 3d 82, 88, this court noted that "since 1974 at the latest, and probably since a much earlier date, the term 'malice' as used in Civil Code section 3294 has been interpreted as including a conscious disregard of the *probability* that the actor's conduct will result in injury to others." (Italics supplied.) Our use of the term "probability" was not intended to effect a change in the law as set forth in *Toole*. Rather, it was meant to reflect correctly what the cases have been stating, albeit in varying ways, as an essential ingredient of the concept of malice in unintentional torts, and to express this essential ingredient in the most precise manner possible. Although the *Toole* formulation of the rule used the expression "possible results," those words were preceded by the pejoratives "wilful," "intentional" and "reckless disregard." Taking the statement as a whole, it is our view that probability that the conduct will result in injury to another is implicit in *Toole*. . . . We agree with Ford, however, that to be as accurate as possible, the rule should be expressed in terms of probability of injury rather than possibility. Viewed in this way, the salient question for this appeal becomes whether the instruction given by the court resulted in a miscarriage of justice because

13. The 1980 revision of BAJI uses the expression "conscious disregard of the plaintiff's rights." The trial court's substitution in the instant case was apparently in response to G. D. Searle & Co. v. Superior Court (1975) 49 Cal. App. 3d 22, 29-32, which criticized the use of the term "reckless" in defining malice and suggested that "conscious disregard" would be a more accurate expression of the required state of mind.

it failed to use "probability." As we explain below, we are convinced that it did not. . . .

Ford has failed to demonstrate prejudice from the claimed defect in the instructions on malice. When the instructions are read as a whole, the jury could not possibly have interpreted the words "conscious disregard of its possible results" to extend to the innocent conduct depicted by Ford. The term "motive and willingness . . . to injure" and the words "wilful," "intentional," and "conscious disregard" signify animus malus or evil motive. . . . The jury was instructed that Ford was not required under the law to produce either the safest possible vehicle or one which was incapable of producing injury. The instructions on malice manifestly referred to conduct constituting conscious and callous disregard of a substantial likelihood of injury to others and not to innocent conduct by the manufacturer. Further, plaintiffs made no attempt in their arguments to the jury to give the instructions on malice the interpretation to which Ford says they are susceptible. Plaintiffs did not argue possibility of injury; they argued that injury was a virtual certainty and that Ford's management knew it from the results of the crash tests. Thus, the instructions on malice, even assuming them to have been erroneous because the word "possible" was used instead of "probable," did not constitute prejudicial error.

(5) Burden of Proof on Issue of Malice

Ford argues that the jury should have been instructed that plaintiff had the burden of proving "malice" by "clear and convincing evidence." Ford's request for such an instruction was denied. Ford relies on cases involving the personal liberty of an individual which are manifestly inapposite. . . . The requested instruction on the burden of proof was properly denied.

(6) Amount of Punitive Damage Award

Ford's final contention is that the amount of punitive damages awarded, even as reduced by the trial court, was so excessive that a new trial on that issue must be granted. Ford argues that its conduct was less reprehensible than those for which punitive damages have been awarded in California in the past; that the $3½ million award is many times over the highest award for such damages ever upheld in California; and that the award exceeds maximum civil penalties that may be enforced under federal or state statutes against a manufacturer for marketing a defective automobile. We are unpersuaded.

In determining whether an award of punitive damages is excessive, comparison of the amount awarded with other awards in other cases is not a valid consideration. . . . In deciding whether an award is excessive as a matter of law or was so grossly disproportionate as to raise the presumption that it was the product of passion or prejudice, the following factors should be weighed: The degree of reprehensibility of defendant's conduct, the wealth of the defendant, the amount of compensatory damages, and an amount which would serve as a deterrent effect on like conduct by defendant and others who may be so inclined. Applying the foregoing criteria to the instant case, the punitive damage award as reduced by the trial court was well within reason.[14]

In assessing the propriety of a punitive damage award, as in assessing the propriety of any other judicial ruling based upon factual determinations, the evidence must be viewed in the light most favorable to the judgment. Viewing the record thusly in the instant case, the conduct of Ford's management was reprehensible in the extreme. It exhibited a conscious and callous disregard of public safety in order to maximize corporate profits. Ford's self-evaluation of its conduct is based on a review of the evidence most favorable to it instead of on the basis of the evidence most favorable to the judgment. Unlike malicious conduct directed toward a single specific individual, Ford's tortious conduct endangered the lives of thousands of Pinto purchasers. Weighed against the factor of reprehensibility, the punitive damage award as reduced by the trial judge was not excessive.

Nor was the reduced award excessive taking into account defendant's wealth and the size of the compensatory award. Ford's net worth was $7.7 billion and its income after taxes for 1976 was over $983 million. The punitive award was approximately .005 percent of Ford's net worth [actually, .05 percent — Ed.] and approximately .03 percent of its 1976 net income [actually, .36 percent — Ed.]. The ratio of the punitive damages to compensatory damages was approximately 1.4 to 1. Significantly, Ford does not quarrel with the amount of the compensatory award to Grimshaw.

Nor was the size of the award excessive in light of its deterrent purpose. An award which is so small that it can be simply written off as a part of the cost of doing business would have no deterrent effect. An award which affects the company's pricing of its product and thereby affects its competitive advantage would serve as a deterrent. The award in question

14. A quantitative formula whereby the amount of punitive damages can be determined in a given case with mathematical certainty is manifestly impossible as well as undesirable. (Mallor & Roberts, Punitive Damages: Towards a Principled Approach, 31 Hastings L.J. 639, 666-667, 670 (1980).) The authors advocate abandonment of the rule that a reasonable relationship must exist between punitive damages and actual damages. They suggest that courts balance society's interest against defendant's interest by focusing on the following factors: Severity of threatened harm; degree of reprehensibility of defendant's conduct, profitability of the conduct, wealth of defendant, amount of compensatory damages (whether it was high in relation to injury), cost of litigation, potential criminal sanctions and other civil actions against defendant based on same conduct. (Id., at pp. 667-669.) In the present case, the amount of the award as reduced by the judge was reasonable under the suggested factors, including the factor of any other potential liability, civil or criminal.

was far from excessive as a deterrent against future wrongful conduct by Ford and others.

Ford complains that the punitive award is far greater than the maximum penalty that may be imposed under California or federal law prohibiting the sale of defective automobiles or other products. For example, Ford notes that California statutes provide a maximum fine of only $50 for the first offense and $100 for a second offense for a dealer who sells an automobile that fails to conform to federal safety laws or is not equipped with required lights or brakes; that a manufacturer who sells brake fluid in this state failing to meet statutory standards is subject to a maximum of only $50; and that the maximum penalty that may be imposed under federal law for violation of automobile safety standards is $1,000 per vehicle up to a maximum of $800,000 for any related series of offenses (15 U.S.C. §§1397-1398). It is precisely because monetary penalties under government regulations prescribing business standards or the criminal law are so inadequate and ineffective as deterrents against a manufacturer and distributor of mass produced defective products that punitive damages must be of sufficient amount to discourage such practices. Instead of showing that the punitive damage award was excessive, the comparison between the award and the maximum penalties under state and federal statutes and regulations governing automotive safety demonstrates the propriety of the amount of punitive damages awarded.

Grimshaw's Appeal

Grimshaw has appealed from the order conditionally granting Ford a new trial on the issue of punitive damages and from the amended judgment entered pursuant to that order.

Grimshaw contends that the new trial order is erroneous because . . . the punitive damages awarded by the jury were not excessive as a matter of law . . . and . . . the court abused its discretion in cutting the award so drastically. For reasons to be stated, we have concluded that the contentions lack merit.

The court prefaced its specification of reasons with a recitation of the judicially established guidelines[16] for determining whether a punitive award is excessive. The court then observed that there was evidence in the record (referring to exhibit 125) which might provide a possible rational basis for the $125 million jury verdict which would dispel any

---

16.   The court stated that

the principles by which the propriety of the amount of punitive damages awarded will be judged are threefold: (1) Is the sum so large as to raise a presumption that the award was the result of passion and prejudice and therefore excessive as a matter of law; (2) Does the award bear a reasonable relationship to the net assets of the defendant; and (3) Does the award bear a reasonable relationship to the compensatory damages awarded.

presumption of passion or prejudice,[17] adding, however, that the court was not suggesting that the amount was warranted "or that the jury did utilize Exhibit 125, or any other exhibits, and if they did, that they were justified in so doing." The court then noted, based on the fact that Ford's net worth was $7.7 billion and its profits during the last quarter of the year referred to in the financial statement introduced into evidence were more than twice the punitive award, that the award was not disproportionate to Ford's net assets or to its profit generating capacity. The court noted, however, that the amount of the punitive award was 44 times the compensatory award, the court stated that while it did not consider that ratio alone to be controlling because aggravating circumstances may justify a ratio as high as the one represented by the jury verdict, it reasoned that the ratio coupled with the amount by which the punitive exceeded the compensatory damages (over $122 million) rendered the jury's punitive award excessive as a matter of law.

Grimshaw contends that the court erred in determining that the ratio of punitive to compensatory damages rendered the punitive excessive as a matter of law. The trial court, however, did not base its decision solely on the ratio of punitive to compensatory. It took into account the ratio, the "aggravating circumstances" (the degree of reprehensibility), the wealth of the defendant and its profit generating capacity, the magnitude of the punitive award, including the amount by which it exceeded the compensatory. Those were proper considerations for determining whether the award was excessive as a matter of law. When a trial court grants a new trial for excessive damages, either conditionally or outright, a presumption of correctness attaches to the order and it will not be reversed unless it plainly appears that the judge abused his discretion. In the case at bench, we find no abuse of discretion. . . .

Finally, Grimshaw contends the court abused its discretion in reducing the award to $3½ million as a condition of its new trial order and urges this court to restore the jury award or at least require a remittitur of substantially less than that required by the trial court.

In ruling on a motion for new trial for excessive damages, the trial court does not sit "in an appellate capacity but as an independent trier of fact." (Neal v. Farmers Ins. Exchange, 21 Cal. 3d 910, 933.) This role as a fact finder is conferred on the trial court by Code of Civil Procedure section 662.5 which provides that if a new trial limited to the issue of damages would be proper after a jury trial,

the trial court may in its discretion: . . . (b) If the ground for granting a new trial is excessive damages, make its order granting the new trial subject to the

17. Exhibit 125 was the report by Ford engineers showing savings which would be realized by deferring design changes to the fuel system of Ford automobiles to meet the proposed governmental standards on the integrity of the fuel systems.

condition that the motion for a new trial is denied if the party in whose favor the verdict has been rendered consents to a reduction of so much thereof as the court *in its independent judgment determines from the evidence to be fair and reasonable.*

(Italics supplied.) An appellate court may reverse the order granting the new trial only when the reasons given by the trial judge reflect a manifest and unmistakable abuse of discretion.

Here, the judge, exercising his independent judgment on the evidence, determined that a punitive award of $3½ million was "fair and reasonable." Evidence pertaining to Ford's conduct, its wealth and the savings it realized in deferring design modifications in the Pinto's fuel system might have persuaded a different fact finder that a larger award should have been allowed to stand. Our role, however, is limited to determining whether the trial judge's action constituted a manifest and unmistakable abuse of discretion. Here, the judge referred to the evidence bearing on those factors in his new trial order and obviously weighed it in deciding what was a "fair and reasonable" award. . . . Finally, while the trial judge may not have taken into account Ford's potential liability for punitive damages in other cases involving the same tortious conduct in reducing the award, it is a factor we may consider in passing on the request to increase the award. Considering such potential liability, we find the amount as reduced by the trial judge to be reasonable and just. We therefore decline the invitation to modify the judgment by reducing the amount of the remittitur.

Disposition

In Grimshaw v. Ford Motor Co., the judgment, the conditional new trial order, and the order denying Ford's motion for judgment notwithstanding the verdict on the issue of punitive damages are affirmed. . . .

MORE NOTES ON PUNITIVE DAMAGES

1. What is the rationale for punitive damages in *Grimshaw*? An economic analysis looks at whether compensation produces adequate deterrence. In *Grimshaw* there was little risk that the wrong would go undetected, and it is unlikely that Ford derived any illicit satisfaction from producing dangerous cars. But the case was expensive to litigate, and despite the enormous incentives to successful litigation, many products cases are lost or settled for less than a jury would award. Moreover, the measure of damage may be systematically undercompensatory.

2. The court does none of this. It simply concludes that punitive damages are necessary to deter conduct that it finds outrageous. What

was so outrageous in *Grimshaw*? Ford's calculating that it would be profit-able to let these accidents happen? The striking thing about *Grimshaw* is its square and utter rejection of the economic view of law. Judge Posner might say that Ford miscalculated costs and benefits, but the basic effort to compare the cost of prevention to the cost of the accidents is exactly what he thinks Ford should do. The law's response is not just that such calculations are negligent, but that they are especially reprehensible and deserving of punitive damages. Note that the jury was instructed that Ford did not have to make the safest possible vehicle or one that was incapable of producing injury. The law balances costs and benefits too, but with a scale tilted in favor of accident prevention. The economic approach would weigh the cost of prevention and the cost of the accident equally. Who has the better of the argument?

3. *Grimshaw* is no oddity. The fear that manufacturers might find accidents profitable if victims are limited to compensatory damages is a recurring theme in the products liability cases awarding punitive dam-ages. The same idea appears in other contexts as well. A stark example is Brown v. Missouri Pacific Railroad, 703 F.2d 1050 (8th Cir. 1983). A driver had been killed in an accident at an unprotected railroad crossing. Although the town had lobbied for a crossing gate for some time, the railroad said that gates were too expensive. A citizen testified to the fol-lowing exchange when a railroad employee spoke to the local Kiwanis Club:

> *The Witness:*   I made the statement that it would be safer and cheaper in the long run to put gates on all the crossings in Prescott, instead of having so many people suing the railroad.
> *Question:*   What was his response?
> *The Witness:*   His response was, the way I understood, is that it was cheaper to have the suits than to put up the gates.

Id. at 858.

The railroad denied such a policy and denied that the local employee knew its policy on such matters. The employee denied making the state-ment. But the jury apparently believed it, and returned a verdict that included $62,000 in punitive damages. The court upheld the verdict, relying largely on this testimony.

4. A defectively designed product is typically mass produced, and it may injure hundreds or thousands of people. Hundreds or thousands of punitive damage awards may be overkill. Coordinating all the lawsuits is difficult, and denying punitive damages to all but the first plaintiff seems to discriminate between plaintiffs. The problem is relatively new, and courts are still grappling with it. They have generally rejected arguments that the only solution is not to award punitive damages in such cases at all. And they have rejected the "first comer" solution — a proposed rule

that after one plaintiff has recovered punitive damages, all others will be barred.

Grimshaw illustrates the dominant approach but not yet a solution. The court took the possibility of additional awards into account in affirming the remittitur. It also indicated that Ford can raise the issue of multiple punitive awards in subsequent cases, but it did not decide what the court should do in those cases. The Supreme Court of Wisconsin has indicated that past awards and likely future awards can be brought to the attention of juries. Wangen v. Ford Motor Co., 97 Wis. 2d 260, 304, 294 N.W.2d 437, 459-460 (1980). (*Wangen* involved an exploding gas tank on the 1967 Mustang.) The *Wangen* rationale was that evidence of other punitive damage awards is relevant to defendant's wealth, and evidence of defendant's wealth has always been admissible. The Wisconsin court also cited studies indicating that catastrophic cumulative punitive damage awards had so far been a theoretical rather than a real problem.

Another solution sometimes suggested is a class action for punitive damages. Class actions are especially attractive in disaster cases where the class of victims is fixed at the beginning of the litigation. But there are obstacles that may be insurmountable.

A good example is In re Federal Skywalk Cases, 93 F.R.D. 415 (W.D. Mo.), *rev'd*, 680 F.2d 1175 (8th Cir.), *cert. denied sub nom.* Stover v. Rau, 459 U.S. 988 (1982). The *Skywalk Cases* all arose from collapse of elevated walkways in a Kansas City hotel. There were 114 deaths and hundreds of injuries. The trial judge certified a class action for punitive damages on the theory that separate punitive damage awards might bankrupt defendants after only some of the victims had been compensated, leaving nothing for plaintiffs whose cases came to trial later. He certified the class under Federal Civil Rule 23(b)(1)(B), finding that "adjudications with respect to individual members" of the class would "substantially impair or impede" the ability of other class members to protect their interests. There is no right to opt out of class actions under Rule 23(b)(1)(B). But there was bitter resistance from many victims, much of it apparently motivated by their lawyers' concerns over attorneys' fees. A divided court of appeals held that the trial court had no authority to enjoin suits already pending in state court before the class certification. Allowing those suits to continue gutted the class. The whole controversy, including the infighting among lawyers, is described in Stewart, Controversy Surrounds Payments to Plaintiffs in Hyatt Regency Case, Wall St. J., July 3, 1984, at 1, col. 1.

Class actions and similar consolidation devices are even less available in products cases, because the injuries happen at intervals over many years and in every state. One case where it was tried is In re Northern District of California "Dalkon Shield" IUD Products Liability Litigation, 526 F. Supp. 887 (N.D. Cal. 1981). There, at defendant's request, the court certified a class action for punitive damages only; the actions for compensatory damages were allowed to proceed individually. But the class was limited to plaintiffs with claims then pending in federal courts in California — a small portion of all the claims. In each of these cases, defendants feared bankruptcy from multiple punitive damage awards, and the court feared that some litigants would not be compensated if defendants' assets were exhausted by earlier punitive damage judgments.

More recently, the manufacturer of the Dalkon shield requested a nationwide class for punitive damages. Walsh, A. H. Robins Seeks a Consolidated Trial for All Dalkon Punitive-Damage Claims, Wall St. J., Oct. 23, 1984, at 4, col. 2. Defendant reported that more than 10,000 Dalkon shield suits had been filed, of which 3,700 were still pending. It had settled most of the rest; about forty had gone to trial. It had won half of those and avoided punitive damages in all but eight cases. But those eight juries had awarded a total of $17.2 million in punitives, including a $6.2 million verdict upheld by the Colorado Supreme Court. Defendant asked a federal court in Richmond, Virginia, to consolidate the remaining 3,700 claims for a single trial on punitive damages before a single jury.

5. Does the California statute, or the jury instructions approved in *Grimshaw*, meaningfully distinguish conduct deserving of punitive damages from ordinary liability? Doesn't the ordinary driver going five miles over the speed limit act in conscious disregard of a heightened risk of injury? The court says that is not enough; there must be conscious disregard of a "probability that the actor's conduct will result in injury to others." What does that mean? 51 percent? It is a virtual certainty that manufacturing cars at all will result in injury to others, and Ford knows that. On the other hand, the probability of any particular Pinto exploding was quite low. Most of them didn't get hit.

There is an older tradition of describing the standard with epithets: fraud, malice, oppression, willful, wanton, outrageous, gross. Such terms aren't very precise, but they don't pretend to be. Is that the best we can do? Doesn't the court rely on such epithets to save the jury instruction in *Grimshaw*?

6. Whatever the standard, what does it mean when applied vicariously? About half the states follow rules like those in *Grimshaw*, requiring that high officials be implicated in the outrageous conduct. The other half apply ordinary respondeat superior rules to punitive damages; the employer is liable for punitives if any employee acting within the course and scope of his employment did something deserving of punitives. Some commentators have been troubled by punishment for vicarious conduct whatever the standard. Ellis, Fairness and Efficiency in the Law of Punitive Damages, 56 S. Cal. L. Rev. 1, 63-71 (1982). Isn't that just a way of saying corporations should be immune from punitive damages? Ford Motor Co. cannot act except vicariously; if punitive damages make sense, they must be imposed for vicarious conduct. What about live

human employers? Should they be immune from punitive damages for the acts of their employees?

7. The Supreme Court has immunized some defendants from punitive damages. Punitive damages are unavailable against municipalities in civil rights suits, City of Newport v. Fact Concerts, 453 U.S. 247 (1981), and against unions in duty of fair representation suits, International Brotherhood of Electrical Workers v. Foust, 442 U.S. 42 (1979). In the municipality case, the Court relied heavily on the vicarious nature of the municipality's liability, and on the fear that the burden would fall on innocent taxpayers. In the union case, the Court was similarly concerned about innocent union members and the union's ability to represent them effectively. Should we be equally concerned about corporate shareholders? Or should they suffer the risks of investing in a badly run company? What about other customers? They can shop elsewhere, but if a whole industry is subjected to punitive damage awards, prices might rise generally. But if deterrence works, higher prices will buy safer products.

NOTES ON THE MEASURE OF PUNITIVE DAMAGES

1. What should we tell juries about how to measure punitive damages? And what criteria should judges apply in reviewing verdicts? *Grimshaw* mentions most of the criteria in common use. Defendant's wealth, the amount of compensatory damages, and the degree of reprehensibility of defendant's conduct are probably the most often cited. None of these is a measure; they are at most factors to be considered. Some of them provide real guidance; some provide little; all leave a vast range of largely unprincipled discretion. It is easy to agree that punitive damages should be higher if conduct is more reprehensible. But it is impossible to agree on a scale; should juries think in hundreds, thousands, or millions?

2. If the jury is to figure out how large an award is necessary to punish and deter the defendant, it surely must know something of his wealth. Judgments that would bankrupt the average citizen many times over would have no effect on Ford. Presumably the verdict should be high enough that the defendant feels it. But is that point reached at 10 percent, 1 percent, or .1 percent of net worth?

Admitting evidence of defendant's wealth is surely prejudicial; we would not allow it in any other context. This dilemma is the strongest argument for bifurcated trials, and some states do have separate punitive damages hearings for this reason.

3. Which way does the amount of compensatory damages cut? Courts often say that punitive damages must be in a reasonable ratio to compensatory damages. The suggestion is that the smaller the compensatories, the smaller the punitives. Does that make any sense? If part of the

rationale for punitives is to deter wrongful conduct that does little measurable harm, and to express and channel outrage at such conduct, aren't small compensatories an argument for larger punitives? In a footnote to the part of the opinion dealing with the Grays' claim for punitive damages in wrongful death, not printed above, the *Grimshaw* court said it agreed with commentators who would eliminate any attention to the ratio between punitive and compensatory damages. 119 Cal. App. 3d at 836 n.30, 174 Cal. Rptr. at 399 n.30. Those commentators would ask whether the compensatories actually awarded were large or small in relation to the injury. Mallor & Roberts, Punitive Damages: Towards a Principled Approach, 31 Hastings L.J. 639, 667-669 (1980).

4. Another rule enforced in many states is that there can be no punitive damages without at least some compensatory damages. Some jurisdictions recognize an exception where compensatory damages are averted by equitable relief. For example, in Fillion v. Troy, 656 S.W.2d 912 (Tex. App. 1983), a twenty-two-year-old woman retained a forty-two-year-old lawyer to expedite the distribution of property from her deceased father's estate. They became sexually involved, and before their relationship ended, she had given him three tracts of real estate worth $95,000, seventeen oil paintings, and substantial sums of cash. The court could not identify any legal services he had performed. She sued to rescind all the transactions for fraud, undue influence, and violation of fiduciary duty. She recovered everything via rescission, no compensatory damages, and $90,000 in punitive damages. Whatever the rationale for denying punitives in the absence of compensatories, it hardly seems to apply to a case like that.

West Virginia recently abandoned the rule altogether. It allows juries to award punitives without awarding compensatories, "provided there is evidence showing an injury to the plaintiff caused by the egregious and tortious conduct of the defendant." Wells v. Smith, 297 S.E.2d 872, 880 (W. Va. 1982). The case involved a successful conspiracy to steal jewelry; the jury awarded compensatory damages against the most active conspirators and punitive damages against them all.

What if there is no injury because plaintiff averts the impact of defendant's outrageous conduct? Should all Pinto owners be able to sue Ford for punitive damages, even though they weren't hurt? Didn't Ford consciously disregard their safety just as much as it disregarded Grimshaw's? An affirmative answer would greatly aggravate the multiple plaintiff problem, and that makes it easy to limit recovery to those actually injured. But suppose the jewel thieves were apprehended breaking into the safe, before they touched a single jewel. There is only one potential plaintiff, and the thieves specifically intended to harm him. Should he be able to recover punitive damages? Or should criminal prosecution be the exclusive remedy? The West Virginia court was concerned that plaintiffs have a remedy that did not depend on possibly "underzealous" prosecutors, but the rule it formulated required an actual injury.

5.   Another factor appearing in some lists is the profitability of the conduct. If one of the reasons for punitive damages is to keep Ford from deciding it is more profitable to pay for accidents than to prevent them, then the jury needs to know how much Ford saved by not building a safer fuel tank. There was evidence in *Grimshaw* that Ford saved $125 million, and that was how much the jury awarded. The court endorsed "profitability of the conduct" as a factor, but it approved the remittitur of all but $3.5 million. Is that because there will be other victims and other punitive damage awards? Would $125 million be the right amount if there were only one victim, or if there were one class action for punitive damages? For another case in which a jury awarded punitive damages based on defendant's savings and the court ordered most of the award remitted, see the Notes on Restitution of Money Not Spent on Safety, supra at 496.

6.   Ford wanted to compare the punitive damage award to criminal and regulatory fines for the same conduct. Was the court right to reject those comparisons as irrelevant? Should juries and judges impose penalties many times greater than those authorized by legislators? Is that a threat to liberty, or to democracy? Or is it sufficient that the legislature could ban or limit punitive damages at any time but chooses not to, that judges are also chosen through the political process, and that jurors are representatives of the people?

Recall the rule that courts will enjoin crime if the criminal penalty is insufficient to deter; that makes the legal remedy inadequate. City of Chicago v. Festival Theatre Corp., supra at 354. The same basic view appears in *Grimshaw*: Punitive damages are needed because other penalties are inadequate to deter. Courts want to stamp out all violations; they implicitly reject the economic view that the optimal level of violations is greater than zero.

NOTE ON PUNITIVE DAMAGES IN WRONGFUL DEATH CASES

Grimshaw also contains a lengthy discussion of punitive damages in death cases. Mrs. Gray was killed, and her heirs cross-appealed from the judgment denying punitive damages in their wrongful death claim. The traditional rule has been that punitive damages are not recoverable for wrongful death, because the claim is statutory and the statute does not authorize punitive damages. That rule has been abandoned in some jurisdictions.

In California and many other states, the heirs cannot recover punitive damages in a wrongful death suit, but the decedent's personal representative can recover punitive damages in a suit for the decedent's pre-death damages. The personal representative is the executor or administrator of the estate; he has no cause of action unless the decedent survived at least briefly after his injury.

Grimshaw reviewed the California authorities and concluded that this strange distinction is indeed the law there. The Grays challenged the distinction on state and federal equal protection grounds. The court found the distinction "difficult to explain on the basis of any conceivable, realistic, rational legislative purpose." However, it found it unnecessary to decide the equal protection claims, because the Grays were not within the group disadvantaged by the statute. Mrs. Gray survived for three days after her accident in the Pinto, but only the heirs' wrongful death claim was presented in this case. The court held that denying punitive damages to heirs when such damages could be recovered by the personal representative was a rational means to avoid double punitive damages.

In the actual case, it is not clear whether the personal representative sued separately, or whether the Grays' attorney bungled the case. Perhaps the heirs and the personal representative were feuding. But more likely, the whole family came to one attorney, and he didn't arrange to have a personal representative appointed or have that representative file a survivor claim. That would seem to be open and shut malpractice, and the award to Grimshaw makes it easy to measure damages. Would they sue him for $3.5 million after he recovered $560,000 for them? Maybe so; don't take a chance.

BRINK'S INC. v. CITY OF NEW YORK
717 F.2d 700 (2d Cir. 1983)

Before OAKES, CARDAMONE and WINTER, Circuit Judges.

OAKES, Circuit Judge.

The City of New York contracted out the collection of its parking meter revenues to Brink's Inc., the well-known national armored car carrier. Under the March 1978 contract, armed, uniformed Brink's personnel were to collect coins from parking meters throughout the City, deposit them into canisters sealed and locked by the City, and return the canisters to the City's parking meter division (PMD) at 42 Franklin Street in Manhattan. On April 9, 1980, seven Brink's collectors were arrested, five of whom were charged with and convicted of stealing parking meter revenues. The City suspended and ultimately cancelled the Brink's contract. On December 5, 1980, Brink's sued the City for money owed under the contract and the City counterclaimed charging breach of contract and negligence based upon lack of due care in hiring, failure to supervise and failure to investigate the parking meter collectors. Brink's served a third-party complaint on the seven employees above mentioned as well as five other employees and their supervisor, William J. Donovan.

The case was tried before a jury in the United States District Court for the Southern District of New York, Edward Weinfeld, Judge. Brink's had preliminarily moved to prevent the City from questioning any Brink's employees about matters with respect to which they could assert their privilege against self-incrimination, but Judge Weinfeld denied the motion. The jury, in a special verdict, found that the City had sustained its claim against Brink's for breach of contract and for negligence in failing to supervise and to investigate, but found for Brink's on the charge of negligence based upon lack of due care in hiring. The jury awarded the City $1 million compensatory and $5 million punitive damages. On the third-party complaint of Brink's Inc. against the individual collectors, ten of them were found severally liable in the amount of $5,000 each. . . .

Judge Weinfeld denied the Brink's motions for a directed verdict on the compensatory and punitive damage claims, for judgment notwithstanding the verdict as to both damage awards, and for a new trial on the ground that the awards were grossly excessive. He did, however, allow a remittitur, to which the City subsequently agreed, of the $5 million punitive damage award to $1.5 million. . . .

Facts

The City of New York owns and operates approximately 70,000 parking meters, mostly on-street, but some in metered parking lots. Daily collections average nearly $50,000. After public bidding in March of 1978, Brink's was awarded the contract to collect coins from these meters and deliver them to the New York City Department of Finance Depository. . . . Brink's was to provide ten three-person collection crews daily, the crews to be rotated in the discretion of the City Department of Finance as a security measure. The City directed that the rotation should be accomplished by a lottery system to prevent the formation of permanent teams, but the City's evidence was that the rotation system was ignored. Daily assignments were frequently made by the collectors themselves and the management of Brink's was aware of this but did nothing to correct it. . . . The contract also provided that Brink's would provide supervisory personnel to oversee the proper performance of its obligations. Although the contract called for two supervisors and one field inspector, the full complement was never assigned.

In response to an anonymous tip, the City's Department of Investigation, in conjunction with the Inspector General's Office of the Department of Finance, began an investigation of parking meter collections. Surveillance of Brink's collectors revealed suspicious activity violative of both the City's and Brink's rules and procedures. The investigators then "salted" parking meters by treating coins with a fluorescent substance and inserting them into specific meters. . . . The "salting" process indicated that a substantial percentage of coins collected by Brink's personnel were not being returned to the City. Surveillance at the 42 Franklin Street depository revealed that at the end of a day Brink's employees would often arrive in personal vehicles following their assigned collection vans, indicating some kind of "drop-off." Brink's employees were also seen entering a parking lot in Manhattan in Brink's vans, removing bags from the vans, placing them in private automobiles and then returning to the vans to continue to the City depository. The City presented video tapes of these transfers at trial; Brink's collectors were shown straining to lift heavy bags into their cars. Brink's employees were also followed to a private residence and again observed carrying heavy bags from their vehicles into the building and emerging empty handed.

James Gargiulo, Trevor Fairweather, Richard Florio, Michael Solomon and John Adams were arrested and charged with grand larceny and criminal possession of stolen property when on April 9 they had in their possession over $4,500 in coins stolen *that day* from parking meter collections. . . .

Discussion

Brink's maintains that its motion for judgment n.o.v. on the punitive damages award should have been granted because, first, the City's claim was essentially one for breach of contract, a claim for which punitive damages are unavailable under New York law and, second, the evidence demonstrated only ordinary negligence and was therefore insufficient to support an award of punitive damages. Brink's also offers several reasons why a new trial should have been granted. At the most general level, Brink's argues that the jury's verdict against it was "excessive" and a result of "passion and prejudice." Brink's contends that the passion and prejudice was a direct result of the introduction of evidence as to its wealth and that of its corporate parent, the City's insistence on calling certain former Brink's employees that the City knew would refuse to testify on Fifth Amendment grounds, and expert testimony as to the City's losses that was so misleading as to be inadmissible. . . .

A. Punitive Damages

In Garrity v. Lyle Stuart, Inc., 40 N.Y.2d 354, 358, 353 N.E.2d 793, 795 (1976), the New York Court of Appeals noted: "It has always been held that punitive damages are not available for mere breach of contract, for in such a case only a private wrong, and not a public right, is involved." This is true even if the breach results from a deliberate breach of good faith. Brink's argument on appeal is based primarily on a sentence drawn from the district court's opinion to the effect that "[c]onceptually, the central core of the City's claims derives from a contract." But we agree with the district court that, "in addition to its claim for negligent breach of contract, the City asserted a separate and independent cause of action for common law negligence." Thus, although the "two claims were interlaced with one another and essentially rested upon the same conduct," New York law does not preclude the award of punitive damages where conduct that gives rise to a contract action is also tortious. The City's theory of the case — that Brink's was negligent in failing to exercise reasonable care in hiring and supervising its employees, some of whom it knew or should have known were stealing — is certainly not a novel negligence claim.

Brink's nevertheless argues that the City has simply sued in tort where the underlying duty breached was contractual. It refers to our own Contemporary Mission, Inc. v. Bonded Mailings, Inc., 671 F.2d 81, 85 (2d Cir. 1982), where the court stated that "[i]f the only interest involved, however, is holding a party to a promise, a plaintiff will not be permitted to transform the contract claim into one for tort." In neither *Contemporary Mission* or another case cited by Brink's, Koufakis v. Carvel, 425 F.2d 892 (2d Cir. 1970), however, did the defendant commit any tort. Here, the jury found that the City proved common law negligence by one contracting party causing injury to the other. Cf. Hargrave v. Oki Nursery, Inc., 636 F.2d 897, 899 (2d Cir. 1980) (fraud inducing a contract creates legal relations separate and distinct from those arising under the contract and constitutes a separate tort). A tort by a defaulting promisor is no less a tort. . . .

Turning to the question of evidentiary support for the award of punitive damages, the test, as we stated in Doralee Estates, Inc. v. Cities Service Oil Co., 569 F.2d 716, 722 (2d Cir. 1977), is whether "the continuing tortious conduct has been brought home to the consciousness of relatively important managerial personnel with authority to make a decision for the corporation that would have prevented the damage." Our review of the evidence bearing on Brink's handling of various incidents implicating security concerns during the course of the contract leaves us with little doubt that the evidence was more than sufficient to support the award under *Doralee Estates*. Indeed, the evidence — some of which we summarize below — indicates not only that "relatively important managerial personnel" had reason to suspect specific employees of theft but also that these officials did not even follow what their own testimony indicated was established Brink's procedure for dealing with security or rules violations, procedures that might well "have prevented the damage" suffered here. . . . For example, Edward Lenehan, vice president of Brink's security division, . . . testified that he did not view the theft of a coin box as a security incident, although such a minor theft would constitute a security incident if it occurred in connection with armored truck operations. Lenehan's surveillance of one collector uncovered that the driver returned three times to his residence during the course of one shift in a Brink's collection van, but Lenehan did not have his notes typed or a report prepared until some nine months later. The collector was never questioned. And after receiving a report from a "confidential source" that another collector was stealing coins, Lenehan ordered surveillance — but the operation lasted only four days and the collector was never observed during the critical period between the last meter collection and arrival at the PMD. Under the basic test set forth in *Doralee Estates*, we think the evidence was sufficient to take the matter of punitive damages to the jury.[4]

B. Motion for a New Trial

1. Evidence of Brink's and Its Corporate Parent's Assets

Under New York law evidence of a defendant's wealth is admissible on the issue of the amount of punitive damages. Rupert v. Sellers, 48 A.D.2d 265, 268-73, 368 N.Y.S.2d 904, 909-13 (App. Div. 1975). *Rupert*, however, alludes to privacy considerations on the one hand, and the ease with which a plausible claim for punitive damage may be made on the other, in pointing out that a rule permitting unlimited examination before trial of a defendant as to his wealth "could have unfortunate results" in terms of exerting pressure to compromise. 48 A.D.2d at 271, 368 N.Y.S.2d at 911. The *Rupert* court therefore prudently adopted the New Jersey rule that, as a "procedural principle," evidence of a defendant's wealth cannot be brought out at trial unless and until the jury has brought in a special verdict that the plaintiff is entitled to punitive damages. Id. at 272, 368 N.Y.S.2d at 912. But Brink's never suggested to the trial court that the *Rupert* practice should be followed; its argument on appeal therefore amounts to a claim that the trial court should have sua sponte ordered a bifurcated trial. Brink's had ample notice from the time the City filed its counterclaim that punitive damages were sought, but bifurcation was never requested. . . . [W]here the issue is not raised below, it will not be considered on appeal.[5] . . .

---

4. The jury was instructed that it had to find by "clear and convincing evidence" that Brink's conduct amounted to gross negligence tantamount to "willful, wanton and reckless" conduct. On the basis of the evidence summarized above, we cannot say either that there was a complete absence of probative evidence to support the verdict or that no reasonable and fair-minded jury could arrive at this verdict.

5. Brink's also complains that evidence of the wealth of its corporate parent, the Pittston Company, was improperly received and referred to in summation, but this point was also not preserved. Herman v. Hess Oil Virgin Islands Corp., 524 F.2d 767, 772 (3d Cir. 1975). We therefore need not reach the question whether annual reports reflecting the income of a parent corporation are admissible for the purpose of assessing punitive damages against a subsidiary. See Mihara v. Dean Witter & Co., 619 F.2d 814, 824 (9th Cir. 1980) (annual reports of parent clearly relevant); Palmer Coal & Rock Co. v. Gulf Oil Co.-U.S., 524 F.2d 884, 887 (10th Cir. 1975), *cert. denied*, 424 U.S. 969 (1976).

[Brink's offered two other grounds for a new trial. First, New York should not have been allowed to call the accused employees as witnesses, forcing them to claim the privilege against self-incrimination in front of the jury. Second, New York's expert testimony on compensatory damages was so speculative that it should not have been admitted. The court rejected both grounds. Judge Winter dissented on the self-incrimination issue. The argument about compensatory damages is summarized supra at 177-178.]

4. *Excessiveness of the Verdict*

Brink's argues that as a result of being

[e]xposed to evidence of massive wealth . . . presented with a stream of witnesses called by the City for the sole purpose of asserting their Fifth Amendment privilege, and misled by expert testimony having the appearance of precision . . . the jury arrived at a verdict awarding excessive compensatory and punitive damages. In this context, the jury's verdict could not have failed to be the result of passion and prejudice.

Our discussion and rejection, supra, of each of these arguments undercuts the contention that the jury's verdict was in any way "tainted." Nevertheless, Brink's argues that the jury's passion and prejudice is demonstrated by the large disparity between the $1 million compensatory verdict awarded the City and the $50,000 verdict awarded Brink's against its former employees.

We note at the outset that there is no legal requirement that the verdicts here be comparable. That the jury did not award as much as it might have against the former employees does not establish that the verdict against Brink's was not "based upon the evidence and the law." Malm v. United States Lines Co., 269 F. Supp. 731, 731-32 (S.D.N.Y.), *aff'd per curiam*, 378 F.2d 941 (2d Cir. 1967). Contrary to Brink's argument, we see no reason why the jury could not infer that there were collectors other than those sued by Brink's that were involved in the thefts. Certainly it was not the City's obligation to establish or negate that possibility. The City's success in its action against Brink's is independent of Brink's success in its suit against its former employees. The cases cited by Brink's involving joint tortfeasors are therefore inapplicable.

Nor are we persuaded that Judge Weinfeld erred in granting remittitur rather than a new trial. In essence, Brink's argument is that if remittitur was appropriate, a new trial should have been granted. We agree with Judge Weinfeld's conclusion that retrial of a case that had "extended over a period of almost four weeks with a record of more than 3,000 pages" would have been unwise, and that the "interests of the parties and justice" were best served by remittitur. We decline to second-guess either this conclusion or his determination that the punitive damages should be reduced to $1.5 million. . . .

Judgments affirmed.

NOTES ON PUNITIVE DAMAGES FOR BREACH OF CONTRACT

1.   It is still the general rule that punitive damages cannot be awarded for breach of contract. But the rule is badly eroded. *Brink's* illustrates the main exception: If an independent tort is committed in a contractual setting, punitive damages can be awarded for the tort. Many breaches of contract involve negligence or fraud, or can be characterized as such. Some jurisdictions recognize a tort of outrage, and some egregious breaches of contract can be fit into that. The most dramatic end run around the rule is the tort of bad faith. The Supreme Court of Alabama defined the tort as follows:

> Every contract contains an implied in law covenant of good faith and fair dealing; this covenant provides that neither party will interfere with the rights of the other to receive the benefits of the agreement. Breach of the covenant provides the injured party with a tort action for "bad faith" notwithstanding that the acts complained of may also constitute a breach of contract.

Childs v. Mississippi Valley Title Insurance Co., 359 So. 2d 1146, 1152 (Ala. 1978).

2.   One technique for transforming breach of contract into fraud is to find that defendant always intended to breach, and that it was fraudulent to induce plaintiff to sign the contract in reliance on the implied representation that defendant intended to perform. A good example of that technique is W-V Enterprises v. Federal Savings & Loan Insurance Corp., 234 Kan. 354, 673 P.2d 1112 (1983). The FSLIC was in the case as receiver of the original defendant, an insolvent savings and loan. The savings and loan had breached a commitment to loan $330,000 to the plaintiffs, inflicting over a million dollars in consequential damages. The jury also found fraud and awarded $250,000 in punitive damages. The court affirmed.

3.   Some jurisdictions have abandoned the independent tort requirement:

> The requirement that an *independent* tort be found serves several purposes. First, it maintains the symmetry of the general rule of not allowing punitive damages in contract actions, because the punitive damages are awarded for the *tort*, not on the contract. Secondly, the independent tort requirement facilitates judicial review of the evidence by limiting the scope of review to a search for the elements of the tort. Neither of these functions of the independence requirement is very compelling when it appears from the evidence as a whole that a serious wrong, tortious in nature, has been committed, but the

wrong does not conveniently fit the confines of a pre-determined tort. The foregoing circumstances alone, however, will not sustain the award of punitive damages. *It must also appear that the public interest will be served by the deterrent effect punitive damages will have upon future conduct of the wrong-doer and parties similarly situated.* Only when these factors coalesce, will the independent tort requirement be abrogated, and the allowance of punitive damages be sustained.

Vernon Fire & Casualty Insurance Co. v. Sharp, 264 Ind. 599, 608-609, 349 N.E.2d 173, 180 (1976).

In *Vernon*, the insured and insurer disagreed about the scope of coverage. The insurer refused to pay the sum it admitted was due until that dispute and another dispute with an associate of the insured were resolved on the insurer's terms. The Indiana court subsequently characterized the insurer's conduct as "'intentional and wanton,' 'oppressive,' and in no way 'privileged' and 'motivated by self interest,' i.e., to extract from Sharp a consideration to which it was not entitled." Travelers Indemnity Co. v. Armstrong, 442 N.E.2d 349, 358 (Ind. 1982), quoting scattered phrases from *Vernon*.

4. *Vernon* was the first Indiana case to award punitive damages without an independent tort. Experience with that rule led the Indiana court to adopt a clear and convincing evidence standard for all punitive damage cases in *Travelers*:

> The propriety of the clear and convincing evidence standard is particularly evident in contract cases, because the breach itself for whatever reason, will almost invariably be regarded by the complaining party as oppressive, if not outright fraudulent. . . .
>
> A rule that would permit an award of punitive damages upon inferences permissibly drawn from evidence of no greater persuasive value than that required to uphold a finding of the breach of contract — which may be nothing more than a refusal to pay the amount demanded and subsequently found to be owing — injects such risks into refusing and defending against questionable claims as to render them, in essence, nondisputable. The public interest cannot be served by any policy that deters resort to the courts for the determination of bona fide commercial disputes. "The infliction of this damage has generally been regarded as privileged, and not compensable, for the simple reason that it is worth more to society than it costs, i.e., the insurer is permitted to dispute its liability in good faith because of the prohibitive social costs of a rule which would make claims nondisputable." Vernon Fire v. Sharp, 264 Ind. 609, 610, 349 N.E.2d 173.

442 N.E.2d at 363.

Recall the concern that even consequential damages for failure to pay money would deter reasonable opposition to claims. Notes on Consequential Damages for Failure to Pay Money, supra at 131 note 9. Certainly the deterrent effect of punitive damages would be much greater. A bad faith requirement would be extraordinary for consequential damages, but it is built into the standard for punitive damages. The clear and convincing evidence requirement beefs up the bad faith requirement and increases judicial control over juries.

5. Many of the cases in these notes involved insurers charged with bad faith refusal to pay claims. This is undoubtedly the largest single category of cases awarding punitive damages for breach of contract. But many other kinds of contracts have been affected too. Brink's is an example; the contract to loan money in note 2 is another.

B. OTHER PUNITIVE REMEDIES

1. Statutory Recoveries by Private Litigants

Common law punitive damages are the best known punitive remedy, and perhaps the most important. But many statutes provide punitive remedies. The best known of these is the treble damage provision of the antitrust laws: Antitrust plaintiffs recover three times their compensatory damages. 15 U.S.C. §15(a) (1982). Many statutes provide for double recovery, either in all cases or in cases of "willful" violations. A good example is the Fair Labor Standards Act. 29 U.S.C. §216(b) (1982).

Other statutes provide for recovery based on a formula, instead of or in addition to compensatory damages. This approach is often used in consumer protection statutes, where there is little at stake in any one transaction and any one violation does little damage. The formula encourages enforcement by creating a minimum recovery that is worth suing for. Indeed, one may argue that these recoveries are not really punitive because they are essential to compensation. In many of these cases, pure compensatory damages would never be collected because the costs of litigation would exceed the recovery. Many of these statutes also authorize recovery of plaintiff's attorneys' fees. Some examples:

- Section 9-507 of the Uniform Commercial Code provides that if a secured party violates any of the rules governing repossession and sale of consumer collateral, the debtor may recover actual damages or all the interest plus ten percent of the principal sum of the transaction.
- Some state usury laws provide Draconian penalties, including forfeiture of all principal and interest to the debtor. See, e.g., Tex. Rev. Civ. Stat. Ann. art. 5069-1.06(2) (Vernon 1971).
- The Truth in Lending Act authorizes recovery of actual damages, plus twice the finance charge, but the recovery based on twice the finance charge cannot be less than $100 nor more than $1,000. 15 U.S.C. §1640(a) (1982).

The advantage of statutory penalties over punitive damages is that they replace a jury's largely unguided discretion with a fixed standard. They ensure that all plaintiffs and all defendants are treated equally. In theory, they can avoid shockingly large or small verdicts, but that is not as easy to do as it first appears. Inevitably there are cases in which the statutory recovery seems inappropriate. Not all antitrust violations are equally reprehensible, or equally difficult to prove; treble damages are more appropriate in some cases than in others. The formula in UCC §9-507 is useless in very small transactions; on a $100 pawnshop loan at 18 percent, payable in three months, the statutory recovery would be $14.50. But on a ten-year mobile home loan of $15,000 at 12 percent, the statutory recovery would be $12,325.20. And this is to be imposed without discretion for any violation, whether egregious or technical.

Griffin v. Oceanic Contractors, 458 U.S. 564 (1982), is an especially dramatic example. 46 U.S.C. §596 (1982) provides that every ship master or owner who fails to pay wages to a seaman without sufficient cause "shall pay to the seaman a sum equal to two days' pay for each and every day during which payment is delayed." On April 1, 1976, Oceanic withheld $412.50 of Griffin's wages, the cost of flying him home from the North Sea. Oceanic was obligated to fly him home at its own expense. Griffin sued, joining his claim for wages with his claim for personal injuries suffered on the job. He eventually won; Oceanic paid the judgment on September 17, 1980. Griffin earned $101.20 per day. Twice his pay for four and a half years came out to $329,912. The lower courts limited the penalty period to the month Griffin was unable to work, but the Supreme Court reversed and ordered the statute enforced as written.

Careful drafting can increase the fit between the statutory formula and the facts of individual cases. But it requires more care than legislatures are usually able to give, and it forfeits much of the certainty that is the supposed advantage of statutory penalty formulas. Consider the history of Truth in Lending penalties. The Truth in Lending formula produced huge liabilities in class actions, because a form with a defective disclosure would be used in thousands of transactions. Congress twice amended the statute to provide special rules for class actions. The penalty in individual actions is still twice the finance charge, but not less than $100 nor more than $1000. In class actions, the statute authorizes the following penalty:

> such amount as the court may allow, except that as to each member of the class no minimum recovery shall be applicable, and the total recovery under this subparagraph in any class action or series of class actions arising out of the same failure to comply by the same creditor shall not be more than the lesser of $500,000 or 1 per centum of the net worth of the creditor.

15 U.S.C. §1640(a)(2)(B) (1982). Then the statute attempts to guide the courts' discretion:

In determining the amount of award in any class action, the court shall consider, among other relevant factors, the amount of any actual damages awarded, the frequency and persistence of failures of compliance by the creditor, the resources of the creditor, the number of persons adversely affected, and the extent to which the creditor's failure of compliance was intentional.

Id.

How different is this from common law punitive damages? There is a cap on recovery and a lower substantive threshold. But between zero and the statutory limit, is the court's discretion any more guided than at common law?

2. Civil Penalties Payable to the Government

In a wide range of situations, government imposes civil penalties for violations of law. In 1979 Professor Diver found 348 statutory civil penalties enforced by twenty-seven federal departments and administrative agencies. Diver, The Assessment and Mitigation of Civil Money Penalties by Federal Administrative Agencies, 79 Colum. L. Rev. 1435, 1438 (1979). He apparently counted only civil fines; many other statutes provide for civil forfeiture of property somehow connected with a crime. Civil penalties are often administratively imposed, subject to judicial review in an ordinary civil proceeding. That procedure is much cheaper and easier for the government than criminal penalties; it is even easier than injunctions and contempt citations.

These penalties clash with the formal doctrine that government cannot punish without the protections of criminal procedure. Civil penalties are unconstitutional if they are "punitive"; they are valid if "remedial." The usage is at least Pickwickian, if not Orwellian.

Some examples: A penalty for tax fraud equal to 50 percent of the tax due is remedial and not punitive. Helvering v. Mitchell, 303 U.S. 391 (1938). A penalty for welfare fraud equal to the amount of aid illegally received, assessed in addition to the obligation to refund the aid, is remedial and not punitive. State v. Greenlee, 61 Ill. App. 3d 649, 378 N.E.2d 579 (1978). A $500 fine for discharging oil into navigable waters is remedial and not punitive. United States v. Ward, 448 U.S. 242 (1980). *Grimshaw* refers to the penalty for violating federal auto safety regulations — $1,000 a car up to a maximum of $800,000 for any related series of violations. 15 U.S.C. §1398 (1982). Congress calls that a civil penalty, so it too must be remedial and not punitive. Unlicensed firearms dealers must forfeit their inventory to the government; this forfeiture is remedial and not punitive. United States v. One Assortment of 89 Firearms, 104 S. Ct. 1099 (1984). Persons caught smuggling goods into the United States forfeit the goods to the government; that forfeiture is remedial and not punitive. One Lot Emerald Cut Stones v. United States, 409 U.S. 232 (1972). The Court solemnly declares that none of these penalties are intended to punish.

But there are some limits. There are no cases allowing imprisonment as a civil penalty. Kennedy v. Mendoza-Martinez, 372 U.S. 144 (1963), refused to allow forfeiture of citizenship as a civil penalty. *Kennedy* lists seven factors for distinguishing civil from criminal penalties, but the factors are amorphous and the Court has said that they are "neither exhaustive nor dispositive," United States v. Ward, 448 U.S. 242, 249 (1980). When a legislature calls a penalty civil, it takes a very clear case for the Court to call it criminal. Civil fines are generally upheld on the ground that they are like liquidated damages for the harm of the violation or the cost of law enforcement. The Court said that forfeiture of firearms was remedial because it kept firearms out of the hands of unlicensed dealers. United States v. One Assortment of 89 Firearms, 104 S. Ct. 1099, 1106 (1984).

Occasionally, the Court has the opposite reaction. Thus, it invalidated civil forfeiture of money used in gambling operations:

> From the relevant constitutional standpoint there is no difference between a man who "forfeits" $8,674 because he has used the money in illegal gambling activities and a man who pays a "criminal fine" of $8,674 as a result of the same course of conduct. In both instances, money liability is predicated upon a finding of the owner's wrongful conduct; in both cases, the Fifth Amendment applies with equal force.

United States v. United States Coin and Currency, 401 U.S. 715, 718 (1971).

Aren't all civil penalties criminal on that reasoning? *Coin and Currency* is not the only case to take that position, but such cases are a minority at least recently. Can *Coin and Currency* be reconciled with the rest of the decisions in this area? In *One Lot Emerald Cut Stones*, the later case upholding civil forfeiture of smuggled goods, the Court distinguished *Coin and Currency* on the ground that gambling money was only forfeit if the government proved a criminal violation. Goods not reported at customs are forfeit for any violation of custom regulations, whether or not the government proves the elements of an offense Congress has labeled criminal. The lesson of *One Lot Emerald Cut Stones* seems to be that if a legislature wants to avoid criminal procedure, it should label the offense civil as well as the penalty. But in other cases it has been enough that Congress provided civil and criminal penalties for the same offense in separate sections of the statute. In the most recent case, *89 Firearms*, the Court cited *One Lot Emerald Cut Stones* heavily and didn't mention *Coin and Currency*.

Classifying a penalty as a criminal penalty or a civil remedy need not be an all-or-nothing proposition. Occasionally, the Court says a penalty is sufficiently punitive to trigger the privilege against self-incrimination, but not sufficiently punitive to trigger other protections, such as the right to counsel, proof beyond a reasonable doubt, or protection from double jeopardy.

The Court has to keep taking these cases because it adheres to the fiction that it will not allow punishment without criminal procedure. It would be more honest to say that criminal procedure is required in all these cases, or that monetary punishments can be imposed civilly. The first alternative would seriously hamper the regulatory process; the second would require the Court to develop a theory that distinguishes civil from criminal punishment.

CHAPTER 8

Enforcing the Judgment:
Ancillary Remedies

Ancillary remedies help implement some other remedy. The line between an ancillary remedy and a procedural practice is indistinct. Some everyday aspects of modern procedure started out as separate remedies requiring an ancillary action; discovery is the best known example. Other examples of remedies cum procedural devices are the equitable devices for avoiding multiple litigation, briefly discussed supra at 346-347. Another example is derivative suits, illustrated in Ross v. Bernhard, infra at 1260. Preliminary injunctions and other interlocutory remedies are often thought of as ancillary to the permanent remedy. All of these remedies are more conveniently discussed elsewhere. This chapter incidentally examines the ancillary remedy of accounting, but it is mainly about the means of enforcing judgments.

The reason that a course in remedies is necessary is that litigation does not end with the liability determination. Neither does it end with the award of a remedy. A wealthy defendant with liquid assets may write a check for the judgment, but many defendants are unable or unwilling to pay. A cooperative defendant may immediately set about fully complying with an injunction, but many are recalcitrant. One of my colleagues is fond of saying that a money judgment is nothing but a handsome piece of paper suitable for framing. He could say the same thing about an injunction. But he would be exaggerating. Judgments come in ordinary typescript on ordinary paper; they are not even suitable for framing. A judgment is an important step toward what plaintiff wants, but it is not what he wants. The judgment still must be enforced.

A. ENFORCING COERCIVE ORDERS: THE CONTEMPT POWER

UNITED STATES v. UNITED MINE WORKERS
330 U.S. 258 (1947)

[In May of 1946 the United States took over most of the nation's bituminous coal mines in order to maintain production that had been disrupted by labor strife. Secretary of the Interior Krug, and John L. Lewis, president of the United Mine Workers, entered into a supplemental labor agreement "for the period of Government possession." The Krug-Lewis agreement gave the miners important new benefits and otherwise incorporated the existing collective bargaining agreement.

The original collective bargaining agreement allowed either side to terminate the contract at any time after a fifteen-day period of bargaining. The Mine Workers invoked that clause in October; the government responded that the Krug-Lewis agreement pre-empted that clause. On November 15, Lewis wrote Krug that the contract was terminated as of midnight on November 20. Lewis circulated that letter to the union membership for their "official information." The union had a long-standing policy of "no contract, no work"; terminating the contract was equivalent to calling a strike.

The United States sued Lewis and the union on November 18. The government sought a declaratory judgment that the contract could not be unilaterally terminated and a temporary restraining order and preliminary injunction ordering Lewis and the union to recall the November 15 notice and refrain from encouraging the miners to strike. The court issued the TRO immediately and without notice to defendants. The order and complaint were served later that day. Some miners began striking on November 18, and by midnight of November 20 the entire union was on strike.

The government promptly filed a contempt citation, and a hearing was set for November 27. Defendants responded that they had ignored the TRO because the Norris-LaGuardia Act says that federal courts have no jurisdiction to enjoin strikes. 29 U.S.C. §§101 et seq. (1982). The court extended the TRO for another ten days, set the jurisdictional motion for full argument, and set the contempt citation for trial. It subsequently rejected the jurisdictional argument. It found both Lewis and the union guilty beyond a reasonable doubt of both civil and criminal contempt. The court entered judgment on December 4, fining Lewis $10,000 and the union $3.5 million. The same day it issued a preliminary injunction in the same terms as the TRO.

Lewis and the union appealed the contempt judgments the next day. On December 7, Lewis ordered the miners to return to work until March

31, 1947. He did not withdraw the November 15 notice terminating the contract.

The Supreme Court granted certiorari before judgment in the Court of Appeals, and decided the case on March 6. Five justices held that the Norris-LaGuardia Act does not apply when the United States is the employer. A different set of five justices held in the alternative that the trial court had power to issue a temporary restraining order while it considered whether the Act applied, and that defendants could be punished for violating an injunction even if it turned out to have been erroneously issued. Two justices found it unnecessary to decide this issue. We will consider this part of the case in connection with Walker v. City of Birmingham, infra at 656. Every opinion discussed at least one of these issues; the separate opinions of Justices Frankfurter, Jackson, and Murphy discussed only these issues. All these discussions are omitted.]

MR. CHIEF JUSTICE VINSON delivered the opinion of the Court. . . .

III

The defendants have pressed upon us the procedural aspects of their trial and allege error so prejudicial as to require reversal of the judgments for civil and criminal contempt. But we have not been persuaded.

The question is whether the proceedings will support judgments for both criminal and civil contempt; and our attention is directed to Rule 42(b) of the Rules of Criminal Procedure. The rule requires criminal contempt to be prosecuted on notice stating the essential facts constituting the contempt charged. In this respect, there was compliance with the rule here. . . .

However, Rule 42(b) requires that the notice issuing to the defendants describe the criminal contempt charged as such. The defendants urge a failure to comply with this rule. The petition alleged a willful violation of the restraining order, and both the petition and the rule to show cause inquired as to why the defendants should not be "punished as and for a contempt" of court. But nowhere was the contempt described as criminal as required by the rule.

Nevertheless, the defendants were quite aware that a criminal contempt was charged. In their motion to discharge and vacate the rule to show cause, the contempt charged was referred to as criminal. And in argument on the motion the defendants stated and were expressly informed that a criminal contempt was to be tried. Yet it is now urged that the omission of the words "criminal contempt" from the petition and rule to show cause was prejudicial error. Rule 42(b) requires no such rigorous application, for it was designed to insure a realization by contemnors that a prosecution for criminal contempt is contemplated. Its purpose was sufficiently fulfilled here, for this failure to observe the rule in all respects has not resulted in substantial prejudice to the defendants.

Not only were the defendants fully informed that a criminal contempt was charged, but we think they enjoyed during the trial itself all the enhanced protections accorded defendants in criminal contempt proceedings. . . .

If the defendants were thus accorded all the rights and privileges owing to defendants in criminal contempt cases, they are put in no better position to complain because their trial included a proceeding in civil contempt and was carried on in the main equity suit. Common sense would recognize that conduct can amount to both civil and criminal contempt. The same acts may justify a court in resorting to coercive and to punitive measures. Disposing of both aspects of the contempt in a single proceeding would seem at least a convenient practice. . . . Even if it be the better practice to try criminal contempt alone and so avoid obscuring the defendant's privileges in any manner, a mingling of civil and criminal contempt proceedings must nevertheless be shown to result in substantial prejudice before a reversal will be required. That the contempt proceeding carried the number and name of the equity suit does not alter this conclusion, especially where, as here, the United States would have been the complaining party in whatever suit the contempt was tried. In so far as the criminal nature of the double proceeding dominates and in so far as the defendants' rights in the criminal trial are not diluted by the mixing of civil with criminal contempt, to that extent is prejudice avoided. . . .

V

It is urged that, in any event, the amount of the fine of $10,000 imposed on the defendant Lewis and of the fine of $3,500,000 imposed on the defendant Union were arbitrary, excessive, and in no way related to the evidence adduced at the hearing.

Sentences for criminal contempt are punitive in their nature and are imposed for the purpose of vindicating the authority of the court. The interests of orderly government demand that respect and compliance be given to orders issued by courts possessed of jurisdiction of persons and subject matter. One who defies the public authority and willfully refuses his obedience, does so at his peril. In imposing a fine for criminal contempt, the trial judge may properly take into consideration the extent of the willful and deliberate defiance of the court's order, the seriousness of the consequences of the contumacious behavior, the necessity of effectively terminating the defendant's defiance as required by the public interest, and the importance of deterring such acts in the future. Because of the nature of these standards, great reliance must be placed upon the discretion of the trial judge.

The trial court properly found the defendants guilty of criminal contempt. Such contempt had continued for 15 days from the issuance of the restraining order until the finding of guilty. Its willfulness had not been qualified by any concurrent attempt on defendants' part to challenge the order by motion to vacate or other appropriate procedures. Immediately following the finding of guilty, defendant Lewis stated openly in court that defendants would adhere to their policy of defiance. This policy, as the evidence showed, was the germ center of an economic paralysis which was rapidly extending itself from the bituminous coal mines into practically every other major industry of the United States. It was an attempt to repudiate and override the instrument of lawful government in the very situation in which governmental action was indispensable.

The trial court also properly found the defendants guilty of civil contempt. Judicial sanctions in civil contempt proceedings may, in a proper case, be employed for either or both of two purposes: to coerce the defendant into compliance with the court's order, and to compensate the complainant for losses sustained. Where compensation is intended, a fine is imposed, payable to the complainant. Such fine must of course be based upon evidence of complainant's actual loss, and his right, as a civil litigant, to the compensatory fine is dependent upon the outcome of the basic controversy.

But where the purpose is to make the defendant comply, the court's discretion is otherwise exercised. It must then consider the character and magnitude of the harm threatened by continued contumacy, and the probable effectiveness of any suggested sanction in bringing about the result desired.

It is a corollary of the above principles that a court which has returned a conviction for contempt must, in fixing the amount of a fine to be imposed as a punishment or as a means of securing future compliance, consider the amount of defendant's financial resources and the consequent seriousness of the burden to that particular defendant.

In the light of these principles, we think the record clearly warrants a fine of $10,000 against defendant Lewis for criminal contempt. A majority of the Court, however, does not think that it warrants the unconditional imposition of a fine of $3,500,000 against the defendant union. A majority feels that, if the court below had assessed a fine of $700,000 against the defendant union, this, under the circumstances, would not be excessive as punishment for the criminal contempt theretofore committed; and feels that, in order to coerce the defendant union into a future compliance with the court's order, it would have been effective to make the other $2,800,000 of the fine conditional on the defendant's failure to purge itself within a reasonable time. Accordingly, the judgment against the defendant union is held to be excessive. It will be modified so as to require the defendant union to pay a fine of $700,000, and further, to pay an additional fine of $2,800,000 unless the defendant union, within five days after the issuance of the mandate herein, shows that it has fully complied with the temporary restraining order issued November 18, 1946, and the preliminary injunction issued December 4, 1946. . . .

The judgment against the defendant Lewis is affirmed. The judgment against the defendant union is modified in accordance with this opinion, and, as modified, that judgment is affirmed.

So ordered.

MR. JUSTICE BLACK and MR. JUSTICE DOUGLAS, concurring in part and dissenting in part. . . .

We agree that the court had power summarily to coerce obedience to those orders and to subject defendants to such conditional sanctions as were necessary to compel obedience. . . . Where the court exercises such coercive power, however, for the purpose of compelling future obedience, those imprisoned "carry the keys of their prison in their own pockets," In re Nevitt, 117 F. 448, 461; by obedience to the court's valid order, they can end their confinement; and the court's coercive power in such a "civil contempt" proceeding ends when its order has been obeyed. The District Court did not enter a conditional decree here. But this Court has modified the District Court's decree to provide as part of the judgment such a coercive sanction in the form of a conditional fine. We agree with the Court's decision in this respect. . . .

Yet the decision of this Court also approves unconditional fines as criminal punishment for past disobedience. We cannot agree to this aspect of the Court's judgment. At a very early date this Court declared, and recently it has reiterated, that in contempt proceedings courts should never exercise more than "the least possible power adequate to the end proposed." Anderson v. Dunn, 6 Wheat. 204, 231.

In certain circumstances criminal contempt culminating in unconditional punishment for past disobedience may well constitute an exercise of "the least possible power adequate to the end proposed." Thus in situations which would warrant only a use of coercive sanctions in the first instance, criminal punishment might be appropriate at a later stage if the defendant should persist in disobeying the order of the court. Without considering the constitutional requisites of such criminal punishment, we believe the application of it inappropriate and improper here. The imposition of criminal punishment here was an exercise of far more than "the least possible power adequate to the end proposed." For here the great and legitimate "end proposed" was affirmative action by the defendants to prevent interruption of coal production pending final adjudication of the controversy. Coercive sanctions sufficient to accomplish this end were justified. From the record we have no doubt but that a conditional civil sanction would bring about at least as prompt and unequivocal obedience to the court's order as would criminal punishment for past disobedience. And this would accomplish a vindication of the District Court's authority against a continuing defiance. Consequently, we do not believe that the accomplishment of the justifiable "end proposed" called for summary criminal punishment which is designed to deter others from disobedience to court orders or to avenge a public wrong, rather than the imposition of a coercive sanction. And for the reasons stated by Mr. Justice Rutledge, we think that the flat $700,000 criminal fine against the defendant union is excessive by constitutional and statutory standards.

In determining whether criminal punishment or coercive sanction should be employed in these proceedings, the question of intent — the motivation of the contumacy — becomes relevant. Difficult questions of law were presented by this case. It is plain that the defendants acted willfully for they knew that they were disobeying the court's order. But they appear to have believed in good faith, though erroneously, that they were acting within their legal rights. Many lawyers would have so advised them. This does not excuse their conduct; the whole situation emphasized the duty of testing the restraining order by orderly appeal instead of disobedience and open defiance. However, as this Court said in Cooke v. United States, 267 U.S. 517, 538, "the intention with which acts of contempt have been committed must necessarily and properly have an important bearing on the degree of guilt and the penalty which should be imposed." . . .

We should modify the District Court's decrees by making the entire amount of the fines payable conditionally. On December 7, 1946, Mr. Lewis directed the mine workers to return to work until midnight, March 31, 1947. But, so far as we are aware, the notice which purported to terminate the contract has not been withdrawn. Thus, there has been, at most, only a partial compliance with the temporary injunction. . . .

MR. JUSTICE RUTLEDGE, dissenting. . . .

III . . .

In any other context than one of contempt, the idea that a criminal prosecution and a civil suit for damages or equitable relief could be hashed together in a single criminal-civil hodgepodge would be shocking to every American lawyer and to most citizens. True, the same act may give rise to all these varied legal consequences. But we have never adopted, rather our Constitution has totally rejected, the continental system of compounding criminal proceedings with civil adjudications. Our tradition is exactly the contrary and few would maintain that this has had no part in bringing about the difference existing today for individual freedom here and in Europe.

I do not think the Constitution contemplated that there should be in any case an admixture of civil and criminal proceedings in one. Such an idea is altogether foreign to its spirit. . . .

This case is characteristic of the long-existing confusion concerning contempts and the manner of their trial, among other things, in that most frequently the question of the nature and character of the proceeding, whether civil or criminal, is determined at its end in the stage of review rather than, as it should be and as in my opinion it must be, at the beginning. And this fact in itself illustrates the complete jeopardy in which rights are placed when the nature of the proceeding remains unknown and unascertainable until the final action on review.

Not only is one thus placed in continuing dilemma throughout the proceedings in the trial court concerning which set of procedural rights he is entitled to stand upon, whether upon the criminal safeguards or only on the civil. He also does not and cannot know until it is too late, that is, until the appellate phase is ended, whether one group or the other of appellate jurisdictional and procedural rules applies. . . .

But we are told that this, and all that followed or may have followed from it, make no difference because there was no prejudice. There are at least two answers. This Court has held that the denial of constitutional guaranties in trials for crime is in itself prejudice. The other, there was prejudice and in the most important thing beyond knowing the nature of the proceeding in advance of trial, namely, in the penalty itself.

IV

Not only was the penalty against the union excessive, as the Court holds. Vice infected both "fines" more deeply. As the proceeding itself is said to have been both civil and criminal, so are the two "fines." Each was imposed in a single lump sum, with no allocation of specific portions as among civil damages, civil coercion and criminal punishment. The Government concedes that some part of each "fine" was laid for each purpose. But the trial court did not state, and the Government has refused to speculate, how much was imposed in either instance for each of those distinct remedial functions.

This was in the teeth of the *Gompers* and other previous decisions here. The law has fixed standards for each remedy, and they are neither identical nor congealable. They are, for damages in civil contempt, the amount of injury proven and no more; for coercion, what may be required to bring obedience and not more, whether by way of imprisonment or fine; for punishment, what is not cruel and unusual or, in the case of a fine, excessive within the Eighth Amendment's prohibition. And for determining excessiveness of criminal fines there are analogies from legislative action which in my opinion are controlling. . . .

Obviously, however, when all these distinct types and functions of relief are lumped together, in a single so-called "fine," none of the long-established bases for measurement can be applied, for there is nothing to which they can apply. . . .

The Court seemingly recognizes this, in part, in the revision it makes of the District Court's penalties. Lewis' fine is affirmed in amount but wholly changed in character. Instead of composite relief as the District Court made it, the Court makes that fine wholly a criminal penalty, thus in effect increasing the amount of his criminal imposition. The union's fine, though held excessive and "reduced," by what standard is not apparent, is replaced by a flat criminal fine of $700,000 plus a contingent penalty of $2,800,000 said to be entirely for civil coercion, although the strike was ended in December. Any award for civil damages allegedly sustained apparently is eliminated.

The Court thus purports to make separate the distinct items of relief commingled in the District Court's action. But in doing so, in my opinion, it wholly disregards the established standard for measuring criminal fines and its own as well as the District Court's function relating to them. If Lewis and the union had been convicted on indictment and jury trial in a proceeding surrounded by all the constitutional and other safeguards of criminal prosecution for violating the War Labor Disputes Act, the maximum fines which could be applied by that Act's terms would be $5,000 for each. In addition, Lewis could have been imprisoned for a year.

In my opinion, when Congress prescribes a maximum penalty for criminal violation of a statute, that penalty fixes the maximum which can be imposed whether the conviction is in a criminal proceeding as such for its violation or is for contempt for violating an order of court to observe it temporarily. If the fine or other penalty in such a case can be multiplied twice or any other number of times, merely by bringing a civil suit, securing a temporary restraining order and then convicting the person who violates it of criminal contempt, regardless of the order's validity and of any of the usual restraints of criminal procedure, the way will have been found to dispense with substantially all of those protections relating not only to the course of the proceedings but to the penalty itself. . . .

No right is absolute. Nor is any power, governmental or other, in our system. There can be no question that it provides power to meet the greatest crises. Equally certain is it that under "a government of laws and not of men" such as we possess, power must be exercised according to law; and government, including the courts, as well as the governed, must move within its limitations. . . .

MR. JUSTICE MURPHY joins in this opinion.

NOTES ON THE THREE KINDS OF CONTEMPT

1. *Mine Workers'* explanation of the separate purposes of criminal contempt, coercive civil contempt, and compensatory civil contempt is settled law in the federal courts and in most states. Of course there is variation with respect to details, and a few states reject the distinctions altogether.

2.   Law can be well settled without being well known. The reports are full of cases in which trial judges confused criminal contempt with coercive civil contempt. Perhaps the most common error is to impose fixed penalties in civil proceedings, but other combinations occur as well. Justice Rutledge's complaint remains true: Courts often wait till the end of contempt proceedings to decide what they are doing. There is also a tendency to think that the distinction has to do with the nature of defendant's act — that some contempts are criminal and others civil. But the distinction is in the proceeding, not in the contempt. Any contempt can be the subject of civil or criminal proceedings or both, just like any assault and battery. The only difference that relates to defendant's act is the rule that contempt is not criminal unless it is willful.

The confusion results partly from carelessness, and partly from ambiguities that creep into orders as they are modified in response to changing circumstances. But there is no reason in principle to be confused. Most of the distinctions among the three kinds of contempt derive directly from their three distinct purposes or from the civil/criminal distinction.

3.   Criminal contempt is prosecuted in the name of the sovereign. The court may ask the prosecutor to prosecute the contempt, or it may appoint plaintiff's attorney or any member of the bar as special prosecutor. The prosecution may be begun by notice rather than indictment, but at trial, defendant gets substantially all the protections of criminal procedure. He cannot be sentenced to more than six months in jail without a jury trial. Bloom v. Illinois, 391 U.S. 194 (1968). Substantial fines can be imposed without jury trial, but there may be some limit based on the proportion between the fine and defendant's wealth. Muniz v. Hoffman, 422 U.S. 454 (1975), upheld a fine of $10,000 against a local labor union convicted of criminal contempt without a jury.

4.   With respect to criminal contempt, plaintiff is in the position of a complaining witness. He can report the contempt, but he cannot require the court to proceed criminally. Any fines are payable to the government.

If plaintiff settles the underlying case, he cannot stop the court from prosecuting the criminal contempt proceeding. Defendants who expect amnesty and plaintiffs who are willing to give it are sometimes surprised to learn that amnesty is not something they can bargain for. The issue commonly arises in public employee strike litigation. A good example is Board of Junior College District No. 508 v. Cook County College Teachers Union, Local 1600, 126 Ill. App. 2d 418, 262 N.E.2d 125 (1970), cert. denied, 402 U.S. 998 (1971). The union defied an antistrike injunction. When collective bargaining settled the strike, the board moved to dissolve the injunction. The court denied the motion and ordered the board's attorney to prosecute the union and its officers for contempt. The board's attorney refused on the ground that he had a conflict of interest. The court asked the county prosecutor to prosecute, but he declined on the ground that this was a civil dispute. The court then appointed a prominent member of the bar to prosecute the contempt as Amicus Curiae. The court convicted defendants, fined the union $5,000, and sentenced its president to thirty days in jail and a $1,000 fine. The court of appeals affirmed, indignantly rejecting the suggestion that the court should "meekly" "condone" contempt at plaintiff's request.

Some courts and prosecutors are willing to go along with amnesty to get the employees back to work; there is always discretion to abandon a prosecution. The important practical point is that this discretion is the court's, not the plaintiff's. How should courts exercise this discretion? What happens if injunctions and criminal contempt become just another bargaining chip? If defendants expect that prosecutions will be abandoned when the underlying dispute is settled, what happens to the effectiveness of injunctions?

5. The Cook County Junior College case also highlights the dual rule of the judge. The judge is not allowed to prosecute the contempt and also decide it; he must get a lawyer to prosecute it for him. But how neutral can he be after he goes to such lengths to initiate the prosecution? Should criminal contempt be decided by a judge other than the one who issued the injunction? That is sometimes done, but it is not the common practice.

6. Civil contempt is prosecuted in the name of the plaintiff, and largely controlled by the plaintiff. He initiates it with a motion, and up to a point he can abandon it or settle it.

Compensatory civil contempt is like an action for damages or restitution. Despite the compensatory label, plaintiff can recover defendant's profits, at least if profits would be an appropriate measure of recovery for the underlying wrong. The leading case is Leman v. Krentler-Arnold Hinge Last Co., 284 U.S. 448 (1932), involving contempt of an injunction against patent infringement.

Because compensatory contempt is ancillary to the injunction suit, there is no jury trial in most jurisdictions. Partly for that reason, about ten states reject compensatory contempt, including California, Illinois, and Texas. Rendleman, Compensatory Contempt: Plaintiff's Remedy When a Defendant Violates an Injunction, 1980 U. Ill. L.F. 971, 982-983 n.49. In those states, plaintiff must file an ordinary action for damages. Plaintiff always has the option of filing an ordinary damage action. He may want a jury too, or he may want to avoid the requirement of clear and convincing evidence that is generally applied in contempt. Does that evidentiary standard make any sense in compensatory contempt?

There is an obvious irony in compensatory contempt. Before it issued the injunction, the court decided that damages would be an inadequate remedy. Now that defendant has violated the injunction, the injury is by hypothesis irreparable. Damages are inadequate, but they are not necessarily useless; recall that adequacy is a comparative judgment. In any event, damages are now the best the court can do. Should the court respond to this irony by measuring damages more generously? By reducing the required degree of certainty? There is no settled doctrine to that effect, but it would be surprising if the court's annoyance at defendant's contempt did not increase the ordinary tendency to resolve doubts against wrongdoers.

7. Criminal contempt looks much like ordinary punishment, and compensatory contempt looks much like ordinary compensation. The unique contribution of the contempt power is coercive civil contempt. Coercive contempt depends on a conditional penalty; defendant is coerced to comply because the penalty will be bigger if he doesn't. In *Mine Workers*, the $2.8 million conditional fine is all or nothing; if the union does not recall the strike notice within five days, it must pay the entire fine. Some have termed this approach "hybrid contempt." United States v. North, 621 F.2d 1255 (3d Cir.) (en banc), *cert. denied*, 449 U.S. 866 (1980). Per diem penalties are more common. An example is the $100 per day fine in the next principal case. Perhaps the most common coercive contempt penalty is imprisonment until compliance.

8. *Mine Workers* found no prejudice in mixing criminal and civil contempt proceedings if criminal safeguards are observed. Justice Rutledge disagreed. Who is more persuasive? Is it true that in any other context "the idea that a criminal prosecution and a civil suit . . . could be hashed together in a single civil-criminal hodgepodge would be shocking to every American lawyer"? At the time Justice Rutledge wrote, there were few other examples of combined civil-criminal proceedings. But centuries before, the law of crime and tort had had common origins.

We may now be coming full circle. A wave of "victims' rights" legislation in the 1980s authorized courts in criminal prosecutions to order compensation to the victim of crime. These provisions are not unprecedented, but they are suddenly much more pervasive. These statutes often refer to making "restitution," but they mean compensation; they do not distinguish defendant's profits from victim's losses. Thus, under the federal statute the judge may order return of stolen property, payment of the value of lost or damaged property, payment of the victim's medical expenses and lost income, and payment of a murder victim's funeral expenses. 18 U.S.C. §3579(b) (1982). The court is directed to consider defendant's ability to pay and the needs of his dependents as well as the amount of the victim's loss. 18 U.S.C. §3580(a) (1982). Crime victims could recover these damages in an ordinary tort suit, but such suits are rarely filed, probably because there is little prospect of collecting damages through the cumbersome means available in civil cases. The judge in the criminal case orders compensation as part of the criminal sentence, or as a condition of probation or parole, thus threatening defendant with more jail time if he fails to pay. We will consider this choice between collection methods in the next section.

One judge has shared Justice Rutledge's reaction to mixing civil and criminal proceedings. The federal victim compensation statute was declared unconstitutional in United States v. Welden, 568 F. Supp. 516 (N.D. Ala. 1983), *rev'd sub nom*. United States v. Satterfield, 743 F.2d 827, 831-843 (11th Cir. 1984). The evidence on damages and ability to pay was submitted in the presentence report, which is now required to include a Victim Impact Statement. It had obviously been done in a slipshod way; Congress did not add to the Justice Department's staff when it enacted this statute. The court held that the procedure denied defendant's right to civil jury trial on damages, and that it was so standardless that it violated due process and equal protection. But the court of appeals reversed, and other courts are enforcing this and similar acts on a regular basis.

9. The Court returned to the question of combined civil and criminal contempt proceedings only three weeks after *Mine Workers*. Penfield Co. v. Securities & Exchange Commission, 330 U.S. 585 (1947). A witness refused to turn over documents in response to an SEC subpoena. He also defied a court order enforcing the subpoena. The SEC filed a motion for coercive civil contempt. The court imposed a fixed fine of $50, which the witness happily paid. On the SEC's appeal, the court of appeals vacated the fine and ordered the witness imprisoned until he complied. The Supreme Court affirmed, holding that the fixed fine was a criminal penalty that could not be imposed in a civil contempt proceeding, and that the SEC was entitled to the coercive relief it had sought. Justices Frankfurter and Jackson dissented, arguing that *Mine Workers* allowed civil and criminal contempt proceedings to be freely mixed. Justice Rutledge concurred in the result, arguing that the case could not be reconciled with *Mine Workers* and celebrating the Court's return to earlier doctrine. He quoted Gompers v. Bucks Stove & Range Co., 221 U.S. 418, 449 (1911), to the effect that imposing criminal punishment in a civil contempt proceedings "was as fundamentally erroneous as if in an action of 'A. vs. B. for assault and battery,' the judgment entered had been that the defendant be confined in prison for twelve months." 330 U.S. at 595. The majority also relied on *Gompers* and *Mine Workers* for the distinction between civil and criminal contempt; it didn't mention the part of *Mine Workers* that let the two proceedings be combined.

Was part III of *Mine Workers* overruled? Or is it all a matter of whose ox is gored? *Mine Workers* was a cause célèbre; the Court may have been determined not to seem to legitimate the strike. In *Penfield*, the procedural foul-up prejudiced the plaintiff and let the contemnor escape through a loophole. Courts generally treat part III of *Mine Workers* as good law, but there is always room to argue that there was insufficient notice of the nature of the proceeding or that criminal penalties were imposed without adequate criminal procedures. The safest course is to be clear about what you are doing from the beginning.

NATIONAL LABOR RELATIONS BOARD v.
BLEVINS POPCORN CO.
659 F.2d 1173 (D.C. Cir. 1981)

Before WRIGHT, TAMM, and WALD, Circuit Judges.

J. SKELLY WRIGHT, Circuit Judge.

In this appeal the National Labor Relations Board . . . seeks review of a determination by a Special Master that the Blevins Popcorn Company . . . did not violate a contempt and purgation order issued by this court on September 16, 1977. . . .

I. Background

A. Enforcement Order and First Contempt Proceeding

On May 4, 1977 this court entered a judgment enforcing in full a decision and order of the NLRB issued against the company on June 19, 1975. In its decision the NLRB found that the company had unjustifiably refused to bargain with the union over rates of pay, wages, hours, and other terms and conditions of employment. The order, as enforced, directed the company to:

1.　Cease and desist from:

    (a)　Refusing to bargain collectively concerning rates of pay, wages, hours, and other terms and conditions of employment with American Federation of Grain Millers, AFL-CIO, as the exclusive bargaining representative of its employees in the following appropriate unit:

    All production and maintenance employees, including truckdrivers employed at the Employer's facility in Ridgeway [sic], Illinois, but excluding office clerical employees, professional employees, guards and supervisors as defined in the Act.

    (b)　In any like or related manner interfering with, restraining, or coercing employees in the exercise of the rights guaranteed them in Section 7 of the Act.

2.　Take the following affirmative action which the Board finds will effectuate the policies of the Act:

    (a)　Upon request, bargain with the above-named labor organization as the exclusive representative of all employees in the aforesaid appropriate unit with respect to rates of pay, wages, hours, and other terms and conditions of employment, and, if an understanding is reached, embody such understanding in a signed agreement.

On September 16, 1977, upon motion of the NLRB, this court entered a second order summarily adjudging the company in civil contempt for willfully continuing to fail and refuse to comply with the court's May 4 order. The September 16 order stated that the company could purge itself of civil contempt by:

> (a) Fully complying with and obeying this court's judgment of May 4, 1977 by, upon request, bargaining collectively in good faith with the union as the exclusive representative of [the company's] employees in the appropriate unit, and, if an understanding is reached, embodying such understanding in a signed agreement, provided, however, that such agreement may be made subject to termination should the United States Supreme Court ultimately decide that [the company] was not obligated to recognize and bargain with the union.
>
> (b) Proceeding with the officials of the union to set an initial meeting date, not to exceed ten days from entry of this order, and thereafter proceeding to bargain upon consecutive days during regular business hours until all contract proposals on mandatory and lawful subjects have been considered and actions taken in relation thereto.

The order further provided:

> 3. That in order to assure against further violations of this court's judgment, this court assesses against [the company] a prospective fine in the amount of one hundred dollars ($100.00) per day if compliance with this order has not been commenced within seven (7) days of the date of this order.
>
> On further motion by the Board the court will take such other and further action and grant such other relief as appears just, reasonable, and necessary at that time. . . .

D. Second Contempt Proceeding

On September 22, 1978, two days before it withdrew recognition from the union, the company asked this court to dissolve the September 16, 1977 contempt and purgation order on the ground that negotiations had reached a bona fide impasse. The NLRB responded to this motion by filing an opposition statement and by moving for another civil contempt adjudication. In its motion the NLRB claimed that the company had violated the September 16, 1977 contempt and purgation order by failing to bargain with the union in good faith and by failing to meet with the union at reasonable intervals during the period September 30, 1977 through June 22, 1978. It further alleged that the company had violated the court's order by refusing to meet with the union after June 22, 1978 and by withdrawing recognition from the union. It asked this court to assess fines and to increase prospective fines.

In March 1979 this court appointed a Special Master to hear evidence and make recommended findings of fact and conclusions of law with respect to the company and NLRB motions. The Master conducted several hearings in September 1979. He issued his report on December 16, 1980. The Master found that the company had bargained in good faith throughout the period September 16, 1977 to June 22, 1978. . . . The Master also found that a bona fide impasse existed as of June 22, 1978, and that the company therefore properly refused to continue bargaining with the union. Finally, he found that . . . the company had reasonable grounds to doubt the union's majority status and properly withdrew recognition. The Master concluded by recommending that the NLRB's motion for a further contempt order be denied and that the company's motion to dissolve the prior contempt order be granted. The NLRB filed exceptions.

II. Discussion

A. The NLRB's Burden of Proof

At the outset of the legal discussion contained in his report the Special Master stated that, to meet its burden of proof, the NLRB is "required to produce clear and convincing evidence in support of its allegations of contemptuous conduct. . . ." Despite this reference to the clear and convincing evidence standard, it appears that the Special Master actually imposed a far heavier burden of proof on the NLRB. Later in his report he suggested that the Board must prove its case beyond a reasonable doubt: he stated that, "if there is ground to doubt the wrongfulness of the conduct, the Company should not be held in contempt." The Master also stated that "the proof must demonstrate that there existed a wilful and deliberate disregard of a court decree." As we explain below, the Master applied the wrong standard of proof; the NLRB should not have been required to do more than produce clear and convincing evidence in support of its allegations.

As a general rule, the "reasonable doubt" standard of proof and the "willfulness" requirement are applicable only in criminal contempt proceedings. In civil contempt proceedings the clear and convincing evidence standard applies and the failure to comply with the court decree need not be intentional. The explanation for this distinction lies in the different purposes of criminal and civil contempt. Criminal contempt is used to punish intentional misconduct. Thus the procedural safeguards that attend any criminal proceeding, including the reasonable doubt standard of proof, come into play. In addition, the recalcitrant party's state of mind is a central issue. Civil contempt, on the other hand, is a remedial sanction used to obtain compliance with a court order or to compensate for damage sustained as a result of noncompliance. Thus criminal procedure safeguards are not applicable. Moreover, the intent of the recalcitrant party is irrelevant.

The Master never disputed these general principles. He noted, however, that this is the third stage of a three-stage civil contempt proceeding. Such proceedings involve (1) issuance of an order; (2) following disobedience of that order, issuance of a conditional order finding the recalcitrant party in contempt and threatening to impose a specified penalty unless the recalcitrant party purges itself of contempt by complying with prescribed purgation conditions; and (3) exaction of the threatened penalty if the purgation conditions are not fulfilled. The Master apparently conceded that the clear and convincing evidence standard should be applied at the second stage, and that no showing of willfulness would be necessary. He suggests, however, that the third stage is punitive in nature since a fine may be assessed. Thus the wrongfulness of the recalcitrant party's conduct must be shown not just by clear and convincing evidence, but beyond any ground for doubt. Moreover, the party's state of mind is crucial.

These conclusions as to burden of proof are erroneous. The third stage of three-stage contempt proceedings does not lose its civil character simply because a penalty may be imposed. The third-stage proceeding is part of the process by which the court obtains compliance with its decrees; it supports the second-stage contempt and purgation order. At the second stage the recalcitrant party is put on notice that unless it obeys the court's decree and purges itself of contempt it will be fined or face other sanctions. At the third stage the court determines whether the party has fulfilled the purgation conditions. If it has, it escapes the threatened penalty; if it has not, the penalty is imposed. To hold that the third-stage proceeding is punitive or criminal would be to hold that a court may never bring about compliance with its orders by imposing prospective penalties in civil proceedings.

In fact, we have already rejected the claim that the third stage of three-stage contempt is criminal in nature, Brhd. of Locomotive Firemen & Enginemen v. Bangor & Aroostook R. Co., 380 F.2d 570 (D.C. Cir.), cert. denied, 389 U.S. 327 (1967).[76] . . .

76. In *Brotherhood*, the amount of the fine that would be assessed in the third stage had been determined at the second stage. Here, on the other hand, the second-stage order says only that $100 will be assessed every day if bargaining did not commence within seven days, and that the NLRB would be able to move for further penalties. The $100 per day fine is no longer applicable. Thus the precise nature of the sanction to be applied at the third stage is uncertain. We do not think this difference is sufficient to distinguish the cases, however. What is important is that at the second stage the recalcitrant party was told that unless it complied with the terms of the court's order it would face sanctions.

Because third-stage proceedings remain civil in character, neither the reasonable doubt standard nor the willfulness requirement are applicable; only the clear and convincing evidence standard should be employed. The Master's decision to impose a more rigorous burden of proof in this case may have had a substantial impact on his findings of fact and conclusions of law. It is quite possible that his decision would not have been in favor of the company if he had not required the NLRB to show that the company had acted in "wilful and deliberate disregard" of the contempt and purgation order and that the company's conduct was wrongful beyond any ground for doubt. . . .

III. Conclusion

We remand this case so that the Special Master may apply the proper standard of proof in determining whether the company violated the September 16, 1977 contempt and purgation order. . . .

TAMM, Circuit Judge, concurring in the result.

Because I believe that the Special Master apparently applied an erroneous standard of proof, I concur in the result reached by the court. . . .

NOTES ON COERCIVE CONTEMPT

1. When conditional fines are used for coercive contempt, the process breaks into three distinct steps. The third step is not easily pigeonholed. When the court threatened to fine Blevins $100 per day, the threat was remedial and prospective. Now that the threats have failed, enforcing the fines looks punitive and retrospective. The fines have lost their coercive effect because they are no longer conditional. But the law must keep its promises, or coercive contempt will no longer coerce. The fines obviously must be collected, but must they be collected with civil procedure? Would the system break down if defendant got the benefit of criminal procedure at this point? Are the issues about fairness and procedure here substantially the same as with punitive damages? Is the clear and convincing evidence standard sufficient recognition of the punitive effects of coercive contempt?

2. What is the purpose of the second step of coercive contempt? When the court issues an injunction, defendant knows he can be fined or imprisoned for violating it. When the court finds defendant in contempt and announces a coercive sanction, it specifies the future penalty. What does that add to the injunction? Is it just that contemplation of a particular punishment concentrates the mind in a way that contemplating the generic possibility of punishment does not? If telling defendant what the penalty is going to be makes injunctions more effective, why not tell him

when the injunction is issued? Is there any need to wait for a violation before specifying the penalty?

3. The three steps of coercive contempt are even more puzzling if the court is not bound to impose the penalty it threatened. Consider Labor Relations Commission v. Fall River Education Association, 382 Mass. 465, 416 N.E.2d 1340 (1981). The trial court had enjoined an illegal teachers' strike, and found the teachers' union in contempt. It announced a coercive penalty of $20,000 per day until the strike ended. The strike lasted thirteen days and the judge imposed a fine of $260,000. The union had net income of $28,000 per year, but the court found it could pay the fine by assessing its members $250 each.

The Supreme Judicial Court ordered the trial court to reconsider the fine in light of the union's ability to pay. It rejected the trial court's suggestion that the union specially assess its members, because the individual members "were not parties to the contempt action and had no reasonable expectation that they would be personally liable for fines assessed against the Association for the failure of its officers to discourage and to disavow the strike." Id. at 483, 416 N.E.2d at 1351. That reasoning is dubious, as we shall see in connection with United States v. Hall, infra at 684. The usual rule is that non-parties in active concert with a party are bound by the injunction and subject to contempt proceedings. But once the individual members were exempted from assessments, it was easy to say the fine was excessive. Even so, the court did not say the threat of $20,000 per day was excessive. Instead, it said that a judge at the third step of coercive contempt "should not feel bound in any way by the specific amount" imposed at the second step. Id. at 482, 416 N.E.2d at 1350.

Can that be right? Does the second step serve any purpose at all in that scenario? The court cited National Labor Relations Board v. Construction & General Laborers' Union Local 1140, 577 F.2d 16, 21 (8th Cir. 1978), cert. denied, 439 U.S. 1070 (1979). In that case, the court imposed the fine it had threatened, but said it did not feel bound to do so. In Hawaii Public Employment Relations Board v. Hawaii State Teachers Association, 55 Hawaii 386, 392-393, 520 P.2d 422, 427 (1974), a coercive fine that had reached $190,000 was reduced to $100,000 for "the promotion of justice."

4. Mine Workers says that defendant's wealth is relevant to the size of coercive fines. The court must ask how much it takes to deter this defendant. Coercive fines against wealthy defendants may be very large. In International Business Machines Corp. v. United States, 493 F.2d 112, 115-117 (2d Cir. 1973), cert. denied, 416 U.S. 995 (1974), IBM was fined $150,000 per day for refusing to produce documents. That turned out to be 5 percent of IBM's daily profits.

Profits are not the only measure of ability to pay. In Perfect Fit Industries v. Acme Quilting Co., 673 F.2d 53 (2d Cir.), cert. denied, 459 U.S.

832 (1982), the court sustained a coercive contempt fine of $5,000 per day against a trademark infringer that claimed to make only $500 per day. But Acme had $20 million per year in sales, so the court thought there was sufficient cash flow to pay the fines even if the profits were as little as claimed. Would it make any difference if Acme were losing money? The injunction still has to be enforced, doesn't it? Acme claimed it would cost $50,000 to change its advertising to comply with the injunction; the court thought it had to make the fines more expensive than that. The court also said that comparing fines to profits was useful mainly when the fines were very large in absolute terms, as in the IBM case.

Per diem fines increase the difficulty of assessing ability to pay. In the *Fall River* school case, it was easy to conclude that the union could not pay $260,000. But when the court set the per diem fine, it did not contemplate waiting thirteen days for compliance. If it set the fine at $2,000 per day, so that the union could afford a two-week strike, would it be inviting a two-week strike? Isn't the plaintiff entitled to a per diem fine that will deter immediately? Does it defeat the purpose if defendant is entitled to have that fine reduced if it accumulates to unduly burdensome levels? Of course, once the fine accumulates beyond the amount of defendant's net worth plus foreseeable income, further accumulations are meaningless anyway.

5. The *Fall River* school case illustrates two other points about coercive fines. They are paid to the state, and not to the plaintiff. The point is not much litigated, but the practice seems to be well settled. Plaintiff is entitled to compensation, and to compliance with the injunction, but not to the fines that result from failed efforts to coerce compliance.

Second, the plaintiff does not control efforts to collect coercive fines. In that respect too, the third step of coercive contempt is like criminal contempt. When the school board and union settled the strike in *Fall River*, the school board agreed not to seek compensation for the expenses caused by the strike and not to seek any penalties for contempt. It could waive its right to compensation, but the fines were imposed anyway.

6. The original and simplest form of coercive contempt is to imprison the contemnor until he complies. This avoids the conundrums of three-step coercive contempt. There are only two steps: First the injunction is issued, and then defendant is found in contempt and sent to jail. He stays there until he indicates that he is willing to comply. Conditional penalties do not accumulate to be collected later, because imprisonment is continuous. Every instant he refuses to comply, and every instant he remains in prison for that refusal. The court is never in the position of enforcing a penalty for an earlier violation of the injunction.

7. But imprisonment has disadvantages in some contexts. Some injunctions can be obeyed only if defendant is at large. Blevins Popcorn can't very well bargain if its officers are in prison. At best the court can imprison them until they promise to bargain, and then let them out and

see if the fear of returning to prison induces them to keep their promise. Imprisonment is expensive to the state, especially if there are many contemnors. Imprisoning a few leaders may create martyrs; few judges have been willing to imprison the rank and file.

8. Why would courts hesitate to imprison the rank and file? Why would they hesitate to enforce announced penalties that accumulate to large sums? The contemnor knowingly allowed the fines to accumulate, and the rank and file knowingly defied the court. Is it just humanitarianism? We don't torture in coercive contempt, and maybe we don't do everything short of torture either. Part of the hesitation may be tactical. There is a lot of psychology and gamesmanship in coercive contempt; the court may think that moderate threats are more likely to be effective than harsher threats. A threat should not be so great that the contemnor doubts the court's will to carry it out. Nor should it be so great that there is no room for further escalation. In strike cases, and other cases where the litigants have a continuing relationship, harsh sanctions may end the contempt but ruin the relationship. The Reagan administration fired all the striking air traffic controllers, but few public employers have been so bold.

9. Such tactical considerations may explain the three steps of coercive fines. Indeed, some judges have stretched the contempt process out into an indefinite number of steps, especially in structural injunctions against government defendants. Early contempt proceedings may result not in a finding of contempt, but in a clarification of the order, making it more specific. Or the court may find defendants in contempt, and indicate that they may purge themselves of contempt by doing A, B, and C, which turn out to be more detailed specifications of the obligations of the original injunction. The court can continue this process indefinitely, slowly tightening the screws. You can get some sense of the process from Hutto v. Finney, supra at 274. The Court summarizes the long series of orders issued to the warden of the Arkansas prisons.

CATENA v. SEIDL
68 N.J. 224, 343 A.2d 744 (1975)

PER CURIAM.

Gerardo Catena, having been found to be in contempt of the State Commission of Investigation (hereinafter S.C.I.), has been confined continuously since March 4, 1970 except for short periods of temporary release for medical treatment and other personal reasons. His confinement has been based on his refusal to answer questions put to him by the S.C.I. concerning organized crime activities, even though he had been granted testimonial immunity pursuant to N.J.S.A. 52:9M-17. Following his refusal to testify, Catena was cited for contempt by the Superior

Court which ordered that he be committed until such time as he purged himself of contempt by testifying. The legality of his confinement was ultimately upheld by the United States Supreme Court in Elias v. Catena, 406 U.S. 952 (1972).

In the meantime, Catena has remained steadfast in his refusal to testify. The present proceedings seeking to effect Catena's release were begun in December 1973. Inter alia it was alleged that despite the fact that Catena had not purged himself of contempt, his confinement should be terminated because it had failed as a coercive measure. The trial court, after a summary hearing and without receiving any testimony or other evidence except for a letter report as to the state of Catena's health, ordered that Catena be released on the grounds that the order holding him in contempt no longer had any coercive impact and had become punitive in nature.

We reversed the aforesaid ruling of the trial court in Catena v. Seidl, 65 N.J. 257 (1974) holding (1) that the test to be applied was whether or not there was a substantial likelihood that continued commitment of Catena would accomplish the purpose of the order upon which the commitment was based, (2) that the S.C.I. was not required to demonstrate the continued efficacy of such order but that Catena had the burden of showing that the commitment, lawful when ordered, had lost its coercive impact and had become punitive and (3) that on the record then presented Catena had not sustained that burden. . . .

When the matter [again] came before the trial court, . . . affidavits were submitted by Catena and three of his attorneys; Catena's wife and one of his daughters also testified. Based on this supplemental proof, as well as Catena's silence since March 1970, his age and condition of health, the trial court again found that Catena's continued confinement had gone beyond the coercive stage and had become punitive and that he should be released.

This Court, in an opinion reported at 66 N.J. 32 (1974), found itself unable to review the correctness of the trial court's ruling because of the inadequacy of the record. We held that use of ex parte proofs in the form of affidavits and a letter report as to the state of Catena's health was improper since it prevented the S.C.I. from testing the veracity and credibility of content. We reiterated that it was Catena who had the burden of proof and that such burden was not sustainable by ex parte affidavits and reports. Accordingly, we remanded the matter to the trial court to afford Catena the opportunity to present live testimony.

Pursuant to the remand, Catena testified, as well as his physician and three of his attorneys. Following the hearing the trial court in an oral decision reviewed all of the evidence and once more found that there was no substantial likelihood that continued confinement of Catena would ever cause him to break his silence and answer the questions put to him by the S.C.I.

The trial court noted Catena's age (73 years old), state of health and confinement since March 1970. It reviewed the reason given by Catena for remaining silent (essentially Catena testified that he believed he had a right of privacy which could not be taken away from him), and while it did not believe him in that regard, concluded that no matter what Catena's real reason was, he had demonstrated such total obstinacy that the trial court was satisfied that he would never answer any questions.

Actually, whether Catena's refusal to testify is based on moral conviction or principle, or whether, as the S.C.I. contends, he is adhering to organized crime's oath of silence is not controlling.[1] Whatever his reason, good or bad, the question is whether there is a substantial likelihood that continued confinement will cause Catena to change his mind and testify.

The great strength of the rule of law in a democratic society is that it applies equally to all persons, the bad as well as the good. True, Catena has refused to cooperate with the S.C.I. in its investigation into organized crime and the statute permits the imposition of sanctions on him as a coercive measure to force him to testify to whatever knowledge and information he has as to the subject matter of the S.C.I.'s investigation. However, his confinement has been for that purpose and that purpose alone. It cannot be used to punish him for remaining silent or for any other shortcoming of which he has not been convicted. As we noted in one of our previous opinions in this matter, "[o]nce it appears that the commitment has lost its coercive power, the legal justification for it ends and further confinement cannot be tolerated." 65 N.J. at p.262.

We have made our own evaluation of the evidence. Catena is now 73 years of age and in the twilight of his life. He has been confined for more than five years in an effort to get him to testify. His condition of health has been deteriorating and his physician has advised him that it is dangerous to his heart condition to remain confined. Despite all this, he has refused to break his silence and has continued to insist that "they'd have to carry me out of there feet first." The trial judge who had the opportunity to see and hear Catena was satisfied that he would never answer any questions for the Commission.

Based on the foregoing, it now appears that there is no substantial likelihood that further confinement will accomplish the purpose of the order upon which Catena's commitment was based. However, we want to make it perfectly clear that in similar circumstances a person's insistence that he will never talk, or confinement for a particular length of time does

1. In In re Farr, 36 Cal. App. 3d 577, 111 Cal. Rptr. 649 (1974), where commitment for disobedience of a court order to testify was involved, it was suggested that it became necessary to determine the point at which the commitment ceased to serve its coercive purpose and became punitive in character only in a situation where the continuous silence was based on "an established articulated moral principle." We reject this limitation as incapable of practical application.

not automatically satisfy the requirement of showing "no substantial likelihood." Each case must be decided on an independent evaluation of all
of the particular facts. Age, state of health and length of confinement are
all factors to be weighed, but the critical question is whether or not
further confinement will serve any coercive purpose.

We are not condoning Catena's defiance of the S.C.I. investigation,
nor are we subscribing to his reasons for remaining silent, whatever they
may be. We hold only that it now appears that there is no substantial
likelihood that further confinement will serve any coercive purpose and
cause him to testify. Since no legal basis for the continued confinement
of Catena exists, such confinement must be terminated. The matter is
remanded to the trial court for entry of an order that Catena be released
from custody forthwith.

SCHREIBER, J. (dissenting).

The majority has held and found that Catena should be released because from Catena's subjective viewpoint his commitment has lost its
coercive impact and become punitive. I must dissent on two grounds: (1)
the test applied is unsound; and (2) even if that standard is used, the
evidence does not justify the result.

I

To view the refusal to testify from Catena's viewpoint is to ignore the
clear legislative mandate. But more than that, it results in the substitution
of Catena's code for that mandate, a code which the majority points out
may well be "organized crime's oath of silence." The effect of the Court's
holding today is to substitute Catena's dogma for the law duly adopted by
society.

The State Commission of Investigation was created to conduct investigations in connection, among other things, with the "faithful execution
and effective enforcement of the laws of the State, with particular reference but not limited to organized crime and racketeering." N.J.S.A.
52:9M-2. . . .

The prime purpose of the act is to satisfy the public need for the
information irrespective of the stubbornness of the witness. The Legislature, fully aware of that need, authorized the Commission to clothe the
witness with immunity so that the data could be obtained. Refusal to
comply with the order justifies a finding of contempt. The statute contemplates that the witness should be incarcerated indefinitely under those
circumstances. Chief Justice Weintraub in In re Zicarelli, 55 N.J. 249,
272 (1970), *aff'd* 406 U.S. 472 (1972), wrote:

> . . . Here we have no doubt that the Legislature intended the S.C.I. to
> obtain the facts, whatever the wish of the person subpoenaed. The very provi-
> sion for a grant of immunity repels the notion that a witness may choose to be
> silent for a price.

The State's primary motive is to obtain information. "[T]he mission of the S.C.I. is to obtain facts for the Legislature and the mere punishment of a recalcitrant witness would not achieve that end." In re Zicarelli, 55 N.J. at 272. In the absence of a showing that the public need for that information no longer exists, the contempt remains unabated. . . . No one has asserted or offered any evidence that the Commission's position has ever been any other than to obtain the information which Catena probably has; and that that information is still presumably useful to the Commission. Catena has conceded for the purpose of this appeal that he is able to testify and possesses information pertinent to the Commission's continuing investigation of organized crime.[1]

The fact that the imprisonment may be for an indefinite period is legally justifiable. Penfield Co. v. Securities & Exchange Commission, 330 U.S. 585 (1947). . . .

One court recently has held that, where the individual had been in jail for one year for failure to comply with a court order to disclose the location of a child, so long as the witness had the power to obey, the incarceration was proper. People ex rel. Feldman v. Warden, 46 A.D. 2d 256, 362 N.Y.S.2d 171 (1974). The court stated:

> The law is clear that one who has been directed by a court to perform an act which the court finds is within that person's power to perform, he may be imprisoned until the act is performed. . . .
> . . . The appellant should not be allowed to bargain and barter with the court on the conditions of her compliance. . . .

362 N.Y.S.2d at 173-174. . . . Catena should not be permitted to substitute his code for the law of society. He should not be permitted to remain "silent for a price."

II

Even applying the subjective standard, namely, when did Catena's incarceration lose its coercive effect, the record here is insufficient to justify his release.

Incarceration has a dual aspect insofar as the prisoner is concerned. It is both coercive and punitive. There can be no doubt that from the outset he must consider his being jailed as punishment. "[I]ncarcerating a man until he does a certain act is as much a punishment of his original refusal to do that same act as it is a coercion of his doing it in the future." Goldfarb, The Contempt Power 60 (1963). The longer he is there, the more extensive the punishment. On the other hand, as time passes the

---

1. Inability to comply with the order would justify release. Maggio v. Zeitz, 333 U.S. 56 (1948). This is not the situation where "[a] man, faced with perpetual imprisonment till he discloses his confederates, will in the end find confederates to disclose." Loubriel v. United States, 9 F.2d 807, 809 (2d Cir. 1926).

coercive force of the desire to open the door to freedom in all likelihood becomes greater too. Age and health do not necessarily detract from and may in fact increase the coercive effect of imprisonment.

At what point the imprisoned person becomes completely adjusted to that life depends on the individual. Certain types of personalities can withstand strain over a longer period of time than others. In considering the effects of imprisonment it has been said that: "The different ways in which punishment is accepted, and the different time taken in the development of the mental processes cause great inequalities." Ohm, Personality Changes During Deprivation of Liberty (1964), summarized in Excerpta Criminologica 219 (1965).

Where, as here, the legislative intent has been expressed to compel the witness to divulge the information in return for immunity, and where the factual issue to be resolved will vary from individual to individual depending upon his personality, psychiatric reactions and adjustment, it is incumbent on him to prove clearly and convincingly that continued incarceration will have no coercive effect. Catena has not met that burden. His continuous legal attacks since incarceration, on many different grounds, until November 1974, reflect a hope which diluted the coercive effect of the order. Conspicuous by its absence was any expert psychiatric evidence. As noted earlier, age and health may well be factors which have primarily a coercive drive — rather than resignation. This Court in Catena v. Seidl, 65 N.J. at 264, in June 1974 wrote:

> The argument is made that Catena's age, condition of health and his persistent silence for four years, without more, establish a prima facie case that his commitment has failed as a coercive measure. We cannot agree. As heretofore noted, Catena's past silence can be rationally attributed to considerations other than an adamant refusal to purge himself of contempt despite the consequences.

There has been nothing more satisfactorily shown in this record to alter the conclusion we made then. Having failed to establish clearly and convincingly that continued imprisonment has lost its coercive import, Catena should not be freed.

I would reverse.

Justice MOUNTAIN joins in this dissent.

NOTES ON PERPETUAL COERCION

1. What has the court made perfectly clear? That determined New Jersey contemnors should be patient? Doesn't this opinion erode judicial power to enforce injunctions, by holding out the hope of release to all contemnors? The erosion may be minor if Catena made the minimum

showing, but some courts are now releasing contemnors on far lesser showings.

2. A federal witness who refuses to testify can be held no more than eighteen months, even in coercive contempt, and even if the testimony is still needed. 18 U.S.C. §1826 (1982). Plainly, he can buy silence for a price. But the announced price is only a maximum. It is becoming common to move for release long before the eighteen months has expired, on the ground that there is no substantial likelihood that the witness will testify, and that the imprisonment has therefore lost its coercive effect. Some of these motions are granted; many are carried through hearings and appeals.

An example is Simkin v. United States, 715 F.2d 34 (2d Cir. 1983), in which the court held that the trial judge had been too concerned about the example set for other witnesses and had not made an individualized determination whether further imprisonment would coerce Simkin. The court of appeals remanded for reconsideration. But in contrast to the New Jersey court's insistence on live testimony, and the New Jersey dissenter's desire for psychiatric evaluation, the Second Circuit said it was enough to take Simkin's affidavit and let his lawyer argue.

Simkin had served ten months at that point; there is no indication that he was not young and in good health. He said he feared retaliation from other drug dealers, and that he had religious scruples against testifying because "Jewish law and liturgy" cast disdain on informants.

3. How can a court make an individualized determination whether a contemnor is incurably recalcitrant? Any contemnor can beat his chest and swear he'll never give in. Those who make these motions generally try to offer a convincing reason for their recalcitrance. Does the court have anything to go on other than the convincing power of the proffered reason and the length of imprisonment already imposed without effect? The most common reasons in witness cases are fear of retaliation and loyalty to some claim of privilege that the court has rejected. Thus, reporters have refused to reveal their sources. In re Farr, 36 Cal. App. 3d 577, 111 Cal. Rptr. 649 (1974). And church workers have claimed that their work in the Hispanic community would be impaired if they testified to a grand jury investigating bombs exploded by the FALN — Armed Forces for the National Liberation of Puerto Rico. In re Cueto, 443 F. Supp. 857 (S.D.N.Y. 1978). Farr and Cueto were both released early.

4. The New Jersey court found it practical to determine whether the contemnor's stubbornness was irrevocable, but impractical to evaluate the moral worth of his reason for being so stubborn. Didn't they get it backwards? And didn't they also sneak in some other considerations? Does Catena's age and medical condition help prove how stubborn he is, or help make a humanitarian case for his release?

5. Think about how these cases change the dynamic of coercive contempt. The imprisoned contemnor can focus his energies on convinc-

ing the judge that he will never obey, and on a series of motions seeking release. He never has to give up hope. The longer he stays in jail, the greater his hope, because the stronger the evidence that his will is unbreakable. If he can just hold out a little longer, surely the judge will realize that further confinement has lost its coercive effect. But if he obeys the injunction now, all this suffering will have gone for nought. A firm resolve to leave him there forever if necessary would surely be more effective.

But what are the costs of such a firm resolve in the case of someone who truly is unbreakable? There are humanitarian reasons to end imprisonment, and economic ones too. While a contemnor is in prison, society loses his production and supports him in expensive quarters. If violation of the injunction were treated as a completed criminal offense, the maximum sentence might be quite short, and would surely be much less than life imprisonment. How much should it matter that the contemnor is seeking release before his offense is completed — that he continues to defy the court even as he seeks its mercy?

6.   Reported opinions releasing contemnors from civil coercion on the ground that it is ineffective are a fairly recent phenomenon. The traditional rhetoric was that defendant could stay in jail forever if he didn't comply. But it is also hard to find cases where that really happened. Perhaps that is because the traditional rhetoric caused most contemnors to eventually obey the injunction.

One case where both court and defendant hung tough involved Daisy Tegtmeyer, a family trustee who refused to turn over trust assets to the beneficiaries and refused to answer questions about the assets. She was committed to jail in 1933, and the court of appeals denied her petition to be released in 1937. Tegtmeyer v. Tegtmeyer, 292 Ill. App. 434, 11 N.E.2d 657 (1937). Another opinion three years later is less clear, but she was apparently still in jail. Tegtmeyer v. Tegtmeyer, 306 Ill. App. 169, 28 N.E.2d 303 (1940). The next opinion is murkiest of all, but the implication is that she was still in jail in 1942. The case seemed to be drawing to a close, and there seemed to be some hope of release. When the case closed, her testimony would no longer be needed, and the court found other grounds to vacate the rest of the coercive contempt order. Tegtmeyer v. Tegtmeyer, 314 Ill. App. 16, 40 N.E.2d 767 (1942).

7.   It is a defense to contempt that defendant is incapable of complying with the injunction. The defense arises most often in the context of injunctions to pay money, which are discussed in the next section. Probably the next most common use of the defense is in cases like *Tegtmeyer*, in which a defendant is ordered to deliver specific assets to plaintiff. In insolvency litigation, these injunctions are called turn-over orders. If defendant no longer has the property, he can't turn it over. That may have been a key element in Daisy Tegtmeyer's eventual release, but the opinion is too cryptic to be sure.

The impossibility defense aggravates the problem of perpetual coercion. The problem is nicely illustrated in People ex rel. Feldman v. Warden, 46 A.D.2d 256, 362 N.Y.S.2d 171 (1974). Feldman led a somewhat unorthodox life with a group in Greenwich Village. Her lover fathered a son, David, by a younger woman in the group. Feldman acted as David's foster mother, and the natural mother acted as his older sister. Later, the natural mother left the group, and sometime after that, sought custody of David.

This group was apparently what social workers would call a multi-problem family. David was thirteen years old and had never attended school. Feldman alleged that the natural mother had once tried to kill David. Feldman herself was confined to a wheelchair with multiple sclerosis.

Feldman refused to produce David in court and was jailed for contempt. After a year she filed a writ of habeas corpus and was released pending hearing of the writ. At the trial, she testified that she had looked for David during her time out of jail and could not find him. The trial judge didn't believe her. He found her testimony evasive, and concluded that "she has certainly not made the kind of an effort that a mother would normally make if her son's whereabouts were unknown to her." (Are the hypothetical efforts of a normal mother a relevant standard for measuring Feldman's credibility?) The trial court sent Feldman back to jail, and the Appellate Division affirmed, 2 to 1. The majority opinion is quoted in Justice Schreiber's dissent in *Catena*.

If Feldman sits in jail long enough, she may tell the truth and bring David to court. But what if her implausible tale is true and she really can't find David? That is certainly possible, and the longer she sits in jail, the more possible it becomes. Must she sit in jail until David is age 21, or until a judge finally believes her? If she had refused to turn over some inanimate thing, she could sit in jail for the rest of her life if no judge ever believed her. Is the option to release her when a judge concludes that imprisonment has lost its coercive effect a necessary protection against the risk of error?

8. The requirement of clear and convincing evidence also reduces the risk of error. But the effectiveness of that standard is reduced in turn-over litigation, because only the defendant knows the facts. To make the turn-over procedure work at all, the trustee in bankruptcy is given the benefit of an inference that if defendant once had the property, he still does. Thus, everything turns on whether the court believes defendant's tale of how he lost or dissipated the property. What does it mean to clearly and convincingly disbelieve somebody? In one of the leading turn-over cases, Justices Black and Rutledge proposed the beyond a reasonable doubt standard for all contempt proceedings that might result in fine or imprisonment. Maggio v. Zeitz, 333 U.S. 57, 79 (1948) (Black, J., dissenting).

9. The majority in *Maggio* offered another way out of the dilemma, at least in turn-over cases. It suggested that if defendant denies having the property despite long imprisonment, the trial judge should eventually believe him even though he did not believe him originally. "His denial of possession is given credit after demonstration that a period in prison does not produce the goods." Id. at 76.

10. Don't forget that a judge who concludes that coercive contempt has lost its coercive power can still turn to criminal contempt. In United States v. Patrick, 542 F.2d 381 (7th Cir. 1976), *cert. denied,* 430 U.S. 931 (1977), defendant was coercively imprisoned throughout a two-month trial, but he refused to testify. When the trial was over, coercive imprisonment ended because his testimony was no longer needed. He was then charged with criminal contempt, convicted by a jury, and sentenced to a fixed term of four years.

Would it be appropriate to give Gerardo Catena four more years after five years of coercion failed? If judges did that on a regular basis, wouldn't it reduce the attractiveness of trying to convince the judge that coercion has failed?

WALKER v. CITY OF BIRMINGHAM
388 U.S. 307 (1967)

MR. JUSTICE STEWART delivered the opinion of the Court.

On Wednesday, April 10, 1963, officials of Birmingham, Alabama, filed a bill of complaint in a state circuit court asking for injunctive relief against 139 individuals and two organizations. The bill and accompanying affidavits stated that during the preceding seven days:

> [R]espondents [had] sponsored and/or participated in and/or conspired to commit and/or to encourage and/or to participate in certain movements, plans or projects commonly called 'sit-in' demonstrations, 'kneel-in' demonstrations, mass street parades, trespasses on private property after being warned to leave the premises by the owners of said property, congregating in mobs upon the public streets and other public places, unlawfully picketing private places of business in the City of Birmingham, Alabama; violation of numerous ordinances and statutes of the City of Birmingham and State of Alabama. . . .

The circuit judge granted a temporary injunction as prayed in the bill, enjoining the petitioners from, among other things, participating in or encouraging mass street parades or mass processions without a permit as required by a Birmingham ordinance.

Five of the eight petitioners were served with copies of the writ early the next morning. Several hours later four of them held a press conference. There a statement was distributed, declaring their intention to disobey the injunction because it was "raw tyranny under the guise of maintaining law and order." At this press conference one of the petitioners stated: "That they had respect for the Federal Courts, or Federal Injunctions, but in the past the State Courts had favored local law enforcement, and if the police couldn't handle it, the mob would."

[There were large marches on April 12, Good Friday, and April 14, Easter Sunday. The marches were largely peaceful, but some members of the crowd threw rocks on Easter Sunday. There was testimony showing that each of the petitioners had marched or helped organize the marches.]

The next day the city officials who had requested the injunction applied to the state circuit court for an order to show cause why the petitioners should not be held in contempt for violating it. At the ensuing hearing the petitioners sought to attack the constitutionality of the injunction on the ground that it was vague and overbroad, and restrained free speech. They also sought to attack the Birmingham parade ordinance upon similar grounds, and upon the further ground that the ordinance had previously been administered in an arbitrary and discriminatory manner.

The circuit judge refused to consider any of these contentions, pointing out that there had been neither a motion to dissolve the injunction, nor an effort to comply with it by applying for a permit from the city commission before engaging in the Good Friday and Easter Sunday parades. Consequently, the court held that the only issues before it were whether it had jurisdiction to issue the temporary injunction, and whether thereafter the petitioners had knowingly violated it. Upon these issues the court found against the petitioners, and imposed upon each of them a sentence of five days in jail and a $50 fine, in accord with an Alabama statute.[3]

The Supreme Court of Alabama affirmed.[4] That court, too, declined to consider the petitioners' constitutional attacks upon the injunction and the underlying Birmingham parade ordinance:

> It is to be remembered that petitioners are charged with violating a temporary injunction. We are not reviewing a denial of a motion to dissolve or discharge a temporary injunction. Petitioners did not file any motion to vacate the temporary injunction until after the Friday and Sunday parades. Instead, petitioners deliberately defied the order of the court and did engage in and incite others to engage in mass street parades without a permit. . . .
> We hold that the circuit court had the duty and authority, in the first instance, to determine the validity of the ordinance, and, until the decision of

3. . . . The circuit court dismissed the contempt proceedings against several individuals on grounds of insufficient evidence. . . .
4. The Alabama Supreme Court quashed the conviction of one defendant because of insufficient proof that he knew of the injunction before violating it, and the convictions of two others because there was no showing that they had disobeyed the order. . . .

the circuit court is reversed for error by orderly review, either by the circuit court or a higher court, the orders of the circuit court based on its decision are to be respected and disobedience of them is contempt of its lawful authority, to be punished. Howat v. State of Kansas, 258 U.S. 181.

279 Ala. 53, 60, 62-63, 181 So. 2d 493, 500, 502.

Howat v. Kansas, 258 U.S. 181, was decided by this Court almost 50 years ago. That was a case in which people had been punished by a Kansas trial court for refusing to obey an antistrike injunction issued under the state industrial relations act. They had claimed a right to disobey the court's order upon the ground that the state statute and the injunction based upon it were invalid under the Federal Constitution. The Supreme Court of Kansas had affirmed the judgment, holding that the trial court

> had general power to issue injunctions in equity and that, even if its exercise of the power was erroneous, the injunction was not void, and the defendants were precluded from attacking it in this collateral proceeding . . . that, if the injunction was erroneous, jurisdiction was not thereby forfeited, that the error was subject to correction only by the ordinary method of appeal, and disobedience to the order constituted contempt.

258 U.S., at 189.

This Court, in dismissing the writ of error, not only unanimously accepted but fully approved the validity of the rule of state law upon which the judgment of the Kansas court was grounded:

> An injunction duly issuing out of a court of general jurisdiction with equity powers upon pleadings properly invoking its action, and served upon persons made parties therein and within the jurisdiction, must be obeyed by them however erroneous the action of the court may be, even if the error be in the assumption of the validity of a seeming but void law going to the merits of the case. It is for the court of first instance to determine the question of the validity of the law, and until its decision is reversed for error by orderly review, either by itself or by a higher court, its orders based on its decision are to be respected, and disobedience of them is contempt of its lawful authority, to be punished.

258 U.S., at 189-190.

The rule of state law accepted and approved in Howat v. Kansas is consistent with the rule of law followed by the federal courts.[5]

In the present case, however, we are asked to hold that this rule of law, upon which the Alabama courts relied, was constitutionally impermissi-

---

5. [Footnote 5 cited twelve cases, concluding with United States v. United Mine Workers. — ED.]

ble. . . . Whatever the limits of Howat v. Kansas,[6] we cannot accept the petitioners' contentions in the circumstances of this case.

Without question the state court that issued the injunction had, as a court of equity, jurisdiction over the petitioners and over the subject matter of the controversy. And this is not a case where the injunction was transparently invalid or had only a frivolous pretense to validity. We have consistently recognized the strong interest of state and local governments in regulating the use of their streets and other public places. When protest takes the form of mass demonstrations, parades, or picketing on public streets and sidewalks, the free passage of traffic and the prevention of public disorder and violence become important objects of legitimate state concern. . . .

The generality of the language contained in the Birmingham parade ordinance upon which the injunction was based would unquestionably raise substantial constitutional issues concerning some of its provisions. The petitioners, however, did not even attempt to apply to the Alabama courts for an authoritative construction of the ordinance. Had they done so, those courts might have given the licensing authority granted in the ordinance a narrow and precise scope. . . . [I]t could not be assumed that this ordinance was void on its face.

The breadth and vagueness of the injunction itself would also unquestionably be subject to substantial constitutional question. But the way to raise that question was to apply to the Alabama courts to have the injunction modified or dissolved. The injunction in all events clearly prohibited mass parading without a permit, and the evidence shows that the petitioners fully understood that prohibition when they violated it.

The petitioners also claim that they were free to disobey the injunction because the parade ordinance on which it was based had been administered in the past in an arbitrary and discriminatory fashion. In support of this claim they sought to introduce evidence that, a few days before the injunction issued, requests for permits to picket had been made to a member of the city commission. One request had been rudely rebuffed, and this same official had later made clear that he was without power to grant the permit alone, since the issuance of such permits was the responsibility of the entire city commission. Assuming the truth of this proffered evidence, it does not follow that the parade ordinance was void on its face. The petitioners, moreover, did not apply for a permit either to the

---

6. In In re Green, 369 U.S. 689, the petitioner was convicted of criminal contempt for violating a labor injunction issued by an Ohio court. Relying on the pre-emptive command of the federal labor law, the Court held that the state courts were required to hear Green's claim that the state court was *without jurisdiction* to issue the injunction. The petitioner in Green, unlike the petitioners here, had attempted to challenge the validity of the injunction *before* violating it by promptly applying to the issuing court for an order vacating the injunction. The petitioner in Green had further offered to prove that the court issuing the injunction had agreed to its violation as an appropriate means of testing its validity.

commission itself or to any commissioner after the injunction issued. Had they done so, and had the permit been refused, it is clear that their claim of arbitrary or discriminatory administration of the ordinance would have been considered by the state circuit court upon a motion to dissolve the injunction.

This case would arise in quite a different constitutional posture if the petitioners, before disobeying the injunction, had challenged it in the Alabama courts, and had been met with delay or frustration of their constitutional claims. But there is no showing that such would have been the fate of a timely motion to modify or dissolve the injunction. There was an interim of two days between the issuance of the injunction and the Good Friday march. The petitioners give absolutely no explanation of why they did not make some application to the state court during that period. The injunction had issued ex parte; if the court had been presented with the petitioners' contentions, it might well have dissolved or at least modified its order in some respects. If it had not done so, Alabama procedure would have provided for an expedited process of appellate review. It cannot be presumed that the Alabama courts would have ignored the petitioners' constitutional claims. Indeed, these contentions were accepted in another case by an Alabama appellate court that struck down on direct review the conviction under this very ordinance of one of these same petitioners.[13]

The rule of law upon which the Alabama courts relied in this case was one firmly established by previous precedents. . . . This is not a case where a procedural requirement has been sprung upon an unwary litigant when prior practice did not give him fair notice of its existence.

The Alabama Supreme Court has apparently never in any criminal contempt case entertained a claim of nonjurisdictional error. In Fields v. City of Fairfield, 273 Ala. 588, 143 So. 2d 177,[15] decided just three years before the present case, the defendants, members of a "White Supremacy" organization who had disobeyed an injunction, sought to challenge the constitutional validity of a permit ordinance upon which the injunction was based. The Supreme Court of Alabama, finding that the trial court had jurisdiction, applied the same rule of law which was followed here. . . .

The rule of law that Alabama followed in this case reflects a belief that in the fair administration of justice no man can be judge in his own case, however exalted his station, however righteous his motives, and irrespective of his race, color, politics, or religion. This Court cannot hold that the petitioners were constitutionally free to ignore all the procedures of the law and carry their battle to the streets. One may sympathize with the petitioners' impatient commitment to their cause. But respect for judicial

---

13. Shuttlesworth v. City of Birmingham, 43 Ala. App. 68, 180 So. 2d 114. The case is presently pending on certiorari review in the Alabama Supreme Court.

15. Reversed on other grounds, 375 U.S. 248.

process is a small price to pay for the civilizing hand of law, which alone can give abiding meaning to constitutional freedom.

Affirmed.

MR. CHIEF JUSTICE WARREN, whom MR. JUSTICE BRENNAN and MR. JUSTICE FORTAS join, dissenting.

Petitioners in this case contend that they were convicted under an ordinance that is unconstitutional on its face because it submits their First and Fourteenth Amendment rights to free speech and peaceful assembly to the unfettered discretion of local officials. They further contend that the ordinance was unconstitutionally applied to them because the local officials used their discretion to prohibit peaceful demonstrations by a group whose political viewpoint the officials opposed. The Court does not dispute these contentions, but holds that petitioners may nonetheless be convicted and sent to jail because the patently unconstitutional ordinance was copied into an injunction — issued ex parte without prior notice or hearing on the request of the Commissioner of Public Safety — forbidding all persons having notice of the injunction to violate the ordinance without any limitation of time. I dissent because I do not believe that the fundamental protections of the Constitution were meant to be so easily evaded, or that "the civilizing hand of law" would be hampered in the slightest by enforcing the First Amendment in this case.

The salient facts can be stated very briefly. Petitioners are Negro ministers who sought to express their concern about racial discrimination in Birmingham, Alabama, by holding peaceful protest demonstrations in that city on Good Friday and Easter Sunday 1963. For obvious reasons, it was important for the significance of the demonstrations that they be held on those particular dates. A representative of petitioners' organization went to the City Hall and asked "to see the person or persons in charge to issue permits, permits for parading, picketing, and demonstrating." She was directed to Public Safety Commissioner Connor, who denied her request for a permit in terms that left no doubt that petitioners were not going to be issued a permit under any circumstances. "He said, 'No, you will not get a permit in Birmingham, Alabama to picket. I will picket you over to the City Jail,' and he repeated that twice." A second, telegraphic request was also summarily denied, in a telegram signed by "Eugene 'Bull' Connor," with the added information that permits could be issued only by the full City Commission, a three-man body consisting of Commissioner Connor and two others.[1] According to petitioners' offer of

---

1. . . . The attitude of the city administration in general and of its Public Safety Commissioner in particular are a matter of public record, of course, and are familiar to this Court from previous litigation. The United States Commission on Civil Rights found continuing abuse of civil rights protesters by the Birmingham police, including use of dogs, clubs, and firehoses. Commissioner Eugene "Bull" Connor, a self-proclaimed white supremacist, made no secret of his personal attitude toward the rights of Negroes and the decisions of this Court. He vowed that racial integration would never come to Birmingham, and wore a button inscribed "Never" to advertise that vow. . . .

proof, the truth of which is assumed for purposes of this case, parade permits had uniformly been issued for all other groups by the city clerk on the request of the traffic bureau of the police department, which was under Commissioner Connor's direction. The requirement that the approval of the full Commission be obtained was applied only to this one group.

Understandably convinced that the City of Birmingham was not going to authorize their demonstrations under any circumstances, petitioners proceeded with their plans despite Commissioner Connor's orders. On Wednesday, April 10, at 9 in the evening, the city filed in a state circuit court a bill of complaint seeking an ex parte injunction. The complaint recited that petitioners were engaging in a series of demonstrations as "part of a massive effort . . . to forcibly integrate all business establishments, churches, and other institutions" in the city, with the result that the police department was strained in its resources and the safety, peace, and tranquility were threatened. It was alleged as particularly menacing that petitioners were planning to conduct "kneel-in" demonstrations at churches where their presence was not wanted. The city's police dogs were said to be in danger of their lives. Faced with these recitals, the Circuit Court issued the injunction in the form requested, and in effect ordered petitioners and all other persons having notice of the order to refrain for an unlimited time from carrying on any demonstrations without a permit. A permit, of course, was clearly unobtainable; the city would not have sought this injunction if it had any intention of issuing one.

Petitioners were served with copies of the injunction at various times on Thursday and on Good Friday. Unable to believe that such a blatant and broadly drawn prior restraint on their First Amendment rights could be valid, they announced their intention to defy it and went ahead with the planned peaceful demonstrations on Easter weekend. On the following Monday, when they promptly filed a motion to dissolve the injunction, the court found them in contempt, holding that they had waived all their First Amendment rights by disobeying the court order.

These facts lend no support to the court's charges that petitioners were presuming to act as judges in their own case, or that they had a disregard for the judicial process. They did not flee the jurisdiction or refuse to appear in the Alabama courts. Having violated the injunction, they promptly submitted themselves to the courts to test the constitutionality of the injunction and the ordinance it parroted. They were in essentially the same position as persons who challenge the constitutionality of a statute by violating it, and then defend the ensuing criminal prosecution on constitutional grounds. It has never been thought that violation of a statute indicated such a disrespect for the legislature that the violator always must be punished even if the statute was unconstitutional. . . .

The Court concedes that "[t]he generality of the language contained in the Birmingham parade ordinance upon which the injunction was based would unquestionably raise substantial constitutional issues concerning some of its provisions." That concession is well-founded but minimal. I believe it is patently unconstitutional on its face. Our decisions have consistently held that picketing and parading are means of expression protected by the First Amendment, and that the right to picket or parade may not be subjected to the unfettered discretion of local officials. . . . The only circumstance that the court can find to justify anything other than a per curiam reversal is that Commissioner Connor had the foresight to have the unconstitutional ordinance included in an ex parte injunction, issued without notice or hearing or any showing that it was impossible to have notice or a hearing, forbidding the world at large (insofar as it knew of the order) to conduct demonstrations in Birmingham without the consent of the city officials. This injunction was such potent magic that it transformed the command of an unconstitutional statute into an impregnable barrier, challengeable only in what likely would have been protracted legal proceedings and entirely superior in the meantime even to the United States Constitution.

I do not believe that giving this Court's seal of approval to such a gross misuse of the judicial process is likely to lead to greater respect for the law any more than it is likely to lead to greater protection for First Amendment freedoms. The ex parte temporary injunction has a long and odious history in this country, and its susceptibility to misuse is all too apparent from the facts of the case. As a weapon against strikes, it proved so effective in the hands of judges friendly to employers that Congress was forced to take the drastic step of removing from federal district courts the jurisdiction to issue injunctions in labor disputes.[6] The labor injunction fell into disrepute largely because it was abused in precisely the same way that the injunctive power was abused in this case. Judges who were not sympathetic to the union cause commonly issued, without notice or hearing, broad restraining orders addressed to large numbers of persons and forbidding them to engage in acts that were either legally permissible or, if illegal, that could better have been left to the regular course of criminal prosecution. The injunctions might later be dissolved, but in the meantime strikes would be crippled because the occasion on which concerted activity might have been effective had passed. Such injunctions, so long discredited as weapons against concerted labor activities, have now been given new life by this Court as weapons against the exercise of First Amendment freedoms. Respect for the courts and for judicial process was not increased by the history of the labor injunction.

Nothing in our prior decisions, or in the doctrine that a party subject to a temporary injunction issued by a court of competent jurisdiction with power to decide a dispute properly before it must normally challenge the injunction in the courts rather than by violating it, requires that we affirm the convictions in this case. The majority opinion in this case rests

6. The Norris-LaGuardia Act, 1932, 47 Stat. 70, 29 U.S.C. §§101-115.

essentially on a single precedent, and that a case the authority of which has clearly been undermined by subsequent decisions. Howat v. Kansas, 258 U.S. 181 (1922), was decided in the days when the labor injunction was in fashion. . . .

Insofar as Howat v. Kansas might be interpreted to approve an absolute rule that any violation of a void court order is punishable as contempt, it has been greatly modified by later decisions. In In re Green, 369 U.S. 689 (1962), we reversed a conviction for contempt of a state injunction forbidding labor picketing because the petitioner was not allowed to present evidence that the labor dispute was arguably subject to the jurisdiction of the National Labor Relations Board and hence not subject to state regulation. If an injunction can be challenged on the ground that it deals with a matter arguably subject to the jurisdiction of the National Labor Relations Board, then a fortiori it can be challenged on First Amendment grounds.[9]

It is not necessary to question the continuing validity of the holding in Howat v. Kansas, however, to demonstrate that neither it nor the *Mine Workers* case supports the holding of the majority in this case. In *Howat* the subpoena and injunction were issued to enable the Kansas Court of Industrial Relations to determine an underlying labor dispute. In the *Mine Workers* case, the District Court issued a temporary antistrike injunction to preserve existing conditions during the time it took to decide whether it had authority to grant the Government relief in a complex and difficult action of enormous importance to the national economy. In both cases the orders were of questionable legality, but in both cases they were reasonably necessary to enable the court or administrative tribunal to decide an underlying controversy of considerable importance before it at the time. This case involves an entirely different situation. The Alabama Circuit Court did not issue this temporary injunction to preserve existing conditions while it proceeded to decide some underlying dispute. There was no underlying dispute before it, and the court in practical effect merely added a judicial signature to a preexisting criminal ordinance. . . .

It is not necessary in this case to decide precisely what limits should be set to the *Mine Workers* doctrine in cases involving violations of the First

---

9. The attempt in footnote 6 of the majority opinion to distinguish In re Green is nothing but an attempt to alter the holding of that case. The opinion of the Court states flatly that "a state court is without power to hold one in contempt for violating an injunction that the state court had no power to enter by reason of federal pre-emption." 369 U.S. at 692 (footnote omitted). The alleged circumstance that the court issuing the injunction had agreed to its violation as an appropriate means of testing its validity was considered only in a concurring opinion. Although the petitioner in *Green* had attempted to challenge the order in court before violating it, we did not rely on that fact in holding that the order was void. Nor is it clear to me why the Court regards this fact as important, unless it means to imply that the petitioners in this case would have been free to violate the court order if they had first made a motion to dissolve in the trial court.

Amendment. Whatever the scope of that doctrine, it plainly was not intended to give a State the power to nullify the United States Constitution by the simple process of incorporating its unconstitutional criminal statutes into judicial decrees. I respectfully dissent.

MR. JUSTICE DOUGLAS, with whom THE CHIEF JUSTICE, MR. JUSTICE BRENNAN, and MR. JUSTICE FORTAS concur, dissenting. . . .

The right to defy an unconstitutional statute is basic in our scheme. Even when an ordinance requires a permit to make a speech, to deliver a sermon, to picket, to parade, or to assemble, it need not be honored when it is invalid on its face.

By like reason, where a permit has been arbitrarily denied, one need not pursue the long and expensive route to this Court to obtain a remedy. The reason is the same in both cases. For if a person must pursue his judicial remedy before he may speak, parade, or assemble, the occasion when protest is desired or needed will have become history and any later speech, parade, or assembly will be futile or pointless.

Howat v. Kansas, 258 U.S. 181, states the general rule that court injunctions are to be obeyed until error is found by normal and orderly review procedures. See United States v. Mine Workers, 330 U.S. 258, 293-294. But there is an exception where "the question of jurisdiction" is "frivolous and not substantial." Id. at 293. Moreover, a state court injunction is not per se sacred where federal constitutional questions are involved. In re Green, 369 U.S. 689, held that contempt could not be imposed without a hearing where the state decree bordered the federal domain in labor relations and only a hearing could determine whether there was federal pre-emption. In the present case the collision between this state court decree and the First Amendment is so obvious that no hearing is needed to determine the issue. . . .

A court does not have *jurisdiction* to do what a city or other agency of a State lacks *jurisdiction* to do. . . . An ordinance — unconstitutional on its face or patently unconstitutional as applied — is not made sacred by an unconstitutional injunction that enforces it. It can and should be flouted in the manner of the ordinance itself. Courts as well as citizens are not free "to ignore all the procedures of the law," to use the Court's language. The "constitutional freedom" of which the Court speaks can be won only if judges honor the Constitution.

MR. JUSTICE BRENNAN, with whom THE CHIEF JUSTICE, MR. JUSTICE DOUGLAS, and MR. JUSTICE FORTAS join, dissenting.

Under cover of exhortation that the Negro exercise "respect for judicial process," the Court empties the Supremacy Clause of its primacy by elevating a state rule of judicial administration above the right of free expression guaranteed by the Federal Constitution. . . .

Like the Court, I start with the premise that States are free to adopt rules of judicial administration designed to require respect for their courts' orders. But this does not mean that this valid state interest does not admit of collision with other and more vital interests.

In the present case we are confronted with a collision between Alabama's interest in requiring adherence to orders of its courts and the constitutional prohibition against abridgement of freedom of speech. . . . The most striking examples of the right to speak first and challenge later, and of peculiar moment for the present case, are the cases concerning the ability of an individual to challenge a permit or licensing statute giving broad discretion to an individual or group, such as the Birmingham permit ordinance, despite the fact that he did not attempt to obtain a permit or license. . . .

Yet by some inscrutable legerdemain these constitutionally secured rights to challenge prior restraints invalid on their face are lost if the State takes the precaution to have some judge append his signature to an ex parte order which recites the words of the invalid statute. . . .

The Court's religious deference to the state court's application of the *Mine Workers'* rule in the present case is in stark contrast to the Court's approach in In re Green, 369 U.S. 689. The state court issued an ex parte injunction against certain labor picketing. Green, counsel for the union, advised the union that the order was invalid and that it should continue to picket so that the order could be tested in a contempt hearing. The court held Green in contempt without allowing any challenge to the order. This Court stated that the issue was "whether the state court was trenching on the federal domain." In re Green, supra, at 692. It remanded for a hearing to determine whether the activity enjoined was "arguably" subject to Labor Board jurisdiction. In *Green*, therefore, we rejected blind effectuation of the State's interest in requiring compliance with its court's ex parte injunctions because of the "arguable" collision with federal labor policy. Yet in the present case the Court affirms the determination of a state court which was willing to assume that its ex parte order and the underlying statute were repugnant on their face to the First Amendment of the Federal Constitution. One must wonder what an odd inversion of values it is to afford greater respect to an "arguable" collision with federal labor policy than an assumedly patent interference with constitutional rights so high in the scale of constitutional values that this Court has described them as being "delicate and vulnerable, as well as supremely precious in our society." NAACP v. Button, 371 U.S. 415, 433. . . .

The Court today lets loose a devastatingly destructive weapon for infringement of freedoms jealously safeguarded not so much for the benefit of any given group of any given persuasion as for the benefit of all of us. We cannot permit fears of "riots" and "civil disobedience" generated by slogans like "Black Power" to divert our attention from what is here at stake — not violence or the right of the State to control its streets and sidewalks, but the insulation from attack of ex parte orders and legislation upon which they are based even when patently impermissible prior restraints on the exercise of First Amendment rights, thus arming the state courts with the power to punish as a "contempt" what they otherwise could not punish at all. Constitutional restrictions against abridgments of First Amendment freedoms limit judicial equally with legislative and executive power. Convictions for contempt of court orders which invalidly abridge First Amendment freedoms must be condemned equally with convictions for violation of statutes which do the same thing. I respectfully dissent.

NOTES ON THE DUTY TO OBEY ERRONEOUS INJUNCTIONS

1. Bull Connor won this battle, but he had long since lost the war. Birmingham was in the national news all through the spring of 1963, and "Bull Connor's police dogs and firehoses" became a catch phrase for bitter resistance to integration. The leader of the marches, Dr. Martin Luther King, won the Nobel Peace Prize for his work in Birmingham and elsewhere. News coverage of Birmingham triggered a massive shift in public opinion that made possible the Civil Rights Act of 1964. The Kennedy administration began work on the bill in May; it had previously believed that such a bill could not be enacted. An assistant attorney general from that administration reviews the political consequences of Birmingham in B. Schlei and P. Grossman, Employment Discrimination Law vii-xiii (1976).

2. Some of the defendants were also prosecuted directly under the parade ordinance. The Supreme Court unanimously held the ordinance unconstitutional in Shuttlesworth v. City of Birmingham, 394 U.S. 147 (1969). Justice Stewart again wrote the opinion. There was no more waffling about the substantiality of the issue or the need to seek a narrowing construction. The ordinance

> fell squarely within the ambit of the many decisions of this Court over the last 30 years, holding that a law subjecting the exercise of First Amendment freedoms to the prior restraint of a license, without narrow, objective, and definite standards to guide the licensing authority, is unconstitutional.

394 U.S. at 150-151. *Shuttlesworth* lets us consider *Walker* without being distracted by lingering doubts about whether the ordinance and injunction were really unconstitutional. The injunction was even broader than the ordinance, and thus even more clearly unconstitutional.

3. Once it is clear that the injunction was unconstitutional, *Walker* depends wholly on the rule that an injunction cannot be collaterally

attacked in a prosecution for criminal contempt. This rule is often called the collateral bar rule. It does not apply in civil contempt. Plaintiff is not entitled to benefit from an erroneous injunction, either by recovering compensation or coercing compliance. But the criminal offense is complete when defendant defies the court. It does not matter whether the court was right or wrong, and the offense is not undone if the injunction is later reversed. The rule is followed nearly everywhere; California is a notable exception. In re Berry, 68 Cal. 2d 137, 436 P.2d 273 (1968).

4. The traditional formulation of the rule is that defendant must obey if the court that issued the injunction had jurisdiction. If the court lacked jurisdiction, the injunction can be ignored. What's so special about jurisdiction? The dissenters in *Walker* argue that surely the first amendment is more important than some technical rule allocating jurisdiction between state courts and the National Labor Relations Board. Would the majority disagree? Does anyone think that jurisdiction is the only value *important* enough to justify disobedience?

5. The jurisdiction exception has a different source. If a drunk claiming to be Warren Burger starts issuing orders, no one is bound to obey. The drunk lacks authority to issue the orders. Similarly, the notion is that a court without jurisdiction lacks authority to enjoin. In Justice Frankfurter's phrase from *Mine Workers*, a judge purporting to exercise jurisdiction that he "unquestionably" lacks "would not be acting as a court. He would be a pretender. . . . " United States v. United Mine Workers, 330 U.S. 258, 310 (1947) (Frankfurter, J., concurring). But unlike a drunk, a court gets the benefit of the doubt. "Only when a court is so obviously traveling outside its orbit as to be merely usurping judicial forms and facilities, may an order issued by a court be disobeyed and treated as though it were a letter to a newspaper." Id. at 309-310.

6. *Mine Workers* carried the collateral bar rule further than *Walker*. The Norris-LaGuardia Act deprives federal courts of jurisdiction to enjoin strikes. 29 U.S.C. §§101 et seq. (1982). There are some express exceptions, but none that apply to the case. Thus, the trial court appeared to lack jurisdiction. The United States argued that the act does not apply when the sovereign is the employer. Justices Vinson, Burton, Reed, Black, and Douglas agreed. It followed that the trial court had had jurisdiction, and that the injunction was proper on the merits. 330 U.S. at 269-289.

A different majority subscribed to an alternative holding based on the collateral bar rule. Justices Frankfurter and Jackson believed, and Justices Vinson, Burton, and Reed assumed arguendo, that the Norris-LaGuardia Act did apply. On that view, the trial court ultimately lacked jurisdiction to enjoin the strike. Still, they said, whether the act applied to the United States was a close question, and the trial court had jurisdiction to decide that question. That is, it had jurisdiction to determine the scope of its own jurisdiction, even if it lacked jurisdiction to determine the merits. And, this majority said, the trial court had power to preserve the status quo while it exercised its power to determine jurisdiction. So it had jurisdiction to issue a temporary restraining order against the strike while it decided whether the Norris-LaGuardia Act applied, even if it ultimately turned out that the act did apply and the court lacked jurisdiction to enjoin the strike. 330 U.S. at 289-295.

Justices Rutledge and Murphy rejected that theory, largely on the ground that the plain language of the Norris-LaGuardia Act permitted no such exception. The majority conceded that Rutledge and Murphy would be right if the claim of an exception for the United States were frivolous. A judge has jurisdiction to consider jurisdiction, but only if there is a nonfrivolous claim of jurisdiction over the merits. Justices Black and Douglas found this whole debate unnecessary to the decision, and expressed no views. So the vote on the alternative holding was 5 to 2.

7. In re Green, 369 U.S. 689 (1962), is much debated in *Walker* and somewhat distorted by both sides. *Green* is easy to reconcile with *Walker* but harder to reconcile with *Mine Workers*. The brief majority opinion rests squarely on the ground that the state court appeared to lack jurisdiction because of federal preemption. And assuming that the state court might have had jurisdiction, the Court said that due process required a hearing where defendant could contest jurisdiction before he was punished for contempt. Justice Harlan concurred on other grounds. He found the majority approach irreconcilable with *Mine Workers*. The state court's claim of jurisdiction was not frivolous, so its orders were binding until jurisdiction was finally determined.

The majority's answer to Harlan was apparently the single sentence about due process. Another answer might be that he overstated the *Mine Workers* rule. If the state court in *Green* went straight to the merits without ever considering jurisdiction, was it exercising jurisdiction to consider jurisdiction? Or was it exercising jurisdiction over the merits? The concept of jurisdiction to consider jurisdiction is central to *Mine Workers*, and arguably requires explicit attention to the jurisdictional issue. Of course, if the court decides that it has jurisdiction, that determination presumably becomes law of the case until reversed. Thus, an erroneous determination of jurisdiction confers jurisdiction over the merits, at least for a while.

8. Is the traditional emphasis on jurisdiction convincing, even on its own terms? If a court that clearly exceeds jurisdictional limits is a pretender, why isn't a court that clearly exceeds constitutional limits a pretender? Don't constitutional limits deprive the whole government of power, just as jurisdictional limits deprive particular courts or agencies of power? If a court has no power to exceed its jurisdiction, why does it have power to violate the constitution?

9. *Walker* holds open the possibility of two exceptions other than lack of jurisdiction. The majority says that "this is not a case where the injunction was transparently invalid or had only a frivolous pretense to validity."

It also says that "this case would arise in quite a different constitutional posture if the petitioners, before disobeying the injunction, had challenged it in the Alabama courts, and had been met with delay or frustration of their constitutional claims." Might either of those disclaimers produce an exception with real content? How "transparently invalid" does the injunction have to be, if the *Walker* injunction isn't transparent enough? How much delay or frustration would you put up with before advising a client to defy an injunction?

Rightly or wrongly, defendants plainly feared delay and frustration in the state courts. What's wrong with a rule that says they have to obey the injunction until it is set aside, but that they can go straight to the federal district court for a counter injunction granting permission to march? The federal court could enjoin Bull Connor from enforcing the state injunction. Whatever the appeal of that solution, the Supreme Court has precluded it in a series of cases beginning with Younger v. Harris, infra at 1182.

10.   The Court says the Alabama trial court "without question" had jurisdiction over defendants. Is that true? How did it acquire jurisdiction? A year after *Walker*, the Court decided Carroll v. President of Princess Anne, supra at 405. Formal service is not required before a temporary restraining order, but the informal notice required by *Carroll* obviously substitutes for formal service. Does it only substitute for the notice function of service, or does it also substitute for the jurisdictional function? Doesn't something have to substitute for the jurisdictional function of service? Shouldn't defendants have argued that the Alabama court lacked personal jurisdiction, because they were not served and there was no effort to notify them or explain why they could not be notified?

11.   One other case you should know about is United States v. Shipp, 203 U.S. 563 (1906). Shipp was the sheriff of Hamilton County, Tennessee. He had custody of a black prisoner, Johnson, sentenced to death for rape of a white woman. Johnson filed a writ of habeas corpus alleging racial discrimination in jury selection and mob domination of his trial. The federal trial court denied the writ, but stayed execution for ten days to permit an appeal to the Supreme Court. Johnson appealed, and on the ninth day, the Court issued a further stay of execution. The order was telegraphed to Shipp and reported in the Chattanooga papers. That night, Johnson was lynched by a mob, and Shipp was charged with aiding the mob instead of protecting his prisoner. Only Tennessee could prosecute him for murder, but the United States prosecuted him for contempt of the Supreme Court's stay order.

Shipp defended on the ground that the Court lacked jurisdiction. The federal courts had jurisdiction only if Johnson presented a substantial federal question. Shipp argued that Johnson's federal claims were "absolutely frivolous" and created a mere pretense of federal jurisdiction. The Court rejected the argument:

It has been held, it is true, that orders made by a court having no jurisdiction to make them may be disregarded without liability or process for contempt. But even if the Circuit Court had no jurisdiction to entertain Johnson's petition, and if this court had no jurisdiction of the appeal, this court, and this court alone, could decide that such was the law. It and it alone necessarily had jurisdiction to decide whether the case was properly before it. . . . Until its judgment declining jurisdiction should be announced, it had authority from the necessity of the case to make orders to preserve the existing conditions and the subject of the petition. . . . [T]he law contemplates the possibility of a decision either way, and therefore must provide for it.

Id. at 573.

12. Should Shipp go unpunished if the Court would have upheld Johnson's conviction? Should he go unpunished if the Court would have concluded that Johnson's claims were so frivolous they conferred only a pretense of jurisdiction? Can the law afford any exception that authorizes litigants to decide for themselves whether to obey court orders? Should defendants be tempted to convince themselves that the court's claim to jurisdiction is frivolous?

13. If Shipp should be punished even if Johnson's claims were frivolous, how is *Walker* different? *Shipp* at least differs in degree; death is the ultimate irreparable injury. But anytime there is an injunction, some court has decided that defendant will suffer irreparable injury if the injunction is violated.

Is it that Walker was exercising a constitutional right but Shipp wasn't? Justice Rehnquist would say that Tennessee's right to enforce the death penalty is as much a constitutional right as Walker's right to speak — that the constitution guarantees state rights as well as individual rights. That is not to say he would defend what Shipp did, but you can't make *Shipp* go away by saying there were no interests on the other side.

Is it that *Shipp* involves a confusion between jurisdiction and the merits? The Supreme Court has always said that frivolous federal questions do not confer federal jurisdiction. The cases are collected in Hagans v. Lavine, 415 U.S. 528, 537-538 (1974). But when a litigant presents a frivolous federal question to a federal court, that court must pronounce it frivolous. That is not a decision that some other court should answer the question — the usual meaning of jurisdiction. It is an answer to the question, a decision on the merits, although labeled jurisdictional. If we accept that reformulation, then the Court unquestionably had jurisdiction in *Shipp*. And there was no error even on the merits in its stay order. It was proper to keep Johnson alive pending final decision, even if the final decision would be adverse. I think this is what Justice Rutledge means in an extraordinarily cryptic passage in his *Mine Workers* dissent. It is a good argument. But it is not what the Court said in *Shipp*, and it is not consistent with the Court's adherence to the fiction that it lacks jurisdiction over frivolous questions. And it doesn't have much to do with the reasons that many people want to punish Sheriff Shipp and exonerate Reverend Walker.

14.   Does the wisdom of the collateral bar rule ultimately come down to predictions about the frequency of cases like *Walker* and cases like *Shipp*? In all cases in which judges issue injunctions that defendants are tempted to violate, will the judges be right more often than the defendants, or will the defendants be right more often than the judges?

15.   The collateral bar rule is designed to discourage defiance. A countervailing rule is applied to cases where it is thought important to discourage appeals. Subpoenas and discovery orders are unappealable. One who receives such an order may move to quash in the trial court, but a denial of the motion to quash is also unappealable. To appeal, the witness or litigant must defy the order and be convicted of criminal contempt. The conviction is appealable, and the validity of the underlying order can be raised on appeal. If the appeal is unsuccessful, appellant faces punishment for contempt. The purpose and effect is to deter appeals by putting a price on failure.

The Supreme Court has explained that *Walker* does not apply to such cases, because it "was based upon the availability of review of [defendants'] claims at an earlier stage." United States v. Ryan, 402 U.S. 530, 532 n.4 (1971). That may not quite capture the distinction. It seems to have been irrelevant that the TRO in *Mine Workers* was unappealable. The order in *Walker* apparently was appealable. But in an unsuccessful petition for rehearing, Walker collected recent reported appeals from Alabama temporary injunctions; even with expedited procedure, it had taken from four and a half to nine months to get an appellate ruling. Petition for Rehearing at 6 n.2.

GRIFFIN v. COUNTY SCHOOL BOARD
363 F.2d 206 (4th Cir.), *cert. denied*, 385 U.S. 960 (1966)

Before HAYNSWORTH, Chief Judge, and SOBELOFF, BOREMAN, BRYAN and BELL, sitting en banc.

BRYAN, Circuit Judge.

A judgment of civil contempt upon the Board of Supervisors of Prince Edward County and its members is moved for by the appellants-plaintiffs. The ground of the motion is that the Board disbursed public funds to private segregated schools while the right to do so was under consideration by this court. A remedial order requiring the Board to restore these moneys to the County Treasurer is also asked. We grant the motion.

The episode developed in the enforcement of decrees of the District Court reopening the Prince Edward County public schools. . . .

[Prince Edward County, Virginia was one of the four school districts in Brown v. Board of Education, 347 U.S. 483 (1954), the original school desegregation suit. Prince Edward County responded by closing its public schools for nine years. During that time, the county made tuition grants to parents of children attending private schools organized for white children.

In 1962, the federal district court ordered the school board to quit paying tuition grants until it reopened the public schools. In the summer of 1964, public schools began registering students for the coming school year. The school board planned to continue paying tuition grants, so that the public schools would be all black and the private schools would be all white.]

After argument of the appeal in regular course, the District Court was directed to enjoin the Board from paying any tuition grants to send children to private schools so long as these schools remained segregated.

Our decision did not pass upon the contempt motion, but remanded it to the District Court for "further inquiries into the facts surrounding the payments." The District Judge was authorized to consider also the charge of the appellants that the defendants had in effect paid 1963-64 grants retrospectively, by authorizing and paying increased amounts for 1964-65, and thus were in contempt of the District Judge's order of July 9, 1964.

Pursuant to the remittitur, the District Court on February 8, 1965 cited the individual members of the Board of Supervisors to show cause, if any, why they should not be held in contempt of the District Court for failure to comply with its injunction of July 9, 1964 against the retroactive payment of the 1963-64 grants. The rule came on for hearing April 23, 1965, at which time all of the parties in interest were present in person and represented by counsel. In addition to the facts heretofore recited, the District Judge made the following undisputed findings in regard to the questioned events of July and August 1964:

> The Board of Supervisors of Prince Edward County held a meeting on the morning of August 4, 1964 at which time Warren Scott and four of the Negro citizens appeared and filed an unsigned petition bearing ten hundred four typewritten names requesting that the Board of Supervisors allocate additional funds to be used for the purpose of public education. No action was then taken.
>
> Shortly after adjournment of the Board meeting, Supervisor Jenkins and Supervisor Steck met with a Mr. Taylor and other interested citizens for the purpose of finding a way to pay the '64-'65 tuition grants prior to the time the Court of Appeals could enter an order staying these payments. (It was then known to Mr. Jenkins and to the other members of the group that there had been discussions between Mr. Gray [counsel for the State Superintendent of Public Instruction] and Mr. Dean [Clerk of the Court of Appeals] in re the possibility of the County agreeing not to make any tuition grant payments during the pendency of the appeal.)
>
> The Commonwealth Attorney and two other members of the Board of Supervisors were then called. Those assembled agreed that if the Board of

Supervisors would increase the tuition grants to $310.00 for high school and $290.00 for elementary school and authorize the immediate payment thereof, this could be done before the Court of Appeals could do anything about it.

The four Board members and the Commonwealth Attorney then went to the home of the chairman of the Board of Supervisors to advise him of what they had in mind and to determine whether or not a special meeting of the Board of Supervisors could be called the next morning for the purpose of expediting the payment of the '64-'65 tuition grants. The chairman, after being advised by the Board's special counsel and the Commonwealth Attorney that such a resolution on the part of the Board of Supervisors would be legal, called a special meeting of the Board for 8:00 A.M. August 5th. At that meeting the Board passed the resolution which provided that the grants should be paid half on or before September 1, 1964 and half on or before January 1, 1965.

In the interim, that is, between the meeting at Chairman Vaughan's house and eight o'clock the next morning, Board Member Jenkins and other members of the citizens' committee made arrangements to telephone the parents of the children then attending the Prince Edward School Foundation schools advising them if they came down that night and made application they could get half the tuition money that morning.

Some twenty or thirty volunteers assisted the secretary of the Board in processing the applications and making out the necessary checks. County bonds were sold in Richmond the next morning to raise the money necessary for the payment of these checks.

Twelve hundred seventeen tuition grant applications were filed during the night of August 4-5. All of these applications were for the '64-'65 school year. Each applicant was paid one-half of the amount applied for. Most, if not all, of the applicants were children enrolled in the Prince Edward School Foundation schools for the year '64-'65.

There being no evidence that the money thus paid covered school years prior to '64-'65, the Court concludes that the payments made August 4-5, 1964 were not violative of the order entered herein July 9, 1964. The show cause order issued against the members of the Board of Supervisors February 8, 1965 will be dismissed, and it is SO ORDERED.

That these acts of the Board of Supervisors constituted a contempt of this court is beyond cavil. The Board undertook to put the money then available for tuition grants — and then wholly subject to its orders — beyond its control as well as that of the court. In doing so the Board took upon itself to decide its right to exercise, in favor of the private school, the Board's general power to appropriate public funds. This use of power was, as the Board was acutely aware, an arrogation of this court's responsibility. Obviously, the aim was to thwart the impact of any adverse decree which might ultimately be forthcoming on the appeal. In effect it was a "resistance to its [this court's] lawful writ, process, order, rule, decree, or command." 18 U.S.C. §401(3). The authorities are quite clear on the point.

The Board would escape the judgment of contempt on the argument that the statute limits the power of the court to violations of orders or decrees then extant. But precedent does not so contract the statute or constrict its intent. Although this court had not issued an injunction against the appropriation of the moneys to tuition grants, the Board knew that if the plaintiffs succeeded this would be its ultimate decree, as in fact it became. That potential decree was thus then within the statute. Furthermore, the appeal was itself a "process" which was alive at the time of the disbursement and was resisted by the disbursement.

In Merrimack River Savings Bank v. Clay Center, 219 U.S. 527 (1911), a temporary injunction had been issued by a Federal District Court to prevent the destruction by a municipality of a public utility's poles and wires, located in the city streets under an authorized franchise. The suit was dismissed on jurisdictional grounds. However, for and during an appeal to the Supreme Court, the injunction was continued in force. On this review the dismissal was upheld. But before the mandate of dismissal had been issued or could issue, and in the period allowed for presenting an application for a rehearing, the city cut down the poles, destroyed a large section of the wires and thus put the utility out of business. This conduct was declared to be contempt of the Supreme Court, Justice Lurton saying at 535-536:

> It does not necessarily follow that disobedience of such an injunction, intended only to preserve the status quo pending an appeal, may not be regarded as a contempt of the appellate jurisdiction of this court, which might be rendered nugatory by conduct calculated to remove the subject-matter of the appeal beyond its control, or by its destruction. This we need not decide, since *irrespective of any such injunction actually issued the wilful removal beyond the reach of the court of the subject-matter of the litigation . . . [on] appeal . . . is, in and of itself, a contempt of the appellate jurisdiction of this court. . . .* Unless this be so, a reversal of the decree would be but a barren victory, since the very result would have been brought about by the lawless act of the defendants which it was the object of the suit to prevent.

(Accent added.)

The contempt power declared in the *Merrimack* case was not suggested to be rooted in the inherent power of the Supreme Court rather than in the statute now embodied in 18 U.S.C. §401(3). Incidentally, the Court has never excluded itself from the statute. But *Merrimack* is not now cited to power. It is cited as warranting our finding that the putting of the subject-matter of this litigation beyond our reach was a defiance of this court, an anticipatory resistance to its ultimate orders or process.

That inferior courts have the same contempt power as the Supreme Court exerted in *Merrimack*, and that similar conduct is contempt of the lower courts, were unequivocally enunciated in Lamb v. Cramer, 285 U.S. 217, 219 (1932). There, as in the case now on review, no injunction or order had been issued restraining disposition of the property in suit. Nevertheless, receipt and possession of a part of the res, pendente lite, by a transferee of the defendant-owner was adjudged a contempt of the trial court. The Court had no difficulty in concluding that there was contempt despite the absence of a current restraining order.

While Lamb v. Cramer did not specifically mention the statute, the Court obviously did not think it barred prosecution of the transferee for contempt. Essentially, the Court followed the statutory terms — "resistance to its [the court's] lawful writ, process, order, rule, decree, or command" — by not limiting its application to an immediately outstanding precept. The anticipated final judgment was not considered to be presently beyond the contemplation of the statute. Indeed, the contrary is implicit in the opinion. The diversion of the res was held to be contumacious because it "tended to defeat any *decree* which the court *might ultimately* make in the cause." (Accent added.)

Civil and not criminal contempt was the gravamen of Lamb v. Cramer and is here too. This was a predominant consideration of the Supreme Court and probably accounts for no advertence to the contempt statute, which seems worded more appropriately for criminal contempt. The omission means nothing, for the primary reasoning of the Court was that the res was in gremio legis [literally, "in the bosom of the law"] and the conveyance of it in part was a disturbance of the constructive possession of the trial court. Whether the decision in Lamb v. Cramer was founded on this conception of judicial custody or on the statute, of which the Court was hardly unaware, is immaterial. Either ground supports our holding that the Board of Supervisors was in contempt.

The present case is quite different factually from Berry v. Midtown Service Corp., 104 F.2d 107 (2 Cir. 1939), relied upon by the Board. There the subject-matter disposed of pending appeal was the leviable assets of the judgment debtor-appellant. The Court distinguished that case from ours when it said that the appeal was not "defeated or impaired" by the defendant's assignment. Further distinction is found in its observation that the suit "was not concerned with any specific property," the judgment on appeal merely establishing a general, personal, financial liability.

In our case the disbursement of the moneys seriously impaired the appeal. The suit and the appeal were directed to a specific subject, the Board's right to apply to a certain purpose moneys within its power. The Board assumed the right in utter and wilful disregard of this court's views. As was said in Merrimack River Savings Bank v. Clay Center, and again in Lamb v. Cramer, such conduct constituted contempt although not formally and explicitly under injunction.

We find the Board of Supervisors and its members guilty of civil contempt. Accordingly, the Board and its constituent individuals, namely, W. W. Vaughan, C. W. Gates, H. M. Jenkins, Charles B. Pickett, John

C. Steck and H. E. Carwile, Jr., personally and in their own right, will be ordered jointly and severally to restore to the County Treasurer of Prince Edward County, through recapture or otherwise, an amount equal to the disbursements authorized and made by their resolutions of August 4-5, 1964. This cause will be continued for a period of 90 days from this date for report by the Board and its members of what has been done towards compliance with this order, as well as for the passage of such further orders as may appear proper. . . .

HAYNSWORTH, Chief Judge, with whom BOREMAN, Circuit Judge, joins (dissenting). . . .

It is clear that this Court has an inherent power to punish contempts. It was originally defined by the seventeenth section of the Judiciary Act of 1789 as the power to punish by fine or imprisonment all contempts of authority in any cause or hearing before the Court. But the power has since been limited and redefined by the Act of Congress of March 2, 1831, now 18 U.S.C. §401. The statute prescribes:

> A court of the United States shall have power to punish by fine or imprisonment, at its discretion, such contempt of its authority, and none other, as —
>
> (1) Misbehavior of any person in its presence or so near thereto as to obstruct the administration of justice;
>
> (2) Misbehavior of any of its officers in their official transactions;
>
> (3) Disobedience or resistance to its lawful writ, process, order, rule, decree, or command.

Considerable doubt was expressed in Ex parte Robinson, 86 U.S. 505, as to whether this statute could limit the contempt power of the Supreme Court, which derives its existence and powers from the Constitution, and it is obvious from *Merrimack* that the Court has since gone beyond the statute. But *Robinson* made it clear that there can be no question about the limiting effect the statute has upon the courts of appeals and the district courts. As courts created, not by the Constitution, but, through the power that document vested in Congress, exercise of their inherent contempt powers must be confined to the bounds that Congress has fixed.

Measuring the facts in the present case by the word of Congress, I am unable to find a basis in the statute for a contempt citation here. Phrases (1) and (2) of the statute are not applicable here. The majority finds, under phrase (3), that there was disobedience or resistance to a lawful writ, process, order, rule, decree, or command of this Court. Yet none in fact existed to be disobeyed or resisted. The plaintiffs sought no temporary restraining order or injunction, and none was issued preventing the action taken by the Supervisors. The stipulation requested of the defendants by this court cannot be expanded to fit into any of the things specified in §401(3).

The word "process," as used in the statute in its context of writs, orders and decrees, obviously means more than the pendency of an appeal or of some other relevant judicial proceeding. It has been traditionally used to encompass such things as a summons, a subpoena, an attachment, a warrant, a mandate, a levy and, generically, other writs and orders. In the context of other orders and writs, "process" can reasonably be understood to mean no more than the sum of more explicit terms, such as "original process," "summary process," "mesne process" and "final process," all of which clearly refer to papers issuing from the court and embodying its commands or judgments, or notice of them. Construed so expansively as the majority's suggestion of equivalence with the pendency of any relevant judicial proceeding, it would entirely contravene the clearly limiting purpose of the congressional act.

Since the suggested construction of the word "process," as used in the statute, is original with the majority, it has never been treated in any reported opinion. The suggestion is inconsistent with the substantially uniform course of decision, however, while the primary theory of the majority is explicitly at odds with the precedents in this and other courts.

This court declared itself in Ex parte Buskirk, 4 Cir., 72 F.14. There it was held not only that an anticipatory, partial avoidance of a potential decree was not a punishable contempt within the confines of the limiting statute; violation of a stipulation made in open court, without which mesne process might, and probably would, have issued, was held not to be. Implicit in the decision is a narrow, literal reading of the word "process."

Buskirk was a party in a judicial proceeding in a district court for a determination of the ownership of a tract of timber. In open court, he entered into a stipulation that none of the timber would be cut until the court had decided the question of ownership. Nevertheless, pending the court's decision, he began cutting the timber and intentionally removed it beyond the reach of the court. This court held because of the statute, "[h]owever reprehensible such conduct . . . may have been . . . it nevertheless did not constitute a contempt to the court or its orders."

My brothers now overrule *Buskirk* without deigning to mention it.

Our own decision in *Buskirk* is not an aberration. It is the exemplar of uniform decision. Four of our sister circuits have embraced the same construction of the statute, and have done so in no uncertain terms.[3] No court of appeals, until now, has toyed with any other reading.

---

3.   Parker v. United States, 1 Cir., 126 F.2d 370, 380; In re Probst, 2 Cir., 205 F.512; Berry v. Midtown Service Corp., 2 Cir., 104 F.2d 107; In re Sixth & Wisconsin Tower, 7 Cir., 108 F.2d 538; Dakota Corp. v. Slope County, 8 Cir., 75 F.2d 584; *and see* United States v. Day, C.C.N.J., 6 Am. L. Reg. 632, 25 Fed. Cas. No. 14,934, p.793; In re Rice, C.C. Ala., 181 F.217.

I cannot dismiss all of these holdings on the basis of an asserted distinction of the Second Circuit's decision in *Berry*. The basis of the asserted distinction of *Berry* was not present in the Second Circuit's earlier *Probst* decision upon which *Berry* depended, or in our decision in *Buskirk* or in those of the First, Seventh and Eighth Circuits.

The holding in Lamb v. Cramer, 285 U.S. 217, is of some comfort to the majority, but I find myself unable to accept it as an authoritative interpretation of a statute which the Supreme Court and the lower courts did not even mention.

Lamb was a lawyer, who, assertedly in payment of accrued legal fees, accepted a transfer of some of the property in litigation, upon which the adverse parties had specific liens. Concurrently, a supplemental bill in equity to require his restoration of the property to the custody of the court was filed and a rule issued against Lamb to show cause why he should not return the property to the custody of the court or be held in contempt. Lamb claimed immunity from service, and the district court upheld him in both cases. In both cases, the Court of Appeals for the Fifth Circuit reversed, holding that service upon Lamb was good, and that the supplemental bill in equity and the citation were each appropriate means to require restoration of the property to the control of the court, and that each means might be pursued concurrently. Lamb appealed both cases to the Supreme Court, which affirmed the Fifth Circuit in each.

Clearly, the only purpose of the citation in *Lamb* was the procurement of the return of property in the actual possession and under the control of the attorney, an officer of the court. It was not to punish him or to compel him to replace out of his own funds dissipated assets or money. The most significant thing about the *Lamb* cases, however, is that attention in both the Court of Appeals for the Fifth Circuit and the Supreme Court was focused upon a very different problem. In neither court was there a citation of the statute with which we are concerned or of the cases which had established a uniform interpretation of it. The Supreme Court wrote in Lamb v. Cramer as if the affront had been to itself. One can only suppose that it did so because the statute had not been called to its attention,[6] for the Supreme Court had made it perfectly clear in *Robinson* that the subordinate, statutory federal courts are subject to the statute, and that their powers to punish contempts are effectively limited by it.

---

6. It was of little moment in any event, for clearly the court had the power to compel the attorney to restore the property which he had taken with notice not only of the pendency of the proceeding, but with notice as well of the specific liens held by the adverse parties.

If the holding in Lamb may be regarded as an interpretation of the unmentioned statute, one may more reasonably conclude that it was an application of §401(2) rather than §401(3) with which, alone, we are concerned.[8]

The large issue in this case was the constitutionality of a continuing program of disbursement of tuition grants allegedly for the purpose of continued maintenance of segregated school systems. The payment of such tuition grants for one-half year did not abort the appeal or frustrate adjudication of the large issue. It was an unwarranted disbursement of public funds, but the Supervisors, themselves, are not now in possession of any part of those moneys. They are not officers of this court punishable under §401(2) for official transgressions. What is attempted here is far from what was accomplished in Lamb v. Cramer, and, to me, is inconsistent with an appropriate deference to an explicit congressional command of unquestioned constitutionality which limits our jurisdiction and authority.

I would not quibble with the majority's finding of fact that the conduct of the Supervisors was contemptible, but I do dissent from their conclusion that it was contemptuous and punishable as such, when the conclusion is dependent upon a reading of the statute which relegates it to meaninglessness. Such an unsympathetic construction is particularly inappropriate when the statute was clearly intended to inhibit our authority, has been declared by the Supreme Court to have that effect and has been uniformly construed by the courts of appeals in accordance with that evident intention. Such a statute limiting the jurisdiction of the federal courts is largely enforceable only by the limited courts, themselves. Above all other statutory commands, courts should be scrupulous to conform themselves to jurisdictional statutes, so that they do not appropriate to themselves powers which have been constitutionally withdrawn from them. . . .

---

8.   It may be that Lamb did not seek protection of the statute because of ignorance of it. More probably, he did not because he thought the court's authority sufficiently clear under §401(2) to warrant his concentration of his defense in an attack upon the service of process. In either event, since, under the plain holdings of the relevant authorities at that time, the contempt proceeding was not arguably authorized by §401(3), but probably was authorized by §401(2), the Supreme Court's opinion, with no reference to either, cannot be construed as an authoritative construction of §401(3). There are too many reasonable explanations of the Supreme Court's action in that case to permit acceptance of the least likely and the most attenuated.

Twenty-four years after Lamb's case was decided, the Supreme Court held that an enrolled attorney was not an officer of the court within the meaning of §401(2), but that was not the prevailing notion when Lamb sought to retain the fruits of his malfeasance. If the explanation of Lamb's failure, and that of the courts which decided his case, to deal with the statute does not lie in an absence of awareness of it, speculation about the reason for ignoring it must be against a background of the law as it was understood at the time.

NOTES ON CONTEMPT OF ANTICIPATED INJUNCTIONS

1. Could the school board members have been punished for criminal contempt? If not, does it matter whether the court can find them in civil contempt? The court had already held that the payments violated the Constitution. Why not base a remedy on violation of the Constitution instead of on violation of an injunction that was never entered?

"It has long been established that where a defendant with notice in an injunction proceeding completes the acts sought to be enjoined the court may by mandatory injunction restore the status quo." Porter v. Lee, 328 U.S. 246, 251 (1946). In *Porter*, a landlord sought to evict his tenants in violation of World War II price controls. The government sued to enjoin the eviction; while the injunction suit was pending, the landlord completed the eviction and the tenants moved out. The Court said the government was entitled to have them moved back in. Isn't that a routine reparative injunction? Why not a similar injunction in *Griffin*? Another alternative would be to seek restitution from the white parents as constructive trustees.

2. It is not clear why the plaintiffs and the court used the contempt remedy in *Griffin*. Perhaps they overlooked the alternative. Perhaps they wanted the court of appeals to control the proceedings. The theory of *Griffin* is that defendants were in contempt of the court of appeals. The district judge had never been very aggressive in this case, and a theory that gave direct access to the court of appeals may have looked too good to pass up.

3. If *Griffin* is rightly decided, what purpose is served by the rules for injunctions pending appeal? If plaintiffs had sought an injunction pending appeal, the court would have had to balance probability of success and risk of irreparable harm before granting it. Does *Griffin* mean that defendants must always act as though there were an injunction pending appeal, even when there isn't? Even when defendant suffers hardship by waiting until the appeal is decided?

Moreover, doesn't the logic of *Griffin* apply equally to the trial court? Does every defendant in an injunction suit have to act as though a TRO were issued? Is he in contempt if he does something plaintiff seeks to have enjoined, even though plaintiff made no motion for a TRO or preliminary injunction?

4. Having said all that, isn't *Griffin* appealing on the facts? Didn't defendants show contempt for the court — in the ordinary English sense of "contempt" — as clearly as if they had violated a direct order?

Is *Griffin*'s theory needed for the occasional case where a reparative injunction won't work? Recall Ex parte Shipp, discussed in the notes to Walker v. City of Birmingham. That was the case where a trial court stayed an execution for ten days to permit appeal to the Supreme Court. Suppose the prisoner filed his appeal on the tenth day, the Supreme Court failed to act, and Shipp executed him at one minute after midnight on the eleventh day. Should that be contempt? Certainly death penalty litigation is conducted on the assumption that the execution can proceed if no stay is in effect; that is why so many orders issue in the middle of the night.

5. Both sides in *Griffin* accurately report the precedents they rely on. Most cases say that defendant is not in contempt unless he knows about a clear order and disobeys it. But every once in a while, when a court gets mad enough, it holds someone in contempt for violating an order that hasn't been made yet. *Merrimack* and *Lamb*, cited by the majority, are still the most relevant holdings from the Supreme Court; there is a similar holding in Toledo Scale Co. v. Computing Scale Co., 261 U.S. 399, 426-428 (1923).

6. If *Griffin* were accepted as good law, what should be its limits? Should it matter how likely the court is to issue the injunction? In *Merrimack*, defendants had already won their case in the Supreme Court of the United States. They were held in contempt because they didn't wait to see if there would be a petition for rehearing. Should it matter that rehearings in the Supreme Court are extraordinarily rare?

Is it more important that if the Supreme Court entered an injunction at all, it would certainly be to preserve the poles? Compare In re Sixth & Wisconsin Tower, 108 F.2d 538 (7th Cir. 1939). One bondholder sent a letter to other bondholders, urging them to reject a reorganization plan. The trial court held the letter writer in civil contempt on the ground that the plan and his objections were then before the court for decision. The court of appeals reversed on the ground that there had been no order not to send the letter. Is that inconsistent with *Griffin*? Did defendant have any way to predict that the court might, if asked, forbid him to send letters to other bondholders?

7. *Griffin* has been cited several times, but none of the decisions citing it actually apply it. There are some cases punishing defendants in criminal contempt for getting rid of documents after receiving an IRS summons and before receiving a court order enforcing the summons. An example is United States v. Asay, 614 F.2d 655 (9th Cir. 1980).

Two cases in the 1970s hold that there can be no contempt for disobedience of the court's command unless there is a written order. In re Stewart, 571 F.2d 958 (5th Cir. 1978); In re LaMarre, 494 F.2d 753 (6th Cir. 1974). Both involved criminal contempt of oral orders communicated through intermediaries. *LaMarre* cites the whole line of cases from the *Griffin* dissent; it does not cite *Griffin* or any of the cases cited by the *Griffin* majority. *Stewart* simply cites *LaMarre*.

8. *Griffin* appears to be inconsistent with cases holding that it is not contempt to violate a judicial decision that does not contain an explicit

command. Thus, violation of a declaratory judgment is not contempt. Steffel v. Thompson, 415 U.S. 452, 471 (1974). Less obviously, an order that "approve[s]" a settlement agreement, without more, does not order the parties to comply with the agreement. H. K. Porter Co. v. National Friction Products Corp., 568 F.2d 24, 25-27 (7th Cir. 1978). The parties can enforce the settlement in a suit for breach of contract, but they cannot enforce it with a contempt citation. Another example: An order "to comply with and to abide by" an arbitration award cannot be enforced by contempt if the arbitration award does not contain "an operative command capable of 'enforcement.'" International Longshoremen's Association, Local 1291 v. Philadelphia Marine Trade Association, 389 U.S. 64, 74 (1967).

Sometimes this rule appears as a mere technicality in the face of a sloppily drafted order. But it is more than that. Litigants often bargain over whether to embody their settlement in a contract or a consent decree. Defendants who successfully insist on contract do so to avoid exposure to the contempt power.

9. In *Griffin*, defendants did something they knew the court would order them not to do. Sometimes it is the other way around: Defendants make themselves incapable of doing something they know the court will order them to do. It is tempting in those cases to order them to do it, and coerce them or punish them for not doing it, rejecting their impossibility defense on the ground that the impossibility is of their own making. That was the rationale in United States v. Asay, a criminal contempt case described in note 7. The Supreme Court denounced the strategy in Maggio v. Zeitz, 333 U.S. 56, 64 (1948), a turn-over case discussed supra at 655-656.

NOTES ON CONTEMPT STATUTES

1. 18 U.S.C. §401 (1982), the contempt statute at issue in *Griffin*, dates from 1831. It was enacted in response to abuses by Judge Peck in St. Louis, who punished as contempts newspaper stories critical of him and his court. The House of Representatives impeached Judge Peck. The Senate acquitted, but Congress promptly enacted the statute in substantially its present language.

2. The statute remains a mystery. It is not even settled whether it applies to civil contempt. It is codified in the title on crimes, and it limits the power to punish. It does not mention the power to coerce or compensate. Judge Peck's scandal involved criminal contempt. But surely Congress would have been just as offended if Judge Peck had jailed his critics until they promised to quite criticizing.

Judge Wyzanski was quite confident that the statute applies only to criminal contempt. H. K. Porter Co. v. National Friction Products

Corp., 568 F.2d 24, 26 (7th Cir. 1978). The Supreme Court assumed arguendo that it applies to both kinds of contempt. Penfield Co. v. SEC, 330 U.S. 585, 594 (1947). But, it held, at most the statute applies to the two kinds of contempt seriatim. The issue was whether a witness could be both fined and imprisoned; the statute authorizes only fine *or* imprisonment. The Court said he could be coercively imprisoned in civil contempt and fined in criminal contempt, even if he couldn't be both fined and imprisoned for the same kind of contempt by itself.

3.   Many statutes impose more effective limits on contempt sanctions. The criminal contempt statute in Walker v. City of Birmingham authorized a maximum sentence of five days and a $50 fine. Courts generally abide by such statutes but sometimes strike them down for infringing the court's "inherent" contempt power. An example is Arnett v. Meade, 462 S.W.2d 940 (Ky. 1971). The Kentucky act allowed coercive imprisonment of a recalcitrant witness for as long as his testimony was needed. But such a witness could be punished for criminal contempt only by a $30 fine and 24 hours in jail.

4.   Statutes also address the problems that arise when the same act violates an injunction and a criminal statute. *Mine Workers* presented an example of this. The strike violated the War Labor Disputes Act, which authorized criminal penalties much smaller than those imposed for contempt. Federal statutes require jury trials in such cases, 18 U.S.C. §3691 (1982), and limit punishment for the contempt to six months in jail and a $1,000 fine, 18 U.S.C. §402 (1982). This limits the total cumulative punishment, and limits the court's ability to evade the maximum statutory punishment by issuing an injunction. Presumably, the statutes do not apply to coercive contempt. More important, they do not apply to cases in which the United States is the plaintiff. Aren't those the cases where they're most likely to be needed?

UNITED STATES v. HALL
472 F.2d 261 (5th Cir. 1972)

Before WISDOM, THORNBERRY and GODBOLD, Circuit Judges.

WISDOM, Circuit Judge.

This case presents the question whether a district court has power to punish for criminal contempt a person who, though neither a party nor bearing any legal relationship to a party, violates a court order designed to protect the court's judgment in a school desegregation case. We uphold the district court's conclusion that in the circumstances of this case it had this power, and affirm the defendant's conviction for contempt.

On June 23, 1971, the district court entered a "Memorandum Opinion and Final Judgment" in the case of Mims v. Duval County School Board.

The court required the Duval County [Jacksonville], Florida school board to complete its desegregation of Duval County schools. . . .

Among the schools marked for desegregation under the plan approved by the district court was Ribault Senior High School, a predominantly white school. . . . After the desegregation order was put into effect racial unrest and violence developed at Ribault, necessitating on one occasion the temporary closing of the school. On March 5, 1972, the superintendent of schools and the sheriff of Jacksonville filed a petition for injunctive relief in the *Mims* case with the district court. This petition alleged that certain black adult "outsiders" had caused or abetted the unrest and violence by their activities both on and off the Ribault campus. The petition identified the appellant Eric Hall, allegedly a member of a militant organization known as the "Black Front," as one of several such outsiders who, in combination with black students and parents, were attempting to prevent the normal operation of Ribault through student boycotts and other activities. . . .

[On March 5 the court issued an ex parte order directed to the population. It forbad anyone to enter the building or grounds of Ribault High, except for students while attending class or official functions, faculty and staff while performing assigned duties, parents with permission from the principal, law enforcement officials, and persons having business obligations that required their presence.]

The order went on to provide that "[a]nyone having notice of this order who violates any of the terms thereof shall be subject to arrest, prosecution and punishment by imprisonment or fine, or both, for criminal contempt under the laws of the United States of America. . . . " The court ordered the sheriff to serve copies of the order on seven named persons, *including Eric Hall.* Hall was neither a party plaintiff nor a party defendant in the *Mims* litigation, and in issuing this order the court did not join Hall or any of the other persons named in the order as parties.

On March 9, 1972, four days after the court issued its order, Hall violated that portion of the order restricting access to Ribault High School by appearing on the Ribault campus. When questioned by a deputy United States marshal as to the reasons for his presence, Hall replied that he was on the grounds of Ribault for the purpose of violating the March 5 order. The marshal then arrested Hall and took him into custody. After a nonjury trial, the district court found Hall guilty of the charge of criminal contempt and sentenced him to sixty days' imprisonment.

On this appeal Hall raises two related contentions. Both contentions depend on the fact that Hall was not a party to the *Mims* litigation and the fact that, in violating the court's order, he was apparently acting independently of the *Mims* parties. He first points to the common law rule that a nonparty who violates an injunction solely in pursuit of his own interests cannot be held in contempt. Not having been before the court as a party or as the surrogate of a party, he argues that in accordance with this common law rule he was not bound by the court's order. Second, he contends that Rule 65(d) of the Federal Rules of Civil Procedure prevents the court's order from binding him, since Rule 65(d) limits the binding effect of injunctive orders to "parties to the action, their officers, agents, servants, employees, and attorneys, and . . . those persons in active concert or participation with them who receive actual notice of the order by personal service or otherwise." We reject both contentions.

I

For his first contention, that a court of equity has no power to punish for contempt a nonparty acting solely in pursuit of his own interests, the appellant relies heavily on the two leading cases of Alemite Manufacturing Corp. v. Staff, 2 Cir. 1930, 42 F.2d 832, and Chase National Bank v. City of Norwalk, 1934, 291 U.S. 431. In *Alemite* the district court had issued an injunction restraining the defendant and his agents, employees, associates, and confederates from infringing the plaintiff's patent. Subsequently a third person, not a party to the original suit and acting entirely on his own initiative, began infringing the plaintiff's patent and was held in contempt by the district court. The Second Circuit reversed in an opinion by Judge Learned Hand, stating that "it is not the act described which the decree may forbid, but only that act when the defendant does it." 42 F.2d at 833. In *Chase National Bank* the plaintiff brought suit against the City of Norwalk to obtain an injunction forbidding the removal of poles, wires, and other electrical equipment belonging to the plaintiff. The district court issued a decree enjoining the City, its officers, agents, and employees, "and all persons whomsoever to whom notice of this order shall come" from removing the equipment or otherwise interfering with the operation of the plaintiff's power plant. The Supreme Court held that the district court had violated "established principles of equity jurisdiction and procedure" insofar as its order applied to persons who were not parties, associates, or confederates of parties, but who merely had notice of the order.

This case is different. In *Alemite* and *Chase National Bank* the activities of third parties, however harmful they might have been to the plaintiffs' interests, would not have disturbed in any way the adjudication of rights and obligations as between the original plaintiffs and defendants. Infringement of the *Alemite* plaintiff's patent by a third party would not have upset the defendant's duty to refrain from infringing or rendered it more difficult for the defendant to perform that duty. Similarly, the defendant's duty in *Chase National Bank* to refrain from removing the plaintiff's equipment would remain undisturbed regardless of the activities of third parties, as would the plaintiff's right not to have its equipment removed by the defendant. The activities of Hall, however, threatened both the plaintiffs' right and the defendant's duty as adjudicated in the *Mims* litigation. In *Mims* the plaintiffs were found to have a constitutional right to attend an integrated school. The defendant school board had a corresponding constitutional obligation to provide them with integrated schools and a right to be free from interference with the performance of that duty. Disruption of the orderly operation of the school system, in the form of a racial dispute, would thus negate the plaintiffs' constitutional right and the defendant's constitutional duty. In short, the activities of persons contributing to racial disorder at Ribault imperiled the court's fundamental power to make a binding adjudication between the parties properly before it.

Courts of equity have inherent jurisdiction to preserve their ability to render judgment in a case such as this. This was the import of the holding in United States v. United Mine Workers of America, 1947, 330 U.S. 258. . . . As an alternative holding the Court stated that the contempt conviction would have been upheld even if the district court had ultimately been found to be without jurisdiction. This holding affirmed the power of a court of equity to issue an order to preserve the status quo in order to protect its ability to render judgment in a case over which it might have jurisdiction.

The integrity of a court's power to render a binding judgment in a case over which it has jurisdiction is at stake in the present case. In *Mine Workers* disruptive conduct prior to the court's decision could have destroyed the court's power to settle a controversy at least potentially within its jurisdiction. Here the conduct of Hall and others, if unrestrained, could have upset the court's ability to bind the parties in *Mims*, a case in which it unquestionably had jurisdiction. Moreover, the court retained jurisdiction in *Mims* to enter such further orders as might be necessary to effectuate its judgment. Thus disruptive conduct would not only jeopardize the effect of the court's judgment already entered but would also undercut its power to enter binding desegregation orders in the future.

The principle that courts have jurisdiction to punish for contempt in order to protect their ability to render judgment is also found in the use of in rem injunctions. Federal courts have issued injunctions binding on all persons, regardless of notice, who come into contact with property which is the subject of a judicial decree. A court entering a decree binding on a particular piece of property is necessarily faced with the danger that its judgment may be disrupted in the future by members of an undefinable class — those who may come into contact with the property. The in rem injunction protects the court's judgment. The district court here faced an analogous problem. The judgment in a school case, as in other civil rights actions, inures to the benefit of a large class of persons, regardless of whether the original action is cast in the form of a class action. At the same time court orders in school cases, affecting as they do large numbers of people, necessarily depend on the cooperation of the entire community for their implementation.

As this Court is well aware, school desegregation orders often strongly excite community passions. School orders are, like in rem orders, particularly vulnerable to disruption by an undefinable class of persons who are neither parties nor acting at the instigation of parties. In such cases, as in voting rights cases, courts must have the power to issue orders similar to that issued in this case, tailored to the exigencies of the situation and directed to protecting the court's judgment. The peculiar problems posed by school cases have required courts to exercise broad and flexible remedial powers. See Swann v. Charlotte-Mecklenburg Board of Education, 1971, 402 U.S. 1, 6, 15. Similarly broad applications of the power to punish for contempt may be necessary, as here, if courts are to protect their ability to design appropriate remedies and make their remedial orders effective.

II

The appellant also asserts that Rule 65(d) of the Federal Rules of Civil Procedure prevents the court's order from binding him.[3] He points out that he was not a party to the original action, nor an officer, agent, servant, employee, or attorney of a party, and denies that he was acting in "active concert or participation" with any party to the original action.

In examining this contention we start with the proposition that Rule 65 was intended to embody "the common-law doctrine that a decree of injunction not only binds the parties defendant but also those identified with them in interest, in 'privity' with them, represented by them or subject to their control." Regal Knitwear Co. v. NLRB, 1945, 324 U.S. 9, 14. Literally read, Rule 65(d) would forbid the issuance of in rem injunctions. But courts have continued to issue in rem injunctions notwithstanding Rule 65(d), since they possessed the power to do so at common law and since Rule 65(d) was intended to embody rather than to limit their common law powers.

Similarly, we conclude that Rule 65(d), as a codification rather than a limitation of courts' common-law powers, cannot be read to restrict the inherent power of a court to protect its ability to render a binding judg-

---

3.   Rule 65(d) is as follows:

Rule 65. Injunctions. . . .

   (d)   Form and Scope of Injunction or Restraining Order. Every order granting an injunction and every restraining order shall set forth the reasons for its issuance; shall be specific in terms; shall describe in reasonable detail, and not by reference to the complaint or other document, the act or acts sought to be restrained; and is binding only upon the parties to the action, their officers, agents, servants, employees, and attorneys, and upon those persons in active concert or participation with them who receive actual notice of the order by personal service or otherwise.

ment. We hold that Hall's relationship to the *Mims* case fell within that contemplated by Rule 65(d). By deciding *Mims* and retaining jurisdiction the district court had, in effect, adjudicated the rights of the entire community with respect to the racial controversy surrounding the school system. Moreover, as we have noted, in the circumstances of this case third parties such as Hall were in a position to upset the court's adjudication. This was not a situation which could have been anticipated by the draftsmen of procedural rules. In meeting the situation as it did, the district court did not overstep its powers.

We do not hold that courts are free to issue permanent injunctions against all the world in school cases. Hall had notice of the court's order. Rather than challenge it by the orderly processes of law, he resorted to conscious, willful defiance. See Walker v. Birmingham, 1967, 388 U.S. 307.

It is true that this order was issued without a hearing, and that ordinarily injunctive relief cannot be granted without a hearing. But we need not hold that this order has the effect of a preliminary or permanent injunction. Rather, the portion of the court's order here complained of may be characterized as a temporary restraining order, which under Rule 65(b) may be issued ex parte. The prohibition directed to restricting access to the school grounds nowhere purported to be an injunction. Moreover, Hall's violation occurred within four days of the issuance of the order, well within the ten-day limitation period for temporary restraining orders. The present case is therefore distinguishable from the situation presented in Harrington v. Colquitt County Board of Education, 5 Cir. 1971, 449 F.2d 161, a direct appeal from a permanent injunction, in which this Court struck language purporting to enjoin persons beyond the scope of Rule 65(d).

We hold, then, that the district court had the inherent power to protect its ability to render a binding judgment between the original parties to the *Mims* litigation by issuing an interim ex parte order against an undefinable class of persons. We further hold that willful violation of that order by one having notice of it constitutes criminal contempt. The judgment of the district court is affirmed.

NOTES ON CONTEMPT CITATIONS AGAINST THIRD PARTIES

1. The issue in *Hall* is whether an injunction can bind persons not parties and not described in Rule 65(d). It does not raise the question whether with proper procedure the court could have made Hall a party and enjoined him from interfering with desegregation. We considered that question supra at 281-294, and there is little doubt that Hall could have been enjoined. He could also have been prosecuted under 18

U.S.C. §1509 (1982). That statute forbids interfering with a federal court decree by threats or force. But under that statute, Hall would have been entitled to indictment and jury trial. And it would not have been enough to prove that Hall entered the school; the government would have had to prove interference by threats or force.

2. Whether Hall is bound by the injunction does not depend on whether he is named or described in it. Agents and persons in active concert with parties are bound even if there is no clause to that effect. It is better practice to say so, because they might not know the rule and think they have found a loophole. But Rule 65(d) is sufficient.

It is essential to the result that Hall had notice of the supplemental injunction. No one is bound by an injunction until he has notice of it. We will take up that issue in a separate set of notes.

3. Rule 65(d) is the main obstacle to the injunction in *Hall*, but the case is full of other problems. Those other problems may cast light on the policies underlying Rule 65(d).

a. Suppose Hall had come on campus on the eleventh day after the injunction. Do you suppose the court would have reversed his conviction on the ground that the TRO had expired, and that Hall could not be bound by a preliminary injunction without notice and a hearing? How would Judge Wisdom have written the opinion then?

b. What about Carroll v. President of Princess Anne, supra at 405? The sheriff found Eric Hall to serve him with the injunction; why couldn't he find him to give notice of his motion?

c. What about potential protestors who had not yet come to the sheriff's attention? These people were included in the injunction. The sheriff couldn't very well give notice to them. But did he have a ripe controversy with them?

4. The court's description of Alemite Manufacturing Corp. v. Staff is a bit misleading. The "third person" prosecuted for contempt in *Alemite* was Joseph Staff, brother of the original defendant John Staff. John had employed Joseph to sell the infringing goods that gave rise to the original suit. The court enjoined John and "his agents, employees, associates and confederates" from infringing or "aiding or abetting or in any way contributing to the infringement." 42 F.2d at 832. Joseph then left John's business and started his own, manufacturing the same infringing product.

Joseph clearly would have been in contempt had he continued to infringe as John's employee, or if his new business was conducted "in active concert" with John. The brothers could not avoid the injunction merely by creating a new entity or rearranging their hierarchy. But at Joseph's contempt hearing, the court found that John had nothing to do with Joseph's business. On those facts, Judge Hand held that there was no more power to punish Joseph "than a third party who had never heard of the suit." Id. at 833. G. & C. Merriam Co. v. Webster Dictionary Co., 639

F.2d 29 (1st Cir. 1980), is astonishingly similar to *Alemite* and reaches the same result.

5. Does Judge Wisdom successfully distinguish *Alemite*? Doesn't it beg the question to say that the *Alemite* injunction established plaintiff's rights against Joseph Staff, but that the *Mims* injunction established plaintiffs' rights against the whole world? Is it more persuasive to say that Hall was trying to keep the school board from obeying the injunction, but that Joseph Staff was not trying to keep John from obeying? Does *Hall* just create a school desegregation exception? An exception for cases that arouse widespread community protest?

6. None of these explanations fits very well with the origins of Rule 65(d). The rule originated in the Clayton Act, and its primary target was the antistrike injunction. Both the strike cases and the school cases involved whole communities bitterly resisting federal courts, with the courts backed up by federal troops when things got really rough. And any third party interfering with the efforts of strike breakers to return to work would be interfering with the very rights adjudicated by the injunction, just as in *Hall*. What would Judge Wisdom say to this history? That in the strike cases the courts were wrong and the community was right, but in the desegregation cases it's the other way around? Won't courts always think they're right when they try to enforce a policy in the face of resistance?

NOTES ON OTHER THEORIES FOR BRINGING THIRD PARTIES WITHIN RULE 65(d)

1. *Parties, officers, agents, servants, employees, and attorneys.* An injunction against a party binds the party's agents. Respondeat superior is enough to tell you that the party is in contempt if his agents violate the injunction. But Rule 65(d) allows the courts to go further. The agents themselves are in contempt, even though they did not have a chance to litigate. The leading case involves a particularly troubling application. In In re Lennon, 166 U.S. 548 (1897), a nonunion railroad got an injunction ordering union railroads to handle its cars. Lennon was a union engineer. He refused to haul a nonunion car and was prosecuted for criminal contempt of the injunction against his employer.

Should agents be bound by injunctions against their employers? Or should the court coerce the defendant, and let him worry about how to control his employees?

2. *Persons in active concert.* An injunction also binds all "persons in active concert or participation with" any of the parties described in note 1. This is a check on subterfuge; defendant cannot get his friends and relatives to violate the injunction for him. Persons in active concert did

not get a chance to litigate either, but at least they have deliberately allied themselves with defendant. Co-conspirator doctrine suggests a rationale for binding people in active concert with a party. Most persons in active concert will also be agents, but that is not required.

3.   *Successors in interest.* Suppose that in *Alemite,* John Staff sold his infringing business to a stranger. Does the stranger take the business subject to the injunction? Is he personally bound? There is no mention of successors or assigns in Rule 65.

The issue has arisen repeatedly under the National Labor Relations Act, and the Supreme Court has been troubled by it. In Regal Knitwear Co. v. NLRB, 324 U.S. 9, 14 (1945), the Court suggested that successors were bound only if they were in active concert with the original employer, as when the successor was "merely a disguised continuance of the old employer," quoting Southport Petroleum Co. v. NLRB, 315 U.S. 100, 106 (1942). But in Golden State Bottling Co. v. NLRB, 414 U.S. 168 (1973), the Court held that a bona fide purchaser who bought with knowledge that a Labor Act violation remained unremedied was bound by the order to remedy it. There was some hint that this was a special rule for labor cases; there was also a *"cf."* citation to *Hall.*

Compare *Golden State* with Swetland v. Curry, 188 F.2d 841 (6th Cir. 1951). A court enjoined Curtiss Airports Corp. and "all persons and corporations, private or municipal . . . deriving title" from Curtis, from operating an airport at a certain location. Fourteen years later, Cuyahoga County acquired the airport by eminent domain, with full knowledge of the injunction. The court held that the county was not in contempt, because it was not a party and was not in active concert with Curtiss.

4.   *Successors to public office.* Federal Rule 25(d) provides that when a litigant who is a public officer leaves office, his successor is automatically substituted as a party. It follows under Rule 65(d) that the successor is automatically bound by injunctions issued against his predecessor, and the cases so hold. An example is Lucy v. Adams, 224 F. Supp. 79 (N.D. Ala. 1963), involving an injunction ordering the registrar of the University of Alabama to admit black applicants.

This is not the same as saying the successor can be ordered to discontinue illegal practices of the predecessor that have not yet been enjoined. That depends on whether there is a likelihood that the successor will continue the illegal practices. See Spomer v. Littleton, 414 U.S. 514 (1974), discussed in notes supra at 234.

5.   *In rem injunctions.* An in rem injunction is an injunction ordering the whole world not to interfere with some property that is in the custody of the court or under supervision by the court. The most common in rem injunction is the automatic stay triggered by the filing of every bankruptcy petition. All the world is enjoined from pursuing claims against the debtor anywhere but in the bankruptcy court. The automatic stay is explicitly authorized by statute, 11 U.S.C. §362 (1982), and that overrides Rule 65(d). But §362 was not enacted until 1978; bankruptcy courts issued

similar stays for decades without statutory authorization. And similar injunctions are issued in analogous nonstatutory contexts. An example is Securities & Exchange Commission v. Wencke, 622 F.2d 1363 (9th Cir. 1980), in which a receiver was appointed to manage Wencke's assets. All the world is enjoined from interfering with the assets in receivership. Judge Wisdom relies heavily on these in rem injunctions in *Hall*.

The automatic stay and its analogs are relatively uncontroversial, perhaps because they are viewed as a means of consolidating litigation in a single court that will continue to honor the substantive rights of the parties. Another form of in rem injunction is much more controversial and much less necessary. Where a building has been used as a brothel, a pornographic movie theater, a gambling hall, or a speakeasy during prohibition, courts have enjoined the whole world from using the building for those purposes. A Texas statute authorizing such injunctions was struck down on prior restraint grounds in Vance v. Universal Amusement Co., 445 U.S. 308 (1980). But *Vance* does not turn on the third party issue, and does not affect in rem injunctions in non-speech contexts.

The talk about the whole world in these injunctions is unnecessary; the targets are successors. But in rem injunctions were used to bind successors who were not in active concert with the original defendant and who were not shown to have taken with notice of the injunction. Some in rem injunctions were issued without statutory authorization. But this was often before the adoption of Rule 65(d) or its equivalent in the relevant state. And some states rejected the concept. Professor Rendleman reviews the history of these injunctions in Rendleman, Beyond Contempt: Obligors to Injunctions, 53 Tex. L. Rev. 873, 911-916 (1975).

6. *Political representation.* An injunction against a state binds its citizens, at least with respect to "public rights." An example is the Washington fishing litigation, in which the Supreme Court also relied on three alternative theories.

In the 1850s, the United States entered into treaties guaranteeing fishing rights to Indian tribes in the Pacific Northwest. The main subject of the treaties were salmon and similar fish that migrate in predictable runs up coastal rivers. The treaties eventually triggered extended litigation.

The courts interpreted the treaties as promising the Indians approximately half the catch unless their needs were fully satisfied by a smaller share. To enforce that right, the trial court had to control all fishing in the watersheds. There were 800 Indian commercial fishermen, 6,600 non-Indian commercial fishermen, and 280,000 licensed sport fishermen, and there was widespread defiance of the court's orders. The court's solution was to monitor the catch from each run, and to close fishing areas to non-Indians whenever non-Indians collectively were about to exceed their share of a run. The court ordered the State of Washington to set up a telephone hot line that would tell non-Indian fishermen what waters were open. Then it issued an injunction against all non-Indians with Washington fishing licenses, ordering them not to fish without first checking the hot line and obeying its directions. This part of the injunction went far beyond Rule 65(d), and associations of commercial fishermen challenged it on that ground. The Supreme Court rejected the argument in a long footnote. It never actually mentioned Rule 65(d):

> The associations advance a third objection as well — that the District Court had no power to enjoin individual nontreaty fishermen, who were not parties to its decisions, from violating the allocations that it has ordered. The reason this issue has arisen is that state officials were either unwilling or unable to enforce the District Court's orders against nontreaty fishermen by way of state regulations and state-law enforcement efforts. Accordingly, nontreaty fishermen were openly violating Indian fishing rights, and, in order to give federal-law enforcement officials the power via contempt to end those violations, the District Court was forced to enjoin them. The commercial fishing organizations, on behalf of their individual members, argue that they should not be bound by these orders because they were not parties to (although the associations all did participate as amici curiae in) the proceedings that led to their issuance.
>
> If all state officials stand by the Attorney General's representations that the State will implement the decision of this Court, this issue will be rendered moot because the District Court no longer will be forced to enforce its own decisions. Nonetheless, the issue is still live since state implementation efforts are now at a standstill and the orders are still in effect. Accordingly, we must decide it.
>
> In our view, the commercial fishing associations and their members are probably subject to injunction under either the rule that nonparties who interfere with the implementation of court orders establishing public rights may be enjoined, e.g., United States v. Hall, 472 F.2d 261 (C.A.5 1972), cited approvingly in Golden State Bottling Co. v. NLRB, 414 U.S. 168, 180, or the rule that a court possessed of the res in a proceeding in rem, such as one to apportion a fishery, may enjoin those who would interfere with that custody. But in any case, these individuals and groups are citizens of the State of Washington, which was a party to the relevant proceedings, and "they, in their public rights as citizens of the State, were represented by the State in those proceedings, and, like it, were bound by the judgment." City of Takoma v. Taxpayers, 357 U.S. 320, 340-341. Moreover, a court clearly may order them to obey that judgment. See Golden State Bottling, supra, at 179-180.

Washington v. Washington State Commercial Passenger Fishing Vessel Association, 443 U.S. 658, 693 n.32 (1979).

7. Does the array of theories in the Washington fishing case leave much of Rule 65(d)? Should the fishermen be bound by the injunction against the state if the state had not vigorously opposed the injunction? Does it follow that all the citizens of a school district are bound by the school district's participation in school desegregation litigation? That would be another way to write *Hall*. Should political representation work for private associations too? Doesn't the Court imply that if the fishing associations had participated as parties, the members would be bound?

8. What about the citation to *Hall*? Has the Supreme Court decided that *Hall* is good law? That it is "probably" good law?

9. *Supplemental injunctions.* Another way to enforce the treaties would be to join non-Indian fishermen as defendants, one by one as they were caught fishing in closed areas. Finding them in closed areas would establish a ripe controversy and justify an injunction; if they were caught again they would be in contempt. Is that too cumbersome to be effective? Does it achieve any real benefits? Every non-Indian fisherman would get one or more free violations, but would he get any more procedural protection?

Supplemental injunctions might be more feasible and more useful in a case like *Hall*. There were fewer independent actors. And all protestors had to come to the school, or at least to bus routes, to do much harm. There were not 6,600 independent fishermen spread out among dozens of rivers, bays, sounds, and inlets. And protestors in *Hall* could raise free speech issues that had not been resolved in the original litigation. But it's safe to predict that no individual fisherman would be allowed to relitigate the meaning of the treaties, and it is hard to think of any individual claims or defenses they might raise.

10. *Defendant class actions.* Another little-explored solution is for plaintiffs to sue some non-Indian fishermen as representatives of a class of all non-Indian fishermen, and for the court to enjoin the class. Is that any better? If you were a defendant, would you want the plaintiffs to pick your representative?

Defendant class actions work fairly well when the class is tightly knit and there is an entity to organize the defense. Examples are suits against union members as a class, or stockholders as a class, or local officials as a class, where the union, the corporation, or the state can organize the defense.

Suits against a more amorphous defendant class are much more troublesome. Their most common use is against patent infringers to adjudicate the validity of the patent. That issue is absolutely identical with respect to every alleged infringer, and the named defendant cannot possibly defend himself without defending all the others as well. The case is typically broken into separate actions to decide whether each class member's product infringes the patent and to assess damages. The cases and problems are sympathetically reviewed in Note, Defendant Class Actions, 91 Harv. L. Rev. 630 (1978).

NOTES ON THE NOTICE REQUIREMENT

1. No one can be in contempt of an injunction he doesn't know about. Hall was personally served with the injunction against coming on school grounds, but that is not required. Knowledge from any source is sufficient. An old but well known case says the standard is any source

"entitled to credit." Cape May & Schellinger's Railroad v. Johnson, 35 N.J. Eq. 422, 425 (1882).

2. Notice was a recurring problem in the Washington fishing litigation. There were hundreds of prosecutions for criminal contempt, and in every one, the government had to prove beyond a reasonable doubt that defendant had had notice of the injunction. Some fishers were personally served; some were sent copies of the injunction by certified mail; some admitted to having heard about it.

The government argued that individual fishers weren't entitled to notice, because they were in privity with the state of Washington. The court of appeals rejected that argument on due process grounds. United States v. Baker, 641 F.2d 1311 (9th Cir. 1981). It also refused to take judicial notice that there had been such widespread publicity that everyone must have heard about it, and it rejected the argument that commercial fishers had a duty of inquiry because their industry was so heavily regulated. Compare In re Jersey City Education Association, 115 N.J. Super. 42, 278 A.2d 206 (1971), in which the court inferred that all members of a teachers' union knew of an antistrike injunction. In that case, plaintiff put in detailed evidence of massive local news coverage.

3. It has been held sufficient for sheriffs to read injunctions to demonstrators over bullhorns. United States v. Gedraitis, 690 F.2d 351 (3d Cir. 1982). In a similar case involving demonstrators at the Seabrook nuclear plant in New Hampshire, some defendants argued that they had been distracted during the announcement and didn't know what had been said. But the court concluded that a posted sign, evidence of discussions of the injunction among the demonstrators, two bullhorn announcements, and a chorus of "no's" to the second bullhorn announcement, were sufficient evidence to support a conviction of everyone there.

4. In the bullhorn cases, defendants learn about the injunction from the other side. It is also enough if plaintiff's attorney tells defendant about the injunction. That was the case in Cape May, supra note 1, and in a modern child visitation case, Ex parte Jackson, 663 S.W.2d 520 (Tex. App. 1983). Should it matter if defendant is represented by counsel and plaintiff communicated directly with defendant? It is unethical for an attorney to communicate directly with an adversary party who is represented by counsel. American Bar Association Model Rules of Professional Conduct, Rule 4.2. Should defendant have a defense to contempt if plaintiff's attorney violated that rule when he gave notice of the injunction? Shouldn't there be an implied exception to the ethical rule if defendant is about to inflict irreparable harm and his attorney can't be found?

5. Consider this war story. In 1972, I was a poll watcher in a working class precinct in Chicago. Charges of vote fraud were rampant. During the morning, volunteers delivered photocopies of a TRO to nearly 5,000

precincts in Cook County. In my precinct, one of the election judges looked at the TRO and said: "This isn't from a court. Things from courts come with seals." She ignored the TRO for the rest of the day.

Was she in contempt? Does that depend on whether the trier of fact believes she was in good faith in rejecting the injunction's authenticity? If she gets off, is it because she didn't have notice or because her violation wasn't willful? If the latter, she's still liable in compensatory contempt; recall that willfulness is required only for criminal contempt.

NOTES ON THE MAXIM THAT EQUITY ACTS IN PERSONAM

1.   What is distinctive about contempt is the attempt to coerce the plaintiff into personally obeying the court's order. This is in sharp contrast to the traditional methods of enforcing money judgments, which we consider in the next section. The law courts traditionally relied on the sheriff to collect judgments, and did not expect defendants to cooperate. This difference is commonly described in the maxim that equity acts in personam; by contrast, the law is said to act in rem. This statement may be more misleading than helpful; certainly it is not helpful unless it is clarified quite substantially.

There are at least five different uses of the distinction between in rem and in personam. The maxim that equity acts in personam is invoked in most of these senses, and courts and commentators often fail to distinguish them.

2.   The distinction may refer to the theory of the plaintiff's substantive right. He may have a personal claim against the defendant, based on defendant's own conduct — the defendant's tort, or breach of contract, or breach of fiduciary duty. Or he may have a property right, good against anyone in the world, without regard to the individual conduct of most of the world's population. The common law has always created both in personam and in rem rights. Equity for a long time claimed to create only in personam rights.

Equity used the distinction in this sense to explain the law of trusts. The trustee owned the assets; he had a property right good against the world. The beneficiary was said to have only a personal right good against the trustee. This personal right was eventually surrounded by so many remedies that it came to be nearly as good as a property right. But the fiction is sometimes useful, so it has not been abandoned.

3.   A second usage refers to the basis of a court's territorial jurisdiction. A suit is in personam if jurisdiction is based on authority over the defendant's person, and in rem if jurisdiction is based on authority over a particular piece of property. This is the sense in which in rem and in personam is encountered in the first-year civil procedure course. In rem

jurisdiction is of limited significance after Shaffer v. Heitner, 433 U.S. 186 (1977). *Shaffer* held that all claims of territorial jurisdiction must be based on authority over persons, and cannot be based solely on authority over their property.

Before *Shaffer* the common law courts asserted jurisdiction both in rem and in personam. Equity claimed to act only in personam. Acting in personam is very helpful when a court has jurisdiction over a defendant and wants to affect property beyond its reach. Thus, an Illinois court can order McDonald's not to cancel a franchise in Paris, France, and enforce its order by holding McDonald's in contempt. Dayan v. McDonald's Corp., 64 Ill. App. 3d 984, 382 N.E.2d 55 (1978). But the notion that equity acted only in personam broke down. Thus, the court where the property is has jurisdiction to foreclose mortgages, even though mortgage foreclosure is equitable. *Shaffer* probably will change only the language and not the results of these cases. See 433 U.S. at 207-208.

4. A third usage refers to the expressed object of a suit. A suit is in personam if plaintiff seeks a judgment against the defendant personally. Such a judgment imposes a personal liability or duty on defendant. A personal liability may be collected out of any of defendant's property; a personal duty may be enforced through contempt proceedings. A suit is in rem if plaintiff seeks to recover or directly affect particular property and no other and not to impose a personal liability or duty on defendant. Actions at law may be either in rem or in personam in this sense. Suits in equity were traditionally said to be only in personam, but again this was abandoned when it became too inconvenient. Thus, Judge Wisdom in *Hall* relies on in rem injunctions, a phrase that would be an oxymoron if we took seriously the notion that equity acts only in personam. What is questionable about in rem injunctions is not that they are in rem, but that they are sometimes directed at people who have not been given their day in court.

5. A fourth usage of in rem and in personam refers to the form of the court's final order. Judgments at law are written as declarations of rights, and this is called in rem. Decrees in equity were historically written as direct orders to the defendant, and this is called in personam. Thus, the law court would say, "Ordered, adjudged, and decreed that plaintiff have judgment for $10," or "that Blackacre belongs to plaintiff and he shall have possession." The equity court would say to defendant, "You pay plaintiff $10," or "You convey and deliver Blackacre to plaintiff."

Equity used the in personam idea in this sense to explain how it could enjoin suits in other courts without being disrespectful. The equity decree never said "The judgment at law is void." Instead, it said to defendant, "You stop enforcing your judgment at law." But acting in personam was a hindrance if defendant refused to do something that the court could do itself if it would only act in rem. For example, it is foolish to imprison defendant indefinitely to coerce him into signing the deed to

Blackacre. It is much easier for the court to transfer Blackacre, and let plaintiff record the judgment, or a deed signed by the sheriff. Federal Civil Rule 70 authorizes courts to do that, and most state rules are similar.

6. The final usage is the one we started with, referring to the traditional means of enforcing judgments and decrees. Common law judgments were enforced by sheriffs and similar officials. They would seize defendant's property and sell it to pay the judgment, or forcibly evict defendant from Blackacre. Equity decrees were traditionally enforced through the contempt power. Dean Ames said this was the fundamental difference between law and equity. J. Ames, Lectures on Legal History and Miscellaneous Legal Essays 76 (1913). But as Professor Cook has pointed out, neither law nor equity used either method of enforcement exclusively. Cook, The Powers of Courts of Equity, 15 Colum. L. Rev. 37, 106-141 (1915). When a defendant refused to obey decrees and stubbornly resisted coercion, equity sent officials called sequestrators to "sequester" his property, sell it, and pay the proceeds to plaintiff. Similarly, common law plaintiffs could often have defendants arrested and imprisoned, a rather obvious effort to coerce payment. Common law imprisonment for debt is now much restricted and little used, but not quite eliminated.

7. The conceptualisms of in rem and in personam are largely in the past. The merger of law and equity makes much of the traditional distinction irrelevant. Today, the notion pops up only occasionally, usually to explain results that could often be better explained some other way. But it is still a useful way to highlight a basic choice about the means of enforcing judgments. It remains true that we coerce defendants to obey injunctions, but we usually do not coerce them to pay money judgments. Even so, there is much more use of coercion in the collection of money judgments than the traditional maxim would lead you to expect. The next two sections explore the means of collecting money judgments, and ask why we don't use the contempt power more generally.

B. COLLECTING MONEY JUDGMENTS

CREDIT BUREAU, INC. v. MONINGER
204 Neb. 679, 284 N.W.2d 855 (1979)

Heard before KRIVOSHA, C.J., and BOSLAUGH, McCOWN, CLINTON, BRODKEY, WHITE and HASTINGS, JJ.

BRODKEY, Justice.

This is an appeal from an order of the District Court for Custer County which affirmed a judgment entered by the county court of Custer

County awarding the proceeds from a sheriff's sale of a 1975 Ford pickup truck to the Broken Bow State Bank. . . . We reverse and remand.

The facts which give rise to this action are not in dispute. The Credit Bureau of Broken Bow, Inc. . . . obtained a default judgment against John Moninger . . . in the amount of $1,518.27 on October 20, 1977. No appeal was taken from this judgment. On May 16, 1978, Moninger renewed his prior note to the Bank in the amount of $2,144.74. The renewed note was to be secured by a security agreement on feeder pigs and a 1975 Ford pickup owned by Moninger, but no security agreement was entered into at that time. On June 27, 1978, at the request of the Bureau, a writ of execution was issued on its judgment in the amount of $1,338.50, the balance remaining due on the judgment.

The deputy county sheriff who received the writ examined the motor vehicle title records on July 7, 1978, to determine if a lien existed as of that date on the pickup owned by Moninger. Finding no encumbrance of record, the deputy sheriff proceeded to Moninger's place of employment to levy on the vehicle. The deputy sheriff found Moninger, served him with a copy of the writ, and informed Moninger that he was executing on the pickup. Moninger testified he informed the officer that there was money borrowed from the Bank against the pickup, and that the Bank had title to the vehicle. Following this conversation, the officer proceeded to the vehicle, "grabbed ahold of the pickup," and stated: "I execute on the pickup for the County of Custer." The officer did not take possession of the vehicle at that time, nor did he ask for the keys to the vehicle.

On July 10, 1978, after being informed of the events which occurred on the 7th, the Bank and Moninger executed a security agreement on the vehicle which was then filed. Notation of the security interest was made on the title to the pickup truck that same day. The vehicle was seized by deputy sheriffs on July 13, 1978, and sold at sheriff's sale on August 14, 1978, for $2,050.

The sheriff filed a motion in the county court for a determination of the division of the proceeds from the sheriff's sale. The Bank joined the action by application for the proceeds of the sheriff's sale, basing its claim on its alleged status as a secured creditor. Prior to a hearing on these matters, a stipulation was entered into by all parties whereby this dispute was limited to the distribution of the proceeds of the sheriff's sale, the pickup having previously been sold. . . .

The Bureau first assigns as error the ruling of the trial court which found the Bank's security interest in the vehicle to be superior to the execution lien of the Bureau. Specifically, the Bureau contends that the actions of the deputy sheriff on July 7, 1978, amounted to a valid levy which bound the vehicle for the satisfaction of the Bureau's judgment against Moninger. §25-1504, R.R.S.1943. On that date, the Bank held

only an unperfected security interest in the vehicle. The Bureau contends that since the levy of execution made the Bureau a lien creditor,
and since the lien creditor has an interest superior to that of an unperfected secured party, the trial court was in error in ruling that the Bank
had a superior interest in the proceeds.

In effect, the Bureau is relying on section 9-301, U.C.C., which relates
to the relative priorities as between unperfected security interests and lien
creditors. "[A]n unperfected security interest is subordinate to the rights
of . . . a person who becomes a lien creditor without knowledge of the
security interest and before it is perfected." §9-301(1)(b), U.C.C. The
correctness of the Bureau's position turns on two issues: (1) Whether the
Bureau was in fact a lien creditor on July 7, 1978; and (2) whether
the Bureau was a lien creditor without knowledge of the Bank's alleged
security interest prior to the perfection of such interest by the Bank.

From an examination of the record, we conclude that the Bureau was
a lien creditor on July 7, 1978. Section 9-301, U.C.C., defines a lien
creditor as "a creditor who has acquired a lien on the property involved by
attachment, levy or the like. . . ." A lien on personal property is acquired
in this state at the time it is "seized in execution." §25-1504, R.R.S.1943.
Therefore, the Bureau became a lien creditor within the meaning of
section 9-301, U.C.C., when the sheriff levied on the vehicle.

The rule by which to test the validity of a levy has been earlier set out
by this court. "'A manual interference with chattels is not essential to a
valid levy thereon. It is sufficient if the property is present and subject for
the time to the control of the officer holding the writ, and that he in
express terms asserts his dominion over it by virtue of such writ.'" Battle
Creek Valley Bank v. First Nat. Bank of Madison, 62 Neb. 825, 88 N.W.
145 (1901). We believe a review of the record makes it clear that a valid
levy did occur before the Bank had perfected its security interest in the
chattel.

The deputy sheriff expressly asserted his dominion over the vehicle by
virtue of the writ. He likewise exerted control over the vehicle as against
all others at the time of levy. At that time the deputy sheriff informed
Moninger that he was sorry that he had to execute on the vehicle but that
it was his job. He further stated that he hoped Moninger would straighten
the problem out with the Bureau. It should be noted that the officer's
report, as well as the return on the writ, clearly indicated that the officer
"executed" on the vehicle on July 7, 1978. On the basis of this evidence,
we conclude that a valid levy took place at that time.

The Bank would have us hold that the pickup should have been physically seized to make the levy valid. We do not believe that failure to take
physical possession in this case goes to the validity of the levy. The deputy
sheriff did all that was required by the laws of this state with regard to
levying under a writ of execution. Whether or not the officer took physi-

cal possession after he levied relates to the ability of the officer to produce the property levied on, and to his possible civil liability for failure to do so, not to the validity of the levy. It is, of course, possible that the failure of a levying officer to protect and preserve the property levied upon might give rise to an action between the officer, or his bonding company, and the judgment creditor. We therefore reject the Bank's contention and conclude that the Bureau was a lien creditor on July 7, 1978, by virtue of the deputy sheriff's levy on the writ of execution.

We now turn to the issue of notice and whether the Bureau was a lien creditor without knowledge of the Bank's interest. The Bank would have us hold that the sheriff was placed on notice of its security interest prior to making the levy on the vehicle, and that such notice would be imputed to the judgment creditor, the Bureau. In 70 Am. Jur. 2d, Sheriffs, Police, and Constables, §1, p.133, it is stated: "Peace officers are agents of the law and ordinarily are not agents of the parties. Thus, a sheriff is not an agent of an execution creditor except for certain purposes, and the latter is bound only by such acts of the sheriff as are within his lawful authority. Nor is he an agent of a party who may purchase at a sale conducted by him." As stated in Riggs v. Gardikas, 78 N.M. 5, 427 P.2d 890 (1967):

> "Notice by a debtor to a sheriff when he was proceeding to attach or to levy upon property is not notice to the creditor for whom the levy is made. . . . '. . . if notice by the debtor to the sheriff was held sufficient, it would almost render nugatory the statute requiring mortgages of personal property to be recorded; for if the mortgagee could depend upon the custody, care, and diligence of the mortgagor, it would not be necessary to record any such mortgage. It would only be necessary, when any one came to attach, that notice should be given.'"

We believe the above rule is applicable in this case.

The position taken by the Bank would place too great a burden upon the sheriffs and constables of this state when levying upon property as it would require them to inquire into the validity of statements made by the debtor, or information from other sources as to any interest claimed by other parties in the property sought to be levied on. This would, in our view, result in unnecessary delays and burdens in the carrying out of their statutory duties. We also note that our statutes already provide for procedures for the resolution of disputes and the adjudication of rights which third parties may have in or claim to the property levied upon. There is no justification to delay the levy of an execution merely on the word of a judgment debtor, who obviously has an interest in retaining possession of the item. We conclude that in levying the execution in this case, the deputy sheriff was carrying out a statutory duty and was acting as an agent of the law, and not as an agent of the judgment creditor. Thus, any information obtained by the deputy sheriff in the performance of his duties would not be imputed to the judgment creditor. We therefore hold that the Bureau was a lien creditor without knowledge of the security interest which the Bank claimed in the vehicle. The Bureau attained this status on July 7, 1978. The record discloses that the Bank did not perfect its security interest in the vehicle until July 10, 1978, when it filed a security agreement entered into on that date. As previously stated, the law of this state is clear that a lien creditor without notice has a superior interest to that of parties holding an unperfected security interest in the property. The Bureau thus has prior rights to the proceeds of the sheriff's sale.

It also seems clear that the Bank itself was responsible for any loss it may suffer because of its own inaction and neglect. Section 60-110, R.R.S.1943, provides for the notation of security interests on certificates of title in order to give notice to third parties of this interest. If the Bank had timely complied with the statute in the instant matter, this dispute would not have arisen. . . .

We hold, therefore, that the Bureau has prior rights to the proceeds of the sheriff's sale. The judgment of the District Court is therefore reversed and the cause remanded for further proceedings not inconsistent with this opinion.

NOTES ON EXECUTION

1. *Credit Bureau* gives you a good look at the mechanics of the execution process. The basic steps are the same everywhere: The court issues a writ, the writ is delivered to the sheriff or constable, he levies on the debtor's property, and eventually sells the property on which he levied. In most states, the writ is called a writ of execution. But some states still use the common law term, writ of fieri facias, or its nickname, fi fa.

The proceeds of the sheriff's sale go first to the sheriff to pay the costs of execution, then to pay off liens on the property. The judgment creditor has an execution lien by virtue of the levy, but he may not have the only lien. There may be a security interest, as in *Credit Bureau*, or a mortgage. There may be mechanics' liens, a landlord's lien, or a variety of other common law or statutory liens. There may be other judgment creditors with execution liens. A trustee in bankruptcy or some other representative of general creditors may claim the property. Someone may claim to be the true owner of the property, or claim a right to restitution of the property. All these claims must be rank ordered from first priority to last priority. Then they will be paid in order until the money runs out. Any money left over is returned to the debtor, but that doesn't happen very often. If a debtor can't pay your client, he probably can't pay a lot of other people either; it is important to be at the head of the line. If you are at the end of the line, you might do better in bankruptcy, where liens acquired in the last ninety days are undone and unsecured creditors share pro rata.

2. The priority contest in *Credit Bureau* is governed in part by the Uniform Commercial Code. Under §9-301, the Credit Bureau wins if it got an execution lien before the Bank perfected its security interest. The Code also tells us that the Bank perfected its interest on July 10, when it noted its interest on the pickup's certificate of title. §9-302(3). But the Code does not tell us when the Credit Bureau got its execution lien. That is left to common law or nonuniform statutes. And the states do not agree on the answer.

3. States disagree on the importance of a levy to the execution lien's priority. In most states the priority of an execution lien on personal property is based on the time at which the sheriff levies on the property. Nebraska is typical in this respect. But in some states, the lien has priority from the time the writ is delivered to the sheriff, at least if a valid levy is made thereafter, from issuance of the writ, from docketing of the judgment, or even from the entry of the judgment. In a handful of states, a judgment creditor can establish priority in personal property by filing a statement for public record; that option is described in note 7. The rules for real estate are generally different: Docketing the judgment in a county where the debtor owns real estate creates a judgment lien on all the debtor's real estate in the county. A judgment docket is generally indexed by the judgment debtor's name, and real estate title searchers must examine the judgment docket as well as the deed records.

All of these statements are somewhat oversimplified. First in time, first in right is the basic priority rule, but there are exceptions, and much depends on the identity of the competing claimant. For example, in many states it is possible to have priority over other execution liens without having priority over bona fide purchasers for value. Some of the complexities are examined in Carlson and Shupack, Judicial Lien Priorities under Article 9 of the Uniform Commercial Code: Part I, 5 Cardozo L. Rev. 287 (1984).

4. Those states that require a levy to establish priority disagree on what constitutes a levy. In Nebraska and several other states, levy is a ceremonial procedure, much like early explorers claiming land for European kings. A Nebraska sheriff cannot stand at the mouth of the Platte and levy on all the land it drains, but it is hard to see what purpose is served by requiring him to announce his levy in the presence of the pickup. Most states require the sheriff to physically take possession if that is possible. If the goods are unmanageable, the seizure may be somewhat symbolic, but the sheriff must exercise as much actual control as the nature of the goods permits. For example, he may disable a large machine, or attach signs to it with chains and padlocks. Many of the cases are conflicting, and many define levy in vague terms that make it hard to know just how much actual control the sheriff has to exercise.

5. The Uniform Commercial Code reflects a strong policy against

secret liens. That is why the Bank's security interest in *Credit Bureau* was not perfected until it noted its interest on the certificate of title. That policy can be traced at least to *Twyne's Case*, 76 Eng. Rep. 809 (Star Ch. 1601). Are execution liens in Nebraska consistent with that policy? What should happen if Moninger sold the pickup to an innocent purchaser after the formal levy and before the actual seizure? Does that purchaser have any way to know about the Credit Bureau's execution lien? Should he be bound by it if he can't know about it? Some states protect good faith purchasers of property subject to secret judicial liens, and some do not. If a good faith purchaser after the levy gets good title, should the sheriff be liable to the Credit Bureau for loss of the pickup?

6.   Sheriff's offices are often overworked and understaffed. Equally important, it is not their money they are trying to collect, and they don't know anything about the debtor. The creditor and his attorney have more time and more incentive to find assets, and more knowledge about where to look. Sheriffs and their deputies will often be quite cooperative about coming to a particular place at a particular time to serve a hard-to-find defendant, or to levy on an asset that is about to disappear. But the creditor or his attorney must find the defendant or the asset and tell the sheriff when and where to go.

7.   California recently enacted legislation that may eliminate most of the problems associated with priorities based on levy. A judgment creditor in California can file a statement in the filing system for security interests under the Uniform Commercial Code. Cal. Civ. Proc. Code §§697.510 et seq. (West 1985 Supp.). Such a filing creates a judgment lien on the debtor's personal property anywhere in the state, including property acquired later. Some kinds of property are excluded from the system. Priority rules are integrated with the UCC priority rules for security interests. It is still possible to get an execution lien by levy on specific assets, and it will still be necessary to eventually seize and sell the property of an uncooperative defendant, but much of the gamesmanship of collection should be eliminated. If creditors use the system, priority will no longer depend on debates about the adequacy of levy. Some of the same results are possible under older and less comprehensive provisions for recording judicial liens on personal property in a handful of states.

8.   *Credit Bureau* is misleading on a collateral issue. The court assumes the Bank had an unperfected security interest before July 10. Actually, the Bank did not have any security interest at all until July 10, because the debtor did not sign a written security agreement until then. UCC §9-203(1)(a). Thus, it was unnecessary to decide whether the Credit Bureau knew about the Bank's security interest. In states that have adopted the 1972 amendments to the UCC, Credit Bureau's knowledge would be irrelevant in any event. In those states, a security interest is junior to all execution liens acquired before the security interest is per-

fected, even if the lien creditor knew about the security interest. Forty states have adopted the 1972 amendments.

NOTES ON EXEMPTIONS

1. All states exempt some property from execution. Judgment debtors can keep their exempt property even if the judgment remains unpaid. There is enormous variation in the generosity of state exemptions. The Nebraska exemptions will illustrate as well as any; they are typical of the kinds of property that is exempted, and somewhere in the middle with respect to amount. In many states, the pickup in *Credit Bureau* would have been exempt, but not in Nebraska.

2. Nebraska exempts the immediate personal possessions of the debtor and his family, $1,500 worth of clothing, furniture, and kitchen utensils, $1,500 worth of tools and equipment, a six-month supply of food and fuel for the debtor and his family, Neb. Rev. Stat. §25-1556 (1979 Reissue), and all rights under life, health, and accident insurance policies, Neb. Rev. Stat. §44-371 (1984 Reissue). In addition, Nebraska homeowners can exempt their homestead. Neb. Rev. Stat. §40-101 (1984 Supp.). The homestead is limited to two city lots or 160 rural acres. Those without a homestead can exempt $2,500 worth of other personal property in addition to the specific exemptions. Neb. Rev. Stat. §25-1552 (1984 Supp.). Thus, if Moninger didn't own a home, and his pickup were worth less than $2,500, he could have exempted the pickup. If it were worth more than $2,500, he could have claimed the first $2,500 in proceeds from sale of the pickup.

Finally, 85 percent of wages are exempt from garnishment in Nebraska. Neb. Rev. Stat. §25-1558 (1979 Reissue). We take up that issue in the next case and set of notes.

3. In states with very generous exemptions, execution is largely ineffective against ordinary citizens. Businesses have nonexempt assets, and individuals with investments have nonexempt assets, but the bulk of the population is judgment proof. For example, Texas exempts household goods, two cars or trucks, food, tools, clothing, sporting equipment, two guns, life insurance, household pets, and specified livestock, up to a total value of $30,000, plus a homestead not to exceed one urban acre or 200 rural acres, plus all current wages. Tex. Prop. Code ch. 41 (1984); Tex. Const. art. 16, §50 (Vernon 1984 Supp.); id. art. 16, §28. For the average family, that leaves only their cash on hand and in the bank. The average family often doesn't have much cash, and what it does have gets spent quickly after each pay day. And cash is easy to hide. A determined creditor can keep after them, picking up a few dollars here and there, but it's often more trouble than it's worth.

WEBB v. ERICKSON
134 Ariz. 182, 655 P.2d 6 (1982)

FELDMAN, Justice. . . .

On August 5, 1975, appellant Webb obtained a default judgment against Carl and Nancy Erickson in the amount of $5,000 plus interest, and $1,500 in attorneys' fees. The judgment was based on two promissory notes and a check for insufficient funds executed by Erickson.

During 1975, Carl Erickson earned commissions by acting as the real estate agent in the sale of several houses. In order to collect on his judgment against Erickson, Webb caused several writs of garnishment to be served on parties whose houses had been sold by Erickson. One of these parties was Bates. On November 22, 1975, Webb served a summons and writ of garnishment on Bates at his home. The process served on Bates designated him as a garnishee-defendant in an action which was based upon the Webb/Erickson judgment.

In a subsequent affidavit, Bates stated that in November of 1975 he had just been released from the hospital after a seven-week stay resulting from injuries sustained in an industrial accident. During a two-year period, Bates had been hospitalized several times for treatment of pain and depression associated with the injury. In addition to his health problems, Bates was involved in divorce proceedings and subsequently lost custody of his two children.

Bates stated that in light of these conditions he did not clearly understand the process served on him in November of 1975. He assumed that the summons was not intended for him because he had never heard of James Webb and was not connected with any dispute between Webb and the Ericksons. While he probably knew that Carl Erickson was the real estate agent involved in the sale of his home, Bates was under the impression that the entire transaction was in escrow at the Minnesota Title Company at that time and that he had no control over payment of the real estate commission. As a result, Bates never answered the writ.

On February 27, 1976, Webb obtained a default judgment against Bates for the full amount of Webb's underlying judgment against Erickson pursuant to A.R.S. §12-1583 (1956) (amended 1981).[1] No copy of the default judgment was mailed to Bates. No execution was attempted.

Bates did not know that a judgment had been entered against him for the full amount of the Webb/Erickson judgment until more than three years later. In late March of 1979, Bates received a telephone call from

---

1. Prior to the 1981 amendment, §12-1583 read:

If a garnishee fails to answer within the time specified in the writ, the court may, after judgment has been rendered against defendant, render judgment by default against the garnishee for the full amount of the judgment against defendant.

Webb's attorney who informed him of the 1976 judgment, that interest had been accruing since that time and that Bates was "in trouble." The attorney told Bates that a reduction of the $6,500 judgment was possible if Bates would be willing to negotiate. Bates immediately contacted an attorney.

The record reflects that some negotiations took place between the parties after Bates was informed of the judgment, but no settlement was reached. On August 7, 1979, Webb served a writ of garnishment on Bates' employer, garnishing Bates' wages on the basis of the 1976 default judgment and seeking to collect the entire amount of Webb's judgment against the Ericksons.

On August 16, 1979, Bates filed a motion to vacate judgment pursuant to Rule 60(c), Rules of Civil Procedure, 16 A.R.S., and a motion to stay the execution of the judgment. After a response and oral argument, the superior court issued an order granting Bates' motion to vacate and set aside the default and quashing the writ of garnishment served on Bates' employer. A formal judgment to this effect was entered on September 19, 1979. Garnisher Webb appealed this decision to the court of appeals, which held that the trial court had abused its discretion, and reversed. Bates then petitioned this court for review. We granted review and now vacate the opinion of the court of appeals and affirm the judgment of the trial court.

Rule 55(c) of the Arizona Rules of Civil Procedure provides that an entry of default or judgment by default may be set aside "for good cause shown." . . . In order to obtain relief, Bates must show each of the following: (1) that his failure to answer was excused by one of the grounds set forth in Rule 60(c); (2) that he acted promptly in seeking relief from the entry of default; and (3) that he had a meritorious defense.

Relief under Rule 60(c)

Rule 60(c) sets forth the grounds upon which a party may be relieved from a default judgment. Rule 60(c) provides, in part:

> On motion and upon such terms as are just the court may relieve a party . . . from a final judgment, order or proceeding for the following reasons: (1) mistake, inadvertence, surprise or excusable neglect; (2) newly discovered evidence . . . ; (3) fraud . . . , misrepresentation or other misconduct of an adverse party; (4) the judgment is void; (5) the judgment has been satisfied, released or discharged, or a prior judgment on which it is based has been reversed or otherwise vacated, or it is no longer equitable that the judgment should have prospective application; or (6) any other reason justifying relief from the operation of the judgment. The motion shall be filed within a reasonable time, and for reasons (1), (2) and (3) not more than six months after the judgment, or order was entered or proceeding was taken. . . .

Rule 60(c)(6) provides that a default judgment may be set aside for "any other reason justifying relief from the operation of the judgment." The wording of this clause places two separate limitations upon its application. First, the reason for setting aside the default must *not* be one of the reasons set forth in the five preceding clauses. Clause 6 and the first five clauses are mutually exclusive. Second, the "other reason" advanced must be one which *justifies* relief.

We must also recognize, however, the broad equitable power of Rule 60(c)(6). It has been stated that clause 6 "vests power in courts adequate to enable them to vacate judgments whenever such action is appropriate to accomplish justice." Klapprott v. United States, 335 U.S. 601, 615 (1949).[2] We realize that clause 6 cannot be used to avoid the six-month limitation which applies to the first three clauses. . . . The need for finality, however, must give way in extraordinary circumstances. Accordingly, clause 6 requires only that the motion be filed "within a reasonable time."

We have examined the record, therefore, to determine whether the facts support the trial court's presumptive discretionary finding that the facts here go beyond the factors enumerated in clauses 1 through 5 of Rule 60(c) and raise extraordinary circumstances of hardship or injustice justifying relief under the residual provision in clause 6. We believe that extraordinary circumstances justifying relief exist in this case.

Bates was a defaulting garnishee. This court has held that more liberality should be shown in setting aside a judgment against a defaulting garnishee than in setting aside a judgment against a defaulting defendant. . . .

Under Arizona law, a judgment can be entered against a defaulting garnishee for the full amount of the judgment against the defendant. The necessary result of such a rule is that a defaulting garnishee often may become liable for a debt which is significantly greater than the debt allegedly owed to the defendant. In light of such a result, it is not difficult to see why the principles relating to the setting aside of default judgments are applied more liberally in the case of a garnishee.

The court of appeals rejected this argument because no distinction between defaulting garnishees and defendants expressly appears in the statutes or rules. We agree with the court of appeals that no such distinction is expressly made; however, the purpose of clause 6 is to enable trial courts to grant equitable relief from default whenever the circumstances are extraordinary and justice requires. The fact that Bates was held responsible for the full amount of another person's debt without a hearing on the merits is certainly a consideration that can properly be taken

---

2.   Rule 60(c) of the Arizona Rules of Civil Procedure is taken from Rule 60(b), Federal Rules of Civil Procedure. The portion of the rule at issue is identical to the federal rule.

into account by the trial court in deciding whether to grant relief under clause 6.

The trial court could also have considered the confusing nature of the entire proceeding as well as the wording contained in the summons and writ served on Bates, a person who was not involved in and knew nothing about the dispute between Webb and Erickson.

The summons served on Bates read as follows:

> In obedience to the Writ of Garnishment served together with this Summons I do hereby summon and require you to appear and answer the accompanying Writ in the manner prescribed by law and within TEN DAYS, exclusive of the day of service, after service of this summons upon you if served within the County of Maricopa, or within TWENTY DAYS, exclusive of the day of service, if served outside the County of Maricopa, and you are hereby notified that in case you fail to so answer, judgment by default may be rendered against you for the full amount of the balance due upon the judgment against the defendant and in favor of plaintiff and not merely for the amount that you may owe to the defendant, and that such judgment may be so rendered in addition to any other matters which may be adjudged against you as prescribed by law.

The writ and summons contained no information with respect to how the garnishee was to "answer" or where and when the garnishee was to "appear." This may have contributed to Bates' failure to appreciate the significance of the documents and his resulting neglect in failing to answer the writ.[3]

An additional factor that could have been considered by the trial court was Bates' physical and mental condition in November of 1975. At that

---

3. The legislature recognized the confusion produced by such notice, and in 1981 amended the statutes accordingly. Section 12-1574(C) was added and reads:

> The plaintiff seeking the writ of garnishment shall serve on the garnishee, together with the summons and writ of garnishment, the form and instructions provided by the clerk of the court or justice of the peace pursuant to §12-1579.

Section 12-1579(B) reads:

> The clerk of the court and justice of the peace shall prepare and furnish without charge answer forms and instructions for completing the forms. The form shall provide information necessary to answer the writ as specified in §12-1574.

The legislature also took notice of the inherent risk of unfairness to garnishee defendants and amended §12-1583. Judgments by default are no longer permitted against garnishees except after further notice and a specific order to the garnishee to appear before the court. Section 12-1583 reads, in pertinent part:

> If a garnishee fails to answer within the time specified in the writ, the party for whom the writ has been issued may petition the court for the issuance of an order requiring the garnishee to appear before the court at a time and place specified in the order to answer the writ. In the event that the garnishee fails to appear after the service of the order requiring the appearance in person upon the garnishee, the court may, after judgment has been rendered against the defendant, render judgment by default against the garnishee for the full amount of the judgment against the defendant.

time, Bates was recovering from an industrial accident and suffering from depression. This condition, added to the confusing nature of the proceedings and notice, could well have contributed to his failure to understand and answer the writ.

The reasons behind Bates' failure to understand and answer relate to the question of excusable neglect. The court of appeals held that excusable neglect alone could not be sufficient grounds to set aside the default under clause 6. We agree. Excusable neglect is listed in clause 1 and therefore must be raised within six months of the judgment. While it is not sufficient grounds alone to authorize relief three and one-half years after judgment, excusable neglect may certainly be an equitable consideration to be weighed with other factors to determine if there are extraordinary circumstances present which justify relief.

The last consideration is the fact that Bates did not receive notice that judgment had been entered against him for the full amount of the Webb/Erickson judgment until some time in March of 1979. Rule 77(g) of the Arizona Rules of Civil Procedure provides that the clerk "shall serve notice of the entry [of judgment] by mail . . . upon *every party* affected thereby who is *not in default for failure to appear.* . . ." (Emphasis supplied.) Since no notice of the entry of judgment is required to be given in the case of default, and since Webb chose not to execute on the judgment until three and one-half years later, Bates was effectively deprived of an opportunity to set the judgment aside under clause 1 of Rule 60(c).

Lack of notice does not toll the six-month limitation, and alone is not sufficient grounds to justify relief under clause 6. . . . [L]ack of notice of the default judgment can be considered among other equities in the application of clause 6.[4]

None of the circumstances of this case alone would have been sufficient to invoke the equitable relief of clause 6. In combination, however, a unique situation was created and we cannot say that the trial court abused its discretion in vacating the default.

Prompt Action . . .

[T]he trial court did not abuse its discretion in presumptively finding that Bates acted promptly to set the default aside. Bates was not even aware of the judgment until March of 1979. After that time, negotiations were in progress to reach a settlement. When his wages were actually garnished and it became clear that no settlement could be reached, Bates promptly

---

4. The record does not reveal the reason for Webb's delay in executing upon the judgment against Bates. Good reasons may exist. It is possible, also, that counsel for a judgment creditor may intentionally delay execution on a default judgment for six months in order to deprive an unwitting, default judgment debtor from asserting the grounds specified in parts (1), (2) or (3) of Rule 60(c) in an attempt to set aside the judgment. We disapprove of such a practice.

and appropriately sought relief from the default. Cf. United Imports & Exports v. Superior Court, 133 Ariz. 43, 653 P.2d 691 (1982) (motion to set aside default judgment was not prompt where motion was not made until after judgment had been subject to several execution proceedings).

Meritorious Defense

In his affidavit, Bates stated that while Carl Erickson was the real estate agent handling the sale of his house, in November of 1975 the entire transaction was in escrow at Minnesota Title Company. Bates claimed that he had no control over the payment of the real estate commission and never owed Erickson any money. It is difficult to tell what Bates meant when he claimed he had "no control" over the payment of the commission. Interpreting this phrase in its broadest sense, however, it could mean that the commission was being paid by someone else or had already been paid.

With respect to the requirement of a meritorious defense, we have recognized that the affidavit asserting such a defense "is not intended to be a substitute for a trial of the facts. It is enough if there is shown from all the material facts set forth in the affidavit . . . that there is a substantial defense to the action." Union Oil of California v. Hudson Oil Co., 131 Ariz. at 289, 640 P.2d at 851. These facts, if proved at trial, would constitute a meritorious defense.

In conclusion, we find that there was sufficient evidence before the trial court from which it could have exercised its discretion to provide Bates relief under clause 6 of Rule 60(c), that Bates had sought relief promptly and had shown a meritorious defense.

Accordingly, the opinion of the court of appeals is vacated, and the judgment of the trial court is affirmed.

HOLOHAN, C.J., GORDON, V.C.J., and HAYS and CAMERON, JJ., concur.

NOTES ON GARNISHMENT

1. Garnishment is an independent action against a third party who owes money to the judgment debtor. The most common garnishees are banks and employers; bank accounts and wages are attractive sources of payment. The garnishee can defend on the ground that it doesn't owe the judgment debtor; it cannot question the underlying judgment. Most commonly, the garnishee appears and admits that it does owe the judgment debtor. Judgment is entered against it, it pays the judgment creditor, and its liability to the judgment debtor is discharged.

2. The garnishee can incur double liability or worse if it ignores the garnishment. If Bates had paid Erickson his real estate commission before he got the summons, he would have no longer owed anything and could have defended on that ground. But a payment to the judgment

debtor after getting the summons would not discharge his liability to the judgment creditor. Bates would have to pay Webb what he had already paid Erickson. But Bates got himself in even worse trouble by ignoring the garnishment proceeding altogether. Because he didn't respond and show how much he actually owed Erickson, the Arizona statute made him liable for the larger amount that Erickson owed Webb.

3. In theory, the garnishee is indifferent between paying his own creditor or paying his creditor's creditor. In practice, he is not indifferent; there is some expense and annoyance to being sued in garnishment, even if there is no disagreement about the amount owed. When the garnishee disputes his liability to the judgment debtor, garnishment turns into a full-scale lawsuit. Some employers discharge employees whose wages are repeatedly garnished. At least one court has held that discharging for garnishment violates the civil rights laws because it disproportionately affects members of minority groups. Johnson v. Pike Corp., 332 F. Supp. 490 (C.D. Cal. 1971).

4. Garnishing wages is a great way to get a debtor's attention. Debtors often respond by paying if they can, and by filing for bankruptcy if they can't. A bankruptcy petition automatically stays all efforts to collect debts outside the bankruptcy court, so it terminates the garnishment order.

Garnishing wages is so effective for creditors because it imposes so much hardship on debtors and their families. Congress responded to that hardship in Title III of the Consumer Credit Protection Act, 15 U.S.C. §§1671-1677 (1982). No more than 25 percent of a worker's take home pay may be withheld pursuant to garnishment orders; an exception authorizes garnishment of up to 60 percent for support of a spouse or dependent child. Texas exempts all current wages from garnishment, except for child support. Tex. Const. art. 16, §28 (Vernon's 1984 Supp.). But as soon as the wages are paid, or as soon as they are overdue, the exemption is lost. Thus, a creditor can garnish a bank account that contains nothing but wages. Sutherland v. Young, 292 S.W. 581 (Tex. Civ. App. 1927). Presumably, a creditor could levy on the paycheck in the employee's pocket.

NOTES ON OTHER MEANS OF COLLECTING MONEY JUDGMENTS

1. Execution and garnishment are the standard means of collecting judgments. Execution is clumsy but workable with respect to tangible property. Garnishment effectively reaches simple money debts owed to the judgment debtor. Both remedies begin to break down in more complicated situations. Much wealth is intangible, and many intangibles are held by trustees, custodians, nominees and other sorts of third parties. Consider corporate stock. To levy on certificated shares of stock, the sheriff must find and take possession of the stock certificates. But certifi-

cates are easy to hide, and defendant may have them registered in the name of his broker, his bank, his brother-in-law, or the trustee for his pension plan.

Or consider Knapp v. McFarland, 462 F.2d 935 (2d Cir. 1972). Knapp tried to collect her New York judgment against McFarland by levying on a half million dollar Treasury bill in possession of Chemical Bank in New York. Chemical held it as custodian for Security National Bank of Washington, D.C. Security acquired it as escrow agent for the proceeds of the sale of an apartment building in Arlington, Virginia. Defendant McFarland owned an undescribed interest in the apartment building; the extent of his interest was the subject of litigation in a Virginia state court. Chemical initially responded that it had never heard of McFarland and could not identify the property the sheriff was trying to levy on. After further investigation, it reported that it had identified McFarland and his Treasury bill, but that Security Bank had a security interest in it.

2.   The common law courts largely refused to get involved in such problems. Execution was available for land and tangible property within the jurisdiction, and that was it. If the common law writs were inadequate to collect the judgment, but the judgment creditor believed the defendant had hidden or intangible assets, he could file a creditor's bill in equity. Today, most of the relief traditionally available in a creditor's bill is available on postjudgment motion in the original action, and from time to time legislatures further simplify the collection process or add to the creditor's tools. These notes are about some of the creditor's options.

3.   The most basic option descended from the creditor's bill is postjudgment discovery. The judgment creditor can ask about the judgment debtor's assets by taking his deposition or serving interrogatories. He can also get discovery from third parties who know about the judgment debtor's assets. The debtor himself is likely to be uncooperative. Unsophisticated or defiant debtors often ignore the discovery notice. The full array of contempt sanctions is available against judgment debtors who ignore a court order compelling discovery. Judgment debtors who respond to discovery sometimes lie. Or they may hide their assets very cleverly and then tell the truth, hoping the creditors won't ask the right questions.

4.   If postjudgment discovery reveals assets readily subject to execution or garnishment, the judgment creditor can proceed with traditional remedies. If discovery reveals less accessible assets, the creditor needs another tool. In many situations, it is often possible to reach assets in the hands of a third party by serving a writ or notice on the third party. For example, investment securities in the hands of financial intermediaries may be reached "by legal process upon the financial intermediary." UCC §8-317(4). And the creditor "is entitled to aid from courts of appropriate jurisdiction, by injunction or otherwise, in reaching the security." UCC §8-317(6).

5.   A variation available in some states is the freezing order. For ex-

ample, the New York Civil Practice Law authorizes an injunction forbidding transfer of the debtor's property. N.Y. Civ. Prac. Law §5222 (McKinney 1978). The injunction may run against the judgment debtor himself, or against a third party in possession of some of the judgment debtor's property. The injunction does not create a lien that gives the judgment creditor priority over other creditors. But it does subject the third party to liability if he fails to retain property of the judgment debtor worth at least twice the amount of the judgment. The injunction is mainly useful to freeze the status quo while waiting for the sheriff to levy.

6.   Sometimes the debtor gives his assets to friends or relatives to put them beyond the reach of execution. The transfer may be a gift, a mortgage, or a sale for less than fair market value. Whatever the form, such a transfer is a fraudulent conveyance; the creditor can set aside the conveyance and levy on the goods in the hands of the third party. Because fraudulent conveyance law is so closely related to constructive trust law, it is more fully explored supra at 559-560.

7.   Perhaps the most powerful collection remedy for ordinary judgments is the appointment of a receiver to collect defendant's assets. Receivers are most important before judgment, and we will study them primarily in that context. Then we'll consider what a receiver can do after judgment.

BEARDEN v. GEORGIA
461 U.S. 660 (1983)

Justice O'CONNOR delivered the opinion of the Court.

The question in this case is whether the Fourteenth Amendment prohibits a State from revoking an indigent defendant's probation for failure to pay a fine and restitution. Its resolution involves a delicate balance between the acceptability, and indeed wisdom, of considering all relevant factors when determining an appropriate sentence for an individual and the impermissibility of imprisoning a defendant solely because of his lack of financial resources. We conclude that the trial court erred in automatically revoking probation because petitioner could not pay his fine, without determining that petitioner had not made sufficient bona fide efforts to pay or that adequate alternative forms of punishment did not exist. . . .

I

In September 1980, petitioner was indicted for the felonies of burglary and theft by receiving stolen property. He pleaded guilty, and was sentenced on October 8, 1980. Pursuant to the Georgia First Offender's Act, the trial court did not enter a judgment of guilt, but deferred further proceedings and sentenced petitioner to three years on probation for the burglary charge and a concurrent one year on probation for the theft charge. As a condition of probation, the trial court ordered petitioner to pay a $500 fine and $250 in restitution. Petitioner was to pay $100 that day, $100 the next day, and the $550 balance within four months.

Petitioner borrowed money from his parents and paid the first $200. About a month later, however, petitioner was laid off from his job. Petitioner, who has only a ninth grade education and cannot read, tried repeatedly to find other work but was unable to do so. The record indicates that petitioner had no income or assets during this period.

Shortly before the balance of the fine and restitution came due in February 1981, petitioner notified the probation office he was going to be late with his payment because he could not find a job. In May 1981, the State filed a petition in the trial court to revoke petitioner's probation because he had not paid the balance. After an evidentiary hearing, the trial court revoked probation for failure to pay the balance of the fine and restitution, entered a conviction and sentenced petitioner to serve the remaining portion of the probationary period in prison. The Georgia Court of Appeals, relying on earlier Georgia Supreme Court cases, rejected petitioner's claim that imprisoning him for inability to pay the fine violated the Equal Protection Clause of the Fourteenth Amendment. The Georgia Supreme Court denied review. Since other courts have held that revoking the probation of indigents for failure to pay fines does violate the Equal Protection Clause, we granted certiorari to resolve this important issue in the administration of criminal justice.

II

This Court has long been sensitive to the treatment of indigents in our criminal justice system. Over a quarter-century ago, Justice Black declared that "there can be no equal justice where the kind of trial a man gets depends on the amount of money he has." Griffin v. Illinois, 351 U.S. 12, 19 (1956) (plurality opinion). . . . Most relevant to the issue here is the holding in Williams v. Illinois, 399 U.S. 235 (1970), that a State cannot subject a certain class of convicted defendants to a period of imprisonment beyond the statutory maximum solely because they are too poor to pay the fine. *Williams* was followed and extended in Tate v. Short, 401 U.S. 395 (1971), which held that a State cannot convert a fine imposed under a fine-only statute into a jail term solely because the defendant is indigent and cannot immediately pay the fine in full. . . .

Most decisions in this area have rested on an equal protection framework, although Justice Harlan in particular has insisted that a due process approach more accurately captures the competing concerns. . . . There is no doubt that the State has treated the petitioner differently from a person who did not fail to pay the imposed fine and therefore did not violate probation. To determine whether this differential treatment violates the Equal Protection Clause, one must determine whether, and under what circumstances, a defendant's indigent status may be considered in the decision whether to revoke probation. This is substantially similar to asking directly the due process question of whether and when it is fundamentally unfair or arbitrary for the State to revoke probation when an indigent is unable to pay the fine. Whether analyzed in terms of equal protection or due process, the issue cannot be resolved by resort to easy slogans or pigeonhole analysis, but rather requires a careful inquiry into such factors as "the nature of the individual interest affected, the extent to which it is affected, the rationality of the connection between legislative means and purpose, [and] the existence of alternative means for effectuating the purpose. . . ." Williams v. Illinois, supra, 399 U.S., at 260 (Harlan, J., concurring).

In analyzing this issue, of course, we do not write on a clean slate, for both *Williams* and *Tate* analyzed similar situations. The reach and limits of their holdings are vital to a proper resolution of the issue here. In *Williams*, a defendant was sentenced to the maximum prison term and fine authorized under the statute. Because of his indigency he could not pay the fine. Pursuant to another statute equating a $5 fine with a day in jail, the defendant was kept in jail for 101 days beyond the maximum prison sentence to "work out" the fine. The Court struck down the practice, holding that "[o]nce the State has defined the outer limits of incarceration necessary to satisfy its penological interests and policies, it may not then subject a certain class of convicted defendants to a period of imprisonment beyond the statutory maximum solely by reason of their indigency." 399 U.S., at 241-242. In Tate v. Short, 401 U.S. 395 (1971), we faced a similar situation, except that the statutory penalty there permitted only a fine. . . .

The rule of *Williams* and *Tate*, then, is that the State cannot "impos[e] a fine as a sentence and then automatically conver[t] it into a jail term solely because the defendant is indigent and cannot forthwith pay the fine in full." *Tate*, supra, at 398. In other words, if the State determines a fine or restitution to be the appropriate and adequate penalty for the crime, it may not thereafter imprison a person solely because he lacked the resources to pay it. Both *Williams* and *Tate* carefully distinguished this substantive limitation on the imprisonment of indigents from the situation where a defendant was at fault in failing to pay the fine. As the Court made clear in *Williams*, "nothing in our decision today precludes imprisonment for willful refusal to pay a fine or court costs." 399 U.S., at 242, n. 19. Likewise in *Tate*, the Court "emphasize[d] that our holding today does not suggest any constitutional infirmity in imprisonment of a defendant with the means to pay a fine who refuses or neglects to do so." 401 U.S., at 400.

This distinction, based on the reasons for non-payment, is of critical importance here. If the probationer has willfully refused to pay the fine or restitution when he has the means to pay, the State is perfectly justified in using imprisonment as a sanction to enforce collection. Similarly, a probationer's failure to make sufficient bona fide efforts to seek employment or borrow money in order to pay the fine or restitution may reflect an insufficient concern for paying the debt he owes to society for his crime. In such a situation, the State is likewise justified in revoking probation and using imprisonment as an appropriate penalty for the offense. But if the probationer has made all reasonable efforts to pay the fine or restitution, and yet cannot do so through no fault of his own, it is fundamentally unfair to revoke probation automatically without considering whether adequate alternative methods of punishing the defendant are available. . . . Cf. Zablocki v. Redhail, 434 U.S. 374, 400 (1978) (Powell, J., concurring) (distinguishing, under both due process and equal protection analyses, persons who shirk their moral and legal obligation to pay child support from those wholly unable to pay).

The State, of course, has a fundamental interest in appropriately punishing persons — rich and poor — who violate its criminal laws. A defendant's poverty in no way immunizes him from punishment. Thus, when determining initially whether the State's penological interests require imposition of a term of imprisonment, the sentencing court can consider the entire background of the defendant, including his employment history and financial resources. . . .

The decision to place the defendant on probation, however, reflects a determination by the sentencing court that the State's penological interests do not require imprisonment. A probationer's failure to make reasonable efforts to repay his debt to society may indicate that this original determination needs reevaluation, and imprisonment may now be required to satisfy the State's interests. But a probationer who has made sufficient bona fide efforts to pay his fine and restitution, and who has complied with the other conditions of probation, has demonstrated a willingness to pay his debt to society and an ability to conform his conduct to social norms. The State nevertheless asserts three reasons why imprisonment is required to further its penal goals.

First, the State argues that revoking probation furthers its interest in ensuring that restitution be paid to the victims of crime. A rule that imprisonment may befall the probationer who fails to make sufficient bona fide efforts to pay restitution may indeed spur probationers to try hard to pay, thereby increasing the number of probationers who make restitution. Such a goal is fully served, however, by revoking probation only for persons who have not made sufficient bona fide efforts to pay. Revoking the probation of someone who through no fault of his own is unable to make restitution will not make restitution suddenly forthcoming. Indeed, such a policy may have the perverse effect of inducing the probationer to use illegal means to acquire funds to pay in order to avoid revocation.

Second, the State asserts that its interest in rehabilitating the probationer and protecting society requires it to remove him from the temptation of committing other crimes. This is no more than a naked assertion that a probationer's poverty by itself indicates he may commit crimes in the future and thus that society needs for him to be incapacitated. . . . [T]he State cannot justify incarcerating a probationer who has demonstrated sufficient bona fide efforts to repay his debt to society, solely by lumping him together with other poor persons and thereby classifying him as dangerous.[11] This would be little more than punishing a person for his poverty.

Third, and most plausibly, the State argues that its interests in punishing the lawbreaker and deterring others from criminal behavior require it to revoke probation for failure to pay a fine or restitution. The State clearly has an interest in punishment and deterrence, but this interest can often be served fully by alternative means. As we said in *Williams*, 399 U.S., at 244, and reiterated in *Tate*, 401 U.S., at 399, "[t]he State is not powerless to enforce judgments against those financially unable to pay a fine." For example, the sentencing court could extend the time for making payments, or reduce the fine, or direct that the probationer perform some form of labor or public service in lieu of the fine. Justice Harlan appropriately observed in his concurring opinion in *Williams* that "the deterrent effect of a fine is apt to derive more from its pinch on the purse than the time of payment." Ibid., 399 U.S., at 265. Indeed, given the general flexibility of tailoring fines to the resources of a defendant, or even permitting the defendant to do specified work to satisfy the fine, a sentencing court can often establish a reduced fine or alternate public service in lieu of a fine that adequately serves the State's goals of punishment and deterrence, given the defendant's diminished financial resources. Only if the sentencing court determines that alternatives to imprisonment are not adequate in a particular situation to meet the State's interest in punishment and deterrence may the State imprison a probationer who has made sufficient bona fide efforts to pay.[12] . . .

---

11. The State emphasizes several empirical studies suggesting a correlation between poverty and crime.

12. As our holding makes clear, we agree with Justice White that poverty does not insulate a criminal defendant from punishment or necessarily prevent revocation of his probation for inability to pay a fine. We reject as impractical, however, the approach suggested by Justice White. He would require a "good-faith effort" by the sentencing court to impose a term of imprisonment that is "roughly equivalent" to the fine and restitution that the defendant failed to pay. Even putting to one side the question of judicial "good faith," we perceive no meaningful standard by which a sentencing or reviewing court could assess whether a given prison sentence has an equivalent sting to the original fine. Under our holding the sentencing court must focus on criteria typically considered daily by sentencing courts throughout the land in probation revocation hearings: whether the defendant has demonstrated sufficient efforts to comply with the terms of probation and whether non-imprisonment alternatives are adequate to satisfy the State's interests in punishment and deterrence. Nor is our requirement that the sentencing court consider alternative forms of punishment a "novel" requirement. In both *Williams* and *Tate*, the Court emphasized the availability of alternate forms of punishment in holding that indigents could not be subjected automatically to imprisonment.

III

We return to the facts of this case. At the parole revocation hearing, the petitioner and his wife testified about their lack of income and assets and of his repeated efforts to obtain work. While the sentencing court commented on the availability of odd jobs such as lawn-mowing, it made no finding that the petitioner had not made sufficient bona fide efforts to find work, and the record as it presently stands would not justify such a finding. This lack of findings is understandable, of course, for under the rulings of the Georgia Supreme Court such an inquiry would have been irrelevant to the constitutionality of revoking probation. The State argues that the sentencing court determined that the petitioner was no longer a good probation risk. In the absence of a determination that the petitioner did not make sufficient bona fide efforts to pay or to obtain employment in order to pay, we cannot read the opinion of the sentencing court as reflecting such a finding. Instead, the court curtly rejected counsel's suggestion that the time for making the payments be extended, saying that "the fallacy in that argument" is that the petitioner has long known he had to pay the $550 and yet did not comply with the court's prior order to pay. The court declared that "I don't know any way to enforce the prior orders of the Court but one way," which was to sentence him to imprisonment.

The focus of the court's concern, then, was that the petitioner had disobeyed a prior court order to pay the fine, and for that reason must be imprisoned. But this is no more than imprisoning a person solely because he lacks funds to pay the fine, a practice we condemned in *Williams* and *Tate*. By sentencing petitioner to imprisonment simply because he could not pay the fine, without considering the reasons for the inability to pay or the propriety of reducing the fine or extending the time for payments or making alternative orders, the court automatically turned a fine into a prison sentence.

We do not suggest by our analysis of the present record that the State may not place the petitioner in prison. If, upon remand, the Georgia courts determine that petitioner did not make sufficient bona fide efforts to pay his fine, or determine that alternate punishment is not adequate to meet the State's interests in punishment and deterrence, imprisonment would be a permissible sentence. Unless such determinations are made, however, fundamental fairness requires that the petitioner remain on probation.

IV

The judgment is reversed, and the case remanded for further proceedings not inconsistent with this opinion.

It is so ordered.

JUSTICE WHITE, with whom THE CHIEF JUSTICE, JUSTICE POWELL, and JUSTICE REHNQUIST join, concurring in the judgment.

We deal here with the recurring situation where a person is convicted under a statute that authorizes fines or imprisonment or both, as well as probation. The defendant is then fined and placed on probation, one of the conditions of which is that he pay the fine and make restitution. In such a situation, the Court takes as a given that the state has decided that imprisonment is inappropriate because it is unnecessary to achieve its penal objectives. But that is true only if the defendant pays the fine and makes restitution and thereby suffers the financial penalty that such payment entails. Had the sentencing judge been quite sure that the defendant could not pay the fine, I cannot believe that the court would not have imposed some jail time or that either the Due Process or Equal Protection Clause of the Constitution would prevent such imposition.

Poverty does not insulate those who break the law from punishment. When probation is revoked for failure to pay a fine, I find nothing in the Constitution to prevent the trial court from revoking probation and imposing a term of imprisonment if revocation does not automatically result in the imposition of a long jail term and if the sentencing court makes a good-faith effort to impose a jail sentence that in terms of the state's sentencing objectives will be roughly equivalent to the fine and restitution that the defendant failed to pay.

The Court holds, however, that if a probationer cannot pay the fine for reasons not of his own fault, the sentencing court must at least consider alternative measures of punishment other than imprisonment, and may imprison the probationer only if the alternative measures are deemed inadequate to meet the State's interests in punishment and deterrence. There is no support in our cases or, in my view, the Constitution, for this novel requirement.

The Court suggests, ante at n.12, that if the sentencing court rejects non-prison alternatives as "inadequate," it is "impractical" to impose a prison term roughly equivalent to the fine in terms of achieving punishment goals. Hence, I take it, that had the trial court in this case rejected non-prison alternatives, the sentence it imposed would be constitutionally impregnable. Indeed, there would be no bounds on the length of the imprisonment that could be imposed, other than those imposed by the Eighth Amendment. But Williams v. Illinois and Tate v. Short stand for the proposition that such "automatic" conversion of a fine into a jail term is forbidden by the Equal Protection Clause, and by so holding, the Court in those cases was surely of the view that there is a way of converting a fine into a jail term that is not "automatic." In building a superstructure of procedural steps that sentencing courts must follow, the Court seems to forget its own concern about imprisoning an indigent person for failure to pay a fine.

In this case, in view of the long prison term imposed, the state court obviously did not find that the sentence was "a rational and necessary trade-off to punish the individual who possessed no accumulated assets," Williams v. Illinois, supra, 399 U.S., at 265 (Harlan, J., concurring). Accordingly, I concur in the judgment.

NOTES ON COERCING PAYMENT OF MONEY

1. *Bearden* is the first Supreme Court case under the modern victim's rights statutes. Defendant was ordered to pay a fine as well as compensation to the victim; our interest is in the compensation to the victim. What are the advantages and disadvantages of ordering defendant to pay and sending him to jail if he doesn't?

2. The other important context in which we order defendants to pay is child support. The typical child support order is an injunction to pay money, enforceable through the contempt power. It differs in some ways from the criminal victim statutes. Most notably, coercive contempt makes it possible to jail a child support defendant indefinitely and conditionally, letting him out when he pays. Presumably, criminal imprisonment for failure to compensate a crime victim will be for a fixed term for the underlying crime. Modern sentencing and parole practices may make it possible to grant earlier release to prisoners who pay, but the tools are not as flexible as coercive contempt. Second, the defense of impossibility is built into injunctions from the beginning; it is not necessary to resort to the Constitution to protect debtors who are unable to pay.

3. A third distinct means of coercing payment is imprisonment for debt. Imprisonment for debt at common law was about as inflexible a remedy as can be imagined. The remedy was exclusive if elected; a creditor could not imprison his debtor and also levy on his property. The debtor could not be released unless he paid or the creditor relented. If the creditor relented, he had no remedy left. And inability to pay was no defense. Poor debtors could languish indefinitely with no hope of ever being able to pay. But imprisoning a wealthy debtor with hidden or intangible assets might well coerce payment. That was a real benefit in a system that refused to levy on intangibles. But the costs in human suffering were enormous. It seems likely that many insolvents were imprisoned for every solvent recalcitrant.

Imprisonment for contract debt has been constitutionally prohibited in a majority of states. But some version of imprisonment for tort debt remains a little used option in many places. Modern debt imprisonment is illustrated in Landrigan v. McElroy, — R.I. — , 457 A.2d 1056 (1983). Plaintiff had a $42,000 judgment for assault and battery. Execution was twice returned unsatisfied. Plaintiff then requested execution on the body of defendant, and defendant was imprisoned. Under the Rhode Island statute, imprisoned debtors could be released by executing a "poor debtor's oath." Contract debtors could sign the oath immediately; tort debtors had to wait six months. Relying on the cases cited in *Bearden*, the court held that all debtors were constitutionally entitled to a pre-incarceration hearing on ability to pay.

4.   By varying routes, ability to pay has become the central issue in all three means of coercing payment of money. The central question is whether ability to pay can be litigated with reasonable fairness and accuracy and at reasonable cost in proceedings where defendant's liberty is at stake.

What should the court examine in determining ability to pay? Is it enough to know defendant's assets and income flow? What if his expenses exceed his income? Doesn't the court have to assess the legitimacy of those expenses? Otherwise, a defendant who is making payments on a Rolls Royce isn't able to pay his child support. There is no way to avoid these inquiries, but they lead to endless wrangling over ability to pay, with state supreme court opinions reviewing personal budgets line by line. The Texas courts say that a defendant must "reduce to the absolute minimum the expenditures for himself and the children in his home," if that is necessary to pay support for other children outside the home. Ex parte Kollenborn, 154 Tex. 223, 227, 276 S.W.2d 251, 254 (1955). Under that standard, one appellate court rejected a mother's claims of inability to pay because she had not explained why it was necessary to live by herself in a $160 a month apartment, or maintain a car that required a $106 monthly payment and $40 a month in gas. Ondrusek v. Ondrusek, 561 S.W.2d 236, 238 (Tex. Civ. App. 1978).

5.   Is it enough to examine expenses? What about the possibility of getting more income? *Bearden* says the court can consider whether defendant has tried hard enough to borrow money or find a job. How far should that inquiry go? Consider Johansen v. State, 491 P.2d 759, 767-769 (Alaska 1971), a child support case:

> Appellant is an Alaskan Native born in the Native village of Ekuk and raised in the nearby Native fishing village of Dillingham. In appellant's brief, it is stated that he is uneducated. Appellant's experience is sharply limited. His whole life, with the exception of four years in the military, has been spent in the village. His only occupation has been fishing, except for some very limited experience as a waiter in Dillingham working a few nights a month as work was available. He has been trained for no other occupation but fishing.
>
> Appellant's last good fishing season, when he cleared $3,200, was in 1965, before his divorce. Since that time he has cleared no more than $700 in any year because of poor fishing conditions. Appellant has been and is heavily in debt to a local cannery in Dillingham. In addition to other sums owed the cannery, appellant owes about $7,200 on his fishing vessel.
>
> Appellant has made attempts to find other employment. But he was unsuc-

cessful, principally, it appears, because prospective employers would not hire fishermen. Appellant testified that he could not quit fishing because he owes so much money to the cannery. He did not know of any way of making more money than as operator of a fishing vessel. In the 1969 fishing season, the year prior to the hearing on this matter, appellant testified that he had gone "in the red." In that year he went deeper in debt to the cannery. Appellant testified that he might have gotten a full time job with Wien Consolidated Airlines in Dillingham if he had given up fishing as his occupation, but that he could not be certain of this. From his testimony, it appears that appellant was continuing his occupation as a fisherman while waiting for a good fishing season to make up his losses and make a profit.

At the conclusion of the hearing, the judge stated that he could not contemplate issuing a judgment which would in effect order the appellant to go somewhere else to live and work at another job. But then the judge reversed his position by stating that appellant had remained in a depressed area year after year hoping for the big strike that had never come, that he ought not to stay in Dillingham, and that he was in contempt of court. The question here is whether one may be required to change his place of residence as a condition of not being held in contempt in a case of this type.

In these circumstances, we cannot agree with the trial judge's suggestion that appellant leave his home in Dillingham and seek employment in an urban community, such as the city of Anchorage. There is no indication from the record that such a move would hold a promise of success within appellant's inherent but unexercised capabilities. Rather, it seems that it would be a gamble, based on little more than hope, that an untrained person could earn more in an urban environment doing an undetermined job than he could in his home locality at his life-long occupation.

We need not close our eyes to the serious problem of unemployment in the city of Anchorage which is more serious for the unskilled. Further, our recent decision in Alvarado v. State, 486 P.2d 891 (Alaska 1971), discusses in detail the wide ranges of difference between life in rural Alaska and life in the city. We found them to be "vastly dissimilar," noting an "order of differences which distinguishes one culture from another."

We hesitate now to adopt a rule allowing a superior court to force a man to move from one community to another, in the process renouncing his life-long occupation to seek an undetermined one, on the penalty of being found in contempt for failure to do so. In short, leaving Dillingham to seek employment elsewhere would be outside the reasonable effort we require of a father in such cases.

We are remanding this case for a trial before a jury. We recognize it is within the function of the jury to make a factual determination as to whether appellant has presented a sufficient excuse for not complying with the order of child support. But we are determining as a matter of law, rather than leaving the question to the jury, that in the circumstances of this case, it is not contempt for a father to refuse to leave his village and seek more promising work in the city.

On the other hand, we hold there is a jury question as to the existence of a lawful excuse for non-compliance with the child support order while the appellant resides in Dillingham. In Houger v. Houger, 449 P.2d 766, 770 (Alaska 1969), we spoke of a father's primary and continuing obligation to support his children and of the fact that the inability of a father to engage in his chosen trade may not excuse him from that obligation. We said:

> But there may be other kinds of work which appellee could engage in despite any disability he may have. He should be required to seek such other work with respect to his obligation to support his children even though such work may not appeal to him, because there is no room for professional or occupational pride where the duty of child support is involved.

We adhere to *Houger* and hold that in a contempt action such as we have here, the father will not be permitted to succeed on the defense of having a legitimate reason or excuse for not complying with an order of child support where he has not made a reasonable effort to employ his earning capacity in directions other than the one he has chosen as his chief means of livelihood.

Should it matter that there was high unemployment in Anchorage? If it were more likely that moving to Anchorage would lead to higher income, should Johansen have to go? Or should courts not intrude into some lifestyle choices? Even if a child is going hungry?

What if Johansen were a professional capable of earning a substantial income, but he quit work and became penniless to avoid paying child support or alimony? Faced with that situation, the New York court ordered alimony based on earning capacity rather than earnings. Hickland v. Hickland, 39 N.Y.2d 1, 346 N.E.2d 243, *cert. denied*, 429 U.S. 941 (1976). A subsequent finding of contempt was reversed because New York guarantees the right to counsel in contempt proceedings that could lead to imprisonment, and Hickland had not been advised of that right. Hickland v. Hickland, 56 A.D.2d 978, 393 N.Y.S. 192 (1977). No further proceedings are reported. In a similar case, a California court reversed a contempt finding on the ground that it imposed involuntary servitude in violation of the thirteenth amendment. In re Jennings, 133 Cal. App. 3d 373, 184 Cal. Rptr. 53 (1982).

6. What if friends or relatives can pay? One of the reasons imprisonment for debt worked is that others would sometimes ransom the debtor. Consider In re MH, 662 S.W.2d 764, 768 (Tex. App. 1983), a probation revocation case. Defendant was a fifteen-year-old unwed mother who had been ordered to attend school as a condition of probation. Her father was in prison and her mother was unemployed. The court rejected her defense of inability to pay on two grounds. First, her mother could have paid a little. Second, her lawyer led the mother through a detailed explanation of the family's financial hardships, but forgot to ask the conclusory question, "Is your daughter able to pay anything at all?" Thus, no one ever testified that the daughter was unable to pay. Judge Gonzalez dissented. The court's absurd view of the evidence is relevant only as a

warning to be meticulous on direct examination. But what about the other holding? Should the daughter be imprisoned because the mother didn't pay?

7.   Whatever the difficulties, coercing payment collects more debts. In the case of child support, there are empirical studies. In Dane County, Wisconsin, where contempt remedies are available but have to be pursued by the custodial parent, about half of all child support is collected in the first year after it is ordered. That declines to about a quarter in the sixth year. By contrast, in Genesee County, Michigan, where a public agency vigorously pursues child support and jails parents who don't pay, 67 percent is collected in the first year and 72 percent in the sixth year. The data are from separate studies by different scholars; they are reported in Chambers, Men Who Know They are Watched: Some Benefits and Costs of Jailing for Nonpayment of Support, 75 Mich. L. Rev. 900, 923, 926 (1977). Chambers found that hardly anyone was so poor that the threat of jail didn't induce him to pay more. D. Chambers, Making Fathers Pay 118-119 (1979).

8.   Is coercive collection worth the cost? Collecting child support may be especially burdensome, because it involves an obligation that accrues monthly for many years rather than a single judgment for a fixed amount. But even allowing for that, one may question whether society should invest the same resources, or impose the same burdens on defendants, to collect ordinary judgments.

Is compensation for crime as compelling a claim as child support? Or are the victim rights laws justified on different grounds? The objections to coercing defendants to pay money are that coercion imposes hardship and risk of error. Are those impositions justified in the case of convicted criminals? Isn't it more productive to impose these hardships than to impose ordinary prison sentences?

9.   Most of the cases involve defendants without substantial assets, who at most could pay a little more each month. What about the defendant who appears to be wealthy but has concealed his assets? Is coercion more appropriate there? Should we coerce him to pay, or coerce him to reveal his assets?

If the assets are beyond the jurisdiction but defendant is before the court, the court may coerce defendant to turn over the assets. Many of the cases are collected in United States v. Ross, 196 F. Supp. 243 (S.D.N.Y. 1961). Ross was the sole shareholder of a Bahamas corporation; the court ordered him to endorse and deliver all the shares of stock to a receiver.

10.   Orders to turn over particular assets differ from an order to pay money. The turn-over order is aimed at specific property that is known to have been in defendant's possession. It may be hard to know whether he still has it, but that inquiry is narrowly focused. It does not lead to a full

review of defendant's income, expenses, and lifestyle. That is why turn-over orders are much more widely used than orders to pay.

Indeed, some statutes make turn-over orders available as a collection device more or less as needed. The Texas act applies in all cases where the debtor owns property that "cannot readily be attached or levied on by ordinary legal process." V.A.T.S. art. 3827a (1984 Supp.).

11. Apart from victim restitution laws, there is widespread informal use of criminal prosecution to coerce payment of money. It is fairly common for a defendant to compensate his victim in exchange for an agreement not to press the prosecution. The agreement is not binding on the prosecutor, and he may be annoyed, but he is not likely to proceed with an uncooperative complaining witness.

For some crimes the informal procedure is institutionalized and the prosecutor cooperates. The most notable example is bad checks. My colleague Robert Dawson tells me that in Texas, bad check prosecutions far outnumber prosecutions for any other crime, even driving while in-toxicated. And in the ten years he has been active in the criminal process, he has never seen a bad check prosecution go to trial. Defendant pays the check, and the prosecutor drops the case.

Can this practice be reconciled with Disciplinary Rule 7-105 of the American Bar Association's Code of Professional Responsibility? That rule provided that "a lawyer shall not present, participate in presenting, or threaten to present criminal charges solely to obtain an advantage in a civil matter." Is the prosecutor implicitly exempt? What if the victim's lawyer tells him to take the check to the prosecutor? There is no corre-sponding rule in the ABA's Model Rules of Professional Conduct adopted in 1983. At this writing there is no way to know how many states will substitute the new Model Rules for the old Code.

12. Bankruptcy coexists uneasily with all these coercive methods of collection. If the legislature decides that a few debts are important enough to justify coercing payment, should the bankruptcy courts pro-vide refuge from coercion? That question arises in many forms, and the lower courts are badly split.

All agree that a crime victim's underlying civil claim is a dischargeable debt. The disagreement begins when the victim pursues that claim through the criminal process, either informally or through a victim resti-tution order. Bankruptcy judges seem to view the widespread use of the criminal process to collect bad checks as an abuse; they are more deferen-tial to legislatively established victim restitution programs. Some courts have held that a victim restitution order from a criminal court is a dis-chargeable debt; others have disagreed. Among those that have held such orders dischargeable, some have enjoined prosecutors from revoking pa-role or probation for nonpayment; others have allowed revocation. Simi-larly, some bankruptcy courts have tried to assess the prosecutor's motive:

If he is trying to collect compensation for the victim, he will be enjoined; if he is trying to punish or rehabilitate the debtor, he will not be enjoined. That question is often unanswerable; often both motives are equally important. But if the crime is serious and the debtor probably would have been jailed but for his promise to pay, shouldn't that matter? Or if the crime is petty and the prosecution would never have been brought but for the victim's desire for restitution, shouldn't that matter? Some bankruptcy courts have tried to test motive without litigating the question. They have allowed prosecution or revocation, but they have enjoined the prosecutor from recommending restitution and enjoined the victim from accepting any money. Is that a workable solution? Most of the approaches are reviewed in In re Brown, 39 Bankr. 820 (Bankr. M.D. Tenn. 1984), and In re Redenbaugh, 37 Bankr. 383 (Bankr. C.D. Ill. 1984).

The Bankruptcy Code explicitly provides that debts for alimony, child support, or spouse support are not dischargeable. 11 U.S.C. §§523(a)(5), 1328(a)(2) (1982). That has traditionally been thought to settle the matter, even if the support is long past due. Some of the cases are collected in In re MacDonald, 41 Bankr. 716 (Bankr. D. Haw. 1984). But a conflicting line of cases originated in In re Warner, 5 Bankr. 434, 438-443 (Bankr. D. Utah). *Warner* was written by Judge Mabey, a well-known and well-respected bankruptcy judge. *Warner* holds that the bankruptcy court must decide whether the support originally ordered is still needed for support; if not, it is dischargeable because it is no longer a debt for support. Isn't that an open invitation to any divorced parent facing contempt charges? File for bankruptcy and make your ex-spouse prove that he or she still needs that back child support.

C.   PRESERVING ASSETS BEFORE JUDGMENT

1.   Attachment and the Like

IN RE CHEMICAL SEPARATIONS CORP.
29 Bankr. 240 (Bankr. E.D. Tenn. 1983)

BARE, Bankruptcy Judge.

. . . I

On June 11, 1982, plaintiff A. G. Campbell & Co., Inc., a pipe fabricator in Chattanooga, filed its complaint in Hamilton County Chancery Court against defendant Chemical Separations Corporation (Chem Seps), a manufacturer of waste and water treatment systems. The affidavit of A. G. Campbell, dated June 18, 1982, in support of plaintiff's petition for an ancillary writ of attachment was filed on June 21, 1982. This affidavit recites in material part:

> 5. That Plaintiff is advised the Defendant is attempting to cease operations at its Knoxville, Tennessee location and that its equipment, some of which is for a project in Mississippi, part of which has been fabricated by Plaintiff, is about to be removed from Tennessee.
>
> 6. Deponent prays that Plaintiff be granted an attachment of One Hundred Six Thousand Four Hundred Eight Dollars ($106,408), together with costs, upon the personal property of Defendant in its bank accounts and at its facilities at One Technology Drive, Knoxville, Knox County, Tennessee, to answer for the indebtedness due Plaintiff in such amount arising from work, labor and services rendered at Defendant's specific request by Plaintiff, which is a just claim and for which attachment should issue under TCA §29-6-101(2).

[handwritten margin note: threatening to move equipment]

On June 21, 1982, based on the averments in Campbell's affidavit, the chancellor in Hamilton County issued a writ of attachment to the Knox County Sheriff, who thereupon attached a bank account of defendant Chem Seps at the former United American Bank of Knoxville. Because there were several outstanding checks issued against and payable from the attached account, defendant necessarily had to either furnish a sufficient bond to obtain a release of the attachment or contend with the payees of the outstanding checks and the concomitant, adverse effect upon its credit reputation. Defendant proffered a surety bond in the amount of $110,000.00 for the discharge of the attachment against its bank account. . . . An order was entered, by the chancellor, on June 28, 1982, providing for the release of the attachment.

Defendant Chem Seps filed its answer and counterclaim in the chancery proceeding on August 20, 1982. Defendant does not deny it was indebted to plaintiff when the attachment was issued. However, in its counterclaim, defendant alleged no legitimate ground existed for the issuance of the writ of attachment because plaintiff either knew or should have known the statements in A. G. Campbell's supporting affidavit were false. As damages for the allegedly wrongful attachment, defendant requested judgment against plaintiff in the amount of $50,000.00.

On or about October 15, 1982, defendant filed its motion to quash the ancillary attachment and release its surety bond. For the first time, defendant specifically raised the issue of the sufficiency of Campbell's supporting affidavit. According to defendant, the affidavit is deficient because Campbell states only that he is advised defendant's equipment is being moved out of the state, as opposed to asserting such removal as a fact based upon personal knowledge. A request was made that defendant be permitted to withdraw the surety bond.

In response, a motion to amend the affidavit given in the ancillary attachment proceeding and a second affidavit of Campbell were filed. This second affidavit recites in material part:

> 2.   That the affidavit of deponent, dated June 18, 1982, was for the purpose of affirmatively stating to this Court that defendant was about to remove its equipment from the State.
>
> 3.   That deponent did not intend to modify or otherwise affect the true and full import of his statement concerning the removal of defendant's equipment from the State by the word "advise" as suggested by the instant motion's papers. Rather, it was deponent's purpose to state he was advised defendant was attempting to cease operations at Knoxville. A clerical error omitted the semicolon which should have followed "location" in paragraph "5" of the deponent's affidavit of June 18, 1982.

An affidavit dated October 28, 1982, of Carl R. Hazen, president of defendant Chem Seps, was offered in support of defendant's motion to quash the ancillary attachment and release the surety bond. Essentially, Hazen averred: (1) defendant Chem Seps did not own any property on or about June 18, 1982, (the date of A. G. Campbell's first affidavit) which was about to be removed from the State of Tennessee; and (2) the equipment which defendant was preparing to ship to Mississippi, a portion of which had been fabricated by plaintiff, actually belonged to TVA and was merely stored on defendant's premises pursuant to a contractual agreement.

Plaintiff, in reply to Hazen's affidavit, submitted an affidavit dated November 1, 1982, of Leon Riggs, vice-president of operations for defendant Chem Seps from April 27, 1981, until June 25, 1982. In apposite part Riggs' affidavit states:

> 4.   On June 18, 1982, to deponent's personal knowledge, equipment was being shipped to the Caterpillar Company in Lafayette, Indiana, and other parts were about to be shipped. Such shipments were continuous until and after deponent left his employee [sic]. This equipment had a value of $50,000.
>
> In addition, Chem-Seps equipment was being fabricated and assembled for shipment to Container Corporation in Fernandina Beach, Florida, of a value of $200,000. This equipment was about to be shipped on June 25, 1982, when deponent left Chem-Seps regular employ, and he has personally returned to Chem-Seps plant since June 25, 1982, and verified the equipment was in fact shipped.

In an effort to clarify the inconsistencies between the averments in the affidavits of Hazen and Riggs, a second affidavit of Carl R. Hazen was submitted by defendant. Hazen's second affidavit, dated February 25, 1983, provides in part:

> 3.   On the 28th day of October, 1982, I made an affidavit in which I stated that on or about June 18, 1982, the Defendant, Chem Seps owned no property

which was about to be removed from the State of Tennessee. This statement was addressed to whether or not sufficient of Chem Seps' property was about to be removed from the State of Tennessee such that a statutory ground authorizing the issuance of an attachment would exist pursuant to T.C.A. §29-6-101(2). The statement was not intended to apply to the work product of Chem Seps which it had contracted with its various customers to design, fabricate and deliver, and which work product was being delivered both to its out-of-state customers and in-state customers in the ordinary course of business. Most of Chem Seps' customers are located outside the State of Tennessee.

4. On or about June 18, 1982, Chem Seps was in the process of finalizing the fabrication of equipment and preparing the same for delivery to its customers Caterpillar Company in Lafayette, Indiana, and Container Corporation in Fernandina Beach, Florida, all of which was being done in the ordinary course of Chem Seps' business and pursuant to its contractual obligations to those customers.

Hazen further averred: (1) the delivery of equipment sold by the defendant generated an account receivable or cash in an amount of greater value to defendant's creditors than the equipment itself; (2) the assets of defendant available in the State of Tennessee at all times when shipments were being made to Caterpillar Company and Container Corporation were more than sufficient to satisfy the claims of creditors.[1]

On October 15, 1982, previous to the submission of the affidavits of Hazen, Riggs, and the second affidavit of Campbell, a voluntary chapter 11 bankruptcy petition was filed by defendant Chem Seps. An application to remove the instant adversary proceeding to this court was filed by defendant on December 2, 1982. See 28 U.S.C.A. §1478 (Supp. 1982).

II

The fundamental issue before the court concerns the sufficiency of A. G. Campbell's affidavit to support the writ of attachment. If the affidavit was insufficient for its purpose, the court must determine whether the insufficiency is either a matter of form cured by corrective amendment or if defendant waived its right to object to the insufficiency by filing an answer to the merits of the complaint without objecting to the sufficiency of the affidavit.

Although the Tennessee attachment statutes are to be liberally construed as a general rule, a strict construction is afforded to the attach-

---

1. In support of Hazen's assertion regarding the presence in Tennessee of assets having a value in excess of liabilities, a balance sheet for the period of June 1982, was attached to his second affidavit. This balance sheet reflects total assets and liabilities in the respective amounts of $8,267,696.82 and $7,448,168.65. However, as observed by plaintiff, this same balance sheet reflects trade payables in the amount of $2,258,778.74 and cash on hand of only $34,326.46.

ment statutes insofar as prescribed causes for which attachment may issue. However, avoidance of an attachment on the basis of a mere technicality appears to be contrary to public policy in Tennessee.

Tenn. Code Ann. §29-6-101 (1980) (Grounds for attachment) provides in relevant part:

> Any person having a debt or demand due at the commencement of an action, or a plaintiff after action for any cause has been brought, and either before or after judgment, may sue out an attachment at law or in equity, against the property of a debtor or defendant in the following cases: . . .
> (2)   Where he is about to remove, or has removed, himself or property from the state. . . .

It is unnecessary for a plaintiff to establish fraud or injury as a consequence of the removal to sustain an attachment on this ground.

Tenn. Code Ann. §29-6-113 (1980) (Plaintiff's affidavit) enacts:

> In order to obtain an attachment, the plaintiff, his agent or attorney, shall make oath in writing, stating the nature and amount of the debt or demand, and that it is a just claim; or, if the action is for a tort, that the damages sued for are justly due the plaintiff or plaintiffs, as affiant believes, but that the true amount of such damages are not ascertained; and, also, that one or more of the causes enumerated in §29-6-101 exists.

Paragraph 5 of the Campbell affidavit is susceptible to two quite different interpretations:

 (1)   Plaintiff is advised both that defendant Chem Seps is attempting to cease its operations in Knoxville and that a portion of its equipment is about to be removed from the State of Tennessee.

 (2)   Plaintiff is advised that defendant Chem Seps is attempting to cease its operations in Knoxville. A portion of defendant's equipment is about to be removed from Tennessee.

Under the first interpretation, averments regarding the cessation of defendant's business and the removal of its equipment are based on Campbell's being advised thereof by another party. The second interpretation is distinguished by the fact the affirmation concerning the imminent out-of-state removal of defendant's equipment is averred as a fact, implicitly based upon Campbell's personal knowledge. The distinction is significant: . . .

> The statement is only that the information had been had, and the belief exists. . . . Again, it may be true that a complainant is informed and believes that a defendant is about fraudulently to dispose of property, but it could not be sufficient to sustain an attachment to show that he had such information,

and believed it without proof, and if proving the allegation made could not sustain the attachment, the allegation is insufficient.

Nelson v. Fuld, 89 Tenn. 466, 468, 14 S.W. 1079 (1891).

Applying the *Nelson* decision in the instant case, it is evident that proof of the verity of Campbell's averments under the first possible interpretation would be insufficient to establish grounds for the writ of attachment. Whether A. G. Campbell was in fact advised defendant was removing or about to remove its equipment out of the state is inconsequential insofar as whether defendant was in fact either removing or about to remove its equipment beyond the state's borders.

Assuming *arguendo* that the former of the two possible interpretations is adopted, may plaintiff correct the deficiency through its motion to clarify and to amend Campbell's first affidavit? Tenn. Code Ann. §29-6-124 (1980) (Correction of defects) enacts:

> The attachment law shall be liberally construed, and the plaintiff, before or during trial, shall be permitted to amend any defect of form in the affidavit, bond, attachment, or other proceedings; and no attachment shall be dismissed for any defect in, or want of, bond, if the plaintiff, his agent, or attorney will substitute a sufficient bond.

This section permits the amendment of any defect in the form of the supporting affidavit, but it does not authorize an amendment affecting the substance of the affidavit. . . .

Plaintiff's request to amend merely involves the insertion of a punctuation mark (a semicolon) to clarify Campbell's averment concerning the imminency of the removal out of the state of defendant's equipment. This request is supported by A. G. Campbell's sworn affidavit that his former supporting affidavit "was for the purpose of affirmatively stating . . . that defendant was about to remove its equipment from the State." . . . Given the susceptibility of the averment in question to two different interpretations, the desirability of the resolution of disputes upon the merits as opposed to technicalities, and the credibility the court believes due the averments of A. G. Campbell in his November 1, 1982, affidavit, the motion to amend Campbell's June 8, 1982, supporting affidavit should be granted.[3]

The question remains whether the amount of defendant's property either being removed or about to be removed was sufficient to support plaintiff's attachment. The removal of an insignificant amount of a debtor's property will not support an attachment. *Freidlander, Stick & Co. v. S. Pollock & Co.*, 45 Tenn. (5 Cold.) 490 (1868).

---

3. The court had the opportunity to observe the testimony of A. G. Campbell during the course of the two-day trial of this adversary proceeding and believes his sworn affidavit is entitled to credibility.

It is not possible to define by precise words, the amount of property re-moved, or about to be removed, which will bring the debtors within the scope of the statute. It need not be all his property, nor will a comparative little suffice. It must be an amount, of substantial consequence in reference to the ability of his estate to bear honestly, the withdrawal of the amount away from his liability, in the domestic court, to his creditors.

Freidlander, 45 Tenn. (5 Cold.) at 493-494. . . .

The affidavit of Leon Riggs clearly supports plaintiff's assertion that property of the defendant was about to be removed beyond the borders of the State of Tennessee when plaintiff sought a writ of attachment. As previously noted, Riggs, former vice-president for operations for the de-fendant, avers that equipment of a value of $50,000.00 was either shipped on June 18, 1982, or was about to be shipped, to Indiana, and that equip-ment of a value of $200,000.00 was about to be shipped to Florida on June 25, 1982, when Riggs left the employ of defendant Chem Seps.

Defendant does not deny its ownership of this equipment. Instead, defendant contends the attachment was wrongful because the amount of its property removed, assuming arguendo a removal occurred, fails to satisfy the *Freidlander* test. Defendant submits its assets substantially exceeded its liabilities at or about the date of the attachment, as evi-denced by the June 1982 balance sheet attached to Hazen's affidavit of February 25, 1983, reflecting total assets and liabilities in the respective amounts of $8,267,696.82 and $7,448,168.65. However, the bankruptcy schedules of the debtor filed some four months later, on October 28, 1982, reflect liabilities of $5,389,993.40 and assets having a value of only $3,991,509.04. Yet, the schedules further reflect:

(1) repayments on loans and installment purchases between June 1, 1982, and September 30, 1982, total only $50,068.76;

(2) no transfer was made other than in the ordinary course of busi-ness during the year preceding the date of the bankruptcy filing;

(3) no fire or theft losses were experienced during the year preceding the date of the filing of the bankruptcy petition.

Under these circumstances it is difficult to understand how the debtor's financial condition declined in a period of four months from a positive equity of $819,528.17 to a negative equity of $1,398,484.36. The figures in the June 1982 balance sheet are rejected by the court as unreliable. Con-sidering the information furnished in the defendant's bankruptcy sched-ules, the court finds an amount of defendant's property of substantial consequence was either being removed or about to be removed when plaintiff sought the attachment writ, when tested against defendant's abil-ity (or inability) to pay plaintiff's debt.

Defendant Chem Seps also insists the equipment it shipped out of the state during June 1982 represented its work product shipped pursuant to contractual obligation in the ordinary course of its business. Defendant further insists the shipments out of the state create accounts receivable of greater value to its creditors than the equipment shipped. The following query is raised by the defendant:

> Can it be that the law of this state is that a business with out-of-state customers which is performing its contractual obligations to those customers in the ordinary course of its business is subjected to prejudgment confiscation of its property simply at the bidding of one of its creditors?

Initially, the court observes that an attaching creditor must furnish a bond, payable to the defendant, providing that, upon failure to prosecute the attachment with effect, the creditor will pay the defendant all costs adjudged against him and all damages sustained as a consequence of any wrongful attachment. Tenn. Code Ann. §29-6-115 (1980). The amount of the bond required is prescribed by Tenn. Code Ann. §29-6-116 (1980). These statutes obviously reduce the probability of any frivolous attachment.

In answer to defendant's query, the court observes Tenn. Code Ann. §29-6-101(2) (1980) makes no exception based on the character of the debtor's property either removed or about to be removed. The creation of an account receivable certainly does not assure subsequent, voluntary payment by the seller to his unpaid creditors. Instead, in interstate sales, it may become necessary for the Tennessee claimant or creditor to prosecute his claim in a foreign forum, remotely situated in some cases, to obtain payment of his debt. This court declines to fashion a judicial exception to Tenn. Code Ann. §29-6-101(2) (1980) immunizing the removal out of the state of a debtor's inventory property.

A/R doesn't = payment → payment

Grounds for attachment pursuant to Tenn. Code Ann. §29-6-101(2) (1980) did exist when plaintiff filed its petition for an ancillary writ of attachment on June 21, 1982, against defendant Chem Seps.

This Memorandum constitutes findings of fact and conclusions of law, Bankruptcy Rule 752.

NOTES ON ATTACHMENT

1.   Usage varies from state to state, but attachment generally refers to a levy or garnishment before judgment. The primary purpose is to keep the assets from disappearing. Another consequence is to establish priority in the assets from the date of the prejudgment attachment instead of from a postjudgment execution or garnishment.

2.   The grounds for attachment are nearly all variations on the theme that assets may be about to disappear. Some states make attachment very

easy; others make it very difficult. The Tennessee statute is a good example, although it tilts toward plaintiffs. In New York, removing assets is not ground for attachment unless there is fraudulent intent. Eaton Factors Co. v. Double Eagle Corp., 17 A.D.2d 135, 232 N.Y.S.2d 901 (1962). That rule is surely more typical than Tennessee's.

In addition to the ground argued in *Chem Seps*, the Tennessee statute authorizes seven other overlapping grounds for attachment:

(a.) Defendant resides out of state;
(b.) He is removing himself "out of the county privately";
(c.) He conceals himself so that the ordinary process of law cannot be served upon him;
(d.) He absconds or conceals himself or property;
(e.) He has fraudulently disposed of his property or is about to do so;
(f.) He resides out of state and dies, leaving property in the state;
(g.) Defendant is a foreign corporation without an agent for service of process within the state.

Tenn. Code Ann. §29-6-101 (1980 Replacement).

3.   It is even easier to get an attachment in Maine. It is enough to show a "reasonable likelihood" that plaintiff will recover judgment in an amount equal to or greater than the amount of the attachment plus any liability insurance. Maine R. Civ. Proc. 4A(c) (1984). There is no need to show risk of fraud or dissipation. A claim meets the "reasonable likelihood" requirement if it is "not of such insubstantial character that its invalidity so clearly appears as to foreclose a reasonable possibility of recovery." Northeast Investment Co. v. Leisure Living Communities, Inc., 351 A.2d 845 (Me. 1976).

Contrast that with Bourque v. Tyler, 401 So. 2d 652 (La. App. 1981). The Bourques sued in wrongful death in Louisiana, alleging that Tyler had murdered their son in Houston, Texas. Tyler had been extradited to Texas to stand trial for murder. The Bourques attached a bank account containing $17,000. The court of appeals vacated the attachment on the ground that although plaintiffs had shown that Tyler had left the state, they had not shown he had left the state permanently. If he's sentenced to 99 years, would that be long enough? The Supreme Court summarily reversed. 410 So. 2d 760 (La. 1981).

4.   In *Chem Seps*, the attachment was not executed because defendant posted a $100,000 bond. Suppose it hadn't been able to post the bond. How could it do business with its bank account frozen and important physical assets in the hands of the sheriff? The amount of the attachment was only $106,000, not much as a percentage of Chem Seps' eight million in assets. But Chem Seps had only $34,000 in cash, so the attachment of the bank account would get all its Tennessee cash. We don't know how much of the eight million in physical assets was in Tennessee,

but there probably wasn't $100,000 worth of surplus equipment sitting idle at the Knoxville plant. The sheriff may have levied on finished products ready for shipment, or on equipment essential to further production. Attachment can push a debtor into bankruptcy even before plaintiff has proved his claim. Is the risk of liability on the bond a sufficient deterrent to unjustified attachments? Does the New York rule requiring fraudulent intent strike a better balance between plaintiffs and defendants?

5. An attachment is one way of getting paid ahead of other creditors. If bankruptcy follows within ninety days, the attaching creditor must return the attached property to the bankrupt estate and share pro rata with other unsecured creditors. 11 U.S.C. §547 (1982).

6. Attachment is a near cousin to replevin. The difference is that in replevin, the plaintiff has some preexisting claim to the particular property replevied. Either he owns it and defendant is wrongfully in possession, or plaintiff has a security interest in it and is entitled to his collateral. Attachment is a more invasive remedy, because it can reach any nonexempt assets defendant owns.

NOTE ON BANKRUPTCY

Chem Seps responded to pressure from its creditors by filing for bankruptcy. The Bankruptcy Code is long, complex, and the subject of a whole separate course. But you should not think of it as something completely apart from the ordinary collection process. All litigators ought to know something about bankruptcy.

Bankruptcy is the debtor's trump card. The mere filing of a petition automatically stays all efforts to collect debts outside of bankruptcy. In this context, debt includes substantially all civil claims, including damage judgments, injunctions, and money judgments in restitution. A debtor may turn over all his nonexempt assets to a court-appointed trustee and receive a discharge of all his debts. Often there are no nonexempt assets; at best, they equal a small percentage of the debts. A business debtor may pay only part of its debts and continue in operation. The threat of bankruptcy hangs over all collection efforts, affecting the tactical calculations of both debtors and creditors. A creditor may do better to accept late payments, or partial payments, if the debtor is willing to make them, rather than force the debtor into bankruptcy with aggressive collection efforts. But the creditor also has to worry that some other creditor will force a bankruptcy. If that happens, he would fare better if he had been more aggressive three months earlier.

Occasionally, it is in a creditor's interest to force a bankruptcy. For example, if one creditor levies on substantially all the debtor's assets, other creditors can undo that levy, and get a share of the assets for themselves, by filing an involuntary bankruptcy petition within ninety days.

2.   Receivership

POULAKIDAS v. CHARALIDIS
68 Ill. App. 3d 610, 386 N.E.2d 405 (1979)

Mr. Justice Linn delivered the opinion of the court.

Plaintiffs, Niko Efstathiou, Thomas Poulakidas and The Maine Lobster House, Inc., brought this action for an accounting and dissolution of an alleged partnership operating The Maine Lobster House, Inc., a restaurant business. Defendant, Elias Charalidis, appeals from an interlocutory order granting plaintiffs' motion for the appointment of a receiver pendente lite to manage the restaurant's financial affairs. Defendant contends, inter alia, that it was error for the trial court to appoint a receiver pendente lite absent a clear showing of fraud or an imminent danger of dissipation or loss to the business assets.

We agree with the defendant, reverse the order appointing the receiver pendente lite, and remand the case for further proceedings.

The Maine Lobster House, Inc., is an Illinois corporation operating a restaurant in Chicago. In December 1975, defendant Charalidis and plaintiff Efstathiou acquired all of the outstanding shares of the corporation. Charalidis is the president of the corporation and Efstathiou, the secretary. Plaintiff Poulakidas is an attorney who represented Charalidis and Efstathiou in the purchase of the restaurant and in other matters relating to the business. . . .

Generally, the complaint alleged that plaintiffs and defendant had entered into an oral partnership agreement to purchase and operate The Maine Lobster House, Inc.; that plaintiffs had performed all their obligations under this agreement; that defendant had ousted plaintiffs from the business and that defendant had secretly appropriated profits and assets of the business without accounting to his partners. Plaintiffs sought an accounting and dissolution of the alleged partnership and requested temporary relief pending the termination of the litigation. . . .

[P]laintiffs moved the trial court for the appointment of a receiver pendente lite and other equitable relief to restrain the transfer or encumbrance of the business assets. . . . The defendant filed an answer to the complaint, denying the material allegations of the complaint and alleging several matters as affirmative defenses. . . .

We will highlight only the relevant testimony.

In September 1975, Charalidis and Efstathiou asked Poulakidas to assist them in acquiring The Maine Lobster House restaurant. Poulakidas and Efstathiou assert that the parties entered into an oral partnership to acquire the corporation and the option to purchase the improved real property containing the restaurant. It is maintained by plaintiffs that Poulakidas was to be an undisclosed partner in the venture. No written documents were presented which evidence a partnership, and defendant denies that the parties entered into such an agreement.

In December 1975, the parties purchased The Maine Lobster House, Inc. The sellers of the restaurant business took back a $50,000 chattel mortgage. . . .

In 1977, the business exercised the option to acquire the real property and building in which the restaurant is operated. . . .

After the business was purchased in 1975, Charalidis and Efstathiou operated the restaurant on a daily basis and each drew a weekly salary of $300. Charalidis, who had more experience in the restaurant business, managed all the financial matters. The restaurant employed an accountant who maintained records and prepared tax returns for the business based only on information given him by Charalidis. This accountant was dismissed by Charalidis prior to the hearing, and a new accountant retained.

There is some dispute regarding the nature of the services rendered to the business by Efstathiou. However, it is undisputed that since November 1977, for health or other reasons, Efstathiou has neither worked in the restaurant nor drawn a salary. Since that time, Charalidis has managed the business exclusively. While Efstathiou was working in the restaurant, he entrusted the financial matters to Charalidis and signed batches of blank checks so that Charalidis could pay the bills. Although he claims to have been locked out of the restaurant by Charalidis, the restaurant is open daily and Efstathiou has made no attempt to return to the business. Several past and present employees of the restaurant testified that Charalidis works long hours and is a competent restauranteur.

The daily business transactions of the restaurant are accounted for by checks turned in by the waitresses at the end of the business day. The waitresses are checked out by Charalidis who records the checks and deposits the money in the bank. Charalidis also handles transactions with the credit card companies. Since Efstathiou has been absent from the business, only Charalidis' signature appears on checks drawn on the accounts of The Maine Lobster House, Inc.

With regard to the financial situation of the restaurant at the time of the hearings, it was undisputed that the business was heavily indebted to the National Bank of Greece. An officer of the bank testified that payments on all the business' obligations to the bank were up to date. Poulakidas stated that he believed the business was several months behind in payments to the former owners of the restaurant. Efstathiou testified that the restaurant owed money to the cheese and fish suppliers. However, another supplier testified that the restaurant had a good credit standing and paid its bills promptly. Charalidis also stated that all of the suppliers were paid up to date.

Plaintiffs attempted to show that Charalidis has monthly personal expenses in excess of his $300 a week salary from the business. Charalidis admitted that he had made substantial improvements to his residence for which he makes monthly payments of $600 to $700.

On April 21, 1978, at the conclusion of the testimony, the trial judge entered an order appointing a receiver pendente lite for the limited purpose of handling the financial affairs of the business. Defendant Charalidis immediately took this interlocutory appeal pursuant to Supreme Court Rule 307(a)(2), and we stayed the appointment of the receiver pendente lite pending a resolution of this matter on appeal.

Opinion

The application for the appointment of a receiver is addressed to the sound discretion of the court. However, in such cases the standards by which the court's appointment of a receiver must be measured are exceptionally stringent. A court of equity has the power to appoint a receiver of a corporation only when conditions of dissension, dispute, fraud or mismanagement exist, which make it impossible for the business to continue or to preserve its assets. It is well recognized that the appointment of a receiver is an extraordinary and drastic remedy to be exercised with great caution. The appointment of a receiver is appropriate only in cases of urgent necessity where there is a present danger to the interests of the investors, consisting of a serious suspension of the business and an imminent danger of dissipation of the corporate assets. Even where the appointment of a receiver is temporary and for the limited purpose of preserving property and continuing the business until the dispute between the parties can be resolved, these rigid standards must be applied.

After reviewing the record in this case, we must conclude that the able trial judge misapprehended the severity of the circumstances which must be shown before the law will sanction the appointment of a receiver pendente lite. The record before us contains no evidence of fraud on the part of defendant Charalidis, nor a sufficient basis upon which to conclude that the business assets are in immediate danger of dissipation or loss.

The major creditor of the business, the National Bank of Greece, is being paid promptly. Some evidence indicates that the business may be indebted to other creditors, but not so severely as to impair its credit standing. Excluding the absence of Efstathiou from the restaurant, the business is being managed by Charalidis as it has been since the parties acquired it. Efstathiou's assertion that he has been locked out of the business is offset by his admission that, although the restaurant is open daily, he has made no attempt to return to work. The testimony relating to Charalidis' income and personal expenses is at this point in the proceedings inconclusive.

Although no accounting has been rendered by Charalidis to the others, there is no evidence in the record that an accounting was requested before this lawsuit was filed. Furthermore, this court has been assured by counsel for defendant that all of the books and records of the business will be made available to the plaintiffs for examination, study and copying.

The most compelling evidence concerns the unsatisfactory records kept by defendant. Although it could be concluded from the evidence that the system of record keeping maintained by defendant is inadequate, this does not, at this point in time, provide proof of wrongdoing or indicate that defendant has appropriated business assets for his own use.

We note that a receiver should not be appointed merely because the measure can do no harm, for this is almost never the case. "The appointment of a receiver impairs the credit of the corporation, interferes [sic] with its management, and imposes upon the court the onerous duty of corporate management which it is not qualified to perform and which it should not undertake except in extreme cases." (16 Fletcher, Cyclopedia Corporations §7697, at 112-13 (perm. ed. 1962).) Mere dissension and dispute between parties is an insufficient cause to invoke the drastic remedy of receivership.

The appointment of a receiver pendente lite is warranted only where there is no other adequate remedy or means of securing the desired result. Where, as here, the dispute between the parties can adequately be resolved by an accounting, that course of action should be followed rather than seeking the appointment of a receiver. We urge the parties to exercise diligence in pursuing this action to a prompt resolution in the trial court.

Reversed and remanded.

JOHNSON and ROMITI, JJ., concur.

NOTES ON RECEIVERSHIP

1. Receivership may be thought of as a very sophisticated form of attachment. You wouldn't want the sheriff to seize a restaurant; the receiver of a restaurant must be prepared to run it. Ideally, receivers are business people with experience in the industry. Often, they are lawyers. Too often, they are friends of the judge.

Receivership is a very expensive remedy, because the receiver must be paid at professional rates. His expenses become a lien against the property; in *Poulakidas*, the restaurant must pay the receiver. He has to do a lot better than Charalidis was doing to justify his pay. The ultimate question in every receivership case is whether a receiver can pay for himself and make everybody better off.

2. A prejudgment receiver manages the property for the court, preserving it for delivery to the true owner once the court decides who the true owner is. Plaintiffs don't always win; the true owner may be the

defendant. Because it is a preliminary remedy based on a showing of probabilities, much of receivership practice is analogous to preliminary injunction practice. Plaintiff must post a bond, and receivership orders are immediately appealable.

3.   *Poulakidas* illustrates one common use of receivership. The litigants are investors in a common enterprise, and one side feels oppressed. Neither side trusts the other to manage the business, and the side that is not in control seeks a receiver. But it's not enough that they aren't getting along; the assets must be in danger. Usually, the charge is that defendant is misappropriating or dissipating them. Sometimes, the charge is that the business is paralyzed by the parties' antagonism, and that it will suffer severe losses unless someone is appointed with power to run it. Poulakidas seems to fear misappropriation, but he doesn't have any evidence.

4.   Receivership is also available for secured creditors whose collateral is in danger of dissipation, and for other plaintiffs with a claim to specific property.

Perhaps the most common use of receivership is in foreclosing mortgages on rental buildings. If it appears that the value of the building is not sufficient to pay the debt, and that it will not be possible to collect the deficiency by execution on the debtor's other assets, the court will appoint a receiver to collect the rents pending foreclosure. If there is also evidence that the debtor is allowing the building to deteriorate, the receiver will be appointed to manage the building. An example with a clear opinion is Garden Homes, Inc. v. United States, 200 F.2d 299 (1st Cir. 1952).

As you might expect, courts vary widely in the strictness with which they enforce these standards. In some places, a receiver is a routine step in most commercial mortgage foreclosures. At the other end of the spectrum, some states with strong debtor protection legislation let the debtor keep the rents through foreclosure and even through the statutory redemption period. Those states will appoint a receiver only if the debtor is damaging the property. A good example of that approach is First Federal Savings & Loan Association v. Moulds, 202 Kan. 557, 451 P.2d 215 (1969).

NOTES ON ACCOUNT AND ACCOUNTING

1.   *Poulakidas* also illustrates an accounting. Plaintiffs want Charalidis to account to them and the court for the proceeds of the restaurant business. The adequacy of that remedy is one ground for denying the receiver.

2.   Accounting can be thought of as a means of trying a claim that raises a particular set of procedural difficulties. But for historical reasons, it is often thought of as a distinct remedy. *Account* was a separate writ at common law. Equity would grant an *accounting* in cases too complicated

for a jury, in cases where discovery was required to get the other side's records, and in cases of fiduciaries. The distinction between the legal and equitable names of substantially the same action persists in some states; for convenience, I will refer to both actions as accounting. In either court the purpose is to review the records of a series of transactions in which both plaintiff and defendant had an interest and determine which one owed the other how much.

3.   An accounting suit seeks a money judgment — either compensation or restitution. The accounting is ancillary to the claim for money. In the case of two merchants who dealt with each other repeatedly, an accounting resolves all disputes growing out of a large number of closely related contracts. In cases like *Poulakidas*, it is a means of forcing a fiduciary to account for his conduct of the business. Another example is Couri v. Couri, infra at 805, where plaintiff gets an accounting for the operations of a grocery store.

Ordinary accountings by business managers and other fiduciaries are closely related to accounting for profits. If the accounting reveals that the fiduciary diverted funds and profited from the diversion, he has to account for those profits. From there it is an easy step to accounting for profits as a general restitutionary remedy. See the notes to Meier Brewing Co. v. Fleischmann Distilling Corp., the case of Black and White beer and Black and White scotch, supra at 472.

4.   It is commonplace that defendant has not kept good records or has refused to let plaintiff see them. Usually, there are disputes about the accuracy of the records, or about the meaning of the records. Often, there are also disputes about some of the underlying transactions. Plaintiff could sue separately on each disputed item, but that would be wasteful. In an accounting, the court looks at the whole series of events in a single litigation. Even so, it would be extraordinarily burdensome to actually litigate every item in a long series of transactions. The parties are encouraged, and often pressured, to settle as much as they can and bring only the disputed items to the court for decision. If necessary, the account can be referred to a master for study. The parties have to pay the master, and that is a good incentive to settle more items.

ADELMAN v. CGS SCIENTIFIC CORP.
332 F. Supp. 137 (E.D. Pa. 1971)

[Adelman controlled Crowell Corp. In 1969, he negotiated the sale of Crowell to CGS, receiving cash and CGS stock for his interest. Adelman and two of his key associates became employees of CGS, in charge of the Crowell Division.

In August 1970, CGS management discovered that one of its divisions had overstated its earnings. Management announced this discovery in

September and released corrected financial statements in December. Adelman then demanded rescission of the Crowell sale, and demanded that he be appointed receiver of the Crowell Division pending rescission. CGS gave notice that Adelman and his associates would be terminated when their contracts expired in October 1971.

The judge made detailed findings of fact at a preliminary hearing. He found that it was "highly probable" that Adelman had relied on the misrepresentations when he agreed to sell Crowell for CGS stock. He also found that Crowell was having problems getting credit because of its association with CGS, and that credit would be wholly unavailable but for the personal reputation and assurances of Adelman and his associates. He issued this opinion and order on August 26, 1971.]

BRODERICK, District Judge. . . .

The granting of preliminary relief rests upon plaintiff's ultimate right to rescission in this action. Indeed, the preliminary relief which plaintiff requests may be granted only on a showing of immediate and irreparable harm for which there cannot be adequate compensation in damages, accompanied by a clear probability of success on the merits. . . .

The plaintiff has, for the purposes of this preliminary relief, shown that he has a clear probability of success in the establishment of all the . . . . elements of fraud in a trial on the merits of this case. . . .

One remedy available to the injured party who has established fraud is rescission of the contract which was fraudulently induced. . . . On the basis of the record as it now stands in this case, it is highly probable that plaintiff can make out a case for rescission under the doctrine of common law fraud and/or the Securities Act. . . .

We also find that plaintiff is likely to suffer irreparable harm if equitable relief is not now granted. It is highly probable that the suppliers of Crowell will cease doing business with Crowell except on a cash in advance basis if the present management is replaced. Moreover, because of the antagonism between the parties it is conceivable that defendants may fire the management of Crowell even though no knowledgeable replacements are available, which action of course would act to the detriment of both parties. Finally, in the event this Court determines that the plaintiff is entitled to rescission, such a determination will be meaningless unless the Crowell division is preserved, and in view of the financial position of CGS it is entirely possible that CGS may sell the assets of Crowell effectively nullifying plaintiff's remedy. Therefore, we find that irreparable injury will result if this court denied preliminary relief. . . .

It is clear that the Court has the power to appoint a Receiver or Custodian in this case. This power is derived from our general and inherent equity power and the grant of authority under the Securities Act of 1933 . . . . and the Securities and Exchange Act of 1934. . . . The basic consideration in appointing a receiver or a custodian is the necessity of protecting, conserving and administering property pending final disposition of a suit.

The interim protection of property fraudulently acquired, and in imminent jeopardy of loss, pending rescission is one of the classic instances where the appointment of a receiver or custodian is proper. . . .

Moreover, the Court deems it unnecessary to make any findings concerning the solvency of CGS for the reason that solvency is not a bar to the appointment of a custodian or receiver. . . .

However, although it is clear this Court has the power to appoint a receiver or custodian and grant other preliminary relief, in determining the appropriate relief we must balance the potential harm of such relief to the parties. . . .

Using such a balancing test we cannot grant the preliminary relief as sought by plaintiff, since it would place Crowell under the control of plaintiff, an adverse party with an obvious conflict of interest, and would create the risk of irreparable harm to CGS. Crowell Division has a net worth on the books of CGS of $2,100,000. It has an assigned value on the bank loan of $1,800,000 and is a division which CGS may sell to a third party. Impairment of this major asset would cause CGS great harm. Furthermore, since it is highly probable that plaintiff has a firm commitment from a third party to provide him with the funds to pay CGS for the Crowell Division, he may be lacking incentive at this time to operate the division more profitably. He may consider it to his advantage to discourage competing prospective buyers so that he would be in a better position to buy Crowell back at a lower price in the event this Court denies rescission. Any harm to the division from plaintiff's self interest will irreparably injure CGS.

There is another reason why this Court cannot appoint the Plaintiff as Receiver. CGS has a bank loan of $2,765,000 secured by the assets of CGS including Crowell. Any impairment in the collateral value of CGS, including Crowell, or any impairment of the net worth of CGS including Crowell gives the bank the right to demand prepayment of the loan. CGS must, therefore, have the continued authority to supervise the division in order to protect its position with the bank. The value assigned to the Crowell Division in the bank loan is $1,800,000. This is over one-third the value of all CGS divisions. Appointing the plaintiff as the Receiver would not be to anyone's best interest. Furthermore, CGS has a clause in its loan agreement with the banks which provides that if a trustee or receiver is appointed for CGS or any of its divisions the banks can take control of the entire corporation.

Moreover, in determining the appropriate relief we must consider the three class actions by shareholders of CGS which are presently before this Court. Each alleges violations of the securities laws in connection with the purchase or sale of CGS stock on the basis of false or misleading statements, primarily in 1970, but also in 1969 and 1968. And no order we issue should unnecessarily prejudice their rights.

Finally, we must note that some relief is necessary because the parties are unable to reach any decisions on the management policy at Crowell.

Since the first hearing in this matter on July 9, 1971, the attorneys for plaintiff and for CGS have been before us numerous times, by letters, telephone calls and in person, in their efforts to arrive at a Stipulation which would preserve the status quo of the parties until this case is heard on the merits. Their last series of discussions began in Chambers on Thursday, August 12, 1971, and counsel for the parties continued their conferences through the next day. The only decision which was reached was that the parties could not agree. It is apparent to us that the parties do not have the present ability to work together or to solve the daily crises which arise in the operation and management of a large corporation. CGS is experiencing financial difficulties; it needs Crowell to continue to operate at a profit. It is imperative that the management of CGS and of Crowell work harmoniously because it is obvious that if the Crowell division is not a financial success, it may destroy the entire corporate structure of CGS. And, by the same token, should CGS be faced with additional financial crises, there is no question but that this would bring about the failure of all its divisions, including Crowell. The need for flexibility in the cash flow between CGS and Crowell makes it impossible to fashion a specific order regulating the cash flow between them and dictates the necessity for a third party to mediate the financial disputes which are now taking place between the parties.

Therefore, in order to avoid irreparable harm to CGS and its shareholders, but at the same time to preserve Crowell's assets and to keep Crowell operational pending a final trial on the merits, we deem it necessary to appoint a Custodian to preserve Crowell and work effectively with both the management of Crowell and of CGS. This Custodian will be given the power to act as an arbitrator when disputes arise between Crowell and CGS and will have the responsibility of working in the best interests of both parties in this action. The primary responsibility of the Custodian will be to preserve the Crowell division as a viable business concern without inflicting harm on CGS, so that if rescission is deemed appropriate Crowell will remain in such financial condition as to make said relief meaningful. In view of the daily financial crises which have confronted both the Crowell division and CGS, the determination of the Custodian will require a constant weighing of the equities in order to preserve the Crowell division without inflicting financial harm on CGS until this Court makes a final determination after trial on the merits, which trial will be scheduled at an early date. . . .

Order

And now, this 26th day of August, 1971, it is hereby ordered and decreed that:

1.   Defendant, their agents, employees, officers, directors and all others acting on their behalf be, and are hereby, enjoined and restrained

until further Order of this Court from doing or causing or permitting to be done any act, transaction or business which will impair the financial condition, assets, credit, good name or trade secrets of the Crowell Division.

2. Plaintiff and all other employees of Crowell Division acting alone or on plaintiff's behalf be, and are hereby, enjoined and restrained until further Order of this Court from doing or causing or permitting to be done any act, transaction or business which will impair the financial condition, assets, credit, good name or trade secrets of the Crowell Division.

3. Harold J. Conner, Esquire, is hereby appointed Custodian of all the assets, property, franchises, rights, privileges and interests of whatsoever kind of Crowell Division with the power to hold, demand, receive and collect all funds, assets and property belonging to Crowell, or in the hands of any debtor, agent, or depository of Crowell, and to account to the Court for the same.

(a) Said Custodian shall have the power and authority to settle all disputes between the management of CGS Scientific Corporation and the Crowell Division of CGS Scientific Corporation and said managements shall be bound by his decisions, which shall be final.

(b) Said Custodian is instructed to consider the best interests of CGS Scientific Corporation and its shareholders as well as the Crowell Division in reaching his decisions; and is further instructed in reaching his decisions to bear in mind that Crowell is a division of CGS and not an independent corporate entity.

(c) Said Custodian shall strive at all times to preserve the integrity, good will and assets of the Crowell Division without impairing the financial condition of CGS.

(d) The Court directs all parties to this proceeding to cooperate fully with the Custodian to ensure efficient, economical and profitable operations at the Crowell Division, such an operation being to the benefit of all parties.

(e) Said Custodian is hereby authorized to employ any professional, secretarial and clerical assistants he deems necessary for the purposes of preserving the assets, property and interests of Crowell.

4. There will be no changes in the management of the Crowell Division as it existed on July 2, 1971 without the consent of the Custodian.

5. The management of Crowell Division is directed to keep the management of CGS Scientific Corporation informed of all significant changes in the operation or financial condition of Crowell; and is further directed to cooperate with CGS management, its agents and employees who came to the Crowell plant to investigate the condition of Crowell.

6. This Order shall remain in effect until final determination of this matter after a hearing on the merits.

7. This case shall proceed to final hearing and trial on the merits before this Court on Wednesday, October 27, 1971, at 10:00 A.M.

(a) All Discovery shall be completed by Friday, October 15, 1971.
(b) A Pre-trial Conference shall be held in Chambers on Friday, October 22, 1971 at 2:00 P.M. A Pre-trial Order shall be completed pursuant to our Standing Order and must be submitted at the Pre-trial Conference.

Memorandum and Order . . .

On August 30, 1971, defendant CGS filed a motion requesting this Court to amend its Order of August 26, 1971, by deletion of paragraph number 3 insofar as that part of said Order appointed a Custodian of the assets of the Crowell Division, but preserving all of the remaining powers conferred on this Custodian and changing his designation from Custodian to Arbitrator. The motion alleges that the naming of a Custodian of the assets of the Crowell Division would place CGS in apparent default under the terms of certain outstanding indentures in the amount of $2,449,000. The terms of this indenture were not placed in evidence during the hearings for the preliminary injunction. Oral argument was heard on this motion on August 31, 1971, at which time CGS placed in the record the terms of said Indenture, which provides in pertinent part:

SECTION 501.   EVENTS OF DEFAULT

"Event of Default," wherever used herein means any one of the following events (whatever the reason for such Event of Default and whether it shall be voluntary or involuntary or be effected by operation of law pursuant to any judgment, decree or order of any court or any order, rule or regulation of any administrative or governmental body): . . .

(4) the entry of a decree or order by a court having jurisdiction in the premises adjudging the Company a bankrupt or insolvent, or approving as properly filed a petition seeking reorganization, arrangement, adjustment or composition of or in respect of the Company under the Federal Bankruptcy Act or any other applicable Federal or State law, *or appointing a receiver, liquidator, assignee, trustee, sequestrator (or other similar official)* of the Company or of any substantial part of its property, or ordering the winding up or liquidation of its affairs, and the continuance of any such decree or order unstayed and *in effect for a period of 60 consecutive days.* . . .

(emphasis added)

CGS claims that the appointment of the Custodian has placed defendant CGS in apparent default under the above quoted sections of the Indenture. CGS argues that "[s]ince all of the officials named in this clause are officials who take title to the assets or part of the assets of the company, an official called a 'custodian' who takes title to the assets of Crowell Division is on the face of the Indenture a 'similar official.'"

On the basis of defendant's title argument, it is questionable whether a Custodian does indeed fit into the above category because under ordinary circumstances a Custodian merely has the care or possession of a res. Moreover, it is possible as plaintiff argues that the appointment of a Custodian is not an event of default under the above Indentures because these particular terms in the Indenture refer only to such officials when appointed in an insolvency proceeding. And, of course, this is not an insolvency proceeding since, as we stated in our Opinion of August 26, 1971, we made no determination as to the solvency or insolvency of CGS. However, even though plaintiff's interpretation is possible, litigation might arise and cause severe harm to CGS.

Since the purpose of this Court's original Order was not only to preserve the assets of Crowell and to keep the Crowell Division operational, but also to avoid irreparable harm to CGS and its shareholders pending a final trial on the merits of this case, we deem some amendment to our Order desirable. In view of this determination, we note from the above quoted language of the Indenture that any order appointing such "other similar official," even if a Custodian could be so construed, must remain "in effect for a period of 60 consecutive days" before such appointment becomes an event of default which can be acted upon by either the Trustee of the Indenture or by the bondholders. Therefore, in order to ensure that our Order is not interpreted as an event of default under the Indenture and to avoid any possibility of irreparable injury to either the plaintiff or the defendant, CGS, in this matter, the Court hereby amends its Order of August 26, 1971, by specifically providing that it shall remain in effect only until midnight of October 23, 1971, the 59th day after its issuance. At the time of the Pre-trial Conference on October 22, 1971, this Court will consider any and all steps which may then be necessary for the maintenance of the status quo in this matter pending final determination after the trial of this case on the merits, which trial has been specially listed for October 27, 1971.

Accordingly, the following Order is entered:

Order

And now, to wit, this 14th day of September 1971, it is hereby ordered and decreed that:

1. The Order of this Court in the above-captioned matter dated August 26, 1971, shall be amended by deleting therefrom paragraph number 6, which reads:

> 6. This Order shall remain in effect until final determination of this matter after a hearing on the merits.

and inserting in place thereof a new paragraph 6 which shall read:

> 6.   This Order shall remain in effect until midnight October 23, 1971.

2.   Security shall be filed by plaintiff in the sum of Twenty-Five Thousand ($25,000.00) Dollars.

MORE NOTES ON RECEIVERSHIP

1.   *Adelman* gives you a sense of what a receiver can accomplish in a complex situation. Calling him a custodian instead of a receiver is largely a cosmetic difference. A custodian is an agent to manage assets, appointed by the owner. Such a custodian often acts in his own name, but generally does not exercise discretion; he typically has less authority than a trustee. Judge Broderick may have wanted a connotation of lesser authority; he clearly wanted some title other than receiver, because he knew that a trustee or receiver would put CGS in default with its banks. But this custodian had all the powers he would have had if he had been called receiver. "Custodian" is not a term of art in this context.

2.   The custodian's powers are limited in one important way in *Adelman*. The custodian does not entirely displace incumbent management and make all decisions himself; he is directed only to resolve disputes between the two factions. That probably makes sense in these circumstances. CGS management has already removed those responsible for the fraud. The parties are deadlocked, but the deadlock affects a semi-autonomous division much more than it affects the whole company. And the court doesn't want to lose Adelman's expertise.

3.   Think about how this order would work out. If CGS and Adelman literally couldn't agree on anything, the custodian would wind up managing Crowell. More likely, CGS took little interest in much of Crowell's day-to-day operation. The most common disputes might have been over cash flow between Crowell and the rest of the company. Those disputes would go to the custodian instead of to the court. The custodian can devote much more time to such disputes than the court could. He can gather information more easily. He is less dependent on adversarial submissions by the parties; he can go directly to the company's records, its bureaucracy, and its data management personnel. He can hire his own staff. He can't make all the problems go away, but he has a better chance of solving them than the judge alone.

4.   In cases where top management is involved in the fraud, the receiver may displace them completely. It is little wonder that receivership has become one of the Securities and Exchange Commission's favorite remedies in cases of serious fraud. Turning the company over to a receiver prevents the suspected wrongdoers from altering or destroying

records, or diverting assets to their personal use. That creates time for the investigation to proceed in a systematic way. The receiver can investigate in much less cumbersome fashion than ordinary discovery or the SEC's subpoena power. His expenses come out of the company's budget instead of the SEC's budget.

In addition, the court appointing the receiver will generally enjoin the company's creditors from suing in other courts. Claims good against the company will still be good against the receiver. But the stay allows those claims to be consolidated and handled in an orderly fashion. There is a good example in SEC v. Wencke, 622 F.2d 1363 (9th Cir. 1980). *Wencke* held that the court had power to issue such an injunction because it had control over the property; it analogized to the automatic stay in bankruptcy and the other examples of in rem injunctions, including United States v. Hall, supra at 684.

The receivership may end with liquidation, reorganization, or with the company being turned over to newly elected management. But receivership is no panacea. Investors are still likely to lose lots of money. The receiver cannot create assets out of nothing; at best, he can prevent further dissipation. The remedy remains expensive and harsh. It tends to freeze the company and the willingness of others to do business with it. And there is always the risk that plaintiff and the court will make a mistake and oust honest management.

5.   In *Adelman*, where the company may still be solvent and may still have a future, the judge limits the custodian's appointment to fifty-nine days to avoid triggering default clauses in its loan agreements. Sixty-day clauses like the one in *Adelman* are common. Their rationale is that a company deserves a chance to get a receiver summarily dismissed if some disgruntled plaintiff convinces an overactive judge to appoint one, but that if he hasn't been dismissed in sixty days, there is probably something to plaintiff's claim.

Appointing a receiver for only fifty-nine days is rare. A fifty-nine-day limit in this case imposes a day and night schedule on the litigants and their lawyers. If the receiver had to investigate all the affairs of a complex business, it would simply be impossible. There is rarely sufficient incentive to incur those burdens. Companies in receivership are often in default on other grounds as well. In that case, a receiver may sink the company's credit rating even lower, and make people even more reluctant to do business with it, but leaving the receiver in office more than sixty days doesn't trigger dramatic new legal consequences. If the world already knows what bad shape the company is in, and a receiver may be able to bring order out of the chaos, appointing a receiver may actually increase confidence in the company.

6.   The receiver operates under supervision of the court, and his decisions are subject to judicial review. But the court generally trusts the receiver more than it trusts the parties, because he is neutral, and be-

cause the court picked him. So challenges to the receiver's routine actions are usually unsuccessful.

On the other hand, the receiver has no authority except what is granted by the court. And he is not supposed to make long-term commitments or decisions that will restrict the court's options or the options of the true owners when the property is returned to them. Some long-term decisions may be essential, but the receiver is supposed to get court approval first. An example is Nulaid Farmers Association v. LaTorre, 252 Cal. App. 2d 788, 60 Cal. Rptr. 821 (1967). The court appointed a receiver to manage a poultry farm pending foreclosure of security interests in the farmer's property. The receiver signed a contract to raise 400,000 fryer chicks; it would take all the resources of the farm a year and a half to raise that many chicks. The court held that the contract was not binding on the court or the property. It also suggested that the receiver might be personally liable to the other party to the contract.

7. Receivers also have an enormously useful power to borrow money. If borrowed money is necessary to preserve the property, the court can authorize the receiver to grant a lien that has priority over existing liens. A dramatic example is Colorado Wool Marketing Association v. Monaghan, 66 F.2d 313 (10th Cir. 1933). The court appointed a receiver to take possession of mortgaged sheep. He found them in deep snow without food. He issued receiver's certificates, a form of promissory note and security agreement granting a prior lien on property in receivership, and used the proceeds to feed and care for the sheep until spring. The decision to borrow money raises the same question as the decision to appoint the receiver: Can this money be spent in a way that pays for itself, so that everyone is made better off? The creditor in Colorado Wool Marketing didn't collect in full, and it collected $3,000 less than it would have if the receiver's certificates didn't have to be paid first. But probably it would have collected nothing if the receiver had not saved the sheep from the winter.

Bankruptcy courts and trustees have a similar power to grant prior liens for new money. 11 U.S.C. §364 (1982). The bankruptcy option is more commonly used in the modern cases. Bankrupt businesses hoping to reorganize must often borrow money to keep operating in bankruptcy.

8. In most states, a receiver will not be appointed at the request of an ordinary unsecured creditor. Generally, a receivership plaintiff must have a claim to the specific property he wants delivered to the receiver. Mintzer v. Arthur L. Wright & Co., 263 F.2d 823, 825 (3d Cir. 1959). Some other plaintiffs can seek receivers on other grounds: For example, the SEC's right to request a receiver is based on its duty to enforce the law, and not on any claim to a company's property.

Shareholders or partners can seek a receiver on the ground that they are being oppressed or that the company is hopelessly deadlocked. Oppression was the theory in *Poulakidas*, but it is unavailable in *Adelman*. As a shareholder, Adelman has no more interest in Crowell than in the rest of the company, and no more interest in CGS than any other shareholder. His right to a receiver or custodian over Crowell is based on his claim for rescission, which is a claim to Crowell itself and not just a claim for compensation.

Secured creditors can seek receivers for their collateral. An unsecured creditor who acquires a judicial lien becomes a secured creditor, eligible to request appointment of a receiver. And a judgment creditor without a judicial lien can get a receiver if it appears that a receiver can reach assets that cannot be reached by more ordinary collection methods. That is the subject of the next set of notes.

NOTES ON RECEIVERS AFTER JUDGMENT

1. In most states, a judgment creditor can get a receiver if it appears that a receiver can reach assets that cannot be reached by more ordinary collection methods. In some states the creditor must first try execution and have the writ returned unsatisfied; in others, it is sufficient to show that execution would be futile. Two examples:

Arndt v. National Supply Co., 650 S.W.2d 547 (Tex. App. 1983). Two writs of execution had been returned unsatisfied. Defendant had twice refused to appear for his deposition, despite sanctions imposed by the court. But plaintiff had somehow acquired defendant's 1976 financial statement, and it showed substantial holdings of corporate stock and accounts receivable. The court appointed a receiver to find the assets, collect them, and sell them.

First National State Bank v. Kron, 190 N.J. Super. 510, 464 A.2d 1146 (1983). Kron was a CPA with an active practice and a luxurious lifestyle. He kept no records, sent no bills, and had no assets. Or so he claimed. From time to time his clients paid him cash, and the cash was always dissipated before the bank could find out about it. After five years of unsuccessful collection efforts, the court appointed a receiver in aid of execution.

2. How will the receivers find the assets in these cases? A receiver obviously has some advantages over a sheriff. But what advantages does he have over the bank? Both have time to spend on the case, and both have financial expertise. Once again, the receiver is no panacea. But the receiver as a representative of the court is more likely to get cooperation and information from third parties. The court's order vests him with title to Kron's property, and that may be of some help in gaining possession. It is contempt of court to interfere with the receiver's possession, and the receiver can seek turnover orders. In addition, the receiver's expenses are

chargeable to the property if it is ever found. Some of the bank's collection expenses would be taxable as costs, but most of them would be paid by the bank.

3. A postjudgment receiver may be useful in some other situations as well. A receiver may be able to sell defendant's assets in an organized way, or sell his whole business as a going concern, getting much more than a series of execution sales of separate assets by competing judgment creditors. Thus, receivership is sometimes used as an insolvency proceeding, to liquidate a debtor's assets and divide the proceeds among the creditors. This use of receivership has been largely replaced by bankruptcy. But some liquidations still occur in receivership proceedings. Often, the receiver is originally appointed for a more limited purpose, and it gradually becomes clear that the debtor must be liquidated. By that time, it may be cheaper to continue the receivership than to start a new case in the bankruptcy court.

If any of the parties file a proper bankruptcy petition, the receiver must turn the assets over to the trustee in bankruptcy. 11 U.S.C. §543 (1982). But the bankruptcy court can defer to the receivership if that benefits the creditors. §543(d). And federal receivership courts have claimed some limited power to tell the parties not to file a bankruptcy petition at all. A good example is Securities & Exchange Commission v. Lincoln Thrift Association, 577 F.2d 600 (9th Cir. 1978). The judge and the receiver had become thoroughly familiar with a massive case, and more than $4 million dollars had already been distributed to creditors. It would have been a waste for a new judge and trustee to learn what was going on. The result makes sense. But it is not at all clear that the receivership court had power to make that decision. The statute provides that all other court proceedings are automatically stayed by the filing of a bankruptcy petition, 11 U.S.C. §362 (1982), and the bankruptcy court decides whether to let other cases proceed.

3. Ne Exeat

1. Perhaps the most extraordinary prejudgment remedy is ne exeat. Ne exeat begins with an injunction not to leave the jurisdiction. An example is United States v. Shaheen, 445 F.2d 6 (7th Cir. 1971). At a time when the government was claiming $450,000 in back taxes, Shaheen sold his house, mortgaged an adjacent lot, shipped his household goods to London, and flew to London with his wife and daughter. The Government could find only nominal assets in the United States, except for trust assets that the trustee refused to turn over. When Shaheen returned to the United States for a hearing on an unrelated criminal charge, the Government obtained ex parte a writ of ne exeat, forbidding Shaheen to leave the Northern District of Illinois.

If that were all, the writ would be ineffective. There is no way to stop defendant from leaving the jurisdiction if he is at large within it, and once he leaves, he's beyond the court's contempt power. That dilemma is solved by requiring defendant to post a bond; Shaheen was ordered to post $450,000. When he refused to post the bond, he was imprisoned. The bonding requirement turns ne exeat into a form of bailable imprisonment for debt, available before or after judgment.

The court of appeals reversed. Drawing on the procedure for preliminary injunctions, the court required the government to show probable success on the merits, and that the tax could not be collected without the writ. The court found the government's showing insufficient. On a motion to quash, Shaheen had testified that publicity from his difficulties with the government had destroyed his financial consulting business, that he was moving to London to start over, that he had voluntarily returned for all court appearances, that three of his children lived in the United States, that most of his assets were held in trust in the United States, and that he wanted to prove that he owed no additional tax.

2.   Ne exeat when sought by the government is historically a legal writ, although *Shaheen* imposes equitable principles on it. As between private litigants, ne exeat is historically equitable. The nearest legal equivalent was the capias ad respondendum, a means of beginning an action by arresting the defendant. Capias is now generally abolished, but ne exeat is still available for equitable money claims. It is still used occasionally, mainly but not exclusively in divorce litigation. Many of the cases are collected in Elkay Steel Co. v. Collins, 392 Pa. 441, 141 A.2d 212 (1958). *Elkay* upheld use of the writ in a suit to recover property taken from plaintiff by fraud and forgery.

3.   Ne exeat has been used to preserve a father's visitation rights by forbidding the mother to leave the state with the child. Palmer v. Palmer, 84 N.J. Eq. 550, 95 A.2d 241 (1915). My family law colleagues tell me that judges still order parents not to take children out of the state without permission, or condition custody on residence within an area approved by the court. But these orders are usually just part of the custody decree; they are not necessarily enforced with ne exeat's bonding requirement.

4.   If defendant posts a ne exeat bond and then leaves the jurisdiction, the bonding company is liable for the judgment, or the accrued arrearage in alimony and support cases, up to the maximum amount of the bond. Plaintiffs in support and alimony cases cannot collect the whole bond at once in anticipation of future accruals. National Automobile & Casualty Insurance Co. v. Queck, 1 Ariz. App. 595, 405 P.2d 905 (1965).

5.   What if an insolvent defendant leaves the jurisdiction? Even if he had stayed, he couldn't have paid, so plaintiff is no worse off. Should the bonding company still have to pay? Yes, says Coursen v. Coursen, 105 N.J. Super. 420, 252 A.2d 738 (App. Div. 1969).

D.   A QUICK LOOK AT IRREPARABLE INJURY IN LIGHT OF THE MEANS OF ENFORCING JUDGMENTS

One argument for the irreparable injury rule is that injunctions impose a greater burden on the court, because they have to be enforced over time. Supra at 336. How persuasive is that now that you know something about enforcing injunctions and collecting damages? Certainly coercion can be difficult, but the "one-time transfer of money" isn't so simple either. Consider the five years of wrangling in First National State Bank v. Kron, supra at 753, and the seven years in Webb v. Erickson, supra at 707. Both cases arose out of simple promises to pay. In *Kron*, the receiver was just beginning to look for assets; in *Webb*, the garnishment had just been remanded for a new trial. There was no prospect of payment any time soon in either case.

Of course, a chapter that illustrates the enforcement of decrees and collection of judgments with appellate cases tends to overemphasize the cases where enforcement and collection are difficult. Some defendants write out a check, just as some defendants promptly obey injunctions. It is a mistake to focus only on the hardest cases; it is a worse mistake to compare the hardest and most publicized injunction cases to the simplest collection cases.

The strongest examples for the argument that damage judgments are easier to enforce are suits against large institutional defendants. Such a defendant cannot very well hide itself or its assets; it may as well pay. It may be quite able to drag its heels in response to a structural injunction. But the irreparable injury rule is irrelevant to structural injunctions; damages are never adequate in those cases. Any attempt to make damages adequate would involve terribly difficult valuation problems, and enormous liability to a large class of plaintiffs. Massive damage judgments for failure to bus school children are not much improvement over busing orders.

PART II

Special Problems Affecting More Than One Kind of Remedy

CHAPTER 9

Some Problems of Implementation

A. THE LIMITS OF PRACTICALITY

BRADLEY v. MILLIKEN
540 F.2d 229 (6th Cir. 1976)

[The district court found that the Detroit school board had deliberately segregated the schools by such means as gerrymandered attendance zones. The court then found that the proportion of black students in Detroit was so great, and the pattern of housing segregation so severe, that desegregation within the city was impossible; accordingly, it announced its intention to consider a metropolitan plan. The Supreme Court held the metropolitan plan beyond the powers of the court and remanded for formulation of a Detroit-only plan. That decision appears supra at 261.

On remand, the district court ordered substantial busing and special remedial programs. But it concluded that three of Detroit's eight administrative regions were impossible to desegregate. It omitted them from the student assignment plan.]

Before PHILLIPS, Chief Judge, and EDWARDS and PECK, Circuit Judges.

PHILLIPS, Chief Judge.

When this school desegregation case was filed in August 1970, Ronald Bradley, one of the black plaintiffs, had been assigned to enter the kindergarten of a Detroit school whose enrollment was 97 percent black. . . .

In September 1976 Ronald Bradley is scheduled to enter the sixth grade of the Clinton School, which now is more than 99 percent black. The decisions of the District Court which we now review do nothing to correct the racial composition of the Clinton School. They grant no relief to Ronald Bradley nor to the majority of the class of black students he represents.

Nevertheless, this court finds itself in the frustrating position of having to leave standing the results reached by the District Judge on the issue of assignment of students, although we disagree with parts of his opinions and orders. Our affirmance is found to be necessary for the simple reason that reversal would be an exercise in futility under the situation now existing in the Detroit school system and the law of this case as established by the Supreme Court in Milliken v. Bradley. . . .

The plan adopted by the District Court became effective as of the beginning of the winter-spring semester, 1976. As of September 26, 1975, the Detroit public schools enrolled 247,774 students, 75.1 percent of whom were black. In broad outline the plan adopted by the District Court required the reassignment of 27,524 students, of whom 21,853 would require bus transportation. The plan changed the racial balance in 105 schools out of approximately 300 zoned schools in the system. Prior to the implementation of the plan, approximately 80 schools had enrollments of a majority of white students. Under the District Court's plan, 67 of these schools received black students through transportation and rezoning. The result of the student reassignments is that no school in Detroit, with two marginal exceptions, will have an enrollment of less than 30 percent black students. Moreover, 47 of the previously white schools have become more than 40 percent black.

In addition, 38 schools, the majority of which previously were at least 80 percent black, received white students via transportation and rezoning. Under the plan, 25 of these schools became 45 to 55 percent black. Furthermore, at least 23 of Detroit's schools, enrolling approximately 22,599 students, contain a substantial mix of black and white students without any student reassignment.

In order to effectuate the reassignment of students, the District Court ordered the purchase of 250 school buses. . . .

Notwithstanding the reassignments effected by the District Court, the percentage of black students in each of the eight regions remains substantially unchanged under the adopted plan. Only twelve of the 157 zoned schools with previous enrollments over 90 percent black have become under 90 percent black. Approximately half of Detroit's schools remain more than 90 percent black. Moreover, the three regions which contain the highest concentration of black students, regions 1, 5 and 8, remain virtually untouched. This means that approximately 83,000 students are granted no relief from unconstitutional de jure segregation. . . .

The Board's burden of justification is particularly heavy in this case because the three regions which the Board has left untouched, in the inner city, are in the area most affected by the acts of de jure segregation of which both the Detroit and State defendants have been found guilty.

The record discloses no adequate justification for excluding regions 1, 5 and 8 from the plan. The principal testimony pertaining to the reasons for excluding the inner city from student reassignments came from Merle Henrickson, Director of Planning and Building Studies for the Detroit Board. Mr. Henrickson stated that the inner city "was beyond the limits of possible treatment." Exclusion of the inner city was necessary, in his view, in order to maintain "the racial mix of desegregated schools." The result of desegregating the inner city, he predicted, would be white flight.

The need for stability in a desegregation plan was emphasized by the Supreme Court in Pasadena City Board of Education v. Spangler, 427 U.S. 424 (1976). Apprehension of white flight, however, cannot be used to deny basic relief from de jure segregation. As said by the Supreme Court in a slightly different context:

> The primary argument made by the respondents in support of Chapter 31 is that the separation of the Scotland Neck schools from those of Halifax County was necessary to avoid "white flight" by Scotland Neck residents into private schools that would follow complete dismantling of the dual school system. Supplemental affidavits were submitted to the Court of Appeals documenting the degree to which the system has undergone a loss of students since the unitary school plan took effect in the fall of 1970. But while this development may be cause for deep concern to the respondents, it cannot, as the Court of Appeals recognized, be accepted as a reason for achieving anything less than complete uprooting of the dual public school system.

United States v. Scotland Neck Board of Education, 407 U.S. 484, 490-91 (1972).

The District Court did not subject the exclusion of these three regions to the close scrutiny required by *Swann*. The District Court merely noted:

> Plaintiffs refuse to acknowledge that the racial composition of these three regions precludes their inclusion in a desegregation plan. . . . Clearly, it would be futile to attempt desegregation within the boundaries of these regions. . . .

402 F. Supp. at 1129.

This perfunctory treatment of the inner city falls far short of the "root and branch" requirements of Green v. County School Board, 391 U.S. 430, 437-438 (1968), and the "all-out desegregation" requirements of Keyes v. School District, 413 U.S. 189, 214 (1973). . . .

Even though we do not approve of that part of the District Court's plan which fails to take any action with respect to schools in Regions 1, 5 and

8, this court finds itself unable to give any direction to the District Court which would accomplish the desegregation of the Detroit school system in light of the realities of the present racial composition of Detroit.

Plaintiffs urge that we reverse and require the District Court to adopt the plan proposed by them. The District Court found that this proposal would require transportation of 77,000 to 81,000 students and the purchase of approximately 840 school buses. Much of the transportation would be of black students from predominately black schools to other predominately black schools and the plan nevertheless would leave a majority of Detroit's students in schools 75 to 90 percent black.

Our considered judgment is that plaintiffs' plan would accelerate the trend toward rendering all or nearly all of Detroit's schools so identifiably black as to represent universal school segregation within the city limits. The anticipated positive results, if any, would not justify the expense and hardship that inevitably would be involved. We agree with the District Judge that plaintiffs' plan would not satisfy the Supreme Court's mandate in this case.

A second alternative would be to reverse and order adoption of the plan originally proposed by the Detroit Board of Education. We have considered this alternative carefully and reject it because the plan originally proposed by the Board is not significantly different from the plan adopted by the court. . . .

A third alternative would be to reverse and direct that the District Court assign the white students now remaining in the Detroit school system among the predominately black schools on a percentage basis somewhat along the lines originally proposed by plaintiffs. It is obvious that such a requirement would accomplish nothing more than token integration, and that of uncertain duration.

Recognizing the absence of alternatives, we affirm the judgment of the District Court on the issue of assignment of students in areas other than Regions 1, 5 and 8. In affirming the District Judge's limited desegregation plan, we observe that the steps which he has taken thus far appear to us to be consistent with the fourteenth amendment, as interpreted by the Supreme Court in Milliken v. Bradley, 418 U.S. 717 (1974). We must, however, remand the case for further consideration in regard to the three central regions of the City of Detroit which both the school board and the District Judge excluded from their proposed remedial plans. We cannot hold that where unconstitutional segregation has been found, a plan can be permitted to stand which fails to deal with the three regions where the majority of the most identifiably black schools are located.

We recognize that it would be appropriate for us at this point to supply guidelines to the District Judge as to what he should do under this remand. Omission of such guidelines is not based on any failure to consider the problem in depth. It is based upon the conviction which this court had at the time of its en banc opinion in this case — and for the reasons carefully spelled out therein — that genuine constitutional desegregation can not be accomplished within the school district boundaries of the Detroit School District. . . .

On remand, the District Court will be empowered to make further alterations in the plan heretofore adopted by it, as the evidence may require, not inconsistent with this opinion.

NOTES ON THE PRACTICAL LIMITS OF REMEDIES

1.   The Supreme Court affirmed the educational components of the district court's remedy. That opinion appears supra at 269. The Supreme Court did not review the student assignment components.

2.   What should the district judge do when he gets this opinion? Bus a few more students? Keep up a perpetual charade of looking for a way to desegregate the three inner-city regions? Enter more detailed findings about why it can't be done? Put the case at the end of his docket and hope it fades away?

3.   As the court of appeals sees the problem, no one has found a practical way to restore plaintiffs to their rightful position. Another way to view it is that the court has grossly misdefined the rightful position. How does the court know that the inner city has been most affected by de jure segregation? Isn't it more likely that the inner city schools would have been all black no matter what the school board did? Recall the standard of *Dayton I*, discussed supra at 272. District courts should eliminate only "the incremental segregative effect" of the school board's violations. *Dayton II* endorsed a chain of presumptions that made *Dayton I* irrelevant, and no one pays much attention to *Dayton I*. If we did, would the problem in the principal case ever arise?

4.   On remand, the district court held that the demographic changes in the city had completely wiped out all lingering effects of de jure segregation. Most of the violations found consisted of deliberately segregating attendance zones in integrated neighborhoods. All those neighborhoods were now completely black. He again concluded that desegregating the three inner-city administrative regions was impossible, noting projections that the district would be 92 percent black by 1981.

The court of appeals held that the finding of no remaining segregative effect was clearly erroneous. Milliken v. Bradley, 620 F.2d 1143 (6th Cir. 1980). It again ordered integration of the inner-city administrative regions. This time it suggested that it was possible to desegregate a few schools in those regions, even though it conceded that most schools in those regions would have to be left alone.

5.   You should not infer from *Milliken* that federal courts generally, or even the Sixth Circuit, have refused to recognize practical limitations

on busing. In Memphis for example, the district judge chose a plan that put 83 percent of students in a desegregated school over a plan that would have put 97 percent of the students in a desegregated school. Under the plan adopted, 38,000 students were bused; 44 percent of them rode more than half an hour each way, but none rode more than 45 minutes each way. Under the more thorough plan, 48,000 students would have been bused, nearly all for more than half an hour, and 9,700 of them would have been bused more than 45 minutes. Elementary school children would have taken most of the longest rides. The district judge found that plan impractical, and the Sixth Circuit deferred to his discretion. Northcross v. Board of Education, 489 F.2d 15 (6th Cir. 1973), *cert. denied*, 416 U.S. 962 (1974).

6. Impracticality is largely a problem of coercive relief, and especially of the structural injunction. But the issue frequently arises in reparative injunctions, specific performance decrees, and class actions for damages. It can even arise in individual actions for monetary relief.

This section does not try to teach a general rule about when a court will give up in the face of practical limitations. There is no such rule, except for the obvious point that there is a strong desire not to leave plaintiff without a remedy. This section offers several illustrations in which courts have taken different approaches.

MORGAN v. McDONOUGH
540 F.2d 527 (1st Cir. 1976), *cert. denied*, 429 U.S. 1042 (1977)

Before COFFIN, Chief Judge, McENTEE and CAMPBELL, Circuit Judges.
CAMPBELL, Circuit Judge.

This appeal was filed on December 10, 1975, by the Boston School Committee (the Committee) from orders of the district court designating a temporary receiver for South Boston High School and ordering the transfer, without reduction in pay, of certain of its staff. The question before us is whether under the extraordinarily difficult and troubled circumstances confronting the School in the fall and early winter of 1975, the district court exceeded its powers in entering such orders. The instant appeal does not deal with how long such a receivership may properly last.

First integrated by court order in 1974 ("Phase I"), the South Boston High School was serving a racially mixed enrollment in 1975-76 under Phase II, a citywide desegregation plan formulated by the district court and upheld on appeal to this court. In November, 1975, the plaintiffs, representing a class of all black Boston public school students and parents, moved to close the School, alleging that black students there were being denied a peaceful, integrated and nondiscriminatory education. Following a lengthy hearing and several visits to the School, the district court found plaintiffs' basic allegations to be correct, but declined to close the School, ordering instead that it be placed in the temporary receivership of the court, effective December 10, 1975. The court first named as receiver a senior official of the Boston School Department, who was, in fact, the assistant superintendent for the district within which the School was located, but on January 9, 1976, after this appeal was filed, the court appointed Boston's Superintendent of Schools, Marion J. Fahey, as temporary receiver in place of the previous receiver. The stated purpose of the receivership was to effectuate as soon as possible "such changes in the administration and operation of South Boston High School as are necessary to bring the School into compliance with the student desegregation plan dated May 10, 1975 [Phase II], and all other remedial orders entered by the court in these proceedings, e.g., desegregation of faculty and staff." The court directed the receiver to (1) arrange for the transfer of the School's headmaster, full-time academic administrators, and football coach, without reduction in compensation, benefits, or seniority; (2) evaluate the qualifications of all faculty and educational personnel and arrange the transfer and replacement of whomever he sees fit for the purposes of desegregation, without reduction in compensation, benefits, or seniority; (3) file a plan with the court for the renovation of the School; (4) try to enroll non-attending students and establish catch-up classes; and (5) make recommendations to the court relative to certain provisions of the plan. It is the receivership order and the foregoing directions, including especially those for transfer of staff, which are the subject of this appeal.[1]

I

As the district court's primary orders requiring South Boston High School and other Boston schools to be desegregated have been reviewed and sustained, the time is no longer ripe to consider arguments against Phase II itself. The questions now before us are simply whether the lower court properly determined that plaintiff's rights under the desegregation plan were being violated at South Boston High School, and if so, whether the temporary remedies ordered were reasonable and lawful. We answer these questions in the affirmative. Given the lawfulness of the court's desegregation decrees, there is little question that it had the power to take reasonable steps to ensure compliance therewith and to protect the students attending the city's desegregated schools. The evidence here does

1. The Committee also appealed the district court's order imposing a moratorium on acting and permanent appointments by the lame duck School Committee (except with court approval) until January 6, 1976, after the terms of office of its members were to expire. On December 19, 1975, this court declined, after hearing, to stay that order. We knew then that, because of the passage of time, we were in practical effect concluding the appeal. To the extent this aspect of the appeal may not now be moot, we affirm the district court's order for reasons given in our Memorandum and Order of December 19, 1975. . . .

not show that the court went beyond what might reasonably be considered necessary to cope with a grave threat to the desegregation plan and to the safety and rights of the black students at South Boston High School.

II

Conditions at South Boston High School which resulted in the challenged receivership and transfer orders are described in the district court's oral and written findings, based on a week-long evidentiary hearing and on affidavits and personal visits to the School. These may be summarized as follows. . . .

A significant black enrollment was introduced for the first time in 1974-75 under Phase I. A litany of the problems that ensued that year is to be found in the district court's findings. Police in large numbers were on hand from the second day of school in September, 1974; there was tension, disruption, violence, and poor attendance. Black students were often the targets of racial slurs and, on occasion, physical abuse. By the fall of 1975, when Phase II went into effect, South Boston High School was known to be an institution where desegregation was experiencing severe difficulty.

These problems did not abate in the 1975-76 academic year. According to some witnesses they increased. The district court found, "Considering the implementation of the Phase One and Phase Two desegregation plans as a whole, the problems experienced at South Boston High School have been unique in their duration and intensity." A major aspect of the troubles was a continued resistance or imperviousness to integration. South Boston High was found to have remained identifiably white notwithstanding its racially mixed student body. All administrative personnel assigned to the main building, approximately 45 persons, were white, and the court concluded that in the opinion of its administration, the School belonged only to the white students residing in the easterly part of the district which it served. Out of 100 teachers, 93 were white. The 1975-76 student handbook, distributed to every student and mailed to parents of all registered students, portrayed the School as if white, ignoring its newly integrated status. The handbook singled out for praise the South Boston High School Home and School Association, an organization whose principal if not sole activity for the past two years was to oppose court-ordered desegregation. There was but a single passing reference to the court-established Multi-Ethnic Councils, designed to facilitate the desegregation process.

The court found that the black students who had been assigned to the School were being intimidated and mistreated. There was evidence that black students had been physically attacked without provocation by larger groups of white students. There was evidence that black students had been disciplined for defending themselves while white attackers went unpunished. Black students were found to have been subjected to continuing verbal abuse, and despite a court-ordered ban on racial epithets school officials did little to intervene. In addition to "familiar racial slurs," white students this year have employed the chant "'2, 4, 6, 8 assassinate the nigger apes,'" and, while changing classes, groups of white students often sing "'bye, bye blackbird' and 'jump down, turn around, pick a bale of cotton.'" The white student caucus, in a list of demands, requested that music be played over the School's public address system during the changing of classes, since "'music soothes the savage beasts.'" On numerous occasions, school staff and police stationed inside the building have heard these remarks and chants and failed to take any corrective or disciplinary action.

The court found, moreover, that racial segregation was persisting inside South Boston High School. Black students failed in attempts to join the football team, due in part to the actions of the coach. Black and white students were kept apart when arriving at or leaving School. The races remained separated in the classrooms and the cafeteria. No administrative policy or directive was issued to desegregate classroom seating; a plan for desegregated assemblies remained unenforced; and no effort was made to initiate desegregation in the cafeteria by, for example, having white and black aides eat together. In fact, the headmaster on one occasion reprimanded a black student who attempted to sit at a table with white students for a "provocative" act. . . . In October, 1975, in response to increasing tensions at the School, the Superintendent's office and the court-created Citywide Coordinating Council sought to send assistance teams into the School. The faculty, however, voted not to cooperate with either group, and the headmaster acquiesced. . . .

III . . .

As the Massachusetts State Board of Education aptly states in its brief,

> The situation at the school was rapidly deteriorating, evidenced both by a falling pupil attendance rate and by the very bringing of the plaintiffs' motion. Black students were being driven from the school by conditions there. . . . The denial of constitutional rights, while from more complex sources, was rapidly becoming as effective as if blacks had been barred from entering the school. . . .

The district court could not shut its eyes to what was taking place.

The question thus boils down to the propriety of the relief that was ordered. A district court's power to fashion and effectuate desegregation decrees is broad and flexible, and the remedies may be "administratively awkward, inconvenient, and even bizarre." Swann v. Charlotte-Mecklenburg Board of Education, 401 U.S. 1, 15-16, 28 (1971). Remedial devices should be effective and relief prompt. While a receivership has been instituted only once in a reported desegregation case, Turner v. Goolsby, 255 F. Supp. 724 (S.D. Ga. 1966), receiverships are and have for years been a familiar equitable mechanism. They are commonly a vehicle for court supervision of distressed businesses, but have not been limited to that role. The Supreme Court indicated many years ago that a receiver might take charge of a company to enforce compliance with the antitrust laws. United States v. American Tobacco Co., 221 U.S. 106, 186 (1911). Receiverships and court-appointed officials with some of the same functions as the receiver here have been approved in other contexts. See, e.g., Inmates of Attica Correctional Facility v. Rockefeller, 453 F.2d 12, 25 (2d Cir. 1971). Masters have been used extensively to formulate plans and recommendations, one of the present receiver's chief functions. Finally, there is precedent for a district court having desegregation responsibilities to order personnel shifts.

We thus find nothing impermissible per se about any of the actions the court took. The test is one of reasonableness under the circumstances. To be sure, direct judicial intervention in the operation of a school system is not to be welcomed, and it should not be continued longer than necessary. But if in extraordinary circumstances it is the only reasonable alternative to noncompliance with a court's plan of desegregation, it may, with appropriate restraint, be ordered.

The receivership here was a means to enlist without delay top Boston School Department leadership to work in conjunction with the court on the troubles of the School. The court utilized the device to ensure priority attention by senior administrators, under court supervision, to South Boston High's unique problems. The more usual remedies — contempt proceedings and further injunctions — were plainly not very promising, as they invited further confrontation and delay; and when the usual remedies are inadequate, a court of equity is justified, particularly in aid of an outstanding injunction, in turning to less common ones, such as a receivership, to get the job done.

Had the School Committee then in office been cooperative, a voluntary approach might have summoned similar resources without need for a formal receivership. However, the then School Committee had continuously resisted desegregation, and its leaders had advised the court on more than one occasion that they would obey nothing but direct orders. . . .

Finally, it bears emphasizing that the principal alternative being suggested to the receivership order was to order that South Boston High be closed. That alternative would not only have involved the abandonment of a large and useful facility but would have necessitated the planning, expense, and inconvenience of finding places for some 2000 students. Without expressing any opinion on the propriety of ordering the School closed, it can be said that the district court demonstrated both restraint and wisdom in selecting the receivership option. For all of the foregoing reasons, therefore, we see the district court's action not as excessive but as reasonably tailored to carrying out the court's responsibilities.

Nor do we find unreasonable the transfer of the headmaster, coach and other staff. Apart from finding overt resistance to the segregation plan by the coach, the court also noted adverse faculty attitudes and a lack of leadership by the School administration in implementing the plan. Given the situation that had developed at the School under existing leadership, the court was entitled to conclude that a change in command was indicated. The change tied into the appointment of the receiver, giving the latter, in conjunction with the court, the opportunity, after study, to bring in administrators and perhaps faculty that seemed best able to cope with the extraordinary difficulties and pressures at the School.

It is true that the court's actions, while not reaching beyond the professional School Department, supplanted the supervisory authority of the elected Committee in this area. However, judicial desegregation necessarily involves some displacement of decision-making powers, as we have already witnessed in other aspects of this case, e.g. drawing of district lines, teacher hiring, and so on. . . . The extent of the court's power is limited to what is required to ensure students their right to a non-segregated education, but within that parameter it may do what reasonably it must. The fact that a school committee is elected, not appointed, cannot put it beyond the reach of the law. Elected officials must obey the Constitution. See, e.g., United States v. Nixon, 418 U.S. 683 (1974).

Here, contrary to the Committee's assertions, we find no evidence of any intrusion by the district court upon the School Committee's right to determine "educational philosophy" except as that philosophy might impermissibly encourage a racially separate school system. The "limited, general purpose of said receivership," as the lower court stated, is only to bring the School into compliance with the desegregation plan and orders. As the receiver is the Superintendent of Schools, we can see little danger that the receivership will introduce educational policies contrary to those prevailing in the system as a whole. The orders in question were, we find, reasonably limited to matters of proper judicial concern, and, given the problems that have arisen, and the history, they do not exceed the court's powers.

We would, however, add a *caveat*. Obviously the substitution of a court's authority for that of elected and appointed officials is an extraordinary step warranted only by the most compelling circumstances. Those circumstances here were the failure of local officials to give effect to the court's desegregation orders in a meaningful manner. The receivership should last no longer than the conditions which justify it make necessary, and the court's utilization of the receivership must not go beyond the constitutional purposes which the device is designed to promote. . . .

Addendum . . .

[T]he Boston School Committee moved to consolidate with the present appeal its appeals from related orders entered by the District Court on December 24, 1975, and December 31, 1975, stipulating "that the only issue presented on such appeals is a determination of the limits of the District Court's remedial powers in a school desegregation case."

Our examination of the record now before us reveals no error. Both orders authorize certain repairs and supplies at South Boston High School that were recommended by appropriate officials of the Boston School Department, including the temporary receiver. The December 24, 1975 order, totalling $23,950, involved such basics as repairs to toilet stalls, water bubblers, torn window shades, and the like; improvements such as painting certain classrooms; and the purchase of certain sports equipment, such as basketballs, mats, and the like. These were to be accomplished before the end of the Christmas recess. More painting, renovation and further repairs were apparently involved in the order of December 31, 1975. . . .

Since absenteeism, complaints of a "prison atmosphere," and poor morale generally were prominent among the difficulties the court faced, we cannot say the court went beyond its desegregation powers in taking prompt steps to achieve these repairs and purchases without delay. There is no evidence as to what, if any better procedure was available that would have secured the necessary results over the Christmas recess or soon thereafter, and we assume that the court knew of none. Quite obviously if the School facilities were maintained at a level way below normal, the difficulty of restoring and maintaining a functioning, desegregated School at which learning of any type could occur would be increased.

NOTES ON CIVIL RIGHTS RECEIVERSHIPS

1. South Boston High remained in receivership for three years. It is probably the most ambitious example of a large group of cases. Federal courts have appointed receivers or special masters with receiver-like powers to manage court ordered reforms in schools, prisons, mental hospitals, and similar institutions. State courts appointed a receiver to run all the public housing in Boston. Spence v. Reeder, 382 Mass. 398, 416 N.E.2d 914 (1981).

2. In traditional usage, receivers are appointed to manage property. Masters are appointed to recommend findings of fact in complex cases too burdensome for the court. Fed. R. Civ. Proc. 53. But the distinction has been blurred in the structural injunction cases. Masters have been appointed to propose desegregation plans and prison reform plans. Masters have been appointed to oversee implementation of the plan, reporting to the court on the extent of progress. The power to report to the

court that defendants are not complying with the decree is an effective club; it often gives de facto power to make defendants do what the master wants. And some courts have explicitly conferred supervisory powers on masters.

It is more common to call these officials masters than receivers. To call them receivers suggests that they should explicitly replace the incumbent state official, and courts rarely do that. Usually, the courts leave that official in place, more or less subject to the master's supervision.

The receiver or master can handle lots of small implementation controversies before they get to the court. The court will still be burdened, especially if the parties object to everything the receiver does: Consider the spectacle of three United States Circuit Judges deciding whether to fix the toilets in South Boston High School. But the court can rely heavily on the receiver's judgment. It is almost inconceivable that the court made an independent decision about the toilets; without someone like a receiver or master, that issue would have come directly to the court on adversarial submissions.

3.   Compare *Morgan* and other civil rights receiverships with Lance v. Plummer, 353 F.2d 585 (5th Cir. 1965), *cert. denied*, 384 U.S. 929 (1966). Lance was ordered to resign his position as an unsalaried deputy sheriff after being found guilty of civil contempt of an injunction against threatening or intimidating blacks. Justice Black dissented from the denial of certiorari. He said that the order came "perilously close to violating the constitutional obligation of the Federal Government to guarantee to every State a republican form of government."

If that's what he thought about displacing an appointed, unsalaried deputy sheriff, who was probably a deputy more for his own convenience than for the state's, what would he say about displacing an elected school board for three years and turning the schools over to a federal receiver? In the Alabama prison litigation, the Fifth Circuit said that federal courts lacked power to remove state officials, fire state employees, or "take over the performance of their functions." Newman v. Alabama, 559 F.2d 283, 288 (5th Cir. 1977), *cert. denied*, 438 U.S. 915 (1978). But it suggested the appointment of a monitor for each prison in the state, under the general supervision of a master. You should not assume that masters are any less active in the Fifth Circuit than elsewhere.

Does the choice of a higher ranking city school official as the receiver ease the federalism problems in *Morgan*? What about the state board of education's apparent support for the order? Courts have turned to higher state officials when that would work, but many receivers and special masters have been private citizens with some relevant expertise; sometimes they have been hired from out-of-state.

4.   Consider how appointing a receiver, or a master with supervisory powers, differs from issuing injunctions to control every detail of school administration. This comparison is relevant both to the federalism and

practicality issues. Such a series of injunctions is arguably as serious an intrusion as the receivership, because it removes the discretion of the elected school officials and leaves them in office only as puppets. It might even be thought more in accord with federalism to transfer authority to another state education official than to a federal judge.

But of course the district judge can never fully reduce the incumbent officials to puppets. There are too many daily administrative decisions for the court to make them all, and many of them are too discretionary to be controlled by general rules laid down in the injunction. The obvious motivation for the receivership is that it is more effective. The receivership makes the desegregation plan more practical exactly to the extent that it reduces the influence of those state officials resisting the injunction. And it is precisely in the discretionary matters hard to control by injunction that the state interest in having decisions made by its duly elected officials and their appointees is greatest.

5.   If the features that make the remedy effective are the very features that displace state authority, there is a real dilemma for anyone who wants to maximize the one while minimizing the other. One proposed solution was a partial receivership — a receiver with authority for desegregation only. There is plenty of precedent for partial receiverships. Recall that in Adelman v. CGS Scientific Corp., supra at 743, the court appointed a custodian for a single division, with authority to resolve disputes but not to manage directly. Courts sometimes appoint receivers to collect rents from a building but not to manage the building. Garden Homes v. United States, discussed in notes supra at 742. And courts in structural injunction cases have appointed masters for single purposes, for example, to supervise all the medical care in a prison.

The United States Civil Rights Commission, which recommended a receiver for the entire Boston school system in 1975, advised against a partial receiver. That would leave personnel decisions to the school board, and employees inclined to cooperate with the receiver might fear job retaliation. The Commission noted that the superintendent of schools had been fired after cooperating with the court. United States Commission on Civil Rights, Desegregating the Boston Public Schools: A Crisis in Civil Responsibility (1975).

Would a full receivership reassure employees who feared retaliation? Wasn't it inevitable that the school would eventually be returned to the control of an elected school committee, and likely that the majority of voters would still be opposed to the court's desegregation plan? Should employees be expected to assume that the receivership would not end until opposition had calmed down, and that there would be no retaliation after that? Or should the injunction include vigorously enforced provisions against retaliations?

6.   Morgan and Adelman v. CGS Scientific Corp. arise in quite different substantive fields. But aren't the remedial problems quite similar?

Weren't both courts trying to protect plaintiffs with a stake in a hopelessly polarized institution? And didn't both courts resort to receivers because injunctions were inadequate to the task? Both courts also tried to protect the interests of defendants — the interest in preserving CGS as a viable company and the interest in local control of schools. The effort to protect defendants' interests was arguably more successful in *Adelman* than in *Morgan*. But isn't that because defendants were more obstreperous in *Morgan*? Whatever the constitutional arguments for and against busing, the administration of South Boston High School as described by the court was flagrantly and unambiguously unconstitutional. Was there any legitimate state interest in that exercise of local control?

NOTE ON THE LIMITS OF THE CONTEMPT POWER IN STRUCTURAL INJUNCTION CASES

In theory, federal injunctions are enforced against state officials rather than the state itself. This is because states are immune from suit in federal court, but state officials are not immune. We will explore immunity in chapter 13. It is relevant here only to define the enforcement problem: It is the state official who is in contempt, and not the state itself.

The full range of contempt sanctions is available against state officials. They can be imprisoned for contempt. Ex parte Young, 209 U.S. 123 (1908). They can be ordered to pay attorney's fees or coercive fines out of their own pocket, or out of official funds. Hutto v. Finney, 437 U.S. 678, 690-692 (1978). Although the contempt remedy is available, it is rarely used. Orders that are labeled "contempt" are often just more detailed injunctions: for example, "Purge yourself of contempt by making the following specific improvements in the prison." The next excerpt explores some of the reasons.

DIVER, THE JUDGE AS POLITICAL POWERBROKER: SUPERINTENDING STRUCTURAL CHANGE IN PUBLIC INSTITUTIONS
65 Va. L. Rev. 43, 99-103 (1979)

Sanctions

To be politically effective, . . . a judge must have access to power. Institutional reform, because of its sheer magnitude, requires cooperation among a multitude of actors. A successful reformer must possess a range of inducements capable of flexible, targeted, and potent application sufficient to influence a wide range of behavior. Most of the direct inducements available to a judge are negative — threats of painful sanctions, the most familiar and feared being civil or criminal contempt. Nevertheless, a judge does have other methods at his disposal, such as awarding attorney's fees, excluding a named defendant from some aspect of remedial planning, closing an institution, removing an officer, or appointing a receiver, that present him with a range of choices for influencing conduct in desired directions.

The utility of sanctions depends upon their severity and credibility. Certainly, all but the most desperate or defiant of defendants perceive citation for contempt or displacement of personal authority as painful enough to overcome their strongest resistance.[278] If a judge could use these sanctions costlessly, he certainly would possess adequate power as a political actor. Nevertheless, much to the consternation of some plaintiffs' advocates, judges seldom threaten and almost never impose sanctions, even in the face of protracted noncompliance. In fact, the only sanction used with any frequency in reported cases is the relatively mild and largely compensatory action of awarding plaintiffs their attorney's fees. Analysis of three other possible penalties — contempt, transfer of authority, and closure of the institution — indicates why these approaches often are not feasible in politicized litigation.

In practice, courts seldom exercise their contempt power against governmental defendants. This reluctance probably reflects a fear of polarizing the dispute by creating a martyr around whom disaffected groups can rally. The imputation of personal guilt inherent in the contempt citation clashes with the perception that nonpersonal and largely systemic factors cause institutional failure. Furthermore, a court often finds as the appropriate object of a potential contempt order a person whose continuing cooperation is indispensable to the implementation process.

Similar concerns explain the reluctance of trial judges to displace the authority of a recalcitrant official by means such as appointing a receiver, transferring operating authority, or removing him outright. Displacement of a central figure not only alienates other political allies, but it also exacerbates the dislocation that reform unavoidably occasions. Some judges, moreover, may entertain doubts that a successor would behave differently, for he will be subject to the same conflicting pressures as his predecessor. Finally, appellate courts are likely to vacate as excessively

---

278. Outright defiance of court orders in institutional reform cases is extremely rare. Even in the celebrated case of school desegregation in Boston, the school committee skirted a direct confrontation. Those who do defy judicial commands, such as leaders of illegally striking labor unions, typically are assured of overwhelming support among their major constituencies.

intrusive an order wholly displacing the authority of a public official because less disruptive sanctions usually are available.

Judged by the frequency with which they threaten to close institutions, courts seem to regard this device as an effective inducement. Closure would inflict on most defendants the inconvenience of having to make alternative arrangements for residents as well as the personal discomfort attendant to adverse publicity or diminution of authority and responsibility. It also redresses directly the violations alleged — closing the institution releases the plaintiffs from the illegal conditions of their confinement. This remedial quality gives the threat of closure further credibility. In practice, however, closing an institution would cause such serious dislocations that it is not a realistic option, and courts virtually never have ordered it. Selective closure, involving particular facilities or buildings or enjoining further admissions, is a more realistic threat, but the prospect that officials simply will reassign residents to other equally deplorable settings diminishes its utility.

In considering what sanctions to use, a judge faces a classic strategic dilemma in bargaining games: whether and how to use a threat of mutually disadvantageous action as an inducement to action. On the one hand, the threatening party must appear committed to carrying out the threat. Still, he would like to maintain enough flexibility to avoid taking mutually damaging action if the threat fails in its objective. Courts typically have avoided making threats that bind them to taking an unattractive future course of action. Fear of losing credibility from not carrying out the threat has outweighed concern for the effectiveness of the threat itself. Judges instead have maintained an almost studied ambiguity, merely hinting at possibilities.[294] In theory, the equivocal threat is useful in bargaining, but only to create the appearance of irrationality. A madman's threat is convincing precisely because his opponent cannot be sure that he will not pursue a mutually damaging course of action. Nevertheless, however uncertain we may be of the range and accuracy of judicial weapons, we expect, instinctively, that judges will not act like madmen. Indeed, the judge is the paradigmatic institutional symbol of rationality. The historical failure of judges to impose harsh sanctions even in the face of protracted noncompliance stands as convincing evidence that they will not do so in the future.

294. A good example is Holt v. Hutto, 363 F. Supp. 194, 217 (E.D. Ark. 1973), aff'd in part, rev'd in part, remanded sub nom. Finney v. Arkansas Bd. of Correction, 505 F.2d 194 (8th Cir. 1974), in which the court listed four sanctions available to it and expressed the "hope" that none need be invoked. Reserving rulings on plaintiffs' motions for coercive orders enables a court to maintain a useful tension. See, e.g., Wyatt v. Stickney, 344 F. Supp. 373, 377 (M.D. Ala. 1972) (reserving rulings on plaintiff's motion ordering a reallocation of the state budget and the sale of public lands as methods of raising funds for remedial implementation), aff'd in part, remanded in part sub nom. Wyatt v. Aderholt, 503 F.2d 1305 (5th Cir. 1974).

NOTES ON COLLECTING MONEY FROM
THE GOVERNMENT

1.   Governments are often immune from damage suits. When they are not immune, they are often willing to pay judgments. But what should a court do when a government refuses to pay a judgment from which it is not immune? We examined the nineteenth century response to these problems in the note on the municipal bond cases, supra at 321. Writs of execution were regularly returned unsatisfied in the nineteenth century bond cases, because substantially all municipal property was exempt from execution. The Supreme Court ordered payment of cash from municipal treasuries, but it never questioned the exemption of "property held for public uses, such as public buildings, streets, squares, parks, promenades, wharves, landing-places, fire-engines, hose and hose-carriages, engine-houses, engineering instruments, and generally everything held for governmental purposes." Meriwether v. Garrett, 102 U.S. (12 Otto) 472, 501 (1880). Collection of judgments against domestic governments requires a remedy other than execution.

2.   The nineteenth century courts ordered officials to pay, and ordered them to levy taxes arguably authorized by state law. I find modern examples only of orders to pay. One good example is Gates v. Collier, 616 F.2d 1268 (5th Cir. 1980), the Mississippi prison litigation. The state refused to pay judgments for attorneys' fees, because the state constitution provided that no judgment could be paid except by special appropriation of the legislature, and the legislature refused to appropriate the money. Finally, the court ordered the auditor and treasurer of Mississippi to pay without an appropriation, holding the state constitutional provision unconstitutional as applied to federal judgments.

3.   Evans v. City of Chicago, 689 F.2d 1286 (7th Cir. 1982), involves a federal order to pay state judgments. Under Illinois law, municipalities are liable for their torts, and obligated to pay the judgments, but they are immune from execution. Chicago appropriated $4.5 million each year to pay tort judgments, but judgments accumulated at a far faster rate. The city paid all judgments under $1,000 immediately, and it paid the rest in the order they accrued, with interest at 6 percent. In September 1979 the city was paying judgments entered in October 1975. Most of the city's judgment creditors sold their judgments to financiers at a substantial discount. The Seventh Circuit held that the discrimination against judgments over $1,000 was irrational and violated equal protection, and that the delay in payment was a taking of property without due process. The federal court ordered the city to pay immediately.

4.   The judgments in Evans were ordinary money judgments. The problem is somewhat different when the court is trying to get the state to raise the money to implement a structural injunction. Those orders are usually written in terms of conditions to be achieved or reforms to be

implemented, and not in terms of a specific amount of money. That makes them easily subject to the process of bargaining and partial compliance described by Professor Diver, and that process blunts head-on collisions with the contempt power. But sometimes an order is sufficiently specific to create the direct collision that courts and defendants usually avoid. *Gates* is such a case; there, the fee award looked just like an ordinary money judgment.

5.   A more finessable confrontation arose in Halderman v. Pennhurst State School & Hospital, 673 F.2d 628 (3d Cir. 1982) (en banc), *cert. denied*, 104 S. Ct. 1315 (1984). Pennhurst was the state school for mentally retarded citizens. The court ordered the Department of Public Welfare to pay a special master appointed to oversee reform of Pennhurst. For several years, the department paid the master out of its general appropriation. In 1981 the Secretary of the department decided to show the master as a separate line item in the appropriations bill. At her legislative testimony on the bill, she ridiculed the need for the special master, said she would take her chances with the federal judge if that was what the legislature decided, and assured the legislators that the judge couldn't do anything to them. The legislature prohibited use of departmental funds to pay the master, and the department obeyed the statute rather than the court.

The trial court held the department and its Secretary in contempt, and imposed a fine of $10,000 per day until compliance. The department paid the fines out of its general appropriation until the trial court suspended the accumulation of the fines. Then the court used the accumulated fines to pay the master. The court of appeals affirmed, partly on the merits and partly on grounds of procedural default.

6.   One feature of these cases is the triangular relationship between the federal court, the state executive, and the state legislature. Most U.S. constitutions, including the federal constitution, prohibit the expenditure of funds without a legislative appropriation. Fortunately, legislatures often appropriate large sums to the general purposes of a department. Thus, the executive has some discretion, and courts can order that discretion used to remedy violations. But what if the legislature focuses on the specific item and denies the appropriation? The court in *Pennhurst* relied heavily on the Secretary's complicity. The court also suggested that the governor should have item vetoed the provision against spending funds on the master. What result if the legislature overrode the veto?

That happened in Delaware Valley Citizens' Council for Clean Air v. Pennsylvania, 678 F.2d 740 (3d Cir.), *cert. denied*, 459 U.S. 969 (1982). The court held the Commonwealth of Pennsylvania in contempt, and cut off federal highway funds as a sanction. That solution is usually unavailable because of sovereign immunity. But there was no immunity in this case because the United States was also a plaintiff.

The Second Circuit backed down in a similar situation. The district court held the governor in contempt for not using his best efforts to get the money from the legislature. The court of appeals reversed. It thought that courts should not try to raise large sums of money to reform institutions; rather, they should give the state the choice of reforming the institution or closing it. New York State Association for Retarded Children v. Carey, 631 F.2d 162 (2d Cir. 1980).

NORTHERN DELAWARE INDUSTRIAL DEVELOPMENT CORP. v. E. W. BLISS CO.
245 A.2d 431 (Del. Ch. 1968)

MARVEL, Vice Chancellor.

Plaintiffs and defendant are parties to a contract dated May 26th, 1966, under the terms of which defendant agreed to furnish all labor, services, materials and equipment necessary to expand and modernize a steel fabricating plant owned by the plaintiff Phoenix Steel Corporation at Claymont, Delaware. A massive undertaking is called for in the contract, the total price for the work to be performed by the defendant being set in the contract at $27,500,000 and the area of contract performance extending over a plant site of approximately sixty acres.

Work on the project has not progressed as rapidly as contemplated in the contract and what plaintiffs now seek is an order compelling defendant to requisition 300 more workmen for a night shift, thus requiring defendant to put on the job, as it allegedly contracted to do, the number of men required to make up a full second shift at the Phoenix plant site during the period when one of the Phoenix mills must be shut down in order that its modernization may be carried out under the contract. And while the present record is sparse, there seems to be no doubt but that defendant has fallen behind the work completion schedules set forth in such contract. What plaintiffs apparently seek is a speeding up of work at the site by means of a court-ordered requisitioning by defendant of more laborers.

The basis for plaintiffs' application for equitable relief is found in a work proposal made by defendant's prime subcontractor, Noble J. Dick, Inc., to the Bliss Company, the terms of which are made part of the contract between plaintiffs and defendant. Such proposal stipulates inter alia:

T.   WORKING SCHEDULE

All work is quoted on a normal 40 hour basis — 5 days per week except for necessary service tie-ins. The only additional premium time included is that required during the shut-down of #1 mill when two turn-week work is contemplated.

According to plaintiffs, the phrase "two turn-week work" is a term used in the steel industry to designate the employment of day and night shifts over a full seven day work week, and defendant does not deny this. Plaintiffs therefor reason that inasmuch as at or about the time of the filing of the complaint defendant was operating one shift at the site ranging in size from 192 to 337 workers per day, whereas paragraph "T" above referred to contemplates two daily shifts, that they are entitled to a court order directing defendant to employ not less than 300 construction workers on each of two shifts, seven days per week. Plaintiffs seek other relief, including damages, but consideration of such other requested relief will be deferred for the present. Defendants earlier moved for dismissal or a stay because the parties are allegedly contractually bound to arbitrate their differences.

However, the sole matter now for decision is a question raised by the Court at argument on defendant's motion, namely whether or not this Court should exercise its jurisdiction to grant plaintiffs' application for an order for specific performance of an alleged contractual right to have more workers placed on the massive construction project here involved, and order the requisitioning of 300 workers for a night shift, this being the number of laborers deemed by plaintiffs to be appropriate properly to bring about prompt completion of the job at hand.

On the basis of the record before me, viewed in the light of the applicable law, I am satisfied that this Court should not, as a result of granting plaintiffs' prayer for specific performance of an alleged term of a building contract, become committed to supervising the carrying out of a massive, complex, and unfinished construction contract, a result which would necessarily follow as a consequence of ordering defendant to requisition laborers as prayed for. Parenthetically, it is noted that if such laborers are in fact available (which appears not to be the case), their presence at the Claymont site might well impede rather than advance the orderly completion of the steel mill renovation work now under way. (See Byrne affidavit).

It is not that a court of equity is without jurisdiction in a proper case to order the completion of an expressly designed and largely completed construction project, particularly where the undertaking to construct is tied in with a contract for the sale of land and the construction in question is largely finished. Furthermore, this is not a case which calls for a building plan so precisely definite as to make compliance therewith subject to effective judicial supervision, but rather an attempt to have the Court as the result of ordering a builder to speed up general work by hiring a night shift of employees (a proposal which was merely "contemplated" by the subcontractor, Dick) to become deeply involved in supervision of a complex construction project located on plaintiffs' property.

The point is that a court of equity should not order specific performance of any building contract in a situation in which it would be impractical to carry out such an order, unless there are special circumstances or the public interest is directly involved. In the case of City Stores v. American (D.C.D.C.) 266 F. Supp. 766, which plaintiffs cite to support their application, specific performance was sought of an agreement which contemplated that plaintiff would become a tenant in a designated section of a shopping center to be constructed by defendant. The plans for such center were quite definite and the court was obviously impressed by the fact that unless the relief sought were to be granted, plaintiff would lose out on a promised opportunity to share in the expected profits of a shopping center located in a burgeoning North Virginia suburb. The ruling while perhaps correct under the circumstances of the case has no application here.

I conclude that to grant specific performance, as prayed for by plaintiffs, would be inappropriate in view of the imprecision of the contract provision relied upon and the impracticability if not impossibility of effective enforcement by the Court of a mandatory order designed to keep a specific number of men on the job at the site of a steel mill which is undergoing extensive modernization and expansion. If plaintiffs have sustained loss as a result of actionable building delays on defendant's part at the Phoenix plant at Claymont, they may, at an appropriate time, resort to law for a fixing of their claimed damages. . . .

On Reargument . . .

In their motion for reargument plaintiffs argue that what they actually seek is not an order which would make the Court the supervisor of a vast building project but rather one directing the performance of a ministerial act, namely the hiring by defendant of more workers. Plaintiffs also contend that they should have an opportunity to supplement the record for the purpose of demonstrating that construction labor is available in the area as well as establishing that perhaps fewer than 300 additional workers could adequately insure defendant's performance of the contract here in issue. These contentions, if factually sustainable, do not, of course, affect the Court's power to decline to exercise its jurisdiction to order specific performance of a construction contract.

Plaintiffs, in seeking specific performance of what they now term defendant's ministerial duty to hire a substantial number of additional laborers, run afoul of the well-established principle that performance of a contract for personal services, even of a unique nature, will not be affirmatively and directly enforced, Lumley v. Wagner, 1 De G. M. & G. 404. This is so, because, as in the closely analogous case of a construction contract, the difficulties involved in compelling performance are such as to make an order for specific performance impractical.

NOTES ON PRACTICALITY AND PRIVATE LITIGATION

1.   Doesn't ordering a second shift on this construction site look like a piece of cake compared to reforming a whole state prison system? Even so, the court's fears are not wholly groundless. Just as a general decision to desegregate Boston's high schools started Judge Garrity down a path that led to his having to decide which toilets to fix, there is a risk that ordering a second shift will lead to the court's deciding how many welders can be efficiently employed on the underside of sheet roller number 3, and dozens of similar details. If the parties accept the basic decision, they can implement it. If they are uncooperative, the court will have to decide everything.

What are the risks of that sort of defiance in a case like *Northern Delaware*, where defendant is trying to make a profit? Does this defendant have the same incentives to litigate as the Boston School Committee?

2.   One immersed in structural injunctions might be tempted to write *Northern Delaware* off as a case from another era. But it is not all that old, and time is not a sufficient explanation. There is good reason to believe many judges would decide it the same way today, and that many judges would have decided it differently in 1968. When complexity becomes impracticality is a matter of discretion. Some judges are scared off easily; others are bolder. To get a more balanced picture, we should compare *Northern Delaware* to the case plaintiff relied on, City Stores Co. v. Ammerman, 266 F. Supp. 766 (D.D.C. 1967), *aff'd*, 394 F.2d 950 (D.C. Cir. 1968). There are scores of cases like *Northern Delaware*, and scores more like *City Stores*; both reflect mainstream approaches.

3.   *Northern Delaware* said the plans in *City Stores* were "quite definite." In fact, defendant had argued that the contract was void for indefiniteness. The only written record of defendant's promise was one sentence in a thank-you note, promising that plaintiff could become a "major tenant" in defendant's planned shopping mall, "with rental and terms at least equal to that of any other major department store in the center." The other stores had more formal contracts, but those contracts said only that the physical plant would be "comparable, at a minimum, to the qualities, values, approaches, and standards" of a particular mall in Los Angeles. The court ordered defendant to build a store for plaintiff.

Northern Delaware focused on the risk that the court would be sucked into supervising the whole project. *City Stores* assumed that everything would be "fairly simple" if the parties deal with each other "in good faith and expeditiously." Is this just a case of the optimist seeing the donut and the pessimist seeing the hole? Or was there more ground for optimism in *City Stores*? The court in *City Stores* ordered the parties to deal with each other in good faith and expeditiously. What are the odds of being held in contempt of that injunction?

The judge in *City Stores* said that if the parties bothered him with details, he would appoint a master to decide how to build the store. Is that overkill? Or a necessary backstop if the court is serious about providing effective remedies?

4.   How do the legal remedies compare in the two cases? In *Northern Delaware* there would be some uncertainty about how much sooner the job would have been done if the second shift had been put on, and about how much plaintiff lost as a result of the delay. But profits need only be calculated for the period of delay, unless plaintiff claims that the delay caused it to lose some customers permanently.

In *City Stores*, damages would be the present value of profits for the life of the mall, a period of many years. In addition, this was to be plaintiff's first suburban store, and the court thought that expanding into that market would bring "almost incalculable future advantages."

Quite likely the uncertainty is great enough to make the legal remedy inadequate in both cases; the court in *Northern Delaware* does not suggest otherwise. But recall that adequacy is a comparative judgment; isn't the damage remedy more inadequate in *City Stores* than in *Northern Delaware*? And wouldn't damages be even worse in the school, prison, and mental health cases, where the values at stake are not dollar values at all? Shouldn't courts balance the problems with the equitable remedy against the problems with the legal remedy? Isn't that what *City Stores* suggests?

5.   More generally, courts might take the view that some rights are more important than others. School desegregation is a constitutional right belonging to the whole public; *Northern Delaware* involves the private rights of one corporation. The Supreme Court is fond of saying that "courts of equity may, and frequently do, go much farther both to give and withhold relief in furtherance of the public interest than they are accustomed to go when only private interests are involved." Golden State Bottling Co. v. National Labor Relations Board, 414 U.S. 168, 179-180 (1973). Is that a legitimate ground for avoiding a difficult injunction? Would it be legitimate in cases where the damage remedy is less adequate than in *Northern Delaware*?

EISEN v. CARLISLE & JACQUELIN
479 F.2d 1005 (2d Cir. 1973)

[This was an antitrust suit for treble damages. Defendants handled the execution of odd lot transactions on the New York Stock Exchange. A round lot is 100 shares or some multiple of 100 shares; an odd lot is a lot of less than 100 shares. Odd lot transactions were handled apart from the regular auction on the Exchange, and defendants handled 99 percent of them. Plaintiff alleged that defendants had monopolized odd lot trading and fixed commissions on odd lots at an excessive level. He sued on behalf of a class of all persons who traded odd lots on the Exchange.

The district judge initially denied class certification. He had several reasons. The most important was that all class members would have to be notified, but that Eisen was unwilling to pay for that. He also thought that Eisen's claim was so small compared to the total claims of the class that he could not adequately represent the class and that individual questions would probably predominate over common questions.

On appeal, the court of appeals first decided that the order denying class certification was an appealable final judgment. The judgment was final in fact, although not in theory, because Eisen claimed only $70 in individual damages. It was therefore economically impossible for the case to proceed on behalf of Eisen individually. 370 F.2d 119 (2d Cir. 1966), cert. denied, 386 U.S. 1035 (1967). That opinion is generally referred to as Eisen I. The rule of Eisen I, known as the "death knell" doctrine, was eventually rejected by the Supreme Court. Coopers & Lybrand v. Livesay, 437 U.S. 463 (1978).

After deciding that it had jurisdiction over the appeal, the court of appeals wrote a separate opinion on whether the case should proceed as a class action. A majority rejected the district court's emphasis on the ratio between Eisen's individual claim and the claims of the class. The majority agreed that notice would be a problem, but concluded that the district court should hold hearings to determine whether it could devise some practical means to decide the case on a class basis. 391 F.2d 555 (2d Cir. 1968). That opinion is generally referred to as Eisen II. Judge Lumbard dissented, calling the case a "Frankenstein monster posing as a class action." Id. at 572.

On remand, the district court eventually concluded that the case could proceed on behalf of all persons who had bought or sold an odd lot between May 1, 1962 and June 30, 1966. This appeal followed, and this opinion became known as Eisen III.]

Before MEDINA, LUMBARD and HAYS, Circuit Judges.

MEDINA, Circuit Judge. . . .

I.   The Decision Below — 52 F.R.D. 253, 1971

In 1968, when the case was previously before us, it was estimated by someone that there were 3,750,000 members of the class, consisting of those who had bought or sold odd lots on the New York Stock Exchange in the period from May 1, 1962 through June 20, 1966. It was then doubtful whether any of the members of the class could be "identified through reasonable effort." Eisen's position then was and now is that, except possibly in the eventuality of the ultimate adoption of Judge Tyler's suggested plan which envisages payment by defendants of 90% of the cost of giving notice, he will not defray any of the expense of giving notice to any of the members of the class, nor will he post any bond to reimburse defendants for any of their disbursements, pursuant to any order of the District Court, made for the purpose of giving any notice.

It now appears that there are 6,000,000 members of the class and of these 2,250,000 can be easily identified. Members of the class reside in every state of the United States and most foreign countries. They speak and understand a great variety of modern languages. The damages sought to be recovered were estimated at the time we last considered the case at something between a maximum of $60,000,000 and a minimum of $22,000,000. Now the estimate has been raised by Eisen's counsel to 120 millions of dollars.

In our prior opinion we stated unequivocally that actual notice must be given to those whose identity could be ascertained with reasonable effort and that "in this type of case" plaintiff must pay the expense of giving notice to these members of the class. We further stated that if this could not be done there might be no other alternative than the dismissal of the case as a class action. For some reason not clear to us Judge Tyler disregarded these holdings and concluded that he had discretion, even with reference to those members of the class who could be easily identified, to provide for such notice as he thought to be reasonable in the light of the facts of this particular case.

Thus he directed actual notice only to "the approximately 2000 or more class members who had ten or more transactions during the relevant period" and to "5000 other class members selected at random" from the 2,500,000 class members who could easily be identified. With respect to the rest of the 6,000,000 members of the class, Judge Tyler ordered what, without reciting all the details concerning the schedule of proposed publications, we consider to be a totally inadequate compliance with the notice requirements of amended Rule 23. One of the reasons for this was perhaps because Judge Tyler thought of these first notices, by mail and by publication, as merely the first of a series of notices. Judge Tyler then deferred the question of who should pay for this first round of notices until after a "brief" preliminary hearing on the merits. This is what is called the "mini-hearing." We shall have more to say later about this preliminary mini-hearing on the merits of Eisen's triple damage antitrust claim. Accordingly, the hearing was held "on the issue of the allocation of the costs of notice" and Judge Tyler concluded that the defendants must bear 90% of these expenses.

To describe Judge Tyler's general scheme as it slowly developed in the series of his many opinions following the remand would be too tedious. The sum and substance of it was that he at last realized that it was highly improbable that any great number of claims would, for a variety of reasons, ultimately be filed by the 6,000,000 members of the class. No claimant in the 6 years of the progress of the action had shown any interest in Eisen's claim. The average odd-lot differential on each transaction had been $5.18. The average individual class member engaging in five trans-actions would have paid a total odd-lot differential of $25.90. Assuming a 5% illegal overcharge the recovery is approximately $1.30, and when trebled the average class member would be entitled to damages of $3.90. As the costs of administration might run into the millions of dollars, it was not likely that a rush of claimants would eventuate no matter how extensive the publication. As he had surmised in the beginning, and as Chief Judge Lumbard stated in his dissent (*Eisen II*), the class action was hopelessly unmanageable. So Judge Tyler tried to pull the case out of this morass by resorting to the "fluid recovery," which had been used as a vehicle for carrying out a voluntary settlement in the Drug Cases, State of West Virginia v. Chas. Pfizer & Co., Inc., et al., 314 F. Supp. 710 (S.D.N.Y.1970).

The concept of this "fluid recovery" is very simple. Having decided that there is no conceivable way in which any substantial number of individual claimants can ever be paid, "the class as a whole" is substituted for the 6,000,000 claimants. Thus the first round of notices becomes relatively unimportant. The scheme adopted envisages the first round of notices as sufficient to get the ball rolling. Little is said about Step Two. This involves a trial of the case to a judge and jury on the merits — not a preliminary mini-trial this time, but a real full scale trial of the private triple damage antitrust case. In some way the damages to "the class as a whole" will be assessed and the defendants, it seems to be assumed, will promptly pay this huge sum into court. This sum is supposed to constitute the "gross damages" to "the class as a whole." With the money in hand, the case begins to resemble the *Drug Cases* and from then on we are to have the real notices soliciting the filing of claims, the processing of these claims, the fixing of counsel fees and the payment of the general expenses of administration. As "the class as a whole" will include all those who had purchased or sold in the period from mid-1962 to mid-1966 and all those who, at the time of assessing the full damages, were presently purchasing or selling, and those who might in the future purchase and sell, securities in lots of less than 100 shares, it is quite apparent that some of the original 6,000,000 claimants will receive nothing, because they have never heard of the case or for other reasons have failed to file claims and have them processed, and many other new traders, who had no transactions in the period from mid-1962 to mid-1966, will receive some payments. According to Judge Tyler, at least those members of the original class of 6,000,000 who "have maintained their odd-lot activity, will reap the benefits of any recovery." As far as we are aware there has never been, nor can there ever be, a reliable or even rational estimate of how many traders, whether speculators or investors, can be said to be expected to continue as such after the lapse of 10 years or so. As it is suspected that relatively few claims will be filed and the damages assessed are supposed to cover the losses of "the class as a whole," there will be a huge residue, similar to the amounts paid to various charities "to advance public health projects" in the *Drug Cases*, and this residue is to be used for the benefit of all odd-lot traders by reducing the odd-lot differential "in an amount determined reasonable by the court until such time as the fund is depleted." We are at a loss to understand how this is to be done, but it is suggested that it "might properly be done under SEC supervision or at least with SEC approval." . . .

II. Disposition of Certain Contentions of the Parties . . .

B . . .

We think the three cases cited by Judge Tyler as "respectable precedent" for fluid class recovery are all distinguishable. These three cases are: Bebchick v. Public Utilities Commission, 115 U.S. App. D.C. 216, 318 F.2d 187, *cert. denied*, 373 U.S. 913 (1963); the *Drug Cases*, 314 F. Supp. 710 (S.D.N.Y.), *aff'd*, 440 F.2d 1079 (2d Cir. 1971); and Daar v. Yellow Cab Company, 67 Cal. 2d 695, 433 P.2d 732 (1967).

Judge Wyatt's extraordinary feat of judicial administration in carrying out the terms of the one hundred million dollar settlement in the *Drug Cases* deserves all the praise it has received. But it was a consensual affair made possible by the agreement of the parties and without objection to the assumption by the District Court of jurisdiction to accept and administer the fund. . . . *Bebchick* was not a class action in any sense of the word. Amended Rule 23 was not involved. In the exercise of its powers of review, the Court of Appeals for the District of Columbia Circuit reversed a judgment of the District Court approving the action of the Public Utilities Commission of the District of Columbia supporting a fare increase by the transit company. In the meantime, the additional cash fares, now found to be illegal, had been collected. There was no way to direct refunds as those who paid these cash fares could not be identified. So, also in the exercise of its powers of review the Court of Appeals directed the amount of these additional cash fares to be set up in the books of the transit company to be used, in the discretion of the regulatory commission "to benefit bus riders as a class in pending or future rate proceedings." We cannot find that this case has any bearing on any of the issues in this amended Rule 23 case. Finally, *Daar* was a case arising under a state class action statute very different in its phraseology from amended Rule 23. . . . Moreover, the court was evidently of the view that the individuals who had been damaged by the alleged overcharge in taxi fares would ultimately have to prove their separate and individual damages. 433 P.2d at 740.

[The court disapproved an earlier district court opinion that had ordered a fluid class recovery. That case was Dolgow v. Anderson, 53 F.R.D. 664 (1971).]

III. Controlling Principles . . .

[C]lichés and rhetorical devices generally miss the mark. Something more substantial is necessary to establish a base for the proper decision of difficult and complex questions of law. . . .

Thus statements about "disgorging" sums of money for which a defendant may be liable, or the "prophylactic" effect of making the wrongdoer suffer the pains of retribution and generally about providing a remedy for the ills of mankind, do little to solve specific legal problems. The result of this approach is almost always confusion of thought and irrational, emotional and unsound decisions. In cases involving claims of money damages all litigation presumes a desire on the part of the judicial establishment to make the wrongdoer pay for the wrongs he has committed, but to do this by applying settled or clearly stated principles of law, rather than by some process of divination. Punishment of wrongdoers is provided by law for criminal acts in statutes making it a crime punishable by fine or imprisonment to violate the antitrust laws. In certain civil suits punitive damages may be awarded; and in private antitrust cases the possible recovery of triple the loss actually suffered by a plaintiff is very properly praised as a supplementary deterrent. But none of these considerations justifies disregarding, nullifying or watering down any of the procedural safeguards established by the Constitution, or by congressional mandate, or by the Federal Rules of Civil Procedure, including amended Rule 23. It is a historical fact that procedural safeguards for the benefit of all litigants constitute some of the most important and salutary protections against oppressions, including oppressions by those whose intentions may be above reproach. . . .

IV. Lack of Individual Notice to "All Members Who Can Be Identified through Reasonable Effort"

Our prior ruling in *Eisen II* is clear and specific. If identification of any number of members of the class can readily be made, individual notice to these members must be given and Eisen must pay the cost. If this cannot be done, the case must be dismissed as a class action. Amended Rule 23(c)(2) unambiguously states that notice to the class generally shall be the "best notice practicable," and then "including individual notice to all members who can be identified through reasonable effort." Moreover, the Advisory Committee's Note states (39 F.R.D. 106-107): "Indeed, under subdivision (c)(2), notice must be ordered, it is not merely discretionary. . . . While Judge Tyler seems to have realized that this phase of amended Rule 23 has decided constitutional overtones, he apparently thought the flexibility of the Rule and our statement that the Rule was to be given a liberal interpretation authorized him to exercise his discretion even if this involved the complete disregard of our specific and unambiguous ruling on the subject of actual individual notice to identifiable members of the class. This ruling alone compels a reversal of the order appealed from and the dismissal of the case as a class action.

V. The Preliminary Mini-Hearing on the Merits Was Not Authorized by Amended Rule 23 and the District Court Had No Jurisdiction or Competence to Hold Such a Hearing

The Federal Rules of Civil Procedure set forth a considerable variety of procedural devices designed for the disposition of cases on the merits. There may be traditional trials to a judge or to a judge and jury; there may be summary judgments, dismissals with or without prejudice for failure to state a claim and so on. But neither in amended Rule 23 nor in any other rule do we find provision for any tentative, provisional or other makeshift determination of the issues of any case on the merits for the avowed purpose of deciding a collateral matter such as which party is to be required to pay for mailing, publishing or otherwise giving any notice required by law. In most cases the so-called tentative findings and conclusions arrived at without the salutary safeguards applicable to all full scale trials on the merits will be extremely prejudicial to one or the other of the parties who bear the brunt of such findings and conclusions, and such prejudice may well be irreparable. . . . No provision is made in amended Rule 23 for any such mini, preliminary or other hearing on the merits. It does violence to the whole concept of summary judgment, and cannot be reconciled with the requirement in Rule 23 that "as soon as practicable after the commencement of the action" the question of class suit *vel non* [or not] be decided. . . .

VI. As a Class Action the Case Is Unmanageable

From the beginning it has been Judge . . . Lumbard's view that as a class action the case is unmanageable and that it should be dismissed as a class action. It turns out that he was right. As soon as the evidence on the remand disclosed the true extent of the membership of the class and the fact that Eisen would not pay for individual notice to the members of the class who could be identified, and the evidence further disclosed that the class membership was of such diversity and was so dispersed that no notice by publication could be devised by the ingenuity of man that could reasonably be expected to notify more than a relatively small proportion of the class, a ruling should have been made forthwith dismissing the case as a class action. This dismissal could have saved several years of hard work by the judge and the lawyers and wholly unnecessary expense running into large figures. The fact that the cost of obtaining proofs of claim by individual members of the class and processing such claims was such as to make it clear that the amounts payable to individual claimants would be so low as to be negligible also should have been enough of itself to warrant dismissal as a class action. Other cases involving millions of diverse and unidentifiable members of an alleged class had been dismissed as unmanageable or altered in composition. And so even Eisen and his counsel conceded that the class was not manageable unless the "fluid recovery" procedures were adopted.

Thus, in the language of Eisen's counsel: . . .

> In both Cherner v. Transitron Electronic Corporation, 201 F. Supp. 934 (D. Mass. 1962) and Illinois Bell Telephone Co. v. Slattery, 102 F.2d 58 (7th Cir. 1939), (the cases included in Stipulation No. 2), the refund process overwhelmed the refunds. And both cases involved, quite obviously, classes much smaller than the class at bar.

Where there are millions of dispersed and unidentifiable members of the class notices by publication giving the essential information required by amended Rule 23 are a farce. And, when it comes to the filing and processing of claims, lawyers specializing in class actions have stated that the only effective way to induce any reasonable number of members of the class to file claims is to conduct full-scale campaigns on TV and radio, solicit appearances by advocates of consumers' rights such as Ralph Nader, letters from Congressmen to their constituents, public statements by various state attorneys general "and coverage in various news media, union newsletters and the like," also to persuade the Federal Communications Commission to classify announcements of this character as "public service announcements."[22]

All the difficulties of management are supposed to disappear once the "fluid recovery" procedure is adopted. The claims of the individual members of the class become of little consequence. If the damages to be paid were only the aggregate of the sums found due to individual members of the class, after their claims had been processed, it is fairly obvious that in cases like Eisen the expenses of giving the notices required by amended Rule 23 and the general costs of administration of the action would exceed the amount due to the few members of the class who filed claims and the individual members of the class would get nothing.

But if the "class as a whole" is or can be substituted for the individual members of the class as claimants, then the number of claims filed is of no consequence and the amount found to be due will be enormous, affording, we are told, plenty of money to pay all expenses, including

---

22. These suggestions were made and discussed in Shapiro, "Consumer Participation in Antitrust Class Action Part II," New York Law Journal, May 31, 1972, p.1.

counsel fees, and a residue so large as to justify reduction of the odd-lot differential for years in the future, for the benefit of all traders, past, present and future, who are to be considered to be members of "the class as a whole."

Even if amended Rule 23 could be read so as to permit any such fantastic procedure, the courts would have to reject it as an unconstitutional violation of the requirement of due process of law. But as it now reads amended Rule 23 contemplates and provides for no such procedure. Nor can amended Rule 23 be construed or interpreted in such fashion as to permit such procedure. We hold the "fluid recovery" concept and practice to be illegal, inadmissible as a solution of the manageability problems of class actions and wholly improper.

Class actions have sprouted and multiplied like the leaves of the green bay tree. No matter how numerous or diverse the so-called class may be or how impossible it may be ever to compensate the individual members of the class, a champion steps forth. Thus class actions have been brought "on behalf of all subscribers of business telephones in New York County, all Master Charge credit card holders similarly situated, all consumers of gasoline in a given state or states, all homeowners in the United States, and even all people in the United States."[24] So far as we are aware not a single one of these class actions including millions of indiscriminate and unidentifiable members has ever been brought to trial and decided on the merits. But the preliminary procedures, including the preliminary mini-hearing on the merits, such as those conducted by Judge Tyler in order to decide whether or not this case was a proper class action, and the huge and unavoidable expense of producing witnesses and documents pursuant to discovery orders, have brought such pressure on defendants as to induce settlements in large amounts as the alternative to complete ruin and disaster, irrespective of the merits of the claim.

The "in terrorem" effects of [these] innovations . . . have been highly praised by those who invented or applied them. But Professor Milton Handler . . . minces no words. He calls these procedures "legalized blackmail."[27] There is reason to believe that the practical effect of these procedures, and the fact that possible recoveries run into astronomical amounts, generate more leverage and pressure on defendants to settle, even for millions of dollars, and in cases where the merits of the class representatives' claim is to say the least doubtful, than did the old-fashioned strike suits made famous a generation or two ago. . . .

And yet, even if amended Rule 23 furnishes no satisfactory solution in situations where immense numbers of consumers have been mulcted in various ways by illegal charges, it would seem that some means should be

24. In the Report and Recommendations of the Special Committee of the American College of Trial Lawyers on Rule 23 of the Federal Rules of Civil Procedure, issued March 15, 1972, this quotation appears on p.6 with supporting citations.

27. Handler, The Shift From Substantive to Procedural Innovations in Antitrust Suits — The 23rd Annual Antitrust Review, 71 Colum. L. Rev. 1, 9 (1971).

provided by law for the redress of these wrongs to the community and to society as a whole. The numerous decisions by courts in these class action cases have at least exposed the lack of adequate remedy under existing laws. From our extensive study of the whole situation in working on this *Eisen* case it would seem that amended Rule 23 provides an excellent and workable procedure in cases where the number of members of the class is not too large. It seems doubtful that further amendments to Rule 23 can be expected to be effective where there are millions of members of the class, without some infringement of constitutional requirements. The problem is really one for solution by the Congress. Numerous administrative agencies protect consumers in various ways. It should, we think, be possible for the Congress to create some public body to do justice in the matter of consumers' claims in such fashion as to afford compensation to the injured consumer. If penalties are to be imposed upon wrongdoers, at least let the Congress decide how the money is to be spent.

Another possibility, suggested by the Report and Recommendations of the Special Committee of the American College of Trial Lawyers, is a further amendment to amended Rule 23 consisting of a new subdivision providing:

> In an action commenced pursuant to subdivision (b)(3), the court shall consider whether justice in the action would be more effectively served by maintenance of the action as a class action pursuant to subdivision (b)(2) in lieu of (b)(3).

[Rule 23(b)(2) authorizes class actions for injunctive or declaratory relief. There is no restriction on the kind of class relief that can be sought under Rule 23(b)(3).] The procedure involved in applying for prospective injunctive relief is relatively simple and inexpensive, social and economic reforms may be implemented and an end put to illegal practices with far more benefit to the community than that derived from minimal or token payments to individual members of a class. Attorney's fees in such cases should also provide adequate incentive to counsel for the representative or representatives of the class.[28]

28. In his recent book Federal Jurisdiction: A General View, . . . Chief Judge Friendly makes this comment on class actions pursuant to amended Rule 23, at page 120:

> Something seems to have gone radically wrong with a well-intentioned effort. Of course, an injured plaintiff should be compensated, but the federal judicial system is not adapted to affording compensation to classes of hundreds of people with $10 or even $50 claims. The important thing is to stop the evil conduct. For this an injunction is the appropriate remedy, and an attorney who obtains one should be properly compensated by the defendant, although not in the astronomical terms fixed when there is a multi-million dollar settlement. If it be said that this still leaves the defendant with the fruits of past wrong-doing, consideration might be given to civil fines, payable to the government, sufficiently substantial to discourage engaging in such conduct but not so colossal as to produce recoveries that would ruin innocent stockholders or, what is more likely, produce blackmail settlements. This is a matter that needs urgent attention.

Conclusion

For the reasons stated in this opinion the findings and conclusions following the mini-hearing are vacated and set aside, the various rulings of the District Court sustaining the prosecution of the case as a class action are reversed and, as a class action, the case is dismissed, without prejudice to the continuance of so much of the claim asserted in the complaint as refers to Eisen's alleged individual rights against the defendants.

HAYS, Circuit Judge (concurring in the result).

I concur in the result because I am unable to accept the ruling of the district court requiring the defendants to pay 90 percent of the cost of notice, since, if the defendants should finally prevail, they would not be reimbursed for this expenditure.

[The court denied rehearing en banc.]

KAUFMAN, Circuit Judge, with whom FRIENDLY, Chief Judge, and FEINBERG, MANSFIELD, and MULLIGAN, Circuit Judges, concur.

I vote against en banc, not because I believe this case is unimportant, but because the case is of such extraordinary consequence that I am confident the Supreme Court will take this matter under its certiorari jurisdiction. . . .

MANSFIELD, Circuit Judge.

I concur in Judge Kaufman's opinion. . . . Otherwise I would agree with Judge Oakes' forceful plea for an en banc hearing.

HAYS, Circuit Judge (dissenting).

I believe that this case should be reconsidered en banc.

OAKES, Circuit Judge (dissenting from the denial of rehearing en banc), with whom TIMBERS, Circuit Judge, concurs.

For this court not to hear a matter of this significance is to render the en banc statute a nullity. . . .

The Case Is of Extreme Importance; It Vitally Affects
Class Actions . . .

The panel opinion defines as unmanageable any case involving a large class where actual notification of readily ascertainable members is expensive. It calls notice by publication to a large class a "farce" and casts constitutional doubts on any other construction of Rule 23. The case accordingly affects adversely much consumer and environmental litigation, as well as all antitrust and other claims by numbers of little people for small amounts. The panel opinion seems on its face to give a green light to monopolies and conglomerates who deal in quantity items selling at small prices to proceed to violate the antitrust laws, unhampered by any realistic threat of private consumer civil proceedings, leaving it to some vague future act of Congress to protect the innocent consumer. The panel opinion as I read it tells polluters that they are pretty safe from class actions because even if a whole city is blanketed in smoke or its water supply contaminated, the plaintiffs can never advance the money for notices to, say, all the people in the city phone book, who certainly are identifiable. I will not belabor the point of importance.

The Panel Opinion Reaches a Very Doubtful Result . . .

Serious questions about the panel's conclusions as to the management of class actions exist. Class actions, I had thought, were "an invention of equity . . . mothered by the practical necessity" of providing a practical procedure to enable large numbers of litigants to enforce their common rights. Montgomery Ward & Co. v. Langer, 168 F.2d 182, 187 (8th Cir. 1948). The panel's decision seems utterly inconsistent with the flexible, equitable spirit that motivated the innovative 1966 amendments to Fed. R. Civ. P. 23. . . .

The view . . . that Rule 23(c)(2) requires individual notice to all members of Eisen's class who can be identified through "reasonable effort" has been criticized as "unnecessarily restrictive. . . . " 7A C. Wright & A. Miller, Federal Practice and Procedure §1786 at 148 (1972). Certainly given the importance of the class action as a means for the little man to bring wealthy or powerful interests into court, Eisen's inability to bear the costs of mailing notice to those 2,000,000 or so "easily identifiable individuals" similarly situated should not necessarily terminate the class action character of this suit. It may be appropriate, as Judge Tyler suggested below, to charge the defendants with a portion of the notification costs. But even if these two questions were decided against the plaintiff, an en banc decision drawing sustenance from the flexible, still developing Rule 23 jurisprudence might embrace one of several other alternatives to the panel's burial of larger-number plaintiff class actions. . . .

The plaintiff class might, for example, be divided into much smaller subclasses, Fed. R. Civ. P. 23(c)(4)(B), of odd lot buyers for particular periods, and one subclass treated as a test case, with the other subclasses held in abeyance. Individual notice at what would probably be a reasonable cost could then be given to all members of the particular small subclass who can be easily identified. . . .

At least as questionable is the panel's conclusion that this class action is unmanageable and should be dismissed because "no notice by publication could be devised by the ingenuity of man that could reasonably be expected to notify more than a relatively small proportion of the class." The panel seems to intimate in a footnote that individualized notice to all

6,000,000 members of the class borders on being a constitutional requirement. This intimation seems to me to be profoundly incorrect. In my
view notice to class members who cannot be identified is not a constitutional requirement and not a prerequisite to a manageable class action.
All that the due process clause requires is a procedure that "fairly insures
the protection of the interests of absent parties who are to be bound by
[the judgment]." Hansberry v. Lee, 311 U.S. 32, 42 (1940) (not cited by
panel decision). The Advisory Committee is a respectable body of procedural experts who did not consider individualized notice to all or a certain
percentage of class members a prerequisite to the maintenance of a Rule
23 class action as a constitutional (or extraconstitutional) requirement.
Advisory Committee Notes, 28 U.S.C.A., Rule 23 Supplementary Note
at 302. The commentators generally agree. Assuming vigorous representation of the class's interests by the representative plaintiff (which is not in
issue here), notice by publication to unidentifiable class members is constitutionally sufficient. Mullane v. Central Hanover Bank and Trust Co.,
339 U.S. at 314. A scheme of notice by publication (with costs perhaps
taxed to the defendants) in financial journals of wide circulation — the
Wall Street Journal, Business Week, Barron's, the New York Times financial section, and the like — would reach most of the class.

To say, as the panel opinion says, that "[w]here there are millions of
dispersed and unidentifiable members of the class notices by publication
. . . are a farce," and to say it without any supporting data or authority,
strikes me as, in the words of the panel opinion, a "rhetorical device." In
this day and age of communications, why are such notices a "farce"? It
may be that most people will not heed them — the sums may be too small
to bother with, for example — but does this make the notices farcical?
Probate notices published in small-town newspapers around the country
are treated as notice to the whole world of possible creditors and heirs
that an estate is being closed, and they are pretty effective for this purpose. Notice by publication of actions such as this in key, spot places can
be, I should think, highly effective. . . . Rule 23 was not looking toward
perfect or total notification; it was — and I write of it in the past tense for
this purpose — reaching out for a practical result that would permit
numbers of little injured people to have their day, too, in court.

NOTES ON THE PRACTICAL LIMITS OF
CLASS ACTIONS

1. The Supreme Court unanimously affirmed. 417 U.S. 156 (1974). It
held that Rule 23 required the plaintiff to pay for individual notice to all
identifiable class members, and that it forbad the mini-hearing held by
the district court. It did not reach the fluid class recovery issue. The

Court noted that Eisen could define a smaller class that he could afford to notify, and three justices emphasized that option in a separate opinion.

2.   Here is the relevant language of Rule 23:

(b)   *Class Actions Maintainable.* An action may be maintained as a class action if the prerequisites of subdivision (a) are satisfied, and in addition: . . .

(3)   the court finds that the questions of law or fact common to the members of the class predominate over any questions affecting only individual members, and that a class action is superior to other available methods for the fair and efficient adjudication of the controversy. The matters pertinent to the findings include: (A) the interest of members of the class in individually controlling the prosecution or defense of separate actions; (B) the extent and nature of any litigation concerning the controversy already commenced by or against members of the class; (C) the desirability or undesirability of concentrating the litigation of the claims in the particular forum; (D) the difficulties likely to be encountered in the management of a class action.

(c)   *Determination by Order Whether Class Action to Be Maintained; Notice; Judgment; Actions Conducted Partially as Class Actions.*

(1)   As soon as practicable after the commencement of an action brought as a class action, the court shall determine by order whether it is to be so maintained. An order under this subdivision may be conditional, and may be altered or amended before the decision on the merits.

(2)   In any class action maintained under subdivision (b)(3), the court shall direct to the members of the class the best notice practicable under the circumstances, including individual notice to all members who can be identified through reasonable effort.

The Supreme Court said that Rule 23(c)(1) precluded a mini-hearing on the merits, because such a hearing would delay determination of the class action issue. Not surprisingly, it said that Rule 23(c)(2) required individual notice and left no discretion about the matter. It said that plaintiff had to pay for the notice "as part of the ordinary burden of financing his own suit." It acknowledged the possibility of making defendant pay for notice where defendant was a fiduciary for the class, as in a shareholder's derivative suit.

3.   Is *Eisen* a license to steal fortunes as long as you steal only a little bit from each of many victims? That's what troubled the dissenters in the court of appeals, and presumably that's what led the majority in *Eisen II* to tell the district court to give it a try. Defining a smaller class will work if there's a class with individual claims substantially larger than the cost of processing those claims. If the average claim in *Eisen* is $3.90, then there is no class plaintiff can afford to notify that has damages big enough to sue for.

4.   One response to Eisen's problem is to deny that it's a problem. If

we consider only the litigation and its immediate consequences, it's a waste of resources to spend $10 on a $3.90 claim. This argument suggests that $3.90 claims should not be filed. When we add in attorneys' fees for both sides and the costs of running the judicial system, antitrust class actions with $70 claims probably shouldn't be filed. Maybe in individual cases, $1,000 claims should not be filed, or should be decided with summary procedures in a justice of the peace court.

How persuasive is that? Certainly we should look for ways to try small cases less expensively, but there are limits to that. Plaintiff has no chance at all of proving many wrongs unless he has access to defendant's records. We have a complex economy with complex regulations; the line between a hard bargain and illegality is often thin. Plaintiff may know he has lost money, and be pretty sure defendant caused the loss, but until he understands defendant's internal operations, he can't know whether the loss was caused legally or illegally. That sort of claim can't be tried for $1,000, no matter how simple the procedures.

Does it follow that small wrongs should go unremedied? An explicit public policy that small wrongs should go unremedied really would be a license to steal small sums. Even from a strictly economic perspective, the balance between costs and benefits cannot focus only on the cost of litigation and the compensation awarded. The balance must also consider the additional violations that would result from a policy of not pursuing small violations.

Beyond that, it seems to me that justice has intrinsic value — that when we remedy a $70 wrong, we do more than $70 worth of good. If Eisen's claims are true, he has not just suffered the loss of $70. He has suffered the indignity of being ripped off. Can society afford to tell him that we don't care about him and his $70, because it's more efficient to let little wrongs go unremedied?

5. Judge Friendly suggests another response to Eisen's problem, and the court of appeals expands on the suggestion in *Eisen III*. He says in effect that we don't care about Eisen's $70, but we do care about not creating a license to steal. His solution is an injunction against further violations, with fees for the plaintiff's attorney and, if necessary, civil fines collected by the government to recover the profits of past wrongdoing.

This proposal assumes that injunction actions are much easier to manage than damage actions. *Eisen III* even says that "the procedure involved in applying for prospective injunctive relief is relatively simple and inexpensive." Contrast that with the argument that we need the irreparable injury rule because injunctions are so much more complicated than damages.

There are some ways in which injunction actions are simpler, but it's not clear they are simple enough to solve Eisen's problem. He still has to prove monopolization or price fixing; the trial on the merits will be complex and expensive. And the case is more likely to be tried; without the risk of damage liability, defendant has less incentive to settle. On the other hand, no one has to measure damages. That means no one has to quantify the amount of the overcharge, or the number or size of transactions to which the overcharge was applied, and no one has to process individual claims.

6. The main attraction of an injunction remedy in *Eisen* is the view that class members would not have to be notified. Rule 23(b)(2) authorizes class actions where "final injunctive relief or corresponding declaratory relief [is appropriate] with respect to the class as a whole." Nothing in Rule 23 requires notice in such class actions. But what about the due process clause? There is a lot of due process talk in *Eisen II* and *III*, and in the Supreme Court's opinion affirming *Eisen III*. *Eisen II* said that "notice is required as a matter of due process in all representative actions," explicitly rejecting the view that actions under (b)(2) were any different for this purpose from those under (b)(3). If the Constitution requires notice to all class members before a court adjudicates their rights, how can (b)(2) class actions be exempt? A few cases require notice in (b)(2) class actions, but a lopsided majority does not. The Second Circuit has not adhered to its dictum in *Eisen II*. The cases are collected in C. Wright & A. Miller, Federal Practice and Procedure §1786 nn.99, 1 (1972 and 1983 Supp.).

Perhaps the best reasoned of these opinions is Wetzel v. Liberty Mutual Insurance Co., 508 F.2d 239, 254-257 (3d Cir.), *cert. denied*, 421 U.S. 1011 (1975). *Wetzel* holds that due process is satisfied if the named plaintiff is an adequate representative, citing dictum in Hansberry v. Lee, 311 U.S. 32, 40-42 (1940). *Hansberry* held that a class was not bound because its representative had been inadequate. *Wetzel* also says that (b)(2) classes are more cohesive than (b)(3) classes, so notice serves less purpose. Lots of cases and commentators say that, but it has never made much sense to me. How would the class of odd lot traders be more cohesive if Eisen sought an injunction than if he sought damages? Doesn't *Wetzel* depend on the view that adequate representation satisfies due process, so that notice is not *constitutionally* required even in (b)(3) class actions?

7. One other difference between a damage judgment and an injunction is that an injunction will not create a fund to pay plaintiff's attorneys' fees. But antitrust plaintiffs can recover their attorneys' fees separately, and Congress could provide generally for attorneys' fees in class actions for injunctions. For such a scheme to work, judges would have to award substantial fees that took into account the complexity of the case and the risks of going unpaid if the case were lost. We will consider attorneys' fee awards in chapter 10.

8. Could Rule 23 be amended to dispense with notice or make it discretionary? How much process is due depends in part on the costs of providing more process. Consider Mullane v. Central Hanover Bank &

Trust Co., 339 U.S. 306 (1950), the case most often cited for the requirement of individual notice. The Bank had pooled many separate trusts into a common trust fund, and it had filed an action to account for its management of the fund. The Court required individual notice to current beneficiaries. But it said the bank did not have to notify future or contingent beneficiaries, because it would be expensive to keep track of who they were, and the expense might dissipate the economies of managing the trusts as a common fund. Id. at 317-318. If the expense of notice and the advantages of combining small interests can be considered in that context, why not in class actions?

9. There is an irony in *Eisen*. Notice is designed to protect class members from losing their claims in a suit they never hear about. In fact, requiring notice took away those claims. This is a special case of an inherent problem. Absent class members are not heard on whether they want to be represented in a class action. But defendant has an enormous stake in defeating class certification. Thus, at the class certification stage, defendant makes himself the de facto representative of absent class members, searching out defects in the official class representative, conflicts within the class, and unachievable procedural protections that can't be dispensed with. Thus, the cases are full of arguments that we must destroy the class in order to save it.

10. It doesn't follow that there are no real questions about the adequacy of representation in class actions. There are good, bad, and indifferent lawyers in the class action business, just as in any other specialty. But for the most part, the bad class actions can't be weeded out by examining the issues defendants raise in opposition to class certification. What the court really needs to know is how the named plaintiff's lawyer will handle the case. The biggest risk is that at some point he will sell out the class for a fat fee. The temptation to do so is enormous, although many lawyers resist it. The court's ability to detect a bad settlement is minimal. If the plaintiff's lawyer says the case has turned out to be weaker than anticipated, the judge has no basis to disagree. He certainly has no time to read the huge volume of material produced in discovery.

But is restricting class actions the solution? Even if some classes recover less than they deserve, they would recover nothing without the class action. And doesn't it seem likely that there will be fewer violations of law in an environment where liability to a class is a live possibility?

11. For any argument that class actions inadequately protect class members, a cure that would significantly restrict class actions is worse than the disease. But what about the argument that class actions are "legal blackmail"? If class actions are unfair to the party opposing the class, there is a real argument for restricting them. Whether the threat of class liability extracts unjustified settlements is an empirical question, and there is not sufficient space to explore it in much depth here. My own experience in a class action practice in the mid-1970s was that reasonable

settlements were harder to achieve in class actions than in individual actions: Defendants were enormously reluctant to pay the huge sums needed to compensate a class. That doesn't mean defendants don't feel they are being blackmailed, but in my experience few of them succumbed.

12.   Could all the notice problems be avoided if we let any member of the class sue for restitution of defendants' profits from the wrong? Could the judgment be held in escrow until the statute of limitations ran out on the claims, and then divided among as many claimants as appeared?

NOTES ON FLUID CLASS RECOVERIES AND AFFIRMATIVE ACTION

1.   Another innovation disapproved in *Eisen* was the fluid class recovery. To avoid the expense of processing individual claims, the district court planned to order defendants to reduce their commissions below the competitive level until all illegal overcharges had been refunded by discounting. The court recognized that these discounts would not necessarily go to the class members who had paid the overcharges, and certainly there would be no relationship between any class member's earlier damage and his subsequent discount. But the court thought that some of the class members who had paid the overcharges would benefit from the subsequent discounts, and that in any event, the class that received the discounts would be similar to the class that paid the overcharges.

The Second Circuit's emphatic rejection of the fluid class recovery has largely disposed of the issue. Even though the Supreme Court did not review that part of the case, there has been no further experimentation with fluid class recoveries.

2.   There has been one widespread exception, largely not recognized as such. Every circuit has ordered racial goals or quotas as a remedy for employment discrimination. In these cases, employers who discriminated against earlier black job applicants are ordered to prefer future black job applicants. Isn't that exactly the fluid class recovery disapproved in *Eisen*?

Most of the cases speak in general terms about eliminating the effects of discrimination. The effect to be eliminated is apparently the racial composition of the employer's work force, and not any effect on a plaintiff. The cases rarely say this explicitly, but there is a square statement in Justice Blackmun's dissent in Firefighters Local Union No. 1784 v. Stotts, 104 S. Ct. 2576 (1984):

In determining the nature of "appropriate" relief under §706(g) [42 U.S.C. §2000e-5(g) (1982)], courts have distinguished between individual relief and race-conscious class relief. . . . [A]n individual plaintiff is entitled to an award of individual relief only if he can establish that he was the victim of discrimination. That requirement grows out of the general equitable principles of "make whole" relief; an individual who has suffered no injury is not entitled to an individual award. . . .

In Title VII class-action suits, the Courts of Appeals are unanimously of the view that race-conscious affirmative relief can also be "appropriate" under §706(g). . . . Because the discrimination sought to be alleviated by race-conscious relief is the classwide effects of past discrimination, rather than discrimination against identified members of the class, such relief is provided to the class as a whole rather than to its individual members. The relief may take many forms, but in class actions it frequently involves percentages . . . that require race to be taken into account when an employer hires or promotes employees. The distinguishing feature of race-conscious relief is that no individual member of the disadvantaged class has a claim to it, and individual beneficiaries of the relief need not show that they were themselves victims of the discrimination for which relief was granted.

104 S. Ct. at 2605-2606.

3.   There are many Second Circuit cases granting such "race-conscious class relief." A fairly thorough opinion that cites many of the others is Association against Discrimination in Employment v. City of Bridgeport, 647 F.2d 256 (2d Cir. 1981), cert. denied sub nom. Bridgeport Firefighters for Merit Employment v. Association against Discrimination in Employment, 455 U.S. 988 (1982). Not one of these cases cites *Eisen* or makes any effort to distinguish it. Is there anything the Second Circuit could say? The reasons for "race-conscious class relief" are substantially the same as the reasons for the fluid class recovery. It is often impractical to identify individual victims of discrimination. They have typically found another job by the time the litigation is over, or they have moved without leaving a forwarding address. A court that wants to create an immediate and substantial black representation in the employer's work force can't do it merely by reinstating identifiable victims. It is also much easier to police compliance with a quota than to police compliance with an order not to discriminate in future hiring. Those reasons weren't enough in *Eisen*. If a fluid class recovery is "fantastic," "illegal," "inadmissible," "unconstitutional," and "wholly improper" in antitrust cases, why is it mandatory in discrimination cases?

4.   The comparison to fluid class recoveries makes clear that much of the bitter national debate over affirmative action is really a debate over the nature of remedies. Proponents of hiring quotas see them as a remedy for widespread and longstanding discrimination. Opponents are quite willing to give identifiable victims of identifiable discrimination back pay, reinstatement with seniority, and anything else needed to make them whole. But these opponents think that "race-conscious class relief" grants

preferences based on race rather than victimization. That is why they see such relief as simply racial discrimination, as evil as the discrimination it is intended to combat.

5. "Race-conscious class relief" and fluid class recoveries take us back to first principles illustrated in United States v. Hatahley, where the plaintiffs' horses were shipped to the glue factory. The district court in *Hatahley* treated the Indians' loss as a loss to the group as a whole; the court of appeals insisted on individual damage determinations. The court of appeals decision reflects our legal system's view that litigation remedies particular wrongs to particular plaintiffs. To change that practice would require a wholly different law of remedies, and perhaps a wholly different role for courts in the constitutional scheme. If a remedy is not designed to restore someone to his rightful position, in what sense is it a remedy? Close attention to the litigants' rightful positions is what differentiates remedial redistribution from legislative redistribution. Professor Chayes and others think courts are breaking free of this tradition in public law litigation; his article is excerpted supra at 294 and 305. But *Eisen*'s reaction to fluid class recoveries illustrates the strength of the tradition and the courts' commitment to it.

6. One can imagine creating an exception or two without abandoning the system. Are the race cases an appropriate exception? On one view they are a highly suspect exception: If the only exception from a fundamental general principle is granted on the basis of race, that looks a lot like race discrimination.

From another perspective, the race cases are a highly appropriate exception: Pervasive racial discrimination has had cumulative effects on its victims and their descendants, and only a tiny portion of those effects will ever be remedied by traditional litigation. The beneficiaries of quotas may not have been discriminated against by the defendant, but surely they are still feeling the effects of discrimination by somebody else. Most obviously, one reason simple nondiscrimination often fails to produce racial balance is that the states have always provided better education to whites than to blacks. *Hatahley* also prefigured this argument: One reading of the district judge's opinion was that the Navajo had suffered many other wrongs, and he was going to remedy as much as he could.

7. Assuming that the beneficiaries of a racial hiring order deserve preference because of some past discrimination by someone else, why must *defendant* remedy that discrimination? Perhaps the answer is that he can't complain because he has been found guilty of discriminating and most of his victims couldn't be identified. That still leaves an even harder question: The burden of a hiring quota falls on new white applicants. What are they guilty of besides being white? Typically they are new entrants to the work force, young and powerless. They didn't design the discriminatory school system. Is it enough that some of them presumably benefitted from it? Are the burdens of quota hiring a rough and ready

form of restitution from third party beneficiaries of a wrong? Are they acceptable on the ground that the whites will have less trouble than the blacks getting a job somewhere else? Don't be too sure: The burden will fall on the least qualified whites.

If all of this is just, it can only be on the theory that gross approximations are good enough and substantial errors in individual cases have to be tolerated. Are the approximations good enough? Are the errors of quota hiring smaller than the errors of denying relief to everyone but identifiable victims of identifiable discrimination? That is, do courts get more people closer to their rightful position by ordering quotas or by insisting on individual proof? There is also an argument that that's not the right question. Some would say it's worse for a court to order discrimination against an innocent third party than to leave a private act of discrimination unremedied for lack of proof. In the first case the court itself is the discriminator; in the second, it is an innocent and helpless bystander. How persuasive is that?

8. A pair of related rules casts light on the courts' attitudes toward these problems. Many courts will not order goals or quotas in promotions if the burden will fall on a small and identifiable group of whites. The *Bridgeport* case, supra note 3, is a good example. Even more striking, no court will displace white incumbents — not even to make room for identifiable victims of discrimination. Firefighters Local Union No. 1784 v. Stotts, 104 S. Ct. 2576, 2588 n.11 (1984). This is so even though the incumbents' union may have urged or demanded the adjudicated discrimination, and the incumbents are likely to have benefitted from it. A finding that a particular black applicant was discriminatorily rejected is a decision that some white incumbent was discriminatorily hired. It may even be possible to identify the very incumbent who was hired on the day the victim was rejected. Then we have an identifiable victim and an identifiable beneficiary of discrimination. It doesn't matter. Even when a company demotes a victim on discriminatory grounds and gives his job to someone else, courts will not displace the beneficiary. Spagnuolo v. Whirlpool Corp., 717 F.2d 114 (4th Cir. 1983). Most courts will compensate the identifiable victim for lost wages while he waits for a position to open up.

The rationale is not that money is an adequate remedy; courts regularly hold that loss of employment on grounds of race is irreparable injury and that reinstatement is the only adequate remedy. Rather, the rationale is that courts should not interfere with the expectations of the white incumbents.

Don't these cases give identifiable victims too little relief? Isn't the identifiable victim entitled to his rightful position immediately? If the courts are so scrupulous about the rights of identifiable incumbents, why are they so cavalier about the rights of white applicants? One answer is that the applicant has not relied on a job with the particular employer but incumbents have. Another is that identifiable incumbents appear in court as real human beings, with lawyers to represent them. Future applicants are unrepresented abstractions.

9. Remedies law is only one perspective from which to consider the debate over affirmative action. Important arguments about the meaning of the Constitution and the civil rights laws, about the wisdom of affirmative action, and about the nature of racial justice are beyond the scope of these notes. But those arguments are also important to a full understanding of affirmative action.

10. Although every circuit has approved injunctions ordering racial goals or quotas in hiring, the Supreme Court has not authoritatively spoken. In International Brotherhood of Teamsters v. United States, 431 U.S. 324, 356-377 (1977), the Supreme Court described in great detail how the district court should fashion a remedy that would restore identifiable victims to their rightful positions. But no goal or quota was before the Court in *Teamsters*, and the lower courts apparently assumed that the opinion was irrelevant to goals and quotas.

The Supreme Court returned to the issue in Firefighters Local Union No. 1784 v. Stotts, 104 S. Ct. 2576 (1984). *Firefighters* involved a quota for layoffs. Layoff quotas are more troubling than hiring quotas, because layoff quotas displace incumbents who would not otherwise have been laid off, and because the Civil Rights Act of 1964 explicitly protects seniority rules. 42 U.S.C. §2000e-2(h) (1982). The Supreme Court held that the layoff quota was improper. It relied partly on the provision protecting seniority rules, and partly on the statute's "policy to provide make-whole relief only to those who have been actual victims of illegal discrimination." Id. at 2589. The Court talked at some length about the clear congressional rejection of relief for plaintiffs who were not identifiable victims. That would seem to reject all the goal and quota cases. But it would not be surprising if the Court changed its mind. There were only five votes for the majority, and one of them joined on the "understanding" that the opinion was consistent with her lengthy concurrence. The opinion is arguably dictum with respect to everything but layoff quotas, and it is entangled in procedural disputes that give additional avenues of attack if five justices decide to get rid of it. The issue of relief for plaintiffs who can't be identified as victims will be with us for a long time.

NOTES ON PARTIALLY IDENTIFIABLE VICTIMS

1. In the fluid class recovery and affirmative action cases, the victims are often impossible to identify. In another important set of cases, the victims can be partly identified. A good example is Hameed v. International Association of Bridge, Structural & Ornamental Iron Workers,

Local Union No. 396, 637 F.2d 506 (8th Cir. 1980). Admission to membership in Local 396 was through an apprentice program that traditionally barred blacks. When the Civil Rights Act of 1964 banned employment discrimination, the union dropped its explicit racial barrier. At about the same time, it adopted a new system for admitting applicants to the apprentice program. The new system had twelve criteria, many of which tended to unnecessarily exclude minorities. The court of appeals eventually held that the new selection system was also illegal. But by that time, it had been in use for many years. What remedy for applicants denied admission under the new system?

2.   *Hameed* presents a common problem in employment discrimination litigation. Plaintiffs are identifiable victims in the sense that we know they were rejected on the basis of discriminatory selection criteria, or that those criteria deterred them from applying. But plaintiffs are not identifiable in the sense that we know they would have been admitted to the apprentice program but for the discrimination. We don't know what criteria the union would have used if it had not used the illegal criteria. Ordering the union to devise a legal selection method, and then applying that method retroactively to see which of the plaintiffs would have been selected, is not very attractive. That approach would involve long delays, because designing legal selection criteria is difficult. And applying those new criteria to decisions made ten or twenty years before would be a grossly uncertain proposition.

In cases where the employer or union had nondiscriminatory selection criteria but didn't apply them to minorities, it is theoretically possible to reconstruct the rightful work history of every applicant and employee. But in practice, this effort often bogs down in "a quagmire of hypothetical judgments." Pettway v. American Cast Iron Pipe Co., 494 F.2d 211, 262 n.152 (5th Cir. 1974). "To assume that employee #242 would have been promoted in three years to such-and-such job instead of employee #354 is so speculative as to unfairly penalize employee #354." Id.

3.   The remedy in cases like *Hameed* and *Pettway* has been pro rata back pay. The basic technique is to determine how much the group of black applicants would have earned but for discrimination. Then, all blacks who had a chance to be selected share in that award pro rata. Where the employer's work force is small and the legitimate hiring and promotion criteria relatively clear, the preferred remedy is to reconstruct actual work histories and award back pay to the plaintiff who would have gotten the job.

4.   There are many ways to prorate in these cases. Courts typically assume that blacks and whites would have had proportionate success under nondiscriminatory criteria, but there is nothing inherent about that assumption. Some courts examine the experience of the whole group; other courts extrapolate from a small sample. Plaintiffs may or may not be divided into subgroups by date of application or job applied

for. All procedures for estimating back pay to the group are uncertain, but no more so than in lost profits cases. What is unique is the ability to identify a small group that contains the victims without being able to identify the victims.

5. Should the courts deny relief in these cases because no plaintiff can show it's more likely than not he would have been selected but for discrimination? But note that these plaintiffs can show a lot more than the beneficiary of a hiring quota. Any black applicant may benefit from a quota, no matter how clear it is that he wasn't around at the time of the discrimination being remedied. Plaintiffs in *Hameed* and similar cases were the targets of the discrimination being remedied, and it's nearly certain some of them would have been admitted but for the discrimination. As long as the employer does not have to pay for the same vacancy more than once, isn't a pro rata payment to all the potential victims the best approximation of the rightful position?

6. Suppose the courts wrote the opinions this way: No one has shown that he lost an apprenticeship. But all plaintiffs lost the opportunity to be fairly considered. That opportunity is worth the pay plaintiff would have earned as an apprentice, discounted by the risk of not being selected. So pro rata back pay is the value of the lost opportunity to be fairly considered. Is that explanation easier to reconcile with the traditional focus on the rightful position?

There is a technical obstacle to that explanation. The statute authorizes "back pay" and "other equitable relief"; it does not authorize damages. 42 U.S.C. §2000e-5(g) (1982). The limitation to equitable relief is designed to avoid jury trial, for fear that white juries might nullify the statute. To make the scheme work, Congress and the courts have said that back pay is equitable restitution. Whether or not that is plausible, compensation for loss of an opportunity to be considered is surely damages, and thus not within the statute.

7. Similar issues arise in other areas. Toxic tort cases often involve a class of plaintiffs who were exposed to a pollutant and have a disease that is caused by the pollutant but also has other causes. It is often nearly certain that many of the plaintiffs would not have gotten the disease but for defendant's pollution, but it can be impossible to tell which ones.

A good example is Allen v. United States, 588 F. Supp. 247 (D. Utah 1984). The government exploded nuclear weapons in the open air in the 1950s and early 1960s. Two decades later, there were unusually high rates of cancer and other radiation related diseases in communities downwind from the test site. *Allen* was a consolidated action involving nearly 1,200 of these disease victims. The district court granted recovery to those plaintiffs who lived in the affected area between 1951 and 1962, and whose disease was of a type caused by radiation. He awarded compensation in ten of the twenty-four test cases initially tried. Apparently these plaintiffs will get full compensation, not pro rata compensation as in *Hameed*. It seems nearly certain that the government will appeal.

8. The partially identifiable victim can also be thought of as the statistical plaintiff. All the black applicants in *Hameed*, and all the cancer victims in *Allen*, could show a statistical chance that they would have been much better off but for defendant's wrongdoing. When the problem is conceived in that way, it can arise in situations with only one possible victim. A recurring example that has split the courts is negligent failure to diagnose cancer or other serious disease. An example is Herskovits v. Group Health Cooperative, 99 Wash. 2d 609, 664 P.2d 474 (1983). Herskovits would have had a 39 percent chance of survival if defendant had not negligently failed to diagnose his lung cancer; by the time another doctor made the diagnosis, his chance of survival was down to 25 percent. Two justices thought a jury could hold defendant liable for the death, but that damages should be limited to those "caused directly by premature death, such as lost earnings and additional medical expenses, etc." What does that mean? Maybe they meant to exclude loss of society. Four justices thought a jury could hold defendant liable for the reduced chance of survival and award prorated death damages; it was not clear whether they meant to allow 14 or 39 percent of usual damages. Three justices would not have allowed any recovery at all. What would you do on remand with that set of opinions?

COURI v. COURI
103 Ill. App. 3d 445, 431 N.E.2d 711 (1982)

Justice HEIPLE delivered the opinion of the court.

The plaintiff, Joseph Couri, and his brother, Anthony Couri, the defendant, jointly operated the Couri Brothers Supermarket. Plaintiff sought an accounting from the defendant for his share of that business. The trial court ordered Anthony Couri to pay $122,690 and convey his interest in a tract of real property to plaintiff. Defendant appeals. Joseph Couri cross-appeals, seeking to increase the amount of the judgment.

The business agreement, or lack thereof, which is the genesis of this controversy spans two generations. This cause, transpiring over almost a decade, consumed the services of several firms of attorneys and two judges. As are many causes involving disgruntled siblings who seek to resolve their economic differences in court, this action has featured uncompromising enmity. The facts follow.

The Couri family opened their supermarket on December 22, 1928, in Peoria. It was a family run business. Everyone helped out. Defendant began working full-time in 1931, a year out of high school: plaintiff worked full-time beginning in 1935. In 1938 the parties' father left the business due to poor health. He died two years later. Anthony, Joseph, and Peter Couri, all brothers, opened the Couri Brothers Supermarket in 1941. They agreed to share equally in the control of the enterprise and its profits and losses for an indefinite period. The agreement was not memorialized by a writing.

In September 1973, Joseph Couri left the store with the resolution of dissolving the partnership with his brother. Thereafter, defendant changed the locks on the doors and reopened the same business as Couri's Supermarket. In June 1980, a court-appointed receiver wound up the affairs of Couri Brothers Supermarket.

The partnership's bookkeeping is unintelligible and inconsistent with acceptable accounting practices. At the end of each business day a daily report was prepared by each grocery checker. The elements of this report consisted of gross receipts less cash paid out for expenses. In short, the figure represented cash on hand at the end of the day, or at least should have. It seems that large expenses often were paid out by check during the day and such disbursements would be deducted from gross receipts. Also, the partners' draws were taken directly from the register. Prior to 1959 no accounting existed for such draws. After 1959 each partner took what he needed and put a chit in the register with his name and the amount taken. The accuracy of this procedure, or that it was even followed, is somewhat dubious since plaintiff did not make a draw according to it until 1962.

Each month these daily reports were compiled in a monthly summary and thereafter a yearly report. The latter two reports were used for sales tax and federal income tax reporting. The defendant was responsible for these records except from 1947 to 1956 when his sister, Gladys Couri, prepared the daily reports. The defendant for the most part was responsible for depositing the cash receipts of the business. Plaintiff did the store's ordering, paid employees, and often toiled as a butcher in the meat department.

After plaintiff decided to dissolve the partnership in September 1973, he went to settle his differences at defendant's home. They agreed that in the previous 14 years that defendant had overdrawn from the business approximately $88,000 more than plaintiff. Since Joseph Couri wanted to sell the business he requested the account books for the prior two years. Defendant gave him the yearly books and told him he would get the "other figures." These latter totals represented a different set of accounts for the business. In any event, settlement could not be reached as to Joseph Couri's share of the partnership. This petition for an accounting resulted.

Six years of litigation and over a dozen hearings later, the trial court decided the case. It concluded that defendant's calculation of store income of $546,143 was wrong. Instead, the trial judge found that between January 1, 1957 and June 30, 1980, the partnership's income was $750,000. Accordingly, defendant was ordered to pay plaintiff $122,690 based on the difference in the brothers' respective draws from the business and the assets of the partnership.

As could be expected, both parties were dissatisfied, and appeal to this court. Plaintiff claims the accounting is inadequate and should be increased to $327,440 since the partnership's gross profits were $1,094,500 from 1957 to 1980. Also, he contends, Anthony Couri was not entitled to $65,000 compensation as a partnership employee after the partnership was dissolved and before it was wound up on June 30, 1980. Defendant cross-appeals, arguing in the alternative that the judgment be reduced or the cause dismissed. . . .

[W]e cannot agree that fashioning an equitable decree is possible. Therefore, we reverse the decision of the trial court and dismiss the bill for want of equity. . . .

[D]efendant cannot be made to account where no evidence exists from which such reckoning can be made.

Both parties agreed that how much income the partnership received from its incipiency until liquidation could be verified reliably from the "daily reports." Such a concession is open to considerable doubt since those reports resulted in only a cash total for each day tabulated. Such figures did not incorporate any balancing from day to day, nor provide figures for cost of goods sold or merchandise sold on credit, even if their method of computation was precise. We have the credit accounts before us. Such records, which plaintiff kept, were inscribed on the backings of cigarette cartons and cracker boxes. They are undated and consist of a name, no address and various amounts. Additionally, over a 20-year period (1955-1975), slightly more than half of such fundamental business records as the business' checking account statements are in the record. Nor prior to 1959 is any recordkeeping system in evidence as to the respective draws each partner took from the business. Money was taken from the till when needed.

The daily reports, which were restated in the monthly summaries and the yearly books, were destroyed two years after the filing of the instant suit. One of the defendant's children, on the urgings of his mother, cleaned out the garage and the attic of defendant's home while the rest of the family was on vacation. The records were in the attic. Thus, with the destruction of the records, even the question of their dubious trustworthiness has become irrelevant.

Accordingly, the parties attempted to re-create or manufacture those records. The defendant submitted the partnership's tax returns. From 1957 through 1973 the defendant produced 10 or 11 returns, the others having been lost or destroyed. The validity of these returns is highly improbable. Defendant apparently kept two sets of books for the partnership. One represented an actual depiction of the business while the other set was used for tax purposes. The latter books misstated income so that tax liability would be reduced. Quite simply, it's anybody's guess what the business took in. The net income from the store for 1974-1980 was computed from the defendant's personal income tax returns. Also, the parties submitted affidavits indicating their calculations as to what the income of the business was from 1957-1980. Defendant indicated the business generated $546,143 in income during such period. His conclusion was not supported by any schedules. Plaintiff, based on compilations made by his nephew, a certified accountant, testified that total payouts made by the partnership were $666,647. Plaintiff contends the imputed net income of the business during this time was $1,442,000. No method existed to verify the draws of either party other than their recollections. The accountant's report had been based on the suspect partnership tax returns, affidavits by each party, and various amounts paid by the partnership to financial institutions concerning other real estate purchases by the brothers. The accountant admitted he had no idea whether any of the reports were correct. The trial court ruled the actual net income of the grocery store for the years 1957 to June 30, 1980, was $750,000. This figure was the basis for calculating plaintiff's award.

The findings of a trial judge will not be disturbed unless against the manifest weight of the evidence. Where the record, however, is barren of evidence to support the trial judge's decision, a judgment based on such decision cannot stand. The record fails to reveal any facts which support the trial judge's conclusion, or his method of computation, that $750,000 was the actual net income of the business over the relevant period. The figure was pure guesswork, perhaps motivated by the trial court's propensity to end an interminable dispute rather than state with certainty an amount actually owed. Although justice is not an exact science, neither can judicial remedies be formed from arbitrary reasoning or calculations. Because plaintiff's award was based on the trial court's determination of the business' actual net income, the judgment which was the result of such erroneous calculation is equally wrong.

An accounting cannot be formulated because the data necessary for such a computation has been destroyed. Although the records from 1971-75 are arguably complete to make some type of accounting, most of the figures the records provide are misstatements. Defendant testified that he understated business income as well as the cost of goods sold during that period. Although the parties have made an effort to extrapolate the truth by re-creating such records, their effort is infected by supposition and hypothesis. Neither is a suitable benchmark for judicial decision-making.

Plaintiff argues that due to the large amount of payouts made by the partnership or the defendant between 1957-1980, it can be determined what income was necessary to make such payments. The infirmity of this reasoning is the fact that both parties had considerable real estate investments as tenants in common which were separate ventures from the supermarket partnership. Such purchases occurred over the life of the partnership, and the business served as the vehicle through which payment was made on the various financing arrangements on these properties. Also, Anthony Couri's statement that his draws exceeded his brother's by $88,000 is nothing more than a fact. Because he withdrew more does not mean he was not entitled to do so. Maybe he had it coming. Perhaps the money was spent on the real estate ventures. Nobody can tell. Over the 37 years the partnership existed, half of that time no system existed of measuring draws against the partnership assets.

We recognize defendant had a duty to account to plaintiff concerning the parties' respective shares. In other words, he had the burden of production. Where no accounts exist it is impossible to say how much is due one party or the other. Nonetheless, defendant's inability to produce does not relieve plaintiff of the ultimate burden of persuasion on the issue of the amount of his share. (Fineman v. Goldberg (1928), 319 Ill. 507, 512.) Attempting to make records or manufacture evidence will not suffice. Once the daily reports were innocuously swept away by a teenager obeying his parent, the accounting for this partnership became not only impracticable, but unattainable. The myriad exhibits, the voluminous, often rambling transcript, and the speculation of the trial judge groping for a resolution, make this abundantly evident.

For the reasons stated, we reverse the judgment of the Circuit Court of Peoria County and dismiss the petition for an accounting.

Reversed.

BARRY and STOUDER, JJ., concur.

MORE NOTES ON PRACTICALITY AND MONEY REMEDIES

1. The Supreme Court of Illinois reversed. 95 Ill. 2d 91, 447 N.E.2d 334 (1983). It relied heavily on the fact that defendant had been responsible for keeping the partnership records; their inadequacy was a breach of his fiduciary duty and all resulting doubts were resolved against him. The Supreme Court said that under the circumstances, the trial court was not "required to detail the nature or method of its calculations."

The Appellate Court had relied on Fineman v. Goldberg, 319 Ill. 507, 161 N.E. 57 (1928). *Fineman* denied an accounting on the ground that "the evidence leaves the account in such doubt and uncertainty that the court is unable to say whether anything is due from either party and how much." Id. at 512, 161 N.E. at 59. The Supreme Court distinguished *Fineman* on two grounds. In *Fineman*, plaintiff had been responsible for keeping the records during his time as a partner. Unfortunately for that rationale, at the time of trial defendant had had possession of the records and refused to produce them. Second, the Supreme Court said that the records in *Couri* were better: "the evidence . . . is not in such a state of uncertainty that it is impossible to determine whether any amount is due." 95 Ill. 2d at 99, 447 N.E.2d at 337. Impossibility may depend on how badly the court wants to grant relief. In a case like *Couri*, the outcome may depend on whether the court is left with a feeling that plaintiff is surely owed something.

2.   In *Couri*, the arguable impracticality of compensation arose out of evidence problems. Damages can also look impractical because of conceptual problems. One of the early wrongful life cases was decided on the ground that it was logically impossible to measure damages:

> This Court cannot weigh the value of life with impairments against the nonexistence of life itself. By asserting that he should not have been born, the infant plaintiff makes it logically impossible for a court to measure his alleged damages because of the impossibility of making the comparison required by compensatory remedies.

Gleitman v. Cosgrove, 49 N.J. 22, 28, 227 A.2d 689, 692 (1967).

3.   Are cases like *Couri* and *Gleitman* just extreme examples of uncertain damages? Is *Gleitman* just an extreme example of a value not measurable in dollars? Isn't it just as impossible to value pain and suffering "logically"? If we can all imagine suffering so bad we would rather be dead, then can't we measure Gleitman's claim as well as we can measure pain and suffering? The later wrongful life cases tend to say that it is against public policy to hold that plaintiff would be better off dead. Is that a better rationale for the result?

NOTES ON APPROACHES TO PRACTICALITY PROBLEMS

1.   One approach to practicality problems is like General Grant's proposal to "fight it out on this line if it takes all summer." The courts of appeals in *Bradley* and *Morgan*, the two school cases, took that approach. Sometimes this approach works, sometimes it fails, sometimes it ends in disaster. Judge Garrity toughed it out in Boston and things calmed down; despite the continued remands, there wasn't much more that could be done in Detroit. The trial court's efforts to complete the accounting in *Couri* also suggest this approach. But another military analogy also comes to mind: the suggestion in the late 1960s that we withdraw from Vietnam and claim we won. The court came up with a number, but there can't be much pretense that it was the right number. But is it closer to the truth than zero was?

Another approach is to avoid risks. *Northern Delaware* denies specific performance because trouble might result. That keeps the court out of messy situations, but it also denies relief in cases where a remedy could have been effective.

An intermediate approach is to take risks but cut losses. The trial court in *Bradley*, and the courts of appeals in *Eisen* and *Couri*, were willing to enter a case and stick with it a long ways, but were also willing to admit defeat and abandon further efforts.

Is any one of these approaches preferable to the others? Or is it all a matter of the odds of success and the costs of denying the remedy? Should there be more deference to trial judges on such practical matters? Or are reversals appropriate because the strength of commitment to particular policy goals is also at stake?

2. A court can accomplish more if it is willing to innovate. Receivers and masters, mini-hearings and fluid class recoveries, quota hiring and prorated back pay are all efforts to create practical remedies when traditional remedies break down. But there are risks to open-ended innovation, and reasons for confining judicial discretion. Is there any reliable way to recognize when an innovation is too threatening to other values, such as due process, democratic control, or individualized justice?

3. Are all these problems so fact specific that any attempt to generalize is doomed?

B. DRAFTING DECREES

INTRODUCTORY NOTES

1. One key to smooth implementation is a well-drafted judgment. A simple damage judgment on a general verdict for a single plaintiff is relatively easy to draft, although a careless lawyer can mess it up. Other judgments are more complex. Injunctions, declaratory judgments, and class action judgments always require very careful drafting. The judge generally asks the parties to draft a decree for his approval. If necessary, a good judge will throw out both parties' drafts and do his own, but he prefers not to. Plaintiff's lawyer can usually write the decree if he does it competently and doesn't overreach. That is an important tactical opportunity; you shouldn't forfeit it with sloppy drafting.

2. In this section you will get to draft an injunction. There are several things to keep in mind as you draft. Perhaps most important is Federal Civil Rule 65(d), and corresponding state rules:

> Every order granting an injunction and every restraining order shall set forth the reasons for its issuance; shall be specific in terms; shall describe in reasonable detail, and not by reference to the complaint or other document, the act or acts sought to be restrained. . . .

In addition, there is the rule that the injunction should not forbid wrongful acts unlike those already committed or threatened. We first encountered Rule 65(d) and the rule against overbroad injunctions at 227-229 supra. Re-read those notes before drafting your own injunction.

3.   There are tactical considerations as well as formal rules. Plaintiff wants an injunction to leave no loopholes for future evasion. He wants it sufficiently precise that contempt sanctions are a meaningful possibility. The problem is highlighted by the Boston School Committee's announcement that it would obey only "direct orders." See Morgan v. McDonough, supra at 767. Sometimes defendants will observe the spirit of the decree, but you can't count on that.

NOTES ON THE REQUIREMENT THAT INJUNCTIONS BE SPECIFIC

1.   Defendants get two chances to attack the specificity of an injunction. They can appeal the order entering the injunction on the ground that it violates Rule 65(d). Or, they can defend the contempt citation on the ground that the injunction failed to specify what they were supposed to do or refrain from doing. In criminal contempt, the collateral bar rule prevents defendants from raising errors in the injunction at the contempt stage. See Walker v. City of Birmingham, supra at 656. But they can still raise specificity claims, on the ground that the violation could not have been willful if defendant could not understand the injunction.

2.   Sloppy drafters might take comfort from McComb v. Jacksonville Paper Co., 336 U.S. 187 (1949). The injunction in *McComb* repeated the minimum wage, overtime pay, and record keeping provisions of the Fair Labor Standards Act, and ordered defendant to comply. Defendant evaded the injunction in imaginative ways; the district court found that defendant used a "false and fictitious" method of computing compensation. But it refused to hold defendant in contempt. Because nothing in the injunction specifically forbad those computations, the trial court thought the violations were not willful. Instead, it amended the injunction to forbid such computations in the future.

The court of appeals affirmed, but the Supreme Court reversed. The Court said that if an injunction is ambiguous, defendant can seek clarification; if he doesn't, he's in contempt if he guesses wrong. That's what *McComb* says, but don't rely too heavily. Consider the circumstances, and the costs to plaintiff. In the first place, lack of specificity always creates a litigable issue that might have been avoided. In *McComb*, that issue went all the way to the Supreme Court. It doesn't usually go that far, but any extra litigation is expensive. And clients don't like to pay you to litigate the meaning of something you could have written more clearly.

Second, the government won in *McComb* because it had the advantage of an injunction as broad as the statute. And the Court noted that the pattern of past violations was broad enough to justify such an injunction. Broad language tends to wipe out errors of underinclusiveness; vagueness or ambiguity in a narrow injunction is much more dangerous to plaintiffs.

Third, although the Court did not formally reject the finding that the violations in *McComb* were not willful, it seems not to have doubted defendant's bad faith. The Court did not view this as a case in which defendant might plausibly have thought its conduct was not forbidden. Willfulness was not required, because the contempt proceeding was civil, not criminal. Indeed, the remedy was limited to compensation. The employees could have sued for compensation under the statute without regard to the injunction.

Fourth, and perhaps most important, the injunction was probably as clear as it could be under the circumstances. It was not possible for the government or the trial court to imagine all the possible ways of violating the act and specifically enjoin each one. The Court feared an endless succession of evasive schemes, none of which would be contempt in the view of the lower courts. That concern has little force in cases where the ambiguity could have been avoided.

Justices Frankfurter and Rutledge dissented. They thought injunctions should be strictly enforced, but that "to be both strict and indefinite is a kind of judicial tyranny." They thought that general language was always dangerous, because it could be plausibly interpreted after the fact to apply to conduct not contemplated when the injunction was issued.

3. *McComb* is the leading case, but other cases have been more sympathetic to defendant's claims that an injunction is ambiguous or not specific. Some examples:

a. Vertex Distributing v. Falcon Foam Plastics, 689 F.2d 885 (9th Cir. 1982). Vertex owned the Falcon Foam trademark, and it sued Falcon Foam for infringement. The case settled and the court entered a consent decree ordering Falcon Foam not to use its corporate name "or any colorable imitation" for promotional purposes. The dispute at the contempt hearing turned on the following exception in the original decree:

> defendants may do business using a trade name which includes the word FALCON providing, however, that when defendants use a trade name incorporating FALCON therein, defendants shall include a falcon bird perched on the "F" of FALCON wherever possible and practical and, in particular, on signs, delivery vehicle markings, letterheads, packaging, product markings, advertising materials, business cards, and Telephone Directory Yellow pages listings.

Defendants thereafter used the name Falcon. They generally included the bird perched on the F. They included the bird logo in large Yellow Pages ads, but omitted it from small Yellow Pages ads. At the contempt hearing, defendants argued that it was not "possible and practical" to include the bird logo in small ads. Plaintiff disagreed. Plaintiff also argued that defendants could not use the name Falcon alone, but only as part of a longer trade name that "includes" the word Falcon.

The court found no contempt. It held that the "possible and practical" language was ambiguous, and that defendants' interpretation was not unreasonable. It issued a clarifying order requiring the bird logo in all Yellow Pages ads henceforth. It held that defendants could use the name Falcon alone, because the decree did not require them to make it part of a longer name. The court was obviously impressed by defendants efforts to comply with the decree.

Did plaintiff get all that it bargained for? Didn't the consent decree already say that it was feasible to include the bird logo in all Yellow Pages ads? What about the other issue? Is "Falcon" a "trade name which includes the word Falcon"? If the parties meant to require that some other word always be used with Falcon, what should they have said?

b.   United States v. Joyce, 498 F.2d 592 (7th Cir. 1974). Joyce was an American, and a corporate officer of a British insurance company that did some business in the United States. The court ordered Joyce to use "his best offices" to produce the corporation's records for inspection by the Internal Revenue Service. The court of appeals held that injunction too vague to support a conviction for criminal contempt. In the alternative, it held that he was not guilty because it was impossible for him to get the documents.

Might the district court have used the "best offices" language to avoid the risk of ordering Joyce to do the impossible? Should the injunction specify the steps Joyce should take to try to get the documents? Would a "best offices" injunction support a finding of civil contempt?

4.   Some jurisdictions take the view of Justice Frankfurter's dissent and require extraordinary specificity in injunctions. Texas is a good example. Consider Ex parte Carpenter, 566 S.W.2d 123 (Tex. Civ. App. 1978). Carpenter's divorce decree ordered him to "timely pay for any medical, dental, and hospital charges with respect to the child to the extent such charges and expenses exceed in-force insurance coverage on such child." The trial court ordered Carpenter imprisoned for ten days and until he purged himself of contempt by paying $650 in back child support and $391 in medical bills. The court of appeals held that "timely" was fatally ambiguous and would not support a finding of contempt. And because a single penalty had been imposed for the child support and the medical bills, the judgment also had to be reversed with respect to the back child support.

The case is typical of the Texas approach to construing injunctions. The decision rests solely on the abstract judgment that "timely" is "imprecise and subjective," and not on any facts specific to the case. The opinion does not indicate whether the medical bills were a few days old or months old; the court does not seem to care whether defendant has acted on any reasonable interpretation of "timely." Nor does the court say that a higher standard is required because the ten-day fixed penalty is a criminal punishment.

Do the procedural shortcuts of a contempt citation justify that kind of strict construction, remitting plaintiff to an independent suit or a motion to clarify if the injunction is not perfectly clear? Or do cases like *Carpenter* just allow defendants to defy injunctions and defend their contempt with word games?

5. Consider one more example. Here is part of what Chief Justice Burger called the "remarkable injunction" in Allee v. Medrano, 416 U.S. 802, 846 (1974) (dissenting). The injunction was entered to prevent the Texas Rangers and other law enforcement officials from abusing and intimidating organizers for a union, the United Farm Workers:

16. It is further ordered, adjudged and decreed by the Court that Defendants, their successors, agents and employees, and persons acting in concert with them, are permanently enjoined and restrained from any of the following acts or conduct directed toward or applied to Plaintiffs and the persons they represent, to-wit:

A. Using in any manner Defendants' authority as peace officers for the purpose of preventing or discouraging peaceful organizational activities without adequate cause.

B. Interfering by stopping, dispersing, arresting, or imprisoning any person, or by any other means, with picketing, assembling, solicitation, or organizational effort without adequate cause.

C. Arresting any person without warrant or without probable cause which probable cause is accompanied by intention to present appropriate written complaint to a court of competent jurisdiction.

D. Stopping, dispersing, arresting or imprisoning any person without adequate cause because of the arrest of some other person.

E. As used in this Paragraph 16, Subparagraphs A, B, and D above, the term 'adequate cause' shall mean (1) actual obstruction of a public or private passway, road, street, or entrance which actually causes unreasonable interference with ingress, egress, or flow of traffic; or (2) force or violence, or the threat of force or violence, actually committed by any person by his own conduct or by actually aiding, abetting, or participating in such conduct by another person; or (3) probable cause which may cause a Defendant to believe in good faith that one or more particular persons did violate a criminal law of the State of Texas other than those specific laws herein declared unconstitutional, or a municipal ordinance.

416 U.S. at 811-812 n.7.

The Chief Justice had many objections to this injunction. Most important, he thought it would not "provide meaningful relief," because contempt proceedings "' would be far too cumbersome and heavy-handed to deal effectively with large numbers of violations.'" 416 U.S. at 858, quoting Comment, The Federal Injunction as a Remedy for Unconstitutional

Police Conduct, 78 Yale L.J. 143, 147 (1968). Justices White and Rehnquist joined the dissent. The majority opinion focused on whether plaintiffs were entitled to any injunction at all, and seemed untroubled by the form and drafting of the injunction.

Are "peaceful organizational activities," "adequate cause," "probable cause," and "good faith" any more specific than the terms that caused trouble in notes 2 and 3 — "possible and practical," "best offices," and "timely"? Does the definition of "adequate cause" solve the problem? It at least helps, and defining terms is often a useful drafting technique.

Is there any way to make this injunction more specific? Is there any way of controlling the enjoined conduct that is less "cumbersome and heavy-handed" than contempt citations?

NOTES ON THE RULE AGAINST INCORPORATING OTHER DOCUMENTS

1. The court in the Washington fishing litigation tried to allocate the fish harvest between thousands of Indian and non-Indian fishers; we first encountered it when we considered how to bind third parties to obey decrees. The injunction also raised difficult drafting problems. Here is the key part of that ingenious injunction:

> 1. All Puget Sound and other marine waters easterly of Donilla Point-Tatoosh line and their watersheds, all Olympic Peninsula watersheds, and all Grays Harbor and its watersheds are hereby closed to all net salmon fishing except during such times and such specific waters as are opened by State or tribal regulations or regulations of the United States conforming to the orders of this Court in this case.
>
> 2. All reef net, gill net and purse seine fishermen licensed by the State of Washington, all other persons who attempt to net or assist in netting salmon in the waters described in paragraph 1, the Puget Sound Gillnetters Association, the Purse Seine Vessel Owners Association, the Grays Harbor Gillnetters Association and all persons in active concert or participation with them are hereby enjoined and prohibited from engaging in taking, possessing, or selling salmon of any species taken from such waters, unless such person has first ascertained from the Washington Department of Fisheries telephone "hot-line," 1-800-562-5672 or 1-800-562-5673, that the area to be fished is open for fishing by non-treaty fishermen at the time the individual intends to fish, *provided*, that this provision shall not apply to persons exercising treaty fishing rights in accordance with the orders of this Court.
>
> 3. The defendant State of Washington is directed to maintain a continuous telephone hot-line service free of charge to any caller from within the State of Washington to provide information on areas within the waters described in paragraph 1 of this order that are open to net salmon fishing by non-treaty fishermen in conformity with the orders of this Court. The defendant

shall furnish to this Court and to the United States Attorney a transcript of the daily hot-line messages.

The court of appeals approved the injunction in Puget Sound Gillnetters Association v. United States District Court, 573 F.2d 1123 (9th Cir. 1978), *vacated on other grounds sub nom.* Washington v. Washington State Commercial Passenger Fishing Vessel Association, 443 U.S. 658 (1979). Subsequently, individual defendants in contempt citations attacked the validity of the injunction. Here is the court of appeals' response:

> All that the injunction requires a fisherman to do is to call the hot-line before going fishing, and then to refrain from fishing in any area which the hot-line tells him is closed. We find paragraph 2 clear, concise, and comprehensible. That is the only paragraph that Dolman was required to obey. We find nothing in paragraph 1 that conflicts with paragraph 2. Paragraph 1 does not purport to authorize fishing in waters declared open by state or tribal or United States regulations. It merely declares that all relevant waters are closed except those opened by such regulations. But it does not do what counsel says it does, that is, require fishermen to know those regulations and follow them. Instead, all it requires is, in paragraph 2, that the fisherman comply with what the hot-line tells him about open or closed waters. If the hot-line tells him that an area is closed, he is not to fish there; if it tells him that an area is open, he may fish there.
>
> The injunction is as specific as the nature of the subject matter — regulation of fishing in Puget Sound — permits.

United States v. Olander, 584 F.2d 876, 880-881 (9th Cir. 1978), *vacated on other grounds sub nom.* Dolman v. United States, 443 U.S. 914 (1979).

Did defendants make the wrong argument? The court is persuasive that the state regulations weren't improperly incorporated into the injunction. But was the hot-line recording improperly incorporated?

Certainly the injunction is not guilty of the abuses at which the incorporation rule was aimed. It does not say, "Don't do any of the things described in the complaint," and it does not do anything that raises comparable vagueness problems. It is hard to see how this injunction could work without the hot line. Yet inescapably, the conduct forbidden is described by reference to something outside the injunction. Might the rule mean hot-line recordings are simply not an available option? Or is it dispositive that the court did the best it could under the circumstances? Does it help to say the telephone recording is not a "document"? (Re-read Rule 65(d).)

If you're uncomfortable with just saying best efforts is good enough, how about this more technical argument: If the court wrote down the contents of each new recording on the hot line, it could produce a new supplemental injunction. And the first injunction could order all fishers to stop by the courthouse and pick up the latest supplemental injunction before going to the water. If that were done, it would surely be OK to also make a hot-line recording available for the convenience of those who chose to use it. If you believe that no one would come to the courthouse rather than call the hot line, then exclusive reliance on the hot line looks like harmless error at most.

2.   Do injunctions to obey the law raise incorporation problems as well as specificity problems? Don't they incorporate the statute and related regulations, and require defendants to know the contents of those external documents? Is that OK because defendants are presumed to know the law anyway? That wasn't the view of the court of appeals in the Washington fishing cases.

One of the contempt charges in *McComb* was that defendants had classified employees as executives in disregard of the relevant regulations. Was there any way to avoid construing the injunction in light of the underlying law? Should the court copy the regulations into every injunction? Classify defendant's employees and specifically list those that are exempt? Classifying all the employees may be burdensome, but isn't the injunction supposed to individuate the law's command? On the other hand, isn't it illusory to think that any injunction can be understood without knowledge of some additional information from somewhere?

Consider the injunction in Allee v. Medrano, discussed in the preceding set of notes. That injunction ordered the Texas Rangers not to arrest Farm Workers without "probable cause." Can defendants know what that injunction means without knowing something about the thousands of precedents on the meaning of probable cause? That doesn't mean the precedents are improperly incorporated does it?

Despite these conceptual problems, I don't know of any cases invalidating obey-the-law injunctions on the ground that they incorporate another document. Most of the litigation is in terms of specificity, ambiguity, and fair notice.

DRAFTING YOUR OWN INJUNCTION

Before drafting your own injunction, you should read the rest of this section and consider the examples of how other drafters responded to difficult situations. You might also want to look at other injunctions reprinted elsewhere in the book. See Adelman v. CGS Scientific Corp., supra at 743, NLRB v. Blevins Popcorn Co., supra at 640, and FMC Corp. v. Varro International, Inc., supra at 219-220.

Try drafting an injunction for Meyer v. Brown & Root Construction Co., 661 F.2d 369 (5th Cir. 1981). *Meyer* is an employment discrimination case; the facts are set out below. Assume that the case was filed as a class action, so that the birth of the named plaintiff's child does not moot the case. And don't worry about the details of employment discrimination law. It is enough to know that the statute reads as follows:

> It shall be . . . unlawful . . . for an employer . . . to discriminate against any individual . . . because of such individual's . . . sex. . . .

42 U.S.C. §2000e-2(a) (1982).

> The terms "because of sex" or "on the basis of sex" include . . . because or on the basis of pregnancy, childbirth, or related medical conditions; and women affected by pregnancy, childbirth, or related medical conditions shall be treated the same for all employment-related purposes . . . as other persons not so affected but similar in their ability or inability to work. . . .

42 U.S.C. §2000e(k) (1982).

You can assume that the statute has been interpreted literally and has no hidden meaning, and that the court is right in finding the employer's conduct to be a violation. Your goal is to forbid discrimination of the sort experienced by Mary Beth Meyer, without giving female employees more protection than the statute requires. Try to describe as precisely as possible what it is you are forbidding. Here are the facts:

> Mary Beth Meyer, a white female, was hired by the Brown and Root Company on July 30, 1976 for employment at its Glen Rose construction site. She was classified as a warehouse helper; her initial duties included coding equipment and furniture and issuing warehouse tickets when equipment arrived. Approximately two years later, she was given the additional duties of preparing accounting records, reports, and inventories. The nature of her position required that she split her workday between the warehouse and the office but she was not engaged in the inventory of heavy equipment in the field after the middle of 1978. In July of 1978, plaintiff was married and in September she informed her supervisor that she was pregnant. She was informed that she would be granted a leave of absence for her pregnancy when she was ready. It is undisputed that Meyer had a good work record and good working relationship with her co-workers at all times during her tenure at Brown & Root.
>
> On January 9, 1979, Meyer arrived at work to find a new person sitting at her desk. She had been informed the day before this that she would be training an individual to replace her during her leave, but was not told that the replacement had actually been hired. When she arrived at work the following day, her supervisor ordered her to clear out her desk because she was going to work in the warehouse. She immediately questioned the supervisor concerning the nature of her duties in the warehouse. He informed her at this point, "you're going to work with Ed and Phil." This concerned plaintiff since the individuals referred to performed heavy manual labor of a type which would be impossible for her to perform without risking harm both to herself and her unborn child. When she told her supervisor of her concern in this regard, he simply snickered. After further discussion, it became clear to plaintiff that he was unconcerned about this problem so she informed her supervisor that she was

quitting. On the termination interview form, Meyer checked the box next to the designation "unable to perform assigned duties" and added that her job duties had been changed. Her employer's representative stated on the form that she had resigned because of her pregnancy. . . .

Despite the testimony of Meyer's supervisor to the effect that only plaintiff's office location was changed, the district court found that the woman hired to replace plaintiff was assigned only clerical duties, leaving plaintiff with the heavier warehouse work. Not only were plaintiff's duties altered but she was denied the opportunity, given to other temporarily disabled workers, of doing lighter work until she recovered from the disability. The court concluded that if she had continued working for defendant she would have faced a reasonable probability of injury to herself and her unborn child. Plaintiff was therefore forced to resign because of this intolerable situation. The district court ordered judgment for the plaintiff in the amount of $23,620 in back pay, $3,500 in attorney fees, and an order enjoining defendant from engaging in this unlawful practice in the future.

CHAPTER 10

Some Problems of Locating the Rightful Position

A. LITIGATION EXPENSES

ALYESKA PIPELINE SERVICE CO. v. WILDERNESS SOCIETY
421 U.S. 240 (1975)

Mr. Justice White delivered the opinion of the Court.

This litigation was initiated by respondents Wilderness Society, Environmental Defense Fund, Inc., and Friends of the Earth in an attempt to prevent the issuance of permits by the Secretary of the Interior which were required for the construction of the trans-Alaska oil pipeline. The Court of Appeals awarded attorneys' fees to respondents against petitioner Alyeska Pipeline Service Co. based upon the court's equitable powers and the theory that respondents were entitled to fees because they were performing the services of a "private attorney general." . . .

I

A major oil field was discovered in the North Slope of Alaska in 1968. In June 1969, the oil companies constituting the consortium owning Alyeska submitted an application to the Department of the Interior for rights-of-way for a pipeline that would transport oil from the North Slope across land in Alaska owned by the United States, a major part of the transport system which would carry the oil to its ultimate markets in the lower 48 States. . . .

Respondents brought this suit in March 1970, and sought declaratory and injunctive relief against the Secretary of the Interior on the grounds that he intended to issue the right-of-way and special land-use permits in violation of §28 of the Mineral Leasing Act of 1920, 30 U.S.C. §185, and without compliance with the National Environmental Policy Act of 1969 (NEPA), 42 U.S.C. §4321 et seq. On the basis of both the Mineral Leasing Act and the NEPA, the District Court granted a preliminary injunction against issuance of the right-of-way and permits.

Subsequently the State of Alaska and petitioner Alyeska were allowed to intervene. On March 20, 1972, the Interior Department released a six-volume Environmental Impact Statement and a three-volume Economic and Security Analysis. After a period of time set aside for public comment, the Secretary announced that the requested permits would be granted to Alyeska. Both the Mineral Leasing Act and the NEPA issues were at that point fully briefed and argued before the District Court. That court then decided to dissolve the preliminary injunction, to deny the permanent injunction, and to dismiss the complaint.

Upon appeal, the Court of Appeals for the District of Columbia Circuit reversed, basing its decision solely on the Mineral Leasing Act. Finding that the NEPA issues were very complex and important, that deciding them was not necessary at that time since pipeline construction would be enjoined as a result of the violation of the Mineral Leasing Act, that they involved issues of fact still in dispute, and that it was desirable to expedite its decision as much as possible, the Court of Appeals declined to decide the merits of respondents' NEPA contentions which had been rejected by the District Court.

Congress then enacted legislation which amended the Mineral Leasing Act to allow the granting of the permits sought by Alyeska and declared that no further action under the NEPA was necessary before construction of the pipeline could proceed.

With the merits of the litigation effectively terminated by this legislation, the Court of Appeals turned to the questions involved in respondents' request for an award of attorneys' fees.[13] Since there was no applicable statutory authorization for such an award, the court proceeded to consider whether the requested fee award fell within any of the exceptions to the general "American rule" that the prevailing party may not recover attorneys' fees as costs or otherwise. The exception for an award against a party who had acted in bad faith was inapposite, since the position taken by the federal and state parties and Alyeska "was manifestly

---

13. Respondents' bill of costs includes a total of 4,455 hours of attorneys' time spent on the litigation.

reasonable and assumed in good faith. . . . " Application of the "common benefit" exception which spreads the cost of litigation to those persons benefiting from it would "stretch it totally outside its basic rationale. . . . " The Court of Appeals nevertheless held that respondents had acted to vindicate "important statutory rights of all citizens . . . ;" had ensured that the governmental system functioned properly; and were entitled to attorneys' fees lest the great cost of litigation of this kind, particularly against well-financed defendants such as Alyeska, deter private parties desiring to see the laws protecting the environment properly enforced. Title 28 U.S.C. §2412 was thought to bar taxing any attorneys' fees against the United States, and it was also deemed inappropriate to burden the State of Alaska with any part of the award. But Alyeska, the Court of Appeals held, could fairly be required to pay one-half of the full award to which respondents were entitled for having performed the functions of a private attorney general. . . .

II

In the United States, the prevailing litigant is ordinarily not entitled to collect a reasonable attorneys' fee from the loser. We are asked to fashion a far-reaching exception to this "American Rule"; but having considered its origin and development, we are convinced that it would be inappropriate for the Judiciary, without legislative guidance, to reallocate the burdens of litigation in the manner and to the extent urged by respondents and approved by the Court of Appeals.

At common law, costs were not allowed; but for centuries in England there has been statutory authorization to award costs, including attorneys' fees. Although the matter is in the discretion of the court, counsel fees are regularly allowed to the prevailing party.[18] . . .

In 1853, Congress undertook to standardize the costs allowable in federal litigation. . . . The result was a far-reaching Act specifying in detail the nature and amount of the taxable items of cost in the federal courts. One of its purposes was to limit allowances for attorneys' fees that were to be charged to the losing parties. . . . The 1853 Act was carried forward . . . in the Revised Code of 1948 as 28 U.S.C. §§1920 and 1923(a). Under §1920, a court may tax as costs the various items specified, including the "docket fees" under §1923(a). That section provides that "[a]ttorney's and proctor's docket fees in courts of the United States may

---

18. ". . . It is now customary in England, after litigation of substantive claims has terminated, to conduct separate hearings before special 'taxing Masters' in order to determine the appropriateness and the size of an award of counsel fees. To prevent the ancillary proceedings from becoming unduly protracted and burdensome, fees which may be included in an award are usually prescribed, even including the amounts that may be recovered for letters drafted on behalf of a client." Fleischmann Distilling Corp. v. Maier Brewing Co., 386 U.S. 714, 717 (1967).

be taxed as costs as follows. . . . ." [The statute then lists specific sums for specific services. The amounts were inadequate even in 1853, and inflation has made them trivial. The recoverable fee for a trial is $20.] Against this background, this Court understandably declared in 1967 that with the exception of the small amounts allowed by §1923, the rule "has long been that attorney's fees are not ordinarily recoverable. . . ." *Fleischmann Distilling Corp.*, 386 U.S., at 717.

To be sure, the fee statutes have been construed to allow, in limited circumstances, a reasonable attorneys' fee to the prevailing party in excess of the small sums permitted by §1923. In Trustees v. Greenough, 105 U.S. 527 (1882), the 1853 Act was read as not interfering with the historic power of equity to permit the trustee of a fund or property, or a party preserving or recovering a fund for the benefit of others in addition to himself, to recover his costs, including his attorneys' fees, from the fund or property itself or directly from the other parties enjoying the benefit. That rule has been consistently followed. Also, a court may assess attorneys' fees for the "willful disobedience of a court order . . . as part of the fine to be levied on the defendant," Fleischmann Distilling Corp. v. Maier Brewing Co., supra, at 718; or when the losing party has "acted in bad faith, vexatiously, wantonly, or for oppressive reasons. . . ." *F.D. Rich Co.*, 417 U.S., at 129. These exceptions are unquestionably assertions of inherent power in the courts to allow attorneys' fees in particular situations, unless forbidden by Congress, but none of the exceptions is involved here. . . .

Congress has not repudiated the judicially fashioned exceptions to the general rule against allowing substantial attorneys' fees; but neither has it retracted, repealed, or modified the limitations on taxable fees contained in the 1853 statute and its successors. Nor has it extended any roving authority to the Judiciary to allow counsel fees as costs or otherwise whenever the courts might deem them warranted. What Congress has done, however, while fully recognizing and accepting the general rule, is to make specific and explicit provisions for the allowance of attorneys' fees under selected statutes granting or protecting various federal rights. These statutory allowances are now available in a variety of circumstances, but they also differ considerably among themselves. Under the antitrust laws, for instance, allowance of attorneys' fees to a plaintiff awarded treble damages is mandatory. In patent litigation, in contrast, "[t]he court in *exceptional* cases *may* award reasonable attorney fees to the prevailing party." 35 U.S.C. §285 (emphasis added). Under Title II of the Civil Rights Act of 1964, 42 U.S.C. §2000a-3(b), the prevailing party is entitled to attorneys' fees, at the discretion of the court, but we have held that Congress intended that the award should be made to the successful plaintiff absent exceptional circumstances. Newman v. Piggie Park Enterprises, Inc., 390 U.S. 400, 402 (1968). Under this scheme of things, it is apparent that the circumstances under which attorneys' fees are to be awarded and the range of discretion of the courts in making those awards are matters for Congress to determine.

It is true that under some, if not most, of the statutes providing for the allowance of reasonable fees, Congress has opted to rely heavily on private enforcement to implement public policy and to allow counsel fees so as to encourage private litigation. . . . But congressional utilization of the private-attorney-general concept can in no sense be construed as a grant of authority to the Judiciary to jettison the traditional rule against nonstatutory allowances to the prevailing party and to award attorneys' fees whenever the courts deem the public policy furthered by a particular statute important enough to warrant the award.

Congress itself presumably has the power and judgment to pick and choose among its statutes and to allow attorneys' fees under some, but not others. But it would be difficult, indeed, for the courts, without legislative guidance, to consider some statutes important and others unimportant and to allow attorneys' fees only in connection with the former. If the statutory limitation of right-of-way widths involved in this case is a matter of the gravest importance, it would appear that a wide range of statutes would arguably satisfy the criterion of public importance and justify an award of attorneys' fees to the private litigant. And, if *any* statutory policy is deemed so important that its enforcement must be encouraged by awards of attorneys' fees, how could a court deny attorneys' fees to private litigants in actions under 42 U.S.C. §1983 seeking to vindicate *constitutional* rights? Moreover, should courts, if they were to embark on the course urged by respondents, opt for awards to the prevailing party, whether plaintiff or defendant, or only to the prevailing plaintiff? Should awards be discretionary or mandatory? Would there be a presumption operating for or against them in the ordinary case?[39]

§1983

---

39. Mr. Justice Marshall, after concluding that the federal courts have equitable power which can be used to create and implement a private-attorney-general rule, attempts to solve the problems of manageability which such a rule would necessarily raise. To do so, however, he emasculates the theory. . . . The theory that he would adopt is not the private-attorney-general rule, but rather an expanded version of the common-fund approach to the awarding of attorneys' fees. When Congress has provided for allowance of attorneys' fees for the private attorney general, it has imposed no such common-fund conditions upon the award. The dissenting opinion not only errs in finding authority in the courts to award attorneys' fees, without legislative guidance, to those plaintiffs the courts are willing to recognize as private attorneys general, but also disserves that basis for fee shifting by imposing a limiting condition characteristic of other justifications.

That condition ill suits litigation in which the purported benefits accrue to the general public. In this Court's common-fund and common-benefit decisions, the classes of beneficiaries were small in number and easily identifiable. The benefits could be traced with some accuracy, and there was reason for confidence that the costs could indeed be shifted with some exactitude to those benefiting. In this case, however, sophisticated economic analysis would be required to gauge the extent to which the general public, the supposed beneficiary, as distinguished from selected elements of it, would bear the costs. The Court of Appeals, very familiar with the litigation and the parties after dealing with the merits of the suit, concluded that "imposing attorneys' fees on Alyeska will not operate to spread the costs of litigation proportionately among these beneficiaries. . . ." . . .

As exemplified by this case itself, it is also evident that the rational application of the private-attorney-general rule would immediately collide with the express provision of 28 U.S.C. §2412. . . . If, as respondents argue, one of the main functions of a private attorney general is to call public officials to account and to insist that they enforce the law, it would follow in such cases that attorneys' fees should be awarded against the Government or the officials themselves. Indeed, that very claim was asserted in this case. But §2412 on its face, and in light of its legislative history, generally bars such awards, which, if allowable at all, must be expressly provided for by statute, as, for example, under Title II of the Civil Rights Act of 1964, 42 U.S.C. §2000a-3(b). . . .

We do not purport to assess the merits or demerits of the "American Rule" with respect to the allowance of attorneys' fees. It has been criticized in recent years, and courts have been urged to find exceptions to it. It is also apparent from our national experience that the encouragement of private action to implement public policy has been viewed as desirable in a variety of circumstances. But the rule followed in our courts with respect to attorneys' fees has survived. It is deeply rooted in our history and in congressional policy; and it is not for us to invade the legislature's province by redistributing litigation costs in the manner suggested by respondents and followed by the Court of Appeals.

The decision below must therefore be reversed.

So ordered.

MR. JUSTICE DOUGLAS and MR. JUSTICE POWELL took no part in the consideration or decision of this case.

MR. JUSTICE BRENNAN, dissenting.

I agree with Mr. Justice Marshall that federal equity courts have the power to award attorneys' fees on a private-attorney-general rationale. Moreover, for the reasons stated by Judge Wright in the Court of Appeals, I would hold that this case was a proper one for the exercise of that power. As Judge Wright concluded:

> Acting as private attorneys general, not only have [respondents] ensured the proper functioning of our system of government, but they have advanced and protected in a very concrete manner substantial public interests. An award of fees would not have unjustly discouraged [petitioner] Alyeska from defending its case in court. And denying fees might well have deterred [respondents] from undertaking the heavy burden of this litigation.

161 U.S. App. D.C. 446, 456, 495 F.2d 1026, 1036.

MR. JUSTICE MARSHALL, dissenting.

In reversing the award of attorneys' fees to the respondent environmentalist groups, the Court today disavows the well-established power of federal equity courts to award attorneys' fees when the interests of justice so require. While under the traditional American Rule the courts ordinarily refrain from allowing attorneys' fees, we have recognized several judicial exceptions to that rule for classes of cases in which equity seemed to favor fee shifting. . . . I see no basis in precedent or policy for holding that the courts cannot award attorneys' fees where the interests of justice require recovery, simply because the claim does not fit comfortably within one of the previously sanctioned judicial exceptions to the American Rule. The Court has not in the past regarded the award of attorneys' fees as a matter reserved for the Legislature, and it has certainly not read the docketing-fees statute as a general bar to judicial fee shifting. The Court's concern with the difficulty of applying meaningful standards in awarding attorneys' fees to successful "public benefit" litigants is a legitimate one, but in my view it overstates the novelty of the "private attorney general" theory. The guidelines developed in closely analogous statutory and nonstatutory attorneys' fee cases could readily be applied in cases such as the one at bar. . . .

I

A

Contrary to the suggestion in the Court's opinion, our cases unequivocally establish that granting or withholding attorneys' fees is not strictly a matter of statutory construction, but has an independent basis in the equitable powers of the courts. In Sprague v. Ticonic National Bank, 307 U.S. 161 (1939), the lower courts had denied a request for attorneys' fees from the proceeds of certain bond sales, which, because of petitioners' success in the litigation, would accrue to the benefit of a number of other similarly situated persons. This Court reversed, holding that the allowance of attorneys' fees and costs beyond those included in the ordinary taxable costs recognized by statute was within the traditional equity jurisdiction of the federal courts. . . .

> Plainly the foundation for the historic practice of granting reimbursement for the costs of litigation other than the conventional [statutory] taxable costs is part of the original authority of the chancellor to do equity in a particular situation.

Id., at 166.

In more recent cases, we have reiterated the same theme: while as a general rule attorneys' fees are not to be awarded to the successful litigant, the courts as well as the Legislature may create exceptions to that rule. . . . While the Court today acknowledges the continued vitality of these exceptions, it turns its back on the theory underlying them, and on the generous construction given to the common-benefit exception in our recent cases.

In Mills v. Electric Auto Lite Co., 396 U.S. 375 (1970), we found the absence of statutory authorization no barrier to extending the common-benefit theory to include nonmonetary benefits as a basis for awarding fees in a stockholders' derivative suit. Discovering nothing in the applicable provisions of the Securities Exchange Act of 1934 to indicate that Congress intended "to circumscribe the courts' power to grant appropriate remedies," 396 U.S., at 391, we concluded that the District Court was free to determine whether special circumstances would justify an award of attorneys' fees and litigation costs in excess of the statutory allotment. Because the petitioners' lawsuit presumably accrued to the benefit of the corporation and the other shareholders, and because permitting the others to benefit from the petitioners' efforts without contributing to the costs of the litigation would result in a form of unjust enrichment, the Court held that the petitioners should be given an attorneys' fee award assessed against the respondent corporation.

We acknowledged in *Mills* that the common-fund exception to the American Rule had undergone considerable expansion since its earliest applications in cases in which the court simply ordered contribution to the litigation costs from a common fund produced for the benefit of a number of nonparty beneficiaries. The doctrine could apply, the Court wrote, where there was no fund at all, id., at 392, but simply a benefit of some sort conferred on the class from which contribution is sought. Id., at 393-394. As long as the court has jurisdiction over an entity through which the contribution can be effected, it is the fairer course to relieve the plaintiff of exclusive responsibility for the burden. Finally, we noted that even where it is impossible to assign monetary value to the benefit conferred, "the stress placed by Congress on the importance of fair and informed corporate suffrage leads to the conclusion that, in vindicating the statutory policy, petitioners have rendered a substantial service to the corporation and its shareholders." Id., at 396. The benefit that we discerned in *Mills* went beyond simple monetary relief: it included the benefit to the shareholders of having available to them "an important means of enforcement of the proxy statute." Ibid.

Only two years ago, in a member's suit against his union under the "free speech" provisions of the Labor-Management Reporting and Disclosure Act, we held that it was within the equitable power of the federal courts to grant attorneys' fees against the union, since the plaintiff had conferred a substantial benefit on all the members of the union by vindicating their free speech interests. Hall v. Cole, 412 U.S. 1 (1973). Because a court-ordered award of attorneys' fees in a suit under the free speech provision of the LMRDA promoted Congress' intention to afford meaningful protection for the rights of employees and the public generally, and because without provision of attorneys' fees an aggrieved union member would be unlikely to be able to finance the necessary litigation, id., at 13, the Court held that the allowance of counsel fees was "consistent with both the [LMRDA] and the historic equitable power of federal courts to grant such relief in the interests of justice." Id., at 14.

In my view, these cases simply cannot be squared with the majority's suggestion that the availability of attorneys' fees is entirely a matter of statutory authority. The cases plainly establish an independent basis for equity courts to grant attorneys' fees under several rather generous rubrics. The Court acknowledges as much when it says that we have independent authority to award fees in cases of bad faith or as a means of taxing costs to special beneficiaries. But I am at a loss to understand how it can also say that this independent judicial power succumbs to Procrustean statutory restrictions — indeed, to statutory silence — as soon as the far from bright line between common benefit and public benefit is crossed. I can only conclude that the Court is willing to tolerate the "equitable" exceptions to its analysis, not because they can be squared with it, but because they are by now too well established to be casually dispensed with.

B

The tension between today's opinion and the less rigid treatment of attorneys' fees in the past is reflected particularly in the Court's analysis of the docketing-fees statute, 28 U.S.C. §1923, as a general statutory embodiment of the American Rule. While the Court has held in the past that Congress can restrict the availability of attorneys' fees under a particular statute either expressly or by implication, see Fleischmann Distilling Corp. v. Maier Brewing Co., 386 U.S. 714 (1967), it has refused to construe §1923 as a plenary restraint on attorneys' fee awards.

Starting with the early common-fund cases, the Court has consistently read the fee-bill statute of 1853 narrowly when that Act has been interposed as a restriction on the Court's equitable powers to award attorneys' fees. In Trustees v. Greenough, 105 U.S. 527 (1881), the Court held that the statute imposed no bar to an award of attorneys' fees from the fund collected as a result of the plaintiff's efforts, since:

> [The fee bill statute addressed] only those fees and costs which are strictly chargeable as between party and party, and [did not] regulate the fees of counsel and other expenses and charges as between solicitor and client. . . . And the act contains nothing which can be fairly construed to deprive the Court of Chancery of its long-established control over the costs and charges of the litigation, to be exercised as equity and justice may require. . . .

Id., at 535-536.

In *Sprague*, supra, the Court again applied this distinction in recognizing "the power of federal courts in equity suits to allow counsel fees and other expenses entailed by the litigation not included in the ordinary taxable costs recognized by statute." 307 U.S., at 164. . . . Whether this award was collected out of a fund in the court or through an assessment against the losing party in the litigation was not deemed controlling. Id., at 166-167; *Mills*, 396 U.S., at 392-394.

More recently, the Court gave its formal sanction to the line of lower court cases holding that the fee statute imposed no restriction on the equity court's power to include attorneys' fees in the plaintiff's award when the defendant has unjustifiably put the plaintiff to the expense of litigation in order to obtain a benefit to which the latter was plainly entitled. Vaughan v. Atkinson, 369 U.S. 527 (1962). *Vaughan* noted that the question was not one of "costs" in the statutory sense, since the attorneys' fee award was legitimately included as a part of the primary relief to which the plaintiff was entitled, rather than an ancillary adjustment of litigation expenses. . . .

In sum, the Court's primary contention — that Congress enjoys hegemony over fee shifting because of the docketing-fee statute and the occasional express provisions for attorneys' fees — will not withstand even the most casual reading of the precedents. . . .

II

The statutory analysis aside, the Court points to the difficulties in formulating a "private attorney general" exception that will not swallow the American Rule. I do not find the problem as vexing as the majority does. In fact, the guidelines to the proper application of the private-attorney-general rationale have been suggested in several of our recent cases, both under statutory attorneys' fee provisions and under the common-benefit exception. . . . The reasonable cost of the plaintiff's representation should be placed upon the defendant if (1) the important right being protected is one actually or necessarily shared by the general public or some class thereof; (2) the plaintiff's pecuniary interest in the outcome, if any, would not normally justify incurring the cost of counsel; and (3) shifting that cost to the defendant would effectively place it on a class that benefits from the litigation.

There is hardly room for doubt that the first of these criteria is met in the present case. Significant public benefits are derived from citizen litigation to vindicate expressions of congressional or constitutional policy. As a result of this litigation, respondents forced Congress to revise the Mineral Leasing Act of 1920 rather than permit its continued evasion. The 1973 amendments impose more stringent safety and liability standards, and they require Alyeska to pay fair market value for the right-of-way and to bear the costs of applying for the permit and monitoring the right-of-way.

Although the NEPA issues were not actually decided, the lawsuit served as a catalyst to ensure a thorough analysis of the pipeline's environmental impact. Requiring the Interior Department to comply with the NEPA and draft an impact statement satisfied the public's statutory right to have information about the environmental consequences of the project, and also forced delay in the construction until safeguards could be included as conditions to the new right-of-way grants. . . .

The second criterion is equally well satisfied in this case. Respondents' willingness to undertake this litigation was largely altruistic. While they did, of course, stand to benefit from the additional protections they sought for the area potentially affected by the pipeline, the direct benefit to these citizen organizations is truly dwarfed by the demands of litigation of this proportion. Extensive factual discovery, expert scientific analysis, and legal research on a broad range of environmental, technological, and land-use issues were required. The disparity between respondents' direct stake in the outcome and the resources required to pursue the case is exceeded only by the disparity between their resources and those of their opponents — the Federal Government and a consortium of giant oil companies.

Respondents' claim also fulfills the third criterion, for Alyeska is the proper party to bear and spread the cost of this litigation undertaken in the interest of the general public. . . .

Before the Department and the courts, Alyeska advocated adoption of the position taken by Interior, playing a major role in all aspects of the case. This litigation conferred direct and concrete economic benefits on Alyeska and its principals in affording protection of the physical integrity of the pipeline. If a court could be reasonably confident that the ultimate incidence of costs imposed upon an applicant for a public permit would indeed be on the general public, it would be equitable to shift those costs to the applicant. In this connection, Alyeska, as a consortium of oil companies that do business in 49 States and account for some 20% of the national oil market, would indeed be able to redistribute the additional cost to the general public. In my view the ability to pass the cost forward to the consuming public warrants an award here. The decision to bypass Congress and avoid analysis of the environmental consequences of the pipeline was made in the first instance by Alyeska's principals and not the Secretary of the Interior. The award does not punish the consortium for these actions but recognizes that it is an effective substitute for the public beneficiaries who successfully challenged these actions. Since the Court of Appeals held Alyeska accountable for a fair share of the fees to ease the burden on the public-minded citizen litigators, I would affirm the judgment below.

NOTES ON PLAINTIFF'S ATTORNEYS' FEES

1. *Alyeska* is the leading case; it definitively recommits the federal judiciary to the American rule for the foreseeable future. Yet it is not an especially good case for testing the underlying question. We will return to *Alyeska*, but let's start with a simpler situation. Suppose Smith cuts

$1,000 worth of timber from Brown's forest. Suppose Brown's lawyer works very efficiently, gets a summary judgment, collects the judgment on the first writ of execution, and sends Brown a bill for $500. Has Brown been restored to the position he would have occupied but for the wrong? Isn't it perfectly clear that he is out $500 and the remedy is undercompensatory?

Moreover, there's an excellent chance that the remedy will cost more than $1,000 and Brown will wind up worse off than if he had swallowed the original loss. Foreseeing that risk, his attorney may advise him that it isn't worth going to trial for only $1,000. But it may be worth bluffing, because Smith faces the risk of paying much more than $1,000 to his attorney. If Smith cut $100,000 worth of timber, it is much less likely that Brown's attorneys' fees would exceed the amount in controversy, although it is not impossible the way some big firms run the meter. Whatever the ratio of fees to judgment, plaintiff is undercompensated if he has to pay his own attorneys' fees.

2. The analysis is substantially the same if Brown hears about Smith's plans in time to get an injunction. If he must spend $500 to save $1,000 worth of timber, he winds up $500 worse off; the injunction has not kept him in the position he would have occupied but for the threatened wrong.

3. Why do we tolerate such a substantial deviation from the usual rule that plaintiff is to be restored to his rightful position? One answer is that we don't tolerate it as much as we used to; exceptions continue to proliferate. The more responsive answers are summarized in Fleischmann Distilling Corp. v. Maier Brewing Co., 386 U.S. 714 (1967). You saw *Fleischmann* in chapter 6; plaintiff recovered defendants' profits from trademark infringement. The lower courts also awarded attorneys' fees under a trademark exception to the American rule. The Supreme Court disapproved the exception:

> In support of the American rule, it has been argued that since litigation is at best uncertain one should not be penalized for merely defending or prosecuting a lawsuit, and that the poor might be unjustly discouraged from instituting actions to vindicate their rights if the penalty for losing included the fees of their opponents' counsel. Also, the time, expense, and difficulties of proof inherent in litigating the question of what constitutes reasonable attorney's fees would pose substantial burdens for judicial administration.

Id. at 718.

Of these two reasons, the fear of deterring litigation has plainly predominated. We will explore that fear in the next principal case. But first, we should explore the exceptions discussed in *Alyeska*.

4. One other question about the general rule: The principal objection to the American rule is that it is undercompensatory. Is that objection irrelevant in restitution cases, where plaintiffs aren't seeking compensation?

NOTES ON THE COMMON BENEFIT RULE

1. The court of appeals in *Alyeska* built on a recognized exception to the American rule, the common benefit rule. When plaintiff collects attorneys' fees from a common fund, he collects not from defendant, but from other plaintiffs or potential plaintiffs similarly situated. The most common application is in class actions, in which the named plaintiff's attorneys are paid from the class recovery. But if plaintiff recovers a fund in which others will share, it does not matter whether he formally filed on behalf of a class.

2. It doesn't even matter whether plaintiff formally recovers the fund, if it is clear that others similarly situated will recover because of his litigation. In Sprague v. Ticonic National Bank, 307 U.S. 161 (1939), plaintiff successfully sued to recover trust funds from an insolvent bank, asserting a preference over ordinary depositors and other general creditors. Fourteen other trusts were similarly situated, and their beneficiaries were also given preferences on the strength of Sprague's precedent. Sprague was allowed to collect pro rata shares of her attorneys' fees from the other trust funds.

3. So far, the common fund rule is simply a special case of restitution. The plaintiff who paid for the litigation has conferred a substantial benefit on all the others, and they would be unjustly enriched if they were allowed to retain the benefit without paying the costs of producing it. The opposing litigant is at most a stakeholder; the award of fees is not added to the judgment; it is taken out of what the defendant owes the class anyway. Thus, it was quite plausible for the Court to say in Trustees v. Greenough, 105 U.S. 527, 535 (1881), that the 1853 legislation on attorneys' fees does not apply to the common fund doctrine.

4. The common fund doctrine begins to look fictional when the court treats defendant as a proxy for the class of beneficiaries. This happened in Mills v. Electric Auto-Lite Co., 396 U.S. 375 (1970), and Hall v. Cole, 412 U.S. 1 (1973). Justice Marshall describes the reasoning of both cases in his dissent in *Alyeska*. *Mills* was a suit challenging misleading proxy statements. The Court held that all shareholders would benefit from the litigation, and that a fee award against the defendant corporation would in effect be borne by the benefitting shareholders. Similar fee awards are common in shareholder derivative suits. *Hall* was a suit against a union for retaliating against a dissident union member. The Court held that all union members and the union itself would benefit from this vindication of union members' rights of free speech, and that an award of attorneys' fees against the union would in effect be borne by the benefitting members.

5. Is common benefit an adequate explanation for *Hall*? Do you suppose the union members considered themselves benefitted? All of them? Some of them? Plaintiff's friends and supporters? Doesn't it seem likely that many of the "beneficiaries" wished there was a way to make

plaintiff shut up? *Hall* looks a lot like making defendant pay. In fact, defendant did pay. But once the Court held that all the members had received a benefit whether they wanted it or not, it was not unreasonable to say that a fee award against the union spread the cost evenly to all members.

6.   How far would *Hall* have to be extended to change the result in *Alyeska*? Who were the beneficiaries in *Alyeska*? The whole population of the United States? Those who care about the environment? Those who hunt, fish, and backpack in the Alaskan wilderness? Nobody, because the pipeline was built anyway, over plaintiffs' objections?

Does it matter that plaintiffs' one clear victory was on a technicality? The old Mineral Leasing Act limited rights-of-way to fifty-four feet, which is not nearly enough for modern construction methods. Alyeska and the Interior Department tried to get around the obsolete statute by granting a fifty-four-foot permanent right-of-way plus a temporary Special Land Use Permit for the construction period. Plaintiffs got an injunction against the Special Land Use Permit.

Plaintiffs' real objections had nothing to do with the width of the right-of-way. They feared the pipeline would do irreversible environmental damage if it were built at all. Congress disagreed and legislated an end to the case; Congress obviously thought the public interest required that the pipeline be built. But the litigation and resulting legislation resulted in some additional environmental safeguards not included in the original plans, and Congress modernized the Mineral Leasing Act rather than let the executive evade it.

7.   Wouldn't *Hall* support a holding that all of this is irrelevant and that everyone benefitted? If the land belonged to the United States, didn't the United States and every citizen benefit from plaintiffs' attempts to protect it? Even if the United States and many citizens thought they would benefit more from the pipeline?

8.   Alyeska was owned by eight big oil companies with 20 percent of the domestic market. Is there any theory under which their customers were the beneficiaries of plaintiffs' suit? Is there any theory under which those customers benefitted in proportion to their use of petroleum products? *Hall* doesn't go that far, does it?

NOTES ON OTHER EXCEPTIONS TO THE AMERICAN RULE

There are many exceptions to the rule that attorneys' fees can't be recovered. Most of the exceptions are widely observed, but in each case there are dissenting jurisdictions.

1.   *The bad faith litigation exception.* Many jurisdictions impose liability for attorneys' fees unnecessarily incurred because of frivolous or

bad faith litigation. The leading federal case is Vaughan v. Atkinson, 369 U.S. 527 (1962), an unfortunately ambiguous admiralty opinion.

Shipowners owe maintenance and cure — financial support and medical expenses for as long as needed — to any seaman who is injured or becomes sick in the ship's service. The illness need not be job related; strict liability is imposed lest a sick sailor be abandoned far from home. In *Vaughan*, a sailor contracted tuberculosis, and defendant ignored his requests for maintenance and cure. The opinion appears to award attorneys' fees as consequential damages, reasoning that if defendant had paid voluntarily, plaintiff would not have had to hire a lawyer. But it also emphasizes defendant's "recalcitrance" and "callous" response, and subsequent Supreme Court cases have treated it as based on defendant's bad faith.

The court may award fees for bad faith litigation against the opposing lawyer instead of the opposing litigant. Roadway Express v. Piper, 447 U.S. 752 (1980), is the leading case. Plaintiffs' attorneys in *Roadway* filed a class action without consulting their clients, failed to answer interrogatories, failed to produce their clients for depositions, failed to file briefs, and ignored orders from the court. The court dismissed the suit for failure to make discovery, and ordered plaintiffs' attorneys to pay all of defendant's attorneys' fees.

2. *The contempt of court exception.* Another exception allows fees in contempt proceedings. The leading Supreme Court case is again ambiguous. Toledo Scale Co. v. Computing Scale Co., 261 U.S. 399 (1923), is always cited for the general rule that a court may assess fees for wilful disobedience of a court order. The contempt consisted of starting litigation in another forum, and the opinion seems to treat the expense of defending the foreign litigation as consequential damages. Id. at 428. But the statement of the case suggests that plaintiff also recovered his fees for the contempt proceeding. Id. at 402. There is an unambiguous modern example in Cook v. Ochsner Foundation Hospital, 559 F.2d 270 (5th Cir. 1977); many other cases are collected in Annotation, Allowance of Attorneys' Fees in Contempt Proceedings, 55 A.L.R.2d 979 (1955), and the supplements to that annotation. The power to award fees in contempt proceedings is discretionary; plaintiffs are not entitled to them as of right.

3. *Statutory exceptions.* There are well over one hundred federal statutory provisions for attorneys' fees; collectively, they account for a large proportion of federal civil litigation. There are many state fee statutes as well. Many of these statutes are based on the private attorney general theory; fees will encourage plaintiffs to enforce the statute. Congress responded to *Alyeska* with the Civil Rights Attorney's Fees Awards Act of 1976, 42 U.S.C. §1988 (1982). It authorizes fee awards to prevailing parties in actions under the Reconstruction civil rights statutes, Title IX of the Education Amendments of 1972, which forbids sex discrimination in federally aided education, and Title VI of the Civil Rights Act of 1964, which forbids race discrimination in federally aided programs. Titles II

and VII of the Civil Rights Act of 1964, which forbid discrimination in public accommodations and employment, already contained similar fee provisions. Some environmental legislation authorizes fee awards, but not the statutes involved in *Alyeska*.

Other fee statutes are harder to explain. An Arizona statute gives courts discretion to award full or partial attorneys' fees to the prevailing party in contract cases, but not in tort cases. Ariz. Rev. Stat. Ann. §12-341.01 (1982). Texas mandates fees to prevailing plaintiffs in suits to collect payment for services rendered, labor done, or material furnished, suits to recover overcharges on freight or express, suits to recover for lost or damaged freight or express or stock killed or injured, suits on sworn accounts, and suits on oral or written contracts, but only if plaintiff first demands payment and payment is not made within thirty days. Texas Rev. Civ. Stat. Ann. art. 2226 (Vernon 1985 Supp.). It has never been clear to me what that list of cases has in common.

Alaska has the most extensive fee provision, authorizing partial fees in all cases unless the court otherwise directs. Alaska Civil Rule 82.

At the time of *Alyeska*, 28 U.S.C. §2412 precluded fee awards against the United States. The Equal Access to Justice Act, enacted in 1980, changed this rule in complex ways. 28 U.S.C. §2412(b) (1982) provides that "unless expressly prohibited by statute," a court "*may*" award fees to the prevailing party in any civil action by or against the United States or one of its agencies or officials in his official capacity. This section also provides that the United States "*shall*" be liable for fees "to the same extent that any other party would be liable" under the common law or a statute that specifically provides for fees.

In addition, §2412(d) provided that the court "*shall*" award fees against the United States in certain circumstances. §2412(d) applied to businesses with fewer than 500 employees and net worth under $5 million and to individuals with net worth under $1 million who prevailed in non-tort civil actions by or against the United States. Fees could not be awarded if the court found "that the position of the United States was substantially justified or that special circumstances make an award unjust." A substantially identical provision applied to administrative proceedings. 5 U.S.C. §504 (1982).

Sections 2412(d) and 504 expired October 1, 1984. The Ninety-Eighth Congress passed a bill to make them permanent and resolve a dispute about their meaning. The dispute was this: The United States argued that it should be immune from fees if it took a substantially justified position after the lawsuit was filed, even if it had forced litigation by taking a wholly unjustified position administratively. The cases went both ways. The extension bill defined the "position of the United States" to include "the actions and omissions of an agency which led to the litigation." H.R. 5479, 98th Cong., 2d Sess. (1984). President Reagan objected to that definition and vetoed the bill. He said he would sign a simple extension, and further action is expected in the Ninety-Ninth Congress.

4. *The contract exception.* Courts will enforce contractual provisions for reasonable attorneys' fees. Promissory notes routinely provide that the debtor will pay the lender's attorneys' fees if the lender sues on the note. They almost never provide that the lender will pay the debtor's attorneys' fees if the debtor prevails in subsequent litigation. Statutes in California, Oregon, and Washington provide that if any contract provides fees for one party, then either party can recover fees if it prevails. Cal. Civ. Code §1717 (West Supp. 1985); Or. Rev. Stat. §20.096 (1983); Wash. Rev. Code Ann. §4.84.330 (West Supp. 1985). Not too many debtors successfully defend collection actions, but some do, and credit buyers sometimes sue credit sellers for breach of warranty, so there are occasions to apply these provisions.

5. *The family law exception.* It is common to award fees in divorce. One spouse may pay the other's fees as part of the property division, or pursuant to the obligation to support the children and dependent spouse. A leading case is Carle v. Carle, 149 Tex. 469, 234 S.W.2d 1002 (1952).

6. *The collateral litigation exception.* When defendant's wrong involves plaintiff in collateral litigation, plaintiff can recover the expenses of that litigation, including attorneys' fees, as consequential damages. Usually the litigation is with third parties, and some cases say the rule applies only to litigation with third parties. A good example is Highlands Underwriters Insurance Co. v. Elegante Inns, 361 So. 2d 1060 (Ala. 1978). Plaintiff's insurance broker improperly endorsed plaintiff's fire insurance policy, and plaintiff had to sue the insurer for reformation. Plaintiff recovered the fees of the reformation suit from the broker. The most common case arises when a seller of property conceals a cloud on the title, or sells property he doesn't own, and the buyer is forced into litigation with another claimant. The buyer may sue his seller for fraud or breach of warranty, depending on the facts, and recover the expenses of the other litigation. Examples are Nalivaika v. Murphy, 120 Ill. App. 3d 773, 458 N.E.2d 995 (1983), and Spillane v. Corey, 323 Mass. 673, 84 N.E.2d 5 (1949).

You can think of these cases as an exception to the American rule, or as outside its scope. Plaintiff does not recover the fees for his suit to collect damages from the primary wrongdoer — the broker in *Highlands Underwriters*, or the sellers in *Nalivaika* and *Spillane*. He recovers only for the collateral litigation caused by the wrong. But sometimes the collateral litigation is with the primary wrongdoer. An example is Anchor Motor Freight v. International Brotherhood of Teamsters, Local Union No. 377, 700 F.2d 1067, 1071-1072 (6th Cir.), *cert. denied*, 104 S. Ct. 81 (1983). The union alleged that the employer's suit was in breach of a covenant not to sue. Attorneys' fees would be the most obvious damages from such a breach, and the court held that the union could recover fees if it won on the merits. *Toledo Scale,* supra note 2, in which defendant was held in contempt for starting additional litigation in another court, could also be explained by the collateral litigation exception.

7. *The private attorney general exception. Alyeska* squarely rejects the notion of a judicially created exception for private litigants who enforce public policy. That decision is binding with respect to federal claims; it may be persuasive, but is not binding, with respect to state claims. California awards fees on a private attorney general theory for state constitutional claims. Serrano v. Priest, 20 Cal. 3d 25, 43-47, 569 P.2d 1303, 1312-1315 (1977).

8. Cumulatively, these exceptions take a huge bite out of the American rule. Class action fee awards and federal statutory fee provisions have been the most visible. Collection cases and family law cases are much more numerous, but the amounts involved are smaller and they cause less debate. Common law tort cases, including personal injury litigation, are the largest remaining domain of the pure American rule.

FRIEDMAN v. DOZORC
412 Mich. 1, 312 N.W.2d 585 (1981)

[Friedman was a urologist who recommended kidney stone surgery on Leona Serafin. Serafin began to bleed uncontrollably on the operating table and died five days later. Autopsy revealed that she had suffered from a rare, incurable, and uniformly fatal blood disease.

Serafin's administrator filed a medical malpractice suit against Friedman and others. He presented no expert evidence that anyone had failed to exercise due care, and the trial court directed a verdict for defendants at the end of plaintiff's case. The court of appeals affirmed, and the state Supreme Court denied review.

Friedman then filed this suit against Dozorc and Golden, the lawyers who represented Serafin's administrator. He alleged that they had negligently and maliciously caused him damages consisting of attorneys' fees, higher malpractice insurance premiums, the loss of two associates who could not afford the higher malpractice premiums charged all associated with him, damage to reputation, and mental anguish. The trial court dismissed all counts; the court of appeals reversed in part and remanded for trial of the malicious prosecution claim. Dozorc and Golden appealed.]

LEVIN, J. . . .

II

A

Plaintiff and amici in support urge this Court to hold that an attorney owes a present or prospective adverse party a duty of care, breach of which will give rise to a cause of action for negligence. We agree with the circuit judge and the Court of Appeals that an attorney owes no actionable duty to an adverse party. . . .

Plaintiff . . . argues that an attorney's separate duty under the Code of Professional Responsibility to zealously represent a client is limited by the requirement that the attorney perform within the bounds of the law. Acting within the bounds of the law is said to encompass refraining from asserting frivolous claims; this charge upon the profession imposes upon counsel a duty to the public, the courts and the adverse party to conduct a reasonable investigation. Assuming that an attorney has an obligation to his client to conduct a reasonable investigation prior to bringing an action, that obligation is not the functional equivalent of a duty of care owed to the client's adversary. We decline to so transform the attorney's obligation because we view such a duty as inconsistent with basic precepts of the adversary system. . . . [T]he public policy of maintaining a vigorous adversary system outweighs the asserted advantages of finding a duty of due care to an attorney's legal opponent. . . . A decision to proceed with a future course of action that involves litigation will necessarily adversely affect a legal opponent. . . .

[C]reation of a duty in favor of an adversary of the attorney's client would create an unacceptable conflict of interest which would seriously hamper an attorney's effectiveness as counsel for his client. Not only would the adversary's interests interfere with the client's interests, the attorney's justifiable concern with being sued for negligence would detrimentally interfere with the attorney-client relationship. . . . We agree with those courts in other jurisdictions which have relied on the policy of encouraging free access to the courts as a reason for declining to recognize a negligence cause of action in physician countersuits. No appellate court has yet approved such a cause of action. . . .

III

To recover upon a theory of abuse of process, a plaintiff must plead and prove (1) an ulterior purpose and (2) an act in the use of process which is improper in the regular prosecution of the proceeding. Spear v. Pendill, 164 Mich. 620, 623; 130 N.W.343 (1911). . . .

The only act in the use of process that plaintiff alleges is the issuance of a summons and complaint in the former malpractice action. However, a summons and complaint are properly employed when used to institute a civil action, and thus plaintiff has failed to satisfy the second element required in *Spear*, supra, 623, where the Court observed "'[t]his action for abuse of process lies for the improper use of process after it has been issued, not for maliciously causing it to issue.'" . . .

IV

Plaintiff relies upon the same allegations respecting defendants' conduct and their failure to meet professional standards which assertedly constitute negligence in contending that he has pled a cause of action for malicious prosecution. He argues that the question of probable cause in a malicious prosecution action against the attorney for an opposing party turns on whether the attorney fulfilled his duty to reasonably investigate the facts and law before initiating and continuing a lawsuit. If the attorney's investigation discloses that the claim is not tenable, then it is his obligation to discontinue the action. . . .

We agree with defendants that under Michigan law special injury remains an essential element of the tort cause of action for malicious prosecution of civil proceedings. . . .

A

The recognition of an action for malicious prosecution developed as an adjunct to the English practice of awarding costs to the prevailing party in certain aggravated cases where the costs remedy was thought to be inadequate and the defendant had suffered damages beyond the expense and travail normally incident to defending a lawsuit. In 1698 three categories of damage which would support an action for malicious prosecution were identified: injury to one's fame (as by a scandalous allegation), injury to one's person or liberty, and injury to one's property. To this day the English courts do not recognize actions for malicious prosecution of either criminal or civil proceedings unless one of these types of injury, as narrowly defined by the cases, is present.

A substantial number of American jurisdictions today follow some form of "English rule" to the effect that "in the absence of an arrest, seizure, or special damage, the successful civil defendant has no remedy, despite the fact that his antagonist proceeded against him maliciously and without probable cause."[23] A larger number of jurisdictions, some say a majority, follow an "American rule" permitting actions for malicious prosecution of civil proceedings without requiring the plaintiff to show special injury.[24]

---

23. 52 Am. Jur. 2d, supra, §10, p.192. The Reporter's Note at 5 Restatement Torts, 2d, Appendix, §674, p.438, identifies 16 states which require some form of special injury in order to support an action for wrongful civil proceedings. O'Toole v. Franklin, 279 Or. 513, 518, fn. 3, 569 P.2d 561 (1977), lists the same 16 states and adds Kentucky.

24. 52 Am. Jur. 2d, supra, §10, p.193; Prosser, Torts (4th ed.), §120, p.853. The Reporter's Note, supra, lists 30 states which purportedly follow this majority rule. O'Toole v. Franklin, supra, pp. 518-519, fn. 4, 569 P.2d 561, identifies 23 states.

Since the Reporter's Note and O'Toole differ over the categorization of Kentucky (see fn. 23, supra), and both include Michigan (see part IVB of this opinion) as a "majority rule" state, the classification of the states does not appear to be entirely reliable.

B

The plaintiff's complaint does not allege special injury. We are satisfied that Michigan has not significantly departed from the English rule and we decline to do so today. . . .

C . . .

Most commentators appear to favor abrogation of the special injury requirement to make the action more available and less difficult to maintain. Their counsel should, however, be evaluated skeptically. The lawyer's remedy for a grievance is a lawsuit, and a law student or tort professor may be particularly predisposed by experience and training to see the preferred remedy for a wrongful tort action as another tort action. In seeking a remedy for the excessive litigiousness of our society, we would do well to cast off the limitations of a perspective which ascribes curative power only to lawsuits.

We turn to a consideration of Dean Prosser's criticisms of the three reasons commonly advanced by courts for adhering to the English rule. First, to the assertion that the costs awarded to the prevailing party are intended as the exclusive remedy for the damages incurred by virtue of the wrongful litigation, Prosser responds that "in the United States, where the costs are set by statute at trivial amounts, and no attorney's fees are allowed, there can be no pretense at compensation even for the expenses of the litigation itself."[35] This argument is compelling, but it does not necessarily justify an award of compensation absent the hardship of special injury or dictate that an award of compensation be assessed in a separate lawsuit. Second, to the arguments that an unrestricted tort of wrongful civil proceedings will deter honest litigants and that an innocent party must bear the costs of litigation as the price of a system which permits free access to the courts, Prosser answers that "there is no policy in favor of vexatious suits known to be groundless, which are a real and often a serious injury."[36] But a tort action is not the only means of deterring groundless litigation, and other devices may be less intimidating to good-faith litigants. Finally, in response to the claim that recognition of the tort action will produce interminable litigation, Prosser argues that the heavy burden of proof which the plaintiff bears in such actions will safeguard bona fide litigants and prevent an endless chain of countersuits. But if few plaintiffs will recover in the subsequent action, one may wonder whether there is any point in recognizing the expanded cause of action. If the subsequent action does not succeed, both parties are left to bear the expenses of two futile lawsuits, and court time has been wasted as well. . . .

35. Prosser, supra, §120, p.851.
36. Id.

[I]f we were to eliminate the special injury requirement, that expansion of the tort of malicious prosecution would not be limited to countersuits against attorneys by aggrieved physicians. . . . In expanding the availability of such an action the Court . . . would arm all prevailing defendants with an instrument of retaliation, whether the prior action sounded in tort, contract or an altogether different area of law.

This is strong medicine — too strong for the affliction it is intended to cure. To be sure, successful defense of the former action is no assurance of recovery in a subsequent tort action, but the unrestricted availability of such an action introduces a new strategic weapon into the arsenal of defense litigators, particularly those whose clients can afford to devote extensive resources to prophylactic intimidation.

At present, a plaintiff and his attorney who know that they have less than an airtight case must, in deciding whether to continue the case or in evaluating a settlement offer, consider whether if they proceed to trial they will invest more and recover less or nothing. If the instant plaintiff's approach is adopted, all plaintiffs and their attorneys henceforth must also weigh the likelihood that if they persevere in the action and receive an unfavorable decision, they will not only take nothing but also be forced to defend an action for malicious prosecution of civil proceedings. Even if the plaintiff and his attorney had abundant cause for bringing and continuing the action and acted without malice, the expense and annoyance foreseeably involved in even a successful defense of the countersuit may induce them to abandon a problematic claim or to settle the case for less than they would otherwise accept. Some will say amen, but this would push the pendulum too far in favor of the defense, more than is necessary to rectify the evil to which this effort is directed.

Because many actions for malicious prosecution of civil proceedings will present questions of fact concerning what measures the former plaintiff and his attorney took, and with what state of mind, the prospect of having the countersuit submitted to a jury capable of returning a large verdict including damages for business loss, injury to reputation and emotional distress will loom large indeed, especially since many parties or attorneys do not have or may be unable to obtain insurance against such liability.

The cost of legal malpractice insurance is bound to increase, assuming coverage against such liability is available. (The currently advertised State Bar group program seems to include such coverage.) Litigators may be excluded from group programs and find that they cannot obtain coverage at reasonable rates. A legal malpractice crisis may arise as serious as the medical malpractice crisis.

Permitting a tort action for wrongful civil proceedings to be maintained absent special injury to the plaintiff could easily generate a surprising number of such actions. Not only doctors, but most defendants, react to a lawsuit with hurt feelings and outrage. They may impute malicious motives to the plaintiff and the opposing attorney and be eager to exact retribution if they prevail. There is no shortage of lawyers who are eager to develop new specialties and would be willing to accept such actions on a contingent fee basis. Some product manufacturers and insurance companies may routinely file countersuits with a view to inhibiting plaintiffs or their attorneys from commencing actions against them or their insureds. The indiscriminate filing of countersuits may lead to actions for wrongfully proceeding with a wrongful civil proceedings action. Embittered litigants whose differences are more emotional than legal will have added opportunities to continue their strife.

The cure for an excess of litigation is not more litigation. Meritorious as well as frivolous claims are likely to be deterred. There are sure to be those who would use the courts and such an expanded tort remedy as a retaliatory or punitive device without regard to the likelihood of recovery or who would seek a means of recovering the actual costs of defending the first action without regard to whether it was truly vexatious.

Other courts have, in the last few years, refused to abandon the special injury requirement [citing cases from Illinois, Oregon, Washington, Rhode Island, and the District of Columbia]. The list of states adhering to the special injury rule includes a number of other major jurisdictions.[42]

V

Apart from special injury, elements of a tort action for malicious prosecution of civil proceedings are (1) prior proceedings terminated in favor of the present plaintiff, (2) absence of probable cause for those proceedings, and (3) "malice," more informatively described by the Restatement as "a purpose other than that of securing the proper adjudication of the claim in which the proceedings are based."[43] . . .

A

The absence of probable cause in bringing a civil action may not be established merely by showing that the action was successfully defended. To require an attorney to advance only those claims that will ultimately be successful would place an intolerable burden on the right of access to the courts.

The Court of Appeals adopted, and plaintiff endorses, the standard for determining whether an attorney had probable cause to initiate and con-

42. The sources cited in fn. 23, supra, agree that New York, Pennsylvania, New Jersey, Maryland, Ohio, Wisconsin and Texas also follow the English rule.
43. Restatement (Second) of Torts §676 (1977).

tinue a lawsuit articulated in Tool Research & Engineering Corp. v. Henigson, 46 Cal. App. 3d 675, 683-684; 120 Cal. Rptr. 291 (1975):

> The attorney is not an insurer to his client's adversary that his client will win in litigation. Rather, he has a duty 'to represent his client zealously . . . [seeking] any lawful objective through legally permissible means . . . [and presenting] for adjudication any lawful claim, issue, or defense.' (ABA, Code of Professional Responsibility, EC 7-1, DR 7-101[A][1]. . . .) So long as the attorney does not abuse that duty by prosecuting a claim which a reasonable lawyer would not regard as tenable or by unreasonably neglecting to investigate the facts and law in making his determination to proceed, his client's adversary has no right to assert malicious prosecution against the attorney if the lawyer's efforts prove unsuccessful. . . .
>
> The attorney's obligation is to represent his client honorably and ethically, and he may, without being guilty of malicious prosecution, vigorously pursue litigation in which he is unsure of whether his client or the client's adversary is truthful, so long as that issue is genuinely in doubt. . . .

In our view, this standard, while well-intentioned, is inconsistent with the role of the attorney in an adversary system.

Our legal system favors the representation of litigants by counsel. Yet the foregoing standard appears skewed in favor of non-representation; the lawyer risks being penalized for undertaking to present the client's claim to a court unless satisfied, after a potentially substantial investment in investigation and research, that the claim is tenable.

A lawyer may be confronted with the choice between allowing the statute of limitation to run upon a claim with which the client has only recently come forward, or promptly filing a lawsuit based on the information in hand. . . .

In medical malpractice actions the facts relevant to an informed assessment of the defendant's liability may not emerge until well into the discovery process. Sometimes the relevant facts are not readily ascertainable. In the instant case, for example, defendants maintain that their efforts to acquire Mrs. Serafin's medical records were rebuffed until they commenced suit and thereupon became able to invoke established discovery procedures and the implicit power of the court to compel disclosure; it may be the practice of some doctors or hospitals to refuse to release medical records until a lawsuit has been commenced.

Moreover, the *Henigson* standard suggests rather ominously that every time a lawyer representing, say, a medical malpractice plaintiff encounters a fact adverse to the client's position or an expert opinion that there was no malpractice, he must immediately question whether to persevere in the action. An attorney's evaluation of the client's case should not be inhibited by the knowledge that perseverance may place the attorney personally at risk; the next fact or the next medical opinion may be the one that makes the case,[50] and such developments may occur even on the eve of trial.

Indeed, a jury-submissible claim of medical malpractice may sometimes be presented even without specific testimony that the defendant physician violated the applicable standard of care. Thus, a lawyer may proceed in the good-faith belief that his proofs will establish a prima facie case of medical malpractice without expert testimony, only to find that the court disagrees. Such conduct is not the equivalent of proceeding without probable cause.

Indeed, whether an attorney acted without probable cause in initiating, defending or continuing proceedings on behalf of a client should not normally depend upon the extent of the investigation conducted. . . .

DR 7-102(A) and the other professional standards to which plaintiff refers consistently incorporate a requirement of scienter as to groundlessness or vexatiousness, not a requirement that the lawyer take affirmative measures to verify the factual basis of his client's position. A lawyer is entitled to accept his client's version of the facts and to proceed on the assumption that they are true absent compelling evidence to the contrary. . . . And, although DR 6-101(A)(2) states that a lawyer shall not "[h]andle a legal matter without preparation adequate in the circumstances," that preparation need not entail verification of the facts related by the client. . . .

B

This Court has said, in opinions addressed to the tort of malicious prosecution, that malice may be inferred from the facts that establish want of probable cause, although the jury is not required to draw that inference. This rule, developed in cases where damages were sought from a layperson who initiated proceedings, fails to make sufficient allowance for the

---

50. Szlinis v. Moulded Fiber Glass Companies, Inc., 80 Mich. App. 55, 263 N.W.2d 282 (1977), *app. dismissed by stipulation* 407 Mich. 893 (1979), . . . illustrates how late-arising developments may provide a plaintiff's lawyer with clear evidence of liability where before there was only suspicion. Four people perished in a boating accident in June, 1969. According to plaintiff-appellant's brief in this Court, the first floating tests and inspections failed to reveal any defects in the hull. Subsequent tests conducted in August and September, 1970 revealed certain abnormalities which of themselves were not striking. It was only in January, 1971, that further tests by naval architects revealed that a combination of defects rendered it virtually impossible to right the boat if it capsized — not an uncommon occurrence in sailing.

In *Szlinis* the complaint was not filed until after the tests were completed. But suppose the complaint had been filed shortly after the accident and subsequent preliminary testing for defects had been unproductive. Had the plaintiff's attorney then evaluated the case in the shadow of a potential tort action or motion to recover litigation expenses by a boat manufacturer claiming injury to business reputation and loss of sales, might he not have decided to discontinue the action rather than conduct additional tests?

lawyer's role as advocate and should not be applied in determining whether a lawyer acted for an improper purpose.

A client's total lack of belief that the action he initiates or continues can succeed is persuasive evidence of intent to harass or injure the defendant by bringing the action. But a lawyer who is unaware of such a client's improper purpose may, despite a personal lack of belief in any possible success of the action, see the client and the claim through to an appropriate conclusion without risking liability. 3 Restatement Torts, 2d, §674, comment d, states:

> An attorney who initiates a civil proceeding on behalf of his client or one who takes any steps in the proceeding is not liable if he has probable cause for his action (see §675); *and even if he has no probable cause and is convinced that his client's claim is unfounded, he is still not liable if he acts primarily for the purpose of aiding his client in obtaining a proper adjudication of his claim.* (See §676.) An attorney is not required or expected to prejudge his client's claim, and although he is fully aware that its chances of success are comparatively slight, it is his responsibility to present it to the court for adjudication if his client so insists after he has explained to the client the nature of the chances.

(Emphasis supplied.) . . .

The Restatement defines the mental element of the tort of wrongful civil proceedings as "a purpose other than that of securing the proper adjudication of the claim in which the proceedings are based." A finding of an improper purpose on the part of the unsuccessful attorney must be supported by evidence independent of the evidence establishing that the action was brought without probable cause.[61]

We affirm that portion of the Court of Appeals decision which upheld summary judgment in favor of defendants on plaintiff's claims sounding in negligence and abuse of process. With respect to plaintiff's claim for malicious prosecution, we reverse the decision of the Court of Appeals and affirm the trial court's grant of summary judgment; we do so on the ground that an action for malicious prosecution of a civil action may not be brought absent special injury and the plaintiff failed to plead special injury.

KAVANAGH, WILLIAMS, and RYAN, JJ., concurred with LEVIN, J.

LEVIN, J. (concurring).

Much of the discussion of the problem of unjustified litigation suffers from an undue focus upon the need to compensate the injury suffered by

---

61. A contingent fee arrangement or the expectation of the attorney that he will ultimately receive a fee for his services is not evidence of an improper purpose. In contrast, a purpose to secure an improper adjudication of the client's claim, as by coercing a settlement unrelated to the merits from an opponent who wishes to avoid the harassment, expense or delay of letting the lawsuit run its course, is an improper purpose. See 3 Restatement Torts, 2d, §674, comment d, p.453.

the defendant subjected to a groundless and malicious action. Groundless civil litigation is, however, more than an affliction visited upon a few scattered individuals; it besets the judicial system as a whole. It is therefore, appropriate to think of it as a systemic problem and to fashion a remedy which preserves and strengthens the integrity of the civil litigation system rather than randomly providing a fortuitous amount of compensation in a handful of isolated cases.

[T]his Court can appropriately devise an approach to wrongful litigation which is capable of providing both an appropriate measure of deterrence and reasonable compensation for wronged litigants without imperiling the right of free access to the courts. The remedy, quite simply, is to recognize the inadequacy of existing provisions for the taxation of costs and to adopt a new and distinct court rule authorizing the judge to whom a civil action is assigned to order payment of the prevailing party's actual expenses, including reasonable attorneys' fees and limited consequential damages, where the action was wrongfully initiated, defended or continued. Depending upon the circumstances, payment might be required of the attorney, the client or both. The factual questions implicit in such an evaluation of the losing side's conduct would be resolved by the judge after a prompt post-termination hearing at which the parties could call witnesses and they and their attorneys could testify. . . .

The sum recoverable should include all fees and administrative charges incurred because of the litigation as well as reasonable attorney's fees. The judge could award a prevailing defendant in a professional malpractice case an additional sum for loss of income-producing time and injury to professional reputation or business resulting from the wrongful action if the amount is capable of being calculated with reasonable certainty.

The rule could provide that the standard to be applied by the judge in determining whether such an award should be made is whether the losing party or his attorney had proceeded without probable cause and for an improper purpose. . . .

Having such a determination made by the judge to whom the original proceeding was assigned would have a number of advantages over assessment of these questions by judge and jury in a separate tort action:

First, a strategy for evaluating the propriety of litigation which is administered exclusively by judges is more susceptible of consistent application and careful supervision than a strategy which relies on a group of laymen chosen at random, often for one day and one trial. . . . Limiting recovery to actual pecuniary loss, thereby eliminating recovery for emotional distress, and relying on a judge to assess damages, combined with the greater control that appellate courts exercise over a judge's findings as compared to a jury's verdict, should tend to avoid awards which might intimidate good-faith litigants.

Second, the judge would usually be familiar with the history of the case; the necessary evidence could be adduced and the relevant findings made in far more efficient fashion than if a new action and a separate trial before a different judge were required.

Third, parties who might be reluctant to initiate further litigation although they felt themselves wronged would be more likely to avail themselves of internal sanctions than of the opportunity to start a separate action which would take its place on the crowded docket and which the defendants would be likely to resist with all available means. . . .

Nothing in the opinion of the Court should . . . be understood as indicating that the Court is unwilling to commit itself to the imposition of sanctions against an attorney where it is appropriate.

WILLIAMS, J., concurred with LEVIN, J.

COLEMAN, C.J. (concurring in part, dissenting in part).

I . . .

Although the majority's stated concern is to protect meritorious claims, it is nowhere contended in the opinion that the special injury requirement serves to distinguish meritorious from frivolous litigation. Nor is there a contention that special injury cases represent injury that is more egregious than in other cases. The majority's position is comprehensible only because of an unstated, although correct, premise: *most litigation does not involve special injury.* . . .

Thus, the arguments that the majority advances in favor of the special injury requirement, in reality, have no basis within the content of the special injury requirement. The same arguments could be advanced as forcefully in favor of abolishing the malicious prosecution action altogether, or even in favor of something so absurd as requiring that all malicious prosecution plaintiffs be from Kansas.

A far more reasonable approach would be to look to other elements of the malicious prosecution cause of action — such as *no probable cause* and an *improper motive* — to provide the necessary protection for bona fide litigants.

However, reliance on an incidental effect of the special injury requirement is not my only objection to the majority position. My colleagues cloud the issue by such statements as, "The cure for an excess of litigation is not more litigation." The issue here is not finding a cure for excessive litigation. *The issue is whether the harm rendered by wrongful litigation is compensable.* . . .

II

Central to this case is the judicial process of weighing two different potential harms. . . . [T]he majority has engaged in much speculation as to what the effects of groundless malicious prosecution suits might be. Little, if any, consideration is given to the harmful effects of other groundless litigation. . . .

If we are to give substance to DR 7-102(A), subds. (1) and (2), which establishes an attorney's duty to the public not to bring frivolous litigation, a viable malicious prosecution action is necessary. . . .

FITZGERALD, J., concurred with COLEMAN, C.J.

BLAIR MOODY, JR., J. (dissenting in part).

I agree with the analysis employed and the result reached by the opinion of the Court, except for part IV which deals with a cause of action for malicious prosecution of civil proceedings. . . .

On balance, the effect which malicious prosecution cases without the special injury requirement would have on access to the courts would be less than the effect which other types of groundless litigation has on society. . . .

A . . .

[O]ur Court today is not bound by explicit decisions that require assertion of the element of special injury. . . .

B

Admittedly, the special injury condition of the "English rule" limits the recovery potential for malicious prosecution of civil proceedings and thereby protects the right of free access to the courts. However, the limitation is too broad. Suits arising out of meritorious as well as vexatious actions are disallowed. The special injury requirement is not logically related to the actual damages incurred by the defendant as a result of a frivolous suit. The injury to reputation or business flowing from any defamatory matter alleged as the basis of the proceedings, and the expense of defending a lawsuit which was brought without probable cause and for an improper purpose do not depend upon a technical interference with person or property. The storekeeper whose property is attached for a few moments certainly suffers no greater injury or harm than the individual whose reputation is tarnished or who suffers a loss of business as a result of a truly vexatious lawsuit.

Furthermore, the requirement of an arrest or seizure of property is in large part an anachronistic one. At an earlier time many actions could be commenced by a writ of *capias ad respondendum*. That writ permitted a civil action to be started by the arrest of the defendant. . . . Civil arrest is now a limited concept and rarely applicable.

The law concerning attachment and garnishment has also changed. See Fuentes v. Shevin, 407 U.S. 67 (1972). The Legislature has abolished, in most situations, attachment and garnishment as prejudgment security devices.

Thus, the likelihood of special injury, as defined by the majority, occurring in a lawsuit brought today is greatly reduced. The element of special injury is now likely to occur in only a limited class and number of cases. . . .

C

The strict requirements of lack of probable cause and malice, i.e., improper purpose, are more appropriate guardians of free access to the courts and of promoting the honest use of the judicial process than the artificial requirement of special injury. . . . Probable cause will be found for bringing or continuing the original action unless counsel proceeded with the knowledge that the client's claim had no factual or legal basis. There should be no requirement that an attorney investigate a claim if the lawyer could reasonably believe the facts to be as alleged by the client. . . .

The element of improper purpose must also be appropriately defined. When a party is sued for malicious prosecution, a jury may infer malice from an absence of probable cause. To permit a jury to infer malice or improper purpose may be appropriate when the defendant is a layperson. However, as explained in 3 Restatement Torts, 2d, §674, comment d, p. 453, it is necessary to make an independent determination of improper purpose when the defendant is the attorney who initiated the original action. . . .

D

As an alternative to a malicious prosecution claim, an ancillary proceeding to occur immediately after judgment in the original action is suggested in a concurring opinion. Such a proposal would offer the advantages of control, availability and efficiency.

However, it may also be anticipated that this procedure could create the potential of adding an ancillary issue to every lawsuit, increase docket congestion, precipitate a conflict of interest between attorney and client, and grant too much power to the trial judge, thereby placing a premium on "judge shopping." The ease of accessibility of such a procedure may increase the likelihood of the prevailing party filing an ancillary proceeding. It could encourage, without reflection or thought, retaliatory claims. Also, since this alternative suggestion would apply to defendant and plaintiff alike, it raises an issue concerning the concept of what is an appropriate defense.

These comments are made only for the purpose of raising initial questions regarding the suggested alternative. This case, nevertheless, raises an issue of significance that should be determined on its own merits. . . .

Accordingly, I would affirm the judgment of the Court of Appeals and remand this cause for further proceedings not inconsistent with this opinion.

NOTES ON DEFENDANT'S ATTORNEYS' FEES

1. *Friedman* is a suit for malicious prosecution, which involves slightly different considerations from a bare request for attorneys' fees. The risk of consequential damages, and especially of liability for emotional distress, would deter more lawsuits than the risk of attorneys' fees. But for plaintiffs of ordinary means, the difference might not be significant. Most personal injury plaintiffs can't pay their own attorneys, and are able to proceed only because of contingent fee arrangements. Now suppose their lawyer said:

> You don't have to pay me if we lose, but you'll have to pay defendant's lawyers, or the insurance company's lawyers. They'll be billing at $150 per hour, and if we go to trial, they may spend hundreds of hours. But don't worry. Even if things go badly we can probably get a settlement that avoids total defeat. And if not, I have a friend who does bankruptcies.

Similarly, Alyeska's fees surely would have bankrupted the Wilderness Society. Many plaintiffs simply couldn't litigate if there were any substantial risk of such liability. Serious claims as well as frivolous ones would be deterred.

2. The risk of liability for malicious prosecution does not deter much litigation, even in states without the anachronistic special injury rule. The reason, of course, is the rest of the *Friedman* opinion, which all the justices agree on. Plaintiff is not liable even for a frivolous suit unless he knows it is frivolous. And his lawyer is not liable even if he does know it's frivolous, unless he also knows his client has some improper motive. A jury can infer the client's improper motive if it finds that he knew the suit was frivolous, but his lawyer apparently is not expected to draw that inference. It is very hard to be found guilty of malicious prosecution. Indeed, if the majority is serious about its view that lawyers can go to trial on untenable claims because something might turn up at the last minute, when could there ever be liability?

3. There is another reason malicious prosecution suits have little deterrent effect. It is burdensome and unwieldy to bring a second lawsuit, with the possibility of a second jury trial. Defendants don't do it very often, and plaintiffs' lawyers don't worry about it much. A provision for awarding attorneys' fees on motion in the original lawsuit has a much greater deterrent effect, even if the substantive standard is based on the

law of malicious prosecution. As a young litigator I was taught never to file a suit under §11 of the Securities Act of 1933, even though it offered plaintiffs some important advantages over the alternative, SEC Rule 10b-5. Under §11, the judge can award fees if he concludes that a claim or defense was "without merit." 15 U.S.C. §77k(e) (1982). A claim is "without merit" only if it is brought in bad faith or "borders on the frivolous"; it is not enough that defendant got a directed verdict. Aid Auto Stores v. Cannon, 525 F.2d 468, 471-472 (2d Cir. 1975). My mentor was a skilled litigator who picked substantial cases from the many that were referred to him. But he thought that no case was strong enough to avoid the risk that some judge would find it "without merit," and that a judgment for defendants' attorneys' fees in a securities fraud case was a risk no client could run. Suits are brought under §11, so not everyone shares his view. And Justice Levin apparently thinks that a risk of liability for fees in the original case will not deter as many lawsuits as a risk of liability for malicious prosecution.

4. Defendant's losses are just as great when the suit is well founded as when it is frivolous. Indeed, he will probably incur more attorneys' fees defending a serious suit. Defendants are almost never restored to the position they would have occupied but for plaintiff's losing lawsuit. Aren't defendants entitled to be made whole too? The problem of defendants' attorneys' fees forces us to choose between two evils: requiring an innocent defendant to suffer substantial losses, or discouraging plaintiff's access to the courts.

5. Probably no other country has a theory of access to the courts as fully developed as ours. Indeed, variations on the English attorneys' fees rule are followed by every industrial democracy except the United States and Japan. Rowe, The Legal Theory of Attorney Fee Shifting: A Critical Overview, 1982 Duke L.J. 651, 651. It is no accident that the English rule discourages litigation. So does the English ban on contingent fee contracts and the smaller size of English damage judgments. The requirement of special injury in malicious prosecution actions serves a quite different purpose in England than in Michigan. The unsuccessful English plaintiff pays defendant's attorneys' fees even if he lost by a whisper, so the restrictions on malicious prosecution actions are not designed to avoid deterring the original lawsuit. Instead, the special damage rule deters the second lawsuit, the malicious prosecution action.

6. Talk of a litigation explosion has brought suggestions that we make losing litigants liable for fees, but *Friedman* is typical of the judicial response. There is some trend to attorneys' fee rules that encourage litigation even more than the American rule, a trend considered in the next set of notes. And although it is easy to collect horrible stories of frivolous lawsuits, and to show that case filings are up, it is hard to show that Americans are generally too quick to litigate. Professor Galanter's survey of empirical studies suggests that contemporary American litigation rates

are not high when compared to the number of grievances resolved some other way, litigation rates in some other countries, or litigation rates at earlier times in our own history. Galanter, Reading the Landscape of Disputes: What We Know and Don't Know (and Think We Know) about Our Allegedly Contentious and Litigious Society, 31 U.C.L.A. L. Rev. 4 (1983).

NOTES ON ONE-WAY FEE SHIFTING

1. It is easy enough to make plaintiffs whole without discouraging them from suing. The solution is to award attorneys' fees to prevailing plaintiffs but not to prevailing defendants. That may seem unfair to defendants. But more and more statutes provide for some variation of that solution.

Some statutes explicitly authorize fees only to prevailing plaintiffs. Federal examples are the antitrust laws, 15 U.S.C. §15 (1982), the Fair Labor Standards Act, 29 U.S.C. §216(b) (1982), and the Truth-in-Lending Act, 15 U.S.C. §1640(a) (1982). Some statutes authorize fees to all prevailing plaintiffs, and authorize fees to prevailing defendants only on a showing akin to malicious prosecution. A typical example is the Texas Deceptive Trade Practices Act, a consumer protection statute, which awards fees to defendants when the action "was groundless and brought in bad faith, or brought for the purpose of harassment." Tex. Bus. & Com. Code Ann. §17.50(c) (Vernon Supp. 1985).

Some statutes that are facially neutral have been construed to favor plaintiffs. The most notable examples here are the federal civil rights laws. The employment discrimination law, for example, provides that "the court, in its discretion, may allow the prevailing party . . . a reasonable attorney's fee. . . . " 42 U.S.C. §2000e-5(k) (1982). The relevant language of the Civil Rights Attorney's Fees Award Act of 1976 is identical. The Supreme Court has held that prevailing plaintiffs should recover fees as a matter of course, unless special circumstances make an award unjust. Albemarle Paper Co. v. Moody, 422 U.S. 405, 415 (1975). But prevailing defendants are to recover fees only when plaintiff's claim was "frivolous, unreasonable, or groundless, or . . . plaintiff continued to litigate after it clearly became so." Christiansburg Garment Co. v. Equal Employment Opportunity Commission, 434 U.S. 412, 422 (1978). The Court emphasized that it was creating an objective standard, and that bad faith was not required. This standard protects defendants more than a malicious prosecution standard, but it still denies fees to defendants' in the overwhelming majority of cases. The claim in *Christiansburg* was very weak, but no one suggested it was frivolous, unreasonable, or groundless.

2. Why should the Court exercise its discretion so differently for

prevailing plaintiffs and prevailing defendants when the statute speaks neutrally of prevailing parties? The Court's answer was that prevailing plaintiffs vindicate federal policy, and losing defendants are adjudicated wrongdoers. But prevailing defendants protect only their own purse, and losing plaintiffs didn't do anything wrong. Of course the conclusion that plaintiff didn't do anything wrong answers an important question that the Court leaves unstated: *Christiansburg* slightly expands the category of wrongful suits, but it shares the prevailing view that most losing litigation is not wrongful and that plaintiffs should not be deterred from suing. The Court feared that liability for defendant's fees would deter "all but the most airtight claims" if the threshold of liability were set too low.

What about defendants' access to the courts? Might one-way fee shifting deter a vigorous defense? Will some defendants settle bad claims rather than risk paying plaintiff's lawyers to try a complicated case and their own lawyers to defend it? The Court says fees will be awarded only against adjudicated wrongdoers. But what if a more vigorous defense would have exonerated defendant?

3.   Even the modest risk of liability for defendant's attorneys' fees created by *Christiansburg* poses substantial risks to plaintiffs of modest means. The lower courts have responded considering plaintiffs' ability to pay and allowing them to pay in installments. Many of the cases are collected in Arnold v. Burger King Corp., 719 F.2d 63 (4th Cir. 1983), *cert. denied*, 105 S. Ct. 108 (1984). Arnold was a restaurant manager, and the court found that with an installment plan he could pay a full fee award — in that case, $10,000. Other cases have awarded partial fees, for example, $100 per month for three years in a case where a reasonable fee would be $12,500. Fisher v. Fashion Institute of Technology, 87 F.R.D. 485 (S.D.N.Y. 1980). But the fee cannot be waived entirely; one court has held that even if plaintiff is impoverished, he must pay some fee for bringing a frivolous action. Durett v. Jenkins Brickyard, 678 F.2d 911, 917 (11th Cir. 1982).

The courts are awarding fees to defendants as though the primary policy is to deter frivolous claims; there is very little sense that defendant should be made whole. Of course, in most of these cases, a make-whole judgment would be uncollectible anyway. Execution could inflict substantial hardship on plaintiff while collecting very little for defendant.

4.   One-way fee shifting epitomizes the American policy of encouraging litigation. Plaintiffs can finance litigation that would be meritorious but uneconomical if they had to pay their own lawyers. They can recover full compensation instead of compensation minus their attorneys' fees. And they don't have to worry much about liability if things go badly. Should we generalize one-way fee shifting? Or is this strong medicine, to be used only in certain kinds of claims? What kinds of claims? *Alyeska* talks about the importance of the substantive policy being enforced. Dean Rowe suggests that an imbalance in the average resources of plaintiffs

and defendants is a better guide. Rowe, The Legal Theory of Attorney Fee Shifting: A Critical Overview, 1982 Duke L.J. 651, 663-665. Certainly that explanation fits most of the examples considered in these notes: civil rights, consumer protection, Truth-in-Lending, and Fair Labor Standards. It fits antitrust less perfectly, but probably well enough.

Some cases tend to involve large plaintiffs and small defendants. The most obvious example is consumer collection suits — Sears Roebuck against a delinquent debtor. How does *Christiansburg's* analysis fit there? Isn't the debtor the wrongdoer? And isn't Sears enforcing public policy in favor of contract? Do we want one-way fee shifting there? That's what we generally get, not by policy but by contract: Creditors almost invariably include an attorneys' fee provision.

5.   A litigant's financial resources are obviously relevant to how much he will be deterred by the risk of liability for the other side's attorneys' fees. Perhaps equally relevant is whether he will litigate once or repeat-

A Taxonomy of Litigation by Strategic Configuration of Parties

Initiator, Claimant

		One-Shotter	Repeat Player
Defendant	One-Shotter	Parent v. Parent (custody) Spouse v. Spouse (divorce) Family v. Family member (insanity commitment) Family v. Family (inheritance) Neighbor v. Neighbor Partner v. Partner **OS v. OS** **I**	Prosecutor v. Accused Finance company v. Debtor Landlord v. Tenant I.R.S. v. Taxpayer Condemnor v. Property owner **RP v. OS** **II**
	Repeat Player	Welfare client v. Agency Auto dealer v. Manufacturer Injury victim v. Insurance company Tenant v. Landlord Bankrupt consumer v. Creditors Defamed v. Publisher **OS v. RP** **III**	Union v. Company Movie distributor v. Censorship board Developer v. Suburban municipality Purchaser v. Supplier Regulatory agency v. Firms of regulated industry **RP v. RP** **IV**

FIGURE 10-1

edly. Professor Galanter's analysis of repeat players and one-shotters casts much light on the debate over attorneys' fees. Galanter, Why the "Haves" Come Out Ahead: Speculation on the Limits of Legal Change, 9 Law & Soc'y Rev. 95, 107 (1974). Sears is a repeat player; it is in court over and over. If it has to pay a debtor's attorney on occasion, it can spread that loss over many cases. The debtor is in court only once, or at most a few times. His risk of paying Sears's lawyer is all-or-nothing; there are no other cases to even things out. Most litigants can be classified as one-shotters or repeat players; consider Galanter's table (see Figure 10-1).

If there is to be one-way fee shifting, should it generally favor plaintiffs? Those parties with the fewest financial resources? One-shotters? What about cases of one-shotter v. one-shotter and repeat player v. repeat player? Should we have a different rule for each cell of Galanter's table? How would you write a statute codifying such a rule? Would the courts have to work it out case by case?

BLUM v. STENSON
104 S. Ct. 1541 (1984)

JUSTICE POWELL announced the opinion for the Court.

Title 42 U.S.C. §1988 provides that in federal civil rights actions "the court, in its discretion, may allow the prevailing party, other than the United States, a reasonable attorney's fee as part of the costs." The initial estimate of a reasonable attorney's fee is properly calculated by multiplying the number of hours reasonably expended on the litigation times a reasonable hourly rate. Hensley v. Eckerhart, 461 U.S. 424 (1983). Adjustments to that fee then may be made as necessary in the particular case. The two issues in this case are whether Congress intended fee awards to nonprofit legal service organizations to be calculated according to cost or to prevailing market rates, and whether, and under what circumstances, an upward adjustment of an award based on prevailing market rates is appropriate under §1988.

I

A

This suit was brought in 1978 by respondents on behalf of a statewide class of Medicaid[1] recipients pursuant to 42 U.S.C. §1983 in the District

---

1. Medicaid is a program providing medical assistance to the needy. It is jointly funded by the state and federal governments. 42 U.S.C. §§1396-1396k; N.Y. Social Services Law §§363-369 (McKinney's 1976).

Court for the Southern District of New York. Under New York law, one who is eligible to receive benefits under the Supplemental Security Income [SSI] program, 42 U.S.C. §1381, et seq. (1976), automatically is eligible to receive Medicaid benefits. N.Y. Social Services Law §363, et seq. (McKinney's 1976). Prior to this suit, persons who qualified for Medicaid in this fashion automatically lost their benefits if they thereafter became ineligible for SSI payments. The case was decided on cross motions for summary judgment after only one set of plaintiff's interrogatories had been served and answered. On these motions, the District Court certified the class and rendered final judgment in favor of respondents.

The court enjoined the prior practice of automatic termination of benefits, and prescribed procedural rights for the certified class that included "(a) an ex parte determination of continued eligibility for Medicaid, independent of eligibility for SSI; (b) timely and adequate notice of such termination; (c) an opportunity for a hearing." The Court of Appeals for the Second Circuit affirmed in an unpublished oral opinion from the bench. Respondents' subsequent request for an award of reasonable attorney's fees under §1988 is the subject of the present case.

B

Throughout this litigation, respondents were represented by attorneys from The Legal Aid Society of New York, a private nonprofit law office. In November 1980, respondents filed a request for attorney's fees for the period December 1978 through the end of the litigation. Their three attorneys sought payment for some 809 hours of work at rates varying from $95 to $105 per hour. This amounted to approximately $79,312. Respondents' total fee request, however, reflected a 50% increase in that fee. In their brief to the District Court, respondents explained that such an increase was necessary to compensate for the complexity of the case, the novelty of the issues, and the "great benefit" achieved. The total requested fee amounted to approximately $118,968. Petitioner opposed the fee award on the grounds that the rates were exorbitant, the number of hours charged were unreasonable and duplicative, and the 50% "bonus" was improper.

The District Court held that both the hours expended and the rates charged were reasonable. It also held that the fee calculated by multiplying the number of hours times the hourly rates should be increased by the requested 50% because of the quality of representation, the complexity of the issues, the riskiness of success, and the "great benefit to the large class" that was achieved. The District Court awarded respondents the requested fee of $118,968.

The Court of Appeals affirmed in an unpublished opinion. We granted certiorari to consider whether it was proper for the District Court to use prevailing market rates in awarding attorney's fees to nonprofit legal services organizations and whether the District Court abused its discretion in increasing the fee award above that based on market rates.[5]

II

Petitioner argues that the use of prevailing market rates to calculate attorney's fees under §1988 leads to exorbitant fee awards and provides windfalls to civil rights counsel contrary to the express intent of Congress. To avoid this result, petitioner urges this Court to require that all fee awards under §1988 be calculated according to the cost of providing legal services rather than according to the prevailing market rate. The Solicitor General, as amicus curiae, urges the Court to adopt a cost-related standard only for fee awards made to nonprofit legal aid organizations. He argues that market rates reflect the level of compensation necessary to attract profit making attorneys, but that such rates provide excessive fees to nonprofit counsel. Because market rates incorporate operating expenses that may exceed the expenses of nonprofit legal services organizations, and include an element of profit unnecessary to attract nonprofit counsel, the Solicitor General argues that fee awards based on market rates "confer an unjustified windfall or subsidy upon legal services organizations."

Resolution of these two arguments begins and ends with an interpretation of the attorney's fee statute. The Civil Rights Attorney's Fees Awards Act of 1976, 42 U.S.C. §1988, authorizes district courts to award a reasonable attorney's fee to prevailing civil rights litigants. In enacting the statute, Congress directed that attorney's fees be calculated according to standards currently in use under other fee-shifting statutes:

> It is intended that the amount of fees awarded under [§1988] be governed by the same standards which prevail in other types of equally complex Federal litigation, such as antitrust cases[,] and not be reduced because the rights involved may be nonpecuniary in nature. The appropriate standards, see Johnson v. Georgia Highway Express, 488 F.2d 714 (5th Cir. 1974), are correctly applied in such cases as Stanford Daily v. Zurcher, 64 F.R.D. 680 (N.D. Cal. 1974); Davis v. County of Los Angeles, 8 E.P.D. ¶9444 (C.D. Cal. 1974); and Swann v. Charlotte-Mecklenburg Board of Education, 66 F.R.D. 483 (W.D.N.C. 1975). These cases have resulted in fees which are adequate to attract competent counsel, but which do not produce windfalls to attorneys.

S. Rept. No. 94-1011, p. 6 (1976), U.S. Code Cong. & Admin. News 1976, pp. 5908, 5913.

5. . . . We decline to consider petitioner's further argument that the hours charged by respondents' counsel were unreasonable. . . . [P]etitioner failed to submit to the District Court any evidence challenging the accuracy and reasonableness of the hours charged, or the facts asserted in the affidavits submitted by respondents' counsel. It therefore waived its right to an evidentiary hearing in the District Court. In view of the trial strategy it chose, petitioner waived its right to challenge in this Court the District Court's determination that the number of hours billed were reasonable for cases of similar complexity.

In all four of the cases cited by the Senate Report, fee awards were calculated according to prevailing market rates. None of these four cases made any mention of a cost-based standard.[10] Petitioner's argument that the use of market rates violates congressional intent, therefore, is flatly contradicted by the legislative history of §1988. . . . [11] The policy arguments advanced in favor of a cost-based standard should be addressed to Congress rather than to this Court.

III

We address now the second question presented: whether a 50% upward adjustment in the fee was — as petitioner argues — an abuse of discretion by the District Court. Petitioner makes two separate but related arguments. First, she asserts that a reasonable attorney's fee is calculated by multiplying the reasonable number of hours expended times a reasonable hourly rate and that any upward adjustment of that fee is improper. In the alternative, she argues that the 50% upward adjustment in this case constitutes a clear abuse of discretion.

In *Hensley*, we reviewed the cases cited in the legislative history of §1988 and concluded that the "product of reasonable hours times a reasonable rate" normally provides a "reasonable" attorney's fee within the meaning of the statute. 461 U.S., at 434. *Hensley* also recognized that "in

---

10. Congress was legislating in light of experience when it enacted the 1976 fee statute. By that time, courts were familiar with calculating fee awards for civil litigation under Title VII of the Civil Rights Act of 1964, 42 U.S.C. §2000e-5(k), and under the judicially established "private attorney general" theory that had prevailed prior to this Court's decision in Alyeska Pipeline Serv. Co. v. Wilderness Society, 421 U.S. 240 (1975). None of the cases decided at that time had adopted a cost-based approach to calculating fees. Reference to market rate was uniform.

11. We recognize, of course, that determining an appropriate "market rate" for the services of a lawyer is inherently difficult. Market prices of commodities and most services are determined by supply and demand. In this traditional sense there is no such thing as a prevailing market rate for the service of lawyers in a particular community. The type of services rendered by lawyers, as well as their experience, skill and reputation, varies extensively — even within a law firm. Accordingly, the hourly rates of lawyers in private practice also vary widely. The fees charged often are based on the product of hours devoted to the representation multiplied by the lawyer's customary rate. But the fee usually is discussed with the client, may be negotiated, and it is the client who pays whether he wins or loses. The §1988 fee determination is made by the court in an entirely different setting: there is no negotiation or even discussion with the prevailing client, as the fee — found to be reasonable by the court — is paid by the losing party. Nevertheless, as shown in the text above, the critical inquiry in determining reasonableness is now generally recognized as the appropriate hourly rate. And the rates charged in private representations may afford relevant comparisons.

In seeking some basis for a standard, courts properly have required prevailing attorneys to justify the reasonableness of the requested rate or rates. To inform and assist the court in the exercise of its discretion, the burden is on the fee applicant to produce satisfactory evidence — in addition to the attorney's own affidavits — that the requested rates are in line with those prevailing in the community for similar services by lawyers of reasonably comparable skill, experience and reputation. A rate determined in this way is normally deemed to be reasonable, and is referred to — for convenience — as the prevailing market rate.

some cases of exceptional success an enhanced award may be justified."
Id., at 434.[14] In view of our recognition that an enhanced award may be
justified "in some cases of exceptional success," we cannot agree with
petitioner's argument that an "upward adjustment" is never permissible.
The statute requires a "reasonable fee," and there may be circumstances
in which the basic standard of reasonable rates multiplied by reasonably
expended hours results in a fee that is either unreasonably low or unreasonably high. When, however, the applicant for a fee has carried his
burden of showing that the claimed rate and number of hours are reasonable, the resulting product is presumed to be the reasonable fee contemplated by §1988.

B

The issue remaining is the appropriateness of an upward adjustment to
the fee award in this case. The burden of proving that such an adjustment
is necessary to the determination of a reasonable fee is on the fee applicant. The record before us contains no evidence supporting an upward
adjustment to fees calculated under the basic standard of reasonable rates
times reasonable hours. The affidavits of respondents' attorneys do not
claim, or even mention, entitlement to a bonus or upward revision. Respondents' brief to the District Court merely states in conclusory fashion
that an upward adjustment to the fee is necessary because the issues were
novel, the litigation was complex, and the results were of far-reaching
significance to a large class of people. The District Court, without elaboration, accepted these conclusory reasons for approving the upward adjustment and supplied additional reasons of its own. In awarding the 50%
increase, the court referred to the complexity of the litigation, the novelty
of the issues, the high quality of representation, the "great benefit" to the
class, and the "riskiness" of the law suit. The Court of Appeals, in affirming, shed no light on why it thought this substantial upward adjustment
was appropriate. In a single sentence, it simply repeated the unsupported
conclusions of the District Court.

The reasons offered by the District Court to support the upward adjustment do not withstand examination. The novelty and complexity of
the issues presumably were fully reflected in the number of billable hours
recorded by counsel and thus do not warrant an upward adjustment in a
fee based on the number of billable hours times reasonable hourly rates.
There may be cases, of course, where the experience and special skill of
the attorney will require the expenditure of fewer hours than counsel
normally would be expected to spend on a particularly novel or complex

14. At another point in *Hensley*, the Court observed that the "product of reasonable
hours times a reasonable rate does not end the inquiry. There remain other considerations
that may lead the District Court to adjust the fee upward or downward, including the
important factor of the 'results obtained.'" 461 U.S., at 434.

issue. In those cases, the special skill and experience of counsel should be reflected in the reasonableness of the hourly rates. Neither complexity nor novelty of the issues, therefore, is an appropriate factor in determining whether to increase the basic fee award.

The District Court, having tried the case, was in the best position to conclude that "the quality of representation was high." In view of the reputation of the Legal Aid Society and its staff, we have no doubt that this was true. The "quality of representation," however, generally is reflected in the reasonable hourly rate. It, therefore, may justify an upward adjustment only in the rare case where the fee applicant offers specific evidence to show that the quality of service rendered was superior to that one reasonably should expect in light of the hourly rates charged and that the success was "exceptional." See *Hensley*, 461 U.S., at 435. Respondents offered no such evidence in this case, and on this record the District Court's rationale for providing an upward adjustment for quality of representation is a clear example of double counting. In justifying the high hourly rates used to calculate the fee award, the District Court explained:

> The rates requested are consonant with fee awards in cases of similar complexity and difficulty. . . . [T]hey are fair in view of these attorneys' experience and expertise. . . . The quality of work performed by counsel throughout this case was high. In view of all these considerations, I do not find the requested rates, from $95 per hour to $105 per hour, excessive.

In justifying the upward adjustment to the fee award, the District Court merely restated these same two factors: "The quality of representation was high. The litigation was complex."

Not only have respondents failed to show that the hourly rates failed to provide a reasonable fee for the quality of representation provided, but they candidly concede that the "fees awarded [to their attorneys] may be at the upper end of the market for awards under §1988. . . . " Absent specific evidence to the contrary, we cannot say that rates from $95 per hour to $105 per hour for these three attorneys do not fully reflect the quality of their representation.

The 50% upward adjustment also was based in part on the District Court's determination that the ultimate outcome of the litigation "was of great benefit to a large class of needy people." The court did not explain, however, exactly how this determination affected the fee award. "Results obtained" is one of the twelve factors identified in Johnson v. Georgia Highway Express, 488 F.2d, at 718, as relevant to the calculation of a reasonable attorney's fee. It is "particularly crucial where a plaintiff is deemed 'prevailing' even though he succeeded on only some of his claims for relief." *Hensley*, 461 U.S., at 434 (fee award must be reduced by the number of hours spent on unsuccessful claims). Because acknowledgment of the "results obtained" generally will be subsumed within other factors used to calculate a reasonable fee, it normally should not provide an independent basis for increasing the fee award.[16] Neither the District Court's opinion nor respondents' briefs have identified record evidence that shows that the benefit achieved requires an upward adjustment to the fee.

Finally, the District Court included among its reasons for an upward adjustment a statement that the "issues presented were novel and the undertaking therefore risky." Absent any claim in the affidavits or briefs submitted in support of respondents' fee request, seeking such an adjustment, we cannot be sure what prompted the court's statement. Nowhere in the affidavits submitted in support of respondents' fee request, nor in their brief to the District Court, did respondents identify any risks associated with the litigation or claim that the risk of nonpayment required an upward adjustment to provide a reasonable fee. On this record, therefore, any upward adjustment for the contingent nature of the litigation was unjustified.[17]

In sum, we reiterate what was said in *Hensley*: "where a plaintiff has obtained excellent results, his attorney should recover a fully compensatory fee. Normally this will encompass all hours reasonably expended on the litigation, and indeed in some cases of exceptional success an enhancement award may be justified." *Hensley*, 461 U.S., at 435. We therefore reject petitioner's argument that an upward adjustment to an attorney's fee is never appropriate under §1988. On the record before us, however, respondent established only that hourly rates ranging from $95 per hour to $105 per hour for the full 809.75 hours billed were reasonable. This resulted in a charge of $79,312. Respondents introduced no evidence that enhancement was necessary to provide fair and reasonable compensation. They therefore have failed to carry their burden of justifying entitlement to an upward adjustment.[19] On this record, we conclude that the fee of $79,312 was "fully compensatory." Accordingly, the judgment below is reversed only insofar as the fee award was increased by the sum of $39,656.

It is so ordered.

16.   Nor do we believe that the *number* of persons benefited is a consideration of significance in calculating fees under §1988. Unlike the calculation of attorney's fees under the "common fund doctrine," where a reasonable fee is based on a percentage of the fund bestowed on the class, a reasonable fee under §1988 reflects the amount of attorney time reasonably expended on the litigation. Presumably, counsel will spend as much time and will be as diligent in litigating a case that benefits a small class of people, or, indeed, in protecting the civil rights of a single individual.

17.   We have no occasion in this case to consider whether the risk of not being the prevailing party in a §1983 case, and therefore not being entitled to an award of attorney's fees from one's adversary, may ever justify an upward fee adjustment.

19.   As we stated in *Hensley*, a "request for attorney's fees should not result in a second major litigation." *Hensley*, supra, at 437. Parties to civil rights litigation in particular should make a conscientious effort, where a fee award is to be made, to resolve any differences. A district court is expressly empowered to exercise discretion in determining whether an award is to be made and if so its reasonableness. The court, with its intimate knowledge of the litigation, has a responsibility to encourage agreement.

Justice Brennan, with whom Justice Marshall joins, concurring.

I join the Court's opinion. I write separately only to reaffirm my view that Congress has clearly indicated that the risk of not prevailing, and therefore the risk of not recovering any attorney's fees, is a proper basis on which a district court may award an upward adjustment to an otherwise compensatory fee. See Hensley v. Eckerhart, 461 U.S. 424, 442-449 (1983) (Brennan, J., concurring in part and dissenting in part).

Although the Court leaves the question unresolved, see ante, n.17, the legislative history that always has controlled our interpretation of §1988, and that proves determinative on the other issues addressed by today's decision, also determines whether an upward adjustment to compensate for the risk of nonpayment may be justified. In particular, Congress referred to Johnson v. Georgia Highway Express, 488 F.2d 714 (C.A.5 1974), for the appropriate standards to be applied by courts awarding attorney's fees under §1988. "Whether the fee is fixed or contingent," 488 F.2d, at 718, was consequently recognized by Congress as a relevant consideration in setting a reasonable fee. Moreover, Congress explicitly cited Stanford Daily v. Zurcher, 64 F.R.D. 680 (N.D. Cal. 1974) (subsequently aff'd, 550 F.2d 464 (C.A.9 1977), rev'd on other grounds, 436 U.S. 547 (1978)), as one of several cases that had "correctly applied" the appropriate standards. S. Rep. No. 94-1011, p.6 (1976). In Stanford Daily, the district court concluded that a court may "increase the fees award obtained by multiplying the number of hours by the average billing rate to reflect the fact that the attorneys' compensation, at least in part, was contingent in nature." 64 F.R.D., at 685-686. It is clear, therefore, that Congress authorized district courts to award upward adjustments to compensate for the contingent nature of success, and thus for the risk of nonpayment in a particular case.

Indeed, allowing district courts to award such upward adjustments is entirely consistent with the market-based approach to hourly rates that is today reaffirmed by the Court. Lawyers operating in the marketplace can be expected to charge a higher hourly rate when their compensation is contingent on success than when they will be promptly paid, irrespective of whether they win or lose. Similarly, it is necessary to account for this risk in fee awards under §1988, either by increasing the appropriate hourly rate or by enhancing the fee otherwise calculated with the use of an hourly rate that does not reflect the risk of not prevailing.* This will

---

* Contingency adjustments under §1988 should not be confused with contingency fee arrangements that are commonly entered into by private attorneys representing plaintiffs in civil litigation. An upward adjustment to compensate for the risk of nonpayment under §1988 is "entirely unrelated to the 'contingent fee' arrangements that are typical in plaintiffs' tort representation. In tort suits, an attorney might receive one-third of whatever amount the plaintiff recovers. In those cases, therefore, the fee is directly proportional to the recovery. Such is not the case in contingency adjustments of the kind . . . describe[d] herein. Th[is] contingency adjustment is a percentage increase in the [amount obtained by multiplying hours expended by hourly rate, and is designed] to reflect the risk that no fee will be obtained." Copeland v. Marshall, 641 F.2d 880, 893 (1980) (en banc).

ensure that fees under §1988 are consistent with prevailing market rates, that nonprofit legal service organizations and private attorneys are treated similarly, and that the attorney's fees awarded are "adequate to attract competent counsel" to represent other clients with civil rights grievances, S. Rep. No. 94-1011, p.6 (1976); H.R. Rep. No. 94-1558, p.9 (1976).

NOTES ON CALCULATING FEE AWARDS

1. The most fundamental debate over the amount of fee awards is whether to use an hourly rate or a percentage of the recovery as a starting point. Percentage of recovery traditionally predominated, but that approach produced offensively large fees after Federal Civil Rule 23 was amended in 1966 to facilitate larger class actions. In City of Detroit v. Grinell Corp., 495 F.2d 448 (2d Cir. 1974), the percentage fee came out to $635 per hour. Counsel defended the fee by alleging that in Sullivan & Cromwell v. Hudson & Manhattan Corp., mem., 35 A.D.2d 1084, 316 N.Y.S.2d 604 (1970), aff'd, 29 N.Y.2d 523, 272 N.E.2d 572 (1971), a percentage fee came out to $3,950 per hour.

The federal courts of appeals responded by insisting on more attention to hourly rates. The leading case was Lindy Brothers Builders v. American Radiator & Standard Sanitary Corp., 487 F.2d 161 (3d Cir. 1973), which coined the unfortunate phrase "lodestar" for the product of hours spent times a reasonable hourly rate. All calculations were to start from the lodestar. The Second Circuit followed Lindy in Grinell, and nearly all the other circuits followed in turn. Blum v. Stenson and Hensley v. Eckerhart, discussed in Blum, appear to commit the Supreme Court to the hourly rate approach in statutory fee award cases. But compare the dictum in footnote 16, stating flatly that fee awards in common benefit cases are based on a percentage of recovery. The dictum inaccurately describes present practice; neither the dictum nor the holding reflects serious consideration of the choice between hourly rates and percentage fees.

2. It is easy to see the problem with an approach that produces $4,000 an hour fees. But the hourly rate approach also has problems. Lawyers may do unnecessary work to pad their hours, or even record hours they never spent. Efforts to control such abuses produce burdensome litigation. It takes only a few seconds to multiply the recovery by 20 percent. But the hourly rate approach invites detailed examination of lawyers' time records. The Supreme Court of Delaware continues to emphasize percentage of recovery, rejecting the "elaborate analyses called for by" Lindy. Sugarland Industries v. Thomas, 420 A.2d 142, 150 (Del. 1980).

3. An extreme example of difficulties with the hourly rate approach is In re Fine Paper Antitrust Litigation, 98 F.R.D. 48 (E.D. Pa. 1983), rev'd

in part, 751 F.2d 562 (3d Cir. 1984). That was a huge collection of cases, with settlements totaling $50 million. Dozens of attorneys filed fee petitions totaling some $20 million. The court held forty-one days of hearings, considered over 1,000 exhibits, wrote an opinion that takes up 190 pages with 161 headnotes in the National Reporter System, and allowed only $4.3 million of the requested fees. The court held that many of the hours spent were unnecessary or duplicative and produced no benefit to the class, that many hours were inadequately documented, that the rates and multipliers claimed were excessive, and that the class should not have to pay for luxury hotels and elaborate meals. Worst for the image of the bar, the court strongly suggested that many of the hours claimed had never been spent at all. None of these findings were disturbed on appeal.

It is easy to be shocked at the thought of a forty-one-day trial on a collateral matter like attorneys' fees. But if you think of the fee petitions as a $20 million lawsuit, with multiple parties on both sides, resulting in a $4.3 million judgment, a forty-one-day trial may not appear so disproportionate. Awarding a percentage of recovery would have been easier, but how should the court pick the percentage?

4. The most visible fee cases involve many hours and large fees. The *Fine Paper* litigation involved tens of thousands of hours. The Legal Aid lawyers in *Blum* spent 809 hours to file a complaint and one set of interrogatories and brief a motion for class certification and summary judgment. Some lawyers practice the way their law teachers taught them, researching every point thoroughly and analyzing it to death. Some cases require that approach; complex and novel issues take lots of hours, and they can arise in a legal aid practice as well as in an elite firm.

But it is misleading to focus on such cases. Most cases are routine, and many lawyers underprepare rather than overprepare. One survey found that the median number of lawyer hours spent on an "ordinary" case is 30.4. Only 12 percent took more than 120 hours, but the big cases raised the mean to 72.9 hours per case. Trubek, Sarat, Felstiner, Kritzer, and Grossman, The Costs of Ordinary Litigation, 31 U.C.L.A. L. Rev. 72, 90 (1983). Extraordinarily large cases — about 2 percent of the sample — were excluded from the study. Cases with less than $1,000 in controversy were also excluded.

If the average case takes thirty to seventy hours, we shouldn't make broad policy judgments about attorneys' fees just on the basis of cases like *Blum* and *Fine Paper*. On the other hand, fee shifting introduces a problem inherent in all third party payment systems: if someone else is going to pay, there is less incentive to hold the cost down. In the case of attorneys' fees, that problem is moderated by the risk that the other side will win and the litigant or his attorney will bear the cost himself.

5. What is a reasonable hourly rate? This is mainly a question of fact; what is the market rate for attorneys with comparable skills and experi-

ence in the relevant market? Some opinions assume that the court should choose an hourly rate in the abstract and then subject the fee to a multiplier to allow for individual factors; *Blum* directs that those factors be considered in setting the hourly rate.

6.   Arguments over hourly rates have also included a policy question that *Blum* seemed to resolve: Should attorneys who work at less than market rates be paid market rates? Before *Blum*, many courts had awarded below market rates to legal aid and public interest lawyers. One explanation was that market rates would confer a windfall on public interest plaintiffs, because public interest lawyers worked for lower salaries in lower rent districts with less support staff and equipment. New York State Association for Retarded Children v. Carey, 711 F.2d 1136, 1148-1153 (2d Cir. 1983). Another explanation was that the purpose of fee award statutes was to attract competent lawyers to enforce statutes, and public interest lawyers were altruists who could be attracted cheaply.

7.   Why do legal aid lawyers make $25,000 while corporate defense lawyers make $250,000? Is it because legal aid lawyers are only one-tenth as valuable? Or is it because legal aid clients have no money to pay their lawyers? And isn't that part of the problem fee awards statutes were supposed to solve? Would the statutes serve their purpose if enforcement of the law still depended on altruism? Why should so many lawyers who charge $200 per hour be offended when public interest lawyers are awarded $100 per hour?

Are market rates less relevant when defendants are state officials? The lawyers defending the state don't make much more than the lawyers for the plaintiffs. Should New York have to pay plaintiffs' lawyers more than it pays its own?

8.   *Blum* was distinguished in Laffey v. Northwest Airlines, 746 F.2d 4 (D.C. Cir. 1984), *cert. denied*, 105 S. Ct. 939 (1985). Plaintiffs in *Laffey* were not represented by salaried legal aid or public interest lawyers. They were represented by a private firm that had paying clients. But those clients did not have deep pockets, and the firm's hourly rates were substantially less than prevailing rates in Washington. The firm characterized itself as a quasi-public interest firm that preferred its existing clients despite their relative inability to pay. Id. at 14 n.69.

The court found that irrelevant. It held that the fee award should be based on the firm's actual billing rate, and not on the higher market rate. Is that consistent with the legislative history cited in *Blum*? Should the firm have to subsidize Northwest Airlines just because it subsidizes its less affluent clients? Judge Wright dissented.

The majority thought altruism should be its own reward. It also thought its rule would simplify fee litigation and encourage settlement. One firm's billing rate is much easier to identify than the prevailing rate for lawyers of comparable skill or the "true value" of the services rendered. There is surely something to that. But what about a firm with different rates for different clients or different kinds of cases?

9. The altruism rationale shows up in reverse in High v. Economics Laboratory, 576 F. Supp. 1365 (W.D.N.C. 1983). There, an "establishment/defendant's" firm handled an employment discrimination case for a plaintiff. The court adjusted the market rate upward because it was so unpleasant for a defense firm to handle the case. If altruism is not its own reward for the establishment, why should it be its own reward for public interest lawyers?

10. Laffey v. Northwest Airlines also dealt with an issue reserved in *Blum* and raised in Justice Brennan's concurrence: Should fee awards be adjusted upward to compensate for the risk of not prevailing and thus recovering no fee? The majority in *Laffey* thought that footnote 17 of *Blum* indicates "grave doubt . . . whether such adjustments should ever be made." 746 F.2d at 28. Is that a fair reading of *Blum*?

Justice Brennan summarizes the arguments in favor of contingency adjustments. What are the arguments against? Full compensation for the risk of not prevailing would require multiplying the lodestar fee by the reciprocal of the original chance of success. That is, the court would double the fee if plaintiff won a case with even odds, or quadruple the fee in a case where the original chances of success were only one in four. *Laffey* explains in some detail what is wrong with that approach. It would reduce the incentive to screen cases, because it would make the expected value of the fee award equal for strong cases and frivolous ones. The largest fees would be paid by defendants who were most reasonable in deciding to litigate but were unlucky enough to lose. The smallest fees would be paid by defendants with the most indefensible positions. The court had less to say about what was wrong with a smaller and less mechanical contingency enhancement. It said only that *Blum* said that enhancements were to be exceptional, and that that statement should be applied to contingency enhancements even though the Supreme Court had reserved the issue. Judge Wright dissented on this issue too.

Laffey did say that the hourly rate underlying the lodestar fee might include an allowance for the contingency risk. 746 F.2d at 29 n.149, quoting Copeland v. Marshall, 641 F.2d 880, 893 (D.C. Cir. 1980) (en banc). Why does it matter whether you increase the rate and then multiply by the number of hours, or multiply by the number of hours and then increase the product? And how would the *Copeland* procedure work given the other holding in *Laffey* — that the lawyers are bound by their own past hourly rates? Should all plaintiffs' lawyers offer clients a choice of a fixed hourly rate and a contingent hourly rate, so they will have an established contingent rate if they ever file a fee petition?

One argument against contingency enhancements is that they are designed to pay the lawyer for other cases that he lost. Is that a fair criticism? Or are they designed to give the lawyer what he would have charged a paying client for the risks of the case he won?

NOTES ON THE PREVAILING PARTY REQUIREMENT

1.   Section 1988 and many other fee provisions authorize fees to a "prevailing party." What about a partially prevailing party, like the plaintiffs in *Alyeska*? They prevailed on their claim under the Mineral Leasing Act, so the court of appeals didn't decide their much more complex claim under the National Environmental Policy Act. If §1988 had applied, should they have gotten fees for all their hours, or only for hours spent on the Mineral Leasing Act? And should it matter that Congress enacted legislation rejecting their position on both claims?

2.   Hensley v. Eckerhart, 461 U.S. 424 (1983), addressed some of these questions. It said that unrelated claims should be treated as separate lawsuits, with fees only for hours spent on successful claims. But the Court acknowledged that most litigation involves related claims, and found it unrealistic to separate them. It directed trial courts to "focus on the significance of the overall relief obtained by the plaintiff in relation to the hours reasonably expended on the litigation." Id. at 435.

The Court said that in *Hensley*, plaintiffs had prevailed on five claims out of six. The Court suggested that in those circumstances it might be reasonable to award fees for all the hours spent, although it remanded for further consideration in light of its vague opinion. But if plaintiffs had prevailed on one claim out of six, the Court thought that compensation for all the hours spent would clearly be excessive.

Not surprisingly, the five claims out of six characterization oversimplifies. Plaintiffs in *Hensley* challenged conditions in a state mental hospital. The complaint listed alleged violations in six general areas, such as physical environment, individual treatment plans, and visitation, phone, and mail privileges. The trial court found violations in five of the six areas. That is not the same as saying plaintiffs prevailed on all their claims in the five areas. The sixth area was staffing; the court found no violation there because defendants had increased staffing during the litigation.

3.   Plaintiff need not get a final judgment to be a prevailing party. A favorable settlement is enough to support a subsequent fee petition. Maher v. Gagne, 448 U.S. 122 (1980). And the lower courts award fees for "catalytic claims" that trigger "voluntary" reform. The additional staffing in *Hensley* might qualify as an example. Another example is Robinson v. Kimbrough, 652 F.2d 458 (5th Cir. 1981). Plaintiffs alleged that defendants systematically excluded blacks and women from jury lists. One month after the suit was filed, the county commissioners compiled a new

list that was 34 percent black and 45 percent women. The trial court then dismissed the complaint on the merits and denied fees. The court of appeals ordered the district court to determine if the lawsuit had been the catalyst that caused jury reform, and if the answer was yes, to award plaintiffs' attorneys' fees.

4. §307(f) of the Clean Air Act, 42 U.S.C. §7607(f) (1982), provides that a court may award fees "whenever it determines that such an award is appropriate." Can it ever be appropriate to award fees to a party who didn't prevail? The D.C. Circuit said yes in Sierra Club v. Gorsuch, 684 F.2d 972 (D.C. Cir. 1982). The Sierra Club and a group of utilities had both challenged the Environmental Protection Agency's standards on sulfur dioxide emissions from coal-burning power plants. The court rejected all challenges and approved the regulation. But it said that the Sierra Club's participation was invaluable, and suggested that it might have accepted some of the utility challenges but for the Sierra Club's argument and evidence. The Supreme Court reversed in Ruckelshaus v. Sierra Club, 103 S. Ct. 3274 (1983). The majority thought that it could never be appropriate to award fees to a party who did not prevail at least in part. There were four dissents.

MIRABAL v. GENERAL MOTORS ACCEPTANCE CORPORATION
576 F.2d 729 (7th Cir.), *cert. denied*, 439 U.S. 1039 (1978)

Before SWYGERT, SPRECHER and WOOD, Circuit Judges.
PER CURIAM. . . .

I

Plaintiffs purchased a new car . . . on a 36-month installment contract. Defendants understated the annual percentage rate applicable to the transaction in the installment contract and GMAC sent a letter to plaintiffs informing them of this error, which letter plaintiffs denied receiving.

Plaintiffs filed an action charging violations of the Truth in Lending Act, 15 U.S.C. §1601 et seq., and two Illinois statutes. The district court found seven violations of the Truth in Lending Act and awarded $1,000 to plaintiffs for each violation. The district court also found violations of both Illinois statutes and awarded damages in excess of $1,000, bringing the total to over $8,000. On appeal, this court held that multiple recovery for multiple errors in a single disclosure statement was impermissible and that defendants had not violated the two Illinois statutes. The judgment was reduced to a total of $2,000 "plus costs and attorney's fees. . . ."

On remand petitioner alleged that he had expended 350 hours on the case, 120 at the trial level and 230 on the appeal. . . . The district court awarded petitioner the total costs requested and attorney's fees in the amount of $2,000. Petitioner appeals from the attorney's fee award.

II

The district court has broad discretion in making an award of attorney's fees because of the advantage of close observation of the work product of an attorney and an understanding of the skill and time required in the suit. Our review is limited to the determination of whether the district court abused this discretion. . . .

Petitioner has received in attorney's fees an amount equal to that which his clients recovered in total.

Although the determination of hours necessary to effectively handle a case is not subject to exact determination, the amount which petitioner claims to have spent on the present case seems clearly out of proportion with the amount in controversy. Moreover, Congress has limited the liability of Truth in Lending Act violators to $1,000 per violation. 15 U.S.C. §1640(a). To grant attorney's fees greatly in excess of a client's recovery requires strong support from the circumstances of the particular case. The instant case involved a one-time individual claim based mainly on a bona fide arithmetical error. . . .

Additionally, to grant large attorney's fee awards on the basis of relatively small injury would encourage suits which do not further the client's interest or the public's interest. The costs of these suits already forces many claims to settlement. Indeed, petitioner himself has inadvertently provided this court with an example of the questionable results in such suits. See Plaintiffs' Reply Memorandum (Document 16), page 4, and the letter attached to it. There petitioner made a settlement in a Truth in Lending case in which his client received $400 while petitioner was paid $12,000 as attorney's fees for the settlement. While such disproportionate sums may be exacted in settlement agreements, we should be loathe to automatically provide judicial approval for such results when these cases reach the courts.

Petitioner also claims that the attorneys for GMAC were paid over $30,000 and that this amount is indicative of what he should be paid. . . . This circuit has held that it is an abuse of discretion to determine attorney's fees solely on the basis of hours spent times billing rate. Petitioner wants us to go a step further and award him a fee based on what the *opposing side* spent in time and money. This ignores the fact that a given case may have greater precedential value for one side than the other. Also, a plaintiff's attorney, by pressing questionable claims and refusing to settle except on outrageous terms, could force a defendant to incur substantial fees which he later uses as a basis for his own fee claim.

Moreover, the amount of fees which one side is paid by its client is a matter involving various motivations in an on-going attorney-client relationship and may, therefore, have little relevance to the value which petitioner has provided to his clients in a given case.

Therefore, for the reasons discussed above, we conclude that the district court properly acted within its discretion in setting the award of attorney's fees at $2,000.

Affirmed.

SWYGERT, Circuit Judge, dissenting.

Despite the thoughtful analysis of the majority's opinion, I am unable to agree with the conclusion it reaches. The enormous disparity between the amount of money received by defendants' attorneys and plaintiffs' attorney disturbs my sense of fairness. Plaintiffs won their lawsuit (though losing part of it on appeal), and yet their counsel received only one-fifteenth of what defendants' counsel was paid for defending the suit. This, together with the summary manner in which the fee proceeding was handled, compels me to dissent.

I . . .

[D]efendants understated the annual percentage rate by almost two percent. Defendants . . . asserted that the error resulted from a bona fide mistake and therefore they were statutorily exempt from liability. The district court disagreed and entered judgment for plaintiffs, finding seven different Truth in Lending violations as well as violations of both Illinois acts. Damages were assessed in the sum of $8,126.80, $1,000 for each violation of the Truth in Lending Act and $1,126.80 for the two state law violations. The defendants appealed and the plaintiffs cross-appealed.

After judgment had been entered but before the case was argued on appeal, Congress amended the Truth in Lending Act by barring multiple recovery for multiple errors committed in a single disclosure statement. . . . [W]e affirmed in part. . . . This court found that defendants had not met their burden of establishing that they were exempt from liability for misstating the annual percentage rate. Because the recently enacted amendment limiting recovery to $1,000 per transaction was held applicable to this pending cause, we did not consider the other six disclosure errors found by the trial court. Moreover, that part of the judgment finding liability under the two Illinois acts was reversed.

Plaintiffs also met with mixed success on their cross-appeal. While this court rejected the argument that defendants were severally liable under the Truth in Lending Act, it did agree with plaintiffs that each debtor was entitled to a separate recovery of $1,000. Because of the statutory change in the Truth in Lending Act, this court reduced the amount of judgment to $2,000 and remanded the cause for a determination of costs and attorney's fees.

On remand plaintiffs' attorney filed a verified petition for award of attorney's fees and costs. . . . Defendants did not answer the petition;[7] they disputed neither the number of hours which counsel had expended nor that these hours were necessary to perform the legal services properly. . . .

A hearing was never held on the fee issue even though one had been requested by petitioner, plaintiffs' attorney. Instead the district court entered a minute order awarding $2,000 in attorney's fees and $690.10 in costs. Petitioner appeals the fee award.

II

In awarding plaintiffs' attorney $2,000 for 350 hours of work, the district court said that the expenditure of this many hours on this case was "utterly unnecessary." In the judge's view, most of these hours were spent in advancing "excessive legal theories." Which theories were excessive and what hours were unnecessary were not specified in the order.

I find it anomalous that the district court, after finding seven different Truth in Lending violations and two state disclosure violations and awarding plaintiffs over $8,000, is now able to say that plaintiffs' counsel advanced excessive legal theories. Moreover, was it "utterly unnecessary" for plaintiffs' counsel to defend the judgment once defendants chose to appeal? And, was it "utterly unnecessary" for plaintiffs to cross-appeal? I believe that plaintiffs not only had the right, but under Canon Seven of the Code of Professional Responsibility,[9] plaintiffs' attorney had the duty to protect the judgment he obtained for his clients. Furthermore, had plaintiffs not cross-appealed, they would have recovered only $1,000 instead of the $2,000 ultimately awarded by this court.

If the district court had held a hearing as plaintiffs requested, we might now know what theories it believed were excessive and what hours were therefore unnecessary. In short, we would be informed how the court arrived at the $2,000 figure. But in the absence of such reasons, the only reasonable inference is that the fee award was matched to the judgment which plaintiffs ultimately obtained. But if it is an abuse of discretion to set fees solely on the basis of a formula applying hours spent times billing rate, Waters v. Wisconsin Steel Works, 502 F.2d 1309, 1322 (7th Cir.

7. Defendants did file a petition for offsetting attorney's fees, wherein they claimed they were entitled to $7,500 in fees for ultimately winning on the counts under the Illinois statutes.

9. Canon Seven provides: "A lawyer should represent a client zealously within the bounds of the law."

1976), I believe it is equally abusive to award fees solely by the amount of recovery obtained.[11]

III

The conclusion reached by the majority seems to be based primarily on the belief that the granting of large attorney fee awards (regardless of the validity of such an award in a particular case) will encourage the filing of questionable claims which defendant-creditors will be forced to settle because the costs of litigation will become too prohibitive. I share this concern and believe it is an important consideration in making a fee award. My difficulty, however, is that it does not fit the facts of this case.

The record here is barren of any evidence that plaintiffs pressed questionable claims or refused to settle except on outrageous terms. If anything, the record proves the contrary. The district court found that defendants had violated two state laws and had violated the Truth in Lending Act in seven different ways. This court affirmed the violation concerning understating the annual percentage rate; it did not have to consider the merits of the other Truth in Lending violations because of the interpretation given the 1974 amendment.

Nor is this a case where the defendants were at the mercy of the plaintiffs, who typically set the perimeters of a lawsuit. At trial it was the defendants who had the burden of establishing their affirmative defense of a bona fide mistake. Furthermore, after losing on all issues, it was defendants who chose to appeal and challenge the findings of the trial court. . . . The defendants were legally justified in electing to make a militant defense; they also had the right to appeal an adverse judgment. But in deliberately choosing such a course of action, they cannot now be heard to complain that it would be unfair to require them to pay a reasonable fee to plaintiffs' attorney.

Defendants are not without weapons to curtail, if not stop entirely, the possibility of "forced settlements." If a plaintiff's settlement demands are unreasonable, a defendant may make an offer of judgment pursuant to Rule 68 of the Federal Rules of Civil Procedure. Once a defendant makes such an offer, he is not liable for plaintiff's costs and attorney's fees if plaintiff does not ultimately recover the amount of the offer. Through such a device a defendant can place on the plaintiff much of the financial risk involved in litigation.

---

11. I too agree that petitioner is not entitled to an award of $30,000 just because defense counsel received such a sum. But I do not agree that such evidence is irrelevant. One of the factors which district courts are to consider in setting a reasonable fee is "[t]he fee customarily charged in the locality for similar legal services." Waters v. Wisconsin Steel Works, 502 F.2d at 1322. What better evidence is there of this information than the fee which defendants paid their attorneys?

Finally, the policy of discouraging the filing of questionable claims must be balanced against the policy underlying the Truth in Lending Act itself. . . . Enforcement of this policy was placed primarily on the private sector through suits for civil penalties. A provision for attorney's fees helps assure that enforcement will take place. But such a provision is rendered meaningless unless attorneys for successful parties are given reasonably adequate compensation for their services.

The need for adequate compensation is particularly important since the statutory penalty is now limited to $1,000 per transaction. If a presumption is imposed that a successful attorney is allowed only that amount recovered by his client — as apparently was done here — creditors can effectively stop the filing of all Truth in Lending actions. By refusing to negotiate even reasonable claims and by litigating every case, creditors can soon force a plaintiff to terminate the litigation, not because his claim is invalid, but because it is no longer economically feasible for his attorney to continue the case. This case is a prime example. I dare say few attorneys will handle a Truth in Lending case when they learn that they may earn only $5.71 an hour.

NOTES ON THE AMOUNT OF THE JUDGMENT AS A CONSTRAINT ON ATTORNEYS' FEES

1. In considering *Mirabal*, it is important to distinguish four arguments. One is that the case wasn't that complicated and the lawyer spent far too many hours. No one argues that either defendants or clients should pay for hours not needed to complete the task. A second argument is that plaintiff filed many claims and prevailed on only one; try analyzing that in light of the notes preceding *Mirabal*. A third argument is that the case wasn't really in the public interest because the violation was inadvertent and GMAC admitted it. The court suggests this argument but doesn't squarely rely on it, presumably because the district court found seven other violations that GMAC didn't admit to.

The fourth argument is that the sum at stake was too small to justify the hours needed to handle the case — that the task was not worth completing. The court of appeals relies mainly on this argument. It raises a recurring issue, especially in individual consumer cases.

2. Not all courts have agreed with the *Mirabal* majority. A dealer who sold a new car that suffered from excessive oil consumption, hard starting, and a rotten egg odor paid $500 in damages and $25,000 in attorneys' fees under the Texas Deceptive Trade Practices Act. Jack Roach Ford v. De Urdanavia, 659 S.W.2d 725 (Tex. App. 1983). A jury had awarded $33,500 in attorneys' fees, but the court found that excessive.

Other courts have waffled. In Republic National Life Insurance Co. v. Heyward, 568 S.W.2d 879 (Tex. Civ. App. 1978), plaintiff's lawyers spent between 750 and 1,000 hours to recover $12,000 in accidental death insurance for the beneficiaries of a murder victim. The case required one trial and a trip to the state Supreme Court on the issue whether death by murder is accidental. The Supreme Court said that depended on whether plaintiff knew he was going to be murdered! Then there was a trial on whether he knew, and on a second defense that he had feloniously assaulted his murderer. The jury rejected both defenses and awarded $57,500 in fees under a fee statute for unpaid insurance claims. The court of appeals noted that "there are 'career cases' where the amount in controversy will not justify the fee that would be required to fully compensate the attorneys. . . ." Id. at 888. It ordered a remittitur, but still allowed $19,000 in fees.

Surprisingly few Truth in Lending cases explicitly address the issue. Truth in Lending fee awards tend to be more generous than in Mirabal, but they generally work out to a much lower hourly rate than in other kinds of litigation. It seems likely that courts are affected by the size of the judgment even though they don't go as far as Mirabal. The Supreme Court of Alaska has squarely rejected basing Truth in Lending fee awards on a percentage of the judgment. Hayer v. National Bank, 663 P.2d 547 (Alaska 1983).

3. The argument in all these cases is whether small claims are worth remedying. We have seen that argument before, in the debate over the practical limits of class actions, supra at 793-798. One way to make it feasible to litigate such claims is to provide that defendant must pay the fees of a prevailing plaintiff. That would seem to be a prime purpose of attorneys' fee provisions in consumer statutes. Don't cases like Mirabal defeat that purpose? Who can try a federal case for $1,000?

4. GMAC found it worthwhile to spend $30,000 on the case. The court explains that by suggesting that the precedent is more important to GMAC than to plaintiffs. Isn't that just because GMAC is a repeat player and plaintiffs are one-shotters? Isn't the precedent just as important to borrowers collectively as to lenders collectively? And isn't that the right comparison if fee statutes are supposed to encourage private enforcement of public policy?

5. Do fully compensatory fees in these cases give plaintiffs too much of a bargaining club? If GMAC can afford to spend $30,000 defending a $1,000 case, will the risk of paying another $30,000 if it loses force it into settlement? What about defendants' settlement leverage under the American rule? Shouldn't defendants always be able to force a less than compensatory settlement, even if liability is absolutely clear, if plaintiff has to pay his own fees for going to trial?

6. Do Blum v. Stenson and Hensley v. Eckerhart cast any light on these issues? The emphasis on hourly rates helps plaintiffs a little bit. But

what about *Hensley's* emphasis on the "significance of the overall relief
. . . . in relation to the hours reasonably expended." Didn't the Court say
that in a quite different context? Should we treat time spent on successful
claims with small recoveries the same way we treat time spent on unsuccessful claims?

7. *Mirabal* limits fees because the claim is too small. Other cases
deny fees because the claim is too large. The leading case is Zarcone v.
Perry, 581 F.2d 1039 (2d Cir. 1978), *cert. denied*, 439 U.S. 1072 (1979), in
which a jury awarded $140,000 against a judge who had a coffee seller
brought before him in handcuffs for selling "putrid" coffee. The court of
appeals held that no fee award was needed, because the case was lucrative
enough to attract private counsel on a contingent fee basis. Subsequent
cases have emphasized that fees can only be denied on this ground only if
the case appeared lucrative enough at the beginning; the ultimate result is
not dispositive. Kerr v. Quinn, 692 F.2d 875 (2d Cir. 1982).

McLean v. Arkansas Board of Education, 723 F.2d 45 (8th Cir. 1983),
presented a combination of the altruism and lucrative case rationales for
denying fees. Plaintiffs challenged a law requiring that "creation science"
be taught in the public schools. The American Civil Liberties Union
sponsored the litigation, and based a fund raising campaign on the case.
Defendants argued that fees should be denied because so many people
were willing to contribute to support the litigation. The court awarded
fees anyway, but one judge dissented.

NOTES ON ETHICAL PROBLEMS IN FEE AWARDS

1.   We have focused on litigated cases, in which the court determines
the damages or other relief to the litigant and also determines the fees to
be awarded his attorney. But most cases are settled, and settlement of fee
claims involves an inherent conflict of interest for the attorney. Defendants are interested only in the total cost of the settlement; they don't
care how much goes to the lawyer and how much to his client. Once
defendant decides how much it is willing to pay, every dollar for the
lawyer comes out of his client's pocket.

2.   In some individual cases, the conflict may be no worse than in any
other attorney-client relationship. It is always the case that the lawyer's
interest is in a high fee and the client's interest is in a low fee. The
settlement negotiations can award a lump sum to the client, and the
client and attorney can divide the sum according to their fee agreement.
The lawyer may take advantage of the client in this division, but that risk
is always present, and the fee award provisions do not aggravate it.

The risk can be aggravated if the lawyer negotiates one sum for the client and a separate sum for himself. Consider the settlement reported in *Mirabal* of $400 for the client and $12,000 for the lawyer. One wonders if the client got the same percentage of his claim as the lawyer got of his.

3. The problems are greatly aggravated in class actions. The class can't agree to a fee, and the lawyer must negotiate both a class recovery and his own fee award. The Third Circuit has suggested that he negotiate the class recovery, get that approved by the court, and then negotiate attorneys' fees. Prandini v. National Tea Co., 557 F.2d 1015 (3d Cir. 1977). That would solve the problem if it worked, but it requires a very cooperative defendant. Defendants frequently won't settle unless they know the bottom line. Who can blame them? If the lawyer for the class steadfastly refuses to discuss fees, it is likely that the case won't settle, or that it will settle for a sum that leaves room for defendant's worst fears of what the fee award might be. Neither result is in the interest of the class. And there is no good way for the court to police the negotiation process. Suppose defendant slips into the conversation that it's willing to spend $100,000 total to get rid of this case. The plaintiff's lawyer may understand that if he settles for $80,000 and requests a $20,000 fee, he'll get no fight on the fee.

Having said all that, it is clear that separating damage negotiations from fee negotiations helps reduce the conflict, and some lawyers try to insist on it.

4. The problem is different in the common fund cases. There, the parties negotiate a lump sum to cover the damages. There is no conflict at this stage, because defendant won't be liable for fees in addition. Then the plaintiff's lawyer petitions the court for fees. Now the problem is obvious: Who represents the class? Often the answer is that nobody does, and the court approves a fee petition without benefit of any adversarial probing. The problem arises whether the damage judgment was litigated or settled. If there are individual class members with a large enough stake, some of them may come forward to object to the fee petition. In the *Fine Paper* litigation, discussed in the notes following Blum v. Stenson, large companies like Xerox were members of the class, and they had huge claims. Even so, the fee petitions might well have gone unchallenged had not one of the lawyers for the class become angry at the excessive fees claimed by many of the others.

5. The fighting among the lawyers in *Fine Paper* illustrates another recurring problem. When a wrong to a large class is discovered, there are many potential plaintiffs and many potential lawyers. Thirty-eight separate lawsuits were consolidated in the *Fine Paper* litigation. Every lawyer wants to be lead counsel, and failing that, most lawyers want a piece of the action. Sometimes lead counsel is elected; sometimes he is appointed by the court. There are no workable standards for selecting lead counsel, and much of the early fighting is plaintiff's lawyer against plaintiff's law-

yer rather than plaintiff class against defendant. Sometimes the pretrial work can be divided among many lawyers, but that often results in wasteful duplication.

If some of the cases are in state court, it is usually impossible to consolidate them all. Then parallel class actions can proceed until one is tried or settled, leaving the other plaintiff at the head of an empty class. It doesn't take a very clever defendant to exploit that risk to achieve enormous settlement leverage. In Lurie v. Canadian Javelin Ltd., 93 Ill. 2d 231, 443 N.E.2d 592 (1982), a state class action was left with twelve class members and a $3,000 settlement when another representative of the original class settled a federal case. Plaintiffs' lawyers sought fees for 2,400 hours of attorney time and 680 hours of law clerk time plus $13,000 in expenses. The trial court awarded $100,000 in fees and $10,600 in expenses, but the Supreme Court vacated and remanded. It said that fees could exceed the judgment, but to exceed it thirty-three-fold was too much. Without any more explicit directions, it ordered reconsideration.

6.   Can the lawyer for the class do anything more than sensitize himself to the risks and bend over backwards to protect the class instead of himself? Can he structure negotiations in ways that reduce the risk? Does defense counsel have an ethical obligation not to exploit class counsel's dilemma? Or does the duty of zealous advocacy obligate defendant to exploit class counsel's dilemma if he can?

NOTES ON COSTS

1.   The federal courts and most states follow something close to the English rule with respect to ordinary court costs. Federal Civil Rule 54(d), for example, provides that "costs shall be allowed as of course to the prevailing party unless the court otherwise directs." Courts do not often deny costs. The most common reasons are indigency of the losing litigant, Badillo v. Central Steel & Wire Co., 717 F.2d 1160 (7th Cir. 1983), and tactics that needlessly inflate costs or prolong the litigation, Jones v. Schellenberger, 225 F.2d 784 (7th Cir. 1955), cert. denied, 350 U.S. 989 (1956).

2.   Taxable costs are generally a small fraction of attorneys' fees, but they can be worth fighting over in substantial litigation. Taxable costs in federal court include fees of the clerk, marshall, court reporter, and witnesses, printing costs, the cost of copying documents "necessarily obtained for use in the case," and fees for court appointed experts and interpreters. 28 U.S.C. §1920 (1982). Allowable witness fees are the statutory fees required by 28 U.S.C. §1821 (1982) — $30 per day plus expenses. Most courts do not tax as costs the fees of expert witnesses. Ramos v. Lamm, 713 F.2d 546 (10th Cir. 1983).

3. Costs are generally taxed administratively by the clerk, but as the litigated cases suggest, judicial review is available.

B. THE PARTIES' POWER TO SPECIFY THE REMEDY

TRUCK RENT-A-CENTER v. PURITAN FARMS 2ND
41 N.Y.2d 420, 361 N.E.2d 1015 (1977)

JASEN, J. The principal issue on this appeal is whether a provision in a truck lease agreement which requires the payment of a specified amount of money to the lessor in the event of the lessee's breach is an enforceable liquidated damages clause, or, instead, provides for an unenforceable penalty.

Defendant Puritan Farms 2nd, Inc. . . . was in the business of furnishing milk and milk products to customers through home delivery. In January, 1969, Puritan leased a fleet of 25 new milk delivery trucks from plaintiff Truck Rent-A-Center for a term of seven years commencing January 15, 1970. . . . [P]laintiff was to supply the trucks and make all necessary repairs. Puritan was to pay an agreed upon weekly rental fee. It was understood that the lessor would finance the purchase of the trucks through a bank, paying the prime rate of interest on the date of the loan plus 2%. The rental charges on the trucks were to be adjusted in the event of a fluctuation in the interest rate above or below specified levels. The lessee was granted the right to purchase the trucks, at any time after 12 months following commencement of the lease, by paying to the lessor the amount then due and owing on the bank loan, plus an additional $100 per truck purchased.

Article 16 of the lease agreement provided that if the agreement should terminate prior to expiration of the term of the lease as a result of the lessee's breach, the lessor would be entitled to damages, "liquidated for all purposes," in the amount of all rents that would have come due from the date of termination to the date of normal expiration of the term less the "re-rental value" of the vehicles, which was set at 50% of the rentals that would have become due. In effect, the lessee would be obligated to pay the lessor, as a consequence of breach, one half of all rentals that would have become due had the agreement run its full course. The agreement recited that, in arriving at the settled amount of damage, "the parties hereto have considered, among other factors, Lessor's substantial initial investment in purchasing or reconditioning for Lessee's service the demised motor vehicles, the uncertainty of Lessor's ability to re-enter [*sic*; *re-rent* may have been intended] the said vehicles, the costs to Lessor during any period the vehicles may remain idle until re-rented, or if sold, the uncertainty of the sales price and its possible attendant loss. The parties have also considered, among other factors, in so liquidating the said damages, Lessor's saving in expenditures for gasoline, oil and other service items."

The bulk of the written agreement was derived from a printed form lease which the parties modified by both filling in blank spaces and typing in alterations. The agreement also contained several typewritten indorsements which also made changes in the provisions of the printed lease. The provision for lessee's purchase of the vehicles for the bank loan balance and $100 per vehicle was contained in one such indorsement. The liquidated damages clause was contained in the body of the printed form.

Puritan tendered plaintiff a security deposit, consisting of four weeks' rent and the lease went into effect. After nearly three years, the lessee sought to terminate the lease agreement. On December 7, 1973, Puritan wrote to the lessor complaining that the lessor had not repaired and maintained the trucks as provided in the lease agreement. Puritan stated that it had "repeatedly notified" plaintiff of these defaults, but plaintiff had not cured them. Puritan, therefore, exercised its right to terminate the agreement "without any penalty and *without purchasing the trucks*." (Emphasis added.) On the date set for termination, December 14, 1973, plaintiff's attorneys replied to Puritan by letter to advise it that plaintiff believed it had fully performed its obligations under the lease and, in the event Puritan adhered to the announced breach, would commence proceedings to obtain the liquidated damages provided for in article 16 of the agreement. Nevertheless, Puritan had its drivers return the trucks to plaintiff's premises, where the bulk of them have remained ever since. At the time of termination, plaintiff owed $45,134.17 on the outstanding bank loan.

Plaintiff followed through on its promise to commence an action for the payment of the liquidated damages. Defendant counterclaimed for the return of its security deposit. At the nonjury trial, plaintiff contended that it had fully performed its obligations to maintain and repair the trucks. Moreover, it was submitted, Puritan sought to cancel the lease because corporations allied with Puritan had acquired the assets, including delivery trucks, of other dairies and Puritan believed it cheaper to utilize this "shadow fleet." The home milk delivery business was on the decline and plaintiff's president testified that efforts to either re-rent or sell the truck fleet to other dairies had not been successful. Even with modifications in the trucks, such as the removal of the milk racks and a change in the floor of the trucks, it was not possible to lease the trucks to other industries, although a few trucks were subsequently sold. The proceeds of the sales were applied to the reduction of the bank balance. The other trucks remained at plaintiff's premises, partially protected by a fence plaintiff erected to discourage vandals. The defendant countered with proof that plaintiff had not repaired the trucks promptly and satisfactorily.

At the close of the trial, the court found, based on the evidence it found to be credible, that plaintiff had substantially performed its obligations under the lease and that defendant was not justified in terminating the agreement. Further, the court held that the provision for liquidated damages was reasonable and represented a fair estimate of actual damages which would be difficult to ascertain precisely. . . . The court calculated that plaintiff would have been entitled to $177,355.20 in rent for the period remaining in the lease and, in accordance with the liquidated damages provision, awarded plaintiff half that amount, $88,677.60. The resulting judgment was affirmed by the Appellate Division, with two Justices dissenting.

The primary issue before us is whether the "liquidated damages" provision is enforceable. Liquidated damages constitute the compensation which, the parties have agreed, should be paid in order to satisfy any loss or injury flowing from a breach of their contract. In effect, a liquidated damage provision is an estimate, made by the parties at the time they enter into their agreement, of the extent of the injury that would be sustained as a result of breach of the agreement. Parties to a contract have the right to agree to such clauses, provided that the clause is neither unconscionable nor contrary to public policy. Provisions for liquidated damage have value in those situations where it would be difficult, if not actually impossible, to calculate the amount of actual damage. In such cases, the contracting parties may agree between themselves as to the amount of damages to be paid upon breach rather than leaving that amount to the calculation of a court or jury.

On the other hand, liquidated damage provisions will not be enforced if it is against public policy to do so and public policy is firmly set against the imposition of penalties or forfeitures for which there is no statutory authority. It is plain that a provision which requires, in the event of contractual breach, the payment of a sum of money grossly disproportionate to the amount of actual damages provides for penalty and is unenforceable. A liquidated damage provision has its basis in the principle of just compensation for loss. A clause which provides for an amount plainly disproportionate to real damage is not intended to provide fair compensation but to secure performance by the compulsion of the very disproportion. A promisor would be compelled, out of fear of economic devastation, to continue performance and his promisee, in the event of default, would reap a windfall well above actual harm sustained. As was stated eloquently long ago, to permit parties, in their unbridled discretion, to utilize penalties as damages, "would lead to the most terrible oppression in pecuniary dealings." (Hoag v. McGinnis, 22 Wend. 163, 166.)

The rule is now well established. A contractual provision fixing damages in the event of breach will be sustained if the amount liquidated bears a reasonable proportion to the probable loss and the amount of actual loss is incapable or difficult of precise estimation. If, however, the amount fixed is plainly or grossly disproportionate to the probable loss, the provision calls for a penalty and will not be enforced. In interpreting a provision fixing damages, it is not material whether the parties themselves have chosen to call the provision one for "liquidated damages," as in this case, or have styled it as a penalty. Such an approach would put too much faith in form and too little in substance. Similarly, the agreement should be interpreted as of the date of its making and not as of the date of its breach.

In applying these principles to the case before us, we conclude that the amount stipulated by the parties as damages bears a reasonable relation to the amount of probable actual harm and is not a penalty. . . .

Looking forward from the date of the lease, the parties could reasonably conclude, as they did, that there might not be an actual market for the sale or re-rental of these specialized vehicles in the event of the lessee's breach. To be sure, plaintiff's lost profit could readily be measured by the amount of the weekly rental fee. However, it was permissible for the parties, in advance, to agree that the re-rental or sale value of the vehicles would be 50% of the weekly rental. Since there was uncertainty as to whether the trucks could be re-rented or sold, the parties could reasonably set, as they did, the value of such mitigation at 50% of the amount the lessee was obligated to pay for rental of the trucks. This would take into consideration the fact that, after being used by the lessee, the vehicles would no longer be "shiny, new trucks," but would be used, possibly battered, trucks, whose value would have declined appreciably. The parties also considered the fact that, although plaintiff, in the event of Puritan's breach, might be spared repair and maintenance costs necessitated by Puritan's use of the trucks, plaintiff would have to assume the cost of storing and maintaining trucks idled by Puritan's refusal to use them. Further, it was by no means certain, at the time of the contract, that lessee would peacefully return the trucks to the lessor after lessee had breached the contract.

With particular reference to the dissent at the Appellate Division, it is true that the lessee might have exercised an option to purchase the trucks. However, lessee would not be purchasing 25 "shiny, new trucks" for a mere $2,500. Rather, lessee, after the passage of one year from the commencement of the term, could have purchased trucks that had been used for at least one year for the amount outstanding on the bank loan, in addition to the $2,500. Of course, the purchase price would be greater if the option were exercised early in the term rather than towards the end of the term since plaintiff would be making payments to the bank all the while. More fundamental, the existence of the option clause has absolutely no bearing on the validity of the discrete, liquidated damages provision. The lessee could have elected to purchase the trucks but elected not to do so. In fact, the lessee's letter of termination made a point of the fact that the lessee did not want to purchase the trucks. The reality is that the lessee sought, by its wrongful termination of the lease, to evade all obligations to the plaintiff, whether for rent or for the agreed upon purchase price. Its effort to do so failed. That lessee could have made a better bargain for itself by purchasing the trucks for $48,134.17 pursuant to the option, instead of paying $92,341.79 in damages for wrongful breach of the lease is not availing to it now. Although the lessee might now wish, with the benefit of hindsight, that it had purchased the trucks rather than default on its lease obligations, the simple fact is that it did not do so.

We attach no significance to the fact that the liquidated damages clause appears on the preprinted form portion of the agreement. The agreement was fully negotiated and the provisions of the form, in many other respects, were amended. There is no indication of any disparity of bargaining power or of unconscionability. The provision for liquidated damages related reasonably to potential harm that was difficult to estimate and did not constitute a disguised penalty. . . .

Chief Judge BREITEL and Judges GABRIELLI, JONES, WACHTLER, FUCHSBERG and COOKE concur.

Order affirmed.

NOTES ON LIQUIDATED DAMAGE AND PENALTY CLAUSES

1.   Here is an excerpt from Justice Shapiro's dissent in the Appellate Division, 51 A.D.2d 786, 788-789, 380 N.Y.S.2d 37, 41-42 (1976):

> The liquidated damage clause is contained in a printed form lease upon which the name of plaintiff is typed, thus making it obvious that the clause was nothing but a printer's boiler-plate provision, having no particular relevance to any party who would use it. The clause in question fixed plaintiff's damages at 50% of the gross rentals it was to receive for the unexpired term of the lease. . . . The evidence adduced by plaintiff clearly shows that its damages, in the event of a breach, could be ascertained with almost mathematical precision. Under such circumstances, reliance on the liquidated damage clause was impermissible since the damages flowing from a breach of this contract can be easily established. As defendants properly point out, the best proof that the clause in question is a penalty clause is that, assuming Puritan had repudiated the lease shortly after it was entered into, plaintiff, which expected to make a profit of 25% of the gross rentals over the life of the lease — seven years — could, under the so-called liquidated damage clause, "claim $2\frac{1}{2}$ times that sum immediately — and would have a fleet of shiny new trucks, which plaintiff could presumably rent or sell to someone else." When a provision gives a party

the right to have its cake and eat it too, it is a penalty and not a legitimate liquidated damage clause. If further proof be needed to establish that we are dealing with a true penalty clause, it is the fact that Puritan, under the terms of the lease agreement, had the right, at any time and for any reason, to acquire title to the trucks and to pay plaintiff $2,500 for them, thereby bringing plaintiff's profits on the transaction down to that nominal sum. Under these circumstances, the judgment, which awards plaintiff damages in excess of $84,000, and still leaves it with title to the trucks, is an unconscionable windfall, which should not receive judicial approval.

2.   Who has the better of the argument? Would you like to know how the 25 percent profit margin was calculated? It may be true that plaintiff's expenses equaled 75 percent of rentals, but it seems unlikely that all those expenses could be eliminated after breach. Presumably part of the expenses were fixed overhead. Certainly plaintiff would still owe the bank, and interest would continue to accrue. If most of the expenses continued, the liquidated damages might have left plaintiff worse off than full performance of the lease.

But what about the option to buy? Why is that irrelevant? Recall the rule that owners of damaged property get lost value or repair costs, whichever is less. O'Brien Brothers v. The Helen B. Moran, supra at 45. Why doesn't the same principle apply here? If defendant could have fully performed by paying the bank note plus $2,500, why isn't that the measure of plaintiff's expectancy and the limit of compensatory damages? And if that's the case, why isn't a provision for nearly twice as much a penalty?

3.   What does it mean to consider the contract "as of the date of its making and not as of the date of its breach"? Justice Shapiro considered the possibility of a breach on the very first day, which would give plaintiff a fleet of shiny new trucks plus three and a half years' rent. The Court of Appeals focused more on the breach that actually occurred, when the trucks were used and battered. Should the clause be invalidated as a penalty if it would have been excessive under some circumstances, but not as the case turned out?

Presumably, the Court of Appeals meant that in deciding whether the estimate of damages was reasonable, courts should focus on what the parties could have predicted at the time of contracting. But the Court of Appeals considers what they could have predicted about the breach that actually occurred, not about the whole range of breaches that might have occurred.

Consider another suit on an equipment lease, Krenek v. Wang Laboratories, 583 S.W.2d 454 (Tex. Civ. App. 1979). There the court refused to enforce the liquidated damage clause, relying on a "rule" that is frequently applied and frequently ignored: that where a contract states several obligations of different importance, and the liquidated damage clause provides the same liability for breach of any of them, the clause is obviously a penalty and not a reasonable attempt to estimate damages. In *Krenek*, the lessee was obligated to maintain the equipment, and not to place any labels on it that might imply a claim of ownership. Because the liquidated damage clause would have plainly been excessive with respect to breaches of these obligations, the court refused to enforce it with respect to a failure to pay rent.

4. As the Court of Appeals viewed *Truck Rent-A-Center*, the clause was reasonable with respect to the actual breach, even though it might not have been reasonable with respect to Justice Shapiro's hypothetical breach on the first day. What about the opposite possibility — a generally reasonable clause that turns out to be clearly excessive in particular circumstances? The clearest case is where plaintiff suffers no damage at all. In Norwalk Door Closer Co. v. Eagle Lock & Screw Co., 153 Conn. 681, 220 A.2d 263 (1966), Eagle went out of business in the middle of a twelve-year contract to produce custom door closers exclusively for Norwalk. Norwalk sued on a $100,000 liquidated damage clause, which might have been reasonable for such a long-term contract. But the company that bought Eagle's assets took over production for Norwalk at the same site with the same local management without interruption, under a new contract more favorable to Norwalk than the old contract with Eagle. The court refused to enforce the liquidated damage clause.

5. One purpose of liquidated damage clauses is to avoid litigation over difficult damage issues. If the court has to determine actual damages to decide whether the liquidated damage clause is reasonable, what has been saved? The Restatement (Second) of Contracts suggests that the court has to determine actual damages only when it is easy to do so. If damages are hard to determine even after breach, the court need decide only that the liquidated damages are a reasonable estimate. §356 comment b (1981). Are *Truck Rent-A-Center* and *Norwalk* consistent with that approach?

6. Suppose the estimate is reasonable but damages are easy to calculate? Should the liquidated damage clause be thrown out on that ground alone? Why shouldn't the parties be able to save themselves the expense of proving actual damages even if the expense is minor? Both the Restatement and §2-718(1) of the Uniform Commercial Code make the certainty factor a guide to application of the reasonableness factor, rather than an independent requirement. Thus, where actual damages are hard to measure, there is a wide range of reasonableness. Where they are easier to measure, the range of reasonableness is narrower. Restatement (Second) of Contracts, §356 comment b (1981).

7. The dissent below said that in doubtful cases, liquidated damage clauses should be invalidated as penalties. The Court of Appeals case cited for that proposition was decided in 1924. Would the Court of Appeals say that today?

8.   Why should the courts second guess the parties' contract at all? If the parties are free to agree on their own contract, why aren't they free to agree on the remedy? Is it likely that enforcing penalty clauses would lead to the "most terrible oppression," as *Truck Rent-A-Center* suggests? Can we control oppression with unconscionability doctrine?

9.   An example of possible oppression is Berlinger v. Suburban Apartment Management Co., 7 Ohio App. 3d 122, 454 N.E.2d 1367 (1982). Berlinger rented an apartment for $210 a month. He kept a motorcycle in violation of the lease. There was a liquidated damage clause that the landlord and court interpreted as specifying $50 per day for each day of violation. The court took judicial notice that motorcycles could annoy other tenants. But it held that $50 per day bore no relation to the landlord's damage and held the clause void as a penalty.

10.   Suppose the landlord had gotten an injunction ordering Berlinger to remove his motorcycle. If that seems unrealistic, suppose that the dispute arose in a condominium project, where eviction is not a likely remedy. If Berlinger defied the injunction, the condominium association could seek coercive sanctions for contempt. One plausible sanction would be a $50 per day fine until Berlinger removed the motorcycle. How is that different from a $50 per day liquidated damage clause in the lease or condominium declaration?

One difference is that defendant would have plenty of notice that coercive sanctions were beginning to accumulate. In *Berlinger*, the landlord enforced the penalty retrospectively. But that difference is not inherent. Suppose the clause provided that the $50 per day penalty would begin to accumulate when the homeowner's association made formal demand to remove the motorcycle and warned the offender that it was invoking the penalty clause. How would that be different from coercive contempt?

In a dissenting opinion in Priebe & Sons v. United States, 332 U.S. 407 (1947), Justice Frankfurter answered that the government reserves to itself the power to impose penalties. Is that an explanation or a restatement of the rule? Might he have meant we trust the court's discretion more than we trust the parties?

11.   Of course it is often fictional to talk about the agreement of the parties. It seems clear there was no bargaining over the lease terms in *Berlinger*, and there is never any bargaining over condominium declarations either. That may be sufficient reason to invalidate a penalty; most of us trust the court more than we trust the plaintiff. But the refusal to enforce penalties is not limited to consumer contracts or adhesion contracts, although liquidated damage clauses in such contracts get closer scrutiny. Are recoveries substantially in excess of compensation unfair even in cases of equal bargaining power? Should we protect United States Steel or IBM when it agrees to an excessive per diem penalty?

12.   Recall the economic notion of efficient breach, and the argu-

ment that damages in excess of compensation will discourage parties from breaching contracts when more profitable opportunities arise. Might that be a reason for invalidating penalty clauses? Those committed to an economic analysis of law think not. Recall that they also think that voluntary transactions are better than court decisions at moving resources to their most valuable use. If one side is worried about unprovable or noncompensable damages, or about the expense of proving damages, it may be willing to pay for a penalty clause. The other side may be willing to accept the risks of the penalty clause to get a higher price. In that scenario, both sides are better off. If a more valuable opportunity comes along, the parties can bargain out of the penalty clause if that makes both sides better off; if it doesn't, then that breach wouldn't be efficient after all. Thus, Professors Goetz and Scott would generally enforce freely bargained liquidated damage and penalty clauses, but they would allow courts to use unconscionability doctrine in cases of seriously unequal bargaining power. Goetz and Scott, Liquidated Damages, Penalties and the Just Compensation Principle: Some Notes on an Enforcement Model and a Theory of Efficient Breach, 77 Colum. L. Rev. 554 (1977).

But Professors Clarkson, Miller, and Muris find an economic reason for distinguishing liquidated damage from penalty clauses. They fear that if a party finds breach more lucrative than performance, he may subtly try to hinder performance and induce breach. Efforts to hinder performance are a complete waste to both sides and to society, and the refusal to enforce penalties avoids tempting parties into such behavior. They would refuse to enforce liquidated damage clauses if, and only if, the amount was unreasonable when compared to actual damages, and the plaintiff had both an incentive and an opportunity to induce breach. Clarkson, Miller, and Muris, Liquidated Damages v. Penalties: Sense or Nonsense?, 1978 Wis. L. Rev. 351.

How would *Truck Rent-A-Center* come out under that test? Could plaintiff try to force breach by cutting corners on maintenance? Would it have an incentive to do so? What if defendant responded by buying instead of breaching?

S. M. WILSON & CO. v. SMITH INTERNATIONAL
587 F.2d 1363 (9th Cir. 1978)

Before WALLACE and SNEED, Circuit Judges, and ENRIGHT, District Judge.
   SNEED, Circuit Judge.
   This case presents the familiar question of the circumstances under which a seller in a commercial sale can limit its liability through contractual exclusions of warranty and remedy.

The district court found that the contract involved here was effective in excluding the buyer's recovery of consequential damages and granted summary or final judgment for defendant Smith International, Inc., on all claims. . . .

I.   Facts . . .

We begin by characterizing the sales contract as one between parties who dealt in a commercial setting from positions of relatively equal bargaining strength and who bargained and negotiated concerning the specifications of the product being sold and the risks of loss arising from any of its defects. The buyer is not "a single inexperienced individual" dealing with a large corporate seller vending a standard product to the general public by means of a standard form, the "fine print" of which purports to relieve the seller of all meaningful liability. More particularly, the contract involves the purchase of a tunnel boring machine by McGuire Shaft & Tunnel Corporation, a predecessor of appellant S. M. Wilson & Company, from the Calweld Division of appellee Smith International, Inc.

In 1971 Wilson contracted to construct a mine shaft in Kennsburg, Illinois, for the Ayrshire Coal Company, a division of American Metal Climax, Inc. To assist in performing that contract, Wilson began negotiations with Smith for the purchase of a tunnel boring machine. In due course Wilson agreed to pay $550,000 for a "Calweld 17'-0" diameter, 600 H.P. rock tunnel boring machine," which Smith agreed to design, build and deliver.

The documents which reflect this agreement are as follows. Smith sent Wilson an April 9, 1971, quotation and an April 16, 1971, revised quotation consisting of virtually the same documents. In these Smith attempted to limit its warranty on the machine and the scope of its liability. . . . In brief, these provisions warranted that the machine would be free from defects in material and workmanship. That warranty was established "expressly in lieu of all other warranties, express or implied . . . not set forth in a writing signed by an authorized representative of Calweld [Smith]." This disclaimer was set forth in capital letters. Smith limited its liability for any breach of warranty to repair or replacement of defective parts. It generally excluded any liability resulting from the use or loss of use of the machine as well as for certain specific instances of such injuries. The proposal also contained a merger clause.

Smith's documents also provided that the contract was to be interpreted in accordance with California law. In addition, Smith agreed to "provide one competent tunnel boring machine specialist free of charge, to supervise installation, to demonstrate initial operation, and train customer's operator, for a period of 30 working days." This provision appears in a paragraph captioned "Installation Personnel" and follows one captioned "Shipping and Installation" which provides in part: "Labor and the use of machinery to complete the erection of the machine will be provided by the Purchaser. Calweld is to provide supervision of erection as outlined under 'Installation Personnel.'" . . . . Attached to the April 9 quotation was a cover letter signed by Brickle, a Smith employee, which estimated that the machine would bore at an approximate rate of 2.5 feet per hour through the hardest material expected to be encountered in the Ayrshire project.

On April 22, 1971, Wilson accepted the proposal by mailing Smith its purchase order. The reverse side of Wilson's purchase order, however, contained a printed liability provision substantially different from that in Smith's proposal. This conflict was resolved by an April 28, 1971, letter in which Smith's vice president for administration objected to the Wilson liability provision and reiterated the terms of Smith's proposal. Wilson, by signing an acceptance of Smith's April 28 letter, acceded to Smith's original terms as to liability as expressed in its April 16 quotation. . . .

The machine did not perform as expected. Wilson alleges that it bored at a rate slower than the expected 2.5 feet per hour, overheated, broke down, and wore out blades faster than had been projected. Smith's representatives visited the mine site but were unable to correct the machine's problems. Owing at least in part to problems with the machine, the Ayrshire project required 210 days to complete, rather than an expected 80 days. Near the completion of the project, Wilson's employees discovered that the machine's thrust rollers had been installed in a reverse position. The thrust rollers are a major link in the delivery of turning pressure to the machine's cutting wheel. Wilson contends that the backward installation of the thrust rollers was a major cause of the machine's poor performance and that such installation had taken place during the machine's reassembly in Illinois under the direction of Smith's supervisor. Smith not only attempted to discover the source of the machine's difficulties but also provided replacement thrust rollers as well as other replacement parts as requested by Wilson.

Problems with the machine continued even after it was removed from the completed Ayrshire project, repaired, and located at a project undertaken by Wilson at United States Steel's Dilworth mine in Pennsylvania. There it was discovered that one of 10 Staffa hydraulic motors was operating in opposition to the other nine because of the reversal of an internal valve in the motor. The Staffa motors had been installed in the machine in factory-built condition.

Wilson alleges that the difficulties with the Calweld machine caused it losses of approximately $1,844,559. . . .

Wilson lists eight causes of action. They are breach of contract for failure to reassemble the machine properly (first cause of action), breach of contract for failure to provide a competent installer (second cause), breach of implied warranty of fitness (third cause), negligence in design, construction, reassembly, and in failure to provide a competent reassembly supervisor (causes four through seven), and misrepresentation as to the machine's boring rate (eighth cause).

The district court held that Wilson could recover on none of its causes of action. This was done in two orders, the first dated March 21, 1975, and the second July 18, 1975. . . .

[The March 21 order granted summary judgment to defendant on counts three through eight.]

The July 18, 1975, order was predicated on a stipulation in open court by counsel for Wilson that it had suffered by reason of the machine's defects "no damages other than consequential damages." The court excluded evidence of such damages with respect to the two remaining causes of action and granted final judgment thereon in favor of Smith.

[The court held that the letter estimating that the machine would bore 2.5 feet per hour was not binding on Smith, because Wilson knew that only certain Smith officials had power to modify the contract. The employee who signed the letter was not one of them.

The court also held that any errors by the Smith employee sent to supervise assembly were defects in workmanship. As such, they were within the clauses limiting Smith's liability to replacement and repair.]

III.   Effect of Inability to Repair

A.   Statutory Background

The contract we must construe, therefore, is one in which the seller warrants the machine to be free of defects in material and workmanship under normal use and service. All other warranties express or implied are disclaimed and the seller limits his liability to replacing or repairing, free of charge, "any defective part or parts of the machine" that the seller manufactured. In addition, the seller is not liable "for any loss or damage resulting, directly or indirectly, from the use or loss of use of the machine."

Wilson alleges that Smith's efforts to repair the machine were unsuccessful. Smith does not allege otherwise. The next issue which we must address is the effect, if any, of this inability to repair on Smith's disclaimers and liability limitations. It is this issue around which Wilson wages his crucial battle. If Smith's inability to repair demolishes his disclaimer and limited liability fortress, Wilson can invoke the implied warranty of fitness and dash to victory by recovering such consequential damages as permitted by section 2715, Cal. Com. Code (West 1964).

To understand the contest four sections of California's Commercial Code must be grasped, viz. §§2316, 2714, 2715 and 2719. . . . Section 2316 permits the exclusion of a warranty of fitness provided it is in writing and conspicuous, as well as the limitation of remedies for breach of warranty. The exclusion of all other warranties in this contract is conspicuous and, of course, is in writing. Thus, section 2316 does not alter the contract we have held the parties intended to make. Section 2714 merely sets forth the measure of damages a buyer is entitled to recover when the goods do not conform to the terms of the contract. The measure provided for breach of warranty "is the difference at the time and place of acceptance between the value of the goods accepted and the value they would have had if they had been as warranted. . . ." Consequential damages may also be recovered in a proper case. Section 2715 defines incidental and consequential damages, the latter including "[a]ny loss resulting from . . . particular requirements . . . of which the seller at the time of contracting had reason to know. . . ."

Section 2719(1)(a) permits the seller to limit the remedy available to a buyer "to repair and replacement of nonconforming goods or parts"; but section 2719(2) permits the buyer the remedies "provided in this code" in those instances "[w]here circumstances cause an exclusive or limited remedy to fail of its essential purpose." Section 2719(3) permits the exclusion of recovery of consequential damages unless the exclusion is unconscionable.

B. Presence of an Implied Warranty

This sketch of the applicable code provisions makes plain that Wilson's attack must consist primarily of invoking either section 2719(2) or (3). In fact, he invokes only 2719(2); no argument is made that the exclusion of consequential damages is unconscionable. He asserts that because Smith was unable to repair the machine the limited remedy of repair failed "of its essential purpose." Such failure, he argues, opens up the remedies available under the Code, including the recovery of consequential damages, and eliminates the disclaimer of implied warranties, making available an implied warranty of fitness. He relies primarily on a line of cases commencing with Adams v. J. I. Case Co., 125 Ill. App. 2d 388, 261 N.E.2d 1 (1970) and including [eleven other cases].

This is an impressive array of authorities. However, Wilson overstates their reach. *Adams*, the common ancestor of them all, did not sweep away entirely the disclaimer of implied warranties upon concluding that the limited remedy of repair had failed of its essential purpose. Such failure raised an implied warranty of "reasonably prompt and timely repairs" notwithstanding a disclaimer, but the existence of an implied warranty "that the tractor [the article sold] was a good, satisfactory tractor capable of doing the work for which it was sold" was prevented by the disclaimer. Hence we do not regard these cases as holding that such failure wipes from the contract entirely a disclaimer of express or implied warranties. They do, however, preclude the existence of an implied warranty of fitness.

C.   The Bar to Recovery of Consequential Damages

This family of cases, however, supports unanimously the proposition that such failure does remove from the contract the bar to the recovery of consequential damages. Against this array Smith relies primarily on American Electric Power Co. v. Westinghouse Electric Corp., 418 F. Supp. 435 (S.D.N.Y. 1976) [and two other cases]. In these cases the clause barring recovery of consequential damages survived the failure of the repair remedy in its essential purpose.

Prior to determining which line of cases should govern our disposition of this case it is necessary to decide whether the repair remedy failed of its essential purpose. Our consideration of this issue has been considerably aided by Eddy, On the "Essential" Purposes of Limited Remedies: The Metaphysics of U.C.C. Section 2-719(2), 65 Calif. L. Rev. 28 (1977). Of particular importance is the following passage:

> This rosy picture of the limited repair warranty, however, rests upon at least three assumptions: that the warrantor will diligently make repairs, that such repairs will indeed "cure" the defects, and that consequential loss in the interim will be negligible. So long as these assumptions hold true, the limited remedy appears to operate fairly and, as noted above, will usually withstand contentions of "unconscionability." But when one of these assumptions proves false in a particular case, the purchaser may find that the substantial benefit of the bargain has been lost.

Id. at 63.

Two of the assumptions suggested by Eddy allegedly have proven false in this case. The repairs did not "cure" the defects and consequential damages are not negligible. However, the warrantor did attempt to repair the machine but was unable to do so. As a result, the buyer lost a substantial benefit of his bargain despite the seller's efforts to provide the limited remedy. We do not weigh the alleged magnitude of consequential damages in determining whether the limited repair remedy failed of its essential purpose, because of the presence of the contractual exclusion of any liability for consequential damages. In any event, the inability to cure substantial defects does indicate that the repair remedy so failed. . . .

The failure of the limited repair warranty to achieve its essential purpose makes available, as indicated above, the remedies as "may be had as provided in this code." This does not mean, however, that the bar to recovery of consequential damages should be eliminated. Wilson, under ordinary circumstances, should be entitled to recover the monetary equivalent of the benefit of his bargain, a recovery precisely described by section 2714(2), Cal. Com. Code (West 1964). That is, a purchaser, upon failure of the limited repair remedy to serve its essential purpose, is entitled to recover the difference between the value of what he should have received and the value of what he got. Wilson, however, has stipulated that he suffered no damages other than consequential. Whatever the reasons for this stipulation, we are confident that it cannot be used to argue that unless consequential damages are allowed no remedy exists to compensate Wilson for Smith's failure to perform. A remedy under section 2714(2) did exist which Wilson chose not to assert. We need not, therefore, reverse and remand to permit Wilson to recover this sum, a course of action we would adopt but for the stipulation.

The issue remains whether the failure of the limited repair remedy to serve its purpose requires permitting the recovery of consequential damages as sections 2714(3) and 2715 permit. We hold it does not. In reaching this conclusion we are influenced heavily by the characteristics of the contract. . . . Parties of relatively equal bargaining power negotiated an allocation of their risks of loss. Consequential damages were assigned to the buyer, Wilson. The machine was a complex piece of equipment designed for the buyer's purposes. The seller Smith did not ignore his obligation to repair; he simply was unable to perform it. This is not enough to require that the seller absorb losses the buyer plainly agreed to bear. Risk shifting is socially expensive and should not be undertaken in the absence of a good reason. An even better reason is required when to so shift is contrary to a contract freely negotiated. The default of the seller is not so total and fundamental as to require that its consequential damage limitation be expunged from the contract.

Our holding is based upon the facts of this case as revealed by the pleadings and record and is not intended to establish that a consequential damage bar always survives a failure of the limited repair remedy to serve its essential purpose. Each case must stand on its own facts. For this reason, although we find encouragement in cases relied upon by Smith, we decline to treat any of them as precisely in point. Supportive California authority consists of Delta Air Lines, Inc. v. Douglas Aircraft Co., 238 Cal. App. 2d 95, 104-05, 47 Cal. Rptr. 518, 524 (1965) (between parties of equal bargaining strength, risk of loss for defective product should be borne by buyer who, as a matter of business judgment, accepted risk associated with bargained-for price; rather than on seller, who neither agreed to bear loss nor was compensated for it).

IV.   Recovery under Negligence Counts

Where the suit is between a nonperforming seller and an aggrieved buyer and the injury consists of damage to the goods themselves and the costs of repair of such damage or a loss of profits that the deal had been expected to yield to the buyer, it would be sensible to limit the buyer's rights to those provided by the Uniform Commercial Code. To treat such a breach as an accident is to confuse disappointment with disaster. Whether the complaint is cast in terms of strict liability in tort or negligence should make no difference. . . .

In a somewhat curious way California law achieves this result by limiting the type of losses recoverable under an action in negligence. Economic losses are not recoverable under negligence. Although the rule is not universally applied, see Union Oil Co. v. Oppen, 501 F.2d 558, 565-67 (9th Cir. 1974), its application in this case by the district court . . . was proper. It serves to limit the parties' rights to those provided by the Uniform Commercial Code, a body of law specifically designed to deal with commercial disputes between sellers and buyers of goods. Therefore, counts four through seven, being based on negligent performance of the contract were properly dismissed.

This conclusion . . . makes it unnecessary to consider whether under California law the contractual bar to recovery of consequential damages also operates to absolve Smith of liability for negligence.

Affirmed.

ENRIGHT, District Judge, sitting by designation, dissenting.

I respectfully dissent. The threshold question presented in this case is whether the parties intended the limited express warranty, with its disclaimer of liability for consequential damages, to govern Smith's obligation to provide "one competent tunnel boring machine specialist . . . to supervise installation." . . .

The specialist furnished by Smith proved to be incompetent. Under his supervision and guidance the thrust rollers of the machine were installed backward. Additionally, one of the machine's ten Staffa motors was installed in such a manner that it rotated backward (while the other nine motors rotated forward). . . .

Wilson bargained for a tunnel boring machine in proper working order. It received a defectively assembled and poorly-working machine. According to the trial court's interpretation of the contract, Wilson's remedy for breach was limited by the terms of the limited express warranty to repair or replacement of defective parts. Since no part of the machine was defective (the malfunctioning being attributable to misassembly), the trial court's construction leaves Wilson remediless. Smith might just as well have provided no assembly specialist at all, furnishing merely a pile of unassembled parts. In that case Wilson would have been relegated to the completely ineffectual remedy of replacement and repair. Such a result would seem anomalous at best and is, in my opinion, in no way compelled by established principles of contract interpretation.

I concur in the majority's finding that recovery is precluded under the negligence counts in Wilson's complaint but would reverse the judgment of the trial court with respect to the contract counts.

NOTES ON LIMITATION OF REMEDY
CLAUSES

1. One of the reasons often offered for invalidating penalty clauses is that the remedy for breach of contract is compensation and the parties cannot deviate from that. But courts have generally been much more sympathetic to clauses limiting remedies to less than full compensation. Why is an undercompensatory remedy more acceptable than an over-compensatory remedy?

2. One answer might be that contracts are intended to allocate risk. The risk that the borer won't work is inherent in the transaction, and a disclaimer of liability allocates that risk to the buyer. But the risk of a $50 a day penalty for keeping a motorcycle is not inherent in the transaction; it is artificially created by the penalty clause. But more than that is going on in these cases and statutes; some allocations of risk are unacceptable.

3. *Wilson* holds that repair and replacement of defective parts fails of its essential purpose when seller is unable to repair, so that Code remedies become available under §2-719(2). How does the court know the essential purpose of the repair and replace remedy? What if the contract recited that the essential purpose of the remedy was to leave the entire risk of loss on buyer except that seller would try in good faith to repair? What if the contract said that whether the product worked depended almost entirely on how buyer took care of it, and consequently, seller would have no liability at all, not even to repair and replace? How could that clause fail of its essential purpose?

The Official Comment to §2-719 implies that a clause whose essential purpose is to leave one side with no remedy at all is unconscionable, even in a commercial setting:

> [I]t is of the very essence of a sales contract that at least minimum adequate remedies be available. If the parties intend to conclude a contract for sale within this Article they must accept the legal consequence that there be at least a fair quantum of remedy for breach of the obligations or duties outlined in the contract. Thus any clause purporting to modify or limit the remedial provisions of this Article in an unconscionable manner is subject to deletion and in that event the remedies made available by this Article are applicable as if the stricken clause had never existed. Similarly, under subsection (2), where an apparently fair and reasonable clause because of circumstances fails in its purpose or operates to deprive either party of the substantial value of the bargain, it must give way to the general remedy provisions of this Article.

Presumably it would be unconscionable for seller to include a clause that denied liability even if it refused to attempt repairs. But what about a clause that says buyer bears the risk that repairs will be impossible? Can the parties contract around cases like *Wilson*?

4.   Why must there be some "minimum quantum of remedy"? Why can't the seller deliver a piece of machinery with absolutely no further obligation if that is what the parties want? Despite the implications of the Comment, they probably can if the machine is already in existence and seller describes the thing to be sold by simply pointing to it. But if they want to write an executory contract that doesn't promise anything, how do they write it? If Smith promises to deliver a seventeen-foot tunnel boring machine, doesn't that inevitably carry implications that might give rise to liability? Suppose Smith adds, "But we don't promise that it will work, and we won't do anything about it if it doesn't work." And then suppose Smith delivers a hand drill. Despite the disclaimers, that's not a seventeen-foot tunnel boring machine, is it? Some remedies may be so strongly implied that it is hard to effectively communicate a total disclaimer.

5.   There is more than one way to limit liability under a contract. A party can limit his substantive obligation or limit his liability for breach. Should we apply the same standards to both kinds of disclaimers? The UCC implies warranties of merchantability and fitness of purpose, and requires that disclaimers of these warranties be conspicuous. If a seller can achieve substantially the same result by making the warranties and limiting liability for their breach, why don't limitation of remedies clauses have to be conspicuous?

On the other hand, if the only substantive constraint on disclaiming warranties and otherwise limiting the scope of the substantive obligation is the general unconscionability section, why are there more specific substantive restrictions on limitation of remedy clauses? Might it be that it is easier to communicate a limited promise than an unlimited promise that is illusory for lack of a remedy?

6.   Did Wilson's lawyer snatch defeat from the jaws of victory by stipulating that his client suffered only consequential damages? The court throws out the clause limiting buyer's remedy to repair and replacement of defective parts, but it leaves in the related clause excluding consequentials. How much would the damages under §2-714(2) be? What was the machine worth "at the time and place of acceptance"? Was it worth almost the whole purchase price, because at the time of acceptance no one knew how hard it would be to repair? Was it worth very little, because in fact it could not be repaired in timely fashion? Or was it worth almost the whole purchase price, because the defects turned out to be easy to fix once they were diagnosed?

Should Wilson's lawyer be liable for malpractice? Or was the court's distinction unforeseeable? Section 2-719(2) says that when an exclusive remedy fails of its essential purpose, "remedy may be had as provided in this Act." Should he have known to imply a proviso? For example: "unless some other clause limits you to only some of the remedies provided by this Act."

7. Both *Wilson* and *Truck Rent-A-Center* emphasize the parties' equal bargaining power. What does that mean? Wilson knew about the limitation of liability, and consciously accepted it, but didn't seem to have much choice about it. Or should we suppose that in a deal of this size, buyer could have gotten its remedy clause for a higher price? Should it matter how many other sellers of seventeen-foot tunnel boring machines there were? Should it matter if the whole industry used the same set of clauses? Sellers routinely disclaim liability for anything other than repair, replacement, or refund, and in small transactions, it is generally impossible to bargain for changes.

Section 2-719(3) makes it prima facie unconscionable to exclude liability for personal injury caused by consumer goods. Tort law also addresses personal injuries and usually refuses to enforce exculpatory agreements. Decisions in other situations are not entirely predictable, but they often turn on the sophistication and financial strength of the buyer and whether the disclaimer of liability was brought to his attention.

8. Compare two cases of lost film. In each case a film developer lost irreplaceable pictures. In each case, the developer had given the customer a receipt that limited liability to replacing the lost pictures with unexposed film. Mieske v. Bartell Drug Co., 92 Wash. 2d 40, 593 P.2d 1308 (1979), held the clause unconscionable and awarded compensatory damages. Carr v. Hoosier Photo Supplies, 441 N.E.2d 450 (Ind. App. 1982), enforced the clause and denied relief; there was one dissent.

Carr didn't read the disclaimer, but from his long experience as an amateur photographer, he knew that such disclaimers were generally printed on receipts for film. The Mieskes also had long experience as amateur photographers, but they claimed not to have learned as much. Mrs. Mieske handled the transaction, and she thought the receipt was only a receipt.

Here's the worst part: The Indiana court thought it important that Carr was an "experienced attorney" who practiced "business law." And he admitted he understood and knew about disclaimers of liability. Have you forfeited a key consumer protection by going to law school?

What good did it do Carr to understand the disclaimer if there was no way to bargain out of it? The court had one suggestion: He could have developed his own film.

NORTHERN ILLINOIS GAS CO. v. ENERGY COOPERATIVE
122 Ill. App. 3d 940, 461 N.E.2d 1049 (1984)

[Northern Illinois Gas promised to buy 56 million barrels of naphtha from Energy Coop over a ten-year period. Northern Illinois converted the naphtha into natural gas. When the United States eased price controls on natural gas, it became cheaper to buy natural gas from drillers and pipe-line companies. Northern Illinois quit buying naphtha, and this litigation resulted. Energy Coop sought damages based on the difference between the market price of naphtha and the contract price plus consequential damages not specified in the opinion.]

HEIPLE, Justice.

NI-Gas argues that the trial court erred in denying its motion for summary judgment on the liquidated damages clause and in striking the liquidated damages defense. The court held that the liquidated damages clause of the contract (section 13) gave the non-breaching party the choice of recovering either actual or liquidated damages. ECI chose to pursue actual damages resulting in a jury award of $305.5 million.

NI-Gas contends that the liquidated damages clause is clear and un-ambiguous and provides the exclusive measure of damages in the event of default:

XIII. LIQUIDATED DAMAGES:

If, prior to the delivery to PURCHASER of the total number of Barrels of Feedstock specified in Section III hereof, this Agreement is terminated by reason of either party's default, prior to the expiration of the term set forth in Section II above, then, upon demand of the party not in default, the default-ing party shall pay to the other as liquidated damages, a sum in cash deter-mined by multiplying one cent ($0.01) by the difference between the total gallons specified in Section III, and the gallons actually delivered to PURCHASER pursuant to this Agreement. . . .

It is further agreed that nothing herein contained shall prejudice the rights of either party to terminate this Agreement as hereinafter provided for and in the event the foregoing provision for liquidated damages is determined to be unenforceable for any reason, the party not in default shall not be precluded from exercising any other rights or remedies to which the party may be enti-tled under the terms of this Agreement or otherwise at law or equity.

According to NI-Gas' calculations, this section would limit ECI's recov-ery to a maximum of $13,576,002.30. . . .

ECI interprets section 13 as being contingent upon a demand for liquidated damages and termination pursuant to section 14 of the con-tract:

XIV. DEFAULT AND TERMINATION

In the event either party is in default of any of its obligations hereunder, in addition to any other rights or remedies available at law or equity, the party not in default may cancel this Agreement by giving not less than thirty (30)

Days prior written notice to the party in default; provided that such notice of default shall not be effective if the party claimed to be in default shall cure such default within thirty (30) Days after having received such notice. Any such termination shall be an additional remedy and shall not prejudice the rights of the party not in default to recover any amounts due it hereunder for any damage or loss suffered by it by virtue of such default, and shall not constitute a waiver of any other remedy to which the party not in default may be entitled for breach of this Agreement. . . .

ECI . . . contends that it has not made a demand for liquidated damages and, therefore, it has the option of seeking actual damages. Failure to demand a contractual right does not create rights greater than those bargained for. A liquidated damages clause is the agreement of the parties as to the amount of damages which must be paid in the event of default. Proof of liability is all that is required to entitle the injured party to recover the liquidated amount. If the non-defaulting party does not wish to demand this amount, he will not be forced to do so. But this does not create the right to seek a greater measure of damages than the amount bargained for.

Next, ECI relies on section 2-719(1)(b) of the Uniform Commercial Code, in arguing that the liquidated damages clause does not provide the exclusive measure of damages unless it is expressly agreed to be exclusive and labeled as such.

§2-719.   CONTRACTUAL MODIFICATION OR LIMITATION
              OF REMEDY

(1) Subject to the provisions of subsections (2) and (3) of this Section and of the preceding section on liquidation and limitation of damages,

(a)   the agreement may provide for remedies in addition to or in substitution for those provided in this Article and may limit or alter the measure of damages recoverable under this Article, as by limiting the buyer's remedies to return of the goods and repayment of the price or to repair and replacement of non-conforming goods or parts; and

(b)   resort to a remedy as provided is optional unless the remedy is expressly agreed to be exclusive, in which case it is the sole remedy.

(Ill. Rev. Stat. 1981, ch. 26, par. 2-719.)

There are no Illinois cases which address the question of whether section 2-719(1)(b) applies to a liquidated damages clause. Other authorities are split on the issue.

NI-Gas takes the position that section 2-719(1)(b) applies only to contract provisions which limit a remedy. A liquidated damages clause does not limit a remedy but instead provides an agreed upon measure of damages. Therefore, section 2-719(1)(b) does not govern the liquidated damages clause in the contract with ECI.

The only reported decision which addresses this precise issue is a North Dakota Supreme Court case. Ray Farmers Union Elevator Co. v. Weyrauch (1975), 238 N.W.2d 47 involved the anticipatory breach of three grain supply contracts which contained liquidated damage clauses. The plaintiffs claimed to have the option of seeking actual damages since the liquidated damage clauses were not declared to be exclusive as allegedly required by section 2-719(1)(a), (b). The court rejected this argument holding that a liquidated damages clause is not a remedy within the portent of section 2-719. In accord with this decision is the commentary found in Bunn, Snead & Speidel, An Introduction to the Uniform Commercial Code 192 (1964) which characterizes section 2-719 as " . . . primarily concerned with *what* remedies are available rather than the monetary amount of damage." (Emphasis in original.)

ECI makes no distinction between a remedy and a measure of damages in arguing that a liquidated damages clause is subject to section 2-719(1)(b). ECI relies on Commonwealth Edison Co. v. Atlantic Richfield Co., No. 76L3951 (N.D. Ill. June 15, 1978), where, in a memorandum opinion, the Federal District Court held that the liquidated damages clause of the contract did not limit the plaintiff's damages to the liquidated amount. The court found that the parties had inserted a provision into the contract which stated that liquidated damages were in addition to any other rights or remedies. Therefore, liquidated damages were optional. Although the court referred to 2-719(1)(b) in reaching its decision, its holding was based primarily on the express terms of the contract which made liquidated damages optional. We do not regard this as a definitive statement requiring liquidated damage clauses to comply with 2-719(1)(b) in order to be exclusive. We also note that this is an unpublished federal trial court decision which has no *stare decisis* effect in this court.

ECI also cites 6 D Willier & Hart, U.C.C. Reporter Digest, §2-719, at 2-666.58 (1983), which is critical of the majority opinion in *Weyrauch*. In this commentary, the authors point to section 1-201(34) of the code which defines "remedy" as "any remedial right to which an aggrieved party is entitled with or without resort to a tribunal." The authors contend that this definition is broad enough to encompass a liquidated damages clause. This is the same position taken by one dissenting justice in *Weyrauch*. For reasons which follow, we prefer the position taken by NI-Gas.

A liquidated damages clause which provides an agreed upon formula for calculating the amount of money damages owed in the event of nonperformance is not a limitation on a remedy. Liquidation or limitation of damages is governed by section 2-718; limitation of remedies falls under

2-719. The concepts are separate and distinct. The only cross reference between the two sections is found in 2-719 which states that it is "subject to" 2-718. If, instead, 2-718 were made subject to 2-719, then the restrictions of 2-719(1)(b) would arguably apply to a liquidated damages clause. But the fact that 2-719 is subject to 2-718 indicates that any restriction on the right to liquidate damages by agreement is contained in 2-718 and nowhere else. We see no reason to impose the additional restraints of 2-719(1)(b).

The trial court erred in finding that the liquidated damages clause did not prevent ECI from seeking an alternate measure of damages. The parties agreed to a liquidated sum as their damages in the event of default. This is often done in order to avoid the difficulty and uncertainty of proving damages by using market value, resale value or otherwise. Such an agreement is binding. Therefore, we reverse the court's order striking the liquidated damages defense. Because of our decision on this issue, it is not necessary for us to review NI-Gas' contention that the jury was improperly instructed on how to calculate ECI's damages. . . .

STOUDER, P.J., and BARRY, J., concur.

NOTES ON UNDERLIQUIDATED DAMAGE CLAUSES

1. We have seen an underliquidated damage clause once before, in Campbell Soup Co. v. Wentz, supra at 364. That case involved a big price swing in Chantenay red cored carrots.

2. A clause that eliminates 96 percent of the damages is a pretty effective limitation of remedy isn't it? Isn't it a mistake to assume that liquidated damage clauses and limitation of remedy clauses are separate categories that never overlap?

3. In the overliquidated damage cases, we asked if the clause were void as a penalty. In the underliquidated damage cases, the question is not whether the clause is void; presumably plaintiff could ask for $13 million even if that's unconscionably low. The question is whether the liquidated damage clause is exclusive: Can Energy Coop sue only for liquidated damages, or can it sue for actual damages in the alternative? Doesn't §2-719(1)(b) speak directly to that?

Does §2-719(1)(b) state a good rule? Won't there inevitably be cases where the parties intend a limited remedy to be exclusive and neglect to "expressly" say so? Consider the fire and burglar alarm cases, such as Atkinson v. Pacific Fire Extinguisher Co., 40 Cal. 2d 192, 253 P.2d 18 (1953). Pacific's contract said that Atkinson could recover liquidated damages of $25 if the system failed to work. Such clauses are standard in the industry. These companies sell alarms; fire and theft insurance must be purchased separately from someone else. Even if some company's form neglected to "expressly" say that the liquidated damage clause is exclusive, would there be any doubt that it should be exclusive anyway?

Or suppose that the clause appears in an adhesion contract drafted by plaintiff. *Campbell Soup* was such a case; another is Farmers Union Grain Terminal Association v. Nelson, 223 N.W.2d 494 (N.D. 1974). Nelson was supposed to sell his wheat to the Terminal Association. Instead, he sold it elsewhere at the market price and tendered a check for liquidated damages. The Terminal Association sued, relying on §2-719(1)(b). The court talked a lot about construing adhesion contracts against their drafters, talked only a little about §2-719, and concluded that the clause "appears clearly intended as an exclusive means of computing the loss." In North Dakota, does "expressly" now include "implicitly"?

4. Can underliquidated damage clauses be attacked under §2-718? Were Energy Coop's damages liquidated in a reasonable amount? The damages obviously aren't a penalty for breach. But the Official Comment notes that an "unreasonably small amount would be subject to similar criticism and might be stricken under the section on unconscionable contracts or clauses." Is $13 million per se unreasonable when compared to $305 million? Or does the court have to know who was to bear the risk of an unexpectedly large swing in the price of naphtha? If so, how is the court supposed to figure that out?

5. *Northern Illinois Gas* doesn't give us much information about the price of naphtha, so consider another price swing case, Carolinas Cotton Growers Association, Inc. v. Arnette, 371 F. Supp. 65 (D.S.C. 1974). *Carolinas Cotton* involved contracts to sell the drought stricken 1973 cotton crop. The contracts specified liquidated damages of $25 per bale for nondelivery. That would have been enough to cover any normal price swings, but in 1973 the price of cotton went from $150 a bale to over $400. The court held that liquidated damages were not the exclusive remedy, relying on §2-719(1)(b). The result is squarely contrary to the North Dakota wheat case, although this also appeared to be an adhesion contract drafted by the buyer.

The clause in *Carolinas Cotton* might have been intended to simplify proof of damage in a normal market but not apply at all to wholly unanticipated conditions. Or it might have been intended to allocate the risk of normal price increases to the farmer and of abnormal price increases to the buyer. Or, quite likely, the parties didn't think about the possibility of abnormal price increases and had no intent whatever. With both sides taking adversarial positions after the fact, how can the court decide? If drafters do have a purpose in mind, should they recite it in the contract?

6. What about the fire and burglar alarm cases? Those underliquidated damage clauses are universally upheld. Annotation, Validity, Construction, and Effect of Limited Liability or Stipulated Damages Clause in Fire or Burglar Alarm Service Contract, 42 A.L.R.2d 591 (1955 and

Supp. 1980 and 1984). But courts have to struggle to make these cases fit within traditional rules about liquidated damages. Is $50 a reasonable estimate of the loss if a burglar alarm fails to function? The California Supreme Court said yes in Better Food Markets v. American District Telegraph Co., 40 Cal. 2d 179, 253 P.2d 10, 15 (1953), a case in which burglars stole $36,000 worth of merchandise. The court said more latitude is allowed where damages are very difficult to estimate, and that many breaches would result in no damage at all, so $50 might be a "fair average." In *Atkinson*, the companion case, the court said $25 was a fair estimate of loss from failure of a fire alarm; actual damages were $97,000. But *Atkinson* also talked about the risk allocation issues that were really at stake. There was one dissent in each case.

It is much easier to reach the right result in the burglar alarm cases if the court recognizes that it is dealing with a limitation of remedy clause, even if it is called an underliquidated damage clause. For a case taking that approach, see General Bargain Center v. American Alarm Co., 430 N.E.2d 407 (Ind. App. 1982).

7. Another consequence of holding that underliquidated damage clauses are limitation of remedy clauses would be that §2-719(2) applies. Does a liquidated damage clause "fail of its essential purpose" if it is undercompensatory? Is that another way of asking whether the clause reasonably estimates damages? Sometimes the parties deliberately underestimate damages, as in the fire and burglar alarm cases. Sometimes they try to estimate reasonably, or even on the high side, and some unexpected development makes the estimate seriously inadequate. *Carolinas Cotton* is a good example. It's not clear from the opinion which category *Northern Illinois Gas* falls into. Doesn't it matter if you're deciding whether the remedy failed of its essential purpose?

8. Now that we've explored what's at stake, let's return to the one question squarely decided in *Northern Illinois Gas*. Should underliquidated damage clauses be governed by §2-718, §2-719, or both? They really do fit in both sections, don't they? Is it dispositive that §2-719(1) is "subject to" §2-718? It's also "subject to" §2-719(2) and (3); that doesn't mean that subsections (2) and (3) deal with separate and distinct kinds of clauses. Is there some more plausible meaning for the "subject to" language? How about this: Even a remedy expressly agreed to be exclusive is not exclusive if it's unconscionable, §2-719(3), if it fails of its essential purpose, §2-719(2), or if it's a liquidated damage clause that is not a reasonable estimate of damages, §2-718. Still, it won't be surprising if many courts try to wiggle out of §2-719(1)(b).

What about the court's other argument — that actual damages and liquidated damages are all one remedy, differing only in measure. Presumably, specific performance and damages are really different remedies. Where does that lead? Doesn't it mean that if §2-719(1)(b) applies and the liquidated damage clause is not exclusive, specific performance is avail-

able but actual damages aren't? That was the court's assumption in
Campbell Soup carrot case, decided before the UCC. Wouldn't Energy
Coop be delighted with specific performance? Does it seem likely that this
court would grant it? What would come next — a holding that liquidated
damages are an adequate remedy? Is $13 million as complete, practical,
and efficient as performance worth $305 million?

9. One other thing to be alert for in these cases is whether the clause
was intended to deal with the kind of breach that actually occurred. Even
a burglar alarm company couldn't collect a $5000 purchase price, fail to
deliver a burglar alarm, and point to a $25 liquidated damage clause as the
exclusive remedy for breach. The example comes from Warren, Formal
and Operative Rules under Common Law and Code, 30 U.C.L.A. L.
Rev. 898, 911 (1983). The title sounds in jurisprudence, but this case
study is also the leading article on underliquidated damage clauses.

NOTES ON CONTRACTING INTO OR OUT OF EQUITABLE REMEDIES

1. Suppose the parties agree that a contract is specifically enforceable. Or that it is not specifically enforceable. Or that a receiver should
be appointed in event of default. Should those clauses be treated any
differently than any other clause specifying or limiting a remedy?

2. Before the merger of law and equity, a clause providing for specific
performance would have been an attempt to confer jurisdiction on the
equity court. This would have run afoul of the usual rule that the litigants
cannot confer subject matter jurisdiction on a court. Some of that attitude persisted after the merger. An example is Stokes v. Moore, 262 Ala.
59, 77 So. 2d 331 (1955), which involved an employment contract in
which the employee promised not to start a competing business. The
contract said the noncompetition clause could be enforced by an injunction. The court said the injunction clause was not binding:

> Such an agreement would serve to oust the inherent jurisdiction of the court
> to determine whether an injunction is appropriate when applied for and to
> require its issuance even though to do so would be contrary to the opinion of
> the court. . . .
>   But . . . the provision for an injunction is important in its influence upon
> an exercise of the discretionary power of the court. . . .

Id. at 64, 77 So. 2d at 335.

The contract also had a liquidated damage clause. The court was not
at all troubled by the possibility that the liquidated damage clause would
oust its jurisdiction to assess damages and force it to award a sum contrary
to its own opinion.

3. Is there any basis for the court's different reactions to the two clauses? Is there enough left to the policy of the irreparable injury rule that the parties should not be able to contract out of it? What if the parties agreed to specific performance of a complex contract that would be burdensome to supervise — say the contract to modernize the steel mill in Northern Delaware Industrial Development Corp. v. E. W. Bliss Co., supra at 777? Can the parties agree to impose that burden on the court without its consent? Do the parties to any other complex litigation have to get the court's consent before they file?

4. It is common for mortgages to provide that a receiver will be appointed for the mortgaged property in the event of default. Courts treat such clauses the same way the injunction clause was treated in Stokes v. Moore: not binding but entitled to weight. An example is Riverside Properties v. Teachers Insurance & Annuity Association, 590 S.W.2d 736 (Tex. Civ. App. 1979). In *Riverside*, the trial court appointed a receiver, and the receiver clause seemed to get enough weight to insulate the appointment from significant appellate review.

5. Parties who are clearly not entitled to specific performance probably don't contract for it very often. If they care enough to put in a clause, they can probably make some plausible argument for the equitable remedy under the traditional criteria, and then it often will be enough for the clause to be given some weight.

6. Clauses excluding equitable remedies that would otherwise be available may be more common. Here there is no residue of historical concerns about conferring jurisdiction, and little sense of imposing on the court. Courts are more likely to view such clauses like any other limitation of remedy clause. An example is Brademas v. Real Estate Development Co., 175 Ind. App. 239, 370 N.E.2d 997 (1977). The contract provided for the sale of thirty-three acres of land for a price to be paid in installments. Seller conveyed the land to a trustee, and the trustee was to convey pro rata portions of the tract to the buyer as it paid the installments. A remedies clause provided that if buyer defaulted in its payments, seller could cancel the contract and reclaim the land still held by the trustee. The court had no trouble concluding that this remedy was exclusive and precluded specific performance, despite the usual rule that real estate contracts are specifically enforceable by both sides.

7. UCC §2-719(1)(a) authorizes the parties to create additional remedies other than those provided by the Code. There is no special provision for equitable remedies. Does that make a specific performance clause binding on the court?

CHAPTER 11

The Equitable Defenses

What are equitable defenses and what are they doing in a book about remedies? Those are fair questions and require a brief answer.

The equitable defenses are here because they are important and there is no better place in the curriculum to put them. They fit here because of their association with equity and because whether they are available sometimes depends on what remedy plaintiff seeks. They don't fit in any substantive course, because except for unconscionability, they are available whatever the substantive claim.

Before the merger of law and equity, equitable defenses were defenses recognized by the chancellors and not by the law courts. The chancellors made some of these defenses available at law by enjoining the opposing litigant from pursuing his claim; fraud is the prime example. Other defenses, such as laches and unclean hands, were available only in equity.

Since the merger, the term "equitable defenses" has no very precise meaning. In common usage it means those defenses that were historically equitable and perhaps others similar to them. This book examines most of the historic equitable defenses, but history was not the criterion for inclusion. I have excluded fraud, because it is so thoroughly assimilated to law and is more important as a tort than as a defense. I have included waiver, because it is so closely related to estoppel. I have never been able to find out whether waiver originated at law or equity, but it no longer matters. The defenses examined here are all discretionary and somewhat overlapping.

Some of these equitable defenses are plainly available whether plaintiff seeks legal or equitable relief. Estoppel and waiver are the clearest examples. The conventional wisdom is that undue hardship, unclean hands, and laches are available only if plaintiff seeks equitable relief. The conventional wisdom is not exactly false, but it is misleading. One of the questions this chapter explores is the extent to which these defenses or near substitutes are available in suits for legal remedies.

Two of the equitable defenses are taken up elsewhere: unconscionability in chapter 4, because it is so closely related to specific performance, and laches in chapter 12, because it is so closely related to statutes of limitation. I am still not sure I put laches in the right place; it is just as closely related to estoppel and waiver. I compromised by putting estoppel, waiver, and laches next to each other even though they are in separate chapters. There is also a sneak preview of laches here in chapter 11.

A.   UNDUE HARDSHIP

BOOMER v. ATLANTIC CEMENT CO.
26 N.Y.2d 219, 257 N.E.2d 870 (1970)

BERGAN, J.

Defendant operates a large cement plant near Albany. These are actions for injunction and damages by neighboring land owners alleging injury to property from dirt, smoke and vibration emanating from the plant. A nuisance has been found after trial, temporary damages have been allowed; but an injunction has been denied. . . .

The ground for the denial of injunction, notwithstanding the finding both that there is a nuisance and that plaintiffs have been damaged substantially, is the large disparity in economic consequences of the nuisance and of the injunction. This theory cannot, however, be sustained without overruling a doctrine which has been consistently reaffirmed in several leading cases in this court and which has never been disavowed here, namely that where a nuisance has been found and where there has been any substantial damage shown by the party complaining an injunction will be granted.

The rule in New York has been that such a nuisance will be enjoined although marked disparity be shown in economic consequence between the effect of the injunction and the effect of the nuisance.

The problem of disparity in economic consequence was sharply in focus in Whalen v. Union Bag & Paper Co. (208 N.Y. 1). A pulp mill entailing an investment of more than a million dollars polluted a stream in which plaintiff, who owned a farm, was "a lower riparian owner." The economic loss to plaintiff from this pollution was small. This court, reversing the Appellate Division, reinstated the injunction granted by the Special Term against the argument of the mill owner that in view of "the slight advantage to plaintiff and the great loss that will be inflicted on defendant" an injunction should not be granted (p.2). "Such a balancing of injuries cannot be justified by the circumstances of this case," Judge Werner noted (p.4). He continued: "Although the damage to the plaintiff may be slight as compared with the defendant's expense of abating the condition, that is not a good reason for refusing an injunction" (p.5).

Thus the unconditional injunction granted at Special Term was reinstated. The rule laid down in that case, then, is that whenever the damage resulting from a nuisance is found not "unsubstantial," viz., $100 a year, injunction would follow. This states a rule that had been followed in this court with marked consistency. . . .

Although the court at Special Term and the Appellate Division held that injunction should be denied, it was found that plaintiffs had been damaged in various specific amounts up to the time of the trial and damages to the respective plaintiffs were awarded for those amounts. The effect of this was, injunction having been denied, plaintiffs could maintain successive actions at law for damages thereafter as further damage was incurred.

The court at Special Term also found the amount of permanent damage attributable to each plaintiff, for the guidance of the parties in the event both sides stipulated to the payment and acceptance of such permanent damage as a settlement of all the controversies among the parties. The total of permanent damages to all plaintiffs thus found was $185,000. This basis of adjustment has not resulted in any stipulation by the parties.

This result at Special Term and at the Appellate Division is a departure from a rule that has become settled; but to follow the rule literally in these cases would be to close down the plant at once. This court is fully agreed to avoid that immediately drastic remedy; the difference in view is how best to avoid it.*

One alternative is to grant the injunction but postpone its effect to a specified future date to give opportunity for technical advances to permit defendant to eliminate the nuisance; another is to grant the injunction conditioned on the payment of permanent damages to plaintiffs which would compensate them for the total economic loss to their property present and future caused by defendant's operations. For reasons which will be developed the court chooses the latter alternative.

If the injunction were to be granted unless within a short period — e.g., 18 months — the nuisance be abated by improved methods, there would be no assurance that any significant technical improvement would occur.

The parties could settle this private litigation at any time if defendant

---

* Respondent's investment in the plant is in excess of $45,000,000. There are over 300 people employed there.

paid enough money and the imminent threat of closing the plant would build up the pressure on defendant. If there were no improved techniques found, there would inevitably be applications to the court at Special Term for extensions of time to perform on showing of good faith efforts to find such techniques.

Moreover, techniques to eliminate dust and other annoying by-products of cement making are unlikely to be developed by any research the defendant can undertake within any short period, but will depend on the total resources of the cement industry Nationwide and throughout the world. The problem is universal wherever cement is made.

For obvious reasons the rate of the research is beyond control of defendant. If at the end of 18 months the whole industry has not found a technical solution a court would be hard put to close down this one cement plant if due regard be given to equitable principles.

On the other hand, to grant the injunction unless defendant pays plaintiffs such permanent damages as may be fixed by the court seems to do justice between the contending parties. All of the attributions of economic loss to the properties on which plaintiffs' complaints are based will have been redressed.

The nuisance complained of by these plaintiffs may have other public or private consequences, but these particular parties are the only ones who have sought remedies and the judgment proposed will fully redress them. The limitation of relief granted is a limitation only within the four corners of these actions and does not foreclose public health or other public agencies from seeking proper relief in a proper court.

It seems reasonable to think that the risk of being required to pay permanent damages to injured property owners by cement plant owners would itself be a reasonable effective spur to research for improved techniques to minimize nuisance.

The power of the court to condition on equitable grounds the continuance of an injunction on the payment of permanent damages seems undoubted.

The damage base here suggested is consistent with the general rule in those nuisance cases where damages are allowed. "Where a nuisance is of such a permanent and unabatable character that a single recovery can be had, including the whole damage past and future resulting therefrom, there can be but one recovery" (66 C.J.S., Nuisances, §140, p.947). It has been said that permanent damages are allowed where the loss recoverable would obviously be small as compared with the cost of removal of the nuisance (Kentucky-Ohio Gas Co. v. Bowling, 264 Ky. 470, 477). . . .

There is some parallel to the conditioning of an injunction on the payment of permanent damages in the noted "elevated railway cases" (Pappenheim v. Metropolitan El. Ry. Co., 128 N.Y. 436, and others which followed). Decisions in these cases were based on the finding that the railways created a nuisance as to adjacent property owners, but in lieu of enjoining their operation, the court allowed permanent damages. . . .

The judgment, by allowance of permanent damages imposing a servitude on land, which is the basis of the actions, would preclude future recovery by plaintiffs or their grantees.

This should be placed beyond debate by a provision of the judgment that the payment by defendant and the acceptance by plaintiffs of permanent damages found by the court shall be in compensation for a servitude on the land. . . .

Jasen, J. (dissenting).

I agree with the majority that a reversal is required here, but I do not subscribe to the newly enunciated doctrine of assessment of permanent damages, in lieu of an injunction, where substantial property rights have been impaired by the creation of a nuisance.

It has long been the rule in this State, as the majority acknowledges, that a nuisance which results in substantial continuing damage to neighbors must be enjoined. To now change the rule to permit the cement company to continue polluting the air indefinitely upon the payment of permanent damages is, in my opinion, compounding the magnitude of a very serious problem in our State and Nation today. . . .

I see grave dangers in overruling our long-established rule of granting an injunction where a nuisance results in substantial continuing damage. In permitting the injunction to become inoperative upon the payment of permanent damages, the majority is, in effect, licensing a continuing wrong. It is the same as saying to the cement company, you may continue to do harm to your neighbors so long as you pay a fee for it. Furthermore, once such permanent damages are assessed and paid, the incentive to alleviate the wrong would be eliminated, thereby continuing air pollution of an area without abatement.

It is true that some courts have sanctioned the remedy here proposed by the majority in a number of cases, but none of the authorities relied upon by the majority are analogous to the situation before us. In those cases, the courts, in denying an injunction and awarding money damages, grounded their decision on a showing that the use to which the property was intended to be put was primarily for the public benefit. Here, on the other hand, it is clearly established that the cement company is creating a continuing air pollution nuisance primarily for its own private interest with no public benefit.

This kind of inverse condemnation may not be invoked by a private person or corporation for private gain or advantage. Inverse condemnation should only be permitted when the public is primarily served in the taking or impairment of property. The promotion of the interests of the polluting cement company has, in my opinion, no public use or benefit.

Nor is it constitutionally permissible to impose servitude on land, without consent of the owner, by payment of permanent damages where the continuing impairment of the land is for a private use. This is made clear by the State Constitution (art. I, §7, subd. [a]) which provides that "[p]rivate property shall not be taken for *public use* without just compensation" (emphasis added). It is, of course, significant that the section makes no mention of taking for a *private* use.

In sum, then, by constitutional mandate as well as by judicial pronouncement, the permanent impairment of private property for private purposes is not authorized in the absence of clearly demonstrated public benefit and use.

I would enjoin the defendant cement company from continuing the discharge of dust particles upon its neighbors' properties unless, within 18 months, the cement company abated this nuisance. . . .

I am aware that the trial court found that the most modern dust control devices available have been installed in defendant's plant, but, I submit, this does not mean that *better* and more effective dust control devices could not be developed within the time allowed to abate the pollution.

Moreover, I believe it is incumbent upon the defendant to develop such devices, since the cement company, at the time the plant commenced production (1962), was well aware of the plaintiffs' presence in the area, as well as the probable consequences of its contemplated operation. Yet, it still chose to build and operate the plant at this site. . . .

Chief Judge FULD and Judges BURKE and SCILEPPI concur with Judge BERGAN; Judge JASEN dissents in part and votes to reverse in a separate opinion; Judges BREITEL and GIBSON taking no part.

NOTES ON UNDUE HARDSHIP

1. There were seven plaintiffs. The $185,000 figure is apparently the court's estimate of the amount by which the cement plant reduces the value of their houses. Is that an adequate remedy? Suppose plaintiffs say their real concern is shortened life expectancy and the risk of lung cancer or emphysema. Has the market valued that risk at $185,000? Should they sell their homes to someone willing to buy at the new market price? What about the rule that money is never an adequate substitute for land?

2. If damages were adequate, plaintiffs would not be entitled to an injunction in the first place. When the court denies an injunction because it would impose too much hardship on defendant, the result will always be that plaintiff gets a remedy the court considered inadequate. But remember that adequacy is comparative. Isn't $185,000 a lot better than nothing?

3. What would happen if the court ordered the plant closed until new technology made it possible to eliminate the pollution? Would the plant close? Or would defendant pay plaintiffs not to enforce the injunction? How much would plaintiffs charge? Certainly not less than $185,000, and not more than $45 million. But is there any way to pick a number in

between? This is a classic bilateral monopoly. The parties can deal only with each other, and they could do a lot of bluffing before reaching a deal. If the cement company were determined not to be blackmailed, and plaintiffs were determined not to move or risk their health unless defendant made them rich, the parties might never reach agreement. If there are other potential plaintiffs, the sheer number of transactions might preclude a deal, or a few holdouts might preclude a deal.

4. Note that the bilateral monopoly is inherent in the situation; the injunction does not create it. If the court denied relief, the parties could still deal only with each other. But bargaining would be futile because a deal would obviously be impossible. Plaintiffs could not pay $45 million for the cement plant, so defendant could ignore plaintiffs' demands.

The numbers could also be the other way around. Suppose a garbage dump were polluting a stream, and a downstream manufacturer of fine specialty papers required a supply of very pure water. The example is suggested by Fletcher v. Bealey, 28 Ch. 688 (1885), a well-known English case. Suppose the garbage business were worth $185,000, and the paper mill were worth $45 million. Then if the court enjoined the garbage business, bargaining would be futile and it would shut down. If the court denied an injunction, the paper mill would have to pay the garbage business to shut down, and the parties would have to bargain in a condition of bilateral monopoly.

Granting or withholding the injunction allocates the power to be unreasonable between bilateral monopolists. A damage remedy eliminates the need to bargain by fixing a price.

5. The court can achieve even more flexibility with a combination of conditional injunctions and damages. Spur Industries v. Del E. Webb Development Co., 108 Ariz. 178, 494 P.2d 700 (1972), is the classic example. A new residential development and defendant's pre-existing feed lot expanded toward each other until the smell of manure became a serious nuisance. As in the hypothetical case of the garbage dump and the paper mill, the value of the feed lot's physical plant was much less than the value of the houses. The court ordered the feed lot to close, but only on condition that the developers and homeowners pay the cost of relocation.

6. The court says that New York had never before refused to enjoin a nuisance, however valuable, if it inflicted "not unsubstantial" damage. Then, without noting any contradiction, it says that it refused to enjoin a nuisance in the elevated railway cases. The dissenter distinguishes those cases on the ground that railways served a public purpose but the cement plant does not. It is true that railways have been thought of as specially affecting the public interest. Railroads generally have eminent domain power, and cement companies do not. But that is surely because cement companies can buy land for plants in ordinary transactions, while railroads could not assemble rights of way without eminent domain. Can

Judge Jasen be serious when he says the cement plant has "no public use or benefit"?

If we required cement companies to buy all the land on which their dust settled, they would need eminent domain power too. In practice, we have let them spread their dust on other people's land, either without paying for the privilege or by paying damages in nuisance actions. Is that eminent domain in disguise? What would Jasen do about it? Would he shut down the whole cement industry? Or would he decide that not all cement plants are nuisances — that it depends on what the plant is close to?

7.   Nuisance law proved to be an ineffective means of regulating pollution. Perhaps most important, nuisance law posed the substantive question in a way that precluded rational planning. Cement plants have to go somewhere, but if the question is whether this plant is hurting this plaintiff, the answer will always be yes. Nuisance law was not well suited to ask whether a plant was in the least objectionable place or using the best possible technology to clean up. It was possible to refocus nuisance law on defendant's efforts to minimize pollution; Learned Hand started in that direction in Smith v. Staso Milling Co., 18 F.2d 736, 738 (2d Cir. 1927). But that was not the traditional approach.

With the substantive question misstated, remedies worked badly. Shutting down industry was too draconian. Permanent damages left industry with no further incentive to clean up once the judgment was paid. Repeated suits for temporary damages were burdensome to courts and litigants, and generally produced small judgments not worth pursuing.

The result is that nuisance law is being pre-empted by regulation. It is hard to imagine enjoining the cement company if it had a permit from the Environmental Protection Agency; indeed, the court would probably lack power to do so. See City of Milwaukee v. Illinois, 451 U.S. 304 (1981). The New York Court of Appeals subsequently refused to apply *Boomer* in a case where the nuisance also violated a valid zoning law. Little Joseph Realty v. Town of Babylon, 41 N.Y.2d 738, 363 N.E.2d 1163 (1977).

Despite the decline of nuisance law, the problem of remedies that do more harm than good is still with us. It can arise in almost any substantive context, but other kinds of land use conflicts account for a large portion of the cases.

ARIOLA v. NIGRO
16 Ill. 2d 46, 156 N.E.2d 536 (1959)

MR. JUSTICE BRISTOW delivered the opinion of the court.

This is a direct appeal by both plaintiffs and defendants from a decree of the circuit court of Cook County allowing plaintiffs damages for a roof drainage system removed by defendants, but denying plaintiffs' request for a mandatory injunction to compel defendants to remove such portion of their building as encroaches on plaintiffs' property and destroys plaintiffs' easement for rain gutters and downspouts. . . .

[P]laintiffs Saverio Ariola and Susanna Ariola were owners in joint tenancy of the property at 818 N. Twenty-third Avenue, Melrose Park, which was improved with a two-story house occupied by them and their children. . . .

Immediately to the west of the Ariola property is the Nigro property, held in joint tenancy by defendants. . . . The property was improved with a one-story building, until October, 1948, when defendants commenced construction of an addition.

According to the testimony of defendants' mason contractor, he excavated right up to plaintiffs' building foundation, put in forms only on one side and poured concrete flush against plaintiffs' foundation, so that the east part of defendants' foundation is flush with the west part of plaintiffs' building.

Special surveys made at plaintiffs' request by registered surveyors before defendants' brick work was superimposed, indicated that defendants' foundation encroached upon plaintiffs' property to the extent of 1 inch at the northeast corner of defendants' foundation and some $2\frac{3}{8}$ inches at the southeast corner of the foundation. Plaintiffs thereupon notified defendants of the encroachment and requested them to discontinue construction. Notice was also given by plaintiffs' attorney to defendant Nigro and to his attorney. Nevertheless, defendants proceeded with the construction of the two-story brick addition, which according to plaintiffs' surveys also encroached to the same extent above ground level. Defendants, however, deny any such encroachment, and their mason contractor testified that the village markers were followed, and that plaintiffs' foundation was irregular and encroached on defendants' property.

It appears further from defendant Daniel Nigro's testimony as an adverse witness that before construction began he had notified plaintiffs that defendants would occupy all of their property, and that it would be necessary for plaintiffs to remove their projecting gutters and downspouts along the west wall.

[The Ariolas' gutters extended six inches over the property line. The gutters had been there since the house was built in 1925, and the court held that the Ariolas had acquired an easement for the gutters by adverse possession.]

[P]laintiffs refused to remove the gutters, and . . . . defendants ordered that they be torn down and that the construction of the building proceed as planned. . . . [U]pon plaintiffs' refusal to pay half the cost of installing a "saddle" type drainage installation, defendants, unbeknown to plaintiffs, installed a tar paper flashing between the east wall of the new building and the west wall of plaintiffs' home, to prevent drainage of rain water and melting snow between the two buildings. This flashing, according to the testimony of both plaintiffs' and defendants' witnesses, was not very effective and caused the accumulation of water along the west wall of the Ariola building, with resulting seepage and rotting of the plaster flashing on the inside of plaintiffs' wall and deterioration of the mortar joints between the bricks. . . .

[T]he master and the trial court found in substance that there were reciprocal foundation encroachments of a minimum nature, which did not warrant equitable intervention; that plaintiffs' building had a roof drainage system which projected into defendants' premises; that since the system existed in open view uninterruptedly from 1925 to 1948, plaintiffs had acquired an easement thereto; that inasmuch as plaintiffs did not claim the existence of such easement until January 13, 1949, when they set up the matter in reply to defendants' counterclaim, after defendants had completed the building, plaintiffs' right to equitable relief was barred by laches. The trial court thereupon allowed plaintiffs damages only for the installation of a new drainage system as good as the one destroyed by defendants, and denied plaintiffs damages for the injury and deterioration to their building. . . .

[T]he remedy of a mandatory injunction has generally been invoked by courts to compel adjoining landowners to remove encroachments. In issuing such injunctions courts have considered such factors as the expense and difficulty of removing an encroachment in relation to the damage resulting therefrom, or the benefit that would accrue from its removal. However, where the encroachment was intentional, in that defendant proceeded despite notice or warning, or where he failed to take proper precautions to ascertain the boundary, the courts, including those of Illinois, have refused to balance the equities, and have issued the mandatory injunction without regard to the relative convenience or hardship involved.

In the *Haverhill* case the Massachusetts court, in ordering the removal of an encroaching heavy masonry wall, stated: "One who knows of a claim to land which he proposes to use as his own proceeds at his peril if he goes forward in the face of protest from the claimant and places structures thereon." Tyler v. Haverhill, 272 Mass. 313, 172 N.E. 342.

The leading Illinois case respecting land encroachments is Pradelt v. Lewis, 297 Ill. 374. The foundation of the defendant's three-story building was placed upon the common lot line, and when one of the walls began to lean, it encroached some 4 inches upon plaintiff's wall, resting upon the wall of plaintiff's frame building, and causing the plaster to crack and other damages. The court, after referring to the rule that an injunction will be denied where the encroachment is slight and the cost of removing it great as compared with any corresponding benefit to the adjoining owner, stated that if the encroachment is intentional, neither the expense involved, nor the absence of damage to the land encroached upon will defeat the right to an injunction. The court then concluded that the encroachment therein was not unintentional as defined by the courts, and issued the mandatory injunction compelling the removal of the encroachment. The court stated at page 378 that "the duty of the courts is to protect rights, and innocent complainants cannot be required to suffer the loss of their rights because of expense to the wrongdoer."

Nitterauer v. Pulley, 401 Ill. 494, expanded the concept of "intent" to include failure to take adequate precautions to ascertain that one is building upon his own property. . . .

In the instant case, while defendants and their mason contractor deny any encroachment upon plaintiffs' property and testified that stakes were set out according to the village survey marks, it is nevertheless undisputed that defendants' contractor excavated up to plaintiffs' foundation, put in forms only on one side and poured concrete between the forms and plaintiffs' foundation, so that plaintiffs' foundation, rather than any survey marks, became the boundary. Moreover, while defendants submitted surveys, they make no reference to the location of the foundation, whereas plaintiffs' professional surveys made before the brick work was superimposed upon the new foundation, indicated that it encroached upon plaintiffs' property to the extent of 1 inch at the northeast corner of the foundation to 2¾ inches at its south end. . . .

[D]efendants had actual notice at the outset of construction that the foundation encroached on plaintiffs' property, and while plaintiffs' gutters did extend onto defendants' property, their continued presence over the years, together with plaintiffs' refusal to remove them, should have apprised defendants that plaintiffs claimed the legal right to maintain them. . . .

We do not find the Colorado case of Golden Press, Inc. v. Rylands, 124 Colo. 122, 235 P.2d 592, determinative. The 2-inch encroachment of the footings of defendant's structure therein, at a point some 7 inches below the surface, was made in good faith, and in no way injured the plaintiff's property, or affected its use, except on the remote contingency that the plaintiff might someday dig a basement. The denial of the injunction under those circumstances would not constitute a precedent for the instant case, where the encroachment was deliberate and caused plaintiffs extensive damages.

Plaintiffs argue further that there is an additional and even more cogent ground for the issuance of an injunction in the instant case, in that defendants' structure destroyed plaintiffs' easement for their projecting roof drainage system along the west wall of their building. . . .

It is firmly established by our case law that a mandatory injunction may be issued to protect the enjoyment of an easement. In the instant case, however, the trial court held that plaintiffs' laches barred such injunctive relief. Inasmuch as defendants failed to set forth that affirmative defense in their answer, . . . it should not properly be considered. However, even if it were available, that defense is without merit.

This court has repeatedly held that mere delay in asserting the easement will not bar the assertion of the right. There must be, in addition, something in the conduct of the complainant which would make it inequitable to permit him to assert his right. In Gerstley v. Globe Wernicke Co., 340 Ill. 270, the court stated that "it is only when by delay or neglect to assert a right the adverse party is lulled into doing that which he would not have done or into omitting to do that which he would have done in reference to the property had the right been properly asserted that the defense of laches can be considered."

In the case at bar plaintiffs at no time lulled defendants into proceeding with the construction of the building. On the contrary, even prior to construction, defendants were put on notice that plaintiffs asserted rights with reference to the projecting gutters and downspouts when they refused to remove them as defendants requested. Moreover, as soon as possible after construction began, plaintiffs sought injunctive relief against the encroaching foundation. The fact that plaintiffs did not also seek a mandatory injunction to protect their easement until January 13, 1949, would in no way constitute laches, as defined by this court, in view of plaintiffs' pending action against the same structure, which affected their easement. As stated in Welton v. 40 E. Oak St. Bldg. Corp. (7th Cir. 1934) 70 F.2d 377, one of the leading cases . . . respecting building encroachments, "The important and determining fact (as to whether the defense of laches will lie) is that appellant at all times protested and challenged the company's right to proceed with the construction of the building."

In the *Welton* case the court went to great lengths to protect an easement. Plaintiffs therein had merely contested the action of the zoning board in varying an ordinance and did not seek a mandatory injunction to protect their easement to light and air across a 16-foot alley, until after defendant's building was completed. Despite the fact that it would cost almost $350,000 to reconstruct the 20-story building, the court issued such a mandatory injunction to protect plaintiffs' easement, and rejected the contention that plaintiffs were guilty of laches for failure to seek such relief, in addition to other remedies, until after the building was completed.

In the light of the foregoing analysis and authorities, it was error for the circuit court to deny plaintiffs' request for a mandatory injunction under the circumstances of defendants' deliberate boundary encroachment and their destruction of plaintiffs' easement.

With reference to the issue of damages, the rule is well established that one who trespasses or assumes control over the property of another without authority is responsible for all the consequences. More specifically, where buildings are damaged, but not totally destroyed by trespasses, the measure of damages is the cost of repair or of restoring the premises to their original condition.

In the instant case the installation of a tar paper flashing to bridge the space between the parapet of defendants' building and the west edge of plaintiffs' roof, made at defendants' direction and without plaintiffs' consent, constituted a continual trespass. There is substantial evidence that as a result of this trespass water accumulated along the west end of the Ariola roof and caused seepage which, in turn, produced extensive damage to plaintiffs' building during the two years before plaintiffs discovered the flashing.

Nevertheless, the trial court limited plaintiffs' damages to the value of a roof drainage system of the same character and extent as the one wrongfully removed by defendants, on the theory that plaintiffs failed to avoid damages by installing an alternative drainage system. That conclusion, however, fails to recognize that it was defendants' intentional trespass and unauthorized installation of the flashing that was the cause of the water accumulating, and the ensuing damage. Plaintiffs should not be compelled to pay for defendants' wrongful act; nor were plaintiffs obliged to pay for half the cost, as requested by defendants, of a saddle-type drainage installation made necessary by defendants' building encroachment and deliberate destruction of plaintiffs' gutters. Their refusal to do so in no way constituted a failure to do equity; hence, the measure of damages adopted by the trial court was improper.

It is our judgment, therefore, that this cause should be reversed and remanded with directions to issue the mandatory injunction as prayed for by plaintiffs, and to award all damages resulting directly from defendants' intentional trespass.

Reversed and remanded, with directions.

MORE NOTES ON UNDUE HARDSHIP

1. If the Nigros installed a working drainage system and paid for all of the Ariolas' water damage, what remaining harm to the Ariolas would there be? How would the Ariolas be harmed by the remaining two-inch encroachment? Not nearly as much as it will cost the Nigros to tear out their wall and foundation and rebuild the whole east end of their house. Does that make sense, even for deliberate wrongdoers?

2. The defense that is allowed in *Boomer* and disallowed in *Ariola* is often called "balancing the equities." Hardship to defendant is common to all the cases, and generally the hardship must be disproportionate to any benefit plaintiff will derive from the injunction. But courts have also considered defendant's culpability, the relationship between the parties, plaintiff's diligence or acquiescence, the risk of creating a private emi-

nent domain power, and especially in the older cases, whether denying relief would allow a public or private benefit.

There are so many factors and so many differences of degree that the cases are highly fact specific. Moreover, what some jurisdictions found culpable others did not. For example, some jurisdictions viewed polluters as deliberate wrongdoers even if they used the best possible anti-pollution technology; other jurisdictions disagreed. Isn't that the principal source of disagreement between Jasen and the majority in *Boomer*?

3. *Ariola* relies on the Illinois "rule" that an "intentional" encroachment will always be removed. But "intentional" does not have its ordinary English meaning. *Ariola* cites Nitterauer v. Pulley, where "intentionally" meant something like "recklessly." Defendant had "no idea" where the boundary was and built a garage without checking; it extended three feet over the line. *Ariola* also describes Pradelt v. Lewis, where "intentionally" meant negligently. When defendant's wall leaned over the line, the court said the encroachment was intentional because one who builds a wall is obligated to build it so it will stand. But in *Pradelt*, the court feared that the leaning wall might eventually crush plaintiff's building. If that were a real risk, then the balance of hardships was not so disproportionate.

4. The cement company intentionally built and operated the plant knowing that the inevitable result would be to pour dust on Boomer's house. Why isn't that an intentional encroachment? Is it just that courts are willing to tear down $30,000 houses but not $45 million factories?

To test that possibility, suppose the cement company had not bought its own land close to Boomer's. Suppose instead it had built a cement plant on the grounds of Boomer's rural estate, without any colorable right to do so, or without using reasonable care to be sure it bought the land from the true owner. And suppose the rural estate were worth $185,000 and the cement plant were still worth $45 million. Should the court still deny an injunction because it would be so wasteful to shut down the plant?

5. One more example is Myers v. Caple, 258 N.W.2d 301 (Iowa 1977). The parties owned adjoining land in a creek bottom. Caple wanted to build a private levee that would protect seventy acres of his land. The levee would aggravate the flood problem on twenty-nine acres of Myers's land, but only under extreme conditions. The court thought the case came down to one question:

> whether Caple should be deprived of the right to reclaim and cultivate some 70 acres of his land year in and year out because in exceptional years 29 acres of Myers' land might suffer additional flooding.

Id. at 305.

The trial court issued the injunction; the Supreme Court reversed. It said that Myers could recover damages. It also said that Myers could renew his request for an injunction if the levee caused more problems than expected. *Myers* really is private eminent domain, isn't it?

6. Is *Myers* more like *Boomer* or *Ariola*? Caple knows he's going to flood Myers's land, Myers is protesting, and Caple is doing it anyway. Suppose plaintiffs in *Boomer* had sued to prevent the cement plant from being built, before the cement company had invested much money in the site. What result then?

In both *Boomer* and *Myers*, the harm to plaintiff is an unavoidable side effect of an otherwise legitimate use of defendant's own land. Nigro was putting part of his house physically on Ariola's land. Should that matter? Isn't a two-inch encroachment trivial compared to a cement plant next door? Is it more important that the Nigros' encroachment was avoidable — that they could have built their house without encroaching at all?

7. Avoidability was plainly more important than physical encroachment in Taubert v. Fluegel, 122 Ill. App. 2d 298, 258 N.E.2d 586 (1970). Defendant's house was entirely within her own lot; the nearest corner was three and a half feet from the boundary. But a restrictive covenant required that she not build closer than eight feet to the line. The court ordered her to remove the part of the house that violated the covenant, even though doing so would reduce the value of the house by 25 percent. As in *Ariola*, the neighbors had objected before the house went up.

8. The presence or absence of physical intrusion has very little to do with the extent of harm inflicted, but it has great symbolic significance. Deep in our common law bones, we "know" that the essence of property is the power to exclude intruders. That common sense notion sometimes overrides economic reality. Thus, in a related context, the Supreme Court has said that New York City took private property when it authorized a cable television company to string wires along the sides and roofs of buildings, because the wires physically intruded. Loretto v. Teleprompter Manhattan CATV Corp., 458 U.S. 419 (1982). But New York City did not take property when it forbad architectural changes at Grand Central Station, even though forbidding a skyscraper on the site cost the owners millions. Penn Central Transportation Co. v. New York City, 438 U.S. 104 (1978).

9. Do not confuse the undue hardship defense with the balancing required for preliminary relief. Courts rule on temporary restraining orders and preliminary injunctions before ruling on the merits. The court must balance harm to defendant if the injunction is improperly issued against harm to plaintiff if the injunction is improperly denied. The interests of both sides are presumptively entitled to equal weight. The court's preliminary prediction about probability of success may tilt the balance one way or the other, but whatever the court predicts, either side may still prevail.

In cases like *Boomer* and *Ariola*, there is no uncertainty about substantive rights. The court has decided that defendant is a wrongdoer and that plaintiff is suffering irreparable injury. In that context, plaintiff gets primary consideration in any balancing. The hardship to defendant must be greatly disproportionate, and defendant must be relatively innocent, for the court to deny relief.

10. The undue hardship defense is the law's most explicit embodiment of the economic approach. If a wrong is too expensive to correct, defendant can pay damages instead. But the doctrine appears as a defense, as a limit on the pursuit of justice, rather than as a first principle. It is not enough for defendant to show that the injunction costs him a little more than it saves plaintiff; defendant's hardship must be greatly disproportionate. And the defense is unavailable if defendant's conduct is too culpable.

There is an economic as well as a moral explanation for the culpability exception. If defendant deliberately builds on plaintiff's land, hoping to invoke undue hardship and pay assessed damages after the fact, he is bypassing the market: He could have dealt directly with plaintiff. But that economic argument is only a partial explanation, because these cases often involve bilateral monopoly. As we saw in the last set of notes, only a damage judgment can break the impasse of bilateral monopoly and avoid the risk that bargaining may fail.

NOTE ON LACHES

The Nigros also claim the Ariolas are barred by laches. Laches has to do with delay, so it is often described as the equitable substitute for statutes of limitation. But there is more to it than that. The Ariolas would be barred by laches if they unreasonably delayed the assertion of their claim *and* the Nigros were prejudiced by the delay. Here, the court finds neither element of the defense. We will consider laches in more detail in section C of this chapter and section A of chapter 12.

PEEVYHOUSE v. GARLAND COAL & MINING CO.
382 P.2d 109 (Okla. 1962), *cert. denied*, 375 U.S. 906 (1963)

JACKSON, JUSTICE.

In the trial court, plaintiffs Willie and Lucille Peevyhouse sued the defendant, Garland Coal and Mining Company, for damages for breach of contract. Judgment was for plaintiffs in an amount considerably less than was sued for. Plaintiffs appeal and defendant cross-appeals.

Briefly stated, the facts are as follows: plaintiffs owned a farm containing coal deposits, and in November, 1954, leased the premises to defendant for a period of five years for coal mining purposes. A "strip-mining" operation was contemplated in which the coal would be taken from pits on the surface of the ground, instead of from underground mine shafts. In addition to the usual covenants found in a coal mining lease, defendant specifically agreed to perform certain restorative and remedial work at the end of the lease period. It is unnecessary to set out the details of the work to be done, other than to say that it would involve the moving of many thousands of cubic yards of dirt, at a cost estimated by expert witnesses at about $29,000.00. . . .

During the trial, it was stipulated that all covenants and agreements in the lease contract had been fully carried out by both parties, except the remedial work mentioned above; defendant conceded that this work had not been done. . . . On the measure of damages, the court instructed the jury that it might consider . . . the "diminution in value" of plaintiffs' farm as well as the cost of "repair work" in determining the amount of damages.

It returned a verdict for plaintiffs for $5000.00 — only a fraction of the "cost of performance," *but more than the total value of the farm even after the remedial work is done.* . . .

[I]t is argued by defendant with some force that the performance of the remedial work defendant agreed to do will add at the most only a few hundred dollars to the value of plaintiffs' farm, and that the damages should be limited to that amount because that is all plaintiffs have lost.

Plaintiffs rely on Groves v. John Wunder Co., 205 Minn. 163, 286 N.W. 235. . . . In that case, the Minnesota court, in a substantially similar situation, adopted the "cost of performance" rule as opposed to the "value" rule. The result was to authorize a jury to give plaintiff damages in the amount of $60,000, where the real estate concerned would have been worth only $12,160, even if the work contracted for had been done. . . .

It may be observed that Groves v. John Wunder Co. is the only case which has come to our attention in which the cost of performance rule has been followed under circumstances where the cost of performance greatly exceeded the diminution in value resulting from the breach of contract. . . .

The explanation may be found in the fact that the situations presented are artificial ones. It is highly unlikely that the ordinary property owner would agree to pay $29,000 (or its equivalent) for the construction of "improvements" upon his property that would increase its value only about three hundred dollars. The result is that we are called upon to apply principles of law theoretically based upon reason and reality to a situation which is basically unreasonable and unrealistic.

In Groves v. John Wunder Co., . . . the Minnesota court apparently considered the contract involved to be analogous to a building and construction contract, and cited authority for the proposition that the cost of performance or completion of the building as contracted is ordinarily the measure of damages in actions for damages for the breach of such a contract. . . .

Even in the case of contracts that are unquestionably building and construction contracts, the authorities are not in agreement as to the factors to be considered in determining whether the cost of performance rule or the value rule should be applied. The American Law Institute's Restatement of the Law, Contracts, Volume 1, Sections 346(1)(a)(i) and (ii) submits the proposition that the cost of performance is the proper measure of damages "if this is possible and does not involve *unreasonable economic waste*"; and that the diminution in value caused by the breach is the proper measure "if construction and completion in accordance with the contract would involve *unreasonable economic waste*." (Emphasis supplied.) In an explanatory comment immediately following the text, the Restatement makes it clear that the "economic waste" referred to consists of the destruction of a substantially completed building or other structure. Of course no such destruction is involved in the case now before us. . . .

On the other hand, in McCormick, Damages, Section 168, it is said with regard to building and construction contracts that " . . . in cases where the defect is one that can be repaired or cured without *undue expense*" the cost of performance is the proper measure of damages, but where " . . . the defect in material or construction is one that cannot be remedied without *an expenditure for reconstruction disproportionate to the end to be attained*" (emphasis supplied) the value rule should be followed. The same idea was expressed in Jacob & Youngs, Inc. v. Kent, 230 N.Y. 239, 129 N.E. 889 as follows:

> The owner is entitled to the money which will permit him to complete, unless the cost of completion is grossly and unfairly out of proportion to the good to be attained. When that is true, the measure is the difference in value.

It thus appears that the prime consideration in the Restatement was "economic waste"; and that the prime consideration in McCormick, Damages, and in Jacob & Youngs, Inc. v. Kent, was the relationship between the expense involved and the "end to be attained" — in other words, the "relative economic benefit." . . .

In view of the unrealistic fact situation in the instant case, and certain Oklahoma statutes to be hereinafter noted, we are of the opinion that the "relative economic benefit" is a proper consideration here. . . .

23 O.S.1961 §§96 and 97 provide as follows:

> §96. . . . . Notwithstanding the provisions of this chapter, no person can recover a greater amount in damages for the breach of an obligation, than he would have gained by the full performance thereof on both sides. . . .

§97. . . . Damages must, in all cases, be reasonable, and where an obligation of any kind appears to create a right to unconscionable and grossly oppressive damages, contrary to substantial justice, no more than reasonable damages can be recovered. . . .

[T]he above sections . . . are peculiarly applicable here where, under the "cost of performance" rule, plaintiffs might recover an amount about nine times the total value of their farm. . . . We therefore hold that where, in a coal mining lease, lessee agrees to perform certain remedial work on the premises concerned at the end of the lease period, and thereafter the contract is fully performed by both parties except that the remedial work is not done, the measure of damages in an action by lessor against lessee for damages for breach of contract is ordinarily the reasonable cost of performance of the work; however, where the contract provision breached was merely incidental to the main purpose in view, and where the economic benefit which would result to lessor by full performance of the work is grossly disproportionate to the cost of performance, the damages which lessor may recover are limited to the diminution in value resulting to the premises because of the non-performance. . . .

[T]he rule as stated does not interfere with the property owner's right to "do what he will with his own" (Chamberlain v. Parker, 45 N.Y. 569), or his right, if he chooses, to contract for "improvements" which will actually have the effect of reducing his property's value. Where such result is in fact contemplated by the parties, and is a main or principal purpose of those contracting, it would seem that the measure of damages for breach would ordinarily be the cost of performance. . . .

Under the most liberal view of the evidence herein, the diminution in value resulting to the premises because of non-performance of the remedial work was $300.00. . . .

[T]he judgment . . . is hereby, modified and reduced to the sum of $300.00, and as so modified it is affirmed.

WELCH, DAVISON, HALLEY, and JOHNSON, JJ., concur.

WILLIAMS, C.J., BLACKBIRD, V.C.J., and IRWIN and BERRY, JJ., dissent.
IRWIN, Justice (dissenting). . . .

Defendant admits that it failed to perform its obligations that it agreed and contracted to perform under the lease contract and there is nothing in the record which indicates that defendant could not perform its obligations. Therefore, in my opinion defendant's breach of the contract was wilful and not in good faith.

Although the contract speaks for itself, there were several negotiations between the plaintiffs and defendant before the contract was executed. Defendant admitted in the trial of the action, that plaintiffs insisted that the above provisions be included in the contract and that they would not agree to the coal mining lease unless the above provisions were included.

In my judgment, we should follow the case of Groves v. John Wunder Company, . . . where the Supreme Court of Minnesota held:

> The owner's or employer's damages for such a breach . . . are to be measured, not in respect to the value of the land to be improved, but by the reasonable cost of doing that which the contractor promised to do and which he left undone.

The hypothesized breach referred to states that where the contractor's breach of a contract is wilful, that is, in bad faith, he is not entitled to any benefit of the equitable doctrine of substantial performance.

In the instant action defendant has made no attempt to even substantially perform. The contract in question is not immoral, is not tainted with fraud, and was not entered into through mistake or accident and is not contrary to public policy. It is clear and unambiguous and the parties understood the terms thereof, and the approximate cost of fulfilling the obligations could have been approximately ascertained. There are no conditions existing now which could not have been reasonably anticipated when the contract was negotiated and executed. The defendant could have performed the contract if it desired. It has accepted and reaped the benefits of its contract and now urges that plaintiffs' benefits under the contract be denied. If plaintiffs' benefits are denied, such benefits would inure to the direct benefit of the defendant.

Therefore, in my opinion, the plaintiffs were entitled to specific performance of the contract and since defendant has failed to perform, the proper measure of damages should be the cost of performance. Any other measure of damage would be holding for naught the express provisions of the contract; would be taking from the plaintiffs the benefits of the contract and placing those benefits in defendant which has failed to perform its obligations; would be granting benefits to defendant without a resulting obligation; and would be completely rescinding the solemn obligation of the contract for the benefit of the defendant to the detriment of the plaintiffs by making an entirely new contract for the parties. . . .

NOTES ON UNDUE HARDSHIP WHERE PLAINTIFF SEEKS MONEY

1. The conventional wisdom is that undue hardship is a problem only of specific relief. In the case of money damages, "there can never be any greater injury inflicted on defendant by allowing recovery than would be inflicted on plaintiff by denying it." H. McClintock, Equity 51 (2d ed. 1948). But isn't *Peevyhouse* an undue hardship case?

Or can *Peevyhouse* be explained as an application of *The Helen B.*

Moran, supra at 45? Recall that the owners of the sunken barge got its value or the cost of repair, whichever was less. That is the general rule in property damage cases. But *Peevyhouse* doesn't say that plaintiffs get the lesser of restoration cost or lost value. It denies restoration cost only because that cost is "grossly disproportionate" to the lost value. Similarly, the Restatement (Second) of Contracts says plaintiffs can recover the cost of completing construction contracts unless that cost is "clearly disproportionate" to benefit. §348(2)(b) (1981).

Suppose it would cost $6,000 to restore the land, and doing so would raise its value by $5,000. If this were a tort case, we would say that $5,000 restores plaintiffs to their rightful position, even though it's not enough to restore their land. Does the contract make any difference? Does the parties' agreement to restore the land suggest that it's worth it to them, even if the market disagrees? Shouldn't there be limits on the court's power to decide the parties made a foolish agreement?

2. Suppose the Peevyhouses sought specific performance. Then the defense would explicitly be undue hardship. It would cost defendant $29,000 to perform, and confer a benefit of only $300 on the plaintiffs. But plaintiffs would respond that equities can't be balanced on behalf of a deliberate wrongdoer. What result? Is a deliberate contract breacher like a deliberate encroacher?

3. There are decisions refusing to balance the equities in specific performance cases on the ground that the parties determined what was fair and reasonable by their contract. One such decision is a federal case applying Oklahoma law, West Edmond Hunton Lime Unit v. Stanolind Oil & Gas Co., 193 F.2d 818 (10th Cir. 1951), *cert. denied*, 343 U.S. 920 (1952). *West Edmond* involved a contract to unitize oil and gas production from a certain geological formation, the Hunton lime formation. All individual owners of land over the formation agreed to turn their wells and production rights over to a new entity, the unit, which would produce on behalf of all. Defendant owned a dual well, a well that produced both from the unitized formation and from a completely separate sand formation directly above it. The unit sued for specific performance of his contract to surrender the dual well. The trial court found that it would cost defendant $80,000 to drill a new well to the sand formation. It found that sharing the dual well would probably cost the unit nothing, and even if all of that well's production from the unitized formation were lost, the unit would lose only $5,600. The trial court balanced the equities and denied relief; the court of appeals ordered specific performance. Did it misstate Oklahoma law in light of the subsequent decision in *Peevyhouse?*

4. There are surely modern decisions contrary to *West Edmond*, but I couldn't find one. The legal encyclopedias all say that a contract will not be specifically enforced where the hardship to defendant greatly outweighs the benefit to plaintiff, but the cases cited are largely not in point.

Either they state the supposed rule without applying it, or the performance is equally valuable to both sides and the hardship is that plaintiff didn't pay a fair price.

One case squarely in point is Sanitary District v. Martin, 227 Ill. 260, 81 N.E. 417 (1907), in which defendant bought part of plaintiff's land for cash and a promise to build a levee that would protect the rest of plaintiff's land from flooding. Defendant refused to build the levee, and plaintiff sued for specific performance. The trial court found that it would cost $60,000 to build the levee and that plaintiff's damages were only $5,600. It awarded damages and denied specific performance, and the Supreme Court affirmed.

A modern but ambiguous case is 3615 Corp. v. New York Life Insurance Co., 717 F.2d 1236 (8th Cir. 1983). The parties agreed to the sale of an empty office building for $35,000; plaintiff planned to renovate it. Before the deal was closed, a broken water main flooded the building's electrical system. Repairs would have cost $1.1 million and weren't covered by insurance. The contract obligated seller to repair "within 30 days if possible"; the court held that was not possible and discharged the contract. In the alternative, it held that specific performance would impose disproportionate hardship on defendant and denied relief on that ground. Should the court have balanced the equities if defendant had an unqualified obligation to repair? Was defendant an "intentional" wrongdoer?

5.   Shouldn't the result in all these cases be the same whether plaintiffs seek specific performance or damages for the cost of completion? Does it matter whether the Peevyhouses really wanted the land restored or wanted $29,000 to spend on other things? If plaintiffs' desire matters, a request for specific performance doesn't prove they really want the land restored, does it?

6.   What if the Peevyhouses had sought restitution? Didn't defendant reap a $29,000 benefit by not performing its promise? But does that benefit come from plaintiff? It certainly doesn't come from a third party; it isn't like $29,000 in profits from a more lucrative contract with someone else.

Does it matter whether the Peevyhouses accepted a lower cash price in exchange for the promise to restore the land? If the cash payment to the Peevyhouses were less than defendant's original offer, or less than the going rate for strip mine leases without promises to restore the land, wouldn't it be clear that defendant was unjustly enriched at plaintiffs' expense? But suppose defendant promised restoration plus the usual cash price. In that case, two things might have happened. Defendant might have badly underestimated the cost of restoration. Or defendant might have estimated accurately and figured the cost would be small in proportion to the value of the coal to be removed. If we're trying to decide whether defendant is unjustly enriched by not restoring the land, does it matter how he came to make the promise?

7.   The Tenth Circuit has predicted in a diversity case that Oklahoma

would no longer follow *Peevyhouse*. Rock Island Improvement Co. v. Helmerich & Payne, 698 F.2d 1075 (10th Cir. 1983). In 1967, Oklahoma enacted the Open Cut Land Reclamation Act, declaring the public policy of the state to be that strip mined land should be reclaimed. The act required mine operators to post a bond with the state to ensure reclamation. In *Rock Island Improvement*, the bond was $50,000 and the cost of reclamation was $375,000. When the mine operator forfeited the bond and refused to reclaim the land, the landowner sued for breach of a contract to reclaim. Defendant relied on *Peevyhouse*, and the parties stipulated that reclamation would add only $6,797 to the value of the land. The court upheld a verdict for $375,000. It thought that the public policy declared in the statute would lead the Oklahoma courts to award the cost of reclamation in all future suits for breach of contracts to reclaim.

B. UNCLEAN HANDS AND IN PARI DELICTO

PRECISION INSTRUMENT MANUFACTURING CO. v. AUTOMOTIVE MAINTENANCE MACHINERY CO.
324 U.S. 806 (1945)

Mr. Justice Murphy delivered the opinion of the Court.

In 1937 and prior thereto Automotive manufactured and sold torque wrenches developed by one of its employees, Herman W. Zimmerman. During this period Snap-On Tools Corporation was one of its customers for these wrenches. Automotive also had in its employ at this time one George B. Thomasma, who worked with Zimmerman and who was well acquainted with his ideas on torque wrenches. In November 1937, Thomasma secretly gave information to an outsider, Kenneth R. Larson, concerning torque wrenches. Together they worked out plans for a new wrench, although Thomasma claimed that it was entirely his own idea.

After unsuccessfully trying to interest other distributors, Larson made arrangements to supply Snap-On with the new torque wrench. On October 1, 1938, Larson filed an application for a patent on the newly-developed wrench, which application had been assigned to Snap-On several days prior thereto. Then in December, 1938, Larson, Thomasma and one Walter A. Carlsen organized the Precision Instrument Manufacturing Company to make the wrenches to supply Snap-On's requirements. . . . Precision succeeded in taking away from Automotive all of Snap-On's business. . . .

Subsequently on October 11, 1939, the Patent Office declared an interference between certain claims in Larson's pending patent application and those in one filed by Zimmerman. Automotive was the owner of Zimmerman's application. . . .

In August, 1940, Larson filed his preliminary statement in the Patent Office proceedings. In it he gave false dates as to the conception, disclosure, drawing, description and reduction to practice of his claimed invention. These dates were designed to antedate those in Zimmerman's application by one to three years. Larson also claimed that he was the sole inventor of his wrench.

[Subsequently, Thomasma revealed the entire scheme. Independent counsel advised Automotive that there was insufficient evidence to prosecute Larson for perjury. The parties entered into a settlement under which Larson assigned his application to Automotive and all parties conceded that Zimmerman was the first inventor. Automotive processed both applications and received patents on both without ever disclosing that the statements filed in support of Larson's application were false.

Precision and Snap-On then began to manufacture a new wrench, allegedly infringing Automotive's patents and violating the settlement agreement. Automotive sued, presumably for specific performance of the settlement, an injunction against infringement, and an accounting.]

The guiding doctrine in this case is the equitable maxim that "he who comes into equity must come with clean hands." This maxim is far more than a mere banality. It is a self-imposed ordinance that closes the doors of a court of equity to one tainted with inequitableness or bad faith relative to the matter in which he seeks relief, however improper may have been the behavior of the defendant. That doctrine is rooted in the historical concept of court of equity as a vehicle for affirmatively enforcing the requirements of conscience and good faith. This presupposes a refusal on its part to be "the abettor of iniquity." Bein v. Heath, 6 How (U.S.) 228, 247. Thus while "equity does not demand that its suitors shall have led blameless lives," Loughran v. Loughran, 292 U.S. 216, 229, as to other matters, it does require that they shall have acted fairly and without fraud or deceit as to the controversy in issue.

This maxim necessarily gives wide range to the equity court's use of discretion in refusing to aid the unclean litigant. It is "not bound by formula or restrained by any limitation that tends to trammel the free and just exercise of discretion." Keystone Driller Co. v. General Excavator Co., 290 U.S. 245, 246. Accordingly one's misconduct need not necessarily have been of such a nature as to be punishable as a crime or as to justify legal proceedings of any character. Any willful act concerning the cause of action which rightfully can be said to transgress equitable standards of conduct is sufficient cause for the invocation of the maxim by the chancellor.

Moreover, where a suit in equity concerns the public interest as well as the private interests of the litigants this doctrine assumes even wider and more significant proportions. For if an equity court properly uses the maxim to withhold its assistance in such a case it not only prevents a wrongdoer from enjoying the fruits of his transgression but averts an injury to the public. The determination of when the maxim should be applied to bar this type of suit thus becomes of vital significance.

In the instant case Automotive has sought to enforce several patents and related contracts. Clearly these are matters concerning far more than the interests of the adverse parties. The possession and assertion of patent rights are "issues of great moment to the public." Hazel-Atlas Glass Co. v. Hartford-Empire Co. 322 U.S. 238, 246. A patent by its very nature is affected with a public interest. As recognized by the Constitution, it is a special privilege designed to serve the public purpose of promoting the "Progress of Science and useful Arts." At the same time, a patent is an exception to the general rule against monopolies and to the right to access to a free and open market. The far-reaching social and economic consequences of a patent, therefore, give the public a paramount interest in seeing that patent monopolies spring from backgrounds free from fraud or other inequitable conduct and that such monopolies are kept within their legitimate scope. The facts of this case must accordingly be measured by both public and private standards of equity. And when such measurements are made, it becomes clear that the District Court's action in dismissing the complaints and counterclaims "for want of equity" was more than justified.

The history of the patents and contracts in issue is steeped in perjury and undisclosed knowledge of perjury. Larson's application was admittedly based upon false data which destroyed whatever just claim it might otherwise have had to the status of a patent. Yet Automotive, with at least moral and actual certainty if not absolute proof of the facts concerning the perjury, chose to act in disregard of the public interest. Instead of doing all within its power to reveal and expose the fraud, it procured an outside settlement of the interference proceedings, acquired the Larson application itself, turned it into a patent and barred the other parties from ever questioning its validity. Such conduct does not conform to minimum ethical standards and does not justify Automotive's present attempt to assert and enforce these perjury-tainted patents and contracts.

Automotive contends that it did not have positive and conclusive knowledge of the perjury until the pleadings in the instant proceedings were filed and until Larson admitted his perjury on pretrial examination. . . .

But Automotive's hands are not automatically cleansed by its alleged failure to possess sufficiently trustworthy evidence of perjury to warrant submission of the case to the District Attorney or to the Patent Office during the pendency of the interference proceedings. The important fact is that Automotive had every reason to believe and did believe that Larson's application was fraudulent and his statements perjured. . . . Thomasma revealed such intimate and detailed facts concerning the perjury as to convince all who heard him. . . .

Automotive knew and suppressed facts that, at the very least, should have been brought in some way to the attention of the Patent Office, especially when it became evident that the interference proceedings would continue no longer. Those who have applications pending with the Patent Office or who are parties to Patent Office proceedings have an uncompromising duty to report to it all facts concerning possible fraud or inequitableness underlying the applications in issue. This duty is not excused by reasonable doubts as to the sufficiency of the proof of the inequitable conduct nor by resort to independent legal advice. Public interest demands that all facts relevant to such matters be submitted formally or informally to the Patent Office, which can then pass upon the sufficiency of the evidence. Only in this way can that agency act to safeguard the public in the first instance against fraudulent patent monopolies. Only in that way can the Patent Office and the public escape from being classed among the "mute and helpless victims of deception and fraud." Hazel-Atlas Glass Co. v. Hartford-Empire Co., 322 U.S. 246. . . . Outside settlements of interference proceedings are not ordinarily illegal. But where, as here, the settlement is grounded upon knowledge or reasonable belief of perjury which is not revealed to the Patent Office or to any other public representative, the settlement lacks that equitable nature which entitles it to be enforced and protected in a court of equity. . . .

By the terms of the settlement, Automotive secured the perjured Larson application and exacted promises from the other parties never to question the validity of any patent that might be issued on that application. Automotive then made numerous changes and expansions as to the claims in the application and eventually secured a patent on it without ever attempting to reveal to the Patent Office or to anyone else the facts it possessed concerning the application's fraudulent ancestry. Automotive thus acted to compound and accentuate the effects of Larson's perjury.

These facts all add up to the inescapable conclusion that Automotive has not displayed that standard of conduct requisite to the maintenance of this suit in equity. That the actions of Larson and Precision may have been more reprehensible is immaterial. The public policy against the assertion and enforcement of patent claims infected with fraud and perjury is too great to be overridden by such a consideration. Automotive knew of and suspected the perjury and failed to act so as to uproot it and destroy its effects. Instead, Automotive acted affirmatively to magnify and increase those effects. Such inequitable conduct impregnated Automotive's entire cause of action and justified dismissal by resort to the unclean hands doctrine. . . .

[The dissenting opinions of JUSTICES ROBERTS and JACKSON are omitted.]

NOTES ON UNCLEAN HANDS AND IN PARI DELICTO

1. The unclean hands defense was traditionally available only in equity. But there is a similar legal doctrine, unfortunately known as in pari delicto (of equal fault). In pari delicto bars one co-conspirator from suing another for damages.

2. The best treatment of the unclean hands doctrine is Chafee, Coming into Equity with Clean Hands, 47 Mich. L. Rev. 877 and 47 Mich. L. Rev. 1065 (1949). His thesis is

> that the clean hands doctrine does not definitely govern anything, that it is a rather recent growth, that it ought not to be called a maxim of equity because it is by no means confined to equity, that its supposed unity is very tenuous and it is really a bundle of rules relating to quite diverse subjects, that insofar as it is a principle it is not very helpful but is at times capable of causing considerable harm.

Id. at 878.

The notes that follow explore the more important of these objections to the conventional wisdom.

3. Did the doctrine do harm in *Precision Instrument*? Certainly if the opinion is taken at face value it was an extreme application. The Court refused to compare plaintiffs' wrongdoing to defendants'. It invalidated not only the patents based on the perjured Larson application, but also the patent based on the Zimmerman application. The primary effect was to allow Larson and Precision to profit from their theft of the Zimmerman-Automotive idea. But the decision also made it legal for any member of the public to manufacture the wrench; theoretically, it follows that the wrench would have to be sold at a competitive rather than a monopoly price. Does this public benefit from deterring misrepresentations to the patent office justify the decision?

Eventually the Court dropped the unclean hands rationale and announced as a substantive rule of patent law that patents procured by fraud are invalid. Invalidity for fraud may be asserted not only as an equitable defense, but in a complaint under the declaratory judgment act or the antitrust laws. Walker Process Equipment v. Food Machinery & Chemical Corp., 382 U.S. 172, 176-177 (1965). But *Precision Instrument* is still the leading Supreme Court case on unclean hands.

4. Patent law is not the only area with a substantive rule very much like unclean hands. A more familiar example is the rule that courts will not enforce illegal contracts. Kaiser Steel Corp. v. Mullins, 455 U.S. 72 (1982).

5. Mechanical application of these doctrines can have unfortunate consequences when defendant's conduct harms the public and not merely the unethical plaintiff. Compare *Precision Instrument* with Worden v. California Fig Syrup Co., 187 U.S. 516 (1903). Both plaintiff and defendant were selling a product called "California Fig Syrup." Plaintiff claimed a trademark in the name and sued to enjoin defendant's infringement. The Court denied relief because of unclean hands: The syrup was not made from figs. The result was that both parties were allowed to continue deceiving the public. Does that make any sense? Is it better that two litigants deceive the public than that one have a monopoly on deception? With the case fully tried, could the court enjoin both litigants from deceiving the public, even though no representative of the public sought that relief against the plaintiff? Is that consistent with our usual conception of the judicial role?

6. Modern decisions refuse to apply unclean hands and in pari delicto when doing so would hamper private enforcement of public policy. The leading case is Perma Life Mufflers v. International Parts Corp., 392 U.S. 134 (1968). Owners of muffler franchises sued the franchisor under the antitrust laws, alleging anticompetitive provisions in the franchise agreement. The lower courts held that plaintiffs were active and eager participants in the antitrust violations they now challenged, and dismissed on in pari delicto. The Supreme Court reversed. It emphasized that plaintiffs were less culpable than defendants, and that if franchisees could not sue, the anticompetitive provisions might go unchallenged.

7. The Eleventh Circuit recently assumed that the fig syrup case is still good law. Shatel Corp. v. Mao Ta Lumber and Yacht Corp., 697 F.2d 1352, 1355 (11th Cir. 1983). Is it consistent with the muffler case? Does that depend on the policy of the trademark laws? Those laws exist to protect investments in trademarks and to prevent deception of the public. But the deception at which the trademark laws are primarily aimed is making the public believe a product was made by someone else.

8. One recurring theme in the cases is that a court will not "serve as referee in an accounting between coconspirators." James v. DuBreuil, 500 F.2d 155 (5th Cir. 1974). This is reminiscent of the Highwaymen's Case, decided in 1725 and unofficially reported in 9 L.Q.R. 197 (1893). Plaintiff alleged a partnership for highway robbery and defendant's failure to account for the partnership profits. The Chancellor dismissed the bill for "scandal and impertinence" and fined plaintiff's solicitors £100 for contempt of court.

Recall Couri v. Couri, supra at 805. Plaintiff sought an accounting for the profits of the family grocery business. One reason the accounting was so difficult is that for twenty years the family had kept phony books for tax purposes. The Illinois Supreme Court allowed an accounting anyway. Is that consistent with the Highwaymen's Case?

9.   One way to allow relief in *Couri* and the fig syrup case is to say that plaintiff's inequitable conduct must not only occur in the transaction sued on, but must be directed at defendant. Many cases say that. Beelman v. Beelman, 121 Ill. App. 3d 684, 460 N.E. 2d 55 (1984), is a good example in the tax context. Plaintiff and her husband fraudulently conveyed their house to his brother to save it from a tax lien. After her husband died and the IRS went away, plaintiff asked for the house back. When her brother-in-law refused to reconvey, the court imposed a constructive trust. It said plaintiff wasn't barred by unclean hands because her fraud on the IRS was not directed at her brother-in-law. The court applied the same rationale in Mascenic v. Anderson, 53 Ill. App. 3d 971, 369, N.E. 2d 172 (1977), where a husband conveyed property to his mistress to keep his wife from claiming it in their divorce.

Are those sound results? Should we give the property to the brother-in-law and the mistress? Might that deter people from making fraudulent conveyances in the first place? But the brother-in-law and the mistress don't look very deserving, do they?

If the results are sound, what about the rationale? Wouldn't the rationale also allow relief in the Highwaymen's Case?

10.   Some cases say the guiding principle is that equity will not help a litigant "in securing or protecting gains from his wrongdoing." Niner v. Hanson, 217 Md. 298, 310, 142 A. 2d 798, 804 (1958). Does that help? The highwayman plaintiff was plainly trying to recover the fruits of his crime. The *Couri* plaintiff was trying to recover some legitimate profits from the sale of groceries and some illegitimate profits from tax fraud. Should he recover one but not the other? That would complicate the accounting even further. *Precision Instrument* is authority for barring Couri altogether; it invalidated both the Zimmerman and the Larson patents. The First Circuit has limited this part of *Precision Instrument* to cases where the separate patent applications have "strong interconnections." Codex Corp. v. Milgo Electronic Corp., 717 F. 2d 622, 633 (1st Cir. 1983), *cert. denied*, 104 S. Ct. 1719 (1984).

What about *Beelman*? Isn't her house the fruits of fraud, because but for the fraudulent conveyance she would have lost it to the IRS?

11.   Another approach is to ask whether defendant is more culpable than plaintiff. *Precision Instrument* refused to consider comparative fault, but most cases go the other way. *Perma Life Mufflers* is a leading example. Gamblers cannot sue to recover their illegal losses, but some states recognize an exception where defendant won by cheating. The cases both ways are collected in Annotation, Recovery of Money or Property Lost through Cheating or Fraud in Forbidden Gambling or Game, 39 A.L.R. 2d 1213 (1955 & Supps.). A patent example is Republic Molding

Corp. v. B. W. Photo Utilities, 319 F.2d 347 (9th Cir. 1963). Plaintiff had marked its goods "patent pending" for six months before it actually applied for a patent, and defendants argued that this created an unclean hands defense. The court disagreed, finding plaintiff's arguable past violation of the patent laws much less egregious than defendant's continuing infringement.

How do you assess comparative fault in *Couri* or the cases in note 9? In each case the defendant participated in the original fraud, although in the cases in note 9 defendants' participation was arguably passive. But then the defendant committed a second wrong by trying to cheat the plaintiff. Does that make defendant more culpable? On that theory, wasn't the defendant highwayman more culpable?

12.   Might courts create so many ways out of the doctrine because the basic premise is unsound? Isn't the unclean hands defense the same as saying two wrongs make a right? Because plaintiff committed some earlier wrong, defendant's wrong goes unremedied. Denying relief may help deter wrongs like plaintiff's, but it only encourages wrongs like defendant's. Shouldn't courts ask whether denying plaintiff relief is a sensible remedy for the earlier wrong, either in the sense that it moves the parties closer to their rightful position, or in the sense that it furthers relevant substantive policies?

13.   "Furthering relevant substantive policies" is a sensible goal, but it doesn't always generate clear answers. Consider the cases on defrauded tippees — plaintiffs who bought securities on the basis of illegal inside tips and then sued when the tip turned out to be misleading. At least two circuits have denied relief on grounds of unclean hands or in pari delicto. Tarasi v. Pittsburgh National Bank, 555 F.2d 1152 (3d Cir.), *cert. denied*, 434 U.S. 565 (1977); James v. DuBreuil, 500 F.2d 155 (5th Cir. 1974). They thought that granting relief would give the tippee his profits if the tip were true and a remedy if it were false, thus encouraging investors to rely on illegal tips. Nathanson v. Weis, Voisin, Cannon, 325 F. Supp. 50 (S.D.N.Y. 1971), went the other way. That court thought it was more important to deter the insider who was giving tips. Is there any way to resolve that argument?

14.   Let me tell you about one more unclean hands case, Powell, Inc. v. Abney, 669 F.2d 348 (5th Cir. 1982). The case is irresistible if you're interested in collecting judgments instead of just getting them. Abney sold Powell $116,000 worth of stolen goods. Abney was convicted of transporting stolen property, and Powell got a judgment for its losses. Most of the money had disappeared, but Powell showed that Abney had used $27,000 of it to buy his family home, which was wholly exempt from execution under Texas law. The court gave Powell a $27,000 equitable lien on the Abney homestead.

Abney then tendered $27,000 into court and moved to discharge the lien. The court of appeals said one who comes into equity must come with clean hands. It also invoked a related maxim: He who seeks equity must do equity. If Abney wanted an order discharging the lien, he must do equity by paying the judgment.

Does that convert a $27,000 lien into a $116,000 lien? Does it undermine the policy behind making the homestead exempt from execution? Is it a great tactical move if the court suspects Abney has the rest of the money concealed somewhere? Presumably Abney could get rid of the lien by selling the homestead, tendering $27,000 of that money to Powell, and investing the remainder in a new homestead within the six months permitted by Texas law.

C. ESTOPPEL AND WAIVER

UNITED STATES v. GEORGIA-PACIFIC CO.
421 F.2d 92 (9th Cir. 1970)

[In 1934, Georgia-Pacific's predecessor entered into a contract with the United States. The contract provided that certain forest lands owned by the private company would be added to the Siskiyou National Forest. Adding this land to the National Forest obligated the government to provide fire protection, but did not transfer ownership of either the land or the timber. In return for fire protection, the company agreed that it would convey the land to the government after cutting the then existing growth of timber.

By 1941 the company had cut and conveyed 6,000 acres. No more sections were cut or conveyed until at least 1958. In that year, the government retracted the bounds of the National Forest, excluding all the land described in the 1934 contract except for sections previously conveyed. Government fire protection was withdrawn.

In 1962 Georgia-Pacific bought the land from the previous owner and undertook an extensive forest management program. In 1967 the government sued for a declaratory judgment that it was entitled to specific performance of the 1934 contract. The district court ruled for Georgia-Pacific on a failure of consideration theory. The Court of Appeals affirmed on other grounds.]

Before HAMLEY and HUFSTEDLER, Circuit Judges, and LEVIN, District Judge.

GERALD S. LEVIN, District Judge. . . .

Equitable Estoppel

Equitable estoppel is a doctrine adjusting the relative rights of parties based upon consideration of justice and good conscience. Pomeroy has defined equitable estoppel as having the effect of absolutely precluding a party, both at law and equity,

> [f]rom asserting rights which might perhaps have otherwise existed, either of property, of contract, or of remedy as against another person, who has in good faith relied upon such conduct, and has been led thereby to change his position for the worse, and who on his part acquires some corresponding right, either of property, of contract, or of remedy.

3 Pomeroy §804, at 189. Equitable estoppel prevents a party from assuming inconsistent positions to the detriment of another party, or, as stated in Bigelow, Law of Estoppel 603 (6th ed. Carter 1913), "'He who keeps silent when duty commands him to speak shall not speak when duty commands him to keep silent.'"

Equitable estoppel is a rule of justice which, in its proper field, prevails over all other rules. An equitable estoppel will be found only where all the elements necessary for its invocation are shown to the court. The test in this circuit was reiterated in Hampton v. Paramount Pictures Corp., 279 F.2d 100, 104 (9th Cir. 1960):

> Four elements must be present to establish the defense of estoppel: (1) The party to be estopped must know the facts; (2) he must intend that his conduct shall be acted on or must so act that the party asserting the estoppel has a right to believe it is so intended; (3) the latter must be ignorant of the true facts; and (4) he must rely on the former's conduct to his injury.

Many kinds of activities — or inactivity — on the part of a defendant may permit the defense of equitable estoppel to be asserted against him. Obviously conduct amounting to fraud would suffice to raise an estoppel against a defendant, but it is clear that conduct far short of actual fraud will also suffice. A party's silence, for example, will work an estoppel if, under the circumstances, he has a duty to speak. A common example of this occurs when a plaintiff knowingly permits a defendant to make expenditures or improvements on property the latter believes to be his, but which in fact the plaintiff knows to be the plaintiff's property. In this case, equity may decree that the plaintiff is estopped from asserting title to the property in question.

In the instant case, the facts show that Government has engaged in just that kind of conduct which would render it liable to the defense of equitable estoppel, subject to the possible immunity therefrom enjoyed by Government, to be discussed hereafter.

Using the test previously enunciated by this Court, we find all the requirements stated there to be met. First, the party to be estopped, Government, certainly "knew the facts" relevant here. As found by the district court below, the 1934 Document was a binding agreement signed by both Georgia-Pacific and a representative of the Government, the Regional Forester. The evidence also makes it clear that Congress was aware of this agreement and knowingly "ratified" it by the passage of the Act of June 13, 1935. Government also knew the facts when another of its representatives, Assistant Secretary of the Interior Sherman, issued P.L.O. 1600, pursuant to a delegation of authority from the President, to effect the retraction of the Siskiyou National Forest northern boundary. Government knew the facts when, by Act of Congress in August, 1958, the exterior boundaries of the Siskiyou National Forest along the Rogue River to the South of the Eden Ridge Tract were extended, but the northern boundary as reduced by P.L.O. 1600 was not disturbed. Finally, Government knew the facts when it permitted Lumber Company and its successor, Georgia-Pacific, to manage and develop the Eden Ridge Tract until 1958 without making any formal demands for conveyance of cut-over lands and when, after P.L.O. 1600 was issued in 1958, the personnel of both Government and the Forest Service treated the boundaries of Siskiyou National Forest as though they had in fact been retracted to the pre-1934 status. Government can hardly claim that it was not aware of the expenditures made by Georgia-Pacific on the lands it thought it owned in the period between 1958 and the Government's bringing suit in 1967.

Second, whether or not Government and its representatives "intended" that Georgia-Pacific act in reliance on Government's actions (and inactions), it is beyond dispute that Georgia-Pacific had a reasonable right to act in reliance thereon. All of Government's actions during the period 1934-1958 were consistent with the belief that Government was not pressing any claims it had under the 1934 Document other than to accept cutover lands as Lumber Company and its successors might convey them. And all of Government's actions during the period 1958-1967 were consistent with Georgia-Pacific's belief that P.L.O. 1600 had in fact reduced the boundaries of Siskiyou National Forest to their status existing prior to the execution of the 1934 Document.

Third, Georgia-Pacific was "ignorant of the true facts," if, as Government claims, the "true facts" are that it never relinquished any claims it had under the 1934 Document and that P.L.O. 1600 was ineffective to cut off Government's rights because its issuance was not validly authorized. There was no explicit statute, ruling, order or case authority to give Georgia-Pacific any indication whatsoever that P.L.O. 1600 might have been issued pursuant to an improper delegation of authority, assuming for the moment such to be the case. Government and its representatives, as discussed above, even treated the Order as binding, changing the pertinent maps and Forest Service routines to coincide with the changes decreed by the Order.

Fourth and finally, it is true that Georgia-Pacific did rely on the representations (or lack of same in some instances) to its injury. Georgia-Pacific spent some $350,000, beginning in 1956, in an intensive forest management program. Georgia-Pacific has maintained a 300-mile road system and has reseeded or planted a new crop of trees. In addition, Georgia-Pacific has continued to pay its annual ad valorem taxes to Coos and Douglas Counties and to pay its annual dues for fire protection to the Fire Patrol Association.

The major issue facing this Court is not whether the facts are sufficient to raise the defense of equitable estoppel, but whether under the circumstances such estoppel can be raised against Government. It has been held generally that the Government is not subject to the same rules of property and estoppel as are private suitors. Such governmental immunity from estoppel is an off-shoot of sovereign immunity. Both the doctrine of sovereign immunity and that of governmental immunity from estoppel have been much discussed, criticized and limited in recent years. While the resulting disfavor with sovereign immunity has resulted in legislation limiting the availability of that defense in certain actions against the Government, a corresponding expansion of the availability of estoppel against the Government has occurred rather more slowly.

In the leading case expressing the limitations of equitable estoppel against the Government, Utah Power & Light Co. v. United States, 243 U.S. 389, 409 (1916), the United States Supreme Court said:

> [T]he United States is neither bound nor estopped by acts of its officers or agents in entering into an arrangement or agreement to do or cause to be done what the law does not sanction or permit. . . .
>
> A suit by the United States to enforce and maintain its policy respecting lands which it holds in trust for all the people stands upon a different plane in this and some other respects from the ordinary private suit to regain the title to real property or to remove a cloud from it.

In Federal Crop Ins. Corp. v. Merrill, 332 U.S. 380 (1947), the Supreme Court declined to find the Federal Crop Insurance Corporation estopped to deny liability on a policy for wheat protection issued to Merrill. Provisions restricting the coverage of certain kinds of wheat having been published in the Federal Register, Merrill was found to have been on constructive notice thereof to the extent that insurance could not be issued to protect his type of crop.

The growth of government and the concomitant increase in its functions, power and contacts with private parties has made many courts increasingly reluctant to deny the defense of equitable estoppel in appropriate situations. The Government, in its caretaker role for all the public, should not be bound by the unauthorized or unlawful acts of its representatives. On the other hand, it is hardly in the public's interest for the Government to deal dishonestly or in an unconscientious manner. This is especially imperative in a time when few individuals and corporations, if any, can escape numerous dealings with the Government and its agents.

Numerous cases reflect the position that equitable estoppels may be found against the Government in certain situations. Thus the courts have held that an equitable estoppel may be found against the Government (1) if the Government is acting in its proprietary rather than sovereign capacity; and (2) if its representative has been acting within the scope of his authority.

(1) While it is said that the Government can be estopped in its proprietary role, but not in its sovereign role, the authorities are not clear about just what activities are encompassed by each. In its proprietary role, the Government is acting as a private concern would; in its sovereign role, the Government is carrying out its unique governmental functions for the benefit of the whole public.

In the instant case, the Government is suing to enforce a contract between it and a third party, and is thus acting as a private party would. The question here is not that of preserving public lands — since Government never had title to the cutover lands it is now claiming — but only of enforcing a private contract to gain new title to lands. *Proprietary role*

In United States v. A. Bentley & Sons Co., 293 F. 229, 235 (S.D. Ohio 1923), a case dealing with commercial paper, the court noted that

> When the government enters into a contract with an individual or corporation, it divests itself of its sovereign character as to that particular transaction and takes that of an ordinary citizen and submits to the same law as governs individuals under like circumstances.

(2) We must also ask whether Assistant Secretary of the Interior Sherman, in issuing P.L.O. 1600 in 1958, was acting beyond the scope of his authority, thus rendering such Order ineffective to bind the Government under the principles discussed above. And if it is found that such Order was ineffective when issued, was it nonetheless ratified and thus binding by the action of Congress in passing the Act of August, 1958?

[The court concluded that Sherman did have authority, and that in any event, Congress had implicitly ratified his order by enacting a bill changing another part of the Forest's boundary without disturbing the boundary at issue here.]

Mr. Justice Holmes once wrote, "Men must turn square corners when they deal with the Government," but it is clear that the Government is itself becoming more reasonable by permitting those corners to be rounded when reason and logic demand that the Government be held to the same standard of rectilinear rectitude that it demands from its citizens. One commentator has summarized the law in this area by saying that, "The claim of the government to an immunity from estoppel is in fact a claim to exemption from the requirements of morals and justice." We agree, and we find that the dictates of both morals and justice indicate that the Government is not entitled to immunity from equitable estoppel in this case.

Clean Hands

A second equitable defense here is that of clean hands, a doctrine some-what akin to, but distinguishable from, that of estoppel. Like estop-pel, the doctrine of clean hands is based on conscience and good faith. . . . Precision Instrument Mfg. Co. v. Automotive Co., 324 U.S. 806 (1945). . . .

The Government comes before this Court seeking the equitable rem-edy of specific performance, a decree for which can be denied if the plaintiff has not come into court with clean hands.

If a court of equity finds the plaintiff to be guilty of unfair conduct or any inequitable advantage it may refuse him the remedy of specific per-formance — even though such conduct would not be sufficient for re-scission of the contract sought to be enforced. . . .

It is clear that in the present case a decree of specific performance in favor of Government will result in an inequitable advantage to it to the extent that Georgia-Pacific has made considerable investment in the Eden Ridge Tract based upon good faith reliance on both the boundary changes of 1958 and the failure of Government to assert any claim to the subject lands until the present suit was instituted.

The Government's actions can hardly be described as comporting with the dictates of good faith, fair dealing, or conscience. Georgia-Pacific was given no indication that the boundary changes effected in 1958 were invalidly made (as Government claims) or that Government would later repudiate such changes to the considerable financial detriment of Georgia-Pacific. It is just these considerations which find Government's hands tained and thus lead this court to deny its claim for specific perfor-mance.

Other Equitable Considerations in Granting Specific Performance

Our final consideration relates to the general rules of equity surround-ing the discretionary remedy of specific performance. Because addressed to the discretion of the court, the remedy may be denied where the equities are such as to convince the court that justice and good con-science requires denial. As this court said over half a century ago in Marks v. Gates, 154 F. 481, 482 (9th Cir. 1907):

> The enforcement of a contract by a decree for its specific performance rests in the sound discretion of the court — a judicial discretion to be exercised in accordance with established principles of equity. A contract may be valid in law and not subject to cancellation in equity, and yet the terms thereof, the attendant circumstances, and in some cases the subsequent events, may be such as to require the court to deny its specific performance.

Courts of equity have long refused to decree specific performance where the result would be unconscionable, unjust, inequitable, oppressive or unduly harsh. . . .

In the instant case, a decree of specific performance would inure to the obvious and substantial hardship of Georgia-Pacific. Georgia-Pacific's program of reseeding and planting would be rendered futile, and its expenditures on the subject land and appurtenant roads and facilities would be lost. A decree of specific performance would result in a severe diminution of the forest reserve assets of Georgia-Pacific, and Georgia-Pacific would have lost any chances it had to purchase similar timberland in the past ten years.

We find it unnecessary to consider the applicability of the doctrine of frustration of contract and of failure of consideration in relation to the 1934 Document briefed and argued by the parties in view of the grounds of our decision.

The judgment of the District Court is affirmed.

NOTES ON ESTOPPEL

1. Other estoppels arose at law. Res judicata is sometimes referred to as estoppel by judgment; the usage survives more commonly in the phrase "collateral estoppel." There is also estoppel by deed, estoppel by contract, and judicial estoppel. Promissory estoppel is an extension of equitable estoppel; plaintiff is allowed to recover because he relied on a defendant's promise. Estoppels have in common that a party is prevented from asserting his present views because some past statement, act or event is held to be determinative.

2. The essence of equitable estoppel is one party's prejudicial reliance on the other party's earlier statement or conduct. There are four-part formulations, as in *Georgia-Pacific*, three-part formulations, as in Central Microfilm Service Corp. v. Basic/Four Corp., 688 F.2d 1206 (8th Cir. 1982), *cert. denied*, 459 U.S. 1204 (1983), and even six-part formulations, as in Beverage v. Harvey, 602 F.2d 657 (4th Cir. 1979). All lead to substantially the same results. The Missouri formulation in *Central Microfilm* is probably the cleanest: an act or statement inconsistent with the right later asserted, reliance, and injury. *Georgia-Pacific*'s reference to the "true facts" is somewhat misleading; the whole point is that it doesn't matter what the true facts were. Whether the government relinquished its rights under the agreement or not, it acted as though it had, and that is what matters.

3. Equitable estoppel is closely related to fraud. All frauds give rise to estoppels and may be relied on defensively. But fraud is also a tort; it gives rise to a cause of action for damages or injunction. The usual distinction is that fraud requires intentional or reckless misrepresentation, but negli-

gent or even inadvertent misrepresentations can give rise to an estoppel. Even good faith representations that become untrue because of changing circumstances can create an estoppel. An example is People v. Kinion, 97 Ill. 2d 322, 331, 454 N.E.2d 625, 629 (1983). A privately retained attorney had his client declared indigent so that the county would pay her psychiatric witnesses. But he told the court that he would continue to represent her without demanding attorneys' fees from the county. He thought that defendant had enough assets to pay him but not enough to pay the experts in addition. Relying on the attorney's representation, the court appointed him instead of the public defender. When it turned out that the defense cost more than defendant could pay, the attorney petitioned for an award of fees from the county. The state Supreme Court held him estopped to seek fees.

The distinction between fraud and estoppel is not always carefully maintained. Some formulations of estoppel require intent to deceive, e.g., United States ex rel. Fogle v. Hal B. Hayes & Associates, 221 F. Supp. 260, 264 (N.D. Cal. 1963), and some jurisdictions have reduced the mental state required for fraud, e.g., Clements Auto Co. v. Service Bureau Corp., 444 F.2d 169, 176 (8th Cir. 1971) (Minnesota law).

4. Estoppel is only a defense; Georgia-Pacific could not sue anyone for estoppel. But one way to think of estoppel is that it is Georgia-Pacific's remedy for the government's misleading conduct. Is it an appropriate remedy? There is a certain intuitive justice in estoppel: You said it, you're stuck with it. Surely the government shouldn't be able to reclaim Georgia-Pacific's forest as if nothing had happened since 1934. But does estoppel confer a windfall on Georgia-Pacific? Why not give the government the land if it compensates Georgia-Pacific for its reliance damages?

Estoppel gives Georgia-Pacific the benefit of whatever the government led it to believe; it is a way of compensating expectancies. Does it make sense to compensate expectancies in a claim based on reliance?

5. The court also relies on unclean hands. Does that add anything to estoppel? Put another way, if the Supreme Court had granted certiorari and reversed on estoppel, is there any chance it would have affirmed on unclean hands?

NOTES ON GENERAL EQUITABLE DISCRETION

1. We have already encountered the notion that equitable remedies are discretionary, and the clarification that equitable discretion is to be exercised in light of fixed principles. See More Notes on the Measure of Injunctive Relief, supra at 249. In *Georgia-Pacific* the court invokes general equitable discretion as something distinct from estoppel and unclean hands. Does that add anything to the opinion, or does it just restate the same considerations under a different heading?

If the government had sued for damages for breach of contract, is there any chance the court would have held Georgia-Pacific liable? If not, why all the talk about how specific performance can be withheld even if the contract is valid?

2. There are cases where courts deny relief for reasons of fairness or reliance that do not squarely fit within any of the established equitable defenses. Perhaps general equitable discretion is as good a label as any for those cases, although certain fact patterns tend to recur. Many of the cases involve harsh and oppressive contracts. They are probably best thought of as unconscionability cases, but not all of them are written that way. These cases are explored in the Notes on Unconscionability and Related Defenses, supra at 380. *Georgia-Pacific* relies on those cases, but there is nothing harsh about the original contract; the harshness comes from the government's reassertion of its rights after apparently abandoning them.

3. Another group of cases involve suits for refunds of money paid by mistake or collected unlawfully. If the recipient has relied on receipt of the money and it would be a hardship to pay it back, he is often allowed to keep it. A typical case is Bush v. Metropolitan Life Insurance Co., 656 F.2d 231 (6th Cir. 1981), involving a disability insurer's attempts to recoup overpayments from disabled workers.

Some of these cases can be explained as estoppels, but in some of them there is little element of reliance and no element of mistake or misrepresentation by the payor. A good example is Thompson v. Washington, 551 F.2d 1316 (D.C. Cir. 1977). A public housing authority imposed a rent increase without proper procedures. Tenants sued to enjoin collection of the higher rents. The trial court denied relief, but the court of appeals reversed. The tenants then sought restitution of the rent that had been illegally collected during the litigation. The court denied restitution, largely on the ground that the housing authority needed the money. Income was already insufficient to pay for maintenance, and the court thought a large judgment would not be in anyone's best interest.

The tenants weren't estopped, were they? They always claimed the rent hike was illegal. Is it undue hardship? The tenants probably need the money as badly as the housing authority; surely the hardship to the housing authority would not be grossly disproportionate to the benefit to the tenants. General equitable discretion?

4. *Thompson* also suggested that granting restitution would apply new procedural requirements retroactively. It relied on Lemon v. Kurtzman, 411 U.S. 192 (1973). *Lemon* allowed Pennsylvania to give one year of financial aid to religious schools under a program the Court had already declared unconstitutional. The schools had already spent the money in reliance on a promise of reimbursement. The Court thought that its prior decisions had not "clearly foreshadowed" the program's unconstitutionality and that it would impose undue hardship to withhold reimbursement after the schools had incurred the expenses. The Court

also suggested that plaintiffs were partly to blame for the choice between undue hardship or unconstitutional payments, because they had not sought a preliminary injunction.

Can you explain *Lemon* on estoppel grounds? Undue hardship? A combination? *Lemon* also builds on a long line of cases about retroactive application of new rules of law.

NOTES ON ESTOPPEL AGAINST THE GOVERNMENT

1. The traditional rule is that the government cannot be estopped. The leading federal case is Federal Crop Insurance Corp. v. Merrill, 332 U.S. 380 (1947), briefly described in *Georgia-Pacific*. The government insured plaintiff's wheat, but when the crop was lost it refused to pay. The variety of wheat that Merrill planted was uninsurable under a regulation published in the Federal Register. The court of appeals held the government estopped to deny coverage, but the Supreme Court reversed. There were four dissents; Justice Jackson was especially outraged. He thought that if any farmer read the Federal Register, "he would never need crop insurance, for he would never get time to plant any crops." Id. at 387.

2. The lower courts are still unhappy with *Merrill. Georgia-Pacific* illustrates one escape route: the distinction between governmental and proprietary activities. The governmental/proprietary distinction appears in a wide range of contexts. Courts alternate between denouncing it and relying on it. The distinction is unworkable, because many government activities can't be classified either way. Was the crop insurance program proprietary, because it was an ordinary insurance contract? Or governmental, because the market couldn't provide adequate crop insurance and the government was solving an important social and economic problem? The majority said it didn't matter, that the government was immune from estoppel in all its activities. "Government is not partly public or partly private, depending upon the governmental pedigree of the type of a particular activity or the manner in which the Government conducts it." 332 U.S. at 383-384.

But the distinction refuses to die, in part because it seems so sensible in extreme cases. There is an intuitive difference between interfering with the President's control over nuclear weapons and interfering with New York's ownership of Yankee Stadium. Professors Wells and Hellerstein think the distinction is a conclusory shorthand for a complex process of interest balancing, and that the terms are helpful as long as we remember they don't mean anything. Wells and Hellerstein, The Governmental-Proprietary Distinction in Constitutional Law, 66 Va. L. Rev. 1073 (1980).

Does the distinction make any sense in *Georgia-Pacific*? How significant is the difference between the government's interest in keeping forest lands it already owns and its interest in acquiring title to forest lands it has purchased? What if it were trying to acquire the Grand Canyon for a national park? Or land for an air force base? Is the answer that the government should use eminent domain if the acquisition is important enough?

3. More recently the lower courts have held that the government can be estopped even in its governmental capacity in certain exceptional cases. They have taken some comfort from repeated statements by the Supreme Court that it has never decided whether the government might be estopped when it is guilty of "affirmative misconduct." The thought first occurs in Montana v. Kennedy, 366 U.S. 308 (1961); the phrase crystallized in United States Immigration & Naturalization Service v. Hibi, 414 U.S. 5 (1973). The courts of appeals have taken that dictum as authority to create exceptions to the general rule — not just an affirmative misconduct exception, but other exceptions as well. They have developed a thriving government estoppel jurisprudence, punctuated by occasional reversals from the Supreme Court.

a. Schweiker v. Hansen, 450 U.S. 785 (1981). A social security field representative erroneously told Hansen she was ineligible for social security. She didn't file an application until she learned the truth eleven months later. Because a written application is a prerequisite to benefits, the field representative's mistake cost her eleven months of benefits. The Second Circuit held the government estopped to deny that she had filed an application the first time. The court of appeals thought the procedural requirement less important than her substantive eligibility. The Supreme Court summarily reversed. It rejected the distinction between substantive and procedural requirements for eligibility, and it held that this mistake fell far short of the affirmative misconduct that would raise a serious question about estoppel against the government.

But for the government's mistake, Hansen would have gotten social security eleven months earlier, which is all she sought by her estoppel argument. But for the government's mistake in *Merrill*, Merrill wouldn't have bought any insurance on his uninsurable crop. But the relief he sought through estoppel was to have the government pay for the loss of his uninsurable crop — a result he could not have obtained any other way. Shouldn't that make a difference? Wasn't Merrill trying to get a windfall from the government's mistake, while Hansen was just trying to get what she was entitled to all along? The Court thought not; in its view, she wasn't eligible because she didn't file a written application.

b. Immigration & Naturalization Service v. Miranda, 459 U.S. 14 (1982). Miranda was an alien married to a citizen. As such, he was entitled to an immigrant visa. INS failed to act on his application for a year and a half; during that time, the marriage ended in divorce. The Ninth Circuit held that the government's delay was affirmative misconduct; the Supreme Court summarily reversed. Once again it held open the possibility of an affirmative misconduct exception. Whatever affirmative misconduct means, bureaucratic delay doesn't seem to be a very good candidate.

c. Heckler v. Community Health Services, 104 S. Ct. 2218 (1984). The government hired Travelers Insurance Companies to manage part of the Medicare program. Community Health asked Travelers whether costs paid under a grant could also be reimbursed under Medicare, and Travelers incorrectly said yes. The government subsequently demanded a $71,000 refund. The demand forced Community Health to the brink of bankruptcy. The court of appeals held that Travelers was guilty of affirmative misconduct in giving erroneous information and not referring the question to the government, and that the government was estopped by the affirmative misconduct of its agent. The Supreme Court reversed, holding that Travelers lacked authority to answer the question and that it was unreasonable to rely on Travelers' advice. Once again, it explicitly refused to hold that the government can never be estopped.

4. The Ninth Circuit's repeated debates over the meaning of affirmative misconduct do not encourage one to believe that the phrase has any real meaning. The cases are collected in Note, Equitable Estoppel of the Government, 79 Colum. L. Rev. 551, 559-560 (1979). Schweiker v. Hansen and Montana v. Kennedy both hold that affirmatively misleading a citizen with erroneous information isn't affirmative misconduct. In both cases, the Supreme Court apparently assumed that the government officer was negligent at worst. Should it be different if he deliberately lied?

5. One case that escaped Supreme Court review is Johnson v. Williford, 682 F.2d 868 (9th Cir. 1982). Johnson was convicted of importing marijuana and sentenced under a statute that precluded parole. He was paroled anyway, went straight, held a job, then started a business, hired five employees, and generally was a model citizen. Fifteen months later the government discovered its mistake and revoked his parole. The court held the government estopped. It relied heavily on the balance of hardships, and didn't refer to the affirmative misconduct test.

Was Johnson ignorant of the true facts? The government thought he was charged with knowledge of the statute just as Merrill was charged with knowledge of the Federal Register. The court of appeals said the government's "active misadvice" kept Johnson from having "even constructive knowledge" of the statute. Didn't Merrill get "active misadvice" too?

Did Johnson rely to his detriment on the mistake? Release from prison isn't a detriment, is it? The court said Johnson relied when he quit his secure job and started a business. How is that reliance on parole? If his parole were revoked, he couldn't have held the "secure" job either.

The Ninth Circuit may have backed off from Johnson in Green v. Christiansen, 732 F.2d 1397 (9th Cir. 1984). Green was serving state and federal sentences concurrently in a state prison. When he came up for state parole, state authorities asked federal authorities if they wanted Green returned to federal prison. They said no. Green successfully completed his parole period and had been at liberty two and a half years when the federal authorities arrested him to complete his federal sentence. The court distinguished *Johnson* on the ground that Johnson's expectations were built up through eight parole reviews; the court seemed to think that Green had no expectations because the government had said only once that he could go. How convincing is that?

6.   One other case that suggests the attitude of the courts of appeals is Portmann v. United States, 674 F.2d 1155 (7th Cir. 1982). Portmann mailed color film separations and paid the Postal Service $31 for "Document Reconstruction Insurance." The clerk assured her that she would be covered for the expense of recreating the film up to a limit of $50,000. The Postal Service lost the package, and she filed a claim for $3,874. The government denied coverage on the ground that color film is "merchandise" and not "documents."

Isn't that on all fours with *Merrill*? The court of appeals thought not. No private company was selling all risk crop insurance of the sort that Merrill bought; Portmann could have gotten insurance through a private carrier. The regulations in *Merrill* were clear; the court thought the regulation in *Portmann* was ambiguous. Thus, examining the regulation might not have helped her. (Justice Jackson didn't think it would have helped Merrill to read the Federal Register either.) Third, the Postal Service is largely self-financed; Merrill's claim would have run directly against the Treasury. Are any of those distinctions convincing?

The court also suggested that the Postal Service is quasi-proprietary. In deciding whether the post office is governmental or proprietary, does it matter that the Postmaster General was one of the original four cabinet officers, long predating the Secretary of Agriculture, to pick an example relevant to *Merrill*? Does it matter that the Federal Crop Insurance Corporation was a quasi-independent corporation much like the Postal Service, and that the Court in *Merrill* insisted that the form in which the government carried out its business was irrelevant?

Portmann was remanded for trial with directions to consider everything and balance interests. Despite the vagueness of the holding, the opinion is one of the most thorough reviews of the present state of the law and the policy arguments for and against estopping the government.

7.   What are those policy arguments? *Georgia-Pacific* says the government is seeking an "exemption from . . . morals and justice." That's true, isn't it? On the other hand, is there a respectable argument that the government should not be bound by the mistakes of every local forest ranger, welfare worker, or GS-7 bureaucrat? Is such a plea any more persuasive when made by the government than when made by IBM or Exxon?

Some have argued that the rule protects separation of powers. If the government is bound by representations of the executive, does that enable the executive to override legislation? Enough to be a practical problem, or only in theory? Consider Doris v. Police Commissioner, 394 Mass. 443, 373 N.E.2d 944 (1978). A Massachusetts statute required police officers to live within ten miles of the city that employed them. For a long time the statute was not enforced, and some 200 Boston police officers lived more than ten miles from the city limits. Then the police commissioner sent them all letters threatening to begin enforcement proceedings in ten days. The 200 officers argued that prior nonenforcement had led them to believe the statute was a "dead letter" and had induced them to buy homes beyond the ten-mile limit. The court held the city not estopped: "It would indeed be a most serious consequence if . . . the inattention or inactivity of government officials could render a statute unenforceable. . . ." Id. at 449, 373 N.E.2d at 949.

Is that the right result? If so, is widespread nullification different from errors in individual cases? Is Doris special because the statute regulated the executive, which might have had an interest in letting it become a dead letter?

8. Professor Braunstein recently offered a different argument: that if the government is held responsible for its advice, it will give less advice. That will make everyone worse off, but especially the ordinary citizen who can't afford private advice. Braunstein, In Defense of a Traditional Immunity — Toward an Economic Rationale for Not Estopping the Government, 14 Rut. L.J. 1 (1982). He thinks most government advice is accurate, and that we're better off letting the victims live with the mistakes than chilling the source of advice. He cites the example of the Federal Reserve Board, which quit giving informal staff interpretations of the Truth in Lending Act after Congress made reliance on such interpretations a defense in private litigation.

It is easy to see how the government can quit giving free legal advice to banks. But is it feasible to cut off the informal opinions that field officers give in government transactions with the public? Is the government likely to instruct social security employees, for example, to take applications and refuse to answer questions? Can postal clerks be ordered to say, "Buy the insurance if you want, but I can't tell you what it covers." Might Congress have something to say about those directives?

UNITED STATES FIDELITY & GUARANTY CO. v. BIMCO IRON & METAL CORP.
464 S.W.2d 353 (Tex. 1971)

[Burglars broke into Bimco's building, dismantled the electrical system, and stole the wiring and transformers. USF&G's policy covered damage to the building by burglars or vandals, but did not cover theft. USF&G offered to pay for the damage done to the door where the burglars broke in, but refused to pay for the stolen equipment. The court ruled that the entire loss was damage to the building and therefore covered.]

McGEE, Justice. . . .

Defendant also relies on the fact that plaintiff failed to timely file a proof of loss. Absent proof of the insurance company's waiver of the necessity for filing a proof of loss, the plaintiff could not recover. The trial court refused to admit certain testimony relating to waiver on the ground that it related to facts occurring after a non-waiver agreement had been executed. The Court of Civil Appeals held that the testimony admitted into evidence did not raise a fact issue as to whether the defendant waived the plaintiff's failure to file a proof, but remanded for a new trial on the ground that testimony developed on a bill of exception raised the issue. The non-waiver agreement provided in part "that any action taken by the Company . . . in investigating said accident shall not operate in any way as a waiver, or invalidate any of the conditions of said policy. . . ."

The plaintiff's bill of exceptions would have shown: that after the time for filing proofs had expired and the non-waiver agreement executed, Mr. Wilson of the General Adjustment Bureau (claim adjuster for defendant) told plaintiff's attorney that the insurance company would not pay the loss from theft but would pay for the damage to the door caused by the breaking in of the burglars. In answer to a request for admission the defendant admitted that it told plaintiff that the damage to the door was covered by the policy but that the loss resulting from the removal of the wiring system was not; and the defendant's counsel made the following statement at the trial: "Your Honor, I think that is certainly what happened, I take the position right now that that is exactly what the policy says, that the door of the building is covered and the wire is not covered."

The total denial of liability on any grounds, after the time for filing the proof of loss had expired would not constitute a waiver of the defense of late filing of the proof of loss.

Mr. Wilson was authorized to adjust this particular loss and to waive notice and formal proofs of loss. "It is generally recognized that an adjuster, authorized to act in the premises, may waive formal proof of loss." 32 Tex. Jur. 2d Insurance §385 at 598 (1962).

Waiver has been defined as an intentional relinquishment of a known right or intentional conduct inconsistent with claiming it. An admission of partial liability for damage to the door after the time for filing proofs of loss had expired is inconsistent with an intention to rely on failure to timely file proofs of loss as a defense. This is not a case where the defendant denied *any* liability after the time allotted for filing proofs of loss. After the time for filing proofs of loss had expired the local agent wrote to the defendant requesting that plaintiff's claim be processed. The recording agent then referred the claim to the General Adjustment Bureau for handling by Mr. Wilson, the adjuster. He never denied liability on the grounds of late filing of proofs of loss. Mr. Wilson had conferences with the insured and through him obtained estimates of the cost of repair of the building damage.

The non-waiver agreement in this case merely states that investigation of the accident will not operate as a waiver. The action of Wilson in attempting to settle the claim by payment of damage to the door is not, in our opinion, a part of the investigation. This conduct was inconsistent with the insurer's known defense of non-filing of proofs of loss. The trial court committed reversible error in excluding this testimony.

The instant case is one of waiver and does not involve estoppel. The time for filing proofs of loss had expired before the action of the insurer constituting an alleged waiver of this defense occurred. Although there is a conflict found in Texas decisions, we adopt the rule that a waiver may be effective *after* expiration of the time for performance of a condition has expired, if the condition which is asserted to have been waived is not a material part of the agreed equivalent of the obligor's promise and its non-performance does not materially affect the value received by the obligor. . . .

The distinction between waiver and estoppel in this situation is again noted in our Massachusetts Bond & Insurance Co. v. Orkin Exterminating Co. opinion, to the effect (416 S.W.2d at page 401): " . . . that waiver is essentially unilateral in its character; it results as a legal consequence from some act or conduct of the party against whom it operates; no act of the party in whose favor it is made is necessary to complete it. It need not be founded upon a new agreement or be supported by consideration, nor is it essential that it be based upon an estoppel."

Waiver need not be founded on a new agreement, nor be supported by a consideration nor based on estoppel. To the extent that . . . cases . . . have held to the contrary and are in conflict with this opinion, they are overruled.

The judgment of the Court of Civil Appeals is affirmed.

NOTES ON WAIVER

1. In what sense did Wilson intentionally waive USF&G's rights? Do you suppose he even thought about the consequences the court attributes to his decision to pay for the door? If he had said explicitly that he was waiving the time limit as to the door, but not as to the electrical equipment, should the case have come out the other way? Suppose he says that's what he thought he was doing? What if he says he routinely waives proof of claim for losses under $500, and that's what this was until the court unexpectedly said the electrical equipment was covered too.

Would paying for the door still be intentional conduct inconsistent with insisting on proof of claim?

Finally, and perhaps most likely, what if he simply didn't notice that the proof of claim hadn't been filed, or lost track of time and didn't realize that the ninety days had expired? That's a pretty inadvertent waiver, isn't it? Does "intentional conduct" just mean that he didn't say the words by accident? Does "known right" just mean that in the abstract he knew the company was entitled to demand proof of loss? Isn't the reality of waiver a long way from "intentional relinquishment of a known right"?

2.   Should we enforce waivers without any consideration or detrimental reliance? Why? Why shouldn't USF&G be able to correct its mistake if no harm has been done? On its face, the doctrine enforces an expectancy even though Bimco gave nothing in exchange. It is as though USF&G made a gift to Bimco, and the gift was complete and enforceable as soon as Wilson offered to pay for the door.

3.   Note 2 describes the doctrine, but does it describe the reality? Won't there nearly always be some kind of reliance on a waiver? Doesn't it seem likely that Bimco relied on the waiver of proof of loss when it continued to spend time and money processing its claim? Likely, but not necessarily so. Perhaps if Wilson had denied liability for failure to file proof of loss, Bimco would have spent just as much time and money arguing the coverage question, and would also have argued that the proof of loss requirement was unenforceable because USF&G had all the information it needed.

4.   Does waiver doctrine make sense as a way of avoiding litigation over attenuated reliance questions? If so, when? Only when the waiver is truly knowing and intentional? Only when the right waived is not very important?

5.   *Bimco* states the prevailing distinction between waiver and estoppel. But usage varies widely. Some cases are just sloppy and use the terms interchangeably. In addition, waivers occur in many contexts and the standards necessarily vary. In addition, some states reject the prevailing formulation. In Pennsylvania, for example, an implied waiver like the one in *Bimco* is effective only if there is reliance. Schifalacqua v. CNA Insurance, 567 F.2d 1255 (3d Cir. 1977). That makes implied waiver indistinguishable from estoppel.

6.   Another recurring source of waiver litigation is loan agreements. Creditors regularly accept late payments for substantial periods before giving up on a debtor and taking legal action. The debtor often argues that the earlier acceptance of late payments precludes the creditor from insisting on prompt payment now. Creditors regularly provide in loan agreements that failure to enforce rights with respect to some payments doesn't waive them with respect to others. The Uniform Commercial Code says that the express terms of an agreement prevail over a course of

dealing between the parties. §1-205(4). But it also says that "the principles of law and equity, including . . . the law relative to . . . estoppel," supplement the Code. §1-103. And courts regularly hold that creditors have waived their right to insist on prompt payment.

But creditors can reclaim the right to prompt payment by telling the debtor that they will insist on it henceforth. An example of the doctrine is Ford Motor Credit Co. v. Washington, 573 S.W.2d 616 (Tex. Civ. App. 1978). Ford sent a letter demanding immediate payment to the wrong address, so that the debtor never received it. The court held Ford had not undone its earlier waiver, so that its subsequent repossession of the debtor's car was a conversion.

Even though the opinion is written in terms of waiver, and even though Texas says reliance is irrelevant to waiver, isn't reliance the key element? What good would a letter demanding immediate payment do if courts weren't primarily concerned about the debtor's reliance on past forbearance?

7. The emphasis on reliance is even more explicit in UCC §2-209, which applies to contracts for the sale of goods. Under §2-209(2), if a contract says it can be modified only in writing, then it can be modified only in writing. But §2-209(4) says that an ineffective attempt to modify orally may operate as a waiver. And §2-209(5) says that a waiver affecting an executory part of the contract may be withdrawn by reasonable notice to the other side, "unless the retraction would be unjust in view of a material change of position in reliance on the waiver." The New York Court of Appeals has applied substantially the same rules to a mortgage, which of course is outside the Code. Nassau Trust Co. v. Montrose Concrete Products Corp., 56 N.Y.2d 175, 436 N.E.2d 1265 (1982).

8. Perhaps the most common use of the waiver notion is in procedure. Courts regularly say that litigants waived a claim, defense, or procedural right by not asserting it at the proper time. The rationale here is clearly that the court and the other litigants relied by completing the litigation; the courts will not retry a case to correct an error that could have been corrected when it was made. For the most part there is no pretense that these waivers are knowing or intentional. Inadvertence is just as binding. But a court so inclined could probably describe most of these waivers as intentional conduct inconsistent with a known right. The conduct is as intentional as Wilson's in Bimco, and the right is often as well known. But at least in the procedure cases, it doesn't matter if the right is known but overlooked, as in Bimco, or if the litigant and his lawyer don't know about it at all.

For a few very important procedural rights that are guaranteed by the Constitution and that affect the accuracy of the fact finding process, the Supreme Court has insisted on the intentional relinquishment of a known right. The distinction is developed in Schneckloth v. Bustamonte, 412 U.S. 218, 235-246 (1973), which holds that a criminal suspect can waive his protection against warrantless searches even though he doesn't know he has such a right.

9. *Bimco* illustrates one other point about equitable defenses. Not only are they not exclusively equitable, they aren't exclusively defenses. Bimco is the plaintiff, asserting that USF&G has waived its defense. Similarly, a defendant can be estopped from asserting a defense; estoppel to assert the statute of limitations is a common example. See Bomba v. W. L. Belvidere, Inc., infra at 999. And a defendant who asks for any kind of relief can be barred by unclean hands. An example is Powell v. Abney, described supra at 936, where defendant asked the court to discharge an equitable lien.

MORE NOTES ON ESTOPPEL AGAINST THE GOVERNMENT AND WAIVERS BY THE GOVERNMENT

1. Even if the government can't be estopped, can it waive its rights? Some courts say yes, but only if the official who waived the rights had authority to do so.

Consider Cinciarelli v. Reagan, 729 F.2d 801 (D.C. Cir. 1984). Cinciarelli was a colonel in the Marine Corps Reserve. He was appointed to a five-year tour of active duty under a written agreement. Regulations provided that such agreements could not be offered to colonels, but the regulation was frequently ignored. The Commandant of the Marine Corps promulgated the regulation; he also approved the agreement with Cinciarelli. But the Marines reneged when Cinciarelli was promoted to general. There were no more slots for active duty generals, and all such slots were reserved for career officers anyway. The Marines sent Cinciarelli back to reserve status, and he sued for five-years' pay as a general. The case eventually settled for $365,000, and then Cinciarelli asked for attorneys' fees under the Equal Access to Justice Act, described supra at 836.

His right to fees turned on whether the government's litigation position was "substantially justified." The court held that it was not:

> Though the law is clear that the government is not bound by the unauthorized acts of its agents, Federal Crop Ins. Co. v. Merrill, the law in this circuit is equally clear that . . . when a government official has authority to waive the regulations allegedly violated, "we look instead to the standards of waiver that would govern between private parties." Molton, Allen & Williams, Inc. v. Harris, 613 F.2d 1176, 1179 (D.C. Cir. 1980). Thus when, in the course of making an agreement, an official with power to waive a regulation that would bar the agreement acts in a way that signals to a private party an objective intent to waive the regulation, and the private party relies on that behavior,

the government official is estopped from voiding the agreement on the basis of the regulation.

729 F.2d at 807-808.

Note the mixture of estoppel and waiver.

2.   How does the court know which government employees have authority to waive regulations? In *Cinciarelli* the government apparently conceded that the Commandant had authority. In *Molton*, the court found authority in regulations of the defendant agency, the Federal National Mortgage Association. One regulation said the agency could "alter or waive" any requirements; another said that the agency's loan officers could do anything the agency could do. And the court thought it was in the agency's interest to grant such power to its loan officers. The agency buys and sells mortgages in the open market, and market conditions often change rapidly; granting authority to field officers enabled the agency to act more efficiently in a fluctuating market. That helped prove that the loan officer really had authority to waive regulations, even though his waiver disadvantaged the government on this particular occasion.

3.   Not even the Supreme Court has been reluctant to hold the government to procedural defaults in litigation. Thus, in Steagald v. United States, 451 U.S. 204, 209-211 (1981), the Court held that the government had waived its right to claim that defendant had no expectation of privacy in a house where it had found incriminating evidence.

4.   One other case you must know about to assess claims of estoppel against the government is Moser v. United States, 341 U.S. 41 (1951). Moser was a Swiss citizen permanently residing in the United States. Under a treaty between the United States and Switzerland, Swiss citizens were exempt from service in the U.S. military. Moser claimed the exemption during World War II, after carefully inquiring whether he would prejudice his right to U.S. citizenship by doing so. The nationalization statute provided that resident aliens who claimed exemptions forfeited any opportunity to become citizens, but the Swiss Legation and the U.S. State Department had negotiated a special exemption application for Swiss nationals. The application form omitted the usual waiver of the right to apply for citizenship, although it contained a footnote referring to the statute. The Swiss Legation's understanding was that Swiss nationals who claimed exemption were still eligible for U.S. citizenship, and it so advised Moser.

After the war, Moser applied for citizenship and the government resisted his application. It said it could not be estopped from enforcing the statute, so that it didn't matter what Moser was told or what his form said.

The Court described the facts, emphasizing Moser's reliance on the government's representations to the Swiss Legation. But the opinion had a surprise ending, suddenly changing the question from the government's estoppel to Moser's waiver:

There is no need to evaluate these circumstances on the basis of any estoppel of the Government or the power of the Swiss Legation to bind the United States by its advice to petitioner. Petitioner did not knowingly and intentionally waive his rights to citizenship. In fact, because of the misleading circumstances of this case, he never had an opportunity to make an intelligent election. . . . Considering all the circumstances of the case, we think that to bar petitioner, nothing less than an intelligent waiver is required by elementary fairness. To hold otherwise would be to entrap petitioner.

Id. at 47.

The judgment was unanimous. The Court didn't cite Federal Crop Insurance Corp. v. Merrill, decided four years before by seven of the same nine justices.

Moser has understandably encouraged the lower courts to believe that there are exceptions to *Merrill*. The Ninth Circuit describes *Moser* as holding "in effect" that "the government was estopped." United States v. Lazy FC Ranch, 481 F.2d 985, 989 (9th Cir. 1973), quoting 2 K. Davis, Administrative Law Treatise §17.03 at 504 (1958). Is that a fair reading?

CHAPTER 12

Some Problems of Timing

A. DENYING A REMEDY BECAUSE OF PLAINTIFF'S DELAY

1. Laches

GULL AIRBORNE INSTRUMENTS v. WEINBERGER
694 F.2d 838 (D.C. Cir. 1982)

Before ROBINSON, Chief Judge, and WRIGHT and WALD, Circuit Judges.
WALD, Circuit Judge.

In October 1977 the United States Navy granted a contract to Consolidated Airborne Systems, Inc. (CAS), for the procurement of certain fuel quantity test sets and data. Following several attempts to obtain administrative relief, appellant, Gull Airborne Instruments, Inc. (Gull), the second low bidder on the contract, filed suit in federal district court, alleging that both the Navy's award and its administration of the contract were illegal and asking that further performance be enjoined. The district court dismissed the case, finding that Gull had standing to protest the contract's award (although not its administration), but that its request for injunctive relief was barred by the equitable doctrine of laches. . . .

D ct.
dismissed

I. Background . . .

In February 1977 Gull filed a preaward protest with the procuring agency, ASO, alleging that CAS had no existing designs that could meet the

959

contract's specifications and that the delivery schedule provided insufficient time for CAS to develop a new design. In April 1977 Gull filed a similar preaward protest with the General Accounting Office (GAO), citing the same allegations and pointing out that [the] contracting officer had relied on the imminent CAS merger with Bendix Corporation as the basis for finding CAS financially responsible. . . .

On October 31, 1977, the contracting officer determined that the equipment involved in the contract was urgently needed and awarded the contract to CAS.[1]

On November 7, 1977, the GAO denied Gull's April protest, finding that an award could properly be made to CAS. Gull promptly requested the GAO to reconsider. In March 1978 the GAO affirmed its prior decision. . . .

Under the contract Bendix was to make its first delivery in April 1978. It failed to do so. A year later, in April 1979, Gull made Freedom of Information Act (FOIA) requests for notes of or any correspondence relating to a June 1978 meeting between the Navy and Bendix. The FOIA documents were received in May 1979 and allegedly indicated that Bendix (as well as CAS) could not comply with either the contract's specifications or its delivery schedule. In July 1979 Gull wrote the Navy's contracting officer, pointing out that CAS' misrepresentations had prompted the contract award and that nonperformance of the contract had directly resulted from these misrepresentations. It therefore requested the officer to terminate the contract for default. The contracting officer once again rejected Gull's protest. In December 1979 Gull renewed its GAO protest, claiming that the contract was void or voidable and that its maladministration had changed it to a new and different procurement. The GAO denied the protest in August 1980.

Gull filed suit in the district court in February 1981, protesting both the award and the administration of the contract and seeking a permanent injunction directing the Navy to terminate the contract. . . .

II. Analysis

B. Laches

The government contends and the district court found that Gull's request for equitable relief on the bid award is barred by the doctrine of laches. The laches doctrine, of course, reflects the principle that "equity aids the vigilant, not those who slumber on their rights," and is designed

---

1. When a written protest is lodged before the award of a contract, the procurement regulations require that the award be withheld until the matter is resolved unless the contracting officer determines that the items to be procured are urgently required, delivery or performance will be unduly delayed by the failure to make an award promptly, or a prompt award will be otherwise advantageous to the government.

Laches defense

to promote diligence and prevent enforcement of stale claims. To establish a successful laches defense, the defendant must show that the plaintiff was guilty of unreasonable delay prejudicial to the defendant. Whether the doctrine bars an action in a particular case depends upon the circumstances of that case.

There are, therefore, two factors to be considered in determining whether laches applies: lack of diligence by the plaintiff and injurious reliance thereon by the defendant. Laches does not depend solely on the time that has elapsed between the alleged wrong and the institution of suit; it is "principally a question of the inequity of permitting the claim to be enforced — an inequity founded upon some change in the condition or relations of the property or the parties." Galliher v. Cadwell, 145 U.S. 368, 373 (1892). It closely tracks the question of whether a defendant suffered prejudice from the delay. If only a short period of time elapses between accrual of the claim and suit, the magnitude of prejudice required before suit would be barred is great; if the delay is lengthy, a lesser showing of prejudice is required.

Gull was diligent

Gull instituted this action three years from the date the contract was awarded, six months from the GAO's denial of its last protest, and three years before the statute of limitations had run on its claim. Gull pursued its administrative remedies diligently throughout this period. It filed a preaward protest with the Navy one month after the bids on the contract were opened in January 1977. In April of the same year it filed a similar protest with the GAO, a request denied in November. Gull thereupon asked the GAO to reconsider its denial; the GAO affirmed its April decision in March 1978. In April 1979 Gull made FOIA requests regarding the Navy's award and administration of the contract. It received the FOIA documents in May 1979. Two months later Gull again requested the Navy to terminate the contract, alleging that it had been illegally awarded and subsequently maladministered. The Navy refused to do so. In December 1979 Gull once again protested to the GAO, which declined to invalidate the contract in August 1980. In February 1981 Gull filed suit in federal district court.

We are mindful that review by the GAO is permissive and is not a prerequisite to judicial review. This court has, however, for obvious reasons, encouraged disappointed bidders to pursue their administrative remedies with the GAO. Although we recognize the need for prompt adjudication of bid challenges, it would be an injustice to unsuccessful bidders if we now penalized them merely for exhausting those administrative remedies.[8]

8. Indeed, Gull's many attempts to receive administrative relief served to put the government on notice that it was not sleeping on its rights. See also Etelson v. Office of Personnel Management, 684 F.2d 918, 924 n.8 (D.C. Cir. 1982) (government attorney challenging method used by government in evaluating candidates for administrative law judge positions had not sat on his rights even though he waited nine years before filing suit since he had been pursuing administrative and legislative remedies during those years).

No
delay

On the basis of delay alone, therefore, we would not bar Gull's suit for injunctive relief, thereby punishing it for its persistent attempts to use the administrative process to resolve its dispute and for its forbearance in not filing suit before it had enough concrete facts to support its allegations. But to determine whether Gull's three-year delay in filing suit was unreasonable, we must also weigh the prejudice the government has suffered as a result of that delay. We find that the grounds on which the district court based its finding of prejudice to the government were insufficient to bar Gull's suit for injunctive relief.

Two kinds of prejudice support a laches defense. Plaintiff's delay in filing suit may have resulted in a loss of evidence or witnesses supporting defendant's position or the defendant may have changed its position in a manner that would not have occurred but for plaintiff's delay.

The district court found that the government had been prejudiced in both ways in this case. First, it stated that the death of the original contracting officer would seriously prejudice the government's ability to combat the charge that the award of the contract was arbitrary and capricious. Second, the court found that if the contract were terminated for default, the government would be liable for all the costs Bendix had incurred in performing the contract up to the date an injunction against further performance issued.

Neither of these grounds supports a finding of laches in this case. The government's own regulations require documentation of all actions taken with respect to a contract. This documentation is sufficient to constitute a full history of the transaction and gives any reviewing body the ability to reconstruct the pertinent events. Thus, the loss of a crucial witness in this case is cured by the documentation required by the government's own regulations.

The district court also found that the government stood to suffer financial prejudice by Gull's delay in bringing suit. Yet, when Gull filed this suit in district court none of the test sets had been delivered to the government. The government could not have, and did not, therefore, argue that it had lost any monies paid to Bendix for performance of the contract. Bendix might, of course, attempt to sue the government for the costs incurred in its attempt to perform up to the time of filing. The Comptroller General has held, however, that if an award is made contrary to statutory or regulatory requirements in reliance on some statement or action of the contractor, or if the contractor is on direct notice that the procedures being followed violate such requirements, then the government may cancel the award without liability except to the extent recovery may be had on the basis of quantum meruit for work done and accepted by the government. See New England Telephone and Telegraph Co., No. B-197297, 80-2 Comptroller's Procurement Decisions at 7-8 (Sept. 25, 1980).

For purposes of reviewing the laches issue on this appeal, we must take as proven Gull's allegations that misrepresentations by CAS secured the award of the contract. Assuming Gull's allegations to be true, the government would have been allowed to cancel the contract without liability because it was illegally awarded except to the extent that Bendix might have sued to recover its costs under a quantum meruit theory. At the time this suit was filed, however, no quantum meruit recovery was likely since Bendix had made no deliveries to the government. Therefore, the government would not have been prejudiced financially if it had rescinded the contract at that point.

In sum, we do not think the district court should have held that the complaint was barred under the doctrine of laches. Gull filed this suit only a few months after the GAO denied its last administrative protest. No deliveries on the contract had been made when it filed. The grounds on which the district court found prejudice to the government were insufficient to support that finding.

C. Mootness

During oral argument before this court, and in a "Suggestion of Mootness" filed shortly thereafter, the government, however, stated that Bendix has now fully performed its contract with the Navy and that the Navy has fully paid for that contract. Gull's request for injunctive relief may therefore very well be moot. . . . Upon the record before us, we are unable to determine whether injunctive relief on the bid award is still realistically a remedy.[9]

If the test sets have been delivered, and satisfactorily fulfill the government's requirements, there is no justification for re-awarding the contract to a more deserving bidder. If, however, the contract has not been fully or satisfactorily performed, then injunctive relief *may* still be available

---

9. [C]ourts have considered several factors in exercising their discretion to issue or refuse to issue an injunction. They have looked carefully at the interests to be affected by injunctive relief, recognizing that substantial harm may accrue to the government and the public when agencies are unable to make necessary procurements without undue delay. Although finding merit in the claims of disappointed bidders, they have struck the balance of equities in favor of the government's interests in the smooth and efficient functioning of the procurement process at the expense of the interests of the unsuccessful bidder in the integrity of the bidding process and equal access to the procurement dollar (and of the public in fairness and competitive bidding).

These courts have also taken into account the availability of a damage remedy in the Court of Claims for bid preparation losses resulting from illegal agency action. And partial performance of a contract has been considered to be a substantial factor in the denial of injunctions to unsuccessful bidders.

and appropriate. We therefore remand the case to the district court for a factual determination on the issue of mootness.[10]

Affirmed in part, reversed in part, and remanded for further proceedings as directed by this opinion.

NOTES ON LACHES

1.   The requirement of prejudice to defendant emphasizes the close link between laches and estoppel. The emphasis in laches is on delay; the emphasis in estoppel is on misleading. But the difference becomes highly attenuated when defendant is misled by plaintiff's silence. Could United States v. Georgia-Pacific, supra at 937, have been decided on laches grounds? Would the argument in *Gull* be any different if the government argued that plaintiff was estopped by its silence? That it waived its rights?

The similarity of the three defenses is more apparent in some contexts than in others. Recall Ariola v. Nigro, supra at 914. Defendants' new house encroached on plaintiffs' easement for gutters. Plaintiffs sued promptly, before defendants could have relied on apparent acquiescence, and the court rejected defendants' laches argument. Suppose plaintiffs had not complained until the construction was complete. It would be entirely plausible to say plaintiffs were estopped by their silence, barred by laches, and that they had waived their rights. And their apparent acquiescence would probably shift the balance of equities on the undue hardship defense as well.

Estoppel, waiver, and laches are conceptually distinct despite their overlap, and you should learn the separate elements of each. Even within the area of overlap, the facts generally fit one of the three defenses better than the other two. But not all judges will keep them straight as well as you will; it is probably sound strategy to put all three labels on your argument.

2.   The most obvious form of prejudice is detrimental reliance. If the government had incurred liability to Bendix before Gull filed suit, that would be prejudice of the same sort that Georgia-Pacific suffered by improving its forest land after the government retracted the bounds of the national forest. Another laches example is Environmental Defense Fund v. Alexander, 614 F.2d 474 (5th Cir.), *cert. denied*, 449 U.S. 919 (1980), in

10.   We are mindful that Gull urges that injunctive relief is the only remedy that will compensate it for the losses it allegedly has sustained. We believe, however, that even if the claim for injunctive relief is extinguished by mootness, Gull may retain a viable claim for damages to the extent of its bid preparation costs, damages clearly not nominal. If these costs are less than $10,000, Gull can seek recovery in the district court, 28 U.S.C. §1346(a)(2); otherwise, its remedy lies in the Court of Claims. Because the claim for damages may survive the completion of performance of the contract under challenge, this litigation is not necessarily moot even if no injunctive relief is appropriate.

which plaintiffs sued to stop construction of a canal after the government had spent $265 million on construction.

3. Lost evidence is a form of prejudice generally seen only in the laches cases. Was the government's prejudice really "cured" in *Gull*? A written record is better than a witness for some things. But what about explaining the contracting officer's exercise of discretionary judgment? Wasn't the government prejudiced despite the written record?

Would the contracting officer's death have been sufficient prejudice if Gull had delayed suit for five years for no good reason? What if Gull had delayed for six months, for no reason except that it took Gull's lawyers that long to get around to drafting the complaint, and the contracting officer dropped dead a week before his deposition? What if Gull's lawyers got to the complaint in only two months, but during those two months the government had foreseeably incurred $10 million in liability to Bendix? Doesn't laches inevitably require the court to balance the reasonableness of the delay against the severity of the prejudice?

4. The balance went in defendant's favor in Equal Employment Opportunity Commission v. Dresser Industries, 668 F.2d 1199 (11th Cir. 1982). The Commission notified Dresser in March 1974 that Doris Smalley had filed a sex discrimination charge. In November 1979 the Commission finally filed a lawsuit based on the charge. But it filed a pattern and practice suit alleging discrimination against all female employees from 1965 to the present. Dresser had retained Doris Smalley's records, but it had destroyed all other records more than five years old. The head of Smalley's department had died. The personnel manager had resigned and was last known to have been working in Libya. The personnel staff had completely turned over. The court held that the Commission's heavy case load and organizational problems did not justify the delay, and that the prejudice to Dresser required that the action be dismissed. It noted that if Dresser were still discriminating, the Commission could file a new suit to end the current violations.

The government generally claims exemption from laches and statutes of limitations, just as it claims exemption from estoppel and waiver. See the notes on using estoppel and waiver against the government, supra at 946 and 955. The EEOC was subject to laches in *Dresser* only because it was suing on behalf of Smalley and the other complainants. Had it sued to enforce the government's own rights, or as it is sometimes formulated, had the government sued in its sovereign capacity, it would have been immune from laches and from any statute of limitations that did not explicitly apply to the government. The distinction is reviewed in Justice Rehnquist's dissent in Occidental Life Insurance Co. v. Equal Employment Opportunity Commission, 432 U.S. 355, 381-384 (1977). Lower courts that have eroded the government's immunity from estoppel have analyzed its immunity from laches in similar terms. An example is United States v. Ruby Co., 588 F.2d 697, 705 n.10 (9th Cir. 1978), *cert. denied*,

442 U.S. 917 (1979). But it is hard to find affirmative misconduct in mere delay, so the assault on laches has made less progress than the assault on estoppel.

5.   A third kind of prejudice occurs when plaintiff's delay shifts a speculative risk to defendant. If plaintiff claims rights in property of a sort that may either rise or fall in value, he cannot wait until the outcome is known and then file suit. The more volatile the value of the property, the sooner any claim will be barred. One classic citation is Twin-Lick Oil Co. v. Marbury, 91 U.S. 587 (1875), an early case involving oil wells:

> Property worth thousands to-day is worth nothing to-morrow; and that which would to-day sell for a thousand dollars as its fair value, may, by the natural changes of a week or the energy and courage of desperate enterprise, in the same time be made to yield that much every day. The injustice, therefore, is obvious, of permitting one holding the right to assert an ownership in such property to voluntarily await the event, and then decide, when the danger which is over has been at the risk of another, to come in and share the profit.

Id. at 592-593.

A modern example is Skeen v. McCarthy, 46 Md. App. 434, 418 A.2d 1214, 1219-1220 (1980). Plaintiffs were pensioners who asserted that their pension plan was entitled to a constructive trust over land purchased with an illegal loan from the plan. There was no evidence that the land was especially speculative, but the appreciation had been extraordinary. The court held the claim barred by laches.

Routine appreciation in routine property is generally not sufficiently prejudicial to trigger laches. An example is Fitzgerald v. O'Connell, 120 R.I. 240, 247-249, 386 A.2d 1384, 1388-1389 (1978), involving an undeveloped residential lot in Newport. The lot increased in value from $500 to $2,800 over a ten-year period, but for much of the ten years, plaintiff's delay was excused.

What if the property fluctuates in value but winds up just where it started? That was the case in Shell v. Strong, 151 F.2d 909 (10th Cir. 1945). Plaintiff acquired a five-year option to purchase land in 1932. He exercised the option in 1937, one day before it expired, but defendant refused to convey. Plaintiff waited five more years, and sued on the day before the statute of limitations ran out in 1942. In 1937 the land was worth $5,000 more than the contract price because of an oil boom, but the boom fizzled and the land declined in value. But there were a series of good crop years beginning in 1940, and by the time plaintiff sued, the land was again worth $5,000 more than the contract price. The trial judge dismissed for laches; a divided court of appeals reversed. The majority found no prejudice because the value in 1942 was the same as in 1937. The dissenter thought that irrelevant; what was important was that plaintiff had shifted the risk of loss to defendant while keeping the prospect of gain for himself. Who's right?

6. The other element of laches is unreasonable delay. Is it clear that Gull's delay was reasonable? Gull spent much of the time exhausting administrative remedies, and courts are always sympathetic to that. Indeed, the court was so sympathetic it didn't examine Gull's actions with much care. Gull knew that Bendix was performing the contract and that the government would begin incurring liability as soon as Bendix began deliveries. Was it reasonable in those circumstances to petition the GAO for rehearing? And what was Gull doing during the thirteen months between the time the GAO denied rehearing and the time Gull filed its Freedom of Information Act requests? Why did Gull wait six months after the final GAO decision before filing its complaint?

Clients think six months is a long time. Lawyers generally don't; they've become accustomed to long delays. Lawyers tend to be overworked and they tend to procrastinate. Once a complaint is filed, judges nag lawyers and set deadlines for lawyers, but they tend not to bar clients because of routine law office delays. Obviously there are limits, and the EEOC went beyond them in *Dresser Industries*.

7. Perhaps the most common source of delay is that plaintiff didn't know he had a claim. If he didn't know and had no reason to know, delay is not unreasonable. If defendant is a fiduciary in whom plaintiff reposed trust and confidence, plaintiff has no duty of inquiry until something happens that ought to arouse his suspicions. But many unsophisticated plaintiffs lose their claims because they aren't sufficiently diligent.

Consider Pyle v. Ferrell, 12 Ill. 2d 547, 147 N.E.2d 341 (1958). In 1932 plaintiff inherited the mineral rights to 80 acres of land. He never got a property tax bill, but he didn't think about that because he didn't know mineral rights were taxed separately from the surface rights. Defendant bought the mineral rights at a tax sale in 1936. Plaintiff first learned of the tax sale when a geologist interested in an oil lease contacted him in 1954. He promptly filed suit alleging defects in the tax sale. The court dismissed for laches, holding that he should have known about the tax sale even if he didn't.

If plaintiff knows the facts, further delay is unexcused whether or not he knows the law or figures out the consequences of putting law and facts together. In Environmental Defense Fund v. Alexander, 614 F.2d 474 (5th Cir.), *cert. denied*, 449 U.S. 919 (1980), plaintiffs alleged that the Army Corps of Engineers was building a canal with a channel 300 feet wide although Congress had authorized a channel only 170 feet wide. Plaintiffs had actively opposed the canal since the 1960s, and they had been at hearings where the 300-foot channel had been mentioned. But apparently they never put the actual width together with the authorized width until they filed an amended complaint in 1978. That was too late, and the delay was not excused.

8. What if plaintiff knows his claim but doesn't know what to do about it? In Saffron v. Department of the Navy, 561 F.2d 938 (D.C. Cir.

1977), *cert. denied*, 434 U.S. 1033 (1978), a civilian aircraft mechanic spent nine years fruitlessly challenging his discharge, largely pro se. Several lawyers refused to represent him. By the time he found a lawyer, the statute of limitations had run. Should his delay have been excused if the case had been governed by laches? There were some indications that the reason he had so much trouble finding a lawyer was that many of the lawyers he contacted thought his case lacked merit. That may tempt the court to get rid of the case on a preliminary motion. But it's not relevant to the reasonableness of his delay, is it?

NOTES ON THE RELATION BETWEEN LACHES AND STATUTES OF LIMITATIONS

1. The conventional statute of limitations creates a fixed time in which suit must be filed. Time begins to run when the cause of action accrues, and the suit is barred when time runs out. It is possible to precisely identify the very last day on which suit can be filed. As we shall see, there are defenses, exceptions, and arguments about how to count that make statutes of limitations less precise than this simple description suggests. But limitations analysis always begins, and often ends, with a fixed period that runs from the day plaintiff is injured by the wrong.

2. Laches is obviously quite different, and it is important to know the relationship between the two rules. The chancellors originally took the position that statutes of limitations applied only to actions at law. Laches was the equitable substitute for statutes of limitations, and the sole time limit on suits in equity. Thus, it was possible for suits in equity to be filed decades after the events giving rise to the claim, if plaintiff's delay were excused or defendant could not show prejudice. That is still the rule in actions subject only to laches. An example is Kay v. Village of Palatine, 126 Ill. App. 2d 308, 261 N.E.2d 823 (1970), where plaintiffs successfully sued in the late 1960s for breaches of trust that began in 1934 and continued into the 1950s.

3. Most equitable claims are now subject both to a statute of limitations and to laches. This came about in two ways. Modern statutes of limitations sometimes explicitly apply to suits in equity. More important, the chancellors began to apply statutes of limitations to suits in equity if the law and equity courts had concurrent jurisdiction. Courts still talk about concurrent jurisdiction long after the merger of law and equity. "Concurrency" provides a handy label for the doctrine, but there is a more informative way to state the idea. If there is both a legal remedy and an equitable remedy for the same underlying wrong, then the statute of limitations applies to both remedies. Cope v. Anderson, 331 U.S. 461, 463-464 (1947). Thus, a suit for damages for breach of contract and a suit

for specific performance are two remedies, but there is only one substantive wrong, the breach of contract. If the statute of limitations would bar the damage action, the specific performance claim is barred as well. Saffron v. Department of the Navy, 561 F.2d 938 (D.C. Cir. 1977), *cert. denied*, 434 U.S. 1033 (1978).

The concurrency doctrine makes statutes of limitations applicable to equitable remedies as well as legal remedies. Laches remains the sole bar only in cases where the substantive right is created by equity, most notably, suits for breach of trust. And even there, there are exceptions. An example is Renz v. Beeman, 589 F.2d 735 (2d Cir. 1978), *cert. denied*, 444 U.S. 834 (1979), applying New York's statute of limitations to a purely equitable claim for breach of an express trust.

Whenever an equitable claim is subject to a statute of limitations, laches is irrelevant unless it bars the claim before the limitations period expires. Thus, in *Gull Airborne*, the statute of limitations for suits against the government was six years. 28 U.S.C. §2401 (1982). Plaintiff sued three years after its claim arose, so the statute plainly didn't apply. As it turned out, laches didn't either. But the issue was whether laches barred the claim even though the statute of limitations didn't.

4.   Notes 2 and 3 summarize the dominant rules, but there are many local variations. The Third Circuit says equitable jurisdiction is exclusive whenever the legal remedy is inadequate. Gruca v. United States Steel Corp., 495 F.2d 1252, 1258 (3d Cir. 1974). That plainly misapplies the Supreme Court cases; it means that no equity claim is ever barred by limitations, because the equitable remedies aren't available at all if the legal remedy is adequate. Some courts apply the statute of limitations by analogy. Others use the statute of limitations to allocate the burden of proof on laches. Either of these variations may be applied to all cases without regard to the concurrency rule, or only to cases where legal and equitable jurisdiction is not concurrent. There are more such cases in jurisdictions that construe the concurrency rule narrowly. Some of the variations are surveyed in Note, Laches in Federal Substantive Law: Relation to Statutes of Limitations, 56 B.U.L. Rev. 970 (1976).

5.   Everyone agrees that laches applies only to equitable claims. Plaintiffs may sue for damages on the last day of the limitations period even if plaintiff had no reason to wait so long and defendant was prejudiced by the delay. Is that distinction just an historical relic, or does it make some sense?

The answer may depend on the nature of the prejudice and a comparison of the legal and equitable remedies in particular circumstances. If the government had already paid Bendix for the test sets, it would surely rather pay Gull's lost profit (damages) than pay the full contract price to have the work done over again (specific performance). But there is no general reason to predict that equitable remedies will be more expensive than legal remedies. Sometimes yes; sometimes no. A preventive injunction is nearly always cheaper than damages for completed violations. But as the next case illustrates, there are other reasons for applying laches to preventive injunctions.

When the prejudice is loss of evidence on the merits, as in Equal Employment Opportunity Commission v. Dresser, the nature of the remedy claimed hardly seems relevant. Should the court say that Dresser can be sued for damages but not for an injunction? That issue didn't arise because the Civil Rights Act of 1964 treats back pay as an equitable remedy.

6. One way to view laches is that it is a trap for the unwary. The statute of limitations says suit can be brought for six years, but the district court said Gull was barred after three. If statutes of limitations represent a rough compromise between defendant's interest in repose and plaintiff's interest in justice, should courts ever second-guess that compromise by applying laches in individual cases? It turns out that there is a large class of cases in which that question makes no sense. Think about how a statute of limitations would apply to the next principal case.

McCARTHY v. BRISCOE
429 U.S. 1317 (1976)

[On September 1, 1975, Texas amended its election laws to provide that independent candidates for President of the United States could not appear on the ballot in Texas or have candidates for elector appear on the ballot. The law was clearly unconstitutional under Storer v. Brown, 415 U.S. 724 (1974). On July 30, 1976, Eugene McCarthy filed suit challenging the law. Defendants claimed that McCarthy was barred by laches, and testified that it would be impossible to verify that McCarthy had substantial support before ballots had to be printed. The district court and the court of appeals both agreed, although recognizing that this permitted a clearly unconstitutional law to be carried out.

McCarthy sought an injunction pending review by the Supreme Court. On September 27, Justice Powell issued the injunction as Circuit Justice for the Fifth Circuit. On September 30, he issued this opinion.]

. . . The District Court, and the Court of Appeals, apparently assumed that the only appropriate remedy was to order implementation of the former statutory procedure permitting independent presidential candidates to demonstrate substantial support by gathering a prescribed number of voters' signatures — a procedure still available to independent candidates for most other elective offices. Since the signature-gathering procedure involved not only a filing deadline which had long since expired but also a lengthy process of signature verification, both lower courts concluded that there was too little time to impose a signature-gathering requirement without undue disruption of the State's electoral process.

This Court will normally accept findings of a district court affirmed by a court of appeals, on factual considerations such as those underlying a determination of laches. But acceptance of findings of fact does not in this case require acceptance of the conclusion that violation of the applicants' constitutional rights must go unremedied. In assuming that a signature-gathering process was the *only* available remedy, the courts below gave too little recognition to the amendment passed by the Texas Legislature making that very process unavailable to independent candidates for the office of President. In taking that action, the Texas Legislature provided no means by which an independent presidential candidate might demonstrate substantial voter support. Given this legislative default, the courts were free to determine on the existing record whether it would be appropriate to order Senator McCarthy's name added to the general election ballot as a remedy for what the District Court properly characterized as an "incomprehensible policy" violative of constitutional rights. This is a course that has been followed before both in this Court, see Williams v. Rhodes, 89 S. Ct. 1 (Opinion of Stewart, J., in-Chambers, 1968), and, more recently, in three District Court decisions involving Senator Mc-Carthy, McCarthy v. Noel, 420 F. Supp. 799 (D.C.R.I. 1976); McCarthy v. Tribbitt, 421 F. Supp. 1193 (D.C. Del. 1976); McCarthy v. Askew, 420 F. Supp. 775 (D.C. Fla. 1976).

In determining whether to order a candidate's name added to the ballot as a remedy for a State's denial of access, a court should be sensitive to the State's legitimate interest in preventing "laundry list" ballots that "discourage voter participation and confuse and frustrate those who do participate." Lubin v. Panish, 415 U.S. at 715. But where a state forecloses independent candidacy in presidential elections by affording no means for a candidate to demonstrate community support, as Texas has done here, a court may properly look to available evidence or to matters subject to judicial notice to determine whether there is reason to assume the requisite community support.

It is not seriously contested that Senator McCarthy is a nationally known figure; that he served two terms in the United States Senate and five in the United States House of Representatives; that he was an active candidate for the Democratic nomination for President in 1968, winning a substantial percentage of the votes cast in the primary elections; and that he has succeeded this year in qualifying for position on the general election ballot in many States. The defendants have made no showing that support for Senator McCarthy is less substantial in Texas than elsewhere.

For the reasons stated, I have ordered that the application be granted and that the Secretary of State place the name of Eugene J. McCarthy on the November 1976 general election ballot in Texas as an independent candidate for the office of President of the United States.[4] I have consulted informally with each of my Brethren and, although no other Justice has participated in the drafting of this opinion, I am authorized to say that a majority of the Court would grant the application.[5]

MORE NOTES ON THE RELATION BETWEEN LACHES AND STATUTES OF LIMITATION

1.   The day after *McCarthy*, Justice Marshall denied a similar order in Fishman v. Schaffer, 429 U.S. 1325 (1976). Fishman circulated petitions for Gus Hall, the Communist Party candidate for President. Connecticut law required petition circulators to swear that each person who signed a petition had satisfactorily identified himself. No one objected to that. But to swear the oath, each petition circulator had to appear personally before the town clerk of every town in which anyone who signed his petition resided. Plaintiffs alleged that this procedure unconstitutionally burdened access to the ballot with excessive and useless travel.

Plaintiffs filed suit on July 2, 1976. The district court dismissed for laches, and the court of appeals affirmed without opinion. Justice Marshall, sitting as Circuit Justice for the Second Circuit, denied an injunction pending certiorari. In part, he acted on the merits. He noted that a single justice should act with restraint, that the merits had not been adjudicated, and that the challenged requirement was not clearly unconstitutional. He concluded that "unlike McCarthy, the question is too novel and uncertain to warrant a single justice's acting unilaterally." Although he did not say so explicitly, this surely must be read in light of the reality that the injunction pending certiorari would be final so far as the 1976 election was concerned.

He then turned to laches as an alternate ground:

[T]he plaintiffs delayed unnecessarily in commencing this suit. The statute is not a new enactment and plaintiffs have, in fact, utilized it before. In 1972, the Communist Party unsuccessfully circulated petitions for presidential electors. And in 1974, Joelle Fishman, one of the plaintiffs-electors in this suit, success-

---

4.   . . . The Texas Election Code does not appear to prescribe a deadline for the printing of ballots for the general election. . . . Political parties are not required to certify their nominees to the Secretary of State until September 28, Art. 11.04 (1967), and the Secretary of State is not required to certify the names of those who have qualified for ballot position to local election officials until October 3, Art. 1.03, Subdiv. 2 (Supp. 1976). Thus there appears to be ample time to add Senator McCarthy's name.

5.   Mr. Justice White, Mr. Justice Marshall, Mr. Justice Blackmun, and Mr. Justice Rehnquist have asked to be recorded as holding a different view.

fully qualified as a petitioning candidate for Congress. Thus plaintiffs were sufficiently familiar with the statute's requirements and could have sued earlier. Moreover, defendants strongly oppose the relief sought, claiming that an injunction at this time would have a chaotic and disruptive effect upon the electoral process. The Presidential and Overseas Ballots have already been printed; some have been distributed. The general absentee ballots are currently being printed. This stands in marked contrast to the situation in Williams v. Rhodes, where Ohio agreed that the Independent Party could be placed on the ballot without disrupting the election. 89 S. Ct. at 2 (1968). It also differs from *McCarthy*, where it appears that Texas had neither printed nor distributed any ballots when the injunction was issued. 429 U.S., at 1324 n.4.

Id. at 1330.

2. These two ballot cases contrast nicely. They also illustrate why statutes of limitations are irrelevant to much injunction litigation. Presumably a cause of action for damages for excluding McCarthy and Hall from the ballot would accrue on election day. Both damages and injunction would protect the same right to appear on the ballot, so under the concurrency doctrine, the statute of limitations would apply to the injunction suit as well. Does that mean they could sue for an injunction anytime up to two years after election day? No court is going to order the 1976 presidential election rerun in 1978. A suit seeking access to the presidential ballot is simply too late if it is not filed in time for the court to grant relief before the election.

You might say that the cause of action for an injunction accrued sometime before election day, as soon as the suit was ripe. But that won't solve the problem; the limitations period still won't expire until well after the election. The Texas statute wasn't even enacted until less than two years before the election, and in any event, the case would not be ripe until the candidate decided to run.

3. A more plausible way to bar a suit seeking a new election is with mootness or impracticality doctrine. That would work in a presidential election. But what about an election that could be rerun? Recall Bell v. Southwell, supra at 234, rerunning the special election for Justice of the Peace of Georgia's 789th Militia District. Mootness and impracticality didn't keep a court from rerunning that election. More generally, any time defendant completes a threatened wrong, plaintiff may seek a reparative injunction undoing the wrong.

Should it be irrelevant whether plaintiff unreasonably delayed suit? In Bell v. Southwell, the wrongdoing occurred without warning on election day; plaintiffs filed suit as quickly as possible. But suppose defendants had passed an ordinance keeping Bell off the ballot. If she wanted an injunction, shouldn't she have to sue as soon as she knew about the ordinance? If delay creates problems that are prejudicial but not insuperable, doesn't it matter who is responsible for the delay? Laches speaks directly to those concerns; mootness, impracticality, and statutes of limitations do not.

(2.) **Statutes of Limitations**

O'BRIEN v. ELI LILLY & CO.
668 F.2d 704 (3d Cir. 1982)

Before ALDISERT, HIGGINBOTHAM and SLOVITER, Circuit Judges.

ALDISERT, Circuit Judge.

The question for decision in this appeal from a summary judgment in favor of four defendant pharmaceutical manufacturers in a diversity action is whether the district court properly applied the Pennsylvania "discovery rule," which modifies the personal injury statute of limitations. The district court determined that, if she had exercised due diligence, appellant Ann O'Brien reasonably could have discovered in February 1976 that her mother had taken Diethylstilbestrol (commonly known as Stilbestrol or DES) during her 1956 pregnancy and that the drug arguably caused appellant's subsequent cancer. She did not file her complaint until December 31, 1979; accordingly, the district court concluded that the suit was barred by the two-year statute of limitations. Appellant contends that whether she possessed the knowledge necessary in 1976 to start the running of the statute was a jury question. Conceding that this is a close case, we nevertheless find no genuine issue of material fact and affirm the grant of summary judgment.

I

The relevant Pennsylvania statute of limitations for personal injury actions states:

> The following actions and proceedings must be commenced within two years: . . .
>
> (2) An action to recover damages for injuries to the person or for the death of an individual caused by the wrongful act or neglect or unlawful violence or negligence of another.

42 Pa. Cons. Stat. Ann. §5524(2). The district court applied this statute in granting appellees' motion for summary judgment. Appellant's warranty claims implicate a four-year statute and are discussed below in Part IV of this opinion.

Statutes of limitation express the legislatures' public policy judgments of how long a plaintiff may delay suit without being unfair to a defendant. "These and similar legislative enactments are expressive of the feeling of mankind that where there are wrongs to be redressed, they should be redressed without unreasonable delay, and where there are rights to be enforced, they should be enforced without unreasonable delay."

Ulakovic v. Metropolitan Life Ins. Co. 339 Pa. 571, 576, 16 A.2d 41, 43 (1940).[1]

Nevertheless, Pennsylvania courts have recognized the potential harshness inherent in a rigid application of the statute and long ago carved out an exception: ignorance of an injury may delay the running of the statute of limitations. Lewey v. Fricke Coke Co., 166 Pa. 536, 31 A. 261 (1895). The judicially created "discovery rule" announced in *Lewey* has been expanded to except the plaintiff who is aware of his injury but not its cause. . . . [T]he rule delays the accrual of a cause of action from the time of a defendant's tortious conduct to a time when the injury and its cause become known or knowable. . . . [I]t avoids potential injustice caused where an injury is "inherently unknowable" at the time of a defendant's conduct, Landis v. Delp, 327 F. Supp. 766, 768 (E.D. Pa. 1971), . . . the legislatively declared desirability for repose and judicial administrative expediency will not be unduly affected by the small number of "inherently unknowable" injuries. . . .

We are not presented with a question of choice or interpretation of the precept; rather the dispute is over the application of the precept to the facts presented to the district court. We will review the facts in detail and in the light most favorable to the appellant, essentially as set forth in her brief.

II

In July 1956, Mary Ann O'Brien, appellant's mother, consulted Dr. Kenneth L. Cooper, a gynecologist and obstetrician, concerning her pregnancy with appellant Ann O'Brien, who was born on February 18, 1957. Because Mrs. O'Brien's previous pregnancy had terminated in a miscarriage, Dr. Cooper on July 26, 1956, prescribed 25 milligrams of Stilbestrol. In her deposition Mrs. O'Brien recalled that Dr. Cooper had

---

1. The Supreme Court of Pennsylvania in *Ulakovic* set forth the following explanation of the policy behind Pennsylvania statutes of limitation:

It has always been the policy of the law to expedite litigation and not to encourage long delays. From this fact arose the various statutes of limitations, and the reasons why the law is unfavorable to delayed litigation are self-evident. If any person has a right which he wishes enforced, he should enforce it promptly. The person against whom the right is to be enforced might be greatly prejudiced by plaintiff's delay. Witnesses disappear or remove to distant parts and the entire aspect of the parties on both sides may change with the lapse of time. In Waring Bros. v. Pennsylvania R.R. Co., 176 Pa. 172, 35 A. 106, 107, this court, in an opinion by Justice Green, quoted with approval what Chief Justice Black said in Huffman's Heirs v. Stiger, 1 Pittsb. Leg. J. 185: "No honest man would be willing to live in a country where the law would require him to prove the actual falsehood and injustice of every stale claim which malice or cupidity might dig up against him. Hence we have statutes of limitation, and, in cases to which they do not apply, we have presumptions which are equally strong."

339 Pa. at 575, 16 A.2d at 42-43.

prescribed some medication during this pregnancy, but she did not know the specific kind. . . .

During the summer of 1971, when she was fourteen years old, appellant experienced unusual vaginal bleeding. In September of that year, upon examination by a gynecologist, Dr. Carl Dorko, and following a recommendation by her pediatrician, Dr. Frank Procopio, she was admitted to the Harrisburg Hospital for diagnosis. Dr. Dorko discovered a tumor and performed a biopsy. In addition to the pathology report prepared by the Harrisburg Hospital pathologist, the biopsy slides were sent for evaluation to Dr. Robert Scully, a pathologist at Massachusetts General Hospital.

Dr. Scully responded that the tumor "fits into the category of clear cell carcinoma occurring in young women that we have found to be frequently associated with maternal Stilbestrol administration." Dr. Dorko informed Mr. and Mrs. O'Brien of the biopsy results and referred their daughter for treatment to Dr. John Mikuta, a gynecologist and oncologist at the Hospital of the University of Pennsylvania. There, in October 1971, appellant underwent a radical hysterectomy, lymph node dissection, and partial vaginectomy. She received radiation therapy for six weeks.

Appellant's parents requested that she not be told that her tumor was malignant. All doctors participating in her diagnosis and treatment cooperated with that wish and her parents did not themselves tell her of the malignancy.

Shortly before appellant's surgery, in the fall of 1971, her mother met with Dr. Mikuta. During this meeting, Dr. Mikuta asked Mrs. O'Brien whether she had ever taken diethylstilbestrol to prevent a miscarriage. Mrs. O'Brien denied taking the medication.

In 1971, Dr. Scully and Dr. Arthur Herbst of Massachusetts General Hospital reported in the medical literature an association between maternal ingestion of diethylstilbestrol during pregnancy and clear cell adenocarcinoma in the female offspring of that pregnancy. . . . Dr. Mikuta was familiar with the work of Drs. Herbst and Scully. . . .

Shortly before her regular appointment with Dr. Mikuta in February 1976, appellant read an article in a January 1976 issue of Newsweek. At this time she knew that her mother had suffered a miscarriage before appellant was born. She also knew that Dr. Cooper was her mother's obstetrician.

In her deposition, Ann recollected the article and her subsequent discussion with Dr. Mikuta:

A. Well, the article talked about a girl whose mother had taken DES and the girl had cancer. And the article talked about the procedure, the surgical procedure . . . that she had gone through. And what happened to her after that and she died.

And everything about the procedure that she had gone through — or almost everything — was what I had gone through. And it was all too close, the cancer, and this was my concern, not DES at that point. And I was quite upset with Doctor Mikuta, I was very adamant that I wanted an answer from him whether I had cancer or not. And he said that I did.

Q. Did you ask him whether it was in any way DES related?
A. Yes. And he said that it pointed to that but they were not sure.
Q. It pointed to DES but they were not sure?
A. Not sure. And we continued to talk about cancer.
Q. Did he tell you why it pointed to DES?
A. No.
Q. Did he tell you why they were not sure?
A. No. . . .
Q. Did Doctor Mikuta indicate to you why he responded that the cancer pointed to DES?
A. Because of the type of cancer that it is or was.
Q. Did he say that to you?
A. Yes.
Q. Did he ever say to you that it pointed to DES because your mother had taken it?
A. I don't think so.

In April 1976, Ann O'Brien confronted her mother about concealing the truth about the tumor. She was very upset with her parents and dissatisfied with Mrs. O'Brien's explanation for withholding the information. During the course of that confrontation, appellant also asked her mother whether she had taken DES during her pregnancy. Her mother denied taking the drug. Although Mrs. O'Brien does not remember her daughter asking prior to September 1979 whether she had taken DES, appellant's recollection of the 1976 conversation is very clear.

Three years later, in the summer of 1979, appellant became aware of additional magazine and newspaper articles on the relationship of DES ingestion by pregnant women to the incidence of cancer in female offspring. Although the record does not set forth the content or text of these articles, she testified that again she was struck by the similarity between her own medical history and the type of cancer and treatment described.

In September 1979, appellant again asked her mother if she had taken DES while pregnant, and Mrs. O'Brien again replied that she had not. This time, however, appellant insisted that her mother call Drs. Cooper and Mikuta in order to determine if in fact she had taken the drug. According to appellant, both doctors confirmed that it had been prescribed for Mrs. O'Brien. Mrs. O'Brien also contacted the Kolb Pharmacy in an attempt to identify the manufacturer of the diethylstilbestrol she had purchased there, but found that any records the pharmacy might have maintained were destroyed in the Hurricane "Agnes" flood of 1972.

Thereafter, on December 31, 1979, appellant filed her complaint against four leading manufacturers of DES.

III

In DaMato v. Turner & Newall, Ltd., 651 F.2d 908 (3d Cir. 1981)(per curiam), we noted Pennsylvania's acceptance of a standard for defining the level of knowledge a plaintiff must have before the period of limitations will start to run. As set forth by Pennsylvania Common Pleas Court Judge Takiff in Volpe v. Johns-Manville Corp., 4 P.C.R. 290 (Phila. C.P. 1980), the standard has three elements:

> With the question of "reasonableness" as a constant qualification running through the decisional law, the principle emerges that three independent phases of knowledge must be known or knowable to plaintiff before the limitations period commences: (1) knowledge of the *injury*; (2) knowledge of the *operative* cause of the injury; and (3) knowledge of the *causative relationship* between the injury and the operative conduct.

4 P.C.R. at 295.

Measuring the instant facts against this three-part standard, we are persuaded that in 1976, when Ann O'Brien was told that she had had cancer, she acquired knowledge of her injury; and that when she read the Newsweek article and consulted with Dr. Mikuta she acquired knowledge from which, by the exercise of due diligence, she could have discovered both the alleged operative cause of her injury — her mother's ingestion of DES — and the causal relationship between the operative conduct and her injury.

Appellant concedes the first element, knowledge of injury by 1976, but she contends that there was sufficient controversy regarding the second and third elements to require submission to a factfinder the issue of when she could have acquired information about the causal relation to DES by the exercise of due diligence. We do not agree. There is no dispute to be resolved by a factfinder. The question is solely whether from the facts presented a jury could reasonably conclude that appellant, if she had exercised due diligence, could not have discovered the operative cause of her injury and the causal relationship in 1976.

Appellant argues that because she did not know that her mother had taken DES until September 1979, she did not acquire actual knowledge of the cause of her injury until then. The acquisition of actual knowledge, however, is not the trigger for the running of the limitations period under Pennsylvania law. The correct inquiry, as appellant recognizes, is not whether she had actual knowledge of all three *Volpe* elements before 1979, but "whether [she] should reasonably be charged with that knowledge before that time." We held in *Bayless* that the statute runs "from the time the plaintiff, through the exercise of due diligence, should have learned" the facts and their relationship. 579 F.2d at 40. The policy enunciated by Judge Takiff in *Volpe* is also applicable:

> Plaintiff's ignorance of his injury or its cause may render knowledge of his cause of action unknown and unknowable. But once he possesses the salient facts concerning the occurrence of his injury and who or what caused it, he has the ability to investigate and pursue his claim. Postponing the commencement of the limitations period until he has actually done so would nullify the justifiable rationale of the statute of limitations and permit the prosecution of stale claims.

Volpe, 4 P.C.R. at 303-04. Although *Volpe* dealt with the relationship of the discovery rule to ignorance of a legal cause of action, the same considerations are present in a case in which a plaintiff has facts sufficient to prompt an investigation but does not investigate.

The flaw in appellant's case is her failure to present evidence sufficient to permit a jury to find that she could not reasonably have possessed "the salient facts concerning the occurrence of [her] injury and who or what caused it" before 1979. The facts recited in Part II of this opinion demonstrate that in 1976 appellant knew the facts necessary to complete her investigation: (1) that her mother had miscarried prior to appellant's birth, (2) that appellant's medical history had a marked similarity to the medical history of other young women whose cancers had been linked to DES ingestion by mothers who had previously miscarried, (3) that her doctors believed her medical history pointed in the direction of DES, and (4) the identity of her mother's obstetrician.

The district court's conclusion that as a matter of law appellant unreasonably delayed investigating is underscored by the similarity of appellant's knowledge in 1976 to her knowledge in 1979. The record shows only two historical events of 1979 supplementing the basic factual matrix of 1976: (1) appellant read some additional articles on DES and (2) she insisted that her mother ask Dr. Cooper if he had prescribed DES to her during her pregnancy. The record does not indicate that appellant acquired knowledge from her reading about the DES-cancer relationship in 1979 that she had not previously acquired in 1976. Indeed, the entire record on this is most scanty:

A. There seemed to be quite a few articles on DES in the [Washington] Post and magazines. . . . and it just seemed like things were really showing up in publications. And I was reading more about it.

The record as to the new information gained from Drs. Cooper and Mikuta in 1979[4] also compels our conclusion that the crucial information

4. . . .

Q. Did your mother report to you about what Dr. Cooper said?
A. That it had been — he told her that it had been indicated on his record that it was prescribed but she nevertheless does not remember taking the drug. . . .

on causation was available upon reasonable inquiry in 1976. The 1976 Newsweek article was specific and presented a case history that paralleled appellant's in many ways. The record fails to show that the articles read by appellant after 1976 contained any new information about either the operative cause or the causal relationship between the operative conduct and the injury that was not contained in the 1976 Newsweek article. Similarly, appellant's mother provided information in 1976 that, in effect, she merely repeated in 1979. When asked by her daughter in 1976, the mother denied having taken DES. When asked again in 1979, the mother persisted in the denial. Given the foregoing circumstances, there appears to be no persuasive reason why appellant in 1976 could not, "through the exercise of due diligence," have requested her mother to call Dr. Cooper then to learn "both the facts in question and that those facts bore some causative relationship to the injury." See *Bayless*, 579 F.2d at 40. . . .

We agree with the district court that, as a matter of law, the crucial knowledge was knowable to the appellant in 1976 and could have been obtained through the exercise of due diligence. Therefore, its conclusion that the action is barred by the statute of limitations must be affirmed.

IV

We need consider only one of appellant's remaining contentions. In her complaint, appellant advanced a claim for breach of warranty. Under the Uniform Commercial Code, the statute of limitations period applicable to breach of warranty actions is four years. 13 Pa. Cons. Stat. Ann. §2725. Thus, if characterized as a breach of warranty complaint, appellant's action would not be barred if her cause of action were deemed to have accrued in 1976.[6] . . .

Except for explicit warranties of future performance, the statute expressly rejects a discovery rule similar to the one that has been developed for personal injury actions. Applying the statute to the facts of this case, appellant's cause of action accrued in 1956 or 1957 when Mrs. O'Brien purchased the drug. Only if the warranty explicitly extended to future performance would appellant's cause of action be deemed to have accrued at the date of discoverability. Nothing in the record provides a satisfactory description of the warranties allegedly made or even specifies whether these warranties were express or implied. In opposing appellees' motion for summary judgment, appellant failed to present evidence that the warranty extended to future performance. . . .

6.   Like the district court, for purposes of this discussion we assume that under 13 Pa. Cons. Stat. Ann. §2318, appellant is a third party beneficiary of any warranty made to her parents. If she is not within the class of plaintiffs contemplated by §2318, her action falls within the rule that personal injury causes of action by non-purchaser third party beneficiaries are governed by the two-year personal injury statute of limitations. . . .

V

The judgment of the district court will be affirmed.

SLOVITER, Circuit Judge, concurring.

The eloquent and sympathetic dissenting opinion of our colleague, Judge Higginbotham, impels me to write separately. I believe that one could make a strong argument that termination of lawsuits on issues which are not related to the merits, such as the statute of limitations, is inherently unjust, and that delay in instituting suit should be considered by the factfinder in making the ultimate decision but that deprivation of a plaintiff's right to recovery on any issue other than the merits is too arbitrary a result to be countenanced under a system of law which seeks to achieve substantial justice. If application of the statute of limitations is often seen as harsh, in this case it is particularly tragic because, as Judge Higginbotham correctly notes, it compounds a great personal tragedy which has befallen the plaintiff.

Our legal system, however, is not premised on the personal view of justice by individual judges, notwithstanding the frequency with which such a charge is leveled by our critics. The statute of limitations is, as the name suggests, a creature of the legislature, not the judiciary, and it is the legislature, as the democratically elected voice of the people, which is uniquely equipped to grapple with the conflicting policies and considerations. Thus the moderating quality of the discovery rule has been read into Pennsylvania's statute of limitations not by judicial compassion but by judicial interpretation of legislative intent. . . .

At oral argument, this court inquired in great detail as to whether plaintiff had acquired additional knowledge by 1979 which had been unknown to her in 1976. Although plaintiff testified at her deposition that she had read additional articles, those articles were not identified and are not in the record, so that the factfinder would have no basis to assume that they were qualitatively different in any way from the Newsweek article plaintiff read in 1976. The following colloquy occurred at oral argument:

The Court: What did she [plaintiff] know, in nineteen — what did she or could she have known in '79 that she didn't know or couldn't have known in 1976?
[Plaintiff's Counsel]: Nothing, your Honor. Everything was knowable at that time.

Since plaintiff admittedly had available to her substantially the same information in 1976 that she had in 1979 when she initiated the inquiry that led to knowledge of the causative relationship between her condition and her mother's ingestion of DES, I concur in the analysis set forth in Judge Aldisert's opinion, and in the unhappy result to which it leads.

A. LEON HIGGINBOTHAM, Jr., Circuit Judge, dissenting. . . .

[T]he majority has stated the applicable precept that we must "review the facts in detail and in the light most favorable to the appellant." . . . Nevertheless, I believe that the majority has . . . imposed on the plaintiff . . . an unrealistic, if not an almost insurmountable burden of knowledge, inquiry and insight. . . . [T]he distilled essence of this case is bottomed on the majority's supposition that in 1976 a nineteen year old girl should have discovered that DES was the cause of her cancer in the face of her experienced surgeon's uncertainty about the cause of her cancer and despite her mother's denial that she had even taken DES. . . .

The "flaw" is not in Ann O'Brien's alleged lack of diligence in ascertaining "what caused" her cancer, rather the flaw is in the majority's erroneous articulation of a far higher requirement of diligence than what a rational jury might expect from a frightened teenage cancer victim who learns for the first time that she had cancer. After learning for the first time in September 1979 that her mother had taken DES, Ann and her parents immediately sought the advice of counsel, and within four months the complaint instituting this action was filed in December, 1979. Rather than being dilatory as the majority finds, I would hold that as a matter of law a rational jury could find that Ann O'Brien was diligent and thus there was a genuine issue of material fact which precluded granting a summary judgment.

I . . .

Mrs. O'Brien denied having taken DES and continued to do so until 1979 when information from her obstetrician revealed otherwise. At no time did Dr. Mikuta explain to Mrs. O'Brien the reason for his questions, or offer information about a suspected connection between Ann's type of cancer and the DES which had been prescribed for Mrs. O'Brien when she was pregnant with Ann. . . .

Shortly before her regularly scheduled appointment with Dr. Mikuta in February 1976, [Ann] read in a January issue of Newsweek magazine of a woman, Grace Malloy, who, while pregnant with one of her daughters, had taken DES. Mrs. Malloy's daughter, Marilyn, died a slow and painful death from cancer when she was eighteen years old. Realizing some similarities between her own medical history and that of the girl in the article, Ann in an emotional encounter with Dr. Mikuta, demanded to know whether she, like the girl in the article, had had cancer. It was then, in February, 1976, that Ann learned *for the first time* that she had had cancer. When questioned by Ann about whether or not her cancer was DES-related, Dr. Mikuta responded that it pointed to DES, but *"they were not sure."*

Significantly, Ann also testified in her deposition that it was the knowledge that she had had cancer and not any equivocal statements about its possible cause by DES which had the greatest impact on her.

A.   Well, I went back to school and I discussed it with my roommate and my other friend. . . . And we discussed cancer, that was my major point.
       I also called Doctor Procopio and just asked why I wasn't told I had cancer and was I going to be all right. *And it was cancer, it was cancer, it was not DES, that was just tremendously upsetting.* I cannot verbalize to you how upset I was.
Q.   Did you and your friend at college and roommate talk about DES at all?
A.   No, no.

Several months later during an upsetting encounter with her mother over why her parents had never told her that she had had cancer, Ann questioned her mother about DES. Mrs. O'Brien denied having taken DES. *Thus, in 1976 Ann had the definitive statement of her mother that she had not taken DES, the equivocal comments of Dr. Mikuta on the etiology of her cancer, and a single magazine article describing the death of a girl whose mother had taken DES.* . . .

The majority's entire theory is predicated on their rigid view of what is the permissible rational conduct of a teenager who has read in a general magazine, a two-column, six paragraph article which is not written by anyone purporting to be a physician or medical expert of any type. Inherent in the majority's holding is the incredible conclusion that, in the mind of Ann O'Brien, the speculative inferences which the majority makes from a Newsweek article on DES should have outweighed the definitive denials of Ann's mother about having taken DES. I believe that it is highly possible that a jury could find that the authoritative voice of Ann's mother dispelled any suspicions or inferences which a Newsweek article, written by strangers, might have raised. The majority, in denying such a possibility, transgresses the principles and application of the "discovery rule" and summary judgment.

II . . .

Only if the defendant companies could have demonstrated that there was no genuine factual issue as to when through the exercise of due diligence Ann should have discovered that DES was the probable cause of her injury and that her mother had taken DES, should the judge have taken the matter away from the jury and granted summary judgment. . . .

III . . .

What is a teenage victim of cancer required to do when the surgeon who operated on her, a distinguished university medical school professor, who specialized in gynecology and oncology, advised her that he was "not sure" of the cause of her cancer? A six paragraph article in Newsweek is the only item in the record other than Dr. Mikuta's equivocal statement by which the majority seeks to justify the conclusion that in 1976 Ann should have discovered that the cause of her cancer was her mother taking DES. . . .

The majority and the lower court's judgment is predicated on the assumption that upon reading those six paragraphs the plaintiff was obligated to discover the fact that her mother had taken DES, and that Ann's conduct after reading the article was so unreasonable that no rational jury could find that she was sufficiently diligent. . . .

The Newsweek case about Grace Malloy is significantly different than Ann's case. First, Mrs. Malloy knew that she had taken DES. . . . Second, the total pathology causing Marilyn Malloy's death was far worse than that of Ann's. Marilyn had suffered from nausea, severe headaches, the cancer reached the pituitary glands, she had had six weeks of "whole head" radiation, all of her hair had fallen out, at night she was moaning in pain, the cancer had spread to her arms, legs, spine and brain and ultimately she was blind and confined to a wheelchair. Certainly a jury could conclude that someone untrained in medicine and with no expertise in the etiology of cancer would not have been put on notice that her condition, (though tragic but not nearly as bad as Marilyn Malloy's), was so analogous to Marilyn Malloy's that it was caused by her mother taking DES.

Patients have always been told to "go to your doctor" for advice, but the majority has now imposed a different standard, which is "disregard your mother and disregard your doctor but go to Newsweek" to learn the etiology of your condition. After reading the Newsweek article Ann went to her physician and asked him whether her condition was DES-related. . . . The trial court found from its analysis of Dr. Mikuta's equivocal statement that "Dr. Mikuta also stated that he was *unsure of the cause* of the plaintiff's" cancer. Ann then went to her mother and asked her whether she had ever taken DES. Her mother responded, just as she continued to up until 1979, that she had not taken DES.

Under these facts what more should have been expected from a teenager who had just learned that she had had cancer? For some unfathomable reason the majority concludes that it was unreasonable for Ann not to have found out in 1976 that her mother had taken DES.

IV

More than three decades ago when speaking in a somewhat different context, Mr. Justice Frankfurter stressed that there was torture of mind as well as body; the will is as much affected by fear as by force. And there comes a point where this Court should not be ignorant as judges of what we know as men.

Watts v. State of Indiana, 338 U.S. 49, 52 (1949). Certainly any teenager who learns for the first time that she had had cancer, sustains a torture of the mind. To fail to comprehend that torture is to "be ignorant as judges of what we know as men [or as persons]." [The bracketed phrase is Judge Higginbotham's. Presumably it is intended to acknowledge that Judge Sloviter is a woman. — ED.] . . .

Every layman knows that the riddle of cancer has not been solved and that its causes are uncertain. Yet, the majority seems to suggest that a nineteen year old who learns that she has suffered this dreaded disease must now be able to ascertain its etiology even when her surgeon, a professor of obstetrics and gynecology, is unsure of its cause. . . .

If we should "not be ignorant as judges of what we know" as men and women, what was the trial court's view of the normal relationship between mother and daughter? Presumably mothers and daughters do not have the inherent antagonism and suspicion which world superpowers might have when negotiating at a bargaining table on disarmament. Wasn't it reasonable for a daughter to believe that her mother spoke the truth when she said in 1976 that she had never taken DES? . . . [T]he majority suggests that a Newsweek article should have caused Ann to disbelieve her mother and probably her surgeon; that such disbelief was the only rational option on the facts of this case; thereafter Ann should have on her own embarked on an investigation to ascertain the etiology of her cancer. . . .

There is a cruel irony in the majority's ruling. The very Newsweek article which they rely on as compelling a teenager to conduct an investigation would never be admitted into evidence if one were attempting to prove that DES causes cancer. It would not have the inherent trustworthiness of a standard reference work or a learned treatise. . . . While Newsweek is an interesting weekly journal, it has no more standing in medicine or oncology than a fortuneteller's forecast. . . .

A reasonable jury could have concluded that, in *insisting* in 1979 that her mother double-check her recollection, Ann made *extraordinary* efforts; that, in fact, she discovered that her mother had taken DES only through the exercise of due diligence. . . .

V

In our own circuit and in other circuits summary judgment has been denied in analogous circumstances. . . .

[T]he trial court in Briskin v. Ernst & Ernst, 589 F.2d 1363 (9th Cir. 1978) concluded that certain documents should have triggered "discovery" by the plaintiffs in that case, despite plaintiffs' denial that the documents had such an effect. In reversing the district court's grant of summary judgment based on limitations, the court of appeals in *Briskin* stated that issues requiring conclusions about the actions and knowledge of a reasonably prudent person in particular circumstances "calls for a review of the documents in question by a trier of fact in light of all the evidence. A trial judge should not assign conclusive legal effect to such documents at the summary-judgment stage when there can be a genuine difference of opinion as to their impact on a reasonable person." Id. at 1368. . . .

No doubt the district court's conclusion . . . is plausible. But because it is just as plausible for a jury to conclude otherwise, the district court's summary disposition, involving as it did resolution of disputed factual inferences, was inappropriate.[4]

NOTES ON THE DISCOVERY RULE

1.   There are three possible dates on which the cause of action can be said to have accrued: the date of defendant's wrongful act, the date of injury, or the date of discovery. There are ambiguities about each date, but these are the basic choices. In a simple car wreck, or an assault and battery, all three dates are the same. For Ann O'Brien, the wrongful act occurred in the 1950s, the injury began insidiously and was first noticed in 1971, and the claim was discovered in the late 1970s. All three dates are in common use. Focus first on the discovery rule.

2.   The majority applies an objective standard: What did she know, and when did she know it? When did she know enough that a reasonable person should have discovered the tort? Judge Higginbotham puts some flesh on the reasonable person: Did plaintiff react reasonably considering all the circumstances, including her youth, her trust in her mother, and the emotional blow of her discoveries? Who has the better of the argument? Would Higginbotham's standard let any plaintiff get to the jury, however long she delayed? Does the majority's standard require superhuman diligence? The usual formulation of the rule is that limitations begins to run when plaintiff knew or *should* have known about her cause of action. Does the majority create a higher standard by overemphasizing when she *could* have known?

3.   The usual formulation of the standard is partly objective and partly subjective: Should a reasonable person, knowing what plaintiff actually knew, have known about the claim? Plaintiff has to actually know enough facts to suggest that there is a claim. She need not know facts to

---

4.   . . . Often it requires the repetition of new or startling ideas before their significance is fully appreciated. Ann testified that from 1976 to 1979 she was not aware of "any DES group or DES daughters action group in Washington" where she was attending college. She testified that she did not become aware of them until August or September, 1979. . . .

support every element of the cause of action, but only enough to make it seem likely that there is a claim. As the Massachusetts court noted, one should not confuse discovery exceptions to statutes of limitations with the discovery rules of civil procedure. If plaintiff discovers the broad outlines of a claim on her own, she should file suit and use the discovery rules to learn the rest. White v. Peabody Construction Co., 386 Mass. 121, 434 N.E.2d 1015 (1982).

4. The focus in *O'Brien* is on plaintiff's knowledge of causation; without the benefits of medical research, nothing in her disease suggested that it was caused by a defective drug given to her mother fifteen years before. But in many cases, the probable cause is apparent from the injury. The Massachusetts case in note 2 is an example. Plaintiffs were tenants of a public housing project that leaked water from the beginning. They didn't sue until the Housing Authority completed an investigation and officially blamed the construction company. By that time the statute of limitations had run. The court said it should have been obvious that widespread leaks in a new building must result from defective design or construction, so plaintiffs could have sued immediately.

5. The discovery rule tolls the statute of limitations until plaintiff knows enough facts; it is irrelevant whether she knows the law. Limitations runs even if she has never heard of tort law, or if she doesn't know the standard of care, or if she doesn't know that she could sue. An example is United States v. Kubrick, 444 U.S. 111 (1979). Kubrick lost his hearing because a Veterans Administration hospital treated an infection with excessive amounts of neomycin. In 1969 a doctor told him that it was "highly possible" that the neomycin he got at the VA caused his hearing loss. In 1971 his doctors told him that the VA should not have administered the neomycin and he should consult an attorney. The Third Circuit held that the statute was tolled until that 1971 conversation; plaintiff knew of his injury and knew of its cause, but he didn't know there was negligence. The Supreme Court reversed. Facts about causation might be in defendant's control and hard for plaintiff to discover, but lots of people knew the standard of care: "he need only ask." 444 U.S. at 122. Incidentally, none of the members of the Third Circuit panel in *Kubrick* were on the panel in *O'Brien*.

6. As noted, the discovery rule does not apply to all statutes of limitations. Probably no jurisdiction applies a discovery rule to all claims. Discovery rules are most common in products liability and professional malpractice actions. They are more common for consumer plaintiffs than for commercial plaintiffs. An excellent opinion reviewing the spread of discovery rules and the arguments for their application in various contexts is Gates Rubber Co. v. USM Corp., 508 F.2d 603 (7th Cir. 1975). *Gates* predicted that Illinois would not apply a discovery rule to sale of a defective industrial machine when the corporate buyer sought only economic damages. The court plainly implied that the answer might be different if one of the buyer's employees sued for personal injuries.

7.   Judges developed the discovery rule; they implied it into some statutes and not into others. Some statutes now codify the discovery rule. Some explicitly reject it, as in the UCC provision on breach of warranty, §2-725. And increasingly, statutes codify or take account of a discovery exception but add an absolute outside limit, often called a statute of repose. For example, the statute in White v. Peabody allowed suits for defective construction for three years after the cause of action accrues, which the Massachusetts court took to mean the time of discovery, but not more than six years after the building was finished.

8.   A rule that the cause of action accrues at the time of the wrongful act, or an outside limit on the discovery rule, can result in a claim being barred before it exists. An example is Mathis v. Eli Lilly & Co., 719 F.2d 134 (6th Cir. 1983), a DES case from Tennessee. The Tennessee statute of limitations for products liability contained an absolute bar of ten years after delivery of the product or one year after the end of the product's anticipated life, whichever was sooner. What was the anticipated life of DES? A few hours for each dose? The duration of the pregnancy? As a practical matter, Lilly has no liability in Tennessee for DES-induced cancer. The court rejected all constitutional challenges.

The Tennessee statute had an exception for asbestos cases, but similar statutes in other states do not. The Indiana statute of limitations for products liability suits has been held to bar suits for asbestosis, which takes twenty to thirty years to appear. Braswell v. Flintkote Mines, 723 F.2d 527 (7th Cir. 1983), cert. denied, 104 S. Ct. 2690 (1984).

9.   These statutes appear to create a right without a remedy. Do they seem any less unjust if we view them as substantive repeals of liability? The UCC statute of limitations on breach of warranty is more or less equivalent to a provision that no warranty lasts more than four years unless explicitly agreed. The products liability statutes can be thought of as repealing liability for any damage done more than ten years after sale. Is that an irrational classification that denies equal protection as between say, victims of DES and victims of poisoned food? The answer is surely no under current federal doctrine; the Supreme Court lets legislatures do whatever they want in areas labeled social and economic regulation.

These statutes have also been attacked on the ground that they discriminate between various classes of defendants, e.g., that doctors are no more deserving of special limitations protection than other professionals, on due process grounds, and under state constitutional provisions guaranteeing a remedy for every wrong. Most state supreme courts have upheld such statutes, but there are exceptions. The cases are collected in McGovern, The Variety, Policy and Constitutionality of Product Liability Statutes of Repose, 30 Am. U.L. Rev. 579 (1981). A more recent opinion striking down such a statute is Lankford v. Sullivan, Long & Hagerty, 416 So. 2d 996 (Ala. 1982). The statute in Lankford barred all products liability suits for injuries suffered more than ten years after the product was sold; the court struck it down under Alabama's remedy for every wrong clause.

Assuming such statutes are constitutional, are they a good idea? Consider that question in light of the next set of notes.

NOTES ON THE POLICY CHOICES IN STATUTES OF LIMITATIONS

1.   It is no accident that most of the plaintiffs in this section are employees, consumers, and small businessmen. Many people know little of courts and lawyers and nothing of statutes of limitations. They frequently arrive in the lawyer's office far too late, after someone or something has forcefully brought to their attention information they had long before, or after they acquired the name of a lawyer through some chance encounter. I once handled a bankruptcy for a husband and wife who seemed barely able to cope with the world. "By the way," they said, "four years ago an ambulance crew brain damaged our child. Can we do anything about that?" The answer was no, because it was a federal government ambulance and the two-year statute of limitations in the Tort Claims Act is not tolled by infancy. The test of diligence is largely objective, and some people are not capable of meeting it. There is much to be said for Judge Sloviter's view that no claim should be barred except on the merits.

2.   Statutes of limitations balance these hardships against the hardships that delayed claims inflict on defendants and the courts. One concern is loss of evidence and fading memories. Another is to let potential defendants quit worrying about litigation after a certain time, often referred to as "repose." Justice Holmes thought these explanations inadequate — that loss of evidence was a "secondary matter," and that as time went on, peace was "increasingly likely to come without the aid of legislation." Holmes, The Path of the Law, 10 Harv. L. Rev. 457, 476 (1897). He thought it more important that potential defendants gradually build up an expectancy that the status quo is permanent and that old questions will not be reopened. As Judge Posner builds on the idea: "[I]t is more painful to lose what you have come to think of as your own than it is gratifying to get back something you wrote off many years ago and have grown accustomed to doing without." Taylor v. Meirick, 712 F.2d 1112, 1119 (7th Cir. 1983).

Another theme in the cases is suspicion that many old claims are fabricated. The notion seems to be that if the alleged events really happened, plaintiff would have sued right away. Years later, the complaint looks like a reconstruction of reality, a product of recent imagination and the likelihood that contrary evidence has been lost. The idea shows up in exaggerated form in footnote 1 of *O'Brien*, in the suggestion that no honest man would live in a country without statutes of limitations. But statutes of limitations bar valid claims as well. Indeed, the Supreme Court has said, "that is their very purpose." United States v. Kubrick, 444 U.S. 111, 125 (1979).

3.   These competing interests are balanced by category, not case by case. The presence or absence of actual prejudice to defendant is irrelevant to limitations, and irrelevant to the tolling doctrines. It is hard to see how Ann O'Brien's cancer claim would be any harder to try in 1979 than in 1976, when she read the Newsweek article. If she had sued in 1971, when her cancer was diagnosed, the pharmacy records would not have been destroyed by a hurricane. That is important but fortuitous. On the other hand, her prognosis would not have been nearly as reliable in 1971. A laches defense would consider and balance these peculiarities of individual cases; a limitations defense does not.

Generalizations about categories of cases sometimes guide legislative and judicial decisions about limitations. Thus, contract claims generally have longer statutes of limitations than tort claims, and written contracts generally have longer statutes of limitations than oral contracts. The discovery rule is much more available in consumer and personal injury claims than in commercial claims. Sometimes these generalizations seem to make sense; sometimes not. If one is worried about fabricated claims, an oral contract is much more suspicious than a serious injury.

Sometimes the legislature is pursuing other goals altogether. A short statute of limitations is a good way to sabotage a statute. The six-month limitations in the employment discrimination laws is an example. Swing Congressmen could tell some constituents they voted for the bill and tell other constituents they made it hard to enforce. Statutes limiting application of the tolling rules in products liability and medical malpractice were a direct response to demands that legislatures reduce liability. Cutting off a few victims altogether is a lot easier than reducing jury verdicts for everyone. But is it fair to extract all the savings from a few of the victims?

NOTE ON CHARACTERIZING CLAIMS

Some statutes of limitations are longer than others, or run from a different date. That is the point of the argument over whether O'Brien can prove breach of warranty instead of tort. The UCC's limitations period for breach of warranty is longer, but it generally runs from an earlier date. In general, any lawyer faced with a limitations problem should consider whether there is some way to plead the claim that will put it under a more favorable statute.

Statutes of limitations are great friends of contract teachers. Limitations periods are generally longer for contract claims than for tort claims, and that creates pressure to expand the boundaries of contract. A large percentage of the cases arguing about the boundary between contract and tort and the limits of implied contract are really limitations cases.

KNAYSI v. A. H. ROBINS CO.
679 F.2d 1366 (11th Cir. 1982)

Before TJOFLAT, HILL and ANDERSON, Circuit Judges.

JAMES C. HILL, Circuit Judge.

Appellants Anita and Ed Knaysi filed suit against appellee A. H. Robins, Inc. . . . and its insurer seeking recovery of damages resulting from injuries to Anita Knaysi allegedly caused by her use of the Dalkon Shield intrauterine device manufactured and distributed by Robins. Mrs. Knaysi became pregnant after insertion of the Dalkon Shield and in the first trimester suffered a spontaneous septic abortion of twin fetuses. The Knaysis' complaint sought recovery on the theories of negligence, breach of warranty, breach of implied contract, strict liability, fraud, conspiracy, and outrageous conduct. Basically the appellants sought to prove that Robins was aware from test results that the effectiveness of the device in preventing pregnancy was lower than it advertised and from both test results and the reports of physicians that spontaneous septic abortions often occurred in connection with its use. They alleged that, despite this adverse information, Robins concealed these reports and continued to issue false advertising to the medical community and the public about the superior efficacy and safety of its contraceptive.

The district court resolved the case in Robins' favor on Robins' motion for summary judgment. In granting that motion the district court addressed two issues: whether the fraud claim was a cause of action separate from the products liability claim for statute of limitations purposes and whether Robins was equitably estopped by its conduct from raising the bar of the statute of limitations. The controlling law on these issues is that of the state of New York. The court ruled that the fraud claim should not be treated separately from the products liability claim and was therefore barred by expiration of the three-year limitation applicable to products liability actions[2] and that the doctrine of equitable estoppel was inapplicable. We reverse the summary judgment in Robins' favor because, appellants having adequately pleaded facts which if proved at trial could

---

2. N.Y.C.P.L.R. §214(5) (McKinney Cum. Supp. 1981-1982) (prescribing a three-year limitation for personal injury actions generally). Mrs. Knaysi's gynecologist inserted the Dalkon Shield on March 15, 1972. On June 26, 1972 Mrs. Knaysi experienced the spontaneous septic abortion. On December 8, 1976 the Knaysis read a newspaper article about reported cases of infected abortions and deaths of pregnant women in connection with the use of the Dalkon Shield. This led them to inquire of Mrs. Knaysi's gynecologist the type of intrauterine device he had inserted. On February 17, 1977 the appellants learned that the doctor had inserted a Dalkon Shield. On June 26, 1978 this suit was filed.

constitute equitable estoppel under New York law, there are genuine issues of material fact with respect to the application of that doctrine.

Under New York law equitable estoppel may arise in either of two ways. "Equitable estoppel sufficient to bar the interposition of the statute of limitations results from representations or conduct which have induced a party to postpone bringing suit on a known cause of action, *or* from fraudulent concealment of an action which is unknown to a party." Parsons v. Department of Transportation, 74 Misc. 2d 828, 344 N.Y.S.2d 19, 24 (Sup. Ct. 1973) (emphasis added). Appellants contend that Robins has engaged in conduct of the latter type. Our review of the New York cases in which equitable estoppel of this kind was determined to apply persuades us that the Knaysis' allegations come within their rationale.

Simcuski v. Saeli, 44 N.Y.2d 442, 377 N.E.2d 713 (1978), was an action by a patient alleging that her physician negligently severed a nerve during surgery and fraudulently concealed this condition. In concluding that the doctrine of equitable estoppel applied to her case, the New York Court of Appeals reasoned: "This complaint . . . alleges that defendant intentionally concealed the alleged malpractice from plaintiff and falsely assured her of effective treatment, as a result of which plaintiff did not discover the injury to the nerve until [four years after the surgery]." Id. at 448, 377 N.E.2d at 716. In General Stencils, Inc. v. Chiappa, 18 N.Y.2d 125, 219 N.E.2d 169, 170 (1966), the New York Court of Appeals held that a plaintiff corporation suing its head bookkeeper for conversion of company funds was entitled to litigate the issue of equitable estoppel because the defendant's wrongdoing — i.e., the theft and manipulation of the books — had fraudulently concealed the wrongdoing from the plaintiff's notice. Finally in Erbe v. Lincoln Rochester Trust Co., 13 A.D.2d 211, 214 N.Y.S.2d 849 (1961), *appeal dismissed,* 11 N.Y.2d 754, 181 N.E.2d 629 (1962), the Appellate Division of the New York Supreme Court held that the trial court had erred in dismissing the trust beneficiaries' complaint for breach of fiduciary duty on the ground of the bar of the statute of limitations. The court reasoned: "In this action . . . it should not be held that a trustee can take advantage of the limitations statute when the beneficiaries of the trust may have been led to believe that there was no breach of the relationship by statements of false facts or concealment of true facts by the fiduciary." Id. at 213, 214 N.Y.S.2d at 852. Specifically, the beneficiaries alleged that the trustee, whom they charged with self-dealing in purchasing trust property, had falsely represented to them: (1) that the trustee had a legal right to purchase the stock, (2) that [a court order] had authorized the trustee to acquire the stock and (3) that the stock was held by the trustee as collateral pledged by the settlor in his lifetime." Id. at 213, 214 N.Y.S.2d at 851.

Two unifying factors appear in these cases. In each case the defendant has control and superior, or exclusive, knowledge of facts necessary for the plaintiff to make out a cause of action. Second, the defendant by affirmative misstatements conceals these essential facts from the plaintiff. In *Simcuski* the patient relied on her physician for proper diagnosis and treatment of the ailment that plagued her after surgery. His false assurances regarding curative treatment precluded the plaintiff's earlier discovery that the physician's malpractice was the cause of her injury and consequently produced the delay in filing suit. In *General Stencils* the plaintiff company had entrusted its bookkeeper with the proper handling of and accounting for company funds. The bookkeeper's manipulation of the books concealed the fact of her conversion. Likewise in *Erbe* the beneficiaries relied on the trustee to honor his duty of loyalty in managing trust property, and the trustee concealed his self-dealing by false statements about the manner in which he acquired or held the trust property and about his legal right to acquire the stock.

The facts of the present case offer no ground for distinction. The medical community and the consuming public, either directly or in justifiable reliance upon medical advice, rely on drug manufacturers for accurate information and assurances regarding the safety and efficacy of their products. The allegation is that Mrs. Knaysi and her gynecologist so relied in this case. Moreover, Robins is alleged to have published information about the Dalkon Shield which it knew to be false and to have suppressed damaging information about the device's danger. These facts were essential to make out the cause of action for products liability, breach of warranty, and other claims put forward by the Knaysis. Hence we conclude that the appellants' allegations, when measured against the standards for equitable estoppel under New York law, are sufficient to invoke the application of that doctrine.

Reliance

Having determined that the facts alleged could, if proved, estop Robins from pleading the bar of the statute of limitations, we further conclude that the issue of equitable estoppel was one inappropriate for summary judgment as there exist genuine issues of material fact to be resolved at trial. First, there are obvious questions of fact regarding the alleged misrepresentations made by Robins. . . .

In addition, the highest state court in New York recently has endorsed the notion that the plaintiff's due diligence in bringing suit must "be demonstrated by the plaintiff when he seeks the shelter of the doctrine [of equitable estoppel]." Simcuski v. Saeli, 44 N.Y.2d at 450, 377 N.E.2d at 717. . . . [P]laintiff's due diligence is a question of fact unsuited for summary judgment. . . . In Erbe v. Lincoln Rochester Trust Co., 3 N.Y.2d 321, 144 N.E.2d 78 (1957), a fraud action, the New York Court of Appeals elaborated on this reasonable diligence test and the inappropriateness of summary disposition:

[T]he plaintiffs will be held to have discovered the fraud when it is established that they were possessed of knowledge of facts from which it could be reasonably inferred, that is, inferred from facts which indicate the alleged fraud.

Ordinarily such an inquiry presents a mixed question of law and fact . . . and, where it does not conclusively appear that the plaintiffs had knowledge of facts of that nature a complaint *should not be dismissed on motion*.

Id. at 326, 144 N.E.2d at 80-81 (citations omitted) (emphasis added). [W]e must conclude that the Knaysis' diligence in pursuing their claims against Robins is a triable issue of fact in this case.

For the foregoing reasons, we reverse the district court's grant of summary judgment for appellee Robins and remand for further proceedings. On remand the appellants are entitled to litigate not only the issue of estoppel but also all other counts raised by their complaint since the Knaysis may prevail on the estoppel issue.[4]

Reversed and remanded.

TJOFLAT, Circuit Judge, dissenting.

Each of the Knaysis' personal injury claims against A. H. Robins, Inc., was brought after the applicable statute of limitations had run.[1] The sole question posed by the majority, therefore, is whether Robins' statute of limitations defense is precluded by equitable estoppel.

Under New York law, an equitable estoppel reply to a statute of limitations defense is in the nature of an affirmative defense and it must be pleaded and proven by the plaintiff. Simcuski v. Saeli, 44 N.Y.2d 442, 377 N.E.2d 713 (1978); see also Fed. R. Civ. P. 8(c) and (d). In this case, the Knaysis pleaded equitable estoppel in the form of a reply to Robins' amended answer.

The burden of proof the Knaysis assumed under their equitable estoppel reply is thoroughly set forth in Jordan v. Ford Motor Co., 73 A.D.2d 422, 426 N.Y.S.2d 359 (1980):

> [W]here a defendant induces a plaintiff to refrain from instituting an action, either by false statements of fact or by active concealment of the true facts, he may be estopped from using the Statute of Limitations to dismiss an otherwise untimely suit against him. *Where the estoppel is based upon an actual misrepresentation by defendant, the plaintiff is required to allege that justified reliance* upon the misrepresentation was the reason for not timely starting the action. Similarly, *where concealment without actual misrepresentation is claimed to have prevented a plaintiff from commencing an action within the Statute of*

---

4. Because of our holding that summary judgment was inappropriate on the issue of estoppel, we need not reach other arguments advanced by the appellants — namely, that the fraud alleged in their complaint is a separate cause of action from the products liability claim for statute of limitations purposes and that summary judgment was inappropriate to resolve disputed issues of fact regarding application of New York's fraud statute of limitations to this case.

1. The majority agrees with this proposition except as it applies to the Knaysis' common law claim of fraud and deceit, which it does not address. See majority opinion at note 4. The district court held that the Knaysis' fraud claim was subsumed by their products liability claim and was time barred. I agree.

Limitations, the courts have invoked estoppel only where there was a fiduciary relationship which gave defendant an obligation to inform plaintiff of facts underlying the claim.

Where the injured party is simply unaware that a cause of action is available to him, either due to lack of diligence on his own part or because of the difficulty of discovering the injury, the courts have not applied the doctrine of equitable estoppel. *A party against whom a claim exists is not, without more, under a duty to inform the injured party thereof,* and such failure to inform does not constitute the kind of fraudulent concealment which gives rise to an estoppel.

73 A.D.2d at 424, 426 N.Y.S.2d at 360-61 (emphasis supplied).

Under the New York law, then, the Knaysis' equitable estoppel reply must proceed on one of two theories. The first requires the Knaysis to prove that Robins made an *actual misrepresentation* to the Knaysis or to Mrs. Knaysi's physician (who I will assume, arguendo, was her agent) that Robins intended would induce the Knaysis to believe that Mrs. Knaysi's septic abortion could not have been caused by the Dalkon Shield; that they, or the physician acting for them, *justifiably relied* on that misrepresentation; and that their reliance on the misrepresentation was the reason the Knaysis did not file a timely suit against Robins. Because this issue arose on Robins' motion for summary judgment, the question for us, as it was for the district court, is whether the record created a question of fact which, if resolved in the Knaysis' favor, would permit them to meet their burden of proof.

The Knaysis concede that Robins never directly or indirectly communicated with them, or vice versa. In Mrs. Knaysi's affidavit and deposition testimony, she insists that she did not know that her IUD was a Dalkon Shield and that she never heard or read anything regarding the Dalkon Shield prior to December 8, 1977, when she read a news report stating that Dalkon Shields *might be a cause* of septic abortions. Moreover, the record contains no evidence that Robins ever communicated in any way with Mrs. Knaysi's physician, or vice versa. The record does not include the testimony of the physician, by way of affidavit or deposition. The record does contain deposition testimony of a Robins representative, but that testimony does not shed any light on any representation that may have been delivered to or received by the physician. The sole evidence in the record of a Robins representation concerning the Dalkon Shield is examples of Robins' advertising literature, which the majority assumes were delivered to and read by Mrs. Knaysi's physician. This literature touts the Dalkon Shield as being "safe," but only in one instance, a brochure published in October 1972, does it contain what could be contended to be a misrepresentation intended to induce someone not to sue Robins over a septic abortion. That brochure, given to physicians for ultimate distribution to patients, stated that if pregnancy should occur with the Dalkon Shield in place, no harm would result if the Shield was not removed. This brochure contains no reference to septic abortion. Nonetheless, an individual who had a septic abortion and read the brochure might be convinced that the Dalkon Shield could not have caused the abortion and might therefore be lulled into not bringing suit against Robins.

I will assume, arguendo, that Mrs. Knaysi's physician received and read Robins' October 1972 brochure. There is absolutely nothing in the record, however, that even suggests that the physician believed what the brochure said or relied on it in any way. More importantly, nothing suggests that the brochure lulled the physician, and in turn the Knaysis, into a state of inaction viz-a-viz Robins. Without the critical link between the alleged misrepresentation and the Knaysis' failure to bring this suit within the limitations period, the Knaysis cannot prevail.

The second equitable estoppel theory available under New York law requires the Knaysis to establish that Robins owed them a fiduciary duty. If Robins did, it could be equitably estopped from raising the statute of limitations defense upon the Knaysis' demonstration that Robins, in violation of that duty, concealed the information they needed in order to bring a timely suit.

Here, the Knaysis make no claim that Robins owed them or their physician a fiduciary duty. Consequently, they simply could not make out a prima facie case under the second theory of equitable estoppel. See Jordan v. Ford Motor Co., 73 A.D.2d at 424, 426 N.Y.S.2d at 361 (automobile manufacturer had no fiduciary duty to automobile owner and therefore could not be estopped from raising statute of limitations where it simply failed to reveal to the public that the placement of the fuel tank in certain of its automobiles increased the seriousness of accidents involving rear end collisions).

Since the Knaysis failed to raise a material issue of fact as to their equitable estoppel reply to Robins' statute of limitations defense, Robins was, and is, entitled to the summary judgment the district court gave it.

I dissent.

NOTES ON FRAUDULENT CONCEALMENT

1. The New York legislature has codified a discovery rule for fraud claims, with an outside limit of six years. N.Y. Civ. Prac. Law §§203(f), 213(8) (McKinney 1972). The New York courts refuse to apply the discovery rule to any other kind of claim. Mrs. Knaysi's causes of action accrued when the shield first began to damage her body, whether or not she could have known about it. The Court of Appeals reaffirmed that doctrine in Martin v. Edwards Laboratories, 60 N.Y.2d 417, 457 N.E.2d 1150 (1983), a case in which the Dalkon Shield caused serious infection leading to sterility.

In both *Knaysi* and *Martin*, there were noticeable symptoms shortly after the onset of injury. But the New York Court of Appeals has applied its accrual rule in cases of slow onset disease that produce no symptoms for years. In Schwartz v. Heyden Newport Chemical Corp., 12 N.Y.2d 212, 188 N.E.2d 142, *cert. denied*, 374 U.S. 808 (1963), plaintiff was given a radioactive substance in 1944 that caused cancer diagnosed in 1957; in Schmidt v. Merchants Despatch Transportation Co., 270 N.Y. 287, 200 N.E. 824 (1936), plaintiff suffered lung disease from long exposure to excessive dust at work. In each case, the court held that the radiation and the dust must have begun to do damage as soon as it entered the body, so that the claim was barred long before the injury was noticeable.

2. Fraudulent concealment is distinct from the discovery rule and should not be confused with it, although some courts inevitably confuse them and there is some blurring as courts reduce the fraud element of fraudulent concealment. New York adds to the potential for confusion by using a different vocabulary from the rest of the country. When defendant conceals the existence of the cause of action, most courts describe that as fraudulent concealment. When defendant induces plaintiff to forbear suing on a known cause of action, he may be estopped to plead limitations. New York follows the same two rules, but treats them as two branches of equitable estoppel.

3. The judges in *Knaysi* do not seem to disagree over the applicable legal standard. Is there anything to Judge Tjoflat's view that plaintiff hasn't shown enough to get to the jury? Robins distributed lots of literature claiming that the shield was "safe"; why doesn't that count? Another panel of the Eleventh Circuit said those advertisements may have fraudulently induced women to use the shield, but they were irrelevant to whether Robins fraudulently concealed its liability from women who had already been injured by the shield. Sellers v. A. H. Robins Co., 715 F.2d 1559, 1561 (11th Cir. 1983). *Sellers* distinguished *Knaysi* on the ground that Alabama law is wholly different from New York law. That is not true; both states recognize fraudulent concealment and neither recognizes the discovery rule. The real source of disagreement between the two panels was over the relevance of general claims of safety not directed at the particular injury plaintiff suffered. If general advertising claims are enough, won't most plaintiffs in products cases be able to show fraudulent concealment?

4. Robins also made a specific claim that the shield would do no harm if left in after pregnancy. Tjoflat says that isn't enough because there is no evidence Knaysi or her doctor relied on it. What further proof might he be looking for? Suppose plaintiff asked her doctor whether she should sue Robins, and he said, "No; I just read a brochure that says the shield is harmless in pregnancy." Surely that would satisfy even Tjoflat. But is it realistic? What if Robins creates such an air of safety about its product that no one's suspicions are ever aroused, and women never ask

whether they should sue? Isn't that the most effective form of concealment?

5. One view of the concealment requirement is that defendant is entitled to the protection of limitations unless he does something in addition to the underlying wrong. Marcus, Fraudulent Concealment in Federal Court: Toward a More Disparate Standard?, 71 Geo. L.J. 829, 856 (1983). In addition, nearly all courts subscribe to the view that mere silence is not fraudulent concealment — that except for fiduciaries, defendants have no duty to disclose their wrongdoing.

The wrong in products liability is selling a defective product. Advertising the product is not an element of the wrong; it is a legally distinct act. But few products can be sold without advertising; realistically, Robins did nothing but sell its product. Should that matter? Should it matter whether Robins believed its product was safe? Should "fraudulent concealment" require Robins to conceal a wrong it knows it committed?

6. One other piece of the Dalkon Shield story is curiously missing from *Knaysi*. In May 1974 Robins warned physicians that the shield might cause septic abortions. In June 1974, under pressure from the Food and Drug Administration, it withdrew the product from the market. The Ninth Circuit held that these acts necessarily ended any fraudulent concealment. Sidney-Vinstein v. A. H. Robins Co., 697 F.2d 880, 884 (9th Cir. 1983). But not until 1984 did Robins recommend that women already using the shield have it removed. Wall Street Journal, Oct. 30, 1984 at 1, col. 3. In the interim, Robins continued to issue statements asserting that the shield was safe and effective. The Ninth Circuit apparently thought the earlier disclosures made these claims irrelevant.

Is that the right result? Aren't safety claims after 1974 more culpable — more "fraudulent" — than safety claims before 1974? On the other hand, must Robins waive the statute of limitations unless it admits liability to the world? If it isn't fraudulent concealment to deny plaintiff's allegations in court, why is it fraudulent concealment to deny them out of court? Should we distinguish general claims of safety from false denials of specific facts? Suppose Robins' statements acknowledged that many users of the shield had experienced gynecological problems. Should that make it OK to say that Robins believed that the shield was safe, and that the reported problems were coincidental and not caused by the shield?

7. A few courts have held that limitations is tolled by fraudulent concealment whether or not plaintiff is diligent, but that is plainly the minority view. Professor Marcus collects the cases at 71 Geo. L.J. 876878. Thus, limitations generally run from the time plaintiff should have known he had a cause of action, even if defendant continues to conceal it. Does that help reconcile the dilemmas explored in note 6? Should a diligent plaintiff proceed despite denials once he has enough information? What if defendant's denial is supported by a false but convincing explanation?

8. Professor Marcus concludes from his extensive survey of the federal cases that plaintiffs' diligence explains results much better than defendants' concealment. That is, he thinks that where plaintiff was diligent and the discovery rule doesn't apply, most courts will find concealment even if there really isn't any. Certainly there are cases where that happens, but I think he exaggerates the trend, even in noncommercial cases. Plaintiffs lost two of the three Dalkon Shield cases considered here, and Knaysi has not yet won, although her chances with a jury seem pretty good.

9. Like the discovery rule, fraudulent concealment doctrine is sometimes codified and sometimes judicially implied. It is usually not subject to any outside limit, but there are exceptions. For example, the Tennessee statute of limitations for products liability cases, discussed in the previous set of notes, recites that it is enacted in response to a products liability crisis and overrides all exceptions to statutes of limitations.

BOMBA v. W. L. BELVIDERE, INC.
579 F.2d 1067 (7th Cir. 1978)

Before FAIRCHILD, Chief Judge, MARKEY, Chief Judge, United States Court of Customs and Patent Appeals, and BAUER, Circuit Judge.
  BAUER, Circuit Judge. . . .

I

Plaintiffs' complaint alleges that the defendant sold them two lots of land on August 4, 1973 without having effective statements of record and without providing plaintiffs with property reports for each lot as required by the Interstate Land Sales Full Disclosure Act, 15 U.S.C. §1703(a)(1). On May 30, 1975, the defendant sent a letter to plaintiffs acknowledging that it had violated the Act, at least with respect to one lot, and informing plaintiffs that they could, if they wished, rescind the sale and receive a refund of any payments made in accordance with the sales contract. Plaintiffs immediately notified defendant that they elected to rescind and wished a refund of their payments. Their letter concluded:

> We expect you to contact us soon with the proper documents to be executed in order to reconvey said lot. . . .

When the defendant did not promptly reply to the letter, plaintiffs telephoned the defendant on several occasions for the purpose of determining when their refund would be forthcoming. According to Annamarie Bomba's deposition, plaintiffs were told in July of 1975 that they would get their money back but that it would take time. This same assurance was made in subsequent phone calls throughout the course of 1975. Finally, in March of 1976, defendant's attorney wrote the Bombas a letter that indicated the defendant, in response to plaintiffs' request for rescission and a refund, would attempt to sell their lot and turn over the "net proceeds of sale" after deduction of various sales costs and commissions. Under the proposed agreement, the Bombas would release defendant from any and all claims in the event their lot was sold, even if the net proceeds of sale did not equal the amount of monies paid by plaintiffs pursuant to the sales agreement with defendant. The Bombas then consulted an attorney, who brought the present suit on May 28, 1977.

II

On appeal, the plaintiffs contend that the defendant is estopped by its conduct from relying on the statute of limitations contained in 15 U.S.C. §1711. According to plaintiffs, by promising them a refund of their money, the defendant lulled them into a false sense of security that led them to refrain from bringing a timely suit. Thus, say plaintiffs, the defendant is estopped from relying on the statute of limitations defense under the principles set out in Glus v. Brooklyn Eastern Dist. Terminal, 359 U.S. 231 (1959).

Defendant responds that the explicit language of 15 U.S.C. §1711 supports the district court's ruling that the statute of limitations contained therein constitutes an absolute bar to plaintiffs' cause of action, for the statute says in no uncertain terms that

> In no event shall any [action to enforce a liability created by this Act] be brought by a purchaser more than three years after the sale or lease to such purchaser.

III . . .

In essence, the district court ruled that the "In no event" wording of 15 U.S.C. §1711 placed an absolute bar on the initiation of suit more than three years after the relevant sale, a limitations period that was not subject to equitable tolling.

Though we might well agree with the district court that the unequivocal language of 15 U.S.C. §1711 presents an insurmountable barrier to the *tolling* of the three-year limitations period contained therein, we cannot agree that the "In no event" terms in which the three-year limitations period is expressed forecloses possible application of the separate and distinct doctrine of equitable estoppel. Tolling, strictly speaking, is concerned with the point at which the limitations period begins to run and with the circumstances in which the running of the limitations period may be suspended. These are matters in large measure governed by the language of the statute of limitations itself, and thus it is not surprising that several district courts have held that the three-year limitations period of 15 U.S.C. §1711 is not subject to being tolled. Equitable estoppel, however, is a different matter. It is not concerned with the running and suspension of the limitations period, but rather comes into play only after the limitations period has run and addresses itself to the circumstances in which a party will be estopped from asserting the statute of limitations as a defense to an admittedly untimely action because his conduct has induced another into forbearing suit within the applicable limitations period. Its application is wholly independent of the limitations period itself and takes its life, not from the language of the statute, but from the equitable principle that no man will be permitted to profit from his own wrongdoing in a court of justice. Thus, because equitable estoppel operates directly on the defendant without abrogating the running of the limitations period as provided by statute, it might apply no matter how unequivocally the applicable limitations period is expressed.

Glus v. Brooklyn Eastern District Terminal, 359 U.S. 231 (1959), is instructive in this regard. In that case, the Supreme Court was confronted with a federal statute of limitations that was just as unequivocal as the one before us now. Yet, notwithstanding the fact that the Federal Employers' Liability Act provided that

> No action shall be maintained under this chapter unless commenced within three years from the day the cause of action accrued,

the Court held that the doctrine of equitable estoppel applied in suits brought under the statute. In so holding, the Court reasoned that the principle that no man may take advantage of his own wrongdoing was so deeply rooted in and integral to our jurisprudence that it should be implied in the interstices of every federal cause of action absent some affirmative indication that Congress expressly intended to exclude the application of equitable estoppel. The Court found no such intent in even the unequivocal language of the statute, and in this respect *Glus* is controlling here. . . .

Having held that the doctrine of equitable estoppel may apply in suits brought under the Interstate Land Sales Full Disclosure Act notwithstanding the terms of 15 U.S.C. §1711, we turn to the question of whether plaintiffs have alleged sufficient facts to possibly warrant the doctrine's application. . . .

In their depositions properly before the district court on defendant's motion for summary judgment, plaintiffs have stated that the defendant's promise to pay them a refund led them to defer seeking legal counsel and bringing suit on their claim. Though it is widely held that mere negotiations concerning a disputed claim, without more, is insufficient to warrant the application of equitable estoppel, the cases are legion that a promise to pay a claim will estop a defendant from asserting the applicable statute of limitations if the plaintiff relied in good faith on defendant's promise in forbearing suit. The oft-quoted rule applicable in such a situation is:

> Estoppel arises where one, by his conduct, lulls another into a false security, and into a position he would not take only because of such conduct. Estoppel, in the event of a disputed claim, arises where one party by words, acts, and conduct led the other to believe that it would acknowledge and pay the claim, if, after investigation, the claim were found to be just, but when, after the time for suit had passed, breaks off negotiations and denies liability and refuses to pay.

Bartlett v. United States, 272 F.2d 291, 296 (10th Cir. 1959). Moreover, it is not necessary that the defendant intentionally mislead or deceive the plaintiff, or even intend by its conduct to induce delay. Rather, all that is necessary for invocation of the doctrine of equitable estoppel is that the plaintiff reasonably rely on the defendant's conduct or representations in forbearing suit.

Accordingly, as we believe that the materials properly before the district court raise a material issue of fact as to whether plaintiffs did in fact reasonably rely on defendant's promise of a refund in forbearing suit within the applicable limitations period, we reverse the district court's judgment and remand the case for further proceeding consistent with this opinion.

Reversed and remanded.

NOTES ON ESTOPPEL TO ASSERT LIMITATIONS

1. The court could have strengthened its opinion by quoting the entire statute of limitations as it then read:

> No action shall be maintained to enforce any liability created under section 1410(a) or (b)(2) unless brought within one year after the discovery of the untrue statement or the omission, or after such discovery should have been made by the exercise of reasonable diligence, or, if the action is to enforce a liability created under section 1410(b)(1), unless brought within two years after the violation upon which it is based. In no event shall any such action be brought by a purchaser more than three years after the sale or lease to such purchaser.

82 Stat. 596.

Doesn't it seem clear in context that the "In no event" clause was intended to put an outside limit on the discovery rule in the first sentence? Was it limited to that? Was there any reason to read it as also putting an outside limit on estoppel? What about fraudulent concealment? The sentence beginning "In no event" was repealed in 1979.

2. Courts have generally taken it upon themselves to imply tolling rules into silent statutes of limitations. The Supreme Court has also said that the fraudulent concealment doctrine is read into every federal statute of limitations. Holmberg v. Armbrecht, 327 U.S. 392, 396-397 (1946). But two circuits applied the three-year outside limit of the Interstate Land Sales Full Disclosure Act to fraudulent concealment. Darms v. McCulloch Oil Corp., 720 F.2d 490, 494 (8th Cir. 1983); Aldrich v. McCulloch Properties, 627 F.2d 1036, 1042-1043 (10th Cir. 1980). Neither case noted the difference between fraudulent concealment and a discovery rule. *Aldrich* cited two district court cases tolling the statute for fraudulent concealment.

3. Compare *Bomba* and *Holmberg* with Borderlon v. Peck, 661 S.W.2d 907 (Tex. 1983). Texas amended the statute of limitations for medical malpractice to read that, "Notwithstanding any other law, no . . . claim may be commenced unless . . . filed within two years from the occurrence. . . . " The court held that this did not abolish fraudulent concealment. And where the doctor knew he had made a mistake, the court found fraudulent concealment in his failure to disclose it; the doctor owed a fiduciary duty to his patient. Four dissenters thought this combination of holdings made the amendment useless.

4. *Bomba* relies on Glus v. Brooklyn Eastern District Terminal, the leading Supreme Court case on estoppel to assert limitations. Plaintiff was an employee with an industrial disease, suing under the Federal Employers' Liability Act. The FELA has a three-year statute of limitations, but the employer repeatedly told Glus he had seven years to sue. The Court held that that could give rise to an estoppel, and that whether it was reasonable to rely on a misrepresentation of law was a jury question. What do you suppose the jury said?

5. Estoppel to assert limitations is simply a special case of the equitable estoppel rules we examined in chapter 11. Any representation that induces plaintiff to refrain from suit might suffice, but three patterns account for the vast bulk of the cases. *Bomba* and *Glus* illustrate two of these patterns.

The third is a promise not to assert limitations. Defendant may urge plaintiff to keep exploring settlement possibilities even though the statute is about to expire, promising not to plead limitations if negotiations fail. In one recent case, defendants promised not to assert the shorter Wisconsin statute if the case were transferred there from New York. When the scope of the litigation expanded in Wisconsin, defendants asserted the

Wisconsin limitations period, but the court held they were estopped. J. H. Cohn & Co. v. American Appraisal Associates, 628 F.2d 994, 999-1001 (7th Cir. 1980).

NOTES ON LIMITATIONS VOCABULARY AND THE EFFECT OF TOLLING

1.   Limitations vocabulary isn't standardized. *Bomba* distinguishes tolling rules from estoppel. It is also common to distinguish tolling rules from accrual rules, although *Bomba* and many other courts lump them together. Other courts use "tolling" to describe anything that delays the running of limitations after the claim has accrued.

It would be useful to agree on terminology, although there is no reason to expect that. It would be clearest to say that a claim accrues when the events giving rise to liability occur. Under this approach, we would say that the statute of limitations runs from that point unless it is tolled by some rule that gives plaintiff extra time in which to sue.

There can be real arguments about both kinds of issues. Even if Ann O'Brien knew everything that happened as soon as it happened, the court would still have to decide whether her claim accrued when her mother took DES, when the DES first affected her body in any way, when she first suffered measurable damage, or when she first had cancer. This is an accrual issue in my usage, and it is a different kind of issue from when she first should have known about her claim. I would say her claim accrued but that limitations was tolled until she should have discovered the claim. Some courts talk that way too; others say the claim does not accrue until it should have been discovered.

2.   Whether the court claims to apply a delayed accrual rule, a tolling rule, or an estoppel rule, the effect of delaying the period of limitations is only a little more standardized than the vocabulary. Common law courts have worked with variations on two possibilities:

a.   The running of limitations may be suspended. Plaintiff gets the full statutory period, not counting periods of suspension. Suppose there is a two-year statute, and defendant fraudulently conceals the claim for three years. Plaintiff could file any time up to two years after the end of the concealment — five years after the claim arose.

b.   A "reasonable time" may be substituted for the statutory period of limitations. Some courts say plaintiff should file promptly after discovering a cause of action on which limitations would have already run but for some tolling rule; some courts use laches doctrine to solve the problem.

3.   Suspension may be little help when a ground for tolling limitations arises some time after the events giving rise to the claim. For example, the statute may have only a few days left to run when defendant promises

not to assert limitations if plaintiff will refrain from filing suit while negotiations continue. In that case, suspending limitations leaves plaintiff
with only a few days to sue when he discovers that defendant plans to
assert limitations anyway. The same problem can arise when the statute is
tolled by the pendency of a suit that for some reason does not resolve the
issue. In American Pipe & Construction Co. v. Utah, 414 U.S. 538
(1974), the Court held that a pending class action tolls limitations for all
members of the class. The class action was filed with eleven days remaining in the limitations period; when the trial court struck the class allegations from the complaint, absent class members had eleven days to find
out what had happened and file individual claims.

Puerto Rico applies a different rule in such cases: After a suspension of
the limitations period, the statute starts over. Under that rule, the American Pipe class members would have a full four years after dismissal of the
class action, not just eleven days. The Supreme Court applied the Puerto
Rican rule to a federal civil rights claim from Puerto Rico in Chardon v.
Fumero Soto, 462 U.S. 650 (1983).

4. When a court talks of tolling or delayed accrual, it is also likely to
talk of suspending the period of limitations. Suspension seems to be less
common in the estoppel cases. But generalizations are dangerous. For
example, in Ott v. Midland-Ross Corp., 600 F.2d 23 (6th Cir. 1979), the
court suspended limitations in an estoppel case. It thought plaintiff was
entitled to at least a full three years to sue, and that any time during
which he relied on defendant's promise of a voluntary remedy shouldn't
count. The court also addressed the problem of American Pipe. Ott says
that after the estoppel ends, plaintiff is entitled to "a reasonable time" or
the remaining period of limitations, whichever is greater. Id. at 34 n.12.

The opposite approach is illustrated by Simcuski v. Saeli, 44 N.Y.2d
442, 377 N.E.2d 713 (1978). Simcuski was a medical malpractice case in
which plaintiff alleged fraudulent concealment. The court held that
plaintiff's duty of diligence required him to sue "within a reasonable
time" after the concealment ended, with the full statutory period as an
outside limit. The court cited an annotation on estoppel to assert limitations; the case may have been affected by New York's use of the estoppel
label to describe fraudulent concealment cases.

5. One other arcane distinction is that between "substantive" and
"procedural" statutes of limitations. This distinction figured in the part of
Glus v. Brooklyn Eastern District Terminal relied on in Bomba. The
distinction is that a limitations rule enacted in a separate statute, and
applying to many kinds of claims, is a procedural statute that bars only
the remedy, and court-made tolling rules are fully applicable. But a limitations rule enacted in the same statute that creates a cause of action, and
applying only to claims under that statute, is a substantive statute that
bars the right, impervious to tolling. Is that a comprehensible distinction?
Is there any reason for it?

The limitations period in *Glus* appeared in the same statute that created the cause of action, and defendant argued that estoppel was therefore unavailable. The Court's insistence that estoppel was so deeply rooted that it had to be implied in every statute of limitations was directed at this substance/procedure distinction. *Glus* squarely rejects the distinction, and one could hope that would be the end of the matter. But it still shows up on occasion. An example is Ott v. Midland-Ross Corp., 523 F.2d 1367 (6th Cir. 1975). *Ott* reads *Glus* as holding that the limitations provision of the Federal Employers Liability Act are procedural even though it appears in the statute creating the cause of action. *Ott* apparently assumes that the underlying distinction survives.

The distinction was not mentioned in Zipes v. Trans World Airlines, 455 U.S. 385 (1982). *Zipes* involved the requirement that victims of employment discrimination file an administrative charge within 180 days of the discrimination, a requirement that appears in the same statute that creates the cause of action. The Court held that the 180-day provision is an ordinary statute of limitations, and that defendant could be estopped from invoking it. This ended a bizarre argument in the lower courts that a charge within 180 days was a prerequisite to subject matter jurisdiction, not subject to tolling, waiver, or estoppel. But the Court did not squarely reject the notion that a limitations provision could be jurisdictional.

6. All arguments about judicial power to imply exceptions to the statute of limitations assume that the legislature didn't address the question. If a statute squarely creates or precludes a tolling rule, the courts are obviously bound. Estoppel, fraudulent concealment, and the discovery rule are all judge-made exceptions, but modern statutes of limitations are more and more likely to address them directly.

Most statutes of limitations codify an older and narrower set of tolling rules. Limitations generally doesn't run against infants or incompetents, or while defendant is beyond the jurisdiction.

RAILING v. UNITED MINE WORKERS
429 F.2d 780 (4th Cir. 1970)

Before BOREMAN, CRAVEN and BUTZNER, Circuit Judges.

CRAVEN, Circuit Judge.

Chester and Paul Railing began this action on June 28, 1961, for injuries to their business and property alleged to have been caused by unfair labor practices of the officers, agents, representatives and members of the United Mine Workers of America. . . .

The Railings conducted a nonunion coal strip-mining operation and coal tipple at Berry Run, West Virginia. In April of 1958, Railings' employees, allegedly instigated by the Union, struck and picketed these operations. The Union's purpose was said to be: (1) to force the Railings to recognize the Union as exclusive bargaining representative, and (2) to force the Railings to cease doing business with other employers or to cease using, selling or otherwise handling the products of other employers, thereby forcing these other employers to recognize the Union as the bargaining representative of their employees. Additionally, the Railings allege that UMW maliciously destroyed specific items of equipment and property[2] and induced employees of other employers to engage in a concerted refusal to handle or otherwise work on any coal produced by Railing. On July 14, 1959, there was a complete cessation of all strike activity and picketing pursuant to an injunction issued by the National Labor Relations Board; however, the Railings did not institute this action until June 28, 1961, one year and approximately eleven and one-half months after such cessation.

The Railings appeal from the partial grant of UMW's motion for summary judgment as it related to the application of the two-year statute of limitations prescribed by W. Va. Code, ch. 55, art. 2, §12 (Michie 1966). The district court held that the statute of limitations began to run on the alleged illegal activities of UMW from each day of their occurrence and not from the time when all such activities ceased. The result is to bar many claims that would be viable if the statute of limitations were adjudged to run from the date of cessation of illegal activity.

In its discussion of the issue now before us, the district court addressed itself to two basic questions: (1) what period of limitation was to be applied, and (2) when the cause of action being sued upon accrued and when the period of limitations began to run.

Section 303 of the Labor Management Relations Act contains no statute of limitations. The district court referred to state law to determine the pertinent period of limitation to be applied. Plaintiffs originally instituted this action in the District Court for the Eastern District of Kentucky, but the action was transferred to the District Court for the Northern District of West Virginia upon motion of UMW. The court below, the transferee district court, determined that it must look to the law of the State of Kentucky, the state from which the transfer was made, including Kentucky's "borrowing statute," KRS 413.060, to determine the statute of limitations applicable to the cause of action sued upon. The Kentucky statute required the application of the West Virginia two-year period of limitation, since it was shorter than the period of limitation prescribed by Kentucky. The Railings do not challenge the correctness of this ruling.

It is the district court's disposition of the problem relating to accrual of the cause of action that is the subject of appeal. In treating this issue of

2. Railing requests compensatory and punitive damages for these common-law torts pursuant to the court's pendent jurisdiction.

accrual the district court correctly determined that federal and not state law must be applied. This is so even though the period of limitation is "borrowed" from the appropriate state. Although it is clear that federal law is to be applied, it is not so clear what that law may be. Since neither the statute nor the reported decisions determine when a cause of action accrues under Section 303, we are faced, as was the court below, with the necessity of fashioning a rule of decision to be applied in determining when such cause of action "accrues."

In undertaking to fashion such a rule we have examined cases involving private causes of action arising under the federal antitrust laws. . . . [I]t has been held that where private causes of action under the antitrust laws are based upon continuous invasions of one's rights, the causes accrue from day to day as the injured party's rights are invaded and damages result. The Union urges us to adopt the principle of the antitrust cases here.

On the other hand, the Railings contend that under the facts of the instant case, where the same illegal activity continued on a daily basis over a definite period, a cause of action should not be held to accrue and the limitation period should not commence to run until cessation of the acts complained of; that it would be impossible to compute damages on a day-to-day basis, and that the decision of the district court requires of a prospective plaintiff "an attempt at prophecy or projecting into the future how long the alleged illegal activities would continue and what their future effect would be"; that it is unfair to put the injured party in the difficult position of having to protect himself from the running of the statute of limitations while the illegal activities continue.

The district court, in holding that the cause of action accrued from day to day, relied directly on the reasoning of the court in Delta Theaters, Inc. v. Paramount Pictures, Inc., 158 F. Supp. 644 (E.D. La. 1958). That case involved a suit under the Clayton Act for damages resulting from conspiracy to destroy competition. The conspiracy had allegedly been going on for ten years before the suit was filed. The plaintiff argued that because the actions of the defendants constituted a continuing conspiracy for a single purpose, the applicable statute of limitations should not be construed to run against the plaintiff's single cause of action as long as the conspiracy continued. As the court viewed plaintiff's argument, if the conspiracy constituted a single cause of action, the statute of limitations would either have run from the first "impact" of the conspiracy, in which case the cause of action would have been barred some nine years before, or from the last, which would mean it had not yet accrued. The plaintiff sought to avoid this result by arguing that it should be able to sue on any part of its claim at any time during the conspiracy, but that defendant should not be able to take advantage of the statute until the conspiracy had ceased. The court rejected plaintiff's position, stating that the conceptual difficulties in attempting to split the type of claim involved were not a sufficient reason for refusing to give effect to the principles underlying the statutes of limitation. "The lapse of time obscures the facts of a continuing conspiracy just as much as those of an intermittent one." 158 F. Supp. at 648.

On its facts, *Delta Theaters* does not reach an unreasonable result. Conspiracy, at best, is an ephemeral concept, and the conspiracy in *Delta Theaters* had allegedly continued over a decade. Certainly the prospect of trying to determine correctly facts spread out over a decade is formidable enough to give pause to any court. The "lapse of time — fading memory — stale claim" arguments underpinning every statute of limitations were, indeed, sufficient reasons for the result the court reached.

But whatever justification existed for applying the day-to-day accrual principle in *Delta Theaters*, we think it does not apply here. The Railings are not charging UMW with conspiracy, but with the virtual destruction of their business through illegal labor activities, including acts of violence. Moreover, the alleged activities continued for only 16 months, from April 1958 to July 14, 1959, and the action was commenced less than two years after the illegal activities ceased. As the Railings point out, the total eventual damage to the business could not be ascertained after each day of illegal activity. Even if all the illegal activity could be broken down into severable, day-to-day "acts," the sum of the damage directly attributable to those acts would likely be less than the total damage resulting from the combination of the acts over 16 months. Thus, for instance, illegal activity during the first month may have caused ascertainable damage at that time, but it may have also caused cumulative damage in the sixteenth month by operating in concert with other illegal activities.

When one views the continuing cause or causes of action in this light, it becomes clear that application of a day-to-day accrual principle is inapposite. Not only would the total damage have been unascertainable before the illegal strike ceased, but also adequate inclusion of all damages resulting from individual, day-to-day acts would have been difficult and cumbersome. To fully protect themselves, plaintiffs would have been forced either to move to amend their complaint frequently to include newly accrued damages, or to speculate as to the total damages that would eventually result from the strike, or both. It would require an unusual degree of prescience to determine when the strike would end and what damage would ultimately result.

Since this is a tort case, it seems to us more sensible to refer to rules of limitation for torts than for antitrust:

> If the continuing nature of the tort and injury is such that damages cannot be determined until cessation of the wrong, the right of action is deemed as continuous as the tort on which it is based so that it accrues at, and limitations begin to run from, the last date rather than from the first date of the wrong, or,

as otherwise expressed, limitations do not apply to such a tort so long as it subsists.

54 C.J.S. Limitations of Actions §169, at p.128 (1948).

Under the circumstances present here, we think the rule most appropriate is that the cause of action accrues on the last date of continuing illegal conduct for purposes of application of a state statute of limitations, but that for separate injury for which damages are earlier ascertainable suit *may* be brought at the date of ascertainment. In other words, the victim of the illegal activity should be entitled to bring suit as soon as he can do so, but should not be required to bring suit until the illegal activity has ceased. Under this rule the West Virginia statute of limitations did not begin to run until the UMW finally ceased its illegal strike activities. We hold the district court erred in ruling that the statute of limitations began to run on the day each unfair labor practice occurred.

The judgment will be reversed and remanded for further proceedings not inconsistent with this opinion.

Reversed and remanded.

BOREMAN, Circuit Judge (dissenting). . . .

The plaintiff demanded judgment for damages in separate amounts: (1) for the destruction of plaintiff's business and the loss of profits therefrom; (2) to plaintiff's physical property, machinery and equipment; (3) for sums expended by plaintiff preparing to resume business operations; and (4) for punitive damages. . . .

The majority takes the view that the pertinent West Virginia statute of limitations did not begin to run until the date of the cessation of strike and picketing activities (July 14, 1959), citing as authority 54 C.J.S. Limitations of Actions §169, at p.128 (1948); but the majority opinion fails to note that text's further comment:

> Where a continuing tort involves separate and successive injuries, the action accrues at, and limitations begin to run as to each injury from, the date thereof, and *there is not only a cause of action for the original wrong, arising when the wrong is committed, but separate and successive causes of action for the consequential damages arise as and when such damages are from time to time sustained*; and, therefore, as long as the cause of the injury exists and the damages continue to occur, plaintiff is not barred of a recovery for such damages as have accrued within the statutory period before the action. Thus an action may lie for an injury recurring within the prescriptive period, even though the first tortious act antedated such period, and a cause of action based solely on the original wrong may be barred; but the recovery is limited to such damages as accrued within the statutory period before the action.

(Emphasis supplied.) §169, at pp. 128-129.

The district court concluded "the most appropriate rule" in cases concerned with the problem of accrual of a cause of action, involving numerous acts resulting in a continuous invasion of a protected interest, is that applied in Delta Theaters, Inc. v. Paramount Pictures, Inc., 158 F. Supp. 644, 648 (E.D. La. 1958), which, although recognizing "conceptual difficulties in attempting to split this type of claim," adopted the Third Circuit's rule in Bluefields S.S. Co. v. United Fruit Co., 243 F. 1, 20 (3 Cir. 1917), as follows:

> The statute began to run when the cause of action arose, and the cause of action arose when the damage occurred. Then action might have been brought.

and, further,

> In the case of successive damages suffered day by day . . . the statute begins to run on each day's damage as it occurs. When suit is brought, the plaintiff may recover only for damages inflicted during the period of limitations immediately preceding the filing of the complaint.

While *Delta Theaters* involved a cause of action based upon a conspiracy violative of the Clayton Act's §4 (15 U.S.C. §15), the court below regarded that analysis "particularly appropriate in an action based on Section 303 of the Act for damages to plaintiff's 'business or property'" since, as the court observed, "determining the actual cause, and the date thereof, of a particular loss for the purpose of establishing the accrual date of a cause of action would normally be impossible except in simple cases where the 'acts are individually related to, and more or less contemporaneous with, the resulting damage.'"

Since the phrase "shall have accrued" is critical in the West Virginia statute of limitations, accrual of a cause of action under West Virginia decisional law becomes a pertinent inquiry.

In Pickens v. Coal River Boom & Timber Company, 66 W. Va. 10, 65 S.E. 865 (1909), the West Virginia Supreme Court held:

> When the operation of a boom causes deposit of sand in a stream, thereby injuring the grinding capacity of a mill, the mill owner may recover in actions from time to time as damage and loss occur, and is not compelled to sue for present and prospective damage in one suit, and the statute of limitations begins to run, not from the construction of the boom, but when the damage occurs in time.

Implementation of *Pickens* came in Guyan Motors v. Williams, 133 W. Va. 630, 634, 57 S.E.2d 529 (1950), where the West Virginia Court recognized that a right of action accrues to a landowner deprived of a lateral support when damage results from a defendant's act and not when the act takes place if that act does not then damage the land in question.

In Harrison v. McOwen, 126 W. Va. 933, 938, 30 S.E.2d 740, 742, the West Virginia Supreme Court, recognizing the validity of its rule in *Pickens*, stated "it is perfectly clear that the result of the alleged acts of the defendant did not happen at the actual time of the blast, but . . . when the alleged slide took place. Then the plaintiff owned this land alleged to have been damaged." . . .

Deponent, Chester Railing, testified that the plaintiff's operation had no coal orders or contracts; that plaintiff was dependent for coal orders upon Pursglove Coal Company, its broker, and that it was only when Pursglove called him daily that he knew what the orders were; that plaintiff had no price contract with Pursglove and that he and the broker "would always keep haggling about the price"; that *plaintiff's losses would go from day to day* because of the way in which the plaintiff's operation shipped and sold its coal.

This testimony is contrary to plaintiff's contention that the alleged illegal activity resulted "in irrevocable loss of coal orders and contracts." Even if there had been contracts (and Chester Railing said there were none), plaintiff's argument that "some coal orders and contracts began and ended at one time and other orders and other contracts began and ended on other dates" is consistent with Railing's testimony that losses would go from "day to day" because of the way plaintiff shipped and sold its coal. If, as admitted, losses occurred on a day-to-day basis, there was no necessity for plaintiff to make an "attempt at prophecy or projecting into the future how long the alleged illegal activities would continue." An instant remedy was available when a right of action accrued.

Furthermore, Chester Railing testified that specific items of mining machinery were dynamited and destroyed on the mine property. He fixed the dates of the occurrences. On the night of November 16, 1958, two "P & H Shovels" were destroyed and an "87 Lorraine" shovel was dynamited on July 9, 1959. . . . Damages for the destruction of this equipment are sought by plaintiff. Mr. Railing knew of the losses almost immediately after they occurred and it would be senseless to hold that the statute of limitations would not begin to operate as to such losses until the alleged unlawful activities had ceased.

I would affirm that portion of the judgment below which relates to and applies the two-year statute of limitations.

NOTES ON CONTINUING VIOLATIONS AND CONTINUING INJURIES

1. Perhaps the classic example of a continuing violation is Hanover Shoe v. United Shoe Machinery Corp., 392 U.S. 481, 502 n.15 (1968).

Hanover filed suit in 1955, alleging that United's restrictive system of distributing shoe machinery violated the antitrust laws. United argued that the claim was barred by limitations because it had applied the challenged policy to Hanover since 1912. Should United be able to continue its illegal conduct forever because no one challenged it during World War I? On the other hand, should Hanover be able to collect forty years of damages with prejudgment interest? The Court thought it obvious that Hanover could sue, but that it could recover only those damages suffered within the period of limitations. This is the day-by-day rule applied in the district court in *Railing*.

2.   Does the majority in *Railing* sufficiently distinguish the day-by-day cases? Is there any reason to believe that Railing's lost profits would be harder to measure day by day than Hanover's? The day-by-day metaphor helps explain the workings of limitations, but it exaggerates the problem of calculating damages. A single cut-off date is established by counting back from the day plaintiff filed suit. The parties would have to allocate all damages to the period before that date or the period after that date, but they would not have to allocate day by day within the two periods.

The majority suggests that the cumulative effect of the sixteen-month violation destroyed plaintiff's business. The dissent suggests that the destruction was only temporary, and that the mine is back in operation. But certainly one can imagine a case in which the business never recovered. Would that damage be impossible to allocate to any particular period? Or would it be enough to say the statute runs from the time at which it became clear that the business could never recover?

Even if lost profits and harm to the business can't be allocated, isn't the dissenter right about the destroyed equipment? There's no trouble identifying the time of that loss, is there? Is *Railing* better explained as a common-sense decision to treat all the events as a single violation when the whole period is short?

3.   The most frequently litigated issue in this area is whether the violation is continuing. Many wrongs inflict continuing harm, but they are not continuing violations because the wrong is finished immediately. The ordinary personal injury case is an obvious example; the claim accrues when the injury first occurs, even if plaintiff's damages continue to accrue for years.

Hanover Shoe noted not only that defendant continuously violated the antitrust laws, but that these violations "inflicted continuing and accumulating harm." There are three distinct requirements tucked into that formulation: The violation must continue, the harm must continue, and the continuing violation must cause the harm.

A pair of Seventh Circuit cases illustrates the causation requirement. In Baker v. F & F Investment Co., 489 F.2d 829 (7th Cir. 1973), plaintiffs alleged that they were forced to buy their homes on disadvantageous installment contracts because the FHA and VA refused to insure mortgages in black neighborhoods. The court held that the complaint alleged continuing violations that lasted until each installment contract was paid off:

> The defendants' wrongful conduct continued after the installment contracts were signed; injury to plaintiffs continued to accrue after the installment contracts were signed; and, had defendants at any time ceased their wrongful conduct, further injury to plaintiffs could have been avoided. . . . [I]f [defendants] had offered mortgage insurance at any time during the life of the installment contracts, plaintiffs could have refinanced the purchase of their homes, possibly reducing further finance charges and ending exposure to other unfavorable terms of the installment contracts. If these claims are proven, it would follow that a new injury was inflicted on plaintiffs each day until the federal defendants abandoned their discriminatory policies or the respective installment contracts were completely performed, whichever occurred first. Consequently, a new limitations period began to run each day as to that day's damage. . . . Of course, plaintiffs cannot recover . . . any items of damage which accrued [more than five years before they filed their complaint.] And they must prove that continuation of the discrimination after that date actually harmed them. It may be, for example, that a non-discriminatory mortgage at the high interest rates of the late sixties would have cost plaintiffs more than their discriminatory installment contracts entered into in the fifties.

Id. at 836.

The court distinguished Baldwin v. Loew's Inc., 312 F.2d 387 (7th Cir. 1963). Baldwin was a victim of the antitrust conspiracy described in Bigelow v. RKO Radio Pictures, supra at 170. He couldn't get good movies on good dates for his independent theater, because the theaters owned by film makers always got priority. Unable to run the theater at a profit, he leased it on unfavorable terms to a chain of theaters owned by a film maker. The first lease began in 1940 and ran five years. The second lease began in 1945, and gave the tenant options to renew for up to twenty years. The court held that the statute of limitations ran from 1945. The conspiracy continued after that date, and Baldwin's damages continued after that date. But all the damage was caused by illegal acts committed in 1945 and before. Once Baldwin committed himself for twenty years, it would not have done him any good if the conspiracy had ended the next day.

4.   The Seventh Circuit recently relied on *Railing* to allow a victim of copyright infringement to recover damages for all infringing sales if at least one of the sales was within the period of limitations. Taylor v. Meirick, 712 F.2d 1112, 1118-1119 (7th Cir. 1983). Is that a correct application of *Railing*? How could there be any problem separating early sales from later sales? The court overlooked *Railing*'s distinction between separable and inseparable damages; it said the general rule is that plaintiff can "reach back and get damages for the entire period of the alleged

violation" if any part of it occurred within the period of limitations. Id. at 1119. All the way back to 1912? Judge Posner wrote the opinion, and Judge Cummings was on the panel. The court didn't cite Cummings's opinion in Baker v. F & F Investment Co. Even more revealing, *Taylor* relied on Berkey Photo v. Eastman Kodak Co., 603 F.2d 263, 295 (2d Cir. 1979). But *Berkey* was a day-by-day case. It seems likely that *Taylor* will cause some confusion, and eventually some backpedaling, in the Seventh Circuit.

5. Often harm continues to accrue even though the violation is complete. *Baldwin* is such a case; personal injury cases are the most common example. The statute of limitations can run out before the damages are fully known. The majority in *Railing* feared that the day-by-day rule would have the same effect, forcing plaintiff to file suit before he knew how much harm he was going to suffer.

The Supreme Court offered a solution in an antitrust case applying the day-by-day rule, Zenith Radio Corp. v. Hazeltine Research, 401 U.S. 321 (1971): "In antitrust and treble-damage actions, refusal to award future profits as too speculative is equivalent to holding that no cause of action has yet accrued for any but those damages already suffered." Id. at 339.

Why should that rule be limited to antitrust actions? Consider Payton v. Abbot Laboratories, 386 Mass. 540, 437 N.E.2d 171 (1982). *Payton* was a class action by DES daughters who did not have cancer, alleging that they suffered severe emotional distress because of their increased risk of cancer. The court held that those whose distress caused physical harm with objective symptoms could recover, and that the others could not. The court also noted that by suing only for emotional distress, plaintiffs had "created a problem" for any suit by class members who subsequently got cancer. Id. at — n.8, 437 N.E.2d at 181 n.8. It cited a typical case barring second suits by plaintiffs who "split" their causes of action. Surely the court would not award damages for cancer to plaintiffs who didn't have cancer. Is there any reason not to say that the claim for emotional distress accrues when the objective symptoms occur, and a separate claim for cancer accrues if and when cancer occurs?

Courts plainly would not allow a personal injury victim to sue for periodic increments of pain and suffering, medical expenses, and lost income; for better or worse, we ask a jury to predict all that in a single trial. We examined some of the resulting problems in Jones & Laughlin Steel v. Pfeifer, supra at 198. How is that different from splitting a DES claim between emotional distress and cancer? Is it just a matter of degree? Is it just that courts award future damages for personal injury despite the difficulties, but surely wouldn't award damages for cancer not yet contracted? *Zenith* speaks only of damages that are too speculative to recover; it doesn't give plaintiff an option to sue now when the facts are clear enough or later when the facts are even clearer. Is that a reasonable place to draw the line?

One other variation: The usual problem in the personal injury cases is uncertainty about the continuing effects of a known injury. What about a personal injury claim with a risk of some dramatic new development? Many DES daughters get abnormal genital growths called adenosis; only a few get cancer. The relationship between adenosis and subsequent cancer is unknown. If an adenosis victim sues, does she jeopardize her claim for any subsequent cancer? If she gets cancer much later and sues for the first time then, has the statute of limitations run out? She knew long before that she had been injured. Suppose she waits until she has passed through the age range in which DES cancers have occurred. If she doesn't get cancer, can she breathe a sigh of relief and sue for her damages from adenosis? Or has the statute of limitations run out?

6.   Finally, reconsider Baldwin and his movie theater. If he sues in 1945, how can the court know whether the lease will expire in five years or be renewed for ten, fifteen, or twenty? Should Baldwin be able to get damages for twenty years by showing that the lease is a good deal for the tenant? Or is a better remedy an injunction against defendants' distribution policies and rescission of the lease?

In the actual case, Baldwin sued in 1953 and his claim was dismissed on limitations grounds. Should that preclude him from suing again in 1965 if the conspiracy continues? Surely the answer is no, although the footnote in Payton v. Abbot Laboratories suggests the Massachusetts court might be troubled.

NOTES ON OTHER ACCRUAL PROBLEMS

1.   Cases of continuing violations and continuing injuries focus attention on when the cause of action accrued. Auto collision cases are at the other extreme. Negligence, injury, and discovery happen almost simultaneously, and there can be no doubt when the cause of action accrued. As usual, there are some in-between cases: cases in which the violation is not continuing, but there is room for argument about when it happened.

2.   An example is Delaware State College v. Ricks, 449 U.S. 250 (1980). Ricks was an untenured college professor. In February 1973, the relevant faculty committee recommended that he be denied tenure. But it agreed to reconsider. In February 1974, it again recommended that he be denied tenure. On March 11, the faculty senate endorsed the recommendation. On March 13, the board of trustees voted to deny tenure. Ricks filed a grievance, and the board's grievance committee held a hearing in May. On June 26, the president of the college formally notified Ricks of the board's decision and offered him a terminal year — a new appointment to expire June 30, 1975. A one-year appointment to allow time for a thorough job search was customary at Delaware State. On September 12, 1974, the board denied his grievance. On April 4, 1975, he

filed a charge with the Equal Employment Opportunity Commission, alleging that he had been denied tenure because of his race. On June 30, 1975, his employment came to an end.

When did his claim accrue? The trial court said June 26, 1974, when Ricks received his formal letter from the president. On that theory, Ricks filed too late. The Third Circuit reversed. It thought the limitations should not run until June 30, 1975, the last day worked, although it did not dispute Ricks's right to file sooner. It thought the tenure decision could have been changed at any time until then, that a bright-line test was preferable, and that an employee should not have to file charges while he was still employed.

The Supreme Court reversed and reinstated the district court's judgment. It thought the decision was final enough by June 26, and that the grievance procedure was merely an alternate remedy and not part of the decision making process. It thought the last day worked completely irrelevant, because this was a case of tenure denial and not a case of discharge.

3. In Chardon v. Fernandez, 454 U.S. 6 (1981), the Court applied *Ricks* to an ordinary discharge case involving untenured employees. Even in that context, the date of notice controlled over the date of discharge.

4. Similar issues can arise anytime the elements of the cause of action do not all arise within a single day. Here is one more example from outside the employment context:

First National Bank misstated the formula it would use to calculate finance charges on its VISA cards. Did the cause of action under the Truth in Lending Act accrue when the bank made its disclosure, or when it first calculated a finance charge on plaintiff's account? In what sense was the disclosure false before a finance charge had been calculated? Goldman v. First National Bank, 532 F.2d 10, 16-22 (7th Cir.), *cert. denied*, 429 U.S. 870 (1976). The majority held that the statute ran from the time of the first finance charge; Justice Stevens dissented. (He had heard argument in the case before his appointment to the Supreme Court.)

5. The only safe course is to assume the cause of action accrued at the earliest possible date. It isn't necessary to file early and often, but it is certainly prudent to file early. Missing the statute of limitations is the biggest single source of attorney malpractice claims.

NOTES ON LIMITATIONS OF FEDERAL CLAIMS

1. Although *Railing* is a federal suit on a federal claim, it turns on a West Virginia statute of limitations. Congress has enacted no general statute of limitations. Sometimes it includes a limitations period when it creates a cause of action; often it does not. Except for Indian claims, the

courts have always rejected the implication that there is no period of limitations. Instead, they have applied the state statute of limitations for the most nearly analogous state law claim. This practice produces huge amounts of wasted litigation; each federal circuit must decide, for each state in the circuit, which statute of limitations is most nearly analogous to each cause of action in the United States Code. A good example is Garcia v. Wilson, 731 F.2d 640 (10th Cir.) (en banc), *aff'd*, 53 U.S.L.W. 4481 (1984), reviewing the decisions of all the other circuits and deciding that henceforth civil rights claims are analogous to personal injury suits.

2.   Federal courts have generally borrowed only the number of years from state statutes of limitation. They have not borrowed state tolling doctrines. In Holmberg v. Armbrecht, the Court said that federal fraudulent concealment law should apply to federal claims, even though the federal court applied a state statute of limitations.

A series of civil rights cases has created some doubts about *Holmberg*. The first of these cases was Johnson v. Railway Express Agency, 421 U.S. 454 (1975). Johnson sued for employment discrimination under the Civil Rights Acts of 1866 and 1964. Johnson did not file suit under either statute until he had exhausted the administrative remedy under the 1964 act. By that time, Tennessee's one-year statute of limitations had run on the claim under the 1866 act. He argued that the statute should be tolled, citing federal cases tolling limitations during the pendency of the same claims in another forum. But the Court disagreed. The Reconstruction era civil rights laws provide that to the extent federal law is silent, courts should apply state law. 42 U.S.C. §1988 (1982). *Johnson* held that this required application of state tolling rules as well as the state's statutory period.

Johnson may be limited to claims controlled by §1988, but some of the language was much broader. The Court said that no statute of limitations could be understood apart from its tolling rules, and implied that states with generous tolling rules might have shorter statutory periods. 421 U.S. at 463-464. That reasoning seems equally applicable to all borrowing of state limitations.

The Court has subsequently applied *Johnson* in Board of Regents v. Tomanio, 446 U.S. 478 (1980) and Chardon v. Fumero Soto, 462 U.S. 650 (1983). Both cases were controlled by §1988; *Tomanio* had more general language about the integral relationship between limitations periods and their tolling rules. None of the three cases says anything explicit about *Holmberg*. *Johnson* does note that "state law may be displaced where . . . inconsistent with the federal policy underlying the cause of action. . . ." 421 U.S. at 465.

Justice Rehnquist, who wrote *Tomanio*, dissented in *Chardon*. Plaintiff in *Chardon* was a member of the alleged class in a case in which the court denied class certification; he subsequently filed an individual claim. Rehnquist thought there was a federal rule for such cases, so that resort to §1988 was unnecessary. (See the discussion of *Chardon* and *American Pipe*, supra at 1005). He relied on *Holmberg*, citing it as another case where an established federal rule made it unncessary to borrow a state rule. A cynic might note that the federal rule would have barred the claim in *Chardon*, while the state rule allowed it to proceed; in *Johnson* and *Tomanio*, it was the other way around.

The lower court response has been mixed. Some courts assume *Holmberg* is dead; others still follow it. Some of the conflicting lower court responses are collected in Marcus, Fraudulent Concealment in Federal Court: Toward a More Disparate Standard?, 71 Geo. L.J. 829, 845-847 (1983). The First Circuit has said that even in cases controlled by §1988, it will apply state tolling rules but federal accrual rules. Rivera Fernandez v. Chardon, 648 F.2d 765 (1st Cir.), *rev'd on other grounds*, 454 U.S. 6 (1981). The Supreme Court disagreed on the content of the federal accrual rule, but no one suggested looking to a state accrual rule. On the other hand, the Sixth Circuit has cited Johnson v. Railway Express Agency, in a case not controlled by §1988, for the proposition that it should apply state accrual rules to all federal claims. Echols v. Chrysler Corp., 633 F.2d 722, 725 (6th Cir. 1980). Federal limitations law is an unsettled mess, and it is likely to remain that way as long as Congress refuses to provide federal statutes of limitations.

3.   All the discussion in this note assumes we are talking about a federal claim. If plaintiff sues in federal court on a state claim, all the elements of state limitations law applies. Guaranty Trust Co. v. York, 326 U.S. 99 (1945).

B.   MODIFYING REMEDIES BECAUSE OF CHANGED CIRCUMSTANCES

UNITED STATES v. SWIFT & CO.
286 U.S. 106 (1932)

Mr. Justice Cardozo delivered the opinion of the Court. . . .

In February, 1920, a bill was filed by the Government under §4 of the Sherman Antitrust Act, against the five leading meat-packers in the United States to dissolve a monopoly. The packers joined as defendants were Swift & Company, Armour & Company, Wilson & Company, the Morris Packing Company, and the Cudahy Packing Company, together with their subsidiaries and also their chief officers. The charge was that by concert of action the defendants had succeeded in suppressing competition both in the purchase of live stock and in the sale of dressed meats, and were even spreading their monopoly into other fields of trade. They had attained this evil eminence through agreements apportioning the percentages of live stock to which the members of the combinations were severally entitled; through the acquisition and control of stockyards and stockyard terminal railroads; through the purchase of trade papers and journals whereby cattle raisers were deprived of accurate and unbiased reports of the demand for live stock; and through other devices directed to unified control. "Having eliminated competition in the meat products, the defendants next took cognizance of the competition which might be expected" from what was characterized as "substitute foods." To that end, so it was charged, they had set about controlling the supply of "fish, vegetables, either fresh or canned, fruits, cereals, milk, poultry, butter, eggs, cheese and other substitute foods ordinarily handled by wholesale grocers or produce dealers." Through their ownership of refrigerator cars and branch houses as well as other facilities, they were in a position to distribute "substitute foods and other unrelated commodities" with substantially no increase of overhead. Whenever these advantages were inadequate, they had recourse to the expedient of fixing prices so low over temporary periods of time as to eliminate competition by rivals less favorably situated. Through these and other devices there came about in the view of the Government an unlawful monopoly of a large part of the food supply of the nation. The prayer was for an injunction appropriate to the case exhibited by the bill.

The defendants consented to dismemberment, though answering the bill and traversing its charges. With their answer there was filed a stipulation which provided for the entry of a decree upon the terms therein set forth and provided also that the decree "shall not constitute or be considered as an adjudication that the defendants, or any of them, have in fact violated any law of the United States." The decree entered on February 27, 1920, enjoined the defendants from maintaining a monopoly and from entering into or continuing any combination in restraint of trade and commerce. In addition they were enjoined both severally and jointly from (1) holding any interest in public stockyard companies, stockyard terminal railroads or market newspapers, (2) engaging in, or holding any interest in, the business of manufacturing, selling or transporting any of 114 enumerated food products, (principally fish, vegetables, fruit and groceries), and thirty other articles unrelated to the meat packing industry, (3) using or permitting others to use their distributive facilities for the handling of any of these enumerated articles, (4) selling meat at retail, (5) holding any interest in any public cold storage plant, and (6) selling fresh milk or cream. No injunction was granted in respect of the sale or distribution of poultry, butter, cheese and eggs, though these had been included in the bill among the substitute foods which the defendants were seeking to engross. The decree closed with a provision whereby jurisdiction of the cause was retained for the purpose of taking such other action or adding at the foot such other relief "as may become necessary or appropriate for the carrying out and enforcement" thereof, "and for the purpose of entertaining at any time hereafter any application which the parties may make" with reference thereto.

The expectation would have been reasonable that a decree entered upon consent would be accepted by the defendants and by those allied with them as a definitive adjudication setting controversy at rest. The events that were to follow recount a different tale. In April, 1922, the California Co-operative Canneries Corporation filed an intervening petition alleging that the effect of the injunction was to interfere with the performance by Armour & Company of a contract by which Armour had agreed to buy large quantities of California canned fruit, and praying that the decree be vacated for lack of jurisdiction. Leave to intervene was granted by the Court of Appeals of the District, which ordered "that such further proceedings thereupon be had as are necessary to determine the issue raised." In November, 1924, motions for like relief were made by Swift and by Armour, their subsidiaries and officers. The motions were denied by the Supreme Court of the District, and thereafter were considered by this court, which upheld the consent decree in the face of a vigorous assault. Swift & Co. v. United States, 276 U.S. 311. In the meantime, however, an order had been made on May 1, 1925, by the Supreme Court of the District at the instance of the California Canneries whereby the operation of the decree as a whole was suspended "until further order of the court to be made, if at all, after a full hearing on the merits according to the usual course of chancery proceedings" (see United States v. California Canneries, 279 U.S. 553, 555). This order of suspension remained in force till May, 1929, when a decision of this court swept the obstacle aside. United States v. California Canneries, supra.

The defendants and their allies had thus been thwarted in the attempt to invalidate the decree as of the date of its entry, and again the expectation would have been reasonable that there would be acquiescence in its restraints. Once more the expectation was belied by the event. The defendants, or some of them, discovered as they thought that during the years that had intervened between the entry of the decree and its final confirmation, conditions in the packing industry and in the sale of groceries and other foods had been transformed so completely that the restraints of the injunction, however appropriate and just in February, 1920, were now useless and oppressive. The discovery or supposed discovery had its fruit in the proceeding now before us. On April 12, 1930, the defendants Swift & Company and Armour & Company and their subsidiaries, being no longer under the shelter of an order suspending the injunction, filed a petition to modify the consent decree and to adapt its restraints to the needs of a new day. The prayer was that the petitioners be permitted (1) to own and operate retail meat markets; (2) to own stock in stockyard companies and terminal railroads; (3) to manufacture, sell and deal in the 144 articles specified in paragraph fourth of the decree, which for convenience will be spoken of as "groceries"; (4) to use or permit others to use their distributive facilities in handling such commodities; and one of the defendants, Swift & Company, asked in addition that the defendants be permitted to hold interests in public cold-storage warehouses and to sell fresh milk and cream. Of the five defendants named in the original suit, one, Morris & Company, sold out to Armour & Company in 1923, and discontinued business. The two other defendants, Wilson and Cudahy, did not join in the petition to modify the decree, but stated in open court that they would consent to such modification as the court might order provided it be made applicable to the defendants equally. All the requests for modification were denied except numbers 3 and 4, of which 4 is merely ancillary to 3 and calls for no separate consideration. The modification in respect of number 3 gave permission to deal at wholesale in groceries and other enumerated commodities, but maintained the injunction against dealing in them at retail. In every other respect, the decree of February 27, 1920, was continued in force as originally entered. The modifying decree, which was entered January 31, 1931, is the subject of this appeal.

We are not doubtful of the power of a court of equity to modify an injunction in adaptation to changed conditions though it was entered by consent. The power is conceded by the Government, and is challenged by the interveners only. . . . Power to modify the decree was reserved by its very terms, and so from the beginning went hand in hand with its restraints. If the reservation had been omitted, power there still would be by force of principles inherent in the jurisdiction of the chancery. A continuing decree of injunction directed to events to come is subject always to adaptation as events may shape the need. The distinction is between restraints that give protection to rights fully accrued upon facts so nearly permanent as to be substantially impervious to change, and those that involve the supervision of changing conduct or conditions and are thus provisional and tentative. The result is all one whether the decree has been entered after litigation or by consent. In either event, a court does not abdicate its power to revoke or modify its mandate if satisfied that what it has been doing has been turned through changing circumstances into an instrument of wrong. We reject the argument for the interveners that a decree entered upon consent is to be treated as a contract and not as a judicial act. A different view would not help them, for they were not parties to the contract, if any there was. All the parties to the consent decree concede the jurisdiction of the court to change it. The interveners gain nothing from the fact that the decree was a contract as to others, if it was not one as to them. But in truth what was then adjudged was not a contract as to any one. The consent is to be read as directed toward events as they then were. It was not an abandonment of the right to exact revision in the future, if revision should become necessary in adaptation to events to be.

Power to modify existing, we are brought to the question whether
enough has been shown to justify its exercise.

The defendants, controlled by experienced business men, renounced
the privilege of trading in groceries, whether in concert or independently,
and did this with their eyes open. Two reasons, and only two, for exacting
the surrender of this adjunct of the business were stated in the bill of
complaint. Whatever persuasiveness the reasons then had, is theirs with
undiminished force today.

The first was that through the ownership of refrigerator cars and
branch houses as well as other facilities, the defendants were in a position
to distribute substitute foods and other unrelated commodities with substantially no increase of overhead. There is no doubt that they are equally
in that position now. Their capacity to make such distribution cheaply by
reason of their existing facilities is one of the chief reasons why the sale of
groceries has been permitted by the modified decree, and this in the face
of the fact that it is also one of the chief reasons why the decree as
originally entered took the privilege away.

The second reason stated in the bill of complaint is the practice followed by the defendants of fixing prices for groceries so low over temporary periods of time as to eliminate competition by rivals less favorably
situated.

Whether the defendants would resume that practice if they were to
deal in groceries again, we do not know. They would certainly have the
temptation to resume it. Their low overhead and their gigantic size, even
when they are viewed as separate units, would still put them in a position
to starve out weaker rivals. Mere size, according to the holding of this
court, is not an offense against the Sherman Act unless magnified to the
point at which it amounts to a monopoly (United States v. United States
Steel Corp., 251 U.S. 417), but size carries with it an opportunity for
abuse that is not to be ignored when the opportunity is proved to have
been utilized in the past. The original decree at all events was framed
upon that theory. It was framed upon the theory that even after the
combination among the packers had been broken up and the monopoly
dissolved, the individual units would be so huge that the capacity to
engage in other forms of business as adjuncts to the sale of meats should
be taken from them altogether. It did not say that the privilege to deal in
groceries should be withdrawn for a limited time, or until the combination in respect of meats had been effectually broken up. It said that the
privilege should be renounced forever, and this whether the units within
the combination were acting collectively or singly. The combination was
to be disintegrated, but relief was not to stop with that. To curb the
aggressions of the huge units that would remain, there was to be a check
upon their power, even though acting independently, to wage a war of
extermination against dealers weaker than themselves. We do not turn
aside to inquire whether some of these restraints upon separate as distin-

guished from joint action could have been opposed with success if the defendants had offered opposition. Instead, they chose to consent, and the injunction, right or wrong, became the judgment of the court. Groceries and other enumerated articles they were not to sell at all, either by wholesale or by retail. Even the things that they were free to sell, meats and meat products, they were not to sell by retail. The court below annulled the restraint upon sales of groceries by wholesale, but retained the prohibition in respect of sale by retail both for groceries and for meats. The one prohibition equally with the other was directed against abuse of power by the individual units after the monopoly was over; and the death of the monopoly, the breaking up of the combination, if an adequate reason for terminating one of them, is an adequate reason for terminating both.

We have said that the defendants are still in a position, even when acting separately, to starve out weaker rivals, or at least that the fear of such abuses, if rational in 1920, is still rational today. The meat monopoly has been broken, for the members now compete with one another. The size of the component units is substantially unchanged. In 1929, the latest year for which any figures are furnished by the record, the sales made by Swift and Armour, each, amounted to over a billion dollars; those made by all the defendants together to over $2,500,000,000; and those made by their thirteen chief competitors to only $407,000,000. Size and past aggressions induced the fear in 1920 that the defendants, if permitted to deal in groceries, would drive their rivals to the wall. Size and past aggressions leave the fear unmoved today. Changes there have been that reduce the likelihood of a monopoly in the business of the sale of meats, but none that bear significantly upon the old-time abuses in the sale of other foods. The question is not whether a modification as to groceries can be made without prejudice to the interests of producers of cattle on the hoof. The question is whether it can be made without prejudice to the interests of the classes whom this particular restraint was intended to protect. Much is made in the defendants' argument of the rise of the chain stores to affluence and power, and especially of chains for the sale of groceries and other foods. Nothing in that development eradicates the ancient peril. Few of the chain stores produce the foods they have for sale, and then chiefly in special lines. Much, indeed most, of what they offer, they are constrained to buy from others. They look to the defendants for their meats, and if the ban of this decree is lifted, they will look to the defendants for other things as well. Meats and groceries today are retailed at the same shops, departments of a single business. The defendants, the largest packers in the country, will thus hold a post of vantage, as compared with other wholesale grocers, in their dealings with the chains. They will hold a post of vantage in their dealings with others outside the chains. When they add groceries to meats, they will do so, they assure us, with substantially no increase of the existing overhead.

Thus in the race of competition they will be able by their own admission to lay a handicap on rivals overweighted at the start. The opportunity will be their to renew the war of extermination that they waged in years gone by.

Sporadic instances of unfair practices even in the meat business are stated in the findings to have occurred since the monopoly was broken, practices as to which the defendants' officers disclaim responsibility or knowledge. It is easy to make such excuses with plausibility when a business is so huge. They become less plausible when the size of the business is moderate. Responsibility is then centered in a few. If the grocery business is added to the meat business, there may be many instances of unfair pressure upon retailers and others with the design of forcing them to buy from the defendants and not from rival grocers. Such at any rate was the rationale of the decree of 1920. Its restraints, whether just or excessive, were born of that fear. The difficulty of ferreting out these evils and repressing them when discovered supplies an additional reason why we should leave the defendants where we find them, especially since the place where we find them is the one where they agreed to be.

There is need to keep in mind steadily the limits of inquiry proper to the case before us. We are not framing a decree. We are asking ourselves whether anything has happened that will justify us now in changing a decree. The injunction, whether right or wrong, is not subject to impeachment in its application to the conditions that existed at its making. We are not at liberty to reverse under the guise of readjusting. Life is never static, and the passing of a decade has brought changes to the grocery business as it has to every other. The inquiry for us is whether the changes are so important that dangers, once substantial, have become attenuated to a shadow. No doubt the defendants will be better off if the injunction is relaxed, but they are not suffering hardship so extreme and unexpected as to justify us in saying that they are the victims of oppression. Nothing less than a clear showing of grievous wrong evoked by new and unforeseen conditions should lead us to change what was decreed after years of litigation with the consent of all concerned.

The case comes down to this: the defendants had abused their powers so grossly and persistently as to lead to the belief that even when they were acting separately, their conduct should be subjected to extraordinary restraints. There was the fear that even when so acting they would still be ready and able to crush their feebler rivals in the sale of groceries and kindred products by forms of competition too ruthless and oppressive to be accepted as fair and just. Wisely or unwisely, they submitted to these restraints upon the exercise of powers that would normally be theirs. They chose to renounce what they might otherwise have claimed, and the decree of a court confirmed the renunciation and placed it beyond recall.

What was then solemnly adjudged as a final composition of an historic litigation will not lightly be undone at the suit of the offenders, and the composition held for nothing.

The decree should be reversed and the petitions dismissed.

Reversed.

THE CHIEF JUSTICE, MR. JUSTICE SUTHERLAND and MR. JUSTICE STONE took no part in the consideration and decision of this case.

MR. JUSTICE BUTLER, dissenting.

The facts on which the District Supreme Court allowed modification of parts of the 1920 consent injunction are set forth in its findings prepared in accordance with Equity Rule No. 70½. They are discussed and amplified in a painstaking opinion contained in the record. I think they are sustained by the evidence and are sufficient to support the decree.

Conditions affecting competition in the lines of business carried on by defendants have changed since 1920. Indeed, the Government, after the introduction of evidence by appellees, formally stipulated that they "are in active competition with each other" etc. The facts negative any suggestion that danger of monopolistic control now exists. Each of the principal packers has suffered discouraging operating losses. One of them, retiring from business, sold its plants to another. The purchaser, in order to avoid failure, was compelled to refinance and has not earned reasonable profits in any year. Another, being embarrassed, passed into the hands of a receiver, was subsequently adjudged bankrupt and later reorganized. Only two have continued able to sustain themselves. It is shown without dispute that defendants' earnings, whether considered in relation to sales or to the worth of property invested, are low and substantially less than those of others carrying on the same lines of business.

Since 1920 the manufacture and distribution of food have grown greatly and to a large extent have come to be carried on by integrated concerns in strong hands, which have taken over and are handling many products from the sources of production to consumers. More and more, meat — formerly distributed through shops selling little if anything else — is sold in stores carrying groceries and other articles of food. The diversification of the business of defendants permitted by the modification of the injunction is in harmony with present legitimate tendencies in the business of producing and selling meat, groceries and other articles of food. In all branches of such activities there is strong and active competition. The use by defendants of their employees and facilities for the sale and distribution of groceries as well as meat would not give them any undue advantage over their competitors. Under present conditions the relief granted below would not enable them to inflict the evils of monopoly upon any part of the food industry. The denial of that relief makes against competition intended to be preserved by the Sherman Act. Defendants should be permitted more efficiently to use their help and equipment to lessen their operating expenses. That makes for lower prices and so is in the public interest.

The wholesale grocers, represented here by objecting interveners, are not entitled to the court's protection against the competition of non-members or of defendants carrying on separately and competing actively. They may not avoid the burden of sustaining themselves in a free and open market by protestation of fear that, if allowed to engage in the grocery business at all, defendants will unfairly compete in violation of the federal antitrust laws. If and whenever shown necessary for the protection of the commerce safeguarded by the original decree, the Government may have the modified provisions restored or new ones added.

There is nothing in the original complaint that makes for reversal here. The Government's allegations were denied by answer. The decree was entered without evidence or findings pursuant to a written stipulation between the Government and the defendants expressly providing that "this stipulation shall not constitute or be considered as an admission, and the rendition or entry of the decree, or the decree itself, shall not constitute or be considered as an adjudication that the defendants, or any of them, have in fact violated any law of the United States." And that provision was in exact words incorporated in and made a part of the decree. Thus the Government consented to, and the court adopted, this provision quite as much as the defendants consented to the other parts of the decree. . . .

I am authorized to say that MR. JUSTICE VAN DEVANTER concurs in this opinion.

NOTES ON MODIFYING JUDGMENTS

1. Why are injunctions more subject to modification than damage judgments? Cardozo gives the obvious answer: that injunctions speak to the future, and justice requires some mechanism for responding to changing conditions. But that answer is insufficient. Many damage judgments also speak to the future, as when juries predict the rate of inflation, or the duration of plaintiff's disability. No one can foresee the future on these questions either, and injustice results if the jury's prediction is inaccurate. Yet the judgment based on the jury's prediction cannot be modified. There is nothing inherent about that practice; the judgment could be modifiable, or it could provide for periodic payments in light of developments. Medical expenses under workers' compensation statutes are generally handled that way, and so is child support, which has its origins in ecclesiastical courts and courts of equity instead of common law.

2. Modifiable judgments or periodic payments have obvious costs in terms of continued litigation. Courts are much more willing to pay those

costs with respect to equitable remedies. Part of the reason may just be the separate traditions of law and equity. Is there any modern justification for the difference?

3.   One possibility is that an injunction that has become unduly harsh or restrictive does more harm than a damage judgment that has turned out to be erroneous. The obsolete injunction may require socially wasteful conduct or forbearance, or it may harm defendant much more than it helps plaintiff. The erroneous damage judgment usually causes a simple transfer payment with no net social consequences. If defendant paid too much, he has suffered his loss and gone on to other things; that is not true if he is still under an overly restrictive injunction.

4.   Once again the distinction between damages and injunctions is not as sharp as the conventional wisdom, but it may be sharp enough. As we saw in chapter 11, damages as well as injunctions can impose undue hardship. And permanent damages for a continuing wrong, as in Boomer v. Atlantic Cement, supra at 908, can license continuing harm and eliminate any incentive to avoid the harm. This problem arises whether the jury predicts damages accurately or inaccurately; it is the inevitable result of permanent damages for a continuing wrong. The problem can be avoided by requiring plaintiff to sue repeatedly for each new increment of damage. Courts required that in cases of temporary nuisance — cases where it was plausible to believe the nuisance might be removed. The temporary nuisance cases are an important example of common law courts measuring damages periodically in light of new developments.

How are they different from the permanent nuisance and personal injury cases? In all these cases there is uncertainty about future damages. But only in the temporary nuisance cases is there uncertainty about future wrongdoing. In the personal injury cases the wrong is over, and in the permanent nuisance cases, the wrong is assumed to be permanent.

5.   Federal Rule 60 authorizes motions to modify judgments. It notes the traditional grounds for modification; to say that it codifies them would be an overstatement. Several of the grounds relate to various errors in the conduct of the litigation: clerical mistakes, mistake, inadvertence, surprise, or excusable neglect, newly discovered evidence, fraud, misrepresentation, or other misconduct. These grounds must be asserted within one year. Some relate to very specific subsequent developments: if the judgment has been paid, released, or discharged, or if it were based on an earlier judgment that has been reversed or vacated. Another applies to void judgments — mainly those issued without jurisdiction. There is a catchall provision for "any other reason justifying relief." Rule 60(b)(6).

The power to modify injunctions is reflected in Rule 60(b)(5), which authorizes modification if "it is no longer equitable that the judgment should have prospective application." This is the only ground examined in this chapter.

A CASE STUDY: NOTES ON THE
MEATPACKER DECREE

1.   The meatpackers were in federal court for most of this century. The Supreme Court's first encounter came in Swift & Co. v. United States, 196 U.S. 375 (1905). The government alleged that the packers had conspired to fix the prices they would pay and the prices they would charge. Defendants did not deny the allegations. The trial court enjoined further price fixing, and the Supreme Court affirmed.

2.   The 1905 decree did not end defendants' domination of the industry. In part it appears not to have been enforced; in part, the packers found means other than price fixing to control the market. The profits of the Big Five packers in 1917 equaled their net worth in 1904. President Wilson directed the Federal Trade Commission to investigate, and its report led to the government's 1920 complaint. The new complaint alleged that the monopoly could be ended only by changing the structure of the industry. The government asked that the packers be ordered to sell their collateral businesses and their distribution facilities. Their meatpacking business would be left intact, but all vertical integration would be forbidden. Defendants would have to rely on independent distributors, independent retailers, and independent stockyards. The case was settled before it was filed.

3.   As Cardozo notes, the packers began to attack the decree almost as soon as they consented to it. The case returned to the Supreme Court in 1928, 1929, and 1932. We can only speculate about why they reneged so quickly, but there is an obvious focus for such speculation. The decree was entered on February 27, 1920. On March 1, the Supreme Court decided United States v. U.S. Steel Corp., 251 U.S. 417 (1920). Certainly both the government and the packers knew the case was pending, and quite possibly much of the impetus to settle came from the risks the case posed to each side.

The district court had found that U.S. Steel dominated the steel industry, and that much of its dominance had been acquired by combining with some competitors and fixing prices with the others. But it also found that the company was no longer actively violating the antitrust laws. The government argued that U.S. Steel's size was the fruit of its past violations, and that the company no longer needed to fix prices because its remaining competitors had no choice but to follow its price leadership. It argued that U.S. Steel should be broken up. It noted that the Supreme Court had not merely ordered American Tobacco and Standard Oil to quit their illegal activities; those companies had been broken up into separate competitors. The government wanted the same remedy for U.S. Steel, but the district court denied relief.

U.S. Steel was obviously relevant to the meatpackers' case. Both sides apparently believed that the packers could maintain their dominance without overt price fixing. If U.S. Steel were broken up to deprive it of the fruits of past price fixing, probably the packers would be broken up as well. If U.S. Steel won, the government could try to distinguish the packers case, but its claim for dissolution would have suffered a serious blow. With U.S. Steel hanging over them, both sides settled for partial dissolution: The packers gave up retailing and most of their collateral businesses in exchange for keeping intact their meatpacking and distribution facilities.

Two days later, the Court affirmed U.S. Steel by a vote of four to three. The majority thought that size alone did not violate the antitrust laws if size were not abused. That present size was a product of past violations was irrelevant; in American Tobacco and Standard Oil, the past violations had been much more egregious. The dissenters would have followed "the well settled practice . . . requiring the dissolution of combinations made in direct violation of the law." 251 U.S. at 458 (Day, J., dissenting).

4.   If we assume that both sides settled for fear of U.S. Steel, should that make any difference to defendants' motion to modify? What if we assume the dissenters were right and that U.S. Steel sharply changed the law? Should the packers be forever barred from collateral businesses if similar relief would be unavailable in any other industry? If the Court modified to avoid that anomaly, wouldn't it also have to modify in the government's direction if U.S. Steel were decided the other way? Why should domination of meatpacking be forever immunized if similar domination could be barred in any other industry? But if the Court said both of those things, what would be left of the consent decree? If a consent decree can be modified as soon as the law is clarified, isn't it futile to settle to avoid the risks of uncertain law?

The standard rule is that a decree can be modified for change in law as well as change in facts. System Federation No. 91 v. Wright, 364 U.S. 642 (1961). We will explore that proposition further in the notes to Pasadena Board of Education v. Spangler, infra at 1047. But the packers did not rely on change in law when they moved to modify.

5.   In 1948 the government filed a new suit seeking to break up the separate meatpacking businesses of the remaining four defendants. The trial court ruled that the government could not rely on any events prior to 1930, when defendants filed their motion to modify. Because the government couldn't prove its case under those conditions, it voluntarily dismissed the action. This litigation is unreported, but it is summarized in United States v. Swift & Co., 189 F. Supp. 885, 907 (N.D. Ill. 1960).

Did the court apply the right standard? Surely the government consented not to seek further relief for violations before the original decree in 1920. But why couldn't it rely on events from the 1920s? Cardozo's opinion held that nothing in the 1920s justified letting defendants sell groceries. Did he also hold that defendants did nothing illegal in the 1920s?

The other obstacle to relying on events from the 1920s and 1930s would be laches and statute of limitations. Recall that they don't apply to the government in its sovereign capacity. Even if they did, the government would presumably claim that market dominance derived from egregious illegal acts was a continuing violation. Once again, *U.S. Steel* would be relevant.

6.   In the late 1950s defendants again moved to modify. The case was transferred to the Northern District of Illinois, and Judge Julius Hoffman heard three and a half months of testimony, admitted more than one thousand exhibits, and received a thousand pages of briefs. His opinion clarifies both the legal standard and the procedure for factfinding announced in Cardozo's opinion. Some excerpts:

> [T]he continued need for the decree and the hardship suffered by the defendants are neither alternative standards for modification, either of which will suffice, as the defendants submit, nor cumulative prerequisites, both of which must be established, as the government claims. As need is diminished, a lesser showing of hardship will tip the scales in favor of modification, and as the defendants' suffering increases, their burden of showing decreased need is correspondingly lightened.

United States v. Swift & Co., 189 F. Supp. 885, 905 (N.D. Ill. 1960), *aff'd mem.*, 367 U.S. 909 (1961).

> The fact that a decree is entered by consent rather than upon litigation does not deprive the court of power to modify. . . . The difference has a profound effect, however, upon the task of the judge in ruling upon a request for modification. Here no evidence was introduced. . . . No findings of fact were made, and no opinion was delivered to explain the legal purposes of the decree. Any attempt to determine now exactly what facts existed in 1920 would be difficult at least, and even if it were possible, the process would involve a trial of issues which the parties solemnly agreed need not be tried. . . .
>
> The task of decision is doubly hypothetical since an unknown past must be compared with a speculative future, involving a prediction of what action the petitioners might take if the decree were relaxed. Nonetheless, if modification is to be possible without impeachment of the decree, its reasons must be identified from the best evidence available. At the same time, unless the solemn judicial act taken upon the considered consent of all the parties is to be stultified, the decree must enjoy a solid presumption that it was founded on fact and supported by reason.

Id. at 905-906.

It didn't matter if the decree were in fact unjustified; "defendants' mistake in giving consent will remain beyond recall" until the standards for modification are met.

If a composition reached after full and deliberate consideration may be set for nought simply because one of the parties on second thought believes he would have fared better at trial, the decree becomes nothing more than a continuance or postponement of the trial, and the mutual benefits which induce this form of disposition will be lost.

Id. at 906-907.

The defendants can gain nothing from the recital in their stipulations to the decree that they consented upon condition that its entry should not be considered an admission or the decree an adjudication that they had in fact violated any law of the United States. By their consent, they relinquished their right to insist that an offense be proved, and the right to show that no violation had been committed. Having accepted a decree drawn on the theory of a violation of the antitrust laws, they cannot now vacate or modify the decree on the ground that the theory was unsound.

Id. at 907.

Like Cardozo, Hoffman looked to the complaint to determine the reasons for the consent decree. But he did not stop there:

[P]leadings in antitrust cases are necessarily general and conclusory. The government is not obliged to set forth all the reasons upon which it relies, and the fact that any appeared was largely fortuitous.

Id. at 908.

Judge Hoffman then tried to draw inferences from the decree itself. He asked what hypothetical conditions would support the restrictions found in the decree. For example, Paragraph Three said defendants could not use their distribution systems for groceries. Paragraph Four said they could not sell groceries. These were independent restrictions; they couldn't sell groceries even if they didn't use the distribution systems. Thus, Hoffman concluded, it was irrelevant that they had largely abandoned their distribution systems, and that the parts that remained were not suited to groceries. The purpose of the decree must have been to keep them out of groceries for as long as they dominated meats.

How reliable is that sort of reasoning? Surely there are other possible explanations for Paragraphs Three and Four. Perhaps the distribution systems were the only reason the government wanted defendants kept out of the grocery business, but the prohibition was absolute because no one on either side could foresee the decline of the distribution systems. Paragraph Three might be a prophylactic backup to Paragraph Four, to prevent defendants from letting "independent" grocery companies use their distribution systems. Cardozo thought Four was "merely ancillary" to Three. Is there any way for a judge to choose between such competing explanations?

7. Judge Hoffman was less persuasive on the facts than he was on the law. He found that defendants still dominated the meat business. Swift and Armour were still the Big Two, but five competitors were now as large as Cudahy. Should that be enough to get Cudahy out from under the injunction? Hoffman didn't think so.

He thought that despite the continued growth of retail chains and cooperative buying associations, and the decline of defendants' distribution systems, there was still a risk that combined sales of meat and groceries would give defendants a competitive advantage. He thought that "offering a full line of products and the economies resulting from large volume and combined managerial and sales staffs would afford the defendants a competitive advantage similar to that which has largely eliminated the butcher shop, the green grocer, and the baker shop from the retail trade." Id. at 912. It was true that defendants handled their few permitted grocery items through divisions separate from their meat operations, and that none of their competitors had found it advantageous to combine the sale of meats and groceries. But the danger was not yet "attenuated to a shadow."

He thought that any hardships were either foreseen or not traceable to the decree:

> [I]t is not enough that the petitioners' profits have been modest, or that other concerns in the food industry have enjoyed greater returns and more rapid growth. To the extent that the petitioners' hardship is only the denial of the opportunity to diversify into more rewarding branches of the food industry, the burden is not new or unforeseen, but was specifically contemplated in the framing of the decree. . . . To the extent the defendants' difficulties, and particularly those of Cudahy, are attributable to causes other than the decree, they may bear on the question of the continued need for the decree, but do not establish hardship.

Id.

Judge Hoffman denied all relief, and the Supreme Court summarily affirmed. 367 U.S. 909 (1961).

8. In the late 1960s, Greyhound Corp. bought a controlling interest in Armour. The government sued to undo the acquisition, arguing that Greyhound sold groceries, and that the acquisition would create a relationship forbidden by the 1920 consent decree. Greyhound owned two subsidiaries that sold products forbidden to Armour. One ran food services for factories, schools, hospitals, and similar places; the other ran restaurants in bus stations and at stops along Greyhound's bus routes. These subsidiaries had combined sales of $110 million in 1968; Armour's sales had been $2 billion in 1960.

The government conceded that Greyhound was not in contempt, because it was not a party to the decree. But it argued that Greyhound should be enjoined from interfering with the decree. The Supreme Court viewed its task as deciding what the decree meant.

The decree prohibited Armour from buying a majority of a grocery company, but it said nothing about a grocery company buying Armour. It prohibited named stockholders in 1920 from buying control of a grocery company, but it said nothing about their successors and assigns. The government conceded all of that. But it argued that the plain purpose of the decree was to keep Armour out of the grocery business, and that that purpose was thwarted just as effectively whether Armour bought Greyhound or Greyhound bought Armour.

The majority disagreed:

> [T]he *decree* itself cannot be said to have a purpose; rather the *parties* have purposes, generally opposed to each other, and the resultant decree embodies as much of those opposing purposes as the respective parties have the bargaining power and skill to achieve. For these reasons, the scope of a consent decree must be discerned within its four corners, and not by reference to what might satisfy the purposes of one of the parties to it.

United States v. Armour & Co., 402 U.S. 673, 681-682 (1971).

How can the decree have a purpose when the Court is deciding whether to modify it, if it has no purpose when the Court is deciding how to construe it? If the courts can deduce the decree's purpose from the four corners on a motion to modify, why not on a motion to construe?

The Court also said that the government could move to modify the decree to prevent Greyhound from acquiring Armour. How should the Court decide that motion? Surely it's not just a matter of changing the label on the government's petition. Must the government argue that no one foresaw the possibility that a grocery company might buy Armour? Won't Armour respond that the parties appear to have carefully bargained to avoid restricting subsequent stockholders?

The decision was four to three. The dissenters argued that when Greyhound acquired Armour, it acquired Armour's legal disabilities, and one of those disabilities was that it couldn't sell groceries.

9. The meatpackers consent decree was gradually dismantled in a series of consent orders in the 1970s and 1980s. Judge Hoffman held a hearing each time, and from 1975 on, he required the parties to publish each proposed modification with notice of the hearing. On November 23, 1981, he vacated all remnants of the decree on joint motion of the government and the defendants. The move came as part of the Reagan administration's review of 1,200 outstanding antitrust injunctions. The modifications and final dismissal are all reported as United States v. Swift & Co. They appear at 1982-1 Trade Cases ¶64,464 (N.D. Ill. 1981); 1983-1 Trade Cases ¶65,250 (N.D. Ill. 1980); 1980-1 Trade Cases ¶63,185 (N.D. Ill. 1980); 1975-1 Trade Cases ¶60,201 (N.D. Ill. 1975); 1971 Trade Cases ¶73,760 (N.D. Ill. 1971).

10.   Two changes contributed to the steady erosion and final elimination of the consent decree. One was that defendants no longer dominated the industry. Swift's market share had declined from 17 percent in 1920 and 1956 to 6 percent in 1980. The other defendants had suffered similar declines. Indeed, the Reagan administration thought that Armour was "struggling for survival" against larger nonunion packers. Newsweek, August 29, 1983, p.51.

The other change was a change in legal attitude. The decree kept the meatpackers out of the grocery business for fear some competitive advantage would let them sell cheaper groceries. But a major purpose of the antitrust laws is to let competition hold down prices. It was clear the decree protected grocers from competition; it was not at all clear it protected the public. The original fear was that the packers would use their distribution advantages to drive out competition and then raise grocery prices to monopoly levels. As Judge Hoffman said in 1960:

> [O]ne of the many paradoxes of the Sherman act [is] that it is sometimes necessary to restrict competition in order to preserve it. The elimination of three or four competitors from the general food industry can hardly be said to harm the public interest, and to whatever extent the defendants would be a significant competitive power in the field, the fears which gave birth to the decree are confirmed.

United States v. Swift & Co., 189 F. Supp. 885, 912-913 (N.D. Ill. 1960), aff'd mem., 367 U.S. 909 (1961).

The original fear wasn't very likely even in 1932, and as the grocery chains and conglomerate food processors like Safeway and General Mills grew stronger, the danger "attenuated to a shadow." The growth of strong competitors in the food industry can be described as a change of fact. But the change in legal attitude was equally significant. Today's antitrust enforcers are much more skeptical of Judge Hoffman's paradox. Especially the Reagan administration's antitrust people think that excluding competition almost never serves antitrust policy. If nothing else had changed, should that change of attitude be ground for modification? Even if the government doesn't consent to the change?

NOTES ON STATUTORY REFORM OF ANTITRUST CONSENT DECREES

1.   In 1974 Congress enacted the Antitrust Procedures and Penalties Act to regulate antitrust consent decrees. 15 U.S.C. §16(b)-(h) (1982). Allegations that the Nixon administration had entered into favorable antitrust settlements in exchange for large campaign contributions led to the act. The act makes it impossible to file a complaint, answer, and

proposed decree and have the judge sign it all in one day, as was done in the meatpackers case. Now the government must file a competitive impact statement and publish it in the Federal Register. The statement must describe the "nature and purpose of the proceeding," the "practices or events giving rise to the alleged violation," the proposed consent decree and its "anticipated effects on competition," the remedies available to private plaintiffs, the procedures available for modification of the consent decree, and a "description and evaluation of alternatives" to the consent decree "actually considered by the United States." Summaries of the competitive impact statement must be published in newspapers. After a sixty-day period for public comments, the court must hold a hearing and determine whether the consent decree is in the public interest.

The act does not apply to modifications, but Judge Hoffman used quite similar procedures on his own authority in reviewing the agreed modifications of the meatpackers decree. Other judges have followed his example. The act also does not apply to consent decrees in any area other than antitrust.

Courts have always had power to refuse to approve consent decrees, but this statute encourages them to use it. Some of them will. The district judge demanded substantial changes in the consent decree that broke up American Telephone and Telegraph.

2. When a consent decree entered under the act comes up for interpretation or modification, there will be a competitive impact statement, public comments, the government's response to the public comments, the record of a trial on whether the decree serves the public interest, and an opinion supporting the decree. What will that do to the *Armour* case? Will it still be true that the decree has no purpose?

What will it do to motions to modify? There will be vastly more information about conditions at the time of the decree; it should no longer be necessary to draw hazy inferences from the complaint and decree.

UNITED STATES v. UNITED SHOE MACHINERY CORP.
391 U.S. 244 (1968)

Mr. Justice Fortas delivered the opinion of the Court.

In 1953, in a civil suit brought by the United States, the District Court for the District of Massachusetts held that appellee had violated §2 of the Sherman Antitrust Act by monopolizing the manufacture of shoe machinery. The court found that "(1) defendant has, and exercises, such overwhelming strength in the shoe machinery market that it controls that market, (2) this strength excludes some potential, and limits some actual, competition, and (3) this strength is not attributable solely to defendant's ability, economies of scale, research, natural advantages, and adaptation to inevitable economic laws." United States v. United Shoe Machinery Corp., 110 F. Supp. 295, 343 (1953). The court did not order the relief requested by the Government — that appellee be dissolved into three separate shoe machinery manufacturing companies. Rather, the court imposed a variety of restrictions and conditions designed "to recreate a competitive market." Appellee appealed to this Court, which affirmed the decision of the District Court. United Shoe Machinery Corp. v. United States, 347 U.S. 521 (1954).

The decree of the District Court, entered on February 18, 1953, and subsequently modified on July 12 and September 17, 1954, provided in paragraph 18 that:

> On [January 1, 1965] both parties shall report to this Court the effect of this decree, and may then petition for its modification, in view of its effect in establishing workable competition. If either party takes advantage of this paragraph by filing a petition, each such petition shall be accompanied by affidavits setting forth the then structure of the shoe machinery market and defendant's power within that market.

110 F. Supp., at 354. Pursuant to this provision, the Government reported to the District Court on January 1, 1965, that appellee continued to dominate the shoe machinery market, that workable competition had not been established in that market, and that additional relief was accordingly necessary. The Government asked that appellee be required to submit to the Court a plan, pursuant to which United's business would be reconstituted so as to form two fully competing companies in the shoe machinery market. It also requested "such other and further relief as may be necessary to establish workable competition in the shoe machinery market."

The District Court, after a hearing, denied the Government's petition. It held that under United States v. Swift & Co., 286 U.S. 106 (1932), its power to modify the original decree was limited to cases involving "(1) a clear showing of (2) grievous wrong (3) evoked by new and unforeseen conditions." United States v. United Shoe Machinery Corp., 266 F. Supp. 328, 330 (1967). Analyzing its 1953 decree, as amended, the court said that the object of the decree was "not to restore so-called workable competition but to move toward establishing it," and that "the 1953 decree has operated in the manner and with the effect intended. It has put in motion forces which, aided by new technology, have eroded United's power and already dissipated much of the effect of United's monopolization." 266 F. Supp., at 330, 334. Accordingly, in view of the stringent requirements of Swift as the court construed that decision, the District Court denied the Government's petition. . . .

I

The District Court misconceived the thrust of this Court's decision in
Swift. . . . *Swift* teaches that a decree may be changed upon an appropriate showing, and it holds that it may *not* be changed in the interests of
the defendants if the purposes of the litigation as incorporated in the
decree (the elimination of monopoly and restrictive practices) have not
been fully achieved.

The present case is the obverse of the situation in *Swift* if the Government's allegations are proved. Here, the Government claims that the
provisions of the decree were specifically designed to achieve the establishment of "workable competition" by various means and that the decree
has failed to accomplish this result. Because time and experience have
demonstrated this fact, according to the Government, it seeks modification of the decree. Nothing in *Swift* precludes this. In *Swift*, the defendants sought relief not to achieve the purposes of the provisions of the
decree, but to escape their impact. Accordingly, we conclude that the
District Court erred in denying the Government's petition "on the authority of United States v. Swift & Co., 286 U.S. 106, 119." 266 F. Supp.
at 334.

II

Decision as to the Government's petition to modify the decree in the
present case must be based upon the specific facts and circumstances that
are presented. In urging affirmance of the 1953 decision, the Government advised this Court that, in framing the decree, the District Court
had "proceeded on the premise that relatively mild remedies should be
tried as a first resort, and that the possibility of more drastic measures
should be held in abeyance." Paragraph 18 of the decree appeared to be
in confirmation of this statement since it expressly required a report after
10 years of experience under the decree and contemplated that petitions
for modification might be filed "in view of [the decree's] effect in establishing workable competition." Paragraph 18 then specifically provided
that any such petition would have to be accompanied by "affidavits setting forth the then structure of the shoe machinery market and defendant's power within that market."

These specifications were peculiarly apt because this is a monopoly
case under §2 of the Sherman Act and because the decree was shaped in
response to findings of monopolization of the shoe machinery market.
That the purpose of the 1953 decree was to eliminate this unlawful market domination was made clear beyond question by the District Court's
statement at the beginning of the section of its opinion dealing with relief.
This read as follows:

> Where a defendant has monopolized commerce in violation of §2, the
> principal objects of the decrees are to extirpate practices that have caused or

may hereafter cause monopolization, and to restore workable competition in the market.

110 F. Supp., at 346-347.

It is of course established that, in a §2 case, upon appropriate findings of violation, it is the duty of the court to prescribe relief which will terminate the illegal monopoly, deny to the defendant the fruits of its statutory violation, and ensure that there remain no practices likely to result in monopolization in the future. The trial court is charged with inescapable responsibility to achieve this objective, although it may, if circumstances warrant, accept a formula for achieving the result by means less drastic than immediate dissolution or divestiture. The decree in the present case was carefully devised within the limits of this principle. Measures short of divestiture were prescribed with provisions for review and possible revision after 10 years.

The District Court has now denied the Government's petition for modification of the decree on the ground that the decree is "still working at its long-range task of freeing the market from all consequences of United's monopolization and keeping the door wide open for the arrival of an adequately provided challenger." According to the court, this was the intended effect of the decree.

If the decree had not contained paragraph 18 — if it had been silent as to the time for submitting reports and, if necessary, petitions for modification — and if after 10 years it were shown that the decree had not achieved the adequate relief to which the Government is entitled in a §2 case, it would have been the duty of the court to modify the decree so as to assure the complete extirpation of the illegal monopoly. The court's power to do this is clear. Its duty is implicit in the findings of violation of §2 and in the decisions of this Court as to the type of remedy which must be prescribed.

We find nothing in the 1953 decree, as amended, or in the District Court's opinion relating thereto which presents an obstacle or embarrassment to the application of this principle in the present case. If the decree has not, after 10 years, achieved its "principal objects," namely, "to extirpate practices that have caused or may hereafter cause monopolization, and to restore workable competition in the market" — the time has come to prescribe other, and if necessary more definitive, means to achieve the result. A decade is enough. Even if we should assume that paragraph 18, as the District Court now states, had only the limited purpose of calling for a 10-year report as to whether the decree was "gradually eroding United's 1953 power to monopolize the market," its specific provisions did not exhaust the District Court's power. Relief in a Sherman Act case "should put an end to the combination and deprive the defendants of any of the benefits of the illegal conduct, and break up or render impotent the monopoly power found to be in violation of the Act." United States v. Grinnell Corp., 384 U.S. 563, 577 (1966). The District Court should proceed to determine whether the relief in this case has met the standards which this Court has prescribed. If it has not, the District Court should modify the decree so as to achieve the required result with all appropriate expedition.

It is so ordered.

MR. JUSTICE MARSHALL took no part in the consideration or decision of this case.

NOTES ON MODIFICATION AT THE REQUEST OF PLAINTIFF

1. What is the standard for modification in *United Shoe*? Has anything changed since 1955? Perhaps the decree isn't working because of some new and unforeseen circumstance; perhaps it isn't working because it never had a chance to work — because the government simply didn't get enough relief. Does the reason matter?

The Court seems to read the 1955 judgment as deciding competition should be restored to the industry. If that were the decision, and the restrictions on United's practices were merely one means, then ordering dissolution in 1968 will not overrule anything decided in 1955. But what if the 1955 decision had been more specific? What if the court had decided that the government's case did not justify dissolution? Should that prevent dissolution in 1968? Should it require the government to prove a violation since 1955 that justifies dissolution? Shouldn't the injunction have some res judicata consequences for the government? What if the court had decided that United had no monopoly and that most of its practices were legal? Wouldn't that be res judicata?

2. What if the 1955 injunction had been entered by consent? Then what should the government have to show to modify it? The court would no longer be obligated to restore competitive conditions, because no one would have proven a monopoly. Should plaintiffs seek recitals about what consent decrees are intended to accomplish? Should defendants resist such recitals?

3. Compare *United Shoe* with International Union of Mine, Mill & Smelter Workers, Local 15 v. Eagle-Picher Mining & Smelting Co., 325 U.S. 335 (1945). Eagle-Picher refused to reinstate a large number of strikers at the end of a strike. The National Labor Relations Board found illegal discrimination against 209 of the strikers. It ordered them reinstated, and it ordered the company to pay back pay according to a formula in the board's order. Eagle-Picher had substantially curtailed its operations after the strike. The board's opinion said that it wanted to restore the victims to the position they would have occupied but for the wrong as nearly as possible, but it believed there would not have been

jobs for many of the 209 victims even if there had been no discrimination. Consequently, it devised a pro rata back pay formula.

The court of appeals enforced the order, so that it became an injunction of the court. Eagle-Picher offered reinstatement to the 209 victims. That made it possible to compute back pay under the board's formula, and Eagle-Picher reported that it owed only $5,400 — about $26 per victim. When it audited Eagle-Picher's calculations, the board discovered that despite the reduction in its operations, Eagle-Picher had had plenty of openings and all 209 victims could have worked continuously from the end of the strike. It also discovered some serious arithmetic errors in its formula. A large group of employees was included in the denominator but inadvertently excluded from the numerator; that greatly reduced the pro rata fraction on which the award was based. The order allowed the victim's earnings at other jobs to be deducted in full although their losses were to be compensated pro rata. The board concluded that the victims' losses totaled $800,000, or about $3,800 each.

The board asked the court of appeals to vacate the back pay part of its order so the board could reconsider it. The board did not accuse Eagle-Picher of fraud, but it said that if Eagle-Picher had explained its situation in more detail, the board would not have made such a mistake. Now that it understood the facts, it wanted to correct its order. The court of appeals denied the request and the Supreme Court affirmed.

The majority opinion is somewhat cryptic. The Court apparently thought the board was claiming an unrestrained power to reconsider its orders whenever it chose; it indignantly rejected the notion. It acknowledged that the board could bring a bill of review to reopen the judgment for fraud or mistake, but it said that was not what the board sought. It is impossible to know what would have happened on a bill of review, but the Court implied that if the board had all the facts, its own mistakes in applying those facts would not count. The Court did not discuss *Swift* or other cases on modifying prospective decrees.

The four dissenters relied heavily on the power to modify prospective decrees. They thought this decree was prospective because the amount of back pay depended in part on future events — on the day Eagle-Picher finally reinstated all the victims, on the total wages it paid up to that day, on the number of applications it received from victims and non-victims up to that day. They thought the decree was not final until "the Board or the courts were satisfied with the application of the formula to the actual facts or until the formula ripened into an executed decree." 325 U.S. at 353 (Murphy, J., dissenting). They would have applied a "reasonableness" standard to requests by the Board to reopen such decrees. Id. at 355.

4. Is *United Shoe* consistent with *Eagle-Picher*? Didn't the *Eagle-Picher* decree even more obviously fail of its purpose? The government was the plaintiff in both cases. The *Eagle-Picher* decree recited its pur-

pose to make the victims whole, but that didn't help. Is it just the difference between money judgments and injunctions again? Even though the
Eagle-Picher decree was prospective when entered, it was no longer prospective when the board sought to modify it. By that time, all back pay
liability had accrued; the parties were arguing over the amount of compensation for a past loss.

5.   Assuming that finality rules should be relaxed for injunctions, why
shouldn't the relaxation be equal for both sides? What is the justification
for *United Shoe*'s distinction between modifications sought by plaintiffs
and modifications sought by defendants? There is no similar distinction in
the res judicata rules applied to money judgments. A judgment for
$10,000 determines "no more than $10,000" just as finally as it determines
"no less." Why shouldn't an injunction have a similarly balanced res
judicata effect?

6.   Part of the answer is that applying the *Swift* standards to all modifications would destroy the working method of the modern equity court. A
modifiable injunction is a much more powerful and effective tool than a
nonmodifiable injunction. It enables a judge to make a series of orders
instead of only one. He can learn by trial and error, adjust the decree in
light of experience, fill loopholes in the original order, and respond more
flexibly to recalcitrance. Consider the four trials in Hutto v. Finney,
supra at 274, and the long series of orders in Milliken v. Bradley, supra at
261, 269, and 758. It is understood in such cases that the first injunction
is merely a start, and that a long series of supplemental orders will follow.
It is hard to see the difference between a modification, a supplemental
decree, a "clarification" that expands the scope of the injunction, and a
contempt order that directs defendants to purge their contempt by complying with new and more specific restrictions.

7.   Why should only plaintiffs get the benefit of experience with the
injunction? If the modern equity court improves its injunctions in light of
experience, why shouldn't both sides be able to call on that experience?
The next case suggests that perhaps they can.

KING-SEELEY THERMOS CO. v.
ALADDIN INDUSTRIES
418 F.2d 31 (2d Cir. 1969)

[King-Seeley sued Aladdin for infringement of its trademarks in the word
Thermos written with an initial capital, all capitals, or in logotype. The
trial court found that *thermos* had become a generic word for any insu-
lated beverage container and was therefore in the public domain, but
that a significant minority of customers still understood the word to refer
only to King-Seeley's products. It enjoined Aladdin from using the word

unless it was printed entirely in lowercase letters and preceded by *Aladdin's*.

Shortly thereafter, Aladdin complained that King-Seeley was misrepresenting the injunction in policing letters sent to Aladdin's retailers who used the word *thermos* in their advertising. Finding that both sides had distorted the injunction, the court issued a second order, referred to as the "policing order," specifying the representations that each side could make to third parties.

Still later, Aladdin moved to modify both the injunction and the policing order. The trial court denied relief and Aladdin appealed.]

Before MOORE, FRIENDLY and HAYS, Circuit Judges.

FRIENDLY, Circuit Judge.

Aladdin . . . proposed that the conditions listed in the original decree be continued only with respect to labels on its products and that in literature, advertising and publicity releases it should be permitted to use "thermos" in solid capitals or with an initial capital "when such typography and/or capitalization are consistent with that of other generic or common words appearing therewith or are in accordance with ordinary rules of grammar," provided only that the material be identified as emanating from Aladdin or its representatives and that Aladdin should be prohibited, as it was in the decree of injunction, from using the words "genuine" or "original" or synonyms thereof relating or referring to "thermos." In support of this it urged that the decree of injunction had handicapped its use of the generic term in various ways, e.g., by preventing publication of testimonial letters from satisfied customers using only the word "thermos," curtailing press releases since newspaper editors tended to reject those which made too frequent mention of the manufacturer, and preventing such effective forms of advertising as "Who makes the best thermos?" It submitted that any possibility of harm to King-Seeley from such advertising or publicity could be avoided by identifying the source, without requirements so severe as those in the decree. Aladdin also sought a modification of the policing order to provide that King-Seeley should not have reasonable cause to believe its trademark rights had been violated by the use of the term "thermos" by persons other than Aladdin in type forms not permitted to Aladdin itself, where such third parties had not used the logotype "THERMOS" and the typographical form and/or capitalization were consistent with that for other generic words. In support of this Aladdin urged that King-Seeley, while ignoring advertisements where dealers used "Thermos" or "THERMOS" without any identification of source, sent policing letters whenever a dealer used the word in one of these forms and identified it with the product of a competitor, with the result that many Aladdin dealers became confused and refrained from advertising which the decree permitted. Finally, Aladdin urged that the policing order be amended in conformity with the changes sought in the decree of injunction, by altering the approved summary of the decision to explain that most of the restrictions applied only to Aladdin's labeling, not to its publicity or advertising.

Judge Anderson denied both branches of the motion. Analyzing United States v. Swift & Co. and United States v. United Shoe Machinery Corp., he thought the applicable rules of law to be:

(1) Where a party seeks a modification which will relieve it of conditions or restrictions imposed by the original decree, it has the burden of showing that there has been such a change in circumstances that the danger at which the decree was directed no longer exists.

(2) Where one party seeks a modification which will impose new and additional restrictions upon the other, it must prove that the provisions of the original decree have failed fully to achieve the objects at which they were directed.

Considering the portion of Aladdin's motion seeking modification of the decree of injunction to be governed by (1), the supposed rule of the *Swift* case, he held that whatever merit there might or might not be in Aladdin's position, it had not sustained the burden of showing a change in circumstances. Viewing the portion of the motion that sought modification of the policing order as governed by (2), the less stringent rule of the *United Shoe* case, he held that Aladdin had not "carried its burden of showing that the injunction dated December 30, 1963, has been ineffective."

Although we admire our brother Anderson's effort to achieve precision, we think he gave the *Swift* decision a rigidity the Court did not intend. The defendants who there sought modification of a consent decree had been obliged by the very nature of the case to stake their claim on drastic changes in conditions and, as pointed out in *United Shoe*, the language "to the effect that 'nothing less than a clear showing of grievous wrong evoked by new and unforeseen conditions should lead us to change' . . . the decree, must, of course, be read in light of this context." . . .

A case like this involves no such sharp conflict between wrong-doing and right-doing as did *Swift*. It presents rather the need for drawing the line between two kinds of right-doing, King-Seeley's legitimate interest in protecting its trademark insofar as this is valid and Aladdin's equally legitimate interest in being free to sell its products by use of a generic term, and their opposites, attempts by King-Seeley to extend its trademark beyond its legal bounds and efforts by Aladdin to encroach upon the protected area. "The source of the power to modify is of course the fact that an injunction often requires continuing supervision by the issuing court and always a continuing willingness to apply its power and processes on behalf of the party who obtained that equitable relief."

System Federation v. Wright, 364 U.S. 642, 647 (1961). Aladdin can be regarded as having obtained equitable relief in the decree of injunction quite as much as King-Seeley. That King-Seeley was the plaintiff was mere accident; the issue could as well have been tendered in a suit by Aladdin for declaratory relief. In that event the decree would very likely have directed that King-Seeley refrain from threatening Aladdin with liability for infringement under the prescribed conditions and Aladdin would now be seeking to "impose new and additional restrictions" upon what King-Seeley could do. While changes in fact or in law afford the clearest bases for altering an injunction, the power of equity has repeatedly been recognized as extending also to cases where a better appreciation of the facts in light of experience indicates that the decree is not properly adapted to accomplishing its purposes. Here, as Aladdin points out, the decree was entered before any experience concerning Aladdin's use of "thermos" had been had.

We think therefore that the court imposed unduly rigid restrictions on its consideration of so much of Aladdin's motion as requested modification of the decree of injunction and that it was free to grant relief if Aladdin could show that, in the light of experience, the detailed provisions of the decree seriously and needlessly impeded its exploitation of the generic term and that modification was necessary to achieve the results intended, even though this would take the form of reducing the restrictions imposed upon it. We express no opinion what the decision should be when that criterion is applied. Although the showing seems sufficient to justify an exercise of discretion in Aladdin's favor, it did not compel this. While we hold there is power to modify an injunction even in the absence of changed conditions, the power should be sparingly exercised. "Firmness and stability must no doubt be attributed to continuing injunctive relief based on adjudicated facts and law, and neither the plaintiff nor the court should be subjected to the unnecessary burden of re-establishing what has once been decided." System Federation v. Wright, supra, 364 U.S. at 647. We thus leave the decision to Judge Anderson under the standard we have enunciated.

Aladdin concedes that the judge applied the correct standard in passing on the branch of its motion that sought to modify the policing order, and we would see no reason for interfering with his refusal to alter this if it stood alone. Since, however, a modification of the decree of injunction might require some changes in the policing order, we vacate the order denying this part of Aladdin's motion so that the judge may have freedom to make such modification of the policing order, if any, as may become appropriate. . . .

MOORE, Circuit Judge, dissenting. . . .

The majority now not only substitute themselves for Judge Anderson in his fact-finding function but also overrule, in effect, the unanimous affirmance by another panel of this court of the original decree. Thus, they say that "where a better appreciation of the facts in light of experience indicates that the decree is not properly adapted to accomplishing its purposes," a power in equity exists to modify. This can only mean that the majority, as two judges, believe that they have a "better appreciation of the facts" than four other judges including, in particular, the judge who saw and heard the witnesses and who has been familiar with the case for over five years. . . .

Nor did Judge Anderson acquire a "rigidity" of mind by a misconstruction of the *Swift* and *United Shoe* cases. To the contrary, his analyses of these cases demonstrate that he was fully aware of the extent of their holdings. Each dealt with an entirely dissimilar situation. Even their judicial generalities are inapplicable except for their teaching "that a decree . . . may not be changed in the interests of the defendants if the purposes of the litigation as incorporated in the decree . . . have not been fully achieved." 286 U.S. at 117-118. . . .

Naturally, Aladdin would like to undo Judge Anderson's original decision and our affirmance thereof. To delete the restraint from "its literature" and from "its advertising" would, in substance, accomplish a reversal of these decisions. . . .

NOTES ON MINOR MODIFICATIONS

1. Is *King-Seeley* consistent with the Supreme Court cases? There's no pretense that circumstances have changed. Aladdin's hardships may be unforeseen, but they certainly weren't unforeseeable. If a "better appreciation" of the facts is enough to justify a modification, is there anything left of res judicata? Even if any issue could be relitigated at any time, a court would deny modification if it understood the law and facts the same way the original court did.

2. Having said all that, doesn't Aladdin have an appealing case? If it's possible to use testimonial letters without confusing anyone about the source of the product, the injunction should permit that. The question is whether the court should fix such a minor glitch in a decree already final.

Is Aladdin's motion equivalent to arguing that a better appreciation of the facts reveals that the judgment should have been for $19,000 instead of $20,000? Should courts fix that error if they won't fix the enormous error in *Eagle-Picher*, described in the notes to *United Shoe*? Wasn't the Board's motion to modify in *Eagle-Picher* also based on a "better appreciation" of the facts?

3. Another way to view these cases is to once again focus on the purpose of the decree. Doesn't *King-Seeley* distinguish modifications that defeat the purpose from modifications that don't? Is that consistent with *Swift* and *United Shoe*? And doesn't it make a lot of sense?

The Supreme Court has repeatedly implied a similar view in cases where defendants attacked injunctions as overbroad or unclear. Where the problem is not egregious, the Court is prone to say that if any problems or uncertainties arise the defendant can move to modify. An example is National Society of Professional Engineers v. United States, 435 U.S. 679 (1978). The trial court had enjoined the society from issuing any statement implying that competitive bidding is unethical. The society feared that the injunction might prevent all statements on ethical matters related to bidding. The Court responded that "the burden is upon the proved transgressor 'to bring any proper claims for relief to the court's attention.'" Id. at 698, quoting International Salt Co. v. United States, 332 U.S. 392, 400 (1947). And it approved the court of appeals' statement that "if the Society wishes to adopt some other ethical guideline more closely confined to the legitimate objective of preventing deceptively low bids, it may move the district court for modification of the decree." 435 U.S. at 699. Wouldn't any such motions to modify have to be controlled by something like the *King-Seeley* standard? They wouldn't do much good under the *Swift* standard, would they?

4.   Focusing on purpose still leaves *Eagle-Picher* unexplained. In *Eagle-Picher*, denying modification defeated the purpose of the decree. But there are two ways to get rid of it. Maybe it's just wrong. Or maybe it's a compensation case, and for better or worse, tradition says compensation cases are different.

PASADENA CITY BOARD OF EDUCATION
v. SPANGLER
427 U.S. 424 (1976)

Mr. Justice Rehnquist delivered the opinion of the Court. . . .

[T]he District Court held a trial on the allegations that the Pasadena school system was unconstitutionally segregated. On January 23, 1970, the court entered a judgment in which it concluded that the defendants' educational policies and procedures were violative of the Fourteenth Amendment. The court ordered the defendants "enjoined from failing to prepare and adopt a plan to correct racial imbalance at all levels in the Pasadena Unified School District." The defendants were further ordered to submit to the District Court a plan for desegregating the Pasadena schools. In addition to requiring provisions for the assignment of staff and the construction and location of facilities, the District Court ordered that

[t]he plan shall provide for student assignments in such a manner that, by or before the beginning of the school year that commences in September of 1970 there shall be no school in the District, elementary or junior high or senior high school, with a majority of any minority students.

The court went on to retain

> jurisdiction of this cause in order to continue to observe and evaluate the plans
> and the execution of the plans of the Pasadena Unified School District in
> regard to the hiring, promotion, and assignment of teachers and professional
> staff members, the construction and location of facilities, and the assignment
> of students.

The defendant school officials voted to comply with the District Court's
decree and not to appeal. They thereupon set out to devise and submit
the plan demanded by the District Court. In February the defendants
submitted their proposed plan, the "Pasadena Plan," and on March 10,
1970, the District Court approved the plan, finding it "to be in conformance with the Judgment entered herein January 23, 1970." The "Pasadena Plan" was implemented the following September, and the Pasadena
schools have been under its terms ever since. . . .

II

Petitioners requested the District Court to dissolve its injunctive order
requiring that there be no school in the PUSD with a majority of any
minority students enrolled. The District Court refused this request, and
ordered the injunction continued. The court apparently based this decision in large part upon its view that petitioners had failed properly to
comply with its original order. This conclusion was in turn premised
upon the fact that although the School Board had reorganized PUSD
attendance patterns in conformity with the court-approved Pasadena
Plan, literal compliance with the terms of the court's order had been
obtained in only the initial year of the plan's operation. Following the
1970-1971 school year, black student enrollment at one Pasadena school
exceeded 50% of that school's total enrollment. The next year, four Pasadena schools exceeded this 50% black enrollment figure; and at the time
of the hearing on petitioners' motion some five schools, in a system of 32
regular schools, were ostensibly in violation of the District Court's "no
majority of any minority" requirement. It was apparently the view of the
majority of the Court of Appeals' panel that this failure to maintain literal
compliance with the 1970 injunction indicated that the District Court
had not abused its discretion in refusing to grant so much of petitioner's
motion for modification as pertained to this aspect of the order. We think
this view was wrong.

We do not have before us any issue as to the validity of the District
Court's original judgment, since petitioners' predecessors did not appeal
from it. The District Court's conclusion that unconstitutional segregation existed in the PUSD; its decision to order a systemwide school reorganization plan based upon the guidelines which it submitted to the
defendants; and the inclusion in those guidelines of the requirement that

the plan contain provisions insuring that there be no majority of any minority in any Pasadena school, all became embodied in the 1970 decree. All that is now before us are the questions of whether the District Court was correct in denying relief when petitioners in 1974 sought to modify the "no majority" requirement as then interpreted by the District Court. . . .

[P]laintiffs never understood the District Court's order to require annual reassignment of pupils in order to accommodate changing demographic residential patterns in Pasadena from year to year, as the Government candidly admits in its brief here.

Petitioners have argued that they never understood the injunction, or the provisions of the plan which they drafted to implement that order, to contain such a requirement either. But at the hearing on petitioners' motion for relief the District Court made it clear that *its* understanding of the decree was quite different from that of the parties. In response to the arguments of petitioners' counsel, the judge stated that his 1970 order "meant to me that at least during my lifetime there would be no majority of any minority in any school in Pasadena."

When the District Court's order in this case, as interpreted and applied by that court, is measured against what this Court said in its intervening decision in Swann v. Charlotte-Mecklenburg Board of Education, 402 U.S. 1 (1971), regarding the scope of the judicially created relief which might be available to remedy violations of the Fourteenth Amendment, we think the inconsistency between the two is clear. The District Court's interpretation of the order appears to contemplate the "substantive constitutional right [to a] particular degree of racial balance or mixing" which the Court in *Swann* expressly disapproved. Id., at 24. It became apparent, at least by the time of the 1974 hearing, that the District Court viewed this portion of its order not merely as a "starting point in the process of shaping a remedy," which *Swann* indicated would be appropriate, id., at 25, but instead as an "inflexible requirement," ibid., to be applied anew each year to the school population within the attendance zone of each school.

The District Court apparently believed it had authority to impose this requirement even though subsequent changes in the racial mix in the Pasadena schools might be caused by factors for which the defendants could not be considered responsible. Whatever may have been the basis for such a belief in 1970, in *Swann* the Court cautioned that "it must be recognized that there are limits" beyond which a court may not go in seeking to dismantle a dual school system. Id., at 28. These limits are in part tied to the necessity of establishing that school authorities have in some manner caused unconstitutional segregation, for "[a]bsent a constitutional violation there would be no basis for judicially ordering assignment of students on a racial basis." Ibid. While the District Court found such a violation in 1970, and while this unappealed finding afforded a basis for its initial requirement that the defendants prepare a plan to remedy such racial segregation, its adoption of the Pasadena Plan in 1970 established a racially neutral system of student assignment in the PUSD. Having done that, we think that in enforcing its order so as to require annual readjustment of attendance zones so that there would not be a majority of any minority in any Pasadena public school, the District Court exceeded its authority.

In so concluding, we think it important to note what this case does not involve. The "no majority of any minority" requirement with respect to attendance zones did not call for defendants to submit "step at a time" plans by definition incomplete at inception. Nor did it call for a plan embodying specific revisions of the attendance zones for particular schools, as well as provisions for later appraisal of whether such discrete individual modifications had achieved the "unitary system" required by Brown v. Board of Education, 349 U.S. 294, 300 (1955). The plan approved in this case applied in general terms to all Pasadena schools, and no one contests that its implementation did "achieve a system of determining admission to the public schools on a nonracial basis," id., at 300-301.

There was also no showing in this case that those post-1971 changes in the racial mix of some Pasadena schools which were focused upon by the lower courts were in any manner caused by segregative actions chargeable to the defendants. The District Court rejected petitioners' assertion that the movement was caused by so-called "white flight" traceable to the decree itself. It stated that the "trends evidenced in Pasadena closely approximate the state-wide trends in California schools, both segregated and desegregated." 375 F. Supp. at 1306. The fact that black student enrollment at 5 out of 32 of the regular Pasadena schools came to exceed 50% during the 4-year period from 1970 to 1974 apparently resulted from people randomly moving into, out of, and around the PUSD area. This quite normal pattern of human migration resulted in some changes in the demographics of Pasadena's residential patterns, with resultant shifts in the racial makeup of some of the schools. But as these shifts were not attributed to any segregative actions on the part of the petitioners, we think this case comes squarely within the sort of situation foreseen in *Swann*:

> It does not follow that the communities served by [unitary] systems will remain demographically stable, for in a growing, mobile society, few will do so. Neither school authorities nor district courts are constitutionally required to make year-by-year adjustments of the racial composition of student bodies once the affirmative duty to desegregate has been accomplished and racial discrimination through official action is eliminated from the system.

402 U.S., at 31-32. . . .

At least one of the judges of the Court of Appeals expressed the view that while all of the petitioners' contentions which we have discussed might be sound, they were barred from asserting them by their predecessors' failure to appeal from the 1970 decree of the District Court. But this observation overlooks well-established rules governing modification of even a final decree entered by a court of equity. See United States v. Swift & Co., 286 U.S. 106 (1932); System Federation v. Wright, 364 U.S. 642 (1961). In the latter case this Court said:

> There is also no dispute but that a sound judicial discretion may call for the modification of the terms of an injunctive decree if the circumstances, whether of law or fact, obtaining at the time of its issuance have changed, or new ones have since arisen. The source of the power to modify is of course the fact that an injunction often requires continuing supervision by the issuing court and always a continuing willingness to apply its powers and processes on behalf of the party who obtained that equitable relief.

Id., at 647. Even had the District Court's decree been unambiguous and clearly understood by the parties to mean what that court declared it to mean in 1974, the "no majority of any minority" provision would, as we have indicated previously, be contrary to the intervening decision of this Court in *Swann*. The ambiguity of the provision itself, and the fact that the parties to the decree interpreted it in a manner contrary to the interpretation ultimately placed upon it by the District Court, is an added factor in support of modification. The two factors taken together make a sufficiently compelling case so that such modification should have been ordered by the District Court. System Federation v. Wright, supra. . . .

MR. JUSTICE STEVENS took no part in the consideration or decision of this case.

MR. JUSTICE MARSHALL, with whom MR. JUSTICE BRENNAN joins, dissenting. . . .

The Court's conclusion that modification of the District Court's order is mandated is apparently largely founded on the fact that during the Pasadena Plan's first year, its implementation did result in no school's having a majority of minority students. According to the Court, it follows from our decision in *Swann* that as soon as the school attendance zone scheme had been successful, even for a very short period, in fulfilling its objectives, the District Court should have relaxed its supervision over that aspect of the desegregation plan. It is irrelevant to the Court that the system may not have achieved "'unitary' status in all other respects such as the hiring and promoting of teachers and administrators." . . .

We have held that "[o]nce a right and a violation have been shown, the scope of a district court's equitable powers to remedy past wrongs is broad, for breadth and flexibility are inherent in equitable remedies." Swann v. Board of Education, 402 U.S., at 15. As the Court recognizes, there is no issue before us as to the validity of the District Court's original judgment that unconstitutional segregation existed in the Pasadena school system. Thus, there is no question as to there being both a "right and a violation." Moreover, at least as of the time that the District Court acted on the request for modification, the violation had not yet been entirely remedied. Particularly, given the breadth of discretion normally accorded a district court in fashioning equitable remedies, I see no reason to require the District Court in a case such as this to modify its order prior to the time that it is clear that the entire violation has been remedied and a unitary system has been achieved. We should not compel the District Court to modify its order unless conditions have changed so much that "dangers, once substantial, have become attenuated to a shadow." United States v. Swift & Co., 286 U.S. 106, 119 (1932). I, for one, cannot say that the District Court was in error in determining that such attenuation had not yet taken place and that modification of the order would "surely be to sign the death warrant of the Pasadena Plan and its objectives." Accordingly, I dissent.

MORE NOTES ON MODIFYING JUDGMENTS

1.   Justice Cardozo's opinion in *Swift* is the most frequently cited case on modification of decrees. Is there anything left of it after *Pasadena*?

2.   Justice Rehnquist relies heavily on the supposed change of law in *Swann*. Compare his description of *Swann* in Rizzo v. Goode, 423 U.S. 362, 376 (1976): "But this case, and the long line of precedents cited therein, simply reaffirmed the body of law originally enunciated in Brown v. Board of Education." In *Rizzo* he was talking about the theory of liability in *Swann*; in *Pasadena* he was talking about the remedy. But the two go hand in hand, especially in Rehnquist's view. The Court has always said that the constitutional right is to be free of state-imposed segregation; nothing before *Swann* suggested a right to any particular racial mix. It is inconceivable that Rehnquist would find any support in pre-*Swann* law for a continuing requirement that no school have a majority of any minority.

Whatever clarification might have come in *Swann* is surely trivial compared to the shift of direction in *U.S. Steel*, described supra at 1029-1030. But then the meatpackers did not rely on change of law in their motion to modify.

3.   *Pasadena* relies on System Federation No. 91 v. Wright, 364 U.S. 642 (1961), the Supreme Court's leading change-of-law case. *System Federation* involved a statutory amendment. Defendants had submitted to a consent decree ordering them not to require railroad employees to join a union. In 1951 Congress amended the Railway Labor Act to permit union

shops. The Court thought it clear this required modification. Three dissenters would have left the decree in effect as to the original plaintiffs, but not as to subsequent employees. The original plaintiffs compromised damage claims for past discrimination in exchange for this decree and partial compensation; as to them, the dissenters thought the Court did an injustice. The majority disagreed:

> The parties cannot, by giving each other consideration, purchase from a court of equity a continuing injunction. . . . [J]ust as the adopting court is free to reject agreed-upon terms as not in furtherance of statutory objectives, so must it be free to modify the terms of a consent decree when a change in law brings those terms in conflict with statutory objectives. In short, it was the Railway Labor Act, and only incidentally the parties, that the District Court served in entering the consent decree now before us.

364 U.S. at 651.

4. Many cases modify injunctions on the basis of a change in case law. An example is Jordan v. School District, 548 F.2d 117 (3d Cir. 1977). Jordan involved a consent decree specifying procedures for suspending or expelling school students. The court ordered the decree modified in light of Goss v. Lopez, 419 U.S. 565 (1975), which required a somewhat different set of procedures.

5. Can Judge Friendly's distinction in *King-Seeley* explain *Pasadena*? Does the modification defeat the purpose of the decree? It certainly defeats the purpose of the judge who entered the decree. On the other hand, it doesn't defeat any purpose Rehnquist will acknowledge as legitimate. Might Cardozo's stringent test survive for modifications that defeat the decree's purpose and that do not depend on intervening change in law? Is it always a "grievous wrong" to subject a litigant to restrictions that have been repealed for everyone else?

6. Rehnquist also suggests a distinction between complete plans and "step-at-a-time plans." A similar but not identical distinction appears in Justice Brennan's dissent in Arizona v. California, 460 U.S. 605, 644-645 n.1 (1983): "[E]ven if changed circumstances are necessary to modify an injunction — and I doubt that an equity court would turn its back on manifest injustice — they have never been the *sine qua non* of adjusting a decree in the process of making it final." Both these distinctions are badly blurred in complex injunction litigation. It is routine to issue a permanent injunction after a full trial and also to explicitly retain jurisdiction. Those injunctions are final judgments for purposes of appeal, but only the naive think the court is done with the case. It is almost inconceivable that the trial judge in *Pasadena* thought he was issuing a once-and-for-all order different in kind from the usual series of orders in structural injunction cases.

7. Whatever the rationalizations, doesn't the Court modify the *Pasadena* injunction because it was wrongly issued? Is it proof of Brennan's later hunch that the Court won't turn its back when the majority thinks it sees a "manifest injustice"? Should we discount the case as a sport, as part of the Court's brief effort to curtail busing? (The mid-1970s saw *Milliken I* in 1974, *Pasadena* in 1976, and *Dayton I*'s "incremental segregative effect" test in 1977.)

CHAPTER 13

Some Problems of Political Power

A. POWER TO CREATE PRIVATE REMEDIES: IMPLIED CAUSES OF ACTION

MERRILL LYNCH, PIERCE, FENNER & SMITH v. CURRAN
456 U.S. 353 (1982)

[In this opinion the Court decided four consolidated suits for violations of the Commodity Exchange Act, 7 U.S.C. §§1 et seq. (1982). The Currans alleged that Merrill Lynch had mismanaged their commodity futures trading account, made material misrepresentations about the account, made excessive trades in the account to generate commissions, and refused to follow the Currans' instructions concerning their account.

The other three cases arose out of a spectacular manipulation of trading in Maine potato futures for May 1976. In the face of a potato shortage, one group of conspirators tried to drive down the price by selling huge numbers of potato contracts short — that is, selling contracts they didn't own, hoping to replace them later at a lower price. Sooner or later they would have to buy; they were obligated to deliver potatoes or a corresponding contract for every contract they had sold short.

A competing group of conspirators thought the "short conspiracy" created a chance to corner the market. They bought potato contracts and tied up all the cars on the Bangor & Aroostook Railroad. When May came and the short conspirators had to cover their short sales, they would have no choice but to pay inflated prices to the "long conspirators." Both conspiracies failed, and the short conspirators defaulted on their contracts. It was the largest default in the history of futures trading.

Plaintiffs were commodities speculators who lost money because of the conspiracies. They sued the New York Mercantile Exchange, alleging that if it had enforced its own rules the conspiracy could not have happened or the damage would have been less. They also sued the brokers who handled trading for the short conspirators, alleging that they were knowing participants in the conspiracy.

In each case the district court dismissed for failure to state a claim and the court of appeals reversed. The issue before the Supreme Court was whether private plaintiffs could sue for violations of the Commodities Exchange Act.]

JUSTICE STEVENS delivered the opinion of the Court. . . .

IV

When Congress intends private litigants to have a cause of action to support their statutory rights, the far better course is for it to specify as much when it creates those rights. But the Court has long recognized that under certain limited circumstances the failure of Congress to do so is not inconsistent with an intent on its part to have such a remedy available to the persons benefited by its legislation.

Cannon v. University of Chicago, 441 U.S. 677, 717 (1979).

Our approach to the task of determining whether Congress intended to authorize a private cause of action has changed significantly, much as the quality and quantity of federal legislation has undergone significant change. When federal statutes were less comprehensive, the Court applied a relatively simple test to determine the availability of an implied private remedy. If a statute was enacted for the benefit of a special class, the judiciary normally recognized a remedy for members of that class. Texas & Pacific R. Co. v. Rigsby, 241 U.S. 33 (1916). Under this approach, federal courts, following a common-law tradition, regarded the denial of a remedy as the exception rather than the rule.

Because the *Rigsby* approach prevailed throughout most of our history, there is no merit to the argument advanced by petitioners that the judicial recognition of an implied private remedy violates the separation of powers doctrine. As Justice Frankfurter explained:

Courts . . . are organs with historic antecedents which bring with them well-defined powers. They do not require explicit statutory authorization for familiar remedies to enforce statutory obligations. A duty declared by Congress does not evaporate for want of a formulated sanction. When Congress has "left the matter at large for judicial determination," our function is to decide what remedies are appropriate in the light of the statutory language and purpose and of the traditional modes by which courts compel performance of legal obligations. If civil liability is appropriate to effectuate the purposes of a statute, courts are not denied this traditional remedy because it is not specifically authorized.

Montana-Dakota Co. v. Northwestern Pub. Serv. Co., 341 U.S. 246, 261-262 (1951) (Frankfurter, J., dissenting).

During the years prior to 1975, the Court occasionally refused to recognize an implied remedy, either because the statute in question was a general regulatory prohibition enacted for the benefit of the public at large, or because there was evidence that Congress intended an express remedy to provide the exclusive method of enforcement. While the *Rigsby* approach prevailed, however, congressional silence or ambiguity was an insufficient reason for the denial of a remedy for a member of the class a statute was enacted to protect.

In 1975 the Court unanimously decided to modify its approach to the question whether a federal statute includes a private right of action. In Cort v. Ash, 422 U.S. 66 (1975), the Court confronted a claim that a private litigant could recover damages for violation of a criminal statute that had never before been thought to include a private remedy. In rejecting that claim the Court outlined criteria that primarily focused on the intent of Congress in enacting the statute under review. The increased complexity of federal legislation and the increased volume of federal litigation strongly supported the desirability of a more careful scrutiny of legislative intent than *Rigsby* had required. Our cases subsequent to Cort v. Ash have plainly stated that our focus must be on "the intent of Congress." Texas Industries, Inc. v. Radcliff Materials, Inc., 451 U.S. 630, 639 (1981). "The key to the inquiry is the intent of the Legislature." Middlesex County Sewerage Auth. v. National Sea Clammers Assn., 453 U.S. 1, 13 (1981). The key to this case is our understanding of the intent of Congress in 1974 when it comprehensively reexamined and strengthened the federal regulation of futures trading.

V

In determining whether a private cause of action is implicit in a federal statutory scheme when the statute by its terms is silent on that issue, the initial focus must be on the state of the law at the time the legislation was enacted. More precisely, we must examine Congress' perception of the law that it was shaping or reshaping. When Congress enacts new legislation, the question is whether Congress intended to create a private remedy as a supplement to the express enforcement provisions of the statute. When Congress acts in a statutory context in which an implied private remedy has already been recognized by the courts, however, the inquiry logically is different. Congress need not have intended to create a new remedy, since one already existed; the question is whether Congress intended to preserve the preexisting remedy.

In Cannon v. University of Chicago, we observed that "[i]t is always appropriate to assume that our elected representatives, like other citizens, know the law." 441 U.S. at 696-697. In considering whether Title IX of the Education Amendments of 1972 included an implied private cause of action for damages, we assumed that the legislators were familiar with the judicial decisions construing comparable language in Title VI of the Civil Rights Act of 1964 as implicitly authorizing a judicial remedy, notwithstanding the fact that the statute expressly included a quite different remedy. We held that even under the "strict approach" dictated by Cort v. Ash, "our evaluation of congressional action in 1972 must take into account its contemporary legal context." Id., at 698-699.

Prior to the comprehensive amendments to the CEA enacted in 1974, the federal courts routinely and consistently had recognized an implied private cause of action on behalf of plaintiffs seeking to enforce and to collect damages for violation of provisions of the CEA or rules and regulations promulgated pursuant to the statute. . . .

In view of the absence of any dispute about the proposition prior to the decision of Cort v. Ash in 1975, it is abundantly clear that an implied cause of action under the CEA was a part of the "contemporary legal context" in which Congress legislated in 1974. In that context, the fact that a comprehensive reexamination and significant amendment of the CEA left intact the statutory provisions under which the federal courts had implied a cause of action is itself evidence that Congress affirmatively intended to preserve that remedy. A review of the legislative history of the statute persuasively indicates that preservation of the remedy was indeed what Congress actually intended.

VI

Congress was, of course, familiar not only with the implied private remedy but also with the long history of federal regulation of commodity futures trading. From the enactment of the original federal legislation, Congress primarily has relied upon the exchanges to regulate the contract markets. The 1922 legislation required for designation as a contract market that an exchange "provide for" the making and filing of reports and records, the prevention of dissemination of false or misleading reports, the prevention of price manipulation and market cornering, and the enforcement of Commission orders. To fulfill these conditions, the exchanges promulgated rules and regulations, but they did not always enforce them. In 1968 Congress attempted to correct this flaw in the self-regulation concept by enacting §5a(8), 7 U.S.C. §7a(8), which requires the exchanges to enforce their own rules.

The enactment of §5a(8), coupled with the recognition by the federal courts of an implied private remedy for violations of the CEA, gave rise to a new problem. As representatives of the exchanges complained during the hearings preceding the 1974 amendments, the exchanges were being sued for not enforcing their rules. The complaint was taken seriously because it implicated the self-regulation premise of the CEA:

> In the few years [§5a(8)] has been in the present Commodity Exchange Act, there is growing evidence to indicate that, as opposed to strengthening the self-regulatory concept in present law, such a provision, coupled with only limited federal authority to require the exchanges to make and issue rules appropriate to enforcement of the Act — may actually have worked to weaken it. With inadequate enforcement personnel the Committee was informed that attorneys to several boards of trade have been advising the boards to *reduce* — not expand exchange regulations designed to insure fair trading, since there is a growing body of opinion that failure to enforce the exchange rules is a violation of the Act which will support suits by private litigants.

House Report at 46 (emphasis in original). Congress could have removed this impediment to exchange rulemaking by eliminating the implied private remedy, but it did not follow that course. Rather, it solved the problem by authorizing the new Commodity Futures Trading Commission to supplement exchange rules. Congress thereby corrected the legal mechanism of self-regulation while preserving a significant incentive for the exchanges to obey the law. Only this course was consistent with the expressed purpose of the 1974 legislation, which was to "amend the Commodity Exchange Act to *strengthen* the regulation of futures trading."

Congress in 1974 created new procedures through which traders might seek relief for violations of the CEA, but the legislative evidence indicates that these informal procedures were intended to supplement rather than supplant the implied judicial remedy. These procedures do not substitute for the private remedy either as a means of compensating injured traders or as a means of enforcing compliance with the statute. The reparations procedure established by §14 is not available against the exchanges, yet we may infer from the above analysis that Congress viewed private litigation against exchanges as a valuable component of the self-regulation concept. Nor is that procedure suited for the adjudication of all other claims. The Commission may, but need not, investigate a complaint, and may, but need not, serve the respondent with the complaint. If the Commission permits the complaint to issue, it need not provide an administrative hearing if the claim does not exceed $5,000. The arbitration procedure mandated by §5a(11) is even narrower in scope. Only members and employees of the contract market are subject to the procedure, and the use of the procedure by a trader is voluntary and is limited to claims of less than $15,000. There are other indications in the legislative history that the two sections were not intended to be exclusive of the implied judicial remedy. It was assumed by hearings witnesses that the informal procedures were supplementary. Indeed, it was urged that complainants be put to the choice between informal and judicial actions. A representative of one exchange urged Congress to place a dollar limit on claims arbitrable under §5a(11) because there was an "economic impediment to Court litigation" only with small claims, and such a limit was enacted. Chairman Poage described the newly enacted informal procedures as "new customer protection features," and Senator Talmadge, the Chairman of the Senate Committee on Agriculture and Forestry, stated that the reparations procedure was "not intended to interfere with the courts in any way," although he hoped that the burden on the courts would be "somewhat lighten[ed]" by the availability of the informal actions.

The late addition of a savings clause in §2(a)(1) provides direct evidence of legislative intent to preserve the implied private remedy federal courts had recognized under the CEA. Along with an increase in powers, the Commission was given exclusive jurisdiction over commodity futures trading. The purpose of the exclusive jurisdiction provision in the bill passed by the House was to separate the functions of the Commission from those of the Securities Exchange Commission and other regulatory agencies. But the provision raised concerns that the jurisdiction of state and federal courts might be affected. Referring to the treble damages action provided in another bill that he and Senator McGovern had introduced, Senator Clark pointed out that "the House bill not only does not authorize them, but section 201 of that bill may prohibit all court actions. The staff of the House Agriculture Committee has said that this was done inadvertently and they hope it can be corrected in the Senate." It was. The Senate added a savings clause to the exclusive jurisdiction provision, providing that "nothing in this section shall supersede or limit the jurisdiction conferred on courts of the United States or of any State." The Conference accepted the Senate amendment.

The inference that Congress intended to preserve the preexisting remedy is compelling. As the Solicitor General argues on behalf of the Commission as amicus curiae, the private cause of action enhances the enforcement mechanism fostered by Congress over the course of sixty years. In an enactment purporting to strengthen the regulation of commodity futures trading, Congress evidenced an affirmative intent to preserve this enforcement tool. It removed an impediment to exchange rulemaking caused in part by the implied private remedy not by disapproving that remedy but rather by giving the Commission the extraordinary power to supplement exchange rules. And when several Members of Congress expressed a concern that the exclusive jurisdiction provision, which was intended only to consolidate federal regulation of commodity futures trading in the Commission, might be construed to affect the implied cause of action as well as other court actions, Congress acted swiftly to dispel any such notion. Congress could have made its intent clearer only by expressly providing for a private cause of action in the statute. In the legal context in which Congress acted, this was unnecessary.

In view of our construction of the intent of the legislature there is no need for us to "trudge through all four of the factors when the dispositive question of legislative intent has been resolved." See California v. Sierra Club, 451 U.S., at 302 (Rehnquist, J., concurring in the judgment). We hold that the private cause of action under the CEA that was previously available to investors survived the 1974 amendments.

VII

In addition to their principal argument that no private remedy is available under the CEA, petitioners also contend that respondents, as speculators, may not maintain such an action and that, in any event, they may not sue an exchange or futures commission merchants for their alleged complicity in the price manipulation effected by a group of short traders. . . .

The cause of action asserted in No. 80-203 is a claim that respondents' broker violated the prohibitions against fraudulent and deceptive conduct in §4b. In the other three cases the respondents allege violations of several other sections of the CEA that are designed to prevent price manipulation. We are satisfied that purchasers and sellers of futures contracts have standing to assert both types of claims.

The characterization of persons who invest in futures contracts as "speculators" does not exclude them from the class of persons protected by the CEA. The statutory scheme could not effectively protect the producers and processors who engage in hedging transactions without also protecting the other participants in the market whose transactions over exchanges necessarily must conform to the same trading rules. This is evident from the text of the statute. The antifraud provision, §4b, 7 U.S.C. §6b, by its terms makes it unlawful for any person to deceive or defraud any other person in connection with any futures contract. . . .

Although §4b compels our holding that an investor defrauded by his broker may maintain a private cause of action for fraud, petitioners in the three manipulation cases correctly point out that the other sections of the CEA that they are accused of violating are framed in general terms and do not purport to confer special rights on any identifiable class of persons. Under Cort v. Ash, the statutory language would be insufficient to imply a private cause of action under these sections. But we are not faced with the Cort v. Ash inquiry. We have held that Congress intended to preserve the preexisting remedy; to determine whether the preexisting remedy encompasses respondents' actions, we must turn once again to the law as it existed in 1974.

Although the first case in which a federal court held that a futures trader could maintain a private action was a fraud claim based on §4b, subsequent decisions drew no distinction between an action against a broker and an action against an exchange. When Congress acted in 1974, courts were recognizing causes of action on behalf of investors against exchanges. . . .

To the extent that the Cort v. Ash inquiry is relevant to the question now before us — whether respondents' claims can be pursued under the implied cause of action that Congress preserved — it is noteworthy that the third and fourth factors of that inquiry support an affirmative answer. As the Solicitor General has argued on behalf of the Commodities Futures Trading Commission, it is "consistent with the underlying purposes of the legislative scheme to imply such a remedy." Moreover, there is no basis for believing that state law will afford an adequate remedy against an exchange. On the contrary, throughout the long history of federal regulation of futures trading it has been federal law that has imposed a stringent duty upon exchanges to police the trading activities in the markets that they are authorized by statute to regulate. Since the amendments to the original legislation regulating futures trading consistently have strengthened that regulatory scheme, the elimination of a significant enforcement tool would clash with this legislative pattern. We therefore may not simply assume that Congress silently withdrew the preexisting private remedy against exchanges.

Having concluded that exchanges can be held accountable for breaching their statutory duties to enforce their own rules prohibiting price manipulation, it necessarily follows that those persons who are participants in a conspiracy to manipulate the market in violation of those rules are also subject to suit by futures traders who can prove injury from these violations. As we said regarding the analogous Rule 10b-5, "privity of dealing or even personal contact between potential defendant and potential plaintiff is the exception and not the rule." Blue Chip Stamps v. Manor Drug Stores, 421 U.S., at 745. Because there is no indication of legislative intent that privity should be an element of the implied remedy under the CEA, we are not prepared to fashion such a limitation. As has been the case with the Rule 10b-5 action, unless and until Congress acts, the federal courts must fill in the interstices of the implied cause of action under the CEA. The elements of liability, of causation, and of damages are likely to raise difficult issues of law and proof in litigation arising from the massive price manipulation that is alleged to have occurred in the May 1976 futures contract in Maine potatoes. We express no opinion about any such question. We hold only that a cause of action exists on behalf of respondents against petitioners. . . .

JUSTICE POWELL, with whom THE CHIEF JUSTICE, JUSTICE REHNQUIST, and JUSTICE O'CONNOR join, dissenting.

The Court today holds that Congress intended the federal courts to recognize implied causes of action under five separate provisions of the Commodity Exchange Act (CEA), 7 U.S.C. §1 et seq. The decision rests on two theories. First, the Court relies on fewer than a dozen cases in which the lower federal courts *erroneously* upheld private rights of action in the years prior to the 1974 Amendments to the CEA. Reasoning that these mistaken decisions constituted "the law" in 1974, the Court holds that Congress must be assumed to have endorsed this path of error when it *failed to amend* certain sections of the CEA in that year. This theory is incompatible with our constitutional separation of powers, and in my view it is without support in logic or in law. Additionally — whether alternatively or cumulatively is unclear — the Court finds that Congress in 1974 "affirmatively" manifested its intent to "preserve" private rights of action by adopting particular amendments to the CEA. This finding is reached without even token deference to established tests for discerning congressional intent.

I

In determining whether an "implied" cause of action exists under a federal statute, "what must ultimately be determined is whether Congress intended to create the private remedy asserted." Transamerica Mortgage Advisors, Inc. (TAMA) v. Lewis, 444 U.S. 11, 15-16 (1979). In this case private rights of action are asserted under five separate provisions of the Commodity Exchange Act — two of them passed initially in 1922, two in 1936, and one adopted for the first time in 1968. The Court does not argue that Congress in 1922, in 1936, or in 1968, intended to authorize private suits for damages in the federal courts. In 1936 — the year in which the CEA was adopted as the successor statute to the Grain Futures Act — Congress did not even provide for federal court jurisdiction to enforce the CEA. And the Court adduces no evidence that congressional views had changed by 1968.

If the Court focused its implication inquiry on the intent of the several Congresses that enacted the statutory provisions involved in this case, it thus is indisputable that the plaintiffs would have no claim. "The dispositive question" in implication cases is whether Congress intended to create the right to sue for damages in federal court. "Having answered that question in the negative, our inquiry [would be] at an end." TAMA, supra, 444 U.S., at 24.

The Court today asserts its fidelity to these principles but shrinks from their application. It does so in the first instance by invoking a novel legal theory — one that relies on congressional inaction and on erroneous decisions by the lower federal courts. In 1967 a federal district court in the Northern District of Illinois upheld the existence of a private right of action under one section of the CEA. Goodman v. H. Hentz & Co., 265 F. Supp. 440 (N.D. Ill. 1967). . . .

The Court does not dispute that the *Goodman* court erred. The *Goodman* court placed primary emphasis on inquiring whether Congress had created a regulatory system for the *benefit* of the plaintiffs' class. As the court's citation of the Restatement of Torts made apparent, this inquiry has been thought appropriate for common law courts of general jurisdiction. But our cases establish that it is *not* appropriate for federal courts possessed only of limited jurisdiction. On the contrary, we have established that an "argument in favor of implication of a private right of action based on tort principles . . . is entirely misplaced." Touche Ross & Co. v. Redington, 442 U.S. 560, 568 (1979). "The dispositive question [is] whether *Congress* intended to create any such [private damages] remedy." *TAMA*, supra, 444 U.S., at 24 (emphasis added). The *Goodman* court did not even ask this question.

About ten cases — none decided by this Court — followed *Goodman*'s mistake. Seven of these found *Goodman* dispositive without further comment. Three remaining cases added to *Goodman*'s analysis only by quoting differing portions of one sentence discussing the CEA's purpose. This single sentence "leaves no doubt that Congress intended to [benefit the named classes of persons by enacting the CEA]. . . . But whether Congress intended additionally that [the CEA] provisions would be enforced through private litigation is a different question." *TAMA*, supra, 444 U.S., at 17-18. Because these cases ignore this "different question," they fail to rectify *Goodman*'s fundamental legal error — that of basing a finding of an implied cause of action under a federal statute on common law principles. "There is, of course, 'no federal general common law.'" Texas Industries, Inc. v. Radcliff Materials, Inc. 451 U.S., at 640, quoting Erie R. Co. v. Tompkins, 304 U.S. 64, 78 (1930).

To the Court, however, this all is irrelevant. The *Goodman* line may have been wrong. The decisions all may have been rendered by lower federal courts. *Goodman* nevertheless was "the law" in 1974. Moreover, the Court reasons, Congress must be presumed to have known of *Goodman* and its progeny, and it could have changed the law if it did not like it. Yet Congress, the Court continues, "left intact the statutory provisions under which the federal courts had implied a cause of action." This legislative *inaction*, the Court concludes, signals a conscious intent to "preserve" the right of action that *Goodman* mistakenly had created. And this unexpressed "affirmative intent" of Congress now is binding on this Court, as well as all other federal courts.

This line of reasoning is inconsistent with fundamental premises of our structure of government. Fewer than a dozen district courts wrongly create a remedy in damages under the CEA; Congress fails to correct the error; and congressional silence binds this Court to follow the erroneous decisions of the district courts and courts of appeals. The Court today does not say that *Goodman* was correctly decided. Congress itself surely would reject emphatically the *Goodman* view that federal courts are free to hold, as a general rule of statutory interpretation, that private rights of action are to be implied unless Congress "evidences a contrary intention." Yet today's decision is predicated in major part on this view.

It is not surprising that the Court — having propounded this novel theory that congressional intent can be inferred from its silence, and that legislative inaction should achieve the force of law — would wish to advance an additional basis for its decision.

II

In 1974 Congress rewrote much of the CEA. It did not, however, reenact or even amend most of the provisions under which the Court today finds implied rights of action. But the Court does not pause over the question how Congress might legislate a right of action merely by remaining silent after the lower federal courts have misstated the law. Instead it argues that at least some of the 1974 amendments evidenced an affirmative congressional intent to "preserve" implied rights of action under the CEA. Fairly read, the evidence fails to sustain this argument.

A

In support of its argument the Court advances no evidence of the kinds generally recognized as most probative of congressional intent. It cites no statutory language stating an intent to preserve judicially created rights. It offers no legislative materials citing *Goodman* or any of its progeny in approving tones. In the hundreds of pages of committee hearings and reports that preceded the 1974 amendments, the Court is unable to discover even a single clear remark to the effect that the 1974 amendments would create or preserve private rights of action.

The Court relies instead on three unrelated additions to the CEA that were adopted by Congress in 1974. First, the Court places weight on the enactment of §8a(7), 7 U.S.C. §12a(7), which authorized the Commodity Futures Trading Commission to supplement the trading regulations established by individual commodity exchanges. The accompanying House Report, H.R. Rep. 93-975, 93d Cong., 2d Sess., 46 (1974), explained that the CEA needed this power to ensure that the local exchanges would establish adequate safeguards. According to the Report, "attorneys to several boards of trade have been advising the boards to reduce — not to expand exchange regulations . . . , since there is a growing body of opinion that failure to enforce the exchange rules is a violation of the Act which will support suits by private litigants." From this observation the Court purports to infer that Congress must have approved of the *Goodman* line of cases.

This single quotation, however, is entirely neutral as to approval or disapproval. Moreover, there is persuasive evidence on the face of the statute that Congress did not contemplate a judicial remedy for damages against the exchanges. The 1974 amendments explicitly subjected the exchanges to fines and other sanctions for nonenforcement of their own rules. But the statute specifies that fines may not exceed $100,000 per violation, and that the Commission must determine whether the amount of any fine will impair an exchange's ability to perform its functions. A private damages action would not be so limited and therefore would expose the exchanges to greater liability than Congress evidently intended.

The second statutory change cited by the Court actually undercuts rather than supports its case. The Court notes that the 1974 Congress enacted two sections creating procedures for reimbursing victims of CEA violations. In its view these sections evidence a further intent to enhance the availability of relief in damages. Yet the Court suggests no reason why the 1974 Congress would have enacted these duplicative channels for damages recovery if it intended at the same time to approve the implied private damages actions permitted by *Goodman*. Rather, the Court flatly contravenes settled rules for the identification of congressional intent. "[I]t is an elemental canon of statutory construction that where a statute expressly provides a particular remedy or remedies, a court must be chary of reading others into it." *TAMA*, supra, 444 U.S., at 19. "In the absence of strong indicia of a contrary congressional intent, we are compelled to conclude that Congress provided precisely the remedies it considered appropriate." *Sea Clammers*, supra, 453 U.S., at 15.

The Court finally relies upon congressional enactment of a so-called jurisdictional saving clause as part of the 1974 amendments:

> Nothing in this section shall supersede or limit the *jurisdiction* conferred on courts of the United States or any State.

Section 201, codified at 7 U.S.C. §2 (emphasis added).

By its terms the saving clause simply is irrelevant to the issue at hand: whether a cause of action should be implied under particular provisions of the CEA. Where judicially cognizable claims do exist, the saving clause makes clear that federal courts retain their jurisdiction. But it neither creates nor preserves any *substantive* right to sue for damages. And it is settled by our cases that "[t]he source of the plaintiffs' rights must be found, if at all, in the substantive provisions of the . . . Act which they seek to enforce, not in the jurisdictional provision." Touche Ross & Co. v. Redington, 442 U.S., at 577. Cf. *Sea Clammers*, supra, 453

U.S., at 15-17 (refusing to imply right of action even from a *substantive* "saving clause").

B

Despite its imaginative use of other sources, the Court neglects the only unambiguous evidence of Congress's intent respecting private actions for civil damages under the CEA. That evidence is a chart that appears in the record of Senate committee hearings. This chart compares features of four proposed bills with the "Present Commodities Exchange Act." It evidently was prepared by the expert committee staff advising the legislators who considered the 1974 amendments.

The chart is detailed. It occupies five pages of the hearing record. Comparing the feature of "civil money penalties" between the different proposed bills, however, the chart does not list "implied damages actions" under the existing Act. Rather, it says there are "none." Neither does the chart make any reference to implied private damages actions under any of the four proposed amending bills. . . .

III

The Court's holding today may reflect its view of desirable policy. If so, this view is doubly mistaken.

First, modern federal regulatory statutes tend to be exceedingly complex. Especially in this context, courts should recognize that intricate policy calculations are necessary to decide when new enforcement measures are desirable additions to a particular regulatory structure. Judicial creation of private rights of action is as likely to disrupt as to assist the functioning of the regulatory schemes developed by Congress.

Today's decision also is disquieting because of its implicit view of the judicial role in the creation of federal law. The Court propounds a test that taxes the legislative branch with a duty to respond to opinions of the lower federal courts. The penalty for silence is the risk of having those erroneous judicial opinions imputed to Congress itself — on the basis of its presumptive knowledge of "the contemporary legal context." Despite the Court's allusion to the lawmaking powers of courts at common law, this view is inconsistent with the theory and structure of our constitutional government.

For reasons that I have expressed before, I remain convinced that "we should not condone the implication of any private right of action from a federal statute absent the most compelling evidence that Congress in fact intended such an action to exist." Cannon v. University of Chicago, supra, 441 U.S., at 749 (Powell, J., dissenting). Here the evidence falls far short of this constitutionally appropriate standard. . . .

NOTES ON IMPLIED REMEDIES FOR
STATUTORY VIOLATIONS

1. *Curran* is the only Supreme Court case to squarely acknowledge
the extent to which the Court has repudiated prior law in this area. The
traditional view was that the intended beneficiaries of a statute could sue
for damages from a violation unless the statute implied that such claims
should not be allowed. The statute created the right; the common law
created the remedy unless the statute negated it.

The four dissenters in *Curran* absolutely reject that view. They think
the federal courts have no power whatever to create remedies, that Congress should do so explicitly, and that only in the most extraordinarily
clear cases should the courts decide that Congress implicitly created a
remedy. Their views generally commanded a majority in the late 1970s
and early 1980s. It is too early to tell whether *Curran* is a new turning
point, a grandfather clause for statutes enacted in an earlier era when the
Court freely implied remedies, or a sport.

2. The Court's turnaround is conventionally dated from Cort v. Ash,
422 U.S. 66 (1975). But that is misleading. The president of Bethlehem
Steel made speeches on issues pending in the 1972 presidential election,
and Bethlehem widely disseminated excerpts of those speeches. A criminal statute provided that corporations could not spend money on presidential elections. Ash owned fifty shares of Bethlehem's stock; he was also
a registered voter. He sued in his own behalf and derivatively on behalf of
Bethlehem, seeking damages and an injunction to prevent further violations of the statute.

Justice Brennan wrote the opinion for a unanimous Court, finding no
implied cause of action. It would have been easy enough to say that the
statute was concerned with the integrity of elections and conferred no
special benefit on Ash or Bethlehem. But Brennan was more thorough;
he identified four "factors" that had been discussed in earlier implied
cause of action cases:

> First, is the plaintiff "one of the class for whose *especial* benefit the statute was
> enacted," Texas & Pacific R. Co. v. Rigsby, 241 U.S. 33, 39 (1916) — that is,
> does the statute create a federal right in favor of the plaintiff? Second, is there
> any indication of legislative intent, explicit or implicit, either to create such a
> remedy or to deny one? Third, is it consistent with the underlying purposes of
> the legislative scheme to imply such a remedy for the plaintiff? And finally, is
> the cause of action one traditionally relegated to state law, in an area basically
> the concern of the States, so that it would be inappropriate to infer a cause of
> action based solely on federal law?

422 U.S. at 78 (emphasis added by Justice Brennan).

There was no sign here of any sharp change of course. Indeed, the
Court noted that where the first factor was clearly established, "it is not

necessary to show an intention to *create* a private cause of action, although an explicit purpose to *deny* such a cause of action would be controlling." Id. at 82.

3. The big shift came in Touche Ross & Co. v. Redington, 442 U.S. 560 (1979), a suit under §17(a) of the Securities Exchange Act of 1934. Section 17(a) requires brokerage houses to file financial statements; plaintiffs sued auditors who certified false statements. The Securities Investor Protection Corporation, the government agency that insures brokerage accounts, urged the Court to find an implied cause of action.

The Court said no; Justice Rehnquist wrote the opinion. Without acknowledging any shift of course, he said that "our task is limited solely to determining whether Congress intended to create the private right of action. . . . " Id. at 568. He admitted that Cort v. Ash mentioned four factors, but he said they were not of equal weight. Subsequent opinions have continued to cite the four factors, but only congressional intent has mattered. And the majority has read legislative history with a strong predisposition to find no intent to create a private remedy. Many of the cases are cited in Justice Powell's dissent in *Curran*.

4. What is wrong with the traditional view? Why shouldn't the intended beneficiaries of a statute be able to enforce it? "The very essence of civil liberty certainly consists in the right of every individual to claim the protection of the laws, whenever he receives an injury." Marbury v. Madison, 5 U.S. (1 Cranch) 137, 163 (1803). If Congress legislates against fraud, why shouldn't the presumption be that it intended compensation for the victims?

5. Justice Stevens suggests that the increasing quantity and complexity of legislation required a change in approach. Justice Powell suggests that damage liability might be counterproductive; for example, it might impoverish the exchanges, who are supposed to be an enforcement agency. How far do these arguments reach? Do they argue for examining each case to make sure there are no strong reasons to deny a remedy? Or do they justify reversing the presumption and cutting off most remedies? The suit against the exchange for not preventing the fraud gives Powell an easy target. When could it ever be counterproductive to impose liability on the primary perpetrators of the fraud?

6. Powell's intense opposition to implied causes of action can only be explained by his separation of powers argument. Whose responsibility is it to make remedies? Certainly Congress could enact a code of federal remedies if it wanted to, or include exclusive remedies provisions in every statute. If it took that route, courts would be bound. But it has not taken that route. Anglo-American law has a rich inventory of common law and equitable remedies, created by the courts and largely left to the courts. I would like to lead you through the argument for both sides, but I can't think of a thing to say on behalf of Powell's view of separation of powers. Surely when the framers vested "the judicial power" in the courts, the

phrase included the power to apply judicial remedies to substantive rights.

Powell's response apparently is that federal courts are different because they have no common law powers. But of course that grossly overstates Erie Railroad Co. v. Tompkins, 304 U.S. 64 (1938). *Erie* held that the federal courts have no general power to make common law on matters left to the states. It said nothing about judicial power to make common law on subjects constitutionally committed to the federal government and not controlled by statute. The federal courts do that all the time. Justice Brandeis announced such an opinion the same day he announced *Erie*, applying federal common law to divide the waters of an interstate stream. Hinderlider v. La Plata River & Cherry Creek Ditch Co., 304 U.S. 92 (1938). The large body of federal common law is reviewed in Friendly, In Praise of *Erie* — And of the New Federal Common Law, 39 N.Y.U.L. Rev. 383, 405-422 (1964). Remedies for violations of federal substantive rights fit well within that function.

7. *Curran* implies a remedy for violations of the Commodities Exchange Act because lower court decisions had implied such a remedy at the time of the most recent amendments to the act. Should it matter whether there were decisions under a specific statute? Isn't it reasonable to assume that Congress relied on the courts to take care of remedies during the era when remedies were freely implied? The Court didn't clearly change the rules until 1979. Shouldn't *Curran*'s reasoning apply to all statutes enacted before then?

8. Presumably Congress can cope with the new regime and include remedies provisions in all its legislation. But think about the implications of that requirement for the legislative process. It is always easier to kill a provision than to enact it. If the courts assume that the intended beneficiaries of a statute may sue for damages under it, the opponents of the remedy have to insert a provision taking that right away. If the courts assume that victims can't sue, the proponents have to insert a section creating a remedy. That is one more battle the proponents have to win. It provides one more target for opponents to shoot at, and one more opportunity for fence sitters to sabotage the bill and then vote for it. There is a bit of deception in this last tactic; on the other hand, there may be a bit of deception in creating liability for damages implicitly instead of explicitly.

9. How do you argue for or against an implied cause of action? Obviously you comb the legislative history for scraps that suggest an answer one way or the other. But the Court has also suggested a more surprising technique. Cannon v. University of Chicago, 441 U.S. 677 (1979), suggested a focus on the statutory language. *Cannon* says that if a statute mentions its beneficiaries, they generally have a cause of action; if it simply declares a standard of conduct, generally no one has a cause of action. For example, "no person shall be denied the right to vote" creates

a private cause of action; "it shall be the duty of every common carrier to establish just and reasonable rates" does not. Id. at 690 n.13.

10.   Lack of a private cause of action does not make a statute a dead letter. There may be criminal penalties for its violation, and there is often an administrative agency to enforce it. But the agency can typically investigate only a handful of cases. For example, the government has told the Supreme Court that every year it can inspect fewer than 4 percent of the employers subject to the Fair Labor Standards Act. Employees of Department of Public Health & Welfare v. Department of Public Health & Welfare, 411 U.S. 279, 287 (1973). A damage action for victims creates a vast army of potential enforcers. Private enforcers will demand compensation; public enforcers often won't or can't. The Commodities Futures Trading Commission investigated the potato conspiracies. The investigation ended in a consent decree under which one short conspirator was suspended from trading for four years, and another for six years. A damage suit against the same two conspirators ended in a jury verdict for $460,000. Hughes, Damages Awarded Over 1976 Default of Potato Futures, Wall St. J., Nov. 21, 1983, at 46, col. 3.

11.   Some regulatory statutes supplement common law. For example, the potato conspirators were probably guilty of common law fraud as well as violations of the Commodities Exchange Act. Victims could have sued for fraud in state court. Most victims find that a much less attractive remedy. The standard of proof is likely to be higher, and there are more likely to be technical obstacles to recovery, such as a privity requirement. The statute often enacts prophylactic measures that facilitate proof. For example, the Commodities Exchange Act provides that no single group of traders may go short more than 150 contracts. The short conspirators were 1,900 contracts short. That is an objective fact, simple to prove, and it is an easy inference that default and resulting losses to other investors were proximate consequences of going so far over the limit. It is easier to prove that violation than to prove fraudulent intent.

On the other hand, the *Curran* dissenters consider it an advantage to keep these cases in state court. They see federal courts as too crowded and too powerful. They want to return power and caseload to state courts, because that is their vision of federalism and because there are a lot more state judges than there are federal judges.

BIVENS v. SIX UNKNOWN NAMED AGENTS OF FEDERAL BUREAU OF NARCOTICS
403 U.S. 388 (1971)

MR. JUSTICE BRENNAN delivered the opinion of the Court.

The Fourth Amendment provides that:

> The right of the people to be secure in their persons, houses, papers, and
> effects, against unreasonable searches and seizures, shall not be violated. . . .

In Bell v. Hood, 327 U.S. 678 (1946), we reserved the question whether
violation of that command by a federal agent acting under color of his
authority gives rise to a cause of action for damages consequent upon his
unconstitutional conduct. Today we hold that it does.

This case has its origin in an arrest and search carried out on the
morning of November 26, 1965. Petitioner's complaint alleged that on
that day respondents, agents of the Federal Bureau of Narcotics acting
under claim of federal authority, entered his apartment and arrested him
for alleged narcotics violations. The agents manacled petitioner in front
of his wife and children, and threatened to arrest the entire family. They
searched the apartment from stem to stern. Thereafter petitioner was
taken to the federal courthouse in Brooklyn, where he was interrogated,
booked, and subjected to a visual strip search.

On July 7, 1967, petitioner brought suit in Federal District Court. In
addition to the allegations above, his complaint asserted that the arrest
and search were effected without a warrant, and that unreasonable force
was employed in making the arrest; fairly read, it alleges as well that the
arrest was made without probable cause. Petitioner claimed to have suffered great humiliation, embarrassment, and mental suffering as a result
of the agents' unlawful conduct, and sought $15,000 damages from each
of them. The District Court, on respondents' motion, dismissed the complaint on the ground, inter alia, that it failed to state a cause of action.
The Court of Appeals, one judge concurring specially, affirmed on that
basis.

We reverse.

I

Respondents do not argue that petitioner should be entirely without remedy for an unconstitutional invasion of his rights by federal agents. In
respondents' view, however, the rights that petitioner asserts — primarily
rights of privacy — are creations of state and not of federal law. Accordingly, they argue, petitioner may obtain money damages to redress invasion of these rights only by an action in tort, under state law, in the state
courts. In this scheme the Fourth Amendment would serve merely to
limit the extent to which the agents could defend the state law tort suit by
asserting that their actions were a valid exercise of federal power: if the
agents were shown to have violated the Fourth Amendment, such a
defense would be lost to them and they would stand before the state law
merely as private individuals. Candidly admitting that it is the policy of
the Department of Justice to remove all such suits from the state to the
federal courts for decision, respondents nevertheless urge that we uphold

dismissal of petitioner's complaint in federal court, and remit him to filing an action in the state courts in order that the case may properly be removed to the federal court for decision on the basis of state law.

We think that respondents' thesis rests upon an unduly restrictive view of the Fourth Amendment's protection against unreasonable searches and seizures by federal agents, a view that has consistently been rejected by this Court. Respondents seek to treat the relationship between a citizen and a federal agent unconstitutionally exercising his authority as no different from the relationship between two private citizens. In so doing, they ignore the fact that power, once granted, does not disappear like a magic gift when it is wrongfully used. An agent acting — albeit unconstitutionally — in the name of the United States possesses a far greater capacity for harm than an individual trespasser exercising no authority other than his own. Accordingly, as our cases make clear, the Fourth Amendment operates as a limitation upon the exercise of federal power regardless of whether the State in whose jurisdiction that power is exercised would prohibit or penalize the identical act if engaged in by a private citizen. It guarantees to citizens of the United States the absolute right to be free from unreasonable searches and seizures carried out by virtue of federal authority. And "where federally protected rights have been invaded, it has been the rule from the beginning that courts will be alert to adjust their remedies so as to grant the necessary relief." Bell v. Hood, 327 U.S., at 684. . . .

That damages may be obtained for injuries consequent upon a violation of the Fourth Amendment by federal officials should hardly seem a surprising proposition. Historically, damages have been regarded as the ordinary remedy for an invasion of personal interests in liberty. Of course, the Fourth Amendment does not in so many words provide for its enforcement by an award of money damages for the consequences of its violation. But "it is . . . well settled that where legal rights have been invaded, and a federal statute provides for a general right to sue for such invasion, federal courts may use any available remedy to make good the wrong done." Bell v. Hood, 327 U.S., at 684. The present case involves no special factors counselling hesitation in the absence of affirmative action by Congress. We are not dealing with a question of "federal fiscal policy," as in United States v. Standard Oil Co., 332 U.S. 301, 311 (1947). In that case we refused to infer from the Government-soldier relationship that the United States could recover damages from one who negligently injured a soldier and thereby caused the Government to pay his medical expenses and lose his services during the course of his hospitalization. Noting that Congress was normally quite solicitous where the federal purse was involved, we pointed out that "the United States [was] the party plaintiff to the suit. And the United States has power at any time to create the liability." Id., at 316. Nor are we asked in this case to impose liability upon a congressional employee for actions contrary to no constitutional prohibition, but merely said to be in excess of the authority delegated to him by the Congress. Wheeldin v. Wheeler, 373 U.S. 647 (1963).

Finally, we cannot accept respondents' formulation of the question as whether the availability of money damages is necessary to enforce the Fourth Amendment. For we have here no explicit congressional declaration that persons injured by a federal officer's violation of the Fourth Amendment may not recover money damages from the agents, but must instead be remitted to another remedy, equally effective in the view of Congress. The question is merely whether petitioner, if he can demonstrate an injury consequent upon the violation by federal agents of his Fourth Amendment rights, is entitled to redress his injury through a particular remedial mechanism normally available in the federal courts. "The very essence of civil liberty certainly consists in the right of every individual to claim the protection of the laws, whenever he receives an injury." Marbury v. Madison, 1 Cranch 137, 163 (1803). Having concluded that petitioner's complaint states a cause of action under the Fourth Amendment, we hold that petitioner is entitled to recover money damages for any injuries he has suffered as a result of the agents' violation of the Amendment. . . .

MR. JUSTICE HARLAN, concurring in the judgment. . . .

I

I turn first to the contention that the constitutional power of federal courts to accord Bivens damages for his claim depends on the passage of a statute creating a "federal cause of action." Although the point is not entirely free of ambiguity, I do not understand either the Government or my dissenting Brothers to maintain that Bivens' contention that he is entitled to be free from the type of official conduct prohibited by the Fourth Amendment depends on a decision by the State in which he resides to accord him a remedy. Such a position would be incompatible with the presumed availability of federal equitable relief, if a proper showing can be made in terms of the ordinary principles governing equitable remedies. However broad a federal court's discretion concerning equitable remedies, it is absolutely clear. . . . that in a nondiversity suit a federal court's power to grant even equitable relief depends on the presence of a substantive right derived from federal law.

Thus the interest which Bivens claims — to be free from official conduct in contravention of the Fourth Amendment — is a federally protected interest. Therefore, the question of judicial *power* to grant Bivens damages is not a problem of the "source" of the "right"; instead, the question is whether the power to authorize damages as a judicial remedy for the vindication of a federal constitutional right is placed by the Constitution itself exclusively in Congress' hands.

II

The contention that the federal courts are powerless to accord a litigant damages for a claimed invasion of his federal constitutional rights until Congress explicitly authorizes the remedy cannot rest on the notion that the decision to grant compensatory relief involves a resolution of policy considerations not susceptible of judicial discernment. Thus, in suits for damages based on violations of federal statutes lacking any express authorization of a damage remedy, this Court has authorized such relief where, in its view, damages are necessary to effectuate the congressional policy underpinning the substantive provisions of the statute.

If it is not the nature of the remedy which is thought to render a judgment as to the appropriateness of damages inherently "legislative," then it must be the nature of the legal interest offered as an occasion for invoking otherwise appropriate judicial relief. But I do not think that the fact that the interest is protected by the Constitution rather than statute or common law justifies the assertion that federal courts are powerless to grant damages in the absence of explicit congressional action authorizing the remedy. Initially, I note that it would be at least anomalous to conclude that the federal judiciary — while competent to choose among the range of traditional judicial remedies to implement statutory and common-law policies, and even to generate substantive rules governing primary behavior in furtherance of broadly formulated policies articulated by statute or Constitution, is powerless to accord a damages remedy to vindicate social policies which, by virtue of their inclusion in the Constitution, are aimed predominantly at restraining the Government as an instrument of the popular will.

More importantly, the presumed availability of federal equitable relief against threatened invasions of constitutional interests appears entirely to negate the contention that the status of an interest as constitutionally protected divests federal courts of the power to grant damages absent express congressional authorization. . . .

If explicit congressional authorization is an absolute prerequisite to the power of a federal court to accord compensatory relief regardless of the necessity or appropriateness of damages as a remedy simply because of the status of a legal interest as constitutionally protected, then it seems to me that explicit congressional authorization is similarly prerequisite to the exercise of equitable remedial discretion in favor of constitutionally protected interests. Conversely, if a general grant of jurisdiction to the federal courts by Congress is thought adequate to empower a federal court to grant equitable relief for all areas of subject-matter jurisdiction enumerated therein, then it seems to me that the same statute is sufficient to empower a federal court to grant a traditional remedy at law. Of course, the special historical traditions governing the federal equity system might still bear on the comparative appropriateness of granting equitable relief as opposed to money damages. That possibility, however, relates, not to whether the federal courts have the power to afford one type of remedy as opposed to the other, but rather to the criteria which should govern the exercise of our power. To that question, I now pass.

III

The major thrust of the Government's position is that, where Congress has not expressly authorized a particular remedy, a federal court should exercise its power to accord a traditional form of judicial relief at the behest of a litigant, who claims a constitutionally protected interest has been invaded, only where the remedy is "essential," or "indispensable for vindicating constitutional rights." While this "essentiality" test is most clearly articulated with respect to damage remedies, apparently the Government believes the same test explains the exercise of equitable remedial powers. It is argued that historically the Court has rarely exercised the power to accord such relief in the absence of an express congressional authorization and that "[i]f Congress had thought that federal officers should be subject to a law different than state law, it would have had no difficulty in saying so, as it did with respect to state officers. . . ." 42 U.S.C. §1983. Although conceding that the standard of determining whether a damage remedy should be utilized to effectuate statutory policies is one of "necessity" or "appropriateness," the Government contends that questions concerning congressional discretion to modify judicial remedies relating to constitutionally protected interests warrant a more stringent constraint on the exercise of judicial power with respect to this class of legally protected interests.

These arguments for a more stringent test to govern the grant of damages in constitutional cases seem to be adequately answered by the point that the judiciary has a particular responsibility to assure the vindication of constitutional interests such as those embraced by the Fourth Amendment. . . . [T]he Bill of Rights is particularly intended to vindicate the interests of the individual in the face of the popular will as expressed in legislative majorities; at the very least, it strikes me as no more appropriate to await express congressional authorization of traditional judicial relief with regard to these legal interests than with respect to interests protected by federal statutes.

The question then, is, as I see it, whether compensatory relief is "necessary" or "appropriate" to the vindication of the interest asserted. In resolving that question, it seems to me that the range of policy considerations we may take into account is at least as broad as the range of those a legislature would consider with respect to an express statutory authorization of a traditional remedy. . . .

I think it is clear that Bivens advances a claim of the sort that, if proved, would be properly compensable in damages. The personal interests protected by the Fourth Amendment are those we attempt to capture by the notion of "privacy"; while the Court today properly points out that the type of harm which officials can inflict when they invade protected zones of an individual's life are different from the types of harm private citizens inflict on one another, the experience of judges in dealing with private trespass and false imprisonment claims supports the conclusion that courts of law are capable of making the types of judgment concerning causation and magnitude of injury necessary to accord meaningful compensation for invasion of Fourth Amendment rights.

On the other hand, the limitations on state remedies for violation of common-law rights by private citizens argue in favor of a federal damages remedy. The injuries inflicted by officials acting under color of law, while no less compensable in damages than those inflicted by private parties, are substantially different in kind, as the Court's opinion today discusses in detail. It seems to me entirely proper that these injuries be compensable according to uniform rules of federal law, especially in light of the very large element of federal law which must in any event control the scope of official defenses to liability. . . .

Putting aside the desirability of leaving the problem of federal official liability to the vagaries of common-law actions, it is apparent that some form of damages is the only possible remedy for someone in Bivens' alleged position. It will be a rare case indeed in which an individual in Bivens' position will be able to obviate the harm by securing injunctive relief from any court. However desirable a direct remedy against the Government might be as a substitute for individual official liability, the sovereign still remains immune to suit. Finally, assuming Bivens' innocence of the crime charged, the "exclusionary rule" is simply irrelevant. For people in Bivens' shoes, it is damages or nothing.

The only substantial policy consideration advanced against recognition of a federal cause of action for violation of Fourth Amendment rights by federal officials is the incremental expenditure of judicial resources that will be necessitated by this class of litigation. There is, however, something ultimately self-defeating about this argument. For if, as the Government contends, damages will rarely be realized by plaintiffs in these cases because of jury hostility, the limited resources of the official concerned, etc., then I am not ready to assume that there will be a significant increase in the expenditure of judicial resources on these claims. Few responsible lawyers and plaintiffs are likely to choose the course of litigation if the statistical chances of success are truly de minimis. And I simply cannot agree with my Brother Black that the possibility of "frivolous" claims — if defined simply as claims with no legal merit — warrants closing the courthouse doors to people in Bivens' situation. There are other ways, short of that, of coping with frivolous lawsuits.

On the other hand, if — as I believe is the case with respect, at least, to the most flagrant abuses of official power — damages to some degree will be available when the option of litigation is chosen, then the question appears to be how Fourth Amendment interests rank on a scale of social values compared with, for example, the interests of stockholders defrauded by misleading proxies. Judicial resources, I am well aware, are increasingly scarce these days. Nonetheless, when we automatically close the courthouse door solely on this basis, we implicitly express a value judgment on the comparative importance of classes of legally protected interests. And current limitations upon the effective functioning of the courts arising from budgetary inadequacies should not be permitted to stand in the way of the recognition of otherwise sound constitutional principles. . . .

MR. CHIEF JUSTICE BURGER, dissenting.

I dissent from today's holding which judicially creates a damage remedy not provided for by the Constitution and not enacted by Congress. We would more surely preserve the important values of the doctrine of separation of powers — and perhaps get a better result — by recommending a solution to the Congress as the branch of government in which the Constitution has vested the legislative power. Legislation is the business of the Congress, and it has the facilities and competence for that task — as we do not. . . .

MR. JUSTICE BLACK, dissenting. . . .

If it wanted to do so, Congress could, of course, create a remedy against federal officials who violate the Fourth Amendment in the performance of their duties. But the point of this case and the fatal weakness in the Court's judgment is that neither Congress nor the State of New York has enacted legislation creating such a right of action. For us to do so is, in my judgment, an exercise of power that the Constitution does not give us.

Even if we had the legislative power to create a remedy, there are many reasons why we should decline to create a cause of action where none has existed since the formation of our Government. The courts of the United States as well as those of the States are choked with lawsuits. . . .

My fellow Justices on this Court and our brethren throughout the federal judiciary know only too well the time-consuming task of conscientiously poring over hundreds of thousands of pages of factual allegations of misconduct by police, judicial, and corrections officials. Of course, there are instances of legitimate grievances, but legislators might well desire to devote judicial resources to other problems of a more serious nature.

We sit at the top of a judicial system accused by some of nearing the point of collapse. Many criminal defendants do not receive speedy trials and neither society nor the accused are assured of justice when inordinate delays occur. Citizens must wait years to litigate their private civil suits. Substantial changes in correctional and parole systems demand the attention of the lawmakers and the judiciary. If I were a legislator I might well find these and other needs so pressing as to make me believe that the resources of lawyers and judges should be devoted to them rather than to civil damage actions against officers who generally strive to perform within constitutional bounds. There is also a real danger that such suits might deter officials from the *proper* and honest performance of their duties.

All of these considerations make imperative careful study and weighing of the arguments both for and against the creation of such a remedy under the Fourth Amendment. I would have great difficulty for myself in resolving the competing policies, goals, and priorities in the use of resources, if I thought it were my job to resolve those questions. But that is not my task. The task of evaluating the pros and cons of creating judicial remedies for particular wrongs is a matter for Congress and the legislatures of the States. . . . Cases could be cited to support the legal proposition which I assert, but it seems to me to be a matter of common understanding that the business of the judiciary is to interpret the laws and not to make them. . . .

MR. JUSTICE BLACKMUN, dissenting.

I too, dissent. I do so largely for the reasons expressed in Chief Judge Lumbard's thoughtful and scholarly opinion for the Court of Appeals. But I also feel that the judicial legislation, which the Court by its opinion today concededly is effectuating, opens the door for another avalanche of new federal cases. . . .

NOTES ON IMPLIED REMEDIES FOR CONSTITUTIONAL VIOLATIONS

1. *Bivens* raises the implied cause of action issue in the constitutional context. It dates from the earlier period when the Court freely implied private remedies for statutory violations. But *Bivens* is still good law; the Court has not retrenched on constitutional remedies nearly as much as it has on statutory remedies.

2. Most constitutional provisions can be violated only by the government and its employees. But the government and its employees are often immune from suit, and that is another obstacle that *Bivens* plaintiffs must overcome. The government's immunity from damages is absolute unless waived, but most of its employees have only partial immunity. Conse-

quently, the implied cause of action for constitutional violations is effective only against the offending employees, and not against the government itself. We will examine these immunities in section C.

3. The lower courts responded warily to *Bivens*. Some thought that *Bivens* announced a rule about the fourth amendment and not a rule about constitutional rights generally. This led to an effort to pick and choose constitutional rights; there was compensation for some rights and not for others.

4. The Supreme Court rejected that approach in Davis v. Passman, 442 U.S. 228 (1979). Otto Passman was a congressman from Louisiana; Shirley Davis worked on his staff. He decided to fire her. Either because he believed it or because he thought it would help cushion the blow, he told her in writing that she was "able, energetic and a very hard worker," but he had decided that it was "essential" to have a man for the job.

She sued him for sex discrimination. But Congress had exempted itself from the employment discrimination statute, so she argued that Passman had violated the equal protection component of the fifth amendment's due process clause. The Fifth Circuit tried to apply the four factors of Cort v. Ash and concluded that "due process" was too vague to support a *Bivens* action.

A majority of the Supreme Court found Cort v. Ash irrelevant:

> the question of who may enforce a *statutory* right is fundamentally different from the question of who may enforce a right that is protected by the Constitution.
>
> Statutory rights and obligations are protected by Congress, and it is entirely appropriate for Congress . . . to determine . . . who may enforce them and in what manner. . . .
>
> At least in the absence of "a textually demonstrable constitutional commitment of [an] issue to a coordinate political department," Baker v. Carr, 369 U.S. 186, 217 (1962), we presume that justiciable constitutional rights are to be enforced through the courts. And, unless such rights are to become merely precatory, the class of those litigants who allege that their own constitutional rights have been violated, and who at the same time have no effective means other than the judiciary to enforce these rights, must be able to invoke the existing jurisdiction of the courts for the protection of their justiciable constitutional rights.

442 U.S. at 241-242.

The Court went on to consider whether damages were an appropriate remedy, and rather easily concluded that they were. Justices Burger, Stewart, Powell, and Rehnquist dissented; the majority was the same five justices who made up the majority in *Curran*.

5. The same majority decided Carlson v. Green, 446 U.S. 14 (1980). Green alleged that that her son had died due to medical neglect in a

federal prison; she asserted claims under the due process, equal protection, and cruel and unusual punishment clauses. The court implied a cause of action. It said broadly that *"Bivens* established that the victims of a constitutional violation by a federal agent have a right to recover damages. . . ." Id. at 18. This right could be defeated if there were "special factors counselling hesitation," or if Congress had "provided an alternative remedy which it explicitly declared to be a *substitute* for recovery directly under the Constitution and viewed as equally effective." Id. at 18-19. Neither exception was met in *Carlson*. Although plaintiff could have sued the United States under the Federal Tort Claims Act, Congress had not indicated that that remedy was a substitute for a constitutional claim against the responsible prison officials. Indeed, the Senate Report on recent amendments to the Tort Claims Act indicated that both remedies would be available.

Justices Powell and Stewart concurred in the judgment but objected to the broad statement that *Bivens* remedies were generally available. Chief Justice Burger indicated a willingness to acquiesce in *Bivens,* but dissented on the ground that the Tort Claims remedy was exclusive. Only Justice Rehnquist continued to argue that *Bivens* was an usurpation that should be repudiated.

6. The Court unanimously refused to imply a *Bivens* remedy for a federal employee discharged for making comments to the press. Bush v. Lucas, 462 U.S. 367 (1983). The Court assumed that plaintiff's first amendment rights had been violated. But Congress had created an elaborate and comprehensive administrative remedy through the Civil Service Commission, and the Court thought that was exclusive. Plaintiff thought the Civil Service remedy inadequate, because it didn't provide for punitive damages, jury trial, attorneys' fees, or compensation for mental suffering. It did provide for reinstatement with back pay.

Justice Marshall's concurrence asked whether the administrative remedy was arguably as good as a damage remedy, and concluded that it was. There were advantages to balance its disadvantages. The employing agency bore the burden of proof before the Commission; plaintiff would bear the burden in a damage action. Supervisors who acted reasonably would have qualified immunity from damages; the government claimed no immunity before the Civil Service Commission. Administrative procedure might be quicker and less expensive than judicial procedure. Marshall thought Congress could reasonably have concluded that the remedy it provided was just as good as a damage remedy. Justice Brennan joined the concurrence; both joined the opinion of the Court.

The Court's opinion took a different approach. It assumed that the administrative remedy was less than complete. The Court thought it should defer to "an elaborate remedial system that has been constructed step by step with careful attention to conflicting policy considerations."

462 U.S. at 388. It noted that Congress often relied on low level federal employees to report on agency malfeasance, so Congress had no reason to be hostile to plaintiff's claim. And it noted the widespread view that government supervisors were already too reluctant to discipline employees, and that the fear of personal liability could aggravate that reluctance. In this part of the opinion the Court seems to be reviewing the congressional judgment for reasonableness. But it never says that is the standard; the only explicit requirement is that Congress consider the matter "careful[ly]."

7. The Court also held unanimously that enlisted military personnel cannot sue their superior officers for constitutional violations. Chappell v. Wallace, 462 U.S. 296 (1983). The case involved five black sailors on a combat vessel who accused their officers of race discrimination. The Court thought that the military's need for unquestioning obedience to superior officers was a "special factor counseling hesitation." It also noted that the Uniform Code of Military Justice provided a mechanism for plaintiffs to complain to their captain's superiors.

8. Justice Black's separation of powers argument in *Bivens* sounds just like Justice Powell's separation of powers argument in *Curran*. Justice Rehnquist elaborates on the separation of powers argument in his dissent in Carlson v. Green. Isn't that argument even weaker in *Bivens* than in *Curran*? If constitutional rights are supposed to protect minorities and isolated individuals from oppressive majorities, how can Congress have power to decide whether these rights ought to be enforced? Could Congress repeal the Bill of Rights by refusing to create remedies?

9. Justice Rehnquist concedes that the Court can enforce the Bill of Rights with injunctions. His dissent in *Carlson* acknowledges that "federal courts have historically had broad authority to fashion equitable remedies." 446 U.S. at 42. But he insists that that is irrelevant to damage remedies, where the history is different. How is authorizing a damage remedy any more an inherently legislative function than authorizing an equitable remedy? Rehnquist doesn't say. And Justice Black's dissent in *Bivens* doesn't even acknowledge the injunction cases.

10. The Court has enforced the constitution by injunction or mandamus from the beginning, in hundreds of cases. Most of the cases involve state defendants, and 42 U.S.C. §1983 (1982) is a general authorization for suits against state officials who violate federal rights. Thus, Justice Black can say in *Bivens* that Congress has authorized the suits against state officials. But the practice is older than §1983. In Osborne v. President of the Bank of the United States, 22 U.S. (9 Wheat.) 738 (1824), the Court enjoined the Treasurer of Ohio from collecting an unconstitutional tax from the Bank.

No one has ever suggested that lack of express statutory authorization is relevant to injunctions ordering federal officials to obey the constitution. Justice Black joined the unanimous opinion in Bolling v. Sharpe,

347 U.S. 497 (1954), ordering the District of Columbia to desegregate its schools. That was an implied cause of action under the fifth amendment due process clause. Surely Black didn't mean to repudiate it as an usurpation. But how is it different from *Bivens*?

On the other hand, if it's no different, why did so many lawyers file injunction cases before anyone filed a damage case? A preventive injunction prevents acts that the constitution forbids. A damage remedy, a reparative injunction, and most structural injunctions remedy a past violation that cannot be wholly undone. Are preventive injunctions more easily deducible directly from the constitutional prohibitions? None of the dissenters has suggested that argument, and none has drawn a line between different kinds of injunctions.

11.   Justice Rehnquist concedes that damage actions have long been available for violation of the just compensation clause. But he says that clause is unique because it specifically requires "compensation." Thus, it too is irrelevant to *Bivens*. How persuasive is that?

Note that the right created by the just compensation clause is narrower than other rights. Compensation is the only right it creates; there is no right not to have your property taken for public use. Thus ordering compensation under that clause is more analogous to ordering agents not to search than to compensating for a completed search. Thus, it may be plausible to say that the just compensation cases are like the equity cases. But Rehnquist still hasn't explained why courts have power to create equitable remedies but no power to create damage remedies.

12.   These notes have assumed that there is no congressional authorization for *Bivens*'s claim. But that is not entirely clear. Plaintiff must clear four separate hurdles to get a remedy against the government: He must identify a substantive right, a grant of jurisdiction, a right of action for a private remedy, and a waiver of immunity. The same four hurdles face a plaintiff suing a government official, although the immunity argument is structured differently. One of the obstacles to creating remedies in this area is that the Court treats the four hurdles as almost entirely independent: that Congress created a substantive right, granted jurisdiction, and waived immunity does not necessarily mean it created a cause of action. United States v. Testan, 424 U.S. 392 (1976).

In *Bivens*, the fourth amendment creates the substantive right. His claim arises under the constitution, so 28 U.S.C. §1331 (1982) confers jurisdiction. The Court subsequently decided that the agents have only qualified immunity. That leaves the question whether Congress said anything about a private remedy or left the courts wholly on their own.

Two statutes suggest that Congress intended that a substantive right plus a grant of jurisdiction should never fail for want of a remedy. These statutes would seem to ensure that federal courts have all the powers they need to handle cases within their jurisdiction. One such statute is the Rules of Decision Act:

The laws of the several states, except where the Constitution or treaties of the United States or Acts of Congress otherwise require or provide, shall be regarded as rules of decision in civil actions in the courts of the United States, in cases where they apply.

28 U.S.C. §1652 (1982). The statutory language of the statute is circular (state law is the rule where it applies), but it has always been understood to direct federal courts to apply state law where federal law is silent. And of course state law would include the whole Anglo-American law of remedies. Another such statute is the All Writs Act:

The Supreme Court and all courts established by Act of Congress may issue all writs necessary or appropriate in aid of their respective jurisdictions and agreeable to the usages and principles of law.

28 U.S.C. §1651(a) (1982).

Most of the case law under the All Writs Act deals with "auxiliary writs" — mandamus, prohibition, ne exeat, and such. But these are merely the survivors of a system in which all common law actions were begun by writ. Why isn't the All Writs Act a general authority to apply all remedies "agreeable to the usages and principles of law"?

Neither side in the implied cause of action debate has relied on either statute. Justice Rehnquist asserted their irrelevance in his *Carlson* dissent. But is it so clear that they are irrelevant?

B. INITIATING CRIMINAL AND ADMINISTRATIVE REMEDIES

LINDA R. S. v. RICHARD D.
410 U.S. 614 (1973)

Mr. Justice Marshall delivered the opinion of the Court.

Appellant, the mother of an illegitimate child, brought this action in United States District Court on behalf of herself, her child, and others similarly situated to enjoin the "discriminatory application" of Art. 602 of the Texas Penal Code. . . .

Article 602, in relevant part, provides:

any parent who shall wilfully desert, neglect or refuse to provide for the support and maintenance of his or her child or children under eighteen years of age, shall be guilty of a misdemeanor, and upon conviction, shall be punished by confinement in the County Jail for not more than two years.

The Texas courts have consistently construed this statute to apply solely to the parents of legitimate children and to impose no duty of support on the parents of illegitimate children. In her complaint, appellant alleges that one Richard D. is the father of her child, that Richard D. has refused to provide support for the child, and that although appellant made application to the local district attorney for enforcement of Art. 602 against Richard D., the district attorney refused to take action for the express reason that, in his view, the fathers of illegitimate children were not within the scope of Art. 602.

Appellant argues that this interpretation of Art 602 discriminates between legitimate and illegitimate children without rational foundation and therefore violates the Equal Protection Clause of the Fourteenth Amendment. Although her complaint is not entirely clear on this point, she apparently seeks an injunction running against the district attorney forbidding him from declining prosecution on the ground that the unsupported child is illegitimate.

Before we can consider the merits of appellant's claim or the propriety of the relief requested, however, appellant must first demonstrate that she is entitled to invoke the judicial process. She must, in other words, show that the facts alleged present the court with a "case or controversy" in the constitutional sense and that she is a proper plaintiff to raise the issues sought to be litigated. The threshold question which must be answered is whether the appellant has "alleged such a personal stake in the outcome of the controversy as to assure that concrete adverseness which sharpens the presentation of issues upon which the court so largely depends for illumination of difficult constitutional questions." Baker v. Carr, 369 U.S. 186, 204 (1962).

Recent decisions by this Court have greatly expanded the types of "personal stake[s]" which are capable of conferring standing on a potential plaintiff. But as we pointed out only last Term, "broadening the categories of injury that may be alleged in support of standing is a different matter from abandoning the requirement that the party seeking review must himself have suffered an injury." Sierra Club v. Morton, 405 U.S. 727, 738 (1972). . . . [F]ederal plaintiffs must allege some threatened or actual injury resulting from the putatively illegal action before a federal court may assume jurisdiction.

Applying this test to the facts of this case, we hold that, in the unique context of a challenge to a criminal statute, appellant has failed to allege a sufficient nexus between her injury and the government action which she attacks to justify judicial intervention. To be sure, appellant no doubt suffered an injury stemming from the failure of her child's father to contribute support payments. But the bare existence of an abstract injury meets only the first half of the standing requirement. "The party who invokes [judicial] power must be able to show . . . that he has sustained or is immediately in danger of sustaining some *direct* injury *as the result of* [a statute's] enforcement." Massachusetts v. Mellon, 262 U.S. 447, 488 (1923) (emphasis added). . . .

Here, appellant has made no showing that her failure to secure support payments results from the nonenforcement, as to her child's father, of Art. 602. Although the Texas statute appears to create a continuing duty, it does not follow the civil contempt model whereby the defendant "keeps the keys to the jail in his own pocket" and may be released whenever he complies with his legal obligations. On the contrary, the statute creates a completed offense with a fixed penalty as soon as a parent fails to support his child. Thus, if appellant were granted the requested relief, it would result only in the jailing of the child's father. The prospect that prosecution will, at least in the future, result in payment of support can, at best, be termed only speculative. Certainly the "direct" relationship between the alleged injury and the claim sought to be adjudicated, which previous decisions of this Court suggest is a prerequisite of standing, is absent in this case.

The Court's prior decisions consistently hold that a citizen lacks standing to contest the policies of the prosecuting authority when he himself is neither prosecuted nor threatened with prosecution. See Younger v. Harris, 401 U.S. 37, 42 (1971). Although these cases arose in a somewhat different context, they demonstrate that, in American jurisprudence at least, a private citizen lacks a judicially cognizable interest in the prosecution or nonprosecution of another. Appellant does have an interest in the support of her child. But given the special status of criminal prosecutions in our system, we hold that appellant has made an insufficient showing of a direct nexus between the vindication of her interest and the enforcement of the State's criminal laws. The District Court was therefore correct in dismissing the action for want of standing,[5] and its judgment must be affirmed.

So ordered.

MR. JUSTICE WHITE, with whom MR. JUSTICE DOUGLAS joins, dissenting. . . .

Obviously, there are serious difficulties with appellant's complaint insofar as it may be construed as seeking to require the official appellees to prosecute Richard D. or others, or to obtain what amounts to a federal child-support order. But those difficulties go to the question of what relief the court may ultimately grant appellant. They do not affect her right to bring this class action. The Court notes, as it must, that the father of a legitimate child, if prosecuted under Art. 602, could properly raise the

5. . . . As the District Court stated, "the proper party to challenge the constitutionality of Article 602 would be a parent of a legitimate child who has been prosecuted under the statute. Such a challenge would allege that because the parents of illegitimate children may not be prosecuted, the statute unfairly discriminates against the parents of legitimate children."

statute's underinclusiveness as an affirmative defense. Presumably, that same father would have standing to affirmatively seek to enjoin enforcement of the statute against him. The question then becomes simply: why should only an actual or potential criminal defendant have a recognizable interest in attacking this allegedly discriminatory statute and not appellant and her class? They are not, after all, in the position of members of the public at large who wish merely to force an enlargement of state criminal laws. Appellant, her daughter, and the children born out of wedlock whom she is attempting to represent have all allegedly been excluded intentionally from the class of persons protected by a particular criminal law. They do not get the protection of the laws that other women and children get. Under Art. 602, they are rendered nonpersons; a father may ignore them with full knowledge that he will be subjected to no penal sanctions. The Court states that the actual coercive effect of those sanctions on Richard D. or others "can, at best, be termed only speculative." This is a very odd statement. I had always thought our civilization has assumed that the threat of penal sanctions had something more than a "speculative" effect on a person's conduct. This Court has long acted on that assumption in demanding that criminal laws be plainly and explicitly worded so that people will know what they mean and be in a position to conform their conduct to the mandates of law. Certainly Texas does not share the Court's surprisingly novel view. It assumes that criminal sanctions are useful in coercing fathers to fulfill their support obligations to their legitimate children.

Unquestionably, Texas prosecutes fathers of legitimate children on the complaint of the mother asserting nonsupport and refuses to entertain like complaints from a mother of an illegitimate child. I see no basis for saying that the latter mother has no standing to demand that the discrimination be ended, one way or the other.

If a State were to pass a law that made only the murder of a white person a crime, I would think that Negroes as a class would have sufficient interest to seek a declaration that that law invidiously discriminated against them. Appellant and her class have no less interest in challenging their exclusion from what their own State perceives as being the beneficial protections that flow from the existence and enforcement of a criminal child-support law. . . .

MR. JUSTICE BLACKMUN, with whom MR. JUSTICE BRENNAN joins, dissenting. . . .

Our decision in Gomez v. Perez, 409 U.S. 535 (1973), announced after oral argument in this case, has important implications for the Texas law governing a man's civil liability for the support of children he has fathered illegitimately. Although appellant's challenge to the civil statute . . . is not procedurally before us, her brief makes it clear that her basic objection to the Texas system concerns the absence of a duty of paternal support for illegitimate children. . . . The decision in Gomez may remove the need for appellant to rely on the criminal law if she continues her quest for paternal contribution.

The standing issue now decided by the Court is, in my opinion, a difficult one with constitutional overtones. I see no reason to decide that question in the absence of a live, ongoing controversy. . . . Under these circumstances, I would remand the case to the District Court for clarification of the status of the litigation.

NOTES ON PRIVATE INITIATION OF CRIMINAL REMEDIES

1. Justice Blackmun argues that Gomez v. Perez may have mooted Linda R. S. Gomez held that the distinction between legitimate and illegitimate children in Texas's civil child support law violated the equal protection clause. Gomez would enable Linda to sue Richard for child support. It would not enable her to force the prosecutor to prosecute him criminally.

2. Is criminal prosecution a remedy for the victim? Or is it a wholly public matter in which the victim has no stake? Does it matter that Texas has a victim restitution law, under which criminal defendants can be ordered to compensate their victims as a condition of probation? Tex. Crim. Proc. Code Ann. Art. 42.12 §6(a)h, n (Vernon Supp. 1984).

3. It is universally the rule that prosecutors have discretion to prosecute or not. But victims can exercise a substantial informal influence. They can nearly always preclude prosecution by refusing to cooperate; only a very determined prosecutor will proceed if he has to coerce the victim's testimony. And a vocal and determined victim can influence the prosecutor to continue with a case he might otherwise have dropped. But all this is informal. Victim restitution laws encourage prosecutors to take more account of the victim's wishes, but they do not give the victim any right to compel prosecution. The use of criminal prosecution to collect compensation is explored more fully in the notes to Bearden v. Georgia, supra at 715.

4. The Court reaffirmed Linda R. S. in Leeke v. Timmerman, 454 U.S. 83 (1981). Leeke involved a South Carolina procedure under which a crime victim could complain directly to a magistrate and request an arrest warrant. The prosecutor retained discretion to pursue the alleged offense further or drop it. Plaintiffs in Leeke were prisoners who sought arrest warrants against their guards; state officials intervened with the magistrate and persuaded him not to issue the warrants. Plaintiffs sued the interfering officials. The Court denied relief, repeating that one citizen has no "cognizable interest in the prosecution . . . of another." Id. at 85-86.

ADAMS v. RICHARDSON
480 F.2d 1159 (D.C. Cir. 1973)

Before BAZELON, Chief Judge, and WRIGHT, McGOWAN, TAMM, LEVEN-
THAL, ROBINSON, MACKINNON, ROBB and WILKEY, Circuit Judges sitting en
banc.

PER CURIAM.

This action was brought to secure declaratory and injunctive relief
against the Secretary of Health, Education, and Welfare, and the Director of HEW's Office of Civil Rights. Appellees, certain black students,
citizens, and taxpayers, allege in their complaint that appellants have
been derelict in their duty to enforce Title VI of the Civil Rights Act of
1964 because they have not taken appropriate action to end segregation in
public educational institutions receiving federal funds. The matter was
before the District Court on cross motions for summary judgment, on an
extensive record consisting of depositions and documentary evidence.

The District Court found appellants' performance to fall below that
required of them under Title VI, and ordered them to (1) institute compliance procedures against ten state-operated systems of higher education, (2) commence enforcement proceedings against seventy-four
secondary and primary school districts found either to have reneged on
previously approved desegregation plans or to be otherwise out of compliance with Title VI, (3) commence enforcement proceedings against forty-
two districts previously deemed by HEW to be in presumptive violation of
the Supreme Court's ruling in Swann v. Charlotte-Mecklenburg Board of
Education, 402 U.S. 1 (1971), (4) demand of eighty-five other secondary
and primary districts an explanation of racial disproportion in apparent
violation of Swann, (5) implement an enforcement program to secure
Title VI compliance with respect to vocational and special schools, (6)
monitor all school districts under court desegregation orders to the extent
that HEW resources permit, and (7) make periodic reports to appellees on
their activities in each of the above areas.

We modify the injunction concerning higher education and affirm the
remainder of the order.

I

Appellants insist that the enforcement of Title VI is committed to agency
discretion, and that review of such action is therefore not within the
jurisdiction of the courts. But the agency discretion exception to the
general rule that agency action is reviewable under the Administrative
Procedure Act, 5 U.S.C. §§701-02, is a narrow one, and is only "applicable in those rare instances where 'statutes are drawn in such broad terms
that in a given case there is no law to apply.' S. Rep. No. 752, 79th Cong.,
1st Sess., 26 (1945)." Citizens to Preserve Overton Park v. Volpe, 401 U.S.

402, 410 (1971). The terms of Title VI are not so broad as to preclude judicial review. A substantial and authoritative body of case law provides the criteria by which noncompliance can be determined, and the statute indicates with precision the measures available to enforce the Act.

Appellants rely almost entirely on cases in which courts have declined to disturb the exercise of prosecutorial discretion by the Attorney General or by United States Attorneys. Georgia v. Mitchell, 146 U.S. App. D.C. 270, 450 F.2d 1317 (1971); Peek v. Mitchell, 419 F.2d 575 (6th Cir. 1970); Powell v. Katzenbach, 123 U.S. App. D.C. 250, 359 F.2d 234 (1965); Moses v. Katzenbach, 342 F.2d 931 (D.C. Cir.1965). Those cases do not support a claim to *absolute* discretion and are, in any event, distinguishable from the case at bar. Title VI not only requires the agency to enforce the Act, but also sets forth specific enforcement procedures. The absence of similar specific legislation requiring particular action by the Attorney General was one factor upon which this court relied in Powell v. Katzenbach to uphold the exercise of discretion in that case.

More significantly, this suit is not brought to challenge HEW's decisions with regard to a few school districts in the course of a generally effective enforcement program. To the contrary, appellants allege that HEW has consciously and expressly adopted a general policy which is in effect an abdication of its statutory duty. We are asked to interpret the statute and determine whether HEW has correctly construed its enforcement obligations.

A final important factor distinguishing this case from the prosecutorial discretion cases cited by HEW is the nature of the relationship between the agency and the institutions in question. HEW is actively supplying segregated institutions with federal funds, contrary to the expressed purposes of Congress. It is one thing to say the Justice Department lacks the resources necessary to locate and prosecute every civil rights violator; it is quite another to say HEW may affirmatively continue to channel federal funds to defaulting schools. The anomaly of this latter assertion fully supports the conclusion that Congress's clear statement of an affirmative enforcement duty should not be discounted.

Appellants attempt to avoid the force of this argument by saying that, although enforcement is required, the means of enforcement is a matter of absolute agency discretion, and that they have chosen to seek voluntary compliance in most cases. This position is untenable in light of the plain language of the statute:

> Each Federal department and agency which is empowered to extend Federal financial assistance to any program or activity . . . is authorized and directed to effectuate the provisions of section 2000d of this title with respect to such program or activity by issuing rules, regulations, or orders of general applicability. . . . Compliance with any requirement adopted pursuant to this section may be effected (1) by the termination of or refusal to grant or to

continue assistance under such program or activity to any recipient as to whom there has been an express finding on the record, after opportunity for hearing, of a failure to comply with such requirement . . . or (2) by any other means authorized by law: *Provided, however,* That no such action shall be taken until the department or agency concerned has advised the appropriate person or persons of the failure to comply with the requirement and has determined that compliance cannot be secured by voluntary means. . . .

42 U.S.C. §2000d-1.

The Act sets forth two alternative courses of action by which enforcement may be effected. In order to avoid unnecessary invocation of formal enforcement procedures, it includes the proviso that the institution must first be notified and given a chance to comply voluntarily. Although the Act does not provide a specific limit to the time period within which voluntary compliance may be sought, it is clear that a request for voluntary compliance, if not followed by responsive action on the part of the institution within a reasonable time, does not relieve the agency of the responsibility to enforce Title VI by one of the two alternative means contemplated by the statute. A consistent failure to do so is a dereliction of duty reviewable in the courts.

II

Although both parties were content to have this case disposed of in the District Court on cross motions for summary judgment, appellants now contend that the case was not one properly to be resolved in that posture. In the District Court, HEW, although denying the contention that it had disregarded its statutory duties, made no claim or showing of disputed material facts relevant to that issue and requiring resolution by trial. Instead, it argued that agency enforcement of Title VI is completely discretionary, and it presses that contention here. That is a legal question involving statutory construction which can be resolved on the record before us. It is true that data concerning the present status of the various school systems is constantly changing, and the record may not identify accurately systems which are currently in compliance. For example, the District Court found, on the basis of the record before it, that seventy-four districts had reneged on previously approved desegregation plans or were otherwise out of compliance. HEW now contends that thirty-nine of these districts were so classified only because of agency error, and that fourteen others are, for various reasons, no longer properly included in that group.

We believe that problems of that nature can be resolved without trial. The District Court went out of its way to note on the first page of its order that it was to be read and interpreted with the staleness of the record in mind. This suggests that, if HEW can demonstrate to the District Court that certain districts are presently in compliance, either interpretation or modification of the order can prevent unnecessary enforcement proceedings. Insofar as the order involves districts as to which HEW lacks sufficient information to determine their current status, an initial purpose of the enforcement proceeding is to obtain that information. Since there was reason in the past to believe that each of these systems was not in compliance with the law, it is not unduly burdensome to require that they now participate in a hearing to determine their present status.

The injunction does not direct the termination of any funds, nor can any funds be terminated prior to a determination of noncompliance. In this suit against the agency, in contrast to actions brought against individual school systems, our purpose, and the purpose of the District Court order as we understand it, is not to resolve particular questions of compliance or noncompliance. It is, rather, to assure that the agency properly construes its statutory obligations, and that the policies it adopts and implements are consistent with those duties and not a negation of them.

III

With this broad purpose in mind, we turn to the substance of the order. We have examined the record in relation to the findings of fact made by the District Court, and can only conclude that they are unassailable. Rule 52(a), Fed. R. Civ. P. Accordingly, with the exception of the higher education problem discussed below, the order must be, and is, affirmed.

In the field of higher education, the District Court found that between January, 1969, and February, 1970, HEW concluded that ten states were operating segregated systems of higher education in violation of Title VI. HEW then directed each state to submit a desegregation plan within 120 days. Five ignored the request, and five submitted unacceptable plans, as to which HEW has not made any formal comments in the intervening years. Nevertheless, HEW has neither instituted any enforcement proceedings itself nor referred any of the cases to the Department of Justice. Although noting HEW's representations that negotiations with the 10 states are still pending, on the basis of these findings the district judge required institution of compliance proceedings within 120 days.

We agree with the District Court's conclusion that HEW may not neglect this area of its responsibility. However, we are also mindful that desegregation problems in colleges and universities differ widely from those in elementary and secondary schools, and that HEW admittedly lacks experience in dealing with them. It has not yet formulated guidelines for desegregating state-wide systems of higher learning, nor has it commented formally upon the desegregation plans of the five states which have submitted them. As regrettable as these revelations are, the stark truth of the matter is that HEW must carefully assess the significance of a variety of new factors as it moves into an unaccustomed area.

None of these factors justifies a failure to comply with a Congressional mandate; they may, however, warrant a more deliberate opportunity to identify and accommodate them.

The problem of integrating higher education must be dealt with on a state-wide rather than a school-by-school basis.[10] Perhaps the most serious problem in this area is the lack of state-wide planning to provide more and better trained minority group doctors, lawyers, engineers and other professionals. A predicate for minority access to quality post-graduate programs is a viable, coordinated state-wide higher education policy that takes into account the special problems of minority students and of Black colleges. As *amicus* points out, these Black institutions currently fulfill a crucial need and will continue to play an important role in Black higher education.[11]

Since some years have elapsed since the initial call was made by HEW for the submission of state higher education plans, we think such a cycle may best be begun by requiring HEW to call upon the states in question — those that have submitted plans earlier as well as those who have not — to submit plans within 120 days, and thereafter to be in active communication with those states whose plans are not acceptable. If an acceptable plan has not been arrived at within an additional period of 180 days, HEW must initiate compliance procedures. As judges well know, the setting down of a case for hearing does not automatically terminate voluntary negotiations nor eliminate the possibility of agreement. The need to prepare for actual hearing frequently causes litigants to focus on their weaknesses as well as their desires.

Some additional comment is desirable with respect to school districts under a court order to desegregate.

Although appellants urge in their brief to this court that "it is difficult to find any legal basis for the imposition upon HEW of a monitoring duty in court-order districts," this injunctive order appears to have been responsive to testimony in the record on behalf of HEW itself. That testimony was that HEW recognized its right and authority, as the responsible disbursing agent of federal funds subject to the standards of compliance in districts under court order; that it was handicapped in this respect by inadequate personnel resources, having only some 38 or 40 inspectors which it thought could be more efficiently used in monitoring compliance with voluntary plans filed with HEW; and that, despite these limitations, whenever a court requested it to monitor compliance with an order

10.   It is important to note that we are not here discussing discriminatory admissions policies of individual institutions. To the extent that such practices are discovered, immediate corrective action is required, but we do not understand HEW to dispute that point. This controversy concerns the more complex problem of system-wide racial imbalance.

11.   The brief is that filed by the National Association for Equal Opportunity in Higher Education, a voluntary association of the presidents of 110 predominantly Negro colleges and universities, both state-supported and private.

issued by that court, it made a special effort to respond and had done so on a number of occasions.

We do not understand the District Court's order to require close surveillance by HEW of all court-order districts, nor that HEW shall be accountable for more than the resources available to it from time to time permit in the good-faith performance of its general obligation not to allow federal funds to be supportive of illegal discrimination. Presumably that good faith would call for a special effort in those instances where significant non-compliance is brought to its attention. So viewed, we do not find this aspect of the District Court's injunction to be unwarranted.

The injunction issued by the District Court relating to state-operated systems of higher education is modified as set forth above. In all other respects, the judgment appealed from is

Affirmed.

NOTES ON PRIVATE INITIATION OF ADMINISTRATIVE REMEDIES

1. *Adams* was decided three months after *Linda R. S.* Are the two cases consistent? Even if they are, doesn't the court have to explain why?

2. The court of appeals does distinguish its own earlier cases refusing to order prosecutors to prosecute. Those cases denied mandamus on the ground that the decision to prosecute was discretionary and not ministerial. The court says that Title VI specifically requires HEW to enforce it and specifies only two methods of enforcement. Unfortunately for the court's argument, one of the two methods is "any other means authorized by law."

Is the directive to HEW any more specific than the directive to United States Attorneys? Their statute provides: "Except as otherwise provided by law, each United States attorney, within his district, shall — (1) prosecute for all offenses against the United States. . . ." 28 U.S.C. §547 (1982).

3. Consider the underlying legal issues in *Linda R. S.* and *Adams*. Which is more appropriate for judicial resolution? There was nothing discretionary about the refusal to prosecute in *Linda R. S.* was there? Wasn't that just an unusual procedure for raising a perfectly justiciable issue? Isn't HEW making a more discretionary claim in *Adams*? What if HEW thinks its enforcement techniques are more likely to work in the long run? What if it thinks there is insufficient evidence to cut off funds? Should either of those decisions be subject to judicial review? What if HEW deliberately failed to enforce Title VI because the Nixon administration didn't like the statute, or because it needed votes in the affected states? Is the remedy for that judicial or political?

One view of the democratic process is that it is perfectly legitimate to elect officials who promise not to enforce unpopular laws. Another view is that the legislature makes the laws, and the laws it makes are binding until repealed. Legislative inertia works against repeal, so it is easier to elect nonenforcers than to repeal. And the presidency changes parties much more often than control of Congress. Requiring a new administration to enforce all the laws it can't repeal ensures stability and respect for law, or it frustrates the popular will, depending on whose ox is gored.

If an administration is free not to enforce unpopular laws, minorities seeking statutory protection must first get enough votes in Congress to enact the law, and then continuously exert enough influence over the executive to get the laws enforced. What if an administration refused to enforce constitutional rights? That's not a legitimate political choice, is it? Should there be a judicial remedy?

4.   Assuming that HEW's duty is sufficiently nondiscretionary to support mandamus, who has standing to enforce the duty? If one citizen has no cognizable interest in the criminal prosecution of another, how can he have an interest in administrative enforcement? Does it matter that HEW may have some ability to directly coerce future compliance, while a criminal prosecution can only punish past violations? Does it matter that HEW is being asked to proceed against other units of government instead of private citizens?

5.   Despite the tension with *Linda R. S.*, there has been a steady trickle of suits demanding more vigorous administrative enforcement. Many of them ended in consent decrees, especially during the Carter administration. Another reported opinion is Legal Aid Society v. Granny Goose Foods, 608 F.2d 1319, 1329-1336 (9th Cir. 1979), *cert. denied sub nom.* Chamber of Commerce v. Legal Aid Society, 447 U.S. 921 (1980). *Legal Aid* ordered the Department of Agriculture to disapprove affirmative action plans filed by its contractors, private corporations in the food and agriculture industries.

6.   Two of these cases have gotten to the Supreme Court. The Court denied standing in both cases. In Simon v. Eastern Kentucky Welfare Rights Organization, 426 U.S. 26 (1976), the Internal Revenue Service had exempted certain hospitals as charitable organizations. Plaintiffs challenged the exemption, alleging that the hospitals weren't charitable because they refused to serve indigents except in their emergency rooms. Relying heavily on *Linda R. S.*, the Court held that there was insufficient reason to believe that denying tax exemptions would benefit plaintiffs by forcing the hospital to serve indigents.

In Allen v. Wright, 104 S. Ct. 3315 (1984), the lower courts ordered the IRS to adopt more stringent standards and procedures for ensuring that tax-exempt private schools did not discriminate on the basis of race. Plaintiffs were black parents and organizations in school districts where the public schools were in the midst of court-ordered desegregation. The lower courts distinguished *Simon* on the ground that plaintiffs there were trying to get into the hospitals, but plaintiffs in *Allen* were not trying to get into the segregated schools.

The Supreme Court reversed, rejecting three standing theories: Plaintiffs did not have an individual right to have the government enforce the law. They were not stigmatized by the government's support of discriminatory programs that did not affect them directly. And there was insufficient reason to believe that denying tax exemptions would force the private schools to integrate or drive white children back to the public schools. Justices Brennan, Blackmun, and Stevens dissented on the last theory; Justice Marshall did not participate.

7.   *Simon* and *Allen* both involve efforts to coerce future compliance, but that didn't seem to matter. Do they cut off all suits to force agencies to enforce the law? Or are criminal cases and tax cases somehow special, so the lower courts can go ahead with other kinds of cases? Will the causal link between enforcement and benefit to plaintiff ever be any clearer than it was in *Linda R. S.?*

8.   It is not clear that the courts can police even egregious refusals to enforce the law. Certainly the courts can't police subtle refusals to enforce. Doesn't that make it all the more important to recognize private causes of action for victims of violations?

C.   GOVERNMENTAL IMMUNITIES

EDELMAN v. JORDAN
415 U.S. 651 (1974)

[Jordan received welfare benefits under Illinois's program of Aid to the Aged, Blind, or Disabled. Illinois accepted federal matching funds for its AABD program, and agreed to run the program in compliance with the Social Security Act and accompanying regulations.

Federal regulations required Illinois to determine eligibility and deliver the first check within forty-five days of an application. Illinois routinely took up to four months to determine eligibility, and paid benefits beginning with the month of its determination. Jordan sued Weaver, the director of the Illinois Department of Public Aid, alleging that Illinois's delays violated federal regulations and the equal protection clause.

The district court entered a permanent injunction ordering the defendant officials to comply with federal regulations in the future. It also ordered the officials to pay all benefits wrongfully withheld since the effective date of the federal regulations. The Court of Appeals affirmed.

Edelman then replaced Weaver as Public Aid Director, and as the defendant in Jordan's lawsuit. The court granted Edelman's petition for certiorari.]

MR. JUSTICE REHNQUIST delivered the opinion of the Court. . . .

The historical basis of the Eleventh Amendment has been oft stated, and it represents one of the more dramatic examples of this Court's effort to derive meaning from the document given to the Nation by the Framers nearly 200 years ago. A leading historian of the Court tells us:

> The right of the Federal Judiciary to summon a State as defendant and to adjudicate its rights and liabilities had been the subject of deep apprehension and of active debate at the time of the adoption of the Constitution; but the existence of any such right had been disclaimed by many of the most eminent advocates of the new Federal Government, and it was largely owing to their successful dissipation of the fear of the existence of such Federal power that the Constitution was finally adopted.

1 C. Warren, The Supreme Court in United States History 91 (rev. ed. 1937).

Despite such disclaimers,[9] the very first suit entered in this Court at its February Term in 1791 was brought against the State of Maryland by a firm of Dutch bankers as creditors. Vanstophorst v. Maryland, see 2 Dall. 401 and Warren, supra, at 91 n.1. The subsequent year brought the

---

9. While the debates of the Constitutional Convention themselves do not disclose a discussion of the question, the prevailing view at the time of the ratification of the Constitution was stated by various of the Framers in the writings and debates of the period. Examples of these views have been assembled by Mr. Chief Justice Hughes:

. . . Madison, in the Virginia Convention, answering objections to the ratification of the Constitution, clearly stated his view as to the purpose and effect of the provision conferring jurisdiction over controversies between States of the Union and foreign States. That purpose was suitably to provide for adjudication in such cases if consent should be given but not otherwise. Madison said: "The next case provides for disputes between a foreign state and one of our states, should such a case ever arise; and between a citizen and a foreign citizen or subject. I do not conceive that any controversy can ever be decided, in these courts, between an American state and a foreign state, without the consent of the parties. If they consent, provision is here made." 3 Elliot's Debates, 533. . . .

Hamilton, in The Federalist, No. 81, made the following emphatic statement of the general principle of immunity: "It is inherent in the nature of sovereignty not to be amenable to the suit of an individual *without its consent*. This is the general sense and the general practice of mankind; and the exemption, as one of the attributes of sovereignty, is now enjoyed by the government of every State in the Union. Unless, therefore, there is a surrender of this immunity in the plan of the convention, it will remain with the States, and the danger intimated must be merely ideal. The circumstances which are necessary to produce an alienation of State sovereignty were discussed in considering the article of taxation and need not be repeated here. A recurrence to the principles there established will satisfy us that there is no color to pretend that the State governments would by the adoption of that plan be divested of the privilege of paying their own debts in their own way, free from every constraint but that which flows from the obligations of good faith. The contracts between a nation and individuals are only binding on the conscience of the sovereign, and have no pretensions to a compulsive force. They confer no right of action independent of the sovereign will. To what purpose would it be to authorize suits against States for the debts they owe? How could recoveries be enforced? It is evident it could not be done without waging war against the contracting State; and to ascribe to the federal courts by mere implication, and in destruction of a pre-existing right of the State governments, a power which would involve such a consequence would be altogether forced and unwarrantable."

Monaco v. Mississippi, 292 U.S. 313, 323-325 (1934) (footnotes omitted).

institution of additional suits against other States, and caused considerable alarm and consternation in the country.

The issue was squarely presented to the Court in a suit brought at the
August 1792 Term by two citizens of South Carolina, executors of a
British creditor, against the State of Georgia. After a year's postponement
for preparation on the part of the State of Georgia, the Court, after
argument, rendered in February 1793, its short-lived decision in
Chisholm v. Georgia, 2 Dall. 419. The decision in that case, that a State
was liable to suit by a citizen of another State or of a foreign country,
literally shocked the Nation. Sentiment for passage of a constitutional
amendment to override the decision rapidly gained momentum, and five
years after *Chisholm* the Eleventh Amendment was officially announced
by President John Adams. Unchanged since then, the Amendment provides:

> The judicial power of the United States shall not be construed to extend to any
> suit in law or equity, commenced or prosecuted against one of the United
> States by Citizens of another State, or by Citizens or Subjects of any Foreign
> State.

While the Amendment by its terms does not bar suits against a State by
its own citizens, this Court has consistently held that an unconsenting
State is immune from suits brought in federal courts by her own citizens
as well as by citizens of another State. Hans v. Louisiana, 134 U.S. 1
(1890); Employees v. Department of Public Health and Welfare, 411 U.S.
279 (1973). It is also well established that even though a State is not
named a party to the action, the suit may nonetheless be barred by the
Eleventh Amendment. In Ford Motor Co. v. Department of Treasury,
323 U.S. 459 (1945), the Court said:

> [W]hen the action is in essence one for the recovery of money from the state,
> the state is the real, substantial party in interest and is entitled to invoke its
> sovereign immunity from suit even though individual officials are nominal
> defendants.

Id., at 464. Thus the rule has evolved that a suit by private parties seeking
to impose a liability which must be paid from public funds in the state
treasury is barred by the Eleventh Amendment. . . .

Ex parte Young, 209 U.S. 123 (1908), was a watershed case in which
this Court held that the Eleventh Amendment did not bar an action in
the federal courts seeking to enjoin the Attorney General of Minnesota
from enforcing a statute claimed to violate the Fourteenth Amendment
of the United States Constitution. This holding has permitted the Civil
War Amendments to the Constitution to serve as a sword, rather than
merely as a shield, for those whom they were designed to protect. But the

relief awarded in Ex parte Young was prospective only; the Attorney General of Minnesota was enjoined to conform his future conduct of that office to the requirement of the Fourteenth Amendment. Such relief is analogous to that awarded by the District Court in the prospective portion of its order under review in this case.

But the retroactive portion of the District Court's order here, which requires the payment of a very substantial amount of money which that court held should have been paid, but was not, stands on quite a different footing. These funds will obviously not be paid out of the pocket of petitioner Edelman. . . . The funds to satisfy the award in this case must inevitably come from the general revenues of the State of Illinois, and thus the award resembles far more closely the monetary award against the State itself than it does the prospective injunctive relief awarded in Ex parte Young.

The Court of Appeals, in upholding the award in this case, held that it was permissible because it was in the form of "equitable restitution" instead of damages, and therefore capable of being tailored in such a way as to minimize disruptions of the state program of categorical assistance. But we must judge the award actually made in this case, and not one which might have been differently tailored in a different case, and we must judge it in the context of the important constitutional principle embodied in the Eleventh Amendment.[11]

We do not read Ex parte Young or subsequent holdings of this Court to indicate that any form of relief may be awarded against a state officer, no matter how closely it may in practice resemble a money judgment payable out of the state treasury, so long as the relief may be labeled "equitable" in nature. The Court's opinion in Ex parte Young hewed to no such line. Its citation of Hagood v. Southern, 117 U.S. 52 (1886), and In re Ayers, 123 U.S. 443 (1887), which were both actions against state officers for specific performance of a contract to which the State was a party, demonstrate that equitable relief may be barred by the Eleventh Amendment.

As in most areas of the law, the difference between the type of relief barred by the Eleventh Amendment and that permitted under Ex parte Young will not in many instances be that between day and night. The

11. . . . [W]e cannot agree that financial impact is the same where a federal court applies Ex parte Young to grant prospective declaratory and injunctive relief, as opposed to an order of retroactive payments as was made in the instant case. . . . [W]here the State has a definable allocation to be used in the payment of public aid benefits, and pursues a certain course of action such as the processing of applications within certain time periods as did Illinois here, the subsequent ordering by a federal court of retroactive payments to correct delays in such processing will invariably mean there is less money available for payments for the continuing obligations of the public aid system.

As stated by Judge McGowan in Rothstein v. Wyman, 467 F.2d 226, 235 (C.A.2 1972): ". . . As time goes by, . . . retroactive payments become compensatory rather than remedial; the coincidence between previously ascertained and existing needs becomes less clear."

injunction issued in Ex parte Young was not totally without effect on the
State's revenues, since the state law which the Attorney General was
enjoined from enforcing provided substantial monetary penalties against
railroads which did not conform to its provisions. Later cases from this
Court have authorized equitable relief which has probably had greater
impact on state treasuries than did that awarded in Ex parte Young. In
Graham v. Richardson, 403 U.S. 365 (1971), Arizona and Pennsylvania
welfare officials were prohibited from denying welfare benefits to otherwise qualified recipients who were aliens. In Goldberg v. Kelly, 397 U.S.
254 (1970), New York City welfare officials were enjoined from following
New York State procedures which authorized the termination of benefits
paid to welfare recipients without prior hearing.[12] But the fiscal consequences to state treasuries in these cases were the necessary result of
compliance with decrees which by their terms were prospective in nature.
State officials, in order to shape their official conduct to the mandate of
the Court's decrees, would more likely have to spend money from the
state treasury than if they had been left free to pursue their previous
course of conduct. Such an ancillary effect on the state treasury is a
permissible and often an inevitable consequence of the principle announced in Ex parte Young.

But that portion of the District Court's decree which petitioner challenges on Eleventh Amendment grounds goes much further than any of
the cases cited. It requires payment of state funds, not as a necessary
consequence of compliance in the future with a substantive federal-question determination, but as a form of compensation to those whose applications were processed on the slower time schedule at a time when
petitioner was under no court-imposed obligation to conform to a different standard. While the Court of Appeals described this retroactive award
of monetary relief as a form of "equitable restitution," it is in practical
effect indistinguishable in many aspects from an award of damages
against the State. It will to a virtual certainty be paid from state funds,
and not from the pockets of the individual state officials who were the
defendants in the action. It is measured in terms of a monetary loss
resulting from a past breach of a legal duty on the part of the defendant
state officials.

Were we to uphold this portion of the District Court's decree, we
would be obligated to overrule the Court's holding in Ford Motor Co. v.

12.   The Court of Appeals considered the Court's decision in Griffin v. School Board,
377 U.S. 218 (1964), to be of like import. But as may be seen from Griffin's citation of
Lincoln County v. Luning, 133 U.S. 529 (1890), a county does not occupy the same position
as a State for purposes of the Eleventh Amendment. The fact that the county policies
executed by the county officials in Griffin were subject to the commands of the Fourteenth
Amendment, but the county was not able to invoke the protection of the Eleventh Amendment, is no more than a recognition of the long-established rule that while county action is
generally state action for purposes of the Fourteenth Amendment, a county defendant is
not necessarily a state defendant for purposes of the Eleventh Amendment.

Department of Treasury, supra. There a taxpayer, who had, under protest, paid taxes to the State of Indiana, sought a refund of those taxes
from the Indiana state officials who were charged with their collection.
The taxpayer claimed that the tax had been imposed in violation of the
United States Constitution. The term "equitable restitution" would seem
even more applicable to the relief sought in that case, since the taxpayer
had at one time had the money, and paid it over to the State pursuant to
an allegedly unconstitutional tax exaction. Yet this Court had no hesitation in holding that the taxpayer's action was a suit against the State,
and barred by the Eleventh Amendment. We reach a similar conclusion
with respect to the retroactive portion of the relief awarded by the District
Court in this case. . . .

Three fairly recent District Court judgments requiring state directors
of public aid to make the type of retroactive payment involved here have
been summarily affirmed by this Court notwithstanding Eleventh
Amendment contentions made by state officers who were appealing from
the District Court judgment. Shapiro v. Thompson, 394 U.S. 618 (1969),
is the only instance in which the Eleventh Amendment objection to such
retroactive relief was actually presented to this Court in a case which was
orally argued. . . . This Court, while affirming the judgment, did not in
its opinion refer to or substantively treat the Eleventh Amendment argument. . . .

This case, therefore, is the first opportunity the Court has taken to
fully explore and treat the Eleventh Amendment aspects of such relief in
a written opinion. Shapiro v. Thompson and these three summary affir-
mances obviously are of precedential value in support of the contention
that the Eleventh Amendment does not bar the relief awarded by the
District Court in this case. Equally obviously, they are not of the same
precedential value as would be an opinion of this Court treating the
question on the merits. Since we deal with a constitutional question, we
are less constrained by the principle of stare decisis than we are in other
areas of the law. Having now had an opportunity to more fully consider
the Eleventh Amendment issue after briefing and argument, we disapprove the Eleventh Amendment holdings of those cases to the extent that
they are inconsistent with our holding today.

The Court of Appeals held in the alternative that even if the Eleventh
Amendment be deemed a bar to the retroactive relief awarded respondent in this case, the State of Illinois had waived its Eleventh Amendment immunity and consented to the bringing of such a suit by
participating in the federal AABD program. The Court of Appeals relied
upon our holdings in Parden v. Terminal R. Co., 377 U.S. 184 (1964),
and Petty v. Tennessee-Missouri Bridge Comm'n, 359 U.S. 275 (1959),
and on the dissenting opinion of Judge Bright in Employees v. Department of Public Health and Welfare, 452 F.2d 820, 827 (C.A.8 1971).
While the holding in the latter case was ultimately affirmed by this Court

in 411 U.S. 279 (1973), we do not think that the answer to the waiver question turns on the distinction between *Parden*, and *Employees*. Both *Parden* and *Employees* involved a congressional enactment which by its terms authorized suit by designated plaintiffs against a general class of defendants which literally included States or state instrumentalities. Similarly, Petty v. Tennessee-Missouri Bridge Comm'n involved congressional approval, pursuant to the Compact Clause, of a compact between Tennessee and Missouri, which provided that each compacting State would have the power "to contract, to sue, and be sued in its own name." The question of waiver or consent under the Eleventh Amendment was found in those cases to turn on whether Congress had intended to abrogate the immunity in question, and whether the State by its participation in the program authorized by Congress had in effect consented to the abrogation of that immunity.

But in this case the threshold fact of congressional authorization to sue a class of defendants which literally includes States is wholly absent. Thus respondent is not only precluded from relying on this Court's holding in *Employees*, but on this Court's holdings in *Parden* and *Petty* as well.

The Court of Appeals held that as a matter of federal law Illinois had "constructively consented" to this suit by participating in the federal AABD program and agreeing to administer federal and state funds in compliance with federal law. Constructive consent is not a doctrine commonly associated with the surrender of constitutional rights, and we see no place for it here. In deciding whether a State has waived its constitutional protection under the Eleventh Amendment, we will find waiver only where stated "by the most express language or by such overwhelming implications from the text as [will] leave no room for any other reasonable construction." Murray v. Wilson Distilling Co., 213 U.S. 151, 171 (1909). . . .

The mere fact that a State participates in a program through which the Federal Government provides assistance for the operation by the State of a system of public aid is not sufficient to establish consent on the part of the State to be sued in the federal courts. And while this Court has, in cases such as J. I. Case Co. v. Borak, 377 U.S. 426 (1964), authorized suits by one private party against another in order to effectuate a statutory purpose, it has never done so in the context of the Eleventh Amendment and a state defendant. Since *Employees*, where Congress had expressly authorized suits against a general class of defendants and the only thing left to implication was whether the described class of defendants included States, was decided adversely to the putative plaintiffs on the waiver question, surely this respondent must also fail on that issue. The only language in the Social Security Act which purported to provide a federal sanction against a State which did not comply with federal requirements for the distribution of federal monies was found in former 42 U.S.C. §1384 (now replaced by substantially similar provisions in 42 U.S.C.

§804), which provided for termination of future allocations of federal funds when a participating State failed to conform with federal law.[16] This provision by its terms did not authorize suit against anyone, and standing alone, fell far short of a waiver by a participating State of its Eleventh Amendment immunity.

Our Brother Marshall argues in dissent, and the Court of Appeals held, that although the Social Security Act itself does not create a private cause of action, the cause of action created by 42 U.S.C. §1983, coupled with the enactment of the AABD program, and the issuance by HEW of regulations which require the States to make corrective payments after successful "fair hearings" and provide for federal matching funds to satisfy federal court orders of retroactive payments, indicate that Congress intended a cause of action for public aid recipients such as respondent. It is, of course, true that Rosado v. Wyman, 397 U.S. 397 (1970), held that suits in federal court under §1983 are proper to secure compliance with the provisions of the Social Security Act on the part of participating States. But it has not heretofore been suggested that §1983 was intended to create a waiver of a State's Eleventh Amendment immunity merely because an action could be brought under that section against state officers, rather than against the State itself. Though a §1983 action may be instituted by public aid recipients such as respondent, a federal court's remedial power, consistent with the Eleventh Amendment, is necessarily limited to prospective injunctive relief, Ex parte Young, and may not include a retroactive award which requires the payment of funds from the state treasury, Ford Motor Co. v. Department of Treasury.

Respondent urges that since the various Illinois officials sued in the District Court failed to raise the Eleventh Amendment as a defense to the relief sought by respondent, petitioner is therefore barred[19] from raising the Eleventh Amendment defense in the Court of Appeals or in this Court. The Court of Appeals apparently felt the defense was properly presented, and dealt with it on the merits. We approve of this resolution, since it has been well settled since the decision in Ford Motor Co. v. Department of Treasury that the Eleventh Amendment defense sufficiently partakes of the nature of a jurisdictional bar so that it need not be raised in the trial court. . . . The judgment of the Court of Appeals is

---

16. HEW sought passage of a bill in the 91st Congress, H.R. 16311, §407(a), which would have given it authority to require retroactive payments to eligible persons denied such benefits. The bill failed to pass the House of Representatives. See H.R. 16311, The Family Assistance Act of 1970, Senate Committee on Finance, 91st Cong., 2d Sess., C169-170 (Comm. Print Nov. 5, 1970).

19. Respondent urges that the State of Illinois has abolished its common-law sovereign immunity in its state courts, and appears to argue that suit in a federal court against the State may thus be maintained. Petitioner contends that sovereign immunity has not been abolished in Illinois as to this type of case. Whether Illinois permits such a suit to be brought against the State in its own courts is not determinative of whether Illinois has relinquished its Eleventh Amendment immunity from suit in the federal courts.

therefore reversed and the cause remanded for further proceedings consistent with this opinion.

So ordered.

MR. JUSTICE DOUGLAS, dissenting. . . .

Most welfare decisions by federal courts have a financial impact on the States. . . . King v. Smith, 392 U.S. 309, required payment to children even though their mother was cohabitating with a man who could not pass muster as a "parent." Rosado v. Wyman, 397 U.S. 397, held that under this state-federal cooperative program a State could not reduce its standard of need in conflict with the federal standard. It is true that *Rosado* did not involve retroactive payments as are involved here. But the distinction is not relevant or material because the result in every welfare case coming here is to increase or reduce the financial responsibility of the participating State. In no case when the responsibility of the State is increased to meet the lawful demand of the beneficiary, is there any levy on state funds. Whether the decree is prospective only or requires payments for the weeks or months wrongfully skipped over by the state officials, the nature of the impact on the state treasury is precisely the same. . . .

What is asked by the instant case is minor compared to the relief granted in Griffin v. School Board, 377 U.S. 218. In that case we authorized entry of an order putting an end to a segregated school system. We held that "the District Court may, if necessary to prevent further racial discrimination, require the Supervisors to exercise the power that is theirs to levy taxes to raise funds adequate to reopen, operate, and maintain without racial discrimination a public school system in Prince Edward County like that operated in other counties in Virginia." Id., at 233. . . .

Griffin is sought to be distinguished on the ground that a "county" is not the "state" for purposes of the Eleventh Amendment. But constitutionally the county in *Griffin* was exercising state policy as are the counties here, because otherwise the claim of denial of equal protection would be of no avail. . . .

Yet petitioner asserts that money damages may not be awarded against state offenses, as such a judgment will expend itself on the state treasury. But we are unable to say that Illinois on entering the federal-state welfare program waived its immunity to suit for injunctions but did not waive its immunity for compensatory awards which remedy its willful defaults of obligations undertaken when it joined the cooperative venture.

It is said however, that the Eleventh Amendment is concerned, not with immunity of States from suit, but with the jurisdiction of the federal courts to entertain the suit. The Eleventh Amendment does not speak of "jurisdiction"; it withholds the "judicial power" of federal courts "to any suit in law or equity . . . against one of the United States. . . ." If that "judicial power," or "jurisdiction" if one prefers that concept, may not be exercised even in "any suit in . . . equity" then Ex parte Young should be overruled. But there is none eager to take the step. Where a State has consented to join a federal-state cooperative project, it is realistic to conclude that the State has agreed to assume its obligations under that legislation. There is nothing in the Eleventh Amendment to suggest a difference between suits at law and suits in equity, for it treats the two without distinction. If common sense has any role to play in constitutional adjudication, once there is a waiver of immunity it must be true that it is complete so far as effective operation of the state-federal joint welfare program is concerned.

We have not always been unanimous in concluding when a State has waived its immunity. In Parden v. Terminal R. Co., 377 U.S. 184, where Alabama was sued by some of its citizens for injuries suffered in the interstate operation of an Alabama railroad, the State defended on the grounds of the Eleventh Amendment. The Court held that Alabama was liable as a carrier under the Federal Employers' Liability Act, saying:

> Our conclusion is simply that Alabama, when it began operation of an interstate railroad approximately 20 years after enactment of the FELA, necessarily consented to such suit as was authorized by that Act,

id., at 192. The Court added:

> Our conclusion that this suit may be maintained is in accord with the common sense of this Nation's federalism. A State's immunity from suit by an individual without its consent has been fully recognized by the Eleventh Amendment and by subsequent decisions of this Court. But when a State leaves the sphere that is exclusively its own and enters into activities subject to congressional regulation, it subjects itself to that regulation as fully as if it were a private person or corporation.

Id., at 196.

As the Court of Appeals in the instant case concluded, Illinois by entering into the joint federal-state welfare plan just as surely "[left] the sphere that is exclusively its own." Ibid.

It is argued that participation in the program of federal financial assistance is not sufficient to establish consent on the part of the State to be sued in federal courts. But it is not merely participation which supports a finding of Eleventh Amendment waiver, but participation in light of the existing state of the law as exhibited in such decisions as Shapiro v. Thompson, 394 U.S. 618, which affirmed judgments ordering retroactive payment of benefits. Today's holding that the Eleventh Amendment forbids court-ordered retroactive payments, as the Court recognizes, necessitates an express overruling of several of our recent decisions. But it was against the background of those decisions that Illinois continued its participation in the federal program, and it can hardly be claimed that such participation was in ignorance of the possibility of court-ordered retroactive payments. The decision to participate against that background of precedent can only be viewed as a waiver of immunity from such judgments.

I would affirm the judgment of the Court of Appeals.

MR. JUSTICE BRENNAN, dissenting.

This suit is brought by Illinois citizens against Illinois officials. In that circumstance, Illinois may not invoke the Eleventh Amendment, since that Amendment bars only federal court suits against States by citizens of other States. Rather, the question is whether Illinois may avail itself of the nonconstitutional but ancient doctrine of sovereign immunity as a bar to respondent's claim for retroactive AABD payments. In my view Illinois may not assert sovereign immunity for the reason I expressed in dissent in Employees v. Department of Public Health and Welfare, 411 U.S. 279, 298 (1973): the States surrendered that immunity in Hamilton's words, "in the plan of the Convention," that formed the Union, at least insofar as the States granted Congress specifically enumerated powers. See id., at 319 n.7; Parden v. Terminal R. Co., 377 U.S. 184 (1964). Congressional authority to enact the Social Security Act, of which AABD is a part, is to be found in Art. I, §8, cl. 1, one of the enumerated powers granted Congress by the States in the Constitution. I remain of the opinion that "because of its surrender, no immunity exists that can be the subject of a congressional declaration or a voluntary waiver," 411 U.S., at 300, and thus have no occasion to inquire whether or not Congress authorized an action for AABD retroactive benefits, or whether or not Illinois voluntarily waived the immunity by its continued participation in the program against the background of precedents which sustained judgments ordering retroactive payments.

I would affirm the judgment of the Court of Appeals.

MR. JUSTICE MARSHALL, with whom MR. JUSTICE BLACKMUN joins, dissenting.

The Social Security Act's categorical assistance programs, including the . . . program involved here, are fundamentally different from most federal legislation. Unlike the Fair Labor Standards Act involved in last Term's decision in Employees v. Department of Public Health and Welfare, 411 U.S. 279 (1973), or the Federal Employers' Liability Act at issue in Parden v. Terminal R. Co., 377 U.S. 184 (1964), the Social Security Act does not impose federal standards and liability upon all who engage in certain regulated activities, including often-unwilling state agencies. Instead, the Act seeks to induce state participation in the federal welfare programs by offering federal matching funds in exchange for the State's voluntary assumption of the Act's requirements. I find this basic distinction crucial: it leads me to conclude that by participation in the programs, the States waive whatever immunity they might otherwise have from federal court orders requiring retroactive payment of welfare benefits.[1] Illinois elected to participate in the AABD program, and received and expended substantial federal funds in the years at issue. It thereby obligated itself to comply with federal law. . . .

In agreeing to comply with the requirements of the Social Security Act and HEW regulations, I believe that Illinois has also agreed to subject itself to suit in the federal courts to enforce these obligations. I recognize, of course, that the Social Security Act does not itself provide for a cause of action to enforce its obligations. As the Court points out, the only sanction expressly provided in the Act for a participating State's failure to comply with federal requirements is the cutoff of federal funding by the Secretary of HEW.

But a cause of action is clearly provided by 42 U.S.C. §1983, which in terms authorizes suits to redress deprivations of rights secured by the "laws" of the United States. And we have already rejected the argument that Congress intended the funding cutoff to be the sole remedy for noncompliance with federal requirements. In Rosado v. Wyman, 397 U.S. 397, 420-423 (1970), we held that suits in federal court under §1983 were proper to enforce the provisions of the Social Security Act against participating States. Mr. Justice Harlan, writing for the Court, examined the legislative history and found "not the slightest indication" that Congress intended to prohibit suits in federal court to enforce compliance with federal standards. Id., at 422.

I believe that Congress also intended the full panoply of traditional judicial remedies to be available to the federal courts in these §1983 suits. There is surely no indication of any congressional intent to restrict the courts' equitable jurisdiction. Yet the Court has held that "[u]nless a statute in so many words, or by a necessary and inescapable inference, restricts the court's jurisdiction in equity, the full scope of that jurisdiction is to be recognized and applied." Porter v. Warner Holding Co., 328 U.S. 395, 398 (1946). "When Congress entrusts to an equity court the enforcement of prohibitions contained in a regulatory enactment, it must be taken to have acted cognizant of the historic power of equity to provide complete relief in light of the statutory purposes." Mitchell v. DeMario Jewelry, 361 U.S. 288, 291-292 (1960).

In particular, I am firmly convinced that Congress intended the restitution of wrongfully withheld assistance payments to be a remedy available to the federal courts in these suits. Benefits under the categorical assistance programs "are a matter of statutory entitlement for persons

---

1. In view of my conclusion on this issue, I find it unnecessary to consider whether the Court correctly treats this suit as one against the State, rather than as a suit against a state officer permissible under the rationale of Ex parte Young, 209 U.S. 123 (1908).

qualified to receive them." Goldberg v. Kelly, 397 U.S. 254, 262 (1970). Retroactive payment of benefits secures for recipients this entitlement which was withheld in violation of federal law. Equally important, the courts' power to order retroactive payments is an essential remedy to insure future state compliance with federal requirements. No other remedy can effectively deter States from the strong temptation to cut welfare budgets by circumventing the stringent requirements of federal law. The funding cutoff is a drastic sanction, one which HEW has proved unwilling or unable to employ to compel strict compliance with the Act and regulations. Moreover, the cutoff operates only prospectively; it in no way deters the States from even a flagrant violation of the Act's requirements for as long as HEW does not discover the violation and threaten to take such action.

Absent any remedy which may act with retroactive effect, state welfare officials have everything to gain and nothing to lose by failing to comply with the congressional mandate that assistance be paid with reasonable promptness to all eligible individuals. This is not idle speculation without basis in practical experience. In this very case, for example, Illinois officials have knowingly violated since 1968 federal regulations on the strength of an argument as to its invalidity which even the majority deems unworthy of discussion. Without a retroactive-payment remedy, we are indeed faced with "the spectre of a state, perhaps calculatingly, defying federal law and thereby depriving welfare recipients of the financial assistance Congress thought it was giving them." Jordan v. Weaver, 472 F.2d 985, 995 (C.A.7 1972). Like the Court of Appeals, I cannot believe that Congress could possibly have intended any such result.

Such indicia of congressional intent as can be gleaned from the statute confirm that Congress intended to authorize retroactive payment of assistance benefits unlawfully withheld. Availability of such payments is implicit in the "fair hearing" requirement, former 42 U.S.C. §1382(a)(4), which permitted welfare recipients to challenge the denial of assistance. The regulations which *require* States to make corrective payments retroactively in the event of a successful fair hearing challenge, 45 C.F.R. §205.10(a)(18), merely confirm the obvious statutory intent. HEW regulations also authorize federal matching funds for retroactive assistance payments made pursuant to court order, 45 C.F.R. §§205.10(b)(2), (b)(3). We should not lightly disregard this explicit recognition by the agency charged with administration of the statute that such a remedy was authorized by Congress.

Illinois chose to participate in the AABD program with its eyes wide open. Drawn by the lure of federal funds, it voluntarily obligated itself to comply with the Social Security Act and HEW regulations, with full knowledge that Congress had authorized assistance recipients to go into federal court to enforce these obligations and to recover benefits wrongfully denied. Any doubts on this score must surely have been removed by our decisions in Rosado v. Wyman and Shapiro v. Thompson, 394 U.S. 618 (1969), where we affirmed a district court retroactive payment order. I cannot avoid the conclusion that, by virtue of its knowing and voluntary decision to nevertheless participate in the program, the State necessarily consented to subject itself to these suits. I have no quarrel with the Court's view that waiver of constitutional rights should not lightly be inferred. But I simply cannot believe that the State could have entered into this essentially contractual agreement with the Federal Government without recognizing that it was subjecting itself to the full scope of the §1983 remedy provided by Congress to enforce the terms of the agreement.

Of course, §1983 suits are nominally brought against state officers, rather than the State itself, and do not ordinarily raise Eleventh Amendment problems in view of this Court's decision in Ex parte Young, 209 U.S. 123 (1908). But to the extent that the relief authorized by Congress in an action under §1983 may be open to Eleventh Amendment objections,[2] these objections are waived when the State agrees to comply with federal requirements enforceable in such an action. I do not find persuasive the Court's reliance in this case on the fact that "congressional authorization to sue a class of defendants which literally includes States" is absent. While true, this fact is irrelevant here, for this is simply not a case "literally" against the State. While the Court successfully knocks down the strawman it has thus set up, it never comes to grips with the undeniable fact that Congress has "literally" authorized this suit within the terms of §1983. Since there is every reason to believe that Congress intended the full panoply of judicial remedies to be available in §1983 equitable actions to enforce the Social Security Act, I think the conclusion is inescapable that Congress authorized and the State consented to §1983 actions in which the relief might otherwise be questioned on Eleventh Amendment grounds.

My conclusion that the State has waived its Eleventh Amendment objections to court-ordered retroactive assistance payments is fully consistent with last Term's decision in Employees v. Department of Public Health and Welfare, 411 U.S. 279 (1973). As I emphasized in my concurring opinion, there was no voluntary action by the State in *Employees* which could reasonably be construed as evidencing its consent to suit in a federal forum.

2.   It should be noted that there has been no determination in this case that state action is unconstitutional under the Fourteenth Amendment. Thus, the Court necessarily does not decide whether the States' Eleventh Amendment sovereign immunity may have been limited by the later enactment of the Fourteenth Amendment to the extent that such a limitation is necessary to effectuate the purposes of that Amendment, an argument advanced by an amicus in this case. In view of my conclusion that any sovereign immunity which may exist has been waived, I also need not reach this issue.

[T]he State was fully engaged in the operation of the affected hospitals and schools at the time of the 1966 amendments. To suggest that the State had the choice of either ceasing operation of these vital public services or 'consenting' to federal suit suffices, I believe, to demonstrate that the State had no true choice at all and thereby that the State did not voluntarily consent to the exercise of federal jurisdiction. . . .

Id., at 296.

A finding of waiver here is also consistent with the reasoning of the majority in *Employees*, which relied on a distinction between "governmental" and "proprietary" functions of state government. Id., at 284-285. This distinction apparently recognizes that if sovereign immunity is to be at all meaningful, the Court must be reluctant to hold a State to have waived its immunity simply by acting in its sovereign capacity — i.e., by merely performing its "governmental" functions. On the other hand, in launching a profitmaking enterprise, "a State leaves the sphere that is exclusively its own," Parden v. Terminal R. Co., 377 U.S., at 196, and a voluntary waiver of sovereign immunity can more easily be found. While conducting an assistance program for the needy is surely a "governmental" function, the State here has done far more than operate its own program in its sovereign capacity. It has voluntarily subordinated its sovereignty in this matter to that of the Federal Government, and agreed to comply with the conditions imposed by Congress upon the expenditure of federal funds. In entering this federal-state cooperative program, the State again "leaves the sphere that is exclusively its own," and similarly may more readily be found to have voluntarily waived its immunity. . . .

I respectfully dissent.

NOTES ON THE EVOLUTION OF ELEVENTH AMENDMENT DOCTRINE

1.   The intent of the framers is not so clear as *Edelman* suggests. Article III of the Constitution authorizes federal jurisdiction over several kinds of cases in which a state might be a defendant:

The judicial Power shall extend to all Cases, in Law and Equity, arising under this Constitution, the Laws of the United States, and Treaties made, or which shall be made, under their Authority; . . . — to Controversies between two or more States; — between a State and Citizens of another State; . . . and between a State, or the Citizens thereof, and foreign States, Citizens or Subjects.

The argument over sovereign immunity in the ratification debates focused on the provisions specifically mentioning states. Opponents of the Constitution argued that these provisions authorized suits against states and that that was a reason for rejecting the Constitution. The Constitution's supporters offered several inconsistent responses. Madison said no state could be a defendant without its consent. Hamilton agreed, "unless . . . there is a surrender of this immunity in the plan of the convention." He found no surrender of immunity from suits to enforce debts; he didn't comment on federal question cases. Other important supporters agreed that the Constitution authorized suits against states and thought this one of its strengths. These included James Wilson and Edmund Randolph, two members of the committee that drafted the jurisdictional provisions. The debates are reviewed in C. Jacobs, The Eleventh Amendment and Sovereign Immunity 22-40 (1972).

Chisholm v. Georgia, 2 U.S. (2 Dall.) 419 (1793), upholding jurisdiction in a suit to collect a debt from a state, was decided by a vote of 4 to 1. Two of the four justices in the majority had been delegates to the constitutional convention — John Wilson and John Blair. Chief Justice Jay cast the third vote for the majority; he had been the third member of the team that wrote the Federalist Papers.

Wilson was the leading legal theorist of the framer's generation; he and Jay wrote the most wide-ranging of the seriatim opinions in Chisholm. Both seemed to think sovereign immunity inconsistent with republican government. Wilson emphasized that under the Constitution the people were sovereign and not their government; Jay emphasized that the new government was committed to equality and justice for all. Wilson also noted that in England sovereign immunity was a mere form; any citizen could sue the King, but he had to do it humbly, by petition instead of by writ. By long tradition, the King was obligated to endorse on the petition, "Let justice be done," and send it to one of his courts for trial. Justice Iredell, dissenting, thought that form was dispositive. Georgia had no King to grant a petition, its legislature had not consented, and so it could not be sued. It is ironic that George III consented to be sued more freely than any of the American states.

Wilson also made the argument that shows up in Brennan's dissent nearly two hundred years later. He thought the case ultimately turned on a question "no less radical than this — 'do the people of the United States form a NATION?'" He answered yes:

[T]he citizens of Georgia, when they acted upon the large scale of the Union, as a part of the "People of the United States," did not surrender the Supreme or sovereign Power to that State; but, as to the purposes of the Union, retained it to themselves. As to the purposes of the Union, therefore, Georgia is NOT a sovereign State.

2 U.S. (2 Dall.) at 457.

2. As in most questions of original intent, the truth is probably that there was no consensus. But there was strong opposition to Chisholm v.

Georgia. The Georgia House of Representatives passed a bill declaring that any federal marshall attempting to enforce the Court's judgment should be hanged. C. Jacobs at 56-57. The bill died in the Senate. But the Eleventh Amendment was proposed and ratified with only token opposition.

3.   As Justice Rehnquist admits, the Eleventh Amendment has nothing to say about *Edelman*. Of the four sources of jurisdiction quoted in note 1, the Eleventh Amendment addresses only the third and part of the fourth:

> The Judicial power of the United States shall not be construed to extend to any suit in law or equity, commenced or prosecuted against one of the United States by Citizens of another State, or by Citizens or Subjects of any Foreign State.

Jordan was a citizen of Illinois. If his suit against Illinois officials was a suit against the state, it was a suit against a state of which he was a citizen. But the accepted doctrine is that that doesn't matter. Most often the Court acts as though the Eleventh Amendment applies to such suits; it simply strikes the last fourteen words from the amendment and enforces most of the rest. The Court has also deleted the phrase, "in law or equity," holding that states are also immune from suits in admiralty. Ex parte New York, 256 U.S. 490, 497-498 (1911). Sometimes it says that *Chisholm* was wrongly decided and that article III does not reach suits against states; sometimes it says that there is an implied constitutional immunity, of which the Eleventh Amendment is simply one example.

4.   The issue first arose in Hans v. Louisiana, 134 U.S. 1 (1890). *Hans* looked just like *Chisholm*; it was a suit to collect on state bonds. Today the Court could dismiss for lack of jurisdiction without reaching any immunity issue. A suit to collect a bond is not a federal claim but a common law contract action. The contract clause was merely Hans's reply to Louisiana's defense. That is not enough for federal jurisdiction; the claim did not "arise under" the Constitution. Louisville & Nashville R.R. v. Mottley, 211 U.S. 149 (1908).

Mottley was not available in 1890, so the Court turned to sovereign immunity. It thought that if anyone had suggested in 1793 that citizens of Georgia could sue Georgia in federal court, the reaction would have been just as outraged as the reaction to *Chisholm*. So states must be immune from suits by their own citizens as well as immune from the suits described in the Eleventh Amendment.

The trouble with that reasoning is that, quite apart from the Eleventh Amendment, no citizen could have sued his own state in federal court in 1793. Most of the jurisdictional authority of article III is not self-executing; Congress must confer jurisdiction. Congress had not conferred federal question jurisdiction, and except for one short-lived experiment, it would not do so until after the Civil War. The Civil War produced a profound change in the role of the federal courts. Three constitutional amendments created vast new federal rights enforceable against states. Four great grants of jurisdiction transferred responsibility for enforcing federal rights to federal courts. These were civil rights removal jurisdiction in 1866, 28 U.S.C. §1443 (1982), modern habeas corpus jurisdiction in 1867, 28 U.S.C. §2241(c)(3) (1982), original civil rights jurisdiction in 1871, 28 U.S.C. §1343 (1982), and finally, general federal question jurisdiction in 1875, 28 U.S.C. §1331 (1982).

Hans assumed it was an unintended oversight that the Eleventh Amendment speaks only to diversity jurisdiction. But maybe it was not an oversight at all. Eliminating diversity jurisdiction against states solved the problem the amendment's framers wanted to solve. They weren't afraid of federal question jurisdiction, because Congress hadn't granted it and they couldn't foresee any circumstances in which Congress might grant it. It would take a Civil War to produce the question raised in *Hans*. If the Eleventh Amendment answers that question, it silently forecloses the range of solutions to a Civil War the framers could not imagine. Isn't it more plausible to assume the framers left the question of immunity in federal question cases to some future generation that might confer federal question jurisdiction? Perhaps they deliberately excluded federal question cases from the amendment; more likely, they didn't say anything about them because they didn't think about them.

5. *Hans* left the Court with the anomaly first noted by Jay and Wilson. How can sovereign immunity be reconciled with republican government? The Constitution guarantees rights against states; how can those rights be enforced if the government is immune from suit? Some constitutional rights can be raised defensively if the government sues the citizen. But what if the government simply acts, without suing? What if it confiscates property, or burns books, or conducts general searches, or imprisons people without trial? A government that cannot be sued can be completely lawless; it can make a bill of rights meaningless. The problem had always been there, but the Civil War amendments vastly increased the number of federal rights enforceable against states, and the new jurisdictional grants brought those cases to federal court.

6. The traditional solution had been suits against officers. These are of two kinds. One may sue the officer in his official capacity, to make him exercise or refrain from exercising some of the powers of his office. Or, one may sue the officer in his personal capacity, to make him pay compensation out of his own pocket. There was historical precedent for both kinds of suits. Mandamus and habeas corpus are both suits against officers in their official capacity. Habeas corpus solves the problem of governments imprisoning people without trial, and the Constitution guarantees its availability.

7. The Court had already used less traditional suits against officers in

their official capacity. In Osborne v. President of the Bank of the United States, 22 U.S. (9 Wheat.) 738 (1824), the Court enjoined the treasurer of Ohio from collecting a tax. He argued that the suit was "really" against Ohio, and therefore barred by the Eleventh Amendment. The Court rejected the argument. Id. at 846-859.

8.   Another early example is United States v. Lee, 106 U.S. (16 Otto) 196 (1882). The United States had not been named as a defendant, but it appears in the case caption because it filed a writ of error in its own name. Nothing in the Constitution explicitly confers sovereign immunity on the United States, and the majority could find no good reason for sovereign immunity in a republican government. But it held that the immunity was well established and could no longer be questioned.

Even so, the Court affirmed writs of ejectment against two federal officers who were holding plaintiff's land for use as a fort and cemetery. During the Civil War, the federal government collected property taxes in confederate states under union control. The United States bought this land at a tax foreclosure sale in 1864. The owner had sent an agent to pay the taxes, but the officials refused payment; they said the owner must pay in person. The owner was Mrs. Robert E. Lee, who obviously could not come to pay in person. The Court held the agent's tender effective and the tax sale void. The government still owns Arlington National Cemetery, but it had to pay for it. Four dissenters would have held that the suit was "really" one against the United States.

9.   Throughout the late nineteenth and early twentieth centuries, the Court continued to experiment with suits against officers in their official capacities. These developments culminated in Ex parte Young, 209 U.S. 123 (1908). Young was the attorney general of Minnesota. A federal court had ordered him not to enforce a railroad rate law. He violated the injunction and was committed to the custody of the federal marshall for contempt. He filed a habeas corpus petition arguing that the court lacked jurisdiction to enjoin him from enforcing state law because such a suit was really against the state of Minnesota, and barred by the Eleventh Amendment.

The majority explained suits against officers in their official capacity with a transparent fiction:

> [T]he use of the name of the State to enforce an unconstitutional act to the injury of complainants is a proceeding without the authority of, and one which does not affect, the State in its sovereign or governmental capacity. It is simply an illegal act upon the part of a state official in attempting, by the use of the name of the State, to enforce a legislative enactment which is void because unconstitutional. . . . [H]e is in that case stripped of his official or representative character and is subjected in his person to the consequences of his individual conduct.

Id. at 159-160.

The Court relied on *Osborne*, on its habeas corpus cases, and on the whole line of less clearly articulated cases involving suits against state officers. Justice Harlan, dissenting, thought it obvious that the only purpose of this suit was to prevent Minnesota from enforcing its rate law. If all the state's legal officers could be enjoined, it was the same as if the state had been enjoined.

Of course he was right; no one pretends otherwise. If the Attorney General were really acting as an individual, there would be no violation of the fourteenth amendment, because his action would not be state action. The Court rejected that argument in Home Telephone & Telegraph Co. v. City of Los Angeles, 227 U.S. 278 (1913).

Similarly, if the Attorney General were really sued as an individual, the suit would continue against him when he left office. But instead his successor is automatically substituted as a defendant; that practice is now codified in Federal Civil Rule 25(d). Because the real point of the suit is to test the state's policy, it makes no difference who the Attorney General is. The occasional exception only underscores the point. When plaintiff seeks to enjoin individual misconduct rather than official policy, the Court demands a showing that the new incumbent will continue the challenged conduct. Spomer v. Littleton, 414 U.S. 514 (1974).

10.   Justice Harlan was less persuasive in his efforts to supply a standard. He defended the habeas corpus cases, the cases against state tax collectors, and some of the others. In those cases, the individual officer was a trespasser, seizing plaintiff's property or holding his person. But the Attorney General going into court on behalf of the state was not a trespasser; to enjoin him was to enjoin the state.

Enforcing laws isn't any more a sovereign function than holding prisoners or collecting taxes, and all of these functions must be conducted through officers. It is hard to see how the fiction is any more or less persuasive in those cases than in *Young*. However transparent the fiction, doesn't *Hans* make some such fiction essential? Would it be more honest to admit that *Hans* was a mistake?

NOTES ON SUITS AGAINST OFFICERS IN THEIR OFFICIAL CAPACITIES

1.   Ex parte Young established the modern framework for sovereign immunity law. But if the Court is not willing to abandon sovereign immunity altogether, it must place limits on *Young*'s fiction. Otherwise, a modern-day Chisholm could sue the treasurer of Georgia under diversity jurisdiction, seeking an injunction ordering payment of the bonds. Any line the Court draws will seem artificial, but some lines are more defensible than others.

2.   *Edelman* represents one line; federal courts can't order state offi-

cers to pay money as compensation for past wrongs. The Court concedes that complying with injunctions may cost money. This is obvious in *Edelman* itself; the Court affirms an order to pay welfare benefits in the future. But the conceptual tension may be greatest in reparative injunctions. The remedial education order in the second Milliken v. Bradley opinion, supra at 269, cost the state of Michigan $6 million. How is that different from a $6 million damage judgment, with damages measured by the cost of paying tutors for remedial education? The Court had no doubt that the remedy was prospective relief permitted by *Edelman*: "That the programs are also 'compensatory' in nature does not change the fact that they are part of a plan that operates *prospectively* to bring about the delayed benefits of a unitary school system." 433 U.S. at 290.

3.   Suppose on remand that Illinois still takes four months to process welfare applications. What can the Court do about it? If it orders defendants to pay back benefits to persons whose applications were delayed after the original injunction, is that a forbidden order for the retrospective payment of money? Or an ancillary effect of securing compliance with the injunction?

Such issues arose in Hutto v. Finney, the Arkansas prison case supra at 274. The Court upheld an award of attorney's fees against defendants as a sanction for bad faith litigation tactics. The Court analogized the fee award to compensatory civil contempt. It said that "Once issued, an injunction may be enforced," and that the Eleventh Amendment did not leave imprisonment of high state officials as the only option. 437 U.S. at 690-691.

4.   Justice Rehnquist dissented in *Hutto*. He found no contempt and no bad faith; if either existed, he would have awarded fees against the responsible officers and let the state decide whether to reimburse them. The trial court had specified that the fees be paid out of Department of Corrections funds. Justice Stevens's opinion for the Court found that to be harmless error at most.

Ten days later the Court corrected such an error in the Alabama prison case. The injunction ran against the relevant prison officials, the Alabama Board of Corrections, and the state of Alabama. The Court granted certiorari to the state and the Board, and summarily reversed. The lower court could enjoin the prison officials in their official capacity, but the state and the board as an entity were immune from suit. The formalities must be observed. Alabama v. Pugh, 438 U.S. 781 (1978). This time Justice Stevens dissented, along with Justices Brennan and Marshall.

5.   *Edelman* also alludes to another limit on the fiction of *Young*. It is easier to pretend that defendant has been stripped of his state authority when the Court orders him to refrain from acting. It is harder to maintain the fiction when the Court orders him to do something that only the state

can do. Thus the Court notes that *Young* approved of Hagood v. Southern, 117 U.S. 52 (1886). As the Court characterized the claim in *Hagood*, plaintiff sought to compel specific performance of a contract with the state. The officer was not a party to the contract; he wasn't obligated to perform. Only the state was obligated to perform, so plaintiff couldn't prove an obligation without admitting that he was suing the state.

6. The authoritative modern statement of this limit on *Young* is Larson v. Domestic & Foreign Commerce Corp., 337 U.S. 682 (1949):

> Of course, a suit may fail, as one against the sovereign, even if it is claimed that the officer being sued has acted unconstitutionally or beyond his statutory powers, if the relief requested cannot be granted by merely ordering the cessation of the conduct complained of but will require affirmative action by the sovereign or the disposition of unquestionably sovereign property.

Id. at 691 n.11.

The facts of *Larson* would seem to be controlled by the "affirmative action" half of footnote 11. The War Assets Administration agreed to sell surplus coal to plaintiff. The contract required plaintiff to pay a deposit in advance. When plaintiff submitted a letter of credit instead of cash, the administrator declared plaintiff in breach and sold the coal to someone else. Plaintiff sued the administrator for specific performance, alleging that the letter of credit was sufficient and that the government was in breach. Isn't that just like Hagood v. Southern? Wouldn't performance of the contract be "affirmative action by the sovereign"?

7. Is footnote 11 consistent with United States v. Lee? What does "unquestionably sovereign property" mean? As between the government and the officers who were the nominal defendants in *Lee*, the property was unquestionably sovereign. Plaintiff questioned whether the property belonged to the sovereign, but so will any plaintiff who asserts that the property is his own. Maybe the Court intended to distinguish property claims from contract claims: Plaintiff in *Larson* asserted title to the coal, but he conceded that it was "unquestionably sovereign property" before the government agreed to sell it.

8. The holding in *Larson* did not turn on footnote 11. Instead, the Court relied on a third limit to the fiction of Ex parte Young. The Court held that even if a letter of credit was sufficient, the officer had not exceeded his authority. If the government were to sell surplus assets on a large scale, someone had to be empowered to decide whether buyers had performed and were entitled to delivery. Sometimes he would be right and sometimes he would be wrong, but either way he was empowered to decide. So the administrator's decision was the government's decision, even if it were wrong; he was not stripped of his authority, and the suit was one against the government.

Perhaps more important, in the Tucker Act Congress had consented to suit for breach of contract. 28 U.S.C. §1491 (1982). But suit could be filed only in the Court of Claims, and plaintiff could only recover damages, not specific performance. A suit against the United States for damages would proceed on the theory that the administrator's breach was the government's breach. Plaintiff could not escape the limitations of the Tucker Act by alleging that the administrator's breach was unauthorized.

9.   This doctrine of discretion to be wrong is a potent limit on claims against the government. Its scope is uncertain. If the officer in *Larson* had discretion to decide whether payment by letter of credit was acceptable, why didn't the officers in United States v. *Lee* have discretion to decide whether payment by an agent was acceptable? Some decisions are committed to the discretion of the officer; some are committed to the courts or expressly resolved by statute. There is no reliable way to tell which; deciding that the officer has discretion to be wrong is often a label for a conclusion that the government should not be sued. Wouldn't the Court have done better to just say that damages in the Court of Claims were a reasonable remedy, and there was no need for fictitious suits against officers when such a remedy was available?

10.   Could the discretion-to-be-wrong doctrine be applied to constitutional claims? Does any official have discretion to be wrong about the Constitution? *Larson's* distinction of *Lee* suggests a negative answer. The Court said that *Lee* involved an unconstitutional taking without compensation. *Larson* didn't; even if the administrator had unlawfully taken coal that had already passed to plaintiff, compensation was available in the Court of Claims. A taking with a right to compensation in the Court of Claims was not an unconstitutional taking. There had been no remedy in the Court of Claims at the time of *Lee*.

11.   The implication that *Lee* would no longer be needed was confirmed in Malone v. Bowdoin, 369 U.S. 643 (1962). Plaintiffs sued a Forest Service Office in ejectment; the Court held the suit barred by sovereign immunity and said their remedy was for money in the Court of Claims.

12.   The Court added a new limit to the fiction of Ex parte Young in Pennhurst State School & Hospital v. Halderman, 104 S. Ct. 900 (1984). *Pennhurst* was a suit to reform Pennsylvania's institution for the mentally retarded. Plaintiffs alleged both state and federal claims. The Court held the state claims barred by the eleventh amendment. An allegation that state officers violated state law did not strip them of their authority; the suit was one against the state. In the Court's view, Ex parte Young is justified only by the need to vindicate federal rights. Id. at 910. For a federal court to tell state officials how to comply with state law would be a gross violation of state sovereignty. Id. at 911. There were four dissents.

NOTES ON OTHER EXCEPTIONS TO
SOVEREIGN IMMUNITY

1. Any state can consent to be sued; the next principal case considers some of the problems that arise in consented suits. These notes consider a variety of involuntary exceptions to the immunity symbolized by the eleventh amendment.

2. One such exception is unsuccessfully argued in *Edelman*. Congress may have some power to coerce states into waiving their immunity. The leading case is Parden v. Terminal Railway, 377 U.S. 184 (1964). Alabama owned the Terminal Railway; Parden was an injured employee who sued under the Federal Employers Liability Act. The act authorized suits against "every" common carrier by rail. The Court held that "by empowering Congress to regulate commerce, . . . the States necessarily surrendered any portion of their sovereignty that would stand in the way of such regulation," that Congress had "conditioned the right to operate a railroad in interstate commerce upon amenability to suit in federal court," and that "by thereafter operating a railroad in interstate commerce, Alabama must be taken to have accepted that condition and thus to have consented to suit." Id. at 192. There were four dissents.

Parden has never been overruled, but there doesn't seem to be much left of it. The Federal Employers Liability Act said nothing explicit about states; its application to Alabama turned on the word "every." Doesn't Justice Marshall make a stronger case for coerced waiver in *Edelman*? Why is that insufficient? Because Congress said only that state officials could be sued in §1983, and never "literally" said states can be sued?

An intervening decision found an even clearer congressional statement insufficient. Employees of the Department of Public Health & Welfare v. Department of Public Health & Welfare, 411 U.S. 279 (1973). Section 16(b) of the Fair Labor Standards Act provided that "any employer" who violates its provisions "shall be liable to the . . . employees affected." 29 U.S.C. §216(b) (1982). "Employer" is a defined term. In 1966, Congress extended the act's coverage to states. It did so by amending the definition of "employer." The Court held that that was not a sufficiently clear statement to authorize suits against state employers because Congress hadn't amended §16(b). The act still applied to states, but only the federal government could enforce the act against states.

Congress promptly amended §16(b), inserting "including any public agency" in parentheses after "employer." Even the right wing of the Court might be hard-pressed to say that isn't clear enough. But the issue couldn't arise for nearly ten years, because the Court soon held that substantive application of the act to state employers violates the tenth amendment. National League of Cities v. Usery, 426 U.S. 833 (1976). But *National League of Cities* was overruled in Garcia v. San Antonio Metropolitan Transit Authority, 105 S. Ct. 1005 (1985). Now the act applies to states again, and employees will surely sue to enforce it. States claiming immunity from those suits have two views: carry the clear-statement rule to a new level of absurdity, or argue that the commerce clause does not authorize Congress to extract waivers of sovereign immunity, thus squarely rejecting the theory of Parden v. Terminal Railway.

3.   Congress may have somewhat greater powers under §5 of the fourteenth amendment. Section 5 authorizes Congress to "enforce by appropriate legislation" the other provisions of the amendment, most notably, the due process and equal protection clauses. Those provisions explicitly apply to states, and the Court concluded that the power to enforce those provisions includes the power to authorize suits to enforce them. Fitzpatrick v. Bitzer, 427 U.S. 445 (1976). "[T]he Eleventh Amendment, and the principle of state sovereignty which it embodies, are necessarily limited by the enforcement provisions of §5." Id. at 456. Justice Rehnquist wrote the opinion.

The plain statement rule also applies to legislation under §5, but the Court has applied the rule more realistically in this context. The Civil Rights Attorney's Fees Awards Act of 1976 does not explicitly mention states; it says plaintiff may recover fees in any suit to enforce certain civil rights laws. 42 U.S.C. §1988 (1976). Most of those suits are suits against officials under §1983. But the legislative history says the fees can be collected from state funds under the official's control, and that was good enough for the majority in Hutto v. Finney, 437 U.S. 678, 693-700 (1978). There were four dissents.

4.   There is no federal barrier to suing one state in the courts of another state. Nevada v. Hall, 440 U.S. 410 (1979). Hall sued Nevada in a California court for injuries suffered in a California collision with a Nevada employee driving a state car. The eleventh amendment speaks only of federal jurisdiction. The majority thought that immunity in California courts is a matter of California law, and California had abolished sovereign immunity. Three dissenters would have found immunity implicit in the Constitution.

5.   The Court has implied some exceptions to state immunity from the nature of the federal system. States are not immune to suit by other states, or by the United States. Judicial resolution of these disputes is thought essential to the peace and permanence of the union. States are immune to suit by foreign states. The distinction is explained in Monaco v. Mississippi, 292 U.S. 313 (1934). The United States can deal with Monaco by diplomacy or war, but the Constitution extinguished those means of dispute resolution between the various governments within the union.

Federal power to sue states occasionally lets the United States provide a remedy for aggrieved citizens. For example, the United States has sued to force states to register black voters. United States v. Mississippi, 380 U.S. 128, 140-141 (1965). And when the Court said state employees couldn't sue under the Fair Labor Standards Act, it said that the Department of Labor could enforce the law against the states. But states cannot sue other states on behalf of their citizens unless "the injury affects the general population of a State in a substantial way." Maryland v. Louisiana, 451 U.S. 725, 737 (1981).

6. "It does not follow that because a State may be sued by the United States without its consent, therefore the United States may be sued by a State without its consent. Public policy forbids that conclusion." Kansas v. United States, 204 U.S. 331, 342 (1907). Perhaps justices who had lived through the Civil War thought no further explanation was needed. But if judicial resolution of disputes between states and the United States is essential to the peace and permanence of the union, why does it matter who initiates the lawsuit?

RISS v. CITY OF NEW YORK
22 N.Y.2d 579, 240 N.E.2d 860 (1968)

BREITEL, J.

This appeal presents, in a very sympathetic framework, the issue of the liability of a municipality for failure to provide special protection to a member of the public who was repeatedly threatened with personal harm and eventually suffered dire personal injuries for lack of such protection. The facts are amply described in the dissenting opinion and no useful purpose would be served by repetition. The issue arises upon the affirmance by a divided Appellate Division of a dismissal of the complaint, after both sides had rested but before submission to the jury.

It is necessary immediately to distinguish those liabilities attendant upon governmental activities which have displaced or supplemented traditionally private enterprises, such as are involved in the operation of rapid transit systems, hospitals, and places of public assembly. Once sovereign immunity was abolished by statute the extension of liability on ordinary principles of tort law logically followed. To be equally distinguished are certain activities of government which provide services and facilities for the use of the public, such as highways, public buildings and the like, in the performance of which the municipality or the State may be liable under ordinary principles of tort law. The ground for liability is the provision of the services or facilities for the direct use by members of the public.

In contrast, this case involves the provision of a governmental service to protect the public generally from external hazards and particularly to control the activities of criminal wrongdoers. The amount of protection that may be provided is limited by the resources of the community and by a considered legislative-executive decision as to how those resources may be deployed. For the courts to proclaim a new and general duty of protection in the law of tort, even to those who may be the particular seekers of protection based on specific hazards, could and would inevitably determine how the limited police resources of the community should be allocated and without predictable limits. This is quite different from the predictable allocation of resources and liabilities when public hospitals, rapid transit systems, or even highways are provided.

Before such extension of responsibilities should be dictated by the indirect imposition of tort liabilities, there should be a legislative determination that that should be the scope of public responsibility.

It is notable that the removal of sovereign immunity for tort liability was accomplished after legislative enactment and not by any judicial arrogation of power (Court of Claims Act, §8). It is equally notable that for many years, since as far back as 1909 in this State, there was by statute municipal liability for losses sustained as a result of riot (General Municipal Law, §71). Yet even this class of liability has for some years been suspended by legislative action (New York State Defense Emergency Act [L. 1951, ch. 784, §113, subd. 3; §121, as last amd. by L. 1968, ch. 115]), a factor of considerable significance.

When one considers the greatly increased amount of crime committed throughout the cities, but especially in certain portions of them, with a repetitive and predictable pattern, it is easy to see the consequences of fixing municipal liability upon a showing of probable need for and request for protection. To be sure these are grave problems at the present time, exciting high priority activity on the part of the national, State and local governments, to which the answers are neither simple, known, or presently within reasonable controls. To foist a presumed cure for these problems by judicial innovation of a new kind of liability in tort would be foolhardy indeed and an assumption of judicial wisdom and power not possessed by the courts.

Nor is the analysis progressed by the analogy to compensation for losses sustained. It is instructive that the Crime Victims Compensation and "Good Samaritan" statutes, compensating limited classes of victims of crime, were enacted only after the most careful study of conditions and the impact of such a scheme upon governmental operations and the public fisc (Executive Law, art. 22, §620 et seq. [L. 1966, ch. 894]; Administrative Code of City of New York, ch. 3, tit. A, §67-3.2). And then the limitations were particular and narrow.

For all of these reasons, there is no warrant in judicial tradition or in the proper allocation of the powers of government for the courts, in the absence of legislation, to carve out an area of tort liability for police protection to members of the public. Quite distinguishable, of course, is the situation where the police authorities undertake responsibilities to particular members of the public and expose them, without adequate protection, to the risks which then materialize into actual losses (Schuster v. City of New York, 5 N.Y.2d 75).

Accordingly, the order of the Appellate Division affirming the judgment of dismissal should be affirmed.

KEATING, J. (dissenting).

Certainly, the record in this case, sound legal analysis, relevant policy considerations and even precedent cannot account for or sustain the result which the majority have here reached. For the result is premised upon a legal rule which long ago should have been abandoned, having lost any justification it might once have had. Despite almost universal condemnation by legal scholars, the rule survives, finding its continuing strength, not in its power to persuade, but in its ability to arouse unwarranted judicial fears of the consequences of overturning it.

Linda Riss, an attractive young woman, was for more than six months terrorized by a rejected suitor well known to the courts of this State, one Burton Pugach. This miscreant, masquerading as a respectable attorney, repeatedly threatened to have Linda killed or maimed if she did not yield to him: "If I can't have you, no one else will have you, and when I get through with you, no one else will want you." In fear for her life, she went to those charged by law with the duty of preserving and safeguarding the lives of the citizens and residents of this State. Linda's repeated and almost pathetic pleas for aid were received with little more than indifference. Whatever help she was given was not commensurate with the identifiable danger. On June 14, 1959 Linda became engaged to another man. At a party held to celebrate the event, she received a phone call warning her that it was her "last chance." Completely distraught, she called the police, begging for help, but was refused. The next day Pugach carried out his dire threats in the very manner he had foretold by having a hired thug throw lye in Linda's face. Linda was blinded in one eye, lost a good portion of her vision in the other, and her face was permanently scarred. After the assault the authorities concluded that there was some basis for Linda's fears, and for the next three and one-half years, she was given around-the-clock protection.

No one questions the proposition that the first duty of government is to assure its citizens the opportunity to live in personal security. And no one who reads the record of Linda's ordeal can reach a conclusion other than that the City of New York, acting through its agents, completely and negligently failed to fulfill this obligation to Linda.

Linda has turned to the courts of this State for redress, asking that the city be held liable in damages for its negligent failure to protect her from harm. With compelling logic, she can point out that, if a stranger, who had absolutely no obligation to aid her, had offered her assistance, and thereafter Burton Pugach was able to injure her as a result of the negligence of the volunteer, the courts would certainly require him to pay damages. (Restatement, 2d, Torts, §323.) Why then should the city, whose duties are imposed by law and include the prevention of crime (New York City Charter, §435) and, consequently, extend far beyond that of the Good Samaritan, not be responsible? If a private detective acts carelessly, no one would deny that a jury could find such conduct unacceptable. Why then is the city not required to live up to at least the same minimal standards of professional competence which would be demanded of a private detective?

Linda's reasoning seems so eminently sensible that surely it must come as a shock to her and to every citizen to hear the city argue and to learn that this court decides that the city has no duty to provide police protection to any given individual. What makes the city's position particularly difficult to understand is that, in conformity to the dictates of the law, Linda did not carry any weapon for self-defense (former Penal Law, §1897). Thus, by a rather bitter irony she was required to rely for protection on the City of New York which now denies all responsibility to her.

It is not a distortion to summarize the essence of the city's case here in the following language: "Because we owe a duty to everybody, we owe it to nobody." Were it not for the fact that this position has been hallowed by much ancient and revered precedent, we would surely dismiss it as preposterous. To say that there is no duty is, of course, to start with the conclusion. The question is whether or not there should be liability for the negligent failure to provide adequate police protection.

The foremost justification repeatedly urged for the existing rule is the claim that the State and the municipalities will be exposed to limitless liability. The city invokes the specter of a "crushing burden" (Steitz v. City of Beacon, 295 N.Y. 51, 55) if we should depart from the existing rule and enunciate even the limited proposition that the State and its municipalities can be held liable for the negligent acts of their police employees in executing whatever police services they do in fact provide.

The fear of financial disaster is a myth. The same argument was made a generation ago in opposition to proposals that the State waive its defense of "sovereign immunity." The prophecy proved false then, and it would now. The supposed astronomical financial burden does not and would not exist. No municipality has gone bankrupt because it has had to respond in damages when a policeman causes injury through carelessly driving a police car or in the thousands of other situations where, by judicial fiat or legislative enactment, the State and its subdivisions have been held liable for the tortious conduct of their employees. Thus, in the past four or five years, New York City has been presented with an average of some 10,000 claims each year. The figure would sound ominous except for the fact the city has been paying out less than $8,000,000 on tort claims each year and this amount includes all those sidewalk defect and snow and ice cases about which the courts fret so often. (Reports submitted by the Comptroller of the City of New York to the Comptroller of the State of New York pursuant to General Municipal Law, §50-f.) . . .

Certainly this is a slight burden in a budget of more than six billion dollars (less than two tenths of 1%) and of no importance as compared to the injustice of permitting unredressed wrongs to continue to go unrepaired. That Linda Riss should be asked to bear the loss, which should properly fall on the city if we assume, as we must, in the present posture of the case, that her injuries resulted from the city's failure to provide sufficient police to protect Linda is contrary to the most elementary notions of justice.

The statement in the majority opinion that there are no predictable limits to the potential liability for failure to provide adequate police protection as compared to other areas of municipal liability is, of course, untenable. When immunity in other areas of governmental activity was removed, the same lack of predictable limits existed. Yet, disaster did not ensue.

Another variation of the "crushing burden" argument is the contention that, every time a crime is committed, the city will be sued and the claim will be made that it resulted from inadequate police protection. Here, again, is an attempt to arouse the "anxiety of the courts about new theories of liability which may have a far-reaching effect." (Spiegler v. City of New Rochelle, 39 Misc. 2d 720, 723, *aff'd on opn. below* 19 A.D.2d 751, *mot. for lv. to app. den.* 13 N.Y.2d 600.) And here too the underlying assumption of the argument is fallacious because it assumes that a strict liability standard is to be imposed and that the courts would prove completely unable to apply general principles of tort liability in a reasonable fashion in the context of actions arising from the negligent acts of police and fire personnel. The argument is also made as if there were no such legal principles as fault, proximate cause or foreseeability, all of which operate to keep liability within reasonable bounds. No one is contending that the police must be at the scene of every potential crime or must provide a personal bodyguard to every person who walks into a police station and claims to have been threatened. They need only act as a reasonable man would under the circumstances. At first there would be a duty to inquire. If the inquiry indicates nothing to substantiate the alleged threat, the matter may be put aside and other matters attended to. If, however, the claims prove to have some basis, appropriate steps would be necessary. . . .

In dismissing the complaint, the trial court noted that there are many crimes being committed daily and the police force is inadequate to deal with its "tremendous responsibilities." The point is not addressed to the facts of this case. Even if it were, however, a distinction must be made. It may be quite reasonable to say that the City of New York is not required to hire sufficient police to protect every piece of property threatened during mass riots. The possibility of riots may even be foreseeable, but the occurrence is sufficiently uncommon that the city should not be required to bear the cost of having a redundancy of men for normal operations. But . . . [if] the police force of the City of New York is so understaffed that it is unable to cope with the everyday problem posed by the relatively few cases where single, known individuals threaten the lives of other persons, then indeed we have reached the danger line and the lives of all of us are in peril. If the police department is in such a deplorable state that the city, because of insufficient manpower, is truly unable to protect persons in Linda Riss' position, then liability not only should, but must be imposed. It will act as an effective inducement for public officials to provide at least a minimally adequate number of police. If local officials are not willing to meet even such a low standard, I see no reason for the courts to abet such irresponsibility.

It is also contended that liability for inadequate police protection will make the courts the arbiters of decisions taken by the Police Commissioner in allocating his manpower and his resources. We are not dealing here with a situation where the injury or loss occurred as a result of a conscious choice of policy made by those exercising high administrative responsibility after a complete and thorough deliberation of various alternatives. There was no major policy decision taken by the Police Commissioner to disregard Linda Riss' appeal for help because there was absolutely no manpower available to deal with Pugach. This "garden variety" negligence case arose in the course of "day-by-day operations of government" (Weiss v. Fote, 7 N.Y.2d 579, 585). Linda Riss' tragedy resulted not from high policy or inadequate manpower, but plain negligence on the part of persons with whom Linda dealt.

More significant, however, is the fundamental flaw in the reasoning behind the argument alleging judicial interference. It is a complete oversimplification of the problem of municipal tort liability. What it ignores is the fact that indirectly courts are reviewing administrative practices in almost every tort case against the State or a municipality, including even decisions of the Police Commissioner. Every time a municipal hospital is held liable for malpractice resulting from inadequate recordkeeping, the courts are in effect making a determination that the municipality should have hired or assigned more clerical help or more competent help to medical records or should have done something to improve its recordkeeping procedures so that the particular injury would not have occurred. Every time a municipality is held liable for a defective sidewalk, it is as if the courts are saying that more money and resources should have been allocated to sidewalk repair, instead of to other public services.

The situation is nowise different in the case of police protection. Whatever effects there may be on police administration will be one of degree, not kind. In McCrink v. City of New York (296 N.Y. 99) we held the city liable where a drunken policeman, while off duty, shot and killed a citizen in an unprovoked assault. The policeman had a long history of being a troublemaker, having been brought up before the Police Commissioner on drunkenness charges on three prior occasions. In imposing liability on the city, were we not in effect overruling the Commissioner's judgment in retaining the policeman on the force and saying his decision was so unreasonable that the city should be required to pay damages?

The truth of the matter, however, is that the courts are not making policy decisions for public officials. In all these municipal negligence cases, the courts are doing two things. First, they apply the principles of vicarious liability to the operations of government. Courts would not insulate the city from liability for the ordinary negligence of members of the highway department. There is no basis for treating the members of the police department differently.

Second, and most important, to the extent that the injury results from the failure to allocate sufficient funds and resources to meet a minimum standard of public administration, public officials are presented with two alternatives: either improve public administration or accept the cost of compensating injured persons. . . . In other words, all the courts do in these municipal negligence cases is require officials to weigh the consequences of their decisions. If Linda Riss' injury resulted from the failure of the city to pay sufficient salaries to attract qualified and sufficient personnel, the full cost of that choice should become acknowledged in the same way as it has in other areas of municipal tort liability. Perhaps officials will find it less costly to choose the alternative of paying damages than changing their existing practices. That may be well and good, but the price for the refusal to provide for an adequate police force should not be borne by Linda Riss and all the other innocent victims of such decisions.

What has existed until now is that the City of New York and other municipalities have been able to engage in a sort of false bookkeeping in which the real costs of inadequate or incompetent police protection have been hidden by charging the expenditures to the individuals who have sustained often catastrophic losses rather than to the community where it belongs, because the latter had the power to prevent the losses.

Although in modern times the compensatory nature of tort law has generally been the one most emphasized, one of its most important functions has been and is its normative aspect. It sets forth standards of conduct which ought to be followed. The penalty for failing to do so is to pay pecuniary damages. At one time the government was completely immunized from this salutary control. This is much less so now, and the imposition of liability has had healthy side effects. In many areas, it has resulted in the adoption of better and more considered procedures just as workmen's compensation resulted in improved industrial safety practices. To visit liability upon the city here will no doubt have similar constructive effects. No "presumed cure" for the problem of crime is being "foisted" upon the city as the majority opinion charges. The methods of dealing with the problem of crime are left completely to the city's discretion. All that the courts can do is make sure that the costs of the city's and its employees' mistakes are placed where they properly belong. Thus, every reason used to sustain the rule that there is no duty to offer police protection to any individual turns out on close analysis to be of little substance.

The city properly cites Motyka v. City of Amsterdam (15 N.Y.2d 134), *Steitz* (supra) and other cases in support of its position. But what is of importance here are cases such as *Bernardine* (infra), *Runkel* (infra) and *Schuster* (infra), for these cases signify the direction in which the law is proceeding. They indicate how, step by step, New York courts are moving . . . toward the day when the government, in carrying out its various functions, will be held equally responsible for the negligent acts of its employees as would a private employer. Bernardine v. City of New York (294 N.Y. 361), one of the earliest cases, is cited generally for the proposition that the State's waiver of "sovereign immunity" is applicable to its subdivisions. What is of greater interest about the case is that it premised liability on pure common-law negligence. But although "sovereign immunity," by that name, supposedly died in Bernardine v. City of New York, it has been revived in a new form. It now goes by the name — "public duty."

Thus, in Steitz v. City of Beacon (295 N.Y. 51), relying on Moch Co. v. Rensselaer Water Co. (247 N.Y. 160), a pre-waiver case, the old rule was revived under a new guise that the duty to furnish police and fire protection runs to the general public and not to any individual. Yet in Runkel v. Homelsky (286 App. Div. 1101, *aff'd* 3 N.Y.2d 857), we held the city liable for failure to order the removal of a vacant building where a city inspector had actual notice that the building was in imminent danger of collapse but did nothing. Logically, there was nothing left to *Steitz* after *Runkel*. Nevertheless, again in Motyka v. City of Amsterdam (15 N.Y.2d 134), in a case involving the failure to enforce a fire safety regulation, we again retreated and held that "liability arises out of a statute only in limited instances where disregard of the command of the statute results in damage to one of the class for whose special benefit the statute was enacted." (Id., p.139.)

The majority opinion would explain the result here as involving the protection of the public from an "external hazard." This attempt to reconcile the case law does not withstand analysis. Is not a blizzard or snowstorm an "external hazard"? Analytically, the problems of providing adequate police protection and snow removal are indistinguishable.

Fortunately, this court has avoided the misfeasance-nonfeasance doctrine.

The rule is Judge made and can be judicially modified. By statute, the judicially created doctrine of "sovereign immunity" was destroyed. It was an unrighteous doctrine, carrying as it did the connotation that the government is above the law. Likewise, the law should be purged of all new evasions, which seek to avoid the full implications of the repeal of sovereign immunity.

No doubt in the future we shall have to draw limitations just as we have done in the area of private litigation, and no doubt some of these limitations will be unique to municipal liability because the problems will not have any counterpart in private tort law. But if the lines are to be drawn, let them be delineated on candid considerations of policy and fairness and not on the fictions or relics of the doctrine of "sovereign immunity." Before reaching such questions, however, we must resolve the fundamental issue raised here and recognize that, having undertaken to provide professional police and fire protection, municipalities cannot escape liability for damages caused by their failure to do even a minimally adequate job of it.

The Appellate Division did not adopt the "no duty" theory, but said there was no negligence here because the danger was not imminent. . . . This finding does not stand examination and to its credit the city does not argue that this record would not support a finding of negligence. The danger to Linda was indeed imminent, and this fact could easily have been confirmed had there been competent police work.

Moreover, since this is an appeal from a dismissal of the complaint, we must give the plaintiff the benefit of every favorable inference. The Appellate Division's conclusion could only have been reached by ignoring the thrust of the plaintiff's claim and the evidence in the record. A few examples of the actions of the police should suffice to show the true state of the record. Linda Riss received a telephone call from a person who warned Linda that Pugach was arranging to have her beaten up. A detective learned the identity of the caller. He offered to arrest the caller, but plaintiff rejected that suggestion for the obvious reason that the informant was trying to help Linda. When Linda requested that Pugach be arrested, the detective said he could not do that because she had not yet been hurt. The statement was not so. It was and is a crime to conspire to injure someone. True there was no basis to arrest Pugach then, but that was only because the necessary leg work had not been done. No one went to speak to the informant, who might have furnished additional leads. Linda claimed to be receiving telephone calls almost every day. These calls could have been monitored for a few days to obtain evidence against Pugach. Any number of reasonable alternatives presented themselves. A case against Pugach could have been developed which would have at least put him away for awhile or altered the situation entirely. But, if necessary, some police protection should have been afforded. . . .

[W]ith actual notice of danger and ample opportunity to confirm and take reasonable remedial steps, a jury could find that the persons involved acted unreasonably and negligently. Linda Riss is entitled to have a jury determine the issue of the city's liability. This right should not be terminated by the adoption of a question-begging conclusion that there is no duty owed to her. The order of the Appellate Division should be reversed and a new trial granted.

Chief Judge FULD and Judges BURKE, SCILEPPI, BERGAN and JASEN concur with Judge BREITEL; Judge KEATING dissents and votes to reverse in a separate opinion.

Order affirmed, without costs.

NOTES ON DAMAGE SUITS AGAINST GOVERNMENTS

1.   Governments often consent to be sued. These consents are often limited to certain kinds of claims; they are often subject to exceptions and special conditions. There is an enormous range of provisions among the states, from very broad consents like New York's, to nearly total immunity, as in South Carolina. Some states have limited or abolished sovereign immunity by judicial decision.

Municipalities are not sovereign, and they have traditionally had much less immunity than the state itself. They do not share the state's immunity from suit in federal court. And in most states they were always liable on their contracts, and liable for torts committed in their proprietary capacities. New York's broad waiver of immunity extends to governmental functions as well as proprietary ones.

2.   Montana declared sovereign immunity unconstitutional in White v. State, 661 P.2d 1272 (Mont. 1983). The opinion rests on equal protection and on a clause of the state constitution guaranteeing a "speedy remedy . . . for every injury." However, the court upheld the state's immunity from punitive damages, and it held out the possibility that some limits on liability might be constitutional.

The Montana decision is heretical in light of the traditional acceptance of sovereign immunity. But aren't the heretics right? Is there any basis to distinguish between a pedestrian run over by a Greyhound bus and a pedestrian run over by a city bus? The Montana court said that "payment of tort judgments is simply a cost of doing business." Certainly the victim's injuries are a cost; immunity doesn't make that cost go away. Is it fair, or even rational, to impose all those costs on the victim instead of distributing them among all the taxpayers?

Suppose the state supported 95 percent of the cost of government through general taxation fairly apportioned, and 5 percent through a negative lottery. Suppose that if your name were drawn in the lottery, you were liable for an additional tax, in a random amount, ranging from $10 to $1 million. Is there any doubt that such a scheme would violate the equal protection clause? How is it any different to impose the cost of government accidents on victims? Or to refuse payment to an occasional creditor?

3.   Even if this reasoning persuades you utterly, abolition of government immunity still raises problems. Government injures people in a vast

variety of ways, and liability for some of these injuries is troubling even to die-hard opponents of immunity. Even Judge Keating concedes that there might have to be some special rules about municipalities.

One of the exclusions in the Federal Tort Claims Act is that the United States shall not be liable for "any claim for damages caused by the fiscal operations of the Treasury or by the regulation of the monetary system." 28 U.S.C. §2680(i) (1982). Probably the courts would not have imposed such liability even without the exclusion. But who can blame Congress for being cautious? Investors make and lose millions every time the Federal Reserve Board meets. And it would not be hard to characterize some of its decisions as negligent or worse. Justice Jackson said that "it is not a tort for government to govern." Dalehite v. United States, 346 U.S. 15, 57 (1953) (dissenting). But how can courts or legislatures reliably draw the line between tortfeasing and governing?

4. One attempt to answer that question is the governmental/proprietary distinction. We first encountered that distinction in United States v. Georgia-Pacific, supra at 937. The distinction persists because it is attractive in clear cases. New York sells bottled mineral water by mail order. New York v. United States, 326 U.S. 572 (1946). Alabama runs a railroad. Parden v. Terminal Railway, 377 U.S. 184 (1964). South Dakota owns a cement plant. Reeves, Inc. v. Stake, 447 U.S. 429 (1980). New York City owns Yankee Stadium; Oakland may own the Raiders if it pursues condemnation proceedings that are pending as I write this chapter. States and cities do many things that could be done by private enterprise. It is often tempting to distinguish such activities from core governmental activities, such as police and fire protection. No matter how often they denounce the distinction, judges keep returning to it.

5. But no matter how often they use the distinction, judges keep denouncing it. No court has ever generated a coherent set of precedents applying the distinction. Many government activities defy classification, and the facts of particular cases and the sympathies of judges influence decisions. Efforts to draw lines in the vast middle sometimes lead to madness. One example will suffice: In Texas, sanitary sewers are governmental, but storm sewers are proprietary. What happens if both kinds of sewer are in the same ditch, and the ditch caves in and kills a worker? It depends on which pipe he was working on at the moment of the cave-in! City of Houston v. Bush, 566 S.W.2d 33 (Tex. Civ. App. 1978).

6. Justice Douglas went to the core of the problem in New York v. United States. He suggested that whatever government does is governmental — that whenever a governmental unit undertakes a nontraditional activity, or an activity "akin to private enterprise," it does so to accomplish some public purpose thought sufficient by its legislature. 326 U.S. at 591 (Douglas, J., dissenting). The majority made the same point in Garcia v. San Antonio Metropolitan Transit Authority, 105 S. Ct. 1005, 1015 (1985). If South Dakota elected a socialist government and

took over all the means of production, wouldn't all the factories be serving governmental functions?

7. The claim in Riss v. City of New York would surely be barred by the governmental/proprietary distinction. Police protection is governmental if anything is. New York's waiver of governmental immunity abolished the distinction. But the Court of Appeals has invoked another traditional limit on governmental liability, the requirement of a duty to the plaintiff. The opinions in *Riss* debate the doctrine but never clearly summarize it; here is a better statement:

> [T]o sustain liability against a municipality, the duty breached must be more than a duty owing to the general public. There must exist a special relationship between the municipality and the plaintiff, resulting in the creation of "a duty to use due care for the benefit of particular persons or classes of persons." (Motyka v. City of Amsterdam, 15 N.Y.2d 134, 139).
>
> For example, as a general rule, a municipality's duty to furnish water to protect its residents against damage caused by fire is a duty inuring to the benefit of the public at large, rather than to individual members of the community. Similarly, a municipality cannot be held liable for the failure to furnish adequate police protection. This duty, like the duty to provide protection against fire, flows only to the general public. [citing *Riss*.]
>
> Where, however, a special relationship exists between a municipality and a plaintiff creating a duty, albeit one normally inuring only to the benefit of the public at large, a municipality may be held liable for damages suffered as a consequence of its negligence. For example, a municipality possesses a special duty to provide police protection to an informer who collaborates with the police in the arrest and prosecution of a criminal. (Schuster v. City of New York, 5 N.Y.2d 75, 82-83).

Florence v. Goldberg, 44 N.Y.2d 189, 195-196, 375 N.E.2d 763, 766 (1978).

Is this a reasoned and workable limit on government liability? Or will the duty doctrine inevitably generate decisions as silly as those under the governmental/proprietary distinction? Is it just the governmental/proprietary distinction in disguise? Why does the duty of care with respect to "rapid transit systems, hospitals, and places of public assembly . . . highways, public buildings and the like" run to individuals, while the duty of care with respect to police and fire protection runs only to the public at large?

8. New York has imposed liability for negligent police protection in a few cases. Florence v. Goldberg involved a six-year-old boy hit by a car while crossing a busy street on the way home from school. His mother had walked him to and from school for the first two weeks, but there was always a crossing guard, so she began letting him go by himself. On the day of the accident, the crossing guard called in sick. Police regulations required the police to cover all designated crossings if they could, to cover

the most dangerous crossings if they couldn't cover them all, and to notify the school principal if they had to leave a crossing unprotected. They left the crossing unprotected and didn't notify the principal. The court affirmed a judgment against the city. It held that the police had voluntarily assumed a duty to "children crossing designated intersections while traveling to and from school at scheduled times" — a special class much narrower than the general public. The court also relied heavily on plaintiff's reliance on the regular performance of this duty.

9.   There was reliance but no special class of persons in De Long v. County of Erie, 60 N.Y.2d 296, 457 N.E.2d 717 (1983). Erie County urged its citizens to call 911 to summon help in emergencies. Mrs. De Long called 911 and said there was a burglar trying to break into her house at 319 Victoria. The "complaint writer" who answered said he would send help right away. But he didn't ask what town she was calling from, and he sent the message to the Buffalo police instead of the police in De Long's suburb. When the responding officer reported that there was no such address, the complaint writer and the police dispatcher both dropped the matter. The operations manual required complaint writers to ask what city the call was coming from at the beginning of each call. It also specified a procedure for checking a list of "duplicate" streets when responding officers reported "no such address."

Fourteen minutes after her call to 911, De Long staggered out of her house, undressed and bleeding, and collapsed on the sidewalk. A neighbor called the local police, who responded in less than a minute. Paramedics came a few minutes later, but she died on the sidewalk. A jury returned an $800,000 verdict against the county and the city of Buffalo, which had trained the complaint writer.

Was there a duty in De Long? The Court of Appeals said yes. The county had advised people not to call the general number for their local police, but to call 911 instead. "In addition, and most significantly, the victim's plea for assistance was not refused. Indeed she was affirmatively assured that help would be there 'right away.'" Id. at 305, 457 N.E.2d at 721. Is that "most significant" because it is the only thing that distinguishes Riss?

10.   Consider a few variations on these cases. In both Florence and De Long, employees failed to comply with specific regulations. The court relied on these regulations to establish duty and to establish negligence. Are the regulations essential? Suppose that in Florence, there were no regulations governing crossing guards, but there had always been one at this corner, and plaintiff had relied on that. Does that create a duty? Does she have to tell someone she's relying on the crossing guard? Shouldn't the city know that parents of small children rely on crossing guards?

Suppose the city withdrew the crossing guards because of a budget crisis. Would that end the duty? Would that be a nonreviewable decision about how to allocate public services? Does the city have to notify people who relied on crossing guards? Notice to school principals would suffice, wouldn't it? What about newspaper coverage of the city's budget problems?

11.   Still another attempt to formulate a limit on government liability is illustrated by the Federal Tort Claims Act. That act consents to tort suits against the United States. But it excludes any claim "based upon the exercise or performance or the failure to exercise or perform a discretionary function or duty on the part of a federal agency or an employee of the Government, whether or not the discretion involved be abused." 28 U.S.C. §2680(a) (1982).

The leading case is Dalehite v. United States, 346 U.S. 15 (1953). *Dalehite* involved enormous liability, and the Court may have felt obliged to stretch the exception. After World War II, the United States tried to feed the populations of Germany, Japan, and Korea. All three countries suffered from shortages of food and fertilizer. At the same time, the United States suddenly had surplus factories for making explosives. Ammonium nitrate, a key ingredient in explosives, can be adapted for use as a fertilizer. Someone thought to convert the explosives plants to fertilizer production. A shipload of this fertilizer exploded in the harbor at Texas City, Texas, destroying the entire dock area and killing 560 people.

The trial court found that the fertilizer was bagged and loaded in a negligent manner and that this negligence caused the explosion. But those who bagged and loaded followed specifications laid down in Washington. Because the fatal decisions were "all responsibly made at a planning rather than operational level and involved considerations more or less important to the practicability of the Government's fertilizer program," they were all within the discretionary function exception. Id. at 42.

There were three dissents:

> The common sense of this matter is that a policy adopted in the exercise of an immune discretion was carried out carelessly by those in charge of detail. We cannot agree that all the way down the line there is immunity for every balancing of care against cost, or safety against production, of warning against silence.

Id. at 58 (Jackson, J., dissenting).

Justice Jackson didn't think decisions about how to bag and load fertilizer had been made at cabinet level. But if they had been, he thought the cabinet should be more careful.

12.   The discretionary function exception is not easy to apply either, and it has generated its share of conflicting decisions. *Dalehite* surely got it off to a bad start. But does it at least focus on the right question? Deciding how much to expand the money supply is a discretionary function, isn't it? What about deciding that New York City needs, or can afford, 30,000 police officers? Should that decision be immune if some crime victim claims that anything fewer than 35,000 was negligent?

Isn't the core concern one of separation of powers? If policy decisions are committed to the political branches and may be taken for political reasons, should courts review those decisions for negligence? One solution would be to say that such decisions simply aren't negligent. But that solution could not function honestly. On the one hand, negligence edges closer and closer to strict liability in private tort cases, and on the other hand, policymakers sometimes make egregious mistakes. Courts would be hard pressed to say that policymakers are never negligent.

13. Is an immunity limited to discretionary functions broad enough? What about safety inspections? The individual inspector surely isn't exercising a discretionary function. Should the government be liable for every injury that would have been prevented if it had competently carried out all its inspection programs? Does that too broadly substitute government for the primary tortfeasor? On the other hand, don't we all rely on governmental inspection programs every day? For example, every time we enter an elevator?

NOTES ON FEDERAL WAIVERS OF IMMUNITY

1. The federal statutory waivers are important because suits against the federal government are so important. They are also as good an example as any of the wide variety of waiver statutes. The pattern of one waiver for contracts, with a specialized court to hear the cases, and a separate waiver for tort, with a lot of exceptions, is a common one. Another common pattern, not illustrated in the federal waivers, is a waiver with a liability limit stated in dollars. For example, Nevada limits its liability to $50,000. Nev. Rev. Stat. §41.035(1) (1983). Montana denied liability for pain and suffering and limited liability to $300,000 for all other damages. This was the provision struck down in White v. State, discussed in the previous set of notes.

Here is a summary of the principal federal waivers of immunity:

2. *The Tucker Act.* The Tucker Act consents to suit on any claim "founded either upon the Constitution, or any Act of Congress, or any regulation of an executive department, or upon any express or implied contract with the United States, or for liquidated or unliquidated damages in cases not sounding in tort." 28 U.S.C. §1491 (1982). Jurisdiction is vested in the United States Claims Court, formerly known as the Court of Claims; claims for less than $10,000 may also be filed in the United States District Courts. The Claims Court also has several less important grants of jurisdiction over miscellaneous suits against the United States.

The reference to the Constitution, statutes, and regulations is misleading. The Tucker Act consents to suit on such claims, but it does not create liability. A law can be enforced in the Claims Court only if the substantive law expressly or by strong implication creates a cause of action for damages. United States v. Testan, 424 U.S. 392 (1976). Thus, the Claims Court hears cases arising under the just compensation clause, but not cases arising under any other part of the Constitution. Implied causes of action for constitutional violations — Bivens claims — run against individual officers. There are no implied causes of action against the sovereign.

In Testan, plaintiffs were civil servants who had been paid less than they would have been paid if their positions had been properly classified. The Classification Act created a substantive right to proper classification, but it did not create any right to damages for improper classification. The Back Pay Act created a right to back pay for unlawful discharge, but not for improper classification. So even though the claim was founded on a federal statute, it was not a statute that created liability for damages, and the Tucker Act was no help.

The most important function of the Claims Court is to enforce government contracts. But it cannot grant specific performance. It is limited to damages and certain kinds of incidental equitable relief that fall short of specific performance.

3.   The Federal Tort Claims Act. The Tort Claims Act consents to suit "for injury or loss of property, or personal injury or death caused by the negligent or wrongful act or omission of any employee of the Government while acting within the scope of his office or employment, under circumstances where the United States, if a private person, would be liable to the claimant in accordance with the law of the place where the act or omission occurred." 28 U.S.C. §1346(b) (1982). The act grants jurisdiction to the district courts.

There are a number of exceptions. The United States is not liable for prejudgment interest or punitive damages. 28 U.S.C. §2674 (1982). We have encountered the ban on punitive damages before, in United States v. Flannery, supra at 78 and 192. There are also substantive exceptions. The Supreme Court has held that the requirement of a "wrongful" act means the United States is not liable under any state rule imposing strict liability. Laird v. Nelms, 406 U.S. 797 (1972). There is no liability for enforcing unconstitutional statutes, for losing letters in the post office, for actions of the military in time of war, for damages caused by fiscal operations of the Treasury or regulation of the monetary system, for claims arising in a foreign country, for most intentional torts, and several other miscellaneous kinds of claims. 28 U.S.C. §2680 (1982). After Bivens, supra at 1071, Congress made the United States liable for most abuses by law enforcement officers, without repealing the liability of the officers themselves.

The most important and troublesome exception is the discretionary function exception, discussed in the preceding set of notes.

4. *The Administrative Procedure Act*. Sovereign immunity is a barrier to ordinary judicial review of administrative action. Most statutes creating administrative agencies provided for judicial review. For those that didn't, mandamus or some other suit against the officers in their official capacity could often be made to work. But sometimes plaintiffs ran up against one of the limits on official capacity suits. The original Administrative Procedure Act was held not to address these problems. Most persons aggrieved by agency action could get review, but a few could not, and the problem generated recurring litigation.

Congress tried to eliminate the whole problem in 1976. It added the following sentences to the Administrative Procedure Act:

> An action in a court of the United States seeking relief other than money damages and stating a claim that an agency or an officer or employee thereof acted or failed to act in an official capacity or under color of legal authority shall not be dismissed nor relief therein be denied on the ground that it is against the United States or that the United States is an indispensable party. The United States may be named as a defendant in any such action, and a judgment or decree may be entered against the United States.

5 U.S.C. §702 (1982).

Incredibly, the Second Circuit initially held that this language was ineffective to waive immunity in a single case. Estate of Watson v. Blumenthal, 586 F.2d 925, 932 (2d Cir. 1978). Several other circuits construed the statute more sensibly, and the Second Circuit rejected *Watson's* reasoning in B.K. Instrument v. United States, 715 F.2d 713, 724-725 (2d Cir. 1983). But there is recurring litigation about the boundaries of §702. An explicit exception provides that nothing in §702 "confers authority to grant relief if any other statute that grants consent to suit expressly or impliedly forbids the relief which is sought." So, for example, §702 can't be used to get around the implied disallowance of specific performance in the Tucker Act.

5. *Other waivers*. There are many more specific waivers scattered through the United States Code. Statutes creating government corporations and independent agencies often say that the entity can "sue and be sued." These clauses are a general waiver of sovereign immunity for suits against that entity. Franchise Tax Board v. United States Postal Service, 104 S. Ct. 2549 (1984). But exceptions to other waivers of immunity have also been read into sue-and-be-sued clauses. The cases are collected in Federal Deposit Insurance Corp. v. Citizens Bank & Trust Co., 592 F.2d 364, 370-372 (7th Cir.), *cert. denied*, 444 U.S. 829 (1979). That case gave the FDIC the benefit of exceptions to the Tort Claims Act.

Another example of the wide ranging effects of sovereign immunity is that it is impossible to garnish the wages of government employees unless the government consents to the garnishment suit. 42 U.S.C. §659(a) (1982) consents to garnishment suits seeking to collect alimony and child support.

STUMP v. SPARKMAN
435 U.S. 349 (1978)

MR. JUSTICE WHITE delivered the opinion of the Court.

This case requires us to consider the scope of a judge's immunity from damages liability when sued under 42 U.S.C. §1983.

I

The relevant facts underlying respondents' suit are not in dispute. On July 9, 1971, Ora Spitler McFarlin, the mother of respondent Linda Kay Spitler Sparkman, presented to Judge Harold D. Stump of the Circuit Court of DeKalb County, Ind., a document captioned "Petition To Have Tubal Ligation Performed On Minor and Indemnity Agreement." The document had been drafted by her attorney, a petitioner here. In this petition Mrs. McFarlin stated under oath that her daughter was 15 years of age and was "somewhat retarded," although she attended public school and had been promoted each year with her class. The petition further stated that Linda had been associating with "older youth or young men" and had stayed out overnight with them on several occasions. As a result of this behavior and Linda's mental capabilities, it was stated that it would be in the daughter's best interest if she underwent a tubal ligation in order "to prevent unfortunate circumstances. . . . " In the same document Mrs. McFarlin also undertook to indemnify and hold harmless Dr. John Hines, who was to perform the operation, and the DeKalb Memorial Hospital, where the operation was to take place, against all causes of action that might arise as a result of the performance of the tubal ligation.

The petition was approved by Judge Stump on the same day. He affixed his signature as "Judge, DeKalb Circuit Court," to the statement that he did "hereby approve the above Petition by affidavit form on behalf of Ora Spitler McFarlin, to have Tubal Ligation performed upon her minor daughter, Linda Spitler, subject to said Ora Spitler McFarlin covenanting and agreeing to indemnify and keep indemnified Dr. John Hines and the DeKalb Memorial Hospital from any matters or causes of action arising therefrom."

On July 15, 1971, Linda Spitler entered the DeKalb Memorial Hospital, having been told that she was to have her appendix removed. The following day a tubal ligation was performed upon her. She was released several days later, unaware of the true nature of her surgery.

Approximately two years after the operation, Linda Spitler was married to respondent Leo Sparkman. Her inability to become pregnant led her to discover that she had been sterilized during the 1971 operation. As a result of this revelation, the Sparkmans filed suit in the United States District Court for the Northern District of Indiana against Mrs. McFarlin, her attorney, Judge Stump, the doctors who had performed and assisted in the tubal ligation, and the DeKalb Memorial Hospital. Respondents sought damages for the alleged violation of Linda Sparksman's constitutional rights; also asserted were pendent state claims for assault and battery, medical malpractice, and loss of potential fatherhood.

Ruling upon the defendants' various motions to dismiss the complaint, the District Court concluded that each of the constitutional claims asserted by respondents required a showing of state action and that the only state action alleged in the complaint was the approval by Judge Stump, acting as Circuit Court Judge, of the petition presented to him by Mrs. McFarlin. The Sparkmans sought to hold the private defendants liable on a theory that they had conspired with Judge Stump to bring about the allegedly unconstitutional acts. The District Court, however, held that no federal action would lie against any of the defendants because Judge Stump, the only state agent, was absolutely immune from suit under the doctrine of judicial immunity. The court stated that "whether or not Judge Stump's 'approval' of the petition may in retrospect appear to have been premised on an erroneous view of the law, Judge Stump surely had jurisdiction to consider the petition and to act thereon."Accordingly, under Bradley v. Fisher, 13 Wall. 335, 351 (1872), Judge Stump was entitled to judicial immunity.[3]

On appeal, the Court of Appeals for the Seventh Circuit reversed the judgment of the District Court, holding that the "crucial issue" was "whether Judge Stump acted within his jurisdiction" and concluding that he had not. He was accordingly not immune from damages liability under the controlling authorities. The Court of Appeals also held that the judge had forfeited his immunity "because of his failure to comply with elementary principles of procedural due process." . . .

II

The governing principle of law is well established and is not questioned by the parties. As early as 1872, the Court recognized that it was "a general principle of the highest importance to the proper administration of justice that a judicial officer, in exercising the authority vested in him, [should]

---

3. The District Court granted the defendants' motion to dismiss the federal claims for that reason and dismissed the remaining pendent state claims for lack of subject-matter jurisdiction.

be free to act upon his own convictions, without apprehension of personal consequences to himself." Bradley v. Fisher, supra, at 347. For that reason the Court held that "judges of courts of superior or general jurisdiction are not liable to civil actions for their judicial acts, even when such acts are in excess of their jurisdiction, and are alleged to have been done maliciously or corruptly." 13 Wall., at 351. Later we held that this doctrine of judicial immunity was applicable in suits under §1 of the Civil Rights Act of 1871, 42 U.S.C. §1983, for the legislative record gave no indication that Congress intended to abolish this long-established principle. Pierson v. Ray, 386 U.S. 547 (1967).

The Court of Appeals correctly recognized that the necessary inquiry in determining whether a defendant judge is immune from suit is whether at the time he took the challenged action he had jurisdiction over the subject matter before him. Because "some of the most difficult and embarrassing questions which a judicial officer is called upon to consider and determine relate to his jurisdiction . . . ," Bradley, supra, at 352, the scope of the judge's jurisdiction must be construed broadly where the issue is the immunity of the judge. A judge will not be deprived of immunity because the action he took was in error, was done maliciously, or was in excess of his authority; rather, he will be subject to liability only when he has acted in the "clear absence of all jurisdiction."[7] 13 Wall., at 351.

We cannot agree that there was a "clear absence of all jurisdiction" in the DeKalb County Circuit Court to consider the petition presented by Mrs. McFarlin. As an Indiana Circuit Court Judge, Judge Stump had "original exclusive jurisdiction in all cases at law and in equity whatsoever . . . , " jurisdiction over the settlement of estates and over guardianships, appellate jurisdiction as conferred by law, and jurisdiction over "all other causes, matters and proceedings where exclusive jurisdiction thereof is not conferred by law upon some other court, board or officer." Ind. Code §33-4-4-3 (1975). This is indeed a broad jurisdictional grant; yet the Court of Appeals concluded that Judge Stump did not have jurisdiction over the petition authorizing Linda Sparkman's sterilization.

In so doing, the Court of Appeals noted that the Indiana statutes provided for the sterilization of institutionalized persons under certain circumstances, but otherwise contained no express authority for judicial approval of tubal ligations. It is true that the statutory grant of general jurisdiction to the Indiana circuit courts does not itemize types of cases those courts may hear and hence does not expressly mention sterilization

---

7. In Bradley, the Court illustrated the distinction between lack of jurisdiction and excess of jurisdiction with the following examples: if a probate judge, with jurisdiction over only wills and estates, should try a criminal case, he would be acting in the clear absence of jurisdiction and would not be immune from liability for his action; on the other hand, if a judge of a criminal court should convict a defendant of a nonexistent crime, he would merely be acting in excess of his jurisdiction and would be immune. Id., at 352.

petitions presented by the parents of a minor. But in our view, it is more significant that there was no Indiana statute and no case law in 1971 prohibiting a circuit court, a court of general jurisdiction, from considering a petition of the type presented to Judge Stump. The statutory authority for the sterilization of institutionalized persons in the custody of the State does not warrant the inference that a court of general jurisdiction has no power to act on a petition for sterilization of a minor in the custody of her parents, particularly where the parents have authority under the Indiana statutes to "consent to and contract for medical or hospital care or treatment of [the minor] including surgery." Ind. Code §16-8-4-2 (1973). The District Court concluded that Judge Stump had jurisdiction under §33-4-4-3 to entertain and act upon Mrs. McFarlin's petition. We agree with the District Court, it appearing that neither by statute nor by case law has the broad jurisdiction granted to the circuit courts of Indiana been circumscribed to foreclose consideration of a petition for authorization of a minor's sterilization.

The Court of Appeals also concluded that support for Judge Stump's actions could not be found in the common law of Indiana, relying in particular on the Indiana Court of Appeals' intervening decision in A. L. v. G. R. H., 163 Ind. App. 636, 325 N.E.2d 501 (1975). In that case the Indiana court held that a parent does not have a common-law right to have a minor child sterilized, even though the parent might "sincerely believe the child's adulthood would benefit therefrom." Id., at 638, 325 N.E.2d, at 502. The opinion, however, speaks only of the rights of the parents to consent to the sterilization of their child and does not question the *jurisdiction* of a circuit judge who is presented with such a petition from a parent. Although under that case a circuit judge would err as a matter of law if he were to approve a parent's petition seeking the sterilization of a child, the opinion in A. L. v. G. R. H. does not indicate that a circuit judge is without jurisdiction to entertain the petition. Indeed, the clear implication of the opinion is that, when presented with such a petition, the circuit judge should deny it on its merits rather than dismiss it for lack of jurisdiction.

Perhaps realizing the broad scope of Judge Stump's jurisdiction, the Court of Appeals stated that, even if the action taken by him was not foreclosed under the Indiana statutory scheme, it would still be "an illegitimate exercise of his common law power because of his failure to comply with elementary principles of procedural due process." 552 F.2d, at 176. This misconceives the doctrine of judicial immunity. A judge is absolutely immune from liability for his judicial acts even if his exercise of authority is flawed by the commission of grave procedural errors. The Court made this point clear in *Bradley*, 13 Wall., at 357, where it stated: "[T]his erroneous manner in which [the court's] jurisdiction was exercised, however it may have affected the validity of the act, did not make the act any less a judicial act; nor did it render the defendant liable to answer in damages for it at the suit of the plaintiff, as though the court had proceeded without having any jurisdiction whatever. . . . "

We conclude that the Court of Appeals, employing an unduly restrictive view of the scope of Judge Stump's jurisdiction, erred in holding that he was not entitled to judicial immunity. Because the court over which Judge Stump presides is one of general jurisdiction, neither the procedural errors he may have committed nor the lack of a specific statute authorizing his approval of the petition in question rendered him liable in damages for the consequences of his actions.

The respondents argue that even if Judge Stump had jurisdiction to consider the petition presented to him by Mrs. McFarlin, he is still not entitled to judicial immunity because his approval of the petition did not constitute a "judicial" act. It is only for acts performed in his "judicial" capacity that a judge is absolutely immune, they say. We do not disagree with this statement of the law, but we cannot characterize the approval of the petition as a nonjudicial act.

Respondents themselves stated in their pleadings before the District Court that Judge Stump was "clothed with the authority of the state" at the time that he approved the petition and that "he was acting as a county circuit court judge." They nevertheless now argue that Judge Stump's approval of the petition was not a judicial act because the petition was not given a docket number, was not placed on file with the clerk's office, and was approved in an ex parte proceeding without notice to the minor, without a hearing, and without the appointment of a guardian ad litem.

This Court has not had occasion to consider, for purposes of the judicial immunity doctrine, the necessary attributes of a judicial act; but it has previously rejected the argument, somewhat similar to the one raised here, that the lack of formality involved in the Illinois Supreme Court's consideration of a petitioner's application for admission to the state bar prevented it from being a "judicial proceeding" and from presenting a case or controversy that could be reviewed by this Court. In re Summers, 325 U.S. 561 (1945). Of particular significance to the present case, the Court in *Summers* noted the following: "The record does not show that any process issued or that any appearance was made. . . . While no entry was placed by the Clerk in the file, on a docket, or in a judgment roll, the Court took cognizance of the petition and passed an order which is validated by the signature of the presiding officer." Id., at 567. Because the Illinois court took cognizance of the petition for admission and acted upon it, the Court held that a case or controversy was presented.

Similarly, the Court of Appeals for the Fifth Circuit has held that a state district judge was entitled to judicial immunity, even though "at the time of the altercation [giving rise to the suit] Judge Brown was not in his judge's robes, he was not in the courtroom itself, and he may well have violated state and/or federal procedural requirements regarding contempt citations." McAlester v. Brown, 469 F.2d 1280, 1282 (1972).[9] Among the factors relied upon by the Court of Appeals in deciding that the judge was acting within his judicial capacity was the fact that "the confrontation arose directly and immediately out of a visit to the judge in his official capacity." Ibid.[10]

The relevant cases demonstrate that the factors determining whether an act by a judge is a "judicial" one relate to the nature of the act itself, i.e., whether it is a function normally performed by a judge, and to the expectations of the parties, i.e., whether they dealt with the judge in his judicial capacity. Here, both factors indicate that Judge Stump's approval of the sterilization petition was a judicial act.[11] State judges with general jurisdiction not infrequently are called upon in their official capacity to approve petitions relating to the affairs of minors, as for example, a petition to settle a minor's claim. Furthermore, as even respondents have admitted, at the time he approved the petition presented to him by Mrs. McFarlin, Judge Stump was "acting as a county circuit court judge." We may infer from the record that it was only because Judge Stump served in that position that Mrs. McFarlin, on the advice of counsel, submitted the petition to him for his approval. Because Judge Stump performed the type of act normally performed only by judges and because he did so in

---

9. In *McAlester* the plaintiffs alleged that they had gone to the courthouse where their son was to be tried by the defendant in order to give the son a fresh set of clothes. When they went into the defendant judge's office, he allegedly ordered them out and had a deputy arrest one of them and place him in jail for the rest of the day. Several months later, the judge issued an order holding the plaintiff in contempt of court, nunc pro tunc.

10. Other Courts of Appeals, presented with different fact situations, have concluded that the challenged actions of defendant judges were not performed as part of the judicial function and that the judges were thus not entitled to rely upon the doctrine of judicial immunity. The Court of Appeals for the Ninth Circuit, for example, has held that a justice of the peace who was accused of forcibly removing a man from his courtroom and physically assaulting him was not absolutely immune. Gregory v. Thompson, 500 F.2d 59 (1974). While the court recognized that a judge has the duty to maintain order in his courtroom, it concluded that the actual eviction of someone from the courtroom by use of physical force, a task normally performed by a sheriff or bailiff, was "simply not an act of a judicial nature." Id., at 64. And the Court of Appeals for the Sixth Circuit held in Lynch v. Johnson, 420 F.2d 818 (1970), that the county judge sued in that case was not entitled to judicial immunity because his service on a board with only legislative and administrative powers did not constitute a judicial act.

11. Mr. Justice Stewart, in dissent, complains that this statement is inaccurate because it nowhere appears that judges are normally asked to approve parents' decisions either with respect to surgical treatment in general or with respect to sterilizations in particular. Of course, the opinion makes neither assertion. Rather, it is said that Judge Stump was performing a "function" normally performed by judges and ·that he was taking "the type of action" judges normally perform. The dissent . . . does [not] dispute that judges normally entertain petitions with respect to the affairs of minors. Even if it is assumed that in a lifetime of judging, a judge has acted on only one petition of a particular kind, this would not indicate that his function in entertaining and acting on it is not the kind of function that a judge normally performs. . . .

his capacity as a Circuit Court Judge, we find no merit to respondents' argument that the informality with which he proceeded rendered his action nonjudicial and deprived him of his absolute immunity.[12]

Both the Court of Appeals and the respondents seem to suggest that, because of the tragic consequences of Judge Stump's actions, he should not be immune. For example, the Court of Appeals noted that "[t]here are actions of purported judicial character that a judge, even when exercising general jurisdiction, is not empowered to take," and respondents argue that Judge Stump's action was "so unfair" and "so totally devoid of judicial concern for the interests and well-being of the young girl involved" as to disqualify it as a judicial act. Disagreement with the action taken by the judge, however, does not justify depriving that judge of his immunity. Despite the unfairness to litigants that sometimes results, the doctrine of judicial immunity is thought to be in the best interests of "the proper administration of justice . . . [, for it allows] a judicial officer, in exercising the authority vested in him [to] be free to act upon his own convictions, without apprehension of personal consequences to himself." Bradley v. Fisher, 13 Wall., at 347. The fact that the issue before the judge is a controversial one is all the more reason that he should be able to act without fear of suit. As the Court pointed out in *Bradley*:

> Controversies involving not merely great pecuniary interests, but the liberty and character of the parties; and consequently exciting the deepest feelings, are being constantly determined in those courts, in which there is great conflict in the evidence and great doubt as to the law which should govern their decision. It is this class of cases which impose upon the judge the severest labor, and often create in his mind a painful sense of responsibility.

Id., at 348.

The Indiana law vested in Judge Stump the power to entertain and act upon the petition for sterilization. He is, therefore, under the controlling cases, immune from damages liability even if his approval of the petition was in error. Accordingly, the judgment of the Court of Appeals is re-

---

12. Mr. Justice Stewart's dissent suggests that Judge Stump's approval of Mrs. McFarlin's petition was not a judicial act because of the absence of what it considers the "normal attributes of a judicial proceeding." These attributes are said to include a "case," with litigants and the opportunity to appeal, in which there is "principled decisionmaking." But under Indiana law, Judge Stump had jurisdiction to act as he did; the proceeding instituted by the petition placed before him was sufficiently a "case" under Indiana law to warrant the exercise of his jurisdiction, whether or not he then proceeded to act erroneously. That there were not two contending litigants did not make Judge Stump's act any less judicial. Courts and judges often act ex parte. They issue search warrants in this manner, for example, often without any "case" having been instituted, without any "case" ever being instituted, and without the issuance of the warrant being subject to appeal. Yet it would not destroy a judge's immunity if it is alleged and offer of proof is made that in issuing a warrant he acted erroneously and without principle.

versed, and the case is remanded for further proceedings consistent with this opinion.[13]

It is so ordered.

MR. JUSTICE BRENNAN took no part in the consideration or decision of this case.

MR. JUSTICE STEWART, with whom MR. JUSTICE MARSHALL and MR. JUSTICE POWELL join, dissenting.

It is established federal law that judges of general jurisdiction are absolutely immune from monetary liability "for their judicial acts, even when such acts are in excess of their jurisdiction, and are alleged to have been done maliciously or corruptly." Bradley v. Fisher, 13 Wall. 335, 351. It is also established that this immunity is in no way diminished in a proceeding under 42 U.S.C. §1983. Pierson v. Ray, 386 U.S. 547. But the scope of judicial immunity is limited to liability for "judicial acts," and I think that what Judge Stump did on July 9, 1971, was beyond the pale of anything that could sensibly be called a judicial act.

Neither in Bradley v. Fisher nor in Pierson v. Ray was there any claim that the conduct in question was not a judicial act, and the Court thus had no occasion in either case to discuss the meaning of that term.[1] Yet the proposition that judicial immunity extends only to liability for "judicial acts" was emphasized no less than seven times in Mr. Justice Field's opinion for the Court in the *Bradley* case. . . .

The Court finds two reasons for holding that Judge Stump's approval of the sterilization petition was a judicial act. First, the Court says, it was "a function normally performed by a judge." Second, the Court says, the act was performed in Judge Stump's "judicial capacity." With all respect, I think that the first of these grounds is factually untrue and that the second is legally unsound.

When the Court says that what Judge Stump did was an act "normally performed by a judge," it is not clear to me whether the Court means that a judge "normally" is asked to approve a mother's decision to have her child given surgical treatment generally, or that a judge "normally" is asked to approve a mother's wish to have her daughter sterilized. But whichever way the Court's statement is to be taken, it is factually inaccurate. In Indiana, as elsewhere in our country, a parent is authorized to arrange for and consent to medical and surgical treatment of his minor child. And when a parent decides to call a physician to care for his sick child or arranges to have a surgeon remove his child's tonsils, he does

---

13. The issue is not presented and we do not decide whether the District Court correctly concluded that the federal claims against the other defendants were required to be dismissed if Judge Stump, the only state agent, was found to be absolutely immune.

1. In the *Bradley* case the plaintiff was a lawyer who had been disbarred; in the *Pierson* case the plaintiffs had been found guilty after a criminal trial.

not, "normally" or otherwise, need to seek the approval of a judge.[3] On the other hand, Indiana did in 1971 have statutory procedures for the sterilization of certain people who were *institutionalized*. But these statutes provided for *administrative proceedings* before a board established by the superintendent of each public hospital. Only if, after notice and an evidentiary hearing, an order of sterilization was entered in these proceedings could there be review in a circuit court.[4]

In sum, what Judge Stump did on July 9, 1971, was in no way an act "normally performed by a judge." Indeed, there is no reason to believe that such an act has ever been performed by *any* other Indiana judge, either before or since.

When the Court says that Judge Stump was acting in "his judicial capacity" in approving Mrs. McFarlin's petition, it is not clear to me whether the Court means that Mrs. McFarlin submitted the petition to him only because he was a judge, or that, in approving it, he *said* that he was acting as a judge. But however the Court's test is to be understood, it is, I think, demonstrably unsound.

It can safely be assumed that the Court is correct in concluding that Mrs. McFarlin came to Judge Stump with her petition because he was a County Circuit Court Judge. But false illusions as to a judge's power can hardly convert a judge's response to those illusions into a judicial act. In short, a judge's approval of a mother's petition to lock her daughter in the attic would hardly be a judicial act simply because the mother had submitted her petition to the judge in his official capacity.

If, on the other hand, the Court's test depends upon the fact that Judge Stump *said* he was acting in his judicial capacity, it is equally invalid. It is true that Judge Stump affixed his signature to the approval of the petition as "Judge, DeKalb Circuit Court." But the conduct of a judge surely does not become a judicial act merely on his own say-so. A judge is not free, like a loose cannon, to inflict indiscriminate damage whenever he announces that he is acting in his judicial capacity.[5]

---

3. This general authority of a parent was held by an Indiana Court of Appeals in 1975 not to include the power to authorize the sterilization of his minor child. A. L. v. G. R. H., 163 Ind. App. 636, 325 N.E.2d 501.

Contrary to the Court's conclusion, that case does not in the least demonstrate that an Indiana judge is or ever was empowered to act on the merits of a petition like Mrs. McFarlin's. The parent in that case did not petition for judicial approval of her decision, but rather "filed a complaint for declaratory judgment seeking declaration of her right under the common-law attributes of the parent-child relationship to have her son . . . sterilized." 163 Ind. App., at 636-637, 325 N.E.2d, at 501. The Indiana Court of Appeals' decision simply established a limitation on the parent's common-law rights. It neither sanctioned nor contemplated any procedure for judicial "approval" of the parent's decision. . . .

4. These statutes were repealed in 1974.

5. Believing that the conduct of Judge Stump on July 9, 1971, was not a judicial act, I do not need to inquire whether he was acting in "the clear absence of all jurisdiction over the subject matter." Bradley v. Fisher, 13 Wall., at 351. "Jurisdiction" is a coat of many colors. I note only that the Court's finding that Judge Stump had jurisdiction to entertain Mrs. McFarlin's petition seems to me to be based upon dangerously broad criteria. Those

If the standard adopted by the Court is invalid, then what is the proper measure of a judicial act? Contrary to implications in the Court's opinion, my conclusion that what Judge Stump did was not a judicial act is not based upon the fact that he acted with informality, or that he may not have been "in his judge's robes," or "in the courtroom itself." And I do not reach this conclusion simply "because the petition was not given a docket number, was not placed on file with the clerk's office, and was approved in an ex parte proceeding without notice to the minor, without a hearing, and without the appointment of a guardian ad litem."

It seems to me, rather, that the concept of what is a judicial act must take its content from a consideration of the factors that support immunity from liability for the performance of such an act. Those factors were accurately summarized by the Court in Pierson v. Ray, 386 U.S., at 554:

> [I]t "is . . . for the benefit of the public, whose interest it is that the judges should be at liberty to exercise their functions with independence and without fear of consequences." . . . It is a judge's duty to decide all cases within his jurisdiction that are brought before him, including controversial cases that arouse the most intense feelings in the litigants. His errors may be corrected on appeal, but he should not have to fear that unsatisfied litigants may hound him with litigation charging malice or corruption. Imposing such a burden on judges would contribute not to principled and fearless decision-making but to intimidation.

Not one of the considerations thus summarized in the *Pierson* opinion was present here. There was no "case," controversial or otherwise. There were no litigants. There was and could be no appeal. And there was not even the pretext of principled decisionmaking. The total absence of *any* of these normal attributes of a judicial proceeding convinces me that the conduct complained of in this case was not a judicial act.

The petitioners' brief speaks of "an aura of deism which surrounds the bench . . . essential to the maintenance of respect for the judicial institution." Though the rhetoric may be overblown, I do not quarrel with it. But if aura there be, it is hardly protected by exonerating from liability such lawless conduct as took place here. And if intimidation would serve to deter its recurrence, that would surely be in the public interest.

Mr. Justice Powell, dissenting.

While I join the opinion of Mr. Justice Stewart, I wish to emphasize what I take to be the central feature of this case — Judge Stump's preclusion of any possibility for the vindication of respondents' rights elsewhere in the judicial system.

---

criteria are simply that an Indiana statute conferred "jurisdiction of all . . . causes, matters and proceedings," and that there was not in 1971 any Indiana law specifically prohibiting what Judge Stump did.

Bradley v. Fisher, 13 Wall. 335 (1872), which established the absolute judicial immunity at issue in this case, recognized that the immunity was designed to further the public interest in an independent judiciary, sometimes at the expense of legitimate individual grievances. The *Bradley* Court accepted those costs to aggrieved individuals because the judicial system itself provided other means for protecting individual rights:

> Against the consequences of [judges'] erroneous or irregular action, from whatever motives proceeding, the law has provided for private parties numerous remedies, and to those remedies they must, in such cases, resort.

13 Wall., at 354. Underlying the *Bradley* immunity, then, is the notion that private rights can be sacrificed in some degree to the achievement of the greater public good deriving from a completely independent judiciary, because there exist alternative forums and methods for vindicating those rights.

But where a judicial officer acts in a manner that precludes all resort to appellate or other judicial remedies that otherwise would be available, the underlying assumption of the *Bradley* doctrine is inoperative. In this case, as Mr. Justice Stewart points out, Judge Stump's unjudicial conduct insured that "[t]here was and could be no appeal." The complete absence of normal judicial process foreclosed resort to any of the "numerous remedies" that "the law has provided for private parties." *Bradley*, supra, at 354.

In sum, I agree with Mr. Justice Stewart that petitioner judge's actions were not "judicial," and that he is entitled to no judicial immunity from suit under 42 U.S.C. §1983.

NOTES ON JUDICIAL IMMUNITY

1. A suit against a public officer in his official capacity seeks to control defendant's exercise of his office. Those suits depend on the fiction of Ex parte Young to escape the bar of sovereign immunity.

Linda Sparkman sued Judge Stump in his personal capacity. There is nothing fictional about her suit. She does not seek damages from the state of Indiana, or the county of De Kalb. She seeks damages from Judge Stump's personal assets. Sovereign immunity does not bar such claims. Sovereign immunity protects only the sovereign, and not the sovereign's officers. But the common law developed various nonconstitutional immunities for officers, and the Supreme Court has read those immunities into statutes like §1983, which authorizes suits against officers.

2. Most government employees have only qualified immunity; we will examine the qualifications in the next principal case. But a few get absolute immunity. Why are judges so special? One answer is that they

would be sued more often if their immunity were qualified. Every case has at least one loser. Many losers will be angry; many will find it hard to believe that any honest judge could have ruled against them. It is easy to allege that the judge was biased, or took a corrupt and malicious dislike to the plaintiff or his lawyer, or took a bribe from the other side. It might be harder to get past a motion for summary judgment, but the plaintiff is entitled to discovery before the court rules on such a motion. The fear has been that the costs of such lawsuits would far outweigh the benefits. Even in cases where the facts are clear, judges might be afraid to extend the law if they could be sued for being wrong.

3. Justice Powell's point may be more important. There are means to correct the errors of judges short of suing them. Indeed, judicial immunity and the right of appeal arose at the same time. The writ of error, under which a higher court reviews the record for errors of law, replaced the writs of false judgment and attaint. The writ of false judgment was a suit against the judge; attaint was a similar procedure against jurors. In neither was the reviewing court limited to the record of the original proceeding, and either could end with an amercement, or money fine, against the judge or juror found to have given false judgment. The amount of amercements was discretionary and generally small. The development is reviewed in Block, *Stump v. Sparkman* and the History of Judicial Immunity, 1980 Duke L.J. 879, 881-885.

4. The traditional formulation of the rule was that a judge is absolutely immune for judicial acts within his jurisdiction. Apparently, the notion is the same one we encountered with respect to the collateral bar rule in Walker v. City of Birmingham, supra at 656. If a judge acts without jurisdiction, he's no longer a judge, but an usurper. But that formalism provides inadequate protection when judges err on debatable questions of jurisdiction. So the Court added that he must act in clear excess of jurisdiction. The example of a probate judge hearing a criminal case may really involve an usurper. But if the criminal defendant can appeal, is there any reason why the usurper should not be immune? What about time in prison pending appeal? Should the usurper be liable for that?

5. Earlier cases had not distinguished between personal jurisdiction and subject matter jurisdiction. Bradley v. Fisher, discussed in *Stump*, said the judge had to have both. Didn't Judge Stump clearly lack jurisdiction over the person of Linda Sparkman? Courts acquire personal jurisdiction by service of process. But she was not served; there was no reason she could not be served; the case did not arguably fall within any exception for ex parte proceedings. Sparkman's lawyer attacked those procedural errors in due process terms; he never argued that they deprived Stump's court of personal jurisdiction. Without even recognizing that it was making a change, the Supreme Court said Stump was immune if he had jurisdiction over the subject matter. That unexamined shift deter-

mined the result. Was it a justified shift? If the standard is clear lack of jurisdiction, isn't personal jurisdiction more relevant to the reasons for immunity than subject matter jurisdiction? Failure to serve Linda Sparkman was an essential step in keeping her ignorant of what was happening and thereby precluding any protest or appeal.

6. Why should jurisdiction be the standard at all? Doesn't Justice Powell have a better approach? My argument for a similar approach appears in Laycock, Civil Rights and Civil Liberties, 54 Chi.-Kent L. Rev. 390, 401-402 (1977).

7. Are there any limits to the immunity in *Stump*? Suppose Judge Stump had approved a petition to lock Linda in the attic, or cut off her hand. Did the majority leave itself a way to deny immunity in such cases? Wouldn't the "controversial" nature of such "tragic consequences" just increase the need for immunity?

8. Consider Zarcone v. Perry, 572 F.2d 52 (2d Cir. 1978), described more fully at 97-98 supra. A deputy sheriff brought Judge Perry a bad cup of coffee. On Perry's orders, the deputy handcuffed the coffee vendor and marched him through the courthouse in full view of dozens of people. Judge Perry then conducted a sort of hearing, in which he threatened the vendor with loss of his livelihood, preserved the coffee as "evidence" and said he would have it "analyzed," and offered to "drop the charges" if the vendor would admit he did something wrong.

The vendor sued the judge, and a jury awarded $140,000 in compensatory and punitive damages. So far as appears, the judge never argued immunity. Was his lawyer guilty of malpractice? How is *Zarcone* different from McAlester v. Brown, described in note 9 of *Stump*? Perhaps Judge Perry "violated . . . procedural requirements regarding contempt citations," but procedural error is irrelevant. Did he act in clear excess of all jurisdiction? Doesn't he have summary power to punish contempts? Didn't he think that the bad coffee disturbed his courtroom? It might matter that Judge Perry sat in traffic court and not in a court of general jurisdiction. But even traffic court judges have to keep order in the courtroom. Did *Stump* immunize Judge Perry? Will the judgment against Judge Perry chill judicial independence or deter any legitimate judicial act?

Would Judge Perry be immune under Justice Powell's test? It is inherent in summary contempt that punishment is imposed before defendant can appeal. Do we need an unstructured exception for conduct so outrageous that liability won't deter anything we are afraid of deterring? But wouldn't that put the courts on a very slippery slope? Lots of losing litigants think the decision was outrageous.

9. Civil liability is essential to compensation. It is not the only way to deter or punish outrageous judicial conduct. Judges are subject to disciplinary proceedings, impeachment, and criminal prosecution; most state judges are subject to periodic election or reappointment. It is generally

thought that these mechanisms are less likely to chill judicial independence, because an aggrieved litigant cannot invoke them at will. Sometimes they work; sometimes they don't. Judge Perry was removed from
office. Judge Stump was re-elected.

10. Judges can also be sued in their official capacity for injunctive
relief. Pulliam v. Allen, 104 S. Ct. 1970 (1984). Judge Allen required
criminal defendants to post bond even when they were charged with
offenses for which they could not be imprisoned. A federal court enjoined that practice. Without deciding whether the particular injunction
was proper, the Supreme Court held that Judge Allen was not immune.
An injunction against a judge was no different from the writs of mandamus and prohibition long issued against judges. The irreparable injury
rule and federal deference to the independence of state judiciaries would
keep such injunctions from becoming tools of harassment.

The four dissenters thought that mandamus and prohibition were
wholly irrelevant. Those writs were consistent with judicial immunity
because they could be used only to correct clear jurisdictional errors;
injunctions were not so limited. The dissenters thought the irreparable
injury rule was an illusory constraint, and that the threat of contempt
proceedings to enforce the injunction would be even more destructive of
judicial independence.

The biggest fight was over attorneys' fees. Plaintiff recovered $7,600
under the Civil Rights Attorney's Fees Award Act, 42 U.S.C. §1988
(1982). The dissenters thought a $7,600 award just as destructive of judi-
cial independence whether it was labelled damages or attorneys' fees. The
majority didn't disagree. But it said that immunity issues were for Congress when it chose to address them. The legislative history indicated that
fees should be awarded even when defendants were immune from damage awards, and that was dispositive. Under Hutto v. Finney, the federal
court could order the fees paid out of official funds. 437 U.S. 678, 693-700
(1978).

11. In *Stump*, the trial court dismissed the suits against the mother,
her lawyer, the doctors, and the hospital. He reasoned that they did not
act under color of law, as required by §1983, unless they conspired with
the judge. Of course, the judge could have joined a conspiracy even if he
were immune, so dismissal of the remaining claims did not follow from
judicial immunity. The Supreme Court so held in Dennis v. Sparks, 449
U.S. 24 (1980). "Immunity does not change the character of the judge's
action or that of his co-conspirators." Id. at 28. The Court also rejected
defendants' argument that they should share the judge's immunity, lest
he be dragged into litigation as a witness.

12. Plaintiffs in *Dennis* alleged that defendants bribed the judge. The
judge was removed from office and subsequently imprisoned for income
tax evasion. If the charges against a judge are proved in a criminal proceeding, should he still be immune from civil liability? Should he be

immune from orders to make compensation in the criminal case under a
victim restitution law?

NOTES ON OTHER ABSOLUTE
IMMUNITIES

1.   Judges are not the only defendants with absolute immunity. Prosecutors are absolutely immune from damage suits for prosecutorial acts.
Imbler v. Pachtman, 424 U.S. 409 (1976). The prosecutor in *Imbler* was
charged with presenting false evidence and concealing exculpatory evidence. Other prosecutors have been sued for malicious prosecution. The
Court offered somewhat inconsistent reasons for making the prosecutor's
immunity absolute: that like judges, he must make a discretionary judgment based on evidence presented to him, and that he must submit weak
cases to juries so they can pass on the evidence. More to the point, the
Court emphasized that the adversary system required uninhibited advocates for both sides. Might it also matter that convicted criminals are
notoriously chronic litigants, so that the risk of marginal and frivolous
claims is very high?

The lower courts have held that prosecutors have only qualified immu-
nity when they act as investigators or administrators, or in other capaci-
ties not directly related to litigation. The cases are collected in
Annotation, When Is Prosecutor Entitled to Absolute Immunity from
Civil Suit for Damages under 42 USCS §1983: Post-*Imbler* Cases, 67
A.L.R. Fed. 640 (1984). An example is Hampton v. Hanrahan, 600 F.2d
600 (7th Cir. 1979), *rev'd in part, on other grounds*, 446 U.S. 754 (1980).
The prosecutor directed a police raid in which the state leader of the
Black Panther party was killed. The Black Panthers were a radical civil
rights organization in the 1960s and 1970s. Plaintiffs alleged that the raid
was an assassination — that the police and prosecutor had planned to
kill. If they prove that allegation, is there any reason to give the prosecutor more immunity than the police? On the other hand, the line between
prosecutorial acts and other acts is not always so clear.

Prosecutors obviously are not immune from injunctive and declaratory suits against them in their official capacity. Prosecutors are nearly
always named as defendants in suits to declare laws unconstitutional.

2.   Legislators are absolutely immune from any kind of suit, including
criminal prosecutions and suits for damages, injunctions, and declaratory
judgments. The origin of this sweeping immunity is in the speech and
debate clauses of state and federal constitutions. The federal version says
that "for any Speech or Debate in either House, they [Senators and
Representatives] shall not be questioned in any other Place." U.S. Const.
art. I, §6. The federal clause does not protect state legislators, and state
clauses can't bind the federal courts. But the Supreme Court read a

similar immunity into §1983, concluding that Congress surely did not intend to disturb the immunities of state legislators. Tenney v. Brandhove, 341 U.S. 367 (1951). Brandhove sued the members of the California Senate Committee on Un-American Activities, alleging that it had used its investigative power to intimidate him and deter him from exercising his first amendment rights. He sought punitive damages and compensatory damages for the expenses of defending himself.

Why is this immunity so much more sweeping than judicial and prosecutorial immunity? The Court has said that any kind of suit would distract legislators from their duties, but the Court could have said the same thing about judges and prosecutors. Perhaps more probative is the Court's reliance on the literal language of the speech and debate clause: Legislators shall not even be "questioned" in any other place. Eastland v. United States Serviceman's Fund, 421 U.S. 491, 501-503 (1975). It may also matter that legislators inherently have the broadest discretion of any government officials, and are most directly accountable to the electorate. In addition, most legislative acts have to be implemented by judges and executives, and the constitutionality of legislation can be decided in suits to prevent its implementation.

The immunity extends to any act that is part of the legislature's deliberative process; it is not literally limited to speeches and debates. The leading case is United States v. Gravel, 408 U.S. 606 (1972). Senator Gravel convened a midnight meeting of the Subcommittee on Buildings and Grounds of the Senate Committee on Public Works, and read the Pentagon Papers into the record. The Pentagon Papers were a secret history of the war in Vietnam. Gravel's aides then arranged to have the Pentagon Papers published by Beacon Press. The Court rejected the government's argument that Gravel was not immune because the committee meeting was a pretense. Id. at 610 n.6, 616. But the Court held that arranging for private publication was not immune legislative business. Id. at 622-627. It noted its earlier holding that legislative lobbying of the executive branch on behalf of constituents was not immune legislative business. United States v. Johnson, 383 U.S. 169 (1966). The Court also held that Gravel's immunity extended to his aides. Id. at 616-622.

Legislative immunity does not preclude remedies against legislators who take bribes. United States v. Brewster, 408 U.S. 501 (1972). The speech and debate clause precludes proof that defendant took any legislative steps on behalf of those who paid the bribe, but proof of such steps is not necessary to conviction. The offense is complete when the legislator takes the bribe, whether or not he delivers what he promised.

Brewster opens the way to a wide range of remedies. Consider In re Leasing Consultants, 592 F.2d 103 (2d Cir. 1979). Leasing bribed a congressman and then went bankrupt. The United States asserted a constructive trust over the bribe money. Leasing's trustee in bankruptcy also sought restitution of the bribe money. The congressman did not bring either case to the attention of the other judge until after both judges had ordered restitution. The court of appeals faced the double restitution issue in the bankruptcy case, and held the congressman bound by his own procedural default. In addition to returning the same money twice, the congressman was convicted of a criminal offense, fined $5,000, sentenced to six months in prison, and forever barred from "any office of honor, trust, or profit under the United States." That combination of remedies is for people who are serious about stamping out wrongdoing.

3.   Absolute immunity for judges, prosecutors, and legislators has not depended on the office held, but on the function performed. Acts are not immune if they are not judicial, not prosecutorial, or not part of the legislative process. Similarly, an official who performs a judicial, prosecutorial, or legislative function acquires absolute immunity even if he does not hold a corresponding title. Thus, in Supreme Court v. Consumers Union, 446 U.S. 719 (1980), the Court held that the Virginia Supreme Court acted legislatively when it promulgated disciplinary rules for the state's lawyers, and that it acted as a prosecutor when it initiated proceedings to enforce those rules. It was entitled to legislative and prosecutorial immunity, respectively, but not to judicial immunity. Similarly, in Butz v. Economou, 438 U.S. 478 (1978), the Court analyzed the functions of federal agency officials. Hearing officers get judicial immunity for adjudicative functions, even though they are in the executive branch. Agency attorneys who prosecute violations in front of such hearing officers get prosecutorial immunity, even though they are not employed in the Department of Justice.

4.   One other official is absolutely immune from damage suits: the President of the United States. Nixon v. Fitzgerald, 457 U.S. 731 (1982). The next principal case is a companion case to *Nixon*; we will consider the President's immunity along with the immunity of other executive officers.

HARLOW v. FITZGERALD
457 U.S. 800 (1982)

JUSTICE POWELL delivered the opinion of the Court.

The issue in this case is the scope of the immunity available to the senior aides and advisers of the President of the United States in a suit for damages based upon their official acts.

I

In this suit for civil damages petitioners Bryce Harlow and Alexander Butterfield are alleged to have participated in a conspiracy to violate the constitutional and statutory rights of the respondent A. Ernest Fitzgerald. Respondent avers that petitioners entered the conspiracy in their capacities as senior White House aides to former President Richard M. Nixon. As the alleged conspiracy is the same as that involved in Nixon v. Fitzgerald, the facts need not be repeated in detail.

[Fitzgerald was a management analyst in the Department of the Air Force. In 1968, he testified to a congressional committee about technical problems and huge cost overruns on the C-5A cargo plane. The revelations were embarrassing to the Defense Department. Harold Brown, the outgoing Secretary of the Air Force, received a staff memo outlining three ways in which he might get rid of Fitzgerald despite his civil service protection. One of the methods was a reduction in force.

Nearly a year later, the Nixon administration carried out the reduction in force, eliminating Fitzgerald's job. A congressional committee held hearings to determine whether the administration had retaliated against Fitzgerald for revealing cost overruns, and a reporter at a press conference asked President Nixon about the charges. Nixon promised to look into it, and there ensued a debate about Fitzgerald among Nixon and the White House staff. Some urged that the administration find another job for Fitzgerald; others objected that he was not "loyal." Fitzgerald was not offered another job.

The Chief Examiner for the Civil Service Commission concluded, after four thousand pages of testimony, that the reduction in force was motivated by "reasons purely personal to" Fitzgerald, but that there was not sufficient evidence to conclude that these reasons included his congressional testimony. Following the Civil Service decision, Fitzgerald filed this suit for damages against Nixon and several high-ranking White House aides.]

Respondent claims that Harlow joined the conspiracy in his role as the Presidential aide principally responsible for congressional relations. At the conclusion of discovery the supporting evidence remained inferential. As evidence of Harlow's conspiratorial activity respondent relies heavily on a series of conversations in which Harlow discussed Fitzgerald's dismissal with Air Force Secretary Robert Seamans. The other evidence most supportive of Fitzgerald's claims consists of a recorded conversation in which the President later voiced a tentative recollection that Harlow was "all for canning" Fitzgerald.

Disputing Fitzgerald's contentions, Harlow argues that exhaustive discovery has adduced no direct evidence of his involvement in any wrongful activity. He avers that Secretary Seamans advised him that considerations of efficiency required Fitzgerald's removal by a reduction in force, despite anticipated adverse congressional reaction. Harlow asserts he had no reason to believe that a conspiracy existed. He contends that he took all his actions in good faith.

Petitioner Butterfield also is alleged to have entered the conspiracy not later than May 1969. Employed as Deputy Assistant to the President and Deputy Chief of Staff to H. R. Haldeman, Butterfield circulated a White House memorandum in that month in which he claimed to have learned that Fitzgerald planned to "blow the whistle" on some "shoddy purchasing practices" by exposing these practices to public view. Fitzgerald characterizes this memorandum as evidence that Butterfield had commenced efforts to secure Fitzgerald's retaliatory dismissal. As evidence that Butterfield participated in the conspiracy to conceal his unlawful discharge and prevent his reemployment, Fitzgerald cites communications between Butterfield and Haldeman in December 1969 and January 1970. After the President had promised at a press conference to inquire into Fitzgerald's dismissal, Haldeman solicited Butterfield's recommendations. In a subsequent memorandum emphasizing the importance of "loyalty," Butterfield counseled against offering Fitzgerald another job in the administration at that time.

For his part, Butterfield denies that he was involved in any decision concerning Fitzgerald's employment status until Haldeman sought his advice in December 1969 — more than a month after Fitzgerald's termination had been scheduled and announced publicly by the Air Force. Butterfield states that he never communicated his views about Fitzgerald to any official of the Defense Department. He argues generally that nearly eight years of discovery have failed to turn up any evidence that he caused injury to Fitzgerald.

Together with their codefendant Richard Nixon, petitioners Harlow and Butterfield moved for summary judgment on February 12, 1980. In denying the motion the District Court upheld the legal sufficiency of Fitzgerald's *Bivens* (Bivens v. Six Unknown Fed. Narcotics Agents, 403 U.S. 388 (1971)) claim under the First Amendment and his "inferred" statutory causes of action under 5 U.S.C. §7211 (1976 ed., Supp. IV) and 18 U.S.C. §1505.[10] The court found that genuine issues of disputed fact remained for resolution at trial. It also ruled that petitioners were not entitled to absolute immunity.

Independently of former President Nixon, petitioners invoked the collateral order doctrine and appealed the denial of their immunity defense

10. The first of these statutes, 5 U.S.C. §7211 (1976 ed., Supp. IV), provides generally that "[t]he right of employees . . . to . . . furnish information to either House of Congress, or to a committee or Member thereof, may not be interfered with or denied." The second, 18 U.S.C. §1505, is a criminal statute making it a crime to obstruct congressional testimony. Neither expressly creates a private right to sue for damages. Petitioners argue that the District Court erred in finding that a private cause of action could be inferred under either statute, and that "special factors" present in the context of the federal employer-employee relationship preclude the recognition of respondent's *Bivens* action under the First Amendment. The legal sufficiency of respondent's asserted causes of action is not, however, a question that we view as properly presented for our decision in the present posture of this case.

to the Court of Appeals for the District of Columbia Circuit. The Court of Appeals dismissed the appeal without opinion. . . .

II

As we reiterated today in Nixon v. Fitzgerald, our decisions consistently have held that Government officials are entitled to some form of immunity from suits for damages. As recognized at common law, public officers require this protection to shield them from undue interference with their duties and from potentially disabling threats of liability.

Our decisions have recognized immunity defenses of two kinds. For officials whose special functions or constitutional status requires complete protection from suit, we have recognized the defense of "absolute immunity." The absolute immunity of legislators, in their legislative functions, see, e.g., Eastland v. United States Servicemen's Fund, 421 U.S. 491 (1975), and of judges, in their judicial functions, see, e.g., Stump v. Sparkman, 435 U.S. 349 (1978), now is well settled. Our decisions also have extended absolute immunity to certain officials of the Executive Branch. These include prosecutors and similar officials, see Butz v. Economou, 438 U.S. 478, 508-512 (1978), executive officers engaged in adjudicative functions, id., at 513-517, and the President of the United States, see Nixon v. Fitzgerald.

For executive officials in general, however, our cases make plain that qualified immunity represents the norm. In Scheuer v. Rhodes, 416 U.S. 232 (1974), we acknowledged that high officials require greater protection than those with less complex discretionary responsibilities. Nonetheless, we held that a governor and his aides could receive the requisite protection from qualified or good-faith immunity. In Butz v. Economou, we extended the approach of *Scheuer* to high federal officials of the Executive Branch. Discussing in detail the considerations that also had underlain our decision in *Scheuer*, we explained that the recognition of a qualified immunity defense for high executives reflected an attempt to balance competing values: not only the importance of a damages remedy to protect the rights of citizens, 438 U.S., at 504-505, but also "the need to protect officials who are required to exercise their discretion and the related public interest in encouraging the vigorous exercise of official authority." Id., at 506. Without discounting the adverse consequences of denying high officials an absolute immunity from private lawsuits alleging constitutional violations — consequences found sufficient in Spalding v. Vilas, 161 U.S. 483 (1896), and Barr v. Matteo, 360 U.S. 564 (1959), to warrant extension to such officials of absolute immunity from suits at common law — we emphasized our expectation that insubstantial suits need not proceed to trial:

> Insubstantial lawsuits can be quickly terminated by federal courts alert to the possibilities of artful pleading. Unless the complaint states a compensable

claim for relief . . . , it should not survive a motion to dismiss. Moreover, the Court recognized in *Scheuer* that damages suits concerning constitutional violations need not proceed to trial, but can be terminated on a properly supported motion for summary judgment based on the defense of immunity. . . . In responding to such a motion, plaintiffs may not play dog in the manger; and firm application of the Federal Rules of Civil Procedure will ensure that federal officials are not harassed by frivolous lawsuits.

438 U.S., at 507-508 (citations omitted).

Butz continued to acknowledge that the special functions of some officials might require absolute immunity. But the Court held that "federal officials who seek absolute exemption from personal liability for unconstitutional conduct must bear the burden of showing that public policy requires an exemption of that scope." Id., at 506. This we reaffirmed today in Nixon v. Fitzgerald.

III

A

Petitioners argue that they are entitled to a blanket protection of absolute immunity as an incident of their offices as Presidential aides. In deciding this claim we do not write on an empty page. In Butz v. Economou, the Secretary of Agriculture — a Cabinet official directly accountable to the President — asserted a defense of absolute official immunity from suit for civil damages. We rejected his claim. In so doing we did not question the power or the importance of the Secretary's office. Nor did we doubt the importance to the President of loyal and efficient subordinates in executing his duties of office. Yet we found these factors, alone, to be insufficient to justify absolute immunity. "[T]he greater power of [high] officials," we reasoned, "affords a greater potential for a regime of lawless conduct." 438 U.S., at 506. Damages actions against high officials were therefore "an important means of vindicating constitutional guarantees." Ibid. Moreover, we concluded that it would be "untenable to draw a distinction for purposes of immunity law between suits brought against state officials under [42 U.S.C.] §1983 and suits brought directly under the Constitution against federal officials." Id., at 504.

Having decided in *Butz* that Members of the Cabinet ordinarily enjoy only qualified immunity from suit, we conclude today that it would be equally untenable to hold absolute immunity an incident of the office of every Presidential subordinate based in the White House. Members of the Cabinet are direct subordinates of the President, frequently with greater responsibilities, both to the President and to the Nation, than White House staff. The considerations that supported our decision in *Butz* apply with equal force to this case. It is no disparagement of the offices held by petitioners to hold that Presidential aides, like Members of the Cabinet, generally are entitled only to a qualified immunity.

B

In disputing the controlling authority of *Butz*, petitioners rely on the principles developed in Gravel v. United States, 408 U.S. 606 (1972). In *Gravel* we endorsed the view that "it is literally impossible . . . for Members of Congress to perform their legislative tasks without the help of aides and assistants" and that "the day-to-day work of such aides is so critical to the Members' performance that they must be treated as the latter's alter egos. . . . " Id., at 616-617. Having done so, we held the Speech and Debate Clause derivatively applicable to the "legislative acts" of a Senator's aide that would have been privileged if performed by the Senator himself. Id., at 621-622.

Petitioners contend that the rationale of *Gravel* mandates a similar "derivative" immunity for the chief aides of the President of the United States. Emphasizing that the President must delegate a large measure of authority to execute the duties of his office, they argue that recognition of derivative absolute immunity is made essential by all the considerations that support absolute immunity for the President himself.

Petitioners' argument is not without force. Ultimately, however, it sweeps too far. If the President's aides are derivatively immune because they are essential to the functioning of the Presidency, so should the Members of the Cabinet — Presidential subordinates some of whose essential roles are acknowledged by the Constitution itself — be absolutely immune. Yet we implicitly rejected such derivative immunity in *Butz*.[14] Moreover, in general our cases have followed a "functional" approach to immunity law. We have recognized that the judicial, prosecutorial, and legislative functions require absolute immunity. But this protection has extended no further than its justification would warrant. In *Gravel*, for example, we emphasized that Senators and their aides were absolutely immune only when performing "acts legislative in nature," and not when taking other acts even "in their official capacity." 408 U.S., at 625. Our cases involving judges and prosecutors have followed a similar line. The undifferentiated extension of absolute "derivative" immunity to the President's aides therefore could not be reconciled with the "functional" ap-

14. The Chief Justice argues that senior Presidential aides work "more intimately with the President on a daily basis than does a Cabinet officer," and that *Butz* therefore is not controlling. In recent years, however, such men as Henry Kissinger and James Schlesinger have served in both Presidential advisory and Cabinet positions. Kissinger held both posts simultaneously. In our view it is impossible to generalize about the role of "offices" in an individual President's administration without reference to the functions that particular officeholders are assigned by the President. Butz v. Economou cannot be distinguished on this basis.

proach that has characterized the immunity decisions of this Court, indeed including *Gravel* itself.[17]

C

Petitioners also assert an entitlement to immunity based on the "special functions" of White House aides. This form of argument accords with the analytical approach of our cases. For aides entrusted with discretionary authority in such sensitive areas as national security or foreign policy, absolute immunity might well be justified to protect the unhesitating performance of functions vital to the national interest. But a "special functions" rationale does not warrant a blanket recognition of absolute immunity for all Presidential aides in the performance of all their duties. This conclusion too follows from our decision in *Butz*, which establishes that an executive official's claim to absolute immunity must be justified by reference to the public interest in the special functions of his office, not the mere fact of high station.

Butz also identifies the location of the burden of proof. The burden of justifying absolute immunity rests on the official asserting the claim. 438 U.S., at 506. We have not of course had occasion to identify how a Presidential aide might carry this burden. But the general requisites are familiar in our cases. In order to establish entitlement to absolute immunity a Presidential aide first must show that the responsibilities of his office embraced a function so sensitive as to require a total shield from liability. He then must demonstrate that he was discharging the protected function when performing the act for which liability is asserted.

Applying these standards to the claims advanced by petitioners Harlow and Butterfield, we cannot conclude on the record before us that either has shown that "public policy requires [for any of the functions of his office] an exemption of [absolute] scope." *Butz*, 438 U.S., at 506. Nor, assuming that petitioners did have functions for which absolute immunity would be warranted, could we now conclude that the acts charged in this lawsuit — if taken at all — would lie within the protected area. We do not, however, foreclose the possibility that petitioners, on remand, could satisfy the standards properly applicable to their claims.

IV

Even if they cannot establish that their official functions require absolute immunity, petitioners assert that public policy at least mandates an appli-

---

17. Our decision today in Nixon v. Fitzgerald, ante, p.731, in no way abrogates this general rule. As we explained in that opinion, the recognition of absolute immunity for all of a President's acts in office derives in principal part from factors unique to his constitutional responsibilities and station. Suits against other officials — including Presidential aides — generally do not invoke separation-of-powers considerations to the same extent as suits against the President himself.

cation of the qualified immunity standard that would permit the defeat of insubstantial claims without resort to trial. We agree.

A

The resolution of immunity questions inherently requires a balance between the evils inevitable in any available alternative. In situations of abuse of office, an action for damages may offer the only realistic avenue for vindication of constitutional guarantees. See Bivens v. Six Unknown Fed. Narcotics Agents, 403 U.S., at 410 ("For people in Bivens' shoes, it is damages or nothing"). It is this recognition that has required the denial of absolute immunity to most public officers. At the same time, however, it cannot be disputed seriously that claims frequently run against the innocent as well as the guilty — at a cost not only to the defendant officials, but to the society as a whole. These social costs include the expenses of litigation, the diversion of official energy from pressing public issues, and the deterrence of able citizens from acceptance of public office. Finally, there is the danger that fear of being sued will "dampen the ardor of all but the most resolute, or the most irresponsible [public officials], in the unflinching discharge of their duties." Gregoire v. Biddle, 177 F.2d 579, 581 (C.A.2 1949), cert. denied, 339 U.S. 949 (1950).

In identifying qualified immunity as the best attainable accommodation of competing values, in Butz, at 507-508, as in Scheuer, 416 U.S., at 245-248, we relied on the assumption that this standard would permit "[i]nsubstantial lawsuits [to] be quickly terminated." 438 U.S., at 507-508. Yet petitioners advance persuasive arguments that the dismissal of insubstantial lawsuits without trial — a factor presupposed in the balance of competing interests struck by our prior cases — requires an adjustment of the "good faith" standard established by our decisions.

B

Qualified or "good faith" immunity is an affirmative defense that must be pleaded by a defendant official. Gomez v. Toledo, 446 U.S. 635 (1980). Decisions of this Court have established that the "good faith" defense has both an "objective" and a "subjective" aspect. The objective element involves a presumptive knowledge of and respect for "basic, unquestioned constitutional rights." Wood v. Strickland, 420 U.S. 308, 322 (1975). The subjective component refers to "permissible intentions." Ibid. Characteristically the Court has defined these elements by identifying the circumstances in which qualified immunity would not be available. Referring both to the objective and subjective elements, we have held that qualified immunity would be defeated if an official "knew or reasonably should have known that the action he took within his sphere of official responsibility would violate the constitutional rights of the [plaintiff], or if he took the action *with the malicious intention* to cause a deprivation of constitutional rights or other injury. . . ." Ibid. (emphasis added).

The subjective element of the good-faith defense frequently has proved incompatible with our admonition in *Butz* that insubstantial claims should not proceed to trial. Rule 56 of the Federal Rules of Civil Procedure provides that disputed questions of fact ordinarily may not be decided on motions for summary judgment. And an official's subjective good faith has been considered to be a question of fact that some courts have regarded as inherently requiring resolution by a jury.

In the context of *Butz*'s attempted balancing of competing values, it now is clear that substantial costs attend the litigation of the subjective good faith of government officials. Not only are there the general costs of subjecting officials to the risks of trial — distraction of officials from their governmental duties, inhibition of discretionary action, and deterrence of able people from public service. There are special costs to "subjective" inquiries of this kind. Immunity generally is available only to officials performing discretionary functions. In contrast with the thought processes accompanying "ministerial" tasks, the judgments surrounding discretionary action almost inevitably are influenced by the decisionmaker's experiences, values, and emotions. These variables explain in part why questions of subjective intent so rarely can be decided by summary judgment. Yet they also frame a background in which there often is no clear end to the relevant evidence. Judicial inquiry into subjective motivation therefore may entail broad-ranging discovery and the deposing of numerous persons, including an official's professional colleagues. Inquiries of this kind can be peculiarly disruptive of effective government.[29]

Consistently with the balance at which we aimed in *Butz*, we conclude today that bare allegations of malice should not suffice to subject government officials either to the costs of trial or to the burden of broad-reaching discovery. We therefore hold that government officials performing discretionary functions generally are shielded from liability for civil damages insofar as their conduct does not violate clearly established statutory or constitutional rights of which a reasonable person would have known.

Reliance on the objective reasonableness of an official's conduct, as measured by reference to clearly established law, should avoid excessive disruption of government and permit the resolution of many insubstantial claims on summary judgment. On summary judgment, the judge

---

29. As Judge Gesell observed in his concurring opinion in Halperin v. Kissinger, 196 U.S. App. D.C. 285, 307, 606 F.2d 1192, 1214 (1979), *aff'd in pertinent part by an equally divided Court*, 452 U.S. 713 (1981):

> . . . A sentence from a casual document or a difference in recollection with regard to a particular policy conversation held long ago would usually, under the normal summary judgment standards, be sufficient [to force a trial]. . . . The effect of this development upon the willingness of individuals to serve their country is obvious.

appropriately may determine, not only the currently applicable law, but whether that law was clearly established at the time an action occurred.[32] If the law at that time was not clearly established, an official could not reasonably be expected to anticipate subsequent legal developments, nor could he fairly be said to "know" that the law forbade conduct not previously identified as unlawful. Until this threshold immunity question is resolved, discovery should not be allowed. If the law was clearly established, the immunity defense ordinarily should fail, since a reasonably competent public official should know the law governing his conduct. Nevertheless, if the official pleading the defense claims extraordinary circumstances and can prove that he neither knew nor should have known of the relevant legal standard, the defense should be sustained. But again, the defense would turn primarily on objective factors.

By defining the limits of qualified immunity essentially in objective terms, we provide no license to lawless conduct. The public interest in deterrence of unlawful conduct and in compensation of victims remains protected by a test that focuses on the objective legal reasonableness of an official's acts. Where an official could be expected to know that certain conduct would violate statutory or constitutional rights, he should be made to hesitate; and a person who suffers injury caused by such conduct may have a cause of action. But where an official's duties legitimately require action in which clearly established rights are not implicated, the public interest may be better served by action taken "with independence and without fear of consequences." Pierson v. Ray, 386 U.S. 547, 554 (1967).[34] . . .

V

The judgment of the Court of Appeals is vacated, and the case is remanded for further action consistent with this opinion.

So ordered.

JUSTICE BRENNAN, with whom JUSTICE MARSHALL and JUSTICE BLACKMUN join, concurring.

I agree with the substantive standard announced by the Court today, imposing liability when a public-official defendant "knew or should have known" of the constitutionally violative effect of his actions. This standard would not allow the official who *actually knows* that he was violating

---

32. As in Procunier v. Navarette, 434 U.S., at 565, we need not define here the circumstances under which "the state of the law" should be "evaluated by reference to the opinions of this Court, of the Courts of Appeals, or of the local District Court."

34. We emphasize that our decision applies only to suits for civil *damages* arising from actions within the scope of an official's duties and in "objective" good faith. We express no view as to the conditions in which injunctive or declaratory relief might be available.

the law to escape liability for his actions, even if he could not "reasonably have been expected" to know what he actually did know. Thus the clever and unusually well-informed violator of constitutional rights will not evade just punishment for his crimes. I also agree that this standard applies "across the board," to all "government officials performing discretionary functions." I write separately only to note that given this standard, it seems inescapable to me that some measure of discovery may sometimes be required to determine exactly what a public-official defendant did "know" at the time of his actions. . . . Of course, as the Court has already noted, summary judgment will be readily available to public-official defendants whenever the state of the law was so ambiguous at the time of the alleged violation that it could not have been "known" then, and thus liability could not ensue. In my view, summary judgment will also be readily available whenever the plaintiff cannot prove, as a threshold matter, that a violation of his constitutional rights actually occurred. I see no reason why discovery of defendants' "knowledge" should not be deferred by the trial judge pending decision of any motion of defendants for summary judgment on grounds such as these.

JUSTICE BRENNAN, JUSTICE WHITE, JUSTICE MARSHALL and JUSTICE BLACKMUN, concurring.

We join the Court's opinion but, having dissented in Nixon v. Fitzgerald, we disassociate ourselves from any implication in the Court's opinion in the present case that Nixon v. Fitzgerald was correctly decided.

JUSTICE REHNQUIST, concurring.

At such time as a majority of the Court is willing to re-examine our holding in Butz v. Economou, 438 U.S. 478 (1978), I shall join in that undertaking with alacrity. But until that time comes, I agree that the Court's opinion in this case properly disposes of the issues presented, and I therefore join it.

CHIEF JUSTICE BURGER, dissenting.

The Court today decides in Nixon v. Fitzgerald what has been taken for granted for 190 years, that it is implicit in the Constitution that a President of the United States has absolute immunity from civil suits arising out of official acts as Chief Executive. I agree fully that absolute immunity for official acts of the President is, like executive privilege, "fundamental to the operation of Government and inextricably rooted in the separation of powers under the Constitution." United States v. Nixon, 418 U.S. 683, 708 (1974).

In this case the Court decides that senior aides of the President do not have derivative immunity from the President. I am at a loss, however, to reconcile this conclusion with our holding in Gravel v. United States, 408 U.S. 606 (1972). The Court reads Butz v. Economou, 438 U.S. 478 (1978), as resolving that question; I do not. *Butz* is clearly distinguishable. . . .

We very properly recognized in *Gravel* that the central purpose of a Member's absolute immunity would be "diminished and frustrated" if the legislative aides were not also protected by the same broad immunity. . . . How can we conceivably hold that a President of the United States, who represents a vastly larger constituency than does any Member of Congress, should not have "alter egos" with comparable immunity? To perform the constitutional duties assigned to the Executive would be "literally impossible, in view of the complexities of the modern [Executive] process, . . . without the help of aides and assistants." *Gravel*, at 616. These words reflect the precise analysis of *Gravel*, and this analysis applies with at least as much force to a President. The primary layer of senior aides of a President — like a Senator's "alter egos" — are literally at a President's elbow, with offices a few feet or at most a few hundred feet from his own desk. The President, like a Member of Congress, may see those personal aides many times in one day. They are indeed the President's "arms" and "fingers" to aid in performing his constitutional duty to see "that the laws [are] faithfully executed." Like a Member of Congress, but on a vastly greater scale, the President cannot personally implement a fraction of his own policies and day-to-day decisions.

For some inexplicable reason the Court declines to recognize the realities in the workings of the Office of a President, despite the Court's cogent recognition in *Gravel* concerning the realities of the workings of 20th-century Members of Congress. Absent equal protection for a President's aides, how will Presidents be free from the risks of "intimidation . . . by [Congress] and accountability before a possibly hostile judiciary?" *Gravel*, 408 U.S., at 617. Under today's holding in this case the functioning of the Presidency will inevitably be "diminished and frustrated." Ibid.

Precisely the same public policy considerations on which the Court now relies in Nixon v. Fitzgerald, and that we relied on only recently in *Gravel*, are fully applicable to senior Presidential aides. The Court's opinion in Nixon v. Fitzgerald correctly points out that if a President were subject to suit, awareness of personal vulnerability to suit "frequently could distract a President from his public duties, to the detriment not only of the President and his office but also the Nation that the Presidency was designed to serve." Ante, at 753. This same negative incentive will permeate the inner workings of the Office of the President if the Chief Executive's "alter egos" are not protected derivatively from the immunity of the President. In addition, exposure to civil liability for official acts will result in constant judicial questioning, through judicial proceedings and pretrial discovery, into the inner workings of the Presidential Office beyond that necessary to maintain the traditional checks and balances of our constitutional structure.[6]

I challenge the Court and the dissenters in Nixon v. Fitzgerald who join in the instant holding to say that the effectiveness of Presidential aides will not "inevitably be diminished and frustrated," *Gravel*, at 617, if they must weigh every act and decision in relation to the risks of future lawsuits. The *Gravel* Court took note of the burdens on congressional aides: the stress of long hours, heavy responsibilities, constant exposure to harassment of the political arena. Is the Court suggesting the stresses are less for Presidential aides? By construing the Constitution to give only qualified immunity to senior Presidential aides we give those key "alter egos" only lawsuits, winnable lawsuits perhaps, but lawsuits nonetheless, with stress and effort that will disperse and drain their energies and their purses.[7] . . .

When we see the myriad irresponsible and frivolous cases regularly filed in American courts, the magnitude of the potential risks attending acceptance of public office emerges. Those potential risks inevitably will be a factor in discouraging able men and women from entering public service. . . .

Butz v. Economou, 438 U.S. 478 (1978), does not dictate that senior Presidential aides be given only qualified immunity. *Butz* held only that a Cabinet officer exercising discretion was not entitled to absolute immunity; we need not abandon that holding. A senior Presidential aide works more intimately with the President on a daily basis than does a Cabinet officer, directly implementing Presidential decisions literally from hour to hour. . . .

The Court's analysis in *Gravel* demonstrates that the question of derivative immunity does not and should not depend on a person's rank or position in the hierarchy, but on the *function* performed by the person and the relationship of that person to the superior. Cabinet officers clearly outrank United States Attorneys, yet qualified immunity is accorded the former and absolute immunity the latter; rank is important only to the extent that the rank determines the function to be performed.

---

6. The same remedies for checks on Presidential abuse also will check abuses by the comparatively small group of senior aides that act as "alter egos" of the President. The aides serve at the pleasure of the President and thus may be removed by the President. Congressional and public scrutiny maintain a constant and pervasive check on abuses, and such aides may be prosecuted criminally. *See Nixon*, at 757. However, a criminal prosecution cannot be commenced absent careful consideration by a grand jury at the request of a prosecutor; the same check is not present with respect to the commencement of civil suits in which advocates are subject to no realistic accountability.

7. The Executive Branch may as a matter of grace supply some legal assistance. The Department of Justice has a longstanding policy of representing federal officers in civil suits involving conduct performed within the scope of their employment. In addition, the Department provides for retention of private legal counsel when necessary. The Congress frequently pays the expenses of defending its Members even as to acts wholly outside the legislative function.

The function of senior Presidential aides, as the "alter egos" of the President, is an integral, inseparable part of the function of the President.[8] . . .

By ignoring *Gravel* and engaging in a wooden application of *Butz*, the Court significantly undermines the functioning of the Office of the President. Under the Court's opinion in *Nixon* today it is clear that Presidential immunity derives from the Constitution as much as congressional immunity comes from that source. Can there rationally be one rule for congressional aides and another for Presidential aides simply because the initial absolute immunity of each derives from different aspects of the Constitution? I find it inexplicable why the Court makes no effort to demonstrate why the Chief Executive of the Nation should not be assured that senior staff aides will have the same protection as the aides of Members of the House and Senate.

NOTES ON QUALIFIED IMMUNITIES

1. Fitzgerald's claim would now be barred by Bush v. Lucas, 462 U.S. 367 (1983), discussed in the notes to *Bivens*, supra at 1081. *Bush* held that the statutory remedy before the Civil Service Commission is exclusive and precludes a *Bivens* remedy.

2. *Harlow* is the authoritative statement of the scope of qualified immunity, not only for presidential aides, but for most executive branch officials of both state and federal governments. It substantially modifies prior law. Will the modification succeed in ending suits without inquiry into motive? What about cases where motive is the essence of the alleged violation?

Consider the claim in *Harlow* itself. It is clearly settled that public employees cannot be fired for criticizing public policy. Pickering v. Board of Education, 391 U.S. 563 (1968). Doesn't that mean that Harlow and Butterfield are not immune under the Court's standard? The hard issue in the case is whether Fitzgerald was fired for criticizing the C-5A or as part of a legitimate reduction in force. How does the Court's standard help cut off discovery on that issue? How does it keep weak claims from going to trial if there is a little bit of evidence to support them?

Bush v. Lucas cuts off such claims for federal civil service employees, but state employees will still bring such claims. Many such employees have no civil service remedy, and even if they do, they can file suit under §1983 without exhausting state remedies. Patsy v. Board of Regents, 457 U.S. 496 (1982).

---

8. This Court had no trouble reconciling *Gravel* with Kilbourn v. Thompson, 103 U.S. 168 (1881). In *Kilbourn* the Sergeant-at-Arms of the House of Representatives was held not to share the absolute immunity enjoyed by the Members of Congress who ordered that officer to act.

Motive is also the key to all equal protection claims, Washington v. Davis, 426 U.S. 229 (1976), and to many free exercise and establishment clause claims. Unless the Court makes officials absolutely immune to all such claims, it cannot cut off inquiry into motive. It might conceivably raise the evidentiary threshold required to survive a motion for summary judgment, but to do that honestly would require amending the Federal Rules of Civil Procedure.

3.   The change of standard in *Harlow* does provide additional protection to public officials in cases where the law is not clearly settled. An example is Wood v. Strickland, 420 U.S. 308 (1975), the previous leading case. Defendants were members of the school board in Mena, Arkansas. Plaintiffs were high school sophomores who spiked the punch at an extracurricular meeting of the Home Economics class. The school board suspended plaintiffs from school for three months. The board made the decision at a meeting that was closed to plaintiffs and their parents, and the reason for suspending all the plaintiffs seemed to be that one of them had gotten in a fight in an unrelated incident. Plaintiffs alleged that the suspensions had been imposed without due process.

The incident occurred in 1972. The Supreme Court first imposed due process requirements on school suspensions in Goss v. Lopez, 419 U.S. 565 (1975). There were some lower court cases, but defendants could plausibly argue that the law was not clearly settled in 1972. If the law were not clearly settled, they would be immune under *Harlow* no matter what their motive. But under Wood v. Strickland, they were liable if they acted with bad motive and in a way that turned out to be illegal, even if the law were unsettled when they acted. The Court said "the official himself must be acting sincerely and with a belief that he is doing right." 420 U.S. at 321. *Harlow* will presumably eliminate those cases before trial.

Justice Powell dissented in Wood v. Strickland. Ironically, he objected to the "clearly settled law" prong of the *Wood* standard. He thought it was a new requirement that defendants would have to meet to establish immunity, and that local officials could not be expected to know even clearly settled law. He would have made motive the sole standard. By the time he wrote the majority opinion in *Harlow*, he had changed his mind about which standard was more protective of public officials.

4.   How is an unpaid school board in Mena, Arkansas, supposed to keep informed of clearly settled law? In 1975 Justice Powell thought it impossible. Can a constitutional republican government be administered on the assumption that it is impossible for public officials to know the constitutional constraints that bind them? If the Court had said they didn't have to know the law, wouldn't that have removed most of their incentive to find out?

School board members don't have to read the advance sheets, or know the whole Constitution. There is a mechanism for keeping them informed of what they need to know. Educational associations publish newsletters summarizing legal developments affecting schools; school board lawyers subscribe to the newsletters. It is not terribly difficult to keep standard operating procedures abreast of "clearly settled" law if the school board cares to do so. Similar newsletters are published for other governmental units.

5. *Harlow* declines to elaborate on what it means by "clearly established" federal rights. Do only Supreme Court cases count? Courts of appeals? District courts? State courts? Courts in other states and circuits? How close do the facts have to be? Is law clearly established only when there is a case on all fours, or do officials have some responsibility to make reasonable applications of clearly established principles? Can one case clearly settle anything? Or does it take three, or five, or fifty?

6. Consider Wood v. Strickland again. There was an Eighth Circuit case involving two students suspended from college for two semesters. The court had said:

> We do hold . . . that procedural due process must be afforded (as Judge Hunter by his first opinion here specifically required) by way of adequate notice, definite charge, and a hearing with opportunity to present one's own side of the case and with all necessary protective measures.

Esteban v. Central Missouri State College, 415 F.2d 1077, 1089 (8th Cir. 1969), *cert. denied*, 398 U.S. 965 (1970). The statement was dictum in the court of appeals, but it had been holding in the district court. In the meantime, the college had held the hearing the district court ordered.

Does that clearly establish the law for the Eighth Circuit? Is it clear that high schools are the same as colleges? Is it clear that three months is the same as two semesters? Does the school board have to read *Esteban* in light of decisions in other circuits, decisions involving high schools and shorter suspensions?

Does it matter that the statement was dictum? What about the district court's holding? Can Arkansas school boards ignore it because it came from the Western District of Missouri? Even if the court of appeals approved the holding in dictum?

On January 11, 1972, the Eighth Circuit decided Tate v. Board of Education, 453 F.2d 975 (8th Cir. 1972). The Mena school board acted on February 18. Is *Tate* relevant to whether the law was clearly established in the Eighth Circuit? What is a reasonable time for officials to find out about new decisions? Could defendants show they "neither knew nor should have known" about *Tate*?

Tate involved a high school and a three-day suspension. Plaintiffs were given a chance to ask questions when their suspensions were announced. The court held that this informal "hearing" satisfied due process because the facts were clear and the penalty was mild. Does that clearly settle that due process applies to high schools? Does it clearly settle how much of a hearing plaintiffs in Wood v. Strickland were entitled to?

7. The Supreme Court's first encounter with these issues came in Davis v. Scherer, 104 S. Ct. 3012 (1984). Plaintiff was fired from a state

civil service position with no formal hearing, although he had several conversations with his superiors in which he presented his side of the story. The district court held that the officials who fired him violated the due process clause. The Supreme Court held them immune. It was clearly established that he was entitled to some kind of hearing, but all the cases had involved either no hearing at all or an adequate hearing. It was not clearly established how much of a hearing he was entitled to, and defendants might have thought the informal conversations were enough. The majority thought it irrelevant to immunity from the constitutional claim that defendants had also violated state civil service regulations.

Four dissenters characterized the case as involving no hearing at all, and thought it had been clearly established for many years that an employee in plaintiff's situation was entitled to a hearing.

8.   The Supreme Court has created the law of governmental immunity largely since 1967. I do not mean that there were no immunities before then; the Court has generally built on common law precedents. But the whole subject got a new impetus from *Bivens* and the expansion of §1983 liability, and the Court has now gone over the whole area with a modern eye. Wood v. Strickland and some of the other early cases attempted to proceed office by office, suggesting the possibility of a different immunity for every official. But the standard in Wood v. Strickland was generalized to all state and federal officers not entitled to absolute immunity, and the *Harlow* standard will presumably be generalized in the same way.

9.   There are occasional suggestions that officials are not immune from suit for errors in the performance of ministerial acts. That was the common law rule, and it sometimes resulted in low ranking officials being held liable for following orders given by immune officials. One example is Kilbourn v. Thompson, 103 U.S. 168 (1881). Kilbourn held that the sergeant-at-arms of the House of Representatives could be liable in damages for imprisoning plaintiff pursuant to unlawful orders of members of the House, who were immune under the speech and debate clause. Chief Justice Burger seems to find nothing wrong with that. See note 8 of his dissent in *Harlow*. Another example is Little v. Barreme, 6 U.S. (2 Cranch) 170 (1804). An American sea captain seized a Danish vessel pursuant to an order of President Jefferson. But Jefferson's order was not authorized by statute, and the captain was held liable.

Such cases are just another device for evading sovereign immunity if the court is confident that the government will reimburse the nominal defendant. But it is not clear that that is what happened. Wouldn't it be outrageous for the liability to rest on the officer who followed orders, while the officer who gave orders is immune? There have been no such incidents in the Supreme Court's modern immunity jurisprudence. But *Harlow*'s statement that "immunity generally is available only to officials performing discretionary functions," supra at 1162, raises the spectre of a repetition.

10. Judges, prosecutors, and legislators are entitled to qualified immunity in cases that fall outside their absolute immunity. An example is Hampton v. Hanrahan, discussed in the Notes on Other Absolute Immunities. What about governmental units themselves? The Court said no in Owen v. City of Independence, 445 U.S. 622 (1980). The Court found no qualified immunity for municipalities at common law in the Reconstruction era, when §1983 was enacted, so it assumed Congress did not intend to include any such immunity in §1983. The common law did recognize immunity in some cases based on the governmental/proprietary distinction, and on a distinction between discretionary and ministerial acts. But the majority found both of these immunities irrelevant; neither bore much resemblance to the qualified immunity it had fashioned in Wood v. Strickland. The city was held liable for firing its chief of police for defamatory reasons without giving him a hearing. He was fired in April 1972; the first Supreme Court decision announcing a right to a hearing in such circumstances came in June 1972. There were four dissents.

However, the Court has also held that §1983 creates no cause of action against municipalities based on respondeat superior. Monell v. New York City Department of Social Services, 436 U.S. 658 (1978). Municipalities are liable only for acts done pursuant to official policy, or by high-ranking officials whose acts "may fairly be said to represent official policy." Id. at 694. Although formulated in terms of cause of action rather than immunity, *Monell* insulates municipalities from liability from many of the most common constitutional violations — police brutality, for example.

11. The traditional reason for both absolute and qualified immunities for government officials is that the threat of liability might deter their exercise of duty. If the governmental unit is worried about that, why can't it indemnify them? If the public wants the benefits of officers who act boldly, why shouldn't it pay for their mistakes?

12. For the ordinary citizen, ignorance of the law is no excuse. Government officials have to know the law only if it is clearly settled. Judges and prosecutors don't have to know any law at all. Does that make any sense? The Fifth Circuit thought not in Folsom Investment Co. v. Moore, 681 F.2d 1032 (5th Cir. 1982). A creditor had seized plaintiff's property pursuant to a prejudgment attachment statute subsequently held unconstitutional. The court gave the creditor qualified immunity.

13. In the cases on implied causes of action, the Court's right wing insisted that federal courts have no common law powers and cannot apply common law remedies where Congress has not codified them. In the cases on immunities of state officials, Congress has created a sweeping cause of action. §1983 says that "every" person who violates federal rights under color of law "shall be liable to the person injured in an action at law, suit in equity, or other proper proceeding for redress." Led by its right wing, the Court has qualified this statute with a body of common law immunities never mentioned by Congress. Is creating an immunity any more or less judicial legislation than creating a cause of action?

NOTES ON PRESIDENTIAL IMMUNITY

1.   As *Harlow* indicates, the Court also held that the President of the United States is absolutely immune from suits for damages. Nixon v. Fitzgerald, 457 U.S. 731 (1982). The majority distinguished the President from governors, cabinet officers, and presidential aides. No other official is as indispensable as the President; no other official is as visible. He would be an obvious target for suits, but he should not be distracted by the need to defend them or deterred in his exercise of office by fear of liability.

2.   Four dissenters insisted that "no man is above the law." They conceded that some government functions deserved absolute immunity. They could hardly do otherwise. Justice White, who wrote the principal dissent, also wrote the majority opinion in Stump v. Sparkman. But White denied that any particular officer could be immune in all his functions. He noted that neither judges, prosecutors, nor legislators would be absolutely immune in a suit challenging the discharge of a staff member, and he saw nothing that required such immunity for the President.

3.   All the justices agreed that the President is not wholly immune from judicial process. In United States v. Nixon, 418 U.S. 683 (1974), the Court unanimously enforced a subpoena against the President. The subpoena was issued in a criminal prosecution of some of the President's aides, but congressional reaction to the evidence disclosed pursuant to the subpoena forced the President to resign.

4.   The Court has also enjoined presidential acts in litigation against his subordinates. The best-known example is Youngstown Sheet & Tube Co. v. Sawyer, 343 U.S. 579 (1952). Secretary of Commerce Sawyer seized the nation's steel mills to continue war production despite a strike against the private owners. He acted pursuant to President Truman's orders, but the Court enjoined the seizure.

D.   FEDERAL INTERFERENCE WITH STATE LAW ENFORCEMENT

EX PARTE YOUNG
209 U.S. 123 (1908)

[Minnesota passed a series of statutes setting maximum rates for railroads. Each set of rates was substantially below the rates previously charged. The railroads complied with the first two such statutes. When a third statute lowered rates even further, the railroads arranged a challenge to the constitutionality of the statutes.

Shareholders of each railroad filed suit against the railroad, representative customers of the railroad, the members of the Minnesota Railroad and Warehouse Commission, and Edward T. Young, Attorney General of Minnesota. The plaintiff shareholders sought an injunction ordering the railroad not to comply with any of the rate laws, and an injunction ordering the various state officials not to enforce the rate laws. Plaintiffs alleged that the rates were confiscatory and took the railroad's property without due process.

The trial court issued first a temporary restraining order, and then a preliminary injunction, against enforcement of the newest rate law. It denied preliminary relief with respect to earlier laws that the railroad had complied with; it indicated that at the trial on the merits, it would consider the constitutionality of all the challenged laws.

The next day, Attorney General Young sought a writ of mandamus from a state court, ordering one of the railroads to comply with the new rate law. The federal court then held Young in contempt of the preliminary injunction. Young was fined $100 and committed to the custody of the United States marshall until he dismissed the mandamus action. Young then filed a petition for habeas corpus in the Supreme Court of the United States.

The Court rejected Young's argument that the suit against him was really a suit against Minnesota, so that the federal trial court lacked jurisdiction. That is the most famous part of the case; it is described in Edelman v. Jordan, supra at 1096.

Young also argued that equity would not enjoin a criminal prosecution, because defense of a state enforcement proceeding would be an adequate remedy at law.

MR. JUSTICE PECKHAM . . . delivered the opinion of the Court. . . .

It is further objected (and the objection really forms part of the contention that the State cannot be sued) that a court of equity has no jurisdiction to enjoin criminal proceedings, by indictment or otherwise, under the state law. This, as a general rule, is true. But there are exceptions. When such indictment or proceeding is brought to enforce an alleged unconstitutional statute, which is the subject matter of inquiry in a suit already pending in a Federal court, the latter court having first obtained jurisdiction over the subject matter, has the right, in both civil and criminal cases, to hold and maintain such jurisdiction, to the exclusion of all other courts, until its duty is fully performed. But the Federal court cannot, of course, interfere in a case where the proceedings were already pending in a state court.

Where one commences a criminal proceeding who is already party to a suit then pending in a court of equity, if the criminal proceedings are brought to enforce the same right that is in issue before that court, the latter may enjoin such criminal proceedings. In Dobbins v. Los Angeles,

195 U.S. 223-241, it is remarked by Mr. Justice Day, in delivering the opinion of the court, that "it is well settled that where property rights will be destroyed, unlawful interference by criminal proceedings under a void law or ordinance may be reached and controlled by a court of equity." Smyth v. Ames distinctly enjoined the proceedings by indictment to compel obedience to the rate act.

These cases show that a court of equity is not always precluded from granting an injunction to stay proceedings in criminal cases, and we have no doubt the principle applies in a case such as the present. In re Sawyer, 124 U.S. 200, 211, is not to the contrary. That case holds that in general a court of equity has no jurisdiction of a bill to stay criminal proceedings, but it expressly states an exception, "unless they are instituted by a party to the suit already pending before it and to try the same right that is in issue there." Various authorities are cited to sustain the exception. The criminal proceedings here that could be commenced by the state authorities would be under the statutes relating to passenger or freight rates, and their validity is the very question involved in the suit in the United States Circuit Court. The right to restrain proceedings by mandamus is based upon the same foundation and governed by the same principles.

It is proper to add that the right to enjoin an individual, even though a state official, from commencing suits under circumstances already stated, does not include the power to restrain a court from acting in any case brought before it, either of a civil or criminal nature, nor does it include power to prevent any investigation or action by a grand jury. The latter body is part of the machinery of a criminal court, and an injunction against a state court would be a violation of the whole scheme of our Government. If an injunction against an individual is disobeyed, and he commences proceedings before a grand jury or in a court, such disobedience is personal only, and the court or jury can proceed without incurring any penalty on that account.

The difference between the power to enjoin an individual from doing certain things, and the power to enjoin courts from proceeding in their own way to exercise jurisdiction is plain, and no power to do the latter exists because of a power to do the former.

It is further objected that there is a plain and adequate remedy at law open to the complainants and that a court of equity, therefore, has no jurisdiction in such case. It has been suggested that the proper way to test the constitutionality of the act is to disobey it, at least once, after which the company might obey the act pending subsequent proceedings to test its validity. But in the event of a single violation the prosecutor might not avail himself of the opportunity to make the test, as obedience to the law was thereafter continued, and he might think it unnecessary to start an inquiry. If, however, he should do so while the company was thereafter obeying the law, several years might elapse before there was a final determination of the question, and if it should be determined that the law was invalid the property of the company would have been taken during that time without due process of law, and there would be no possibility of its recovery.

Another obstacle to making the test on the part of the company might be to find an agent or employé who would disobey the law, with a possible fine and imprisonment staring him in the face if the act should be held valid. Take the passenger rate act, for instance: A sale of a single ticket above the price mentioned in that act might subject the ticket agent to a charge of felony, and upon conviction to a fine of five thousand dollars and imprisonment for five years. It is true the company might pay the fine, but the imprisonment the agent would have to suffer personally. It would not be wonderful if, under such circumstances, there would not be a crowd of agents offering to disobey the law. The wonder would be that a single agent should be found ready to take the risk.

If, however, one should be found and the prosecutor should elect to proceed against him, the defense that the act was invalid, because the rates established by it were too low, would require a long and difficult examination of quite complicated facts upon which the validity of the act depended. Such investigation it would be almost impossible to make before a jury, as such body could not intelligently pass upon the matter. Questions of the cost of transportation of passengers and freight, the net earnings of the road, the separation of the cost and earnings, within the State from those arising beyond its boundaries, all depending upon the testimony of experts and the examination of figures relating to these subjects, as well, possibly, as the expenses attending the building and proper cost of the road, would necessarily form the chief matter of inquiry, and intelligent answers could only be given after a careful and prolonged examination of the whole evidence, and the making of calculations based thereon. All material evidence having been taken upon these issues, it has been held that it ought to be referred to the most competent and reliable master to make all needed computations and to find therefrom the necessary facts upon which a judgment might be rendered that might be reviewed by this court. From all these considerations it is plain that this is not a proper suit for investigation by a jury. Suits for penalties, or indictment or other criminal proceedings for a violation of the act, would therefore furnish no reasonable or adequate opportunity for the presentation of a defense founded upon the assertion that the rates were too low and therefore the act invalid.

We do not say the company could not interpose this defense in an action to recover penalties or upon the trial of an indictment, but the facility of proving it in either case falls so far below that which would obtain in a court of equity that comparison is scarcely possible.

To await proceedings against the company in a state court grounded upon a disobedience of the act, and then, if necessary, obtain a review in this court by writ of error to the highest state court, would place the company in peril of large loss and its agents in great risk of fines and imprisonment if it should be finally determined that the act was valid. This risk the company ought not to be required to take. Over eleven thousand millions of dollars, it is estimated, are invested in railroad property, owned by many thousands of people who are scattered over the whole country from ocean to ocean, and they are entitled to equal protection from the laws and from the courts, with the owners of all other kinds of property, no more, no less. The courts having jurisdiction, Federal or state, should at all times be open to them as well as to others, for the purpose of protecting their property and their legal rights.

All the objections to a remedy at law as being plainly inadequate are obviated by a suit in equity, making all who are directly interested parties to the suit, and enjoining the enforcement of the act until the decision of the court upon the legal question. . . .

Finally it is objected that the necessary result of upholding this suit in the Circuit Court will be to draw to the lower Federal courts a great flood of litigation of this character, where one Federal judge would have it in his power to enjoin proceedings by state officials to enforce the legislative acts of the State, either by criminal or civil actions. To this it may be answered, in the first place, that no injunction ought to be granted unless in a case reasonably free from doubt. We think such rule is, and will be, followed by all the judges of the Federal courts. . . .

The rule to show cause is discharged and the petition for writs of habeas corpus and certiorari is dismissed.

So ordered.

MR. JUSTICE HARLAN, dissenting. . . .

Too little consequence has been attached to the fact that the courts of the States are under an obligation equally strong with that resting upon the courts of the Union to respect and enforce the provisions of the Federal Constitution as the Supreme Law of the Land, and to guard rights secured or guaranteed by that instrument. We must assume — a decent respect for the States requires us to assume — that the state courts will enforce every right secured by the Constitution. If they fail to do so, the party complaining has a clear remedy for the protection of his rights; for, he can come by writ of error, in an orderly, judicial way, from the highest court of the State to this tribunal for redress in respect of every right granted or secured by that instrument and denied by the state court. The state courts, it should be remembered, have jurisdiction concurrent with the courts of the United States of all suits of a civil nature, at common law or equity involving a prescribed amount, arising under the Constitution or laws of the United States. . . .

At the argument of this case counsel for the railway company insisted that the provisions of the act in question were so drastic that they could be enforced by the State in its own courts with such persistency and in such a manner as, in a very brief period, to have the railway officers and agents all in jail, the business of the company destroyed and its property confiscated by heavy and successive penalties, before a final judicial decision as to the constitutionality of the act could be obtained. I infer from some language in the court's opinion that these apprehensions are shared by some of my brethren. And this supposed danger to the railway company and its shareholders seems to have been the basis of the action of the Federal Circuit Court when, by its order directed against the Attorney General of Minnesota, it practically excluded the State from its own courts in respect of the issues here involved. . . .

It is to be observed that when the State was in effect prohibited by the order of the Federal court from appearing in its own courts, there was no danger, absolutely none whatever, from anything that the Attorney General had ever done or proposed to do, that the property of the railway company would be confiscated and its officers and agents imprisoned, beyond the power of that company to stay any wrong done *by bringing to this court, in regular order, any final judgment of the state court, in the mandamus suit, which may have been in derogation of a Federal right.* When the Attorney General instituted the mandamus proceeding in the state court against the railway company there was in force, it must not be forgotten, an order of injunction by the Federal court which prevented that company from obeying the state law. There was consequently no danger from that direction. Besides, the mandamus proceeding was not instituted for the recovery of any of the penalties prescribed by the state law, and therefore no judgment in that case could operate directly upon the property of the railway company or upon the persons of its officers or agents. The Attorney General in his response to the rule against him assured the Federal court that he did not contemplate any proceeding whatever against the railway company except the one in mandamus. Suppose the mandamus case had been finally decided in the state court, the way was open for the railway company to preserve any question it made as to its rights under the Constitution, and, in the event of a decision adverse to it in that court, at once to carry the case to the highest court of Minnesota and thence by a writ of error bring it to this court. That course would have served to determine every question of constitutional law raised by the suit in the Federal court in an orderly way without trampling upon the State, and without interfering, in the meantime, with the operation of the railway property in the accustomed way. Instead of adopting that course — so manifestly consistent with the dignity and authority of both the Federal and state judicial tribunals — the Federal court practically closed the state courts against the State itself when it adjudged that the Attorney General, without regard to the wishes of the Governor of Minnesota, and without reference to his duties as prescribed by the laws of that State, should stand in the custody of the Marshal, unless he dismissed the mandamus suit. . . .

NOTES ON THE *YOUNG* DILEMMA

1.   *Young* identifies a special form of irreparable injury imposed by
allegedly unconstitutional statutes. You cannot understand this irreparable injury by focusing only on what happens if the statute is unconstitutional. There is no way to know for sure whether the statute is
constitutional until a court decides; persons subject to the statute must
act on their own judgment, and the irreparable injury is a product of their
uncertainty.

If the railroad complies with the rate law, it forfeits its asserted constitutional rights. Loss of constitutional rights is nearly always irreparable
injury, because constitutional rights are usually hard to value, and because even if they can be valued, all the defendants are immune from
suit. It is inconceivable that the railroad could recover lost freight charges
from Minnesota or from any state officer.

The railroad can avoid this irreparable harm by violating the statute.
But the statute might be constitutional; the railroad can violate the statute only by risking criminal penalties for the railroad and its agents.
Criminal penalties also inflict irreparable injury. That is their point, and
usually the injury is deserved. But if defendant thought the statute was
unconstitutional, criminal penalties may be the price of a court ruling.

The choice between forfeiting asserted constitutional rights or risking
penalties is the *Young* dilemma. A suit to enjoin enforcement of the
statute avoids the dilemma; it allows the railroad to obtain a ruling on the
statute's constitutionality without risking penalties.

2.   How serious is the *Young* dilemma? The majority focused on what
might happen: $5,000 fines and five years' imprisonment for the sale of a
single ticket, cumulative penalties for every violation, prosecutions of
ticket agents as well as the railroad itself. Justice Harlan focused on the
Attorney General's promise not to seek penalties until the law was upheld
in the state mandamus proceeding.

Which view is more realistic? Minnesota isn't really going to imprison
ticket agents, is it? But if you were a ticket agent, would you want to take a
chance? This is the railroad's fight; ticket agents don't have much stake in
it. What about the railroad? Does it matter that the railroad could afford a
few $5,000 fines?

3.   What is the Attorney General's promise worth? Remember that
the government generally cannot be estopped, see notes supra at 946 and
955, and that violation of a stipulation is not contempt of court, Ex parte
Buskirk, 72 F. 14 (4th Cir. 1896), discussed in Griffin v. Board of Education, supra at 672. The traditional rule was that a criminal defendant can
be convicted even though the prosecutor erroneously told him his proposed conduct did not violate the statute. Hopkins v. State, 193 Md. 489,
498-499, 69 A.2d 456, *appeal dismissed,* 339 U.S. 940 (1950). Young's
promise was surely worthless in 1908. It is conceivable that it might be

enforced today. The Supreme Court has enforced plea bargains, Santobello v. New York, 404 U.S. 257 (1971), and it has invalidated a conviction for refusing to testify to a committee that assured the witness he could invoke the privilege against self-incrimination, Raley v. Ohio, 360 U.S. 423, 437-440 (1959). And the Court has said in dictum that "Ordinarily, citizens may not be punished for actions undertaken in good faith reliance upon authoritative assurance that punishment will not attach." United States v. Laub, 385 U.S. 475, 487 (1967). If the Court had converted the prosecutor's promise not to seek penalties into an enforceable grant of immunity for all violations committed before the statute's constitutionality had been determined, wouldn't that be as good as the preliminary injunction actually issued? Should the railroad have to rely on the prosecutor's promise if no one knows whether the promise is enforceable?

4. Try not to let your assessment of the remedy issues be colored by lack of sympathy with the railroad's constitutional claim or by assumptions about the railroad's power or wealth. Congress has largely repealed federal court jurisdiction to interfere with state rate orders. But the same remedy issues arise in quite different substantive contexts. In Cameron v. Johnson, the plaintiffs were civil rights workers trying to register black voters in Mississippi. 390 U.S. 611 (1968). In Allee v. Medrano, they were migrant farm workers trying to organize a union. 416 U.S. 802 (1974). Litigants such as these have no reason to trust the prosecutor. Even a small fine may be more than they can pay. Even if the fine is trivial, why should individuals have to risk the stigma of a criminal conviction? What if they want to go to law school some day?

5. Subsequent cases applying Ex parte Young did not rely on the severity of the penalties. It was enough that without an injunction against prosecution, plaintiffs would have to risk prosecution to learn their constitutional rights. In the Sunday closing cases, the Court heard suits to enjoin enforcement of statutes enforceable only by small fines — $100 for one section, and $4 for another section. Two Guys v. McGinley, 366 U.S. 582, 585-586, 589 (1961).

6. Congress responded to Ex parte Young with the Three-Judge Court Act. This statute required special trial courts composed of three judges to decide requests for injunctions against enforcement of state laws, and it authorized direct appeals to the Supreme Court. Act of June 18, 1910, Chap. 309 §17, 36 Stat. 539, 557. The act was repealed in 1976. 90 Stat. 1119.

NOTES ON FEDERAL JURISDICTION

1. Plaintiffs facing the *Young* dilemma want a chance to litigate their constitutional claim without risking penalties. They also generally want to litigate that claim in federal court. It was probably no accident that the

federal court promptly issued a temporary restraining order against enforcement of the rate law and the state court promptly issued a writ of mandamus enforcing it. Both state and federal judges swear to uphold the Constitution, and most judges take that oath seriously. Some state courts construe some constitutional rights more vigorously than some federal courts; that has especially been true during the time of the Burger Court. But historically, most litigants with constitutional claims have preferred federal court, and historically, they have had good reason. Professor Neuborne argues that this is not just a long-running coincidence. Rather, he thinks there are structural differences that predispose federal judges to be more sympathetic to federal constitutional claims. These include life tenure, an historical sense of special responsibility for the Constitution, and greater technical competence arising from fewer judges, lighter caseloads, higher pay, and the assistance of able law clerks. Neuborne, The Myth of Parity, 90 Harv. L. Rev. 1105, 1115-1130 (1977). James Madison predicted the federal judiciary's sense of special responsibility for constitutional rights in Federalist No. 10.

2.   The structure of federal jurisdiction links the right to a federal forum with the argument whether defense of an enforcement proceeding is an adequate remedy. This linkage was probably inadvertent. To understand it requires a brief review of the relevant statutes.

42 U.S.C. §1983 (1982) creates a cause of action for legal or equitable relief against state officials who violate federal rights. This broad language includes suits to enjoin enforcement of unconstitutional state laws. 28 U.S.C. §1343 (1982) grants federal jurisdiction over suits to enforce constitutional rights. In addition, 28 U.S.C. §1331 (1982) grants federal jurisdiction over all claims arising under federal law. Before 1980, §1331 applied only to claims over $10,000. Section 1343(3) applied to claims of any size. Now that §1331's jurisdictional amount requirement has been repealed, §1343 is probably redundant. But its history helps clarify congressional intent.

All these statutes date from Reconstruction, a time when some state courts were openly hostile to federal rights. The legislative history is quite clear that Congress created federal jurisdiction because it didn't trust state courts. Congress intended that plaintiffs with constitutional claims have an option to go directly to federal court, and the Supreme Court has held that plaintiffs need not exhaust state remedies before suing state officials under §1983. Monroe v. Pape, 365 U.S. 167 (1961). Sections 1983 and 1343 were part of the Civil Rights Act of 1871, and it is the legislative history of that act that is best known. That history is reviewed in Monroe at 172-183, and in Mitchum v. Foster, 407 U.S. 225, 238-242 (1972).

3.   The Reconstruction Congresses also authorized state defendants to remove state cases to federal courts if they could not enforce in the state courts "any law providing for equal civil rights of citizens," and to remove prosecutions for "any act under color of authority derived from

any law providing for equal rights." 28 U.S.C. §1443 (1982). And they authorized federal habeas corpus for any person held "in custody in violation of the Constitution." 28 U.S.C. §2241(c)(3) (1982). Professor Amsterdam has argued that these provisions were intended to permit state defendants to freely remove a wide array of state cases to federal courts. Amsterdam, Criminal Prosecutions Affecting Federally Guaranteed Civil Rights: Federal Removal and Habeas Corpus Jurisdiction to Abort State Court Trial, 113 U. Pa. L. Rev. 793 (1965). However that may be, the effect was quite different. Narrow construction has made the civil rights removal jurisdiction substantially useless; that construction was reaffirmed in City of Greenwood v. Peacock, 384 U.S. 808 (1966). Habeas corpus has become a postjudgment remedy only.

4.   The combined effect of these developments is that a plaintiff who asserts a claim arising under federal law has a right to file in federal court, but a defendant who asserts a federal defense has no right to remove to federal court. So a suit to enjoin enforcement of an invalid state law can be heard in federal court, but any proceeding to enforce the state law will be in state court. So the right to sue for an injunction becomes the key to federal jurisdiction.

But the right to any injunction depends on the inadequacy of legal remedies. So if defending an enforcement proceeding is an adequate remedy, plaintiff can't get an injunction, and he is left to his state court defense. If defending an enforcement proceeding is not an adequate remedy, plaintiff can file suit in either state or federal court to enjoin enforcement. He can choose federal court as of right, and need not show that there is anything inadequate about suing to enjoin enforcement in state court.

5.   Two other jurisdictional provisions break this linkage for certain categories of cases. The Tax Injunction Act denies federal courts jurisdiction to enjoin the assessment, levy, or collection of state taxes. 28 U.S.C. §1341 (1982). The Johnson Act denies federal courts jurisdiction to enjoin state rate orders. 28 U.S.C. §1342 (1982). Both provisions were enacted during the New Deal, and both are conditioned on the availability of a "plain, speedy and efficient remedy" in state court. Typically, the state remedy is to pay the tax and sue for a refund, or to seek direct judicial review of the rate order. Thus, plaintiff can initiate a remedy to assert his federal claim, and this avoids or greatly eases the *Young* dilemma. But he is required to file his federal claim in state court. With respect to other constitutional claims, the congressional commitment to federal jurisdiction has not wavered.

6.   One other arguably relevant jurisdictional provision turns out to have no direct effect on these cases. The anti-injunction act provides that no federal court may "grant an injunction to stay proceedings in a State court except as expressly authorized by Act of Congress, or where necessary in aid of its jurisdiction, or to protect or effectuate its judgments." 28

U.S.C. §2283 (1982). It appears that everyone assumed the statute to be irrelevant in Ex parte Young. The Court eventually held that the statute applies only to state proceedings that are already pending; it is irrelevant to injunctions against threatened prosecutions. Dombrowski v. Pfister, 380 U.S. 479, 484 n.2 (1965). Then it held that §1983 is an expressly authorized exception, so that in §1983 suits federal courts may enjoin even pending state proceedings. Mitchum v. Foster, 407 U.S. 225 (1972). With some basis in precedent and legislative history, the Court held that "expressly" authorized meant "implicitly" authorized. Section 1983 "created a specific and uniquely federal right or remedy, enforceable in a federal court of equity, that could be frustrated if the federal court were not empowered to enjoin a state court proceeding." Id. at 237. The Court relied heavily on legislative history showing that Congress created the §1983 remedy because it profoundly distrusted state courts. Some judges continue to invoke the anti-injunction act as a policy guide that counsels deference toward state courts and restraint in enjoining state proceedings. But the act of its own force is irrelevant to suits to enjoin enforcement of unconstitutional statutes.

7. Many discussions of Ex parte Young and the modern cases that question its holding emphasize the choice between state and federal court. Certainly that is an important perspective; it is probably the most important perspective if one is studying these cases in a course on federal jurisdiction. This book will not ignore that choice, but it will emphasize the choice between the two kinds of remedies: injunction against enforcement or defense of an enforcement proceeding. The link between federalism issues and remedies issues is not inherent. The Tax Injunction Act and the Johnson Act break the link; removal jurisdiction for federal defenses would break the link. The same remedial choice can and often does arise in unitary court systems. For an example of a suit in federal court to enjoin enforcement of federal law, see United States Postal Service v. Council of Greenburgh Civic Associations, 453 U.S. 114 (1981). For examples of suits in state court to enjoin enforcement of state laws, see New York State Liquor Authority v. Bellanca, 452 U.S. 714 (1981), or Bio-Medical Laboratories v. Trainor, 68 Ill. 2d 540, 370 N.E.2d 223 (1977).

YOUNGER v. HARRIS
401 U.S. 37 (1971)

MR. JUSTICE BLACK delivered the opinion of the Court.

Appellee, John Harris, Jr., was indicted in a California state court, charged with violation of the California Penal Code §§11400 and 11401, known as the California Criminal Syndicalism Act. . . . He then filed a complaint in the Federal District Court, asking that court to enjoin the appellant, Younger, the District Attorney of Los Angeles County, from prosecuting him, and alleging that the prosecution and even the presence of the Act inhibited him in the exercise of his rights of free speech and press, rights guaranteed him by the First and Fourteenth Amendments. Appellees Jim Dan and Diane Hirsch intervened as plaintiffs in the suit, claiming that the prosecution of Harris would inhibit them as members of the Progressive Labor Party from peacefully advocating the program of their party, which was to replace capitalism with socialism and to abolish the profit system of production in this country. Appellee Farrell Broslawsky, an instructor in history at Los Angeles Valley College, also intervened claiming that the prosecution of Harris made him uncertain as to whether he could teach about the doctrines of Karl Marx or read from the Communist Manifesto as part of his classwork. All claimed that unless the United States court restrained the state prosecution of Harris each would suffer immediate and irreparable injury. A three-judge Federal District Court, convened pursuant to 28 U.S.C. §2284, held that it had jurisdiction and power to restrain the District Attorney from prosecuting, held that the State's Criminal Syndicalism Act was void for vagueness and overbreadth in violation of the First and Fourteenth Amendments, and accordingly restrained the District Attorney from "further prosecution of the currently pending action against plaintiff Harris for alleged violation of the Act." . . .

[T]he judgment of the District Court, enjoining appellant Younger from prosecuting under these California statutes, must be reversed as a violation of the national policy forbidding federal courts to stay or enjoin pending state court proceedings except under special circumstances. We express no view about the circumstances under which federal courts may act when there is no prosecution pending in state courts at the time the federal proceeding is begun.

I

Appellee Harris has been indicted, and was actually being prosecuted by California for a violation of its Criminal Syndicalism Act at the time this suit was filed. He thus has an acute, live controversy with the State and its prosecutor. But none of the other parties plaintiff in the District Court, Dan, Hirsch, or Broslawsky, has such a controversy. None has been indicted, arrested, or even threatened by the prosecutor. . . .

If these three had alleged that they would be prosecuted for the conduct they planned to engage in, and if the District Court had found this allegation to be true — either on the admission of the State's district attorney or on any other evidence — then a genuine controversy might be said to exist. But here appellees Dan, Hirsch, and Broslawsky do not claim that they have ever been threatened with prosecution, that a prosecution is likely, or even that a prosecution is remotely possible. They claim the right to bring this suit solely because, in the language of their complaint, they "feel inhibited." We do not think this allegation, even if true, is sufficient to bring the equitable jurisdiction of the federal courts into play to enjoin a pending state prosecution. A federal lawsuit to stop a prosecution in a state court is a serious matter. And persons having no fears of state prosecution except those that are imaginary or speculative, are not to be accepted as appropriate plaintiffs in such cases. Since Harris is actually being prosecuted under the challenged laws, however, we proceed with him as a proper party.

II

Since the beginning of this country's history Congress has, subject to few exceptions, manifested a desire to permit state courts to try state cases free from interference by federal courts. In 1793 an Act unconditionally provided: "[N]or shall a writ of injunction be granted to stay proceedings in any court of a state. . . . " 1 Stat. 335, c.22, §5. A comparison of the 1793 Act with 28 U.S.C. §2283, its present-day successor, graphically illustrates how few and minor have been the exceptions granted from the flat, prohibitory language of the old Act. During all this lapse of years from 1793 to 1970 the statutory exceptions to the 1793 congressional enactment have been only three: (1) "except as expressly authorized by Act of Congress"; (2) "where necessary in aid of its jurisdiction"; and (3) "to protect or effectuate its judgments." In addition, a judicial exception to the longstanding policy evidenced by the statute has been made where a person about to be prosecuted in a state court can show that he will, if the proceeding in the state court is not enjoined, suffer irreparable damages. See Ex parte Young, 209 U.S. 123 (1908).

The precise reasons for this longstanding public policy against federal court interference with state court proceedings have never been specifically identified but the primary sources of the policy are plain. One is the basic doctrine of equity jurisprudence that courts of equity should not act, and particularly should not act to restrain a criminal prosecution, when the moving party has an adequate remedy at law and will not suffer irreparable injury if denied equitable relief. The doctrine may originally have grown out of circumstances peculiar to the English judicial system and not applicable in this country, but its fundamental purpose of restraining equity jurisdiction within narrow limits is equally important under our Constitution, in order to prevent erosion of the role of the jury and avoid a duplication of legal proceedings and legal sanctions where a single suit would be adequate to protect the rights asserted. This underlying reason for restraining courts of equity from interfering with criminal prosecutions is reinforced by an even more vital consideration, the notion of "comity," that is, a proper respect for state functions, a recognition of the fact that the entire country is made up of a Union of separate state governments, and a continuance of the belief that the National Government will fare best if the States and their institutions are left free to perform their separate functions in their separate ways. This, perhaps for lack of a better and clearer way to describe it, is referred to by many as "Our Federalism," and one familiar with the profound debates that ushered our Federal Constitution into existence is bound to respect those who remain loyal to the ideals and dreams of "Our Federalism." The concept does not mean blind deference to "States' Rights" any more than it means centralization of control over every important issue in our National Government and its courts. The Framers rejected both these courses. What the concept does represent is a system in which there is sensitivity to the legitimate interests of both State and National Governments, and in which the National Government, anxious though it may be to vindicate and protect federal rights and federal interests, always endeavors to do so in ways that will not unduly interfere with the legitimate activities of the States. It should never be forgotten that this slogan, "Our Federalism," born in the early struggling days of our Union of States, occupies a highly important place in our Nation's history and its future.

This brief discussion should be enough to suggest some of the reasons why it has been perfectly natural for our cases to repeat time and time again that the normal thing to do when federal courts are asked to enjoin pending proceedings in state courts is not to issue such injunctions. In Fenner v. Boykin, 271 U.S. 240 (1926), suit had been brought in the Federal District Court seeking to enjoin state prosecutions under a recently enacted state law that allegedly interfered with the free flow of interstate commerce. The Court, in a unanimous opinion made clear that such a suit, even with respect to state criminal proceedings not yet formally instituted, could be proper only under very special circumstances. . . . These principles, made clear in the *Fenner* case, have been repeatedly followed and reaffirmed in other cases involving threatened prosecutions. See, e.g., Spielman Motor Sales Co. v. Dodge, 295 U.S. 89 (1935); Beal v. Missouri Pac. R. Co., 312 U.S. 45 (1941); Watson v. Buck, 313 U.S. 387 (1941); Williams v. Miller, 317 U.S. 599 (1942); Douglas v. City of Jeannette, 319 U.S. 157 (1943).

In all of these cases the Court stressed the importance of showing irreparable injury, the traditional prerequisite to obtaining an injunction. In addition, however, the Court also made clear that in view of the fundamental policy against federal interference with state criminal prosecutions, even irreparable injury is insufficient unless it is "both great and immediate." *Fenner*, supra. Certain types of injury, in particular, the cost, anxiety, and inconvenience of having to defend against a single criminal prosecution, could not by themselves be considered "irreparable" in the special legal sense of that term. Instead, the threat to the plaintiff's federally protected rights must be one that cannot be eliminated by his defense against a single criminal prosecution. See, e.g., Ex parte Young, supra, at 145-147. . . . And similarly, in *Douglas*, supra, we made clear, after reaffirming this rule, that:

> It does not appear from the record that petitioners have been threatened with any injury other than that incidental to every criminal proceeding brought lawfully and in good faith. . . .

319 U.S., at 164.

This is where the law stood when the Court decided Dombrowski v. Pfister, 380 U.S. 479 (1965), and held that an injunction against the enforcement of certain state criminal statutes could properly issue under the circumstances presented in that case. In *Dombrowski*, unlike many of the earlier cases denying injunctions, the complaint made substantial allegations that:

> the threats to enforce the statutes against appellants are not made with any expectation of securing valid convictions, but rather are part of a plan to employ arrests, seizures, and threats of prosecution under color of the statutes to harass appellants and discourage them and their supporters from asserting and attempting to vindicate the constitutional rights of Negro citizens of Louisiana.

380 U.S., at 482. The appellants in *Dombrowski* had offered to prove that their offices had been raided and all their files and records seized pursuant to search and arrest warrants that were later summarily vacated by a state judge for lack of probable cause. They also offered to prove that despite the state court order quashing the warrants and suppressing the evidence seized, the prosecutor was continuing to threaten to initiate new prosecutions of appellants under the same statutes, was holding public hearings at which photostatic copies of the illegally seized documents were being used, and was threatening to use other copies of the illegally seized documents to obtain grand jury indictments against the appellants on charges of violating the same statutes. These circumstances, as viewed by the Court sufficiently establish the kind of irreparable injury, above and beyond that associated with the defense of a single prosecution brought in good faith, that had always been considered sufficient to justify federal intervention. Indeed, after quoting the Court's statement in *Douglas* concerning the very restricted circumstances under which an injunction could be justified, the Court in *Dombrowski* went on to say:

> But the allegations in this complaint depict a situation in which defense of the State's criminal prosecution will not assure adequate vindication of constitutional rights. They suggest that a substantial loss of or impairment of freedoms of expression will occur if appellants must await the state court's

disposition and ultimate review in this Court of any adverse determination. These allegations, if true, clearly show irreparable injury.

380 U.S., at 485-486.

It is against the background of these principles that we must judge the propriety of an injunction under the circumstances of the present case. Here a proceeding was already pending in the state court, affording Harris an opportunity to raise his constitutional claims. There is no suggestion that this single prosecution against Harris is brought in bad faith or is only one of a series of repeated prosecutions to which he will be subjected. In other words, the injury that Harris faces is solely "that incidental to every criminal proceeding brought lawfully and in good faith," *Douglas*, supra, and therefore under the settled doctrine we have already described he is not entitled to equitable relief "even if such statutes are unconstitutional," *Buck*, supra.

The District Court, however, thought that the *Dombrowski* decision substantially broadened the availability of injunctions against state criminal prosecutions and that under that decision the federal courts may give equitable relief, without regard to any showing of bad faith or harassment, whenever a state statute is found "on its face" to be vague or overly broad, in violation of the First Amendment. We recognize that there are some statements in the *Dombrowski* opinion that would seem to support this argument. But, as we have already seen, such statements were unnecessary to the decision of that case, because the Court found that the plaintiffs had alleged a basis for equitable relief under the long-established standards. In addition, we do not regard the reasons adduced to support this position as sufficient to justify such a substantial departure from the established doctrines regarding the availability of injunctive relief. It is undoubtedly true, as the Court stated in *Dombrowski*, that "[a] criminal prosecution under a statute regulating expression usually involves imponderables and contingencies that themselves may inhibit the full exercise of First Amendment freedoms." 380 U.S., at 486. But this sort of "chilling effect," as the Court called it, should not by itself justify federal intervention. In the first place, the chilling effect cannot be satisfactorily eliminated by federal injunctive relief. In *Dombrowski* itself the Court stated that the injunction to be issued there could be lifted if the State obtained an "acceptable limiting construction" from the state courts. The Court then made clear that once this was done, prosecutions could then be brought for conduct occurring before the narrowing construction was made, and proper convictions could stand so long as the defendants were not deprived of fair warning. 380 U.S., at 491 n.7. The kind of relief granted in *Dombrowski* thus does not effectively eliminate uncertainty as to the coverage of the state statute and leaves most citizens with virtually the same doubts as before regarding the danger that their conduct might eventually be subjected to criminal sanctions. The chilling effect can, of course, be eliminated by an injunction that would prohibit any prosecution whatever for conduct occurring prior to a satisfactory rewriting of the statute. But the States would then be stripped of all power to prosecute even the socially dangerous and constitutionally unprotected conduct that had been covered by the statute, until a new statute could be passed by the state legislature and approved by the federal courts in potentially lengthy trial and appellate proceedings. Thus, in *Dombrowski* itself the Court carefully reaffirmed the principle that even in the direct prosecution in the State's own courts, a valid narrowing construction can be applied to conduct occurring prior to the date when the narrowing construction was made, in the absence of fair warning problems.

Moreover, the existence of a "chilling effect," even in the area of First Amendment rights, has never been considered a sufficient basis, in and of itself, for prohibiting state action. Where a statute does not directly abridge free speech, but — while regulating a subject within the State's power — tends to have the incidental effect of inhibiting First Amendment rights, it is well settled that the statute can be upheld if the effect on speech is minor in relation to the need for control of the conduct and the lack of alternative means for doing so. Just as the incidental "chilling effect" of such statutes does not automatically render them unconstitutional, so the chilling effect that admittedly can result from the very existence of certain laws on the statute books does not in itself justify prohibiting the State from carrying out the important and necessary task of enforcing these laws against socially harmful conduct that the State believes in good faith to be punishable under its laws and the Constitution.

Beyond all this is another, more basic consideration. Procedures for testing the constitutionality of a statute "on its face" in the manner apparently contemplated by *Dombrowski*, and for then enjoining all action to enforce the statute until the State can obtain court approval for a modified version, are fundamentally at odds with the function of the federal courts in our constitutional plan. The power and duty of the judiciary to declare laws unconstitutional is in the final analysis derived from its responsibility for resolving concrete disputes brought before the courts for decision; a statute apparently governing a dispute cannot be applied by judges, consistently with their obligations under the Supremacy Clause, when such an application of the statute would conflict with the Constitution. Marbury v. Madison, 1 Cranch 137 (1803). But this vital responsibility, broad as it is, does not amount to an unlimited power to survey the statute books and pass judgment on laws before the courts are called upon to enforce them. . . . [T]he task of analyzing a proposed statute, pinpointing its deficiencies, and requiring correction of these deficiencies before the statute is put into effect, is rarely if ever an appropriate task for the judiciary. The combination of the relative remoteness of the controversy, the impact on the legislative process of the relief sought, and above all the speculative and amorphous nature of the required line-by-line analysis of detailed statutes, ordinarily results in a kind of case that is wholly unsatisfactory for deciding constitutional questions, whichever way they might be decided. In light of this fundamental conception of the Framers as to the proper place of the federal courts in the governmental processes of passing and enforcing laws, it can seldom be appropriate for these courts to exercise any such power of prior approval or veto over the legislative process.

For these reasons, fundamental not only to our federal system but also to the basic functions of the Judicial Branch of the National Government under our Constitution, we hold that the *Dombrowski* decision should not be regarded as having upset the settled doctrines that have always confined very narrowly the availability of injunctive relief against state criminal prosecutions. We do not think that opinion stands for the proposition that a federal court can properly enjoin enforcement of a statute solely on the basis of a showing that the statute "on its face" abridges First Amendment rights. There may, of course, be extraordinary circumstances in which the necessary irreparable injury can be shown even in the absence of the usual prerequisites of bad faith and harassment. For example, as long ago as the *Buck* case, supra, we indicated:

> It is of course conceivable that a statute might be flagrantly and patently violative of express constitutional prohibitions in every clause, sentence and paragraph, and in whatever manner and against whomever an effort might be made to apply it.

313 U.S., at 402. Other unusual situations calling for federal intervention might also arise, but there is no point in our attempting now to specify what they might be. It is sufficient for purposes of the present case to hold, as we do, that the possible unconstitutionality of a statute "on its face" does not in itself justify an injunction against good-faith attempts to enforce it, and that appellee Harris has failed to make any showing of bad faith, harassment, or any other unusual circumstance that would call for equitable relief. Because our holding rests on the absence of the factors necessary under equitable principles to justify federal intervention, we have no occasion to consider whether 28 U.S.C. §2283, which prohibits an injunction against state court proceedings "except as expressly authorized by Act of Congress" would in and of itself be controlling under the circumstances of this case.

The judgment of the District Court is reversed, and the case is remanded for further proceedings not inconsistent with this opinion.

Reversed.

MR. JUSTICE STEWART, with whom MR. JUSTICE HARLAN joins, concurring.

The questions the Court decides today are important ones. Perhaps as important, however, is a recognition of the areas into which today's holdings do not necessarily extend. . . .

In basing its decisions on policy grounds, the Court does not reach any questions concerning the independent force of the federal anti-injunction statute, 28 U.S.C. §2283. Thus we do not decide whether the word "injunction" in §2283 should be interpreted to include a declaratory judgment, or whether an injunction to stay proceedings in a state court is "expressly authorized" by §1 of the Civil Rights Act of 1871, now 42 U.S.C. §1983. And since all these cases involve state criminal prosecutions, we do not deal with the considerations that should govern a federal court when it is asked to intervene in state civil proceedings, where, for various reasons, the balance might be struck differently. Finally, the Court today does not resolve the problems involved when a federal court is asked to give injunctive or declaratory relief from *future* state criminal prosecutions. . . .

MR. JUSTICE BRENNAN, with whom MR. JUSTICE WHITE and MR. JUSTICE MARSHALL join, concurring in the result.

I agree that the judgment of the District Court should be reversed. Appellee Harris had been indicted for violations of the California Criminal Syndicalism Act before he sued in federal court. He has not alleged that the prosecution was brought in bad faith to harass him. His constitutional contentions may be adequately adjudicated in the state criminal proceeding, and federal intervention at his instance was therefore improper.

Appellees Hirsch and Dan have alleged that they "feel inhibited" by the statute and the prosecution of Harris from advocating the program of the Progressive Labor Party. Appellee Broslawsky has alleged that he "is uncertain" whether as an instructor in college history he can under the statute give instruction relating to the Communist Manifesto and similar revolutionary works. None of these appellees has stated any ground for a reasonable expectation that he will actually be prosecuted under the statute for taking the actions contemplated. . . .

MR. JUSTICE DOUGLAS, dissenting.

The fact that we are in a period of history when enormous extrajudicial sanctions are imposed on those who assert their First Amendment rights in unpopular causes emphasizes the wisdom of Dombrowski v. Pfister, 380 U.S. 479. . . .

Dombrowski represents an exception to the general rule that federal courts should not interfere with state criminal prosecutions. The exception does not arise merely because prosecutions are threatened to which the First Amendment will be the proffered defense. *Dombrowski* governs

statutes which are a blunderbuss by themselves or when used *en masse* —
those that have an "overbroad" sweep. "If the rule were otherwise, the
contours of regulation would have to be hammered out case by case —
and tested only by those hardy enough to risk criminal prosecution to
determine the proper scope of regulation." Id., at 487. It was in the
context of overbroad state statutes that we spoke of the "chilling effect
upon the exercise of First Amendment rights" caused by state prosecutions. Ibid. . . .

The special circumstances when federal intervention in a state criminal proceeding is permissible are not restricted to bad faith on the part of
state officials or the threat of multiple prosecutions. They also exist where
for any reason the state statute being enforced is unconstitutional on its
face. As Mr. Justice Butler, writing for the Court, said in Terrace v.
Thompson, 263 U.S. 197, 214:

> Equity jurisdiction will be exercised to enjoin the threatened enforcement of a
> state law which contravenes the Federal Constitution wherever it is essential
> in order effectually to protect property rights and the rights of persons against
> injuries otherwise irremediable; and in such a case a person, who as an officer
> of the State is clothed with the duty of enforcing its laws and who threatens
> and is about to commence proceedings, either civil or criminal, to enforce
> such a law against parties affected, may be enjoined from such action by a
> federal court of equity. . . .

In *Younger*, "criminal syndicalism" is defined so broadly as to jeopardize "teaching" that socialism is preferable to free enterprise.

Harris' "crime" was distributing leaflets advocating change in industrial
ownership through political action. . . .

Whatever the balance of the pressures of localism and nationalism
prior to the Civil War, they were fundamentally altered by the war. The
Civil War Amendments made civil rights a national concern. Those
Amendments, especially §5 of the Fourteenth Amendment, cemented
the change in American federalism brought on by the war. Congress
immediately commenced to use its new powers to pass legislation. Just as
the first Judiciary Act, 1 Stat. 73, and the "anti-injunction" statute represented the early views of American federalism, the Reconstruction statutes, including the enlargement of federal jurisdiction, represent a later
view of American federalism. . . .

The "anti-injunction" statute, 28 U.S.C. §2283, is not a bar to a federal
injunction under these circumstances. . . .

I hold to the view that §1983 is included in the "expressly authorized"
exception to §2283, a point not raised or considered in the much-discussed
Douglas v. City of Jeannette, 319 U.S. 157. There is no more good reason
for allowing a general statute dealing with federalism passed at the end of
the 18th century to control another statute also dealing with federalism,

passed almost 80 years later, than to conclude that the early concepts of federalism were not changed by the Civil War. . . .

HISTORICAL NOTE: FROM *YOUNG* TO *YOUNGER*

As Justice Black summarizes the law, Ex parte Young was a minor exception to a general practice of refusing to enjoin enforcement of unconstitutional state laws. For him, the general practice is represented by Fenner v. Boykin and the five cases he cites as in accord. The best known of those cases is Douglas v. City of Jeannette, 319 U.S. 157 (1943). In Black's history, Dombrowski v. Pfister was a bit of sixties radicalism that unwisely expanded the Ex parte Young exception, but the expansion was dictum and should be disregarded.

Justice Brennan's version of history in *Dombrowski* was only slightly different. He acknowledged that *Young* made injunctions against prosecution generally available. 380 U.S. at 483. But he thought *Young* had been modified by *Douglas* and similar cases so that injunctions against prosecution were now generally unavailable. Id. at 484-485. He cited five of the six cases Black cited in *Younger*; the sixth, Williams v. Miller, is a summary order citing some of the others.

This version of history helps Black get where he wants to go; it is less clear why Brennan told a similar tale. The truth is dramatically different. Ex parte Young was always the law before *Dombrowski*; Black's six cases were freaks when they were decided, and derelicts shortly thereafter. Here is a more accurate history; the many cases referred to are all cited in the notes of the original article.

LAYCOCK, FEDERAL INTERFERENCE WITH STATE PROSECUTIONS: THE CASES *DOMBROWSKI* FORGOT
46 U. Chi. L. Rev. 636 (1979)

Providing relief from the *Young* dilemma has been at the heart of legislative and judicial policy in this area throughout the century. Congress early on made special provision for *Young*-based injunctions in the Three-Judge Court Act and later provided an alternative remedy in the Declaratory Judgment Act. The legislative history of the latter makes clear that Congress accepted the basic premise first elaborated in *Young* and later championed by Professor Borchard — a person should not have to risk penalties to learn his rights. More importantly for our purposes, this same insight accounts for an almost unbroken line of pre-*Dom-*

browski Supreme Court cases granting prospective relief to persons facing the *Young* dilemma. . . .

In the period following Ex parte Young, the *Young* dilemma was frequently explained, and the *Young* remedy even more frequently applied. From *Young* to *Douglas*, the Supreme Court decided by opinion at least ninety-four cases seeking injunctions against enforcement of state statutes. In thirty-three of these cases, the injunction issued. Forty-two injunctions were denied on the merits, and six cases were remanded for further factual development. Because the federal court decided the constitutional merits under each of these dispositions, each is inconsistent with the view that the merits should be left to state courts in enforcement proceedings. Another six cases were dismissed for procedural reasons, and two because plaintiff faced no risk of prosecution.

The remaining five cases are the five *Dombrowski* cited to illustrate the "rule" that cases seeking such injunctions should normally be dismissed without reaching the merits because a state enforcement proceeding would provide an adequate remedy. Although the language of the five cases — which will be referred to as the *Douglas* dictum — strongly suggests such a rule, none of the cases squarely so holds. Spielman Motor Sales Co. v. Dodge comes the closest, but is limited by the Court's reliance on the plaintiff's failure to allege how it would be injured by compliance or to dispute the prosecutor's avowed intention to bring only a single test prosecution. Fenner v. Boykin actually affirmed a decision on the merits of a motion for preliminary injunction. In Beal v. Missouri Pacific Railroad, a diversity case in which the railroad alleged that a concededly constitutional statute was being misconstrued by a state prosecutor, the Court emphasized that only a state court could authoritatively resolve the controversy and that the state had promised it would bring only a single test prosecution. Watson v. Buck held prospective relief unavailable with respect to some sections of the challenged statute, but reached the merits of the plaintiff's challenge to the most important section without explaining why it was different from the others. Finally, in Douglas v. City of Jeannette, the plaintiffs were not required to risk further penalties to exercise their first amendment rights because the challenged ordinance was held unconstitutional in the companion case of Murdock v. Pennsylvania. Since there was no reason to believe that the state prosecutor and courts would not adhere to the Court's ruling in *Murdock*, the plaintiffs no longer faced the *Young* dilemma, prospective relief was unnecessary, and federal interference inappropriate.

These are the five cases that *Dombrowski* maintained had substantially modified *Young* and its scores of uncited progeny. If *Young* had been modified, one would expect to find that injunctive relief became relatively unavailable in the years following *Douglas*. But this is not what happened. . . .

Even in the early forties, the dominant line of cases freely granting injunctions did not die out. On the day that *Beal* was decided, the Court enjoined enforcement of a state alien registration law without making any reference to *Beal* or suggesting that any special showing of the need for prospective relief was required or had been made.[63] Between Watson v. Buck and *Douglas*, two requests for injunctions against state enforcement proceedings were denied on the merits. The first case[64] did not refer to the remedies issue, but in the second,[65] the Court summarily rejected the defendants' contention that the plaintiff's opportunity to raise his constitutional claim as a defense in the enforcement proceeding afforded him an adequate remedy.[66]

Following *Douglas*, the Court continued to give conflicting signals. In West Virginia State Board of Education v. Barnette,[67] it enjoined state enforcement proceedings without making any reference to the *Douglas* line of cases. Another opinion referred to "the traditional use of equity proceedings to enjoin criminal proceedings."[68] But in three other opinions, the *Douglas* dictum was restated, each time in sweeping terms and in further dictum.[69] *Douglas* was also cited as an alternative ground for decision in one affirmance without opinion.[70] These conflicting indications apparently represented real division on the Court. Although the *Douglas* dictum appeared six times in the early forties, all of these opinions were written by only two Justices: two were written by Justice Black[71] and four, including *Douglas* itself, by Chief Justice Stone.[72] This division came into the open and was resolved against the *Douglas* dictum in AFL v. Watson,[73] a result reinforced two years later — after Chief Justice Stone's death — by a unanimous Court in Toomer v. Witsell.[74] . . .

Toomer v. Witsell completed the restoration of Ex parte Young. In *Toomer*, plaintiffs sought to enjoin enforcement of South Carolina laws requiring out-of-state fishermen either to pay local taxes and license fees

---

63.   Hines v. Davidowitz, 312 U.S. 52 (1941).
64.   Reitz v. Mealey, 314 U.S. 33 (1941).
65.   Parker v. Brown, 317 U.S. 341 (1943).
66.   Id. at 349-50.
67.   319 U.S. 624 (1943).
68.   Switchmen's Union v. National Mediation Bd., 320 U.S. 297, 306 (1943).
69.   Yakus v. United States, 321 U.S. 414, 444 (1944); Meredith v. Winter Haven, 320 U.S. 228, 235 (1943); Burford v. Sun Oil Co., 319 U.S. 315, 333 n.29 (1943).
70.   Ryan v. Thompson, 324 U.S. 821 (1945).
71.   Burford v. Sun Oil Co., 319 U.S. 315, 333 n.29 (1943); Watson v. Buck, 313 U.S. 387, 400-02 (1941). *But see* Hines v. Davidowitz, 312 U.S. 52 (1941) (Black, J., for the Court) (enjoining enforcement of state alien registration law).
72.   Yakus v. United States, 321 U.S. 414, 444 (1944); Meredith v. Winter Haven, 320 U.S. 228, 235 (1943); Douglas v. City of Jeannette, 319 U.S. 157, 162-163 (1943); Beal v. Missouri Pac. R.R., 312 U.S. 45, 49-51 (1941). *But see* Parker v. Brown, 317 U.S. 341, 349-50 (1943) (Stone, C.J., for the Court) ("The majority of the Court is also of opinion that the suit is within the equity jurisdiction of the Court since the complaint alleges and the evidence shows threatened irreparable injury to respondent's business").
73.   327 U.S. 582 (1946).
74.   334 U.S. 385 (1948).

and use South Carolina port facilities or to stay out of South Carolina waters. A unanimous Court rejected the defendants' argument that the *Douglas* line of cases barred prospective relief:

> It is also clear that compliance . . . would have required payment of large sums of money for which South Carolina provides no means of recovery, that defiance would have carried with it the risk of heavy fines and long imprisonment, and that withdrawal from further fishing until a test case had been taken through the South Carolina courts and perhaps to this Court would have resulted in a substantial loss of business for which no compensation could be obtained.[85]

This is a straightforward description of the *Young* dilemma. The two alternatives to risking penalties — paying fees or withdrawing from South Carolina waters — were merely alternative means of compliance. *Toomer* thus went beyond *Watson* in two ways. First, the risk-of-penalties branch of the *Young* dilemma was once again made explicit. Second, it held that even when the cost of compliance can be measured in money, the legal remedy is inadequate unless the state has waived its immunity from suit. This holding was important since few states were likely to acknowledge liability for consequential damages caused by compliance with invalid statutes.

There are few prospective challenges to statutes that could not be brought under the *Toomer* standard. Its analysis of the *Young* dilemma would apply to any statute carrying penalties, for compliance always costs something and defiance is never risk-free. . . . *Toomer*'s reasoning fully repudiates the *Douglas* dictum. Its only ambiguity is that this consequence was left implicit: *Douglas* was not cited. . . .

After AFL v. Watson and *Toomer*, injunctions against threatened enforcement of state statutes again issued routinely. In the twenty-two years from *Douglas* to *Dombrowski*, the Court ordered or affirmed at least fifty-six district court injunctions or declaratory judgments preventing enforcement of state constitutions, statutes, or local ordinances. To be sure, many of these laws — those relating to voting rights, school administration, and public employment — would not ordinarily have been enforced by judicial proceedings, so that *Douglas* was not directly implicated. Moreover, those in which the United States was the plaintiff can perhaps be explained away as special treatment for the sovereign, even though the Court itself has never offered such an explanation. There remain, however, twenty-one cases in which the Court enjoined state enforcement proceedings against federal plaintiffs or prevented such proceedings by declaring the statute invalid. This latter group of cases was not merely, as one commentator has suggested, a civil rights exception to *Douglas*. Ten cases did involve racial discrimination, and

85. 334 U.S. at 391-92.

one was a free speech case. But nine struck down economic regulation and one voided a state tax. Moreover, there were at least sixteen additional cases in which the Court failed to grant prospective relief for reasons other than irreparable injury — cases in which, contrary to the *Douglas* dictum, the Court resolved the constitutional merits or authorized their resolution in federal court on remand.

Although the Court did not discuss the irreparable injury issue at length after *Toomer*, it alluded to it or closely related issues with sufficient frequency to negate any argument that the requirement was simply overlooked for two decades. . . .

These opinions, together with the numerous decisions granting prospective relief without raising the issue, strongly suggest that *Young* and *Toomer* were the law, and that the *Douglas* dictum was not. There was no contrary line of cases; the Court did not invoke *Douglas* to deny prospective relief in some cases and not in others according to a hidden agenda of its own. But neither did it explicitly overrule or limit *Douglas*. In fact, *Douglas* continued to be cited from time to time.

Many of these citations to *Douglas* are plainly irrelevant to the issues here, but at times the Court cited the dictum as if it were still good law. The most important of these citations appear in a line of cases involving requests for federal injunctions preventing the admission of improperly obtained evidence in state criminal trials. These cases presented considerations quite different from those of *Young* and *Douglas*. In particular, the federal plaintiffs had no need for prospective relief because their evidentiary claim could be presented in the state criminal court without repeating their violation or otherwise exposing themselves to additional risk. Moreover, federal interference with evidentiary rulings in a state trial would have split control of the trial between two courts, a result more disruptive than enjoining intitiation of the state proceeding.

Douglas was thus not implicated in any of these cases. Yet in three of them, the Court spoke generally of equitable restraint with respect to criminal prosecutions, cited *Douglas*, and restated its dictum in sweeping terms. Justice Douglas, on the other hand, in a dissenting opinion to another of these cases,[128] noted that "[i]njunction against the *commencement* of state court criminal proceedings has long been the first line of defense for federally secured rights,"[129] citing *Douglas* but apparently only as an unexplained deviation from the general rule.[130] . . .

Careful research has not disclosed a single case in the Supreme Court

128.   Pugach v. Dollinger, 365 U.S. 458 (1961).
129.   Id. at 462 n.3 (Douglas, J., dissenting) (emphasis in original).
130.   Id. *See also* Larson v. Domestic & Foreign Commerce Corp., 337 U.S. 682, 690 (1949) (Vinson, C.J., for the Court) ("injunctions against the threatened enforcement of unconstitutional statutes are familiar examples of" relief not barred by sovereign immunity) (dictum).

during the twenty-two year period from *Douglas* to *Dombrowski* in which the *Douglas* dictum was unambiguously applied to deny prospective relief in the face of threatened enforcement proceedings. *Stainback*[134] comes the closest and would be a clear exception but for the emphasis on the equitable nature of the enforcement proceedings. After 1949, the *Douglas* dictum survived in only three or four bits of dicta, while holding after holding went the other way.

The lower courts responded to these developments with considerable confusion. Some concluded that *Douglas* had been modified; some read it narrowly; some simply ignored it; some gave it lip service but decided prospective-relief cases on the merits anyway. Some concluded that *Douglas* did not apply to cases involving "vital" or "fundamental human liberties." But others considered and rejected the argument that it had been modified; still others applied it vigorously without acknowledging that anything had happened to cast doubt on it, or restated its dictum broadly in situations where it did not apply.

Simply counting these cases may underestimate the frequency with which prospective relief was granted, for the decisions that ignore *Douglas* cannot be found in any systematic way. But it is clear that lower federal courts decided claims for prospective relief on the merits considerably more often than not and that the Supreme Court routinely entertained such claims whenever they otherwise deserved plenary review. Thus, it is simply not true that the "doors of the federal equity court" were "long shut by *Douglas*."[154] Some courts were closed, but many others were not. What should have been important in the long run was that the doors to the Supreme Court stood open. These are the forgotten precedents; since *Dombrowski*, they have disappeared from the cases and the literature.

NOTES ON INJUNCTIONS WHILE A CRIMINAL PROSECUTION IS PENDING

1. Justice Black's history sweeps indiscriminately over all suits to enjoin enforcement of a state statute, whether or not a criminal prosecution is pending. But plaintiff sought an injunction against a pending prosecution, and *Younger*'s holding is limited to that situation. In a companion case, the Court held that a pending prosecution also bars a federal suit for a declaratory judgment that the state statute is unconstitutional. Samuels v. Mackell, 401 U.S. 66 (1971). The Court said that even though such a declaratory judgment would not mention the pending prosecution, it

---

134. Stainback v. Mo Hock Ke Lok Po, 336 U.S. 368 (1949).
154. Fiss, *Dombrowski*, 86 Yale L.J. 1103, 1163 (1977).

would have the same effect as an injunction: It would effectively preclude further prosecution.

2. Does a pending prosecution eliminate the *Young* dilemma? If plaintiff has already violated the statute, hasn't he already incurred the risk of penalties? If the statute is constitutional, he can be punished for that violation; if not, he can't be. In terms of the *Young* dilemma, it doesn't matter whether the constitutional issue is decided in the criminal case or a separate injunction case.

3. But what if he wants to pass out leaflets again? Doesn't he still face the choice between risking additional penalties or forfeiting his asserted constitutional rights? Isn't that exactly the *Young* dilemma? Isn't that dilemma especially acute if he wants to pass out leaflets without waiting for the end of the criminal prosecution? There has been no ruling on his constitutional claim, and the prosecutor's attention is focused on him.

That issue was raised in Roe v. Wade, 410 U.S. 113 (1973). One of the plaintiffs, Dr. Hallford, had been indicted for performing abortions. He conceded that the federal court could not enjoin his pending prosecution. But he sought injunctions against any additional prosecutions for future violations. Every day patients came to his clinic. Every day he had to decide whether to risk additional felony prosecutions or turn those patients away, knowing that long before his criminal case was decided, it would be too late for those patients to abort. Without analysis, the Court found "no merit" in the distinction between past and future violations. Id. at 126.

4. How did the pending prosecution help Dr. Hallford? Isn't the prosecution for past violations irrelevant to the *Young* dilemma with respect to future violations? Doesn't he really need a preliminary injunction? Consider this analysis of the difference between the equitable and criminal remedies:

> Three important powers of equity courts are not available to criminal courts in Anglo-American jurisprudence: the power to give interlocutory relief, the power to give prospective relief, and the power to give class relief. Interlocutory relief is used here to mean relief available before the end of litigation, based on a tentative assessment of the law and facts, to minimize hardship pending final adjudication of the merits. . . . Class relief means relief given to a defined class of litigants, as under Federal Civil Rule of Procedure 23 or comparable state procedures. . . .
>
> Prospective relief in this context means relief directed to contemplated future violations of the challenged statute — an injunction against enforcement or a binding judgment that the statute cannot constitutionally be applied to the contemplated conduct.

Laycock, Federal Interference with State Prosecutions: The Need for Prospective Relief, 1977 Sup. Ct. Rev. 193, 199-200.

5. How significant are those differences? Is Hallford's case different from Ex parte Young because the pending prosecution promises an eventual end to his *Young* dilemma? Relief may not be as quick as a preliminary injunction, and he and some patients may suffer irreparable injury pending final judgment. But that is only temporary. Doesn't the criminal case virtually ensure that the constitutional challenge will soon be decided? Once there is a final judgment, Dr. Hallford will know his constitutional rights.

6. There is something to that argument, but not as much as appears at first reading. Why should the criminal defendant have to suffer irreparable injury pending trial? Does "Our Federalism" justify the irreparable loss of constitutional rights? Where does it say that in the Constitution? Doesn't Black need a new amendment: "The rights guaranteed by this constitution shall not be enforced when to do so would be offensive to state sensibilities and the loss of rights is only temporary."

This temporary irreparable injury may last a long time. The criminal case may not reach the constitutional issue; the court is obligated to decide on nonconstitutional grounds if it can. Consider the case of Sanford Zwickler, who made two trips to the Supreme Court of the United States and a separate trip to the New York Court of Appeals without getting a ruling on his constitutional claim. Zwickler was convicted of passing out anonymous leaflets opposing a congressman's campaign for re-election in 1964. The Appellate Division reversed his conviction on the facts of the particular violation: The state failed to prove he passed out leaflets "in quantity" as the statute required. The New York Court of Appeals affirmed on the same ground. People v. Zwickler, 16 N.Y.2d 1069, 213 N.E.2d 467 (1965). Even so, the federal district court thought he should keep trying state remedies. Zwickler v. Koota, 261 F. Supp. 985 (E.D.N.Y. 1966). The Supreme Court reversed and remanded for consideration of the merits. 389 U.S. 241 (1967). By the time the case got back to the Supreme Court again, two more congressional elections had come and gone, the congressman had become a judge, and the Court held the case moot. Golden v. Zwickler, 394 U.S. 103 (1969).

Like *Zwickler,* a large proportion of all *Younger* cases involve political speech, where time is of the essence. It doesn't do much good to pass out election leaflets after the election.

7. Even if the criminal court holds the law unconstitutional, it cannot enjoin future prosecutions. The acquitted defendant must rely on stare decisis and res judicata for protection. That will often be sufficient. But often it won't be. Trial court decisions have no stare decisis effect, and the state is unlikely to be barred by res judicata on a question of law it could not appeal. The prosecutor may acquiesce, but then again he may not.

Consider the following examples:

It is easy . . . to overestimate the informal consequences of a criminal judgment. Many *Younger* cases involve bitter disputes. Dombrowski v. Pfister,[46] Cameron v. Johnson,[47] O'Shea v. Littleton,[48] and Allee v. Medrano[49] involved prolonged battles between entrenched local power structures and political activists seeking a share of that power. Huffman v. Pursue, Ltd.,[50] Hicks v. Miranda,[51] and Doran v. Salem Inn, Inc.[52] pitted profitable businesses against officials determined to shut them down. In Gibson v. Berryhill,[53] a substantial portion of the income of every independent optometrist in Alabama was believed to be at stake. In such litigation, neither side is likely to give up until every legal possibility is exhausted or until the federal plaintiffs are financially unable to continue. Dombrowski[54] and Cameron v. Johnson[55] went to the Supreme Court twice. *Allee*[56] spent eight years getting there the first time, and there was a related state appeal.[57] After two opinions indicating the probable unconstitutionality of one ordinance regulating the Salem Inn,[58] the Town of North Hempstead enacted another.[59] After that was struck down,[60] the State of New York initiated liquor license revocation proceedings.[61] With nothing but principle at stake for either side, the plaintiff in Wooley v. Maynard was arrested three times in five weeks.[62]

When passengers sought to integrate the Jackson, Mississippi, bus terminal, more than 300 prosecutions were brought.[63] There were fifteen directed acquittals,[64] and the Supreme Court ordered a single judge to hold the statute unconstitutional, finding the state's contentions so frivolous that a three-judge court was not required.[65] But these developments did not cause the prosecutor to acquiesce, and due to standing problems the prosecutions were not enjoined.[66] There were 300 convictions. Many defendants gave up for lack of

46. 380 U.S. 479 (1965).
47. 390 U.S. 611 (1968).
48. 414 U.S. 488 (1974).
49. 416 U.S. 802 (1974).
50. 420 U.S. 592 (1975).
51. 422 U.S. 332 (1975).
52. 422 U.S. 922 (1975).
53. 411 U.S. 564 (1973).
54. Dombrowski v. Eastland, 387 U.S. 82 (1967); Dombrowski v. Pfister, 380 U.S. 479 (1965).
55. 390 U.S. 611 (1968); 381 U.S. 741 (1965).
56. 416 U.S. at 805-11.
57. United Farm Wkrs. Organ. Comm. v. La Casita Farms, Inc., 439 S.W.2d 398 (Tex. Civ. App. 1968).
58. Salem Inn, Inc. v. Frank, 501 F.2d 18 (2d Cir. 1974).
59. Salem Inn, Inc. v. Frank, 522 F.2d 1045, 1046 (2d Cir. 1975).
60. Id. at 1047.
61. Salem Inn, Inc. v. Frank, 408 F. Supp. 852 (E.D.N.Y. 1976).
62. 430 U.S. 705, 712 (1977).
63. Lusky, Racial Discrimination and The Federal Law: A Problem in Nullification, 63 Colum. L. Rev. 1163, 1179-1180 (1963).
64. Id. at 1180.
65. Bailey v. Patterson, 369 U.S. 31, 33-34 (1962).
66. Id. at 32-33.

funds, and the appeals of the others dragged through the state courts[67] while various federal litigants made two more trips to the Court of Appeals.[68]

The Supreme Court's docket includes an unusually high percentage of such bitterly fought cases, but they exist throughout the system. The press reported recently that the United States attorney for the District of New Mexico pledged to prosecute violations of the Antiquities Act of 1906[69] "with vigor, wherever they occur,"[70] despite repeated rulings that the act was unconstitutionally vague.[71] Chicago's disorderly-house ordinance[72] is still enforced[73] after having been held unconstitutional.[74] Professor Amsterdam has collected his own set of examples.[75] Where a challenge is to a statute as applied, the prosecutor may find it especially easy to justify not acquiescing in an initial adverse decision. The point is not that judgments have no informal effects but that such effects cannot be relied on in place of judicial prospective relief.

Laycock, Federal Interference with State Prosecutions: The Need for Prospective Relief, 1977 Sup. Ct. Rev. 193, 200-202.

8.   What is the significance of class relief? Consider Allee v. Medrano, 416 U.S. 802 (1974), a case involving migrant farm workers and their attempts to organize a union. Is it an adequate remedy to acquit Medrano? Even if he is free to speak and picket, isn't he helpless if the rest of his movement is not free to do so as well? If there is some doubt whether Medrano can safely rely on an acquittal, there is even less reason to believe others similarly situated can safely rely on it.

9.   Quite apart from any difference between state and federal courts, isn't it clear that equitable remedies are better than defense of a criminal prosecution? And isn't that the traditional test of irreparable injury?

The Court might have argued that these defects in the criminal remedy are simply costs that must be paid to preserve the independence of the state courts. It didn't make that argument; instead, it overlooked the defects and pretended that defense of a criminal prosecution was an

67.   Lusky, note 63 supra, at 1180.

68.   Bailey v. Patterson, 323 F.2d 201 (5th Cir. 1963); United States v. City of Jackson, 318 F.2d 1 (5th Cir. 1963).

69.   16 U.S.C. §433 (1970).

70.   "Warn artifact diggers on U.S. land despite court ruling," Chicago Sun-Times, 29 Aug. 1977, p.26, col. 1, reporting United States v. Camazine (D.N.M. 1977).

71.   United States v. Diaz, 499 F.2d 113 (9th Cir. 1974); United States v. Camazine, Chicago Sun-Times, 29 Aug. 1977, p.26, col. 1 (D.N.M. 1977).

72.   See Foster v. Zeeko, 540 F.2d 1310, 1311 (7th Cir. 1976).

73.   Counsel in Foster v. Zeeko, note 72 supra, stated in an interview that he has been retained by another client arrested in a situation substantially identical with the one there.

74.   Foster v. Zeeko, No. 73 C 891 (N.D. Ill. 1975), rev'd in part, on other grounds, 540 F.2d 1310 (7th Cir. 1976).

75.   Amsterdam, Criminal Prosecution Affecting Federally Guaranteed Civil Rights: Federal Removal and Habeas Corpus Jurisdiction to Abort State Court Trial, 113 U. Pa. L. Rev. 793, 841-42 (1965).

adequate remedy. When Justice Black talks about chilling effect in *Younger*, he refers only to the special case of the overbreadth doctrine — the rule that litigants whose speech was not constitutionally protected may nonetheless be acquitted if they are prosecuted under a law that forbids lots of protected speech as well. Broadrick v. Oklahoma, 413 U.S. 601 (1973). In his discussion of the general rule that defense of a criminal prosecution is an adequate remedy, he refers only to the "cost, anxiety, and inconvenience of having to defend." In all the litigation over prospective relief, only Chief Justice Stone ever squarely acknowledged the *Young* dilemma and argued that other considerations outweigh the need to relieve from it. AFL v. Watson, 327 U.S. 582, 600 (1946) (dissenting).

10. How plausible is the argument that federalism requires litigants to put up with inadequacies in the criminal defense? Professor Fiss has suggested that the important federalism decisions were made in the supremacy clause, the Judiciary Act of 1789, and the Reconstruction amendments: Federal constitutional rights control, and the Supreme Court has the last word. Fiss, *Dombrowski*, 86 Yale L.J. 1103, 1107 (1977). He thinks it is a cosmetic deference to give state courts the first word. Justice Black does not question that federal law controls. Why is it so important for the state to be the judge in its own case?

Might federalism considerations actually argue in favor of plaintiffs? The Constitution defines the structure of federalism. If the Constitution authorizes Congress to confer jurisdiction on federal courts, and if it authorizes Congress to enforce the fourteenth amendment against the states, and if pursuant to those powers Congress finds that state courts are actively hostile to federal rights and that it is essential to give citizens an option to litigate these claims in federal court, shouldn't the Court honor the resulting grant of jurisdiction? In short, are the premises of *Younger* consistent with the premises of Mitchum v. Foster? *Mitchum* is discussed in the notes immediately preceding *Younger*; it held that §1983 is an expressly authorized exception to the anti-injunction act.

11. Suppose plaintiffs sue in state court to enjoin enforcement of state law. Would there be any reason to defer to the criminal remedy? What about Justice Black's fear that suits to enjoin enforcement lead to abstract decisions of constitutional questions? That too seems mainly directed at the overbreadth doctrine. The overbreadth doctrine makes a law unenforceable if a litigant can imagine situations in which the law would be unconstitutional, even though those situations are not his situation. That is a clear invitation to hypothetical decision making. That is why the overbreadth doctrine was substantially narrowed in *Broadrick*.

Is there any problem apart from the overbreadth doctrine? If plaintiff plans a specific course of conduct, isn't there a real and concrete controversy about whether that conduct can be punished? Can plaintiff's plans ever be as concrete as his past violation? But can't the court deny relief in particular cases where plaintiff's plans aren't concrete enough for sound adjudication?

STEFFEL v. THOMPSON
415 U.S. 452 (1974)

[Steffel and his friend Becker were passing out antiwar leaflets in a shopping center. They were threatened with arrest and prosecution for trespassing if they persisted. Steffel quit passing out leaflets; Becker continued and was prosecuted. Both then filed this action seeking an injunction against enforcement and a declaratory judgment that the criminal trespass statute was being applied in violation of their first amendment rights. The state court voluntarily stayed Becker's prosecution pending the federal case.

The Fifth Circuit denied relief. It read *Younger* to preclude an injunction whether or not a state prosecution was pending, and it thought that Samuels v. Mackell barred declaratory judgments in any case in which *Younger* barred injunctions. Only Steffel petitioned for certiorari, and he sought review only as to the declaratory judgment.]

MR. JUSTICE BRENNAN delivered the opinion of the Court. . . .

When no state criminal proceeding is pending at the time the federal complaint is filed, federal intervention does not result in duplicative legal proceedings or disruption of the state criminal justice system; nor can federal intervention, in that circumstance, be interpreted as reflecting negatively upon the state court's ability to enforce constitutional principles. In addition, while a pending state prosecution provides the federal plaintiff with a concrete opportunity to vindicate his constitutional rights, a refusal on the part of the federal courts to intervene when no state proceeding is pending may place the hapless plaintiff between the Scylla of intentionally flouting state law and the Charybdis of forgoing what he believes to be constitutionally protected activity in order to avoid becoming enmeshed in a criminal proceeding. Cf. Dombrowski v. Pfister, 380 U.S. 479, 490 (1965).

When no state proceeding is pending and thus considerations of equity, comity, and federalism have little vitality, the propriety of granting federal declaratory relief may properly be considered independently of a request for injunctive relief. Here, the Court of Appeals held that, because injunctive relief would not be appropriate since petitioner failed to demonstrate irreparable injury — a traditional prerequisite to injunctive relief, e.g., Dombrowski v. Pfister, supra — it followed that declaratory relief was also inappropriate. Even if the Court of Appeals correctly viewed injunctive relief as inappropriate — a question we need not reach today since petitioner has abandoned his request for that remedy[12] — the court erred in treating the requests for injunctive and declaratory relief as a single issue. "[W]hen no state prosecution is pending and the only question is whether declaratory relief is appropriate[,] . . . the congressional scheme that makes the federal courts the primary guardians of constitutional rights, and the express congressional authorization of declaratory relief, afforded because it is a less harsh and abrasive remedy than the injunction, become the factors of primary significance." Perez v. Ledesma, 401 U.S. 82, 104 (1971) (separate opinion of Brennan, J.).

The subject matter jurisdiction of the lower federal courts was greatly expanded in the wake of the Civil War. A pervasive sense of nationalism led to enactment of the Civil Rights Act of 1871, empowering the lower federal courts to determine the constitutionality of actions, taken by persons under color of state law, allegedly depriving other individuals of rights guaranteed by the Constitution and federal law, see 42 U.S.C. §1983, 28 U.S.C. §1343(3). Four years later, in the Judiciary Act of March 3, 1875, Congress conferred upon the lower federal courts, for but the second time in their nearly century-old history, general federal-question jurisdiction subject only to a jurisdictional-amount requirement, see 28 U.S.C. §1331. With this latter enactment, the lower federal courts "ceased to be restricted tribunals of fair dealing between citizens of different states and became the *primary* and powerful reliances for vindicating every right given by the Constitution, the laws, and treaties of the United States." F. Frankfurter & J. Landis, The Business of the Supreme Court 65 (1928) (emphasis added). These two statutes, together with the Court's decision in Ex parte Young, 209 U.S. 123 (1908) — holding that state officials who threaten to enforce an unconstitutional state statute may be enjoined by a federal court of equity and that a federal court may, in appropriate circumstances, enjoin future state criminal prosecutions under the unconstitutional Act — have "established the modern framework for federal protection of constitutional rights from state interference." Perez v. Ledesma, supra, at 107 (separate opinion of Brennan, J.). . . .

Congress in 1934 enacted the Declaratory Judgment Act, 28 U.S.C. §§2201-2202. That Congress plainly intended declaratory relief to act as an alternative to the strong medicine of the injunction and to be utilized to test the constitutionality of state criminal statutes in cases where in-

---

12. We note that, in those cases where injunctive relief has been sought to restrain an imminent, but not yet pending, prosecution *for past conduct*, sufficient injury has not been found to warrant injunctive relief, see Beal v. Missouri Pacific R. Co., 312 U.S. 45 (1941); Spielman Motor Sales Co. v. Dodge, 295 U.S. 89 (1935); Fenner v. Boykin, 271 U.S. 240 (1926). There is some question, however, whether a showing of irreparable injury might be made in a case where, although no prosecution is pending or impending, an individual demonstrates that he will be required to forgo constitutionally protected activity in order to avoid arrest. Compare Dombrowski v. Pfister, 380 U.S. 479 (1965); Hygrade Provision Co. v. Sherman, 266 U.S. 497 (1925); and Terrace v. Thompson, 263 U.S. 197, 214, 216 (1923), with Douglas v. City of Jeannette, 319 U.S. 157 (1943).

junctive relief would be unavailable is amply evidenced by the legislative history of the Act, traced in full detail in Perez v. Ledesma, supra, at 111-115 (separate opinion of Brennan, J.). . . .

The "different considerations" entering into a decision whether to grant declaratory relief have their origins in the preceding historical summary. First, as Congress recognized in 1934, a declaratory judgment will have a less intrusive effect on the administration of state criminal laws. As was observed in Perez v. Ledesma, 401 U.S., at 124-126 (separate opinion of Brennan, J.):

> Of course, a favorable declaratory judgment may nevertheless be valuable to the plaintiff though it cannot make even an unconstitutional statute disappear. A state statute may be declared unconstitutional in toto — that is, incapable of having constitutional applications; or it may be declared unconstitutionally vague or overbroad — that is, incapable of being constitutionally applied to the full extent of its purport. In either case, a federal declaration of unconstitutionality reflects the opinion of the federal court that the statute cannot be fully enforced. If a declaration of total unconstitutionality is affirmed by this Court, it follows that this Court stands ready to reverse any conviction under the statute. If a declaration of partial unconstitutionality is affirmed by this Court, the implication is that this Court will overturn particular applications of the statute, but that if the statute is narrowly construed by the state courts it will not be incapable of constitutional applications. Accordingly, the declaration does not necessarily bar prosecutions under the statute, as a broad injunction would. Thus, where the highest court of a State has had an opportunity to give a statute regulating expression a narrowing or clarifying construction but has failed to do so, and later a federal court declares the statute unconstitutionally vague or overbroad, it may well be open to a state prosecutor, after the federal court decision, to bring a prosecution under the statute if he reasonably believes that the defendant's conduct is not constitutionally protected and that the state courts may give the statute a construction so as to yield a constitutionally valid conviction. Even where a declaration of unconstitutionality is not reviewed by this Court, the declaration may still be able to cut down the deterrent effect of an unconstitutional state statute. The persuasive force of the court's opinion and judgment may lead state prosecutors, courts, and legislators to reconsider their respective responsibilities toward the statute. Enforcement policies or judicial construction may be changed, or the legislature may repeal the statute and start anew. Finally, the federal court judgment may have some res judicata effect, though this point is not free from difficulty and the governing rules remain to be developed with a view to the proper workings of a federal system. What is clear, however, is that even though a declaratory judgment has "the force and effect of a final judgment," 28 U.S.C. §2201, it is a much milder form of relief than an injunction. Though it may be persuasive, it is not ultimately coercive; noncompliance with it may be inappropriate, but is not contempt.

(Footnote omitted.)

Second, engrafting upon the Declaratory Judgment Act a requirement that all of the traditional equitable prerequisites to the issuance of an injunction be satisfied before the issuance of a declaratory judgment is considered would defy Congress' intent to make declaratory relief available in cases where an injunction would be inappropriate. . . . Thus, the Court of Appeals was in error when it ruled that a failure to demonstrate irreparable injury — a traditional prerequisite to injunctive relief, having no equivalent in the law of declaratory judgments, see Aetna Life Ins. Co. v. Haworth, 300 U.S. 227, 241 (1937); Nashville, C. & St. L.R. Co. v. Wallace, 288 U.S. 249, 264 (1933) — precluded the granting of declaratory relief.

The only occasions where this Court has disregarded these "different considerations" and found that a preclusion of injunctive relief inevitably led to a denial of declaratory relief have been cases in which principles of federalism militated altogether against federal intervention in a class of adjudications. See Great Lakes Co. v. Huffman, 319 U.S. 293 (1943) (federal policy against interfering with the enforcement of state tax laws); Samuels v. Mackell, 401 U.S. 66 (1971). In the instant case, principles of federalism not only do not preclude federal intervention, they compel it. Requiring the federal courts totally to step aside when no state criminal prosecution is pending against the federal plaintiff would turn federalism on its head. When federal claims are premised on 42 U.S.C. §1983 and 28 U.S.C. §1343(3) — as they are here — we have not required exhaustion of state judicial or administrative remedies, recognizing the paramount role Congress has assigned to the federal courts to protect constitutional rights. See, e.g., Monroe v. Pape, 365 U.S. 167 (1961). But exhaustion of state remedies is precisely what would be required if both federal injunctive and declaratory relief were unavailable in a case where no state prosecution had been commenced. . . .

We therefore hold that, regardless of whether injunctive relief may be appropriate, federal declaratory relief is not precluded when no state prosecution is pending and a federal plaintiff demonstrates a genuine threat of enforcement of a disputed state criminal statute, whether an attack is made on the constitutionality of the statute on its face or as applied. The judgment of the Court of Appeals is reversed, and the case is remanded for further proceedings consistent with this opinion.

It is so ordered.

MR. JUSTICE REHNQUIST, with whom THE CHIEF JUSTICE joins, concurring.

I concur in the opinion of the Court. Although my reading of the legislative history of the Declaratory Judgment Act of 1934 suggests that its primary purpose was to enable persons to obtain a definition of their rights before an actual injury had occurred, rather than to palliate any controversy arising from Ex parte Young, 209 U.S. 123 (1908). Congress apparently was aware at the time it passed the Act that persons threatened with state criminal prosecutions might choose to forgo the offending conduct and instead seek a federal declaration of their rights. Use of the declaratory judgment procedure in the circumstances presented by this case seems consistent with that congressional expectation. . . .

First, the legislative history of the Declaratory Judgment Act and the Court's opinion in this case both recognize that the declaratory judgment procedure is an alternative to pursuit of the arguably illegal activity. There is nothing in the Act's history to suggest that Congress intended to provide persons wishing to violate state laws with a federal shield behind which they could carry on their contemplated conduct. Thus I do not believe that a federal plaintiff in a declaratory judgment action can avoid, by the mere filing of a complaint, the principles so firmly expressed in *Samuels*, supra. The plaintiff who continues to violate a state statute after the filing of his federal complaint does so both at the risk of state prosecution and at the risk of dismissal of his federal lawsuit. For any arrest prior to resolution of the federal action would constitute a pending prosecution and bar declaratory relief under the principles of *Samuels*.

Second, I do not believe that today's decision can properly be raised to support the issuance of a federal injunction based upon a favorable declaratory judgment. The Court's description of declaratory relief as "'a milder alternative to the injunction remedy,'" having a "less intrusive effect on the administration of state criminal laws" than an injunction, indicates to me critical distinctions which make declaratory relief appropriate where injunctive relief would not be. It would all but totally obscure these important distinctions if a successful application for declaratory relief came to be regarded, not as the conclusion of a lawsuit, but as a giant step toward obtaining an injunction against a subsequent criminal prosecution. The availability of injunctive relief must be considered with an eye toward the important policies of federalism which this Court has often recognized. . . .

A declaratory judgment is simply a statement of rights, not a binding order supplemented by continuing sanctions. State authorities may choose to be guided by the judgment of a lower federal court, but they are not compelled to follow the decision by threat of contempt or other penalties. If the federal plaintiff pursues the conduct for which he was previously threatened with arrest and is in fact arrested, he may not return the controversy to federal court, although he may, of course, raise the federal declaratory judgment in the state court for whatever value it may prove to have.[3] In any event, the defendant at that point is able to

3. The Court's opinion notes that the possible res judicata effect of a federal declaratory judgment in a subsequent state court prosecution is a question "'not free from difficulty.'" I express no opinion on that issue here. However, I do note that the federal decision would not be accorded the stare decisis effect in state court that it would have in a subsequent proceeding within the same federal jurisdiction. Although the state court would not be compelled to follow the federal holding, the opinion might, of course, be viewed as highly persuasive.

present his case for full consideration by a state court charged, as are the federal courts, to preserve the defendant's constitutional rights. Federal interference with this process would involve precisely the same concerns discussed in *Younger* and recited in the Court's opinion in this case.

Third, attempts to circumvent *Younger* by claiming that enforcement of a statute declared unconstitutional by a federal court is per se evidence of bad faith should not find support in the Court's decision in this case. As the Court notes, quoting my Brother Brennan's separate opinion in Perez v. Ledesma, 401 U.S. 82, 125:

> The persuasive force of the [federal] court's opinion and judgment *may* lead state prosecutors, courts, and legislators to reconsider their respective responsibilities toward the statute. Enforcement policies or judicial construction *may* be changed, or the legislature *may* repeal the statute and start anew.

(Emphasis added.) This language clearly recognizes that continued belief in the constitutionality of the statute by state prosecutorial officials would not commonly be indicative of bad faith and that such allegations, in the absence of highly unusual circumstances, would not justify a federal court's departure from the general principles of restraint discussed in *Younger*.

If the declaratory judgment remains, as I think the Declaratory Judgment Act intended, a simple declaration of rights without more, it will not be used merely as a dramatic tactical maneuver on the part of any state defendant seeking extended delays. Nor will it force state officials to try cases time after time, first in the federal courts and then in the state courts. I do not believe Congress desired such unnecessary results, and I do not think that today's decision should be read to sanction them. Rather the Act, and the decision, stand for the sensible proposition that both a potential state defendant, threatened with prosecution but not charged, and the State itself, confronted by a possible violation of its criminal laws, may benefit from a procedure which provides for a declaration of rights without activation of the criminal process. If the federal court finds that the threatened prosecution would depend upon a statute it judges unconstitutional, the State may decide to forgo prosecution of similar conduct in the future, believing the judgment persuasive. Should the state prosecutors not find the decision persuasive enough to justify forbearance, the successful federal plaintiff will at least be able to bolster his allegations of unconstitutionality in the state trial with a decision of the federal district court in the immediate locality. The state courts may find the reasoning convincing even though the prosecutors did not. Finally, of course, the state legislature may decide, on the basis of the federal decision, that the statute would be better amended or repealed. All these possible avenues of relief would be reached voluntarily by the States and would be completely consistent with the concepts of federalism discussed above. Other more intrusive forms of relief should not be routinely available. . . .

[JUSTICE WHITE concurred for the sole purpose of responding to JUSTICE REHNQUIST.]. . .

It should be noted, first, that his views on these issues are neither expressly nor impliedly embraced by the Court's opinion filed today. Second, my own tentative views on these questions are somewhat contrary to my Brother's.

At this writing at least, I would anticipate that a final declaratory judgment entered by a federal court holding particular conduct of the federal plaintiff to be immune on federal constitutional grounds from prosecution under state law should be accorded res judicata effect in any later prosecution of that very conduct. There would also, I think, be additional circumstances in which the federal judgment should be considered as more than a mere precedent bearing on the issue before the state court.

Neither can I at this stage agree that the federal court, having rendered a declaratory judgment in favor of the plaintiff, could not enjoin a later state prosecution for conduct that the federal court has declared immune. The Declaratory Judgment Act itself provides that a "declaration shall have the force and effect of a final judgment or decree," 28 U.S.C. §2201; eminent authority anticipated that declaratory judgments would be res judicata, E. Borchard, Declaratory Judgments 10-11 (2d ed. 1941); and there is every reason for not reducing declaratory judgments to mere advisory opinions. Toucey v. New York Life Insurance Co., 314 U.S. 118 (1941), once expressed the view that 28 U.S.C. §2283 forbade injunctions against relitigation in state courts of federally decided issues, but the section was then amended to overrule that case, the consequence being that "[i]t is clear that the Toucey rule is gone, and that to protect or effectuate its judgment a federal court may enjoin relitigation in the state court." C. Wright, Federal Courts 180 (2d ed. 1970). I see no more reason here to hold that the federal plaintiff must always rely solely on his plea of res judicata in the state courts. The statute provides for "[f]urther necessary or proper relief . . . against any adverse party whose rights have been determined by such judgment," 28 U.S.C. §2202, and it would not seem improper to enjoin local prosecutors who refuse to observe adverse federal judgments.

Finally, I would think that a federal suit challenging a state criminal statute on federal constitutional grounds could be sufficiently far along so that ordinary consideration of economy would warrant refusal to dismiss the federal case solely because a state prosecution has subsequently been filed and the federal question may be litigated there.

NOTES ON PROSPECTIVE RELIEF WHEN NO PROSECUTION IS PENDING

1. Isn't *Steffel* just a watered down version of Ex parte Young? Isr' Justice Brennan's Scylla and Charybdis just a restatement of the Yo'g

dilemma? Why isn't that dilemma irreparable injury anymore? But does it matter whether the Court calls the injury irreparable, as long as it provides a remedy?

2. In Samuels v. Mackell, 401 U.S. 66 (1971), the Court said that a pending prosecution bars a declaratory judgment that the statute is unconstitutional, because the declaratory judgment would stop the prosecution as effectively as an injunction. Is that consistent with *Steffel's* elaborate explanation of the differences between the two remedies? Is it consistent with the limits Justice Rehnquist would put on the declaratory judgment? In Rehnquist's view, what's the difference between a declaratory judgment and a law review article?

Which of these views of the declaratory judgment is closest to reality? In practice, declaratory judgments that statutes are unconstitutional appear to have been as effective as injunctions against enforcement. And such declaratory judgments have once again become routine. The cases from the late 1970s are collected in Laycock, Federal Interference with State Prosecutions: The Cases *Dombrowski* Forgot, 46 U. Chi. L. Rev. 636, 665 n.191 (1979).

3. Justices Rehnquist and White debate the effect of a criminal prosecution initiated after plaintiff filed his federal suit for a declaratory judgment. The Court faced that issue in Hicks v. Miranda, 422 U.S. 332 (1975). White wrote the opinion, and he and Rehnquist resolved their disagreements. The Court held that the federal proceeding must be dismissed if a prosecution is commenced "before any proceedings of substance on the merits." Id. at 349. Any other rule would "trivialize the principles of Younger v. Harris." Id. at 350. Four dissenters thought the majority trivialized *Steffel*. Id. at 353 (Stewart, J., dissenting).

Professor Fiss has described *Hicks* as creating a "reverse removal power." Fiss, *Dombrowski*, 86 Yale L.J. 1103, 1134-1136 (1977). He refers to federal statutes authorizing state-court defendants to remove state cases to federal court if they could have been filed there originally, 28 U.S.C. §1441 (1982), or in certain other circumstances enumerated in §1441 to §1451 of Title 28.

4. There is nothing in *Hicks* to prevent the prosecutor from routinely prosecuting anyone who files a suit challenging the constitutionality of a state statute. Is there anything the federal plaintiff can do to counteract this reverse removal power? Doesn't the prosecutor have to have some colorable violation to charge in the indictment or information? Should persons challenging the constitutionality of state laws sue early, and refrain from violations until there have been "proceedings of substance on the merits" in the federal case?

5. What are "proceedings of substance on the merits"? The Court didn't say. In *Hicks*, the trial court had denied a temporary restraining order, in part because plaintiffs had failed to show probability of success on the merits. Each side had filed substantial written submissions on the motion for TRO, and the court had held it under advisement for nearly a

month. Presumably these were not "substantial proceedings on the merits," but the majority did not explain why not, or how much more was required.

NOTES ON RIPENESS

1. *Steffel* requires the federal plaintiff to beat the prosecutor to the courthouse, and *Hicks* requires him to win the race by a wide margin. But the ripeness requirement prevents him from getting there too early; he must show a real threat of prosecution. These rules have a potential for squeezing litigants out of federal court altogether, with half the cases being dismissed as unripe and the rest being dismissed because there is a pending prosecution.

2. Whether this happens largely depends on the administration of the ripeness requirement. Most of the Court's cases hold or assume that a suit to enjoin enforcement is ripe when the statute is on the books and plaintiff wants to violate it. But a few cases suggest that plaintiff must receive something equivalent to a personal threat from the prosecutor before he can sue. Justice Stewart filed a concurrence in *Steffel* that suggested an extraordinarily stringent ripeness requirement; Chief Justice Burger joined in that concurrence:

> Our decision today must not be understood as authorizing the invocation of federal declaratory judgment jurisdiction by a person who thinks a state criminal law is unconstitutional, even if he genuinely feels "chilled" in his freedom of action by the law's existence, and even if he honestly entertains the subjective belief that he may now or in the future be prosecuted under it. . . .
>
> The petitioner in this case has succeeded in objectively showing that the threat of imminent arrest, corroborated by the actual arrest of his companion, has created an actual concrete controversy between himself and the agents of the State. He has, therefore, demonstrated "a genuine threat of enforcement of a disputed state criminal statute. . . ." Cases where such a "genuine threat" can be demonstrated will, I think, be exceedingly rare.

415 U.S. at 476.

3. Is there any justification for such a stringent ripeness requirement? Isn't plaintiff's *Young* dilemma just as real whether or not the prosecutor has focused attention on him? Re-read the Note on Constitutional and Remedial Ripeness, supra at 223.

4. Stewart's concurrence has not carried the day. The Court continues to routinely entertain suits to declare statutes unconstitutional, invoking the ripeness requirement only occasionally. Justice Powell attempted to explain why in a dissenting opinion in Ellis v. Dyson, 421 U.S. 426, 447-449 (1975). Plaintiffs in *Ellis* challenged a Dallas loitering ordinance. Justice Stewart and Chief Justice Burger joined in this dissent:

In several cases we have found constitutional challenges to state and federal statutes justiciable despite the absence of actual threats of enforcement directed personally to the plaintiff. In each such case, however, the challenged statute applied particularly and unambiguously to activities in which the plaintiff regularly engaged or sought to engage. In each case the plaintiff claimed that the State or Federal Government, by prohibiting such activities, had exceeded substantive constitutional limitations on the reach of its powers. The plaintiffs, therefore, were put to a choice.[13] Unless declaratory relief was available, they were compelled to choose between a genuine risk of criminal prosecution and conformity to the challenged statute, a conformity that would require them to incur substantial deprivation either in tangible form or in forgoing the exercise of asserted constitutional rights. In such circumstances we have recognized that the challenged statute causes the plaintiff present harm, and that the "controversy is both immediate and real." Lake Carriers' Assn. v. MacMullan, 406 U.S. 498, 508 (1972).

Steffel does not depart from this general analysis. The difference between *Steffel* and the above cases lies in the nature of the statute involved. *Steffel* concerned a general trespass ordinance that did not, on its face, apply particularly to activities in which Steffel engaged or sought to engage. The statute was susceptible of a multitude of applications that would not even arguably exceed constitutional limitations on state power. But the threatened prosecution of Steffel, following the arrest and prosecution of his companion, demonstrated that the state officials construed the statute to apply to the precise activities in which Steffel had engaged and proposed to engage in the future. There was, therefore, no question that Steffel was confronted with a choice identical in principle and practical consequence to that faced by plaintiffs in the above cases: he could either risk criminal prosecution or forgo engaging in specific activities that he believed were protected by the First Amendment. Whichever choice he made, the harm to Steffel was real and immediate.

The pleadings in this case reveal no like circumstances. They merely aver that the Dallas ordinance has a "chilling" effect on First Amendment rights of speech and association. This averment, moreover, is related not to petitioners specifically, but rather to the "citizens of Dallas." While it is theoretically possible that the ordinance may be applied to infringe petitioners' First Amendment rights, nothing in the facts relating to their respective prior arrests and convictions indicates that the ordinance has been so applied to petitioners or indeed to anyone else. In short, petitioners rely entirely on a speculative deterrent effect that the Dallas ordinance conceivably could have on the exercise of constitutional rights by all Dallas citizens. The complaint nowhere alleges that the ordinance has been applied to particular activities, assertedly within the scope of First Amendment protection, in which *petitioners* regularly engage or in which they would engage but do not because of fear of prosecution.

421 U.S. at 447-449.

---

13. In all of these cases the statutes were not, through lack of enforcement, practical and legal nullities. *See* Poe v. Ullman, 367 U.S. 497 (1961).

The majority vacated *Ellis* for reconsideration in light of *Steffel* without reaching the ripeness issue or any other issue.

5.   If we take the Powell dissent in *Ellis* as the hard-liners' position on ripeness, ripeness isn't much of a problem, is it? Doesn't any plaintiff who clearly faces the *Young* dilemma have a ripe controversy? Isn't that the way it should be? Is it unreasonable to require the state to assert improbable applications of a statute before deciding the constitutionality of such applications?

6.   In Poe v. Ullman, cited in Justice Powell's footnote 13, the Court refused to decide a challenge to Connecticut's law forbidding the use of birth control. The statute had been on the books since 1879, and repeated modern attempts to repeal it had failed, but no one had ever been convicted of violating it. Condoms were openly sold in drugstores, but there were no birth control clinics anywhere in Connecticut. Plaintiffs were a private physician and some of his patients, who alleged that the law prevented him from giving them information about birth control. There were four dissents: Justices Black, Douglas, Harlan, and Stewart thought the case ripe. Weren't they right? Should plaintiffs have to worry about some prosecutor dusting off an old law and trying to enforce it?

The plurality relied in part on the tiny likelihood that these plaintiffs could ever be caught. Suppose the physician had alleged that he wished to open a birth control clinic. That violation could obviously have been detected, but the Court might still have thought the statute a dead letter. It would also have upset the plaintiffs' litigation strategy on the merits. Each of the plaintiff patients was carefully selected. One mother had given birth to three fatally deformed children in a row; the other had nearly died from her first pregnancy.

Poe was decided in June 1961. In November, the physician did open a birth control clinic. Ten days later he was arrested and closed the clinic. He was convicted and fined $100. On appeal, the Supreme Court held the statute unconstitutional. Griswold v. Connecticut, 381 U.S. 479 (1965).

DORAN v. SALEM INN
422 U.S. 922 (1975)

[Plaintiffs Salem Inn, Tim-Rob Bar, and M & L Restaurant all featured topless dancers. The Town of North Hempstead passed a new ordinance forbidding such entertainment. All three plaintiffs initially complied. On August 9, 1973, they filed this suit in federal court seeking a declaratory judgment that the ordinance was unconstitutional and a temporary restraining order and preliminary injunction against its enforcement. On August 10, M & L resumed topless dancing. The ordinance provided that each day's show was a separate offense; M & L and its dancers were served with criminal summonses on August 10, 11, 12, and 13. On Sep-

tember 6, the federal court held the ordinance unconstitutional and preliminarily enjoined its enforcement. It recognized that M & L's
complaint was barred by *Younger*, but thought it would be anomalous to
grant relief to two plaintiffs without granting it to the third. The Second
Circuit affirmed, noting that it was much more efficient to resolve all
three claims in one case instead of two.]

MR. JUSTICE REHNQUIST delivered the opinion of the Court. . . .

Turning to the *Younger* issues raised by petitioner, we are faced with
the necessity of determining whether the holdings of *Younger*, *Steffel*,
and Samuels v. Mackell, 401 U.S. 66 (1971), must give way before such
interests in efficient judicial administration as were relied upon by the
Court of Appeals. We think that the interest of avoiding conflicting out-
comes in the litigation of similar issues, while entitled to substantial deference in a unitary system, must of necessity be subordinated to the claims
of federalism in this particular area of the law. The classic example is the
petitioner in *Steffel* and his companion. Both were warned that failure to
cease pamphleteering would result in their arrest, but while the petitioner
in *Steffel* ceased and brought an action in the federal court, his companion did not cease and was prosecuted on a charge of criminal trespass in
the state court. The same may be said of the interest in conservation of
judicial manpower. As worthy a value as this is in a unitary system, the
very existence of one system of federal courts and 50 systems of state
courts, all charged with the responsibility for interpreting the United
States Constitution, suggests that on occasion there will be duplicating
and overlapping adjudication of cases which are sufficiently similar in
content, time, and location to justify being heard before a single judge
had they arisen within a unitary system.

We do not agree with the Court of Appeals, therefore, that all three
plaintiffs should automatically be thrown into the same hopper for *Younger* purposes, and should thereby each be entitled to injunctive relief. We
cannot accept that view, any more than we can accept petitioner's
equally Procrustean view that because M & L would have been barred
from injunctive relief had it been the sole plaintiff, Salem and Tim-Rob
should likewise be barred not only from injunctive relief but from declaratory relief as well. While there plainly may be some circumstances in
which legally distinct parties are so closely related that they should all be
subject to the *Younger* considerations which govern any one of them, this
is not such a case — while respondents are represented by common
counsel, and have similar business activities and problems, they are apparently unrelated in terms of ownership, control, and management. We
thus think that each of the respondents should be placed in the position
required by our cases as if that respondent stood alone.

Respondent M & L could have pursued the course taken by the other
respondents after the denial of their request for a temporary restraining

order. Had it done so, it would not have subjected itself to prosecution for violation of the ordinance in the state court. When the criminal summonses issued against M & L on the days immediately following the filing of the federal complaint, the federal litigation was in an embryonic stage and no contested matter had been decided. In this posture, M & L's prayer for injunction is squarely governed by *Younger*.

We likewise believe that for the same reasons Samuels v. Mackell bars M & L from obtaining declaratory relief, absent a showing of *Younger*'s special circumstances, even though the state prosecution was commenced the day following the filing of the federal complaint. Having violated the ordinance, rather than awaiting the normal development of its federal lawsuit, M & L cannot now be heard to complain that its constitutional contentions are being resolved in a state court. Thus M & L's prayers for both injunctive and declaratory relief are subject to *Younger*'s restrictions.

The rule with regard to the coplaintiffs, Salem and Tim-Rob, is equally clear, insofar as they seek declaratory relief. Salem and Tim-Rob were not subject to state criminal prosecution at any time prior to the issuance of a preliminary injunction by the District Court. Under *Steffel* they thus could at least have obtained a declaratory judgment upon an ordinary showing of entitlement to that relief. The District Court, however, did not grant declaratory relief to Salem and Tim-Rob, but instead granted them preliminary injunctive relief. Whether injunctions of future criminal prosecutions are governed by *Younger* standards is a question which we reserved in both *Steffel* and Younger v. Harris. We now hold that on the facts of this case the issuance of a preliminary injunction is not subject to the restrictions of *Younger*. The principle underlying *Younger* and *Samuels* is that state courts are fully competent to adjudicate constitutional claims, and therefore a federal court should, in all but the most exceptional circumstances, refuse to interfere with an ongoing state criminal proceeding. In the absence of such a proceeding, however, as we recognized in *Steffel*, a plaintiff may challenge the constitutionality of the state statute in federal court, assuming he can satisfy the requirements for federal jurisdiction.

No state proceedings were pending against either Salem or Tim-Rob at the time the District Court issued its preliminary injunction. Nor was there any question that they satisfied the requirements for federal jurisdiction. As we have already stated, they were assuredly entitled to declaratory relief, and since we have previously recognized that "[o]rdinarily . . . the practical effect of [injunctive and declaratory] relief will be virtually identical," *Samuels*, 401 U.S., at 73, we think that Salem and Tim-Rob were entitled to have their claims for preliminary injunctive relief considered without regard to *Younger*'s restrictions. At the conclusion of a successful federal challenge to a state statute or local ordinance, a district court can generally protect the interests of a federal plaintiff by entering a declaratory judgment, and therefore the stronger injunctive medicine will be unnecessary. But prior to final judgment there is no established declaratory remedy comparable to a preliminary injunction; unless preliminary relief is available upon a proper showing, plaintiffs in some situations may suffer unnecessary and substantial irreparable harm. Moreover, neither declaratory nor injunctive relief can directly interfere with enforcement of contested statutes or ordinances except with respect to the particular federal plaintiffs, and the State is free to prosecute others who may violate the statute. . . .

While we regard the question as a close one, we believe that the issuance of a preliminary injunction in behalf of respondents Salem and Tim-Rob was not an abuse of the District Court's discretion. As required to support such relief, these respondents alleged (and petitioner did not deny) that absent preliminary relief they would suffer a substantial loss of business and perhaps even bankruptcy. Certainly the latter type of injury sufficiently meets the standards for granting interim relief, for otherwise a favorable final judgment might well be useless.

The other inquiry relevant to preliminary relief is whether respondents made a sufficient showing of the likelihood of ultimate success on the merits. Both the District Court and the Court of Appeals found such a likelihood. The order of the District Court spoke in terms of actually holding the ordinance unconstitutional, but in the context of a preliminary injunction the court must have intended to refer only to the likelihood that respondents ultimately would prevail. The Court of Appeals properly clarified this point.

Although the customary "barroom" type of nude dancing may involve only the barest minimum of protected expression, we recognized in California v. LaRue, 409 U.S. 109, 118 (1972), that this form of entertainment might be entitled to First and Fourteenth Amendment protection under some circumstances. . . .

In these circumstances, and in the light of existing case law, we cannot conclude that the District Court abused its discretion by granting preliminary injunctive relief. . . . The judgment of the Court of Appeals is reversed as to respondent M & L, and affirmed as to respondents Salem and Tim-Rob.

It is so ordered.

NOTES ON PRELIMINARY INJUNCTIONS AGAINST PROSECUTION

1.   Justice Douglas dissented from the denial of relief to M & L.

2.   If Salem Inn might go bankrupt without a preliminary injunction, doesn't M & L face the same risk? Indeed, isn't M & L even more likely to

go bankrupt if its competitors continue to offer topless entertainment while it is deterred by repeated prosecutions? Does the Court satisfactorily explain why M & L shouldn't get the same preliminary protection Salem Inn gets?

3.   If you're representing a client who believes a statute is unconstitutional, how do you advise him after *Salem Inn*? How do you proceed if you're the prosecutor?

NOTES ON RELATED LITIGANTS IN *YOUNGER* LITIGATION

1.   The Court held that M & L's prosecution was irrelevant to Salem Inn. Similarly, it assumed that Becker's prosecution was irrelevant to Steffel. It apparently assumed that Dr. Hallford's prosecution was irrelevant to Jane Roe, the pregnant woman who got an injunction against enforcement of the Texas abortion statute in Roe v. Wade, 410 U.S. 113 (1973).

2.   The Court took a different view in Hicks v. Miranda, 422 U.S. 332 (1975). Miranda owned a theater that showed sexually explicit films. On November 26, the state seized four copies of the film "Deep Throat" and filed criminal charges against two of Miranda's employees, presumably the ticket seller and the projectionist. On November 29, Miranda filed his federal lawsuit seeking to enjoin enforcement of the statute. On January 15, the state prosecuted Miranda and his wholly owned corporation.

Hicks v. Miranda is best known for its holding that the federal action should have been dismissed when Miranda became a state defendant on January 15. But there was also an alternate holding. The Court thought that the interests of Miranda and his employees were "obviously . . . intertwined." 332 U.S. at 348-349. Miranda's lawyers represented his employees. "Absent a clear showing that appellees [Miranda and his corporation] . . . could not seek the return of their property in the state proceedings and see to it that their federal claims were presented there, the requirements of Younger v. Harris could not be avoided on the ground that no criminal prosecution was pending against appellees on the date the federal complaint was filed." Id. at 349.

3.   Should the same lawyers have represented both Miranda and his employees? Can those lawyers consider Miranda's interests when representing the employees? If the employees have a chance to plea bargain, should their lawyers consider that Miranda may want to use their prosecution to raise constitutional claims? The answer to all these questions is no. Miranda and his employees have conflicting interests, because they have vastly different stakes in the controversy. Why aren't their claims as independent as Becker's and Steffel's, or Salem Inn's and M & L's?

4.   In Allee v. Medrano, 416 U.S. 802 (1974), a union and its members

sued to enjoin police harassment, and to enjoin enforcement of Texas statutes that had been used to harass them. The record in the Supreme Court did not show whether any prosecutions were pending; the majority remanded for consideration in light of *Younger* and *Steffel*.

Chief Justice Burger filed a concurrence, in which Justices White and Rehnquist joined. The union had standing to assert the rights of its members; the Chief Justice thought it followed that the union was barred by *Younger* if there were a pending prosecution against any of its members. "Any other result would allow the easy circumvention of *Younger* by individuals who could assert their claims of First Amendment violations through an unincorporated association of those same individuals if the association is immune from *Younger* burdens." Id. at 831.

5.   Is the Chief Justice right? Compare the Court's view in *Salem Inn*: "[N]either declaratory nor injunctive relief can directly interfere with enforcement of statutes or ordinances except with respect to the particular federal plaintiffs, and the State is free to prosecute others who may violate the statute." Justices Burger, Rehnquist, and White joined both opinions. Can they be right both times? Can it be that the union is barred from suing by the prosecution of its members but gets no benefit if its members are acquitted on constitutional grounds? Should the *Salem Inn* dictum be limited to cases where the prosecution of one litigant does not bar a federal claim by the others?

Would prosecution of one union member forbid suits by all other union members? What result in a class action on behalf of all unprosecuted union members? What result in a suit by the union? The Chief Justice was only concurring, after all.

6.   Doesn't the *Salem Inn* dictum make clear that class relief is often needed in these cases? Doesn't the union in Allee v. Medrano need an order that protects the organization and the whole membership? What result if Salem Inn filed a class action on behalf of all establishments offering sexual entertainment?

7.   In Wooley v. Maynard, infra at 1230, plaintiffs were a husband and wife. The husband had been prosecuted three times for defacing the license plate on the family car. Are the prosecutions against him relevant to her suit in federal court?

8.   Can you identify any kind of rule to determine when a prosecution against one litigant will bar a federal suit by another litigant?

EDGAR v. MITE CORP.
457 U.S. 624 (1982)

JUSTICE WHITE delivered an opinion, Parts I, II, and V-B of which are the opinion of the Court.

The issue in this case is whether the Illinois Business Take-Over Act is unconstitutional under the Supremacy and Commerce Clauses of the Federal Constitution.

I

Appellee MITE Corporation and its wholly-owned subsidiary, MITE Holdings, Inc., are corporations organized under the laws of Delaware with their principal executive offices in Connecticut. Appellant James Edgar is the Secretary of State of Illinois and is charged with the administration and enforcement of the Illinois Act. Under the Illinois Act any takeover offer for the shares of a target company must be registered with the Secretary of State. . . .

On January 19, 1979, MITE initiated a cash tender offer for all outstanding shares of Chicago Rivet and Machine Co., a publicly held Illinois corporation, by filing a Schedule 14D-1 with the Securities and Exchange Commission in order to comply with the Williams Act. The Schedule 14D-1 indicated that MITE was willing to pay $28.00 per share for any and all outstanding shares of Chicago Rivet, a premium of approximately $4.00 over the then-prevailing market price. MITE did not comply with the Illinois Act, however, and commenced this litigation on the same day by filing an action in the United States District Court for the Northern District of Illinois. The complaint asked for a declaratory judgment that the Illinois Act was preempted by the Williams Act and violated the Commerce Clause. In addition, MITE sought a temporary restraining order and preliminary and permanent injunctions prohibiting the Illinois Secretary of State from enforcing the Illinois Act. . . .

On February 1, 1979, the Secretary of State notified MITE that he intended to issue an order requiring it to cease and desist further efforts to make a tender offer for Chicago Rivet. On February 2, 1979, Chicago Rivet notified MITE by letter that it would file suit in Illinois state court to enjoin the proposed tender offer. MITE renewed its request for injunctive relief in the District Court and on February 2 the District Court issued a preliminary injunction prohibiting the Secretary of State from enforcing the Illinois Act against MITE's tender offer for Chicago Rivet.

MITE then published its tender offer in the February 5 edition of the Wall Street Journal. The offer was made to all shareholders of Chicago Rivet residing throughout the United States. The outstanding stock was worth over $23 million at the offering price. On the same day Chicago Rivet made an offer for approximately 40% of its own shares at $30.00 per share. The District Court entered final judgment on February 9, declaring that the Illinois Act was preempted by the Williams Act and that it violated the Commerce Clause. Accordingly, the District Court permanently enjoined enforcement of the Illinois statute against MITE. Shortly after final judgment was entered, MITE and Chicago Rivet entered into an agreement whereby both tender offers were withdrawn. . . .

II

The Court of Appeals specifically found that this case was not moot, reasoning that because the Secretary has indicated he intends to enforce the Act against MITE, a reversal of the judgment of the District Court would expose MITE to civil and criminal liability for making the February 5, 1979 offer in violation of the Illinois Act. We agree. It is urged that the preliminary injunction issued by the District Court is a complete defense to civil or criminal penalties. While, as Justice Stevens' concurrence indicates, that is not a frivolous question by any means, it is an issue to be decided when and if the Secretary of State initiates an action. That action would be foreclosed if we agree with the Court of Appeals that the Illinois Act is unconstitutional. Accordingly, the case is not moot. . . .

V . . .

B . . .

We conclude with the Court of Appeals that the Illinois Act imposes a substantial burden on interstate commerce which outweighs its putative local benefits. It is accordingly invalid under the Commerce Clause. . . .

JUSTICE POWELL, concurring in part.

I agree with Justice Marshall that this case is moot. In view, however, of the decision of a majority of the Court to reach the merits, I join Parts I and V-B of the Court's opinion.

JUSTICE O'CONNOR, concurring in part.

I agree with the Court that the case is not moot. . . . I join only Parts I, II and V of the Court's opinion. . . .

JUSTICE STEVENS, concurring in part and concurring in the judgment.

The question whether this case is moot depends on the effect of the preliminary injunction entered on February 2, 1979, restraining the Illinois Secretary of State from enforcing the Illinois Business Take-Over Act while the injunction remained in effect. If, as Justice Marshall contends in his dissenting opinion, the injunction granted the MITE Corporation a complete immunity from state sanctions for any acts performed while the injunction was outstanding, I would agree that the case is moot. On the other hand, if the injunction did no more than it purported to do, setting aside the injunction would remove its protection and MITE would be subject to sanctions in the state courts. Those courts might regard the fact that an injunction was outstanding at the time MITE violated the Illinois statute as a defense to any enforcement proceeding, but unless the federal injunction was tantamount to a grant of immunity, there is no federal rule of law that would require the state courts to absolve MITE from liability. I believe, therefore, that to resolve the mootness issue — which, of course, is jurisdictional — we must answer the question that Justice Marshall's dissent raises.

Justice Marshall advances various reasons for adopting a rule that will give federal judges the power to grant complete immunity to persons who desire to test the constitutionality of a state statute. His proposed rule would treat any federal judge's preliminary injunction restraining enforcement of a state statute on federal grounds as a grant of immunity with respect to any conduct undertaken while the injunction was outstanding. Under the rule he proposes, "if the statute is later determined to be valid, the State will never be able to prosecute the individual that obtained the preliminary injunction for action taken while the injunction was in effect." For me, the question is not whether such a rule would be wise; the question is whether federal judges possess the power to grant such immunity. In my opinion they do not.

I . . .

Neither the terms of the preliminary injunction nor prior equity practice provides any support for an interpretation of the District Court's order as a grant of total immunity from future prosecution. More fundamentally, federal judges have no power to grant such blanket dispensation from the requirements of valid legislative enactments.

A

An injunction restrains conduct. Its effect is normally limited to the parties named in the instrument. Since a preliminary injunction may be granted on a mere probability of success on the merits, generally the moving party must demonstrate confidence in his legal position by posting bond in an amount sufficient to protect his adversary from loss in the event that future proceedings prove that the injunction issued wrongfully. The bond, in effect, is the moving party's warranty that the law will uphold the issuance of the injunction.

These features of injunctive relief are inconsistent with a blanket grant of immunity, as this case demonstrates. The preliminary injunction did not purport to provide permanent immunity for violations of the statute that occurred during its effective period. It merely provided that the Secretary of State was enjoined from "issuing any cease and desist order or notice of hearing or from otherwise invoking, applying, or enforcing the Illinois Business Take-Over Act" against MITE. It did not enjoin other parties who are authorized by the Act to enforce its provisions. Moreover, the preliminary injunction was entered without any declara-

tion that the Illinois statute was unconstitutional. There simply is no basis
on which to conclude that the preliminary injunction issued by the District Court should be construed as having granted MITE permanent
immunity from future proceedings brought under the Illinois statute.

In Steffel v. Thompson, the Court unanimously held that an individual who wished to engage in "constitutionally protected activity" but was
threatened with prosecution under a state criminal statute could obtain a
declaratory judgment in federal court declaring the statute invalid. The
Court did not suggest that, armed with such a judgment from a federal
district court, the individual could violate the statute with impunity; indeed, it stated just the opposite:

> [A] federal declaration of unconstitutionality reflects the opinion of the federal
> court that the statute cannot be fully enforced. If a declaration of total uncon-
> stitutionality is affirmed by this Court, it follows that this Court stands ready to
> reverse any conviction under the statute.

Id., at 469-470 (quoting Perez v. Ledesma, 401 U.S. 82, 124 (separate
opinion of Brennan, J.)). Justice White attached possibly the greatest
significance to a federal declaratory judgment, writing separately in *Steffel* that "I would anticipate that a final declaratory judgment entered by a
federal court holding particular conduct of the federal plaintiff to be
immune on federal constitutional grounds from prosecution under state
law should be accorded res judicata effect in any later prosecution of that
very conduct." 415 U.S., at 477 (White, J., concurring). A declaratory
judgment reversed on appeal, however, certainly would not have such res
judicata effect.

An individual who is imminently threatened with prosecution for conduct that he believes is constitutionally protected should not be forced to
act at his peril. One purpose of the federal declaratory judgment statute is
to permit such an individual to test the legality of a state statute before
engaging in conduct that is prohibited by its terms. Recognition of this
fact, however, does not determine the point at which an individual may
act with absolute assurance that he may not be punished for his contemplated activity. The fact that a federal judge has entered a declaration that
the law is invalid does not provide that assurance; every litigant is pain-
fully aware of the possibility that a favorable judgment of a trial court may
be reversed on appeal. . . . Since a final judgment declaring a state
statute unconstitutional would not grant immunity for actions taken in
reliance on the court's decision, certainly a preliminary injunction —
which on its face does nothing more than temporarily restrain conduct —
should not accomplish that result. Neither the preliminary injunction
nor the subsequent judgment declaring the statute unconstitutional can
fairly be construed as a grant of absolute immunity from enforcement of
the Illinois statute.

B

My conclusions concerning the proper nature of injunctive and declaratory relief are not based upon arcane interpretations of common law. Federal courts are courts of limited jurisdiction. . . . There simply is no constitutional or statutory authority that permits a federal judge to grant dispensation from a valid state law.[6] . . . The District Court in this case entered both an injunction restraining certain conduct by the Illinois Secretary of State and a judgment declaring a state statute unconstitutional. It did not — because it could not — grant immunity from the requirements of a valid state law. As a result, this Court has jurisdiction to consider whether the judgment and relief entered by the District Court were proper.[8]

II

On the merits, I agree with the Court. . . . I therefore join part V of its opinion. . . .

JUSTICE MARSHALL, with whom JUSTICE BRENNAN joins, dissenting. . . . The parties to this appeal have no adversary interest in the outcome of this case. Their positions would be the same, whether the Court approved the Illinois Business Take-Over Act or struck it down. Because the Court finds that the Illinois Act is unconstitutional, there will be no further litigation. However, even if the Court had held that the Illinois Act is constitutional, and had lifted the permanent injunction that now restrains enforcement of the Act against MITE, there would be no basis for continued litigation. . . .

I

The Secretary argues that the case is not moot because the preliminary injunction would not be a complete defense to a state enforcement action. He contends that the preliminary injunction merely barred him from commencing an enforcement action during the period the injunction was in effect. Thus, if this Court had decided that the statute is constitutional and had lifted the permanent injunction, the State would

6. I do not suggest that, if the state law is valid, a federal court lacks jurisdiction to enter an injunction restraining state officials from enforcing the statute. Such an injunction may be appropriate — and would be binding on the parties — to permit the federal court to preserve its jurisdiction pending a final decision on the constitutionality of the statute. . . . Such an injunction does not *continue* to be binding on the parties, however, if it is vacated on appeal. . . .

8. Justice Rehnquist concludes that this case is moot because the injunction restrains an enforcement proceeding that has not yet begun. If his view were accepted, an injunction against a threatened criminal proceeding would never be appropriate, for the controversy between the parties would not yet be "ripe."

have been able to commence an action seeking penalties for any violations that occurred during the period the preliminary injunction was in effect. In other words, argues the Secretary, the preliminary injunction only provided temporary security. It enabled MITE to go forward with the tender offer — subject to the risk that at some later stage, the constitutionality of the statute would be upheld, and the state would commence enforcement proceedings.

Federal courts undoubtedly have the power to issue a preliminary injunction that restrains enforcement of a state statute, subject to the condition that if the statute is later found to be valid, the state is free to seek penalties for violations that occurred during the period the injunction was in effect. In my view, however, federal courts also have the power to issue a preliminary injunction that offers permanent protection from penalties for violations of the statute that occurred during the period the injunction was in effect. Determining whether a particular injunction provides temporary or permanent protection becomes a question of interpretation.

I believe that in the ordinary case, unless the order contains specific language to the contrary, it should be presumed that an injunction secures permanent protection from penalties for violations that occurred during the period it was in effect; the burden should be on the State to show that the injunction provided only temporary security. A presumption in favor of permanent protection is likely to reflect the intentions of the court that granted the motion. In acting upon a request for an injunction, it will recognize that short-term protection is often only marginally better than no protection at all. Parties seek to restrain the enforcement of a state statute, not just because they want short-term protection, but because they desire permanent immunity for actions they take in reliance on the injunction. If they are contemplating action that might violate a state statute, they will take little solace from temporary immunity — when they know that if they decide to act, enforcement proceedings might be initiated at some later stage.

Here, the preliminary injunction does not expressly state that it provides permanent immunity from penalties for violations of the Illinois Act that may occur during its effective period. The injunction provides only that the Secretary of State is enjoined from "issuing any cease and desist order or notice of hearing or from otherwise invoking, applying, or enforcing the Illinois Business Take-Over Act" against MITE.

However, I see no reason why the presumption in favor of permanent protection should not be applied here. In this context, as the District Court must have recognized, permanent protection was needed. MITE sought an injunction, not just because it desired protection from enforcement actions during the period it was actually making the tender offer, but also because it desired protection from such actions in the future. The Act provides for substantial civil and criminal penalties. MITE would have been reluctant to go forward with its offer, which entailed considerable expense, if there were some risk that it would be penalized later. Indeed, in the Schedule 14D-1 filed with the SEC, MITE expressly stated that it would not commence the tender offer unless it obtained injunctive relief. It also reserved the right to withdraw its offer if injunctive relief were initially granted, but later withdrawn.

Interpreting the injunction to provide permanent protection also ensures that MITE could never be penalized for acting in reliance on the injunction. MITE went forward with the tender offer, reasonably believing that the District Court's order provided complete immunity. Under the circumstances, it would be improper to permit the State to penalize action taken while the injunction was in effect. In the past, this Court has recognized that reasonable reliance on judicial pronouncements may constitute a valid defense to criminal prosecution. See, e.g., Marks v. United States, 430 U.S. 188 (1977).[6] . . . [10] . . .

II

The majority disposes of the mootness issue in a short paragraph. It concedes that the only possible basis for continued litigation in this case would be a state action for penalties. It further concedes that the preliminary injunction issued by the District Court may be a complete defense to an action for civil or criminal penalties. It argues, however, that the effect to be given the preliminary injunction should not be reached in this case. Rather, that question should be decided in a state enforcement action, if it is raised as a defense. Thus, contends the majority, the case is not moot.

I am completely unpersuaded by the majority's facile analysis. . . . It may be true that the State could file a complaint if this Court were to lift the permanent injunction. However, this fact is not enough to keep the case alive where, as a matter of federal law, the complaint *must* be dismissed. If the action that the State plans to commence in state court lacks

---

6. In *Marks*, a conviction for transporting obscene materials was overturned, where the materials were not obscene at time of transportation, but were rendered obscene at time of trial by intervening decision of this Court. *See also* Cox v. Louisiana, 379 U.S. 559, 569-571 (1965) (conviction for illegal picketing reversed where defendant had relied on permission from police officer); Raley v. Ohio, 360 U.S. 423, 437-439 (1959) (conviction for refusal to testify before state commission reversed because witness had relied on opinion of commission chairman that he was privileged to remain silent); United States v. Mancuso, 139 F.2d 90 (C.A.3 1943) (defendant could not be held liable for ignoring induction notices issued while ex parte order staying induction was in effect).

10. . . . I believe that injunctions should ordinarily be interpreted only as providing permanent protection from *penalties*. The state should be barred from penalizing the offeror for acts that took place during the period the injunction was in effect. However, if a court determines that the state statute is valid, the state should be free to provide a remedy for the continuing effects of acts that violated the statute. In particular, a state should be permitted to dismantle a successful acquisition that violated a valid statute.

any merit — if MITE has an automatic defense to that action — then there simply is no controversy.

This case is made more difficult because the Court has never before decided what effect should be given to preliminary injunctions. But the fact that we must decide a novel question does not make the case any less moot. Certainly, if the Court had already held that a preliminary injunction provides permanent immunity, the case would be moot even though the State could go into state court and seek penalties. Such a suit, which would be clearly frivolous, could not keep the dispute alive. . . .

JUSTICE REHNQUIST, dissenting.

I agree with JUSTICE MARSHALL that this case does not present a justiciable controversy, but for a different reason. . . . The possibility of a future enforcement action . . . is insufficient for me to conclude that the controversy that is before the Court is not moot.[1]

This Court has no power over a suit not pending before it. . . . A case pending in this Court may not be kept alive simply because similar or identical issues are currently ripe for decision in a controversy between the same parties in another court. MITE is not presently engaging in activity that is regulated by the Illinois statute, and there is no indication that MITE intends to engage in any such activity in the future. Therefore, the facts that gave rise to *this controversy* over the constitutionality of Illinois' anti-takeover statutes no longer exist and it is unlikely that they will be repeated in the future. As the tender offer has met its demise for reasons having nothing to do with the validity of the Illinois statute, the injunction is no longer necessary to accomplish the purposes for which it was obtained. MITE no longer needs an injunction in order to effect a tender offer for the shares of Chicago Rivet or any other corporation subject to the Illinois Act. Nor does MITE need the injunction in order to preclude the Secretary from rescinding a completed tender offer. . . . A fortiori, this case may not be kept alive simply because there may exist a presently unripened controversy between these same parties over the constitutionality of the same Act. This is so even if our resolution of the merits of the instant case will resolve certain defenses that MITE could raise in an enforcement action were one to be brought by the Secretary. It follows that this case is not alive simply because a decision on the merits in this case will determine whether or not the Secretary's threatened enforcement action may ever ripen into a live controversy.

If an enforcement action were brought by the Secretary, "there is no way to know what the outcome of such a proceeding in the [Illinois]

---

1. This case is unlike those in which this Court has found justiciable an action to enjoin a threatened criminal prosecution. The plaintiff in the present posture of this case no longer intends to engage in, or is presently engaging in, what is asserted to be federally-protected activity.

courts might be." Oil Workers Unions v. Missouri, 361 U.S., at 371. The Illinois courts may well conclude that the injunction constitutes a defense either on state law grounds or upon the grounds suggested by Justice Marshall in his dissent. The Illinois courts may also agree with MITE that the Business Take-Over Act is preempted by the Williams Act or that Illinois' regulation of interstate tender offers runs afoul of the Commerce Clause. The possibility that this Court might disagree with the Illinois courts' ultimate resolution of the issues arising in a presently unripe, but threatened enforcement action hardly justifies the Court's resolution of important constitutional issues in the abstract posture in which they are currently presented. . . .

NOTES ON THE EFFECT OF A
PRELIMINARY INJUNCTION AGAINST
PROSECUTION

1.   What good is a preliminary injunction against prosecution if plaintiff can be prosecuted later? Would MITE have gone ahead with its tender offer if it had known the preliminary injunction might not protect it against prosecution? If a preliminary injunction doesn't confer temporary immunity, doesn't it leave plaintiffs in the *Young* dilemma?

2.   A preliminary injunction that doesn't preclude prosecutions after trial may still have some uses. When it issues the injunction, the court must determine the probability of success on the merits. If the court says the statute is probably unconstitutional, or almost certainly unconstitutional, plaintiffs may feel safer relying on the court's opinion than on their own, even though they know the court might change its mind or get reversed.

Second, without the preliminary injunction, plaintiffs might be in jail pending trial. They may be willing to risk prosecution later in order to continue their course of conduct. But if they are jailed at the first violation, they don't have that choice. As Professor Amsterdam said of the desegregation and voter registration campaigns of the 1960s, "The battle is for the streets, and on the streets conviction now is worth a hundred times reversal later." Amsterdam, Criminal Prosecutions Affecting Federally Guaranteed Civil Rights: Federal Removal and Habeas Corpus Jurisdiction to Abort State Court Trial, 113 U. Pa. L. Rev. 793, 801 (1965). Sometimes the opposite is also true; freedom to speak now may be well worth the price of conviction later.

These considerations mean that a preliminary injunction that doesn't confer immunity is better than nothing. Even so, doesn't it fail to achieve the central purpose of prospective relief against unconstitutional statutes?

3.   What is the court's inquiry at the preliminary injunction stage? What irreparable harms does it balance? *Doran* casts more light on that

question than *Edgar*, but neither opinion goes into much detail. Shouldn't the court balance the harm to the public and to any victims if violations continue until trial, against the harm to plaintiff if he has to comply until trial? If that balance of hardships tips toward plaintiff when considered in light of the probability of success, isn't that a judgment that it's better for the statute to be violated until trial, even if the statute turns out to be valid? The form of the preliminary injunction is that there can be no prosecutions until after trial. But what is the substance of the court's decision? Isn't it that irreparable injury to both sides will be minimized by permitting violations until trial? Doesn't it defeat that decision to permit later prosecutions? The risk of subsequent prosecutions will deter violations in cases where the court has found that irreparable injury to all sides will be minimized by permitting violations. Won't that inevitably increase irreparable injury? This argument was first developed by my student, James Newsom, in an unpublished paper.

4. On the other hand, isn't Justice Stevens right that the federal courts have no power to enjoin enforcement of a constitutional statute? He could have cited Milliken v. Bradley, supra at 261, for the proposition that the scope of the violation determines the scope of the remedy. And recall Swann v. Charlotte-Mecklenburg's statement that "judicial powers may be exercised only on the basis of a constitutional violation." Where's the constitutional violation if the statute isn't unconstitutional? Does Justice Marshall's footnote 6 succeed in showing that a prosecution of MITE would violate the due process clause? Does it matter that the trial court told MITE only that the statute was *probably* unconstitutional?

5. If there's no constitutional violation, where did the federal court get authority to issue the preliminary injunction? Is a probable constitutional violation enough? Justice Stevens argues in his footnote 6 that the preliminary injunction is based on an alleged violation plus the federal court's authority to preserve its jurisdiction. We first encountered that theory in United States v. United Mine Workers, supra at 628.

Does all that authority disappear as soon as the statute is upheld on the merits? Under *Mine Workers*, the federal court could punish the state prosecutor for enforcing a valid statute while the preliminary injunction was in effect. If it can do that, why can't it permanently enjoin prosecutions for violations committed while the preliminary injunction was in effect?

6. None of the justices found Oklahoma Operating Co. v. Love, 252 U.S. 331 (1920). That was an appeal from an order denying a preliminary injunction against a rate law. In a unanimous opinion by Justice Brandeis, the Court held that plaintiff was entitled to a preliminary injunction, and if the rates were ultimately found confiscatory, a permanent injunction. Then it said: "If upon final hearing the maximum rates fixed should be found not to be confiscatory, a permanent injunction should, nevertheless, issue to restrain enforcement of penalties accrued *pendente lite*

[pending litigation], provided that it also be found that the plaintiff had reasonable ground to contest them as being confiscatory." Id. at 338.

Is that a reasonable compromise? What does it rest on? The power to do complete equity in the case? Is there anything left of that power after *Milliken?* What about Hutto v. Finney, supra at 274? Is there anything in *Hutto* that would support a permanent injunction in *Edgar?* If *Love* wasn't implicitly overruled in *Milliken*, was it wiped out by the Court's fresh start in *Younger* and *Steffel?*

7.   How persuasive is Justice Stevens's analogy to liability on the injunction bond? Relying on a preliminary injunction always involves some risk. But isn't the risk of punishment qualitatively different from the risk of having to pay compensation up to a fixed limit? And doesn't it matter that the court that issued the preliminary injunction retains control over the bond, and has discretion to waive the bond or waive its enforcement?

8.   What does the majority hold? There are at least three possible interpretations of its cryptic opinion:

   a.   There is no constitutional power to enjoin prosecution of acts done in reliance on a preliminary injunction that is subsequently vacated.

   b.   Whether or not there is constitutional power to enjoin such prosecutions, the issue is not ripe until a prosecution is actually filed. (Wouldn't an injunction suit after a prosecution is filed be barred by *Younger?*)

   c.   Whether or not there is constitutional power to enjoin such prosecutions, there is no irreparable injury. Plaintiff no longer wishes to continue his course of conduct, so he no longer faces the *Young* dilemma. Defense of a criminal prosecution is a perfectly adequate remedy for any constitutional claims with respect to past violations.

9.   Suppose that the Court had upheld the Illinois law, that MITE were prosecuted in an Illinois court, and that it pled its reliance on the preliminary injunction as an affirmative defense. Is that a state or federal defense? Could the Supreme Court reverse a conviction? If one of MITE's officers were imprisoned, could he raise the preliminary injunction defense on federal habeas corpus?

The federal courts can vacate a state conviction only on the basis of a constitutional violation. If the Supreme Court could reverse a subsequent conviction, why can't it enjoin prosecution? The ripeness and irreparable injury explanations of its opinion can explain such a distinction. But if it meant there is no constitutional power to enjoin prosecutions, there probably is no constitutional power to overturn convictions either.

10.   Does a criminal defendant who relied on a preliminary injunction have any state law defenses? It is important to distinguish federally enforceable due process arguments from mistake of law defenses that are part of the substantive criminal law of the prosecuting state. The Model Penal Code contains the following provision:

A belief that conduct does not legally constitute an offense is a defense to a prosecution for the offense based upon such conduct when: . . .

(b) [defendant] acts in a reasonable reliance upon an official statement of the law, afterward determined to be invalid or erroneous, contained in (i) a statute or other enactment; (ii) a judicial decision, opinion or judgment; (iii) an administrative order or grant of permission; or (iv) an official interpretation of the public officer or body charged by law with responsibility for the interpretation, administration or enforcement of the law defining the offense.

Model Penal Code §2.04(3), 10 U.L.A. 468 (1974).

Provisions based on this section have been enacted in a number of states, beginning with Illinois in 1961. Is it reasonable to rely on a statement of law in an opinion granting a preliminary injunction? Is it reasonable after *Edgar*? A 1978 article reports that not a single case has substantively construed this provision. Cremer, The Ironies of Law Reform: A History of Reliance on Officials as a Defense in American Criminal Law, 14 Cal. W.L. Rev. 48, 78 (1978).

The Illinois enactment of the Model Penal Code modified §2.04(3)(ii) in a way that is probably dispositive of MITE's claim. Defendant must have relied on "an order or opinion of an Illinois Appellate or Supreme Court, or a United States appellate court later overruled or reversed." Ill. Ann. Stat. ch. 38, §4-8(b)(3) (Smith-Hurd 1972). Doesn't that mean reliance on a federal district court is no defense? What about reliance on a subsequently overruled opinion of the Supreme Court of the United States?

There are cases going both ways on whether reliance on a preliminary injunction is a defense when the statute is silent. Such a defense was allowed in United States v. Mancuso, 139 F.2d 90 (3d Cir. 1943), and State v. Chicago, Milwaukee & St. Paul Railway, 130 Minn. 144, 153 N.W. 320 (1915). It was disallowed in State v. Wadhams Oil Co., 149 Wis. 58, 134 N.W. 1121 (1912), and State v. Keller, 8 Idaho 699, 70 P. 1051 (1902).

WOOLEY v. MAYNARD
430 U.S. 705 (1977)

[Mr. and Mrs. Maynard were Jehovah's Witnesses who objected on moral, religious, and political grounds to the state motto, "Live Free or Die," which appeared on all New Hampshire license plates. It was a misdemeanor to knowingly obscure the figures or letters on a license plate. Mr. Maynard was prosecuted three times for covering the motto. Each time he defended pro se, explained his objections, and was convicted. He took no appeals. He served fifteen days in jail for one offense. His last conviction was continued for sentence, which meant that no consequences attached unless he was again convicted.

The Maynards then filed this suit seeking a declaratory judgment that the statute was unconstitutional and an injunction against its enforcement. The trial court held that the statute required the Maynards to involuntarily affirm a political view and thus violated the first amendment. It enjoined further prosecutions.]

MR. CHIEF JUSTICE BURGER delivered the opinion of the Court. . . .

Mr. Maynard now finds himself placed "between the Scylla of intentionally flouting state law and the Charybdis of forgoing what he believes to be constitutionally protected activity in order to avoid becoming enmeshed in [another] criminal proceeding." Steffel v. Thompson. Mrs. Maynard, as joint owner of the family automobiles, is no less likely than her husband to be subjected to state prosecution. Under these circumstances he cannot be denied consideration of a federal remedy.

Appellants, however, point out that Maynard failed to seek review of his criminal convictions and cite Huffman v. Pursue, Ltd., for the propositions that "a necessary concomitant of *Younger* is that a party in appellee's posture must exhaust his state appellate remedies before seeking relief in the District Court," 420 U.S., at 608, and that "*Younger* standards must be met to justify federal intervention in a state judicial proceeding as to which a losing litigant has not exhausted his state appellate remedies," id., at 609. *Huffman*, however, is inapposite. There the appellee was seeking to prevent, by means of federal intervention, enforcement of a state-court judgment declaring its theater a nuisance. We held that appellee's failure to exhaust its state appeals barred federal intervention under the principles of *Younger*: "Federal posttrial intervention, in a fashion designed to annul the results of a state trial . . . deprives the States of a function which quite legitimately is left to them, that of overseeing trial court dispositions of constitutional issues which arise in civil litigation over which they have jurisdiction." Ibid.

Here, however, the suit is in no way "designed to annul the results of a state trial" since the relief sought is wholly prospective, to preclude further prosecution under a statute alleged to violate appellees' constitutional rights. Maynard has already sustained convictions and has served a sentence of imprisonment for his prior offenses. He does not seek to have his record expunged, or to annul any collateral effects those convictions may have, e.g., upon his driving privileges. The Maynards seek only to be free from prosecutions for future violations of the same statutes. *Younger* does not bar federal jurisdiction.

In their complaint, the Maynards sought both declaratory and injunctive relief against the enforcement of the New Hampshire statutes. We have recognized that although " '[o]rdinarily . . . the practical effect of [injunctive and declaratory] relief will be virtually identical,' " Doran v. Salem Inn, supra, at 931, quoting Samuels v. Mackell, 401 U.S. 66, 73 (1971), a "district court can generally protect the interests of a federal plaintiff by entering a declaratory judgment, and therefore the stronger injunctive medicine will be unnecessary." *Doran*, supra, at 931. It is correct that generally a court will not enjoin "the enforcement of a criminal statute even though unconstitutional," Spielman Motor Co. v. Dodge, 295 U.S. 89, 95 (1935), since "[s]uch a result seriously impairs the State's interest in enforcing its criminal laws, and implicates the concerns for federalism which lie at the heart of *Younger*," *Doran*, supra, at 931. But this is not an absolute policy and in some circumstances injunctive relief may be appropriate. "To justify such interference there must be exceptional circumstances and a clear showing that an injunction is necessary in order to afford adequate protection of constitutional rights." *Spielman Motor Co.*, supra, at 95.

We have such a situation here for, as we have noted, three successive prosecutions were undertaken against Mr. Maynard in the span of five weeks. This is quite different from a claim for federal equitable relief when a prosecution is threatened for the first time. The threat of repeated prosecutions in the future against both him and his wife, and the effect of such a continuing threat on their ability to perform the ordinary tasks of daily life which require an automobile, is sufficient to justify injunctive relief. Cf. Douglas v. City of Jeannette, 319 U.S. 157 (1943). We are therefore unwilling to say that the District Court was limited to granting declaratory relief. Having determined that the District Court was not required to stay its hand as to either appellee,[9] we turn to the merits of the Maynards' claim. . . .

We conclude that the State of New Hampshire may not require appellees to display the state motto upon their vehicle license plates; and, accordingly, we affirm the judgment of the District Court.

Affirmed.

MR. JUSTICE WHITE, with whom MR. JUSTICE BLACKMUN and MR. JUSTICE REHNQUIST join in part, dissenting in part. . . .

The whole point of Douglas v. City of Jeannette's admonition against injunctive relief was that once a declaratory judgment had issued, further equitable relief would depend on the existence of unusual circumstances thereafter. Here the State's enforcement of its statute prior to the declaration of unconstitutionality by the federal court would appear to be no more than the performance of their duty by the State's law enforcement officers. If doing this much prior to the declaration of unconstitutionality amounts to unusual circumstances sufficient to warrant an injunction, the standard is obviously seriously eroded.

Under our cases, therefore, more is required to be shown than the

9.   If the totality of appellants' arguments were accepted, a §1983 action could never be brought to enjoin state criminal prosecutions. According to appellants, *Younger* principles bar Mr. Maynard from seeking an injunction because he has already been subjected to prosecution. As to Mrs. Maynard, they argue, in effect, that the action is premature because no such prosecution has been instituted. Since the two spouses were similarly situated but for the fact that one has been prosecuted and one has not, we fail to see where appellants' argument would ever leave room for federal intervention under §1983.

Court's opinion reveals to affirm the issuance of the injunction. To that extent I dissent.

NOTES ON PROSPECTIVE RELIEF AFTER A STATE PROSECUTION

1. In Huffman v. Pursue, Ltd., 420 U.S. 592 (1975), the state proceeding was not a criminal prosecution but a civil nuisance action. The state court enjoined operation of Pursue's theater for a year. Such injunctions are invalid as prior restraints, and the Court so held in Vance v. Universal Amusement Co., 445 U.S. 308 (1980). But Universal Amusement filed its suit before any enforcement proceedings were commenced. Pursue missed that opportunity, and it did not appeal through the state courts. Instead, it asked the federal district court to enjoin enforcement of the state court injunction. That is the sense in which Pursue sought to "annul the effects of a state trial." Huffman v. Pursue also emphasized the importance of the state's interest in providing appellate review of judgments in its courts.

2. Is *Wooley* just a case in which no prosecution is pending? That isn't what the Court says, is it? The Court says: "The Maynards seek only to be free from prosecutions for future violations of the same statutes. *Younger* does not bar federal jurisdiction." Suppose the state had commenced a fourth prosecution promptly after the Maynards filed their federal suit. Would that require dismissal under Hicks v. Miranda? Even if the Maynards continued to seek only prospective relief? Suppose they said they didn't want to interfere with the pending prosecution and were willing to serve their sentence if convicted?

Wouldn't it still be true that they sought "only to be free from prosecutions for future violations." Wouldn't they still face the *Young* dilemma as to future violations? Isn't *Wooley* ultimately inconsistent with the rejection of Dr. Hallford's claim in Roe v. Wade? See Notes on Injunctions while a Criminal Prosecution Is Pending, supra at 1197. And if that is true, can't any state criminal defendant file a federal suit seeking relief with respect to future violations, while continuing to litigate the past violation in state court? That's how the Third Circuit read *Wooley* in Spartacus, Inc. v. Borough of McKees Rocks, 694 F.2d 947, 949 n.3 (3d Cir. 1982).

3. Samuels v. Mackell reasoned that a declaratory judgment aimed at future violations will inevitably interfere with a pending prosecution. Does that help reconcile *Wooley* with *Roe*? This might be a case where an injunction is a more finely tuned remedy than a declaratory judgment. In Cline v. Frink Dairy Co., 274 U.S. 445 (1927), the Court affirmed injunctions against future prosecutions but vacated injunctions against pending prosecutions. Will that work? Or does the injunction wipe out the pending prosecutions via res judicata?

4.   At the very least an injunction against future prosecutions is less disruptive of state proceedings than an injunction against pending prosecutions. A preliminary injunction against future prosecutions would have no res judicata effect and need not disrupt anything. The state prosecution might reach final judgment before the federal injunction suit, in which case the prosecution would not have been disrupted at all. If not, the state court would still decide the facts of the criminal case and decide whether the past violation was distinguishable from the proposed violations protected by the injunction. If even this is thought too disruptive of the state prosecution, the injunction against future prosecutions could be conditioned on the federal plaintiff waiving any plea of res judicata or collateral estoppel in prosecutions for past violations. Why can't an injunction against future prosecutions protect the federal plaintiff from the *Young* dilemma while also respecting the dignity of the state courts?

5.   The prosecutors did not plead res judicata in either *Huffman* or *Wooley*. Was that a mistake? Professor Currie thinks so. Currie, Res Judicata: The Neglected Defense, 45 U. Chi. L. Rev. 317 (1978). He would apparently bar both claims. But he concedes that the Maynards may have an argument. The full faith and credit statute, 28 U.S.C. §1738 (1982), requires that state judgments be given "the same full faith and credit in every court within the United States . . . as they have by law or usage in the courts of such State . . . from which they are taken." New Hampshire follows the traditional rule that issues not actually litigated are not binding in subsequent litigation on a separate cause of action, and its precedents seem to take a narrow view of what is an issue and what is a cause of action. 45 U. Chi. L. Rev. at 350 n.216.

The trial court in *Wooley* raised res judicata on its own motion, and rejected it on the ground that the constitutional defense had not been litigated in the criminal case. 406 F. Supp. 1381, 1385 n.6 (D.N.H. 1976) (three-judge court).

6.   Maynard did tell the judge about his political and religious objections to displaying the state motto on his car. Does that mean he litigated the issue? Whether or not he litigated the issue, should one conviction bind him with respect to future violations? Should he permanently forfeit his constitutional rights because of one bad decision or procedural default? The D.C. Circuit has held that a conviction is res judicata as to that violation, but not as to future violations at issue in a suit under *Wooley*. Kaplan v. Hess, 694 F.2d 847, 852 (D.C. Cir. 1982). Would one conviction be binding on the constitutional issue in a subsequent prosecution? Should it matter that Maynard wasn't represented by counsel at any of his convictions?

7.   Compare Montana v. United States, 440 U.S. 147 (1979). Montana levied a gross receipts tax on contractors on public construction projects. The United States alleged that the tax violated its sovereign immunity from taxation. One of its contractors paid $8,000 in taxes and sued for a refund. The United States funded and controlled this litiga-

tion. The Montana Supreme Court rejected the claim, and the Solicitor General asked the contractor to withdraw its petition for certiorari. Then the United States itself sued in federal court, seeking a declaratory judgment that the tax was unconstitutional, an injunction against further enforcement, and a refund of taxes paid by its contractors and passed through to the government. The district court struck down the tax; the Supreme Court held the United States barred by res judicata. The constitutional issue was the same as in the state court litigation it had controlled, and there had been no intervening change in "legal climate." Id. at 161.

Does that suggest that Maynard should be barred if he had actually litigated his constitutional claim? Is *Montana* distinguishable? If Mr. Maynard is barred, should Mrs. Maynard be barred too?

8. Should the answer to these questions turn on state law? Section 1738 unequivocally refers to state law, but state law may not be clear. If there is no state decision on the effect of a conviction in a subsequent prosecution or suit to declare the statute unconstitutional, should the federal court try to deduce a state rule from civil cases about the scope of a cause of action? Or should it assume the state would apply a rule consistent with the policy of extricating litigants from the *Young* dilemma?

Section 1738 is one of the more neglected federal statutes. Federal judges apparently would prefer to develop their own law of res judicata and don't want to be bothered with state law. The Supreme Court in *Montana*, the D.C. Circuit in *Kaplan*, and the trial court in *Wooley*, all ignored §1738 and local law. But in Kremer v. Chemical Construction Corp., 456 U.S. 461 (1982), the Court did invoke §1738, directed the parties to state law, and refused to apply a federal exception denying preclusive effect where there was not a "full and fair" opportunity to litigate in the earlier case. It held §1738 binding unless the earlier proceedings failed to satisfy due process. *Kremer* also extended the holding of Allen v. McCurry, 449 U.S. 90 (1980): There is no civil rights exception to §1738, either under §1983 (*Allen*) or the employment title of the Civil Rights Act of 1964 (*Kremer*).

9. There isn't any escape from res judicata in *Huffman*, is there? Doesn't the effort to annul the effects of the state judgment strike at the core of res judicata policy?

NOTE ON THE DISTINCTION BETWEEN INJUNCTIONS AND DECLARATORY JUDGMENTS

Why is the Court still fighting over the distinction between injunctions and declaratory judgments? Isn't that a purely formal distinction that happened to help the Court work its way out of the excesses of Justice

Black's opinion in *Younger*? Does anything still turn on it? Are the dissenters in *Wooley* just protecting the state's tactical advantage in being one step further away from a contempt citation? Compare the Notes on Ripeness and Preventive Injunctions, supra at 215.

In some apparently routine cases the Court has affirmed an injunction against enforcement without comment and without dissent. Examples are Bellotti v. Baird, 443 U.S. 622, 651 (1979), Ray v. Atlantic Richfield Co., 435 U.S. 151, 156-157, 180 (1978), and Zablocki v. Redhail, 434 U.S. 374, 377 (1978).

NOTES ON PROSPECTIVE RELIEF WHEN CIVIL PROCEEDINGS ARE PENDING

1. In Huffman v. Pursue, Ltd., 420 U.S. 592 (1975), the pending state proceeding was not a criminal prosecution but a civil nuisance action. This prompted a debate on the scope of *Younger*. Three dissenters thought *Younger* was based on the maxim that equity will not enjoin a criminal prosecution, and that it should apply only to criminal cases. They noted that there was a long tradition of enjoining other civil litigation. The majority conceded that criminal cases were special, but thought that federalism also required deference to civil proceedings. Whatever the result might be in civil litigation involving private parties, the nuisance action in *Huffman* was "in aid of and closely related to criminal statutes which prohibit the dissemination of obscene materials." The state was a party; the proceeding was "akin to a criminal prosecution," and the state's interest in the case "is likely to be every bit as great if it would be were this a criminal proceeding." So *Younger* was fully applicable.

2. Subsequent cases have applied *Younger* to suits to recover fraudulently collected welfare payments, Trainor v. Hernandez, 431 U.S. 434 (1977), to suits to terminate parental rights because of child abuse, Moore v. Sims, 442 U.S. 415 (1979), to attorney disciplinary proceedings, Middlesex County Ethics Committee v. Garden State Bar Association, 457 U.S. 423 (1982), and to coercive contempt in ordinary civil cases, Juidice v. Vail, 430 U.S. 327 (1977). But the Court has not fulfilled Justice Brennan's outraged prediction that it would apply *Younger* even to ordinary civil litigation between private parties. The courts of appeals have split on that question. Diaz v. Stathis, 576 F.2d 9 (1st Cir. 1978) says no; Louisville Area Inter-Faith Committee for United Farm Workers v. Nottingham Liquors, 542 F.2d 652 (6th Cir. 1976), says yes.

3. The Sixth Circuit may not be committed to *Louisville*. Consider WXYZ v. Hand, 658 F.2d 420 (6th Cir. 1981). Hand was a state court judge presiding over the trial of a priest charged with sexual assault.

Relying on a Michigan statute, he ordered the press not to report the names of the victim or the defendant. Television station WXYZ reported both names on its evening news; then it sued to enjoin Judge Hand from enforcing his order and to have the underlying statute declared unconstitutional. The federal court granted relief. The Sixth Circuit affirmed, reasoning that contempt proceedings were threatened but not yet instituted when the federal trial court acted.

Why doesn't the proceeding leading to issuance of the gag order count? It can't be because it was over. Huffman v. Pursue rejects that argument, and there is no doubt that the federal injunction in WXYZ annulled the state gag order. Either everybody overlooked the underlying proceeding, or the court thought it was private civil litigation to which Younger didn't apply. One way to view the gag order is that it arises out of a dispute between the victim and defendant, on the one hand, and the press on the other. Is that the right way to look at it? Or is the state the implicit plaintiff in a gag order proceeding? Or is Younger directly applicable because the gag order is issued in a pending criminal case?

Quite apart from Younger, is there any basis for an injunction in WXYZ? Is anything at stake other than sanctions for a past violation? The TV station may have faced the Young dilemma with respect to future newscasts, but that did not appear to be its concern. Is there any basis for letting it effectively remove the contempt proceeding to federal court?

4. The argument over applying Younger to civil cases has focused on the strength of the state's interest. But that may not be the most important variable. What is plaintiff's interest? In Stainback v. Mo Hock Ke Lok Po, 336 U.S. 368 (1949), the Supreme Court refused to enjoin enforcement of a statute that could be enforced only by injunction. The Court emphasized that the federal plaintiffs had "no reason to fear a court of equity," id. at 383, and that the "lack of coercion by fine or imprisonment" was "important" to its decision, id. at 373. Plaintiff might still want to be in federal court because he fears that the state court is hostile to his rights. Consider, for example, the benefits of a federal temporary restraining order allowing Martin Luther King and his followers to march in Walker v. City of Birmingham, supra at 656. But apart from that preference for federal court, isn't a state civil remedy much more likely to be adequate than a state criminal remedy? If a litigant is in a court with equity powers, does he still face the Young dilemma?

What if the federal plaintiff would have to file a state court permissive counterclaim to get an adequate remedy? Shouldn't he be able to file in federal court instead? That is the clear implication of the jurisdictional statutes, but the Supreme Court held otherwise in Moore v. Sims, 442 U.S. 415 (1979). Moore involved such a procedural tangle in both state and federal court, and such a wide ranging and intrusive federal review of the state statute, that it is hard to generalize from Moore to other litigation.

NOTES ON INJUNCTIONS AGAINST STATE COURT PROCEDURE

1. In several of the civil cases in the last set of notes, plaintiff plainly did not face the *Young* dilemma, quite apart from any question about the remedial powers of the state court. In *Juidice*, *Trainor*, and *Moore*, in the Supreme Court, and in Diaz v. Stathis in the First Circuit, plaintiffs challenged only the procedures used in state court; they did not challenge any substantive restriction on their own behavior. Criminal defendants can also raise collateral challenges to state court procedure. The Supreme Court has always denied relief. A pre-*Younger* example is Pugach v. Dollinger, 365 U.S. 458 (1961); a post-*Younger* example is Kugler v. Helfant, 421 U.S. 117 (1975). Is there any reason for using injunctions to control the procedure in litigation pending in another court?

2. There are two possible reasons. One is to save litigation costs by getting the procedural issue resolved early rather than after an appeal. Injunctions on this rationale are an end run around the policy against interlocutory appeals; they raise the debate over whether more time will be wasted on unsuccessful interlocutory challenges or on litigating cases that eventually have to be reversed because of some error early on. Injunctions on this ground run counter to the Supreme Court's holdings that litigation expense is never sufficient irreparable injury to justify bypassing administrative proceedings. Renegotiation Board v. Bannercraft Clothing Co., 415 U.S. 1, 23-24 (1974). It is in this context, and not in the context of the *Young* dilemma, that *Younger*'s treatment of irreparable injury makes sense: "[T]he cost, anxiety, and inconvenience of having to defend against a single prosecution" do not justify enjoining the prosecution. You may agree or disagree, but at least with respect to this kind of case, *Younger* accurately stated the harm of denying federal relief.

3. The other argument for federal injunctions against unconstitutional state procedure is to assure a federal forum in a district court, for fear the Supreme Court will be too busy to grant certiorari. That argument turns squarely on the argument that the state courts can't be trusted and that all plaintiffs are entitled to a federal forum. However appealing the argument may be to those who want to maximize the litigant's options, it has little appeal to the present Supreme Court.

NOTES ON *YOUNGER'S* EXCEPTIONS

1. *Younger* held out the possibility that there might be exceptional cases in which federal courts could enjoin state prosecutions. Not much has come of those exceptions. They are occasionally invoked successfully in the lower courts, but the Supreme Court precedents make clear that they are exceptions with virtually no content.

These notes also consider the argument that the constitutional claim cannot be raised in the state case. This argument has been somewhat more successful.

2. Bad faith harassment is impossible to prove. That had been established in Cameron v. Johnson, 390 U.S. 611 (1968). Civil rights workers picketed the Hattiesburg, Mississippi, courthouse to encourage registration of black voters. They stayed within a line of march designated by the local sheriff. On April 8, the legislature passed a new statute making it a crime to block the entrance to a courthouse. The statute was delivered to Hattiesburg by messenger on April 9, and beginning on April 10, pickets were repeatedly arrested until they abandoned picketing. Justices Fortas and Douglas, dissenting, found no evidence that pickets had left the designated line of march or blocked the entrance to the courthouse. They thought it clear the prosecutions were brought with no hope of ultimate success and solely to intimidate the picketers, and that the new statute was a legislative directive to break up the picket line. The majority found no evidence of bad faith harassment.

3. Younger also noted an exception for statutes that are "flagrantly and patently violative of express constitutional prohibitions in every clause, sentence and paragraph, and in whatever manner and against whomever an effort might be made to apply" them. The exception makes no sense in terms of the Young dilemma; if a statute is that unconstitutional, the federal plaintiffs will be less deterred than if the constitutional question were fairly debatable. The phrase originated in Watson v. Buck, 313 U.S. 387, 402 (1941), where the district court had enjoined an entire statute because certain sections were unconstitutional. In that context, the phrase was a sensible reminder that constitutional sections of statutes can generally be severed from unconstitutional sections.

In Trainor v. Hernandez, 431 U.S. 434 (1977), the district court held the Illinois garnishment statute "flagrantly and patently unconstitutional." Without explanation, the Supreme Court suggested that such a finding did not satisfy the exception, apparently because it didn't refer to "every clause, sentence and paragraph." Justice Stevens, dissenting, interpreted this to mean that the exception would be unavailable if the statute had a constitutional title, or a constitutional severability clause. What about a constitutional recital that it was enacted by the People of Illinois in General Assembly? It is hard to imagine a statute that would satisfy this exception if the Illinois garnishment law didn't satisfy it.

4. Younger hints at a possible exception for multiple prosecutions. Perhaps that is the basis for granting an injunction instead of a declaratory judgment in Wooley v. Maynard. In Doran v. Salem Inn, M & L Tavern argued that multiple arrests proved bad faith harassment. The Court left that issue open on remand, but Cameron v. Johnson would seem to foreclose it. The multiple prosecution exception has not been heard from again in the Supreme Court.

5. The only exception successfully invoked in the Supreme Court is one not mentioned in *Younger*. In Gibson v. Berryhill, plaintiffs sought to enjoin an administrative proceeding before the Alabama Board of Optometry. The Board was made up exclusively of independent optometrists; the proceeding was aimed at eliminating the competition of defendants, optometrists employed by a corporation with a chain of outlets. The district court found that the Board was biased by prejudgment and monetary interest, and that this justified an exception to *Younger*. The Supreme Court affirmed. 411 U.S. 564, 578-579 (1973).

6. The *Younger* doctrine is inapplicable if the constitutional claim cannot be raised in the state case. This is not so much an exception as a definitional limitation on the scope of the doctrine. The whole rationale was that the state proceeding provides an adequate remedy; in these cases the state proceeding does not purport to provide a remedy. Often the remedy is not to enjoin the state proceeding, but rather to enjoin some collateral feature of the state proceeding.

An example is Fuentes v. Shevin, 407 U.S. 67, 71 n.3 (1972). *Fuentes* was a suit to enjoin prejudgment replevin without due process. The Court held that this was not a suit to enjoin the state proceedings "as such," because the writs of replevin were issued by the clerk. The Court rejected a similar argument in Trainor v. Hernandez, 431 U.S. 434 (1977), a challenge to the Illinois prejudgment garnishment law. But it left open the issue whether there was any way to challenge the garnishment in the state proceeding. On remand, the district court found that the issue could not be raised in the state proceeding and enjoined enforcement of the statute. Hernandez v. Finley, 471 F. Supp. 516 (N.D. Ill. 1978), *aff'd mem. sub nom.* Quern v. Hernandez, 440 U.S. 951 (1979).

Another example is Gerstein v. Pugh, 420 U.S. 103, 108 n.9 (1975). *Gerstein* was a suit to enjoin pretrial detention without a finding of probable cause. The injunction did not interfere with the ultimate criminal trials of the class members, and the issue could not be raised in defense of the criminal prosecution.

RIZZO v. GOODE
423 U.S. 362 (1976)

[Plaintiffs in these class actions were citizens and community organizations suing on behalf of all citizens of Philadelphia and an included class of all black citizens of Philadelphia. Defendants were high-ranking city officials, including the mayor and the police commissioner.

Plaintiffs alleged a pattern of brutality by rank and file police officers, especially in black neighborhoods. They attempted to prove some forty individual incidents of police brutality. The trial court made findings with respect to each incident; as the Supreme Court viewed the record, approximately half these incidents involved constitutional violations.

Plaintiffs also alleged that defendants condoned these violations. The trial court did not find any official policy of police brutality. It did find that the police department discouraged citizens from filing complaints about officers and took few steps against guilty officers.]

MR. JUSTICE REHNQUIST delivered the opinion of the Court. . . .

The District Court concluded by directing petitioners to draft, for the court's approval, "a comprehensive program for dealing adequately with civilian complaints," to be formulated along the following "guidelines" suggested by the court:

> (1) Appropriate revision of police manuals and rules of procedure spelling out in some detail, in simple language, the "dos and don'ts" of permissible conduct in dealing with civilians (for example, manifestations of racial bias, derogatory remarks, offensive language, etc.; unnecessary damage to property and other unreasonable conduct in executing search warrants; limitations on pursuit of persons charged only with summary offenses; recording and processing civilian complaints, etc.). (2) Revision of procedures for processing complaints against police, including (a) ready availability of forms for use by civilians in lodging complaints against police officers; (b) a screening procedure for eliminating frivolous complaints; (c) prompt and adequate investigation of complaints; (d) adjudication of nonfrivolous complaints by an impartial individual or body, insulated so far as practicable from chain of command pressures, with a fair opportunity afforded the complainant to present his complaint, and to the police officer to present his defense; and (3) prompt notification to the concerned parties, informing them of the outcome.

While noting that the "guidelines" were consistent with "generally recognized minimum standards" and imposed "no substantial burdens" on the police department, the District Court emphasized that respondents had no constitutional *right* to improved police procedures for handling civilian complaints. But given that violations of constitutional rights of citizens occur in "unacceptably" high numbers, and are likely to continue to occur, the court-mandated revision was a "necessary first step" in attempting to prevent future abuses.

II

These actions were brought, and the affirmative equitable relief fashioned, under the Civil Rights Act of 1871, 42 U.S.C. §1983. It provides that

> [e]very person who, under color of [law] subjects, or causes to be subjected, any . . . person within the jurisdiction [of the United States] to the deprivation of any rights . . . secured by the Constitution and laws, shall be liable to the party injured in an action at law [or] suit in equity. . . . "

The plain words of the statute impose liability — whether in the form of payment of redressive damages or being placed under an injunction —

only for conduct which "subjects, or causes to be subjected" the complainant to a deprivation of a right secured by the Constitution and laws.

The findings of fact made by the District Court at the conclusion of these two parallel trials — in sharp contrast to that which respondents sought to prove with respect to petitioners — disclose a central paradox which permeates that court's legal conclusions. Individual police officers *not named as parties* to the action were found to have violated the constitutional rights of particular individuals, only a few of whom were parties plaintiff. As the facts developed, there was no affirmative link between the occurrence of the various incidents of police misconduct and the adoption of any plan or policy by petitioners — express or otherwise — showing their authorization or approval of such misconduct. Instead, the *sole* causal connection found by the District Court between petitioners and the individual respondents was that in the absence of a change in police disciplinary procedures, the incidents were likely to continue to occur, *not* with respect to them, but as to the members of the classes they represented. In sum, the genesis of this lawsuit — a heated dispute between individual citizens and certain policemen — has evolved into an attempt by the federal judiciary to resolve a "controversy" between the entire citizenry of Philadelphia and the petitioning elected and appointed officials over what steps might, in the Court of Appeals' words, "[appear] to have the potential for prevention of future police misconduct." 506 F.2d, at 548. The lower courts have, we think, overlooked several significant decisions of this Court in validating this type of litigation and the relief ultimately granted.

A

We first of all entertain serious doubts whether on the facts as found there was made out the requisite Art. III case or controversy between the individually named respondents and petitioners. In O'Shea v. Littleton, 414 U.S. 488 (1974), the individual respondents, plaintiffs in the District Court, alleged that petitioners, a county magistrate and judge, had embarked on a continuing, intentional practice of racially discriminatory bond setting, sentencing, and assessing of jury fees. No specific instances involving the individual respondents were set forth in the prayer for injunctive relief against the judicial officers. And even though respondents' counsel at oral argument had stated that some of the named respondents had in fact "suffered from the alleged unconstitutional practices," the Court concluded that "[p]ast exposure to illegal conduct does not in itself show a present case or controversy regarding injunctive relief, however, if unaccompanied by any continuing, present adverse effects." Id., at 495-496. The Court further recognized that while "past wrongs are evidence bearing on whether there is a real and immediate threat of repeated injury," the attempt to anticipate under what circumstances the respondents there would be made to appear in the future before petitioners "takes us into the area of speculation and conjecture." Id., at 496-497. These observations apply here with even more force, for the individual respondents' claim to "real and immediate" injury rests not upon what the named petitioners might do to them in the future — such as set a bond on the basis of race — but upon what one of a small, unnamed minority of policemen might do to them in the future because of that unknown policeman's perception of departmental disciplinary procedures. This hypothesis is even more attenuated than those allegations of future injury found insufficient in O'Shea to warrant invocation of federal jurisdiction. Thus, insofar as the individual respondents were concerned, we think they lacked the requisite "personal stake in the outcome," Baker v. Carr, 369 U.S. 186, 204 (1962), i.e., the order overhauling police disciplinary procedures.

B

That conclusion alone might appear to end the matter, for O'Shea also noted that "if none of the named plaintiffs . . . establishes the requisite of a case or controversy with the defendants, none may seek relief on behalf of himself or any other member of the class" which they purport to represent. 414 U.S., at 494. But, unlike O'Shea, this case did not arise on the pleadings. The District Court, having certified the plaintiff classes, bridged the gap between the facts shown at trial and the classwide relief sought with an unprecedented theory of §1983 liability. It held that the classes' §1983 actions for equitable relief against petitioners were made out on a showing of an "unacceptably high" number of those incidents of constitutional dimension — some 20 in all — occurring at large in a city of three million inhabitants, with 7,500 policemen.

Nothing in Hague v. CIO, 307 U.S. 496 (1939), the only decision of this Court cited by the District Court, or any other case from this Court, supports such an open-ended construction of §1983. In *Hague*, the pattern of police misconduct upon which liability and injunctive relief were grounded was the adoption and enforcement of deliberate policies by the defendants there (including the Mayor and the Chief of Police) of excluding and removing the plaintiff's labor organizers and forbidding peaceful communication of their views to the citizens of Jersey City. These policies were implemented "by force and violence" on the part of individual policemen. There was no mistaking that the defendants proposed to continue their unconstitutional policies against the members of this discrete group.

Likewise, in Allee v. Medrano, 416 U.S. 802 (1974), relied upon by the Court of Appeals and respondents here, we noted:

> The complaint charged that the enjoined conduct was but one part of a *single plan* by the defendants, and the District Court found a *pervasive pattern of intimidation* in which the law enforcement authorities sought to suppress appellees' constitutional rights. In this blunderbuss effort the police not only

> relied on statutes . . . found constitutionally deficient, but concurrently exercised their authority under valid laws in an unconstitutional manner.

Id., at 812 (emphasis added). The numerous incidents of misconduct on the part of the *named* Texas Rangers, as found by the District Court and summarized in this Court's opinion, established beyond peradventure not only a "persistent pattern" but one which flowed from an intentional, concerted, and indeed conspiratorial effort to deprive the organizers of their First Amendment rights and place them in fear of coming back. Id., at 814-815.

Respondents stress that the District Court not only found an "unacceptably high" number of incidents but held, as did the Court of Appeals, that "when a *pattern* of frequent police violations of rights is shown, the law is clear that injunctive relief may be granted." However, there was no showing that the behavior of the Philadelphia police was different in kind or degree from that which exists elsewhere; indeed, the District Court found "that the problems disclosed by the record . . . are fairly typical of [those] afflicting police departments in major urban areas." Thus, invocation of the word "pattern" in a case where, unlike *Hague* and *Medrano*, the defendants are not causally linked to it, is but a distant echo of the findings in those cases. The focus in *Hague* and *Medrano* was not simply on the number of violations which occurred but on the common thread running through them: a "pervasive pattern of intimidation" flowing from a deliberate plan by the *named* defendants to crush the nascent labor organizations. *Medrano*, supra, at 812. The District Court's unadorned finding of a statistical pattern is quite dissimilar to the factual settings of these two cases.

The theory of liability underlying the District Court's opinion, and urged upon us by respondents, is that even without a showing of direct responsibility for the actions of a small percentage of the police force, petitioners' *failure* to act in the face of a statistical pattern is indistinguishable from the active conduct enjoined in *Hague* and *Medrano*. Respondents posit a constitutional "duty" on the part of petitioners (and a corresponding "right" of the citizens of Philadelphia) to "eliminate" future police misconduct; a "default" of that affirmative duty being shown by the statistical pattern, the District Court is empowered to act in petitioners' stead and take whatever preventive measures are necessary, within its discretion, to secure the "right" at issue. Such reasoning, however, blurs accepted usages and meanings in the English language in a way which would be quite inconsistent with the words Congress chose in §1983. We have never subscribed to these amorphous propositions, and we decline to do so now.

C

Going beyond considerations concerning the existence of a live controversy and threshold statutory liability, we must address an additional and novel claim advanced by respondent classes. They assert that given the citizenry's "right" to be protected from unconstitutional exercises of police power, and the "need for protection from such abuses," respondents have a right to mandatory equitable relief in some form when those in supervisory positions do not institute steps to reduce the incidence of unconstitutional police misconduct. The scope of federal equity power, it is proposed, should be extended to the fashioning of prophylactic procedures for a state agency designed to minimize this kind of misconduct on the part of a handful of its employees. However, on the facts of this case, not only is this novel claim quite at odds with the settled rule that in federal equity cases "the nature of the violation determines the scope of the remedy," but important considerations of federalism are additional factors weighing against it. Where, as here, the exercise of authority by state officials is attacked, federal courts must be constantly mindful of the "special delicacy of the adjustment to be preserved between federal equitable power and State administration of its own law." Stefanelli v. Minard, 342 U.S. 117, 120 (1951), quoted in O'Shea v. Littleton, 414 U.S., at 500. Even in an action between private individuals, it has long been held that an injunction is "to be used sparingly, and only in a clear and plain case." Irwin v. Dixon, 9 How. 10, 33 (1850). When a plaintiff seeks to enjoin the activity of a government agency, even within a unitary court system, his case must contend with "the well-established rule that the Government has traditionally been granted the widest latitude in the 'dispatch of its own internal affairs,' Cafeteria Workers v. McElroy, 367 U.S. 886, 896 (1961)," quoted in Sampson v. Murray, 415 U.S. 61, 83 (1974). The District Court's injunctive order here, significantly revising the internal procedures of the Philadelphia police department, was indisputably a sharp limitation on the department's "latitude in the 'dispatch of its own internal affairs.' "

When the frame of reference moves from a unitary court system, governed by the principles just stated, to a system of federal courts representing the Nation, subsisting side by side with 50 state judicial, legislative, and executive branches, appropriate consideration must be given to principles of federalism in determining the availability and scope of equitable relief. Doran v. Salem Inn, Inc., 422 U.S. 922, 928 (1975).

So strongly has Congress weighted this factor of federalism in the case of a state criminal proceeding that it has enacted 28 U.S.C. §2283 to actually deny to the district courts the authority to issue injunctions against such proceedings unless the proceedings come within narrowly specified exceptions. Even though an action brought under §1983, as this was, is within those exceptions, Mitchum v. Foster, 407 U.S. 225 (1972), the underlying notions of federalism which Congress has recognized in dealing with the relationships between federal and state courts still have weight. Where an injunction against a criminal proceeding is sought under §1983, "the principles of equity, comity, and federalism" must nonetheless restrain a federal court. 407 U.S., at 243.

But even where the prayer for injunctive relief does not seek to enjoin the state criminal proceedings themselves, we have held that the principles of equity nonetheless militate heavily against the grant of an injunction except in the most extraordinary circumstances. In O'Shea v. Littleton, supra, at 502, we held that "a major continuing intrusion of the equitable power of the federal courts into the daily conduct of state criminal proceedings is in sharp conflict with the principles of equitable restraint which this Court has recognized in the decisions previously noted." And the same principles of federalism may prevent the injunction by a federal court of a state civil proceeding once begun. Huffman v. Pursue, Ltd., 420 U.S. 592 (1975).

Thus the principles of federalism which play such an important part in governing the relationship between federal courts and state governments, though initially expounded and perhaps entitled to their greatest weight in cases where it was sought to enjoin a criminal prosecution in progress, have not been limited either to that situation or indeed to a criminal proceeding itself. We think these principles likewise have applicability where injunctive relief is sought, not against the judicial branch of the state government, but against those in charge of an executive branch of an agency of state or local governments such as petitioners here. Indeed, in the recent case of Mayor v. Educational Equality League, 415 U.S. 605 (1974), in which private individuals sought injunctive relief against the Mayor of Philadelphia, we expressly noted the existence of such considerations, saying: "There are also delicate issues of federal-state relationships underlying this case." Id., at 615.

Contrary to the District Court's flat pronouncement that a federal court's legal power to "supervise the functioning of the police department . . . is firmly established," it is the foregoing cases and principles that must govern consideration of the type of injunctive relief granted here. When it injected itself by injunctive decree into the internal disciplinary affairs of this state agency, the District Court departed from these precepts.

For the foregoing reasons the judgment of the Court of Appeals which affirmed the decree of the District Court is reversed.

MR. JUSTICE STEVENS took no part in the consideration or decision of this case.

MR. JUSTICE BLACKMUN, with whom MR. JUSTICE BRENNAN and MR. JUSTICE MARSHALL join, dissenting.

To be sure, federal-court intervention in the daily operation of a large city's police department, as the Court intimates, is undesirable and to be avoided if at all possible. The Court appropriately observes, however, that what the Federal District Court did here was to engage in a careful and conscientious resolution of often sharply conflicting testimony and to make detailed findings of fact, now accepted by both sides, that attack the problem that is the subject of the respondents' complaint. The remedy was one evolved with the defendant officials' assent, reluctant though that assent may have been, and it was one that the police department concededly could live with. Indeed, the District Court, in its memorandum of December 18, 1973, stated that "the resolution of all the disputed items was more nearly in accord with the defendants' position than with the plaintiffs' position," and that the relief contemplated by the earlier orders of March 14, 1973 "did not go beyond what the defendants had always been willing to accept." No one, not even this Court's majority, disputes the apparent efficacy of the relief or the fact that it effectuated a betterment in the system and should serve to lessen the number of instances of deprival of constitutional rights of members of the respondent classes. What is worrisome to the Court is abstract principle, and, of course, the Court has a right to be concerned with abstract principle that, when extended to the limits of logic, may produce untoward results in other circumstances on a future day.

But the District Court here, with detailed, careful, and sympathetic findings, ascertained the existence of violations of citizens' *constitutional* rights, of a *pattern* of that type of activity, of its likely continuance and recurrence, and of an official indifference as to doing anything about it. The case, accordingly, plainly fits the mold of Allee v. Medrano, 416 U.S. 802 (1974), and Hague v. CIO, 307 U.S. 496 (1939), despite the observation, 357 F. Supp., at 1319, that the evidence "does not establish the existence of any overall Police Department *policy* to violate the legal and constitutional rights of citizens, nor to discriminate on the basis of race" (emphasis supplied). I am not persuaded that the Court's attempt to distinguish those cases from this one is at all successful. There must be federal relief available against persistent deprival of federal constitutional rights even by (or, perhaps I should say, particularly by) constituted authority on the state side.

The Court entertains "serious doubts" as to whether there is a case or controversy here, citing O'Shea v. Littleton, 414 U.S. 488 (1974). *O'Shea*, however, presented quite different facts. There, the plaintiff-respondents had alleged a fear of injury from actions that would be subsequent to some future, valid arrest. The Court said:

> We assume that respondents will conduct their activities within the law and so avoid prosecution and conviction as well as exposure to the challenged course of conduct said to be followed by petitioners. . . . Under these circumstances, where respondents do not claim any constitutional right to engage in conduct proscribed by therefore presumably permissible state laws, or indicate that it is otherwise their intention to so conduct themselves, the threat of injury from the alleged course of conduct they attack is simply too remote to satisfy the case-or-controversy requirement and permit adjudication by a federal court.

Id., at 497-498. Here, by contrast, plaintiff-respondents are persons injured by past unconstitutional conduct (an allegation not made in the

O'Shea complaint) and fear injury at the hands of the police regardless of whether they have violated a valid law.

To the extent that Part II-A of the Court's opinion today indicates that some constitutional violations might be spread so extremely thin as to prevent any individual from showing the requisite case or controversy, I must agree. I do not agree, however, with the Court's substitution of its judgment for that of the District Court on what the evidence here shows. The Court's criticism about numbers would be just as forceful, or would miss the mark just as much, with 100 incidents or 500 or even 3,000, when compared with the overall number of arrests made in the city of Philadelphia. The pattern line will appear somewhere. The District Court drew it this side of the number of proved instances. One properly may wonder how many more instances actually existed but were unproved because of the pressure of time upon the trial court, or because of reluctant witnesses, or because of inherent fear to question constituted authority in any degree, or because of a despairing belief, unfounded though it may be, that nothing can be done about it anyway and that it is not worth the effort. That it was worth the effort is convincingly demonstrated by the result in the District Court, by the affirmance, on the issues before us, by a unanimous panel of the Third Circuit, and by the support given the result below by the Commonwealth of Pennsylvania, the Philadelphia Bar Association, the Greater Philadelphia Movement, and the other entities that have filed briefs as amici curiae here in support of the respondents.

The Court today appears to assert that a state official is not subject to the strictures of 42 U.S.C. §1983 unless he directs the deprivation of constitutional rights. In so holding, it seems to me, the Court ignores both the language of §1983 and the case law interpreting that language. Section 1983 provides a cause of action where a person acting under color of state law "subjects, or causes to be subjected," any other person to a deprivation of rights secured by the Constitution and laws of the United States. By its very words, §1983 reaches not only the acts of an official, but also the acts of subordinates for whom he is responsible.

I do not find it necessary to reach the question under what circumstances failure to supervise will justify an award of money damages, or whether an injunction is authorized where the superior has no consciousness of the wrongs being perpetrated by his subordinates.[1] It is clear that an official may be enjoined from consciously permitting his subordinates, in the course of their duties, to violate the constitutional rights of persons with whom they deal. In rejecting the concept that the official may be

---

1. In this regard, however, this Court recently has approved the imposition of criminal liability without "consciousness of wrongdoing" for failure to supervise subordinates. United States v. Park, 421 U.S. 658 (1975). The concept, thus, is far from novel doctrine.

responsible under §1983, the Court today casts aside reasoned conclusions to the contrary reached by the Courts of Appeals of 10 Circuits.

In the instant case, the District Court found that although there was no departmental policy of racial discrimination, "such violations do occur, with such frequency that they cannot be dismissed as rare, isolated instances; and that little or nothing is done by the city authorities to punish such infractions, or to prevent their recurrence," and that it "is the policy of the department to discourage the filing of such complaints, to avoid or minimize the consequences of proven police misconduct, and to resist disclosure of the final disposition of such complaints."

Further, the applicability of §1983 to controlling officers allows the district courts to avoid the necessity of injunctions issued against individual officers and the consequent continuing supervision by the federal courts of the day-to-day activities of the men on the street.

I would regard what was accomplished in this case as one of those rightly rare but nevertheless justified instances — just as *Allee* and *Hague* — of federal-court "intervention" in a state or municipal executive area. The facts, the deprival of constitutional rights, and the pattern are all proved in sufficient degree. And the remedy is carefully delineated, worked out within the administrative structure rather than superimposed by edict upon it, and essentially, and concededly, "livable."

NOTES ON INTERFERENCE WITH STATE ADMINISTRATION

1. *Rizzo* has three alternate holdings. The first is jurisdictional — that there is no ripe threat of harm to plaintiffs that can be cured by an injunction against these defendants. The second is substantive — that supervisors do not "cause" constitutional violations, within the meaning of §1983, by doing nothing about them and creating a climate in which they are tolerated. The third is an expansion of *Younger* to include state administration. As you think about each holding, try to keep it disentangled from the other two.

2. Consider the third holding first. Is it limited to state law enforcement agencies? To internal disciplinary matters? To remedies ordering "prophylactic procedures"? If it is not limited in some such way, doesn't it threaten all structural injunctions? Didn't Brown v. Board of Education interfere with "State administration of its own law"?

3. *Rizzo* did not mark the end of structural injunctions, even in the Supreme Court. You have already read two more recent examples: Hutto v. Finney, the Arkansas prison case, supra at 274, and Milliken v. Bradley, the Court's second encounter with the Detroit school case, supra at 269. The injunction in *Hutto* ran against a state law enforcement agency,

and Justice Rehnquist in dissent thought the injunction improperly established a prophylactic procedure. The injunction in *Milliken II* ordered remedial education programs and teacher training programs that were related to segregation, but surely no more so than the disciplinary procedures were related to police brutality in *Rizzo*. And the teacher training programs were surely matters of internal administration. Indeed, the injunction disapproved in *Rizzo* ordered training programs. Neither *Hutto* nor *Milliken II* discusses *Rizzo*. Might *Rizzo* be a wild card, to be pulled out only when some lower court does something that deeply offends the Supreme Court majority?

4.   Might the third holding in *Rizzo* best be understood as a caution against unnecessary intrusiveness? Does it add anything to the three-part test of *Milliken II*? *Milliken* said a remedy must be determined by the nature and scope of the violation, that it must restore plaintiffs to the position they would have occupied but for the wrong, and that "the federal courts in devising a remedy must take into account the interests of state and local authorities in managing their own affairs."

5.   The jurisdictional holding reflects a ripeness theory that we have encountered before. See Notes on Ripeness and Preventive Injunctions, supra at 215. It showed up again in City of Los Angeles v. Lyons, 461 U.S. 95 (1983), refusing to enjoin police chokeholds because there was no particular threat that any individual plaintiff would be choked again.

6.   It is consistent with long-established doctrine to say that a threat against all the citizens of Los Angeles or Philadelphia is not a threat against anybody in particular, so that no one has standing to challenge the threat judicially. But in *Rizzo*, there was also a class of all blacks, who were alleged to face a separate threat. Why isn't that claim justiciable? How are all blacks in Philadelphia different from all union organizers in Jersey City? Is it just a matter of the odds? Or is it a matter of defendants' motive, with statistics at best evidentiary? Suppose the number of actual incidents was unchanged, but plaintiffs found an inside witness to testify that Rizzo thought intermittent police violence in black neighborhoods would help keep gangs off the street, and that he conveyed that belief to rank and file police officers. Would there be a case or controversy then?

7.   The substantive holding must be read in conjunction with Monell v. New York City Department of Social Services, 436 U.S. 658 (1978), which held that municipalities are not liable under §1983 for constitutional violations of employees not authorized to make official policy. If the employer isn't liable under respondeat superior, and neither the employer nor the supervisor is liable for failing to supervise, the only §1983 remedy for police violence is against the individual officer. If you are ever beaten by a police officer, be sure to ask for his badge number. You should also hope he has plenty of assets, and that the jury doesn't feel sorry for him. Does the language of §1983 really require such a narrow

remedy? Keep in mind that official and unofficial violence against blacks was one of the prime evils against which §1983 was directed.

E. THE RIGHT TO JURY TRIAL

BEACON THEATRES v. WESTOVER
359 U.S. 500 (1959)

MR. JUSTICE BLACK delivered the opinion of the Court.

Petitioner, Beacon Theatres, Inc., sought by mandamus to require a district judge in the Southern District of California to vacate certain orders alleged to deprive it of a jury trial of issues arising in a suit brought against it by Fox West Coast Theatres, Inc. . . .

Fox operates a movie theatre in San Bernardino, California, and has long been exhibiting films under contracts with movie distributors. These contracts grant it the exclusive right to show "first run" pictures in the "San Bernardino competitive area" and provide for "clearance" — a period of time during which no other theatre can exhibit the same pictures. After building a drive-in theatre about 11 miles from San Bernardino, Beacon notified Fox that it considered contracts barring simultaneous exhibitions of first-run films in the two theatres to be overt acts in violation of the antitrust laws. Fox's complaint alleged that this notification, together with threats of treble damage suits against Fox and its distributors, gave rise to "duress and coercion" which deprived Fox of a valuable property right, the right to negotiate for exclusive first-run contracts. Unless Beacon was restrained, the complaint continued, irreparable harm would result. Accordingly, while its pleading was styled a "Complaint for Declaratory Relief," Fox prayed both for a declaration that a grant of clearance between the Fox and Beacon theatres is reasonable and not in violation of the antitrust laws, and for an injunction, pending final resolution of the litigation, to prevent Beacon from instituting any action under the antitrust laws against Fox and its distributors arising out of the controversy alleged in the complaint. Beacon filed an answer, a counterclaim against Fox, and a cross-claim against an exhibitor who had intervened. . . .

The District Court . . . viewed the issues raised by the "Complaint for Declaratory Relief," including the question of competition between the two theatres, as essentially equitable. . . . [I]t directed that these issues be tried to the court before jury determination of the validity of the charges of antitrust violations made in the counterclaim and cross-claim. A common issue of the "Complaint for Declaratory Relief," the counterclaim, and the cross-claim was the reasonableness of the clearances granted to Fox, which depended, in part, on the existence of competition

between the two theatres. Thus the effect of the action of the District
Court could be, as the Court of Appeals believed, "to limit the petitioner's
opportunity fully to try to a jury every issue which has a bearing upon its
treble damage suit," for determination of the issue of clearances by the
judge might "operate either by way of res judicata or collateral estoppel so
as to conclude both parties with respect thereto at the subsequent trial of
the treble damage claim." . . .

Nevertheless the Court of Appeals refused to upset the order of the
district judge. . . . A party who is entitled to maintain a suit in equity for
an injunction, said the court, may have all the issues in his suit determined by the judge without a jury regardless of whether legal rights are
involved. The court then rejected the argument that equitable relief,
traditionally available only when legal remedies are inadequate, was rendered unnecessary in this case by the filing of the counterclaim and cross-
claim which presented all the issues necessary to a determination of the
right to injunctive relief. Relying on American L. Ins. Co. v. Stewart,
300 U.S. 203, 215, decided before the enactment of the Federal Rules
of Civil Procedure, it invoked the principle that a court sitting in
equity could retain jurisdiction even though later a legal remedy became
available. . . .

[A]ssuming . . . that the complaint can be read as alleging the kind of
harrassment by a multiplicity of lawsuits which would *traditionally* have
justified equity to take jurisdiction and settle the case in one suit we are
nevertheless of the opinion that, under the Declaratory Judgment Act
and the Federal Rules of Civil Procedure, neither claim can justify denying Beacon a trial by jury of all the issues in the antitrust controversy.

The basis of injunctive relief in the federal courts has always been
irreparable harm and inadequacy of legal remedies. At least as much is
required to justify a trial court in using its discretion under the Federal
Rules to allow claims of equitable origins to be tried ahead of legal ones,
since this has the same effect as an equitable injunction of the legal
claims. And it is immaterial, in judging if that discretion is properly employed, that before the Federal Rules and the Declaratory Judgment Act
were passed, courts of equity, exercising a jurisdiction separate from
courts of law, were, in some cases, allowed to enjoin subsequent legal
actions between the same parties involving the same controversy. This
was because the subsequent legal action, though providing an opportunity to try the case to a jury, might not protect the right of the equity
plaintiff to a fair and orderly adjudication of the controversy. Under such
circumstances the legal remedy could quite naturally be deemed inadequate. Inadequacy of remedy and irreparable harm are practical terms,
however. As such their existence today must be determined, not by precedents decided under discarded procedures, but in the light of the remedies now made available by the Declaratory Judgment Act and the
Federal Rules.

Viewed in this manner, the use of discretion by the trial court under Rule 42(b) to deprive Beacon of a full jury trial on its counterclaim and cross-claim, as well as on Fox's plea for declaratory relief, cannot be justified. Under the Federal Rules the same court may try both legal and equitable causes in the same action. Fed. Rules Civ. Proc. 1, 2, 18. Thus any defenses, equitable or legal, Fox may have to charges of antitrust violations can be raised either in its suit for declaratory relief or in answer to Beacon's counterclaim. On proper showing, harassment by threats of other suits, or other suits actually brought, involving the issues being tried in this case, could be temporarily enjoined pending the outcome of this litigation. Whatever permanent injunctive relief Fox might be entitled to on the basis of the decision in this case could, of course, be given by the court after the jury renders its verdict. In this way the issues between these parties could be settled in one suit giving Beacon a full jury trial of every antitrust issue. By contrast, the holding of the court below while granting Fox no additional protection unless the avoidance of jury trial be considered as such, would compel Beacon to split his antitrust case, trying part to a judge and part to a jury. Such a result, which involves the postponement and subordination of Fox's own legal claim for declaratory relief as well as of the counterclaim which Beacon was compelled by the Federal Rules to bring, is not permissible.

Our decision is consistent with the plan of the Federal Rules and the Declaratory Judgment Act to effect substantial procedural reform while retaining a distinction between jury and nonjury issues and leaving substantive rights unchanged. Since in the federal courts equity has always acted only when legal remedies were inadequate, the expansion of adequate legal remedies provided by the Declaratory Judgment Act and the Federal Rules necessarily affects the scope of equity. Thus, the justification for equity's deciding legal issues once it obtains jurisdiction, and refusing to dismiss a case, merely because subsequently a legal remedy becomes available, must be re-evaluated in the light of the liberal joinder provisions of the Federal Rules which allow legal and equitable causes to be brought and resolved in one civil action. Similarly the need for, and therefore, the availability of such equitable remedies as Bills of Peace, Quia Timet and Injunction must be reconsidered in view of the existence of the Declaratory Judgment Act as well as the liberal joinder provision of the Rules.[15] This is not only in accord with the spirit of the Rules and the Act but is required by the provision in the Rules that "[t]he right to trial by jury as declared by the Seventh Amendment to the Constitution or as given by a statute of the United States shall be preserved . . . inviolate."

If there should be cases where the availability of declaratory judgment

---

15. . . . Of course, unless there is an issue of a right to jury trial or of other rights which depend on whether the cause is a "legal" or "equitable" one, the question of adequacy of legal remedies is purely academic and need not arise.

or joinder in one suit of legal and equitable causes would not in all respects protect the plaintiff seeking equitable relief from irreparable harm while affording a jury trial in the legal cause, the trial court will necessarily have to use its discretion in deciding whether the legal or equitable cause should be tried first. Since the right to jury trial is a constitutional one, however, while no similar requirement protects trials by the court, that discretion is very narrowly limited and must, wherever possible, be exercised to preserve jury trial. As this Court said in Scott v. Neely, 140 U.S. 106, 109, 110: "In the Federal courts this [jury] right cannot be dispensed with, except by the assent of the parties entitled to it, nor can it be impaired by any blending with a claim, properly cognizable at law, of a demand for equitable relief in aid of the legal action or during its pendency." This long-standing principle of equity dictates that only under the most imperative circumstances, circumstances which in view of the flexible procedures of the Federal Rules we cannot now anticipate, can the right to a jury trial of legal issues be lost through prior determination of equitable claims. As we have shown, this is far from being such a case. . . .

MR. JUSTICE FRANKFURTER took no part in the consideration or decision of this case. . . .

MR. JUSTICE STEWART, with whom MR. JUSTICE HARLAN and MR. JUSTICE WHITTAKER concur, dissenting. . . .

I

The Court suggests that "the expansion of adequate legal remedies provided by the Declaratory Judgment Act . . . necessarily affects the scope of equity." Does the Court mean to say that the mere availability of an action for a declaratory judgment operates to furnish "an adequate remedy at law" so as to deprive a court of equity of the power to act? That novel line of reasoning is at least implied in the Court's opinion. But the Declaratory Judgment Act did not "expand" the substantive law. That Act merely provided a new statutory remedy, neither legal nor equitable, but available in the areas of both equity and law. When declaratory relief is sought, the right to trial by jury depends upon the basic context in which the issues are presented. If the basic issues in an action for declaratory relief are of a kind traditionally cognizable in equity, e.g., a suit for cancellation of a written instrument, the declaratory judgment is not a "remedy at law." If, on the other hand, the issues arise in a context traditionally cognizable at common law, the right to a jury trial of course remains unimpaired, even though the only relief demanded is a declaratory judgment.

Thus, if in this case the complaint had asked merely for a judgment declaring that the plaintiff's specified manner of business dealings with

distributors and other exhibitors did not render it liable to Beacon under
the antitrust laws, this would have been simply a "juxtaposition of parties"
case in which Beacon could have demanded a jury trial. But the complaint in the present case, as the Court recognizes, presented issues of
exclusively equitable cognizance, going well beyond a mere defense to
any subsequent action at law. Fox sought from the court protection
against Beacon's allegedly unlawful interference with its business relationships — protection which this Court seems to recognize might not
have been afforded by a declaratory judgment, unsupplemented by equitable relief. The availability of a declaratory judgment did not, therefore,
operate to confer upon Beacon the right to trial by jury with respect to the
issues raised by the complaint.

II

The Court's opinion does not, of course, hold or even suggest that a court
of equity may never determine "legal rights." For indeed it is precisely
such rights which the Chancellor, when his jurisdiction has been properly invoked, has often been called upon to decide. Issues of fact are
rarely either "legal" or "equitable." All depends upon the context in
which they arise. The examples cited by Chief Judge Pope in his thorough opinion in the Court of Appeals in this case are illustrative: " . . .
[I]n a suit by one in possession of real property to quiet title, or to remove
a cloud on title, the court of equity may determine the legal title. In a suit
for specific performance of a contract, the court may determine the
making, validity and the terms of the contract involved. In a suit for an
injunction against trespass to real property the court may determine the
legal right of the plaintiff to the possession of that property."

Though apparently not disputing these principles, the Court holds,
quite apart from its reliance upon the Declaratory Judgment Act, that
Beacon by filing its counterclaim and cross-claim acquired a right to trial
by jury of issues which otherwise would have been properly triable to the
court. Support for this position is found in the principle that, "in the
federal courts equity has always acted only when legal remedies were
inadequate. . . . " Yet that principle is not employed in its traditional
sense as a limitation upon the exercise of power by a court of equity. This
is apparent in the Court's recognition that the allegations of the complaint entitled Fox to equitable relief — relief to which Fox would not
have been entitled if it had had an adequate remedy at law. Instead, the
principle is employed today to mean that because it is possible under the
counterclaim to have a jury trial of the factual issue of substantial competition, that issue must be tried by a jury, even though the issue was
primarily presented in the original claim for equitable relief. This is a
marked departure from long-settled principles.

It has been an established rule "that equitable jurisdiction existing at the filing of a bill is not destroyed because an adequate legal remedy may have become available thereafter."[8] American L. Ins. Co. v. Stewart, 300 U.S. 203, 215. It has also been long settled that the District Court in its discretion may order the trial of a suit in equity in advance of an action at law between the same parties, even if there is a factual issue common to both. In the words of Mr. Justice Cardozo, writing for a unanimous Court in American L. Ins. Co. v. Stewart: "A court has control over its own docket. . . . In the exercise of a sound discretion it may hold one lawsuit in abeyance to abide the outcome of another. . . ."

III

The Court today sweeps away these basic principles as "precedents decided under discarded procedures." It suggests that the Federal Rules of Civil Procedure have somehow worked an "expansion of adequate legal remedies" so as to oust the District Courts of equitable jurisdiction, as well as to deprive them of their traditional power to control their own dockets. But obviously the Federal Rules could not and did not "expand" the substantive law one whit. . . .

NOTES ON JURY TRIAL IN CASES COMBINING LEGAL AND EQUITABLE CLAIMS

1.   Fox Theatre's claim of irreparable injury was like the claims of the plaintiffs in the *Younger* cases. Each time Fox acquired exclusive local rights to a new movie, it ran the risk of incurring additional liability for treble damages. Can the trial court protect Fox against that harm while preserving Beacon's right to jury trial? Does the Court restrict Fox's remedy? Or does it say only that Fox can't use its need for an equitable remedy to avoid jury trial of the rest of the case?

2.   Westover was the trial judge. After he denied Beacon's demand for jury trial, Beacon sued the judge in the court of appeals for a writ of mandamus ordering him to try the jury parts of the case first. It is well settled that mandamus is available to protect the right to jury trial, although it is not clear how this practice fits into the usual tests for mandamus against judges. Those tests are discussed supra at 432.

3.   The dissenters in *Beacon* were right about recent historical practice. Equity courts asserted jurisdiction to decide all issues in a case, including damage issues, if the case were once properly in equity. And

---

8.   The suggestion by the Court that "This was because the subsequent legal action, though providing an opportunity to try the case to a jury, might not protect the right of the equity plaintiff to a fair and orderly adjudication of the controversy" is plainly inconsistent with many of the cases in which the rule has been applied.

they would retain a jurisdiction once asserted, even if a legal remedy subsequently became available. This practice was not limited to cases where the legal remedy might not provide a fair and orderly adjudication. For example, in American Life Insurance Co. v. Stewart, 300 U.S. 203 (1937), the insurer sued to cancel a life insurance policy for fraud. Then the insured died and the beneficiary sued on the policy. Fraud was a defense to the policy, and there was no risk the beneficiary's suit would be abandoned or fail to resolve the controversy. The beneficiary's suit was for breach of contract, plainly a suit at law and triable to a jury. But as Justice Stewart notes, the Court unanimously affirmed the trial court's decision to first decide the insurer's equitable claim himself.

4. The seventh amendment says that "in suits at common law," the right to jury trial shall be "preserved." The amendment does not guarantee jury trial in equity or admiralty, and the incorporation of that historical distinction, plus the verb "preserved," has always been thought to impose an historical test: The Constitution guarantees the right to jury trial as it existed in 1791. But the Court has never let the seventh amendment freeze the procedural system. So it has upheld modern procedural devices that take cases away from juries, such as motions for directed verdict and summary judgment; each had a clumsier counterpart in 1791. The Court reasoned that the seventh amendment "was designed to preserve the basic institution of jury trial in only its most fundamental elements, not the great mass of procedural forms and details, varying even then so widely among common-law jurisdictions." Galloway v. United States, 319 U.S. 372, 392 (1943).

5. The standard is thus historical but flexible. The problem in *Beacon* and similar cases is how to apply that standard to the merger of law and equity, a procedural reform that completely undermines the premise on which the seventh amendment was based. Justice Black's answer is that the one constant is the irreparable injury rule, and that as the law becomes capable of repairing more injuries, the scope of equity will shrink and the scope of jury trial will expand. Does a clause requiring that the right to jury trial be "preserved" also require that the right expand? That's not ordinary English usage, is it? On the other hand, are incidental expansions necessary to offset the incidental contractions caused by things like motions for summary judgment?

The dissenters take a more fixed view of history. They are inclined to ask, "Would this case have been tried to a jury in 1791?" The answer is presumably no; once the equity court took jurisdiction of Beacon's suit, it would have enjoined Fox from starting any new suits at law. But if Fox had simply filed its lawsuit instead of writing threatening letters, it could have sued for damages at law in 1791.

6. Which approach is better? The further we get from 1791, the harder it is to reconstruct what would have happened then. Is it possible to forever decide jury issues in a merged system as though the merger had

never happened? Is it worth the trouble? Is it compelled by the constitutional text?

7. Does it matter that jury trial is slower and more expensive, and that many federal judges consider civil juries a nuisance? The seventh amendment applies to all cases where the amount in controversy is over $20; it costs far more than that to empanel a jury. Is it legitimate to lock the seventh amendment in the basement with the second (the right to bear arms) and any others that we no longer believe in? If that's not legitimate, is it at least legitimate and wise to avoid expanding the scope of the right?

As you may infer from *Beacon*, Justice Black shared none of these doubts. He was a stout believer in the benefits of jury trial. So is the plaintiffs' bar. Plaintiffs generally demand juries even in complex securities and antitrust cases where there is a substantial risk the jury will never understand the claim. Lawyers believe that juries are more likely to be influenced by sympathy for victims, and more likely to measure damages generously. In a few kinds of cases, it is defendants who prefer jury trial. Examples are individuals sued by large institutions, and police officers sued by suspected criminals. Litigators aren't always right about who will benefit from jury trial, but their generalizations have substantial basis in experience and at least some basis in empirical research. Aren't these expected advantages the substance of the constitutional right to jury trial? Is trial efficiency a sufficient reason to construe such a right narrowly? It's not much of a safeguard that judges trust their own fairness, is it?

8. The Court applied *Beacon* in Dairy Queen v. Wood, 369 U.S. 469 (1962). A Dairy Queen franchisee failed to pay all the royalties promised to the owner of the trademark. The trademark owner sued for infringement, alleging that it had cancelled the contract for material breach, so that the franchisee was no longer entitled to use the Dairy Queen name. Plaintiff sought an accounting for the unpaid royalties and an injunction against further use of the trademark. It argued that defendant had no right to jury trial, because injunction and accounting were equitable remedies.

In another opinion by Justice Black, the Court held that whatever the label, the suit was an ordinary claim for money damages. It didn't matter whether the suit was characterized as one for breach of contract or for the tort of trademark infringement. The legal remedy would be inadequate only if the accounts were so complicated that a jury could not untangle them even with the aid of a special master. As in *Beacon*, the Court said the trial judge could issue a preliminary injunction against infringement pending the jury's decision, and a permanent injunction thereafter if the jury found infringement.

9. The Court limited *Beacon* and *Dairy Queen* in Katchen v. Landy, 382 U.S. 323 (1966). *Katchen* was a bankruptcy case, in which a creditor

filed a claim and the trustee in bankruptcy sought to recover a preferential payment the creditor had already received. The Court had held earlier that a suit to recover a preference was legal and triable to a jury. Schoenthal v. Irving Trust Co., 287 U.S. 92 (1932). But Congress had provided that if a creditor who had received a preference filed a bankruptcy claim for the amount still due, the bankruptcy court could determine the amount of his preference, offset the two claims, and enter judgment for the creditor or the trustee as the case might be. And bankruptcy courts are courts of equity, sitting without juries.

The Court held that this procedure did not violate the creditor's right to jury trial. The creditor argued that *Beacon* and *Dairy Queen* controlled: His equitable claim for a pro rata share of the bankruptcy estate was irrelevant to the right of jury trial on the trustee's legal claim to recover a preference. The Court's response is not perfectly clear. It emphasizes that independent suits to recover preferences are slow and expensive, and that they disrupt the bankruptcy policy of summary adjudication and quick distribution. Perhaps it just holds that this is a case where separating out the legal claim for jury trial would inflict irreparable injury. At one point the Court notes that *Beacon* acknowledged the possibility of "imperative circumstances" in which the right to jury trial could be lost through prior determination of equitable claims. *Beacon* couldn't imagine what such circumstances might be, but *Katchen* implies that it has found some. But are the circumstances really "imperative"? Jury trial nearly always causes delay, and litigants can often argue that delay causes irreparable injury. In some big city state courts, a jury demand puts a case at the end of a five-year waiting list. Is delay any less imperative for an unemployed personal injury victim than for a bankrupt business?

At another point, the Court says that requiring jury trial would "dismember a scheme which Congress has prescribed." Deference to Congress may be the real ground of decision. But if the scheme violates the seventh amendment, how can Congress authorize it? Might the gap between Justice Stewart's fixed historical test and Justice Black's expanding historical test be a zone of discretion, in which Congress can provide for juries or not? Justices Black and Douglas dissented on the basis of *Beacon* and *Dairy Queen*.

10.   *Beacon, Dairy Queen,* and *Katchen* all assumed that the decision of the judge or jury, whichever comes first, will bind the other decision maker. The Court finally so held in Parklane Hosiery Co. v. Shore, 439 U.S. 322 (1979). In an enforcement proceeding brought by the Securities and Exchange Commission, the district court held that Parklane and thirteen of its officers, directors, and controlling stockholders had issued a materially misleading proxy statement. Plaintiffs in a pending damage action then moved for partial summary judgment, asserting that defen-

dants were bound by the judgment in the SEC case and could no longer litigate whether the proxy was misleading. The Supreme Court agreed, rejecting arguments that the right to jury trial should override collateral estoppel.

The Court thought it irrelevant that in 1791 a decision against Parklane would not have been binding in a separate suit by different plaintiffs; the evolution of collateral estoppel doctrine was no different from the evolution of motions for summary judgment. There was a strong dissent, full of democratic rhetoric about the virtues of juries and the right to jury nullification. "[A]s with other provisions of the Bill of Rights, the onerous nature of the protection is no license for contracting the rights secured by the Amendment." Id. at 346. It wasn't Black or Douglas; they were off the Court. And it wasn't Brennan or Marshall. It was that famous expander of constitutional rights, Justice Rehnquist.

ROSS v. BERNHARD
396 U.S. 531 (1970)

MR. JUSTICE WHITE delivered the opinion of the Court.

The Seventh Amendment to the Constitution provides that in "[s]uits at common law, where the value in controversy shall exceed twenty dollars, the right of trial by jury shall be preserved." Whether the Amendment guarantees the right to a jury trial in stockholders' derivative actions is the issue now before us. . . .

What can be gleaned from this Court's opinions is not inconsistent with the general understanding, reflected by the state court decisions and secondary sources, that equity could properly resolve corporate claims of any kind without a jury when properly pleaded in derivative suits complying with the equity rules.

Such was the prevailing opinion when the Federal Rules of Civil Procedure were adopted in 1938. It continued until 1963 when the Court of Appeals for the Ninth Circuit, relying on the Federal Rules as construed and applied in Beacon Theatres, Inc. v. Westover, 359 U.S. 500 (1959), and Dairy Queen, Inc. v. Wood, 369 U.S. 469 (1962), required the legal issues in a derivative suit to be tried to a jury. De Pinto v. Provident Security Life Ins. Co., 323 F.2d 826. It was this decision that the District Court followed in the case before us and that the Court of Appeals rejected.

Beacon and Dairy Queen presaged De Pinto. Under those cases, where equitable and legal claims are joined in the same action, there is a right to jury trial on the legal claims which must not be infringed either by trying the legal issues as incidental to the equitable ones or by a court trial of a common issue existing between the claims. The Seventh Amendment question depends on the nature of the issue to be tried rather than the character of the overall action.[10] The principle of these cases bears heavily on derivative actions.

We have noted that the derivative suit has dual aspects: first, the stockholder's right to sue on behalf of the corporation, historically an equitable matter; second, the claim of the corporation against directors or third parties on which, if the corporation had sued and the claim presented legal issues, the company could demand a jury trial. As implied by Mr. Justice Holmes in Fleitmann v. Welsbach Street Lighting Co., 240 U.S. 27 (1916), legal claims are not magically converted into equitable issues by their presentation to a court of equity in a derivative suit. The claim pressed by the stockholder against directors or third parties "is not his own but the corporation's." Koster v. Lumbermens Mut. Cas. Co., 330 U.S. 518, 522 (1947). The corporation is a necessary party to the action; without it the case cannot proceed. Although named a defendant, it is the real party in interest, the stockholder being at best the nominal plaintiff. The proceeds of the action belong to the corporation and it is bound by the result of the suit. The heart of the action is the corporate claim. If it presents a legal issue, one entitling the corporation to a jury trial under the Seventh Amendment, the right to a jury is not forfeited merely because the stockholder's right to sue must first be adjudicated as an equitable issue triable to the court. *Beacon* and *Dairy Queen* require no less.

If under older procedures, now discarded, a court of equity could properly try the legal claims of the corporation presented in a derivative suit, it was because irreparable injury was threatened and no remedy at law existed as long as the stockholder was without standing to sue and the corporation itself refused to pursue its own remedies. Indeed, from 1789 until 1938, the judicial code expressly forbade courts of equity from entertaining any suit for which there was an adequate remedy at law. This provision served "to guard the right of trial by jury preserved by the Seventh Amendment and to that end it should be liberally construed." Schoenthal v. Irving Trust Co., 287 U.S. 92, 94 (1932). If, before 1938, the law had borrowed from equity, as it borrowed other things, the idea that stockholders could litigate for their recalcitrant corporation, the corporate claim, if legal, would undoubtedly have been tried to a jury.

Of course, this did not occur, but the Federal Rules had a similar impact. Actions are no longer brought as actions at law or suits in equity. Under the Rules there is only one action — a "civil action" — in which all claims may be joined and all remedies are available. Purely procedural impediments to the presentation of any issue by any party, based on the difference between law and equity, were destroyed. In a civil action pre-

---

10. As our cases indicate, the "legal" nature of an issue is determined by considering, first, the pre-merger custom with reference to such questions; second, the remedy sought; and, third, the practical abilities and limitations of juries. Of these factors, the first, requiring extensive and possibly abstruse historical inquiry, is obviously the most difficult to apply.

senting a stockholder's derivative claim, the court after passing upon the plaintiff's right to sue on behalf of the corporation is now able to try the corporate claim for damages with the aid of a jury. Separable claims may be tried separately, Fed. Rule Civ. Proc. 42(b), or legal and equitable issues may be handled in the same trial. The historical rule preventing a court of law from entertaining a shareholder's suit on behalf of the corporation is obsolete; it is no longer tenable for a district court, administering both law and equity in the same action, to deny legal remedies to a corporation, merely because the corporation's spokesmen are its shareholders rather than its directors. Under the rules, law and equity are procedurally combined; nothing turns now upon the form of the action or the procedural devices by which the parties happen to come before the court. The "expansion of adequate legal remedies provided by . . . the Federal Rules necessarily affects the scope of equity." Beacon Theatres, Inc. v. Westover, 359 U.S. at 509.

Thus, for example, before-merger class actions were largely a device of equity, and there was no right to a jury even on issues that might, under other circumstances, have been tried to a jury. Although at least one post-merger court held that the device was not available to try legal issues, it now seems settled in lower federal courts that class action plaintiffs may obtain a jury trial on any legal issues they present.

Derivative suits have been described as one kind of "true" class action. We are inclined to agree with the description, at least to the extent it recognizes that the derivative suit and the class action were both ways of allowing parties to be heard in equity who could not speak at law.[15] After adoption of the rules there is no longer any procedural obstacle to the assertion of legal rights before juries, however the party may have acquired standing to assert those rights. Given the availability in a derivative action of both legal and equitable remedies, we think the Seventh Amendment preserves to the parties in a stockholder's suit the same right to a jury trial that historically belonged to the corporation and to those against whom the corporation pressed its legal claims.

In the instant case we have no doubt that the corporation's claim is, at least in part, a legal one. The relief sought is money damages. There are allegations in the complaint of a breach of fiduciary duty, but there are also allegations of ordinary breach of contract and gross negligence. The

---

15. Other equitable devices are used under the rules without depriving the parties employing them of the right to a jury trial on legal issues. For example, although the right to intervene may in some cases be limited, when an intervention is permitted generally, the intervenor has a right to a jury trial on any legal issues he presents. A similar development seems to be taking place in the lower courts in interpleader actions. Before merger interpleader actions lay only in equity, and there was no right to a jury even on issues that might, under other circumstances, have been tried to a jury. This view continued for some time after merger, but numerous courts and commentators have now come to the conclusion that the right to a jury should not turn on how the parties happen to be brought into court.

corporation, had it sued on its own behalf, would have been entitled to a jury's determination, at a minimum, of its damages against its broker under the brokerage contract and of its rights against its own directors because of their negligence. Under these circumstances it is unnecessary to decide whether the corporation's other claims are also properly triable to a jury. Dairy Queen, Inc. v. Wood, 369 U.S. 469 (1962). The decision of the Court of Appeals is reversed.

It is so ordered.

MR. JUSTICE STEWART, with whom THE CHIEF JUSTICE and MR. JUSTICE HARLAN join, dissenting.

In holding as it does that the plaintiff in a shareholder's derivative suit is constitutionally entitled to a jury trial, the Court today seems to rely upon some sort of ill-defined combination of the Seventh Amendment and the Federal Rules of Civil Procedure. Somehow the Amendment and the Rules magically interact to do what each separately was expressly intended not to do, namely, to enlarge the right to a jury trial in civil actions brought in the courts of the United States.

The Seventh Amendment, by its terms, does not extend, but merely *preserves* the right to a jury trial "[i]n Suits at common law." All agree that this means the reach of the Amendment is limited to those actions that were tried to the jury in 1791 when the Amendment was adopted. Suits in equity, which were historically tried to the court, were therefore unaffected by it. Similarly, Rule 38 of the Federal Rules has no bearing on the right to a jury trial in suits in equity, for it simply preserves inviolate "[t]he right of trial by jury as declared by the Seventh Amendment.". . . Since, as the Court concedes, a shareholder's derivative suit could be brought only in equity, it would seem to me to follow by the most elementary logic that in such suits there is no constitutional right to a trial by jury. Today the Court tosses aside history, logic, and over 100 years of firm precedent to hold that the plaintiff in a shareholder's derivative suit does indeed have a constitutional right to a trial by jury. This holding has a questionable basis in policy[5] and no basis whatever in the Constitution.

The Court begins by assuming the "dual nature" of the shareholder's action. While the plaintiff's right to get into court at all is conceded to be equitable, once he is there the Court says his claim is to be viewed as though it were the claim of the corporation itself. If the corporation would have been entitled to a jury trial on such a claim, then, it is said, so would the shareholder. This conceptualization is without any historical

---

5. *See, e.g.*, J. Frank, Courts on Trial 110-111 (1949). Certainly there is no consensus among commentators on the desirability of jury trials in civil actions generally. Particularly where the issues in the case are complex — as they are likely to be in a derivative suit — much can be said for allowing the court discretion to try the case itself. *See* discussion in 5 J. Moore, Federal Practice ¶38.02[1].

basis. For the fact is that a shareholder's suit was not originally viewed in this country, or in England, as a suit to enforce a *corporate* cause of action. Rather, the shareholder's suit was initially permitted only against the managers of the corporation — not third parties — and it was conceived of as an equitable action to enforce the right of a beneficiary against his trustee. The shareholder was not, therefore, in court to enforce indirectly the corporate right of action, but to enforce directly his own equitable right of action against an unfaithful fiduciary. Later the rights of the shareholder were enlarged to encompass suits against third parties harming the corporation, but "the postulated 'corporate cause of action' has never been thought to describe an actual historical class of suit which was recognized by courts of law."[7] Indeed the commentators, including those cited by the Court as postulating the analytic duality of the shareholder's derivative suit, recognize that historically the suit has in practice always been treated as a single cause tried exclusively in equity. They agree that there is therefore no constitutional right to a jury trial even where there might have been one had the corporation itself brought the suit.

This has been not simply the "general" or "prevailing" view in the federal courts as the Court says, but the unanimous view with the single exception of the Ninth Circuit's 1963 decision in De Pinto v. Provident Security Life Ins. Co., 323 F.2d 826, a decision that has since been followed by no court until the present case. . . .

It is true that in *Beacon Theatres* it was stated that the 1938 Rules did diminish the scope of federal equity jurisdiction in certain particulars. But the Court's effort to force the facts of this case into the mold of *Beacon Theatres* and *Dairy Queen* simply does not succeed. Those cases involved a combination of historically separable suits, one in law and one in equity. Their facts fit the pattern of cases where, before the Rules, the equity court would have disposed of the equitable claim and would then have either retained jurisdiction over the suit, despite the availability of adequate legal remedies, or enjoined a subsequent legal action between the same parties involving the same controversy.

But the present case is not one involving traditionally equitable claims by one party, and traditionally legal claims by the other. Nor is it a suit in which the plaintiff is asserting a combination of legal and equitable claims. For, as we have seen, a derivative suit has always been conceived of as a single, unitary, equitable cause of action. It is for this reason, and not because of "procedural impediments," that the courts of equity did not transfer derivative suits to the law side. In short, the cause of action is wholly a creature of equity. And whatever else can be said of *Beacon*

7. Note, The Right to a Jury Trial in a Stockholder's Derivative Action, 74 Yale L.J. 725, 730.

Theatres and *Dairy Queen*, they did not cast aside altogether the historic division between equity and law.

If history is to be so cavalierly dismissed, the derivative suit can, of course, be artificially broken down into separable elements. But so then can any traditionally equitable cause of action, and the logic of the Court's position would lead to the virtual elimination of all equity jurisdiction. An equitable suit for an injunction, for instance, often involves issues of fact which, if damages had been sought, would have been triable to a jury. Does this mean that in a suit asking only for injunctive relief these factual issues *must* be tried to the jury, with the judge left to decide only whether, given the jury's findings, an injunction is the appropriate remedy? Certainly the Federal Rules make it *possible* to try a suit for an injunction in that way, but even more certainly they were not intended to have any such effect. Yet the Court's approach, it seems, would require that if any "legal issue" procedurally *could* be tried to a jury, it constitutionally *must* be tried to a jury.

The fact is, of course, that there are, for the most part, no such things as inherently "legal issues" or inherently "equitable issues." There are only factual issues, and, "like chameleons [they] take their color from surrounding circumstances."[12] Thus the Court's "nature of the issue" approach is hardly meaningful.

As a final ground for its conclusion, the Court points to a supposed analogy to suits involving class actions. . . . [T]he analogy to derivative suits is wholly unpersuasive. For it is clear that the draftsmen of the Federal Rules intended that Rule 23 as it pertained to class actions should be applicable, like other rules governing joinder of claims and parties, "to all actions, whether formerly denominated legal or equitable."[13] This does not mean that a formerly equitable action is triable to a jury simply *because* it is brought on behalf of a class, but only that a historically legal cause of action can be tried to a jury *even if* it is brought as a class action. Since a derivative suit is historically wholly a creation of equity, the class action "analogy" is in truth no analogy at all. . . .

MORE NOTES ON JURY TRIAL IN CASES COMBINING LEGAL AND EQUITABLE CLAIMS

1. The majority distinguishes the corporation's substantive claim from the plaintiff's claim to sue on the corporation's behalf. Isn't that a plausible analysis of the modern derivative suit, whether or not it has any

12. James, Right to a Jury Trial in Civil Actions, 72 Yale L.J. 655, 692. . . .
13. Original Committee Note of 1937 to Rule 23. . . .

basis in history? But does that matter? Does it make any sense to start with an historical test and then rewrite it in light of modern analysis?

2. No matter how one analyzes the derivative suit, the historical practice is clear. There isn't the slightest doubt that in 1791 this suit could have been filed only in a court of equity. If the corporation had sued on its own behalf, it could have sued at law. Does that make any difference? Or is that just the dissent from *Beacon* again?

3. Assuming that the majority is correct to conceive of the derivative suit as two separate claims, is *Ross* controlled by *Beacon* and *Dairy Queen*? Derivative suits, class actions, and interpleader are at most ancillary remedies; in some ways they are more like procedural devices than independent remedies. Is a legal claim asserted in an equitable procedure the same as legal and equitable claims asserted in the same suit? Isn't the substantive claim wholly independent of the procedural device that brings it to court? On the other hand, but for Fox's suit to enjoin Beacon from suing, Beacon could have sued at law and tried its case to a jury in 1791. No matter what anybody else did, there is no way that plaintiffs in *Ross* could have gotten a jury trial in 1791. Does that matter?

4. The dissenters say there is no limit to the process of breaking lawsuits down into issues. A specific performance suit raises issues of offer, acceptance, consideration, and breach that could be tried to a jury; if the jury found for plaintiff, the judge could decide whether to grant specific performance. Presumably the majority doesn't intend to go that far, but it doesn't answer the argument. Is there an answer? Was "issue" a poor choice of words in the text at footnote 10? Would the majority do better to characterize "claims" instead of "issues"? Footnote 10 says an "issue" is characterized as legal or equitable in part by the remedy sought. Can you seek a remedy for an "issue"?

5. Professor Fiss has proposed that we abolish the irreparable injury rule, and give plaintiff the best remedy available, whether legal or equitable. See Reprise on Irreparable Injury, supra at 434. Would that proposal violate the seventh amendment? Do *Beacon*, *Dairy Queen*, and *Ross* constitutionalize the irreparable injury rule? Consider this response:

> In . . . Schoenthal v. Irving Trust Co. and Ross v. Bernhard, the relief sought was a money judgment. . . . Dairy Queen, Inc. v. Wood was similar: the issue was whether plaintiff could avoid jury trial of a claim for money by demanding an accounting for trademark infringement rather than damages for breach of a contract licensing the trademark. The Court noted that the judge should decide plaintiff's claims for temporary and permanent injunctions against further use of the trademark.
>
> Beacon Theatres, Inc. v. Westover was . . . no different. . . . The Court held that the counterclaim must be tried first, and to a jury. But it emphasized that if plaintiff needed temporary or permanent injunctions against defendant's suits or threats, the judge could give this relief and that plaintiff was entitled to protection "in all respects . . . from irreparable harm."

Thus, despite the emphasis in these cases on adequacy of the legal remedy, none of them addresses the question of how adequate the legal remedy must be. In each the legal remedy was identical to — not merely as good as — all or some substantial part of the equitable remedy; to the extent of any difference, plaintiff was entitled to the equitable remedy. The Court could plausibly view each of these cases as an attempt to avoid a jury by artful pleading, even though the insistence that the case was in equity had no effect on relief.

These cases do not constitutionalize any rule concerning the quite different situation that Fiss' proposal addresses: the case in which there is a difference between the legal and equitable remedies, and in which one remedy seems about as good as the other, but the plaintiff claims that on close analysis the equitable remedy is slightly better. So long as that claim is not a transparent attempt to avoid jury trial, courts should consider it on its own merits, without a bias in favor of the legal remedy.

Laycock, Injunctions and the Irreparable Injury Rule, 57 Tex. L. Rev. 1065, 1081-1082 (1979).

Would Justice Black have been persuaded by that? Should five justices be persuaded by it? Do *Beacon* and *Ross* demand that the trial judge do anything more than preserve jury trial where that can be done without prejudice to either party?

NOTES ON CHARACTERIZING CLAIMS

1.   Footnote 10 of *Ross* attempts to summarize the tests for characterizing issues as legal or equitable. It does not appear to be a very careful job. Does the remedy sought have any relevance apart from the premerger custom? Are the practical limitations of juries relevant if the issue were clearly triable to a jury in 1791? Might the policy arguments for and against jury trial in a particular kind of case be a tie breaker when the 1791 practice is unclear?

2.   Historical analysis has dominated in practice. And except for a handful of exclusively equitable substantive areas, such as breach of trust, analysis has largely focused on the remedy. Suits for common law wrongs seeking damages or injunctions are easy; such suits existed in 1791 and the practice was clear. Suits on new substantive rights that didn't exist in 1791 are classified according to the most nearly analogous cause of action that did exist in 1791. The Court has rejected the argument that the seventh amendment reference to "common law" excludes statutory claims. As a practical matter, new claims are largely categorized on the basis of the remedy. Thus in Curtis v. Loether, 415 U.S. 189 (1974), the Court held that the seventh amendment required jury trial in damage suits for racial discrimination in housing. The statute defined a new legal duty, and thus created a new tort; but "more important," the relief sought was compensatory and punitive damages. Id. at 195-196.

3. *Beacon* assumes that declaratory judgments are a legal remedy. Doesn't that ignore the historical analogy approach? Before the declaratory judgment acts, most of the declaratory remedies were equitable: bills to quiet title, cancel documents, and such. Often the declaratory judgment substitutes for an injunction. Aren't these the relevant analogies, and don't they make most declaratory judgments equitable?

Most courts have so held, but with an important exception relevant to *Beacon*. If the declaratory judgment is brought in a context in which no declaratory remedy exists apart from the declaratory judgment act, and the primary effect of suing for declaratory judgment is to reverse the alignment of the parties in a suit that would have been brought anyway, then the legal or equitable character of the suit that would have been brought anyway will control the characterization of the declaratory suit. You can't deprive your opponent of jury trial in an ordinary contract or tort action by suing for a declaratory judgment that you aren't liable. The cases are collected in Annotation, Jury Trial in Action for Declaratory Relief, 13 A.L.R.2d 777 (1950 & Supps.). If *Beacon* had been decided on that ground, it probably wouldn't be in very many case books.

4. Not all monetary relief is legal. Some equitable remedies ended in money decrees, most notably accounting for profits and some other examples of restitution. Restitution was available at both law and equity, under different conditions and different theories; only a legal historian after lengthy study could claim to know much about the location of the boundary in 1791. It seems nearly certain that the scope of legal restitution has expanded since then. If the logic of *Beacon* and *Dairy Queen* is followed out, legal forms of restitution such as quasi-contract must be used whenever possible, because the right to jury trial has expanded with the scope of legal remedies.

The courts have not taken that view. Consider Securities & Exchange Commission v. Commonwealth Chemical Securities, 574 F.2d 90 (2d Cir. 1978). The SEC sought restitution of profits from securities fraud; it planned to disburse the disgorged profits to the victims of the fraud. Judge Friendly held that defendants were not entitled to jury trial. "The court is not awarding damages to which plaintiff is legally entitled but is exercising the chancellor's discretion to prevent unjust enrichment." Id. at 95. He quoted Moore's Federal Practice for the proposition that there is no right to jury trial "when restitution is sought in the form and in the situations allowed in equity prior to the rules or authorized by valid statutes." Is that emphasis on form consistent with the Supreme Court's cases? Dictum in Curtis v. Loether lends support to Friendly's holding. Justice Black was the moving force behind *Beacon* and *Dairy Queen*, and perhaps *Ross* as well; it would not be surprising if the Court quit building on those cases.

5. The unexamined view that restitution is equitable has been decisive in employment discrimination suits under Title VII of the Civil Rights Act of 1964. Title VII authorizes injunctions against discrimina-

tion, and such "affirmative action as may be appropriate, which may include . . . reinstatement . . . with or without back pay" and any "other equitable relief" the court "deems appropriate." 42 U.S.C. §2000e-5(g) (1982). The lower courts have uniformly concluded that back pay under this provision is a form of equitable restitution. There is a sense in which the employer saved the wages by his wrong, but usually he has paid the savings out to a replacement employee; he hasn't really profited. And to the extent this remedy is restitutionary, quasi-contract would surely fit as well as constructive trust.

But Congress feared, and the courts have feared, that jury trials would nullify the statute. That may not be true today, but surely it would have been true in much of the country in 1964. The statutory talk of equitable relief was a deliberate attempt to avoid jury trial, recognized as such at the time; one of the arguments against the statute was that it eroded the right to jury trial. The Supreme Court has not decided whether the effort to avoid jury trial succeeded, but it is fair to consider the matter settled. *Curtis* reserved the issue, but it carefully explained the reasoning of the lower court cases and said that the language of Title VII "contrasts sharply" with the language of the Fair Housing Act. Other cases have held that the right to back pay is equitable and therefore discretionary, although discretion to deny back pay is quite narrow. City of Los Angeles v. Manhart, 435 U.S. 702, 718-723 (1978); Albemarle Paper Co. v. Moody, 422 U.S. 405, 413-425 (1975).

Is it legitimate to let Congress evade the seventh amendment in this way? The amendment was as much aimed at Congress as at the judiciary; its drafters feared that Congress would entrust the enforcement of un-popular laws to courts without juries. Wolfram, The Constitutional History of the Seventh Amendment, 57 Minn. L. Rev. 639, 664-665, 706-707 (1973). Isn't that exactly what Congress did, and consciously so, in the Civil Rights Act of 1964? Is there implied authorization for such evasion in the enforcement provisions of the thirteenth, fourteenth, and fifteenth amendments? If constitutional rights in a democracy are intended to protect minorities from oppressive majorities, how can juries be expected to enforce constitutional rights? Can the seventh amendment be reconciled with the others by the power to enforce constitutional rights by injunction, and the power to set aside jury verdicts that are unsupported by the evidence?

Civil rights plaintiffs pay a price for avoiding jury trial. Back pay is the only monetary remedy available under Title VII. Because the statute doesn't authorize damages, plaintiffs can't recover for mental distress, or consequential damages, or punitive damages. Does that make the provision constitutional, by proving that it isn't really a damage remedy in disguise? Plaintiffs can recover these items under 42 U.S.C. §1981 (1982), one of the Reconstruction civil rights acts; suits under that section are tried to juries.

6. Congress also has broad power to commit claims to administrative

agencies without juries. The rationale has varied somewhat over the years. But the current leading case rests on the recurring view that actions before administrative agencies are not suits at common law, so the seventh amendment is simply irrelevant. Atlas Roofing Co. v. Occupational Safety & Health Review Commission, 430 U.S. 442 (1977). On that rationale, can't Congress avoid jury trial at will by committing everything to agencies instead of courts? No, the Court said:

> Our prior cases support administrative factfinding in only those situations involving "public rights," e.g., where the Government is involved in its sovereign capacity under an otherwise valid statute creating enforceable public rights. Wholly private tort, contract, and property cases, as well as a vast range of other cases, are not at all implicated.

Id. at 458.

Even so, it is hard to find any limit to the concept of public rights. Back pay to individual workers under the National Labor Relations Act is a public right, presumably because the National Labor Relations Board brings suit on the worker's behalf. NLRB v. Jones & Laughlin Steel Corp., 301 U.S. 1 (1937). Can Congress make any private right public by providing that the action be brought in the name of the agency? Compensation of injured workers is often entrusted to administrative agencies; how is that different from "wholly private tort" cases? And Atlas Roofing repeats the dictum of Pernell v. Southall Realty, 416 U.S. 363, 383 (1974): "We may assume that the Seventh Amendment would not be a bar to a congressional effort to entrust landlord-tenant disputes, including those over the right to possession, to an administrative agency." My colleagues in administrative law view Atlas Roofing's "public rights" dictum as wholly inconsistent with modern administrative law; they don't expect much to ever come of it.

7.   There has been much litigation and scholarship over whether the Constitution requires jury trial in cases too complex for juries to understand. This has sometimes been argued as a characterization issue: Would equity have taken jurisdiction on the ground of complexity in 1791? It has sometimes been argued as an implied exception to the seventh amendment. And it has sometimes been argued as a due process override: The seventh amendment does not require jury trial in cases where the resulting decision would be so irrational that it denied due process. The cases are collected in Annotation, Complexity of Civil Action as Affecting Seventh Amendment Right to Trial by Jury, 54 A.L.R. Fed. 733 (1981 & 1984 Supps.).

The two leading cases are squarely in conflict. The Ninth Circuit rejected any complexity exception in a case in which the trial judge estimated that the factfinder would have to read 100,000 pages of documents and that the trial would last two years. In re U.S. Financial Securities Litigation, 609 F.2d 411 (9th Cir. 1979), *cert. denied sub nom.* Gant v. Union Bank, 446 U.S. 929 (1980). The court was confident the lawyers could find a way to explain the case to jurors.

The Third Circuit disagreed, holding that due process requires bench trial in cases beyond the ability of jurors. In re Japanese Electronic Products Antitrust Litigation, 631 F.2d 1069 (3d Cir. 1980). The trial court predicted that trial would last a year; nine years of discovery had produced a million pages of documents and 100,000 pages of depositions. The court remanded for the trial court to determine whether jurors could comprehend the case. Without reconsidering the jury trial issue, the district court granted summary judgment to defendants. The Court of Appeals reversed in part and remanded for trial. 723 F.2d 238 (3d Cir. 1983).

The Japanese antitrust litigation graphically illustrated the problems an historical test can create both for judges and scholars. IBM and Zenith were on opposite sides of the jury trial issue in that case. Each commissioned one of the world's leading legal historians to write a law review article supporting its view of whether complexity was a ground of equity jurisdiction in 1791. Each scholar reached the conclusion he promised. Devlin, Jury Trial of Complex Cases: English Practice at the Time of the Seventh Amendment, 80 Colum. L. Rev. 43 (1980); Arnold, A Historical Inquiry into the Right to Trial by Jury in Complex Civil Litigation, 128 U. Pa. L. Rev. 829 (1980). IBM's lawyers then published a reply to Professor Arnold, and Professor Arnold published a replication. Campbell and Le Poidevin, Complex Cases and Jury Trials: A Reply to Professor Arnold, 128 U. Pa. L. Rev. 965 (1980); Arnold, A Modest Replication to a Lengthy Discourse, 128 U. Pa. L. Rev. 986 (1980). The court considered some of these articles but didn't rely on any of them.

John Langbein of the University of Chicago has argued orally that the whole historical inquiry in the case was misdirected. In his view, there was no such thing as a complex common law case in 1791. The common law's narrow joinder rules, and the requirement of pleading to a single issue, meant that common law juries decided only simple cases. If a case couldn't fit within those rules, it could not be brought at common law. It might go to equity, or it might be abandoned, but in Langbein's view, the issue whether equity should interfere to take a complex case away from a jury could never arise.

NOTES ON THE RIGHT TO JURY TRIAL IN STATE COURT

1.   The seventh amendment does not apply to the states, and the fourteenth amendment's due process clause does not require juries in civil cases. Every state except Louisiana guarantees civil jury trial in its

own constitution, generally in terms similar to the seventh amendment. But these provisions have been construed in disparate ways. Some states have adopted rules similar to *Beacon* and *Dairy Queen*; other states still adhere to earlier rules allowing equity to preempt jury trial of legal claims related to equitable claims.

A survey of state cases citing *Beacon* reveals an almost even split between these two general approaches. Of course, there is room for many variations within each approach; this sampling of cases only scratches the surface of state jury trial law.

2.   One way to avoid the whole problem is to provide jury trial in equity cases. Several states have experimented with the practice; a few have declared it unconstitutional. The history is reviewed state by state in Van Hecke, Trial by Jury in Equity Cases, 31 N.C.L. Rev. 157 (1953). In Georgia, North Carolina, Tennessee, and Texas, jury trial in equity has become the norm. All four states submit equity cases on special verdicts or interrogatories, preserving issues of equitable discretion for the court. The line between fact and discretion is thin. In Texas, for example, whether there is a sufficient threat of future violations to justify an injunction is for the judge. State v. Texas Pet Foods, 591 S.W.2d 800 (Tex. 1979). Whether the cost of the injunction so far outweighs its benefits that relief should be denied is also for the judge. Merrick v. Evergreen Helicopters, 649 S.W.2d 807 (Tex. App. 1983).

NOTE ON ADVISORY JURIES

Any equity case can be tried to an advisory jury, and some judges view that as a compromise solution to these problems. But it doesn't avoid the need to decide whether the claims are legal or equitable. If the claims are legal, the verdict is binding; if the claims are equitable, it is only advisory. So litigants can appeal on the ground that the verdict was given the wrong weight. An example is Abner A. Wolf, Inc. v. Walch, 385 Mich. 253, 188 N.W.2d 544 (1971). The trial judge in that case correctly held the verdict advisory, adopted it as his own, and entered judgment on the verdict without making his own findings of fact and conclusions of law. The state Supreme Court reversed for findings and conclusions, holding that it couldn't review the judgment without them. Id. at 266-267, 188 N.W.2d at 550-551. Federal Civil Rule 52(a) explicitly requires federal judges to enter their own findings and conclusions in cases tried to an advisory jury; many state rules are similar.

APPENDIX

Present Value Tables

Present value tables are useful in determining the present value of a worker's lost income or the present value of the income produced by a capital asset. The example here is taken from R. Wixon, Accountant's Handbook 29.58-29.59, fig. 25 (4th ed. 1960). It shows the present value of $1 at interest rates ranging from 1 to 6 percent over periods from 0 to 100 years. If you read across the row for any period, to the column for any interest rate, you will find the present value of $1 at that time and interest rate. Some examples:

The present value of $1 paid immediately — period 0 — is $1; that is true at any interest rate. The present value of $1 paid in one year is 99.009901 cents at an interest rate of 1 percent, or 94.339623 cents at an interest rate of 6 percent. The present value of $1 paid in thirty years is 74.192292 cents at an interest rate of 1 percent, or 17.411013 cents at an interest rate of 6 percent.

For larger amounts, simply multiply. Thus, the present value of $10,000 to be paid in thirty years is $7,419.23 at an interest rate of 1 percent, or $1,741.10 at an interest rate of 6 percent.

To calculate the present value of a stream of income, you have to treat each year separately. Find the value of the first year's income, the second year's income, etc., to the end of the expected stream. Then add up the present value of each year's income to get the present value of the whole stream of income.

If you want to work with interest rates higher than 6 percent, you can use periods of less than a year. For example, ten years at 12 percent is equal to twenty six-month periods at 6 percent.

Present Value of 1 at Compound Interest

Value for period n and interest rate $= \dfrac{1}{(1+i)^n} = (1+i)^{-n}$

Periods	1%	1.25%	1.5%	1.75%	2%	2.25%	2.5%
0	1.	1.	1.	1.	1.	1.	1.
1	0.99009901	0.98765432	0.98522167	0.98280098	0.98039216	0.97799511	0.97560976
2	0.98029605	0.97546106	0.97066175	0.96589777	0.96116878	0.95647444	0.95181440
3	0.97059015	0.96341833	0.95631699	0.94928528	0.94232233	0.93542732	0.92859941
4	0.96098034	0.95152428	0.94218423	0.93295851	0.92384543	0.91484335	0.90595064
5	0.95146569	0.93977706	0.92826033	0.91691254	0.90573081	0.89471232	0.88385429
6	0.94204524	0.92817488	0.91454219	0.90114254	0.88797138	0.87502427	0.86229687
7	0.93271805	0.91671593	0.90102679	0.88564378	0.87056018	0.85576946	0.84126524
8	0.92348322	0.90539845	0.88771112	0.87041157	0.85349037	0.83693835	0.82074657
9	0.91433982	0.89422069	0.87459224	0.85544135	0.83675527	0.81852161	0.80072836
10	0.90528695	0.88318093	0.86166723	0.84072860	0.82034830	0.80051013	0.78119840
11	0.89632372	0.87227746	0.84893323	0.82626889	0.80426304	0.78289499	0.76214478
12	0.88744923	0.86150860	0.83638742	0.81205788	0.78849318	0.76566748	0.74355589
13	0.87866260	0.85087269	0.82402702	0.79809128	0.77303253	0.74881905	0.72542038
14	0.86996297	0.84036809	0.81184928	0.78436490	0.75787502	0.73234137	0.70772720
15	0.86134947	0.82999318	0.79985150	0.77087459	0.74301473	0.71622628	0.69046556
16	0.85282126	0.81974635	0.78803104	0.75761631	0.72844581	0.70046580	0.67362493
17	0.84437749	0.80962602	0.77638526	0.74458605	0.71416256	0.68505212	0.65719506
18	0.83601731	0.79963064	0.76491159	0.73177990	0.70015937	0.66997763	0.64116591
19	0.82773992	0.78975866	0.75360747	0.71919401	0.68643076	0.65523484	0.62552772
20	0.81954447	0.78000855	0.74247042	0.70682458	0.67297133	0.64081647	0.61027094
21	0.81143017	0.77037881	0.73149795	0.69466789	0.65977582	0.62671538	0.59538629
22	0.80339621	0.76086796	0.72068763	0.68272028	0.64683904	0.61292457	0.58086467
23	0.79544179	0.75147453	0.71003708	0.67097817	0.63415592	0.59943724	0.56669724
24	0.78756613	0.74219707	0.69954392	0.65943800	0.62172149	0.58624668	0.55287535
25	0.77976844	0.73303414	0.68920583	0.64809632	0.60953087	0.57334639	0.53939059
26	0.77204796	0.72398434	0.67902052	0.63694970	0.59757928	0.56072997	0.52623472
27	0.76440392	0.71504626	0.66898574	0.62599479	0.58586204	0.54839117	0.51339973
28	0.75683557	0.70621853	0.65909925	0.61522829	0.57437455	0.53632388	0.50087778
29	0.74934215	0.69749978	0.64935887	0.60464697	0.56311231	0.52452213	0.48866125
30	0.74192292	0.68888867	0.63976243	0.59424764	0.55207089	0.51298008	0.47674269
31	0.73457715	0.68038387	0.63030781	0.58402716	0.54124597	0.50169201	0.46511481
32	0.72730411	0.67198407	0.62099292	0.57398247	0.53063330	0.49065233	0.45377055
33	0.72010307	0.66368797	0.61181568	0.56411053	0.52022873	0.47985558	0.44270298
34	0.71297334	0.65549429	0.60277407	0.55440839	0.51002817	0.46929641	0.43190534
35	0.70591420	0.64740177	0.59386608	0.54487311	0.50002761	0.45896960	0.42137107
36	0.69892495	0.63940916	0.58508974	0.53550183	0.49022315	0.44887002	0.41109372
37	0.69200490	0.63151522	0.57644309	0.52629172	0.48061093	0.43899268	0.40106705
38	0.68515337	0.62371873	0.56792423	0.51724002	0.47118719	0.42933270	0.39128492
39	0.67836967	0.61601850	0.55953126	0.50834400	0.46194822	0.41988528	0.38174139
40	0.67165314	0.60841334	0.55126232	0.49960098	0.45289042	0.41064575	0.37243062
41	0.66500311	0.60090206	0.54311559	0.49100834	0.44401021	0.40160954	0.36334695
42	0.65841892	0.59348352	0.53508925	0.48256348	0.43530413	0.39277216	0.35448483
43	0.65189992	0.58615656	0.52718153	0.47426386	0.42676875	0.38412925	0.34583886
44	0.64544546	0.57892006	0.51939067	0.46610699	0.41840074	0.37567653	0.33740376
45	0.63905492	0.57177290	0.51171494	0.45809040	0.41019680	0.36740981	0.32917440
46	0.63272764	0.56471397	0.50415265	0.45021170	0.40215373	0.35932500	0.32114576
47	0.62646301	0.55774219	0.49670212	0.44246850	0.39426836	0.35141809	0.31331294
48	0.62026041	0.55085649	0.48936170	0.43485848	0.38653761	0.34368518	0.30567116
49	0.61411921	0.54405579	0.48212975	0.42737934	0.37895844	0.33612242	0.29821576
50	0.60803882	0.53733905	0.47500468	0.42002883	0.37152788	0.32872608	0.29094221
55	0.57852808	0.50497892	0.44092800	0.38512970	0.33650425	0.29411528	0.25715052
60	0.55044962	0.47456760	0.40929597	0.35313025	0.30478227	0.26314856	0.22728359
65	0.52373392	0.44598775	0.37993321	0.32378956	0.27605069	0.23544226	0.20088557
70	0.49831486	0.41912905	0.35267692	0.29688670	0.25002761	0.21065309	0.17755358
75	0.47412949	0.39388787	0.32737599	0.27221914	0.22645771	0.18847391	0.15693149
80	0.45111794	0.37016679	0.30389015	0.24960114	0.20510973	0.16862993	0.13870457
85	0.42922324	0.34787426	0.28208917	0.22886242	0.18577420	0.15087528	0.12259463
90	0.40839119	0.32692425	0.26185218	0.20984682	0.16826142	0.13498997	0.10835579
95	0.38857020	0.30723591	0.24306699	0.19241118	0.15239955	0.12077719	0.09477073
100	0.36971121	0.28873326	0.22562944	0.17642422	0.13803297	0.10806084	0.08464737

2.75%	3%	3.5%	4%	4.5%	5%	6%
1.	1.	1.	1.	1.	1.	1.
0.97323601	0.97087379	0.96618357	0.96153846	0.95693780	0.95238095	0.94339623
0.94718833	0.94259591	0.93351070	0.92455621	0.91572995	0.90702948	0.88999644
0.92183779	0.91514166	0.90194271	0.88899636	0.87629660	0.86383760	0.83961928
0.89716573	0.88848705	0.87144223	0.85480419	0.83856134	0.82270247	0.79209366
0.87315400	0.86260878	0.84197317	0.82192711	0.80245105	0.78352617	0.74725817
0.84978491	0.83748426	0.81350064	0.79031453	0.76789574	0.74621540	0.70496054
0.82704128	0.81309151	0.78599096	0.75991781	0.73482846	0.71068133	0.66505711
0.80490635	0.78940923	0.75941156	0.73069021	0.70318513	0.67683936	0.62741237
0.78336385	0.76641673	0.73373097	0.70258674	0.67290443	0.64460892	0.59189846
0.76239791	0.74409391	0.70891881	0.67556417	0.64392768	0.61391325	0.55839478
0.74199310	0.72242128	0.68494571	0.64958093	0.61619874	0.58467929	0.52678753
0.72213440	0.70137988	0.66178330	0.62459705	0.58966386	0.55683742	0.49696936
0.70280720	0.66095134	0.63940415	0.60057409	0.56427164	0.53032135	0.46883902
0.68399728	0.66111781	0.61778179	0.57747508	0.53997286	0.50506795	0.44230096
0.66569078	0.64186195	0.59689062	0.55526450	0.51672044	0.48101710	0.41726506
0.64787424	0.62316694	0.57670591	0.53390818	0.49446932	0.45811152	0.39364628
0.63053454	0.60501645	0.55720378	0.51337325	0.47317639	0.43629669	0.37136442
0.61365892	0.58739461	0.53836114	0.49362812	0.45280037	0.41552065	0.35034379
0.59723496	0.57028603	0.52015569	0.47464242	0.43330179	0.39573396	0.33051301
0.58125057	0.55367575	0.50256588	0.45638695	0.41464286	0.37688948	0.31180473
0.56569398	0.53754928	0.48557090	0.43883360	0.39678743	0.35894236	0.29415540
0.55055375	0.52189250	0.46915063	0.42195539	0.37970089	0.34184987	0.27750510
0.53581874	0.50669175	0.45328563	0.40572633	0.36335013	0.32557131	0.26179726
0.52147809	0.49193374	0.43795713	0.39012147	0.34770347	0.31006791	0.24697855
0.50752126	0.47760557	0.42314699	0.37511680	0.33273060	0.29530277	0.23299863
0.49393796	0.46369473	0.40883767	0.36068923	0.31840248	0.28124073	0.21981003
0.48071821	0.45018906	0.39501224	0.34681657	0.30469137	0.26784832	0.20736795
0.46785227	0.43707675	0.38165434	0.33347747	0.29157069	0.25509364	0.19563014
0.45533068	0.42434636	0.36874815	0.32065141	0.27901502	0.24294632	0.18455674
0.44314421	0.41198676	0.35627841	0.30831867	0.26700002	0.23137745	0.17411013
0.43128391	0.39998715	0.34423035	0.29646026	0.25550241	0.22035947	0.16425484
0.41974103	0.38833703	0.33258971	0.28505794	0.24449991	0.20986617	0.15495740
0.40850708	0.37702625	0.32134271	0.27409417	0.23397121	0.19987254	0.14618622
0.39757380	0.36604490	0.31047605	0.26355209	0.22389589	0.19035480	0.13791153
0.38693314	0.35538340	0.29997686	0.25341547	0.21425444	0.18129029	0.13010522
0.37657727	0.34503243	0.28983272	0.24366872	0.20502817	0.17265741	0.12274077
0.36649856	0.33498294	0.28003161	0.23429685	0.19619921	0.16443563	0.11579318
0.35668959	0.32522615	0.27056194	0.22528543	0.18775044	0.15660536	0.10923885
0.34714316	0.31575355	0.26141250	0.21662061	0.17966549	0.14914797	0.10305552
0.33785222	0.30655684	0.25257247	0.20828904	0.17192870	0.14204568	0.09722219
0.32880995	0.29762800	0.24403137	0.20027793	0.16452507	0.13528160	0.09171905
0.32000968	0.28895922	0.23577910	0.19257493	0.15744026	0.12883962	0.08652740
0.31144495	0.28054294	0.22780590	0.18516820	0.15066054	0.12270440	0.08162962
0.30310944	0.27237178	0.22010231	0.17804635	0.14417276	0.11686133	0.07700908
0.29499702	0.26443862	0.21265924	0.17119841	0.13796437	0.11129651	0.07265007
0.28710172	0.25673653	0.20546787	0.16461386	0.13202332	0.10599668	0.06853781
0.27941773	0.24925876	0.19851968	0.15828256	0.12633810	0.10094921	0.06465831
0.27193940	0.24199880	0.19180645	0.15219476	0.12089771	0.09614211	0.06099840
0.26466122	0.23495029	0.18532024	0.14634112	0.11569158	0.09156391	0.05754566
0.25757783	0.22810708	0.17905337	0.14071262	0.11070965	0.08720373	0.05428836
0.22490511	0.19676717	0.15075814	0.11565551	0.08883907	0.06832640	0.04056742
0.19637679	0.16973309	0.12693431	0.09506040	0.07128901	0.05353552	0.03031434
0.17146718	0.14641325	0.10687528	0.07813272	0.05720594	0.04194648	0.02265264
0.14971726	0.12629736	0.08998612	0.06421940	0.04590497	0.03286617	0.01692737
0.13072622	0.10894521	0.07576590	0.05278367	0.03683649	0.02575150	0.01264911
0.11414412	0.09397710	0.06379285	0.04338433	0.02955948	0.02017698	0.00945215
0.09966540	0.08106547	0.05371187	0.03565875	0.02372003	0.01580919	0.00706320
0.08702324	0.06992779	0.04522395	0.02930890	0.01903417	0.01238691	0.00527803
0.07598469	0.06032032	0.03807735	0.02408978	0.01527399	0.00970547	0.00394405
0.06634634	0.05203284	0.03206011	0.01980004	0.01225663	0.00760449	0.00294723

Table of Cases

Index